S0-BXX-033

Frommer's®
Hawaii

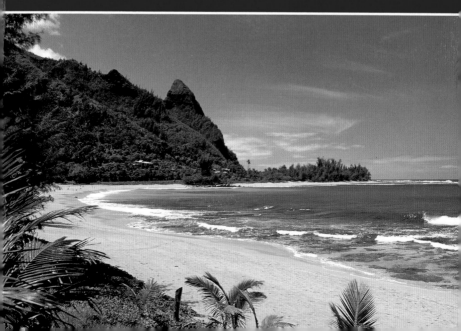

My Hawaii
by Jeanette Foster

I'VE ALWAYS BEEN IN LOVE WITH HAWAII. AS A YOUNG CHILD, I LIVED ON the island of Oahu. The overwhelming tropical beauty, the vibrant colors of the flowers, the sweet smell in the air, and the reflection of light haunted my dreams long after I left the state. Later, I moved back to Hawaii, this time to Maui. As soon as my feet touched the ground, I could feel it—that sense of place unique to Hawaii.

Hawaii is the most isolated land mass in the world. It's taken eons to develop the exotic splendor of these isles, where gigantic mountains rise above the clouds; earth-scented rainforests contain perfect ecosystems; and the slow, gentle island lifestyle holds promises of rest and rejuvenation.

After more than a decade, I watched Maui go from obscurity to fame. I decided to move to the Big Island of Hawaii, where Pele, the volcano goddess, still creates new land through the continuous eruption of lava, and where white, gold, black, and even green sand beaches beckon travelers from around the globe.

Hawaii is a place of dreams. Dreams the ancient Polynesians had when they paddled thousands of miles to get here. Dreams millions of visitors have of venturing into this sacred land to experience its beauty, breathe the fragrant perfume of its flowers, and walk the soft sand of its beaches. Hawaii is my home; and through these pictures, I hope to share this ethereal sense of place with you.

Since the current eruption of **KILAUEA** **(left)** began on January 3, 1983, lava has covered some 16,000 acres of the Big Island. Some areas have been mantled repeatedly and are now buried underneath 80 feet of lava. But Kilauea hasn't just destroyed parts of the island, it has also added to it—more than 560 acres of new land. The "quiet" nature of Kilauea's eruptions produces slow-moving, oozing lava that provides excellent, safe viewing most of the time, making the volcano the state's premier natural attraction. In Hawaii, people run to volcanoes instead of fleeing from them.

Driving, hiking, or biking through the otherworldly landscape of Maui's **HALEAKALA NATIONAL PARK (above)** is an experience not to be missed. Here you can take a hike above the clouds and peer down into Haleakala crater, which is big enough to swallow Manhattan. To the Hawaiians, 10,000-foot Haleakala, a dormant volcano, was a very spiritual place where kahuna (priests) performed rituals. Today it's home to two of Hawaii's most endangered species: nene (Hawaiian geese) and silversword plants.

The spectacular beauty of Kauai's Na Pali Coast is unmatched anywhere in the world. Hanging valleys open like green-velvet accordions, and waterfalls like **HANAKAPIAI FALLS (left)** tumble to the sea from the 4,120-foot-high cliffs. The remote, rugged nature of the region makes it difficult to experience—serious hikers should head for the Na Pali Coast State Park, which includes a 22-mile stretch of fluted cliffs that wrap around the northwest shore of Kauai between Kee Beach and Polihale State Park. Others can see the coast by boat or helicopter.

Some five million tourists visit Oahu every year, and 9 out of 10 of them stay in **WAIKIKI (above)**. This urban beach is where all the action is; it's backed by 175 high-rise hotels with more than 33,000 guest rooms and hundreds of bars and restaurants, all in a 1½-square-mile beach zone. Waikiki means honeymooners and sun seekers, bikinis and bare buns, a round-the-clock beach party every day of the year—and it's all because of a thin crescent of sand that was shipped over from Molokai.

The massive waves off the coast of Maui at **PEAHI (left)**, which the local residents call Jaws (as in, the waves can eat you up), have always been there, but for years, they were just too far off shore, too big, and coming in too fast for surfers to climb aboard and ride them. About a decade ago, surfers started using jet boats to tow a surfer to the waves, get the surfer up to speed, and then let him go to ride these giants (some as high as 60 ft.). Jaws has been conquered.

In ancient Hawaii, skilled artisans were able to carve an **OUTRIGGER CANOE (below)** from a single log of koa with just a stone adze. Used for transportation, the canoes ranged from small family-sized canoes used for fishing to huge canoes that could carry up to 200. Today canoe paddling is still one of Hawaii's most popular sports, with races nearly every weekend between May and September.

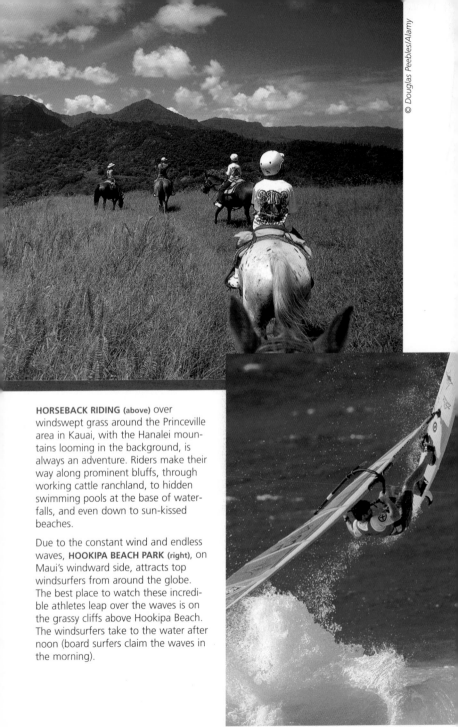

HORSEBACK RIDING (above) over windswept grass around the Princeville area in Kauai, with the Hanalei mountains looming in the background, is always an adventure. Riders make their way along prominent bluffs, through working cattle ranchland, to hidden swimming pools at the base of waterfalls, and even down to sun-kissed beaches.

Due to the constant wind and endless waves, **HOOKIPA BEACH PARK (right),** on Maui's windward side, attracts top windsurfers from around the globe. The best place to watch these incredible athletes leap over the waves is on the grassy cliffs above Hookipa Beach. The windsurfers take to the water after noon (board surfers claim the waves in the morning).

© D. Hurst/Alamy

The main feature at every luau is the **EARTH-ROASTED PIG (left)**, known as kalua pork. A whole pig is roasted all day in a pit called an imu.

Hawaii's largest visitors—the **HUMP-BACK WHALES (below)**—arrive every year around December and stay until April. You can spot the frolicking leviathans from shore.

The **PROTEA (top right)** comes in more than 40 different varieties, including pincushions (pictured). They're grown on the slopes of Haleakala.

Old Hawaii lives on at **PUUHONUA O HONAUAU NATIONAL HISTORIC PARK (bottom right)**, on the Big Island of Hawaii. This sacred site was once a refuge for ancient Hawaiian warriors. Today you can walk the consecrated grounds and glimpse a former way of life in a partially restored 16th-century village.

© Michael S. Nolan/AGE Fotostock

Standing on the deck of the **USS ARIZONA MEMORIAL AT PEARL HARBOR, OAHU (left)**, with the ship underneath, is an unforgettable experience. On December 7, 1941 the 608-foot Arizona sank in just 9 minutes, killing 1,177 of the men onboard, after being bombed during the Japanese air raid that sent the United States to war.

Only 38 miles from end to end and just 10 miles wide, **MOLOKAI (above)** stands like a big green wedge in the blue Pacific. Some of the most spectacular scenery is along the north shore of the island, where emerald-green cliffs plunge into a lurid aquamarine sea. These breathtaking 3,250-foot sea cliffs, the highest in the world, stretch 14 majestic miles, laced by waterfalls and creased by five valleys.

Hawaii History and Legend

Kaulakahi Channel

Hanalei   Princeville

KAUAI ④

Puuwai ①   ②   Lihue

NIIHAU   Poipu ③

Kauai Channel

22° N

21° N

20° N

19° N

MOLOKAI

11 Kalaupapa Leper Colony
On Jan. 6, 1866, King Kamehameha V sent the 9 people who had contracted *ma'i hookaawale* (separating sickness), or leprosy, to this lonely peninsula. In the next 10 years some 11,000 more victims would be sent here.

Laie

Haleiwa ⑤   ⑩

Makaha ⑥ **OAHU**   Kailua

⑥ ⑦ ⑧ ⑨ Waikiki

Honolulu

Kaiwi

KAUAI

1 Niihau
In 1864 Eliza Sinclair bought the 18×6 mile island from King Kamehameha for $10,000. It's been closed to the public ever since.

2 Captain Cook Arrives
Captain James Cook became the first Westerner to step foot in Hawaii in 1778, in Waimea.

3 Menehune Fish Pond
According to legend, the first people to live on Kauai were a race of small people, Menehune, who worked at night to accomplish magnificent feats like building this 25-mile fish pond in just one night.

4 Wailua Heiau
Seven sacred *heiau* (temples), ranging from royal birthing stones to a sacrificial site, lined this district, from the mouth of the Wailua River to Mt. Waialeale. Some remains of the *heiau* can still be seen.

OAHU

5 Kaena Point
At the tip of Oahu, according to legend, souls depart this world for the next.

6 Pearl Harbor
On Dec. 7,1941, the Japanese bombed Pearl Harbor, killing 2,403 Americans and propelling the United States into World War II.

7 Hawaiian Kingdom Overthrown
On January 17, 1893, a coup led by U.S. sugar planters and missionary descendants, and backed by U.S. Marines, overthrew the Hawaiian Monarchy.

8 Hawaii Calls
Beginning in 1935, and continuing for 40 years, the weekly radio show Hawaii Calls was broadcast live from Waikiki to millions of listeners in the U.S., Canada and Australia.

9 Merrie Times
The "Merrie Monarch" King Kavid Kalakaua, who reinstituted numerous cultural practices like the return of the hula, which the missionaries had forbidden, also gave his people Kapiolani Park, a 140-acre oasis next to Waikiki.

10 Kukaniloko Birthing Stones
In ancient times, women of *alii* (royal) status came to these sacred *pohaku* (rocks) to give birth, while 48 chiefs pounded drums to announce the newborn's arrival.

MAUI

12 Black Rock
According to legend, souls depart Maui for the next life at this rocky point off Kaanapali Beach.

13 Lahaina
Lahaina was the royal capital of Hawaii from the turn of the 19th century until 1845, when Kamehameha III moved it to the larger port of Honolulu.

14 Kepaniwai
In 1790, in his effort to gain control of all the Hawaiian islands, Kamehameha and his men fought and won the bloody battle in Iao Valley, which left the Iao Stream blocked with fallen bodies, giving the area the name Kepaniwai, or "damming of the waters."

15 Piilanihale Heiau
This *heiau* (temple), the largest in the state, was named for one of Maui's greatest chiefs, Piilani, who united the island of Maui in the 15th century.

16 Kahoolawe
The U.S. military took over this island, a sacred site to Hawaiians, during World War II and used it as a bombing target until 1993, when it was returned to the state.

```
0          30 mi
0      30 km
```

THE BIG ISLAND

17 Mo'okini Heiau
According to legend, this massive temple was erected in 480 A.D. by 18,000 men in just one night. Workers lined up for 14 miles to pass stones from Pololu Valley to build the sacred temple, where human sacrifices were once held.

18 Kamehameha's Birthplace
A *kuhuna* (priest) predicted that the child born to the chief of Kohala and a chieftess from Kona would be a killer of chiefs. Fearing the local chiefs would kill her child, Kamehama's mother traveled gave birth to him in secret, then gave him to a manservant to raise him in the remote area of Kapaau.

19 Puukohola Heiau
Kamehameha built this mammoth temple in 1791 after a prophet told him he would conquer and unite the islands if he built this shrine and dedicated it to Ku, the god of war.

20 Mauna Kea
The world's tallest mountain from its base under the ocean, and an impressive 13,796 feet above sea level, Mauna Kea was sacred to the Hawaiians (it is where their gods lived). Today it is home to a host of high-tech telescopes from 11 nations.

21 Puako Petroglyph Archaeological District
Thousands of petroglyphs are carved in rocks throughout this district, which covers several acres. Unfortunately the language of these petroglyphs or rock carvings is lost to us.

22 Ahuena Heiau
After Kamehameha conquered the islands he built this great compound in 1812, where he focused on governing in peace. After he died, this was the site where his son Liloliho broke a major *kapu* (taboo) by eating with women—his mother, Keopuolani, and another one of Kamehameha's wives, Kaahumanu. It was the beginning of the end of the *kapu* system.

23 Puuhonua O Honaunau
During ancient times anyone who broke a *kapu* (law) was immediately put to death unless they could escape to a "city of refuge" like this 16th century *heiau*.

24 Laupahoehoe
On a sunny day in 1946, one of the most ferocious tidal waves in history hit the eastern coast of the state, killing 20 students and four teachers in this village and nearly wiping out the town of Hilo. The event resulted in the establishment of the Pacific Tsunami Warning System.

25 Kilauea Eruption
On January 3, 1983, the southeast flank of Kilauea erupted with a curtain of lava. Since then, the still-continuing eruption has blanketed more than 20,000 acres with lava, destroyed more than 200 homes and businesses, and wiped out entire towns and subdivisions.

**Map labels:**

Channel

11 MOLOKAI
Kaunakakai

Pailolo Channel

Kalohi Channel

12 Kaanapali
14
13 Lanai City Lahaina Kahului **15**
LANAI Kihei **MAUI** Hana

Kealaikahiki Channel

16 Haleakala National Park
KAHOOLAWE

Alenuihaha Channel

17 Upolu Point Halawa
18 Hawi Nakapala
19
21 Waimea **24**
Keahole Point *Mauna Kea* **20** Hilo
22 Kailua-Kona **HAWAII "The Big Island"**
Captain Cook *Mauna* **25** Cape Kumukahi
23 *Loa* Kilauea Crater
Hawaii Volcanoes National Park
Pahala **27**
Kaalualu
Ka Lea (South Point)

Hawaii Volcanoes National Park

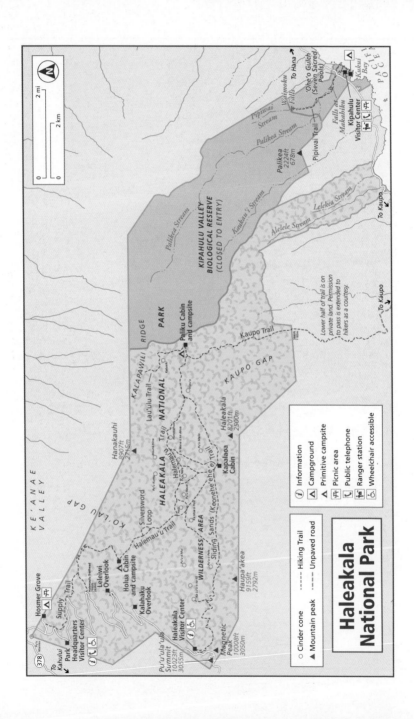

Haleakala National Park

Frommer's®

Hawaii

2008

by Jeanette Foster

Here's what the critics say about Frommer's:

"Amazingly easy to use. Very portable, very complete."

—*Booklist*

"Detailed, accurate, and easy-to-read information for all price ranges."
—*Glamour Magazine*

"Hotel information is close to encyclopedic."

—*Des Moines Sunday Register*

"Frommer's Guides have a way of giving you a real feel for a place."
—*Knight Ridder Newspapers*

Wiley Publishing, Inc.

Published by:

Wiley Publishing, Inc.
111 River St.
Hoboken, NJ 07030-5774

ISBN: 978-0-470-13478-8

Editor: Christine Ryan
Production Editor: Michael Brumitt
Cartographer: Roberta Stockwell
Photo Editor: Richard Fox
Anniversary Logo Design: Richard Pacifico
Production by Wiley Indianapolis Composition Services

For information on our other products and services or to obtain technical support, please contact our Customer Care Department within the U.S. at 800/762-2974, outside the U.S. at 317/572-3993 or fax 317/572-4002.

Wiley also publishes its books in a variety of electronic formats. Some content that appears in print may not be available in electronic formats.

Manufactured in the United States of America

5 4 3 2 1

Contents

3 Suggested Hawaii Itineraries 82

4 Oahu, the Gathering Place 95

8 Lanai, a Different Kind of Paradise   515

9 Kauai, the Garden Isle   537

Appendix: Hawaii in Depth   624

Index   643

List of Maps

Acknowledgments

Special thanks to Priscilla Life, the best researcher in Hawaii.

An Invitation to the Reader

In researching this book, we discovered many wonderful places—hotels, restaurants, shops, and more. We're sure you'll find others. Please tell us about them, so we can share the information with your fellow travelers in upcoming editions. If you were disappointed with a recommendation, we'd love to know that, too. Please write to:

Frommer's Hawaii 2008
Wiley Publishing, Inc. • 111 River St. • Hoboken, NJ 07030-5774

An Additional Note

Please be advised that travel information is subject to change at any time—and this is especially true of prices. We therefore suggest that you write or call ahead for confirmation when making your travel plans. The authors, editors, and publisher cannot be held responsible for the experiences of readers while traveling. Your safety is important to us, however, so we encourage you to stay alert and be aware of your surroundings. Keep a close eye on cameras, purses, and wallets, all favorite targets of thieves and pickpockets.

About the Author

A resident of the Big Island, **Jeanette Foster** has skied the slopes of Mauna Kea—during a Fourth of July ski meet, no less—and gone scuba diving with manta rays off the Kona Coast. A prolific writer widely published in travel, sports, and adventure magazines, she's also a contributing editor to *Hawaii* magazine, the editor of *Zagat's Survey to Hawaii's Top Restaurants,* and the Hawaii chapter author of *1,000 Places to See in the U.S.A. and Canada Before You Die.* In addition to writing this guide, Jeanette is the author of *Frommer's Maui 2008; Frommer's Kauai; Frommer's Hawaii with Kids; Frommer's Portable Big Island of Hawaii; Frommer's Honolulu, Waikiki & Oahu; Frommer's Maui Day by Day;* and *Frommer's Honolulu & Oahu Day by Day.*

Other Great Guides for Your Trip:

Frommer's Maui 2008
Frommer's Honolulu, Waikiki & Oahu
Frommer's Portable Big Island of Hawaii
Frommer's Portable Maui
Frommer's Kauai
Frommer's Hawaii with Kids
Frommer's Maui Day by Day
Frommer's Honolulu & Oahu Day by Day
Hawaii For Dummies

Frommer's Star Ratings, Icons & Abbreviations

Every hotel, restaurant, and attraction listing in this guide has been ranked for quality, value, service, amenities, and special features using a **star-rating system.** In country, state, and regional guides, we also rate towns and regions to help you narrow down your choices and budget your time accordingly. Hotels and restaurants are rated on a scale of zero (recommended) to three stars (exceptional). Attractions, shopping, nightlife, towns, and regions are rated according to the following scale: zero stars (recommended), one star (highly recommended), two stars (very highly recommended), and three stars (must-see).

In addition to the star-rating system, we also use **seven feature icons** that point you to the great deals, in-the-know advice, and unique experiences that separate travelers from tourists. Throughout the book, look for:

Finds	Special finds—those places only insiders know about
Fun Fact	Fun facts—details that make travelers more informed and their trips more fun
Kids	Best bets for kids and advice for the whole family
Moments	Special moments—those experiences that memories are made of
Overrated	Places or experiences not worth your time or money
Tips	Insider tips—great ways to save time and money
Value	Great values—where to get the best deals

The following **abbreviations** are used for credit cards:

AE American Express	DISC Discover	V Visa	
DC Diners Club	MC MasterCard		

Frommers.com

Now that you have this guidebook to help you plan a great trip, visit our website at **www. frommers.com** for additional travel information on more than 3,500 destinations. We update features regularly to give you instant access to the most current trip-planning information available. At Frommers.com, you'll find scoops on the best airfares, lodging rates, and car rental bargains. You can even book your travel online through our reliable travel booking partners. Other popular features include:

- Online updates of our most popular guidebooks
- Vacation sweepstakes and contest giveaways
- Newsletters highlighting the hottest travel trends
- Online travel message boards with featured travel discussions

What's New in Hawaii

Nearing the end of the first decade of the 21st century, Hawaii is reinventing itself with big upgrades and renovations at all the major resort areas, improved air transportation to and within the state, more outdoor and ocean activities, and great eateries for every kind of cuisine, from gourmet to plate lunch, to shrimp trucks parked by the side of the road.

And more people are coming to the 50th state—some 8.45 million people visited Hawaii in the last year, 4% more than the previous year.

Below is a brief overview of the Aloha State's latest changes that can make your vacation to Hawaii better than ever.

PLANNING YOUR TRIP Getting Around Joining **Hawaiian Airlines** and **Aloha Air** as interisland air carriers is **go!** (© 888/IFLYGO2; www.iflygo.com), owned by Mesa Air Group (which has more than 1,000 flights to 166 cities across the U.S., Canada, and Mexico). The new airline began service with 50-passenger Bombardier CRJ 200 jets with service from Honolulu to Maui, Kauai, and the Big Island (both Hilo and Kona). go! offers the cheapest interisland fares in Hawaii.

In 2007, visitors to Molokai and Lanai got not one, but two new commuter airlines which began flying from Honolulu to Molokai and Lanai. go! airline started a new commuter service from Honolulu to Molokai and Lanai, under the name, **go!Express,** on their new fleet of Cessna Grand Caravan 208B planes. Another commuter airline, **Pacific Wings,** started operating their discount airline, **PW Express** (© **888/866-5022** or 808/873-0877; www.flypwx.com), with daily non-stop flights between Honolulu and Molokai and Lanai, plus flights from Kahului, Maui, and Molokai.

As we went to press, on the horizon was the proposed **Hawaii Superferry** (www.hawaiisuperferry.com), a 350-foot vessel which could carry 866 passengers and 282 cars and trucks between Honolulu and Kauai, Maui, and the Big Island at speeds up to 35 knots. The State of Hawaii has committed some $40 million for harbor improvements to accommodate the new ferry service. Hawaii briefly had a ferry service (Super Flite) in the 1970s, but the high winds and waves took its toll on the hydrofoil boat and it lasted only a few years. Proposed fares range from $42 to $62 for passengers and $55 to $75 for cars.

However, environmentalists have been fighting the Superferry for years because the company was not required to do an environmental impact statement. Recently Hawaii legislators have gotten into the flight and have called for a more thorough review of the impact of the Superferry, and Maui County has joined a lawsuit with environmentalists on whether state improvements to Kahului Harbor are adequate to handle increased traffic from the Superferry. Stay tuned . . . .

Ocean Safety Sharks may make the headlines, but drownings claim far more lives. The City and County of Honolulu has a staff of 200 professional lifeguards (the largest in the nation), but most of the drownings occur at beaches where there are no lifeguards. To educate people about ocean safety and how that beautiful blue ocean may look calm but have numerous dangers under the waves, the state has launched several websites, including **Hawaii Beach Hazard Forecast** (http://oceansafety.soest.hawaii.edu), a partnership between the University of Hawaii and Honolulu's city ocean safety office. The site informs beachgoers statewide (you can click on the island of your choice) on ocean conditions at hundreds of beaches, including whether they are safe for swimming. The island of Kauai has an even better website, **www.kauaiexplorer.com**, with daily updates from lifeguards around Kauai on the beach conditions.

Hawaiian Airlines airs a brief water safety video on all flights from the mainland explaining what those warning signs posted at beaches in Hawaii mean.

Tips on Accommodations For the first time, the number of new hotel units is down and the number of new time shares and condotels (condominium units in a hotel which are sold to private ownership but remain in the hotel's rental pool) is up. Since the arrival of the big boys of the vacation industry into timeshares (Hilton, Marriott, Ritz-Carlton, etc.), the industry has taken off in Hawaii. Statewide, Hawaii has some 15,000 condotel rooms and more than 7,000 timeshare units. Even the Ritz-Carlton Kapalua is selling some of its suites (some will stay in the hotel rental pool). Also, at Kapalua Resort on Maui, a new concept called fractional ownership on luxury homes and condominiums allows you to stay there 21 days per year. Units are priced in the high six figures.

Not to worry—there are still 73,000 hotel rooms statewide, and the majority of visitors (63%) prefer the old-fashioned way of traveling versus staying in a condotel (21%), a timeshare (10%), a vacation rental (3.3%), or a B&B (1%).

OAHU Where to Stay One of the biggest projects to take place in Waikiki in decades is the total renovation of an 8-acre area (bound by Saratoga Rd., Kalakaua Ave., Lewers St., and Kalia Rd.) called the **"Waikiki Beach Walk."** The project, by Outrigger Hotels & Resorts, cost some $460 million.

Phase 1, completed in 2007, reconfigured the formerly very congested area (narrow streets with double-parked delivery trucks, crowded sidewalks, and no vegetation) into an oasis of broad sidewalks, tropical foliage, water features, open space, and new, totally renovated hotels. Eleven hotels were razed, upgraded, or changed to suites or condos. Five hotels and one unit of timeshare condominiums remain.

The bad news is, most of the budget hotels, neighborhood eateries, and small independent shops in the area have been replaced with luxury (higher-priced) properties and swank shops and trendy restaurants to match, all linked through pedestrian bridges and connecting walkways.

These changes inspired other hotel groups to make changes of their own (details in the Oahu chapter, p. 116 and 124). Aqua Hotels and Resorts entered the Waikiki market by upgrading and rebranding several off-the-beach properties. **Hilton** added a property—the former Radisson Waikiki Prince Kuhio, after massive renovations, was rebranded the **Hilton Waikiki Prince Kuhio Hotel.**

Not to be outdone, **Starwood** announced renovations, demolition, and additions to their Waikiki hotels (see p. 117 for details).

And finally, the other new property coming to Waikiki is the **Trump International Hotel,** estimated to open in 2009. When the hotel-condominium went on sale in December 2006, every one of the 460 luxury units sold out within just a few hours. The ultra-upscale property will have hotel suites available and offer 24-hour concierge and room service. Other amenities will include a lobby bar, cafe, outdoor swimming pool, private fitness center, and separate lobbies for hotel guests and residents.

Beaches You may notice on your next trip to **Waikiki Beach** that it seems bigger and better. Yes, it is bigger—about 40% bigger than it has been in years. Waikiki, like lots of other beaches on Oahu and Maui, has faced chronic erosion problems for the past 50 years. A pilot project in Waikiki (costing $425,000) dredged up 9,500 cubic yards of sand from a half mile off the shore, and then pumped the sand, underwater, back to Kuhio Beach, fronting the Duke Kahanamoku statue. The former 20-foot-wide shoreline is now 40 feet wide.

BIG ISLAND Golf For those interested in improving their golf game, **Darrin Gee's Spirit of Golf Academy** (© 866-GOLF-433; www.spiritofgolf hawaii.com) has developed a 2½-hour clinic that helps golfers gain focus and relax under pressure, among other skills. Classes meet at the Big Island Country Club or Mauna Kea Resort's Hapuna course.

Shopping New shopping and dining opportunities are underway with the opening of the **Queen's MarketPlace** (www.waikoloabeachresort.com), located across the street from the Kings' Shops in the Waikoloa Beach Resort.

Seeing the Sights Don't leave Hilo without visiting **Imiloa: Astronomy Center of Hawaii,** University of Hawaii at Hilo Science and Technology Park campus, 600 Imiloa Pl. (© **808/969-9700;** www.imiloahawaii.org). Some 300 exhibits in the 12,000-square-foot gallery connect the Hawaiian culture and its

explorers, who discovered the Hawaiian Islands, with the astronomers who explore the heavens from the observatories atop Mauna Kea. *Imiloa,* which means "explorer" or "seeker of profound truth," is the perfect name. The center's stunning architecture, featuring titanium cones, sits on 9 landscaped acres overlooking Hilo Bay. Allow at least a half a day to wander around.

The Big Island After Dark The **Sheraton Keauhou Bay Resort & Spa** has a new luau and show: **Kamaha'o, The Wondrous Myths of Hawaii** (© **808/930-4828;** www.kaikehawaii.com), featuring lavish theatrics woven into Hawaiian chants, legends, and hula, with acrobatic performing arts. This is definitely not a typical, tired Polynesian revue.

MAUI Several new restaurants have opened on the Valley Isle. **E&O Trading Company,** Lahaina Cannery Mall, 1221 Honoapiilani Hwy. (© **808/667-1818;** www.eotrading.com), serves eclectic Southeast Asian cuisine in an elaborate setting (p. 404). At **Mala Ocean Tavern,** 1307 Front St., in Lahaina (© **808/667-9394;** www.malaoceantavern.com), you can enjoy an ocean view as you dine on "tavern food" such as ahi burgers or cheeseburgers, one of the tempting salads (the beet and Kula goat cheese salad is divine), or something off the "big plate" menu (perhaps wok-fried moi fish or glazed baby back ribs). **Tastings Wine Bar & Grill,** Kihei Kalama Village, 1912 S. Kihei Rd. (© **808/879-8711**), a tiny, tiny hole in the wall, produces "island-inspired American Cuisine" and features excellent food and wine pairings.

Maui now has an organic vodka, **OCEAN Vodka** (www.oceanvodka.com). It's made from water 3,000 feet beneath the ocean off the Kona coast of the Big Island which is shipped to Maui, where it's blended with organic corn and rye to produce this one-of-a-kind libation. A

Smoke-Free State

Hawaii has gone smoke-free with one of the toughest smoking laws in the country: It's against the law to smoke in public buildings, including airports, shopping malls, grocery stores, retail shops, buses, movie theaters, banks, convention facilities, and all government buildings and facilities. There is no smoking in restaurants, bars, or nightclubs. You cannot smoke in parking garages, public lobbies (anywhere where there are employees is considered public), lanais, patios, covered walkways, or bus stops that have a roof or have two sides enclosed. The fine is $50.

Most bed-and-breakfasts prohibit smoking indoors; more and more hotels and resorts are becoming nonsmoking even in public areas. Also, there is no smoking within 20 feet of a doorway, window, or ventilation intake (so no hanging around outside a bar to smoke—you must go 20 ft. away).

Where *can* you smoke? Curbside along the street (but not within 20 ft. of a door or window), in your car, or in a tobacco shop. Even some beaches have no-smoking policies. On those that do allow smoking, you'd better pick up your butts instead of using the sand as your own private ashtray, or you could face a stiff fine.

number of Maui restaurants serve OCEAN Vodka—visit the website to find out where to try it.

LANAI The **Lodge at Koele** has joined its sister hotel, **Manele Bay Resort,** in being rebranded a **Four Season Resort** (© **800/321-4666** or 808/565-2000; www.fourseasons.com/koele), with plans for a free-standing Wellness Center and Spa to be built in 2008.

KAUAI Where to Stay The **Outrigger Waipouli Beach Resort & Spa** (© **800/ OUTRIGGER** or 808/823-8300; www. outrigger.com), a $200-million luxury condominium project on 12.6 acres between the historic towns of Wailua and Kapaa, opened recently with high-end one- and two-bedroom units and a long list of amenities, such as a 4,000-square-foot

Aveda spa and a 300,000-gallon heated saltwater fantasy pool complete with flowing river, garden, dual serpentine waterslides, a sand-bottom children's pool, and three sand-bottom whirlpool tubs.

Hilton renovated and rebranded the old Radisson Kauai, opening as the **Hilton Kauai Beach Hotel Resort** (© **800/ HILTONS** or 808/245-1955; www.hilton kauairesort.com), one of the few hotels on Kauai offering complimentary airport shuttle service.

Where to Dine In the culinary world, **Mediterranean Gourmet** (© **808/826-9875**), located next door to the Hanalei Colony Resort, was awarded "Best New Restaurant" on Kauai for chef/owner Imad Beydoun's Middle Eastern dishes, which he embellishes with an island twist.

1

The Best of Hawaii

There's no place on earth quite like this handful of sun-drenched, mid-Pacific islands. The Hawaii of South Seas literature and Hollywood films really does exist. Here you'll find palm-fringed blue lagoons, lush rainforests, hidden gardens, cascading waterfalls, wild rivers running through rugged canyons, and soaring volcanoes. And oh, those beaches—gold, red, black, and even green sands caressed by an endless surf. The possibilities for adventure—and relaxation—are endless. Each of the six main islands is separate, distinct, and infinitely complex. There's far too much to see and do on any 2-week vacation, which is why so many people return to the Aloha State year after year.

Unfortunately, even paradise has its share of stifling crowds and tourist schlock. If you're not careful, your trip to Hawaii could turn into a nightmare of tourist traps selling shells from the Philippines, hokey faux culture like cellophane-skirted hula dancers, overpriced exotic drinks, and a 4-hour timeshare lecture before you get on that "free" snorkeling trip. That's where this guide comes in. As a Hawaii resident, I can tell the extraordinary from the merely ordinary. This book will steer you away from the crowded, the overrated, and the overpriced—and toward the best Hawaii has to offer. No matter what your budget, this guide will help ensure that every dollar is well spent.

1 The Best Beaches

- **Lanikai Beach** (Oahu): Too gorgeous to be real, this stretch along the Windward Coast is one of Hawaii's postcard-perfect beaches—a mile of golden sand as soft as powdered sugar bordering translucent turquoise waters. The waters are calm year-round and excellent for swimming, snorkeling, and kayaking. Two tiny offshore islands complete the picture, functioning not only as scenic backdrops, but also as bird sanctuaries. See p. 178.
- **Hapuna Beach** (Big Island): This ½-mile-long crescent regularly wins kudos in the world's top travel magazines as the most beautiful beach in Hawaii—some consider it one of the

most beautiful beaches in the world. One look and you'll see why: Perfect cream-colored sand slopes down to crystal-clear waters that are great for swimming, snorkeling, and bodysurfing in summer; come winter, waves thunder in like stampeding horses. The facilities for picnicking and camping are top-notch, and there's plenty of parking. See p. 298.
- **Kapalua Beach** (Maui): On an island with many great beaches, Kapalua takes the prize. This golden crescent with swaying palms is protected from strong winds and currents by two outstretched lava-rock promontories. Its calm waters are perfect for snorkeling, swimming,

and kayaking. Facilities include showers, restrooms, and lifeguards. See p. 424.

- **Papohaku Beach** (Molokai): These gold sands stretch on for some 3 miles (it's one of Hawaii's longest beaches) and are about as wide as a football field. Offshore the ocean churns mightily in winter, but the waves die down in summer, making the calm waters inviting for swimming. It's also great for picnicking, walking, and watching sunsets. See p. 496.

- **Hulopoe Beach** (Lanai): This golden, palm-fringed beach off the south coast of Lanai gently slopes down to the azure waters of a Marine Life Conservation District, where clouds of tropical fish flourish and spinner dolphins come to play. A tide pool in the lava rocks defines one side

of the bay, while the other is lorded over by the Manele Bay Hotel, which sits prominently on the hill above. Offshore you'll find good swimming, snorkeling, and diving; onshore there's a full complement of beach facilities, from restrooms to camping areas. See p. 526.

- **Haena Beach** (Kauai): Backed by verdant cliffs, this curvaceous North Shore beach has starred as Paradise in many a movie. It's easy to see why Hollywood loves Haena Beach, with its grainy golden sand and translucent turquoise waters. Summer months bring calm waters for swimming and snorkeling, and winter brings mighty waves for surfers. There are plenty of facilities on hand, including picnic tables, restrooms, and showers. See p. 587.

2 The Best Island Experiences

- **Hitting the Beach:** A beach is a beach is a beach, right? Not in Hawaii. With 132 islets, shoals, and reefs, plus a general coastline of 750 miles, Hawaii has beaches in all different shapes, sizes, and colors, including black. The variety on the six major islands is astonishing; you could go to a different beach every day for years and still not see them all. For the best of a spectacular bunch, see "The Best Beaches," above.

- **Taking the Plunge:** Don mask, fin, and snorkel, and explore Hawaii's magical underwater world, where exotic corals and kaleidoscopic clouds of tropical fish await you—a sea turtle may even come over to check you out. Can't swim? That's no excuse— take one of the many submarine tours offered by **Atlantis Submarines** (ⓒ **800/548-6262;** www.go-atlantis. com) on Oahu, the Big Island, and

Maui. Check out the "Watersports" section in each island chapter for more information on all these underwater adventures.

- **Meeting Local Folks:** If you go to Hawaii and see only people like the ones back home, you might as well not have come. Extend yourself— leave your hotel, go out and meet the locals, and learn about Hawaii and its people. Just smile and say "Owzit?"— which means "How is it?" ("It's good," is the usual response)—and you're on your way to making a new friend. Hawaii is remarkably cosmopolitan; every ethnic group in the world seems to be represented here. There's a huge diversity of food, culture, language, and customs.

- **Feeling History Come Alive at Pearl Harbor** (Oahu): The United States could turn its back on World War II no longer after December 7, 1941, when Japanese warplanes

The Hawaiian Islands

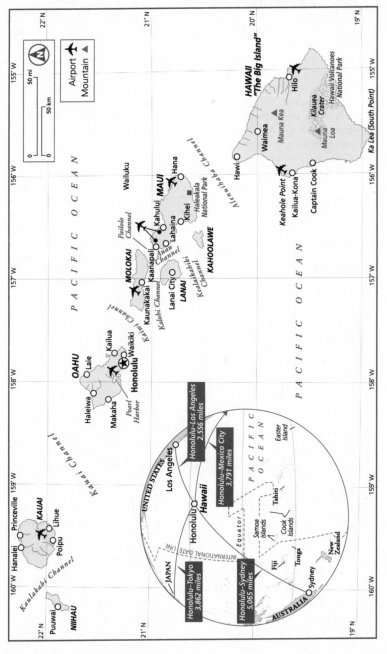

Airport ✈
Mountain ▲

50 mi
50 km

PACIFIC OCEAN

22° N
21° N
20° N
19° N

155° W
156° W
157° W
158° W
159° W
160° W

NIIHAU
Puuwai

KAUAI
Hanalei
Princeville
Lihue
Poipu

Kauai Channel
Kaulakahi Channel

OAHU
Laie
Kailua
Haleiwa
Makaha
Honolulu Waikiki
Pearl Harbor

Kaiwi Channel

MOLOKAI
Kaunakakai
Kaluaaha

LANAI
Lanai City

KAHOOLAWE

MAUI
Wailuku
Kahului
Lahaina
Kaanapali
Kihei
Hana
Haleakala National Park

Pailolo Channel
Auau Channel
Kealaikahiki Channel
Kalohi Channel
Alenuihaha Channel

Haleakala National Park Channel

HAWAII "The Big Island"
Hawi
Waimea
Keahole Point
Kailua-Kona
Captain Cook
Keauhou Point
Hilo
Mauna Kea
Mauna Loa
Kilauea Crater
Hawaii Volcanoes National Park
Ka Lea (South Point)

UNITED STATES
Los Angeles

Hawaii
Honolulu

INTERNATIONAL DATE LINE
JAPAN
Equator

PACIFIC OCEAN

Easter Island
Tahiti
Samoa Islands
Cook Islands
Fiji
Tonga
New Zealand
Sydney

AUSTRALIA

Honolulu–Los Angeles 2,556 miles
Honolulu–Mexico City 3,791 miles
Honolulu–Tokyo 3,862 miles
Honolulu–Sydney 5,065 miles

bombed Pearl Harbor. Standing on the deck of the USS *Arizona* Memorial (© **808/422-0561;** www.nps.gov/usar)—the eternal tomb for the 1,177 sailors and Marines trapped below when the battleship sank in just 9 minutes—is a moving experience you'll never forget. Also in Pearl Harbor, you can visit the USS *Missouri* Memorial, where World War II came to an end. The Japanese signed their surrender on the deck of this 58,000-ton battleship on September 2, 1945. See p. 204.

- **Watching for Whales:** If you happen to be in Hawaii during humpback-whale season (roughly Dec–Apr), don't miss the opportunity to see these gentle giants. A host of boats—from small inflatables to high-tech, high-speed sailing catamarans—offer a range of whale-watching cruises on every island. One of my favorites is along the Big Island's Kona Coast, where **Capt. Dan McSweeney's Year-Round Whale-Watching Adventures** (© **808/322-0028;** www.ilovewhales.com) takes you right to the whales year-round (pilot, sperm, false killer, melon-headed, pygmy killer, and beaked whales call Hawaii home even when humpbacks aren't in residence). A whale researcher for more than 25 years, Captain Dan frequently drops an underwater microphone or video camera into the depths so you can listen to whale songs and maybe actually see what's going on. See p. 300.

- **Creeping up to the Ooze** (Big Island): Kilauea volcano has been adding land to the Big Island continuously since 1983. If conditions are right, you can walk up to the red-hot lava and see it ooze along, or you can stand at the shoreline and watch with awe as 2,000°F (1,092°C) molten fire pours into the ocean. You can also take to the air in a helicopter and see the Volcano Goddess's work from above. See "Hawaii Volcanoes National Park," under "Seeing the Sights," in chapter 5.

- **Going Big-Game Fishing off the Kona Coast** (Big Island): Don't pass up the opportunity to try your luck in the sportfishing capital of the world, where 1,000-pound marlin are taken from the sea just about every month of the year. Not looking to set a world record? Kona's charter-boat captains specialize in conservation and will be glad to tag any fish you angle, and then let it go so someone else can have the fun of fighting a big-game fish tomorrow. See "Sportfishing: The Hunt for Granders," under "Watersports," in chapter 5.

- **Greeting the Rising Sun from atop Haleakala** (Maui): Bundle up in warm clothing, fill a thermos full of hot java, and drive up to the summit to watch the sky turn from inky black to muted charcoal as a small sliver of orange light forms on the horizon. There's something about standing at 10,000 feet, breathing in the rarefied air, and watching the first rays of sun streak across the sky. This is a mystical experience of the first magnitude. See "House of the Sun: Haleakala National Park," under "Seeing the Sights," in chapter 6.

- **Riding a Mule to Kalaupapa** (Molokai): If you have only a day to spend on Molokai, spend it on a mule. The trek from "topside" Molokai to Kalaupapa National Historic Park (Father Damien's world-famous leper colony) with **Molokai Mule Ride** (© **800/567-7550;** www.muleride.com) is a once-in-a-lifetime adventure. The cliffs are taller than 300-story skyscrapers, but Buzzy Sproat's surefooted mules go up and down the narrow 2.9-mile trail daily, rain or shine, and he's never lost a rider or a mount on the 26 switchbacks. Even if you can't afford to mule or helicopter in, don't pass up the opportunity to see this hauntingly beautiful peninsula. If you're in good shape and brought hiking boots with you, you can get a permit (available at the trail head) and hike down the trail. The views are breathtaking: You'll see the world's highest sea cliffs and waterfalls plunging thousands of feet into the ocean. See "The Legacy of Father Damien: Kalaupapa National Historic Park," under "Seeing the Sights," in chapter 7.

- **Taking a Day Trip to Lanai** (Maui): If you'd like to visit Lanai but have only a day to spare, consider taking a day trip. **Trilogy** (© 888/MAUI-800; www.sailtrilogy.com) offers an all-day sailing, snorkeling, and whale-watching adventure. Trilogy is the only outfitter with rights to Hulopoe Beach, and the trip includes a minivan tour

of the little isle (pop. 3,500). See p. 429. You can also take **Expeditions Lahaina/ Lanai Passenger Ferry** (© 808/661-3756; www.go-lanai.com) from Maui to Lanai, and then rent a four-wheel-drive vehicle from **Dollar Rent-A-Car** (© 800/588-7808) for a day of backcountry exploring and beach fun. See p. 430.

- **Soaring over the Na Pali Coast** (Kauai): This is the only way to see the spectacular, surreal beauty of Kauai. Your helicopter will dip low over razor-thin cliffs, fluttering past sparkling waterfalls and swooping down into the canyons and valleys of the fabled Na Pali Coast. The only problem is that there's too much beauty to absorb, and it all goes by in a rush. See "Helicopter Rides over Waimea Canyon & the Na Pali Coast," under "Seeing the Sights," in chapter 9.

3 The Best of Natural Hawaii

- **Volcanoes:** The entire island chain is made of volcanoes; don't miss the opportunity to see one. On Oahu the entire family can hike to the top of ancient, world-famous **Diamond Head** (see "Diamond Head Crater," under "Nature Hikes," in chapter 4). At the other end of the spectrum is fire-breathing Kilauea at **Hawaii Volcanoes National Park,** on the Big Island, where you can get an up-close-and-personal experience with the red-hot lava ooze (see "Hawaii Volcanoes National Park," under "Seeing the Sights," in chapter 5). On Maui, **Haleakala National Park** provides a bird's-eye view into a long-dormant volcanic crater (see "House of the Sun: Haleakala National Park," under "Seeing the Sights," in chapter 6).

- **Waterfalls:** Rushing waterfalls thundering downward into sparkling freshwater pools are some of Hawaii's most beautiful natural wonders. If you're on the Big Island, stop by **Rainbow Falls** (p. 333) in Hilo or the spectacular 442-foot **Akaka Falls** (p. 327), just outside the city. On Maui the Road to Hana offers numerous viewing opportunities; at the end of the drive, you'll find **Oheo Gulch** (also known as the Seven Sacred Pools), with some of the most dramatic and accessible waterfalls on the islands (see "Tropical Haleakala: Oheo Gulch at Kipahulu," under "Seeing the Sights," in chapter 6). Kauai is loaded with waterfalls, especially along the North Shore and in the Wailua area, where you'll find 40-foot **Opaekaa Falls,** probably the best-looking drive-up waterfall on Kauai (see "Wailua River State Park," under "Seeing the Sights," in chapter 9). With scenic mountain peaks in the background and a restored Hawaiian village on the nearby riverbanks, the Opaekaa Falls are what the tourist-bureau folks call an eye-popping photo op.

- **Gardens:** The islands are redolent with the sweet scent of flowers. For a glimpse of the full breadth and beauty of Hawaii's spectacular range of tropical flora, we suggest spending an afternoon at a lush garden. On Oahu, amid the high-rises of downtown Honolulu, the leafy oasis of **Foster Botanical Garden** (p. 206) showcases 26 native Hawaiian trees and the last stand of several rare trees, including an East African, whose white flowers bloom only at night. On the Big Island, **Liliuokalani Gardens** (p. 330), the largest formal Japanese garden this side of Tokyo, resembles a postcard from Asia, with bonsai, carp ponds, pagodas, and even a moon-gate bridge. At Maui's **Kula Botanical Garden** (p. 457), you can take a leisurely self-guided stroll through more than 700 native and exotic plants, including orchids, proteas, and bromeliads. On lush Kauai, **Na Aina Kai Botanical Gardens** (p. 614), on some 240 acres, is sprinkled with some 70 life-size (some larger than life-size) whimsical bronze statues, hidden off the beaten path of the North Shore.

- **Marine Life Conservation Areas:** Nine underwater parks are spread across Hawaii, most notably **Waikiki Beach** (p. 172) and **Hanauma Bay** (p. 173) on Oahu; the Big Island's **Kealakekua Bay** (p. 304); **Molokini,** just off the coast of Maui (see "Watersports," in chapter 6); and Lanai's **Manele and Hulopoe bays** (see "Beaches," in chapter 8). Be sure to bring snorkel gear to at least one of these wonderful places during your vacation.

- **Garden of the Gods** (Lanai): Out on Lanai's north shore lies the ultimate rock garden: a rugged, barren, beautiful place full of rocks strewn by volcanic forces and molded by the elements into a variety of shapes and colors—brilliant reds, oranges, ochers, and yellows. Scientists use phrases such as "ongoing posterosional event" or "plain and simple badlands" to describe the desolate, windswept place. The ancient Hawaiians, however, considered the Garden of the Gods to be an entirely supernatural phenomenon. Natural badlands or mystical garden? Take a four-wheel-drive trip out here and decide for yourself. See p. 531.

- **Waimea Canyon** (Kauai): This valley, known for its reddish lava beds, reminds everyone who sees it of Arizona's Grand Canyon. Kauai's version is bursting with ever-changing color, just like its namesake, but it's smaller—only a mile wide, 3,567 feet deep, and 12 miles long. All this grandeur was caused by a massive earthquake that sent all the streams flowing into a single river, which then carved this picturesque canyon. You can stop by the road and look at it, hike down into it, or swoop through it by helicopter. See p. 606.

4 The Best of Underwater Hawaii

- **Hanauma Bay** (Oahu): It can get crowded, but for clear, warm, calm waters; an abundance of fish that are so friendly they'll swim right up to your face mask; a beautiful setting; and easy access, there's no place like Hanauma Bay. Just wade in waist-deep and look down to see more than 50 species of reef and inshore fish. Snorkelers hug the safe, shallow inner bay—it's like swimming in an outdoor aquarium. Serious divers shoot "the slot," a passage through the reef, to enter Witch's Brew, a turbulent cove. See p. 173.

- **Kahaluu Beach** (Big Island): The calm, shallow waters of Kahaluu are perfect for beginning snorkelers or those who are unsure of their swimming abilities and want the comfort of being able to stand up at any time. The sunlight through the shallow waters casts a dazzling spotlight on the colorful sea life and coral formations. If you listen closely, you can actually hear the parrotfish feeding. See p. 295.

- **Kealakekua Bay** (Big Island): Mile-wide Kealakekua Bay, at the foot of massive U-shaped sea cliffs, is rich with marine life, snorkelers, and history. A white obelisk marks the spot where, in 1778, the great British navigator Capt.

James Cook, who charted most of the Pacific, was killed by Hawaiians. The bay itself is a marine sanctuary that teems with schools of polychromatic tropical fish. See p. 304.

- **Molokini** (Maui): The islet of Molokini is shaped like a crescent moon that fell from the sky. Its shallow concave side serves as a sheltering backstop against sea currents for tiny tropical fish; its opposite side is a deepwater cliff inhabited by spiny lobsters, moray eels, and white-tipped sharks. Neophyte snorkelers should report to the concave side, experienced scuba divers the other. The clear water and abundant marine life make this islet off the Makena Coast one of Hawaii's most popular dive spots, so expect crowds. See "Watersports," in chapter 6.

- **Kee Beach** (Kauai): Where the road ends on the North Shore, you'll find a dandy little reddish-gold sand beach almost too beautiful to be real. It borders a reef-protected cove at the foot of fluted volcanic cliffs. Swimming and snorkeling are safe inside the reef, where long-nosed butterfly fish flitter about and schools of taape (bluestripe snapper) swarm over the coral. See p. 587.

5 The Best Golf Courses

- **Mauna Kea's Beach and Hapuna Courses** (Big Island; ✆ **808/882-5400** for Beach Course, ✆ **808/880-3000** for Hapuna Course): The Mauna Kea Golf Course (p. 310), located out on the Kohala Coast, is everyone's old favorite. One of the first fields of play to be carved out of the black lava, the dramatic, always-challenging, par-72, 18-hole championship course is still one of Hawaii's

top three. The Arnold Palmer/Ed Seay–designed Hapuna Golf Course (p. 310) rests in the rolling foothills above Hapuna Beach Prince Hotel and provides a memorable links-style golf experience along with one of the best views of this unusual coast (p. 261).

- **Mauna Lani Frances I'i Brown Championship Courses** (Big Island; ✆ **808/885-6655**): Mauna Lani's two resort courses, North and South, feature a combination of oceanfront and interior lava-lined holes; both offer wonderful scenery accompanied by strategic, championship-level golf. See p. 310.

- **Kapalua Resort Courses** (Maui; ℂ 877/KAPALUA): Kapalua is probably the best nationally known golf resort in Hawaii, thanks to the PGA Kapalua Mercedes Championship played here each January. The Bay and Village courses are vintage Arnold Palmer designs; the Plantation Course is a strong Ben Crenshaw/Bill Coore design. See p. 442.

- **Wailea Courses** (Maui; ℂ 808/875-7450): On Maui's sunbaked south shore stands Wailea Resort, *the* hot spot for golf in the islands. Three resort courses complement a string of beachfront hotels: The Blue Course is an Arthur Jack Snyder design, while Robert Trent Jones, Jr., is the mastermind behind the Emerald and Gold courses. All three boast outstanding views of the Pacific and the mid-Hawaiian islands. See p. 443.

- **The Lanai Courses** (Lanai): For quality and seclusion, nothing in Hawaii can touch Lanai's two resort offerings. **The Experience at Koele** (p. 530), designed by Ted Robinson

and Greg Norman, and **The Challenge at Manele** (p. 530), a wonderful Jack Nicklaus effort with ocean views from every hole, both rate among Hawaii's best courses.

- **Poipu Bay Golf Course** (Kauai; ℂ 808/742-8711): On Kauai's flat, dry south shore is a 210-acre, links-style course designed by Robert Trent Jones, Jr. The course, which for years hosted the PGA Tour's Grand Slam of Golf, is not only scenically spectacular, but is also a lot of fun to play. A flock of native Hawaiian nene geese frequents the course's lakes, and you can often see whales, monk seals, and green sea turtles along the shore. See p. 601.

- **Princeville Golf Club** (Kauai; ℂ 800/826-1105): Here you'll find 45 of the best tropical holes of golf in the world, all the work of Robert Trent Jones, Jr. They range along green bluffs below sharp mountain peaks and offer stunning views in every direction. The 18-hole Prince course, one of the top three courses in Hawaii, provides a round of golf few ever forget. It winds along 390 acres of scenic tableland bisected by tropical jungles, waterfalls, streams, and ravines. See p. 601.

6 The Best Ways to Immerse Yourself in Hawaiian Culture

- **Experiencing the Hula:** For a real, authentic hula experience on Oahu, check out the **Bishop Museum** (p. 198), which has excellent performances on weekdays, or head to the Halekulani's **House Without a Key** (p. 237) at sunset to watch the enchanting Kanoelehua Miller dance beautiful hula under a century-old kiawe tree. The first week after Easter brings Hawaii's biggest and most prestigious hula extravaganza, the **Merrie Monarch Hula Festival**

(p. 35), at Hilo on the Big Island; tickets sell out by January 30, so reserve early. In May there's the **Molokai Ka Hula Piko Festival** (p. 500), at Molokai's Papohaku Beach Park, a wonderful day-long festival that celebrates the hula on the island where it was born.

- **Watching the Ancient Hawaiian Sport of Canoe Paddling** (Oahu): From February to September, on weekday evenings and weekend days, hundreds of canoe paddlers gather at

Ala Wai Canal and practice the Hawaiian sport of canoe paddling. Find a comfortable spot at Ala Wai Park, next to the canal, and watch this ancient sport come to life.

- **Attending a Hawaiian-Language Church Service** (Oahu): **Kawaiahao Church** (© 808/522-1333) is the Westminster Abbey of Hawaii. The vestibule is lined with portraits of the Hawaiian monarchy, many of whom were crowned in this very building. The coral church is a perfect setting in which to experience an all-Hawaiian service, held every Sunday at 9am, complete with Hawaiian song. Admission is free; let your conscience be your guide as to a donation. See p. 203.

- **Buying a Lei in Chinatown** (Oahu): There's actually a host of cultural sights and experiences to be had in Honolulu's Chinatown. Wander through this several-square-block area with its jumble of exotic shops offering herbs, Chinese groceries, and acupuncture services. Before you leave, be sure to check out the lei sellers on Maunakea Street (near N. Hotel St.), where Hawaii's finest leis go for as little as $5. If you'd like a little guidance, you can follow the walking tour on p. 210.

- **Listening to Old-Fashioned "Talk Story" with Hawaiian Song and Dance** (Big Island): Once a month, under a full moon, **"Twilight at Kalahuipua'a,"** a celebration of the Hawaiian culture that includes storytelling, singing, and dancing, takes place ocean-side at Mauna Lani Bay Resort (© **808/885-6622;** www.maunalaniculture.org/twilight). It hearkens back to another time in Hawaii when family and neighbors would gather on back porches to sing, dance, and "talk story." See the box "Old-Style Hawaiian Entertainment," in chapter 5.

- **Visiting Ancient Hawaii's Most Sacred Temple** (Big Island): On the Kohala Coast, where King Kamehameha the Great was born, stands Hawaii's oldest, largest, and most sacred religious site: the 1,500-year-old Mo'okini Heiau, used by kings to pray and offer human sacrifices. This massive three-story stone temple, dedicated to Ku, the Hawaiian god of war, was erected in A.D. 480. It's said that each stone was passed from hand to hand from Pololu Valley, 14 miles away, by 18,000 men who worked from sunset to sunrise. The best way to see this sacred site is to help out with the monthly cleanups when the *Kahuna Nui* (high priestess), Momi Mo'okini Lum, is on-site. See p. 322.

- **Hunting for Petroglyphs** (Big Island): Archaeologists are still uncertain exactly what these ancient rock carvings—the majority of which are found in the 233-acre Puako Petroglyph Archaeological District, near Mauna Lani Resort on the Kohala Coast—mean. The best time to hunt for these intricate depictions of ancient life is either early in the morning or late afternoon, when the angle of the sun lets you see the forms clearly. See "Kohala Coast Petroglyphs," under "Seeing the Sights," in chapter 5.

- **Exploring Puuhonua O Honaunau National Historical Park** (Big Island): This sacred site on the South Kona Coast was once a place of refuge and a revered place of rejuvenation. You can walk the same consecrated grounds where priests once conducted holy ceremonies and glimpse the ancient way of life in precontact Hawaii in the re-created 180-acre village. See p. 320.

The Welcoming Lei

There's nothing like a lei. The stunning tropical beauty of the delicate garland, the deliciously sweet fragrance of the blossoms, the sensual way the flowers curl softly around your neck. There's no doubt about it: Getting lei'd in Hawaii is a sensuous experience.

Leis are much more than just a decorative necklace of flowers; they're also one of the nicest ways to say hello, goodbye, congratulations, I salute you, my sympathies are with you, or I love you. The custom of giving leis can be traced back to Hawaii's very roots; according to chants, the first lei was given by Hiiaka, the sister of the volcano goddess Pele, who presented Pele with a lei of lehua blossoms on a beach in Puna.

During ancient times, leis given to *alii* (high-ranking chiefs) were accompanied by a bow, since it was *kapu* (forbidden) for a commoner to raise his arms higher than the king's head. The presentation of a kiss with a lei didn't come about until World War II; it's generally attributed to an entertainer who kissed an officer on a dare and then quickly presented him with her lei, saying it was an old Hawaiian custom. It wasn't then, but it sure caught on fast.

Lei making is a tropical art form. All leis are fashioned by hand in a variety of traditional patterns; some are sewn with hundreds of tiny blooms or shells, or bits of ferns and leaves. Some are twisted, some braided, some strung; all are presented with love. Every island has its own special flower lei—the lei of the land, so to speak. On Oahu the choice is *ilima*, a small orange flower. Big Islanders prefer the *lehua*, a large, delicate red puff. On Maui it's the *lokelani*, a small rose; on Kauai, it's the *mokihana*, a fragrant green vine and berry; on Molokai it's the *kukui*, the white blossom of a candlenut tree; and on Lanai it's the *kaunaoa,* a bright yellow moss. Residents of Niihau use the island's abundant seashells to make leis that were once prized by royalty and are now worth a small fortune.

Leis are available at all of the islands' airports. Other places to get wonderful, inexpensive leis are the half-dozen lei shops on **Maunakea Street** in Honolulu's Chinatown, and **Greene Acres Leis** (© 808/329-2399), off Kaimiminani Drive in the Kona Palisades subdivision, across from the Kona International Airport on the Big Island. If you plan ahead, you can also arrange to have a lei-greeter meet you and your travel party as you deplane; **Greeters of Hawaii** (© **800/366-8559,** 808/836-0161, or 808/836-3246) serves Honolulu, Kona (on the Big Island), Kahului (Maui), and Lihue (Kauai) airports.

Leis are the perfect symbol for the islands: They're given in the moment and their fragrance and beauty are enjoyed in the moment, but even after they fade, their spirit of aloha lives on. Welcome to Hawaii!

- **Visiting the Most Hawaiian Isle:** A time capsule of old Hawaii, Molokai allows you to experience real Hawaiian life in its most unsullied form. The island's people have woven the cultural values of ancient times into modern life. In addition to this rich community, you'll find the magnificent natural wonders it so cherishes: Hawaii's highest waterfall, its greatest collection of fish ponds, and the world's tallest sea cliffs, as well as sand dunes, coral reefs, rainforests, and gloriously empty beaches. The island is pretty much the same Molokai of generations ago. See chapter 7.

7 The Best Luxury Hotels & Resorts

- **Halekulani** (Oahu; © 800/367-2343; www.halekulani.com): When price is no object, this is really the only place to stay. An oasis of calm amid the buzz, this beach hotel is the finest Waikiki has to offer (heck, I think it's the finest in the state). Even if you don't stay here, pop by for a sunset mai tai to hear Sonny Kamehele sing the old *hapa-haole* tunes of the 1930s and 1940s while a lovely hula dancer sways to the music. See p. 119.

- **Royal Hawaiian** (Oahu; © 800/325-3535; www.sheraton.com): This flamingo-pink oasis, hidden away among blooming gardens within the concrete jungle of Waikiki, is a symbol of luxury. You can step back in time by staying in the rooms in the Historic Wing, which contain carved wooden doors, four-poster canopy beds, flowered wallpaper, and period furniture. One of Waikiki's best spas, **Abhasa** (© 808/922-8200; www.abhasa.com), is located on the property. See p. 121.

- **Kahala Hotel & Resort** (Oahu; © 800/367-2525; www.kahalaresort.com): After 11 years under the helm of the Mandarin Oriental Group, this grand old hotel changed management firms in 2006. The new firm promised to restore this elegant property to what it once was. The location alone offers a similarly wonderful compromise: Situated in one of Oahu's most prestigious residential areas, the Kahala offers the peace and serenity of a neighbor-island vacation, but with the conveniences of Waikiki just a 10-minute drive away. The lush, tropical grounds include an 800-foot crescent-shaped beach and a 26,000-square-foot lagoon (home to two bottle-nosed dolphins, sea turtles, and tropical fish). See p. 135.

- **Mauna Lani Bay Hotel & Bungalows** (Big Island; © 800/367-2323; www.maunalani.com): Burned out? In need of tranquillity and gorgeous surroundings? Look no further. Sandy beaches and lava tide pools are the focus of this serene seaside resort, where gracious hospitality is dispensed in a historic setting. From the lounge chairs on the pristine beach to the turndown service at night, everything here is done impeccably. The rooms are arranged to capture maximum ocean views, and they surround interior atrium gardens and pools in which endangered baby sea turtles are raised. A shoreline trail leads across the whole 3,200-acre resort, giving you an intimate glimpse into the ancient past, when people lived in lava caves and tended the large complex of fish ponds. See p. 262.

- **Four Seasons Resort Hualalai at Historic Kaupulehu** (Big Island; © 888/340-5662; www.fourseasons.com/hualalai): Private pools, unimpeded ocean views, excellent food, and a new 18-hole championship golf course—what more could any mortal want? This new low-impact, high-ticket hideaway under the dormant Hualalai Volcano ups the ante with its residential resort of two-story bungalows clustered around five seaside swimming pools on a black lagoon. See p. 252.

- **Hotel Hana-Maui** (Maui; © 800/321-HANA; www.hotelhanamaui.com): Picture Shangri-La, Hawaiian-style: 66 acres rolling down to the sea in a remote Hawaiian village, with a wellness center, two pools, and access to one of the best beaches in Hana. Cathedral ceilings, a plush feather bed, a giant-size soaking tub, Hawaiian artwork, bamboo hardwood floors—this is luxury. The white-sand beach (just a 5-min. shuttle away), a top-notch wellness center with some of the best massage therapists in Hawaii, and numerous activities (horseback riding, mountain biking, tennis, pitch-and-putt golf) all add up to make this one of the top resorts in the state. I highly recommend this little slice of paradise. See p. 394.

- **The Fairmont Kea Lani Maui** (Maui; ✆ **800/659-4100;** www. fairmont.com/kealani): This is the place to get your money's worth: For the price of a hotel room, you get an entire suite—plus a few extras. Each unit in this all-suite luxury hotel has a kitchenette, a living room with entertainment center and sofa bed (great if you have the kids in tow), a marble wet bar, an oversize marble bathroom with separate shower big enough for a party, a spacious bedroom, and a large lanai that overlooks the pools, lawns, and white-sand beach. See p. 387.

- **Four Seasons Resort Maui at Wailea** (Maui; ✆ **800/334-MAUI;** www. fourseasons.com/maui): This is the ultimate beach hotel for latter-day royals, with excellent cuisine, spacious rooms, gracious service, and Wailea Beach, one of Maui's best gold-sand strips, out the front door. Every guest room has at least a partial ocean view from a private lanai. The luxury suites, as big as some Honolulu condos, are full of marble and deluxe appointments. See p. 388.

- **The Lodge at Molokai Ranch** (Molokai; ✆ **888/627-8082;** www. molokairanch.com): This quaint

22-room inn in Maunaloa sits on 8 nicely landscaped acres in the rolling hills of Maunaloa town. Designed to resemble a 1930s-style Hawaii ranch owner's private home, the Lodge features a giant fireplace, huge wooden beam construction, panoramic views, and lots of details (cuffed cowboy boots beside the door, old books lining the shelves) to make it look and feel like a real ranch. Guests step back in time to a Hawaii of yesteryear. The beach is 6 miles and about a 20-minute car ride away. See p. 488.

- **Four Seasons Resort Lana'i at Manele Bay** (Lanai; ✆ **800/321-4666;** www. fourseasons.com/lanai): The well-known luxury hotel chain Four Seasons took over management of this 236-unit resort after a multimillion-dollar makeover in 2005. Perched on a sun-washed southern bluff overlooking Hulopoe Beach, one of Hawaii's best stretches of golden sand, this U-shaped hotel steps down the hillside to the pool and the beach. Designed as a traditional luxury beachfront hotel, the Manele Bay features open, airy, oversize rooms, each with a breath-taking view of the big blue Pacific. The guest rooms have been redone in a clean, crisp style of an elegant oceanside Hawaiian resort with 40-inch, flatscreen LCD TVs, huge marble bathrooms, and semiprivate lanais. See p. 520.

- **Four Seasons Resort Lana'i The Lodge at Koele** (Lanai; ✆ **800/321-4666;** www.fourseasons.com/lanai): The sister hotel to Manele Bay (see above), this luxury resort was renovated and rebranded a Four Seasons in 2006. A $50-million renovation gave all 102 guest rooms new carpeting, glass bath partitions, signature Four Seasons beds, 42-inch LCD flatscreen TVs, new furniture, new fabrics, and high-speed Internet. This small inn, which resembles a grand English country estate, was built in 1991 and needed the renovation—the new look is spectacular. See p. 521.

- **Grand Hyatt Kauai Resort & Spa** (Kauai; ℭ **800/55-HYATT;** www. kauai.hyatt.com): This Art Deco beach hotel recalls Hawaii in the 1920s—before the crash—when gentlemen in blue blazers and ladies in summer frocks came to the islands to learn to surf and play the ukulele. The hotel's architecture and location, on the sunny side of Kauai, make this the island's best hotel. The beach is a bit too rough for swimming, but the saltwater swimming pool is the biggest on the island. An old-fashioned reading room by the sea houses club chairs, billiards, and a bar well

stocked with cognac and port. Nearby diversions include golf, horseback riding, and the shops of Koloa, a former plantation town. See p. 547.

- **Princeville Resort Kauai** (Kauai; ℭ **800/826-4400;** www.princeville. com): This palace of green marble and sparkling chandeliers recalls Hawaii's monarchy period of the 19th century. It's set in one of the most remarkable locations in the world, on a cliff between the crystal-blue waters of Hanalei Bay and steepled mountains; you arrive on the ninth floor and go down to get to the beach. Opulent rooms with magnificent views and all the activities of Princeville and Hanalei make this one of Hawaii's finest resorts. See p. 560.

8 The Best Moderately Priced Accommodations

- **New Otani Kaimana Beach Hotel** (Oahu; ℭ **800/356-8264;** www. kaimana.com): This is one of Waikiki's best-kept secrets: a boutique hotel nestled right on a lovely stretch of beach at the foot of Diamond Head, with Kapiolani Park just across the street. The Waikiki-side guest rooms are teeny-tiny, with barely room for two, but are tastefully decorated and open onto lanais with ocean and park views (plus they start at just $150 a night). A good budget buy is the park-view studio with kitchen. You can stock up with provisions from the on-site Mini-Mart. See p. 131.

- **Ke Iki Beach Bungalows** (Oahu; ℭ **866/638-8229;** www.keikibeach. com): This collection of studio, one-, and two-bedroom cottages snuggled on a large lot with its own 200-foot stretch of white-sand beach between two legendary surf spots (Waimea Bay and Banzai Pipeline) has been totally renovated to the tune of $1

million. Most units are compact—the kitchens and living rooms are small and the bedrooms even smaller—but they're affordable, with rates starting at $120 a night. And with the ocean just outside, how much time are you going to spend inside anyway? The winter waves are too rough for most swimmers, but there's a large lava reef nearby with tide pools to explore and, on the other side, Shark's Cove, a relatively protected snorkeling area. Nearby are tennis courts and a jogging path. All units have full kitchens and their own barbecue areas. See p. 139.

- **Holualoa Inn** (Big Island; ℭ **800/ 392-1812;** www.holualoainn.com): The quiet, secluded setting of this B&B—on 40 pastoral acres just off the main drag of the artsy village of Holualoa, 1,350 feet above Kailua-Kona—provides stunning panoramic views of the entire coast. This contemporary 7,000-square-foot Hawaiian home built of golden woods has six private suites (starting at $225) and window-walls that roll back to embrace the gardens and views. Cows graze on the bucolic pastures below the garden Jacuzzi and pool, and the coffee plantation on the property is the source of the morning brew. See p. 257.

- **Kona Tiki Hotel** (Big Island; ✆ 808/ 329-1425; www.konatiki.com): Right on the ocean, away from the hustle and bustle of downtown Kailua-Kona, is one of the hottest budget deals in Hawaii: tastefully decorated rooms with private lanais overlooking the ocean, starting at just $66 a night! Although it's called a hotel, this small, family-run operation is more like a large B&B, with plenty of friendly conversation around the pool at the morning continental breakfast buffet. See p. 256.

- **Waipio Wayside B&B Inn** (Big Island; ✆ 800/833-8849; www.waipio wayside.com): Jackie Horne renovated this 1938 Hamakua sugar supervisor's home—nestled among fruit trees and surrounded with sweet-smelling ginger, fragile orchids, and blooming birds of paradise—and transformed it into a gracious B&B. Just minutes from the Waipio Valley Lookout and Honokaa village, this comfy five-bedroom house abounds with thoughtful touches, such as a help-yourself tea-and-cookies bar with 26 different kinds of tea. Jackie's friendly hospitality and excellent continental breakfasts really round out the experience. Rooms start at $99 for two. See p. 267.

- **Old Wailuku Inn at Ulupono** (Maui; ✆ 800/305-4899; www.maui inn.com): This 1924 former plantation manager's home, lovingly restored, offers a genuine old Hawaii experience. The theme is Hawaii of the 1920s and 1930s, with decor, design, and landscaping to match. The spacious rooms are gorgeously outfitted with exotic ohia-wood floors, high ceilings, and traditional Hawaiian quilts. A full gourmet breakfast is served on the enclosed back lanai or, if you prefer, delivered to your room. The inn is located in the old historic area of Wailuku, about 10 to 15 minutes to the beach. Once you settle in, you may not want to leave—and with rooms starting at $140 for a double, you can afford to stay a while. See p. 366.

- **Pineapple Inn Maui** (Maui; ✆ 877/ 212-MAUI [6284]; www.pineapple innmaui.com): This charming inn (only four rooms, plus a cottage) is not only an exquisite find, but a terrific value. Located in the residential Maui Meadows area, with panoramic ocean views, this two-story inn is expertly landscaped in tropical flowers and plants with a lily pond in the front and a giant saltwater pool and Jacuzzi overlooking the ocean. Each of the soundproof rooms is expertly decorated with a small kitchenette, a comfy bed, free wireless Internet access, TV/VCR, and an incredible view off your own private lanai. Prices start at $109. If you need more room, they also offer a darling two-bedroom, one-bathroom cottage. See p. 385.

- **Dunbar Beachfront Cottages** (Molokai; ✆ 800/673-0520; www.molokai-beachfront-cottages.com): Each of these green-and-white plantation-style cottages sits on its own secluded beach—you'll feel like you're on your own private island. Impeccable decor, a magical setting, and reasonable rates ($170 for two) make these cottages a must-stay. See p. 491.

- **Hotel Lanai** (Lanai; ✆ 800/795-7211; www.hotellanai.com): Lanai's only budget lodging is a simple, down-home, plantation-era relic that has recently been Laura Ashley–ized. The Hotel Lanai is homey, funky, and fun—and, best of all, a real bargain (starting at $125 for two) compared to its ritzy neighbors. See p. 521.

- **Hanalei Surf Board House** (Kauai; **808/826-9825;** www.hanaleisurfboard house.com): Book well in advance—this place is so fabulous, it will go fast! Just a block from the beach, these two incredibly decorated studio units are a steal at $150. Host Simon Potts, a former record company executive from England, has filled his two studios (with kitchenettes) with imaginative decor choices: One of them sports a whimsical cowgirl theme, the other is filled with Elvis Presley memorabilia. But the best reason to stay here (besides the 2-min. walk to the beach or a 10-min.

walk to downtown Hanalei) is Simon himself—his stories about the record industry will keep you howling with laughter for hours. See p. 563.

- **Kauai Country Inn** (Kauai; ℂ **808/ 821-0207;** www.kauaicountryinn. com): This old-fashioned country inn, nestled in the rolling hills behind Kapaa, seems too good to be true. Each of the four suites (starting at just $99) is uniquely decorated in Hawaiian Art Deco, complete with hardwood floors, private bathrooms, kitchen or kitchenette, your own computer with high-speed Internet connection, and lots of little extra amenities. Everything is top-drawer, from the furniture to the Sub-Zero refrigerator. They recently added a two-bedroom country cottage for families with young children. The grounds are immaculate, and you can pick as much organic fruit as you want. See p. 558.

9 The Best Places to Stay with the Kids

- **Hilton Hawaiian Village Beach Resort & Spa** (Oahu; ℂ **800/ HILTONS;** www.hawaiianvillage. hilton.com): The Rainbow Express, Hilton's year-round daily program of activities for children ages 5 to 12, offers a wide range of educational and fun activities for $56 a day, including lunch. Everything about this hotel is kid-friendly, from the wildlife parading about the grounds to the submarine dives offered just out front. In three of the resort's restaurants, kids ages 4 to 11 eat free. See p. 114.

- **J. W. Marriott Ihilani Resort & Spa at Ko Olina Resort** (Oahu; ℂ **800/ 626-4446;** www.ihilani.com): This resort on Oahu's virgin leeward coast is a haven of relaxation and tropical fun for travelers of all ages. The Keiki Beachcomber Club, for children ages 5 to 12, is available daily. Activities

(9am–3pm) range from kite-flying, tide-pool exploration, and snorkeling to Hawaiian cultural activities. The cost is $58 per child. See p. 140.

- **Kona Village Resort** (Big Island; ℂ **800/367-5290;** www.konavillage. com): This is a parent's dream: custom-designed programs to entertain your kids, from tots to teenagers, from dawn to well after dusk, all at no charge. There's even a dinner seating for children, so Mom and Dad can enjoy an intimate dinner for two later in the evening. See p. 252.

- **The Fairmont Orchid, Hawaii** (Big Island; ℂ **800/845-9905;** www. fairmont.com/orchid): The Keiki Aloha program, for kids 5 to 12 years old, features supervised activities from watersports to Hawaiian cultural games for $85 for the full day. The resort has some great money-saving deals; for example, children 5 and under eat free at various restaurants in the resort. See p. 263.

- **Four Seasons Resort Maui at Wailea** (Maui; ℭ 800/334-MAUI; www.four seasons.com/maui): The most kid-friendly hotel on Maui not only offers a complimentary kids program year-round and an everyday activities center (daily 9am–5pm), but also makes children feel welcome with extras such as complimentary milk and cookies on their first day and children's menus at all resort restaurants and even from room service. See p. 388.

- **Hyatt Regency Maui** (Maui; ℭ 800/233-1234; www.maui.hyatt.com): The Camp Hyatt program, for kids 5 to 12 years old, operates daily from 9am to 3pm and offers young guests a range of activities, from "Olympic Games" to a scavenger hunt. The cost is $65 to $80 for a full day. See p. 371.

- **Aloha Beach House** (Molokai; ℭ 888/828-1008; www.molokai vacation.com): This Hawaiian-style beach house sits right on the white-sand beach of Waialua on the lush East End. Perfect for families, this impeccably decorated, two-bedroom, 1,600-square-foot beach house has a huge, airy living/dining/kitchen area that opens out to an old-fashioned porch perfect for meals or just sitting in the comfy chairs and watching the clouds roll by. It's fully equipped, from the complete kitchen to a VCR (and library of videos), to all the beach toys you can think of. A family of five can stay here for just $240 to $280. See p. 490.

- **Grand Hyatt Kauai Resort & Spa** (Kauai; ℭ 800/55-HYATT; www. kauai.hyatt.com): In addition to the Camp Hyatt program (for kids 3–12; $70 for a full day), it's the collection of swimming pools—freshwater and salt, with slides, waterfalls, and secret lagoons—that makes this oceanfront Hyatt a real kids' paradise. During the summer months and the holiday season, there's Rock Hyatt, an activity room for teens to gather in and play electronic games. Summertime also boasts Family Fun Theatre Nights, when the whole family can enjoy a showing of one of the more than 400 movies filmed on Kauai. See p. 547.

10 The Best Resort Spas

- **SpaHalekulani, Halekulani hotel** (Oahu; ℭ 808/923-2311; www. halekulani.com): This is Waikiki's first spa to explore the healing traditions of the Pacific islands, as well as Hawaii. Like everything else at the top-rated Halekulani hotel, the spa is truly a heavenly experience, from the time you step into the elegantly appointed, intimate spa and experience the foot massage to the last whiff of fragrant maile, their signature scent. Spa connoisseurs should try something unique, like the Polynesian Nonu, a Samoan-inspired massage using stones. See p. 119.

- **Spa Suites at the Kahala** (Oahu; ℭ 808/739-8938): The Kahala has taken the concept of spa as a journey into relaxation to a new level, with former garden rooms converted to individual spas, each with a glass-enclosed shower, private changing area, infinity-edge deep soaking Jacuzzi tub, and personal relaxation area. No detail is overlooked, from the warm foot bath when you arrive to the refreshing hot tea served on your personal enclosed garden lanai after your relaxation treatment. See p. 135.

- **Turtle Bay Resort** (Oahu; ℭ 800/203-3650; www.turtlebayresort.com):

This Zen-like spa positioned on the ground floor facing the ocean has six treatment rooms, a meditation waiting area, an outdoor workout area, plus a complete fitness center and a private elevator to the rooms on the second floor, reserved for guests getting spa treatments. See p. 138.

- **Ihilani Spa at the J. W. Marriott Ihilani Resort & Spa** (Oahu; ✆ 800/626-4446; www.ihilani.com): An oasis by the sea, this free-standing 35,000-square-foot facility is dedicated to the traditional spa definition of "health by water." This modern, multistoried spa, filled with floor-to-ceiling glass looking out on green tropical plants, combines Hawaiian products with traditional therapies to produce some of the best water treatments in the state. You'll also find a fitness center, tennis courts, and a bevy of aerobic and stretching classes. See p. 140.

- **Hualalai Sports Club and Spa at Four Seasons Resort Hualalai at Historic Kaupulehu** (Big Island; ✆ 888/340-5662; www.fourseasons.com/hualalai): It's easy to see why some 6,000 *Condé Nast* readers voted this 13,000-square-foot facility their favorite resort spa. Five of its 16 treatment rooms are thatched huts (with bamboo privacy screens) nestled into a tropical garden. This is the place to come to be pampered. The fitness facilities, classes, and adventure activities are all excellent, but the attentive service and dreamy spa facilities are what you will remember long after your vacation. See p. 252.

- **Kohala Spa at the Hilton Waikoloa Village** (Big Island; ✆ 800/HILTONS; www.hiltonwaikoloavillage.com): The Big Island's oldest (since 1989) spa has something for everyone, including 33 treatment rooms, 50 classes, and a variety of sports ranging from racquetball to indoor rock climbing. Treatments are on the cutting edge and include such unique therapies as acupuncture facials and astrological readings. Spend the day luxuriating in the lava whirlpool, steam room, and sauna before or after your treatment. See p. 264.

- **Spa Grande at the Grand Wailea Resort Hotel & Spa** (Maui; ✆ 800/888-6100; www.grandwailea.com): This is Hawaii's biggest spa, at 50,000 square feet, with 40 treatment rooms. The spa incorporates the best of the Old World (romantic ceiling murals, larger-than-life Roman-style sculptures, mammoth Greek columns, huge European tubs), the finest Eastern traditions (a full Japanese-style traditional bath and various exotic treatments from India), and the lure of the islands (tropical foliage, ancient Hawaiian treatments, and island products). This spa has everything from a top fitness center to a menu of classes and is constantly on the cutting edge of the latest trends. See p. 388.

- **The Spa at Four Seasons Resort Maui at Wailea** (Maui; ✆ 800/334-MAUI; www.fourseasons.com/maui): This relaxing oasis in the luxurious Four Seasons offers a menu of pampering—traditional Hawaii massage to Ayurvedic, plus Vichy shower treatments, body wraps, body scrubs, facials, even ocean aquacranial massage for the ultimate in relaxation. You don't just get a massage here; you can choose from a list of therapies: hot stone, reiki, jin shin do, Swedish, aromatherapy, shiatsu, reflexology, and Thai. See p. 388.

- **Spa Moana at the Hyatt Regency Maui** (Maui; ✆ 800/233-1234; www.maui.hyatt.com): You cannot match the location—this is Hawaii's only oceanfront spa. The 20,000-square-foot spa houses 15 relaxing

Pampering in Paradise

Hawaii's spas have raised the art of relaxation and healing to a new level. The traditional Greco-Roman-style spas have evolved into airy, open facilities that embrace the Tropics. Spa-goers in Hawaii want to hear the sound of the ocean, smell the salt air, and feel the caress of the warm breeze. They want to experience Hawaiian products and traditional treatments they can get only here.

Today's spas offer a wide diversity of treatments. Massage options include Hawaiian lomilomi, Swedish, aromatherapy, craniosacral (massaging the head), shiatsu (no oil, just deep thumb pressure on acupuncture points), Thai (another oilless massage involving stretching), and hot stone. There are even side-by-side massages for couples, and duo massages—two massage therapists working on you at once.

Body treatments, for the entire body or just the face, involve a variety of herbal wraps, masks, or scrubs using a range of ingredients from seaweed to salt to mud, with or without accompanying aromatherapy.

After you have been rubbed and scrubbed, most spas offer an array of water treatments—a sort of hydromassage in a tub with jets and an assortment of colored crystals, oils, and scents.

Those are just the traditional treatments. Most spas also offer a range of alternative healthcare like acupuncture and chiropractic, and more exotic treatments like ayurvedic and siddha from India or reiki from Japan. Some offer cutting-edge treatments, like the Grand Wailea Resort's full-spectrum color-light therapy pod (based on NASA's work with astronauts).

Spas also offer a range of fitness facilities (weights, racquetball, tennis, golf) and classes (yoga, aerobics, spinning, tai chi, kickboxing). Several even offer adventure fitness packages (from bicycling to snorkeling). For the less active, most spas have salons dedicated to hair and nail care.

Of course, all this pampering doesn't come cheap. Massages are generally $150 to $250 for 50 minutes and $250 to $295 for 80 minutes; body treatments are in the $150-to-$250 range; and alternative healthcare treatments can be as high as $200 to $300. But you may think it's worth the expense to banish your tension and stress.

treatment rooms and features one of the island's best full-service fitness centers, plus a relaxation lounge, a romantic couples' treatment room, a salon/retail shop, and new treatments for kids and teenagers. See p. 371.

- **Spa Kea Lani at The Fairmont Kea Lani Maui** (Maui; ② 800/659-4100; www.fairmont.com/kealani): Come to this intimate Art Deco boutique spa

(just a little over 5,000 sq. ft., with nine treatment rooms) for personal and private attention. The fitness center is just next door. See p. 387.

- **ANARA Spa at the Grand Hyatt Kauai Resort & Spa** (Kauai; ② 808/240-6440; www.anaraspa.com): Come here to get rid of stress and to be soothed and pampered in a Hawaiian atmosphere, where the spirit of aloha reigns. An elegant 25,000-square-foot spa, ANARA (A New Age Restorative Approach) focuses on Hawaiian culture and healing, with some 16 treatment rooms, a lap pool, fitness facilities, lava rock showers that open to the tropical air, outdoor whirlpools, a 24-head Swiss shower, Turkish steam rooms, Finnish saunas, and botanical soaking tubs. Recent renovations make this spa even more serene and relaxing. The four-handed massage (two therapists at once) is not be missed. See p. 547.

11 The Best Dining, Hawaii Style

• **Tropical Fruit: Mangosteen,** the queen of fruit in Indonesia, is the sensation at the Hilo Farmers Market on the Big Island. Mangosteen's elegant purple skin and soft, white, floral-flavored flesh (like litchi, but more custardlike) make this fruit a sure winner.

The **mango** is always a much-anticipated feature of late spring and summer. **Hayden mangoes** are universally loved for their plump, juicy flesh and brilliant skins. **White Piries,** with their resinous flavor and fine, fiberless flesh, are even better; this rare and ambrosial variety can be found in Honolulu's Chinatown or at roadside fruit stands in rural Oahu. Watch for the **Rapoza,** a new large, sweet, fiberless mango introduced to Hawaii several years ago.

Kahuku papayas—firm, fleshy, dark orange, and so juicy they sometimes squirt—are the ones to watch for on menus and in markets; check out the roadside stands in Kahuku on Oahu, and at supermarkets. **Sunrise papayas** from Kapoho and Kauai are also top-notch.

White, acid-free, extra-sweet, and grown on Kauai and the Big Island, **Sugarloaf pineapples** are the new rage. Hilo is the town for **litchis** (also known as lychees) in summer, but Honolulu's Chinatown markets carry them, too. **Ka'u oranges,** grown in the volcanic soil of the southern Big Island, are available in supermarkets and health-food stores. Don't be fooled by their brown, ugly skin—they're juicy, thin-skinned, and sweet as honey.

• **Noodles:** Ramen, udon, saimin, pho, pasta, chow mein—Hawaii is the epicenter of ethnic noodle stands and houses, with many recommendable and inexpensive choices. **Jimbo's Restaurant** (Oahu; ☎ 808/947-2211), a neighborhood staple, is tops for freshly made udon with generous toppings and a homemade broth (p. 164). On the neighbor islands, noodle-mania prevails at **Hamura's Saimin Stand** (Kauai; ☎ 808/245-3271), where saimin and teriyaki sticks have replaced hamburgers and pizza as the late-night comfort-food tradition (p. 566). **Nori's Saimin & Snacks** (Big Island; ☎ 808/935-9133) is the place in charming Hilo for consummate saimin of every stripe (p. 293).

• **Plate Lunches: Zippy's** (21 locations throughout Oahu; call ☎ 808/973-0880 for the one nearest you) is a household word in Hawaii. Other favorite plate-lunch spots on Oahu include **Kakaako Kitchen** (☎ 808/596-7488), Ward Centre (p. 233), serving dinner at indoor and outdoor tables; **I ♥ Country Cafe** (☎ 808/596-8108); and **Yama's Fish Market** (☎ 808/941-9994), where the chocolate/macadamia nut cookies and chocolate biscotti have legions of fans. On Maui, **Pauwela Cafe** (☎ 808/575-9242; p. 420) serves gourmet feasts from a tiny kitchen, and **Aloha Mixed Plate** (© 808/661-3322; p. 405) lets you nosh on fabulous shoyu chicken at ocean's edge—and with a mai tai, too. On Kauai, **Pono Market** (© 808/822-4581; p. 567), **Fish Express** (© 808/245-9918; p. 566), and **Koloa Fish Market** (© 808/742-6199; p. 566) are at the top of the plate-lunch pyramid.

- **Shave Ice:** Like surfing, shave ice is synonymous with Haleiwa, the North Shore Oahu town where **Matsumoto Shave Ice** (© 808/637-4827; p. 223) serves mounds of the icy treat. Shave ice is even better over ice cream and adzuki beans.
- **Other Mighty Morsels:** Poi biscotti from the **Poi Company,** available at supermarkets and gourmet outlets, is the consummate accompaniment to another island phenomenon, Kona

coffee. Coffee growers of highest esteem (all based on the Big Island, of course), include: **Rooster Farms** (© 808/328-9173), which sells and ships only organic coffees; **Bong Brothers** (© 808/328-9289); **Kona Blue Sky Coffee Company** (© 808/322-1700); **Langenstein Farms** (© 808/328-8356); and **Holualoa Kona Coffee Company** (© 800/334-0348). See the box "Kona Coffee Craze!" on p. 281.

The buttery, chocolate-dipped shortbread cookies of **Big Island Candies** (Big Island; © 808/935-8890; p. 349) are worth every calorie and every dollar. From Kauai, Hanapepe town's venerable **Taro Ko taro chips** (© 808/335-5586 for the factory; p. 619) are a crunchy snack neighbor islanders drive long miles to find.

12 The Best Restaurants

- **Alan Wong's Restaurant** (Oahu; © 808/949-2526): Master strokes at this shrine of Hawaii Regional Cuisine include warm California rolls made with salmon roe, wasabi, and Kona lobster instead of rice; luau lumpia with butterfish and *kalua* pig; and ginger-crusted fresh onaga. Opihi shooters and day-boat scallops in season are a must, and grilled lamb chops are a perennial special. The menu changes daily, but the flavors never lose their sizzle. See p. 163.
- **Chef Mavro Restaurant** (Oahu; © 808/944-4714): Honolulu is abuzz over the wine pairings and elegant cuisine of George Mavrothalassitis, the culinary wizard and James Beard Award–winner from Provence who turned La Mer (at the Halekulani) and Seasons (at the Four Seasons Resort Wailea) into temples of fine dining. He brought his award-winning signature dishes with him

and continues to prove his ingenuity with dazzling a la carte and prix-fixe ($66–$93) menus. See p. 162.
- **Hoku's** (Oahu; © 808/739-8780): Elegant without being stuffy, and creative without being overwrought, the fine-dining room of the Kahala offers elegant lunches and dinners, and one of Oahu's best Sunday brunches. This is fusion that really works—European finesse with an island touch. The ocean view, open kitchen, and astonishing bamboo floor are stellar features. Reflecting the restaurant's cross-cultural influences, the kitchen is equipped with a kiawe grill, an Indian tandoori oven, and Szechuan woks. See p. 167.
- **La Mer** (Oahu; © 808/923-2311): This romantic, elegant dining room at Waikiki's Halekulani is the only AAA Five-Diamond restaurant in the state. The second-floor, open-sided room, with views of Diamond Head

and the sound of trade winds rustling the nearby coconut fronds, is the epitome of fine dining. Michelin award–winning chef Yves Garnier melds classical French influences with fresh island ingredients. It's pricey but worth it. Men are required to wear jackets (they have a selection if you didn't pack one). See p. 141.

- **3660 on the Rise** (Oahu; © 808/ 737-1177): Ever since *Wine Spectator* gave this restaurant its "Award of Excellence," this place has been packed, and with good reason. In his 200-seat restaurant, chef Russell Siu adds an Asian or local touch to the basics: rack of lamb with macadamia nuts, filet of catfish in *ponzu* sauce, and seared ahi salad with grilled shiitake mushrooms, a local favorite. See p. 165.

- **Roy's Restaurant** (Oahu; © 808/ 396-7697): Good food still reigns at this busy, noisy flagship dining room in Hawaii Kai with the trademark open kitchen. Roy Yamaguchi's deft way with local ingredients, nostalgic ethnic preparations, and fresh fish makes his menu, which changes daily, a novel experience every time. See p. 168.

- **Merriman's** (Big Island; © 808/885-6822): Chef Peter Merriman, one of the founders of Hawaii Regional Cuisine, displays his creativity at this Waimea eatery, a premier Hawaii attraction. Dishes include his signature wok-charred ahi, kung pao shrimp, or lamb from nearby Kahua Ranch. His famous platters of seafood and meats are among the many reasons this is still the best— and busiest—dining spot in Waimea. See p. 286.

- **Son'z Maui at Swan Court** (Maui; © 808/667-4506; www.sonzmaui. com): For 30 years, the Swan Court was *the* dining experience at the Hyatt Regency Maui. When Tri-Star Restaurant Group CEO Aaron Placourakis (who also owns Nick's Fishmarket, see p. 144) took over this restaurant, he and executive chef Geno Sarmiento knew they wanted to hit a home run every night with the cuisine. The restaurant already had perhaps the most romantic location in Maui, overlooking a manmade lagoon with white and black swans swimming by and the rolling surf of the Pacific in the distance. The culinary team's creative dishes, made with fresh local ingredients (Kula corn and strawberries, Ono Farms avocados, Hana hearts of palm, Maui Cattle Company beef, fresh Hawaiian fish, and sweet Maui onions) plus top-notch service and a relaxing atmosphere make this gem one of Maui's best restaurants. See p. 406.

- **Haliimaile General Store** (Maui; © 808/572-2666): Bev Gannon, one of the 12 original Hawaii Regional Cuisine chefs, is still going strong at her foodie haven in the pineapple fields. You'll dine at tables set on old wood floors under high ceilings, in a peach-colored room emblazoned with works by local artists. Gannon's Texas roots shine through in her food, a blend of eclectic American with ethnic touches that puts an innovative spin on Hawaii Regional Cuisine. See p. 416.

- **Pineapple Grill Kapalua** (Maui; © 808/669-9600): If you have only 1 night to eat on the island of Maui, this is the place to go. In fact, if you eat here at the beginning of your Maui trip, you are definitely going to want to come back! Executive chef Joey Macadangdang (a protégé of Roy Yamaguchi of Roy's Restaurant p. 168), is a genius, combining Asian/Filipino ingredients into culinary masterpieces. You'll find lots of tasty sandwiches and salads at lunch, and a continental-style breakfast in the morning—all served in a very Maui-like atmosphere overlooking the rolling hills of the Kapalua Golf Course out to the Pacific Ocean. See p. 409.

- **Ihilani** (Lanai; © **808/565-2296**): A number of top Hawaii chefs (such as Phillippe Padovani and Edwin Goto) have each added a bit of their own style during their tenure here, but the common denominator is the melding of Mediterranean with Island cuisine. The result is Lanai's top gourmet restaurant, in a formal atmosphere with inspiring food. The latest incarnation of this classy restaurant, overlooking the resort and the ocean beyond, is traditional Italian cuisine, priced moderately for the Four Seasons Resort Lana'i at Manele Bay. See p. 522.

- **Hanapepe Cafe & Espresso Bar** (Kauai; © **808/335-5011**): This is one of those places that locals know about and generally visitors are not aware of. Nestled in the quaint little town on the west side of Kauai, this small, wholesome cafe boasts a casual, winning ambience and some of the most creative cuisine around. See p. 573.

- **Dondero's** (Kauai; © **808/742-1234**): If you're looking for a romantic dinner, Dondero's is hard to beat. Dine either under the stars overlooking the ocean or tucked away at an intimate table surrounded by inlaid marble floors, ornate imported floor tiles, and Franciscan murals. You get all this atmosphere plus the best Italian cuisine on the island, served with efficiency. It's hard to have a bad experience here. Dinners are pricey but worth every penny. See p. 569.

13 The Best Spots for Sunset Cocktails

- **Duke's Canoe Club,** at the Outrigger Waikiki (Oahu; © **808/922-2268**): It's crowded in the evening, but who can resist Hawaiian music with Waikiki sand still on your feet? Come in from the beach or the street—it's always a party at Duke's. Entertainment here is tops, reaching a crescendo at sunset. See p. 237.

- **House Without a Key,** at the Halekulani (Oahu; © **808/923-2311**): Oahu's quintessential sunset oasis offers a view of Diamond Head, great hula and steel-guitar music, and the best mai tais on the island—all under a century-old kiawe tree. Even jaded locals are unable to resist the lure. See p. 237.

- **Mai Tai Bar,** at the Royal Hawaiian Hotel (Oahu; © **808/923-7311**): This bar without walls is perched a few feet from the sand, with pleasing views of the south shore and the Waianae Mountains. Surfers and paddlers ride the waves while Diamond Head acquires a golden sunset halo. Sip a mighty mai tai while Carmen and Keith Haugen serenade you. See p. 237.

- **Sunset Lanai Lounge,** at the New Otani Kaimana Beach Hotel (Oahu; © **808/923-1555**): The hau tree here shaded Robert Louis Stevenson as he wrote poems to Princess Kaiulani; today it frames the ocean view from the Sunset Lanai Lounge. This lounge is the favorite watering hole of Diamond Head–area beachgoers, who love Sans Souci beach, the ocean view, the mai tais, and the live music during weekend sunset hours. See p. 131.

- **Jameson's by the Sea** (Oahu; © **808/637-6272**): The mai tais here are dubbed the best in surf city, and the view, though not perfect, doesn't hurt, either. Across the street from the harbor, this open-air roadside oasis is a happy stop for North Shore wave-watchers and sunset-savvy sightseers. See p. 170.

- **Huggo's on the Rocks** (Big Island; (C) **808/329-1493**): Here's a thatched-bar fantasy that's *really* on the rocks. This mound of thatch, rock, and grassy-sandy ground right next to Huggo's restaurant is a sunset lover's nirvana. Sip a tropical drink while reclining on a chaise and nosh on Island-style appetizers while the ocean laps at your feet. See p. 276.
- **Beach Tree Bar & Grill,** at the Four Seasons Resort Hualalai (Big Island; (C) **808/325-8000**): The bar on the beach seats only a handful, but the restaurant will accept the overflow.

This is the finest sunset perch in North Kona, with consummate people-watching, tasty drinks, and the gorgeous ocean. The open-air restaurant, with Hawaiian music and hula dancing at sunset, also serves excellent fare. See p. 276.

- **Kimo's** (Maui; (C) **808/661-4811**): An oceanfront dining room and deck, upstairs dining, and happy-hour drinks draw a fun-loving Lahaina crowd. Nibble on sashimi or nachos and take in the views of Lanai and Molokai. See p. 404.
- **Hula Grill** (Maui; (C) **808/667-6636**): Sit outdoors at the Barefoot Bar, order drinks and macadamia nut and crab won tons, and marvel at the wonders of West Maui, where the sun sets slowly and Lanai looks like a giant whale offshore. It's simply magical. See p. 407.

Planning Your Trip to Hawaii

Hawaii has so many places to explore, things to do, sights to see—it can be bewildering to plan your trip with so much vying for your attention. Where to start? That's where I come in. In the pages that follow, I've compiled everything you need to know to plan your ideal trip to Hawaii.

The first thing to do: Decide where you want to go. Read through each chapter (especially each chapter introduction) to see which islands fit the profile and offer the activities that you're looking for. I strongly recommend that you **limit your island-hopping to one island per week.** If you decide to go to more than one in a week, be warned: You could spend much of your precious vacation time in airports and checking in and out of hotels. Not much fun!

My second tip is to **fly directly to the island of your choice;** doing so can save you a 2-hour layover in Honolulu and another plane ride. Oahu, the Big Island, Maui, and Kauai now all receive direct flights from the mainland; if you're heading to Molokai or Lanai, you'll have the easiest connections if you fly into Honolulu.

So let's get on with the process of planning your trip. Searching out the best deals and planning your dream vacation to Hawaii should be half the fun.

1 Visitor Information & Maps

For information about traveling in Hawaii, contact the **Hawaii Visitors and Convention Bureau (HVCB),** Suite 801, Waikiki Business Plaza, 2270 Kalakaua Ave., Honolulu, HI 96815 (© **800/GO-HAWAII** or 808/923-1811; www.go hawaii.com). The bureau publishes the helpful *Accommodations and Car Rental Guide* and supplies free brochures, maps, and *Islands of Aloha* magazine, the official HVCB magazine. If you want information about working and living in Hawaii, contact the **Chamber of Commerce of Hawaii,** 1132 Bishop St., Suite 402, Honolulu, HI 96813 (© **808/545-4300;** www.cochawaii.com).

INFORMATION ON HAWAII'S PARKS

Hawaii has several national parks and historical sites—four on the Big Island, one each on Maui, Oahu, and Molokai. The following offices can supply you with hiking and camping information (or check online at www.nps.gov):

• On the **Big Island: Hawaii Volcanoes National Park,** P.O. Box 52, Hawaii National Park, HI 96718 (© **808/985-6000**); **Puuhonua o Honaunau National Historical Park,** P.O. Box 129, Honaunau, HI 96726 (© **808/328-2326**); **Puukohola Heiau National Historic Site,**

Hawaii on the Web

Listed below are some of the most useful Hawaii sites.

- Hawaii Visitors and Convention Bureau: www.gohawaii.com
- Hawaii State Vacation Planner: www.hshawaii.com
- The Hawaiian Language Website: www.geocities.com/~olelo
- Planet Hawaii: www.planet-hawaii.com
- Oahu Visitors Bureau: www.visit-oahu.com
- Big Island's Kona-Kohala Resort Association: www.kohalacoastresorts.com
- Big Island Visitors Bureau: www.bigisland.org
- Maui Visitors Bureau: www.visitmaui.com
- Maui Net: www.maui.net
- Maui's Kaanapali Beach Resort Association: www.kaanapaliresort.com
- Maui Island Currents (arts and culture): www.islandcurrents.com
- Molokai information: www.molokai-hawaii.com
- Kauai Visitors Bureau: www.kauaivisitorsbureau.org
- Kauai County Vacation Information: www.kauai-hawaii.com
- Kauai's Poipu Beach Resort Association: www.poipu-beach.org
- Lanai Visitors Bureau: www.visitlanai.net

P.O. Box 44340, Kawaihae, HI 96743 (© **808/882-7218**); and **Kaloko-Honokohau National Historical Park,** 72–4786 Kanalani St., Kailua-Kona, HI 96740 (© **808/329-6881**).

- On **Maui: Haleakala National Park,** P.O. Box 369, Makawao, HI 96768 (© **808/572-9306**).
- On **Molokai: Kalaupapa National Historical Park,** P.O. Box 2222, Kalaupapa, HI 96742 (© **808/567-6802**).
- On **Oahu:** USS *Arizona* **Memorial at Pearl Harbor** (© **808/422-0561**).

To find out more about Hawaii's state parks, contact the **Hawaii State Department of Land and Natural Resources,** 1151 Punchbowl St., No. 130, Honolulu, HI 96813 (© **808/587-0300;** www.hawaii.gov). The office can provide you with information on hiking and camping at the parks and will send you free topographic trail maps.

WHAT TO PACK

Hawaii is very informal. Shorts, T-shirts, and tennis shoes will get you by at most restaurants and attractions; a casual dress or a polo shirt and khakis are fine even in the most expensive places. Dinner jackets for men are required only in some of the fine-dining rooms of a very few ultraexclusive resorts, such as the Halekulani on Oahu, the Big Island's Mauna Kea Beach Hotel, and the Lodge at Koele on Lanai—and they'll cordially provide you with a jacket if you don't bring your own. Aloha wear is acceptable everywhere, so you may want to plan on buying an aloha shirt or a muumuu (a Hawaiian-style dress) while you're in the islands.

So bring T-shirts, shorts, long pants, a couple of bathing suits, a long-sleeve cover-up (to throw on at the beach when you've had enough sun for the day), tennis shoes, rubber water shoes or flip-flops, and hiking boots and good socks, if you plan on hiking.

The tropical sun poses the greatest threat to anyone who ventures into the great outdoors, so be sure to bring **sun protection:** a good pair of sunglasses, strong sunscreen, a light hat, and a canteen or water bottle if you'll be hiking—you'll easily dehydrate in the tropical heat, so figure on carrying 2 liters of water per day on any hike. Campers should bring water-purification tablets or devices. Also see "Health" and "Safety," later in this chapter.

One last thing: **It really can get cold in Hawaii.** If you plan to see the sunrise from the top of Maui's Haleakala Crater, venture into the Big Island's Hawaii Volcanoes National Park, or spend time in Kokee State Park on Kauai, bring a warm jacket; 40°F (4°C) upcountry temperatures, even in summer when it's 80°F (27°C) at the beach, are not uncommon. It's always a good idea to bring at least a windbreaker, a sweater, or a light jacket. And be sure to toss some **rain gear** into your suitcase if you'll be in Hawaii between November and March.

2 Entry Requirements

PASSPORTS

For information on how to get a passport, go to **"Passports"** in the **"Fast Facts"** section of this chapter—the websites listed provide downloadable passport applications as well as the current fees for processing passport applications. For an up-to-date, country-by-country listing of passport requirements around the world, go to the "Foreign Entry Requirement" Web page of the U.S. State Department at **http://travel.state.gov**. International visitors can obtain a visa application at the same website. *Note:* Children are required to present a passport when entering the United States at airports. More information on obtaining a passport for a minor can be found at http://travel.state.gov.

VISAS

For specifics on how to get a visa, go to **"Visas"** in the **"Fast Facts"** section of this chapter.

The U.S. State Department has a **Visa Waiver Program (VWP)** allowing citizens of the following countries (at press time) to enter the United States without a visa for stays of up to 90 days: Andorra, Australia, Austria, Belgium, Brunei, Denmark, Finland, France, Germany, Iceland, Ireland, Italy, Japan, Liechtenstein, Luxembourg, Monaco, the Netherlands, New Zealand, Norway, Portugal, San Marino, Singapore, Slovenia, Spain, Sweden, Switzerland, and the United Kingdom. Canadian citizens may enter the United States without visas; they will need to show passports and proof of residence, however. *Note:* Any passport issued on or after October 26, 2006, by a VWP country must be an **e-Passport** for VWP travelers to be eligible to enter the U.S. without a visa. Citizens of these nations also need to present a round-trip air or cruise ticket upon arrival. E-Passports contain computer chips capable of storing biometric information, such as the required digital photograph of the holder. (You can identify an e-Passport by the symbol on the bottom center cover of your passport.) If your passport doesn't have this feature, you can still travel without a visa if it is a valid passport issued before October 26, 2005, and includes a machine-readable zone, or between October 26, 2005, and October 25, 2006, and includes a digital photograph. For more information, go to **www.travel.state. gov/visa**.

Citizens of all other countries must have (1) a valid passport that expires at least 6 months later than the scheduled end of their visit to the United States and

U.S. Entry: Passport Required

New regulations issued by the Homeland Security Department now require virtually every air traveler entering the U.S. to show a passport—and future regulations will cover land and sea entry as well. As of January 23, 2007, all persons, including U.S. citizens, traveling by air between the United States and Canada, Mexico, Central and South America, the Caribbean, and Bermuda are required to present a valid passport. Similar regulations for those traveling by land or sea (including ferries) are expected as early as January 1, 2008.

(2) a tourist visa, which may be obtained without charge from any U.S. consulate.

As of January 2004, many international visitors traveling on visas to the United States will be photographed and fingerprinted on arrival at Customs in airports and on cruise ships in a program created by the Department of Homeland Security called **US-VISIT.** Exempt from the extra scrutiny are visitors entering by land or those (mostly in Europe; see p. 81) that don't require a visa for short-term visits. For more information, go to the Homeland Security website at **www.dhs.gov/dhspublic**.

MEDICAL REQUIREMENTS

Unless you're arriving from an area known to be suffering from an epidemic (particularly cholera or yellow fever), inoculations or vaccinations are not required for entry into the United States. If you have a medical condition that requires **syringe-administered medications,** carry a valid signed prescription from your physician; syringes in carry-on baggage will be inspected. Insulin in any form should have the proper pharmaceutical documentation. If you have a disease that requires treatment with **narcotics,** you should also carry documented proof with you—smuggling narcotics aboard a plane carries severe penalties in the U.S.

For **HIV-positive visitors,** requirements for entering the United States are somewhat vague and change frequently. For up-to-the-minute information, contact **AIDSinfo** (© **800/448-0440** or 301/519-6616 outside the U.S.; www.aidsinfo.nih.gov) or the **Gay Men's Health Crisis** (© **212/367-1000;** www.gmhc.org).

CUSTOMS

For information on what you can bring into and take out of Hawaii, go to **"Customs"** in the **"Fast Facts"** section of this chapter.

3 When to Go

Most visitors don't come to Hawaii when the weather's best in the islands; rather, they come when it's at its worst everywhere else. Thus, the **high season**—when prices are up and resorts are often booked to capacity—is generally from mid-December through March or mid-April. The last 2 weeks of December, in particular, are the prime time for travel to Hawaii. If you're planning a holiday trip, make your reservations as early as possible, expect crowds, and prepare to pay top dollar for accommodations, car rentals, and airfare.

The **off season,** when the best rates are available and the islands are less crowded, is spring (mid-Apr to mid-June) and fall (Sept to mid-Dec)—a paradox because these are the best seasons to be in Hawaii, in terms of reliably great weather. If you're looking to save money, or if you just want to avoid the crowds, this is the time to visit. Hotel rates and airfares tend to be

---

> **Tips Travel Tip**
>
> Your best bets for total year-round sun are **Waikiki Beach** and the **Ko Olina** (southwest) coast of Oahu, the Big Island's **Kona-Kohala Coast,** the south **(Kihei/Wailea)** and west **(Lahaina/Kapalua)** Maui coasts, and **Poipu Beach** and the southwest coast of Kauai.

---

significantly lower, and good packages are often available.

Note: If you plan to come to Hawaii between the last week in April and early May, be sure you book your accommodations, interisland air reservations, and car rentals in advance. In Japan, the last week of April is called **Golden Week** because three Japanese holidays take place one after the other. Waikiki is especially busy with Japanese tourists during this time, but the neighboring islands also see dramatic increases.

Due to the large number of families traveling in **summer** (June–Aug), you won't get the fantastic bargains of spring and fall. However, you'll still do much better on packages, airfare, and accommodations than you will in the winter months.

CLIMATE

Because Hawaii lies at the edge of the tropical zone, it technically has only two seasons, both of them warm. There's a dry season that corresponds to **summer** (Apr–Oct) and a rainy season in **winter** (Nov–Mar). It rains every day somewhere in the islands any time of the year, but the rainy season sometimes brings enough gray weather to spoil your tanning opportunities. Fortunately, it seldom rains in one spot for more than 3 days straight.

The **year-round temperature** doesn't vary much. At the beach, the average daytime high in summer is 85°F (29°C), while the average daytime high in winter is 78°F (26°C); nighttime lows are usually about 10°F cooler. But how warm it is on any given day really depends on *where* you are on the island.

Each island has a leeward side (the side sheltered from the wind) and a windward side (the side that gets the wind's full force). The **leeward** sides (the west and south) are usually hot and dry, while the **windward** sides (east and north) are generally cooler and moist. When you want arid, sunbaked, desertlike weather, go leeward. When you want lush, wet, junglelike weather, go windward.

Hawaii is also full of **microclimates,** thanks to its interior valleys, coastal plains, and mountain peaks. Kauai's Mount Waialeale is the wettest spot on earth, yet Waimea Canyon, just a few miles away, is almost a desert. On the Big Island, Hilo is one of the wettest cities in the nation, with 180 inches of rainfall a year, but at Puako, only 60 miles away, it rains less than 6 inches a year. If you travel into the mountains, the climate can change from summer to winter in a matter of hours because it's cooler the higher you go. So if the weather doesn't suit you, just go to the other side of the island—or head into the hills.

On rare occasions, the weather can be disastrous, as when Hurricane Iniki crushed Kauai in September 1992 with 225-mph winds. Tsunamis have swept Hilo and the south shore of Oahu. But those are extreme exceptions. Mostly, one day follows another here in glorious, sunny procession, each quite like the other.

HOLIDAYS

When Hawaii observes holidays (especially those over a long weekend), travel between the islands increases, interisland airline seats are fully booked, rental cars are at a premium, and hotels and restaurants are busier.

Federal, state, and county government offices are closed on all federal holidays: January 1 (New Year's Day), the third Monday in January (Martin Luther King, Jr., Day), the third Monday in February (Presidents' Day, Washington's Birthday), the last Monday in May (Memorial Day), July 4 (Independence Day), the first Monday in September (Labor Day), the second Monday in October (Columbus Day), November 11 (Veterans Day), the fourth Thursday in November (Thanksgiving Day), and December 25 (Christmas).

State and county offices are also closed on local holidays, including Prince Kuhio Day (Mar 26), honoring the birthday of Hawaii's first delegate to the U.S. Congress; King Kamehameha Day (June 11), a statewide holiday commemorating Kamehameha the Great, who united the islands and ruled from 1795 to 1819; and Admissions Day (third Fri in Aug), which honors the admittance of Hawaii as the 50th state on August 21, 1959.

Other special days celebrated in Hawaii by many people but which involve no closing of federal, state, and county offices are the Chinese New Year (which can fall in Jan or Feb; in 2008, it's Feb 7), Girls' Day (Mar 3), Buddha's Birthday (Apr 8), Father Damien's Day (Apr 15), Boys' Day (May 5), Samoan Flag Day (in Aug), Aloha Festivals (in Sept and Oct), and Pearl Harbor Day (Dec 7).

HAWAII CALENDAR OF EVENTS

Please note that, as with any schedule of upcoming events, the following information is subject to change; always confirm the details before you plan your trip around an event.

For an exhaustive list of events beyond those mentioned here, check www.calendar.gohawaii. com for a list of events throughout the islands, or http://events.frommers.com, where you'll find a searchable, up-to-the-minute roster of what's happening in cities all over the world.

January

Rockstar Games Pipeline Pro 2008, Banzai Pipeline, North Shore, Oahu. Competition is judged on the best wave selection and maneuvers on the wave. Call © **732/528-0621;** www. usbatour.org. Early January.

PGA Kapalua Mercedes Championship, Kapalua Resort, Maui. Top PGA golfers compete for $1 million. Call © **808/669-2440;** www.kapalua maui.com. December 31, 2007, to January 6, 2008.

Sony Open, Waialae Country Club, Oahu. A $1.2-million PGA golf event featuring the top men in golf. Call © **808/792-9300.** Early to mid-January.

Pacific Islands Arts Festival at Thomas Square, across from Honolulu Academy of the Arts, Honolulu, Oahu. Over 100 artists and handicraft artists, entertainment, food, and demonstrations fill the day. Admission is free. Call © **808/696-6717.** Mid-January.

Ka Molokai Makahiki, Kaunakakai Town Baseball Park, Mitchell Pauole Center, Kaunakakai, Molokai. Makahiki, a traditional time of peace in ancient Hawaii, is re-created with performances by Hawaiian music groups and hula halau, ancient Hawaiian games, a sporting competition, and Hawaiian crafts and food. It's a wonderful chance to experience the Hawaii of yesteryear. Call © **800/800-6367** or 808/553-3876; www.molokai-hawaii.com. Late January.

Ala Wai Challenge, Ala Wai Park, Waikiki, Oahu. This all-day event features ancient Hawaiian games, like *ulu maika* (bowling a round stone through pegs), *oo ihe* (spear throwing at an upright target), *huki kaula* (tug of war), and a ¼-mile outrigger canoe race. It's also a great place to hear

Hawaiian music. Call ℂ **808/923-1802;** www.waikikicommunitycenter. org. Last week-end in January.

Hula Bowl Football All-Star Classic, Aloha Stadium, Honolulu, Oahu. An annual all-star football classic featuring America's top college players. Call ℂ **800-971-1232;** www.hulabowl hawaii.com. Ticket orders are processed beginning April 1 for the next year's game. Mid- to late January.

February

NFL Pro Bowl, Aloha Stadium, Honolulu, Oahu. The National Football League's best pro players square off in this annual gridiron all-star game. Call ℂ **212/450-2000** or 808/486-9555; www.nfl.com. Early February (a week after the Super Bowl).

Chinese New Year, Maui. Lahaina town rolls out the red carpet for this important event with a traditional lion dance at the historic Wo Hing Temple on Front Street, accompanied by fireworks, food booths, and a host of activities. Call ℂ **888/310-1117** or 808/667-9175. Also on Market Street in Wailuku; call ℂ **808/244-3888.** On Oahu a big celebration takes place in Chinatown; call ℂ **808/533-3181** for details. February 7, 2008, starts the year of the rat.

Narcissus Festival, Honolulu, Oahu. Taking place around the Chinese New Year, this cultural festival includes a queen pageant, cooking demonstrations, and a cultural fair. Call ℂ **808/533-3181** for details.

Waimea Town Celebration, Waimea, Kauai. This annual 2-day party on Kauai's west side celebrates the Hawaiian and multiethnic history of the town where Captain Cook first landed. This is the island's biggest event, drawing some 10,000 people. Top Hawaiian entertainers, sporting events, rodeo, and lots of food are on tap

during the weekend celebration. Call ℂ **808/338-1332;** www.wkbpa.org/ events.html. Weekend after Presidents' Day Weekend.

Sand Castle Building Contest, Kailua Beach Park, Oahu. Students from the University of Hawaii School of Architecture compete against professional architects to see who can build the best, most unusual, and most outrageous sand sculpture. Call ℂ **808/956-956-3518.**

Punahou School Carnival, Punahou School, Honolulu. This event has everything you can imagine in a school carnival, from high-speed rides to homemade jellies. All proceeds go to scholarship funds for Hawaii's most prestigious high school. Call ℂ **808/944-5753.** Early to mid-February.

The Great Aloha Run, Oahu. Thousands run 8.25 miles from Aloha Tower to Aloha Stadium. Call ℂ **808/528-7388.** Presidents' Day (third Mon in Feb).

Buffalo's Big Board Classic, Makaha Beach, Oahu. This contest involves traditional Hawaiian surfing, long boarding, and canoe-surfing. Call ℂ **808/951-7877.** Depending on surf conditions, it can be held in February or March.

March

Daylight saving time begins. Since 1966, most of the United States has observed daylight saving time from 2am on the first Sunday of April to 2am on the last Sunday of October. In 2007, these dates changed, and now daylight saving time lasts from 2am on the second Sunday in March to 2am on the first Sunday in November. Hawaii does *not* observe daylight saving time. So beginning on March 9, 2008, Hawaii is 3 hours behind the West Coast and 6 hours behind the East Coast.

Kona Brewer's Festival, King Kamehameha's Kona Beach Hotel Luau Grounds, Kailua-Kona, Big Island. This annual event features microbreweries from around the world, with beer tastings, food, and entertainment. Call © **808/334-1133.** Second Saturday in March.

Annual St. Patrick's Day Parade, Waikiki (Fort DeRussy to Kapiolani Park), Oahu. Bagpipers, bands, clowns, and marching groups parade through the heart of Waikiki, with lots of Irish-style celebrating all day. Call © **808/ 536-4612** (O'Toole's Pub). March 17.

Annual Kona Chocolate Festival, Kona, Big Island. A 3-day celebration of the chocolate (cacao) that is grown and produced in Hawaii. Days 1 and 2 are filled with symposiums and seminars on chocolate and its uses. Day 3 features a Gala party with samples of chocolate creations by Big Island chefs, caterers, and ice cream and candy makers. A chocoholic's dream! For information and tickets, call © **808/ 324-4606** or visit www.konachocolate festival.com. Mid- to late March.

Prince Kuhio Day Celebrations, all islands. State holiday. Various festivals throughout the state celebrate the birth of Jonah Kuhio Kalanianaole, who was born on March 26, 1871, and elected to Congress in 1902. Kauai, his birthplace, stages a huge celebration in Lihue; call © **808/240-6369** for details. Molokai also hosts a 2-day-long celebration; call © **808/553-3876** to learn more. March 26.

April

East Maui Taro Festival, Hana, Maui. Taro, a Hawaiian staple food, is celebrated through music, hula, arts, crafts, and, of course, food. Call © **808/ 264-3336;** www.tarofestival.org. Generally late April.

Buddha Day, Lahaina Jodo Mission, Lahaina, Maui. Each year this historic mission holds a flower festival pageant honoring the birth of Buddha. First Saturday in April.

Annual Ritz-Carlton Kapalua Celebration of the Arts, Ritz-Carlton Kapalua, Maui. Contemporary and traditional artists give free hands-on lessons. Call © **808/669-6200.** The 4-day festival begins the Thursday before Easter (Mar 20–23, 2008).

Annual Easter Sunrise Service, National Cemetery of the Pacific, Punchbowl Crater, Honolulu, Oahu. For a century, people have gathered at this famous cemetery for Easter sunrise services. Call © **808/566-1430.** March 23, 2008.

Merrie Monarch Hula Festival, Hilo, Big Island. Hawaii's biggest hula festival features 3 nights of modern *(auana)* and ancient *(kahiko)* dance competition in honor of King David Kalakaua, the "Merrie Monarch" who revived the dance. Tickets sell out by January 30, so reserve early. Call © **808/935-9168;** www.merriemonarchfestival.org. The week after Easter (Mar 23–30, 2008).

David Malo Day, Lahainaluna High School, Lahaina, Maui. This daylong event with hula and other Hawaiian cultural celebrations commemorates Hawaii's famous scholar and ends with a luau. Call © **808/662-4000.** Mid-April.

May

Outrigger Canoe Season, all islands. From May to September, canoe paddlers across the state participate in outrigger canoe races nearly every weekend. Call © **808/383-7798,** or go to www.y2kanu.com for this year's schedule of events.

Annual Lei Day Celebrations, various locations on all islands. May Day is Lei Day in Hawaii, celebrated with lei-making contests, pageantry, arts and crafts, and the real highlight, a Brothers Cazimero concert at the Waikiki Shell. Call © **808/692-5118** or visit www.honolulu.gov/parks/programs/lei day for Oahu events (© **808/597-1888,** ext. 232, for the Brothers Cazimero show; © **808/886-1655** for Big Island events; © **808/224-6042** for Maui events; or © **808/245-6931** for Kauai events). May 1.

World Fire-Knife Dance Championships and Samoan Festival, Polynesian Cultural Center, Laie, Oahu. Junior and adult fire-knife dancers from around the world converge on the center for one of the most amazing performances you'll ever see. Authentic Samoan food and cultural festivities round out the fun. Call © **808/293-3333;** www.polynesianculturalcenter. com. Mid-May.

International Festival of Canoes, West Maui. Celebration of the Pacific islands' seafaring heritage. Events include canoe paddling and sailing regattas, a luau feast, cultural arts demonstrations, canoe-building exhibits, and music. Call © **888/310-1117;** www.Maui CanoeFest.com. Mid- to late May.

Memorial Day, National Memorial Cemetery of the Pacific, Punchbowl, Honolulu, Oahu. The armed forces hold a ceremony recognizing those who died for their country, beginning at 9am. Call © **808/532-3720.** Memorial Day (last Mon in May).

June

Hawaiian Slack-Key Guitar Festival, Maui Arts and Cultural Center, Kahului, Maui. Great music performed by the best musicians in Hawaii. It's 5 hours long and absolutely free. Call © **808/242-SHOW** or 808/226-2697, or e-mail kahokuproductions@yahoo. com. June 22, 2008.

King Kamehameha Celebration, all islands. This state holiday features a massive floral parade, *hoolaulea* (party), and much more. Call © **808/586-0333** for Oahu and Kauai events, © **808/886-1655** for Big Island events, © **808/667-9194** for Maui events, or © **808/553-3876** for Molokai events; or visit www.state.hi.us/dags/ kkcc. June 6 and 7, 2008, on Oahu; each island celebrates on different dates.

Great Waikoloa Food, Wine & Music Festival, Hilton Waikoloa Village, Big Island. One of the Big Island's best food and wine festivals features Hawaii's top chefs (and a few mainland chefs) showing off their culinary talents, wines from around the world, and an excellent jazz concert with fireworks. Not to be missed. Call © **808/886-1234** or visit www.hilton waikoloavillage.com or www.dolphin days.com. Mid-June

Maui Film Festival, Wailea Resort, Maui. Five days and nights of screenings of premieres and special films, along with traditional Hawaiian storytelling, chants, hula, and contemporary music. Call © **808/572-3456;** www.mauifilmfestival.com. June.

King Kamehameha Hula Competition, Neal Blaisdell Center, Honolulu, Oahu. This is one of the top hula competitions in the world, with dancers from as far away as Japan. Call © **808/ 586-0333** or visit www.hawaii.gov/ dags/king_kamehameha_commission for information. Third weekend in June (June 21–22, 2008).

July

Makawao Parade and Rodeo, Makawao, Maui. The annual parade and rodeo event have been taking place in this upcountry cowboy town for generations. www.visitmaui.com. July 4.

Lanai Pineapple Festival, Lanai City, Lanai. Celebrates Lanai's history of pineapple plantations and ranching, and includes a pineapple-eating contest, a pineapple-cooking contest, entertainment, arts and crafts, food, and fireworks. Call ✆ **808/565-7600** or visit www.visitlanai.net. First Saturday in July (July 5, 2008).

Kapalua Wine and Food Festival, Kapalua, Maui. Famous wine and food experts and oenophiles gather at the Ritz-Carlton and Kapalua Bay hotels for formal tastings, panel discussions, and samplings of new releases. Call ✆ **800/KAPALUA** or go to www. kapaluaresort.com. Early July.

Fourth of July Fireworks, Desiderio and Sills Field, Schofield Barracks, Oahu. A free daylong celebration, with entertainment, food, and games, ends with a spectacular fireworks show. Call ✆ **808/655-0110.**

Prince Lot Hula Festival, Moanalua Gardens, Honolulu, Oahu. Authentic ancient and modern hula, as well as demonstrations and arts and crafts, are some of the things you'll encounter at this festival. It's a good alternative to April's much better-known (and much more crowded) Merrie Monarch Hula Festival. Call ✆ **808/839-5334** or visit www.mgf-hawaii.org. Third Saturday in July (July 19, 2008).

Ukulele Festival, Kapiolani Park Bandstand, Waikiki, Oahu. This free concert features a ukulele orchestra of some 600 students (ages 4–92). Hawaii's top musicians all pitch in. Call ✆ **808/ 732-3739;** www.roysakuma.net. Late July.

Queen Liliuokalani Keiki Hula Competition, Neal Blaisdell Center, Honolulu, Oahu. More than 500 *keiki* (children) representing 22 halau (hula schools) from the islands compete in this dance fest. The event is broadcast a week later on KITV-TV. Call ✆ **808/ 521-6905.** Late July.

Hawaii State Farm Fair, Aloha Stadium, Honolulu, Oahu. The annual state fair is a great one: It features displays of Hawaii agricultural products (including orchids), educational and cultural exhibits, entertainment, and local-style food. Call ✆ **808/682-5767** or visit www.ekfernandez.com. Late July or early August.

August

Hawaii International Jazz Festival, The Hawaii Theatre, Honolulu, Oahu. This festival includes evening concerts and daily jam sessions, plus scholarship giveaways, the University of Southern California jazz band, and many popular jazz and blues artists. Call ✆ **808/ 941-9974** or visit www.hawaiijazz. com. August 9 and 10.

Puukohola Heiau National Historic Site Anniversary Celebration, Kawaihae, Big Island. This is a weekend of Hawaiian crafts, workshops, and games. Call ✆ **808/882-7218.** Mid-August (Aug 16–17, 2008).

Admissions Day, all islands. Hawaii became the 50th state on August 21, 1959. The state takes a holiday (all state-related facilities are closed) on the third Friday in August (Aug 15, 2008).

September

Queen Liliuokalani Canoe Race, Kailua-Kona to Honaunau, Big Island. The world's largest long-distance canoe race takes places over Labor Day weekend, with hundreds participating. Call ✆ **808/331-8849** or visit www. kaiopua.org.

Parker Ranch Rodeo, Waimea, Big Island. This is a hot rodeo competition in the heart of cowboy country. Call ✆ **808/885-7311** or go to www. parkerranch.com. Labor Day Weekend (Aug 30–Sept 1, 2008).

Hawaiian Slack-Key Guitar Festival, Sheraton Keauhou Bay Resort & Spa, Kona, Big Island. The best of Hawaii's folk music (slack-key guitar) performed by the best musicians in Hawaii. It's 5 hours long and absolutely free. Call ⓒ **808/239-4336** or e-mail kahoku productions@yahoo.com. September 7, 2008.

Aloha Festivals, various locations statewide. Parades and other events celebrate Hawaiian culture and friendliness throughout the state. Call ⓒ **808-589-1771** or visit www.alohafestivals. com for a schedule of events.

Aloha Festivals Poke Recipe Contest, Hapuna Beach Prince Hotel, Mauna Kea Beach Resort, Kohala Coast, Big Island. Top chefs from across Hawaii and the U.S. mainland, as well as local amateurs, compete in making this Hawaiian delicacy, poke (pronounced po-*kay*): chopped raw fish mixed with seaweed and spices. Here's your chance to sample poke at its best. Call ⓒ **808/880-3424** or visit www.pokecontest. com.

A Taste of Lahaina, Lahaina Civic Center, Maui. Some 30,000 people show up to sample 40 signature entrees from Maui's premier chefs during this weekend festival, which includes cooking demonstrations, wine tastings, and live entertainment. The event begins Friday night with Maui Chefs Present, a dinner/cocktail party featuring about a dozen of Maui's best chefs. Call ⓒ **888/310-1117** or go to www.visit maui.com. Second weekend in September (Sept 13–14, 2008).

LifeFest Kapalua, Kapalua, Maui. An all-new health-and-wellness 3-day event featuring lectures and panel presentations by leaders in the health-and-wellness field (Dr. Deepak Chopra, Bob Greene, Dr. Julian Whitaker, and others), plus ocean sporting events, fitness activities, a health-and-wellness expo, and sumptuous culinary gala dinners. Call ⓒ **800/KAPALUA;** www.lifefest kapalua.com. Early September.

Na Wahine O Ke Kai, Molokai to Oahu. Women's 32-mile canoe race. Watch the sunrise and the start of the race beginning at 7am on Sunday morning. The finish line fronts the shores of the Hilton Hawaiian Village. Call ⓒ **808/259-7112;** www.na wahineokekai.com. Mid-September.

Maui County Fair, War Memorial Complex, Wailuku, Maui. The oldest county fair in Hawaii features a parade, amusement rides, live entertainment, and exhibits. Call ⓒ **808/270-7626** or visit www.calendarmaui.com. Last weekend in September.

October

Emalani Festival, Kokee State Park, Kauai. This festival honors Her Majesty Queen Emma, an inveterate gardener and Hawaii's first environmental queen, who made a forest trek to Kokee with 100 friends in 1871. Call ⓒ **808/245-3971.** Second Saturday in October.

Aloha Classic World Wavesailing Championship, Hookipa Beach, Maui. The top windsurfers in the world gather for this final event in the Pro Boardsailing World Tour. If you're on Maui, don't miss it—it's spectacular to watch. Call ⓒ **808/298-3560;** www.alohaclassicwindsurfing.com.

Hamakua Music Festival, Hamakua, Big Island. This event features a surprisingly eclectic mix of well-known musicians, ranging from blues and jazz to rock 'n' roll, Hawaiian, and even classical. At press time, the festival was in the midst of reorganization, so first call ⓒ **808/775-3378** or check at www.hamakuamusicfestival.org.

Ironman Triathlon World Championship, Kailua-Kona, Big Island. Some 1,500-plus world-class athletes run a full marathon, swim 2½ miles, and bike 112 miles on the Kona-Kohala coast of the Big Island. Spectators can watch the action along the route for free. The best place to see the 7am start is along the seawall on Alii Drive, facing Kailua Bay; arrive before 5:30am to get a seat. The best place to see the bike-and-run portion is along Alii Drive (which will be closed to traffic; park on a side street and walk down). To watch the finishers come in, line up along Alii Drive from Holualoa Street to the finish at Palani Road/Alii Drive; the first finisher can come as early as 2:30pm, and the course closes at midnight. Call ℂ **808/329-0063** or visit www.ironman.com. October. (As we went to press, they did not have a confirmed date, so check the website.)

Halloween in Lahaina, Maui. There's Carnival in Rio, Mardi Gras in New Orleans, and Halloween in Lahaina. Come to this giant costume party (some 20,000 people show up) on the streets of Lahaina; Front Street is closed off for the festivities. Call ℂ **808/667-9175** or go to www.visitmaui.com. October 31.

November

Daylight saving time ends. Beginning in 2007, most of the U.S. will revert to standard time on the first Sunday in November. Since Hawaii does not observe daylight saving time, starting on November 4, 2008, Hawaii will be 2 hours behind the West Coast and 5 hours behind the East Coast.

Hula O Na Keiki, Ka'anapali Beach Hotel, Ka'anapali, Maui. This solo hula competition for children ages 5 to 17 is in its 18th year. A weekend festival of Hawaiian dance, arts and music.

Call ℂ **808/661-0011;** www.kbhmaui.com. Early November.

Hawaiian Slack-Key Guitar Festival, Kauai Marriott Resort, Lihue, Kauai. The best of Hawaii's folk music (slack-key guitar) performed by the best musicians in Hawaii. It's 5 hours long and absolutely free. Call ℂ **808/226-2697** or e-mail kahokuproductions@yahoo.com. November 16, 2008.

Annual Kona Coffee Cultural Festival, Kailua-Kona, Big Island. Celebrate the coffee harvest with a bean-picking contest, lei contests, song and dance, and the Miss Kona Coffee pageant. Call ℂ **808/326-7820** or go to www.konacoffeefest.com for this year's schedule.

Hawaii International Film Festival, various locations throughout the state. This cinema festival with a cross-cultural spin features filmmakers from Asia, the Pacific Islands, and the United States. Call ℂ **808/550-8457** or visit www.hiff.org. First 2 weeks in November.

Annual Invitational Wreath Exhibit, Volcano Art Center, Volcano National Park, Big Island. Thirty-two artists, including painters, sculptors, glass artists, fiber artists, and potters, produce both whimsical and traditional "wreaths" for this exhibit. Park entrance fees apply. Call ℂ **866/967-7565** or 808/967-7565; www.volcanoartcenter.org. Mid-November through the first of January.

Triple Crown of Surfing, North Shore, Oahu. The world's top professional surfers compete in events for more than $1 million in prize money. Call ℂ **808/739-3965;** www.triplecrownofsurfing.com. Held between mid-November and mid-December, whenever conditions are best.

December

Festival of Trees, Honolulu, Oahu. This downtown display of one-of-a-kind decorated trees, wreaths, and decorations benefits Queen's Medical Center. Call (© **808/667-9194;** www.visitlahaina.com. The lighting takes place the first or second week of December.

Na Mele O Maui, Ka'anapali, Maui. Traditional Hawaiian song competition for children in kindergarten through twelfth grade. $2 admission. Takes place in the ballroom of one of the Kaanapali resort hotels. Call (© **808/661-3271;** www.kaanapaliresort.com. First Friday in December.

Old-Fashioned Holiday Celebration, Lahaina, Maui. This day of Christmas carolers, Santa Claus, live music and entertainment, a crafts fair, Christmas baked goods, and activities for children takes place in the Banyan Tree Park on Front Street. Call (© **888/310-1117;** www.visitlahaina.com. Second Saturday in December (Dec 8, 2007).

Billabong Pro Maui, Honolua Bay at Kapalua Resort, Maui. The final triple Crown women's surfing contest of the year, bringing together the best of the women's international surfing community. Call (© **808/669-2440** or visit www.kapalua.com.

Festival of Lights, all islands. On Oahu, the mayor throws the switch to light up the 40-foot-tall Norfolk pine and other trees in front of Honolulu Hale, while on Maui, marching bands, floats, and Santa roll down Lahaina's Front Street in an annual parade. Molokai celebrates with a host of activities in Kaunakakai; on Kauai the lighting ceremony takes place in front of the former county building on Rice Street, Lihue. Call (© **808/523-4385** on Oahu, (© **808/667-9175** on Maui, (© **808/552-2800** on Molokai, or (© **808/828-0014** on Kauai. Early December.

Honolulu Marathon, Honolulu, Oahu. This is one of the largest marathons in the world, with more than 30,000 competitors. Call (© **808/734-7200;** www.honolulumarathon. org. Second Sunday in December (Dec 14, 2008).

Aloha Bowl, Aloha Stadium, Honolulu, Oahu. A Pac-10 team plays a Big 12 team in this nationally televised collegiate football classic. Call (© **808/483-2500.** Christmas Day.

Rainbow Classic, University of Hawaii, Manoa Valley, Oahu. Eight of the best NCAA basketball teams compete at the Special Events Arena. Call (© **808/956-7523.** The week after Christmas.

First Light, Maui Arts and Cultural Center, Maui. Major films are screened at this festival (past films have included *The Lord of the Rings: Return of the King, Mystic River, Aviator, Hotel Rwanda,* and many others). Not to be missed. Call (© **808/573-3456** or visit www.mauifilmfestival.com. End of December and early January.

4 Getting There

BY PLANE

Most major U.S. and many international carriers fly to Honolulu International Airport. Some also offer direct flights to Kailua-Kona, on the Big Island; Kahului, Maui; and Lihue, Kauai.

United Airlines (© **800/225-5825;** www.ual.com) offers the most frequent service from the U.S. mainland, flying not only to Honolulu, but also offering nonstop flights from Los Angeles and San Francisco to the Big Island, Maui, and Kauai. **Aloha Airlines** (② **800/ 367-5250** or 808/484-1111; www.aloha airlines.com) has direct flights from Oakland to Maui, Kona, and Honolulu, and from Orange County, California, to Honolulu, Kona, and Maui. Aloha also offers connecting flights from Las Vegas to Oakland and Orange County. **American Airlines** (② **800/433-7300;** www. americanair.com) offers flights from Dallas, Chicago, San Francisco, San Jose, Los Angeles, and St. Louis to Honolulu, plus several direct flights to Maui and Kona. ATA/code sharing with **Southwest Airlines** (② **800/I-FLY-ATA** or 800/ 435-9282; www.ata.com) has direct flights to Honolulu from Oakland, Los Angeles, Orange County, Las Vegas, and Phoenix; direct flights to Maui from Oakland, Orange County, and Phoenix; and direct flights from Oakland to Kona, Hilo, and Lihue. **Continental Airlines** (② **800/231-0856;** www.continental. com) offers the only daily nonstop from the New York area (Newark) to Honolulu. **Delta Air Lines** (② **800/221- 1212;** www.delta.com) flies nonstop from the West Coast and from Houston and Cincinnati. **Hawaiian Airlines** (② **800/367-5320;** www.hawaiianair. com) offers nonstop flights to Honolulu from several West Coast cities (including new service from San Diego), plus nonstop flights from Los Angeles to Maui. **Northwest Airlines** (② **800/225-2525;** www.nwa.com) has a daily nonstop from Detroit to Honolulu.

Airlines serving Hawaii from places other than the U.S. mainland include **Air Canada** (② 800/776-3000; www.air canada.ca); **Air New Zealand** (② 0800/ 737-000 in Auckland, 643/379-5200 in Christchurch, 800/926-7255 in the U.S.; www.airnewzealand.com); **Qantas** (② 008/177-767 in Australia, 800/227- 4500 in the U.S.; www.qantas.com.au); **Japan Air Lines** (② 03/5489-1111 in Tokyo, 800/525-3663 in the U.S.;

www.japanair.com); **All Nippon Airways** (**ANA;** ② 03/5489-1212 in Tokyo, 800/235-9262 in the U.S.; www.fly-ana. com); **China Airlines** (② 02/715-1212 in Taipei, 800/227-5118 in the U.S.; www.china-airlines.com); **Air Pacific,** serving Fiji, Australia, New Zealand, and the South Pacific (② 800/227-4446; www.airpacific.com); **Korean Air** (② 02/ 656-2000 in Seoul, 800/223-1155 on the East Coast, 800/421-8200 on the West Coast, 800/438-5000 from Hawaii; www. koreanair.com); and **Philippine Airlines** (② 631/816-6691 in Manila, 800/435- 9725 in the U.S.; www.philippineairlines. com).

Operated by the European Travel Network, **www.discount-tickets.com** is a great online source for regular and discounted airfares to destinations around the world. You can also use this site to compare rates and book accommodations, car rentals, and tours.

If you're traveling in the United States beyond Hawaii, some large American airlines—such as **American, Delta, Northwest,** and **United**—offer travelers on transatlantic or transpacific flights special discount tickets under the name **Visit USA,** allowing travel between any U.S. destinations at reduced rates. These tickets must be purchased before you leave your foreign point of departure. This system is the best, easiest, and fastest way to see the United States at low cost. You should obtain information well in advance from your travel agent or the office of the airline concerned, since the conditions attached to these discount tickets can change without advance notice.

Locally, **Hawaiian Airlines** (② **800/ 367-5320;** www.hawaiianair.com) flies nonstop to Sydney, Tahiti, and American Samoa.

Visitors arriving by air should cultivate patience and resignation before setting foot on U.S. soil. Getting through immigration control may take as long as 2

Tips Getting through the Airport

- Arrive at the airport 1 hour before a domestic flight and 2 hours before an international flight; if you show up late, tell an airline employee and he or she will probably whisk you to the front of the line.
- Beat the ticket-counter lines by using airport electronic kiosks or even online check-in from your home computers, from where you can print out boarding passes in advance. Curbside check-in is also a good way to avoid lines.
- Bring a current, government-issued photo ID such as a driver's license or passport. Children under 18 do not need government-issued photo IDs for flights within the U.S., but they do for international flights to most countries.
- Speed up security by removing your jacket and shoes before you're screened. In addition, remove metal objects such as big belt buckles. If you've got metallic body parts, a note from your doctor can prevent a long chat with the security screeners.
- Use a TSA-approved lock for your checked luggage. Look for Travel Sentry certified locks at luggage or travel shops and Brookstone stores (or online at www.brookstone.com).

hours on some days, especially summer weekends. Add the time it takes to clear Customs, and you'll see that you should make a very generous allowance for delay in planning connections between international and domestic flights—an average of 2 to 3 hours at least.

AGRICULTURAL SCREENING AT THE AIRPORTS At Honolulu International and the neighbor-island airports, baggage and passengers bound for the mainland must be screened by agricultural officials. Officials will confiscate local produce like fresh avocados, bananas, and mangoes, in the name of fruit-fly control. Pineapples, coconuts, and papayas inspected and certified for export; boxed flowers; leis without seeds; and processed foods (macadamia nuts, coffee, jams, dried fruit, and the like) will pass.

FLYING FOR LESS: TIPS FOR GETTING THE BEST AIRFARE

- Passengers who can book their ticket either **long in advance or at the last minute,** or who **fly midweek** or **at less-trafficked hours** may pay a fraction of the full fare. If your schedule is flexible, say so, and ask if you can secure a cheaper fare by changing your flight plans.
- Search **the Internet** for cheap fares. The most popular online travel agencies are **Travelocity.com** (www.travelocity.co.uk), **Expedia.com** (www.expedia.co.uk and www.expedia.ca), and **Orbitz.com.** In the U.K., go to **Travelsupermarket** (© **0845/345-5708;** www.travelsupermarket.com), a flight search engine that offers flight comparisons for the budget airlines whose seats

often end up in bucket-shop sales. Other websites for booking airline tickets online include **Cheapflights. com, SmarterTravel.com, Priceline. com,** and **Opodo** (www.opodo.co. uk). Meta search sites (which find and then direct you to airline and hotel websites for booking) include **Sidestep.com** and **Kayak.com**—the latter includes fares for budget carriers like Jet Blue and Spirit as well as the major airlines. **Site59.com** is a great source for last-minute flights and getaways. In addition, most **airlines** offer online-only fares that even their phone agents know nothing about. British travelers should check **Flights International** (© **0800/ 0187050;** www.flights-international. com) for deals on flights all over the world.

- Watch local newspapers for **promotional specials** or **fare wars,** when airlines lower prices on their most popular routes. Also keep an eye on price fluctuations and deals at websites such as **Airfarewatchdog.com** and **Farecast.com.**

- Try to book a ticket **in its country of origin.** If you're planning a one-way flight from Johannesburg to New York, a South Africa–based travel agent will probably have the lowest fares. For foreign travelers on multileg trips, book in the country of the first leg; for example, book New York–Chicago–Montreal–New York in the U.S.

- **Consolidators,** also known as bucket shops, are wholesale brokers in the airline-ticket game. Consolidators buy deeply discounted tickets ("distressed" inventories of unsold seats) from airlines and sell them to online ticket agencies, travel agents, tour operators, corporations, and, to a lesser degree,

the general public. Consolidators advertise in Sunday newspaper travel sections (often in small ads with tiny type), in both the U.S. and the U.K. They can be great sources for cheap international tickets. On the down side, bucket-shop tickets are often rigged with restrictions, such as stiff cancellation penalties (as high as 50–75% of the ticket price). And keep in mind that most of what you see advertised is of limited availability. Several reliable consolidators are worldwide and available online. **STA Travel** (www.statravel.com) has been the world's leading consolidator for students since purchasing Council Travel, but their fares are competitive for travelers of all ages. **Flights.com** (© **800/TRAV-800;** www.flights. com) has excellent fares worldwide, particularly to Europe. They also have "local" websites in 12 countries. **Fly-Cheap** (© **800/FLY-CHEAP;** www. 1800flycheap.com) has especially good fares to sunny destinations. **Air Tickets Direct** (© **800/778-3447;** www.airticketsdirect.com) is based in Montreal and leverages the currently weak Canadian dollar for low fares; they also book trips to places that U.S. travel agents won't touch, such as Cuba.

- Join **frequent-flier clubs.** Frequent-flier membership doesn't cost a cent, but it does entitle you to free tickets or upgrades when you amass the airline's required number of frequent-flier points. You don't even have to fly to earn points; **frequent-flier credit cards** can earn you thousands of miles for doing your everyday shopping. But keep in mind that award seats are limited, seats on popular routes are hard to snag, and more and more major airlines are cutting their

---

Tips **Don't Stow It—Ship It**

Though pricey, it's sometimes worthwhile to travel luggage free. Specialists in door-to-door luggage delivery include **Virtual Bellhop** (www.virtualbellhop. com), **SkyCap International** (www.skycapinternational.com), **Luggage Express** (www.usxpluggageexpress.com), and **Sports Express** (www.sportsexpress.com).

---

expiration periods for mileage points—so check your airline's frequent-flier program so you don't lose your miles before you use them. *Inside tip:* Award seats are offered almost a year in advance, but seats also open up at the last minute, so if your travel plans are flexible, you may strike gold. To play the frequent-flier game to your best advantage, consult the community bulletin boards on **FlyerTalk** (www.flyertalk.com) or go to Randy Petersen's **Inside Flyer** (www.insideflyer.com). Petersen and friends review all the programs in detail and post regular updates on changes in policies and trends.

ARRIVING AT THE AIRPORT
IMMIGRATION & CUSTOMS CLEARANCE   Foreign visitors arriving by air, no matter what the port of entry, should cultivate patience and resignation before setting foot on U.S. soil. U.S. airports have considerably beefed up security clearances in the years since the terrorist attacks of 9/11, and clearing Customs and Immigration can take as long as 2 hours.

People traveling by air from Canada, Bermuda, and certain Caribbean countries can sometimes clear Customs and Immigration at the point of departure, which is much faster.

LONG-HAUL FLIGHTS: HOW TO STAY COMFORTABLE

- Your choice of airline and airplane will definitely affect your legroom. Find more details about U.S. airlines at **www.seatguru.com**. For international airlines, the research firm Skytrax has posted a list of average seat pitches at **www.airlinequality.com**.

- Emergency exit seats and bulkhead seats typically have the most legroom. Emergency exit seats are usually left unassigned until the day of a flight (to ensure that someone able-bodied fills the seats); it's worth getting to the ticket counter early to snag one of these spots for a long flight. Many passengers find that bulkhead seating (the row facing the wall at the front of the cabin) offers more legroom, but keep in mind that bulkhead seats have no storage space on the floor in front of you.

- To have two seats for yourself in a three-seat row, try for an aisle seat in a center section toward the back of coach. If you're traveling with a companion, book an aisle and a window seat. Middle seats are usually booked last, so chances are good you'll end up with three seats to yourselves. And in the event that a third passenger is assigned the middle seat, he or she will probably be more than happy to trade for a window or an aisle.

- Ask about entertainment options. Many airlines offer seatback video systems where you get to choose your movies or play video games—but only on some of their planes. (Boeing 777s are your best bet.)

- To sleep, avoid the last row of any section or the row in front of an emergency exit, as these seats are the

Tips Coping with Jet Lag

Jet lag is a pitfall of traveling across time zones. If you're flying north–south and you feel sluggish when you touch down, your symptoms will be the result of dehydration and the general stress of air travel. When you travel east–west or vice versa, however, your body becomes thoroughly confused about what time it is, and everything from your digestive system to your brain is knocked for a loop. Traveling east—say, from San Francisco to Boston—is more difficult on your internal clock than traveling west—say, from Atlanta to Hawaii— because most people's bodies are more inclined to stay up late than fall asleep early.

Here are some tips for combating jet lag:

- **Reset your watch** to your destination time before you board the plane.
- **Drink lots of water** before, during, and after your flight. Avoid alcohol.
- **Exercise and sleep well** for a few days before your trip.
- If you have trouble sleeping on planes, **fly eastward on morning flights.**
- **Daylight** is the key to resetting your body clock. At the website for **Outside In** (www.bodyclock.com), you can get a customized plan of when to seek and avoid light.

least likely to recline. Avoid seats near highly trafficked toilet areas. Avoid seats in the back of many jets—these can be narrower than those in the rest of coach. Or reserve a window seat so you can rest your head and avoid being bumped in the aisle.

- Get up, walk around, and stretch every 60 to 90 minutes to keep your blood flowing. This helps avoid **deep vein thrombosis,** or "economy-class syndrome."

- Drink water before, during, and after your flight to combat the lack of humidity in airplane cabins. Avoid caffeine and alcohol, which will dehydrate you.
- If you're flying with kids, don't forget to carry on toys, books, pacifiers, and snacks and chewing gum to help them relieve ear pressure buildup during ascent and descent.

5 Money

It's always advisable to bring money in a variety of forms on a vacation: a mix of cash, credit cards, and traveler's checks. You should also exchange enough petty cash to cover airport incidentals, tipping, and transportation to your hotel before you leave home, or withdraw money upon arrival at an airport ATM.

ATMS

Nationwide, the easiest and best way to get cash away from home is from an ATM (automated teller machine), sometimes referred to as a "cash machine" or "cashpoint." ATMs are everywhere in Hawaii—at banks, supermarkets, Long's Drugs, and Honolulu International Airport, and in some resorts and shopping centers. The **Cirrus** (✆ **800/424-7787;** www.mastercard.com) and **PLUS** (✆ **800/ 843-7587;** www.visa.com) networks span the country; you can find them even in remote regions. Go to your bank card's

Why Oahu Is More Expensive

No, it's not your imagination—Oahu is more expensive than the other islands. That's the result of the Hawaii State Legislature passing a bill allowing the City and County of Honolulu (which is the entire island of Oahu) to add an additional .05% tax on to the state general excise tax of 4%. Everything you buy on Oahu will have this tax, and so will your hotel bill. The funds from this additional tax are earmarked for mass transit for Oahu.

website to find ATM locations at your destination. Be sure you know your daily withdrawal limit before you depart.

Note: Many banks impose a fee every time you use a card at another bank's ATM, and that fee is often higher for international transactions (up to $5 or more) than for domestic ones (where they're rarely more than $2). In addition, the bank from which you withdraw cash may charge its own fee. To compare banks' ATM fees within the U.S., use **www.bankrate.com**. Visitors from outside the U.S. should also find out whether their bank assesses a 1% to 3% fee on charges incurred abroad.

CREDIT CARDS & DEBIT CARDS

Credit cards are the most widely used form of payment in the United States: **Visa** (Barclaycard in Britain), **Master-Card** (EuroCard in Europe, Access in Britain, Chargex in Canada), **American Express, Diners Club,** and **Discover.** They also provide a convenient record of all your expenses and offer relatively good exchange rates. You can withdraw cash advances from your credit cards at banks or ATMs, but high fees make credit card cash advances a pricey way to get cash.

It's highly recommended that you travel with at least one major credit card. You must have a credit card to rent a car, and hotels and airlines usually require a credit card imprint as a deposit against expenses.

ATM cards with major credit card backing, known as **"debit cards,"** are now a commonly acceptable form of payment in most stores and restaurants.

Debit cards draw money directly from your checking account. Some stores enable you to receive cash back on your debit card purchases as well. The same is true at most U.S. post offices.

TRAVELER'S CHECKS

Though credit cards and debit cards are more often used, traveler's checks are still widely accepted in the U.S. Foreign visitors should make sure that traveler's checks are denominated in U.S. dollars; foreign-currency checks are often difficult to exchange.

You can buy traveler's checks at most banks. Most are offered in denominations of $20, $50, $100, $500, and sometimes $1,000. Generally, you'll pay a service charge ranging from 1% to 4%.

The most popular traveler's checks are offered by **American Express** (© 800/807-6233; © 800/221-7282 for card holders—this number accepts collect calls, offers service in several foreign languages, and exempts Amex gold and platinum cardholders from the 1% fee.); **Visa** (© 800/732-1322—AAA members can obtain Visa checks for a $9.95 fee for checks up to $1,500 at most AAA offices or by calling © 866/339-3378); and **MasterCard** (© 800/223-9920).

Be sure to keep a copy of the traveler's checks serial numbers separate from your checks in case they are stolen or lost. You'll get a refund faster if you know the numbers.

Another option is the new **prepaid traveler's check cards,** reloadable cards that work much like debit cards but aren't linked to your checking account. The **American Express Travelers Cheque Card,** for example, requires a minimum deposit ($300), sets a maximum balance ($2,750), and has a one-time issuance fee of $14.95. You can withdraw money from an ATM ($2.50 per transaction, not including bank fees), and the funds can be purchased in dollars, euros, or pounds. If you lose the card, your available funds will be refunded within 24 hours.

6 Travel Insurance

The cost of travel insurance varies widely, depending on the cost and length of your trip, your age and health, and the type of trip you're taking, but expect to pay between 5% and 8% of the vacation itself. You can get estimates from various providers through **InsureMyTrip.com.** Enter your trip cost and dates, your age, and other information, for prices from more than a dozen companies.

For **U.K. citizens,** insurance is always advisable when traveling in the States. Travelers or families who make more than one trip abroad per year may find an annual travel insurance policy works out cheaper. Check **www.moneysupermarket.com**, which compares prices across a wide range of providers for single- and multitrip policies.

Most big travel agents offer their own insurance and will probably try to sell you their package when you book a holiday. Think before you sign. **Britain's Consumers' Association** recommends that you insist on seeing the policy and reading the fine print before buying travel insurance. **The Association of British Insurers** (© 020/7600-3333; www.abi.org.uk) gives advice by phone and publishes *Holiday Insurance,* a free guide to policy provisions and prices. You might also shop around for better deals: Try **Columbus Direct** (© 0870/033-9988; www.columbusdirect.net).

TRIP-CANCELLATION INSURANCE

Trip-cancellation insurance will help retrieve your money if you have to back out of a trip or depart early, or if your travel supplier goes bankrupt. Trip cancellation traditionally covers such events as sickness, natural disasters, and State Department advisories. The latest news in trip-cancellation insurance is the availability of **expanded hurricane coverage** and the **"any-reason"** cancellation coverage—which costs more but covers cancellations made for any reason. You won't get back 100% of your prepaid trip cost, but you'll be refunded a substantial portion. **TravelSafe** (© **888/885-7233;** www.travelsafe.com) offers both types of coverage. Expedia also offers any-reason cancellation coverage for its air-hotel packages.

For details, contact one of the following recommended insurers: **Access America** (© 866/807-3982; www.accessamerica.com), **Travel Guard International** (© 800/826-4919; www.travelguard.com), **Travel Insured International** (© 800/243-3174; www.travelinsured.com), and **Travelex Insurance Services** (© 888/457-4602; www.travelex-insurance.com).

MEDICAL INSURANCE

Although it's not required of travelers, health insurance is highly recommended. Most health insurance policies cover you if you get sick away from home—but check your coverage before you leave.

International visitors should note that, unlike many European countries, the United States does not usually offer free or low-cost medical care to its citizens or visitors. Doctors and hospitals are expensive and, in most cases, will require advance payment or proof of coverage before they render their services. Good policies will cover the costs of an accident, repatriation, or death. Packages such as **Europ Assistance's "Worldwide Healthcare Plan"** are sold by European automobile clubs and travel agencies at attractive rates. **Worldwide Assistance Services, Inc.** (© 800/777-8710; www.worldwideassistance.com), is the agent for Europ Assistance in the United States.

Though lack of health insurance may prevent you from being admitted to a hospital in nonemergencies, don't worry about being left on a street corner to die: The American way is to fix you now and bill the living daylights out of you later.

If you're ever hospitalized more than 150 miles from home, **MedjetAssist** (© 800/527-7478; www.medjetassistance.com) will pick you up and fly you to the hospital of your choice in a medically equipped and staffed aircraft 24 hours day, 7 days a week. Annual memberships are $225 individual, $350 family; you can also purchase short-term memberships.

Canadians should check with their provincial health plan offices or call **Health Canada** (© 866/225-0709; www.hc-sc.gc.ca) to find out the extent of their coverage and what documentation and receipts they must take home in case they are treated in the United States.

LOST-LUGGAGE INSURANCE

On flights within the U.S., checked baggage is covered up to $2,500 per ticketed passenger. On flights outside the U.S. (and on U.S. portions of international trips), baggage coverage is limited to approximately $9.07 per pound, up to approximately $635 per checked bag. If you plan to check items more valuable than what's covered by the standard liability, see if your homeowner's policy covers your valuables, get baggage insurance as part of your comprehensive travel-insurance package, or buy Travel Guard's "BagTrak" product.

If your luggage is lost, immediately file a lost-luggage claim at the airport, detailing the luggage contents. Most airlines require that you report delayed, damaged, or lost baggage within 4 hours of arrival. The airlines are required to deliver luggage, once found, directly to your house or destination free of charge.

7 Health

STAYING HEALTHY
GENERAL AVAILABILITY OF HEALTH CARE

Contact the **International Association for Medical Assistance to Travelers** (IAMAT; © 716/754-4883 or, in Canada, 416/652-0137; **www.iamat.org**) for tips on travel and health concerns in the countries you're visiting, and for lists of local, English-speaking doctors. The United States **Centers for Disease Control and Prevention** (© 800/311-3435; www.cdc.gov) provides up-to-date information on health hazards by region or country and offers tips on food safety. The website **www.tripprep.com**, sponsored by a consortium of travel medicine practitioners, **Travel Health Online,** may also offer helpful advice on traveling abroad. You can find listings of reliable clinics overseas at the **International Society of Travel Medicine** (www.istm.org).

INSECTS

Like any tropical climate, Hawaii is home to lots of bugs. Most of them won't harm you. However, watch out for mosquitoes, centipedes, and scorpions, which do sting and may cause anything from mild annoyance to severe swelling and pain.

MOSQUITOES These pesky insects are not native to Hawaii but arrived as larvae stowed away in water barrels on

---

⌐Tips Don't Get Burned: Smart Tanning Tips

Hawaii's Caucasian population has the highest incidence of malignant melanoma (deadly skin cancer) in the world. And nobody is completely safe from the sun's harmful rays: All skin types and races can burn. To ensure that your vacation won't be ruined by a painful sunburn, be sure to wear a strong sunscreen that protects against both UVA and UVB rays at all times (look for Zinc oxide, benzophenone, oxybenzone, sulisobenzone, titanium dioxide, or avobenzone in the ingredients list). Wear a wide-brimmed hat and sunglasses. Keep infants under 6 months out of the sun completely and slather older babies and children with strong sunscreen frequently.

If you do get a burn, aloe vera, cool compresses, cold baths, and benzocaine can help with the pain. Stay out of the sun until the burn is completely gone.

---

the ship *Wellington* in 1826, when it anchored in Lahaina. There's not a whole lot you can do about them, except to apply commercial repellent, which you can pick up at any drugstore.

CENTIPEDES   These segmented bugs with a jillion legs come in two varieties: 6- to 8-inch-long brown ones and 2- to 3-inch-long blue guys. Both can really pack a wallop with their sting. Centipedes are generally found in damp, wet places, such as under wood piles or compost heaps; wearing closed-toe shoes can help prevent stings. If you're stung, apply ice at once to prevent swelling. See a doctor if you experience extreme pain, swelling, nausea, or any other severe reaction.

SCORPIONS   Rarely seen, scorpions are found in arid, warm regions; their stings can be serious. Campers in dry areas should always check their boots before putting them on and shake out sleeping bags and bed rolls. Symptoms of a scorpion sting include shortness of breath, hives, swelling, and nausea. In the unlikely event that you're stung, apply diluted household ammonia and cold compresses to the area of the sting and seek medical help immediately.

HIKING SAFETY
In addition to taking the appropriate precautions regarding Hawaii's bug population, hikers should always let someone know where they're heading, when they're going, and when they plan to return; too many hikers get lost in Hawaii because they don't let others know their basic plans.

Always check weather conditions with the **National Weather Service (© 808/ 973-4381** on Oahu; see individual island chapters for local weather information) before you go. Hike with a pal, never alone. Wear hiking boots, a sun hat, clothes to protect you from the sun and from getting scratches, and high-SPF sunscreen on all exposed areas of skin. Take water. Stay on the trail. Watch your step. It's easy to slip off precipitous trails and into steep canyons. Many experienced hikers and boaters today pack a cellphone in case of emergency; just dial © **911.**

VOG
The volcanic haze dubbed *vog* is caused by gases released when molten lava—from the continuous eruption of Kilauea volcano on the Big Island—pours into

Everything You've Always Wanted to Know about Sharks

The Hawaii State Department of Land and Natural Resources has launched a website, www.hawaiisharks.com, that covers the biology, history, and culture of these carnivores. It also provides information on safety and data on shark bites in Hawaii.

the ocean. Some people claim that long-term exposure to the hazy, smoglike air has caused bronchial ailments, but it's highly unlikely to cause you any harm in the course of your visit.

There actually is a vog season in Hawaii: the fall and winter months, when the trade winds that blow the fumes out to sea die down. The vog is felt not only on the Big Island, but also as far away as Maui and Oahu.

One more word of caution: If you're pregnant or have heart or breathing problems, you should avoid exposure to the sulfuric fumes that are ever present in and around the Big Island's Hawaii Volcanoes National Park.

OCEAN SAFETY

Because most people coming to Hawaii are unfamiliar with the ocean environment, they're often unaware of the natural hazards it holds. With just a few precautions, your ocean experience can be a safe and happy one. An excellent book is *All Stings Considered: First Aid and Medical Treatment of Hawaii's Marine Injuries* (University of Hawaii Press, 1997), by Craig Thomas and Susan Scott.

Note that sharks are not a big problem in Hawaii; in fact, they appear so infrequently that locals look forward to seeing them. Since records have been kept, starting in 1779, there have been only about 100 shark attacks in Hawaii, of which 40% have been fatal. Most attacks occurred after someone fell into the ocean from the shore or from a boat; in these cases, the sharks probably attacked after the person was dead. But general rules for

avoiding sharks are: Don't swim at sunrise, at sunset, or where the water is murky due to stream runoff—sharks may mistake you for one of their usual meals. And don't swim where there are bloody fish in the water, as sharks become aggressive around blood.

SEASICKNESS The waters in Hawaii can range from as calm as glass (off the Kona Coast on the Big Island) to downright frightening (in storm conditions), and they usually fall somewhere in between. In general, expect rougher conditions in winter than in summer. Some 90% of the population tends toward seasickness. If you've never been out on a boat, or if you've been seasick in the past, you might want to heed the following suggestions:

- The day before you go out on the boat, avoid alcohol, caffeine, citrus and other acidic juices, and greasy, spicy, or hard-to-digest foods.
- Get a good night's sleep the night before.
- Take or use whatever seasickness prevention works best for you—medication, an acupressure wristband, gingerroot tea or capsules, or any combination. But do it *before* **you board;** once you set sail, it's generally too late.
- While you're on the boat, stay as low and as near the center of the boat as possible. Avoid the fumes (especially if it's a diesel boat); stay out in the fresh air and watch the horizon. Do not read.

- If you start to feel queasy, drink clear fluids like water, and eat something bland, such as a soda cracker.

STINGS The most common stings in Hawaii come from jellyfish, particularly Portuguese man-of-war and box jellyfish. Since the poisons they inject are very different, you need to treat each sting differently.

A bluish-purple floating bubble with a long tail, the **Portuguese man-of-war** causes some 6,500 stings a year on Oahu alone. These stings, although painful and a nuisance, are rarely harmful; fewer than 1 in 1,000 requires medical treatment. The best prevention is to watch for these floating bubbles as you snorkel (look for the hanging tentacles below the surface). Get out of the water if anyone near you spots these jellyfish.

Reactions to stings range from mild burning and reddening to severe welts and blisters. *All Stings Considered* recommends the following treatment: First, pick off any visible tentacles with a gloved hand, a stick, or anything handy; then rinse the sting with salt- or fresh water, and apply ice to prevent swelling and to help control pain. Avoid folk remedies like vinegar, baking soda, or urinating on the wound, which may actually cause further damage. Most Portuguese man-of-war stings will disappear by themselves within 15 to 20 minutes if you do nothing at all to treat them. Still, be sure to see a doctor if pain persists or a rash or other symptoms develop.

Transparent, square-shaped **box jelly-fish** are nearly impossible to see in the water. Fortunately, they seem to follow a monthly cycle: 8 to 10 days after the full moon, they appear in the waters on the leeward side of each island and hang around for about 3 days. Also, they seem to sting more in the morning hours, when they're on or near the surface.

The stings can cause anything from no visible marks to red, hivelike welts; blisters; and pain lasting from 10 minutes to 8 hours. *All Stings Considered* recommends the following treatment: First, pour regular household vinegar on the sting; this will stop additional burning. Do not rub the area. Pick off any vinegar-soaked tentacles with a stick. For pain, apply an ice pack. Seek additional medical treatment if you experience shortness of breath, weakness, palpitations, muscle cramps, or any other severe symptoms. Most box jellyfish stings disappear by themselves without any treatment.

PUNCTURES Most sea-related punctures come from stepping on or brushing against the needlelike spines of sea urchins (known locally as *wana*). Be careful when you're in the water; don't put your foot down (even if you have booties or fins on) if you can't clearly see the bottom. Waves can push you into *wana* in a surge zone in shallow water. The spines can even puncture a wet suit.

A sea-urchin puncture can result in burning, aching, swelling, and discoloration (black or purple) around the area where the spines entered your skin. The best thing to do is to pull any protruding spines out. The body will absorb the spines within 24 hours to 3 weeks, or the remainder of the spines will work themselves out. Again, contrary to popular wisdom, do not urinate or pour vinegar on the embedded spines—this will not help.

CUTS All cuts obtained in the marine environment must be taken seriously because the high level of bacteria present in the water can quickly cause the cut to become infected. The best way to prevent cuts is to wear a wet suit, gloves, and reef shoes. Never touch coral; not only can you get cut, but you can also damage a living organism that took decades to grow.

Tips **Enjoying the Ocean & Avoiding Mishaps**

The Pacific Whale Foundation has a free brochure called "Enjoying Maui's Unique Ocean Environment" that introduces visitors to Hawaii's ocean, beaches, tide pools, and reefs. Although written for Maui (with maps showing Maui's beaches) it's a great resource on how to stay safe around the ocean, with hints on how to assess weather before you jump into the water and the best ways to view the marine wildlife. To get the brochure, contact the Pacific Whale Foundation at ℂ 808/244-8390, or visit www.pacificwhale.org.

The symptoms of a coral cut can range from a slight scratch to severe welts and blisters. *All Stings Considered* recommends gently pulling the edges of the skin open and removing any embedded coral or grains of sand with tweezers. Next, scrub the cut well with fresh water. If pressing a clean cloth against the wound doesn't stop the bleeding, or the edges of the injury are jagged or gaping, seek medical treatment.

WHAT TO DO IF YOU GET SICK AWAY FROM HOME

We list **hospitals** and **emergency numbers** under "Fast Facts," p. 76.

If you suffer from a chronic illness, consult your doctor before your departure. Pack **prescription medications** in your carry-on luggage, and carry them in their original containers, with pharmacy labels—otherwise, they won't make it through airport security. Visitors from outside the U.S. should carry generic names of prescription drugs. For U.S. travelers, most reliable health-care plans provide coverage if you get sick away from home. Foreign visitors may have to pay all medical costs up front and be reimbursed later. See "Medical Insurance," under "Travel Insurance," earlier.

8 Safety

GENERAL SAFETY

Although tourist areas are generally safe, visitors should always stay alert, even in laid-back Hawaii (and especially in Waikiki). It's wise to ask the island tourist office if you're in doubt about which neighborhoods are safe. Avoid deserted areas, especially at night. Don't go into any city park at night unless there's an event that attracts crowds—for example, the Waikiki Shell concerts in Kapiolani Park. Generally speaking, you can feel safe in areas where there are many people and open establishments.

Avoid carrying valuables with you on the street, and don't display expensive cameras or electronic equipment. Hold on to your pocketbook, and place your billfold in an inside pocket. In theaters, restaurants, and other public places, keep your possessions in sight.

There has been a series of purse-snatching incidents in Oahu. Thieves in slow-moving cars or on foot have snatched handbags from female pedestrians. The Honolulu police department advises women to carry their purses on the shoulder away from the street or, better yet, to wear the strap across the chest instead of on one shoulder. Women with clutch bags should hold them close to their chest.

Remember also that hotels are open to the public and that in a large hotel, security may not be able to screen everyone entering. Always lock your room door—don't assume that once inside your hotel, you're automatically safe.

DRIVING SAFETY

Recently, burglaries of tourist rental cars in hotel parking structures and at beach parking lots have become more common. Park in well-lighted and well-traveled areas, if possible. Never leave any packages or valuables visible in the car. If someone attempts to rob you or steal your car, do not try to resist the thief or carjacker—report the incident to the police department immediately. Ask your rental agency about personal safety, and get written directions or a map with the route to your destination clearly marked.

9 Specialized Travel Resources

TRAVELERS WITH DISABILITIES

Most disabilities shouldn't stop anyone from traveling in the U.S. There are more options and resources out there than ever before.

Travelers with disabilities are made to feel very welcome in Hawaii. There are more than 2,000 ramped curbs in Oahu alone, hotels are usually equipped with wheelchair-accessible rooms, and tour companies provide many special services. The **Hawaii Center for Independent Living,** 414 Kauwili St., Suite 102, Honolulu, HI 96817 (© **808/522-5400;** fax 808/586-8129), can provide information.

The only travel agency in Hawaii specializing in needs for travelers with disabilities is **Access Aloha Travel** (© **800/ 480-1143;** www.accessalohatravel.com), which can book anything, including rental vans (available on Maui and Oahu only), accommodations, tours, cruises, airfare, and anything else you can think of. For more details on wheelchair transportation and tours around the islands, see "Getting Around," in the island chapters.

The **America the Beautiful— National Park and Federal Recreational Lands Pass—Access Pass** (formerly the **Golden Access Passport**) gives the visually impaired persons or those with permanent disabilities (regardless of age) free lifetime entrance to federal recreation sites administered by the National Park Service, including the Fish and Wildlife Service, the Forest Service, the Bureau of Land Management, and the Bureau of Reclamation. This may include national parks, monuments, historic sites, recreation areas, and national wildlife refuges.

The America the Beautiful Access Pass can be obtained only in person at any NPS facility that charges an entrance fee. You need to show proof of medically determined disability. Besides free entry, the pass offers a 50% discount on some federal-use fees charged for such facilities as camping, swimming, parking, boat launching, and tours. For more information, go to www.nps.gov/fees_passes.htm or call © **888/467-2757.**

Organizations that offer a vast range of resources and assistance to travelers with disabilities include **MossRehab** (© **800/ CALL-MOSS;** www.mossresourcenet. org), the **American Foundation for the Blind** (AFB; © 800/232-5463; www. afb.org), and **SATH (Society for Accessible Travel & Hospitality;** © 212/447-7284; www.sath.org). **AirAmbulance-Card.com** is now partnered with SATH and allows you to preselect top-notch hospitals in case of an emergency.

Access-Able Travel Source (© **303/ 232-2979;** www.access-able.com) offers a comprehensive database on travel agents from around the world with experience in accessible travel, destination-specific access information, and links to such resources as service animals, equipment rentals, and access guides.

Many travel agencies offer customized tours and itineraries for travelers with disabilities. Among them are **Flying Wheels Travel** (© 507/451-5005; www.

flyingwheelstravel.com) and **Accessible Journeys** (© 800/846-4537 or 610/521-0339;www.disabilitytravel.com).

Flying with Disability (www.flying-with-disability.org) is a comprehensive information source on airplane travel. **Avis Rent a Car** (© 888/879-4273) has an "Avis Access" program that offers services for customers with special travel needs. These include specially outfitted vehicles with swivel seats, spinner knobs, and hand controls; mobility scooter rentals; and accessible bus service. Be sure to reserve well in advance.

Also check out the quarterly magazine *Emerging Horizons* (www.emerginghorizons.com), available by subscription ($16.95 year U.S.; $21.95 outside U.S.). The "Accessible Travel" link at **Mobility-Advisor.com** (www.mobility-advisor.com) offers a variety of travel resources to persons with disabilities.

British travelers should contact **Holiday Care** (© 0845-124-9971 in U.K. only; www.holidaycare.org.uk) to access a wide range of travel information and resources for elderly people and those with disabilities.

GAY & LESBIAN TRAVELERS

Hawaii is known for its acceptance of all groups. The number of gay- or lesbian-specific accommodations on the islands is limited, but most properties welcome gays and lesbians like any other travelers.

The Center, mailing address P.O. Box 22718, Honolulu, 96823, or 2424 S. Beretania St., between Isenberg and University, Honolulu (© 808/951-7000; fax 808/951-7001; www.thecenterhawaii.org), open Monday through Friday from 10am to 6pm and on Saturday from noon to 4pm, is a referral center for nearly every kind of gay-related service you can think of, including the latest happenings on Oahu. Check out their community newspaper, *Outlook* (published quarterly), for information on local

issues in the gay community in the islands.

For information on Kauai's gay community and related events, contact the **Gay/Lesbian/Bisexual/Transgender Audio Bulletin Board** (© 808/823-6248).

For the Big Island, Oahu, Maui, and Kauai, check out the website for **Out in Hawaii,** www.outinhawaii.com, for vacation ideas and a calendar of events.

The International Gay and Lesbian Travel Association (IGLTA; © 800/448-8550 or 954/776-2626; www.iglta.org) is the trade association for the gay and lesbian travel industry, and offers an online directory of gay- and lesbian-friendly travel businesses and tour operators.

Many agencies offer tours and travel itineraries specifically for gay and lesbian travelers. **Above and Beyond Tours** (© 800/397-2681; www.abovebeyondtours.com) are gay Australia tour specialists. San Francisco–based **Now, Voyager** (© 800/255-6951; www.nowvoyager.com) offers worldwide trips and cruises, and **Olivia** (© 800/631-6277; www.olivia.com) offers lesbian cruises and resort vacations. **Pacific Ocean Holidays** (© 800/735-6600 or 808/944-4700; www.gayhawaiivacations.com) offers vacation packages that feature gay-owned and gay-friendly lodgings. Also on their website is *A Guide for Gay Visitors & Kamaaina.*

Gay.com Travel (© 800/929-2268 or 415/644-8044; www.gay.com/travel or www.outandabout.com), is an excellent online successor to the popular *Out & About* print magazine. It provides regularly updated information about gay-owned, gay-oriented, and gay-friendly lodging, dining, sightseeing, nightlife, and shopping establishments in every important destination worldwide. British travelers should click on the "Travel" link at **www.uk.gay.com** for advice and gay-friendly trip ideas.

The Canadian website **GayTraveler** (**gaytraveler.ca**) offers ideas and advice for gay travel all over the world.

The following travel guides are available at many bookstores, or you can order them from any online bookseller: *Spartacus International Gay Guide, 35th Edition* (Bruno Gmünder Verlag; www.spartacus world.com/gayguide/) and *Odysseus: The International Gay Travel Planner, 17th Edition* (www.odyusa.com); and the *Damron* guides (www.damron.com), with separate annual books for gay men and lesbians.

SENIOR TRAVEL

Discounts for seniors are available at almost all of Hawaii's major attractions and occasionally at hotels and restaurants. The Outrigger hotel chain, for instance, offers travelers ages 50 and older a 20% discount off regular published rates—and an additional 5% off for members of AARP. Always ask when making hotel reservations or buying tickets. And always carry identification with proof of your age—it can really pay off.

Members of **AARP,** 601 E St. NW, Washington, DC 20049 (© **888/687-2277;** www.aarp.org), get discounts on hotels, airfares, and car rentals. AARP offers members a wide range of benefits, including *AARP: The Magazine* and a monthly newsletter. Anyone over 50 can join.

The U.S. National Park Service offers an **America the Beautiful—National Park and Federal Recreational Lands Pass—Senior Pass** (formerly the **Golden Age Passport**), which gives seniors 62 years or older lifetime entrance to all properties administered by the National Park Service—national parks, monuments, historic sites, recreation areas, and national wildlife refuges—for a one-time processing fee of $10. The pass must be purchased in person at any NPS facility that charges an entrance fee. Besides free entry, the America the Beautiful Senior Pass offers a 50% discount on some federal-use fees charged for such facilities as camping, swimming, parking, boat launching, and tours. For more information, go to www.nps.gov/fees_passes.htm or call © **888/467-2757.**

Many reliable agencies and organizations target the 50-plus market. **Elderhostel** (© **800/454-5768;** www.elder hostel.org) arranges worldwide study programs for those aged 55 and over. **ElderTreks** (© **800/741-7956** or 416/558-5000 outside North America; www.eldertreks.com) offers small-group tours to off-the-beaten-path or adventure-travel locations, restricted to travelers 50 and older.

Recommended publications offering travel resources and discounts for seniors include the quarterly magazine *Travel 50 & Beyond* (www.travel50andbeyond.com) and the bestselling paperback *Unbelievably Good Deals and Great Adventures That You Absolutely Can't Get Unless You're Over 50 2005–2006, 16th Edition* (McGraw-Hill), by Joann Rattner Heilman.

FAMILY TRAVEL

Hawaii is paradise for children: beaches to run on, water to splash in, and unusual sights to see. Be sure to check out the boxes in each island chapter for kid-friendly places to stay and family activities.

The larger hotels and resorts offer supervised programs for children and can refer you to qualified babysitters. By state law, hotels can accept only children ages 5 to 12 in supervised activities programs, but they often accommodate younger children by simply hiring babysitters to watch over them. You can also contact **People Attentive to Children (PATCH),** which can refer you to babysitters who have taken a training course on child care. On Oahu call © 808/839-1988; on the Big Island call © 808/325-3864 in Kona or © 808/961-3169 in Hilo; on Maui call © 808/242-9232; on Kauai call

ⓒ 808/246-0622; on Molokai and Lanai call ⓒ 800/498-4145; or visit www.patch hawaii.org.

Baby's Away (www.babysaway.com) rents cribs, strollers, highchairs, playpens, infant seats, and the like on Maui (ⓒ 800/942-9030 or 808/875-9030), the Big Island (ⓒ 800/996-9030 or 808/987-9236), and Oahu (ⓒ 800/496-6386 or 808/222-6041). The staff will deliver whatever you need to wherever you're staying and pick it up when you're done.

To locate accommodations, restaurants, and attractions that are particularly kid-friendly, refer to the "Kids" icon throughout this guide.

Recommended family travel websites include **Family Travel Forum** (www.familytravelforum.com), a comprehensive site that offers customized trip planning; **Family Travel Network** (www.familytravelnetwork.com), an online magazine providing travel tips; and **TravelWithYourKids.com** (www.travelwithyourkids.com), a comprehensive site written by parents for parents offering sound advice for long-distance and international travel with children.

Also look for *Frommer's Hawaii with Kids* (Wiley Publishing, Inc.).

10 Sustainable Tourism/Ecotourism

Each time you take a flight or drive a car, CO_2 is released into the atmosphere. You can help neutralize this danger to our planet through "carbon offsetting"—paying someone to reduce your CO_2 emissions by the same amount you've added. Carbon offsets can be purchased in the U.S. from companies such as **Carbonfund.org** (www.carbonfund.org) and **TerraPass** (www.terrapass.org), and from **Climate Care** (www.climatecare.org) in the U.K.

Although one could argue that any vacation that includes an airplane flight can't be truly "green," you can go on holiday and still contribute positively to the environment. In addition to purchasing carbon offsets from the companies mentioned above, you can take other steps toward responsible travel. Choose forward-looking companies who embrace responsible development practices, helping preserve destinations for the future by working alongside local people. An increasing number of sustainable tourism initiatives can help you plan a family trip and leave as small a "footprint" as possible on the places you visit.

Responsible Travel (www.responsibletravel.com), run by a spokesperson for responsible tourism in the travel industry, contains a great source of sustainable travel ideas.

You can find eco-friendly travel tips, statistics, and touring companies and associations—listed by destination under "Travel Choice"—at the TIES website, **www.ecotourism.org**. Also check out **Conservation International** (www.conservation.org), which, with *National Geographic Traveler,* annually presents **World Legacy Awards** (www.wlaward.org) to those travel tour operators, businesses, organizations, and places that have made a significant contribution to sustainable tourism. **Ecotravel.com** is part online magazine and part ecodirectory that lets you search for touring companies in several categories (water-based, land-based, spiritually oriented, and so on).

In the U.K., **Tourism Concern** (www.tourismconcern.org.uk) works to reduce social and environmental problems connected to tourism and find ways of improving tourism so that local benefits are increased.

Frommers.com: The Complete Travel Resource

It should go without saying, but we highly recommend **Frommers.com,** voted Best Travel Site by *PC Magazine.* We think you'll find our expert advice and tips; independent reviews of hotels, restaurants, attractions, and preferred shopping and nightlife venues; vacation giveaways; and an online booking tool indispensable before, during, and after your travels. We publish the complete contents of over 128 travel guides in our **Destinations** section, covering nearly 3,800 places worldwide to help you plan your trip. Each weekday, we publish original articles reporting on **Deals and News** via our free **Frommers.com Newsletter** to help you save time and money and travel smarter. We're betting you'll find our new **Events** listings (http://events.frommers.com) an invaluable resource; it's an up-to-the-minute roster of what's happening in cities everywhere—including concerts, festivals, lectures, and more. We've also added weekly **Podcasts, interactive maps,** and hundreds of new images across the site. Check out our **Travel Talk** area, featuring **Message Boards** where you can join in conversations with thousands of fellow Frommer's travelers and post your trip report once you return.

The **Association of British Travel Agents (ABTA;** www.abtamembers.org) acts as a focal point for the U.K. travel industry and is one of the leading groups spearheading responsible tourism.

The **Association of Independent Tour Operators (AITO;** www.aito.co. uk) is a group of interesting specialist operators leading the field in making holidays sustainable.

For information about the ethics of swimming with dolphins and other outdoor activities, visit the **Whale and Dolphin Conservation Society** (www.wdcs. org) and **Tread Lightly** (www.tread lightly.org).

11 Staying Connected

TELEPHONES

Generally, hotel surcharges on long-distance and local calls are astronomical, so you're better off using your **cellphone** or a **public pay telephone.** Many convenience groceries and packaging services sell **prepaid calling cards** in denominations up to $50; for international visitors, these can be the least expensive way to call home. Many public pay phones at airports now accept American Express, MasterCard, and Visa credit cards. **Local calls** made from pay phones in most locales cost either 25¢ or 35¢ (no pennies, please).

Most long-distance and international calls can be dialed directly from any phone. **For calls within the United States and to Canada,** dial 1 followed by the area code and the seven-digit number. **For other international calls,** dial 011 followed by the country code, city code, and number you are calling.

Calls to area codes **800, 888, 877,** and **866** are toll-free. However, calls to area codes **700** and **900** (chat lines, bulletin boards, "dating" services, and so on) can be very expensive—usually a charge of 95¢ to $3 or more per minute, and they sometimes have minimum charges that can run as high as $15 or more.

For **reversed-charge or collect calls,** and for person-to-person calls, dial the number 0 and then the area code and number; an operator will come on the line, and you should specify whether you are calling collect, person-to-person, or both. If your operator-assisted call is international, ask for the overseas operator.

For **local directory assistance** ("information"), dial 411; for long-distance information, dial 1, then the appropriate area code, and 555-1212.

CELLPHONES

Just because your cellphone works at home doesn't mean it'll work everywhere in the U.S. (thanks to our nation's fragmented cellphone system). It's a good bet that your phone will work in major cities, but take a look at your wireless company's coverage map on its website before heading out; T-Mobile, Sprint, and Nextel are particularly weak in rural areas. If you need to stay in touch at a destination where you know your phone won't work, **rent** a phone that does from **InTouch USA** (© 800/ 872-7626; www.intouchglobal.com) or a rental car location, but beware that you'll pay $1 a minute or more for airtime.

If you're not from the U.S., you'll be appalled at the poor reach of our **GSM (Global System for Mobile Communications) wireless network,** which is used by much of the rest of the world. Your phone will probably work in most major U.S. cities; it definitely won't work in many rural areas. To see where GSM phones work in the U.S., check out www.t-mobile.com/coverage/national_popup.asp. And you may or may not be able to send SMS (text messaging) home.

VOICE OVER INTERNET PROTOCOL (VOIP)

If you have Web access while traveling, you might consider a broadband-based telephone service (in technical terms, Voice over Internet protocol, or VoIP) such as Skype (www.skype.com) or Vonage (www.vonage.com), which allows you to make free international calls if you use their services from your laptop or in a cybercafe. The people you're calling must also use the service for it to work; check the sites for details.

INTERNET/E-MAIL WITHOUT YOUR OWN COMPUTER

To find cybercafes in your destination, check www.cybercaptive.com and www.cybercafe.com.

Most major airports have **Internet kiosks** that provide basic Web access for a per-minute fee that's usually higher than cybercafe prices. Check out copy shops like **Kinko's** (FedEx Kinkos), which offers computer stations with fully loaded software (as well as Wi-Fi).

WITH YOUR OWN COMPUTER

More and more hotels, resorts, airports, cafes, and retailers are going Wi-Fi (wireless fidelity), becoming "hotspots" that offer free high-speed Wi-Fi access or charge a small fee for usage. Wi-Fi is even found in campgrounds, RV parks, and entire towns. Most laptops sold today have built-in wireless capability. To find public Wi-Fi hotspots at your destination, go to www.jiwire.com; its Hotspot Finder holds the world's largest directory of public wireless hotspots.

For dial-up access, most business-class hotels in the U.S. offer dataports for laptop modems, and a few thousand hotels in the U.S. and Europe now offer free high-speed Internet access.

Wherever you go, bring a **connection kit** of the right power and phone adapters, a spare phone cord, and a spare Ethernet network cable—or find out whether your hotel supplies them to guests.

For information on electrical currency conversions, see "Electricity," in the "Fast Facts" section at the end of this chapter.

12 Packages for the Independent Traveler

Package tours are simply a way to buy the airfare, accommodations, and other elements of your trip (such as car rentals, airport transfers, and sometimes even activities) at the same time and often at discounted prices.

One good source of package deals is the airlines themselves. Most major airlines offer air/land packages, including **American Airlines Vacations** (© 800/321-2121; www.aavacations.com), **Delta Vacations** (© 800/654-6559; www.delta vacations.com), **Continental Airlines Vacations** (© 800/301-3800; www.co vacations.com), and **United Vacations** (© 888/854-3899; www.unitedvacations. com). Several big **online travel agencies**—Expedia, Travelocity, Orbitz, Site59, and Lastminute.com—also do a brisk business in packages.

Some packagers specialize in Hawaiian vacations. **Pleasant Holidays** (© 800/2-HAWAII or 800/242-9244; www.pleasant holidays.com) is by far the biggest and most comprehensive packager to Hawaii; it offers an extensive, high-quality collection of 50 condos and hotels in every price range. **Travelzoo** (www.travelzoo.

com) often has package deals to Hawaii as well.

Hawaii's **top hotel chains** offer package deals and special rates as well. Packages may be available for families, seniors, honeymooners, and golfers, and some offer discounts on rental cars or multi-night stays. Check with **Outrigger**'s "Ohana" (Hawaiian for "family") Hotels (© **800/462-6262;** www.ohanahotels. com) and the more upscale "Outrigger" resorts and condominiums (© **800/ OUTRIGGER;** www.outrigger.com), the ResortQuest chain (© **1800/GO-RELAX;** www.resortquest.com), **Marc Resorts Hawaii** (© **800/535-0085;** fax 800/633-5085; www.marcresorts.com), and **Castle Resorts and Hotels** (© **800/ 367-5004;** fax 800/477-2329; www. castleresorts.com).

Travel packages are also listed in the travel section of your local Sunday newspaper. Or check ads in the national travel magazines such as *Arthur Frommer's Budget Travel Magazine, Travel + Leisure, National Geographic Traveler,* and *Condé Nast Traveler.*

Tips **Ask Before You Go**

Before you invest in a package deal or an escorted tour:

- Always ask about the **cancellation policy.** Can you get your money back? Is there a deposit required?
- Ask about the **accommodations choices and prices** for each. Then look up the hotels' reviews in a Frommer's guide and check their rates online for your specific dates of travel. Also find out what types of rooms are offered.
- Request a complete **schedule** (escorted tours only).
- Ask about the **size** and demographics of the group (escorted tours only).
- Discuss what is included in the **price** (transportation, meals, tips, airport transfers, etc.; escorted tours only).
- Finally, look for **hidden expenses.** Ask whether airport departure fees and taxes, for example, are included in the total cost—they rarely are.

13 Special-Interest Trips

If all you want is a fabulous beach and a perfectly mixed mai tai, then Hawaii has what you're looking for. But the islands' wealth of natural wonders is equally hard to resist; the year-round tropical climate and spectacular scenery tend to inspire almost everyone to get outside and explore.

If you don't have your own snorkel gear or other watersports equipment, or if you just don't feel like packing it, don't fret: Everything you'll need is available for rent in the islands. We discuss all kinds of places to rent or buy gear in the island chapters that follow.

SETTING OUT ON YOUR OWN VS. USING AN OUTFITTER

There are two ways to go: Plan all the details before you leave and either rent gear or schlep your stuff 2,500 miles across the Pacific, or go with an outfitter or a guide and let someone else worry about the details.

Experienced outdoors enthusiasts may head to coastal campgrounds or even trek to the 13,796-foot-high summit of Mauna Loa on their own. But in Hawaii, it's often preferable to go with a local guide who is familiar with the conditions at both sea level and summit peaks, knows the land and its flora and fauna in detail, and has all the gear you'll need. It's also good to go with a guide if time is an issue or if you have specialized interests. If you really want to see native birds, for instance, an experienced guide will take you directly to the best areas for sightings. And many forests and valleys in the interior of the islands are either on private property or in wilderness preserves accessible only on guided tours. The downside? If you go with a guide, plan on spending at least $100 a day per person. We've recommended the best local outfitters and tour-guide operators on each island in the chapters that follow.

But if you have the time, already own the gear, and love doing the research and planning, try exploring on your own. Each island chapter discusses the best spots to set out on your own, from the top offshore snorkel and dive spots to great day-long hikes, as well as the federal, state, and county agencies that can help you with hikes on public property; we also list references for spotting birds, plants, and sea life. We recommend that you always use the resources available to inquire about weather, trail, or surf conditions; water availability; and other conditions before you take off on your adventure.

For hikers, a great alternative to hiring a private guide is taking a guided hike offered by the **Nature Conservancy of Hawaii,** PO Box 96, Honolulu, HI 96759 (© **808/572-7849** on Maui, 808/621-2008 on Oahu, or 808/553-5236 on Molokai); or the **Hawaii Chapter of the Sierra Club,** P.O. Box 2577, Honolulu, HI 96813 (© **808/579-9802** on Oahu; www.hi.sierraclub.org). Both organizations offer guided hikes in preserves and special areas during the year, as well as day- to week-long work trips to restore habitats and trails and to root out invasive plants. It might not sound like a dream vacation to everyone, but it's a chance to see the "real" Hawaii—including wilderness areas that are ordinarily off-limits.

All Nature Conservancy hikes and work trips are free (donations are appreciated). However, you must reserve a spot for yourself, and a deposit is required for guided hikes to ensure that you'll show up; your deposit is refunded once you do. The hikes are generally offered once a month on Maui, Molokai, and Lanai, and twice a month on Oahu. For all islands, call the Oahu office for reservations. Write for a schedule of guided hikes and other programs.

Outdoor Etiquette

Act locally, think globally, and carry out what you carry in. Find a trash container for all your litter (including cigarette butts; it's *very* bad form to throw them out of your car window or to use the beach as an ashtray). Observe KAPU (taboo) and NO TRESPASSING signs. Don't climb on ancient Hawaiian *heiau* (temple) walls or carry home rocks, all of which belong to the Hawaiian volcano goddess Pele. Some say it's just a silly superstition, but each year the national and state park services get boxes of lava rocks in the mail that have been sent back to Hawaii by visitors who've experienced unusually bad luck.

The Sierra Club offers weekly hikes on Oahu and Maui. Hikes are led by certified Sierra Club volunteers and are classified as easy, moderate, or strenuous. These half-day or all-day affairs cost $1 for Sierra Club members and $3 for nonmembers (bring exact change). For a copy of the club newsletter, which lists all outings and trail-repair work, send $2 to the address above.

Local eco-tourism opportunities are also discussed in each island chapter. For more information, contact the **Hawaii Ecotourism Association** (✆ 877/300-7058; www.hawaiiecotourism.org).

USING ACTIVITIES DESKS TO BOOK YOUR ISLAND FUN

If you're unsure of which activity or which outfitter or guide is the right one for you and your family, you might want to consider booking through a discount activities center or activities desk. Not only will they save you money, but good activities centers should also be able to help you find, say, the snorkel cruise that's right for you, or the luau that's most suitable for both you *and* the kids.

Remember, however, that it's in the activities agent's best interest to sign you up with outfitters from which they earn the most commission. Some agents have no qualms about booking you into any activity if it means an extra buck for them. If an agent tries to push a particular outfitter or activity too hard, be skeptical. Conversely, they'll try to steer you away from outfitters who don't offer big commissions. For example, Trilogy, the company that offers Maui's most popular snorkel cruises to Lanai (and the only one with rights to land at Lanai's Hulopoe Beach), offers only minimum commissions to agents and does not allow agents to offer any discounts at all. As a result, most activities desks will automatically try to steer you away from Trilogy.

Another important word of warning: Stay away from activities centers that offer discounts as fronts for timeshare sales presentations. Using a free or discounted snorkel cruise or luau tickets as bait, they'll suck you into a 90-minute presentation—and try to get you to buy into a Hawaii timeshare in the process. Because their business is timeshares, not activities, they won't be as interested, or as knowledgeable, about which activities might be right for you. These shady deals seem to be particularly rampant on Maui.

There are also a number of very reliable local activities centers on each of the neighbor islands. On Maui your best bet is **Tom Barefoot's Cashback Tours** (✆ 800/895-2040 or 808/661-8889; www.tombarefoot.com), 834 Front St., Lahaina. Tom offers a 10% discount on all tours, activities, and adventures if you pay using cash, a personal check, or traveler's checks. If you use a credit card, you'll get a 7% discount.

On the Big Island, check out the **Activity Connection,** Bougainvillea Plaza Suite 102, 75-5656 Kuakini Hwy.,

Kailua-Kona (© **800/459-7156** or 808/ 329-1038; www.beachactivityguide.com); it offers up to 15% off on various island activities.

Finally, you can book activities yourself and get the commission by booking via the Internet. Most activities offer from 10% to 25% off their prices if you book online.

OUTDOOR ACTIVITIES A TO Z

Here's a brief rundown of the many outdoor activities available in Hawaii. For our recommendations on the best places to go, the best shops for renting equipment, and the best outfitters to use, see the individual island chapters later in this book.

BIRDING Many of Hawaii's tropical birds are found nowhere else on earth. There are curved-bill honeycreepers, black-winged red birds, and the rare o'o, whose yellow feathers Hawaiians once plucked to make royal capes. When you go birding, take along *A Field Guide to the Birds of Hawaii and the Tropical Pacific,* by H. Douglas Pratt, Phillip L. Bruner, and Delwyn G. Berett (Princeton University Press, 1987).

Kauai and **Molokai,** in particular, are great places to go birding. On Kauai large colonies of seabirds nest at Kilauea National Wildlife Refuge and along the Na Pali Coast. Be sure to take along a copy of *The Birds of Kauai* (University of Hawaii Press), by Jim Denny. The lush rainforest of Molokai's Kamakou Preserve is home to the Molokai thrush and Molokai creeper, which live only on this 30-mile-long island. For details, see "Birding," in chapters 5 and 9, as well as the discussion of the Kamakou Preserve under "Seeing the Sights," in chapter 7.

BOATING Almost every type of nautical experience is available in the islands, from old-fashioned Polynesian outrigger canoes to America's Cup racing sloops to submarines. You'll find details on all these seafaring experiences in the individual island chapters.

No matter which type of vessel you choose, be sure to see the Hawaiian islands from offshore if you can afford it. It's easy to combine multiple activities into one cruise: Lots of snorkel boats double as sightseeing cruises and, in winter, whale-watching cruises. The main harbors for visitor activities are Kewalo Basin, Oahu; Honokohau, Kailua-Kona, and Kawaihae on the Big Island; Lahaina and Maaalea, Maui; Nawiliwili and Port Allen, Kauai; and Kaunakakai, Molokai.

BODY BOARDING (BOOGIE BOARDING) & BODYSURFING

Bodysurfing—riding the waves without a board, becoming one with the rolling water—is a way of life in Hawaii. Some bodysurfers just rely on hands to ride the waves; others use hand boards (flat, paddlelike gloves). For additional maneuverability, try a boogie board or body board (also known as belly boards or *paipo* boards). These 3-foot-long boards support the upper part of your body and are very maneuverable in the water. Both bodysurfing and body boarding require a pair of open-heeled swim fins to help propel you through the water. The equipment is inexpensive and easy to carry, and both sports can be practiced in the small, gentle waves. See the individual island chapters for details on where to rent boards and where to go.

CAMPING Hawaii's year-round balmy climate makes camping a breeze. However, tropical campers should always be ready for rain, especially in Hawaii's winter wet season, but even in the dry summer season as well. And remember to bring a good mosquito repellent. If you're heading to the top of Hawaii's volcanoes, you'll need a down mummy bag. If you plan to camp on the beach, bring a mosquito net and a rain poncho. Always be prepared to deal with contaminated water (purify it by boiling, through filtration,

---

Tips **Travel Tip**

When planning sunset activities, be aware that Hawaii, like other places close to the Equator, has a very short (5–10 min.) twilight period after the sun sets. After that, it's dark. If you hike out to watch the sunset, be sure you can make it back quickly, or take a flashlight.

---

or by using iodine tablets) and the tropical sun (protect yourself with sunscreen, a hat, and a long-sleeved shirt). Also be sure to check out "Health," earlier in this chapter, for hiking and camping tips.

There are many established campgrounds at beach parks, including Kauai's Anini Beach, Oahu's Malaekahana Beach, Maui's Waianapanapa Beach, and the Big Island's Hapuna Beach. Campgrounds are also located in the interior at Maui's Haleakala National Park and the Big Island's Hawaii Volcanoes National Park, as well as at Kalalau Beach on Kauai's Na Pali Coast and in the cool uplands of Kokee State Park. See "Beaches" or "Hiking & Camping," in the individual island chapters, for the best places to camp. For more details on getting regulations and camping information for any of Hawaii's national or state parks, see the "Visitor Information & Maps" section at the beginning of this chapter.

Hawaiian Trail and Mountain Club, P.O. Box 2238, Honolulu, HI 96804, offers an information packet on hiking and camping throughout the islands. Send $2 and a legal-size, self-addressed, stamped envelope for information. Another good source is the *Hiking/Camping Information Packet,* available from **Hawaii Geographic Maps and Books,** 49 S. Hotel St., Honolulu, HI 96813 (© **800/538-3950** or 808/538-3952), for $7. The **University of Hawaii Press,** 2840 Kolowalu St., Honolulu, HI 96822 (© **888/847-7737;** www.uhpress.hawaii. edu), has an excellent selection of hiking, backpacking, and bird-watching guides,

especially Stuart M. Ball, Jr.'s, *The Hikers Guide to the Hawaiian Islands.*

GOLF Nowhere else on earth can you tee off to whale spouts, putt under rainbows, and play around a live volcano. Hawaii has some of the world's top-rated golf courses. But be forewarned: Each course features hellish natural hazards, like razor-sharp lava, gusty trade winds, an occasional wild pig, and the tropical heat. And greens fees tend to be very expensive. Still, golfers flock here from around the world and love every minute of it. See the individual island chapters for coverage of the resort courses most worth splurging on (with details, where applicable, on money-saving twilight rates), as well as the best budget and municipal courses.

A few tips on golfing in Hawaii: There's generally wind—10 to 30 mph is not unusual between 10am and 2pm—so you may have to play two to three clubs up or down to compensate. Bring extra balls: The rough is thick, water hazards are everywhere, and the wind wreaks havoc with your game. On the greens, your putt will *always* break toward the ocean. Hit deeper and more aggressively in the sand because the type of sand used on most Hawaii courses is firmer and more compact than on mainland courses (lighter sand would blow away in the constant wind). And bring a camera— you'll kick yourself if you don't capture those spectacular views.

See our coverage in each island chapter, and see also "The Best Golf Courses," in chapter 1.

(Value) Fun for Less: Don't Leave Home without a Gold Card

Almost any activity you can think of, from submarine rides to Polynesian luau, can be purchased at a discount by using the **Activities and Attractions Association of Hawaii Gold Card,** 355 Hukilike St., No. 202, Kahului, HI 96732 (② 800/398-9698 or 808/871-7947; fax 808/877-3104; www.hawaii-ifun.org). The Gold Card, accepted by members on all islands, offers a discount of 10% to 25% off activities and meals for up to four people; it's good for a year from the purchase date and costs $30.

Your Gold Card can lower the regular $149 price of a helicopter ride to only $119, saving you almost $120 for a group of four. And there are hundreds of activities to choose from: dinner cruises, horseback riding, watersports, and more—plus savings on rental cars, restaurants, and golf.

Contact Activities and Attractions to purchase your card; you then contact the outfitter, restaurant, rental-car agency, or other proprietor directly; supply your card number; and receive the discount.

HIKING   Hiking in Hawaii is a breathtaking experience. The islands have hundreds of miles of trails, many of which reward you with a hidden beach, a private waterfall, an Eden-like valley, or simply an unforgettable view. However, rock climbers are out of luck: Most of Hawaii's volcanic cliffs are too steep and brittle to scale.

Hawaiian Trail and Mountain Club, P.O. Box 2238, Honolulu, HI 96804, offers an information packet on hiking and camping in Hawaii; to receive a copy, send $2 and a legal-size, self-addressed, stamped envelope. **Hawaii Geographic Maps and Books,** 49 S. Hotel St., Honolulu, HI 96813 (② **800/538-3950** or 808/538-3952), offers the *Hiking/Camping Information Packet* for $7. Also note that the **Hawaii State Department of Land and Natural Resources,** 1151 Punchbowl St., No. 131, Honolulu, HI 96809 (② **808/587-0300;** www.hawaii.gov), will send you free topographical trail maps.

The **Nature Conservancy of Hawaii** (② **808/537-4508** on Oahu, ② **808/572-7849** on Maui, or ② **808/553-5236** on Molokai; www.tnc.org/hawaii) and the **Hawaii Chapter of the Sierra Club,** P.O. Box 2577, Honolulu, HI 96803 (② **808/538-6616**), both offer guided hikes in preserves and special areas during the year. Also see the individual island chapters for complete details on the best hikes for all ability levels.

A couple of terrific books on hiking are Stuart M. Ball, Jr.'s, *The Hiking Guide to the Hawaiian Islands,* published by the University of Hawaii Press, and his book on Oahu, *The Hikers Guide to Oahu,* also from University of Hawaii Press.

Before you set out on the trail, see "Health," earlier in this chapter, for tips on hiking safety, as well as "What to Pack," earlier in this chapter.

HORSEBACK RIDING   One of the best ways to see Hawaii is on horseback; almost all the islands offer riding opportunities for just about every age and level of experience. You can ride into Maui's

Haleakala Crater, along Kauai's Mahaulepu Beach, or through Oahu's remote windward valleys on Kualoa Ranch, or you can gallop across the wide-open spaces of the Big Island's Parker Ranch, one of the largest privately owned ranches in the United States. See the individual island chapters for details. Be sure to bring a pair of jeans and closed-toed shoes to wear on your ride.

KAYAKING Hawaii is one of the world's most popular destinations for ocean kayaking. Beginners can paddle across a tropical lagoon to two uninhabited islets off Lanikai Beach on Oahu, and more experienced kayakers can take on Kauai's awesome Na Pali Coast. In summer, experts take advantage of the usually flat conditions on the north shore of Molokai, where the sea cliffs are the steepest on earth and the remote valleys can be reached only by sea. See "Watersports," in chapters 5 through 9, for local outfitters and tour guides.

SCUBA DIVING Some people come to the islands solely to take the plunge into the tropical Pacific and explore the underwater world. Hawaii is one of the world's top 10 dive destinations, according to *Rodale's Scuba Diving Magazine.* Here you can see the great variety of tropical marine life (more than 100 endemic species found nowhere else on the planet), explore sea caves, and swim with sea turtles and monk seals in clear, tropical water. If you're not certified, try to take classes before you come to Hawaii so you don't waste time learning and can dive right in.

If you dive, **go early in the morning.** Trade winds often rough up the seas in the afternoon, especially on Maui, so most operators schedule early-morning dives that end at noon. To organize a dive on your own, order **The Oahu Snorkelers and Shore Divers Guide,** by Francisco B. de Carvalho, from University of Hawaii Press.

Tip: It's usually worth the extra bucks to go with a good dive operator. Check "Scuba Diving" in the island chapters; we've listed the operators that'll give you the most for your money.

SNORKELING Snorkeling is one of Hawaii's main attractions, and almost anyone can do it. All you need is a mask, a snorkel, fins, and some basic swimming skills. In many places, all you have to do is wade into the water and look down at the magical underwater world.

If you've never snorkeled before, most resorts and excursion boats offer snorkeling equipment and lessons. You don't really need lessons, however; it's plenty easy to figure out for yourself, especially once you're at the beach, where everybody around you will be doing it. If you don't have your own gear, you can rent it from one of dozens of dive shops and activity booths, discussed in the individual island chapters that follow.

While everyone heads for Oahu's Hanauma Bay—the perfect spot for first-timers—other favorite snorkel spots include Kee Beach on Kauai, Kahaluu Beach on the Big Island, Hulopoe Bay on Lanai, and Kapalua Bay on Maui. Although snorkeling is excellent on all the islands, the Big Island, with its recent lava formations and abrupt drop-offs, offers some particularly spectacular opportunities. Some of the best snorkel spots in the islands—notably, the Big Island's Kealakekua Bay and Molokini Crater just off Maui—are accessible only by boat; for tips on the islands' top snorkel boats, see "Watersports" in chapters 5, 6, 7, and 9.

Some snorkel tips: Always snorkel with a buddy. Look up every once in a while to see where you are and if there's any boat traffic. Don't touch anything; not only can you damage coral, but camouflaged fish and shells with poisonous spines may surprise you. Always check with a dive shop, lifeguards, or others on

> ### *Tips* Snorkel Bob's
>
> If you're planning on visiting several islands and would like to rent snorkel gear on one island and keep it with you for your whole trip, try **Snorkel Bob's** (www.snorkelbob.com), which lets you rent snorkel gear, boogie boards, life jackets, and wet suits on any one island and return them on another. A basic set of snorkel gear costs $3.50 a day or $9 a week—a very good deal. The best gear is $6.50 a day or $29 a week; if you're nearsighted and need a prescription mask, it's $9 a day or $39 a week.
>
> You can find Snorkel Bob's on **Oahu** at 702 Kapahulu Ave. (at Date St.), Honolulu (© **808/735-7944**); on **Maui** at 1217 Front St., in Lahaina (© **808/661-4421**), at Napili Village, 5425-C Lower Honoapiilani Hwy., Napili (© **808/669-9603**), and in South Maui at Kamole Beach Center, 2411 S. Kihei Rd., Kihei (© **808/879-7449**); on the **Big Island** at 75–5831 Kahakai St. (off Alii Dr., next to Huggo's and the Royal Kona Resort), in Kailua-Kona (© **808/329-0770**); and on **Kauai** at 4–734 Kuhio Hwy. (just north of Coconut Plantation Marketplace), in Kapaa (© **808/823-9433**), and in Koloa at 3236 Poipu Rd., near Poipu Beach (© **808/742-2206**).

the beach about the area in which you plan to snorkel and ask if there are any dangerous conditions you should know about.

SPORT-FISHING   Big-game fishing at its best is found off the Big Island of Hawaii at **Kailua-Kona,** where the deep blue waters offshore yield trophy marlin year-round. You can also try for spearfish, swordfish, various tuna, mahimahi (dorado), rainbow runners, wahoo, barracuda, trevallies, bonefish, and various bottom fish like snappers and groupers. Each island offers deep-sea boat charters for good-eating fish like tuna, wahoo, and mahimahi. Visiting anglers currently need no license.

Charter fishing boats range widely both in size—from small 24-foot open skiffs to luxurious 50-foot-plus yachts—and in price—from about $100 per person to "share" a boat with other anglers for a half-day to $900 a day to book an entire luxury sport-fishing yacht on an exclusive basis. Shop around. Prices vary according to the boat, the crowd, and the captain. See the individual island chapters for details. Also, many boat captains

tag and release marlin or keep the fish for themselves (sorry, that's Hawaii style). If you want to eat your mahimahi for dinner or have your marlin mounted, tell the captain before you go.

Money-saving tip: Try contacting the charter boat captain directly and bargaining. Many charter captains pay a 20% to 30% commission to charter-booking agencies and may be willing to give you a discount if you book directly.

SURFING   The ancient Hawaiian practice of *hee nalu* (wave sliding) is probably the sport most people picture when they think of Hawaii. Believe it or not, you, too, can do some wave sliding—just sign up at any one of the numerous surfing schools located throughout the islands; see "Surfing" in chapters 5, 6, 7, and 9. On world-famous Waikiki Beach, just head over to one of the surf stands that line the sand; these guys say they can get anybody up and standing on a board. If you're already a big Kahuna in surfing, check the same chapters listed above for the best deals on rental equipment and the best places to hang ten.

Not So Close! They Hardly Know You

In the excitement of seeing a whale or a school of dolphins, don't forget that they're protected under the Marine Mammals Protection Act. You must stay at least 300 feet (the length of a football field) away from all whales, dolphins, and other marine mammals. This applies to swimmers, kayakers, and windsurfers. And, yes, visitors have been prosecuted for swimming with dolphins! If you have any questions, call the **National Marine Fisheries Service** (℅ **808/541-2727**) or the **Hawaiian Islands Humpback Whale National Marine Sanctuary** (℅ **800/831-4888**).

TENNIS   Tennis is a popular sport in the islands. Each island chapter lists details on free municipal courts as well as the best deals on private courts. The etiquette at the free county courts is to play only 45 minutes if someone is waiting.

WHALE-WATCHING   Every winter, pods of Pacific humpback whales make the 3,000-mile swim from the chilly waters of Alaska to bask in Hawaii's summery shallows, fluking, spy hopping, spouting, breaching, and having an all-around swell time. About 1,500 to 3,000 humpback whales appear in Hawaiian waters each year.

Humpbacks are one of the world's oldest, most impressive inhabitants. Adults grow to be about 45 feet long and weigh a hefty 40 tons. Humpbacks are officially an endangered species; in 1992 the waters around Maui, Molokai, and Lanai were designated a Humpback Whale National Marine Sanctuary. Despite the world's newfound ecological awareness, humpbacks and their habitats and food resources are still under threat from whalers and pollution.

The season's first whale is usually spotted in November, but the best time to see humpback whales in Hawaii is between **January and April,** from any island. Just look out to sea. Each island also offers a variety of whale-watching cruises, which will bring you up close and personal with the mammoth mammals; see the individual island chapters for details.

Money-saving tip: Book a snorkeling cruise during the winter whale-watching months. The captain of the boat will often take you through the best local whale-watching areas on the way, and you'll get two activities for the price of one. It's well worth the money.

WINDSURFING   Maui is Hawaii's top windsurfing destination. World-class windsurfers head for Hookipa Beach, where the wind roars through Maui's isthmus and creates some of the best windsurfing conditions in the world. Funky Paia, a derelict sugar town saved from extinction by surfers, is now the world capital of big-wave board sailing. And along Maui's Hana Highway, there are lookouts where you can watch the pros flip off the lip of 10-foot waves and gain hang time in the air.

Others, especially beginners, set their sails for Oahu's Kailua Bay or Kauai's Anini Beach, where gentle onshore breezes make learning this sport a snap. See the individual island chapters for outfitters and local instructors.

14 Getting Around Hawaii

For additional advice on travel within each island, see "Getting Around" in the individual island chapters that follow.

INTERISLAND FLIGHTS

Since September 11, 2001, the major interisland carriers have cut way, way, way

A Cruise through the Islands

If you're looking for a taste of several islands in a single week, consider taking a cruise with **Norwegian Cruise Line** (© 800/327-7030; www.ncl.com), the only cruise line that operates year-round in the Hawaiian Islands.

Norwegian Cruise Line's 2,240-passenger ships *Pride of Aloha* and *Pride of Hawaii* have itineraries that circle the Hawaii islands, stopping on the Big Island, Maui, Kauai, and Oahu, and some that actually go to Fanning Island in the Republic of Kiribati before returning to Honolulu.

The disadvantage of a cruise is that you won't be able to see any of the islands in depth or at leisure; the advantage is that you can spend your days exploring the island where the ship is docked and your nights aboard ship sailing to the next port of call.

---

back on the number of interisland flights. The airlines warn you to show up at least 90 minutes before your flight, and believe me, with all the security inspections, you will need all 90 minutes to catch your flight.

In 2006, a new airline entered the Hawaiian market: **go!** (© 888/IFLYGO2; www.iflygo.com), owned by Mesa Air Group (which has more than 1,000 flights to 166 cities across the U.S., Canada, and Mexico). The new airline began service with 50-passenger Bombardier CRJ 200 jets with service from Honolulu to Maui, Kauai, and both Hilo and Kona on the Big Island. go! offers the cheapest interisland fares in Hawaii.

Aloha Airlines (© 800/367-5250 or 808/484-1111; www.alohaairlines.com) is the state's largest provider of interisland air transport service. It offers daily flights throughout Hawaii, using an all-jet fleet of Boeing 737 aircraft. **Hawaiian Airlines** (© 800/367-5320 or 808/835-3700; www.hawaiianair.com), Hawaii's first interisland airline, has carried more than 100 million passengers to and around the state.

In 2007, visitors to Molokai and Lanai got not one, but two new commuter airlines, which began flying from Honolulu to Molokai and Lanai. go! started a new commuter service from Honolulu to Molokai and Lanai, under the name **go!Express,** on their new fleet of Cessna Grand Caravan 208B planes. Another commuter airline, **Pacific Wings,** started operating a discount airline, **PW Express** (© 888/866-5022 or 808/873-0877; www.flypwx.com), with daily nonstop flights between Honolulu and Molokai and Lanai, plus flights from Kahului, Maui, and Molokai.

Island Air (© 800/323-3345 or 808/484-2222) serves Hawaii's small interisland airports on Maui, Molokai, and Lanai. However, I have to tell you that I have not had stellar service from Island Air and recommend that you book on go!Express or PW Express if you are headed to Molokai or Lanai.

Overseas visitors can take advantage of the APEX (Advance Purchase Excursion) reductions offered by all major U.S. and European carriers. In addition, some large airlines offer transatlantic or transpacific passengers special discount tickets under the name **Visit USA,** which allows mostly one-way travel from one U.S. destination to another at very low prices. Unavailable in the U.S., these discount tickets must be purchased abroad in conjunction with your international fare. This system is the easiest, fastest, cheapest way to see the country.

BY CAR

Hawaii has some of the lowest car-rental rates in the country. (An exception is the island of Lanai, where they're very expensive.) To rent a car in Hawaii, you must be at least 25 years of age and have a valid driver's license and credit card. *Note:* Foreign driver's licenses are usually recognized in the U.S., but you should get an international one if your home license is not in English.

At Honolulu International Airport and most neighbor-island airports, you'll find most major car-rental agencies, including **Alamo** (© 800/327-9633; www.goalamo.com), **Avis** (© 800/321-3712; www.avis.com), **Budget** (© 800/572-0700; www.budget.com), **Dollar** (© 800/800-4000; www.dollarcar.com), **Enterprise** (© 800/325-8007; www.enterprise.com), **Hertz** (© 800/654-3011; www.hertz.com), **National** (© 800/227-7368; www.nationalcar.com), and **Thrifty** (© 800/367-2277; www.thrifty.com). It's almost always cheaper to rent a car at the airport than in Waikiki or through your hotel (unless there's one already included in your package deal).

Rental cars are usually at a premium on Kauai, Molokai, and Lanai, and may be sold out on the neighbor islands on holiday weekends, so be sure to book well ahead.

INSURANCE Hawaii is a no-fault state, which means that if you don't have collision-damage insurance, you are required to pay for all damages before you leave the state, whether or not the accident was your fault. Your personal car insurance may provide rental-car coverage; check before you leave home. Bring your insurance identification card if you decline the optional insurance, which usually costs from $12 to $20 a day. Obtain the name of your company's local claim representative before you go. Some credit card companies also provide collision-damage

insurance for their customers; check with yours before you rent.

DRIVING RULES Hawaiian state law mandates that all car passengers must wear a **seat belt** and all infants must be strapped into car seats. You'll pay a $50 fine if you don't buckle up. **Pedestrians** always have the right of way, even if they're not in the crosswalk. You can turn **right on red** after a full and complete stop, unless otherwise posted.

ROAD MAPS The best and most detailed maps for activities are published by **Franko Maps** (www.frankosmaps.com); they feature a host of island maps, plus a terrific "Hawaiian Reef Creatures Guide" for snorkelers curious about those fish they spot under water. Free road maps are published by *This Week Magazine,* a free visitor publication available on Oahu, the Big Island, Maui, and Kauai. For even greater road map detail, check out Odyssey Publishing (© **888/729-1074;** www.hawaiimapsource.com). They have very detailed maps of East and West Hawaii, Maui, and Kauai. Another source of good maps is the University of Hawaii Press maps, which include a detailed network of island roads, large-scale insets of towns, historical and contemporary points of interest, parks, beaches, and hiking trails. If you can't find them in a bookstore near you, contact **University of Hawaii Press,** 2840 Kolowalu St., Honolulu, HI 96822 (© **888/847-7737;** www.uhpress.hawaii.edu). For topographic and other maps of the islands, go to the **Hawaii Geographic Society,** 49 S. Hotel St., Honolulu, or contact P.O. Box 1698, Honolulu, HI 96806 (© **800/538-3950** or 808/538-3952).

BY FERRY

As we went to press, the Hawaii legislature approved the long-awaited Sperferry (www.hawaiisuperferry.com), scheduled to begin service between Honolulu and

Kauai and Honolulu and Maui in summer 2007. If you buy tickets online at least 14 days in advance, fares are $44 off-peak (Tues–Thurs), $55 peak (Fri–Mon) one-way. The regular fare is $52 off-peak or $62 peak. Tickets for children (2–12) and seniors (62 and over) cost $41 off-peak, $51 peak. Tickets for infants under 2 cost $17.

Vehicles are charged separately, in addition to the passenger fares above. The fare for a car or SUV is $59 off-peak, $69 peak.

The 3-hour trip from Honolulu to Maui or Kauai will be offered once daily 6 days a week (no Sat service). The company hopes to add a second ferry in 2009 and a 4½-hour service from Honolulu to the Big Island.

15 Tips on Accommodations

Hawaii offers all kinds of accommodations, from simple rooms in restored plantation homes and quaint cottages on the beach to luxurious oceanview condo units and opulent suites in beachfront resorts. Each type has its pluses and minuses, so before you book, make sure you know what you're getting into.

TYPES OF ACCOMMODATIONS

HOTELS   In Hawaii, "hotel" can indicate a wide range of options, from few or no on-site amenities to enough extras to qualify as a miniresort. Generally, a hotel offers daily maid service and has a restaurant, on-site laundry facilities, a pool, and a sundries/convenience–type shop. Top hotels also have activities desks, concierge and valet service, room service, business centers, airport shuttles, bars and/or lounges, and perhaps a few more shops.

The advantages of staying in a hotel are privacy and convenience; the disadvantage is generally noise (either thin walls between rooms or loud music from a lobby lounge late into the night). Hotels

are often a short walk from the beach rather than right on the beachfront (although there are exceptions).

RESORTS   In Hawaii a resort offers everything a hotel does—and more. You can expect direct beach access, with beach cabanas and lounge chairs; pools and a Jacuzzi; a spa and fitness center; restaurants, bars, and lounges; a 24-hour front desk; concierge, valet, and bellhop services; room service (often 'round-the-clock); an activities desk; tennis and golf; ocean activities; a business center; kids' programs; and more.

The advantages of a resort are that you have everything you could possibly want in the way of services and things to do; the disadvantage is that the price generally reflects this. And don't be misled by a name—just because a place is called "ABC Resort" doesn't mean it actually *is* a resort. Make sure you're getting what you pay for.

CONDOS   The roominess and convenience of a condo—which is usually a fully

---

Nickel-&-Dime Charges at High-Priced Hotels

Several upscale resorts in Hawaii engage in a practice that I find distasteful and dishonest: charging a so-called "resort fee." This daily fee is added on to your bill for such "complimentary" items as a daily newspaper, local phone calls, and use of the fitness facilities—amenities that the resort has been happily providing free to its guests for years. In most cases, you do not have an option to decline the resort fee—in other words, this is a sneaky way to increase the nightly rate without telling you.

Tips **B&B Etiquette**

In Hawaii it is traditional and customary to remove your shoes before entering anyone's home. The same is true for most bed-and-breakfast facilities. If this custom is unpleasant to you, a B&B may not be for you.

Hawaii has a very strict no-smoking law (no smoking in public buildings, restaurants, bars, retail stores, etc.), and more and more hotels, resorts, condos, and vacation rentals generally do *not* allow smoking in the guest rooms (if a hotel does allow smoking—they all have nonsmoking rooms available), but the majority of bed-and-breakfast units forbid smoking in the rooms. Be sure to check the policy of your accommodations before you book.

---

equipped, multiple-bedroom apartment—makes this a great choice for families. Condominium properties in Hawaii generally consist of several apartments set in either a single high-rise or a cluster of low-rise units. Condos usually have amenities such as some maid service (ranging from daily to weekly; it may or may not be included in your rate), a pool, and an on-site front desk or a live-in property manager. Condos tend to be clustered in resort areas. There are some very high-end condos, but most are quite affordable, especially if you're traveling in a group.

The advantages of a condo are privacy, space, and conveniences—which usually include a full kitchen, a washer and dryer, a private phone, and more. The downsides are the standard lack of an on-site restaurant and the density of the units (vs. the privacy of a single-unit vacation rental).

BED & BREAKFASTS Hawaii has a wide range of places that call themselves B&Bs: everything from a traditional B&B—several bedrooms in a home, with breakfast served in the morning—to what is essentially a vacation rental on an owner's property that comes with fixings for you to make your own breakfast. Make sure that the B&B you're booking matches your own mental picture. Note that laundry facilities and private phones are not always available. I've reviewed lots of wonderful B&Bs in the island chapters that follow. If you have to share a bathroom, I've spelled it out in the listings; otherwise, you can assume that you will have your own.

The advantages of a traditional B&B are its individual style and congenial atmosphere, with a host who's often happy to act as your own private concierge. In addition, they're usually an affordable way to go. The disadvantages are lack of privacy, usually a set time for breakfast, few amenities, and generally no maid service. Also, B&B owners usually require a minimum stay of 2 or 3 nights, and it's often a drive to the beach.

VACATION RENTALS This is another great choice for families and for long-term stays. "Vacation rental" usually means that there will be no one on the property where you're staying. The actual accommodations can range from an apartment to an entire fully equipped house. Generally, vacation rentals allow you to settle in and make yourself at home for a while. They have kitchen facilities (at least a kitchenette), on-site laundry facilities, and a phone; some also come with such extras as a TV, VCR, and stereo.

The advantages of a vacation rental are complete privacy, your own kitchen (which can save you money on meals), and lots of conveniences. The disadvantages are a lack of an on-site property manager and generally no maid service; often a minimum stay is required (sometimes as much as a week). If you book a vacation rental, be sure that you have a 24-hour contact to call if the toilet won't flush or you can't figure out how to turn on the air-conditioning.

USING A BOOKING AGENCY VS. DOING IT YOURSELF

If you don't have the time to call several places yourself to make sure they offer the amenities you'd like, you might consider a booking agency.

A statewide booking agent for B&Bs is **Bed & Breakfast Hawaii** (© 800/733-1632 or 808/822-7771; fax 808/822-2723; www.bandb-hawaii.com), offering a range of accommodations from vacation homes to B&Bs, starting at $65 a night. For vacation rentals, contact **Hawaii Beachfront Vacation Homes** (© 808/247-3637; fax 808/235-2644). **Hawaii Condo Exchange** (© 800/442-0404; www.myhawaiibeachfront.com) acts as a consolidator for condo and vacation-rental properties.

SURFING FOR HOTELS

In addition to the online travel booking sites **Travelocity, Expedia, Orbitz, Priceline,** and **Hotwire,** you can book hotels through **Hotels.com, Quikbook** (www.quikbook.com), and **Travelaxe** (www.travelaxe.com).

HotelChatter.com is a daily webzine offering smart coverage and critiques of hotels worldwide. Go to **TripAdvisor.com** or **HotelShark.com** for helpful independent consumer reviews of hotels and resort properties.

It's a good idea to **get a confirmation number** and **make a printout** of any online booking transaction.

SAVING ON YOUR HOTEL ROOM

The **rack rate** is the maximum rate that a hotel charges for a room. Hardly anybody pays this price, however, except in high season or on holidays.

Rates can sometimes be bargained down, but it depends on the place. The best bargaining can be had at **hotels** and **resorts.** If business is slow and you book directly, some places may give you at least part of the commission they'd normally pay a travel agent. Most hotels and resorts also have local rates for islanders, which they may extend to visitors during slow periods. It never hurts to ask about discounted or local rates; a host of special rates are available for the military, seniors, members of the travel industry, families, corporate travelers, and long-term stays. Also ask about **package deals,** which might include a car rental or free breakfast for the same price as a room by itself. Hotels and resorts offer packages for everyone: golfers, tennis players, families, honeymooners, and more (see "Packages for the Independent Traveler," earlier in this chapter). I've found that it's worth the extra few cents to make a local call to the hotel; sometimes the local reservations person knows about package deals that the toll-free operators are unaware of. If all else fails, try to get the hotel or resort to upgrade you to a better room for the same price as a budget room, or waive the parking fee or extra fees for children. Persistence and polite inquiries can pay off.

It's harder to bargain at **bed-and-breakfasts.** You may be able to negotiate down the minimum stay or get a discount if you're staying a week or longer. But generally, a B&B owner has only a few rooms and has already priced the property at a competitive rate; expect to pay what's asked.

You have somewhat more leeway to negotiate at **vacation rentals** and **condos.** In addition to asking for a discount on a multinight stay, ask if they can throw in a rental car to sweeten the deal; believe it or not, they often will.

To lower the cost of your room:

- **Ask about special rates or other discounts.** You may qualify for corporate, student, military, senior, frequent flier, trade union, or other discounts.
- **Dial direct.** When booking a room in a chain hotel, you'll often get a better deal by calling the individual hotel's reservation desk rather than the chain's main number.
- **Book online.** Many hotels offer Internet-only discounts or supply rooms to Priceline, Hotwire, or Expedia at rates much lower than the ones you can get through the hotel itself.
- **Remember the law of supply and demand.** Resort hotels are most crowded and, therefore, most expensive on weekends, so discounts are usually available for midweek stays. Business hotels in downtown locations are busiest during the week, so you can expect big discounts over the weekend.
- **Look into group or long-stay discounts.** If you come as part of a large group, you should be able to negotiate a bargain rate. Likewise, if you're planning a long stay (at least 5 days), you might qualify for a discount. As a general rule, expect 1 night free after a 7-night stay.
- **Sidestep excess surcharges and hidden costs.** Many hotels have the unpleasant practice of nickel-and-diming its guests with opaque surcharges. When you book a room, ask what is included in the room rate and what is extra. Avoid dialing direct from hotel phones, which can have exorbitant rates. And don't be tempted by the room's minibar offerings: Most hotels charge through the nose for water, soda, and snacks. Finally, ask about local taxes and service charges, which can increase the cost of a room by 15% or more.

- **Carefully consider your hotel's meal plan.** If you enjoy eating out and sampling the local cuisine, it makes sense to choose a **Continental Plan (CP),** which includes breakfast only, or a **European Plan (EP),** which doesn't include any meals and allows you maximum flexibility. If you're more interested in saving money, opt for a **Modified American Plan (MAP),** which includes breakfast and one meal, or the **American Plan (AP),** which includes three meals. If you must choose a MAP, see if you can get a free lunch at your hotel if you decide to do dinner out.
- **Book an efficiency.** A room with a kitchenette allows you to shop for groceries and cook your own meals. This is a big money saver, especially for families on long stays.
- **Consider enrolling in hotel "frequent-stay" programs,** which are upping the ante lately to win the loyalty of repeat customers. Frequent guests can now accumulate points or credits to earn free hotel nights, airline miles, in-room amenities, merchandise, tickets to concerts and events, discounts on sporting facilities—and even credit toward stock in the participating hotel, in the case of the Jameson Inn hotel group. Perks are awarded not only by many chain hotels and motels (Hilton HHonors, Marriott Rewards, Wyndham ByRequest, to name a few), but also individual inns and B&Bs. Many chain hotels partner with other hotel chains, car-rental firms, airlines, and credit card companies to give consumers additional incentive to do repeat business.

LANDING THE BEST ROOM

Somebody has to get the best room in the house. It might as well be you. You can start by joining the hotel's frequent-guest program, which may make you eligible for upgrades. A hotel-branded credit card usually gives its owner "silver" or "gold" status in frequent-guest programs for free. Always ask about a corner room. They're often larger and quieter, with more windows and light, and they often cost the same as standard rooms. When you make your reservation, ask if the hotel is renovating; if it is, request a room away from the construction. If you're a light sleeper, request a quiet room away from vending or ice machines, elevators, restaurants, bars, and discos. Ask for a room that has most recently been renovated or redecorated.

If you aren't happy with your room when you arrive, notify the front desk or booking agency immediately. Approach the management in a calm, reasonable manner and suggest a solution (like moving to another unit). Be willing to compromise. Do not leave; if you do, you may not get your deposit back.

In resort areas, particularly in warm climates, ask the following questions before you book a room:

- What's the view like? Cost-conscious travelers may be willing to pay less for a back room facing the parking lot, especially if they don't plan to spend much time in their room.
- Does the room have air-conditioning or ceiling fans? Do the windows open? If they do, and the nighttime entertainment takes place alfresco, you may want to find out when show time is over.
- What's included in the price? Your room may be moderately priced, but if you're charged for beach chairs, towels, sports equipment, and other amenities, you could end up spending more than you bargained for.
- How far is the room from the beach and other amenities? If it's far, is there transportation to and from the beach, and is it free?

16 Getting Married in the Islands

Hawaii is a great place for a wedding. The islands exude romance and natural beauty, and after the ceremony, you're already on your honeymoon. And the members of your wedding party will most likely be delighted, since you've given them the perfect excuse for their own island vacation.

More than 20,000 marriages are performed annually on the islands, mostly on Oahu; nearly half are for couples from somewhere else. The booming wedding business has spawned more than 70 companies that can help you organize a long-distance event and stage an unforgettable wedding, Hawaiian style or your style. However, you can also plan your own island wedding, even from afar, and not spend a fortune doing it.

THE PAPERWORK

The state of Hawaii has some very minimal procedures for obtaining a marriage license. The first thing you should do is contact the **Honolulu Marriage License Office,** State Department of Health Building, 1250 Punchbowl St., Honolulu, HI 96813 (© **808/586-4545;** www.state.hi.us/doh/records/vr_marri.html), which is open Monday through Friday from 8am to 4pm. The office no longer will mail you the brochure *Getting Married;* you can download it from the website or contact a marriage-licensing agent closest to where you'll be staying in Hawaii (also listed on the website).

Once in Hawaii, the prospective bride and groom must go together to the marriage-licensing agent to get the license, which costs $60 and is good for 30 days. Both parties must be 15 years of age or older (couples 15–17 years old must have proof of age, written consent of both parents, and written approval of the judge of the family court) and not more closely related than first cousins. That's it.

Gay couples cannot marry in Hawaii. After a protracted legal battle and much discussion in the state legislature, the Hawaii Supreme Court ruled that the state will not issue marriage licenses to same-sex couples.

PLANNING THE WEDDING

DOING IT YOURSELF The marriage-licensing agents, who range from employees of the governor's satellite office in Kona to private individuals, are usually friendly, helpful people who can steer you to a nondenominational minister or marriage performer who's licensed by the state of Hawaii. These marriage performers are great sources of information for budget weddings. They usually know wonderful places to have the ceremony for free or for a nominal fee. For the names and addresses of marriage-licensing agents on Hawaii (Big Island), call ⊙ **808/974-6008;** on Kauai, ⊙ **808/ 241-3498;** on Maui, ⊙ **808/984-8210;** on Molokai, ⊙ **808/553-3663;** and on Lanai, ⊙ **808/565-6411.**

If you don't want to use a wedding planner (see below), but you do want to make arrangements before you arrive in Hawaii, our best advice is to get a copy of the daily newspapers on the island where you want to have the wedding. People willing and qualified to conduct weddings advertise in the classifieds. They're great sources of information, as they know the best places to have the ceremony and can recommend caterers, florists, and everything else you'll need. If you want to have your wedding on the Kona/Waimea side of the Big Island, get *West Hawaii Today,* P.O. Box 789, Kailua-Kona, HI 96745 (⊙ 808/329-9311; www.westhawaiitoday.com); for the Hilo/Puna side, try the *Hawaii Tribune Herald,* P.O. Box 767, Hilo, HI 96720 (⊙ 808/935-6621; www.hilo-hawaiitribune.com). On Maui, get the *Maui News,* P.O. Box 550, Wailuku, HI 96793 (⊙ 808/244-3981; www.maui news.com). On Kauai, try the *Garden Island,* 3137 Kuhio Hwy., Lihue, HI 96766 (⊙ 808/245-3681; www.kauai-world.com). And on Oahu, check out the *Honolulu Advertiser,* P.O. Box 3110, Honolulu, HI 96802 (⊙ 808/525-8000; www.honoluluadvertiser.com); the *Honolulu Star Bulletin,* 7 Waterfront Plaza, Suite 500, Honolulu, HI 96813 (⊙ 808/ 529-4700; www.honolulustarbulletin. com); and *MidWeek,* 45–525 Luluku Rd., Kaneohe, HI 96744 (⊙ 808/235-5881; www.midweek.com).

USING A WEDDING PLANNER Wedding planners—many of whom are marriage-licensing agents as well—can arrange everything for you, from a small, private, outdoor affair to a full-blown formal ceremony in a tropical setting. They charge anywhere from $225 to a small fortune—it all depends on what you want. On the Big Island, contact **Paradise Weddings Hawaii** (⊙ 800/428-5844 or 808/883-9067; www.paradise weddingshawaii.com); on Maui contact **First Class Weddings** (⊙ 800/262-8433 or 808/877-1411; www.firstclassweddings. com); on Kauai try **Coconut Coast Weddings & Honeymoons** (⊙ 800/585-5595 or 808/826-5557; www.kauai wedding.com); on Oahu contact Rev. Toni Baran and Rev. Jerry Le Lesch at **Love Hawaii** (⊙ 808/235-6966; www. lovehawaii.com), which offers wedding services starting at $95. The Hawaii Visitors and Convention Bureau (see section 1 of this chapter) can provide contact information for other wedding coordinators, and many of the big resorts have their own coordinators on staff.

FAST FACTS: The Hawaiian Islands

American Express For 24-hour traveler's-check refunds and purchase information, call ✆ **800/221-7282.** For local offices, see the "Fast Facts" sections in the individual island chapters.

Area Code All the Hawaiian Islands are in the **808** area code. Note that if you're calling one island from another, you'll have to dial 1-808 first.

ATM Networks See "Money," p. 45.

Automobile Organizations Auto clubs will supply maps, suggested routes, guidebooks, accident and bail-bond insurance, and emergency road service. The **American Automobile Association (AAA)** is the major auto club in the United States. If you belong to an auto club in your home country, inquire about AAA reciprocity before you leave. You may be able to join AAA even if you're not a member of a reciprocal club; to inquire, call AAA (✆ **800/222-4357**). AAA is actually an organization of regional auto clubs, so look under "AAA Automobile Club" in the White Pages of the telephone directory. AAA has a nationwide emergency road service telephone number (✆ 800/AAA-HELP).

Business Hours Most offices are open Monday through Friday from 8am to 5pm. Bank hours are Monday through Thursday from 8:30am to 3pm and Friday from 8:30am to 6pm; some banks are open on Saturday as well. Shopping centers are open Monday through Friday from 10am to 9pm, Saturday 10am to 5:30pm, and Sunday from noon to 5 or 6pm.

Car Rentals See "Getting Around Hawaii," p. 67.

Cashpoints See "ATM Networks," above.

Currency The most common bills are the $1 (a "buck"), $5, $10, and $20 denominations. There are also $2 bills (seldom encountered), $50 bills, and $100 bills (the last two are usually not welcome as payment for small purchases).

Coins come in seven denominations: 1¢ (1 cent, or a penny); 5¢ (5 cents, or a nickel); 10¢ (10 cents, or a dime); 25¢ (25 cents, or a quarter); 50¢ (50 cents, or a half-dollar); the gold-colored Sacagawea coin, worth $1; and the rare silver dollar.

For additional information, see "Money," p. 45.

Customs **What You Can Bring into Hawaii** Every visitor more than 21 years of age may bring in, free of duty, the following: (1) 1 liter of wine or hard liquor; (2) 200 cigarettes, 100 cigars (but not from Cuba), or 3 pounds of smoking tobacco; and (3) $100 worth of gifts. These exemptions are offered to travelers who spend at least 72 hours in the United States and who have not claimed them within the preceding 6 months. It is altogether forbidden to bring into the country foodstuffs (particularly fruit, cooked meats, and canned goods) and plants (vegetables, seeds, tropical plants, and the like). Foreign tourists may carry in or out up to $10,000 in U.S. or foreign currency with no formalities; larger sums must be declared to U.S. Customs on entering or leaving, which includes filing form CM 4790. For details regarding U.S. Customs and Border Protection, consult your nearest U.S. embassy or consulate, or **U.S. Customs** (✆ **202/927-1770;** www.customs.ustreas.gov).

What You Can Take Home from Hawaii:

Canadian Citizens: For a clear summary of Canadian rules, write for the booklet *I Declare,* issued by the **Canada Border Services Agency** (📞 **800/461-9999** in Canada, or 204/983-3500; **www.cbsa-asfc.gc.ca**).

U.K. Citizens: For information, contact **HM Customs & Excise** at 📞 **0845/010-9000** (from outside the U.K., 020/8929-0152), or consult their website at **www.hmce.gov.uk**.

Australian Citizens: A helpful brochure available from Australian consulates or Customs offices is *Know Before You Go.* For more information, call the **Australian Customs Service** at 📞 **1300/363-263,** or log on to **www.customs. gov.au**.

New Zealand Citizens: Most questions are answered in a free pamphlet available at New Zealand consulates and Customs offices: *New Zealand Customs Guide for Travellers, Notice no. 4.* For more information, contact **New Zealand Customs,** The Customhouse, 17–21 Whitmore St., Box 2218, Wellington (📞 **04/473-6099** or 0800/428-786; **www.customs.govt.nz**).

Drinking Laws The legal drinking age in Hawaii is 21. Bars are allowed to stay open daily until 2am; places with cabaret licenses are able to keep the booze flowing until 4am. Grocery and convenience stores are allowed to sell beer, wine, and liquor 7 days a week. Proof of age is required and often requested at bars, nightclubs, and restaurants, so it's always a good idea to bring ID when you go out.

Do not carry open containers of alcohol in your car or any public area that isn't zoned for alcohol consumption. The police can fine you on the spot. And nothing will ruin your trip faster than getting a citation for DUI ("driving under the influence"), so don't even think about driving while intoxicated.

Driving Rules See "Getting Around Hawaii," p. 67.

Electricity Like Canada, the United States uses 110 to 120 volts AC (60 cycles), compared to 220 to 240 volts AC (50 cycles) in most of Europe, Australia, and New Zealand. Downward converters that change 220–240 volts to 110–120 volts are difficult to find in the United States, so bring one with you.

Embassies & Consulates All embassies are located in the nation's capital, Washington, D.C. Some consulates are located in major U.S. cities, and most nations have a mission to the United Nations in New York City. If your country isn't listed below, call for directory information in Washington, D.C. (📞 **202/555-1212**), or log on to **www.embassy.org/embassies**.

The embassy of **Australia** is at 1601 Massachusetts Ave. NW, Washington, DC 20036 (📞 **202/797-3000**; www.austemb.org). There are consulates in New York, Honolulu, Houston, Los Angeles, and San Francisco.

The embassy of **Canada** is at 501 Pennsylvania Ave. NW, Washington, DC 20001 (📞 **202/682-1740**; www.canadianembassy.org). Other Canadian consulates are in Buffalo (New York), Detroit, Los Angeles, New York, and Seattle.

The embassy of **Ireland** is at 2234 Massachusetts Ave. NW, Washington, DC 20008 (📞 **202/462-3939**; www.irelandemb.org). Irish consulates are in Boston, Chicago, New York, San Francisco, and other cities. See the website for complete listing.

The embassy of **New Zealand** is at 37 Observatory Circle NW, Washington, DC 20008 (② **202/328-4800;** www.nzemb.org). New Zealand consulates are in Los Angeles, Salt Lake City, San Francisco, and Seattle.

The embassy of the **United Kingdom** is at 3100 Massachusetts Ave. NW, Washington, DC 20008 (② **202/588-7800;** www.britainusa.com). Other British consulates are in Atlanta, Boston, Chicago, Cleveland, Houston, Los Angeles, New York, San Francisco, and Seattle.

Emergencies Dial ② **911** for police, fire, or ambulance.

Gasoline (Petrol)/[en]At press time, in the U.S., the cost of gasoline (also known as gas, but never petrol), is abnormally high. Taxes are already included in the printed price. One U.S. gallon equals 3.8 liters or .85 imperial gallons. Fill-up locations are known as gas or service stations.

Holidays Banks, government offices, post offices, and many stores, restaurants, and museums are closed on the following legal national holidays: January 1 (New Year's Day), the third Monday in January (Martin Luther King, Jr., Day), the third Monday in February (Presidents' Day), the last Monday in May (Memorial Day), July 4 (Independence Day), the first Monday in September (Labor Day), the second Monday in October (Columbus Day), November 11 (Veterans Day/Armistice Day), the fourth Thursday in November (Thanksgiving Day), and December 25 (Christmas). The Tuesday after the first Monday in November is Election Day, a federal government holiday in presidential-election years (held every 4 years, and next in 2008).

For more information on holidays, see "Hawaii Calendar of Events," earlier in this chapter.

Hospitals For information on doctors, dentists, and hospitals, see the "Fast Facts" sections in the individual island chapters.

Internet Access See the "Fast Facts" sections in the individual island chapters.

Legal Aid If you are "pulled over" for a minor infraction (such as speeding), never attempt to pay the fine directly to a police officer; this could be construed as attempted bribery, a much more serious crime. Pay fines by mail or directly into the hands of the clerk of the court. If accused of a more serious offense, say and do nothing before consulting a lawyer. Here the burden is on the state to prove a person's guilt beyond a reasonable doubt, and everyone has the right to remain silent, whether he or she is suspected of a crime or actually arrested. Once arrested, a person can make one telephone call to a party of his or her choice. International visitors should call their embassy or consulate.

Lost & Found Be sure to tell all of your credit card companies the minute you discover your wallet has been lost or stolen, and file a report at the nearest police precinct. Your credit card company or insurer may require a police report number or record of the loss. Most credit card companies have an emergency toll-free number to call if your card is lost or stolen; they may be able to wire you a cash advance immediately or deliver an emergency credit card in a day or two. Visa's U.S. emergency number is ② **800/847-2911** or 410/581-9994.

American Express cardholders and traveler's check holders should call ⓒ 800/221-7282. MasterCard holders should call ⓒ 800/307-7309 or 636/722-7111. For other credit cards, call the toll-free number directory at ⓒ 800/555-1212.

If you need emergency cash over the weekend when all banks and American Express offices are closed, you can have money wired to you via **Western Union** (ⓒ 800/325-6000; www.westernunion.com).

Mail At press time, domestic postage rates were 26¢ for a postcard and 41¢ for a letter. For international mail, a postcard or first-class letter of up to 1 ounce costs 90¢ (69¢ to Canada and Mexico). For more information, go to **www.usps.com** and click on "Calculate Postage."

If you aren't sure what your address will be in the United States, mail can be sent to you, in your name, c/o General Delivery at the main post office of the city or region where you expect to be. (Call ⓒ 800/275-8777 for information on the nearest post office.) The addressee must pick up mail in person and must produce proof of identity (driver's license, passport, etc.). Most post offices will hold your mail for up to 1 month and are open Monday to Friday from 8am to 6pm and Saturday from 9am to 3pm.

Always include zip codes when mailing items in the U.S. If you don't know your zip code, visit www.usps.com/zip4.

Maps See "Getting Around Hawaii," p. 67.

Measurements See the chart on the inside front cover of this book for details on converting metric measurements to U.S. equivalents.

Newspapers & Magazines See the "Fast Facts" sections in the individual island chapters.

Passports **For Residents of Australia:** You can pick up an application from your local post office or any branch of Passports Australia, but you must schedule an interview at the passport office to present your application materials. Call the **Australian Passport Information Service** at ⓒ 131-232, or visit the government website at www.passports.gov.au.

For Residents of Canada: Passport applications are available at travel agencies throughout Canada or from the central **Passport Office,** Department of Foreign Affairs and International Trade, Ottawa, ON K1A 0G3 (ⓒ 800/567-6868; www.ppt.gc.ca). *Note:* Canadian children who travel must have their own passport. However, if you hold a valid Canadian passport issued before December 11, 2001, that bears the name of your child, the passport remains valid for you and your child until it expires.

For Residents of Ireland: You can apply for a 10-year passport at the **Passport Office,** Setanta Centre, Molesworth Street, Dublin 2 (ⓒ 01/671-1633; www.irl-gov.ie/iveagh). Those under age 18 and over 65 must apply for a 3-year passport. You can also apply at 1A South Mall, Cork (ⓒ 021/272-525), or at most main post offices.

For Residents of New Zealand: You can pick up a passport application at any New Zealand Passports Office or download it from their website. Contact the **Passports Office** at ⓒ 0800/225-050 in New Zealand or 04/474-8100, or log on to www.passports.govt.nz.

For Residents of the United Kingdom: To pick up an application for a standard 10-year passport (5-yr. passport for children under 16), visit your nearest passport office, major post office, or travel agency, or contact the **United Kingdom Passport Service** at ✆ **0870/521-0410** or search its website at www.ukpa.gov.uk.

For Residents of the United States: Here are some useful phone numbers:
U.S. Dept. of State Travel Advisory: ✆ 202/647-5225 (manned 24 hr.)
U.S. Passport Agency: ✆ 202/647-0518
U.S. Centers for Disease Control International Traveler's Hotline: ✆ 404/332-4559

Police Dial ✆ **911** for police.

Safety See "Safety," earlier in this chapter.

Smoking It's against the law to smoke in public buildings, including airports, shopping malls, grocery stores, retail shops, buses, movie theaters, banks, convention facilities, and all government buildings and facilities. There is no smoking in restaurants, bars, and nightclubs. Most bed-and-breakfasts prohibit smoking indoors, and more and more hotels and resorts are becoming nonsmoking even in public area. Also, there is no smoking within 20 feet of a doorway, window, or ventilation intake (no hanging around outside a bar to smoke—you must go 20 feet away).

Taxes The United States has no value-added tax (VAT) or other indirect tax at the national level. Every state, county, and city may levy its own local tax on all purchases, including hotel and restaurant checks and airline tickets. These taxes will not appear on price tags.

Telegraph, Telex & Fax **Telegraph and telex services** are provided primarily by Western Union. You can telegraph money, or have it telegraphed to you, very quickly over the Western Union system, but this service can cost as much as 15% to 20% of the amount sent.

Most hotels have **fax machines** available for guest use (be sure to ask about the charge to use it). Many hotel rooms are even wired for guests' fax machines. A less expensive way to send and receive faxes may be at stores such as **The UPS Store** (formerly Mail Boxes Etc.),

Time The continental United States is divided into **four time zones:** Eastern Standard Time (EST), Central Standard Time (CST), Mountain Standard Time (MST), and Pacific Standard Time (PST). Alaska and Hawaii have their own zones. For example, when it's 9am in Los Angeles (PST), it's 7am in Honolulu (HST),10am in Denver (MST), 11am in Chicago (CST), noon in New York City (EST), 5pm in London (GMT), and 2am the next day in Sydney.

Daylight saving time is in effect from 1am on the second Sunday in March to 1am on the first Sunday in November, except in Arizona, Hawaii, the U.S. Virgin Islands, and Puerto Rico. Daylight saving time moves the clock 1 hour ahead of standard time.

Tipping Tips are a very important part of certain workers' income, and gratuities are the standard way of showing appreciation for services provided. (Tipping is certainly not compulsory if the service is poor!) In hotels, tip **bellhops** at least $1 per bag ($2–$3 if you have a lot of luggage) and tip the **chamber staff** $1 to $2 per day (more if you've left a disaster area for him or her to clean up). Tip the **doorman** or **concierge** only if he or she has provided you with some specific service (for example, calling a cab for you or obtaining difficult-to-get theater tickets). Tip the **valet-parking attendant** $1 every time you get your car.

In restaurants, bars, and nightclubs, tip **service staff** 15% to 20% of the check, tip **bartenders** 10% to 15%, tip **checkroom attendants** $1 per garment, and tip **valet-parking attendants** $1 per vehicle.

As for other service personnel, tip **cab drivers** 15% of the fare; tip **skycaps** at airports at least $1 per bag ($2–$3 if you have a lot of luggage); and tip **hairdressers** and **barbers** 15% to 20%.

Toilets You won't find public toilets or "restrooms" on the streets in most U.S. cities, but they can be found in hotel lobbies, bars, restaurants, museums, department stores, railway and bus stations, and service stations. Large hotels and fast-food restaurants are often the best bet for clean facilities. If possible, avoid the toilets at parks and beaches, which tend to be dirty; some may be unsafe. Restaurants and bars in resorts or heavily visited areas may reserve their restrooms for patrons.

Visas For information about U.S. visas, go to **http://travel.state.gov** and click on "Visas." Or go to one of the following websites:

Australian citizens can obtain up-to-date visa information from the **U.S. Embassy Canberra,** Moonah Place, Yarralumla, ACT 2600 (② **02/6214-5600**), or by checking the U.S. Diplomatic Mission's website at **http://usembassy-australia.state.gov/consular**.

British subjects can obtain up-to-date visa information by calling the **U.S. Embassy Visa Information Line** (② **0891/200-290**) or by visiting the "Visas to the U.S." section of the American Embassy London's website at **www.usembassy.org.uk**.

Irish citizens can obtain up-to-date visa information through the **Embassy of the USA Dublin,** 42 Elgin Rd., Dublin 4, Ireland (② **353/1-668-8777**) or by checking the "Consular Services" section of the website at **http://dublin.usembassy.gov**.

Citizens of **New Zealand** can obtain up-to-date visa information by contacting the **U.S. Embassy New Zealand,** 29 Fitzherbert Terrace, Thorndon, Wellington (② **644/472-2068**), or get the information directly from the website at **http://wellington.usembassy.gov**.

3

Suggested Hawaii Itineraries

What should I do in Hawaii? This is the most common question that readers ask me. The purpose of this chapter is to give you my expert advice on the best things to see and do on each island, and how to do them in an orderly fashion so you are not driving madly from one end of the island to the other.

First, here's the best advice I can give you: **Do not plan to see more than one island per week.** With the exception of the ferry between Maui and Lanai, getting from one island to another is an all-day affair once you figure in packing, checking out of and into hotels, driving to and from airports, and dealing with rental cars, not to mention time actually spent at the airport and on the flight. Don't waste a day of your vacation seeing our interisland air terminals.

Second, don't max out your days. This is Hawaii—allow some time to do nothing but relax. Remember that you most likely will arrive jet-lagged, so it's a good idea to ease into your vacation. In fact, exposure to sunlight can help reset your internal clock, so I include time at the beach on the first day of most of these itineraries.

Third, if this is your first trip to Hawaii, think of this as a "scouting" trip. Hawaii is too beautiful, too sensual, too enticing to see just once in a lifetime. You'll be back. You don't need to see and do everything on this trip.

Finally, keep in mind that the following itineraries are designed to appeal to a wide range of people. If you're a golf fan or a scuba diver, check out chapter 1, "The Best of Hawaii," to plan your trip around your passion.

One last thing—you will need a car to get around the islands. Oahu has an adequate public transportation service, but even so, it's set up for Hawaii residents, not tourists carrying coolers and beach toys (all carry-ons must fit under the bus seat). So plan to rent a car. But also plan to get out of the car as much as possible. Hawaii is not a place to view from your car window. You have to get out to smell the sweet perfume of plumerias, to hear the sound of the wind through a bamboo forest, and to plunge into the gentle waters of the Pacific.

1 A Week on Oahu

The island of Oahu is so stunning that the *alii,* the kings of Hawaii, made it the capital of the island nation. I've presumed that you are staying in Waikiki—if you are in another location, be sure to factor in the time for traveling.

Day ❶: Arrival & Waikiki Beach 🐝🐝

After you get off the plane, lather up in sunscreen, grab your sunglasses and hat, and head for the most famous beach in the world—Waikiki Beach (p. 172). If you have kids in tow or you can't handle a whole afternoon in Hawaii's intense sun, you might consider checking out Hawaii's water world by dropping by the **Waikiki Aquarium** (p. 207), or gaining

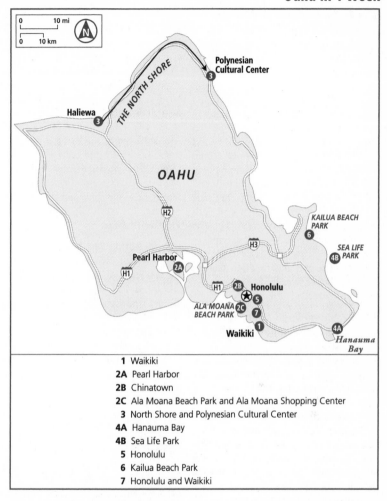

1   Waikiki
2A Pearl Harbor
2B Chinatown
2C Ala Moana Beach Park and Ala Moana Shopping Center
3   North Shore and Polynesian Cultural Center
4A Hanauma Bay
4B Sea Life Park
5   Honolulu
6   Kailua Beach Park
7   Honolulu and Waikiki

insight into Waikiki's past on the **Waikiki Historic Trail** (p. 198), a 2-mile trail marked with bronzed surfboards. Be sure to catch the sunset (anywhere on Waikiki Beach will do), and get an early dinner.

Day ❷: Pearl Harbor ✮✮✮ & Honolulu's Chinatown ✮✮✮

Head to the **USS *Arizona* Memorial at Pearl Harbor** (p. 203). Get there as early as possible—by the afternoon, the lines are 2 hours long. While you are there, be

sure to see the **USS *Missouri* Memorial** (p. 204) and the **USS *Bowfin* Submarine Museum & Park** (p. 204). On your way back, stop in **Chinatown** for lunch and take my self-guided walking tour (p. 210) of this unique area. In the afternoon, take a nap or head for the beach at **Ala Moana Beach Park** (p. 172) or a shopping spree across the street at the **Ala Moana Center** (p. 231). Plan to have dinner in Honolulu or the surrounding area.

Day ❸: North Shore _RRR_ **& the**
Polynesian Cultural Center _R_
Start your day with a drive to the **North**
Shore (see "Central Oahu & the North
Shore," in chapter 4). If you're up early
enough, have breakfast in the quaint
town of **Haleiwa;** if not, at least stop and
get a picnic lunch before you beach-hop
down the coast of the North Shore and
choose from some of the world's most
beautiful beaches, like **Waimea Beach**
Park, which is calm for swimming in
summer but gets pounded with 30- and
40-foot waves in winter. Any time after
12:30pm, head for the **Polynesian Cul-**
tural Center in Laie (p. 219). Allow at
least 2 hours to tour this miniglimpse of
the Pacific. Continue driving down the
coast road to the small town of **Kailua.**
Stay for dinner here to avoid the traffic
back to Waikiki.

Day ❹: Snorkeling in Hanauma
Bay _RR_ **& Watching Marine Life**
at Sea Life Park _R_
If it's not Tuesday (when the park is
closed), head out in the morning for the
spectacular snorkeling at **Hanauma Bay**
(p. 173). After a couple of hours, wander
down the coast to **Sea Life Park** (p. 207).
If you have kids, this is a must-stop. Otherwise, you can continue "beach-hop-
ping" down the coastline—check out
Sandy Beach (p. 178) and **Makapuu**
Beach Park (p. 178) to see which one
appeals to you. Then turn back to take
the Pali Highway back to Waikiki (be
sure to stop at the **Pali Lookout,** p. 208).

Day ❺: Rainforest Hike _RR_,
Historic Honolulu & Hawaiian
Culture
You probably could use a day out of the
sun by now, so try a short hike into the
rainforest, just a 15-minute drive from
downtown Honolulu. Be sure to wear

good hiking or trail shoes for the **Manoa**
Falls Trail (p. 187), and bring mosquito
repellent. Next, head for downtown
Honolulu to see some of the city's historic
sites, including the **Iolani Palace** (p. 202),
Kawaiahao Church (p. 203), **Mission**
Houses Museum (p. 203), and **Hawaii**
Maritime Center (p. 202). For a view of
where you've been, go to the top of the
Aloha Tower, at the Aloha Tower Mar-
ketplace, for a bird's-eye view of Hon-
olulu. Stop for lunch at either the
Marketplace or one of the nearby restau-
rants. Spend the afternoon at the **Bishop**
Museum (p. 198) to immerse yourself in
Hawaiian culture.

Day ❻: Kailua Beach _RRR_
On your last full day on Oahu, travel over
the Pali Highway to the windward side of
the island and spend a day at **Kailua**
Beach. Before you leave Waikiki, drop by
MAC 24-7 (p. 146) and pick up a picnic
lunch. Kailua is the perfect beach to just
relax or snorkel or try something different, such as kayaking or windsurfing. You
can spend the entire day here, or you can
take an afternoon hike at the **Hooma-**
luhia Botanical Gardens (p. 189).

Day ❼: Final Day: Shopping & Art
Been having too much fun to shop for
gifts for your friends back home? You can
find a great selection of stores in Waikiki
at the **Ala Moana Shopping Center,** the
DFS Galleria, and the **Royal Hawaiian**
Shopping Center. If you're more interested in looking than buying, check
out the **Honolulu Academy of Arts**
(p. 208), **The Contemporary Museum**
(p. 208), or the **Hawaii State Art**
Museum (p. 208). On your way back to
the airport, be sure to stop at one of the
Maunakea Street lei shops (p. 213) in
Chinatown to buy a sweet-smelling souvenir of your trip.

2 A Week on the Big Island of Hawaii

A week is barely enough time to see the entire Big Island of Hawaii; 2 weeks would be better. But if your schedule doesn't allow more time, this tour will let you see the highlights of this huge island (twice the size of all the other islands combined). The itinerary is set up for people staying either in Kailua-Kona or on the Kohala Coast, and I suggest you spend at least 2 nights in Volcano Village to enjoy one of the stars of the Big Island, Hawaii Volcanoes National Park.

Day ❶: Arrival & Beach Time

After you settle into your hotel, head for the beach: Snorkelers should go to **Kahaluu Beach Park** (p. 295), surfers to **White Sands Beach** (p. 295), privacy buffs to **Kekaha Kai State Park (Kona Coast State Park;** p. 295), and beach aficionados can choose from **Anaehoomalu Bay, Hapuna Beach,** and **Kaunaoa Beach (Mauna Kea Beach),** depending on whether you want to snorkel, bodyboard, or just relax (see reviews starting on p. 299 to help you decide). When the sun starts to wane, head for old **Kailua-Kona** town and wander through the **Hulihee Palace, Mokuaikaua Church,** and **Kamehameha's Compound at Kamakahonu Bay** (p. 316). Find a spot to watch the sunset (either on the pier or along the seawall), and then head for dinner in either **Kailua-Kona** or **Keauhou.**

Day ❷: Out on the Water, Then Drive to Hawaii Volcanoes National Park ✹✹✹

Since you most likely will be up early your first day in Hawaii (and still on mainland time), take advantage of it and book a morning sailing/snorkeling tour on the *Fair Wind* (p. 302) to **Kealakekua Bay,** a marine-life preserve. Spend the morning floating in a rainbowed sea of fish and enjoy a terrific lunch on board the sailing catamaran. After you return to Keauhou, start driving south. Great stops along the way are **Puuhonua O Honaunau National Historical Park** (p. 320), **South Point** (p. 320), and **Green Sand Beach (Papakolea Beach;** p. 298). Then head up **Mauna Kea** to the **Hawaii Volcanoes National Park** (p. 307) and stay at one of the many quaint bed-and-breakfasts in the tiny village of **Volcano** (a list of recommended accommodations starts on p. 270).

Day ❸: Exploring an Active Volcano ✹✹✹

The highlight of your trip most likely will be the time you spend in the incredible **Hawaii Volcanoes National Park** (p. 333). I recommend spending the morning exploring the park and taking hikes. Your first stop should be the Kilauea Visitors Center. Then explore **Halemaumau Crater, Thurston Lava Tube, Devastation Trail,** and all the other sites in the crater. Find out from the rangers how to get to the current lava flow. In the afternoon, drive down to the current flow and walk out as far as the rangers will allow. Go eat a nice dinner in Volcano and return to the flow after dark, armed with a flashlight, water bottle, and jacket. Since you were there during the day, the path to the volcano after dark will be familiar to you. Seeing the ribbon of red lava snake its way down the side of the mountain and then thunder into the ocean is a sight you will never forget. You are going to be tired after this full day, so I recommend spending another night in Volcano.

Day ❹: Touring Old Hawaii: Hilo Town ✹✹✹, Akaka Falls ✹✹✹, Waipio Valley ✹✹✹ & Cowboy Country

It's just a 45-minute drive from Volcano to **Hilo** (p. 330), so plan to arrive early in

The Big Island in 1 Week

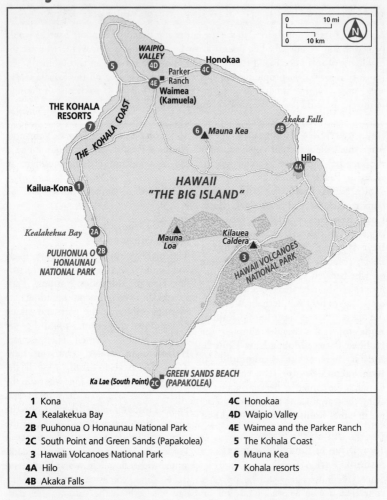

1 Kona
2A Kealakekua Bay
2B Puuhonua O Honaunau National Park
2C South Point and Green Sands (Papakolea)
3 Hawaii Volcanoes National Park
4A Hilo
4B Akaka Falls
4C Honokaa
4D Waipio Valley
4E Waimea and the Parker Ranch
5 The Kohala Coast
6 Mauna Kea
7 Kohala resorts

the morning, grab a cup of coffee at **Bears' Coffee** (p. 281), and wander through the old town, being sure to see **Banyan Drive, Liliuokalani Gardens, Lyman Museum & Mission House,** the **Pacific Tsunami Museum,** and one of the wonderful botanical gardens such as **Nani Mau Gardens** (p. 332), **Hawaii Tropical Botanical Garden** (p. 328), or **World Botanical Garden** (p. 328). Head up the Hamakua Coast, stopping at **Akaka Falls** (p. 327) and planning a lunch stop in **Honokaa.** After lunch, be sure to see **Waipio Valley** (p. 329), the birthplace of Hawaii's kings, before heading for **Waimea** (p. 345). Spend some time in this cowboy town and at the **Parker Ranch Visitor Center and Museum** (p. 323). Spend the night along the Kohala Coast.

Day ❺: The Kohala Coast: Stepping Back in Time ✸✸✸

Get an early start on your trip back in time. The first stop is just south of Kawaihae, at the **Puukohola Heiau National Historic Site** (p. 320), the temple Kamehameha built to the war god to ensure his success in battle. Allow at least an hour to view the temple and wander through the visitor center. Keep driving up Highway 270 to the **Lapakahi State Historical Park** (p. 322) for a view of a typical 14th-century Hawaiian village and the **Mo'okini Luakini Heiau** (p. 322). Plan a lunch stop in Hawi or Kapaau at either **Bamboo** (p. 285) or **Kohala Rainbow Cafe** (p. 286), and stop by **The Original King Kamehameha Statue** (p. 322) in Kapaau. The final stop on your northward journey is the **Pololu Valley Lookout** (p. 322). On your way back, in the late afternoon (the best time for viewing), be sure to stop at the **Puako Petroglyph Archaeological District** (p. 321). If it's Friday, make reservations at the **Kona Village Luau** (p. 351) for the perfect ending to your trip back in time.

Day ❻: Mauna Kea: Where the Gods Live ✸✸✸

Sleep in, have a lazy morning at the beach, and, in the afternoon, plan to explore Hawaii's tallest mountain (and dormant volcano), **Mauna Kea** (p. 324). You need a four-wheel-drive vehicle to climb to the top of the 13,796-foot Mauna Kea, so I recommend you book with the experts, **Mauna Kea Summit Adventures** (p. 326), for a 7- to 8-hour visit to this mountain, sacred to the Hawaiians and treasured by astronomers around the globe.

Day ❼: Relaxing or Shopping

Depending on how much time you have on your final day, I recommend either relaxing on the beach or being pampered in a spa. Spa-goers have a range of terrific spas among the **Kohala resorts** (reviews start on p. 261) to choose from. Shoppers have lots to choose from—see my recommendations starting on p. 343.

3 A Week on Maui

I've outlined the highlights of Maui for those who just have 7 days and want to see everything. Two things I suggest: First, spend 2 nights in Hana, a decision you will not regret, and second, take the Trilogy boat trip to Lanai for the day. I've designed this itinerary assuming you'll stay in West Maui for 5 days. If you are staying elsewhere (like Wailea or Kihei), allow extra driving time.

Day ❶: Arrival & Kapalua Beach ✸✸✸

Check into your hotel, and then head for **Kapalua Beach** (p. 424). Don't overdo the sun on your first day. After an hour or two at the beach, drive to **Lahaina** (p. 449) and spend a couple of hours walking the historic old town. To really feel like you are in Hawaii, go to the **Old Lahaina Luau** (p. 476) at sunset to immerse yourself in Hawaiian culture.

Day ❷: Up a 10,000-Foot Dormant Volcano & Down Again ✸✸✸

You'll likely wake up early on your first day in Hawaii, so take advantage of it and head up to the 10,000-foot (dormant) volcano, **Haleakala.** You can **hike in the crater** (p. 437), **speed down the mountain on a bicycle** (p. 444), or just wander about **Haleakala National Park.** You don't have to be at the top for sunrise; in

Maui in 1 Week

1A Kaanapali Beach or Kapalua Beach
1B Lahaina
2 Haleakala National Park
3 Hana Highway
4 Hana

5A Ulapalukua Ranch, the Tedeschi Winery
    and Grandma's Coffee House
5B Haliimaile General Store
5C Maui Ocean Center
6 Lanai
7 Iao Valley

fact, it has gotten so crowded and congested at sunrise you may not have quite the awe-inspiring experience you were hoping for if you are fighting the crowds. I'd suggest wandering up any time during the day. On your way back down, stop and tour **Upcountry Maui** (p. 457), particularly the communities of **Kula, Makawao,** and **Paia.** Plan for a sunset dinner in **Paia** or **Kuau.**

Day ❸: Hana Highway ✦✦✦

Pack a lunch and spend the entire day driving the scenic **Hana Highway** (p. 458). Pull over often and get out to take photos, smell the flowers, and jump in the mountain stream pools. Wave to everyone, move off the road for those speeding by, and breathe in Hawaii. Plan to spend

at least 2 nights in Hana (hotel recommendations start on p. 394).

Day ❹: A Day in Heavenly Hana ✦✦✦

An entire day in paradise, so many things to do. Take an early-morning hike along the black sands of **Waianapanapa State Park** (p. 427); then explore the tiny town of **Hana** (coverage starts on p. 461). Be sure to see the **Hana Museum Cultural Center, Hasegawa General Store,** and **Hana Coast Gallery.** Get a picnic lunch and drive out to the Kipihulu end of Haleakala National Park at **Oheo Gulch** (p. 462). Hike to the waterfalls and swim in the pools. Splurge on dinner at the dining room at the **Hotel Hana-Maui.** Spend another night in Hana.

Day ❺: Wine, Food & (Hawaiian) Song

Check to see if the road past Hana is open (it closed after the 2006 earthquake); if it is, continue driving around the island, past **Kaupo** and up to the **Ulupalakua Ranch** (p. 457) and the **Tedeschi Vineyards and Winery** (p. 457). Stop at **Grandma's Coffee House** (p. 417) for a cup of java and head down the mountain, with a stop for lunch at **Haliimaile General Store** (p. 416). Spend the afternoon at the **Maui Ocean Center** in Maalaea (p. 451) checking out the marine life, especially the sharks. Plan a dinner in Lahaina and see the drama/dance/music show **Ulalena** (p. 476). If the road past Hana is closed, go back along the Hana Highway the way you came, stopping for lunch at Haliimaile, and then follow the rest of the itinerary from there.

Day ❻: Sailing to Lanai 👍👍👍

Trilogy (p. 429) is the best sailing/snorkeling trip in Hawaii, so don't miss it. You'll spend the day (breakfast and lunch included) sailing to the island of Lanai, snorkeling, touring the island, and sailing back to Lahaina. Plus, you still have the afternoon to go shopping for souvenirs or take a nap.

Day ❼: Relaxing & Shopping

Depending on how much time you have on your final day, you can choose from relaxing on the beach, being pampered in a spa, or shopping for souvenirs and bargains. Spa-goers have a range of terrific **spas,** and **shopping** aficionados should check out some of my favorite stores (recommendations start on p. 463). If you have a late flight, you might want to check out **Iao Valley** (p. 448).

4 A Week on Molokai

The island of Molokai is for people trying to get away from everything or those looking for adventure. There are no direct flights from the mainland to Molokai, so you will have to fly into Honolulu and then take a commuter plane to Molokai.

Day ❶: Arrival & Kaunakakai

If you are staying in a condo or a vacation rental, head into **Kaunakakai** and stock up on groceries and supplies. While you're there, wander around the old two-street town and check out the stores. Be sure to stop at the **Kapuaiwa Coconut Grove/Kiowea Park** (p. 503) and watch the sunset.

Day ❷: Ride a Mule to Kalaupapa 👍👍👍

Your internal clock will still be set to mainland time, so you should have no problem getting up early and getting out to the **Molokai Mule Ride** (p. 507). This adventure will take you through 26 switchbacks on a 1,600-foot cliff and give you a chance to tour the **Kalaupapa Peninsula,** where people suffering from leprosy have lived for decades.

Day ❸: Head for the Beach

Molokai not only has terrific beaches, but on weekdays they generally are empty! Depending on the time of year and the weather, great beaches for snorkeling are **Murphy Beach Park (Kumimi Beach Park)** and **Sandy Beach** (p. 496) on the East End, and **Kapukahehu (Dixie Maru) Beach** (p. 498) on the West End. Pack a picnic lunch or stop by the **Outpost Natural Foods** or the **Sundown Deli** in Kaunakakai (p. 494). Stay all day. Relax.

Molokai in 1 Week

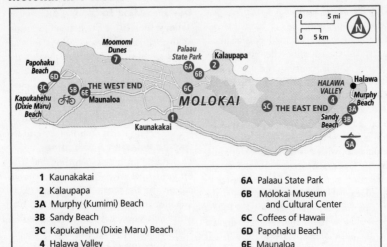

Day ❹: Hike in a Tropical Valley & Venture into Paradise ⚘

After a day at the beach, you'll be ready for a hike into the tropical jungle of **Halawa Valley**. Book with **The Lodge at Molokai Ranch** (p. 488) before you head out, as you cannot venture into the valley on your own without trespassing. Bring a picnic lunch for after the hike, and then spend the rest of the day on the beach at Halawa. Stop to see the **fish ponds** (p. 509) before you leave the East End.

Day ❺: Outdoor Adventure ⚘

Spend a day kayaking, bicycling, or hiking on this Hawaiian oasis. **Molokai Outdoors Activities** (p. 497) can set you up with whatever equipment you need: kayaks, mountain bikes, or maps for hiking. My choice would be kayaking along the shallow water of the East End. Mountain bikers can find the best off-road bicycle trails in the state on the **Molokai Ranch** (p. 503), and hikers should check out **Pepeopae Trail** (p. 499) or the **Kamakou Preserve** (p. 509).

Day ❻: Touring the West End ⚘⚘

Since you've already seen the East End, spend a day touring the rest of the island. Start out with a tour of the central part of the island by driving out to **Palaau State Park** (p. 504), which overlooks the Kalaupapa Peninsula, then stop off at the **Molokai Museum and Cultural Center** (p. 504), and take a coffee break at **Coffees of Hawaii Plantation Store and Espresso Bar** (p. 512). Next head for the 3-mile-long, white-sand **Papohaku Beach** (p. 496). After an hour or so at the beach, drive up to the cool air in **Maunaloa** town to see the best store on the island: the **Big Wind Kite Factory & the Plantation Gallery** (p. 513).

Day ❼: Moomomi Dunes: Archaeology Heaven

Before you catch your plane back, stop by the **Moomomi Dunes** (p. 507), located close to the Hoolehua Airport. This wild, sand-covered coast is a treasure trove for archaeologists. Buried in the mounds are ancient Hawaiian burial sites, fossils,

Hawaiian artifacts, and even the bones of prehistoric birds. If you have enough time, take the 20-minute easy walk west to **Kawaaloa Bay,** the perfect place to say aloha to Molokai.

5 A Week on Lanai

The smallest of all the Hawaiian islands, Lanai was once a big pineapple plantation and now is home to two exclusive resorts, hundreds of years of history, and just one small town with some of the friendliest people you will ever meet. Like the island of Molokai, there are no direct flights from the mainland to Lanai. You will have to fly into Honolulu and then take a commuter plane to Lanai.

Day ❶: Arrival & Hulopoe Bay 🐠🐠

After you settle into your hotel, head for the beach. The best beach on the island is the marine preserve at **Hulopoe Bay** (p. 526). It's generally safe for swimming, and because it's a marine preserve, no one can take the fish, which means snorkeling is terrific and the fish are so friendly you practically have to shoo them away.

Day ❷: Tour the Island in a Four-Wheel-Drive Vehicle

Lanai is a fantastic place to go four-wheeling. Generally you will not need a car if you are staying at one of the two resorts or at the Hotel Lanai (they provide shuttle bus service). So splurge and rent a four-wheel-drive vehicle for 2 or 3 days. Get a picnic lunch from **Pele's Other Garden** (p. 525) and head out of Lanai City to the **Kanepuu Preserve** (p. 533), a 590-acre dry-land forest. Next stop is **Garden of the Gods** (p. 531) and a picnic lunch at **Polihua Beach** (p. 527), Lanai's largest white-sand beach. The beach generally is not safe for swimming and it can be windy here, but it most likely will be deserted and you'll have a great view of Molokai in the distance. After lunch, reverse directions and head to **Shipwreck Beach** (p. 527) and then on to **Keomoku Village** (p. 533).

Day ❸: A Day at the Beach

Plan a lazy day at **Hulopoe Beach** (p. 526). Get a good book, watch the kids play in the surf, or take a long slow walk around the crescent-shaped bay. Wander over to the **Manele Bay Hotel** for lunch poolside at the **Ocean Grill** (p. 523) or over to the **Manele Bay Clubhouse** (p. 524). Plan a nap for the afternoon or try your hand at some Island crafts at the **Lanai Arts Program** (p. 532).

Day ❹: Hike (or Drive) the Munro Trail

If it has not been raining and the ground is dry, do a little exploring. The adventurous can spend the day (plan on at least 7 hr.) climbing to the top of Lanai at Lanaihale on the **Munro Trail** (p. 528). The not-so-adventurous can take a four-wheel-drive vehicle. Pencil in a soak in a hot tub on your return.

Day ❺: A Day on the Ocean 🐠🐠

Ring up **Trilogy Lanai Ocean Sports** (p. 527) and book a sailing/snorkeling, whale-watching, or scuba trip. Or go on a surfing safari with **Lanai Surf School & Surf Safari** (p. 528) to a secluded beach.

Day ❻: Horseback Riding, Followed by a Trip Back in Time

Saddle up: Horse lovers should arrange a tour of Lanai through the **Stables at Koele** (p. 530) in the morning. Then plan a four-wheel-drive in the afternoon to the historic ruins of the old **Kaunolu Village** (p. 533), on the southwestern side of the island.

Day ❼: Biking & Shopping

The best way to get around the tiny village of Lanai City is via bicycle. Rent one

Lanai in 1 Week

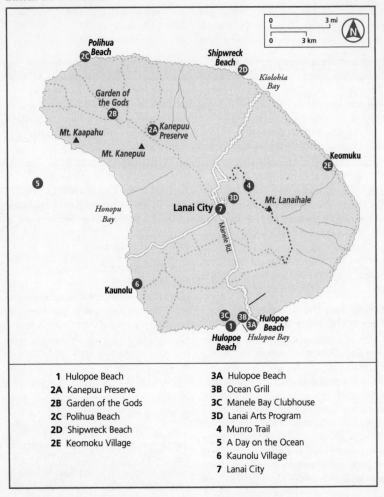

1	Hulopoe Beach	**3A**	Hulopoe Beach
2A	Kanepuu Preserve	**3B**	Ocean Grill
2B	Garden of the Gods	**3C**	Manele Bay Clubhouse
2C	Polihua Beach	**3D**	Lanai Arts Program
2D	Shipwreck Beach	**4**	Munro Trail
2E	Keomuku Village	**5**	A Day on the Ocean
		6	Kaunolu Village
		7	Lanai City

from **The Lodge at Koele** (p. 521) and ride (downhill) into town. Lanai City has some terrific boutique shops that you'll find nowhere else (descriptions of my favorites start on p. 534).

6 A Week on Kauai

Hawaii's oldest island, ringed with white-sand beaches, is small and easy to circum-navigate in a week. But there are so many wonderful things to do and see that you may find yourself wishing you had more time.

Day ❶: Arrival & Beach Time

After you settle in at your hotel, head for the beach. If you are staying on the south side, **Poipu Beach** (p. 582) is your best bet; on the east in the Coconut Coast area, go to **Lydgate State Park** (p. 585);

1A Poipu Beach	**3B** Coconut Coast
1B Lydgate State Beach	**4A** Kokee State Park
1C Anini Beach	**4B** Waimea Canyon
1D Hanalei Beach	**4C** Menehune Ditch
1E Haena Beach	**4D** Russian Fort Elizabeth
1F Ke'e Beach	**4E** Art Night in Hanapepe and
2A Na Pali Coast Trail	Hanapepe Café and Espresso Bar
2B Ka Ulu O Laka Heiau	**5A** Allerton Gardens
2C Hanalei	**5B** Spouting Horn
2D Hanalei Bay	**6** Kauai Museum
2E Na Aina Kai Botanical Gardens	**7A** ANARA Spa at the Hyatt Regency Kauai
3A Helicopter Tour	**7B** Princeville Health Club & Spa

and if you are on the North Shore, try **Anini, Hanalei, Haena,** or **Kee beaches** (p. 586).

Day ❷: Tour the North Shore ★★

It rains often on the Garden Isle of Kauai, so the first sunny day, head out for the **North Shore** (p. 599). Drive all the way to the end of the road to Kee Beach. Plan to hike a little on the famous Kalalau trail in **Na Pali Coast State Park** (p. 599)— bring hiking shoes or closed-toed tennis shoes. A half-hour on the trail will give

you an idea of the spectacular coastline. The hearty may want to hike all the way to **Hanakapiai Beach,** a 2-hour trip one-way. After your hike, take a look at **Ka Ulu O Laka Heiau** (p. 613) at Kee Beach. Head into **Hanalei** (p. 564) for lunch, and then drive down to **Hanalei Bay** (p. 586) for a quiet afternoon on the beach, or book at tour with **Na Aina Kai Botanical Gardens** (p. 614) to see one of Kauai's most beautiful (and whimsical) gardens. Plan to have dinner on the

North Shore—my recommendations start on p. 578.

Day ❸: See Kauai from the Air: Book a Helicopter Tour 🌴🌴🌴

Book a **helicopter tour** (p. 605) for Day 3, but not until 10 or 11am at the earliest, to avoid the bumper-to-bumper commuter traffic. After your tour, head to the **Coconut Coast** for lunch (my dining recommendations start on p. 575). After lunch, go back in Hawaiian history at the **Wailua River State Park** (p. 609). Since you are already in the area, book a luau at the **ResortQuest Kauai Beach at Makaiwa** (p. 557).

Day ❹: Hiking Kokee State Park 🌴🌴 & Waimea Canyon 🌴🌴🌴

Get an early start and drive up to the 4,640-acre **Kokee State Park** (p. 596), where you will find a range of hiking trails to fit every ability. Birders, hikers, and sightseers will love wandering around this park. You can get lunch at the **Kokee Lodge Restaurant** (p. 597), open from 9am to 3:30pm. Be sure to stop by the **Kokee Natural History Museum** (p. 607), which is full of great information as well as trail maps. In the afternoon, stop at the "Grand Canyon of the Pacific," **Waimea Canyon** (p. 606), with more great hiking. After you've had enough hiking for the day, don't miss the **Kiki a Ola (Menehune Ditch;** p. 606) and the **Russian Fort Elizabeth State Historical Park** (p. 606) on your way out of Waimea town. *Tip:* A great time to plan this trip to Kokee and Waimea is on a Friday. Since you are already on the west side, you can attend Friday night's Hanapepe **Art Night** (p. 623), and the terrific **Hanapepe Cafe & Espresso Bar** (p. 575) will be open for dinner.

Day ❺: Beach Day 🌴🌴

Kauai has the best beaches in Hawaii, so you should devote at least 1 day to them. Check out our **beach recommendations,** starting on p. 581. If you're not the type to just lie around, you can book a kayak or snorkel tour (watersports options start on p. 587—I particularly recommend a tour of the Na Pali Coast). If you've had enough sun to last you awhile, then be sure to book a tour at **Allerton Garden of the National Tropical Botanical Garden** (p. 605). On your way back from the Garden, stop and marvel at the very unusual **Spouting Horn** (p. 605).

Day ❻: Getting out of the Rain (or Sun)

It's best to plan for at least 1 rainy day on Kauai, but my rainy-day suggestions are just as much fun to do when it's not rainy. The first thing I would do is book a **Hawaii Movie Tour** (p. 610). An air-conditioned van takes you to some of the many spots on Kauai where films have been made, showing you clips of the movie on the spot it was made. Another great rainy-day activity is exploring the treasure-filled **Kauai Museum** (p. 604) in Lihue, or **shopping** at Kauai's unique markets (see my recommendations starting on p. 614).

Day ❼: Spa Day

A treatment at a rejuvenating spa is a great way to end your trip. Kauai's best spa is the **Grand Hyatt Kauai Resort & Spa** (p. 547). In addition to the fabulous menu of treatments, they have a great area to relax, take a steam or a sauna, or just hang out in the hot tub. On the North Shore, try the **Princeville Resort Kauai Health Club & Spa** (p. 560), which is small but very good.

4

Oahu, the Gathering Place

A wise Hawaiian kahuna once told me that the islands are like children—each is special yet different, and each is to be loved for its individual qualities. One thing's for sure: You'll never find another island like Oahu, the commercial and population center of Hawaii.

Honolulu offers a fast-paced urban setting with Hawaii's hottest nightlife, its best shopping, and a huge array of restaurants. But the North Shore and the windward side of the island present a different face: miles of white-sand beaches and a slower, country way of life. If just the thought of rush-hour traffic, freeways, high-rise towers, and having to pay for parking makes your back molars hurt, then either head for the North Shore or take the next plane out to a quieter neighbor island.

It's astounding to spend hours flying across the barren blue of the Pacific and then suddenly see the most remote big city on earth, a 26-mile-long metropolis of some 903,000 souls living in the middle of nowhere. Once on its streets, you'll find bright city lights, excellent restaurants, nightclubs, world-class shopping, a vibrant arts scene, and grand old hotels.

Nine out of 10 visitors to Hawaii—some five million people a year—stop on Oahu, and most of them end up along the canyonlike streets of Waikiki, Honolulu's well-known hotel district and its most densely populated neighborhood.

Some days it seems like the entire world is sunning itself on Waikiki's famous beach. Beyond Waikiki, Honolulu is clean and easy to enjoy. The city is coming of age for the 21st century: The old port town opened a new convention center in 1998 and is reshaping its waterfront, altering its skyline, opening new world-class hotels, and all the while trying to preserve its historical roots and revive its Polynesian heritage.

Out in the country, Oahu can be as down-home as a slack-key guitar. This is where you'll find a big blue sky, perfect waves, empty beaches, rainbows and waterfalls, sweet tropical flowers, and fiery Pacific sunsets. In fact, nowhere else within 60 minutes of a major American city can you snorkel in a crystal-clear lagoon, climb an old volcano, surf monster waves, kayak to a desert isle, picnic on a sandbar, soar in a glider over tide pools, skin-dive over a sunken airplane, bicycle through a rainforest, golf a championship course, and sail into the setting sun.

And in terms of weather, no other Hawaiian island has it as fine as Oahu. The Big Island is hotter, Kauai is wetter, Maui has more wind, and Molokai and Lanai are drier. But Oahu enjoys a kind of perpetual late spring, with light trade winds and 82°F (28°C) days almost year-round. In fact, the climate is supposed to be the best on the planet. Once you have that, the rest is easy.

1 Orientation

ARRIVING

Honolulu is your gateway to the Hawaiian Islands; even though more and more transpacific flights are going directly to the neighbor islands these days, chances are still good that you'll touch down on Oahu first. **Honolulu International Airport** sits on the south shore of Oahu, west of downtown Honolulu and Waikiki near Pearl Harbor. Many major American and international carriers fly to Honolulu from the mainland; see "Getting There," in chapter 2, for a list of carriers and their toll-free numbers.

LANDING AT HONOLULU INTERNATIONAL AIRPORT

The airport at Honolulu is probably the most cosmopolitan spot in the Pacific, with passengers from every corner of the globe. You can walk or take the free airport shuttle from your arrival gate to the main terminal and baggage claim, on the ground level. After collecting your bags, unless you're getting on an interisland flight immediately, you'll exit to the palm-lined street, where uniformed attendants can either flag down a taxi or direct you to **TheBus** (for transportation information, see below). For Waikiki shuttles and rental-car vans, cross the street to the center island and wait at the designated stop.

Passengers connecting to neighbor-island flights take the free shuttle or walk to the large interisland terminal serving Aloha and Hawaiian airlines or the more distant commuter terminal, which serves the smaller Island Air. (For details on interisland flights, see "Getting Around Hawaii," in chapter 2.)

GETTING TO & FROM THE AIRPORT

BY RENTAL CAR   All major rental companies have cars available at the airport (see "By Car," under "Getting Around Hawaii," in chapter 2). Rental-agency vans will pick you up curbside at the center island outside baggage claim and take you to their off-site lot.

BY TAXI   Taxis are abundant at the airport; an attendant will be happy to flag one down for you. Taxi fare is about $20 from Honolulu International to downtown Honolulu, about $25 to $35 to Waikiki. If you need to call a taxi, see "Getting Around," below, for a list of cab companies.

BY AIRPORT SHUTTLE   **Airport Waikiki Express** (© **808/566-7333;** www. hawaii.gov/dot/airports/hnl/hnl_ground_trans.htm) offers 24-hour service every day of the year between the airport and all 350 hotels and condos in Waikiki. A one-way trip from the airport to Waikiki in one of the company's air-conditioned vans costs just $9 per person (it's $15 round-trip). You'll find the shuttle at street level outside baggage claim. You can board with two pieces of luggage and a carry-on at no extra charge. Tips are welcome. For advance purchase of group tickets, call the number above.

BY BUS   TheBus nos. 19 and 20 (Waikiki Beach and Hotels) run from the airport to downtown Honolulu and Waikiki. The first bus from Waikiki to the airport leaves at 4:50am Monday through Friday and 5:25am Saturday and Sunday; the last bus departs the airport for Waikiki at 11:45pm Monday through Friday, 11:25pm Saturday and Sunday. There are two bus stops on the main terminal's upper level; a third is on the second level of the interisland terminal. You can board TheBus with a carry-on or small suitcase, as long as it fits under the seat and doesn't disrupt other passengers; otherwise, you'll have to take a shuttle or taxi. The approximate travel time to Waikiki is an hour. The one-way fare is $2 for adults and $1 for children ages 6 to 17, exact change only. For more information on TheBus, see "Getting Around," below.

VISITOR INFORMATION

The **Hawaii Visitors and Convention Bureau (HVCB),** 2270 Kalakaua Ave., Seventh Floor, Honolulu, HI 96815 (© **800/GO-HAWAII** or 808/923-1811; www.go hawaii.com), supplies free brochures, maps, accommodations guides, and *Islands of Aloha,* the official HVCB magazine. The **Oahu Visitors Bureau,** 735 Bishop St., Suite 1872, Honolulu, HI 96813 (© **877/525-OAHU** or 808/524-0722; fax 808/ 521-1620; www.visit-oahu.com), distributes a free travel planner and map.

A number of free publications, such as *This Week Oahu,* are packed with money-saving coupons and good regional maps; look for them on racks at the airport and around town.

THE ISLAND IN BRIEF

Honolulu

Hawaii's largest city looks like any other big metropolitan center with tall buildings. In fact, some cynics refer to it as "Los Angeles West." But within Honolulu's boundaries, you'll find rainforests, deep canyons, valleys, waterfalls, a nearly mile-high mountain range, coral reefs, and gold-sand beaches. The city proper—where most of Honolulu's residents live—is approximately 12 miles wide and 26 miles long, running east-west roughly between Diamond Head and Pearl Harbor. Within the city are seven hills laced by seven streams that run to Mamala Bay.

A plethora of neighborhoods surrounds the central area, from the quiet suburbs of **Hawaii Kai** to kamaaina (native-born) neighborhoods like **Manoa.** These areas are generally quieter and more residential than Waikiki, but they're still within minutes of beaches, shopping, and all the activities Oahu has to offer.

WAIKIKI 🌀🌀🌀 Some say that Waikiki is past its prime—that everybody goes to Maui now. If it has fallen out of favor, you couldn't prove it by me. Waikiki is the very incarnation of Yogi Berra's comment about Toots

Shor's famous New York restaurant: "Nobody goes there anymore. It's too crowded."

When King Kalakaua played in Waikiki, it was "a hamlet of plain cottages . . . its excitements caused by the activity of insect tribes and the occasional fall of a coconut." The Merrie Monarch, who gave his name to Waikiki's main street, would love the scene today. Some five million tourists visit Oahu every year, and 9 out of 10 of them stay in Waikiki. This urban beach is where all the action is; it's backed by 175 high-rise hotels with more than 33,000 guest rooms and hundreds of bars and restaurants, all in a 1½-square-mile beach zone. Waikiki means honeymooners and sun seekers, bikinis and bare buns, a 'round-the-clock beach party every day of the year—and it's all because of a thin crescent of sand that was shipped over from Molokai. Staying in Waikiki puts you in the heart of it all, but also be aware that this is an on-the-go place with traffic noise 24 hours a day and its share of crime—and it's almost always crowded.

ALA MOANA 🌀🌀 A great beach as well as a famous shopping mall, Ala Moana is the retail and transportation

Oahu

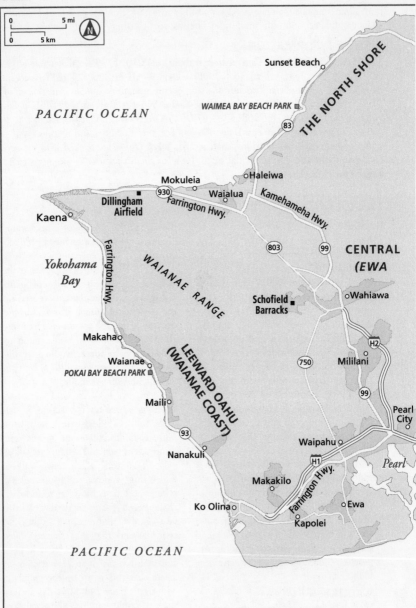

PACIFIC OCEAN

Yokohama Bay

Kaena

Dillingham Airfield

Mokuleia

Waialua

Haleiwa

Sunset Beach

THE NORTH SHORE

WAIMEA BAY BEACH PARK

Farrington Hwy.

Kamehameha Hwy.

WAIANAE RANGE

Farrington Hwy.

Makaha

Waianae

POKAI BAY BEACH PARK

Maili

LEEWARD OAHU (WAIANAE COAST)

Schofield Barracks

CENTRAL (EWA

Wahiawa

Mililani

Pearl City

Nanakuli

Waipahu

Makakilo

Pearl

Ko Olina

Kapolei

Ewa

Farrington Hwy.

PACIFIC OCEAN

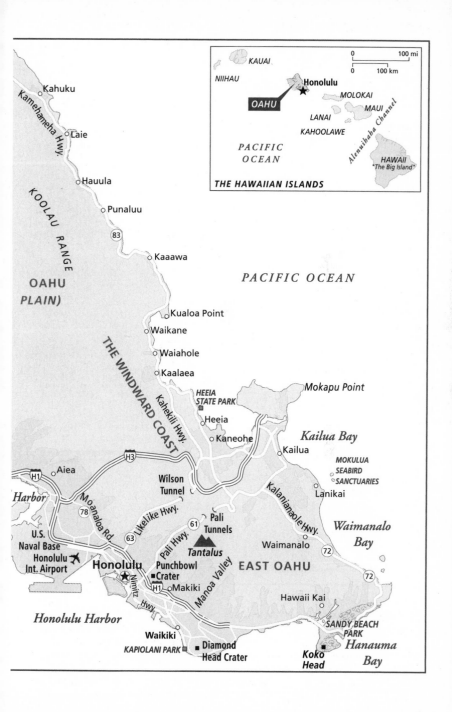

Honolulu Neighborhoods in Brief

Kamehameha IV Rd.

School St.

Likelike Hwy.

78

Kaua St.

63

Alewa Dr.

Wyllie St.

Judd St.

Nuuanu Stream

Fort Shafter Military Res.

H1 Lunalilo Fwy.

Houghtailing St.

Halona St.

Liliha St.

Iolani Ave.

61

Booth Rd.

Middle St.

92

Puuhale Rd.

Kalihi St.

Waiakamilo Rd.

N. King St.

Palama St.

Pali Hwy.

Puowaina Dr.

Punchbowl Crater

Nimitz Hwy.

Dillingham Blvd.

CHINATOWN

Iwilei Rd.

Vineyard Blvd.

Prospect St.

DOWNTOWN

Kapalama Military Res.

Sand Island Access Rd.

Kapalama Basin

Nuuanu Ave.

Bishop St.

N. Richards St.

N. King

N. Beretania St.

S. King St.

Pensacola St.

U.S. Coast Guard Res.

Honolulu Harbor

Punchbowl St.

South St.

Queen St.

Ward St.

Kewalo Basin

92

Mokauea Island

Sand Island

SAND ISLAND STATE REC. AREA

ALA MOANA PARK

KAKAAKO WATERFRONT STATE REC. AREA

See "Downtown Honolulu" map

Mamala Bay

OAHU

Honolulu ★

Airport ✈
Information ⓘ
Mountain ▲

heart of Honolulu, a place where you can both shop and suntan in one afternoon. All bus routes lead to the open-air **Ala Moana Shopping Center,** across the street from **Ala Moana Beach Park.** This 50-acre, 200-shop behemoth attracts 56 million customers a year (people fly up from Tahiti just to buy their Christmas gifts here). Every European designer from Armani to Vuitton is represented in Honolulu's answer to Beverly Hills's Rodeo Drive. For our purposes, the neighborhood called "Ala Moana" extends along Ala

Moana Boulevard from Waikiki in the direction of Diamond Head to downtown Honolulu in the Ewa direction (west) and includes the **Ward Centre** and **Ward Warehouse** complexes, as well as **Restaurant Row.**

DOWNTOWN A tiny cluster of high-rises west of Waikiki, downtown Honolulu is the financial, business, and government center of Hawaii. On the waterfront stands the iconic 1926 Aloha Tower, now the centerpiece of a harborfront shopping and

Waikiki Orientation

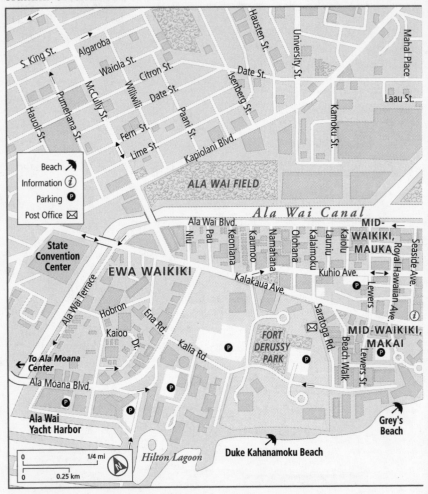

Legend:
- Beach ↗
- Information ⓘ
- Parking Ⓟ
- Post Office ✉

**Map labels:**

S. King St., Algaroba, Waiola St., Citron St., Date St., Hausten St., University St., Mahai Place, Hauoli St., Pumehana St., McCully St., Wiliwili, Date St., Isenberg St., Laau St., Fern St., Paani St., Lime St., Kapiolani Blvd., Kamoku St.

ALA WAI FIELD

Ala Wai Canal

State Convention Center

Ala Wai Blvd., Niu, Pau, Keoniana, Kaumoko, Namahana, Olohana, Kalaimoku, Launiu, Kaiolu, Kaiolu

MID-WAIKIKI, MAUKA

Seaside Ave., Royal Hawaiian Ave.

EWA WAIKIKI

Kalakaua Ave., Kuhio Ave., Lewers

Ala Wai Terrace, Hobron, Ena Rd., Saratoga Rd., Beach Walk

Kaioo Dr., Kalia Rd., FORT DERUSSY PARK

MID-WAIKIKI, MAKAI

Lewers St.

To Ala Moana Center

Ala Moana Blvd.

Ala Wai Yacht Harbor

Grey's Beach

0   1/4 mi
0   0.25 km

Hilton Lagoon   Duke Kahanamoku Beach

---

restaurant complex known as the **Aloha Tower Marketplace.** The whole history of Honolulu can be seen in just a few short blocks: Street vendors sell papayas from trucks on skyscraper-lined concrete canyons; joggers and BMWs rush by a lacy palace where U.S. Marines overthrew Hawaii's last queen and stole her kingdom; burly bus drivers sport fragrant white ginger flowers on their dashboards; Methodist churches look like Asian temples; and

businessmen wear aloha shirts to billion-dollar meetings.

On the edge of downtown is the **Chinatown Historic District** ✦✦✦, the oldest Chinatown in America and still one of Honolulu's liveliest neighborhoods, a nonstop pageant of people, sights, sounds, smells, and tastes—not all Chinese, now that Southeast Asians, including many Vietnamese, share the old storefronts. Go on Saturday morning, when everyone shops for fresh goods such as gingerroot, fern shoots, and hogs' heads.

Among the historic buildings and Pan-Pacific corporate headquarters are a few hotels, geared mainly toward business travelers. Most visitors prefer the excitement of Waikiki or choose a quieter neighborhood outside the city.

MANOA VALLEY First inhabited by white settlers, the Manoa Valley, above Waikiki, still has vintage kamaaina

(native-born) homes, one of Hawaii's premier botanical gardens (the Lyon Arboretum), the ever-gushing Manoa Falls, and the 320-acre campus of the University of Hawaii, where 50,000 students hit the books when they're not on the beach.

TO THE EAST: KAHALA Except for the estates of millionaires and the luxurious Kahala hotel (home of Hoku's, an outstanding beachfront

Downtown Honolulu

restaurant), there's not much out this way that's of interest to visitors.

East Oahu

Beyond Kahala lies East Honolulu and suburban bedroom communities like Aina Haina, Niu Valley, and Hawaii Kai, among others, all linked by the Kalanianaole Highway and loaded with homes, condos, fast-food joints, and shopping malls. It looks like Southern California on a good day. There are only a few reasons to come here: to have dinner at **Roy's,** the original and still-outstanding Hawaii

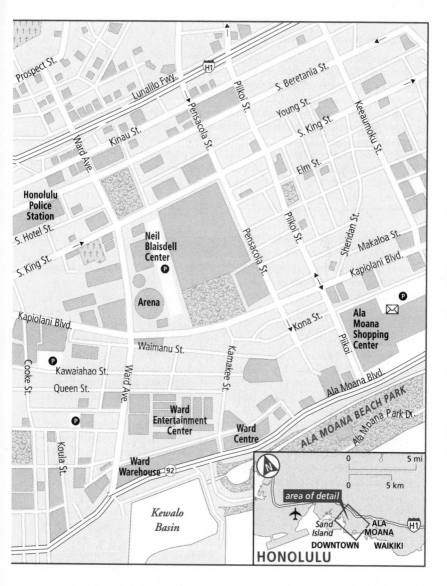

Regional Cuisine restaurant, in Hawaii Kai; to snorkel at **Hanauma Bay** or watch daredevil surfers at **Sandy Beach;** or just to enjoy the natural splendor of the lovely coastline, which might include a hike to **Makapuu Lighthouse.**

The Windward Coast

The windward side is the opposite side of the island from Waikiki. On this coast, trade winds blow cooling breezes over gorgeous beaches; rain squalls inspire lush, tropical vegetation; and miles of subdivisions dot the landscape.

Tips **Finding Your Way Around, Oahu Style**

Mainlanders sometimes find the directions given by locals a bit confusing. Seldom will you hear the terms *east, west, north,* and *south;* instead, islanders refer to directions as either **makai** (ma-*kae*), meaning toward the sea, or **mauka** (*mow*-kah), toward the mountains. In Honolulu, people use **Diamond Head** as a direction meaning to the east (in the direction of the world-famous crater called Diamond Head), and **Ewa** as a direction meaning to the west (toward the town called Ewa, on the other side of Pearl Harbor).

So if you ask a local for directions, this is what you're likely to hear: "Drive 2 blocks makai (toward the sea), and then turn Diamond Head (east) at the stoplight. Go 1 block, and turn mauka (toward the mountains). It's on the Ewa (western) side of the street."

Bed-and-breakfasts, ranging from oceanfront estates to tiny cottages on quiet residential streets, are everywhere. Vacations here are spent enjoying ocean activities and exploring the surrounding areas. Waikiki is just a 15-minute drive away.

KAILUA ✿ The biggest little beach town in Hawaii, Kailua sits at the foot of the sheer green Koolau Mountains, on a great bay with two of Hawaii's best beaches. The town itself is a funky low-rise cluster of timeworn shops and homes. Kailua has become the B&B capital of Hawaii; it's an affordable alternative to Waikiki, with rooms and vacation rentals starting at $60 a day. With the prevailing trade winds whipping up a cooling breeze, Kailua attracts windsurfers from around the world.

KANEOHE BAY ✿ Helter-skelter suburbia sprawls around the edges of Kaneohe, one of the most scenic bays in the Pacific. A handful of B&Bs dots its edge. After you clear the trafficky maze of town, Oahu returns to its more natural state. This great bay beckons you to get out on the water; you can depart from Heeia Boat Harbor on snorkel or fishing charters and visit Ahu a Laka a, the sandbar that

appears and disappears in the middle of the bay. From here, you'll have a panoramic view of the Koolau Range.

KUALOA/LAIE ✿✿ The upper-northeast shore is one of Oahu's most sacred places, an early Hawaiian landing spot where kings dipped their sails, cliffs hold ancient burial sites, and ghosts still march in the night. Sheer cliffs stab the reef-fringed seacoast, while old fish ponds are tucked along the two-lane coast road that winds past empty gold-sand beaches around beautiful Kahana Bay. Thousands "explore" the South Pacific at the **Polynesian Cultural Center,** in Laie, a Mormon settlement with its own Tabernacle Choir of sweet Samoan harmony.

The North Shore ✿✿✿

Here's the Hawaii of Hollywood—giant waves, surfers galore, tropical jungles, waterfalls, and mysterious Hawaiian temples. If you're looking for a quieter vacation that's closer to nature and filled with swimming, snorkeling, diving, and surfing, or just plain hanging out on some of the world's most beautiful beaches, the North Shore is your place. The artsy little beach town of **Haleiwa** ✿✿ and the surrounding shoreline seem a world away from Waikiki. The North

Shore boasts good restaurants, shopping, and cultural activities—but here they come with the quiet of country living. Bed-and-breakfasts are the most common accommodations, but there's one first-class hotel and some vacation rentals as well. Be forewarned: It's a long trip—nearly an hour's drive—to Honolulu and Waikiki, and it's about twice as rainy on the North Shore as in Honolulu.

Central Oahu: The Ewa Plain

Flanked by the Koolau and Waianae mountain ranges, the hot, sunbaked Ewa Plain runs up and down the center of Oahu. Once covered with sandalwood forests (hacked down for the China trade) and later the sugar-cane and pineapple backbone of Hawaii, Ewa today sports a new crop: suburban houses stretching to the sea. But let your eye wander west to the Waianae Range and Mount Kaala, at 4,020 feet the highest summit on Oahu; up there in the misty rainforest, native birds thrive in the hummocky bog. In 1914 the U.S. Army pitched a tent camp on the plain; author James Jones would later call **Schofield Barracks** "the most beautiful army post in the world." Hollywood filmed Jones's *From Here to Eternity* here.

Leeward Oahu: The Waianae Coast

The west coast of Oahu is a hot and dry place of dramatic beauty: white-sand beaches bordering the deep blue ocean, steep verdant green cliffs, and miles of Mother Nature's wildness. Except for the luxurious J. W. Marriott Ihilani Resort and Spa, and Roy's Restaurant, in the Ko Olina Resort and the Makaha Golf Course, you'll find virtually no tourist services out here. The funky west coast villages of Nanakuli, Waianae, and Makaha are the last stands of native Hawaiians. This side of Oahu is seldom visited, except by surfers bound for **Yokohama Bay** and those coming to see needle-nose **Kaena Point** (the island's westernmost outpost), which has a coastal wilderness park.

2 Getting Around

BY CAR   Oahu residents own 686,696 registered vehicles, but they have only 1,500 miles of mostly two-lane roads to use. That's 400 cars for every mile, a fact that becomes abundantly clear during morning and evening rush hours. You can avoid the gridlock by driving between 9am and 3pm or after 6pm.

All the major car-rental firms have agencies on Oahu, at the airport and in Waikiki. For a complete list, as well as tips on insurance and driving rules, see "By Car," under "Getting Around Hawaii," in chapter 2.

BY BUS   One of the best deals anywhere, **TheBus** will take you around the whole island for $2. In fact, every day more than 260,000 people use the system's 68 lines and 4,000 bus stops. TheBus goes almost everywhere almost all the time. The most popular route is **no. 8,** which arrives every 10 minutes or so to shuttle people between Waikiki and Ala Moana Center (the ride takes 15–20 min.); the **no. 19** (Airport/ Hickam), **no. 20** (Airport/Halawa Gate), **no. 47** (Waipahu), and **no. 58** (Waikiki/Ala Moana) also cover the same stretch. Waikiki service begins daily at 5am and runs until midnight; most buses run about every 15 minutes during the day and every 30 minutes in the evening.

The Circle Island–North Shore route is no. 52 (Wahiawa/Circle Island); the Circle Island–South Shore route is no. 55 (Kaneohe/Circle Island). Both routes leave Ala

TheBus

Fare $2 per ride, $1 for children 5–17. Exact change only; children under 5 ride free.

A **Visitor Pass** is available for $10 at any ABC Store in Waikiki. It's good for unlimited rides for four consecutive days.

Express and shuttle routes not shown.

Common Bus Routes:

Academy of Arts: Take #2 bus (School/Middle St) to Beretania St. and Ward Ave.

Ala Moana Shopping Center: Take bus #19 & #20 AIRPORT. Return via #19 WAIKIKI, or cross Ala Moana Blvd. for #20.

Bishop Museum: Take #2 SCHOOL STREET. Get off at Kapalama St., cross School St., walk down Bernice St. Return to School St. and take #2 WAIKIKI.

Byodo-In Temple: Take bus #2 to Hotel-Alakea St. (TRF) to #55 KANEOHE-KAHALUU. Get off at Valley of the Temple cemetery. Also #19 and #20 AIRPORT to King-Alakea St., (TRF) on Alakea St. to #55 KANEOHE-KAHALUU.

Circle Island: Take a bus to ALA MOANA CENTER (TRF) to #52 WAHIAWA CIRCLE ISLAND or #55 KANEOHE CIRCLE ISLAND. This is a 4-hour bus ride.

Chinatown or Downtown: Take any #2 bus going out of Waikiki to Hotel St. Return, take #2 WAIKIKI on Hotel St., or #19 or #20 on King St.

The Contemporary Museum & Punchbowl (National Cemetery of the Pacific): Take #2 bus (TRF) at Alapai St. to #15 MAKIKI-PACIFIC HGTS. Return, take #15 and get off at King St., area (TRF) #2 WAIKIKI.

Diamond Head Crater: Take #22 HAWAII KAI-SEA LIFE PARK to the crater. Take a flashlight. Return to the same area and take #22 WAIKIKI.

Dole Plantation: Take bus to ALA MOANA CENTER (TRF) to #52 WAHIAWA CIRCLE ISLAND.

Foster Botanic Gardens: Take #2 bus to Hotel-Riviera St. Walk to Vineyard Blvd. Return to Hotel St. Take #2 WAIKIKI, or take #4 NUUANU and get off at Nuuanu-Vineyard. Cross Nuuanu Ave. and walk one block to the gardens.

Hanauma Bay: Take #22 Beach Bus.

For further information, call ☎ **808/848-5555** daily between 5:30am and 10pm. Recorded information is available 24 hours a day; dial ☎ **808/296-1818,** then press **8287.**

on the web at **www.thebus.org**

Aloha Tower Marketplace & Hawaii Maritime Center: Take #19-#20 AIRPORT and get off at Alakea–Ala Moana. Cross the street to the Aloha Tower.

Honolulu Zoo: Take any bus on Kuhio Ave. going DIAMOND HEAD direction to Kapahulu Ave.

Iolani Palace (also **State Capitol, Honolulu Hale, Kawaihao Church, Mission Houses, Queen's Hospital, King Kamehameha Statue, State Judiciary Bldg.**) Take any #2 bus and get off at Punchbowl and Beretania St. Walk to King St. Return #2 WAIKIKI on King St.

Kahala Mall: Take #22 HAWAII KAI–SEA LIFE PARK to Kilauea Ave. Return, #22 WAIKIKI.

Pearl Harbor (*Arizona* Memorial): Take #20 AIRPORT. Get off across from Memorial, or take a bus to ALA MOANA CENTER (TRF) to #52.

Polynesian Cultural Center: Take a bus to ALA MOANA CENTER (TRF) to #55 KANEOHE CIRCLE ISLAND. Bus ride takes 2 hours one-way.

Queen Emma's Summer Home: Take #4 NUUANU, or board a bus to ALA MOANA CENTER (TRF) to #55 KANEOHE.

Sea Life Park: Take #22 HAWAII KAI-SEA LIFE PARK. #22 will stop at Hanauma Bay en route to the park.

University of Hawaii: Take #4 NUUANU. The bus will go to the University en route to Nuuanu.

Waimea Valley Audobon Center: Take a bus to ALA MOANA CENTER (TRF) to #52 WAHIAWA CIRCLE ISLAND or #55 KANEOHE CIRCLE ISLAND.

Waikele Premium Outlets: Take bus #42 from Waikiki to Wapahu Transit Center, then bus #433 to Waikele.

Moana Shopping Center every 30 minutes and take about 4½ hours to circle the island. Be aware that at Turtle Bay Resort, just outside of Kahuku, the 52 becomes the 55 and returns to Honolulu via the coast, and the 55 becomes the 52 and returns to Honolulu on the inland route. (Translation: You have to get off and switch buses to complete your island tour.) There are express buses available to some areas (for example, no. 54 to Pearl City, no. 46 to Kailua-Kaneohe, and nos. 57 and 58 to Sea Life Park).

For more information on routes and schedules, call **TheBus** (© **808/848-5555,** or 808/296-1818 for recorded information) or check out **www.thebus.org**, which provides timetables and maps for all routes, plus directions to many local attractions and a list of upcoming events. Taking TheBus is often easier than parking your car.

BY TROLLEY   It's fun to ride the 34-seat, open-air, motorized **Waikiki Trolley** (© **800/824-8804** or 808/593-2822; www.waikikitrolley.com), which looks like a San Francisco cable car (see "Orientation Tours," later in this chapter). The trolley loops around Waikiki and downtown Honolulu, stopping every 40 minutes at 12 key places like Iolani Palace, Chinatown, the State Capitol, King Kamehameha's Statue, the Mission House Museum, the Aloha Tower, the Honolulu Academy of Arts, the Hawaii Maritime Museum, Fisherman's Wharf, and Restaurant Row. The driver provides commentary along the way. Stops on the new 2-hour, fully narrated Ocean Coast Line (the blue line) of the southeast side of Oahu include Sea Life Park, Diamond Head, and Waikiki Beach. A 1-day trolley pass—which costs $25 for adults, $18 for seniors over 62, and $12 for kids ages 4 to 11—allows you to jump on and off all day long (8:30am–11:35pm). Four-day passes cost $45 for adults, $27 for seniors, and $18 for kids 4 to 11.

BY TAXI   Oahu's major cab companies offer islandwide, 24-hour, radio-dispatched service, with multilingual drivers and air-conditioned cars, limos, and vans, and vehicles equipped with wheelchair lifts (there's a $5 charge for wheelchairs). Fares are standard for all taxi firms; from the airport, expect to pay about $28 to $35 to Waikiki, about $25 to downtown, $45 and up to Kailua, about $40 to $45 to Hawaii Kai, and about $85 to $95 to the North Shore (plus tip). For a flat fee of $25, **Star Taxi** ⊛ (© **800/671-2999** or 808/942-STAR; www.hawaiistartaxi.net) will take up to five passengers from the airport to Waikiki (with no extra charge for baggage); however, you must book in advance, and call Star again after you've arrived and before you pick up your luggage to make sure a cab will be outside waiting for you.

For a metered cab, try **Charley's Taxi & Tours** (© 808/531-1333), **Elite Limousine Service** (© 808/735-2431), and **V.I.P. Transportation** (© 808/836-0317). **Robert's Taxi and Shuttle** (© 808/261-8555) serves windward Oahu, and **Hawaii Kai Hui/Koko Head Taxi** (© 808/396-6633) serves east Honolulu/southeast Oahu.

WHEELCHAIR TRANSPORTATION   Handicabs of the Pacific (© **808/524-3866**) is a private company offering wheelchair taxi services in air-conditioned vehicles that are specially equipped with ramps and wheelchair lockdowns. Handicabs offers a range of taxi services (airport pickup to Waikiki hotels is $47 one-way for two). To rent wheelchair-accessible vans, contact **Accessible Vans of Hawaii** (© **800/303-3750;** www.accessiblevanshawaii.com/index.htm).

FAST FACTS: Oahu

American Express The Honolulu office is at 1440 Kapiolani Blvd., Suite 104 (℃ **808/946-7741**), and is open Monday through Friday from 8am to 5pm. There's also an office at **Hilton Hawaiian Village**, 2005 Kalia Rd. (℃ **808/947-2607** or 808/951-0644), and one at the **Hyatt Regency Waikiki**, 2424 Kalakaua Ave. (℃ **808/926-5441**); both offer financial services daily from 8am to 8pm.

Dentists If you need dental attention on Oahu, contact the **Hawaii Dental Association** (℃ **808/593-2135**).

Doctors **Straub Doctors on Call**, 2222 Kalakaua Ave., at Lewers Street, Honolulu (℃ **808/971-6000**), can dispatch a van if you need help getting to the main clinic or to any of their additional clinics at the Royal Hawaiian Hotel, Hyatt Regency Waikiki, Hawaiian Regent Hotel, Hilton Hawaiian Village, Kahala Hotel & Resort, and Ihilani Resort and Spa.

Emergencies Call ℃ **911** for police, fire, and ambulance. The **Poison Control Center** (℃ **808/941-4411**) is at 1319 Punahou St.

Hospitals Hospitals offering 24-hour emergency care include **Queens Medical Center**, 1301 Punchbowl St. (℃ 808/538-9011); **Kuakini Medical Center**, 347 Kuakini St. (℃ 808/536-2236); **Straub Clinic and Hospital**, 888 S. King St. (℃ 808/522-4000); **Moanalua Medical Center**, 3288 Moanalua Rd. (℃ 808/834-5333); **Kapiolani Medical Center for Women and Children**, 1319 Punahou St. (℃ 808/973-8511); and **Kapiolani Medical Center** at Pali Momi, 98–1079 Moanalua Rd. (℃ 808/486-6000). Central Oahu has **Wahiawa General Hospital**, 128 Lehua St. (℃ 808/621-8411). On the windward side is **Castle Medical Center**, 640 Ulukahiki St., Kailua (℃ 808/263-5500).

Internet Access ShakaNet, Hawaii's largest wireless Internet service provider, has completed the first phase of its free Wireless Waikiki network. Phase 1 covers a significant portion of Waikiki and includes an estimated 1,000 hotel rooms, portions of the Honolulu Zoo, Kapi'olani Park, Queens Beach, Kuhio Beach, and the adjacent shoreline. The boundaries of Phase 1 are roughly Kalakaua Ave from Liliuokalani Ave to Queen's Beach in the Diamond Head direction, and Liliuokalani Ave./Kuhio Ave. on the Ewa side, down Kuhio Ave across Kapiolani Park to Monsarrat Ave

Newspapers The *Honolulu Advertiser* and *Honolulu Star-Bulletin* are Oahu's daily papers. *Pacific Business News* and *Honolulu Weekly* are weekly papers. *Honolulu Weekly,* available free at restaurants, clubs, shops, and newspaper racks around Oahu, is the best source for what's going on around town.

Post Office To find the location nearest you, call ℃ **800/275-8777**. The downtown location is in the old U.S. Post Office, Customs, and Court House Building (referred to as the Old Federal Building) at 335 Merchant St., across from Iolani Palace and next to the Kamehameha Statue (bus no. 2). Other branch offices include the Waikiki Post Office, 330 Saratoga Ave. (Diamond Head side of Fort DeRussy; bus no. 19 or 20), and in the Ala Moana Shopping Center (bus no. 8, 19, or 20).

Safety Recently there has been a series of purse-snatching incidents in Oahu. Thieves work from slow-moving cars or on foot. The Honolulu police department advises that you carry your purse on the shoulder away from the street or, better yet, wear the strap across your chest instead of on one shoulder. If you're carrying a clutch bag, hold it close to your chest.

Weather For National Weather Service recorded forecasts for Honolulu, call ℭ **808/973-4380**; for elsewhere on the island, call ℭ **808/973-4381**. For marine reports, call ℭ **808/973-4382**. For surf reports, call ℭ **808/973-4383**.

3 Where to Stay

Before you reach for the phone to book a place to stay, consider when you'll be visiting. The high season, when hotels are full and rates are at their highest, is mid-December to March. The secondary high season, when rates are high but rooms are somewhat easier to come by, is June to September. The low seasons—when you can expect fewer tourists and better deals—are April to June and September to mid-December. (For more on Hawaii's travel seasons, see "When to Go," in chapter 2.) No matter when you travel, you can often get the best rate at many of Waikiki's hotels by booking a package; for details, see "Packages for the Independent Traveler," in chapter 2.

See "The Island in Brief," earlier in this chapter, for a description of each neighborhood. It can help you decide where you'd like to base yourself.

Remember that **hotel and room taxes** of 11.962% will be added to your bill (Oahu has a .005% additional tax that the other islands do not have). And don't forget about parking charges—at up to $25 a day Waikiki, they can add up quickly.

BED & BREAKFASTS   For a more intimate experience, try staying in a B&B. Accommodations on Oahu calling themselves bed-and-breakfasts vary from a room in a house (sometimes with a shared bathroom) to a vacation rental in a private cottage. Breakfast can be anything from coffee, pastries, and fruit to a home-cooked gourmet meal with just-caught fresh fish. Due to space limitations, I can include only a handful of Oahu's best B&Bs below; for a wider selection, check out *Frommer's Honolulu, Waikiki & Oahu,* or call one of the statewide booking agencies recommended in "Tips on Accommodations" in chapter 2.

AIRPORT HOTELS   If you're arriving late at night or leaving early in the morning, consider a hotel near the airport (just for a night—this is not the place to spend your whole vacation). **Best Western—The Plaza Hotel,** 3253 N. Nimitz Hwy., Honolulu (ℭ **800/800-4683** or 808/836-0661; www.bestwestern.com), has rooms from $145 up; and the **Honolulu Airport Hotel** (ℭ **800/836-0661** or 808/833-1738; www. ohanahotels.com) has rooms from $145. Both offer free airport shuttle service.

WAIKIKI
EWA WAIKIKI
All the hotels listed below are located from the ocean to Kalakaua Avenue, and between Ala Wai Terrace in the Ewa (western) direction and Olohana Street and Fort DeRussy Park in the Diamond Head (eastern) direction.

Very Expensive
Hawaii Prince Hotel Waikiki 𝕮𝕮   For a vacation with a view and the feel of a palace, stay in this striking $150-million modern structure (actually, twin 33-story high-tech towers). The high-ceilinged lobby is a mass of pink Italian marble with English slate accents; a grand piano sits in the midst of the raised seating area, where high

(Tips) Affordable Parking in Waikiki

It is possible to find affordable parking in Waikiki if you know where to look. I've divided up the parking in Waikiki into free or metered parking, cheap parking, and carry-a-big-wallet parking.

Free or Metered Parking:

- All side streets in Waikiki
- Ala Wai Boulevard along the Ala Wai Canal, 180 stalls
- Waikiki Zoo, 217 stalls
- Kuhio Avenue (at Lewers)—this 65-stall metered parking lot is the "best secret" in Waikiki

Cheap Parking:

- Ohana East, 150 Kaiulani Ave., 238 stalls, $1 per hour, maximum 5 hours
- King Kalakaua Plaza, 2080 Kalakaua Ave., 195 stalls, $1 per hour, maximum 5 hours
- Hilton Waikiki Prince Kuhio, 2500 Khuio Ave., 190 stalls, $1 per hour, maximum 5 hours
- Waikiki Parking Garage, 336 stalls, $6 flat rate for the day
- Waikiki Parc and Halekulani, 2199 Kalia Rd., just tip valet (no parking fee)

Carry-a-Big-Wallet Parking:

- Hilton Hawaiian Village, 2005 Kalia Rd., free if you eat there (up to 4 hr.), not so free if you don't ($7 an hour)
- Waikiki Beach Marriott, 2552 Kalakaua Ave. (entrance on Ohua Ave.), validated and reduced fee if you eat there; flat fee: $5 self parking, $10 valet if you don't
- Sheraton Princess Kaiulani, 120 Kaiulani Ave., validated and reduced fee if you eat there, otherwise $5 an hour
- Sheraton Waikiki and Royal Hawaiian, 2365 Kalakaua Ave., 4 hours free with validation from one of the resort's restaurants, otherwise $5 per hour
- Hawaii Prince Hotel, 100 Holomoana St., $3 self park or $5 valet park with validation from hotel restaurant; otherwise $5 per hour
- Renaissance Ilikani Waikiki Hotel, 1777 Ala Moana Blvd., with validation from restaurant $6 flat fee (up to 4 hrs), otherwise $7 per hour

---

tea is served every afternoon. Culinary options include two great restaurants, one with award-winning Japanese cuisine and one with Euro-Asian buffets, plus a lobby cafe coffee bar in the morning and a wine bar in the afternoon. The outdoor pool is one of the few saltwater pools in Waikiki, with no chemicals or chlorine added. A glass-encased elevator with views of Honolulu whisks you up to your room. All bedrooms face the Ala Wai Yacht Harbor, with floor-to-ceiling sliding-glass windows that let you enjoy the view (sorry, no lanais). All of the comfortably appointed rooms are basically the same, but the higher the floor, the higher the price. In 2006 the hotel added flatscreen TVs, new beds and soft goods, and high-speed Internet (fee of $11 per day) to every room.

Following Japanese standards, the level of service is impeccable; no detail is ignored, and no request is too small. The location is perfect for shopping—Ala Moana Center

Where to Stay in Waikiki

Ala Moana Hotel **1**

Aloha Punawai **10**

Aqua Bamboo **29**

Aqua Coconut Plaza **8**

Aqua Waikiki Wave **21**

The Breakers **12**

The Cabana at Waikiki **35**

Diamond Head Bed & Breakfast **37**

DoubleTree Alana Waikiki **6**

Embassy Suites Hotel–Waikiki Beach Walk **18**

Equus **2**

Halekulani **16**

Hawaii Prince Hotel Waikiki **3**

Hawaiiana Hotel **11**

Hilton Hawaiian Village Beach Resort & Spa **5**

Hilton Waikiki Prince Kuhio **31**

Holiday Inn Waikiki **4**

Hotel Renew **36**

Hyatt Regency Waikiki **27**

Ilima Hotel **19**

is a 10-minute walk away—and Waikiki's beaches are just a 5-minute walk away (both are also accessible via the hotel's own shuttle bus).

100 Holomoana St. (just across Ala Wai Canal Bridge, on the ocean side of Ala Moana Blvd.), Honolulu, HI 96815. ☎ **800/321-OAHU** or 808/956-1111. Fax 808/946-0811. www.princeresortshawaii.com. 521 units. $375–$520 double; from $610 suite. Extra person $60. Children 17 and under stay free in parent's room using existing bedding. AE, DC, DISC, MC, V. Valet parking $21, self-parking $15. Bus: 19 or 20. **Amenities:** 2 excellent restaurants (Japanese, Hawaii Regional Cuisine, and a terrific buffet at a great price—see Prince Court review on p. 145); outdoor bar; outdoor pool; 27-hole golf club a 40-min. drive away in Ewa Beach (reached by hotel shuttle); small but newly renovated fitness room; small day spa; Jacuzzi; concierge; car-rental desk; business center; room service; babysitting; dry cleaning; executive-level rooms. *In room:* A/C, TV, high-speed Internet ($11/day), fridge, coffeemaker, hair dryer, iron (on request), safe.

Hilton Hawaiian Village Beach Resort & Spa ★★ *Kids* Sprawling over 20 acres, this is Waikiki's biggest resort—a minicity unto itself, so big it even has its own post office.

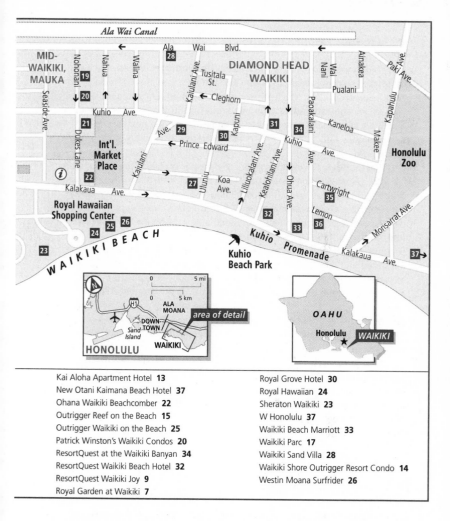

MID-WAIKIKI, MAUKA

DIAMOND HEAD WAIKIKI

Ala Wai Canal

Ala Wai Blvd.

Nohonani
Nahua
Walina

Kaiulani Ave.
Tusitala St.
← Cleghorn

Kapuni

Wai Nani
Ainakea
Paki Ave.
Pualani
Kanaloa

Makee
Kapahulu
Lunalilo Ave.

Kuhio Ave.

Seaside Ave.
Dukes Lane
Kaiulani
Ave.
← Prince Edward
Uluniu
Koa Ave.
Kalakaua Ave.

Int'l. Market Place

Kuhio Ave.

Liliuokalani Ave.
Kealohilani Ave.
Ohua Ave.

Paoakalani Ave.

Cartwright
Lemon

Honolulu Zoo

Royal Hawaiian Shopping Center

WAIKIKI BEACH

Kuhio Promenade

Kuhio Beach Park

Kalakaua Ave.

Monsarrat Ave.

0   5 mi
0   5 km

ALA MOANA

area of detail

HONOLULU
DOWNTOWN
Sand Island
WAIKIKI

OAHU

Honolulu ★   WAIKIKI

Kai Aloha Apartment Hotel **13**
New Otani Kaimana Beach Hotel **37**
Ohana Waikiki Beachcomber **22**
Outrigger Reef on the Beach **15**
Outrigger Waikiki on the Beach **25**
Patrick Winston's Waikiki Condos **20**
ResortQuest at the Waikiki Banyan **34**
ResortQuest Waikiki Beach Hotel **32**
ResortQuest Waikiki Joy **9**
Royal Garden at Waikiki **7**

Royal Grove Hotel **30**
Royal Hawaiian **24**
Sheraton Waikiki **23**
W Honolulu **37**
Waikiki Beach Marriott **33**
Waikiki Parc **17**
Waikiki Sand Villa **28**
Waikiki Shore Outrigger Resort Condo **14**
Westin Moana Surfrider **26**

If you are looking for a big resort "village" that has everything you could possibly dream of, this is your place. You'll find tropical gardens dotted with exotic wildlife (flamingos, peacocks, and even tropical penguins), award-winning restaurants (the Golden Dragon, p. 144, and Bali by the Sea, p. 141), 100 different shops, a secluded lagoon, two minigolf courses, and a gorgeous stretch of Waikiki Beach. This is a great place to stay with the kids—the children's program, one of Waikiki's best, offers a wide range of educational and fun activities, and at three of the resort's restaurants, kids ages 4 to 11 eat free.

There's a wide choice of accommodations. Rooms, which range from simply lovely to ultradeluxe, are housed in five towers, each with its own restaurants and shopping. This division cuts down on the chaotic, impersonal feeling you can get from a resort this size. Still, this is the place for a lively, activity-packed vacation; those seeking a more intimate experience might want to look elsewhere.

It's Not Your Father's Waikiki

More big changes are in store for Waikiki. The Outrigger is nearly done with its $500-million-plus Waikiki Beach Walk project (see the "Waikiki Beach Walk" box on p. 124), which seems to have inspired a host of renovations, upgrading, and rebranding of other properties in Waikiki. The upshot is that Waikiki is going through major changes, and in the next few years the world-famous resort area will be even more beautiful, with more upscale properties.

Hilton took over the moderately priced Radisson Waikiki Prince Kuhio Hotel (now the Hilton Waikiki Prince Kuhio Hotel) and put some $55 million into renovations. Most of it went into upgrading the rooms, which now feature amenities like 42-inch plasma-screen TVs that link to laptops, portable DVD players, and MP3 players. They also added a new 24-hour eatery, MAC 24-7 (reviewed on p. 146). Of course, room rates went from $250 a night to $439.

Aqua Hotels and Resorts, which specializes in boutique properties, upgraded and rebranded several off-the-beach properties in Waikiki. Their 10 hotels are divided into three levels (Elite, Moderate, and Lite), all offering such amenities as spas and fitness centers, daily continental breakfast, minikitchens, and free wireless and high-speed Internet in each room. **Hotel Renew** (formerly the Mauka Tower of ResortQuest Waikiki Beach Hotel), a 72-room property, underwent a $5-million renovation. Formerly a low-end property with rates of $169 a night, Hotel Renew now fits into Aqua's Elite category, with rates starting at $300 a night. The fabulous Zen-like rooms resemble the equally high-end W Honolulu. The company spent $7.5 million renovating the 247-room **Aqua Wave** (formerly the Coral Reef), which fits in Aqua's Moderate category, with rates starting at $200. In the Lite category, there's **Aqua Coconut Plaza,** with rates from $135.

All rooms are large and beautifully furnished; if you can afford it, I highly recommend the ones in the Alii Tower, located right on the ocean. Guests in these 348 amenity-laden rooms and suites get the royal treatment, including in-room registration, an exclusive health club and pool, and the full attention of a multilingual staff. But if you choose a room in one of the more affordable towers, you'll still be happy.

Included in this "village" is the **Holistica Hawaii** ★★, a wellness center with high-tech body-scanning equipment (see the box "Take a Healthy Vacation: Have Your Next Medical Checkup in Waikiki," later), and **Mandara Spa** ★★, a state-of-the-art fitness center and traditional body-treatment spa. Also new at the Hilton is a 24-hour hotel business center, located on the ground floor of the Diamond Head tower.

The latest addition was the recently opened $6-million **Ocean Crystal Chapel,** Waikiki's only free-standing resort wedding chapel, ready for couples to say "I do."

For guests in a hurry to get on with their vacation, the Hilton became the first hotel in Hawaii to offer self-service kiosks for arriving passengers at the Honolulu Airport to check into the hotel and get their room keys before they even claim their baggage and leave the airport.

Not to be outdone, four of Starwood's five properties in Waikiki (the **Royal Hawaiian Hotel, Sheraton Waikiki, Moana Surfrider,** and **Sheraton Princess Kailani**) are in the midst of a $500-milion renovation, which calls for demolition of parts of one hotel, an addition of a new hotel, and a possible timeshare property. Tentative renovations include:

- **Royal Hawaiian Hotel:** Renovations to the Historic Wing (my favorite part of this hotel) and upgrades to the Surf Room, the pool/beachfront area, and the Monarch Room.
- **Moana Surfrider:** Rebranded in 2007 from a Sheraton, with plans for renovation of the Banyan Wing, the addition of a spa on the entire second floor, and the possible replacement of the Diamond Wing with a separate 200- to 250-room hotel.
- **Sheraton Waikiki:** Continued room renovations and upgrades.
- **Sheraton Princess Kaiulani:** In the discussion stages of a demolition of the Princess Wing, Kalulani Wing, and Kalakaua Avenue stores to build a new timeshare condominium and renovate the Ainahau Tower into a free-standing Sheraton hotel.

The other new property coming to Waikiki is the **Trump International Hotel,** estimated to open in 2009. When the hotel-condominium went on sale in December 2006, every one of the 460 luxury units sold out within just a few hours. The ultraupscale property will have hotel suites available and offer 24-hour concierge and room service. Other amenities will include a lobby bar, cafe, outdoor swimming pool, private fitness center, and separate lobbies for hotel guests and residents.

2005 Kalia Rd. (at Ala Moana Blvd.), Honolulu, HI 96815. (②) **800/HILTONS** or 808/949-4321. Fax 808/951-5458. www.hiltonhawaiianvillage.com. 2,860 units. $229–$609 double; from $559 suite. Extra person $50. Children 18 and under stay free in parent's room. AE, DISC, MC, V. Valet parking $25, self-parking $20. Bus: 19 or 20. **Amenities:** 16 restaurants (including the Golden Dragon, p. 144, and Bali by the Sea, p. 141); 5 bars; 6 outdoor pools; fitness center w/high-tech equipment; superplush Mandara Spa; watersports equipment rentals; year-round children's program; concierge; activities desk; car-rental desk; 24-hr. business center; huge shopping arcade; salon; room service; in-room massage; babysitting; same-day laundry service; dry cleaning; concierge-level rooms. *In room:* A/C, TV, dataport, fridge, coffeemaker, hair dryer, iron, safe.

Expensive

DoubleTree Alana Hotel Waikiki ⭐   This boutique hotel is a welcome oasis of beauty, comfort, and prompt service (operated by the Hilton Hawaiian Village). It's an intimate choice, offering the amenities of a much larger, more luxurious hotel at more affordable prices. The guest rooms last underwent a $2.9-million renovation a couple of years ago, with new carpet, wallpaper, woven-palm-frond curtains, refinished and reupholstered furniture, 25-inch TVs, and "Sweet Dream" pillow-top beds. Guests can enjoy wireless "g" Internet service throughout the hotel and hard-wired

DSL service on four floors. Some of the rooms are small but make good use of space and offer all the amenities you'd expect from a more expensive hotel. Many guests are business travelers who expect top-drawer service—and the Alana Waikiki delivers. The staff is attentive to detail and willing to go to any lengths to make you happy. Waikiki Beach is a 10-minute walk away, and the convention center is about a 7-minute walk.

1956 Ala Moana Blvd. (on the Ewa side, near Kalakaua Ave.), Honolulu, HI 96815. © 800/222-TREE or 808/941-7275. Fax 808/949-0996. www.doubletree.com. Managed by Hilton. 317 units. $169–$349 double; from $309 suite. Extra person $40. Children under 18 stay free in parent's room. AE, DC, DISC, MC, V. Valet parking $18. Bus: 19 or 20. **Amenities:** Bar; outdoor heated pool; poolside fitness center; concierge; activities desk; business center; room service; laundry service; dry cleaning. *In room:* A/C, TV, dataport, high-speed Internet ($10/day), fridge, coffeemaker, hair dryer, iron, safe.

Moderate
Holiday Inn—Waikiki Just 2 blocks from the beach, 2 blocks from Ala Moana Shopping Center, and a 7-minute walk from the convention center, this Holiday Inn has a great location and offers this chain's usual amenities for prices that are quite reasonable (for Waikiki, anyway). All rooms, which have a modern Japanese look, come with either a king-size or two double beds. The property sits back from the street, so noise is at a minimum. The staff is unbelievably friendly.

1830 Ala Moana Blvd. (between Hobron Lane and Kalia Rd.), Honolulu, HI 96815. © 888/992-4545 or 808/955-1111. Fax 808/947-1799. www.holidayinn.com. 199 units. $138–$158 double. Suites from $300. Children 19 and under stay free in parent's room using existing bedding. AE, DC, DISC, MC, V. Parking $13. Bus: 19 or 20. **Amenities:** Restaurant; outdoor pool; small fitness room; activities desk; room service; coin-op washer/dryers; laundry service; dry cleaning. *In room:* A/C, TV, dataport, high-speed Internet ($10/day), fridge, coffeemaker, hair dryer, iron, safe.

Royal Hotel & Spa ⟨R⟩ *(Finds* Formerly Royal Garden at Waikiki, this quiet, elegant boutique hotel, tucked away on a tree-lined side street, was purchased in 2007 and as we went to press, plans for a "quiet" multi-million renovations (no structural changes, just replacement of furniture, drapes, carpets, etc.) were underway. Rates went up considerably (the standard room rate went from $150 to $185 and deluxe rooms jumped from $250 to $350), a bit of a stretch for new furniture and drapes, in my opinion. Because the beach is a few blocks away (about a 10–15 minute walk), I'd recommend you only book here if you can get a deal on the Internet; otherwise, $350 for a deluxe room is high for this location.

440 Olohana St. (between Kuhio Ave. and Ala Wai Blvd.), Honolulu, HI 96815. © 800/367-5666 or 808/943-0202. Fax 808/946-8777. www.royalgardens.com. 210 units. $185–$350 double; from $650 suite. Packages galore, and Internet rates starting at $120. Extra person $25. Children under 12 stay free in parent's room. AE, DC, DISC, MC, V. Parking $18. Bus: 19 or 20. **Amenities:** Restaurant; lounge (w/DJ); 2 outdoor pools (1 w/cascading waterfall); small fitness room; 2 Jacuzzis; 2 saunas; small business center; coin-op washer/dryers; laundry service; dry cleaning. *In room:* A/C, TV, dataport, kitchenette, fridge, coffeemaker, hair dryer, iron, safe.

Inexpensive
The Equus Formerly the Hawaii Polo Inn, now owned by Aqua Hotels and Resorts, this small boutique hotel has been renovated and upgraded into a very comfortable inn within walking distance to the Ala Moana Shopping Center, Waikiki Beach, and the Hawaii Convention Center. The suites have microwaves and hot plates. A few years ago, the management added more studio units (with kitchenettes, two-burner stove, dishwasher, microwave, and such) next door at the Aqua Marina Hotel. *Warning:* Ala Moana Boulevard is very noisy; ask for a room in the back or bring ear plugs.

1696 Ala Moana Blvd. (between Hobron Lane and Ala Wai Canal), Honolulu, HI 96815. © 866/406-2782 or 808/949-0061. Fax 808/949-4906. http://aquaresorts.com/aqua-equus. Managed by Aqua Hotels and Resorts. 68 units, with shower only. $109–$139 double; $187–$205 studios with kitchenettes in Aqua Marina next door. Extra person

— I don't speak sign language.

A hotel can close for all kinds of reasons.
Our Guarantee ensures that if your hotel's undergoing construction, we'll let you know in advance. In fact, we cover your entire travel experience. See www.travelocity.com/guarantee for details.

You'll never roam alone.

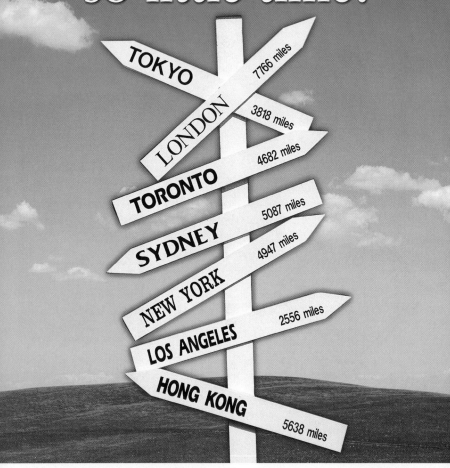

$12. Children 18 and under stay free in parent's room. AE, DC, DISC, MC, V. Parking $15. Bus: 19 or 20. **Amenities:** Tiny outdoor wading pool; activity desk; car-rental desk; coin-op washer/dryers. *In room:* A/C, TV, free Internet access, fridge, coffeemaker, microwave, hair dryers, iron, safe.

MID-WAIKIKI, MAKAI

All the hotels listed below are between Kalakaua Avenue and the ocean, and between Fort DeRussy in the Ewa (western) direction and Kaiulani Street in the Diamond Head (eastern) direction.

Very Expensive

Embassy Suites Hotel–Waikiki Beach Walk ★★★ *Kids*   This ultraluxurious one- and two-bedroom suite hotel chain, famous for its complimentary all-you-can-eat, "cooked to order" breakfast and evening manager's cocktail reception, just opened in 2007 at one of the best locations in Waikiki. The beach is just a block away, and the hotel sits in the midst of the shops and restaurants of the newly opened Waikiki Beach Walk (see box on p. 124). The amenities here are numerous. First there's the wonderful one- and two-bedroom suites (some with unbelievable ocean views) plus a separate living room, with flat-panel LCD-TV, telephone in each bedroom and living room, minirefrigerator, wet bar, microwave, coffeemaker, and lots of entertainment electronics to keep the teenagers happy. Suites feature top-of-the-line furniture, Hawaiian décor such as bronze hula lamps, plush mattresses, expensive linen, granite bathroom counter tops, and great views from every window. The two-towered property is connected via a huge lobby area (with sun deck, swimming pool, waterfall, and covered terrace for those yummy breakfasts). At first glance, the prices may seem high, but when you add in the free breakfast, evening reception, and all the amenities, it pencils out to quite a deal for families.

201 Beachwalk St., Honolulu, HI 96815 ⓒ **800/EMBASSY** or 808/921-2345. Fax 808/921-2343. www.waikikibeach. embassysuites.com. 421 suites. $399–$469 1-bedroom; $549–$649 2-bedroom. AE, DC, DISC, MC, V. Parking $25. Bus: 19 or 20. **Amenities:** Complimentary "cooked to order" breakfast and cocktail party daily; nearby restaurants and bars; outdoor pool and whirlpool spa; 24-hour fitness center; watersports equipment rentals; bike rentals; children's program during the summer and at Christmas; 24-hr. concierge; activities desk; 24-hour business center; top-drawer shops; lunch and dinner room service; same-day laundry service and dry cleaning. *In room:* A/C, TV/DVD, CD/MP3 player, complimentary local and long-distance phone calls, complimentary high-speed wireless Internet, coffeemaker, microwave, small fridge, hair dryer, iron, safe.

Halekulani ★★★ *Kids*   Here's the ultimate heavenly Hawaii vacation. *Halekulani* translates as "House Befitting Heaven"—an apt description of this luxury resort. It's spread over 5 acres of prime Waikiki beachfront in five buildings that are connected by open courtyards and lush, tropical gardens. Upon arrival, you're immediately greeted and escorted to your room, where registration is handled in comfort and privacy.

There are so many things that set this luxury hotel apart from the others, the most important being the rooms: About 90% face the ocean, and they're big (averaging 620 sq. ft.), each with a separate sitting area and a large, furnished lanai. Each bathroom features a deep soaking tub, a separate glassed-in shower, and a marble basin. Recent renovations to this luxury property include total refurbishment of the rooms, new entertainment centers with DVD players, a bedside control panel, wireless Internet service, and a new spa.

Other perks include complimentary tickets to any or all of the following: Ihilani Palace, Bishop Museum, Contemporary Art Museum, Honolulu Academy of Arts, and the Honolulu Symphony (a combined value of about $100 per person), and a great children's program during the summer and at Christmas. The hotel's restaurants are outstanding, and the **House Without a Key** 🦆🦆 is surely one of the world's most romantic spots for sunset cocktails, light meals, and entertainment. You can't find a better location on Waikiki Beach or a more luxurious hotel.

2199 Kalia Rd. (at the ocean end of Lewers St.), Honolulu, HI 96815. © **800/367-2343** or 808/923-2311. Fax 808/926-8004. www.halekulani.com. 455 units. $405–$705 double; from $875 suite. Extra person $125. 1 child under 17 stays free in parent's room using existing bedding; additional rollaway bed $40. Maximum 3 people per room. AE, DC, MC, V. Self-parking $22; complimentary valet. Bus: 19 or 20. **Amenities:** 3 superb restaurants (including La Mer and Orchids, p. 141, and p. 145); 2 bars; gorgeous outdoor pool; fitness center; spa; watersports equipment rentals; bike rentals; children's program during the summer and at Christmas; 24-hr. concierge; activities desk; complete business center; top-drawer shops; salon; room service; in-room massage; babysitting; same-day laundry service and dry cleaning. *In room:* A/C, TV/DVD, complimentary high-speed wireless Internet, minibar, hair dryer, iron, safe.

Moana Surfrider, a Westin Resort 🦆🦆   In 2007 this wonderful momentous property, Waikiki's first hotel, which dates from 1901 and is listed on the National Register of Historic Places, completed renovations (including installing Westin's Heavenly Beds and flatscreen TVs); added the Westin Kids Club childcare program; started construction of a new spa, which will fill most of the second floor; and was rebranded a Westin (it was a Sheraton). It's hard to get a bad room here (even before the renovations); most have ocean views and all come with bedside controls, luxury amenities, and comfy, plush bathrobes. My pick is the Banyan Wing rooms. These historic rooms are a modern replica of the hotel's first rooms. They are small and don't have lanais, but they all carry that feeling of Hawaii of 1901, when steam ship travel with big trunks was the only way to see Hawaii. Be sure to stop by the Historical room and peruse through Waikiki's past. Speaking of the past, when the hotel was built, it was considered an innovation in the travel industry because the Moana featured a private bathroom and a telephone in each guest room—an unheard-of luxury in the early 20th century. Yesteryear lives on at this grand hotel, from the main entry through the original colonial porte-cochere to the highly polished front porch dotted with rocking chairs, to the perfectly restored lobby with detailed millwork and intricate plasterwork. The female employees even wear traditional Victorian-era muumuu. The aloha spirit that pervades this classy and charming place is infectious.

One of the best reasons to stay here is the hotel's prime stretch of beach, with a lifeguard, beach chairs, towels, and any other service you desire. The Beach Bar and a poolside snack bar are located in an oceanfront courtyard centered around a 100-year-old banyan tree, where there's live music in the evenings.

2365 Kalakaua Ave. (ocean side of the street, across from Kaiulani St.), Honolulu, HI 96815. © **800/325-3535** or 808/922-3111. Fax 808/923-0308. www.moana-surfrider.com. 793 units. $380–$710 double; from $1,150 suite. Extra person and rollaway bed $65. Children under 18 stay free in parent's room using existing bedding. AE, DC, MC, V. Valet parking $25, self-parking at sister property $15. Bus: 19 or 20. **Amenities:** 3 restaurants; bar; outdoor pool; nearby fitness room (about a 2-min. walk down the beach at the Sheraton Waikiki); watersports equipment rentals; children's program; nearby game room (a stroll down the beach at the Sheraton Waikiki); concierge; activities desk; car-rental desk; nearby business center (a few minutes away at the Sheraton Waikiki); very upscale shopping arcade; salon; room service; massage; babysitting; coin-op washer/dryers; same-day laundry service and dry cleaning. *In room:* A/C, TV, dataport, fridge, coffeemaker, hair dryer, iron, safe.

Outrigger Waikiki on the Beach 🦆 *(Kids)*   The same value and quality that I've come to expect in every Outrigger hotel is definitely in evidence here, only multiplied by a factor of 10. Even the standard rooms in this 16-story oceanfront hotel are large and comfortable. In 2004 the Outrigger poured some $20 million into the guest rooms, upgrading the furniture and sprucing up the bathrooms with new granite vanity tops, ceramic floor tiles, and new lighted makeup mirrors. The prime beachfront location and loads of facilities help make this one of the chain's most attractive properties. Even if you aren't staying here, wander through the renovated lobby, filled with rare and historic Hawaiian artifacts (like a century-old canoe made of koa). The guest rooms all have huge closets, roomy bathrooms, and plenty of amenities, plus a spacious lanai; the price is entirely dependent on the view. Just added: free high-speed Internet (most hotels charge $10 a day) and free phone calls to Hawaii and the U.S. mainland (very, very unusual for Waikiki). If money is no object, book the Deluxe Oceanfront units, which feature oversize Jacuzzi bathtubs that have an ocean view of Waikiki Beach. Don't miss the Hula Grill Waikiki (p. 148).

2335 Kalakaua Ave. (between the Royal Hawaiian Shopping Center and the Moana Surfrider), Honolulu, HI 96815. (©) 800/OUTRIGGER or 808/923-0711. Fax 800/622-4852. www.outrigger.com. 525 units. $359–$749 double; from $999 suite. Ask about other package deals, like 5th night free, seniors over 50 discount rates, or add a rental car for $28 more a day. Extra person $50. Children 17 and under stay free in parent's room using existing bedding. AE, DC, DISC, MC, V. Valet-only parking $25. Bus: 19 or 20. **Amenities:** 3 restaurants (including Hula Grill Waikiki, p. 148, and Duke's Canoe Club, p. 147); 3 bars; showroom w/nightly entertainment; giant outdoor pool; fitness center; new Waikiki Plantation Spa; Jacuzzi; watersports equipment rentals; year-round children's program; concierge; activities desk; car-rental desk; fully automated business center; large shopping arcade; salon; room service; babysitting; coin-op washer/dryers; laundry service; dry cleaning; concierge-level rooms. *In room:* A/C, TV, complimentary high-speed Internet, kitchenette (in some rooms), fridge, coffeemaker, hair dryer, iron, safe.

Royal Hawaiian 𝄞𝄞 This flamingo-pink oasis, hidden away among blooming gardens within the concrete jungle of Waikiki, is a symbol of luxury. Built by Matson steamship lines, the Spanish/Moorish "Pink Palace" opened in 1927 on the same spot where Queen Kaahumanu had her summer palace—on one of the best stretches of Waikiki Beach.

On your way into the hotel, you pass the lush gardens, with their spectacular banyan tree, and then step into the black terrazzo-marble lobby, which features hand-woven pink carpets and giant floral arrangements. My heart was won over by the rooms in the Historic Wing, which contain carved wooden doors, four-poster canopy beds, flowered wallpaper, and period furniture. Historic touches abound, including Hawaiian craft displays (quilts, leis, weaving, and more) by local artists every Monday, Wednesday, and Friday. Another plus: 24-hour medical services on the property. If you prefer the nonhistorical, newer rooms, the latest decor is a la Tommy Bahama, with a tropical palm tree motif.

One of Waikiki's best spas, **Abhasa** 𝄞𝄞 ((©) 808/922-8200; www.abhasa.com), is located on the property. This contemporary spa, spread out over 7,000 square feet, concentrates on natural, organic treatments in a soothing atmosphere (the smell of eucalyptus wafts through the air) with everything from the latest aromatherapy thalassotherapy (soaking in a sweet-smelling hot bath of salt water) to shiatsu massages. Its specialty is a cold-laser, antiaging treatment that promises to give you a refreshed, revitalized face in just 30 minutes.

In the culinary department, the Surf Room is known for its elaborate seafood buffets; the casual Beach Club features an oceanfront patio that's a great place to start your day. The Royal Hawaiian luau is done in grand style on Monday nights. The hotel's **Mai Tai Bar** 𝄞𝄞 is one of the most popular places in Waikiki for its namesake drink, which supposedly originated here.

2259 Kalakaua Ave. (at Royal Hawaiian Ave., on the ocean side of the Royal Hawaiian Shopping Center), Honolulu, HI 96815. (©) 800/325-3535 or 808/923-7311. Fax 808/924-7098. www.sheraton.com. 527 units. $445–$775 double; from $925 suite. Extra person $100. Ask about the "Royal Treatment" package: 4 nights, 2 spa treatments, and $100 dining credit for $695 a night. AE, MC, V. Valet parking $25, self-parking at Sheraton Waikiki $15. Bus: 19 or 20.

A Room for Everyone in Waikiki: The Outrigger & Ohana Hotels Dynasty

Among the largest hotel chains in Waikiki, Outrigger and Ohana hotels offer excellent accommodations across the board. The Outrigger properties are more resort oriented, with amenities like concierge service, children's programs, and a variety of restaurants and shops. You'll be comfortable at any of their outposts: **Outrigger Waikiki on the Beach** (see complete review, above), **Outrigger Reef on the Beach** (rooms from $289), and **Outrigger Waikiki Shore Resort Condo** (condominiums from $265). Plus, there are plenty of package deals available for these properties. Ask about other package deals, like a fifth night free, discount rates for seniors over 50, a rental car for $28 more a day, family plans (children 17 and under stay free in parent's room using existing bedding), even romance and honeymoon packages. To ask about current offerings and make reservations at any of the Outrigger properties throughout the islands, contact **Outrigger Hotels & Resorts** (✆ 800/OUTRIGGER or 808/942-7722; www.outrigger.com).

The Ohana Hotels offer dependable, clean, moderately priced, and well-appointed rooms in central locations. The chain's price structure (from $179) is based entirely on location, room size, and amenities. Check the Internet site where "best available rates" start at $99 (true bargain in Waikiki!). The **Ohana Hotels & Resorts** also offer other deals, including air and car-rental packages; for information, contact **Ohana Hotels** (✆ 800/462-6262; www.ohanahotels.com).

Amenities: 2 restaurants; landmark bar; good-size outdoor pool; preferential tee times at various golf courses; nearby fitness room (next door at the Sheraton Waikiki); excellent full-service spa (Abhasa); watersports equipment rentals; bike rentals; excellent year-round children's program; game room; multilingual concierge desk; activities desk; car-rental desk; business center; elegant shopping arcade; room service; in-room massage; babysitting; 24-hr. laundry service and dry cleaning (except Sun). *In room:* A/C, TV, high-speed Internet $14/day, fridge, hair dryer, iron, safe.

Sheraton Waikiki ✦ *Kids*   Occupying two 30-story towers, this is by far the biggest of the four Sheratons on the beach. The lobby is immense and filled with shops, travel desks, and people. Not surprisingly, this hotel hosts numerous conventions; if you're not comfortable with crowds and conventioneers, book elsewhere. However, size has its advantages: The Sheraton has everything from a fabulous kids' program (boogie boarding, kite flying, nightly movies, and more) to historical walks and cooking demonstrations for Mom and Dad. Plus, you can "play and charge" at Waikiki's other Sheraton hotels.

It's hard to get a bad room here. A whopping 1,200 units have some sort of ocean view, and 650 rooms overlook Diamond Head. Accommodations are spacious, with big lanais to take in those magnificent views. In 2007 Sheraton renovated all the rooms, putting a "Sheraton Sweet Sleeper bed" in each room, adding big LCD flatscreen TVs, putting in high-speed Internet ($14/day), cutting new windows out of the bathroom wall over the sink to make the room feel more expansive, and creating a clean interior design in the room with an uncluttered look and minimalist furniture. For the budget-conscious, the Sheraton Manor Hotel occupies a separate adjacent wing and offers all the services and beachfront of the main hotel. The views aren't the best, and the rooms are small (156 sq. ft., just enough room for two people, max) and modestly appointed (no lanai), but the price is hard to beat.

2255 Kalakaua Ave. (at Royal Hawaiian Ave., on the ocean side of the Royal Hawaiian Shopping Center and west of the Royal Hawaiian), Honolulu, HI 96815. © **800/325-3535** or 808/922-4422. Fax 808/923-8785. www.sheraton. com. 1,852 units. $350–$680 double (Sheraton Manor Hotel Annex $160 double); from $1,000 suite. Extra person $70. Children under 18 stay free in parent's room. AE, DC, DISC, MC, V. Valet parking $25, self-parking $15. Bus: 19 or 20. **Amenities:** 4 restaurants; 3 bars; nightclub; 2 large outdoor pools, including one of the biggest and sunniest along the Waikiki beachfront; access to Makaha Golf Club's golf and tennis facilities (about 1 hr. away); fitness center; watersports equipment rentals; bike rentals; children's program; game room; concierge; activities desk; car-rental desk; business center; shopping arcade; room service; in-room massage; babysitting; coin-op washer/dryers; same-day laundry service and dry cleaning (except holidays). *In room:* A/C, TV, high-speed Internet ($14/day), kitchenette, minibar, fridge, coffeemaker, hair dryer, iron, safe.

Expensive

Waikiki Parc 🏝🏝   Recently redesigned and renovated with an eye to attracting the 20s and 30s crowd, this hotel offers lots of bonuses: It has a terrific location, just 100 yards from the beach, and it's managed and run by the ultraluxury Halekulani Hotel, but at a more reasonable price. The compact, beautifully appointed rooms underwent complete renovation in 2006 with new modern, Hawaiian-Zen decor. Superfluous furniture was removed to make the rooms look more spacious, and wired Internet access was installed (the thick concrete walls, plus the density of Waikiki buildings, make wireless reception practically impossible). All rooms have lanais with an ocean, mountain, or city view. Nice extras include adjustable floor-to-ceiling shutters for those who want to sleep in. The Parc features the same level of service that has made the Halekulani famous. A branch of internationally famous chef Nobu Matsuhisa's Nobu restaurant was not yet open as we went to press but should be by the time you're reading this.

2233 Helumoa Rd. (at Lewers St.), Honolulu, HI 96815. © **800/422-0450** or 808/921-7272. Fax 808/923-1336. www.waikikiparchotel.com. 297 units. $275–$415 double. Extra person $65. Children 17 and under stay free in parent's room. Ask about the room and package deal that starts at just $215 a night. AE, DC, MC, V. Self- or valet parking $20. Bus: 19 or 20. **Amenities:** 2 restaurants; 8th-floor pool deck; fitness center; concierge; business center; room service; babysitting; same-day laundry service and dry cleaning; weekly wine receptions. *In room:* A/C, TV, dataport, high-speed Internet access ($11/day), fridge, hair dryer, safe.

Inexpensive

Aloha Punawai *(Value)*   Here's one of Waikiki's best-kept secrets: a low-profile, family-operated (since 1959) apartment hotel just 2 blocks from the beach and within walking distance of most Waikiki attractions. With the Waikiki Beach Walk renovations well under way, it seems Waikiki is going upscale and expensive; who knows how much longer the old-fashioned accommodations along Saratoga Road and Beach Walk will remain? The Aloha Punawai offers some of the lowest prices in Waikiki; if you stay a week, prices drop even more. And the location is great, just across the street from Fort DeRussy Park and 2 blocks to Grey's Beach—the same great beach facing the luxury Halekulani and Sheraton Waikiki hotels. The apartments contain a mishmash of furniture and come with full kitchens and lanais. Don't expect the Ritz (or any interior decoration to speak of, for that matter)—just sparkling clean accommodations in a great location. Towels and linens are provided. Phones are not, so bring your cellphone.

305 Saratoga Rd. (across from Fort DeRussy and the Waikiki Post Office, between Kalia Rd. and Kalakaua Ave.), Honolulu, HI 96815. © **808/923-5211.** Fax 808/622-4688. www.alternative-hawaii.com/alohapunawai. 19 units, studios

Waikiki Beach Walk

One of the biggest projects to take place in Waikiki in decades is the total renovation of an 8-acre area (bound by Saratoga Road, Kalakaua Avenue, Lewers Street, and Kalia Road) called the Waikiki Beach Walk. The project, by Outrigger Hotels & Resorts, cost some $460 million.

Phase 1, completed in 2007, reconfigured the formerly very congested area (narrow streets, with lots of delivery trucks double-parked, crowded sidewalks, and no vegetation) into an oasis of broad sidewalks, tropical foliage, water features, open space, and new, totally renovated hotels. Eleven hotels were razed, upgraded, or changed to suites or condos. Five hotels and one timeshare condominium remain. The bad news is that the near-oceanfront budget hotels, neighborhood eateries, and small independent shops have been replaced with luxury (higher-priced) properties and 90,000 square feet of swank shops and trendy restaurants to match, all linked through pedestrian bridges and connecting walkways.

Changes to the hotels in this area include:

- The former 480-room Ohana Reef Towers is now a 193-condominium unit timeshare, operated by Outrigger and renamed **Wyndham Waikiki Beach Walk.**
- The Ohana Edgewater and Ohana Coral Seas were razed and replaced by the 90,000-square-foot **Waikiki Beach Walk** retail/entertainment complex. It features 40 retail shops, four major restaurants, three or four smaller food and beverage places, and an open pedestrian plaza.
- The former Ohana Waikiki Village and the Ohana Waikiki Tower hotels, which had a total of 881 rooms, were demolished and replaced by **Embassy Suites Hotel–Waikiki Beach Walk** (reviewed earlier), which offers 421 suites.
- The **Outrigger Reef on the Beach** totally refurbished its 858 rooms.
- The **Ohana Islander Waikiki,** on the corner of Kalakaua Avenue and Lewers Street, is renovating its 280 units.

have shower only. $110–$135 studio double; $140–$150 1-bedroom double (sleeps up to 5). Children 16 and under stay free in parent's room with existing bedding. Extra person $10. Discounts for week-long (or longer) stays. MC, V. Parking $15. Bus: 19 or 20. **Amenities:** Coin-op washer/dryers. *In room:* A/C, TV, kitchen, fridge, coffeemaker.

The Breakers *(Value* Another great buy just a 2-minute walk to Waikiki Beach, The Breakers is full of old-fashioned Hawaiian aloha, comfortable budget accommodations, and family-friendly prices. This two-story 1950s hotel has an accommodating staff and a loyal following. Its six buildings are set around a pool and a tropical garden blooming with brilliant red and yellow hibiscus; wooden jalousies and shoji doors further the tropical ambience. Each of the tastefully decorated, slightly oversize rooms comes with a lanai and a kitchenette. Every Wednesday and Friday, you're invited to a formal Japanese tea ceremony from 10am to noon at the Urasenke Tea House next door. One of the best things about The Breakers is the location—easy walking distance to numerous restaurants, shopping, and Waikiki Beach.

250 Beach Walk (between Kalakaua Ave. and Kalia Rd.), Honolulu, HI 96815. ℭ **800/426-0494** or 808/923-3181. Fax 808/923-7174. www.breakers-hawaii.com. 64 units, shower only. $125–$135 double and extra person $20 per day; $185 garden studio double ($205 for 3, $225 for 4, and $245 for 5). AE, DC, MC, V. Limited free parking (just 7 stalls), additional parking across the street $11/day. Bus: 19 or 20. **Amenities:** Restaurant (poolside bar open Mon–Fri, and grill for lunch on Fri only); outdoor pool; coin-op washer/dryers; dry cleaning. *In room:* A/C, TV, kitchenette, fridge, hair dryer (on request), iron (on request), safe.

Hawaiiana Hotel 🛝 *(Kids* *(Finds* The hotel's slogan—"The spirit of old Hawaii"—says it all. The lush tropical flowers and carved Tiki at the entrance on Beach Walk set the tone for this intimate low-rise hotel. From the moment you arrive, you'll be embraced by the aloha spirit: At check-in, you're given a pineapple, and every morning, complimentary Kona coffee and tropical juice are served poolside. The concrete, hollow-tiled guest rooms feature kitchenettes and two beds (a double and a single or a queen-size plus a sofa bed), which makes the Hawaiiana a great choice for families (as does the welcoming, helpful staff). All rooms have a view of the gardens and two swimming pools. Hawaiian entertainment is featured every week. The hotel is about a block from the beach and within walking distance of Waikiki shopping and nightlife.

260 Beach Walk (near Kalakaua Ave.), Honolulu, HI 96815. ℭ **800/367-5122** or 808/923-3811. Fax 808/926-5728. www.hawaiianahotelatwaikiki.com. 95 units, some with shower only. $125–$215 double; $235 1-bedroom with kitchenette (sleeps up to 4). Extra person $25. AE, DC, DISC, MC, V. Parking $15. Bus: 19 or 20. **Amenities:** 2 good-size outdoor pools; barbecue; coin-op washer/dryers. *In room:* A/C, TV, kitchenette, fridge, coffeemaker, iron, safe.

Kai Aloha Apartment Hotel *(Value* If you want to experience what Waikiki was like 40 years ago, stay here. This small apartment hotel just a block from the beach is reminiscent of the low-key hotels that used to line the blocks of Waikiki in the good old days. It offers one-bedroom apartments and studios, all furnished in modest rattan and colorful island prints. Each of the one-bedroom units has a bedroom with either a queen-size bed or two twins, a living room with a couch and two additional twins (Hawaiian houses of 40 years ago all had extra beds in the living room, called punee, for guests to sleep on), a full kitchen, a dining table, and even voice mail. These rooms are large enough to accommodate a roll-away bed for a fifth person. Glass jalousies take advantage of the cooling trade winds, but there's also air-conditioning for very hot days. The studios have two twin beds, a kitchenette, a balcony, a Plexiglas roof in the bathroom (the forerunner of the skylight), and a screen door for ventilation. The units aren't exactly designer showrooms, but they do have a homey, comfortable feel and provide daily maid service. You're sure to forgive the lack of aesthetics when you're presented with the bill. A large deck on the second floor is a great place to sip early-morning coffee or watch the sun sink into the Pacific.

235 Saratoga Rd. (across from Fort DeRussy and Waikiki Post Office, between Kalakaua Ave. and Kalia Rd.), Honolulu, HI 96815. ℭ **808/923-6723.** Fax 808/922-7592. www.magickhawaii.com/kaialoha. 18 units. $76 studio double; $85 1-bedroom double ($100 for 3, $115 for 4, $130 for 5). 3-night minimum. AE, MC, V. Parking at separate pay lot across the street for $15. Bus: 19 or 20. **Amenities:** Coin-op washer/dryers. *In room:* A/C, TV, kitchenette, fridge, coffeemaker.

MID-WAIKIKI, MAUKA

These mid-Waikiki hotels, on the mountain side of Kalakaua Avenue, are a little farther away from the beach than those listed above. All are between Kalakaua Avenue and Ala Wai Canal, and between Kalaimaku Street in the Ewa (western) direction and Kaiulani Street in the Diamond Head (eastern) direction.

Expensive

Ohana Waikiki Beachcomber   Management of this high-rise property has been taken over by Ohana Hotels & Resorts. One of the best features of this property is the great location—a block from Waikiki Beach, across the street from the upscale Royal Hawaiian Shopping Center, and next door to bargain shopping at the International Market Place. The rooms feature Berber carpets, contemporary furniture, and voice mail. This is one of the few hotels in Waikiki with great night life—*The Magic of Polynesia*, a show with illusionist John Hirokana, plays nightly.

2300 Kalakaua Ave. (at Duke's Lane), Honolulu, HI 96815. © 800/462-6262 or 808/922-4646. Fax 808/926-9973. www.ohanahotels.com. 492 units, shower only. $269–$339 double; from $459 suite. Extra person $30. Check the website for Internet rates from $129. AE, DC, MC, V. Parking $18. Bus: 19 or 20. **Amenities:** Restaurant (poolside coffee shop); outdoor pool; activities desk; coin-op washer/dryers; laundry service; dry cleaning; valet; complimentary wireless Internet access in lobby. *In room:* A/C, TV, complimentary high-speed Internet access (most rooms), fridge, coffeemaker, hair dryer, iron (on request), safe (fee), complimentary newspaper delivery.

Moderate/Inexpensive

Aqua Coconut Plaza   Aqua Resorts and Hotels have taken Waikiki by storm. They specialize in turning old, tired properties into fabulous boutique inns with modern decor and amenities such as free high-speed Internet and flatscreen TVs in every room. This property, built in 1962 and last renovated in 1992, is no exception. Over the years, it has been managed by a host of companies, from Aston to ResortQuest, but in January 2007, Aqua took over. Thank goodness. As we went to press, the renovation teams were swarming over this once-quaint oasis and gutting the rooms completely. The rates below are good during the construction period—my guess is that once the people at Aqua work their magic and turn this old toad of a hotel into the hip, modern type of place they're known for, rates will go up.

450 Lewers St. (at Ala Wai Blvd.), Honolulu, HI 96815. © 866/406-2782 or 808/923-8828. Fax 808/923-3473. www. aquaresorts.com/aqua-coconut-plaza. 80 units. $135 hotel room; $150–$160 double studio with kitchenette; $210 junior suite. Rates include continental breakfast. Extra person $20. AE, DC, MC, V. Valet parking $15. Bus: 19 or 20. **Amenities:** Tiny outdoor pool w/sun deck; coin-op washer/dryers, complimentary high-speed Internet in lobby. *In room:* A/C, TV, dataport; kitchenette, fridge, coffeemaker, hair dryer, iron, safe.

Aqua Waikiki Wave *(Finds)*   It's hard to believe that this sleek, modern oasis could emerge from the old Coral Reef—a wreck of a hotel. Aqua completely gutted the old hotel, spending $7.63 million in renovations. The result is a clean, hip decor with bright white walls, offset by the burnt orange fabric on the bed headboard, which extends up to the ceiling. Potted plants and live orchids liven up the rooms. The 21st century has arrived at the Wave—guests here enjoy flatscreen TVs and free Wi-Fi and high-speed Internet. About a 10-minute walk to the beach and located next door to the International Market Place, the rooms at the Wave have either two queen beds or a king (with comfy Serta mattresses). The decades-old bathrooms have new plumbing, modern fixtures, and resurfaced tiles and tubs.

2299 Kuhio Ave (at Duke's Lane), Honolulu, HI 96815. © 866/406-2782 or 808/922-1262. Fax 808/922-5048. www. aquaresorts.com. 247 units. $200–$265 double; from $280 suites. Rates include continental breakfast. Extra person $25. AE, DISC, MC, V. Parking $15. Bus: 19 or 20. **Amenities:** 2 restaurants; outdoor pool; fitness room; spa; activities desk; babysitting; laundry service; dry cleaning. *In room:* A/C, flatscreen TV, DVD, complimentary Wi-Fi and high-speed Internet, fridge, coffeemaker, hair dryer, iron, safe.

Ilima Hotel *(Kids)*   The Teruya brothers, former owners of Hawaii's Times Supermarket, wanted to offer comfortable accommodations that Hawaii residents could afford, and they've succeeded. One of Hawaii's small, well-located condo-style hotels, the 17-story, pale-pink Ilima (named for the native orange flower used in royal leis) offers value for your money. Rooms are huge, the location (near the International Market Place and the Royal Hawaiian Shopping Center; 2 blocks to Waikiki Beach) is great, and prices are low. A tasteful koa-wood lobby lined with works by Hawaiian artists greets you upon arrival. Perks include free local phone calls and a full kitchen in every unit; in addition, all the couches fold out into beds, making this a particularly good deal for families (kids will appreciate the Nintendo games in each room). The one-bedroom units now have Jacuzzi tubs. There are three sun decks, a dry sauna, and truly nice people staffing the front desk to help you enjoy your vacation. The only caveat: no ocean views.

445 Nohonani St. (near Ala Wai Blvd.), Honolulu, HI 96815. ℂ 800/801-9366 or 808/923-1877. Fax 808/924-2617. www.HotelWaikiki.com. 99 units. $135–$165 double; $169–$219 1-bedroom (rate for 4); $245–$285 2-bedroom (rate for 4, sleeps up to 6); $375–$395 3-bedroom (rate for 6, sleeps up to 8). Extra person $10. Discounts available for seniors and business travelers. AE, DC, DISC, MC, V. Limited free parking on-site, $10 across the street. Bus: 19 or 20. **Amenities:** Outdoor pool w/sauna; exercise room; tour desk; coin-op washer/dryers. *In room:* A/C, TV, free high-speed Internet for deluxe rooms (floors 10–16), kitchen, fridge, coffeemaker, hair dryer, iron, safe (fee).

Patrick Winston's Waikiki Condos *(Finds*   Looking for a condo priced to fit a tight budget, with a hefty dose of old-fashioned aloha thrown in? Try Patrick Winston's rentals, located on a quiet side street. When this five-story condominium hotel was built in 1981, Winston bought one unit; he has since acquired 24 more, spent hundreds of thousands of dollars on refurbishment, and put his spacious suites on the market at frugal prices. Staying here is like having a personal concierge; Winston has lots of terrific tips on where to eat, where to shop, and how to get the most for your money, and he can book any activity you want.

Three types of units are available: standard/budget rooms, one-bedroom suites, and ground-floor junior business suites. All have sofa beds, separate bedrooms, lanais with breakfast table and chairs, ceiling fans, and full kitchens; most have a washer and dryer. All are individually decorated. Eight units are "standard budget," which means the carpet has not been replaced or the walls need repainting, but they're otherwise a terrific deal for those looking for a condominium unit at a penny-pincher price. Waikiki Beach is just a 10- to 15-minute walk away, shopping is a ½ block away, and restaurants are within a 5- to 10-minute walk. This area of Waikiki is a little scary at night—not totally safe for a single woman to be wandering about by herself. Also be aware there is *no* maid service (you are the maid) and that there is a cleaning fee.

Hawaiian King Building, 417 Nohonani St., Suite 409 (between Kuhio Ave. and Ala Wai Blvd.), Honolulu, HI 96815. ℂ 800/545-1948 or 808/924-3332. Fax 808/922-3894. www.winstonswaikikicondos.com. 24 units, shower only. $125–$145 1-bedroom; $145–$165 business suite; $165–$185 1 bedroom with den; plus $60 cleaning fee for all units. Extra person $10. 7-night minimum. Ask for the Frommer's readers' discount. AE, DC, DISC, MC, V. Limited parking $10. Bus: 19 or 20. **Amenities:** Bar; small outdoor pool surrounded by a tropical courtyard; babysitting; coin-op washer/dryers. *In room:* A/C, TV, dataport, kitchen, fridge, coffeemaker, hair dryer, iron, washer/dryer (in most units).

ResortQuest Waikiki Joy   Tucked away down a narrow path on a side street, this boutique hotel offers not only outstanding personal service, but also a Jacuzzi in every room. Complimentary continental breakfast is included in the price. The Italian marble–accented open-air lobby and the tropical veranda set the scene for the beautifully decorated guest rooms, each with a marble entry, tropical-island decor, and a lanai wide enough for you to sit and enjoy the views. Another plus: All the rooms are soundproof. The suites are even more luxurious: either a king-size bed or two doubles, a fridge, a microwave, a coffeemaker, and a wet bar. Executive suites come with two

Take a Healthy Vacation: Have Your Next Medical Checkup in Waikiki

Souvenirs from your next vacation to Waikiki could include more than pictures of the sunset: How about photos of your colon? Holistica Hawaii Health Center, Hawaii's only high-tech, preventative medical facility, offers a way for you to see the full picture (literally, in CD format) of your "inner" self.

Set in the tropical resort atmosphere of the Hilton Hawaiian Village Beach Resort and Spa, the Holistica features the Electron Beam Tomography scanner, which offers a safe, rapid, and noninvasive way to detect heart disease, lung cancer, aneurysm, stroke, osteoporosis, colorectal disorders, cancerous abnormalities, and other diseases—all without even taking your clothes off.

This $2-million EBT scanner is considered the "gold standard" in detection. The doctors at Holistica can cite case histories where the scanner revealed potential problems that 10 years down the road could have been fatal, but thanks to early detection, the clients had time to change high-risk behaviors and to reverse the harmful effects. For more information, call ⓒ **808/951-6546**, or visit www.holistica.com.

double beds and a kitchen with microwave and full fridge; the executive king suites add a separate living room and bedroom. Every unit comes with voice mail, as well as fax and modem hookups. There are, however, a couple of downsides: The 1960 hotel has had some renovations, such as new carpet in the rooms and fresh paint, but you won't mistake it for a new hotel. The rack rates are on the high side, considering the 10- to 15-minute walk to the beach, and although there's a sandwich/coffee shop on-site, the food's nothing to brag about. *Tip:* Check the website under "E-Specials" for rooms starting at $125.

320 Lewers St. (between Kuhio and Kalakaua aves.), Honolulu, HI 96815. ⓒ **866/77-HAWAII** or 808/923-2300. Fax 808/924-4010. www.ResortQuestHawaii.com. 94 units. $175–$205 double; $215–$225 double club suite; $255–$265 junior suite with kitchen (sleeps up to 4); $300–$310 1-bedroom executive suite with kitchen (up to 4). Rates include continental breakfast. Extra person $30. AE, DC, DISC, MC, V. Valet-only parking $10. Bus: 19 or 20. **Amenities:** Restaurant; bar (karaoke); minuscule outdoor pool w/dry sauna; concierge; coin-op washer/dryers. *In room:* A/C, TV, dataport, kitchenette (full kitchen in suites), fridge, coffeemaker, hair dryer, iron, safe (fee).

DIAMOND HEAD WAIKIKI
You'll find all these hotels between Ala Wai Boulevard and the ocean, and between Kaiulani Street (1 block east of the International Market Place) and world-famous Diamond Head itself.

Very Expensive
Hilton Waikiki Prince Kuhio   Hilton took over this 37-floor hotel, several long blocks from the beach and a couple of blocks from the zoo, in 2007. After spending $50 million on renovations, Hilton has taken this former midpriced, moderate Radisson hotel into a high-tech, 21st-century luxury hotel. However, I find the rack rates ridiculously high. This hotel is a 5-minute walk to the beach, and at these rates, you could stay at a beachfront hotel. If you can find a good rate on the Internet (a good

rate would be in the $200 range), then go for it; otherwise, you can do better for the money. The sleek, modern rooms all have high-speed Internet (for a fee), a flatscreen 42-inch plasma high-def TV with multimedia monitor that you can use with a laptop computer, a game station console, a camera, or an MP3 player. The contemporary rooms feature Hilton's comfy beds, and the bathrooms feature marble and natural stone and top-end amenities. All of the rooms are the same; the floor and the view determine the price (from the 18th floor and up, the mountain views overlooking the Ala Wai Canal are spectacular and not as pricey as the oceanview rooms). Hilton has added a 24-hour eatery, MAC 24-7 (see p. 146), which comes in handy if you arrive late at night.

2500 Kuhio Ave. (Liliuokalani Ave.), Honolulu, HI 96815. ℰ **800-HILTONS** or 808/922-0811. Fax 808/921-5511. www.waikikiprincekuhio.hilton.com. 601 units. $439–$509 double, from $689 suite for 4. Extra person $40. AE, DC, DISC, MC, V. Valet-only parking $20. Bus: 19 or 20. **Amenities:** Restaurant; bar; outdoor pool; small fitness room; Jacuzzi; concierge; activities desk; small business center; shopping arcade; room service; coin-op washer/dryers; laundry service; dry cleaning; concierge-level rooms. *In room:* A/C, TV, dataport, high-speed Internet ($11/day) fridge, coffeemaker, hair dryer, iron, safe.

Waikiki Beach Marriott Resort & Spa   This 1,310-room hotel, which was completely renovated in 2002 (to the tune of $60 million) has a lot to offer, including a terrific location just across the street from Waikiki Beach, great restaurants (including renowned Maui chef D. K. Kodama's Sansei Seafood Restaurant & Sushi Bar, p. 147, and d.k Steakhouse, p. 148), a terrific spa, and lots of nightly entertainment.

The 5¼-acre property has two towers (one 33 stories, the other 25 stories) and a long list of amenities to keep guests happy, from an espresso bar to an array of shops. The newly done rooms feature comfortable island-style decor, marble flooring, and granite counters in the bathroom. When they opened in 2002, they had moderate prices, but they've been creeping up every year. Don't pay the rack rates—you can do better elsewhere in Waikiki for that kind of money. But if you get a good deal, go for it. *Tip:* Check the Internet for specials; rooms sometimes go for half-price.

Even if you don't stay here, spa aficionados won't want to miss the **Spa Olakino & Salon** ⚘. Conceived and managed by Paul Brown, a well-known hairstylist with numerous salons in Hawaii, this boutique spa offers a unique experience: The spa looks directly out onto Waikiki Beach (technically, Kuhio Beach, at the far end of Waikiki). Comfy cushioned chairs allow you to sit and stare at the rolling surf of Waikiki before or after your treatment. The spa "menu" of treatments is one of the most enchanting I have seen. I recommend the Na La'au, which starts with a Hawaiian lomilomi massage (using traditional native Hawaiian plants like kukui nut oil), then goes on to a noni-plant-and-ti-leaf body wrap, and concludes with a private steam room and shower.

2552 Kalakaua Ave. (entrance on Ohua Ave.), Honolulu, HI 96815. ℰ **800/367-5370** or 808/922-6611. Fax 808/921-5255. www.marriottwaikiki.com. 1,310 units. $425–$700 double; from $1,500 suite. Extra person $30. Children under 18 stay free in parent's room using existing bedding. AE, DC, DISC, MC, V. Valet parking $25, self-parking $18. Bus: 19 or 20. **Amenities:** 5 restaurants; 2 bars; outdoor pool w/view of Waikiki; fitness room; elegant spa; Jacuzzi; concierge; activities desk; car-rental desk; business center; shopping arcade; salon; room service; in-room massage; babysitting; coin-op washer/dryers; same-day laundry service and dry cleaning; Doctors On Call, a 24-hour medical service. *In room:* A/C, TV, dataport, high-speed wireless Internet ($13/day), coffeemaker, hair dryer, iron, safe.

W Honolulu ⚘⚘⚘   It's ultraexpensive, but this luxury hotel located on the outskirts of Waikiki, in a quieter, more residential neighborhood, will make your stay in Waikiki a memorable one. If you're craving peace and quiet away from the crowds of

Waikiki but want to be close enough (about a 15-min. walk) to shops and restaurants, this is a perfect location. The hotel lobby looks like an elegant living room, and check-in occurs in the privacy of the guest rooms, which are decorated with handmade teak furniture from Bali. In addition to the large balconies with great views of Diamond Head, there are numerous excellent touches, from Hawaiian-music CDs to dual-line cordless phones, plush robes, top-drawer bathroom amenities, twice-daily maid service, and various business equipment available on request. Although the W is not on the beach, guests have access to the small, private beach in front of the Colony Surf (great swimming here), less than a 60-second walk away; Kapiolani Park is across the street, and the Waikiki Aquarium is just a few steps away. The famous W pledge (whatever, whenever) still lives up to its reputation. I asked for the best place to get a manicure and pedicure late at night, and not only did they make an immediate appointment, but they Googled a map and directions for me. Within 10 minutes of making my request, I was soaking my feet in warm bubbling water. If this is too pricey for you, book at the Hotel Renew (see below), where the same philosophy and decor prevails but rates are about 40% less.

2885 Kalakaua Ave. (on the ocean side between the Waikiki Aquarium and Outrigger Canoe Club), Honolulu, HI 96815. (C) **888/528-9465** or 808/922-1700. Fax 808/923-2249. www.starwood.com/hawaii. 51 units. $495–$610 double; $4,000 2-bedroom ocean penthouse suite. Extra person $65. Children under 18 stay free in parent's room. AE, DC, DISC, MC, V. Valet parking $18 (no self-parking available). Bus: 19 or 20. **Amenities:** Restaurant (Diamond Head Grill, p. 142); elegant bar (entertainment nightly); concierge service; laundry service; dry cleaning. *In room:* A/C, TV/DVD, dataport, high-speed Internet ($11/day), minibar, coffeemaker, hair dryer, iron, safe.

Expensive

Hyatt Regency Waikiki ✪   This is one of Waikiki's biggest hotels, a $100-million project sporting two 40-story towers and covering nearly an entire city block, just across the street from the Diamond Head end of Waikiki Beach. Some may love the location, but others will find this behemoth too big and impersonal—you can get lost just trying to find the registration desk. The second-floor lobby is huge, decorated in koa, and wraps around an atrium that rises *40 floors* from the ground level. It's filled with the squawks of parrots, tumbling waterfalls, and traffic noise from busy Kalakaua Avenue outside.

The guest rooms are spacious and luxuriously furnished. But please, at these prices, why does the hotel have to charge you an extra couple of bucks for coffee to be used in the "free coffeemaker" in your room? (Not only that, but if you want to empty your minibar to use it as a fridge, the cost is $12!) The deluxe oceanview rooms overlooking Waikiki Beach are fabulous but can be noisy (traffic on Kalakaua is constant). For a few dollars more (well, actually more than a few dollars), you can upgrade to the Regency Club floors, where the rooms are nicer (and the coffee is free); you'll also be entitled to an expedited check-in and entry to a private rooftop sun deck and Jacuzzi, as well as the Regency Club, which has concierge service all day and serves complimentary continental breakfast and afternoon pupu.

The 10,000-square-foot, two-story luxury spa offers all the massage services, body treatments, and facials you can imagine.

2424 Kalakaua Ave. (at Kaiulani St., across the street from the beach), Honolulu, HI 96815. (C) **800/233-1234** or 808/923-1234. Fax 808/923-7839. www.waikiki.hyatt.com. 1,230 units. $260–$610 double; $460–$730 Regency Club double; from $785 suite. Extra person $50 ($75 Regency Club). Children under 18 stay free in parent's room using existing bedding. AE, DC, DISC, MC, V. Valet parking $25, self-parking $18. Bus: 19 or 20. **Amenities:** 4 restaurants (including Ciao Mein, p. 147); elegant poolside bar; outdoor pool with view of Waikiki; fitness room; spa; Jacuzzi; children's program (Fri–Sat year-round and daily in summer); concierge; activities desk; car-rental desk; business center; large shopping arcade; salon; room service; babysitting; coin-op washer/dryers; same-day laundry service and dry cleaning; concierge-level rooms. *In room:* A/C, TV, high-speed Internet ($10/day), minibar, coffeemaker, hair dryer, iron, safe.

Moderate

Hotel Renew *Finds* Once upon a time, this now-70-room boutique hotel was one of the towers to the ResortQuest Waikiki Beach Hotel (see below)—that was the before. The after is an oasis of tranquillity and excellent taste in a sea of tired, aging Waikiki hotels. After several million dollars in renovations (every single surface was redone), the Hotel Renew offers a quiet, relaxing vacation just a block from the beach. Guests are seated at the front desks to check in while their luggage is whisked to their rooms. The new rooms are designed with a clean, Zen-like decor, with black and white walls, discreet lighting, and a hint of scented candles in the air (it reminds me of the W Hotel chain, but for a fraction of the price). But it's the high-tech electronics that won me over—a DVD player that projects onto a 6×4-foot screen (and can work with your computer), a 42-inch high-definition flatscreen TV, complimentary high-speed Internet, a library of over 500 movies, and even an iPod docking station. The final touch: a fresh flower lei when you depart to remember your sweet time here.

129 Paoakalani Ave (at Lemon Rd.), Honolulu, HI 96815. *C* **866-406-2782** or 808/687-7700. Fax 808/687-7701. www.aquaresorts.com. 70 units. $300–$350; suites from $595. Extra person $25. AE, DC, MC, V. Valet-only parking $15. Bus: 19 or 20. **Amenities:** Cafe and lounge; complimentary gourmet breakfast; fitness center (including free yoga classes); spa; concierge; business services; laundry service; dry cleaning. *In room:* A/C, flatscreen high-definition TV, DVD, CD, complimentary high-speed Internet, fridge, coffeemaker, hair dryer, iron, safe.

New Otani Kaimana Beach Hotel *Finds* This is one of Waikiki's best-kept secrets: a boutique hotel nestled right on a lovely stretch of beach at the foot of Diamond Head, with Kapiolani Park just across the street. Robert Louis Stevenson's description of Sans Souci, the beach fronting the hotel, still holds true: "If anyone desires lovely scenery, pure air, clear sea water, good food, and heavenly sunsets, I recommend him cordially to the Sans Souci." The Waikiki-side guest rooms are teeny-tiny, barely with room for two, but tastefully decorated in pale pastels; they open onto lanais with ocean and park views. A good budget buy is the park-view studio with kitchen. You can stock up with provisions from the on-site Mini-Mart, open until 11pm.

Because the hotel overlooks Kapiolani Park, guests have easy access to activities such as golf, tennis, jogging, and bicycling; kayaking and snorkeling are available at the beach. The hotel also arranges for visitors to climb to the top of Diamond Head. The airy lobby opens onto the al fresco Hau Tree Lanai restaurant (p. 147) and features music nightly. The beachfront **Sunset Lanai Lounge** *is great for cocktails and has live Hawaiian music at lunch on Friday.

2863 Kalakaua Ave. (ocean side of the street just Diamond Head of the Waikiki Aquarium, across from Kapiolani Park), Honolulu, HI 96815. *C* **800/356-8264** or 808/923-1555. Fax 808/922-9404. www.kaimana.com. 124 units. $150–$375 double; from $250 junior suites; from $460 regular suites. Extra person $30. Children 12 and under stay free in parent's room using existing bedding. AE, DC, DISC, MC, V. Valet parking $15. Bus: 2 or 14. **Amenities:** 2 restaurants (including the Hau Tree Lanai, p. 147); beachfront bar; fitness room; watersports equipment rentals; concierge; activities desk; small shopping arcade; salon; room service; in-room massage; babysitting; coin-op washer/dryers; laundry service; dry cleaning. *In room:* A/C, TV, dataport, kitchenette (in some rooms), minibar (on request), fridge, coffeemaker (on request), hair dryer, iron (on request), safe.

ResortQuest at the Waikiki Banyan *Kids* The one-bedrooms here combine the homey comforts of a condo apartment with the amenities of a hotel. You'll get daily maid service, bellhop service, the assistance of the front desk, and much more, including an enormous sixth-floor recreation deck with a panoramic mountain view, complete with sauna, barbecue areas, snack bar, and children's play area—a great boon for families (kids 12 and under get a toy when you check in), plus there's a kid's library with games and terrific Hawaiian books for children. Your introduction to this complex is through the open-air lobby with impressive lacquer artwork, hand-carved and painted in Hong Kong. All units have a fully equipped full-size kitchen, a breakfast bar that opens to a comfortably furnished living room (with sofa bed), and a separate bedroom with two double beds or a king-size bed. The one I stayed in had an old-fashioned air conditioner in the wall, but it did the job. Each apartment opens onto a fairly good-size lanai with chairs and a small table; there's a partial ocean view, with some buildings blocking the way. *Tip:* For apartments starting at $155, check the website under "Specials & Offers," then click "E-Specials."

201 Ohua Ave. (on mountain side, at Kuhio Ave.), Honolulu, HI 96815. © **86677-HAWAII** or 808/922-0555. Fax 808/922-0906. www.ResortQuestHawaii.com. 307 units. $205–$280 for up to 5. AE, DC, DISC, MC, V. Self-parking $8. Bus: 19 or 20. **Amenities:** Huge outdoor pool; free tennis courts; 2 whirlpools; children's playground; activity desk; coin-op washer/dryers; barbecue. *In room:* A/C, TV, dataport, kitchen, fridge, coffeemaker, hair dryer, iron, safe (fee).

ResortQuest Waikiki Beach Hotel   After a $30-million renovation on a very old and tired hotel, this former Aston resort opened in late 2002. The location, directly across the street from the beach, couldn't be better, but the rooms couldn't be smaller—averaging 225 to 266 square feet (though 85% of them have ocean views). When ResortQuest took over in 2006, they immediately got rid of the Hawaiian "kitschy nostalgia" theme and repainted (the horrible garish colors are gone, replaced with wooden baseboards and bamboo trim over a floral carpet), installed 32-inch flatscreen TVs and bamboo dressers, and punched up the decor with bright floral headboards and accents. One of the good ideas ResortQuest kept was the "Breakfast on the Beach" deal—you get a free breakfast, which you can pack up in an insulated carrying bag and walk across the street to eat. This is a full, hot breakfast, too, with several food stations offering everything from burritos (veggie, ham, or cheese), pastries, fruit, and cereals to a Japanese breakfast of miso, rice, and fish. *Tip:* For the best rate, check the website, under "Specials & Offers," or choose one of their package deals.

2570 Kalakaua Ave. (at Paoakalani St.), Honolulu, HI 96815. © 866/77-HAWAII or 808/922-2511. Fax 808/923-3656. www.ResortQuestHawaii.com. 717 units. $265–$430 double; $450 suite. Extra person $35. AE, DC, DISC, MC, V. Valet parking $20. Bus: 19 or 20. **Amenities:** 2 restaurants (including Tiki's Grill & Bar, p. 149); bar; outdoor pool; activities desk; coin-op washer/dryers; dry cleaning. In room: A/C, TV, dataport, fridge, coffeemaker, hair dryer, iron, safe (fee).

Inexpensive

Aqua Bamboo ✶ *Value*   Formerly a very neglected budget hotel just a block from Waikiki Beach, Bamboo has been transformed into a contemporary condotel (a condominium/hotel) decorated with an Asian flair. The rooms are stylish and functional, with modern furniture, marble bathrooms, and kitchenettes or kitchens. The location is good, too—it's within walking distance to numerous restaurants, shopping, and the Honolulu Zoo, and just 3 minutes to the beach. Because it's small, the staff gives guests personalized attention. Like all the Aqua Resort properties, there's a complimentary continental breakfast every morning, but this hotel has its own spa on property. When booking, be sure to reserve a parking space if you need one—the parking lot has a limited number of spaces.

2425 Kuhio Ave. (Kaiulani Ave.), Honolulu, HI 96815. © **800/367-5004** or 808/922-7777. Fax 808/922-9473. www.aquaresorts.com. 90 units. $195–$207 double; $218–$253 studio double; $276–$310 1-bedroom; from $350 luxury suites. Extra person $25. AE, DC, DISC, MC, V. Parking $15. Bus: 19 or 20. **Amenities:** Complimentary continental breakfast; outdoor pool; fitness center; spa; Jacuzzi; sauna; concierge; coin-op washer/dryers; laundry service;

dry cleaning. *In room:* A/C, flatscreen TV, complimentary high-speed Internet access, kitchenette or kitchen, fridge, coffeemaker, hair dryer, iron, safe.

The Cabana at Waikiki   Located on a quiet street in Waikiki, this boutique hotel caters to a clientele of gay men and features exquisitely decorated rooms. Each has a queen-size bed and pull-out sofa bed, entertainment center with VCR and CD player, lanai, and well-equipped kitchenette. A free continental breakfast is served every morning. Free Internet access is available in the lobby. A giant, eight-person spa also is on the property. The Cabana is within walking distance of gay nightclubs and the gay scene at Queen's Surf Beach.

2551 Cartwright Rd. (between Paoakalani and Kapahulu aves.), Honolulu, HI 96815. © 877/902-2121 or 808/926-5555. Fax 808/926-5566. www.cabana-waikiki.com. 15 units. $149–$225 double. Rates include continental breakfast. Extra person $15. Check the Internet for rates as low as $99. AE, DC, DISC, MC, V. Parking $8. Bus: 19 or 20. **Amenities:** Complimentary access to nearby (about a 15-min. walk) fitness complex; Jacuzzi; concierge; coin-op washer/dryers. *In room:* A/C, TV, dataport, kitchenette, fridge, coffeemaker, hair dryer, iron, safe.

Diamond Head Bed & Breakfast *Finds*   Hostess Joanne offers a quiet, relaxing place to stay on the far side of Kapiolani Park, away from the hustle and bustle of Waikiki. Staying here is like venturing back 50 years to a time when kamaaina (native-born) families built huge houses with airy rooms opening onto big lanais and tropical gardens. The house is filled with family heirlooms and Joanne's artwork. One of the two rooms features the beyond-king-size carved koa bed that once belonged to Princess Ruth, a member of Hawaii's royal family.

Noela Dr. (at Paki Ave.), off Diamond Head Rd.), Honolulu. c/o Hawaii's Best Bed & Breakfasts, 571 Pauku St,. Kailua, HI 96734. © 800/262-9912 or 808/263-3100. Fax 808/62-5030. www.bestbnb.com. 2 units. $130 double. Rates include large breakfast. Extra person $30. 2-night minimum. No credit cards. Free parking. Bus: 2. *In room:* TV, fridge, hair dryer.

Royal Grove Hotel *Value*   This is a great bargain for frugal travelers. You can't miss the Royal Grove—it's bright pink. Among Waikiki's canyons of corporate-owned high-rises, it's also a rarity in another way: The Royal Grove is a small, family-owned hotel. What you get here is old-fashioned aloha in cozy accommodations along the lines of Motel 6—basic and clean. For years *Frommer's* readers have written about the aloha spirit of the Fong family; they love the potluck dinners and get-togethers the Fongs have organized so their guests can get to know one another. And you can't do better for the price—this has to be *the* bargain of Waikiki. For $47 (about the same price a couple would pay to stay in a private room at the hostel in Waikiki), you get a clean room in the older Mauka Wing, with two twin beds, plus a kitchenette with refrigerator and stove. I suggest that you spend a few dollars more and go for an air-conditioned room ($64) to help drown out the street noise. Even the most expensive unit, a one-bedroom suite with three beds and kitchenette for $80, is half the price of similar accommodations elsewhere. At these rates, you won't mind that maid service is only twice a week.

The hotel is built around a courtyard pool, and the beach is just a 3-minute walk away. All of Waikiki's attractions are within walking distance. *Tip:* If you book 7 nights or more from April to November, you'll get a discount on the already low rates.

151 Uluniu Ave. (between Prince Edward and Kuhio aves.), Honolulu, HI 96815. © 808/923-7691. Fax 808/922-7508. www.royalgrovehotel.com. 85 units. $47 double (no A/C); $64 standard double; $80 standard 1-bedroom. Children 5 years and under no charge. Extra person $10. Crib charge $10/day. AE, DC, DISC, MC, V. Parking nearby $10. Bus: 19 or 20. **Amenities:** Pool; activities desk; coin-op washer/dryers. *In room:* A/C (most rooms), TV, kitchen, fridge.

Waikiki Sand Villa   Budget travelers, take note: This very affordable hotel is located on the quieter side of Waikiki, across the street from the Ala Wai Canal. The 10-story tower has medium-size rooms, most with a double bed plus a single bed (convenient for families) and a lanai with great views of the green mountains. The adjacent three-story building features studio apartments with kitchenettes (fridge, stove, and micro-wave). Another plus for families is the Nintendo system in every room ($7.86/hr.). For guests arriving early or catching a late flight, there's a hospitality room (complete with shower) for late checkout and a luggage-storage area.

2375 Ala Wai Blvd. (entrance on Kanekapolei Ave.), Honolulu, HI 96815. ⓒ 800/247-1903 or 808/922-4744. Fax 808/923-2541. www.waikikisandvillahotel.com. 214 units. $139–$205 double; $261–$347 studio with kitchenette; suites from $405. Rates include continental breakfast served poolside every morning. Extra person $25. Children under 17 stay free in parent's room using existing bedding. Internet specials start as low as $81. AE, DC, DISC, MC, V. Valet-only parking $9. Bus: 19 or 20. **Amenities:** 70-ft. outdoor pool w/adjoining whirlpool spa; activities desk; coin-op washer/dryers; laundry service; dry cleaning. In room: A/C, TV w/Nintendo, complimentary high-speed Internet, kitch-enette (in some rooms), fridge (in some rooms), coffeemaker (in some rooms), safe, microwave (in some rooms).

HONOLULU BEYOND WAIKIKI
ALA MOANA
Ala Moana Hotel This former 1,152-room hotel (on 36 floors) recently went through a multimillion-dollar renovation that converted it into a hotel-condominium (sometimes called a condotel), where the units are individually owned, but most are put back into the rental pool for guests. Renovations include redone suites and a new pool, sun deck, and fitness center/spa. It's run by the Outrigger/Ohana Resort group. The main advantage of staying here is its proximity to Waikiki, the downtown finan-cial and business district, the new convention center, and Hawaii's largest mall, Ala Moana Shopping Center. If you are headed for a convention at the convention cen-ter, this hotel is your best bet. The rooms vary in price according to size: The cheaper rooms are small, but all come with two double beds and all the amenities you'll need to make your stay comfortable. The views of Waikiki and Honolulu from the upper floors are spectacular. *Tip:* Book on the website, where rooms start at $129.

410 Atkinson Dr. (at Kona St., next to Ala Moana Center), Honolulu, HI 96814. ⓒ 800/367-6025 or 808/955-4811. Fax 808/944-6839. www.alamoanahotel.com. 1,152 units. $229–$299 double; from $429 suite. Extra person $40. Chil-dren under 18 stay free in parent's room. Internet specials as low as $129. AE, DC, DISC, MC, V. Valet parking $18, self-parking $15. Bus: 19 or 20. **Amenities:** 5 restaurants; 2 bars (plus a Polynesian show); large outdoor pool; small fitness room; game room; concierge; activities desk; business center; shopping arcade; salon; limited room service; coin-op washer/dryers; laundry service; dry cleaning. In room: A/C, TV, dataport, fridge, coffeemaker, hair dryer, iron, safe.

Pagoda Hotel This is where local residents from neighbor islands stay when they come to Honolulu. Close to shopping and downtown, the Pagoda has been serving Hawaii's island community for decades. This modest hotel has very plain (motel-like) rooms: clean and utilitarian, with no extra frills. Ask for a mountain-view room to avoid the street noise. There's easy access to Waikiki via TheBus—the nearest stop is just half a block away. Ask about rental-car packages. Studios and one- and two-bed-room units have kitchenettes. *Tip:* Check the website for Internet rates from $90 and excellent room/car package deals.

1525 Rycroft St. (between Keeaumoku and Kaheka sts.), Honolulu, HI 96814. ⓒ 800/367-6060 or 808/923-4511. Fax 808/922-8061. www.pagodahotel.com. 361 units. $120 double hotel room Sun–Thurs, $141 Fri–Sat; $146–$173 1-bedroom double Sun–Thurs, $167–$205 Fri–Sat; $183 2-bedroom double (sleeps up to 5) Sun–Thurs, $215 Fri–Sat. Extra person $25. Free cribs available. Ask about car/room deals. AE, DC, DISC, MC, V. Parking $10. Bus: 5 or 6. **Ameni-ties:** Restaurant; bar; 2 outdoor pools; activities desk; salon; babysitting; coin-op washer/dryers; laundry service; dry cleaning. In room: A/C, TV, dataport, kitchenette (some units), fridge, coffeemaker, hair dryer, iron, safe.

DOWNTOWN

ResortQuest at the Executive Centre Hotel 🟊   Located in the heart of down-town, this is the perfect hotel for the business traveler. Not only is it close to the business and financial center of Honolulu, but the staff also goes out of its way to meet every need. The hotel occupies the top 10 floors of a 40-story, multiuse, glass-walled tower. Every room is a spacious suite, with three phones, a whirlpool bathtub, and unobstructed views of the city, the mountains, and Honolulu Harbor. Executive suites add a full kitchen, washer/dryer, and VCR. All guests awaken to the local newspaper outside their doors. Local phone calls are free. The only downside is that the suites are privately owned, so quality is inconsistent—some are fantastic, but some need work.

1088 Bishop St. (at S. Hotel St.), Honolulu, HI 96813. ℂ **866/77-HAWAII** or 808/539-3000. Fax 808/523-1088. www. ResortQuestHawaii.com. 114 suites. $290–$320 suite; $280–$295 1-bedroom. Rates include continental breakfast. Extra person $30. Children under 17 stay free in parent's room. AE, DC, DISC, MC, V. Parking $15. Bus: 1, 2, 3, 9, or 12. **Amenities:** Restaurant; outdoor pool; 24-hr. fitness center w/free weights and aerobic equipment; concierge; business center; shopping arcade; coin-op washer/dryers. *In room:* A/C, TV, dataport, high-speed Internet ($11/day), kitchenette, fridge, coffeemaker, hair dryer, iron, safe, washer/dryer (some rooms), in-room jet spa.

MANOA VALLEY

Manoa Valley Inn *Overrated*   The 2006 earthquake hit this place hard (the entire chimney collapsed); that unfortunate event, coupled with years of neglected mainte-nance, has left this once–grande dame in a state of sadly needed renovations and gen-eral sprucing up. As we went to press, we spoke with the management and they said they have no plans for any renovations except the necessary repairs to the building from the fallen chimney. Although once a fabulous place to stay (it's completely off the tourist trail), this historic 1915 Gothic home, on a quiet residential street near the University of Hawaii, needs some more work before I can give it my endorsement. If you have your heart set on staying in an inn on the National Register of Historic Places, you will find the rooms charming, complete with a parlor with antiques, old-fashioned rose wallpaper, and king-size koa beds. The bathroom features an old-style tub as well as a separate modern shower. The three top-floor rooms share a full bath-room; the others have private bathrooms. As we went to press, the owner has put his historic property on the market. I hope that the new owners will restore the B&B back to its glory days.

2001 Vancouver Dr. (at University Ave.), Honolulu, HI 96822. ℂ **808/947-6019.** Fax 808/946-6168. www.manoavalley inn.com. 10 units, 3 with shared bathroom. $99–$125 double with shared bathroom; $140–$170 double with private bathroom (shower only); $150 cottage double. Rates include continental breakfast. MC, V. Free parking. Bus: 4 or 6. Children 8 and older preferred. **Amenities:** In-room massage; laundry service. *In room:* A/C (some rooms), TV (some rooms), dataport, safe.

TO THE EAST: KAHALA

Kahala Hotel & Resort 🟊🟊 *Kids*   After 11 years under the helm of the Mandarin Oriental Group, this grand old hotel changed management firms in 2006. At press time, the new administrative team, Landmark Hotels, said they plan "extensive" ren-ovations: every room will be refurnished with new window treatments and shutters, new carpets, and wood floors, and those wonderful four-poster beds will still be there but replaced with a new, stylish, "tropical" four-poster bed. The management prom-ises to restore this elegant property to what it once was. The location alone offers a similarly wonderful compromise: Situated in one of Oahu's most prestigious residen-tial areas, the Kahala offers the peace and serenity of a neighbor-island vacation, but with the conveniences of Waikiki just a 10-minute drive away. The lush, tropical grounds include an 800-foot crescent-shaped beach and a 26,000-square-foot lagoon (home to two bottle-nosed dolphins, sea turtles, and tropical fish).

All guest rooms feature 19th-century mahogany reproductions, teak parquet floors with hand-loomed Tibetan rugs, overstuffed chairs, canopy beds covered with soft throw pillows, and works by local artists adorning the grasscloth-covered walls. Views from the floor-to-ceiling sliding-glass doors are of the ocean, Diamond Head, and Koko Head. In-room amenities include two-line phones, 27-inch TVs, large bathrooms with vintage fixtures, free-standing glass showers, large soaking tubs, and "his" and "hers" dressing areas.

Other extras that make this property outstanding: Hawaiian cultural programs, shuttle service to Waikiki and major shopping centers, free scuba lessons in the pool, daily dolphin-education talks by a trainer from Sea Life Park, and a great year-round children's program. The recently added spa offers treatments such as massages, body scrubs, rubs, wraps, and other pampering therapies.

5000 Kahala Ave. (next to the Waialae Country Club), Honolulu, HI 96816. (℃) **800/367-2525** or 808/739-8888. Fax 808/739-8800. www.kahalaresort.com. 343 units. $405–$820 double; from $1,600 suite. Extra person $140. Children 17 and under stay free in parent's room. AE, DC, DISC, MC, V. Parking $22. **Amenities:** 5 restaurants (including Hoku's, p. 167); 4 bars; large outdoor pool; nearby golf course; tennis courts; great fitness center w/steam rooms, Jacuzzis, and dry sauna; watersports equipment rentals; complimentary use of bikes; children's program; game room; concierge; activities desk; car-rental desk; multilingual business center; shopping arcade; salon; room service; in-room massage; babysitting; laundry service; dry cleaning. *In room:* A/C, TV, dataport, high-speed Internet ($15/day), minibar, hair dryer, iron, safe.

THE WINDWARD COAST

Windward Coast accommodations are located on the "Eastern Oahu & the Windward Coast" map on p. 215.

KAILUA

Pat O'Malley of **Pat's Kailua Beach Properties,** 204 S. Kalaheo Ave., Kailua, HI 96734 (℃ **808/261-1653** or 808/262-4128; fax 808/261-0893; www.patskailua.com), books a wide range of houses and cottages on or near Kailua Beach. Rates start at $100 a day for a studio cottage 33 feet from the beach and go up to $500 per day for a multimillion-dollar home right on the sand with room to sleep eight. All units are fully furnished, with everything from cooking utensils to telephone and TV, even washer/dryers.

Ingrid's 🎀 Ingrid has impeccable taste. Decorated in modern Japanese style, her cute one-bedroom apartment is straight out of a magazine. The pristine white walls and cabinets are accented with such dramatic touches as black tile counters, black-and-white shoji doors, and a black Oriental screen behind a king-size bed dressed in white quilts and red throw pillows. The tiled bathroom has a luxurious soaking tub. The kitchenette has a microwave, a refrigerator, cooking utensils, and even a dishwasher. A huge tiled deck extends out from the apartment, and a small alcove off the bedroom can house a third person or serve as a reading nook. Fresh flowers are everywhere. The apartment is located upstairs, past the Japanese garden and through a private entrance.

Pauku St. (across from Enchanted Lakes School), Kailua. c/o Hawaii's Best Bed & Breakfasts, 571 Pauku St,. Kailua, HI 96734. (℃ **800/262-9912** or 808/263-3100. Fax 808/62-5030. www.bestbnb.com. 1 unit. $150 double, plus one-time $100 cleaning fee. Extra person $25. 4-night minimum. MC, V. Free parking. Bus: 52, 55, or 56. *In room:* A/C, TV, high-speed Internet, kitchenette, fridge, coffeemaker, hair dryer, iron.

Lanikai Bed & Breakfast ⭐ *(Finds)*   This old-time bed-and-breakfast, a kamaaina (native) home that reflects the Hawaii of yesteryear, is now into its second generation of owners. The 1,000-square-foot upstairs apartment, which easily accommodates four, is decorated in old Hawaii bungalow style. There's a king-size bed in one bedroom, twin beds in the other bedroom, a large living/dining room, a big bathroom, a kitchenette, and all the modern conveniences—VCR, cordless phone with answering machine—plus oversize windows to let you enjoy wonderful views. Or you can follow the ginger- and ti-lined path to a 540-square-foot honeymooner's delight, a quaint studio with a huge patio outside and queen-size bed and sitting area with VCR, cordless phone, answering machine, and recently remodeled full-size kitchen inside. The units are stocked with breakfast fixings (bagels, juice, fruit, coffee, tea) and all the beach equipment you'll need (towels, mats, chairs, coolers, water jugs).

1277 Mokulua Dr. (between Onekea and Aala Dr. in Lanikai), Kailua, HI 96734. ℂ **800/258-7895** or 808/261-1059. Fax 808/262-2181. www.lanikaibb.com. 2 units. $155 studio double; $175 apt double or $225 for 3 or 4. Rates include breakfast items in fridge. 5-night minimum. MC, V. Free parking. Bus: 52, 55, or 56. **Amenities:** Washer/dryer. *In room:* TV/DVD, complimentary high-speed Internet, kitchenette or kitchen, fridge, coffeemaker, hair dryer, iron.

Sheffield House *(Kids)*   If you have kids or someone needing handicapped-accessible rooms, here's your place in the suburbs of Kailua. Unlike many other B&Bs, Sheffield House welcomes children. The owners, Paul Sheffield and his wife, Rachel, have three kids, so things like a portable baby bed are no problem. There are two units here, a one-bedroom and a studio (which is fully wheelchair-accessible), each with a private entry (through elaborately landscaped tropical gardens) and a full kitchen. The two units can be combined and rented as two-bedroom/two-bathroom accommodations.

131 Kuulei Rd. (at Kalaheo Dr.), Kailua, HI 96734. ℂ/fax **808/262-0721.** www.hawaiisheffieldhouse.com. 2 units. $85 double studio (shower only); $105 apt for 4; $200 2-bedroom for 6. Some lower rates, depending on the season. Rates include 1st day's continental breakfast. 3-night minimum. MC, V. Free parking. Bus: 56 or 57. *In room:* TV, kitchen, fridge, coffeemaker.

KANEOHE

Alii Bluffs Windward Bed & Breakfast   Located on a quiet residential street just 15 minutes from the beach, this traditional B&B is filled with antiques and collectibles, as well as the owners' original art. The guest wing has two rooms, one with a double bed and adjacent bathroom, the other with two extra-long twins and a bathroom across the hall. The yard blooms with tropical plants, and the view of Kaneohe Bay from the pool area is breathtaking. Lots of extras make this B&B stand out from the crowd: daily maid service, a large breakfast served on the poolside lanai, afternoon tea, and sewing kits in the bathroom—they'll even lend you anything you need for the beach.

46-251 Ikiiki St. (off Kamehameha Hwy.), Kaneohe, HI 96744. ℂ **800/235-1151** or 808/235-1124. Fax 808/236-4877. www.hawaiiscene.com/aliibluffs. 2 units. $60–$75 double. Rates include continental breakfast. 3-night minimum. MC, V. Free parking. Bus: 55 or 65. Children must be 16 or older. **Amenities:** Outdoor pool. *In room:* Hair dryer, no phone.

Schrader's Windward Country Inn   Despite the name, the ambience here is more motel than resort, but Schrader's offers a good alternative for families. The property is nestled in a tranquil, tropical setting on Kaneohe Bay, only a 30-minute drive from Waikiki. The complex is made up of cottage-style motels and a collection of older homes. Cottages contain either a kitchenette with refrigerator and microwave or a full kitchen. There's also a picnic area with barbecue grills. Prices are based on the views; depending on how much you're willing to pay, you can look out over a Kahuluu fish pond, the Koolau Mountains, or Kaneohe Bay. Lots of watersports are available at an additional cost; don't miss the complimentary 2-hour boat cruise with snorkeling and kayaking. Evening activities include Hawaiian music night and karaoke night, both with free pupu (Hawaii-style appetizers). *Tip:* When booking, ask for a unit with a lanai; that way, you'll end up with at least a partial view of the bay.

47–039 Lihikai Dr. (off Kamehameha Hwy.), Kaneohe, HI 96744. © 800/735-5071 or 808/239-5711. Fax 808/239-6658. www.hawaiiscene.com/schrader. 20 units. $72–$143 1-bedroom double; $127–$215 2-bedroom for 4; $226–$358 3-bedroom for 6; $446–$501 4-bedroom for 8. Rates include continental breakfast. Additional person $7.50. 2-night minimum. AE, DC, DISC, MC, V. Free parking. Bus: 52, 55, or 56. **Amenities:** Outdoor pool; watersports equipment rentals. *In room:* TV, kitchenette, fridge, coffeemaker.

THE NORTH SHORE

The North Shore doesn't have many accommodations or an abundance of tourist facilities—some say that is its charm. **Team Real Estate,** 66–250 Kamehameha Hwy., Suite D-103, Haleiwa, HI 96712 (© **800/982-8602** or 808/637-3507; fax 808/637-8881; www.teamrealestate.com), manages vacation rentals on the North Shore. Its units range from affordable cottages to condos, to oceanfront homes, at rates ranging from $65 for a condo unit and $120 for a one-bedroom apartment to $1,035/night for an 11-bedroom oceanfront luxury home. A minimum stay of 1 week is required for some properties, but shorter stays are available as well.

North Shore accommodations are located on the "Oahu's North Shore" map on p. 224.

Very Expensive

Turtle Bay Resort 🎯🎯 This property recently completed a massive $35-million renovation. When the resort was built 30 years ago, there was hope that it would become a "gaming operation" (Las Vegas–type gambling). That never materialized, but the dark interior, closed to the awe-inspiring view, remained. With the renovations, the lobby is now open and airy, with floor-to-ceiling windows overlooking the dramatic ocean shoreline view. The resort is spectacular: an hour's drive from Waikiki, but eons away in its country feeling. Sitting on 808 acres, this place is loaded with activities and 5 miles of shoreline with secluded white-sand coves. It's located on Kalaeokaunu Point ("Point of the Altar"), where ancient Hawaiians built a small altar to the fish gods (the altar's remains are now at the Bishop Museum).

All the rooms have ocean views and balconies. The rooms feature marble floors and countertops in the bathroom, and comfy bedding. It's a big improvement, but unfortunately the improvements don't justify the rack rates—for these prices, you can stay in true luxury at the Halekulani in Waikiki, where you will get much better accommodations and much-improved service. If you can afford it, book the separate beach cottages. Positioned right on the ocean (the views alone are worth the price), the 42 bungalows boast hardwood floors, poster beds with feather comforters, and butler service, and have their own check-in and private concierge (like a hotel within a hotel).

The biggest change is the new Zen-like Spa Luana, with six treatment rooms, a meditation waiting area, an outdoor workout area, plus a complete fitness center and a private elevator to the rooms on the second floor, reserved for guests getting spa treatments. The new restaurant, 21 Degrees North (p. 169), is so fabulous people are driving from all over the island to eat there.

57-091 Kamehameha Hwy. (Hwy. 83)], Kahuku, HI 96731. © **800/203-3650** or 808/293-6000. Fax 808/293-9147. www.turtlebayresort.com. 443 units. $440–$520 double; $900–$2,400 cottage; from $650 suite. Additional person $50. Children 17 and under stay free in parent's room. Daily resort fee of $15. AE, DC, DISC, MC, V. Valet parking $8.

Bus: 52 or 55. **Amenities:** 4 restaurants (including 21 Degrees North, p. 169); 2 bars (live entertainment Fri–Sat at the Bay Club Lounge, plus a poolside bar); 2 outdoor heated pools (w/80-ft. water slide); 36 holes of golf; 10 Plexipave tennis courts; spa w/fitness center; 2 Jacuzzis; watersports equipment rentals; concierge; activities desk; business center; salon; room service; babysitting; coin-op washer/dryers; laundry service; dry cleaning; stable w/horseback riding. *In room:* A/C, TV, fridge, coffeemaker, hair dryer, iron.

Moderate

Santa's by the Sea ⟨K⟩ *Finds*   This certainly must be where Santa Claus comes to vacation: St. Nick knows a bargain when he sees it. The location, price, and style make this a must-stay if you plan to see the North Shore. It's one of the few North Shore B&Bs right on the beach—and not just any beach, but the famous Banzai Pipeline. You can go from your bed to the sand in less than 30 seconds to watch the sun rise over the Pacific. Hosts Gary and Cyndie offer an impeccable one-bedroom unit with finely crafted woodwork, bay windows, and a collection of unique Santa figurines and one-of-a-kind Christmas items. It may sound schlocky, but somehow it gives the apartment a country charm. Honeymooners, take note: There's lots of privacy here. The unit has its own entrance, a living room with VCR and stereo, and a full kitchen with everything a cook could need. There's also a barbecue area. Fruit, cereal, bread, coffee, tea, and juice are provided on the first morning, to get you started.

Ke Waena Rd. (off Kamehameha Hwy.), Haleiwa. c/o Hawaii's Best Bed & Breakfasts, 571 Pauku St,. Kailua, HI 96734. ⓒ 800/262-9912 or 808/263-3100. Fax 808/62-5030. www.bestbnb.com. 1 unit, shower only. $225 double. Rates include breakfast items in refrigerator. Additional person $15. 2-night minimum. No credit cards. Free parking. Bus: 52 or 55. **Amenities:** Washer/dryer; ocean-side gazebo. *In room:* A/C (in bedroom), TV/VCR, kitchen, fridge, coffeemaker, hair dryer.

Inexpensive

Ke Iki Beach Bungalows   This collection of studio, one-, and two-bedroom cottages, located on a beautiful white-sand beach, has been totally renovated, to the tune of $1 million. Snuggled on a large lot with its own 200-foot stretch of white-sand beach between two legendary surf spots (Waimea Bay and Banzai Pipeline), the units are still affordable (if you can live without being right on the ocean, the garden units are very affordable for the location). Most units are compact: a small kitchen with all the necessary essentials and living room with very small bedrooms. But, hey, with the ocean just outside, just how much time are you going to spend inside? The winter waves are too rough for most swimmers, but there's a large lava reef nearby with tide pools to explore and, on the other side, Shark's Cove, a relatively protected snorkeling area. Nearby are tennis courts and a jogging path. All units have full kitchens and their own barbecue areas. *Tip:* Stay on the beach side, where the views are well worth the extra bucks.

59–579 Ke Iki Rd. (off Kamehameha Hwy.), Haleiwa, HI 96712. ⓒ 866/638-8229 or 808/638-8829. Fax 808/637-6100. www.keikibeach.com. 11 units. $120–$135 double garden-view studio; $135–$150 double 1-bedroom garden-view; $180–$210 double 1-bedroom beachfront; $155–$190 double 2-bedroom garden-view; $205–$230 double 2-bedroom beachfront. Additional person stays free. 3-night minimum. AE, MC, V. Free parking. Bus: 52. **Amenities:** Complimentary watersports equipment and bikes; in-room massage; coin-op washer/dryers. *In room:* TV, kitchen, fridge, coffeemaker, CD player.

Laie Inn   This two-story plantation-style hotel, within walking distance of the Polynesian Cultural Center, Brigham Young University Hawaii, and the Mormon Temple, has been scheduled (for several years now) to be torn down and replaced with four separate three-story buildings on the 8-acre site. As we went to press, the "latest" discussion called for the old inn to be torn down "sometime" in 2008. Of course, we've heard this all before. If you would like a place to stay to enjoy the nearby Polynesian

Cultural Center or just to get away from urban Waikiki, you will either love or hate this tiny motel. The very old Laie Inn is badly in need of renovation (bedding and towels are old and worn, carpet is dirty, pillows are either lumpy or flat as pancakes, paint is peeling, some bathrooms are moldy and musty, some of the air conditioners sound like they are on their last legs, etc.). However, people who love this place all point to the extremely caring staff (as friendly as you will find anywhere in Hawaii), who know that the old place is not up to par, and they make up for it in cheerfulness and helpfulness. The other plus: It is unbelievably cheap! Plus, the rates include a small continental breakfast (if you are still hungry, there's a McDonald's nearby). The beach is just across the street.

55–109 Laniloa St. (off Kamehameha Hwy., near the Polynesian Cultural Center), Laie, HI 96762. © **800/526-4562** or 808/293-9282. Fax 808/293-8115. www.laieinn.com. 49 units. $89–$99 double. Additional person $10. Children under 18 stay free in parent's room. AE, DISC, MC, V. Free parking. Bus: 52 or 55. **Amenities:** Outdoor pool; activities desk; coin-op washer/dryers. In room: A/C, TV, fridge.

LEEWARD OAHU: THE WAIANAE COAST

J. W. Marriott Ihilani Resort & Spa at Ko Olina Resort ★★★ (Kids   When the 640-acre Ko Olina Resort community opened, some 17 miles and 25 minutes west of Honolulu Airport (and worlds away from the tourist scene of Waikiki), critics wondered who would want to stay so far from the city. Lots of people, it turns out. Ihilani ("Heavenly Splendor") is nestled in a quiet location between the Pacific Ocean and the first of four man-made beach lagoons. Featuring a luxury spa and fitness center, plus tennis and one of Hawaii's premier golf courses, it's a haven of relaxation and well-being. The spa alone is reason enough to come here. Treatments include thalassic treatments, Swiss showers, Vichy showers, Roman pools, and various kinds of massages. You can even have a fitness-and-relaxation program custom designed.

Marriott took over management of the resort in late 1999. It's hard to get a bad room in the 15-story building—some 85% of the units enjoy lagoon or ocean views. Accommodations are luxuriously appointed and spacious (680 sq. ft.), and come with huge lanais outfitted with very comfortable, cushioned teak furniture. There's even a state-of-the-art comfort-control-system panel to operate the ceiling fans, air-conditioning, lights, and so on. Luxurious marble bathrooms have deep soaking tubs, separate glass-enclosed showers, and many more amenities. Other extras include a daily newspaper, transportation to Waikiki and Ala Moana Shopping Center, a 3-mile coastal fitness trail, and a stretch of four white-sand beaches for ocean activities. In 2004 the entire hotel was recarpeted.

The Ihilani's children's program puts all others to shame, offering year-round outdoor adventures and indoor learning activities for toddlers and teens alike. There's a Computer Learning Center, a 125-gallon fish tank, an evening lounge for teen-themed parties, and more.

92–1001 Olani St., Kapolei, HI 96707. © **800/626-4446** or 808/679-0079. Fax 808/679-0080. www.ihilani.com. 387 units. $465–$750 double; from $850 suite. Additional person $50. Children (maximum 2) under 17 stay free in parent's room using existing bedding. Ask about Paradise Plus package rates, which include a free car rental or daily breakfast for 2 starting at $329. AE, DC, MC, V. Parking $15. No bus service. Take H-1 west toward Pearl City/Ewa Beach; stay on H-1 until it becomes Hwy. 93 (Farrington Hwy.); look for the exit sign for Ko Olina Resort; turn right on Olani St. **Amenities:** 3 restaurants; 2 bars (w/nightly entertainment poolside); 2 outdoor pools; championship 18-hole Ko Olina Golf Course, designed by Ted Robinson; tennis club w/pro shop; world-class spa; watersports equipment rentals; excellent children's program; game room; concierge; activities desk; 24-hr. business center; shopping arcade; salon; room service; in-room massage; babysitting; same-day laundry service and dry cleaning. In room: A/C, TV, dataport, wireless high-speed Internet ($13/day), minibar, hair dryer, iron, safe.

4 Where to Dine

On Oahu, the full range of dining choices includes chef-owned glamour restaurants, neighborhood eateries, fast-food joints, ethnic spots, and food courts in shopping malls.

The recommendations below are organized by location, beginning with Waikiki, then neighborhoods west of Waikiki, neighborhoods east of Waikiki, and finally the Windward Coast and the North Shore.

WAIKIKI
VERY EXPENSIVE

La Mer ✹✹✹ NEOCLASSIC FRENCH   This is the splurge restaurant of Hawaii, the oceanfront bastion of haute cuisine, where two of the state's finest chefs (George Mavrothalassitis and Philippe Padovani, each with his own eponymous restaurant now) quietly redefined fine dining in Hawaii. La Mer is romantic, elegant, and expensive; dress up not to be seen, but to match the ambience and food. It's the only AAA Five-Diamond restaurant in the state, with a second-floor, open-sided room with views of Diamond Head, and the sound of trade winds rustling the nearby coconut fronds. Michelin award–winning chef Yves Garnier melds classical French influences with fresh island ingredients: elegant soups with saffron, chanterelles, and savory fresh fish filets (winners include the signature crispy skin fillet of onaga with truffle jus, tomato confit, and fresh basil, and the delightful hamachi with pistachio and shrimp on black risotto). The wine list, desserts, and service—formal without being stiff—complete the dining experience.

In the Halekulani, 2199 Kalia Rd. © **808/923-2311.** www.halekulani.com. Reservations recommended. Jackets or long-sleeved shirts required for men. Main courses $39–$58; 9-course prix-fixe menu $125 (with occasion special dinners like a designer dinner with Remy Martin VVSOP for $155), 4-course prix-fixe menu $89. AE, DC, MC, V. Daily 6–10pm.

Michel's ✹✹ FRENCH/HAWAII REGIONAL   This room on the sand at Sans Souci Beach has windows that open to the ocean air. One side opens to the sunset, with torches on the breakwater and a hula moon above the palm fronds; the entire Waikiki skyline is visible on the other. All tables have an ocean view, and dining here is less stiff and more welcoming than in bygone years. Jackets are no longer required for men, but collared shirts and long pants are preferred, and the live music (6:30–9:30pm weekdays and until 10pm weekends) attracts sunset- and music-lovers, too. Chef Hardy Kintscher has added his touch to the classics (onion soup, steak tartare, chateaubriand, bouillabaisse) and prepares fresh seafood, vegetarian creations, and rack of lamb with restraint and creativity.

In the Colony Surf Hotel, 2895 Kalakaua Ave. © **808/923-6552.** www.michelshawaii.com. Reservations recommended. No shorts or beachwear. Main courses $36–$49. AE, DC, DISC, MC, V. Sun–Thurs 5:30–9:30pm; Fri–Sat 5:30–10pm.

EXPENSIVE
Bali by the Sea ✹✹ CONTINENTAL/PACIFIC RIM   This is another memorable oceanfront dining room—pale and full of light, with a white grand piano at the entrance and sweeping views of the ocean (ask for a table by the window). The menu merges island cooking styles and ingredients: Their signature sautéed opakapaka with crusted mac nuts and cilantro comes with ginger scented jasmine rice with a kaffir lime sauce. Or try the wonderful seafood duo—tempura ahi with orange miso–glazed

Where to Dine in Waikiki

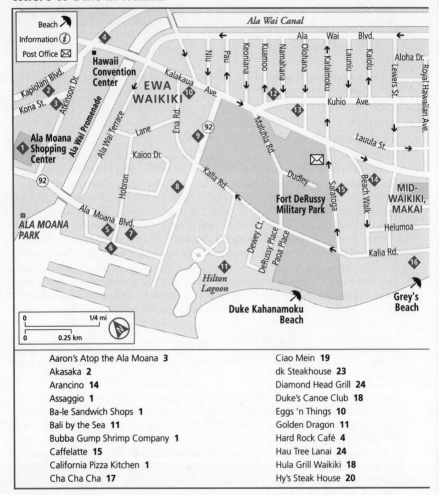

Aaron's Atop the Ala Moana **3**
Akasaka **2**
Arancino **14**
Assaggio **1**
Ba-le Sandwich Shops **1**
Bali by the Sea **11**
Bubba Gump Shrimp Company **1**
Caffelatte **15**
California Pizza Kitchen **1**
Cha Cha Cha **17**

Ciao Mein **19**
dk Steakhouse **23**
Diamond Head Grill **24**
Duke's Canoe Club **18**
Eggs 'n Things **10**
Golden Dragon **11**
Hard Rock Café **4**
Hau Tree Lanai **24**
Hula Grill Waikiki **18**
Hy's Steak House **20**

Kona kampachi, served with Molokai sweet potatoes and Big Island hearts of palm salad. The popular Bali trio features the signature opakapaka, grilled filet mignon, and lemon-grass prawns with spicy mango coulis. The menu also features "heart-healthy" items such as angel hair pasta with Big Island mushrooms, asparagus, and basil tomato sauce. Leave room for their mouth-watering desserts.

In the Hilton Hawaiian Village, 2005 Kalia Rd. ☎ 808/941-2254. Reservations recommended. Main courses $23–$62. AE, DC, DISC, MC, V. Mon–Thurs 6–9:30pm; Fri–Sat 5:30–9:30pm.

Diamond Head Grill ✯✯ ECLECTIC   Talk about buzz. Everyone from judges to fashionistas, to politicos, to the boy next door comes to the W Honolulu's restaurant, either to eat in the sleek and stylish dining room or to be seen at the "bar with the bed," the serpentine DHG Bar that is the social nexus of Friday-night Honolulu.

But it's not all flash at the Diamond Head Grill—this is some serious food. New executive chef Eric Sakai has designed a menu that begins with a foie gras torchon with frisée salad and toasted brioche, or, for fish fans, cold, smoked hamachi crudo with avocado and orange, topped with extra virgin olive oil. My pick for the best salad is the delightful chicory with persimmons, Gorgonzola, hazelnuts, and apple cider vinaigrette. His main courses range from house-made pastas (bruitti ma buni, a fried ricotta and parmigiano dumpling) to fish (slow-cooked Hawaiian walu with braised artichokes and mushrooms), to meat and game (organic chicken with creamy polenta). Don't pass up the desserts—the "Way Too Much Chocolate" is a must-try. At 10pm on Friday and Saturday, the place turns into a very hot nightspot, jammed with beautiful people listening and dancing to DJs.

Room Service from 50 Different Restaurants

You are not limited to the room service menu in your hotel room; **Room Service in Paradise** (© 808/941-DINE; www.941-dine.com) delivers almost a dozen different cuisines (from American/Pacific Rim to Italian to burgers) from oodles of restaurants to your hotel room. All you do is select a restaurant and order what you want (see the online menu or pick up one of its magazines in various Waikiki locations). You are charged for the food, a $6.50 delivery charge in Waikiki (more in outlying areas), and a tip for the driver. Best of all, you can pay with your credit card. Both lunch and dinner are available; you can call in advance, and they will deliver your food whenever you want.

In the W Honolulu, 2885 Kalakaua Ave. © **808/922-3734**. Reservations recommended. Main courses $23–$39 dinner. AE, DC, DISC, MC, V. Sun–Thurs 6–10pm, Fri–Sat 6–9:30pm; bistro menu nightly 10–11:30pm; live entertainment Wed–Thurs 7–11pm, DJ Fri–Sat 10pm–2am.

Golden Dragon 𝒜𝒜 CHINESE   For a second, you might think you've been transported to one of Hong Kong's finest Chinese restaurants—until you notice you can see Waikiki Beach from the outdoor terrace. This is where local residents go if they want to celebrate a special occasion or just enjoy the finest Chinese cooking in Hawaii. Chef Steve Chiang has an extraordinary light touch, turning well-known Chinese cuisine into a rare exotic treat. Several items from the Golden Dragon's original chef, Dai Hoy Chiang, remain on the menu (like the lobster tail stir-fry with curry sauce served with haupia, a coconut pudding). Chiang's own creations include beggar's chicken (wrapped in lotus leaves, covered with clay, baked, and then broken open at your table), which you must order 24 hours in advance. For a real treat, get the nine-course "lotus dinner," which showcases the restaurant's finest dishes.

In the Hilton Hawaiian Village Beach Resort & Spa, 2005 Kalia Rd. © **808/946-5336**. Reservations recommended. Main courses $12–$35; prix-fixe dinners $38–$54. AE, DC, DISC, MC, V. Wed–Sun 6–9pm.

Hy's Steak House AMERICAN   This is as good as it gets in steakhouses. Think dark, clubby, lots of leather, good Scotch, and filet mignon. This is a great choice for steak lovers with hefty pocketbooks or for those who have tired of Hawaii Regional Cuisine. Hy's has demonstrated admirable staying power in the cult of the low fat, still scoring high among carnivores while offering ample alternatives, such as a grilled vegetable platter and excellent salads prepared tableside (the spinach and Caesar are textbook-perfect). "The Only" is its classic best, a kiawe-grilled New York strip steak served with a mysterious signature sauce. Garlic lovers swear by the "Garlic Steak Diane," a richly endowed rib-eye with sliced mushrooms.

2440 Kuhio Ave. © **808/922-5555**. Reservations recommended. Main courses $21–$60 or market price. AE, DC, DISC, MC, V. Mon–Fri 6–10pm; Sat–Sun 5:30–10pm.

Nick's Fishmarket 𝒜 SEAFOOD   With its extensive fish and lobster specialties, Nick's is the restaurant for seafood lovers with upscale tastes. It's a bit of a time warp (extravagant '80s), and the atmosphere is unremarkable, but you will find first-rate seafood and professional service from crisp, formally clad servers. Come here for the classics: bouillabaisse, Alaskan crab legs, lobster tail (prepared six different ways), and fresh fish in a medley of preparations. Meat lovers can order rack of lamb, chicken, New York steak, or filet mignon; appetizers range from escargots to ahi and salmon tartare, oysters Rockefeller, and blackened sashimi. The kids' menu appeals to families, the pasta and risotto to less formal tastes. The Kalakaua Room has a window for people-watching, but I prefer the intimacy of the banquettes on the opposite side of the room. Live entertainment and dancing in the lounge attract the after-dinner crowd.

In the Waikiki Gateway Hotel, 2070 Kalakaua Ave. © **808/955-6333**. Reservations recommended. Main courses $33 or market price. AE, DC, DISC, MC, V. Sun–Thurs 5:30–10pm; Fri–Sat 5:30–11pm.

Orchids 𝕽𝕽 INTERNATIONAL/SEAFOOD   Orchids highlights fresh local produce and seafood in elegant presentations and in a fantasy setting with consummate service. It's an extraordinary setting, and the food ranges from good to excellent. Blinding white linens and a view of Diamond Head from the open oceanfront dining room will start you off with a smile. (The parade of oiled bodies traversing the seawall is part of the entertainment.) At lunch, the seafood and vegetable curries, though pricey, are winners, and the steamed ehu (short-tail red snapper) is an Orchids signature. The executive lunch specials are an excellent way to sample this fare without breaking the bank: $22 for two courses and $26 for three. For dinner, onaga (ruby snapper) is steamed with ginger, Chinese parsley, shiitake mushrooms, and soy sauce, and is then drizzled with hot sesame oil—delightful. Delicately textured opakapaka (pink snapper) is sautéed and presented with wasabi mashed potatoes and wasabi cream, another pleaser with Asian undertones. There are lamb, chicken, and beef entrees as well, and the desserts, especially the chocolate hazelnut dacquoise and the Halekulani signature coconut cake, are extraordinary. **Sunday brunch** 𝕽𝕽𝕽, with its outstanding selection of dishes, is one of the best in Hawaii.

In the Halekulani, 2199 Kalia Rd. © **808/923-2311**. Reservations recommended. Dinner main courses $24–$40; 5-course chef's prix-fixe dinner $53. AE, DC, MC, V. Mon–Sat 7:30–11am, 11:30am–2pm, and 6–10pm; Sun 9:30am–2:30pm and 6–10pm.

Prince Court 𝕽 CONTEMPORARY ISLAND CUISINE   Floor-to-ceiling windows, sunny views of the harbor, and top-notch buffets are Prince Court's attractions, especially at lunch, when locals and visitors line up at the international buffet. Chef Khamtan Tanhchaleun keeps the menu fresh and the dining room busy. The harbor view is particularly pleasing at sunset or on Friday nights when fireworks light up the sky. Wednesday and Thursday, diners can sample everything from island seafood to Hawaii Regional specialties (like melt-in-your-mouth ahi carpaccio), to excellent grilled and roasted meats at the buffet. Desserts, too, are legendary, especially the custard-drenched bread pudding and the macadamia nut pie.

In the Hawaii Prince Hotel Waikiki, 100 Holomoana St. © **808/944-4494**. Reservations recommended. Main courses $18–$28; breakfast buffet $20; weekend brunch $33; luncheon buffet $24; dinner buffets $40–$42. AE, DC, MC, V. Daily 6–10:30am; Mon–Fri 11:30am–2pm; Sat–Sun brunch 11am–1pm; Mon–Thurs 6–9:30pm; Fri–Sun 5:30–9:30pm.

Sarento's Top of the I 𝕽 ITALIAN   The ride up in the glass elevator at this special-occasion Italian restaurant is an event in itself, but Sarento's is not all show. Diners rave about the romantic view of the city, the stellar Greek salad (a trademark of this restaurant chain, whose president is Aaron Placourakis), the opakapaka portofino (with asparagus, in a lemon-dill-butter sauce), and the seafood *fra diavolo* in marinara sauce. Things can be buttery here, so leave your inhibitions at the door. The pasta selections include lobster ravioli and the simple (and divine) capellini pomodoro. Veal lovers come for the *osso buco* with saffron risotto.

Dining in Waikiki 24-7

If your flight to Honolulu arrives late and you are starving, there now is help in Waikiki with the newly opened **MAC 24-7** (which stands for Modern American Cooking, 24 hours a day, 7 days a week), at the **Hilton Waikiki Prince Kuhio Hotel,** 2500 Kuhio Ave., at Liliuokalani Ave. (*(C)* **808/921-5564**). All day, every day, the menu has everything from breakfast, lunch, and dinner to snacks and desserts (though the bar stops pouring drinks between 4 and 6am for some reason). It's not just for late-night dining (although it comes in handy, as Waikiki eateries shut down by 10 or 11pm), but it's also a great place to get picnic lunches during the day. The view from the floor-to-ceiling windows is of the landscaped gardens in the lobby, the interior design is the new "in" decor—sophisticated but sparse in a Zen-like way, with splashes of bright color—and the waitstaff is friendly and helpful.

The cuisine is hotel coffee shop/diner "comfort" food, reasonably priced for Waikiki ($4–$28, with most entrees in the $11–$16 range), and plenty of it. The portion sizes can feed two and, in some cases, three people (even three hungry people). My pick for best meal of the day is breakfast, where the six-pack of buttery cinnamon rolls ($6) will feed three and the yummy wild blueberry pancakes ($11) are supersized (3 pancakes, each one 14 inches in diameter), plenty for two hungry people. Another "must-try" from the menu: the delicious meatloaf with garlic mashed potatoes and mushroom gravy ($16).

In the Renaissance Ilikai Waikiki hotel, 1777 Ala Moana Blvd. *(C)* **808/955-5559**. Reservations recommended. Main courses $25–$37. AE, DC, DISC, MC, V. Sun–Thurs 5:30–9pm; Fri–Sat 5:30–9:30pm.

MODERATE

Arancino ITALIAN   When jaded Honolulu residents venture into Waikiki for dinner, it had better be good. Arancino is worth the hunt. Here's what you'll find: a cheerful cafe of Monet-yellow walls and tile floors, respectable pastas, wonderful pizzas, fabulous red-pepper salsa and rock-salt focaccia, we-try-harder service, and reasonable prices. The risotto changes daily. Don't miss the Gorgonzola-asparagus pizza if it's on the menu. The line on the sidewalk to get in is worth the wait.

255 Beach Walk. *(C)* **808/923-5557**. Main courses $12–$25. AE, DC, DISC, MC, V. Daily 11:00am–2:30pm and 5–10:00pm.

Caffelatte ✿ NORTHERN ITALIAN   Chef/owner Laura Proserpio makes everything from scratch and to order; you won't catch her near a microwave oven. As a result, you won't find a better bruschetta, pasta carbonara, or risotto in Waikiki. The menu is built on uncompromising basics such as generations-old recipes and soups and sauces that simmer for hours. Dinner is a prix-fixe menu consisting of appetizer or salad, soup (usually fish, lentil, or vegetable, and always good), and entree, which could be a porcini risotto, homemade ravioli, or any of several veal selections.

339 Saratoga Rd. *(C)* **808/924-1414**. Reservations recommended. Prix-fixe menu $35. MC, V. Wed–Sun 6:30–10pm.

Ciao Mein ITALIAN/CHINESE   Risotto with chopsticks, fried rice with a fork—such is the cross-cultural way of Ciao Mein, a dozen years old and still going strong. The large, pleasant dining room; efficient service; surprisingly good Chinese food (especially for a hotel restaurant); and award-winning menu items have made this a haven for noodle lovers. The honey-walnut shrimp, with snap peas and honey-glazed walnuts, is a hit. The angel-hair pasta with spicy ginger-garlic shrimp is a big seller, and few who have tasted Ciao Mein's tiramisu will forget its creamy, ambrosial kick. The antipasto is Italian, and the seafood funn lasagna (as in chow funn) is a form of what Ciao Mein calls "collision cuisine"—a mix of Chinese and Italian. Choose from six different pastas and six sauces.

In the Hyatt Regency Waikiki, 2424 Kalakaua Ave. (808/923-2426. www.ciaomein.com. Reservations recommended. Main courses $16–$35; prix-fixe menu $42–$76. AE, DC, DISC, MC, V. Daily 6–10pm.

d.k Steakhouse STEAK   Attention carnivores: This steakhouse opened in 2004 to rave reviews, giving the national steakhouse chains and the top local steakhouses a run for their money. Locally known chef D. K. Kodama (of Sansei Seafood Restaurant & Sushi Bar, p. 148, and Vino Italian Tapas & Wine Bar, p. 160) and Hawaii's top sommelier, Chuck Furuya, have created the ultimate steakhouse for the 21st century at very reasonable prices (especially for Waikiki). Purists will love the prime grade and dry-aged (in-house for 10 days) New York strip and filet mignon, served either unadorned or with one of the following toppings: sauce au poivre with three types of peppercorns; blue crab and béarnaise sauce; shiitake mushroom demi-glace; or D. K.'s own sesame seed–miso sauce. The ultimate treat is the 22-ounce, bone-in rib-eye (aged for 15 days): Every bite has a melt-in-your-mouth richness that steak fans will remember forever. I recommend coming early and booking a table outside on the lanai to watch the sun set on Waikiki Beach. The decor inside is romantic, with dim lighting, intimate wooden booths, and tiny bar lights. For the non–steak lovers, the menu also includes a fresh catch, lamb chops, and chicken.

Waikiki Beach Marriott Resort, 2552 Kalakaua Ave., 3rd Floor. (808/931-6280. http://dksteakhouse.com. Reservations recommended. Main courses $19–$59. AE, DISC, MC, V. Daily 5:30–10pm.

Duke's Canoe Club *Value* STEAK/SEAFOOD   Hip, busy, and on the ocean—this is what dining in Waikiki should be. There's hardly a time when the open-air dining room isn't filled with good Hawaiian music. Just because Duke's is popular among singles, don't dismiss it as a pickup bar—its ambience is stellar. Named after fabled surfer Duke Kahanamoku, this casual, upbeat hot spot buzzes with diners and Hawaiian-music lovers throughout the day. Lunch and the Barefoot Bar menu include pizza, sandwiches, burgers, salads, and appetizers such as mac-nut and crab won tons and the ever-popular grilled chicken quesadillas. Dinner fare is steak and seafood, with decent marks for the fresh catch, prepared in your choice of five styles. There's live entertainment nightly from 4pm to midnight, with no cover. Be prepared to fight the crowds if you come at sunset.

In the Outrigger Waikiki on the Beach, 2335 Kalakaua Ave. (808/922-2268. www.hulapie.com. Reservations recommended for dinner. Main courses $18–$38; breakfast buffet $15. AE, DC, DISC, MC, V. Daily 7am–midnight.

Hau Tree Lanai PACIFIC RIM   Informal and delightful, this Honolulu institution scores higher on ambience than on food. The outdoor setting and earnest menu make it a popular informal dining spot; an ancient hau tree provides shade and charm for diners. A diverse parade of beachgoers at Sans Souci Beach (called "Dig Me Beach" for its eye-candy sunbathers) is part of the scenery. Breakfast here is a must: Choices include salmon Florentine, served with a fresh-baked scone; poi pancakes; Belgian waffles; eggs Benedict; and the Hawaiian platter of miniature poi pancakes, eggs, and a medley of island sausages. Lunchtime offerings include an assortment of burgers, sandwiches, salads, fish, and pasta. Dinner selections are more ambitious and less reliable: fresh moonfish, red snapper, opakapaka, ahi, and chef's specials, in preparations ranging from plain grilled to stuffed and over-the-top rich.

In the New Otani Kaimana Beach Hotel, 2863 Kalakaua Ave. © **808/921-7066.** Reservations recommended. Main courses $18–$39. AE, DC, DISC, MC, V. Mon–Sat 7–11am, 11:30am–2pm, and 5:30–9pm; Sun 7–11am, noon–2pm, and 5:30–9pm. Late lunch in the open-air bar daily 2–4pm.

Hula Grill Waikiki 𝔸𝔸 *(Value* HAWAIIAN REGIONAL   This is the best place for breakfast in Waikiki: Not only does it have a terrific view of all of Waikiki (clear to Diamond Head), but the food is fabulous and a great value. Breakfast is a generous selection of pancakes (banana, mac nut, pineapple, even coconut) and eggs (from crab cake eggs Benedict to a ham, bacon, and Portuguese sausage omelet with cheddar). Come back for a romantic dinner—the restaurant is decorated in a 1930s Hawaii waterfront home theme, with touches like the ohia log bar, a hula doll collection, slate flooring, and lauhala pine–soffited ceilings. Signature dinner dishes at this beachside bistro include Hawaiian seviche, fire-grilled ono (wahoo), oven-roasted sesame opah (moonfish), and a nightly collection of specials.

In the Outrigger Waikiki on the Beach, 2335 Kalakaua Ave. © **808/923-HULA.** www.hulagrillwaikiki.com. Reservations recommended for dinner. Breakfast $5–$11; main courses $17–$29. AE, DC, MC, V. Daily breakfast 6:30–10:30am; happy hour 4–6pm with light menu; dinner 5–10pm.

Keo's in Waikiki 𝔸 THAI   With fresh spices, spirited dishes, and a familiar menu of Thai delights, Keo's arrived in Waikiki with a splashy tropical ambience and a menu that islanders and visitors love. Owner Keo Sananikone grows his own herbs, fruits, and vegetables without pesticides on his North Shore farm. Satay shrimp, basil-infused eggplant with tofu, evil jungle prince (shrimp, chicken, or vegetables in a basil-coconut-chile sauce), Thai garlic shrimp with mushrooms, pad Thai noodles, and the ever-delectable panang, green, and yellow curries are among his abiding delights.

2028 Kuhio Ave. © **808/951-9355.** www.keosthaicuisine.com. Reservations recommended. Main courses $15–$30; prix-fixe menu $35. AE, DC, DISC, MC, V. Daily 7am–2pm; Sun–Thurs 5–10:30pm; Fri–Sat 5–11pm.

Sansei Seafood Restaurant & Sushi Bar 𝔸𝔸 SUSHI/ASIAN–PACIFIC RIM Perpetual award-winner D. K. Kodama, who built Kapalua's Sansei into one of Maui's most popular eateries, has become something of a local legend with his exuberant brand of sushi and fusion cooking. Although some of the flavors (sweet Thai chile sauce with cilantro, for example) may be too fussy for sushi purists, there are ample choices. On the extensive menu appear Sansei's award-winning trademark Asian rock shrimp cake and Sansei special sushi (crab, cilantro, cucumber, and avocado with a sweet chile sauce), as well as seared foie gras nigiri sushi (lightly seared duck liver over sushi rice, accompanied by caramelized onion and ripe mango) or the wonderful mango crab salad hand roll with mango, blue crab, greens, and peanuts served with a sweet Thai chili vinaigrette. More traditional selections range from very fresh yellowtail sushi to Japanese miso eggplant.

Waikiki Beach Marriott Resort, 2552 Kalakaua Ave., 3rd Floor. © **808/931-6286.** www.sanseihawaii.com. Reservations recommended. Sushi $3–$17; entrees $17–$40. AE, DISC, MC, V. Sun–Thurs 5:30–10pm; Fri–Sat 5:30pm–1am.

Moments Tasty Tours for the Hungry Traveler

See Honolulu—one restaurant at a time. Former Honolulu newspaper food critic and chef Mathew Gray has put together **"Hawaii Food Tours"** to show you a side of Hawaii that you would not discover on your own. He offers three different types of tours, all with transportation from your Waikiki hotel in an air-conditioned van and all with running commentary on Hawaii's history, culture, and architecture. Our favorite was the "Hole-in-the-Wall Tour," a lunch tour, from 10am to 2pm, for $99 per person, where you visit at least four different ethnic restaurants (Vietnamese, Indian, local food, and dessert). Mathew has already preordered the best dishes from their menus. He also has the "Hawaiian Feast in Paradise," a three-course feast in contemporary Hawaiian foods for $149, and a "Gourmet Trilogy Tour" of three different restaurants with everything from champagne to a decadent dessert, for $199 per person. For information and booking, call © **800/715-2468** or 808/926-FOOD, or go to www.hawaiifoodtours.com.

Singha Thai Cuisine THAI   The Royal Thai dancers arch their graceful fingers nightly in classical Thai dance on the small center stage, but you may be too busy tucking into your blackened ahi summer rolls to notice. Imaginative combination dinners and the use of local organic ingredients are among the special touches of this Thai-Hawaiian fusion restaurant. Complete dinners for two to five cover many tastes and are an ideal way for the uninitiated to sample this cuisine, as well as some elements of Hawaii Regional Cuisine, which has had considerable influence on the chef. Some highlights: local fresh catch with Thai chile and light black-bean sauce; red, green, yellow, and vegetarian curries; spicy lemon grass soup with shrimp; and many seafood dishes. Such extensive use of fresh fish (mahimahi, ono, ahi, opakapaka, onaga, and uku) in traditional Thai preparations is unusual for a Thai restaurant. The entertainment and indoor-outdoor dining add to this first-class experience.

1910 Ala Moana Blvd. (at the Ala Moana end of Waikiki). © 808/941-2898. www.singhathai.com. Reservations recommended. Main courses $15–$36. AE, DC, DISC, MC, V. Daily 4–11pm.

Tiki's Grill & Bar AMERICAN/PACIFIC RIM   Located on the second floor of the ResortQuest Waikiki Beach Hotel, overlooking Waikiki Beach (get an outside table on the lanai at sunset), this casual eatery is decorated in palm wood flooring with fish nets hanging from the ceiling and lava-rock walls. A 30-foot volcano is the showpiece in the bar (where you can snack on pupu). Chef Ron Villoria's cuisine is good ol' American, with his particular touch of Pacific Rim, apparent in all his fish dishes. Tiki's signature dish is king salmon glazed with lemon grass beurre blanc. Also high on the list is the opah grilled with a spicy seafood salsa. Save room for Tiki's chocolate lava flow, brownie s'mores, and outstanding *lilikoi* (yellow passion fruit) cheesecake with basil syrup. There's live Hawaiian music in the bar every night and on Saturday and Sunday afternoons.

Aston Waikiki Beach Hotel, 2570 Kalakaua Ave. (at Paoakalani St.). © 808/923-TIKI. Lunch entrees $9–$13; dinner main courses $11–$28. AE, DC, DISC, MC, V. Daily 10:30am–midnight.

INEXPENSIVE

Cha Cha Cha MEXICAN/CARIBBEAN   Its heroic margaritas, cheap happy-hour beer, pupu, excellent homemade chips, and all-around lovable menu make this a Waikiki treasure. From the beans to the salsa, to the grilled Jamaican chicken, there's nothing wimpy about the flavors here. The lime, coconut, and Caribbean spices make Cha Cha Cha more than plain ol' Mex, adding zing to the blackened mahimahi and fresh fish burritos, the jerk chicken breast, and the grilled veggies in a spinach tortilla. Tacos, tamales, quesadillas, soups, enchiladas, chimichangas, and a host of spicy pork, chicken, and fish ensembles are real pleasers. Ask about the specials because they're likely to be wonderful. Blackened swordfish, shrimp fajitas, and homemade desserts (including a creamy toasted coconut custard you won't want to miss) are some of the highlights. Its location, across from two of Waikiki's three movie theaters, makes it a choice spot for pre- and post-theater dining.

342 Seaside Ave. Ⓒ 808/923-7797. Complete dinners $7.95–$16. MC, V. Daily 11:30am–11pm; happy hour 4–6pm and 9–11pm.

Eggs 'n Things ✸✸ BREAKFAST   This popular breakfast-only eatery is famous not only for its great food, but also for its all-night hours (drop in at 3am and check out the clientele scarfing down the humongous breakfasts). You'll find the fluffiest omelets (which come with pancakes, potatoes, and toast) and melt-in-your-mouth waffles (piled high with fruit and whipped cream). Prices are surprisingly reasonable, making this place worth standing in line for.

1911-B Kalakaua Ave. (at Ala Moana Blvd.). Ⓒ 808/949-0820. www.eggsnthings.com. Breakfast entrees $7–$12. No credit cards. Mon–Wed 6am–2pm; Thurs–Sun 11pm–2pm the next day.

HONOLULU BEYOND WAIKIKI
ALA MOANA & KAKAAKO
Expensive

Aaron's Atop the Ala Moana AMERICAN/CONTINENTAL/SEAFOOD   Take the express elevator to the 36th floor, where the circular dining room reveals the city in its mountain-to-sea splendor. This may be the best view from a Honolulu restaurant that isn't on the beach. Tables line the sweeping windows and intimate banquettes curve around the interior. A private dining room next to the wine cellar serves parties of up to 10. Aaron's offers its famous black-and-blue ahi (seared in Cajun spices) and seafood entrees such as opakapaka Gabriella, with lemon butter and capers. This is rich Continental fare with some lively local touches and some heavy sauces. Among the excellent salads, the Greek Maui Wowie—chopped tomatoes, bay shrimp, avocado, Maui onions, feta cheese, lettuce—is tops.

Ala Moana Hotel, 410 Atkinson Dr. Ⓒ 808/955-4466. www.tri-star-restaurants.com. Reservations recommended. Main courses $26–$65. AE, DC, DISC, MC, V. Sun–Thurs 5:30–10:30pm; Fri–Sat 5:30–11pm.

Longhi's ITALIAN/MEDITERRANEAN   Bob Longhi, who opened Longhi's in Lahaina in 1976, opened this swank, open-air, Italian-Mediterranean restaurant overlooking romantic sunset views of the ocean. It features the family's famous cooking—lobster Longhi over linguine, prawns Amaretto, and *puttana,* a spicy calamari pasta dish with 35 whole garlic cloves. Meals can be pricey, in part because everything comes a la carte, but the view is spectacular and the service is prompt. It also is a great place for breakfast (their French toast with a "touch" of Grand Marnier is wickedly divine, and their baked goods are delicious), with surprisingly moderate prices and that terrific view. Lunch, which can get crowded, features yummy salads, sandwiches, pastas, and excellent fish entrees.

Ala Moana Shopping Center, 1450 Ala Moana Blvd. (✆ **808/947-9899.** www.longhis.com. Reservations recommended for dinner. Breakfast main courses $9–$23; lunch main courses $9–$14; dinner main courses $24–$36. AE, DISC, MC, V. Mon–Fri 8am–10pm; Sat–Sun 7:30am–10pm.

Mariposa 🟊🟊 PACIFIC RIM/SOUTHWESTERN   Once you get past the gourmet food department of the new Neiman Marcus, you'll be in Mariposa, a popular lunch spot in town. High ceilings and tables on the deck with views of Ala Moana Park and its Art Deco bridges add up to a pleasing ambience, with or without the shopping. You'll find cordial service, nearly four dozen reasonably priced wines by the glass, and a menu of Pacific and American (called "heritage cuisine") specialties that include everything from a king crab, shrimp, and mussel risotto to pan-roasted Hawaiian snapper, to New York striploin. Chef Jason Kagihara's creativity comes out in dishes like the Laksa seafood curry, which, unfortunately, is available only at lunch. Another lunchtime favorite is the towering, eggy popover with *poha* (cape gooseberry) butter. Save room for my favorite dessert, the Valrhona chocolate fudge cake (four layers of devil's food cake with Valrhona's chocolate ganache and raspberry compote)— heaven on earth!

In Neiman Marcus, Ala Moana Center, 1450 Ala Moana Blvd. (✆ **808/951-3420.** Reservations recommended. Lunch main courses $12–$24; dinner main courses $25–$58. AE, DC, MC, V. Sun–Thurs 11am–9pm; Fri–Sat 11am–10pm.

The Pineapple Room 🟊🟊 HAWAII REGIONAL   Yes, it's in a Macy's department store, but the chef is Alan Wong, a culinary icon. The food is terrific, particularly anything with fresh island fish or *kalua* pig (like the *kalua* pig BLT). Wong conjures culinary masterpieces that will probably leave you wanting to come back and try breakfast, lunch, and dinner, just to see what else he will present. The room features an open kitchen with a lava-rock wall and abundant natural light, but the food takes center stage. The menu changes regularly, but keep an eye out for the fresh Big Island moi (served whole and steamed Chinese style), the crispy Asian slaw (with cilantro and mac nuts), the miso-glazed salmon, the black-pepper ahi (with risotto), and pineapple barbecued baby back ribs (with garlic mashed potatoes and sautéed corn). Last time I was there, I salivated over the apple curry glazed pork chop with pumpkin and mascarpone purée and mango chutney. Alan Wong is a culinary master.

Macy's, 1450 Ala Moana Blvd. (✆ **808/945-6573.** www.alanwongs.com. Reservations recommended for lunch and dinner. Main courses $11–$18 lunch; prix-fixe lunch $24–$29; main courses $26–$38 dinner; sampling dinner $60. AE, DC, MC, V. Mon–Fri 11am–8:30pm; Sat 8am–8:30pm; Sun 9am–3pm.

Sushi Sasabune 🟊🟊 *(Finds)* SUSHI   This elegant sushi restaurant, tucked away among nondescript shops along a very busy street, is one of the marvels of the edible world. If you wish to order from the regular menu, by all means grab a table. But if you sit at the sushi bar, you must submit to the Japanese version of the *Seinfeld* Soup Nazi, otherwise known as *omakase*. You obey the chef and eat what's served, and God help you if you drop a grain of rice or dip something in wasabi without permission. The payoff is that whatever you eat is freshly shipped in that day and often exotic. Whether it's salmon from Nova Scotia, sea urchin from Japan, halibut from Boston, blue crab from Louisiana, or farmed oyster from Washington, chef Seiji Kumagawa's sushi comes with a strict protocol: Dip only with permission, and then with restraint. This is an extraordinary experience for sushi aficionados—a journey into new tastes, textures, and sensations. It's expensive but well worth it.

Honolulu Dining Beyond Waikiki

Ocean Club **12**
Olive Tree Cafe **42**
OnJin's Café **17**
Palomino **10**
Panda Cuisine **24**
The Pineapple Room at Macy's **20**
Roy's Restaurant **42**
Ruth's Chris Steak House **12**
Sam Choy's Breakfast, Lunch,
   Crab & Big Aloha Brewery **3**
Sam Choy's Diamond Head Restaurant **35**
Shaduko **23**
Side Street Inn **19**
Spices **32**

Sushi King **33**
Sushi Sasabune **25**
3660 On the Rise **41**
To Chau **4**
Town **37**
12th Avenue Grill **39**
Vino Italian Tapas & Wine Bar **12**
Willows **31**
Yanagi Sushi **13**

1417 S. King St. ℂ **808/947-3800.** Reservations recommended. Sushi $4–$15; sashimi $7–$15. AE, DC, DISC, MC, V. Tues–Fri noon–2pm; Mon–Sat 5:30–10pm.

Moderate

Akasaka ⍢ JAPANESE/SUSHI BAR   Akasaka is difficult to find, and once you do find it, you enter through a back door, but this cozy, casual, and always busy restaurant wins high marks for sushi, sizzling tofu and scallops, miso-clam soup, and the overall quality of its cuisine. Highlights include the zesty spicy tuna hand roll *(temaki)*, scallop roll with flying-fish roe, yellowtail *(hamachi)*, and soft-shell crab in season. Lunch and dinner specials help ease the bite of the bill, and ordering noodles or other less expensive a la carte items can also reduce the cost considerably. The staff is efficient but not necessarily accommodating.

1646B Kona St. ℂ **808/942-4466.** Reservations recommended. Main courses $10–$25. AE, DC, DISC, MC, V. Mon–Sat 11am–2:30pm and 5pm–2am; Sun 5pm–midnight.

Assaggio ⍢ ITALIAN   This wildly popular chain, until recently the toast of suburban Oahu (see p. 168 for the Kailua location), moved into Ala Moana Center to a roar of approval and immediate success. Townies can now enjoy Assaggio's extensive, high-quality Italian offerings—at good prices. The lighter lunch menu features pasta dishes and house specialties (shrimp scampi, rigatoni alla ricotta) at prices around $15 and less. At dinner a panoply of pastas and specialties streams out of the kitchen: at least nine chicken entrees, pasta dishes ranging from mushroom and clam to linguine primavera, and eight veal choices. One of Assaggio's best features is its prodigious seafood selection: shrimp, scallops, mussels, calamari, and fresh fish in many preparations, ranging from plain garlic and olive oil to spicy tomato and wine sauces. Assaggio's excellent service paired with entrees priced under $20 deserves applause.

In the Ala Moana Center, 1450 Ala Moana Blvd. ℂ **808/942-3446.** Reservations recommended. Main courses $9–$15 lunch, $11–$21 dinner. AE, DC, DISC, MC, V. Daily 11am–3pm and 4:30–9:30pm (until 10pm Fri–Sat).

Kincaid's Fish, Chop, and Steakhouse ⍢ SEAFOOD/STEAKS   Kincaid's always wins surveys for one thing or another—best place for a business lunch, best seafood restaurant—because it pleases wide-ranging tastes and budgets. Brisk service, a harbor view, and an extensive seafood menu keep the large dining room full. Fresh fish sandwiches, seafood chowders, and French onion soups top the menu. They also serve a memorable rack-salted prime rib, pepper-crusted steak, and, if you can't make up your mind, a combo plate of center-cut filet mignon with Australian lobster tail. You might want to save room for the true-blue Key lime pie. Kincaid's is also a popular happy-hour rendezvous, with inexpensive beer and appetizers and live entertainment from 8:30 to 11:30pm Friday and Saturday nights.

In the Ward Warehouse, 1050 Ala Moana Blvd. ℂ **808/591-2005.** Reservations recommended. Lunch $9–$15; dinner main courses $13–$50. AE, DC, DISC, MC, V. Sun–Thurs 11am–10pm; Fri–Sat 11am–11pm.

OnJin's Café ⍢⍢ *Value* FRENCH/ASIAN   OnJin's can be either a "moderate" or "inexpensive" choice because it's fabulously inexpensive for lunch (gourmet fare at plate-lunch prices) and, although more expensive for dinner, is still a noteworthy value. OnJin Kim is a brilliant chef (formerly of Bagwell's in the Hyatt Regency and her own restaurant, Hanatei) who serves excellent fare at excellent prices. Expect long lines at lunch, a more relaxed mood at dinner, pleasant service, and an indoor/outdoor ambience in a rapidly developing part of Kakaako. At lunch you order and pay at the counter, but your superbly prepared snapper with lemon caper beurre blanc or salmon misoyaki arrives on a real plate—for under $8.75. Specials (crispy calamari, braised short ribs Milanaise) change daily. For dinner, there's charred ahi with seven Japanese spices and a selection of dishes, such as lobster ravioli or the top-of-the-line bouillabaisse (an OnJin signature), that are remarkable not only for their friendly prices, but also for the sophisticated execution.

401 Kamakee St. ℂ 808/589-1666. Lunch reservations accepted for 6 or more. Dinner reservations suggested. Lunch main courses $7.25–$13; dinner main courses $13–$22. MC, V. Daily 11am–9pm.

Inexpensive

Angelo Pietro PIZZA/SPAGHETTI   This restaurant has a quirky take on Italian food that could come only from Japan. You can order raw potato salad with any of four dressings—shoyu, ginger, *ume* (plum), or sesame-miso—and chase it with one of more than four dozen spaghetti choices, with sauces and toppings ranging from several types each of mushroom, shrimp, chicken, spinach, and sausage to squid ink and eggplant—everything is grist for the spaghetti mill at the hands of Angelo Pietro. Garlic lovers adore the crisp garlic chips that are heaped atop some of the selections.

1585 Kapiolani Blvd. ℂ 808/941-0555. Reservations accepted for groups of 5 or more. Main courses $7.50–$14. AE, DC, DISC, MC, V. Sun–Thurs 11am–10pm; Fri–Sat 11am–11pm.

Dixie Grill *Kids* AMERICAN   Popcorn, video games, a TV bar, and a lusty, noisy atmosphere—that's Dixie Grill, the busiest (and perhaps noisiest) spot on Ward Avenue. You can't miss it—just look for the fire-engine-red walls and fence. You can sit outside on wooden tables (with a view of Sports Authority) or indoors in a high-decibel, quirky atmosphere much loved by families with kids. The all-American menu features barbecued ribs, burgers, shrimp, salads, sandwiches, and a "mess o' crabs." Watch for the Screamin' Mai Tais.

404 Ward Ave. ℂ 808/596-8359. Reservations accepted for groups of 8 or more. Sandwiches and entrees $7–$20. AE, DC, DISC, MC, V. Mon–Thurs 11am–10pm; Fri 11am–11pm; Sat 10am–11pm; Sun 10am–10pm.

I ♥ Country Café INTERNATIONAL   Give yourself time to peruse the lengthy list of specials posted on the menu board, as well as the prodigious printed menu. Stand in line at the counter, place your order and pay, and find a Formica-topped table; or wait about 10 minutes for your takeout order to appear on a Styrofoam plate heaped with salad and other accompaniments. The small cafe is filled with families and people in terrific shape (athlete and bodybuilder types). The menu ranges from virtually fatless vegetarian meals to regular local–style plate-lunch specials with plenty of gravy. If you're looking for something healthful, it's a good place to be virtuous.

In Ala Moana Plaza, 451 Piikoi St. ℂ 808/596-8108. Main courses $5–$9.25. AE, DC, DISC, MC, V. Daily 8am–9pm.

Kaka'ako Kitchen *Kids* *Finds* GOURMET PLATE LUNCHES   This popular industrial-style plate-lunch haven is busier than ever since it moved to the trendy Ward Centre in March 2000, with an expanded concept that includes dinner and breakfast service. It's owned by chef Russell Siu, of 3660 on the Rise (p. 165). You'll get excellent home-style cooking served on Styrofoam plates in a warehouse ambience. The menu, which changes every 3 to 4 months, includes a seared ahi sandwich with *tobiko* (flying-fish roe) aioli, sandwiches, beef stew, five-spice shoyu chicken, the very popular meatloaf, and other multiethnic entrees, all at budget prices.

In Ward Centre, 1200 Ala Moana Blvd. ℂ 808/596-7488. Breakfast $5–$8; lunch and dinner main courses $7–$13. AE, MC, V. Mon–Thurs 7am–9pm; Fri–Sat 7am–10pm; Sun 7am–5pm.

Kua Aina 🇰 *Value* AMERICAN   This popular branch of the ultimate sandwich shop (the original is a North Shore fixture) is in the Ward Centre area (near Borders and Starbucks). Phone in your order, if you can. During lunch and dinner hours, people wait patiently in long lines for the famous burgers and sandwiches: the beef burgers with heroic toppings, mahimahi with Ortega chile and cheese (a legend), grilled eggplant and peppers, roast turkey, tuna and avocado, roast beef and avocado, and about a dozen other selections. The sandwiches and fries are excellent, and the outdoor section with tables has grown (thank goodness)—but there still may be a wait during lunch hour. The takeout business is brisk.

In Ward Village, 1116 Auahi St. ⓒ **808/591-9133.** Sandwiches and burgers $4.40–$7.15. No credit cards. Mon–Sat 10:30am–9pm; Sun 10:30am–8:00pm

Panda Cuisine 🇰 DIM SUM/SEAFOOD/HONG KONG–STYLE CHINESE This is dim sum heaven, not only for the selection, but for the late-night (after 10pm) dim sum service, a rare thing for what is a morning and lunchtime tradition in Hong Kong. Panda's dim sum selection—spinach-scallop, chive, taro, shrimp dumplings, pork hash, and some 50-plus others—is a real pleaser. (*Tip:* The spinach-scallop and taro puff varieties are a cut above.) The reckless can spring for the live Maine lobster and Dungeness crab in season, or the king clam and steamed fresh fish, but the steaming bamboo carts yielding toothsome surprises are hard to resist. Noodles and sizzling platters make good accompaniments.

641 Keeaumoku St. ⓒ **808/947-1688.** Main courses $8–$29. MC, V. Mon–Sat 10:30am–2:30pm and 5pm–2am; Sun 5–10pm.

Shokudo 🇰 *Finds* JAPANESE   *Shokudo* means "dining room" in Japanese, and this large, beautifully designed but casual dining room is the first U.S. restaurant of this very popular Japanese chain. It attracts local families and hip, young 20-somethings more than tourists. This eatery is a cross between an izakaya (Japanese pub where people eat appetizers and have a beer or two) and a sushi bar. The place is huge and looks even larger with the high ceiling, tiered seating, and central bar. The food comes on small plates, so bring a crowd to taste several items. The 60-item menu (complete with vivid color photos and an English translation of the food with detailed descriptions of each dish) includes appetizers, tofu, salad, fish and meat, rice, soup, sushi, sashimi, nabe, ishiyaki, noodles, and desserts. The waitstaff is extremely knowledgeable, but during the busy dinner hours, there just aren't enough of them and service suffers. Here are my picks: deep-fried battered tofu ($5.75), grilled herb-spiced chicken ($8.75), garlic tuna seared on a hot plate ($7.75), and the honey toast dessert ($6.75), a sumo-sized serving of soft, toasted bread drizzled with honey and topped with vanilla ice cream.

Ala Moana Pacific Center, 1585 Kapiolani Blvd. (at Kaheka St.) ⓒ **808/941-3701.** www.shokudojapanese.com. Entrees $7.75–$20. MC, V. Sun–Thurs 11:30am–1am; Fri–Sat 11:30am–2am.

Side Street Inn 🇰 *Finds* LOCAL   After their own fancy kitchens have closed, some of Honolulu's top chefs head to this off-the-beaten-track neighborhood bar with TV sets on the walls and a back room with a dart board and neon beer signs. Very camp. This small side street near Ala Moana Center is noted more for its seedy bars than for pesto-crusted ahi and gourmet Nalo greens, which makes Side Street Inn such a pleasant surprise. The grinds (that's local slang for eats) are fabulous, with no pretensions and a spirited local feeling. The barbecued baby back ribs in *lilikoi* (yellow passion fruit) sauce are tender, flavorful, and a steal at $14, and you can find 12-ounce steaks, charbroiled or on sizzling platters. My faves are the blackened ahi, pesto-crusted ahi, tender fresh-steamed Manila clams in a wine-garlic broth, shrimp scampi, and escargots. By the end of the meal, you'll be planning when to return.

1225 Hopaka St. Ⓒ **808/591-0253.** Reservations accepted, usually for parties of 4 or more. Plate lunches $4.50–$7.50; dinner main courses $7–$20. AE, DC, MC, V. Mon–Fri 10:30am–1:30pm; daily 4pm–midnight.

ALOHA TOWER MARKETPLACE

Chai's Island Bistro ⓕ PACIFIC RIM/ASIAN   I give Chai's high marks for food but have less enthusiasm for service and ambience, especially at dinner, when the over-amped music can detract from the dining experience (the nightly entertainment, usually live music, can be excruciatingly loud). Also, the dinner entree prices have risen significantly. But the food is generally of high quality and creativity. The 200-seat restaurant has high ceilings, a good location (though not on the waterfront), indoor/outdoor seating, and a discreetly placed open kitchen. The appetizer sampler for two appears on a boat-size platter—a feast of ahi katsu with yellow curry sauce and wasabi; crisp duck lumpia, tasty and greaseless; macadamia nut–crusted tiger prawns; and Alaskan king crab cakes. This is an appetizer that could be an entree and is my favorite item on the menu. The fusion dishes include steamed, fresh, Asian-style moi and an ample selection of vegetarian dishes.

Aloha Tower Marketplace, 1 Aloha Tower Dr. Ⓒ **808/585-0011.** Reservations recommended. Main courses $12–$25 lunch, $26–$43 dinner. AE, DC, MC, V. Tues–Fri 11am–10pm; Sat–Mon 4–10pm.

Don Ho's Island Grill HAWAIIAN/CONTEMPORARY ISLAND   This shrine to Don Ho, who passed away in 2007, mixes a number of nostalgic interior elements: koa paneling, thatched roof, split-bamboo ceilings, old pictures of Ho with celebrities, faux palm trees, and open sides looking out onto the harbor. It's kitschy and charming, down to the vinyl pareu-printed tablecloths and the flower behind the server's ear. The Hawaiian food served here is perfectly fine, but people come here more for the atmosphere than the cuisine.

Aloha Tower Marketplace, 1 Aloha Tower Dr. Ⓒ **808/528-0807.** Reservations recommended. Main courses $11–$26. AE, DC, DISC, MC, V. Daily 10am–10pm; nightclub (days vary) open until 2am.

Gordon Biersch Brewery Restaurant NEW AMERICAN/PACIFIC RIM   German-style lagers brewed on the premises would be enough of a draw, but the food is also a lure at Gordon Biersch, one of Honolulu's liveliest after-work hangouts. Fresh Pacific and Island seafood highlights the eclectic menu. The lanai bar and the brewery bar—open until 1am—are the brightest spots in the marketplace, teeming with downtown types who nosh on pot stickers, grilled steaks, baby back ribs, chicken pizza, garlic fries, and any number of American classics with deft cross-cultural touches. Extensive renovations in 1999 created a stage area for live music, a popular weekend feature.

Aloha Tower Marketplace, 1 Aloha Tower Dr. Ⓒ **808/599-4877.** Reservations recommended. Main courses $8–$20. AE, DC, DISC, MC, V. Sun–Thurs 10am–10pm; Fri–Sat 10am–11pm; late-night menu Sun–Thurs 10–11pm; Fri–Sat 11pm–midnight.

DOWNTOWN

Downtowners love the informal walk-in cafes lining one side of attractive **Bishop Square,** at 1001 Bishop St. (at King St.), in the middle of the business district, where free entertainment is offered every Friday during lunch hour. The popular **Che Pasta** is a stalwart here, chic enough for business meetings and not too formal (or expensive) for a spontaneous rendezvous over pasta and minestrone. Some places in Bishop Square open for breakfast and lunch, others just for lunch, but most close when business offices empty.

Note: Keep in mind that **Restaurant Row** (Ala Moana Blvd., between Punchbowl and South sts.), which features several hot new establishments, offers free validated parking in the evening.

Duc's Bistro 🌴🌴 *Finds* FRENCH/VIETNAMESE   Surrounded by lei stands and marked by a cheery neon sign, this cozy 80-seater stands out at the mauka end of Maunakea in Chinatown. Narrow and quietly elegant, the restaurant has three components: the front room, with windows looking out to Maunakea Street; the windowless back room; and the tiny bar. It has an edgy chic feeling that's more like Manhattan than Honolulu, and the food is beautifully prepared and presented. Sauces for the meats hint of Grand Marnier (duck supreme), Bordeaux (lamb Raymond Oliver), cognac (steak au poivre), Pernod (prawns and oysters), and fresh herbs and vegetables. From the seafood spring rolls with shrimp, taro, and mushrooms to the excellent "meal in a bowl" (rice noodles heaped with fresh herbs and julienne vegetables, topped with lime dressing), creative touches abound. There's live music nightly, and surprise vocalists and hula dancers are known to join in the fun.

1188 Maunakea St., Chinatown. ✆ 808/531-6325. Reservations recommended. Main dishes $13–$22 lunch, $15–$33 dinner. AE, DC, DISC, MC, V. Mon–Fri 11:30am–2pm; Mon–Sat 5–10pm.

Hiroshi Eurasian Tapas 🌴🌴 EURO-ASIAN FUSION   Part of the new trend in cuisine, tapas, or small plates (named after the appetizers served in Spanish bars), make up most of the menu here. Star chef Hiroshi Fukui opened this restaurant in 2004, along with Hawaii's only master sommelier, Chuck Furuya, and manager Cheryle Gomez. The result is fabulous, especially for foodies who want to sample several items off the menu (the staff recommends three dishes per person). These small plates offer a range of tastes, from the simple sizzling Koa kampachi carpaccio with ginger, tomato, tofu, and ponza vinaigrette; to foie gras sushi with a teriyaki glaze; to Portuguese sausage pot stickers with sweet corn, garlic chili foam, and truffled ponzu sauce; to crab cannelloni with shitake mushrooms, dill pesto, mozzarella cheese, and saikyo miso sauce. Go with as many people as possible so you can sample more items. They also serve larger plates, like the dreamy crab-stuffed mahimahi, catch of the day, and an oven-roasted lamb "T-bone." Try to hold out for the desserts: a delicious green tea crème brûlée, a wicked chocolate cake with chocolate ooze, and a great panna cotta.

Restaurant Row, 500 Ala Moana Blvd. ✆ 808/533-HIRO. Reservations recommended. Tapas $6.95–$12; larger plates $19–$22. AE, DISC, MC, V. Daily 5:30–9:30pm.

Indigo Eurasian Cuisine 🌴🌴 EURASIAN   Hardwood floors, red brick, wicker, high ceilings, and an overall feeling of Indochine luxury give Indigo a stylish edge. You can dine indoors or in a garden setting on menu offerings such as pot stickers, Buddhist *bao* buns, savory brochettes, tandoori chicken breast, Asian-style noodles and dumplings, plum-glazed baby back ribs, and cleverly named offerings from both East and West. Chef Glenn Chu is popular, but many claim that Indigo is more style than flavor. I disagree—this is a great restaurant.

1121 Nuuanu Ave. ✆ 808/521-2900. www.indigo-hawaii.com. Reservations recommended. Lunch $17–$23; dinner main dishes $23–$37. DC, DISC, MC, V. Tues–Fri 11:30am–2pm; Tues–Sat 6–9:30pm; martini time in the Green Room Tues–Fri 4–7pm.

Legend Seafood Restaurant ☆ DIM SUM/SEAFOOD   It's like dining in Hong Kong here, with a Chinese-speaking clientele poring over Chinese newspapers and the clatter of chopsticks punctuating conversations. Excellent dim sum comes in bamboo steamers that beckon seductively from carts. Although dining here is a form of assertiveness training (you must wave madly to catch the server's eye and then point to what you want), the system doesn't deter fans from returning. Among my favorites: deep-fried taro puffs, prawn dumplings, shrimp dim sum, vegetable dumplings, and the open-faced seafood (with shiitake, scallops, and a tofu product called *aburage*). Dim sum is served only at lunch, but dinnertime seafood dishes comfort sufficiently. Not a very elegant restaurant, but the food is serious and great.

In the Chinese Cultural Plaza, 100 N. Beretania St. ℭ **808/532-1868.** Reservations recommended for dinner. Most items under $15. AE, DC, MC, V. Mon–Fri 10:30am–2pm and 5:30–10pm; Sat–Sun 8am–2pm and 5:30–10pm.

Little Village Noodle House CHINESE   Don't let the decor throw you—the interior design here reminds me of a small French bistro in Provence. No matter, the food here is "simple and healthy" (its motto) and authentic Chinese (Northern, Canton, and Hong Kong–style). My picks are the Shanghai noodles with stir-fried veggies, the walnut shrimp, and the butterfish in black-bean sauce. The menu is eclectic and offers some interesting selections you don't often see. The service is not only friendly (a rarity in Chinatown), but the waitstaff is quite knowledgeable about the dishes. Even more unique (for Chinatown), there's parking in the back! It's BYOB, but there's an excellent wine store just around the corner (the staff will point it out to you) that delivers to the restaurant.

1113 Smith St. ℭ **808/545-3008.** Most items under $10. AE, DISC, MC, V. Sun–Thurs 10:30am–10:30pm; Fri–Sat 10am–midnight.

Ocean Club ☆ SEAFOOD   Ocean Club could be listed as a restaurant or a nightclub. This sleek, chic spot has redefined happy hour with its extended hours of slashed prices, excellent appetizer-only seafood menu, and ultracool ambience for the 30-and-under set. Galvanized steel counters, mahogany bars lined with shoyu bottles, linoleum tile floors, and oddly attractive pillars resembling pahu (Hawaiian drums) make for a wonderfully eclectic mix. Add DJs spinning hip-hop, and you get the picture. The menu of appetizers lives up to its "ultimate cocktail hour" claim, especially from 4:30 to 8pm nightly, when many items are slashed to half-price and the upbeat mood starts spiraling. A happy-hour sampling: toothsome dips of spinach, artichoke, or crab served with tortilla chips, salsa, and sour cream; ahi tacos and sashimi for a pittance; and standards such as Buffalo wings and fried calamari.

On Restaurant Row, 500 Ala Moana Blvd. ℭ **808/526-9888.** www.oceanclubonline.com. No T-shirts, athletic wear, or beachwear (including rubber slippers) allowed. Minimum age 23. Appetizers $1–$5 before 8pm and $2–$9 after 8pm. AE, DISC, MC, V. Tues and Fri 4:30pm–2am; Thurs 4:30pm–4am; Sat 7pm–4am.

Palomino ☆☆ AMERICAN REGIONAL   Palomino offers splendid harbor views, interesting architecture, conscientious service, and excellent food. It's more Chicago than Hawaii but proffers dishes that will likely bring you back (and it's within walking distance from Hawaii Theatre). Don't miss the cedar-plank roasted salmon. The pizzas (one with caramelized onion and spinach), shrimp in grape leaves, and grilled fish get high marks, as does the devastating dessert called Caffè Affogato (white-chocolate ice cream, espresso, and whipped cream).

In the Harbor Court Building, 66 Queen St., mezzanine. ℭ **808/528-2400.** Reservations recommended. Main dishes $7–$27. AE, DC, DISC, MC, V. Mon–Fri 11am–2:30pm; Sun–Thurs 5–10pm; Fri–Sat 5–11pm. Late-night bar menu Mon–Fri until 11pm; Fri–Sat until 1am.

To Chau ✿✿ *Value* VIETNAMESE PHO   The two stars are strictly for the pho (noodle soup), which many think is the best in a city studded with pho houses. Ambience is nil; you'll have to stand in line, and service can be brusque. But that is all part of the charm of this no-nonsense Formica-style pho house, located in Chinatown and marked, without fail, by a queue of Asian diners. The anticipation is heightened by the view of diners relishing their steaming, long-awaited orders, visible through the windows as you wait your turn on the sidewalk. There are shrimp and spring rolls and chicken and pork chop plates, but I've never seen anyone order anything but pho. And what a soup this is! The broth is clear, hearty, and marvelously flavored with hints of cinnamon and spice. You can order it with several choices of meat, and it comes with a heaping platter of fresh bean sprouts, basil, hot green peppers, and an Asian green called *boke* (bo-*kay*). It's worth the wait, and so inexpensive.

1007 River St., Chinatown. ✆ **808/533-4549.** Reservations not accepted. Pho $4.50–$6.50. No credit cards. Daily 8:30am–2:30pm (or until they run out of food).

Vino Italian Tapas & Wine Bar ✿ *Finds* ITALIAN   Two Japanese guys, D. K. Kodama (chef and owner of Sansei Seafood Restaurant & Sushi Bar and d.k Steakhouse, reviewed earlier) and Chuck Furuya (Hawaii's top master sommelier), teamed up to create this culinary adventure for foodies. The cozy room, with murals of a vineyard and a kitchen with barrels of wine on the walls, makes you ready for the mouthwatering Italian creations by chef Tom Selman. The menu, similar to Vino on Maui, features tapas, or small plates. I'd recommend any ravioli on the menu, but signature dishes include roasted peppers with grilled focaccia, tender crispy calamari, seared foie gras, and petite *osso buco*. Don't pass up the house-made gnocchi or the daily pizza. Furuyu has put together an amazing array of wines by the glass, dispensed from a custom-crafted 20-spigot wine cruvinet. The idea here is to enjoy great wines and be able to taste great Italian food.

Restaurant Row, 500 Ala Moana Blvd. ✆ **808/524-8466.** Reservations recommended. Tapas $5–$17. AE, DISC, MC, V. Wed–Thurs 5:30–9:30pm; Fri–Sat 5:30–10:30pm.

Yanagi Sushi ✿ JAPANESE   I love the late-night hours, the sushi bar, and the extensive choices of combination lunches and dinners. But I also love the a la carte Japanese menu, which covers everything from *chazuke* (a comfort food of rice with tea, salmon, seaweed, and other condiments) to *shabu-shabu* and other steaming earthenware-pot dishes. Complete dinners come with choices of sashimi, shrimp tempura, broiled salmon, New York steak, and many other possibilities. You can dine here affordably or extravagantly, on $7 noodles or a $33 lobster *nabe* (cooked in seasoned broth). Consistently crisp tempura and fine spicy ahi hand-rolled sushi also make Yanagi worth remembering.

762 Kapiolani Blvd. ✆ **808/597-1525.** Reservations recommended. Main courses $8–$33; complete dinners $16–$23. AE, DC, DISC, MC, V. Daily 11am–2pm; Mon–Sat 5:30pm–2am; Sun 5:30–10pm.

KALIHI/SAND ISLAND

La Mariana AMERICAN   Just try to find a spot more evocative or nostalgic than this South Seas oasis at lagoon's edge in the bowels of industrial Honolulu, with carved Tikis, glass balls suspended in fishing nets, shell chandeliers, and old tables made from koa trees. In the back section, the entire ceiling is made of tree limbs. This unique, nearly 50-year-old restaurant is popular for lunch, sunset appetizers, and impromptu Friday- and Saturday-night sing-alongs at the piano bar, where a colorful crowd

Local Chains & Familiar Names

Todai, 1910 Ala Moana Blvd. ((C) **808/947-1000**), part of a string of Japanese seafood buffet restaurants with locations ranging from Dallas to Portland to Beverly Center, is packing 'em in at the gateway to Waikiki with bountiful tables of sushi (40 kinds), hot seafood entrees (tempura, calamari, fresh fish, gyoza, king crab legs, teppanyaki), and delectable desserts. There's not much ambience, but no one cares; the food is terrific, the selection impressive, and the operation as smooth as the green tea cake, and the prices eyepopping: Lunch is $15 weekdays and $18 on weekends; dinner is $28 weekdays and $29 on weekends.

Ala Moana Center's third floor is a mecca for dining and schmoozing. The open-air **Mai Tai Bar** is a popular watering hole. Next door are the boisterous **Bubba Gump Shrimp Company** ((C) **808/949-4867**) and the **California Pizza Kitchen** ((C) **808/941-7715;** I have to note that on my last visit, it was surprisingly very dirty), which also maintains branches in Waikiki at 2284 Kalakaua Ave., next door to the Waikiki Beachcomber Hotel ((C) **808/924-2000**); Kahala Mall, 4211 Waialae Ave. ((C) **808/737-9446**); and Pearlridge, 98–1005 Moanalua Rd. ((C) **808/487-7741**).

L&L Drive-Inn is a plate-lunch bonanza, with 45 locations in Hawaii (36 on Oahu alone). **Zippy's Restaurants** *(C)*, the maestros of quick meals, offer a surprisingly good selection of fresh seafood, saimin, chili, and local fare, plus the wholesome new low-fat, vegetarian "Shintani Cuisine" (based on the dietary principles of Hawaiian doctor Terry Shintani). Every restaurant (21 of them on Oahu, at last count) offers a daily Shintani special, and some locations (Kahala, Vineyard, Pearlridge, Kapolei, Waipio) sell cold Shintani items in 2-pound portions to take home and heat up.

It's hard to spend more than $7 for the French and Vietnamese specials at the **Ba-le Sandwich Shops:** pho, croissants as good as the espresso, and wonderful taro/tapioca desserts. Among Ba-le's 20 locations are those at Ala Moana Center ((C) **808/944-4752**) and 333 Ward Ave. ((C) **808/591-0935**). For smoothies, head to **Jamba Juice,** with 11 locations in and around Honolulu at last count, including Kahala Mall ((C) **808/734-7988**) and Ward Gateway ((C) **808/593-2043**). The ubiquitous **Boston's North End Pizza Bakery** chain claims an enthusiastic following with its reasonable prices and generous toppings. Boston's can be found in Kaimuki, Kaneohe, and Makakilo.

For Italian food, **Buca di Beppo** ((C) **808/591-0880**) is in the Ward Entertainment Center, 1030 Auahi St. Heaping plates of Italian food, enough to feed a very hungry family, make this place quite popular, along with the reasonable prices. Reservations are a must.

In Waikiki, the local **Hard Rock Cafe** is at 1837 Kapiolani Blvd. ((C) **808/955-7383**), and at the Ala Moana end of Waikiki, **Outback Steakhouse,** 1765 Ala Moana Blvd. ((C) **808/951-6274**), serves great steaks and is always full. In downtown's Restaurant Row, beef eaters can also chow down at swanky **Ruth's Chris Steak House,** 500 Ala Moana Blvd. ((C) **808/599-3860**).

(including some Don Ho look-alikes) gathers to sing Hawaiian classics like a 1950s high school glee club. It is delightful. The seared Cajun-style ahi is your best bet as an appetizer or entree; La Mariana is more about spirit and ambience than food.

50 Sand Island Rd. ℂ **808/848-2800.** Reservations recommended, especially on weekends. Main courses $6–$12 lunch, $10–$22 dinner. AE, MC, V. Daily 11am–3pm, 3–5pm (pupu), and 5–9pm. Turn makai (toward the ocean) on Sand Island Rd. from Nimitz Hwy.; immediately after the first stoplight on Sand Island, take a right and drive toward the ocean; it's not far from the airport.

Nico's at Pier 38 ⚝⚝ *Finds* FRESH FISH Gourmet French cuisine produced island style on Styrofoam takeout containers at local plate lunch prices—you can't get better than this tiny takeout place. French-born chef Nicolas "Nico" Chize has cooked at such upscale eateries as Michel's and the Bistro At Century Center, but his own tiny, oddly located eatery is so popular you'll have to stand in line during the crowded lunch hour (where you will see commercial fishermen, business executives, and a small smattering of tourists). My favorite is the furikake pan-seared ahi with the addicting ginger garlic cilantro dip, served with greens or macaroni salad for $8.75. They also have a wicked catch of the day (grilled swordfish with a fennel-cream sauce was on the menu when I were there), a double cheese burger to die for, and a mean beef stew. Hearty breakfasts are served to 9:30am weekdays and 10:30am on Saturday. You can munch on your goodies at plastic tables under an awning at the edge of the pier.

Pier 38, 1133 N. Nimitz Hwy. ℂ **808/540-137.** www.nicospier38.com. No reservations, but they do take orders over the phone. Breakfast $2.45–$6.95; lunch $5.75–$8.75. Mon–Fri 6:30am–6pm; Sat 6:30am–2:30pm.

Sam Choy's Breakfast, Lunch, Crab & Big Aloha Brewery ISLAND CUISINE/ SEAFOOD This is a happy, carefree eatery—elegance and cholesterol be damned. Chef/restaurateur Sam Choy's crab house features great fun and gigantic meals (a Choy trademark). Imagine dining in an all-wood sampan (a type of boat; it's the centerpiece of the 11,000-sq.-ft. restaurant) and washing your hands in an oversize wok in the center of the room. A 2,000-gallon tank containing a live assortment of crabs in season (Kona, Maryland, Samoan, Dungeness, Florida stone) lines the open kitchen. Clam chowder, seafood gumbos, oysters from the oyster bar, and assorted poke (chunks of marinated raw fish) are also offered at dinner, which comes complete with soup, salad, and entree. Children's menus are an attractive feature for families. Several varieties of Big Aloha beer, brewed on-site, go well with the crab and poke.

580 Nimitz Hwy., Iwilei. ℂ **808/545-7979.** www.samchoy.com. Reservations recommended for lunch and dinner. Main courses $5–$13 breakfast, $9–$40 lunch, and $19–$45 dinner. AE, DC, DISC, MC, V. Sun–Thurs 7am–9:30pm; Fri–Sat 7am–10pm. Located in the Iwilei industrial area near Honolulu Harbor, across the street from Gentry Pacific Center.

MANOA VALLEY/MOILIILI/MAKIKI
Very Expensive
Chef Mavro Restaurant ⚝⚝⚝ PROVENÇAL/HAWAII REGIONAL If you have only 1 night on Oahu, this is the restaurant to go to. Chef/owner George Mavrothalassitis, a native of Provence (and winner of the 2003 prestigious James Beard Award for Best Chef for Hawaii and the Pacific Northwest), has fans all over the world who have admired his creativity since his days at Halekulani's La Mer and the Four Seasons Resort Wailea's Seasons. His restaurant resides in a convenient, nontouristy neighborhood in McCully. You can order prix fixe or a la carte, with or without wine pairings (which are dazzling). The list of signature items includes filet of poached fresh catch, sago-coconut nage Thai herbs, pousse-tied seaweed, and lime

froth; and award-winning onaga marinated with fennel served with "Big Wave" tomatoes, vegetables a la Grecque, and sauce raite. Recently added: sautéed foie gras with poha berries, spiced kabocha bread, braised leeks, and balsamic foie gras glaze. Hints of Tahitian vanilla, lemon grass, ogo (a type of seaweed), rosemary, and Madras curry add exotic flavors to the French-inspired cooking and fresh island ingredients. The desserts are extraordinary; his latest is a Maui lavender soup with Hawaiian vanilla pearls, confit white pineapple, and Maui pineapple wine granite (Provence cuisine marries Maui produce). The split-level room is quietly cordial, and the menu changes monthly to highlight seasonal ingredients. As we went to press, Chef Mavro just returned from Chili with great ideas for his next menu.

1969 S. King St. *C* **808/944-4714.** www.chefmavro.com. Reservations recommended. Prix-fixe menu $66–$102 ($99–$208 with wine pairings). AE, DC, DISC, MC, V. Tues–Sun 6–9:30pm.

Expensive

Alan Wong's Restaurant ★★★ HAWAII REGIONAL CUISINE   Alan Wong is one of Hawaii's most popular chefs, as proved by the worshipful foodies who come from all over the state to wait for a table at this bustling eatery, and recently *Gourmet* magazine named this restaurant the eighth best in the "Top 50 Best Restaurants in America." And deservedly so—the food here is brilliant and the menu irresistible. The 90-seat room has a glassed-in terrace and open kitchen. Sensitive lighting and curly koa wall panels accent an unobtrusively pleasing environment—casual, but not too. The menu's cutting-edge offerings sizzle with the Asian flavors of lemon grass, sweet-and-sour, garlic, and wasabi, deftly melded with the fresh seafood and produce of the islands. The California roll is a triumph, made with salmon roe, wasabi, and Kona lobster instead of rice, and served warm. I love the opihi (limpet) shooters, day-boat scallops, and fresh fish preparations. But don't get attached to any one item—the menu changes daily. The only warning is this place is very noisy.

1857 S. King St., 3rd floor. *C* **808/949-2526.** www.alanwongs.com. Reservations recommended. Main courses $26–$48; 5-course sampling menu $65 ($90 with wine); chef's tasting menu $85 ($120 with wine). AE, DC, MC, V. Daily 5–10pm.

Moderate

Contemporary Museum Cafe ★ *Finds* HEALTHFUL GOURMET   The surroundings are an integral part of the dining experience at this tiny lunchtime cafe, part of an art museum nestled on the slopes of Tantalus amid carefully cultivated Asian gardens, with a breathtaking view of Diamond Head and priceless contemporary artwork displayed indoors and out. The menu is limited to sandwiches, soups, salads, and appetizers, but you won't leave disappointed: They're perfect lunchtime fare. Try the day's crostini, hummus and pita, lentil burger, shrimp roasted shallot and tarragon salad, or fresh fish specials. Crown your meal with flourless chocolate cake or fresh, local-made gelato.

In The Contemporary Museum, 2411 Makiki Heights Dr. *C* **808/523-3362.** www.tcmhi.org. Reservations recommended. Main courses $9–$12. AE, MC, V. Tues–Sat 11:30am–2:30pm; Sun noon–2:30pm.

Maple Garden SZECHUAN   It hums like a top and rarely disappoints. Maple Garden is known for its garlic eggplant, Peking duck, and Chinaman's Hat, a version of mu shu pork, available in vegetarian form as well. The crisp green beans are out of this world. Other hits: braised scallops with Chinese mushrooms, sautéed spinach, and prawns in chile sauce. There are ample vegetarian selections and dozens of seafood entrees—everything from sea cucumbers and braised salmon to lobster with black-bean sauce. An ever-expanding visual feast adorns the dining-room walls, which are covered with original drawings, sketches, and murals by noted artist John Young. The staff is unbelievably friendly, and service is top-notch.

909 Isenberg St. ✆ **808/941-6641.** Main courses $5–$23 (most $8–$9). DC, DISC, MC, V. Daily 11am–2pm and 5:30–10pm.

Sushi King *Value* JAPANESE   This is a top value for lovers of Japanese food. Brusque service can't deter the throngs that arrive for the excellent lunch specials. It's tricky to find, located in a small mini-mall (look for University Flower Shop). Don't pass up the jumbo platters—soup, pickles, California roll sushi, and your choice of chicken teriyaki, beef teriyaki, shrimp and vegetable tempura, or calamari and vegetable tempura, all at arrestingly low prices. Other combination lunches offer generous choices that include sashimi, tempura, butterfish, fried oysters, and noodles hot and cold. Early-bird specials are offered daily from 5:30 to 6:30pm.

2700 S. King St. ✆ **808/947-2836.** Reservations recommended, especially for 5 or more on weekends. Lunch $8–$15; dinner main courses $14–$21. AE, DC, DISC, MC, V. Daily 11:30am–2pm; Wed–Mon 5:30pm–2am; Tues 5:30–10pm.

Willows LOCAL   Food is not the headliner here; the ambience is. There just aren't many places in Hawaii anymore with this kind of tropical setting. Shoes click on hardwood floors in rooms surrounded by lush foliage and fountains fed by the natural springs of the area. The dining rooms are open-air, with private umbrella tables scattered about. Willows will never regain the charm and nostalgia of its early kamaaina days, but it has been beautifully restored, and the food is more than adequate, with some of the Hawaiian dishes (laulau, lomi salmon, poke) quite good. Everything is served buffet style.

817 Hausten St. ✆ **808/952-9200.** www.willowshawaii.com. Reservations recommended. Lunch buffet $20 Mon–Fri, $22 Sat, $30 Sun; dinner buffet $30 daily. AE, DC, DISC, MC, V. Mon–Fri 11am–2pm and 5:30–9pm; Sat–Sun 10am–2pm and 5–9pm. No parking in the neighborhood; valet parking $3, self-parking $3.

Inexpensive

Chiang Mai Thai Cuisine THAI   Chiang Mai made sticky rice famous in Honolulu, serving it in bamboo steamers with fish and exotic curries. Menu items include toothsome red, green, and yellow curries; the signature Cornish game hen in lemon grass and spices; and a garlic-infused green papaya salad marinated in tamarind sauce. Spicy shrimp soup, eggplant with basil and tofu, and the vegetarian green curry are favorites.

2239 S. King St. ✆ **808/941-1151.** Reservations recommended for dinner. Main courses $8–$14. AE, DC, DISC, MC, V. Mon–Fri 11am–2pm; daily 5:30–9:30pm.

Jimbo's Restaurant ✿ *Value* JAPANESE   Jimbo's is the quintessential neighborhood restaurant—small, with a line of regulars outside, fantastic house-made noodles and broths, and everything good and affordable. A must for any noodle lover, Jimbo's serves homemade udon in a flawless broth with a subtly smoky flavor and then tops it with shrimp tempura, chicken, eggs, vegetables, seaweed, roasted mochi, and a variety of accompaniments of your choice. Cold noodles (the Tanuki salad is wonderful!), stir-fried noodles, *donburi* (rice dishes with assorted toppings), and combination dinners are other delights. The earthenware pot of noodles, with shiitake mushrooms, vegetables, and udon, plus a platter of tempura on the side, is the top-of-the-line combo. But my favorite is the *nabeyaki* (an earthenware pot of udon with tempura on top). Owner Jimbo Motojima, a perfectionist, uses only the finest ingredients from Japan.

1936 S. King St. ℂ 808/947-2211. Reservations not accepted. Main courses $7–$14. AE, DC, MC, V. Daily 11am–2:50pm; Sun–Thurs 5–9:50pm; Fri–Sat 5–10:30pm.

Spices *Value* SOUTHEAST ASIAN   Located in a small building near the university, this delicious, tiny Asian bistro specializes in tantalizing traditional dishes from Viet Nam, Laos, Thailand, and Burma (now known as Myanmar) using local Hawaii ingredients. True to the restaurant's name, the smell of pungent spices greets you as you enter; the walls, painted in saffron orange, mustard yellow, and green basil trim, let you know that you are in for a treat. A cornucopia of Southeast Asian specialties (with plenty of vegetarian dishes) ranges from curries (green, yellow, Malaysian, and Laotian) to noodles (pad Thai), to soups. But the best are the homemade ice creams, with such unusual flavors as durian, pandanus, or chile/lemon grass. Limited parking (about eight stalls) behind the restaurant.

2671 S. King St. (at University Ave.) ℂ 808/949-2679. Curries $14–$16; rice and noodle dishes $12–$42. MC, V. Tues–Fri 11:30am–2pm and 5:30–10pm; Sat 5:30–10pm; Sun 5–9pm.

KAIMUKI/KAPAHULU
Expensive
Ninniku-Ya Garlic Restaurant EURO-ASIAN   This great restaurant is a paean to the stinking rose. Ninniku-Ya is located in a cozy old home, with tables in a split-level dining room and outdoors under venerable trees. The menu titillates with many garlic surprises and specials. The seasonal specialties are fine, but the staples are quite wonderful. The four-mushroom pasta is sublime, the hot-stone filet mignon tender and tasty, and the garlic rice a meal in itself. Every garlic lover should experience the garlic toast and the roasted garlic with blue cheese. Everything contains garlic, even the house-made garlic gelato, but it doesn't overpower. Yes, that's garlic gelato—and it gets high marks from me. Look for the festive fairy lights lining the building.

3196 Waialae Ave. ℂ 808/735-0784. Reservations recommended. Main dishes $15–$30. AE, DC, DISC, MC, V. Tues–Sun 5:30–9:30pm (last seating).

Sam Choy's Diamond Head Restaurant ✦ HAWAII REGIONAL   You'll know you're in the right place if you see a parade of diners leaving the restaurant clutching Styrofoam bundles—leftovers are de rigueur at any Sam Choy operation. The servings here are gargantuan, verging on off-putting. Choy has won over a sizable chunk of Hawaii's dining population with his noisy, informal, and gourmet-cum-local style of cooking. Now his kitchen is also the set for his cooking show. The master of poke (marinated raw fish), Choy serves several of the best versions to be had (including fried poke, poke and chips, and the famous traditional poke). I recommend the fried brie won tons, the seafood laulau, and seared ahi.

449 Kapahulu Ave. ℂ 808/732-8645. www.samchoy.com. Reservations recommended. Main courses $28–$53; prix-fixe menu $55; Sun brunch buffet $26 adults, $17 ages 5–12 years. AE, DC, DISC, MC, V. Daily 5:30–10pm; Sun brunch 9:30am–1:30pm.

3660 On the Rise ✦✦✦ EURO-ISLAND   Ever since *Wine Spectator* gave this restaurant its Award of Excellence, this place has been packed, and with good reason. In his 200-seat restaurant, chef Russell Siu adds an Asian or local touch to the basics: rack of lamb with macadamia nuts, filets of catfish in *ponzu* (a Japanese sauce), and seared ahi salad with grilled shiitake mushrooms, a local favorite. The ahi katsu, wrapped in nori and fried medium rare, is a main attraction in the appetizer department. Diners rave over chef Gilbert Crisostomo's desserts, especially the warm chocolate cake.

3660 Waialae Ave. ℭ **808/737-1177.** www.3660.com. Reservations suggested. Main courses $25–$55; prix-fixe menu $40. AE, DC, DISC, MC, V. Tues–Sun 5:30–8:30pm.

Moderate

C & C Pasta ★★ *Finds* ITALIAN   Just as we went to press, Sun Hendricks, a restaurateur from the U.S. mainland, fell in love with this quaint Italian bistro and bought it. She swore that she would not change anything on the beloved menu and would only add "more fresh fish dishes" prepared in the classic and contemporary style. This tiny neighborhood gem, Honolulu's best Italian eatery, really sizzles. Dress casually and relax to the opera playing in the background, but be sure to make a reservation—there's always a line for dinner. Diners are an eclectic crowd of pasta lovers who will go to any lengths to tuck into toe-tingling feasts: a *sublime* mushroom risotto with truffle butter, excellent bruschetta and raviolis, and my perpetual favorites, linguine with clams and spaghetti puttanesca. Other excellent choices include the lasagna (meat and vegetarian) or penne with roasted eggplant. If that's not enough, try one of the specials on the blackboard, like the linguine I had recently that was generously flavored with spinach and roasted garlic. Also on the menu are pizzas (with garlic, Gorgonzola, and other such tasty toppings) and a heroic salad of mixed greens, Gorgonzola, hazelnuts, and roasted onions and peppers, with fig-balsamic dressing. Although service can lag when it's busy, the quality is tops at C & C, the atmosphere is casual, and even the pickiest palates should find something to rave about. *Tip:* The bread pudding and the tiramisu, if on the menu, are must-haves.

3605 Waialae Ave. ℭ **808/732-5999.** Reservations required for dinner. Main courses $15–$28. MC, V. Tues–Sat 11am–3pm; Tues–Thurs and Sun 5–9pm; Fri–Sat 5–10pm.

Genki Sushi ★ SUSHI   Take your place in line for a seat at one of the U-shaped counters. Conveyor belts parade by with freshly made sushi, usually two pieces per color-coded plate, priced inexpensively. The possibilities are dizzying: spicy tuna topped with scallions, ahi, scallops with mayonnaise, Canadian roll (like a California roll, except with salmon), sea urchin, flavored octopus, sweet shrimp, surf clam, corn, tuna salad, and so on. Genki starts with a Japanese culinary tradition and takes liberties with it, so don't be a purist. By the end of the meal, the piled-high plates are tallied up by color and, presto, your bill appears. Combination platters are available for takeout.

900 Kapahulu Ave. ℭ **808/735-7700.** A la carte sushi from $1.25 for 2 pieces; combination platters $8–$42. AE, DC, DISC, MC, V. Sun–Thurs 11am–9pm; Fri–Sat 11am–10pm; takeout available daily 11am–9pm.

Town ★ *Finds* CONTEMPORARY ITALIAN   The latest hip restaurant along Waialae's miracle mile of "in" spots is a surprisingly delicious place to eat (generally the new hot spots tend more toward pretense than lip-smacking food). Ignore the metro high-tech atmosphere of highly polished concrete floors, stainless steel tables, and incredibly uncomfortable chairs, and ask for a table outside on the lanai (where the noise level will be bearable). The hand-typed (who the heck still has a typewriter these days?), incredibly creative menu changes daily but promises "local first, organic whenever possible, with aloha always" and delivers. At my last visit, I sampled the ahi tartar on risotto cakes and frito misto, and an Italian tempura of scallops, celery, lemon, and white beans. Entrees range from braised lamb to crispy moi (a highly prized Hawaiian fish) to excellent gnocchi. Desserts (around $6) range from buttermilk panna cotta to chocolate banini (panini of toast, chocolate, and bananas—yum).

Lunches are along the lines of sandwiches, salads, and pastas. Breakfast (frittata of the day, eggs, wonderful baked goods) has recently been added.

3435 Waialae Ave. (at 9th St.). (C) **808/735-5900.** Dinner reservations a must. Lunch entrees $7.50–$13; dinner entrees $15–$24. AE, MC, V. Mon–Thurs 6:30–9:30am, 11:30am–2pm, and 5:30–9:30pm; Fri–Sat 6:30–10am, 11:30am–2pm, and 5:30–10pm.

12th Avenue Grill (R (Finds RETRO-AMERICAN Since the doors opened in 2004, this tiny (14 tables) upscale neighborhood diner is packed every night. Chef Kevin Hanney whips up gourmet versions of American classics, such as macaroni and cheese (with smoked Parmesan), and the restaurant's signature dish of kim-chee steak (beef marinated in a sweet-hot sauce and grilled). A chalkboard menu lists the specials of the night (the smoked trout is a must). Diners are packed in close, so noise is a problem, but the food more than makes up for this one flaw. Whatever you order, leave room for desserts, done by chef Samantha Choy (who also bakes for Sam Choy Restaurants). The fruit crisp of the day is a good bet. They recently added a full bar.

1145-C 12th Ave. (at Wailalea Ave.). (C) **808/732-9469.** Reservations recommended. Small plates $6–$11; large plates $17–$27. MC, V. Mon–Thurs 5:30–9pm; Fri–Sat 5:30–10pm.

Inexpensive
Cafe Laufer (R BAKERY/SANDWICH SHOP This small, cheerful cafe features frilly decor and sublime pastries—from apple scones and Linzer tortes to fruit flan, decadent chocolate mousse, and carrot cake—to accompany the latte and espresso. Fans drop in for simple soups and deli sandwiches on fresh-baked breads; biscotti during coffee break; or a hearty loaf of seven-grain, rye, pumpernickel, or French. The small but satisfying lunch menu includes soup-salad-sandwich specials for a song, a fabulous spinach salad with dried cranberries and Gorgonzola, and gourmet greens with mango-infused, honey-mustard dressing. The orange-seared shrimp salad and the Chinese chicken salad are hits for the light eater, and the smoked Atlantic salmon with fresh pumpernickel bread and cream cheese, Maui onions, and capers is excellent. The special Saturday-night desserts draw a brisk postmovie business.

3565 Waialae Ave. (C) **808/735-7717.** www.cafelaufer.com. Most items less than $10. AE, DC, DISC, MC, V. Sun–Mon and Wed–Thurs 10am–9pm; Fri–Sat 10am–10pm.

EAST OF WAIKIKI: KAHALA

Hoku's (R(R(R HAWAIIAN REGIONAL Elegant without being stuffy, and creative without being overwrought, the upscale dining room of the Kahala Hotel & Resort underwent a $700,000 renovation of the elegant restaurant. Dinners combine European finesse with an island touch. This is fusion that really works. The ocean view, open kitchen, and astonishing bamboo floor are stellar features. Reflecting the restaurant's cross-cultural influences, the kitchen is equipped with a kiawe grill and Szechuan woks for the prawn, lobster, tofu, and other stir-fried specialties. The steamed Hong Kong–style whole fresh fish is worthy of a special occasion. The chef's daily selection of appetizers could include pan-seared Hudson Valley foie gras, sashimi, slow-braised pork belly, and other dainty tastings, and is a good choice for the curious. Rack of lamb, pan-seared ahi steak, and the full range of East-West specialties appeal to many tastes. Sunday brunch is not to be missed.

In the Kahala Hotel, 5000 Kahala Ave. (C) **808/739-8780.** Reservations recommended. Main courses $32–$94. AE, DC, DISC, MC, V. Daily 5:30–10pm. Sunday brunch 10:30am–2pm.

Olive Tree Cafe ★★ *Finds* GREEK/EASTERN MEDITERRANEAN Delectables at bargain prices stream out of the tiny open kitchen here. Recently voted Best Restaurant in Hawaii Under $20 in a local survey, Olive Tree is every neighborhood's dream—a totally hip restaurant with divine Greek fare and friendly prices. There are umbrella tables outside and a few seats indoors, and you order and pay at the counter. The mussel seviche is broke-the-mouth fabulous, with lemon, lime, capers, herbs, and olive oil—a perfect blend of flavors. The creamy, tender chicken saffron, a frequent special, always elicits groans of pleasure, as does the robust and generous Greek salad. I also love the souvlaki, ranging from fresh fish to chicken and lamb, spruced up with the chef's homemade yogurt-dill sauce. A large group can dine here like sultans without breaking the bank and take in a movie next door, too. BYOB.

4614 Kilauea Ave., next to Kahala Mall. ⓒ 808/737-0303. Main courses $8–$15. No credit cards; checks accepted. Daily 5–10pm.

EAST OAHU

HAWAII KAI

Roy's Restaurant ★★★ EUROPEAN/ASIAN This is the first of Roy Yamaguchi's six signature restaurants in Hawaii (he has two dozen all over the world). It is still the flagship and many people's favorite, true to its Euro-Asian roots and Yamaguchi's winning formula: open kitchen, fresh ingredients, ethnic touches, and a good dose of nostalgia mingled with European techniques. The menu changes nightly, but you can generally count on individual pizzas, a varied appetizer menu (Szechuan spiced baby back ribs, blackened ahi), a small pasta selection, and entrees such as garlic-mustard short ribs, hibachi-style salmon in *ponzu* sauce, and several types of fresh catch. One of Hawaii's most popular restaurants, Roy's is lit up at night with Tiki torches outside; the view from within is of scenic Maunalua Bay. Roy's is also renowned for its high-decibel style of dining—it's always full and noisy. Other Roy's restaurants in Hawaii are located in Ko Olina, Oahu; Poipu, Kauai; Waikoloa, Big Island; and Kihei and Napili, Maui. There's also live music Friday and Saturday evenings from 7:30 to 10pm and Sunday from 6 to 9pm.

6600 Kalanianaole Hwy. ⓒ 808/396-7697. www.roysrestaurant.com. Reservations recommended. Main courses $25–$70. AE, DC, DISC, MC, V. Mon–Thurs 5:30–9pm; Fri 5:30–9:30pm; Sat–Sun 5–9:30pm.

THE WINDWARD COAST

The following restaurants are located on the "Eastern Oahu & the Windward Coast" map on p. 215.

MODERATE

Assaggio ★ ITALIAN This was the mother ship of the Assaggio empire before the Ala Moana branch (p. 154) opened in December 1999. The affordable prices, attentive service, and winning menu items have attracted loyal fans throughout the years. The best-selling homemade hot antipasto has jumbo shrimp, fresh clams, mussels, and calamari in a sauce of cayenne pepper, white wine, and garlic. You can choose linguine, fettuccine, or ziti with 10 different sauces in small or regular portions or any of nine chicken pastas (the chicken Assaggio, with garlic, peppers, and mushrooms, is especially flavorful). Equally impressive is the extensive list of seafood pastas, including the garlic/olive oil sauté. A plus is that, at dinner, servings come in two sizes and prices.

354 Uluniu St., Kailua. ⓒ 808/261-2772. Reservations recommended. Main courses $10–$25. AE, DC, DISC, MC, V. Mon–Fri 11:30am–2:30pm; Sun–Thurs 5–9:30pm; Fri–Sat 5–10pm.

Lucy's Grill 'n Bar ★★ HAWAII REGIONAL CUISINE   This is one of Kailua's most popular restaurants, not just because of the open-air bar and the outdoor lanai seating, but because of the terrific food. The menu is eclectic Hawaii Regional Cuisine, with lots of choices and giant-size portions. The dress is casual, and the clientele is local. Be sure to order the spicy ahi tower with sushi rice, avocado, wasabi cream, and roasted nori to get you started. Any of the fresh fish and seafood is wonderful, especially the Szechuan-spiced jumbo tiger prawns with black-bean cream and penne pasta, or the lemon grass–crusted scallops with yellow Thai curry. Save room for desserts: crème brûlée with Tahitian vanilla bean, dark chocolate soufflé cake, or their "damn fine" apple crisp—a la mode, of course. *Budget tip:* The Early Bird Special (5–6:30pm nightly) is a terrific dinner for just $14.

33 Aulike St., Kailua. © 808/230-8188. Reservations recommended. Main courses $14–$28. MC, V. Daily 5–10pm.

THE NORTH SHORE
The following restaurants can be located on the "Oahu's North Shore" map on p. 224.

EXPENSIVE
21 Degrees North ★★★ PACIFIC RIM CUISINE   *Foodies alert:* It is well worth the drive from Waikiki (45–60 min.) to the North Shore to enjoy this impressive signature restaurant at Turtle Bay Resort (p. 138). Not only is it visually inspiring, with floor-to-ceiling windows overlooking the North Shore's famous rolling surf, but chef Hector Morales's Pacific Rim cuisine is outstanding. The dishes emerging from the kitchen take Hawaiian dining to a new level. The chef has taken contemporary Island cuisine and made it fresh and interesting. The ever-changing menu has such unusual combinations as crab-crusted Hawaiian sea bass with a lemon grass coulis, salmon with Molokai mashed sweet potatoes and an orange and soy glaze, and roasted Peking

---

The Shrimp Trucks

Maybe it's a Hawaii thing, but the best, sweetest, juiciest shrimp you are ever going to eat will be from a shrimp truck on Oahu's North Shore. Several trucks line up around the entry to Haleiwa, just off the Kamehameha Hwy, but our two favorites are **Giovanni's Original White Shrimp Truck** and **Holy Smokes: Hawaiian Meats and Seafood.**

Giovanni's (© **808/293-1839**), which usually parks across the street from the Halewai Senior Housing, claims to be the first shrimp truck to serve the delicious aquaculture shrimp farmed in the surrounding area. The menu is simple—spicy, garlic, or lemon-and-butter shrimp. Skip the lemon-and-butter shrimp (boring), and go to the garlic (my fave) or the spicy (but beware—it really packs a punch.) The battered white truck has picnic tables under the awning outside, so you can munch away right there.

The other truck parked in the same area, Holy Smokes, has a bit more extensive menu; in addition to the famous shrimp, they also have pork spare ribs ($8.95), smoked chicken ($7.95), and a steak plate ($11).

The trucks are usually in place before noon and stay until about sunset. Depending on how much shrimp you can down, expect to spend no more than $12 per person.

duck with a vanilla and plum sweet and sour glaze. Or try numerous creations with the five-course tasting menu.

57–091 Kamehameha Hwy., Kahuku. ℂ **800/203-3650** or 808/293-8811. www.turtlebayresort.com. Reservations a must. Main courses $29–$42; 5-course tasting menu $76 without wine, $95 with wine. AE, DC, DISC, MC, V. Tues–Sat 6–10pm.

MODERATE

Haleiwa Joe's AMERICAN/SEAFOOD   Next to the Haleiwa bridge, with a great harbor and sunset view, Haleiwa Joe's serves up fresh local seafood such as whole Hawaiian moi, opakapaka, ahi, and whatever comes in fresh that day. This is a steak-and-seafood harborside restaurant with indoor-outdoor seating and a surf-and-turf menu that could include New York steak, coconut shrimp, and black-and-blue sashimi. Sandwiches and salads make it a great lunch stop, too. There are only two Haleiwa restaurants close to the ocean, and this is one of them.

66–011 Kamehameha Hwy., Haleiwa. ℂ **808/637-8005.** Reservations not accepted. Main courses $14–$27. MC, V. Mon–Thurs 11:30am–9:30pm (limited menu 4:15–5:30pm); Fri–Sat 11:30am–10:30pm (limited menu 4:15–5:30pm, bar until midnight); Sun 11:30am–9:30pm (limited menu 3:45–5pm).

Jameson's by the Sea SEAFOOD   Duck into this roadside watering hole across the street from the ocean for cocktails, sashimi, and its celebrated salmon pâté, or for other hot and cold appetizers, salads, and sandwiches. The grilled crab-and-shrimp sandwich on sourdough bread is a perennial, and it's hard to go wrong with the fresh-fish sandwich of the day, grilled plain and simple. The dinner menu offers the usual surf-and-turf choices: fresh opakapaka ulua (Hawaiian jackfish), mahimahi, scallops in lemon butter and capers, lobster tail, and steaks.

62–540 Kamehameha Hwy., Haleiwa. ℂ **808/637-4336.** Reservations recommended. Main courses lunch $7–$19; dinner $9–$39. AE, DC, DISC, MC, V. Mon–Fri 10:30am–9pm; Sat–Sun 9am–9pm.

Ola at Turtle Bay Resort ☆☆ *Finds* HAWAIIAN/SEAFOOD   Even if you are staying in Waikiki, plan a day at the beach on the North Shore and eat here for dinner. You will not regret it. First, there's the location—literally on the sand on the beach next door to the Turtle Bay Resort. Second, the restaurant is an open-air ("open" as in no walls) beach pavilion, made from ironwood trees harvested from the surrounding area. The view is the lapping waves of the Pacific on to the sand. The atmosphere when they light the Tiki torches at sunset is very, very romantic. Third, and best of all, is the food! Chef Fred DeAngelo named his restaurant Ola, which means "alive" or "healthy" in Hawaii, and he insists on only the freshest of ingredients. The menu is filled with creative selections (the ahi and lobster poke served with a wonton spoon) and some of the best food you will eat in Hawaii. My favorites are the incredible slow-poached togarashi salmon with a sweet, sugar cane crust served with Okinawan sweet potato and locally grown corn; the Lawai'a fishermen's stew with lobster, shrimp, scallops and fresh fish; and an unforgettable kiawe smoked beef tenderloin.

Turtle Bay Resort, 57-091 Kamehamehaha Hwy., Kahuku. ℂ **808/293-0801.** www.turtlebayresort.com/Dining/ Ola.asp. Reservations recommended at dinner. Lunch entrees $9–$16; dinner entrees $17–$53. AE, DC, DISC, MC, V. Sun–Thurs 11am–3pm and 5:30–9:30pm; Fri–Sat 5:30–10pm.

INEXPENSIVE

Cafe Haleiwa BREAKFAST/LUNCH/MEXICAN   Haleiwa's legendary breakfast joint is a big hit with surfers, urban gentry with weekend country homes, reclusive artists, and anyone who loves mahimahi plate lunches and heroic sandwiches. It's a wake-up-and-hit-the-beach kind of place, serving generous omelets with names like Off the Wall, Off the Lip, and Breakfast in a Barrel. Surf pictures line the walls, and the ambience is Formica-style casual. Hit the espresso bar for a caffeine fix.

66–460 Kamehameha Hwy., Haleiwa. © 808/637-5516. Reservations not accepted. Main courses $6–$11. AE, MC, V. Daily 7am–2pm.

Cholos Homestyle Mexican II *(Value* MEXICAN   There's usually a wait at this popular North Shore eatery, where some of the tables have leather stools without backs, and great home-style Mexican food is presented with so-so service. Still, this is the unhurried North Shore, and the biggest rush for most folks is getting to and from the beach. I recommend the spinach quesadilla, a generous serving filled with black beans, cheese, and fresh vegetables; the chicken fajita plate; and the fish taco plate, a steal at $8 (just $4.75 a la carte). There are tables and stools outdoors; indoors, it's dark and cavelike, with loud music and Mexican handicrafts all over the place.

North Shore Marketplace, 66–250 Kamehameha Hwy. © 808/637-3059. Combination plates $7–$12. AE, DISC, MC, V. Daily 10:30am–9:30pm.

Kua Aina *(Value* AMERICAN   "What's the name of that sandwich shop on the North Shore?" I hear that often. After 29 years at the same spot, Kua Aina moved a few years ago down the street and to a larger, 75-seat eatery. It's as busy as ever, and many diners get their burgers to go and head for the beach. Kua Aina's thin and spindly french fries are renowned islandwide and are the perfect accompaniment to its legendary burgers. Fat, moist, and homemade, the burgers can be ordered with avocado, bacon, and many other accompaniments, including Ortega chiles and cheese. The roast turkey, mahimahi, and tuna and avocado sandwiches are excellent alternatives to the burgers. Kua Aina is unparalleled on the island and is a North Shore must, eclipsing its fancier competitors at lunch.

66–160 Kamehameha Hwy., Haleiwa. © 808/637-6067. Sandwiches and burgers $4.20–$7.35. No credit cards. Daily 11am–8pm.

Paradise Found Cafe VEGETARIAN   A tiny cafe behind Celestial Natural Foods, Paradise Found is a bit of a hunt, but stick with it. For more than a few townies, the North Shore sojourn begins at Paradise, the only pure vegetarian restaurant in these parts. Breakfasts feature the "up & at 'em" (scrambled eggs, veggies, and home fries wrapped in a cheese quesadilla) and the "nanna nutty" (peanut butter, banana, honey, granola, and cinnamon wrapped in a flour tortilla and grilled). Their smoothies (especially the Waimea Shorebreak) are legendary, and their organic soups, fresh-pressed vegetable juices, sandwiches, and healthy plate lunches are a great launch to a Haleiwa day. Vegan substitutes are willingly made in place of dairy products.

66–443 Kamehameha Hwy., Haleiwa. © 808/637-4540. All items less than $12. No credit cards. Mon–Sat 9am–5pm; Sun 9am–4pm.

LEEWARD OAHU

Roy's Ko Olina ★★★ *(Finds* EUROPEAN/ASIAN   The latest in the Roy's empire of excellent restaurants opened in 2004 in Ko Olina Resort on the leeward coast of Oahu, some 16 years after the flagship first restaurant (p. 168) opened in Hawaii Kai. One of some nearly three dozen locations around the globe, Roy's Ko Olina perches in a peerless location overlooking the lagoon, waterfalls, and 18th hole of the Ko Olina Golf Club. You'll find Roy's famous display kitchen here and floor-to-ceiling windows that showcase the view. Roy's usual high-decibel style of dining has been

---

(*Moments* **Luau!**

The sun is setting, the Tiki torches are lit, the pig is taken from the imu (an oven in the earth), the drums begin pounding—it's luau time. Recently three new luau have started from across the island in Waikiki, on the North Shore and in windward Oahu at Sea Life Park.

On the North Shore, the **Turtle Bay Resort** presents **"Legends of the North Shore Luau,"** on the lawn overlooking the ocean with a "Taste of the Islands" luau buffet and a Polynesian revue featuring the songs and dances of the Tuamotu Islands, Samoa, Tahiti, Fiji, and Hawaii. Tickets for the dinner and show are $75 adults and $45 children ages 4 to 11; tickets for the show only are $50 for adults and $30 for children ages 4 to 11. To book, call ⓒ **808/293-6000.**

On the Windward side, by Makapuu Point, **Sea Life Park** has the **"Sea Life Park Luau,"** every night except Tuesday and Saturday, which offers a dolphin show, Hawaiian food, and Polynesian revue. Prices are $80 for adults and $48 for kids ages 4 to 12 years old. For information, call ⓒ **808/259-7933.**

---

replaced by a relaxing, romantic atmosphere where you can have a conversation without shouting while enjoying the incredible cuisine. The menu changes daily, but you can generally count on Roy's classics: blackened ahi, hibachi salmon, and Szechuan baby back ribs. Some great additions include Asian pesto steamed fresh fish, cilantro-dusted papio (jack trevally), kiawe-grilled filet mignon, and roasted chicken with huli-huli sauce. Ko Olina also is open for lunch, and after that you can get appetizers at the bar. It's worth the drive for this incredible dining experience.

92–1220 Aliinui Dr., Kapolei, in the Ko Olina Resort. ⓒ 808/676-7697. www.roysrestaurant.com. Reservations recommended. Lunch $8.50–$16; appetizers at the bar $8.50–$14; dinner entrees $23–$35. AE, DC, DISC, MC, V. Daily 11am–9:30pm (appetizers only 2–5:30pm).

5 Beaches

THE WAIKIKI COAST

ALA MOANA BEACH PARK 🐟🐟

Gold-sand Ala Moana ("by the sea"), on sunny Mamala Bay, stretches for more than a mile along Honolulu's coast between downtown and Waikiki. This 76-acre midtown beach park, with spreading lawns shaded by banyans and palms, is one of the island's most popular playgrounds. It has a man-made beach, created in the 1930s by filling a coral reef with Waianae Coast sand, as well as its own lagoon, yacht harbor, tennis courts, music pavilion, bathhouses, picnic tables, and enough wide-open green spaces to accommodate four million visitors a year. The water is calm almost year-round, protected by black lava rocks set offshore. There's a large parking lot as well as metered street parking.

WAIKIKI BEACH 🐟🐟🐟

No beach anywhere is so widely known or so universally sought after as this narrow, 1½-mile-long crescent of imported sand (from Molokai) at the foot of a string of high-rise hotels. Home to the world's longest-running beach party, Waikiki attracts nearly five million visitors a year from every corner of the planet. First-timers are always amazed to discover how small Waikiki Beach actually is, but there's always a place for them under the tropical sun here.

Waikiki is actually a string of beaches that extends between **Sans Souci State Recreational Area,** near Diamond Head to the east, and **Duke Kahanamoku Beach,** in front of the Hilton Hawaiian Village, to the west. Great stretches along Waikiki include **Kuhio Beach,** next to the Moana Surfrider, which provides the quickest access to the Waikiki shoreline; the stretch in front of the Royal Hawaiian Hotel known as **Grey's Beach,** which is canted so it catches the rays perfectly; and **Sans Souci,** the small, popular beach in front of the New Otani Kaimana Beach Hotel that's locally known as "Dig Me" Beach because of all the gorgeous bods who strut their stuff here.

Waikiki is fabulous for swimming, board surfing and bodysurfing, outrigger canoeing, diving, sailing, snorkeling, and pole fishing. Every imaginable type of marine equipment is available for rent here. Facilities include showers, lifeguards, restrooms, grills, picnic tables, and pavilions at the **Queen's Surf** end of the beach (at Kapiolani Park, between the zoo and the aquarium). The best place to park is at Kapiolani Park, near Sans Souci.

EAST OAHU
HANAUMA BAY ⊀⊀

Oahu's most popular snorkeling spot is this volcanic crater with a broken sea wall; its small, curved, 2,000-foot gold-sand beach is packed elbow-to-elbow with people year-round. The bay's shallow shoreline water and abundant marine life are the main attractions, but this good-looking beach is also popular for sunbathing and people-watching. Serious divers shoot "the slot" (a passage through the reef) to get to Witch's Brew, a turbulent cove, and then brave strong currents in 70-foot depths at the bay mouth to see coral gardens, turtles, and even sharks. (*Divers:* Beware of the Molokai Express, a strong current.) You can snorkel in the safe, shallow (10-ft.) inner bay, which, along with the beach, is almost always crowded. Because Hanauma Bay is a conservation district, you cannot touch or take any marine life here. Feeding the fish is also prohibited.

A $13-million Marine Education Center features exhibits and a 7-minute video orienting visitors on this Marine Life Sanctuary. The 10,000-square-foot center includes a training room, gift shop, public restrooms, snack bar, and staging area for the motorized tram, which, for a fee (50¢ for one ride, or $2 for an all-day pass), will take you down the steep road to the beach. Facilities include parking, restrooms, a pavilion, a grass volleyball court, lifeguards, barbecues, picnic tables, and food concessions. Alcohol is prohibited in the park; there is no smoking past the visitor center. Expect to pay $1 per vehicle to park and a $5 per-person entrance fee (free for children 12 and under). If you're driving, take Kalanianaole Highway to Koko Head Regional Park. Avoid the crowds by going early, about 8am, on a weekday morning; once the parking lot's full, you're out of luck. Alternatively, take TheBus to escape the parking problem: The Hanauma Bay Shuttle runs from Waikiki to Hanauma Bay every half-hour from 8:45am to 1pm; you can catch it at the Ala Moana Hotel, the Ilikai Hotel, or any city bus stop. It returns every hour from noon to 4pm. Hanauma Bay is closed on Tuesday so the fish can have a day off.

Beaches & Outdoor Activities on Oahu

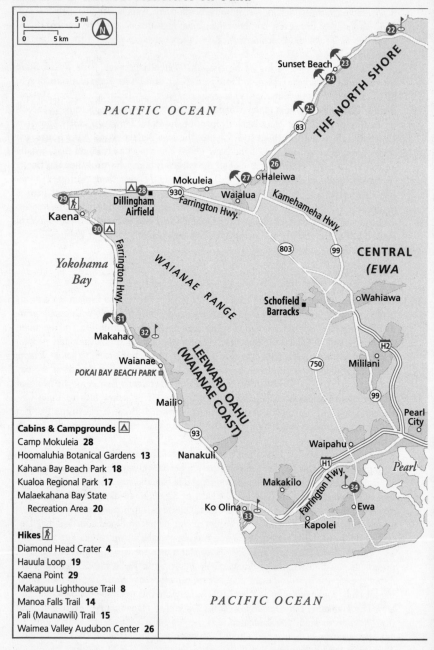

PACIFIC OCEAN

THE NORTH SHORE

Sunset Beach

Mokuleia
Dillingham Airfield
Kaena
Yokohama Bay
Farrington Hwy.
WAIANAE RANGE

Waialua
Haleiwa
Farrington Hwy.
Kamehameha Hwy.

CENTRAL (EWA

Wahiawa

Schofield Barracks

Makaha
Waianae
POKAI BAY BEACH PARK
Maili

LEEWARD OAHU (WAIANAE COAST)

Mililani

Pearl City

Cabins & Campgrounds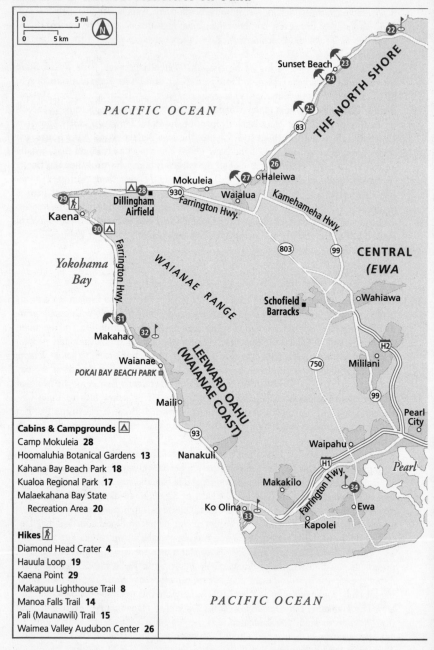
Camp Mokuleia **28**
Hoomaluhia Botanical Gardens **13**
Kahana Bay Beach Park **18**
Kualoa Regional Park **17**
Malaekahana Bay State
Recreation Area **20**

Hikes
Diamond Head Crater **4**
Hauula Loop **19**
Kaena Point **29**
Makapuu Lighthouse Trail **8**
Manoa Falls Trail **14**
Pali (Maunawili) Trail **15**
Waimea Valley Audubon Center **26**

Nanakuli
Waipahu
Makakilo
Ko Olina
Ewa
Kapolei
Farrington Hwy.

Pearl

PACIFIC OCEAN

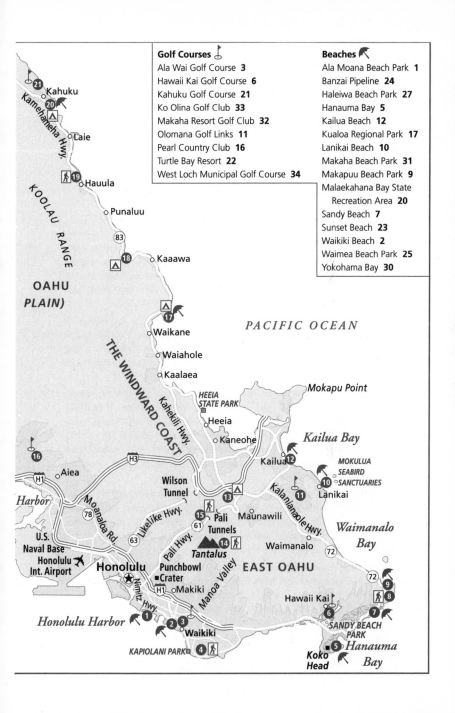

Golf Courses
Ala Wai Golf Course **3**
Hawaii Kai Golf Course **6**
Kahuku Golf Course **21**
Ko Olina Golf Club **33**
Makaha Resort Golf Club **32**
Olomana Golf Links **11**
Pearl Country Club **16**
Turtle Bay Resort **22**
West Loch Municipal Golf Course **34**

Beaches
Ala Moana Beach Park **1**
Banzai Pipeline **24**
Haleiwa Beach Park **27**
Hanauma Bay **5**
Kailua Beach **12**
Kualoa Regional Park **17**
Lanikai Beach **10**
Makaha Beach Park **31**
Makapuu Beach Park **9**
Malaekahana Bay State
   Recreation Area **20**
Sandy Beach **7**
Sunset Beach **23**
Waikiki Beach **2**
Waimea Beach Park **25**
Yokohama Bay **30**

Frommer's Favorite Oahu Experiences

Getting a Tan on Waikiki Beach. The best spot for catching the rays on the world-famous beach is in front of the big pink Royal Hawaiian Hotel—the beach here is set at the perfect angle for sunning. It's also a great spot for people-watching. Get here early; by midday, it's towel-to-towel out there.

Exploring Oahu's Rainforests. In the misty sunbeams, colorful birds flit among giant ferns and hanging vines, while towering tropical trees form a thick canopy that shelters all below in cool shadows. This emerald world is a true Eden. For the full experience, try Manoa Falls Trail, a walk of about a mile that ends at a freshwater pool and waterfall.

Snorkeling the Glistening Waters of Hanauma Bay. This underwater park, once a volcanic crater, is teeming with a rainbow of tropical fish. Bordered by a 2,000-foot gold-sand beach, the bay's shallow water (10 ft. in places) is perfect for neophyte snorkelers. Arrive early to beat the crowds—and don't forget that the bay is closed on Tuesday. **Aloha Dive Shop,** Koko Marina Shopping Center (℘ 808/395-5922), can set you up with fins, mask, and snorkel for just $7 a day.

Hiking to the Top of Diamond Head Crater. Almost everyone can make this easy hike to the top of Hawaii's most famous landmark. The 1½-mile round-trip goes up to the top of the 750-foot volcanic cone, where you have a 360-degree view of Oahu. Allow an hour for the trip up and back, bring a buck for the entry fee, and don't forget your camera.

Heading to Waimea Bay when the Surf's up. From November to March, monstrous waves—some 50 feet tall—roll into Waimea. When they break on the shore, the ground actually shakes and everyone on the beach is covered with salt spray mist. The best surfers in the world paddle out to challenge these freight trains. It's amazing to see how small they appear in the lip of the giant waves. This is an experience you'll never forget—and the show won't cost you a dime.

Hearing the Sounds of History. The Royal Hawaiian Band (℘ 808/527-5666; www.royalhawaiianband.com), which has been performing since being commissioned by King Kamehameha III in 1836, plays every Friday at noon in front of the Iolani Palace and every Sunday, 2pm, in the bandstand in Kapiolani Park. Both events are free.

Watching the Ancient Hawaiian Sport of Canoe Paddling. On weekday evenings and weekend days from February to September, hundreds of paddlers gather at Ala Wai Canal and practice taking traditional Hawaiian canoes out to sea. Find a comfortable spot at Ala Wai Park, next to the canal, and watch the canoe paddlers re-create this centuries-old sport.

Finding a Bargain at the Aloha Flea Market. Just 50¢ will get you into this all-day show at the Aloha Stadium parking lot, where more than 1,000 vendors sell everything from junk to jewels. Go early for the best deals. Open Wednesday, Saturday, and Sunday from 6am to 3pm.

Attending a Hawaiian-Language Church Service. Built in 1842, Kawaiahao Church, 957 Punchbowl St. (near King St.), is the Westminster Abbey of Hawaii; the vestibule is lined with portraits of the Hawaiian monarchy, many of whom were coronated in this very building. The coral church is a perfect setting to experience an all-Hawaiian service, complete with Hawaiian song. Hawaiian-language services are held every Sunday, 9am, and admission is free (donations appreciated).

Visiting the Lei Sellers in Chinatown. There's a host of cultural sights and experiences to be had in Honolulu's Chinatown. Wander through this several-square-block area with its jumble of exotic shops offering herbs, Chinese groceries, and acupuncture services. Be sure to check out the lei sellers on Maunakea Street (near N. Hotel St.), where Hawaii's finest leis go for as little as $2.50.

Experiencing a Turning Point in America's History: The Bombing of Pearl Harbor. Standing on the deck of the USS *Arizona* Memorial at Pearl Harbor, with the ship underneath, is an unforgettable experience. On that fateful day—December 7, 1941—the 608-foot *Arizona* sank in just 9 minutes, killing 1,177 of the men onboard, after being bombed during the Japanese air raid that sent the United States to war. Go early; you'll wait 2 to 3 hours if you visit at midday. You must wear closed-toed shoes; no sandals allowed.

Watching the Sun Sink into the Pacific from a Hill Named after a Sweet Potato. Actually, it's more romantic than it sounds. Puu Ualakaa State Park, at the end of Round Hill Drive, translates into "rolling sweet potato hill." This majestic view of the sunset is not to be missed.

Ordering a Shave Ice in a Tropical Flavor You Can Hardly Pronounce. In Haleiwa stop at Matsumoto Shave Ice, 66–087 Kamehameha Hwy., for a snow cone with an exotic flavor poured over the top, such as the local favorite, the fruity *li hing mui,* or try one with sweet Japanese adzuki beans hidden inside. This taste of tropical paradise goes for just $1.

Listening to the Soothing Sounds of Hawaiian Music. Sit under the huge banyan tree at the Moana Surfrider's Banyan Veranda in Waikiki, order a cocktail, and sway to live Hawaiian music any night of the week. Another quintessential sunset oasis is the Halekulani's House Without a Key, a sophisticated oceanfront lounge with wonderful hula and steel-guitar music, a great view of Diamond Head, and the best mai tais on the island.

SANDY BEACH 𝒢

Sandy Beach is one of the best bodysurfing beaches on Oahu; it's also one of the most dangerous. It's better to just stand and watch the daredevils literally risk their necks at this 1,200-foot-long gold-sand beach that's pounded by wild waves and haunted by a dangerous shore break and strong backwash. Weak swimmers and children should definitely stay out of the water here; Sandy Beach's heroic lifeguards make more rescues in a year than those at any other beach. Visitors, easily fooled by experienced bodysurfers who make wave riding look easy, often fall victim to the bone-crunching waves. Lifeguards post flags to alert beachgoers to the day's surf: Green means safe, yellow means caution, and red indicates very dangerous water conditions.

Facilities include restrooms and parking. Go weekdays to avoid the crowds and weekends to catch the bodysurfers in action. From Waikiki, drive east on the H-1, which becomes Kalanianaole Highway; proceed past Hawaii Kai, up the hill to Hanauma Bay, past the Halona Blow Hole, and along the coast. The next big gold beach on the right is Sandy Beach. TheBus no. 22 will also bring you here.

MAKAPUU BEACH PARK 𝒢

Makapuu Beach, the most famous bodysurfing beach in Hawaii, is a beautiful 1,000-foot-long gold-sand beach cupped in the stark black Koolau cliffs on Oahu's easternmost point. Even if you never venture into the water, it's worth a visit just to enjoy the great natural beauty of this classic Hawaiian beach. You've probably already seen it in countless TV shows, from *Hawaii Five-O* to *Magnum, P.I.*

In summer the ocean here is as gentle as a Jacuzzi, and swimming and diving are perfect; come winter, however, Makapuu is a hit with expert bodysurfers, who come for big, pounding waves that are too dangerous for regular swimmers. Small boards—3 feet or less with no skeg (bottom fin)—are permitted; no regular board surfing allowed.

Facilities include restrooms, lifeguards, barbecue grills, picnic tables, and parking. To get here, follow Kalanianaole Highway toward Waimanalo, or take TheBus no. 57 or 58.

THE WINDWARD COAST
LANIKAI BEACH 𝒢𝒢

One of Hawaii's best spots for swimming, gold-sand Lanikai's crystal-clear lagoon is like a giant saltwater swimming pool that you're lucky enough to be able to share with the resident tropical fish and sea turtles. Too gorgeous to be real, this is one of Hawaii's postcard-perfect beaches: It's a mile long and thin in places, but the sand's as soft as talcum powder. Prevailing onshore trade winds make this an excellent place for sailing and windsurfing. Kayakers often paddle out to the two tiny offshore Mokulua islands, which are seabird sanctuaries. Because Lanikai is in a residential neighborhood, it's less crowded than other Oahu beaches, the perfect place to enjoy a quiet day. Sun worshipers should arrive in the morning, though, as the Koolau Range blocks the afternoon rays.

There are no facilities here, just off-street parking. From Waikiki, take the H-1 to the Pali Highway (Hwy. 61) through the Nuuanu Pali Tunnel to Kailua, where the Pali Highway becomes Kailua Road as it proceeds through town. At Kalaheo Avenue, turn right and follow the coast about 2 miles to Kailua Beach Park; just past it, turn left at the T intersection and drive uphill on Aalapapa Drive, a one-way street that loops back as Mokulua Drive. Park on Mokulua Drive and walk down any of the eight public-access lanes to the shore. Or take TheBus no. 56 or 57 (Kailua) and then transfer to the shuttle bus.

Impressions

The boldness and address with which we saw them perform these difficult
and dangerous maneuvers was altogether astonishing.
                    —Capt. James Cook's observations of Hawaiian surfers

KAILUA BEACH ✦✦✦

Windward Oahu's premier beach is a 2-mile-long, wide golden strand with dunes, palm trees, panoramic views, and offshore islets that are home to seabirds. The swimming is excellent, and the azure waters are usually decorated with bright sails; this is Oahu's premier windsurfing beach as well. It's also a favorite spot to sail catamarans, bodysurf the gentle waves, or paddle a kayak. Water conditions are quite safe, especially at the mouth of Kaelepulu Stream, where toddlers play in the freshwater shallows at the middle of the beach park. The water's usually about 78°F (26°C), the views are spectacular, and the setting, at the foot of the sheer, green Koolaus, is idyllic. Best of all, the crowds haven't found it yet.

The 35-acre beach park is intersected by a freshwater stream and watched over by lifeguards. Facilities include picnic tables, barbecues, restrooms, a volleyball court, a public boat ramp, free parking, and an open-air cafe. Kailua's new bike path weaves through the park, and windsurfer and kayak rentals are available as well. To get here, take Pali Highway (Hwy. 61) to Kailua, drive through town, turn right on Kalaheo Avenue, and go a mile until you see the beach on your left. Or take TheBus no. 56 or 57 into Kailua, and then the no. 70 shuttle.

KUALOA REGIONAL PARK ✦✦

This 150-acre coco palm–fringed peninsula is the biggest beach park on the windward side and one of Hawaii's most scenic. It's located on Kaneohe Bay's north shore, at the foot of the spiky Koolau Ridge. The park has a broad, grassy lawn and a long, narrow white-sand beach ideal for swimming, walking, beachcombing, kite-flying, or just enjoying the natural beauty of this once-sacred Hawaiian shore, listed on the National Register of Historic Places. The waters are shallow and safe for swimming year-round (lifeguards are on duty). Offshore is Mokolii, the picturesque islet otherwise known as Chinaman's Hat. At low tide, you can swim or wade out to the island, which has a small sandy beach and is a bird preserve—so don't spook the red-footed boobies.

The park is located on Kamehameha Highway (Hwy. 83) in Kualoa; you can get here via TheBus no. 55.

THE NORTH SHORE

MALAEKAHANA BAY STATE RECREATION AREA ✦✦

This white-sand crescent, almost a mile long, lives up to just about everyone's image of the perfect Hawaii beach. It's excellent for swimming. On a weekday you may be the only one here; but should some net fisherman—or kindred soul—intrude upon your delicious privacy, you can swim out to Goat Island (or wade across at low tide), a sanctuary for seabirds and turtles (so don't chase 'em, brah.) Facilities include restrooms, barbecue grills, picnic tables, outdoor showers, and parking.

To get here, take Kamehameha Highway (Hwy. 83) 2 miles north of the Polynesian Cultural Center; as you enter the main gate, you'll come upon the wooded beach park. Or you can take TheBus no. 52.

WAIMEA BEACH PARK 🌟🌟

This deep, sandy bowl has gentle summer waves that are excellent for swimming, snorkeling, and bodysurfing. To one side of the bay is a huge rock that local kids like to climb up and dive from. In this placid scene, the only clues of what's to come in winter are those evacuation whistles on poles beside the road. But what a difference a season makes: Winter waves pound the narrow bay, sometimes rising to 50 feet high. When the surf's really up, very strong currents and shore breaks sweep the bay—and it seems like everyone on Oahu drives out to Waimea to get a look at the monster waves and those who ride them. Weekends are great for watching the surfers; to avoid the crowds, go on weekdays.

Facilities include lifeguards, restrooms, showers, parking, and nearby restaurants and shops in Haleiwa town. The beach is located on Kamehameha Highway (Hwy. 83); from Waikiki, you can take TheBus no. 52.

LEEWARD OAHU/THE WAIANAE COAST

MAKAHA BEACH PARK 🌟🌟

When surf's up here, it's spectacular: Monstrous waves pound the beach. This is the original home of Hawaii's big-wave surfing championship; surfers today know it as the home of Buffalo's Big Board Surf Classic, where surfers ride the waves on 10-foot-long wooden boards in the old Hawaiian style of surfing. Nearly a mile long, this half-moon, gold-sand beach is tucked between 231-foot Lahilahi Point, which locals call Black Rock, and Kepuhi Point, a toe of the Waianae mountain range. Summer is the best time to hit this beach—the waves are small, the sand abundant, and the water safe for swimming. Children hug the shore on the north side of the beach, near the lifeguard stand, while surfers dodge the rocks and divers seek an offshore channel full of big fish. *A caveat:* This is a "local" beach; you are welcome, of course, but you can expect "stink eye" (mild approbation) if you are not respectful of the beach and the local residents who use the facility all the time.

Facilities include restrooms, lifeguards, and parking. To get here, take the H-1 freeway to the end of the line, where it becomes Farrington Highway (Hwy. 93), and follow it to the beach; or you can take TheBus no. 51.

YOKOHAMA BAY 🌟

Where Farrington Highway (Hwy. 93) ends, the wilderness of Kaena Point State Park begins. It's a remote 853-acre coastline park of empty beaches, sand dunes, cliffs, and deep-blue water. This is the last sandy stretch of shore on the northwest coast of Oahu. Sometimes it's known as Keawalua Beach or Puau Beach, but everybody here calls it Yokohama, after the Japanese immigrants who came from that port city to work the cane fields and fished along this shoreline. When the surf's calm—mainly in summer—this is a good area for snorkeling, diving, swimming, shore fishing, and picnicking. When surf's up, board surfers and bodysurfers are out in droves; don't go in the water then unless you're an expert. There are no lifeguards or facilities, except at the park entrance, where there's a restroom and lifeguard stand. No bus service.

6 Watersports

For general advice on the activities listed below, see "Special-Interest Trips," in chapter 2.

If you want to rent beach toys (snorkeling equipment, boogie boards, surfboards, kayaks, and more), check out the following rental shops: **Snorkel Bob's,** on the way to Hanauma Bay at 700 Kapahulu Ave. (at Date St.), Honolulu (© **808/735-7944;**

www.snorkelbob.com); and **Aloha Beach Service,** in the Moana Surfrider Hotel, 2365 Kalakaua Ave. (② **808/922-3111,** ext. 2341), in Waikiki. On Oahu's windward side, try **Kailua Sailboards & Kayaks,** 130 Kailua Rd., a block from the Kailua Beach Park (② **808/262-2555;** www.kailuasailboards.com). On the North Shore, get equipment from **Surf-N-Sea,** 62–595 Kamehameha Hwy., Haleiwa (② **808/637-9887;** www.surfnsea.com).

BOATING

A funny thing happens to people when they come to Hawaii: Maybe it's the salt air, the warm tropical nights, or the blue Hawaiian moonlight, but otherwise-rational people who have never set foot on a boat in their life suddenly want to go out to sea. You can opt for a "booze cruise," jammed with loud, rum-soaked strangers, or you can sail on one of these special yachts, all of which will take you out **whale-watching** in season (roughly Jan–Apr). For fishing charters, see "Sportfishing" below.

Captain Bob's Adventure Cruises ⚐   See the majestic Windward Coast the way it should be seen—from a boat. Captain Bob will take you on a 4-hour lazy-day sail of Kaneohe Bay aboard his 42-foot catamaran, which skims across the almost always calm water above the shallow coral reef, lands at the disappearing sandbar Ahu o Laka, and takes you past two small islands to snorkel spots full of tropical fish and sometimes turtles. The color of the water alone is worth the price. This is an all-day affair, but, hey, getting out on the water is the reason you came to Hawaii, right? A shuttle will pick you up at your Waikiki hotel between 9 and 9:30am and bring you back at about 4pm—it's a lot quicker than taking TheBus.

Kaneohe Bay. ② 808/942-5077. $79 adults, $60 children 3–14, free for under 3. Rates include all-you-can-eat barbecue lunch and transportation from Waikiki hotels. No cruises Sun and holidays. Bus: 55 or 56.

Navatek I ⚐⚐   You've never been on a boat, you don't want to be on a boat, but here you are being dragged aboard one. Why are you boarding this weird-looking vessel? It guarantees that you'll be "seasick-free," that's why. The 140-foot-long *Navatek I* isn't even a boat; it's actually a SWATH (Small Waterplane Area Twin Hull) vessel. That means the ship's superstructure—the part you ride on—rests on twin torpedo-like hulls that cut through the water so you don't bob like a cork and spill your mai tai. It's the smoothest ride on Mamala Bay. In fact, *Navatek I* is the only dinner cruise ship to receive U.S. Coast Guard certification to travel beyond Diamond Head.

   Sunset dinner cruises leave Pier 6 (across from the Hawaii Maritime Museum) nightly. If you have your heart set on seeing the city lights, take the Royal Sunset Dinner Cruise, which runs from 5:15 to 7:15pm. The best deal is the **lunch cruise,** with full buffet lunch and a great view of Oahu offshore. During the **whale season** (roughly Jan–Apr), you get whales, to boot. The lunch cruise lasts from 11:30am to 2pm. Both cruises include live Hawaiian music.

Aloha Tower Marketplace, Pier 6, c/o Hawaiian Cruises Ltd. ② 808/973-1311. www.atlantisadventures.com/oahu. cfm. Dinner cruises $80–$112 adults, $74–$95 children 2–12; lunch cruises $63 adults, $56 children 2–11. Validated parking before 4:30pm $3, after 4:30pm flat parking fee of $2. Bus: 8, 19, 20, 55, 56, or 57.

Wild Side Tours   Picture this: floating in the calm waters off the Waianae coast, where your 42-foot sailing catamaran has just dropped you off. Below, in the reef, are turtles, and suddenly in the distance, you see spinner dolphins. Happens every day on the 4-hour tours operated by the Cullins family, who have swum in these waters for decades. In the winter, you may spot humpback whales on the morning cruise, which also includes continental breakfast, snorkel gear, instruction, and a floatation device. They also have an afternoon/sunset whale-watching sail in the winter for $75 per person, and a sunset/full-moon/star-gazing sail for $95.

Waianae Boat Harbor, 87-1286 Farrington Hwy., Waianae, HI 96792. ℂ 808/306-7273. www.sailhawaii.com. Morning sail/snorkel $95 (ages 6 and up, not recommended for younger children). MC, V. Check in 7:30am, tour 8am–noon. Bus: 19 or 20 to Ala Moana Shopping Center, then the 40 or 40A.

BODY BOARDING (BOOGIE BOARDING) & BODYSURFING

Good places to learn to body-board are in the small waves of **Waikiki Beach** and **Kailua Beach** (both reviewed under "Beaches," earlier in this chapter), and **Bellows Field Beach Park,** off Kalanianaole Highway (Hwy. 72) in Waimanalo, which is open to the public on weekends (noon Fri to midnight Sun and holidays). To get here, turn toward the ocean on Hughs Road, and then right on Tinker Road, which takes you right to the park.

See the introduction to this section for a list of rental shops where you can get a boogie board.

OCEAN KAYAKING

For a wonderful adventure, rent a kayak, arrive at Lanikai Beach just as the sun is appearing, and paddle across the emerald lagoon to the pyramid-shaped islands called Mokulua—it's an experience you won't forget. Kayak equipment rental starts at $10 an hour for a single kayak and $16 an hour for a double kayak. In Waikiki try **Prime Time Sports,** Fort DeRussy Beach (℃ **808/949-8952**); on the windward side, check out **Kailua Sailboards & Kayaks,** 130 Kailua Rd., a block from Kailua Beach Park (℃ **808/262-2555;** www.kailuasailboards.com), where single kayaks rent for $39 for a half-day and double kayaks rent for $49 for a half-day. On the North Shore, **Surf-N-Sea,** 62–595 Kamehameha Hwy., Haleiwa (℃ **808/637-9887;** fax 808/637-3008; www.surfnsea.com), rents kayaks at $7 for the first hour, $5 after that.

First-timers should go to Kailua Sailboards & Kayaks (see above). The company offers a guided tour ($69) with the novice in mind in a safe, protected environment. Lunch, all equipment, and transportation from Waikiki hotels are included. Kayak lessons and self-guided trips are also available.

SCUBA DIVING

Oahu is a wonderful place to scuba-dive, especially for those interested in wreck diving. One of the more famous wrecks in Hawaii is the *Mahi,* a 185-foot former minesweeper easily accessible just south of Waianae. Abundant marine life makes this a great place to shoot photos—schools of lemon butterfly fish and taape (blue-lined snapper) are so comfortable with divers and photographers that they practically pose. Eagle rays, green sea turtles, manta rays, and white-tipped sharks occasionally cruise by as well, and eels peer out from the wreck.

For non–wreck diving, one of the best dive spots in summer is **Kahuna Canyon.** In Hawaiian, *kahuna* means priest, wise man, or sorcerer; this massive amphitheater, located near Mokuleia, is a perfect example of something a sorcerer might conjure up. Walls rising from the ocean floor create the illusion of an underwater Grand Canyon. Inside the amphitheater, crabs, octopi, slippers, and spiny lobsters abound (be aware that taking them in summer is illegal), and giant trevally, parrotfish, and unicorn fish congregate as well. Outside the amphitheater, you're likely to see an occasional shark in the distance.

Because Oahu's greatest dives are offshore, your best bet is to book a two-tank dive from a dive boat. Hawaii's oldest and largest outfitter is **Aaron's Dive Shop,** 307 Hahani St., Kailua (© **808/262-2333;** www.hawaii-scuba.com), which offers boat and beach dive excursions off the coast. The boat dives cost from $115 per person ($99 if you book on their website), including two tanks and transportation from the Kailua shop. The beach dive off the North Shore in summer or the Waianae Coast in winter is the same price as a boat dive, including all gear and transportation, so Aaron's recommends the boat dive.

In Waikiki, **Dive Oahu,** 1085 Ala Moana (© **808/922-3483;** www.diveoahu.com), offers everything from shipwreck dives in Waikiki to World War II Corsair plane dives in Hawaii Kai for just $129 for a two-tank boat dive (friends or family members can tag along for just $35 each to snorkel). Captain Brian, who has a couple of decades of diving, loves to help beginners feel comfortable scuba diving, as well as showing experienced scuba divers what the Waikiki coast has to offer. On the North Shore, **Surf-N-Sea,** 62–595 Kamehameha Hwy., Haleiwa (© **808/637-9887;** fax 808/637-3008; www.surfnsea.com), has dive tours from the shore (starting at $75 for one tank), from a boat ($110 for two tanks), and at night ($100 for one tank). Surf-N-Sea also rents equipment and can point you to the best dive sites in the area.

Another great resource for diving on your own is the University of Hawaii Sea Grant's *Dive Hawaii Guide,* which describes 44 dive sites at the various Hawaiian

---

Moments **Experiencing Jaws: Up Close & Personal**

You're 4 miles out from land, surrounded by open ocean. Suddenly from out of the blue depths a shape emerges: the sleek, pale shadow of a 6-foot-long gray reef shark, followed quickly by a couple of 10-foot-long Galapagos sharks. Within moments, you are surrounded by sharks on all sides. Do you panic? No, you paid $120 to be in the midst of these jaws of the deep. And, of course, you have a 6×6×10-foot aluminum shark cage separating you from all those teeth.

It happens every day at **North Shore Shark Adventures** (© **808/256-2769;** www.hawaiisharkadventures.com), the dream of Capt. Joe Pavsek, who decided after some 30 years of surfing and diving to share the experience of seeing a shark with visitors. To make sure that the predators of the deep will show up for the viewing, Captain Pavsek heaves "chum," a not very appetizing concoction of fish trimmings and entrails, over the side of his 26-foot boat, *Kailolo.* After a few minutes, the sharks (generally gray reef, Galapagos, and sandbars, ranging 5–15 ft.) show up—sometimes just a few, sometimes a couple dozen. Depending on the sea conditions and the weather, snorkelers can stay in the cage as long as they wish, with the sharks just inches away. The shark cage, connected to the boat with wire line, holds up to four snorkelers (it's comfortable with two but pretty snug at full capacity). You can stay on the boat and view the sharks from a more respectable distance for just $60. The more adventurous, down in the cage with just thin aluminum separating them from the sharks, are sure to create a memory they won't forget.

islands, including Oahu. Send $2 to UH/SGES, Attn: Dive Guide, 2525 Correa Rd., HIG 237, Honolulu, HI 96822.

SNORKELING

Some of the best snorkeling in Oahu is at **Hanauma Bay** 🍂🍂. It's crowded—sometimes it seems there are more people than fish—but Hanauma has clear, warm, protected waters and an abundance of friendly reef fish, including Moorish idols, scores of butterfly fish, damselfish, and wrasses. Hanauma Bay has two reefs, an inner and an outer—the first for novices, the other for experts. The inner reef is calm and shallow (less than 10 ft.); in some places, you can just wade and put your face in the water. Go early: It's packed by 10am (closed Tues). For details, see "Beaches," earlier in this chapter.

Braver snorkelers may want to head to **Shark's Cove,** on the North Shore just off Kamehameha Highway, between Haleiwa and Pupukea. Sounds risky, I know, but I've never seen or heard of any sharks in this cove, and in summer this big, lava-edged pool is one of Oahu's best snorkel spots. Waves splash over the natural lava grotto and cascade like waterfalls into the pool full of tropical fish. To the right of the cove are deep-sea caves to explore.

The uninitiated might prefer a lesson and a snorkel tour. **Surf-N-Sea,** 62–595 Kamehameha Hwy., Haleiwa (© **808/637-9887**), has 2-hour tours, with equipment, starting at $45.

SPORTFISHING

Kewalo Basin, located between the Honolulu International Airport and Waikiki, is the main location for charter fishing boats on Oahu. From Waikiki, take Kalakaua Ewa (west) beyond Ala Moana Center; Kewalo Basin is on the left, across from Ward Centre. Look for charter boats all in a row in their slips; when the fish are biting, the captains display the catch of the day in the afternoon. You can also take TheBus no. 19 or 20 (Airport).

The best sportfishing booking desk in the state is **Sportfish Hawaii** 🍂 (© **877/ 388-1376** or 808/396-2607; www.sportfishhawaii.com), which books boats on all the islands. These fishing vessels have been inspected and must meet rigorous criteria to guarantee that you will have a great time. Prices range from $750 to $932 for a full-day exclusive charter (you plus five friends get the entire boat to yourself); $621 to $717 for a half-day exclusive; or from $187 for a full-day share charter (you share the boat with five other people).

SUBMARINE DIVES

Here's your chance to play Jules Verne and experience the underwater world from the comfort of a submarine, which will take you on an adventure below the surface in high-tech comfort. The entire trip is narrated as you watch tropical fish and sunken ships just outside the sub; if swimming's not your thing, this is a great way to see Hawaii's spectacular sea life. Shuttle boats to the sub leave from Hilton Hawaiian Village Pier. The cost is $90 to $113 for adults, $80 to $98 for kids 12 and under (children must be at least 36 in. tall). *Budget tip:* Book online for discount rates of $84 adults and $78 kids. Call **Atlantis Submarines** 🍂 (© **800/548-6262** or 808/973-9811; www.atlantissubmarines.org) to reserve. *Warning:* Skip this if you suffer from claustrophobia.

SURFING

In summer, when the water's warm and there's a soft breeze in the air, the south swell comes up. It's surf season in Waikiki, the best place on Oahu to learn how to surf. For lessons, go early to **Aloha Beach Service,** next to the Moana Surfrider, 2365 Kalakaua Ave., Waikiki (② **808/922-3111**). The beach boys offer surfing lessons for $30 an hour; board rentals are $10 for the first hour and $5 for every hour after that. You must know how to swim.

On the North Shore, there's no excuse not to learn to surf in Hawaii: Hans Hedemann, a champion surfer for some 34 years, has opened the **Hans Hedemann Surf School** at the Turtle Bay Resort (② **808/924-7778;** www.hhsurf.com). His classes range from one-on-one private sessions to group lessons (four students to one teacher) and begin at $50 an hour. If you aren't staying at the Turtle Bay, he will provide complimentary hotel transportation from Waikiki hotels to one of his locations on the North Shore, in Waikiki, or at the Kahala Hotel & Resort.

Surfboards are also available for rent on the North Shore at **Surf-N-Sea,** 62–595 Kamehameha Hwy., Haleiwa (② **808/637-9887;** www.surfnsea.com), for $5 to $7 an hour. They also offer lessons for $75 for 2 hours. For the best surf shops, where you can soak in the culture as well as pick up gear, also see "Shopping A to Z," later in this chapter.

On the windward side, call **Kimo's Surf Hut,** 151 Hekili St., across from Don Quijote, in Kailua (② **808/262-1644**). Kimo and his wife, Ruth, couldn't be more friendly and helpful. In addition to surfboards ($30 a day) for rent, Kimo has his own personal collection of vintage surfboards, lovingly displayed on the walls of his shop. If you have the time, Kimo will gladly tell you the pedigree and history of each board. Although Kimo doesn't offer formal surfing lessons, he'd be happy to give you pointers.

More experienced surfers should drop in on any surf shop around Oahu, or call the **Surf News Network Surfline** (② **808/596-SURF**) to get the latest surf conditions. **The Cliffs,** at the base of Diamond Head, is a good spot for advanced surfers; 4- to 6-foot waves churn here, allowing high-performance surfing.

If you're in Hawaii in winter and want to see the serious surfers catch the really big waves, bring your binoculars and grab a front-row seat on the beach near **Kalalua Point.** To get there from Waikiki, take the H-1 toward the North Shore, veering off at H-2, which becomes Kamehameha Highway (Hwy. 83). Keep going to the funky surf town of Haleiwa and Waimea Bay; the big waves will be on your left, just past Pupukea Beach Park.

WINDSURFING AND KITESURFING

Windward Oahu's **Kailua Beach** is the home of champion and pioneer windsurfer Robbie Naish; it's also the best place to learn to windsurf. The oldest and most established windsurfing business in Hawaii is **Naish Hawaii/Naish Windsurfing Hawaii,** 155-A Hamakua Dr., Kailua (② **800/767-6068** or 808/262-6068; www.naish.com). The company offers everything: sales, rentals, instruction, repair, and free advice on where to go when the wind and waves are happening. Private lessons start at $75 for one, $100 for two for a 90-minute lesson; beginner equipment rental is $25 for 2 hours and $35 for a full day. Kitesurfing lessons are also available ($125 for 1½ hr.). Kite board rentals are $25 a day (boards only). **Kailua Sailboards & Kayaks,** 130 Kailua Rd., a block from the Kailua Beach Park (② **808/262-2555;** www.kailuasailboards.com), offers 3-hour small-group lessons windsurfing ($89 per person, including all gear, plus lunch) and rentals of kitesurfing boards, windsurfing equipment, surfboards, snorkel gear, and ocean kayaks.

Windsurfer wannabes on the North Shore can contact **Surf-N-Sea,** 62–595 Kamehameha Hwy., Haleiwa (② **808/637-9887;** www.surfnsea.com), which offers equipment rental ($12 for the first hour, then $8 an hour), as well as private lessons (beginning at $75 for 2 hr.).

7 Nature Hikes

People are often surprised to discover that the great outdoors is less than an hour away from downtown Honolulu. The island's 33 major hiking trails traverse razor-thin ridgebacks, deep waterfall valleys, and more. The best source of hiking information on Oahu is the state's **Na Ala Hele (Trails to Go On) Program** (© **808/973-9782;** www.hawaiitrails.org). The website has everything you need: detailed maps and descriptions of 40 trails in the state's Na Ala Hele, a hiking safety brochure, updates on the trails, hyperlinks to weather information, health warnings on the trails, info on native plants, how to volunteer for trail upkeep, and more.

The **Hawaiian Trail and Mountain Club,** P.O. Box 2238, Honolulu, HI 96804 (http://htmclub.org), offers regular hikes on Oahu. Bring a couple of bucks for the donation, your own lunch, and drinking water, and meet up with the club members at the scheduled location to join them on a hike. In addition, the club meets for Saturday and Sunday hikes at the Iolani Palace, King Street, between Richard and Punchbowl streets in downtown Honolulu. Generally they meet at 8am; look for a group of people dressed in hiking clothes and boots at the left rear of the Palace.

Other organizations that offer regularly scheduled hikes are the **Sierra Club,** P.O. Box 2577, Honolulu, HI 96803 (www.hi.sierraclub.org); the **Nature Conservancy,** 1116 Smith St., Suite 201, Honolulu, HI 96817 (© **808/537-4508,** ext. 220; www. nature.org/wherewework/northamerica/states/hawaii); and the **Hawaii Nature Center,** 2131 Makiki Heights Dr. (© **808/955-0100;** www.hawaiinaturecenter.org).

HONOLULU-AREA HIKES
DIAMOND HEAD CRATER ✹✹✹

This is a moderate but steep walk to the summit of Hawaii's most famous landmark. Kids love to look out from the top of the 760-foot volcanic cone, where they have 360-degree views of Oahu up the leeward coast from Waikiki. The 1.5-mile round-trip takes about 1½ hours, and the entry fee is $1.

Diamond Head was created by a volcanic explosion about half a million years ago. The Hawaiians called the crater *Leahi* (meaning the brow of the ahi, or tuna, referring to the shape of the crater). Diamond Head was considered a sacred spot; King Kamehameha offered human sacrifices at a *heiau* (temple) on the western slope. It wasn't until the 19th century that Mount Leahi got its current name: A group of sailors found what they thought were diamonds in the crater; it turned out they were just worthless calcite crystals, but the name stuck.

Before you begin your journey to the top of the crater, put on some decent shoes (rubber-soled tennies are fine) and pack a flashlight (you'll walk through several dark tunnels, which are not always lighted), binoculars (for better viewing at the top), water (very important), a hat to protect you from the sun, and a camera. You might want to put all your gear in a pack to leave your hands free for the climb. If you don't have a flashlight or your hotel can't lend you one, you can buy a small one for a few dollars as part of a Diamond Head climbers' "kit" at the gift shop at the **New Otani Kaimana Beach Hotel,** on the Diamond Head end of Kalakaua Avenue, just past the Waikiki Aquarium and across from Kapiolani Park.

Go early, preferably just after the 6:30am opening, before the midday sun starts beating down. The hike to the summit of Diamond Head starts at Monsarrat and 18th avenues on the crater's inland (or mauka) side. To get here, take TheBus no. 58 from the Ala Moana Shopping Center or drive to the intersection of Diamond Head

Road and 18th Avenue. Follow the road through the tunnel (which is closed 6pm–6am) and park in the lot. The trail head starts in the parking lot and proceeds along a paved walkway (with handrails) as it climbs up the slope. You'll pass old World War I and II pillboxes, gun emplacements, and tunnels built as part of the Pacific defense network. Several steps take you up to the top observation post on Point Leahi. The views are incredible.

If you want to go with a guide, the Clean Air Team leads a guided hike to the top of Diamond Head every Saturday. The group gathers at 9am, near the front entrance to the Honolulu Zoo (look for the rainbow windsock). Hikers should bring a flashlight and a $5 fee. Each person will be given a bag and asked to help keep the trail clean by picking up litter. For more information, call © **808/948-3299.**

MANOA FALLS TRAIL 🐸🐸

This easy .75-mile (one-way) hike is terrific for families; it takes less than an hour to reach idyllic Manoa Falls. The trail head, marked by a footbridge, is at the end of Manoa Road, past Lyon Arboretum. The staff at the arboretum prefers that hikers do not park in their lot, so the best place to park is in the residential area below Paradise Park; you can also get to the arboretum via TheBus no. 5. The often-muddy trail follows Waihi Stream and meanders through the forest reserve past guavas, mountain apples, and wild ginger. The forest is moist and humid and is inhabited by giant bloodthirsty mosquitoes, so bring repellent. If it has rained recently, stay on the trail and step carefully, as it can be very slippery (and it's a long way down if you slide off the side). The trail sometimes closes due to unsafe conditions; before you venture out, call © **808/587-0300** to check if it's open.

EAST OAHU HIKES
MAKAPUU LIGHTHOUSE TRAIL 🐸

You've seen this famous old lighthouse on episodes of *Magnum, P.I.* and *Hawaii Five-O.* No longer manned by the Coast Guard (it's fully automated now), the lighthouse sits at the end of a precipitous cliff trail on an airy perch over the Windward Coast, Manana (Rabbit) Island, and the azure Pacific. It's about a 45-minute, mile-long hike from Kalanianaole Highway (Hwy. 72), along a paved road that begins across from Hawaii Kai Executive Golf Course and winds around the 646-foot-high sea bluff to the lighthouse lookout.

To get to the trail head from Waikiki, take Kalanianaole Highway (Hwy. 72) past Hanauma Bay and Sandy Beach to Makapuu Head, the southeastern tip of the island; you can also take TheBus no. 57 or 58. Look for a sign that says NO VEHICLES ALLOWED on a gate to the right, a few hundred yards past the entrance to the golf course. The trail isn't marked, but it's fairly obvious: Just follow the abandoned road that leads gradually uphill to a trail that wraps around Makapuu Point. It's a little precarious, but anyone in reasonably good shape can handle it.

Blowhole alert: When the south swell is running, usually in summer, there are a couple of blowholes on the south side of Makapuu Head that put the famous Halona blowhole to shame.

WINDWARD OAHU HIKES
HAUULA LOOP 🐸

For one of the best views of the coast and the ocean, follow the Hauula Loop Trail on the windward side of the island. It's an easy 2.5-mile loop on a well-maintained path that passes through a whispering ironwood forest and a grove of tall Norfolk pines. The trip takes about 3 hours and gains some 600 feet in elevation.

To get to the trail, take TheBus no. 55 or follow Highway 83 to Hauula Beach Park. Turn toward the mountains on Hauula Homestead Road; when it forks to the left at Maakua Road, park on the side of the road. Walk along Maakua Road to the wide, grassy trail that begins the hike into the mountains. The climb is fairly steep for about 900 feet but turns into easier-on-the-calves switchbacks as you go up the ridge. Look down as you climb: You'll spot wildflowers and mushrooms among the matted needles. The trail continues up, crossing Waipilopilo Gulch, where you'll see several forms of native plant life. Eventually, you reach the top of the ridge, where the views are spectacular.

Camping is permitted along the trail, but it's difficult to find a place to pitch a tent on the steep slopes and in the dense forest growth. There are a few places along the ridge, however, that are wide enough for a tent. Contact the **Division of Forestry and Wildlife,** 1151 Punchbowl St., Honolulu, HI 96813 (© **808/587-0166**), www.dofaw.net, for information on camping permits.

PALI (MAUNAWILI) TRAIL ௸

For a million-dollar view of the Windward Coast, take this 11-mile (one-way) foothill trail. The trail head is about 6 miles from downtown Honolulu, on the windward side of the Nuuanu Pali Tunnel, at the scenic lookout just beyond the hairpin turn of the Pali Highway (Hwy. 61). Just as you begin the turn, look for the scenic overlook sign, slow down, and pull off the highway into the parking lot (sorry, no bus service available).

The mostly flat, well-marked, easy-to-moderate trail goes through the forest on the lower slopes of the 3,000-foot Koolau Mountain range and ends up in the backyard of the coastal Hawaiian village of Waimanalo. Go halfway to get the view and then return to your car, or have someone meet you in 'Nalo.

NORTH SHORE HIKES
WAIMEA VALLEY AUDUBON CENTER

For nearly 3 decades, 1,875-acre Waimea Falls Park has lured visitors with activities from cliff diving and hula performances to kayaking and ATV tours. In 2003 the City and County of Honolulu awarded the lease to the valley to the National Audubon Society. The Audubon Society has renamed the park **Waimea Valley Audubon Center** (59–864 Kamehameha Hwy., Haleiwa; © **808/638-9199;** www.audubon.org) and is focusing on protecting and interpreting the valley's cultural, botanical, and ecological resources. Activities have been eliminated; instead, the emphasis is on education and preservation of the park's 6,000 species of plants and trees. The public is invited to hike the trails and spend a day in this quiet oasis. Admission prices have been lowered to $8 for adults, $5 for children 4 to 12, and $5 for seniors (and parking now is free).

TO LAND'S END: A LEEWARD OAHU HIKE
KAENA POINT ௸

At the very western tip of Oahu lie the dry, barren lands of Kaena Point State Park, 853 acres of jagged sea cliffs, deep gulches, sand dunes, endangered plant life, and a remote, wild, wind- and surf-battered coastline. *Kaena* means "red-hot" or "glowing" in Hawaiian; the name refers to the brilliant sunsets visible from the point.

Kaena is steeped in numerous legends. A popular one concerns the demigod Maui: Maui had a famous hook that he used to raise islands from the sea. He decided that he wanted to bring the islands of Oahu and Kauai closer together, so one day he threw his hook across the Kauai Channel and snagged Kauai (which is actually visible from Kaena Point on clear days). Using all his might, Maui was able to pull loose a huge boulder, which fell into the waters very close to the present lighthouse at Kaena. The rock is still called *Pohaku o Kauai* (the rock from Kauai). Like Black Rock in Kaanapali on Maui, Kaena is thought of as the point on Oahu from which souls depart.

To hike out to the departing place, take the clearly marked trail from the parking lot of Kaena Point State Park. The moderate, 5-mile, round-trip hike to the point will take a couple of hours. The trail along the cliff passes tide pools abundant in marine life and rugged protrusions of lava reaching out to the turbulent sea; seabirds circle overhead. Stay on the trail. Do *not* go off the trail; there are buried birds eggs you might step on. There are no sandy beaches, and the water is nearly always turbulent. In winter, when a big north swell is running, the waves at Kaena are the biggest in the state, averaging heights of 30 to 40 feet. Even when the water appears calm, offshore currents are powerful, so don't plan to swim. Go early in the morning to see the schools of porpoises that frequent the area just offshore.

To get to the trail head from Honolulu or Waikiki, take the H-1 west to its end; continue on Highway 93 past Makaha and follow Highway 930 to the end of the road. There's no bus service.

8 Camping & Wilderness Cabins

If you plan to camp, you must bring your own gear or buy it here—no one on Oahu rents gear. If you are bringing your own equipment, remember that you can't transport fuel (even in a canister) on the plane. Also, if your equipment runs on butane, don't bother bringing it—butane is very difficult to find here.

The best places to camp on Oahu are listed below. TheBus's Circle Island route can get you to or near all these sites, but remember: On TheBus, you're allowed only one bag, which has to fit under the seat. If you have more gear, you're going to have to drive or take a cab.

WINDWARD OAHU
HOOMALUHIA BOTANICAL GARDENS &
This little-known windward campground outside Kaneohe is a real treasure. It's hard to believe that you're just half an hour from downtown Honolulu.

The name *Hoomaluhia,* or "peace and tranquillity," accurately describes this 400-acre botanical garden at the foot of the jagged Koolaus. In this lush, tropical setting, gardens are devoted to plants specific to tropical America, native Hawaii, Polynesia, India, Sri Lanka, and Africa. A 32-acre lake sits in the middle of the scenic park (no swimming or boating allowed), and there are numerous hiking trails. The visitor center offers free guided walks Saturday at 10am and Sunday at 1pm (call the number below to register).

Facilities for this tent-camp area include restrooms, cold showers, dish-washing stations, picnic tables, and water. A public phone is available at the visitor center. Shopping and gas are available in Kaneohe, 2 miles away. Permits are free, but stays are limited to 3 nights (Fri–Sun only); the office is closed on Sunday. The gate is locked at 4pm and doesn't open again until 9am, so you're locked in for the night. To get a permit, contact **Parks Permit Section,** Honolulu Municipal Building, 650 South

King St., Honolulu, HI 96713 (© **808/523-4525;** www.co.honolulu.hi.us/parks/
permits.htm), or any Satellite City Halls (www.honolulu.gov/csd/satellite). For inquiries
and reservations, contact **Hoomaluhia Botanical Gardens,** 45–680 Luluku Rd. (at
Kamehameha Hwy.), Kaneohe, HI 96744 (© **808/233-7323;** www.co.honolulu.hi.
us/parks/hbg/hmbg.htm). From Waikiki, take H-1 to the Pali Highway (Hwy. 61);
turn left on Kamehameha Highway (Hwy. 83); at the fourth light, turn left on Luluku
Road. TheBus nos. 55 and 56 stop nearby on Kamehameha Highway; from here, you
have to walk 2 miles to the visitor center.

KAHANA BAY BEACH PARK ★★

Lying under Tahiti-like cliffs, with a beautiful gold-sand crescent beach framed by
pine-needle casuarina trees, Kahana Bay Beach Park is a place of serene beauty. You
can swim, bodysurf, fish, hike, and picnic, or just sit and listen to the trade winds
whistle through the beach pines. Only tent and vehicle camping are allowed at this
ocean-side oasis. Facilities include restrooms, picnic tables, drinking water, public
phones, and a boat-launching ramp. *Note:* The restrooms are located at the north end
of the beach, far away from the camping area, and there are no showers.

There's a $5 fee for camping, and you must get a permit. Permits are limited to 5
nights (Fri–Wed); contact the **Department of Land and Natural Resources,** State
Parks Division, P.O. Box 621, Honolulu, HI 96809 (© **808/587-0300;** www.state.hi.
us/dlnr/dsp/oahu.html). Kahana Bay Beach Park is located in the 52–222 block of
Kamehameha Highway (Hwy. 83) in Kahana. From Waikiki, take the H-1 west to the
Likelike Highway (Hwy. 63). Continue north on the Likelike, through the Wilson
Tunnel, turning left on Highway 83; Kahana Bay is 13 miles down the road on the
right. You can also get here via TheBus no. 55.

KUALOA REGIONAL PARK ★★

This park has a spectacular setting on a peninsula on Kaneohe Bay. The gold-sand
beach is excellent for snorkeling, and fishing can be rewarding as well (see the
"Beaches" section, earlier in this chapter). There are two campgrounds: Campground
A—located in a wooded area with a sandy beach and palm, ironwood, kamani, and
monkeypod trees—is mainly used for groups. It does have a few sites for families,
except during the summer (June–Aug), when the Department of Parks and Recreation
conducts a children's camping program here. Campground B is on the main beach; it
has fewer shade trees but a great view of Mokolii Island. Facilities at both sites include
restrooms, showers, picnic tables, drinking fountains, and a public phone. Campground A also has sinks for dish washing, a volleyball court, and a kitchen building.
Gas and groceries are available in Kaaawa, 2½ miles away. The gate hours at Kualoa
Regional Park are 7am to 8pm.

Permits are free but limited to 5 days (no camping Wed–Thurs). Contact the
Honolulu Department of Parks and Recreation, 650 S. King St., Honolulu, HI
96713 (© **808/523-4525;** www.co.honolulu.hi.us/parks), for information and permits. To get to the park, take the Likelike Highway (Hwy. 63); after the Wilson Tunnel, get in the right lane and turn off on Kahakili Highway (Hwy. 83). Or take
TheBus no. 55.

THE NORTH SHORE
CAMP MOKULEIA ★

The centerpiece of this 9-acre campground is a quiet, isolated beach on Oahu's North
Shore, 4 miles from Kaena Point. Camping is available on the beach or in a grassy,

wooded area. Activities include swimming, surfing, shore fishing, and beachcombing. This place makes a great getaway. Facilities include tent camping, cabins, and lodge accommodations. The tent-camping site has portable chemical toilets, a water spigot, and outdoor showers; there are no picnic tables or barbecue grills, so come prepared. The cabins sleep up to 22 people in bunk beds. The cabins are $160 to $170 per night for the 14-bed cabin and $240 to $250 per night for the 22-bed cabin. Rooms at the lodge are $65 to $70 for a shared bathroom and $75 to $80 for a private bathroom. A studio cottage rents for $85 to $90 and sleeps two; a three-bedroom beach house goes for $200 to $210 and sleeps six. Tent camping is $10 per person, per night. Many groups use the camp, but there's a real sense of privacy. Reservations are required; contact **Camp Mokuleia,** 68–729 Farrington Hwy., Waialua, HI 96791 (✆ **808/637-6241;** www.campmokuleia.org).

Camp Mokuleia is located on Farrington Highway, west of Haleiwa. From Waikiki, take the H-1 to the H-2 exit; stay on H-2 until the end. Where the road forks, bear left to Waialua on Highway 803, which turns into Highway 930 to Kaena Point. Look for the green fence on the right, where a small sign at the driveway reads CAMP MOKULEIA, EPISCOPAL CHURCH OF HAWAII.

MALAEKAHANA BAY STATE RECREATION AREA ★★

This is one of the most beautiful beach-camping areas in the state, with a mile-long, gold-sand beach on Oahu's Windward Coast (see "Beaches," earlier in this chapter, for details). There are two areas for tent camping. Facilities include picnic tables, restrooms, showers, sinks, drinking water, and a phone. For your safety, the park gate is closed between 6:45pm and 7am; vehicles cannot enter or exit during those hours. Groceries and gas are available in Laie and Kahuku, each less than a mile away.

Permits are $5 and limited to 5 nights (Fri–Wed); they can be obtained at any state park office, including the **Department of Land and Natural Resources,** State Parks Division, P.O. Box 621, Honolulu, HI 96809 (✆ **808/587-0300;** www.state.hi.us/dlnr/dsp/oahu.html). The recreation area is located on Kamehameha Highway (Hwy. 83) between Laie and Kahuku. Take the H-2 to Highway 99 to Highway 83 (both roads are called Kamehameha Hwy.); continue on Highway 83 just past Kahuku. You can also get here via TheBus no. 55.

9 Golf & Other Outdoor Activities

GOLF

Oahu has nearly three dozen golf courses, ranging from bare-bones municipal courses to exclusive country-club courses with membership fees running to six figures a year. Below are the best of a great bunch.

As you play Oahu's courses, you'll come to know that the windward courses play much differently than the leeward courses. On the windward side, the prevailing winds blow from the ocean to shore, and the grain direction of the greens tends to run the same way—from the ocean to the mountains. Leeward golf courses have the opposite tendency: The winds usually blow from the mountains to the ocean, with the grain direction of the greens corresponding.

Tips on beating the crowds and saving money: Oahu's golf courses tend to be crowded, so I suggest that you go midweek if you can. Also, most island courses have twilight rates that offer substantial discounts if you're willing to tee off in the afternoon; these are included in the listings below, where applicable.

Tips **Insider Tip**

For last-minute and discount tee times, call **Stand-by Golf** (© 888/645-BOOK; www.stand-bygolf.com), which offers discounted tee times for same-day or next-day golfing. Call between 7am and 11pm for a guaranteed tee time with up to a 50% discount off greens fees.

Transportation note: TheBus does not allow golf-club bags onboard, so if you want to use TheBus to get to a course, you're going to have to rent clubs there.

WAIKIKI

Ala Wai Municipal Golf Course   The *Guinness Book of World Records* lists this as the busiest golf course in the world; some 500 rounds a day are played on this 18-hole municipal course within walking distance of Waikiki's hotels. For years I've held off recommending this par-70, 6,020-yard course because it was so busy (tee times taken by local retirees), but a recent scandal, involving telephone company employees tapping into the tee time reservation system to get tee times has shaken up the old system, and visitors now have a better chance of playing here. It still is a challenge to get a tee time, and the computerized tee reservations system for all of Oahu's municipal courses will allow you to book only 3 days in advance, but keep trying. Ala Wai has a flat layout bordered by the Ala Wai Canal on one side and the Manoa-Palolo Stream on the other. It's less windy than most Oahu courses, but pay attention to the 372-yard, par-4 1st hole, which demands a straight and long shot to the very tiny green. If you miss, you can make it up on the 478-yard, par-5, 10th hole—the green is reachable in two, so with a two-putt, a birdie is within reach.

404 Kapahulu Ave., Waikiki. © **808/733-7387** (golf course), or 808/296-2000 tee time reservations. www.co. honolulu.hi.us/des/golf/alawai.htm. Greens fees $42; twilight rate $21. From Waikiki, turn left on Kapahulu Ave.; the course is on the mauka side of Ala Wai Canal. Bus: 19, 20, or 22.

EAST OAHU

Hawaii Kai Golf Course   This is actually two golf courses in one. The par-72, 6,222-yard **Hawaii Kai Championship Golf Course** is moderately challenging, with scenic vistas. The course is forgiving to high-handicap golfers, although it does have a few surprises. The par-55 **Hawaii Kai Executive Golf Course** is fun for beginners and those just getting back in the game after a few years. The course has lots of hills and valleys, with no water hazards and only a few sand traps. Lockers are available.

8902 Kalanianaole Hwy., Honolulu. © **808/395-2358.** www.hawaiikaigolf.com. Greens fees: Champion Course $100 ($90 early-bird Internet special—book 7 days in advance) Mon–Fri, $110 ($100 when booked on Internet) Sat–Sun, twilight rates $70; Executive Course $37 Mon–Fri, $42 Sat–Sun. Take H-1 east past Hawaii Kai; it's immediately past Sandy Beach on the left. Bus: 58.

THE WINDWARD COAST

Olomana Golf Links   Low-handicap golfers may not find this gorgeous course difficult, but the striking views of the craggy Koolau mountain ridge alone are worth the fees. The par-72, 6,326-yard course is popular with locals and visitors alike. The course starts off a bit hilly on the front 9 but flattens out by the back 9, where there are some tricky water hazards. The 1st hole, a 384-yard par-4 that tees downhill and approaches uphill, is definitely a warm-up. The next hole is a 160-yard par-3 that starts from an elevated tee to an elevated green over a severely banked V-shaped gully.

Shoot long here—it's longer than you think, and short shots tend to roll all the way back down the fairway to the base of the gully. This course is very, very green; the rain gods bless it regularly with brief passing showers. You can spot the regular players here—they all carry umbrellas, wait patiently for the squalls to pass, and then resume play. Reservations are a must. Facilities include a driving range, practice greens, club rental, a pro shop, and a restaurant.

41–1801 Kalanianaole Hwy., Waimanalo. (✆) **808/259-7926**. www.olomanagolflinks.com. Greens fees $80; twilight fees $26 weekdays, $28 weekends. Take H-1 to the Pali Hwy. (Hwy. 61); turn right on Kalanianaole Hwy.; after 5 miles, it will be on the left. Bus: 57.

THE NORTH SHORE

Kahuku Golf Course *(Finds)*   This 9-hole budget golf course is a bit funky. There are no club rentals, no clubhouse, and no facilities other than a few pull carts that disappear with the first handful of golfers. But a round at this scenic ocean-side course amid the tranquillity of the North Shore is quite an experience nonetheless. Duffers will love the ease of this recreational course, and weight watchers will be happy to walk the gently sloping greens. Don't forget to bring your camera for the views (especially at holes 3, 4, 7, and 8, which are right on the ocean). No reservations are taken; tee times are first come, first served, and with plenty of retirees happy to sit and wait, the competition is fierce for early tee times. Bring your own clubs and call ahead to check the weather. The cost for this experience? Ten bucks!

56–501 Kamehameha Hwy., Kahuku. (✆) **808/293-5842**. Greens fees $10 for 9 holes. Take H-1 west to H-2; follow H-2 through Wahiawa to Kamehameha Hwy. (Hwy. 99, then Hwy. 83); follow it to Kahuku.

Turtle Bay Resort *(★)*   This North Shore resort is home to two of Hawaii's top golf courses. The 18-hole **Arnold Palmer Course** (formerly the Links at Kuilima) was designed by Arnold Palmer and Ed Seay. Now that the casuarina (ironwood) trees have matured, it's not as windy as it used to be, but this is still a challenging course. The front 9, with rolling terrain, only a few trees, and lots of wind, play like a British Isles course. The back 9 have narrower, tree-lined fairways and water. The course circles Punahoolapa Marsh, a protected wetland for endangered Hawaiian waterfowl.

Another option is the par-71, 6,200-yard **George Fazio**–designed course—the only Fazio course in Hawaii. Larry Keil, pro at Turtle Bay, says that people like the Fazio course because it's a more forgiving course, without all the water hazards and bunkers of the Palmer course. The 6th hole has two greens, so you can play the hole as a par-3 or a par-4. The toughest hole has to be the par-3, 176-yard 2nd hole, where you tee off across a lake with a mean crosswind. The most scenic hole is the 7th, where the ocean is on your left; in winter, you might get lucky and see some whales. Facilities include a pro shop, driving range, putting and chipping green, and snack bar. Weekdays are best for tee times.

57–049 Kamehameha Hwy., Kahuku. (✆) **808/293-8574** or 808/293-9094. www.turtlebayresort.com. Greens fees: Palmer Course $175 (Turtle Bay guests pay $145); Fazio Course $155 (guests pay $115). Take H-1 west past Pearl City; when the freeway splits, take H-2 and follow the signs to Haleiwa; at Haleiwa, take Hwy. 83 to Turtle Bay Resort. Bus: 52 or 55.

LEEWARD OAHU

Ko Olina Golf Club *(★★★)*   *Golf Digest* named this 6,867-yard, par-72 course one of "America's Top 75 Resort Courses" in 1992. The Ted Robinson–designed course has rolling fairways and elevated tee and water features. The signature hole—the 12th, a par-3—has an elevated tee that sits on a rock garden with a cascading waterfall. At the

18th hole, you'll see and hear water all around you—seven pools begin on the right side of the fairway and slope down to a lake. A waterfall is on your left off the elevated green. You'll have no choice but to play the left and approach the green over the water. Book in advance; this course is crowded all the time. Facilities include a driving range, locker rooms, a Jacuzzi, steam rooms, and a restaurant and bar. Lessons are available.

92–1220 Aliinui Dr., Kapolei. ✆ **808/676-5309.** www.koolinagolf.com. Greens fees $170 ($150 for Ihilani Resort guests); twilight rates (after 1pm in winter and 2:30pm in summer) $110 ($90 for guests). Men and woman are asked to wear a collared shirt. Take H-1 west until it becomes Hwy. 93 (Farrington Hwy.); turn off at the Ko Olina exit; take the exit road (Aliinui Dr.) into Ko Olina Resort; turn left into the clubhouse. No bus service.

Makaha Resort Golf Club 🏌🏌 This challenging course sits some 45 miles west of Honolulu, in Makaha Valley. Designed by William Bell, the par-72, 7,091-yard course meanders toward the ocean before turning and heading into the valley. Sheer volcanic walls tower 1,500 feet above the course, which is surrounded by swaying palm trees and neon-bright bougainvillea; an occasional peacock will even strut across the fairways. The beauty here could make it difficult to keep your mind on the game if it weren't for the course's many challenges: eight water hazards, 107 bunkers, and frequent brisk winds. This course is packed on weekends, so it's best to try weekdays. Facilities include a pro shop, bag storage, and a snack shop.

84–627 Makaha Valley Rd., Waianae. ✆ **808/695-7111** or 808/695-5239. www.makahavalleyycc.com. Greens fees $80 (check the website for specials). Take H-1 west until it turns into Hwy. 93, which winds through the coastal towns of Nanakuli, Waianae, and Makaha. Turn right on Makaha Valley Rd. and follow it to the fork; the course is on the left. Bus: 51.

West Loch Municipal Golf Course *(Value)* This par-72, 6,615-yard course located just 30 minutes from Waikiki, in Ewa Beach, offers golfers a challenge at bargain rates. The difficulties on this unusual municipal course, designed by Robin Nelson and Rodney Wright, are water (lots of hazards), constant trade winds, and narrow fairways. To help you out, the course features a "water" driving range (with a lake) to practice your drives. In addition to the driving range, West Loch has practice greens, a pro shop, and a restaurant.

91–1126 Okupe St., Ewa Beach. ✆ **808/675-6076.** Greens fees $50; $25 after 4pm. Book a week in advance. Take H-1 west to the Hwy. 76 exit; stay in the left lane and turn left at West Loch Estates, just opposite St. Francis Medical Center. To park, take 2 immediate right turns. Bus: 50.

CENTRAL OAHU

Pearl Country Club Looking for a challenge? You'll find one at this popular public course, located just above Pearl City in Aiea. Sure, the 6,230-yard, par-72 looks harmless enough, and the views of Pearl Harbor and the USS *Arizona* Memorial are gorgeous, but around the 5th hole, you'll start to see what you're in for. That par-5, a blind 472-yard hole, doglegs seriously to the left (with a small margin of error between the tee and the steep out-of-bounds hillside on the entire left side of the fairway). A water hazard and a forest await your next two shots. Suddenly, this nice public course becomes not so nice. Oahu residents can't get enough of it, so don't even try to get a tee time on weekends. Stick to weekdays—Mondays are usually the best bet. Facilities include a driving range, practice greens, club rental, a pro shop, and a restaurant.

98–535 Kaonohi St., Aiea. ✆ **808/487-3802.** www.pearlcc.com. Greens fees $75 Mon–Fri; $85 Sat–Sun; after 4pm 9 holes are $25. Book at least a week in advance. Take H-1 past Pearl Harbor to the Hwy. 78 (Moanalua Fwy.), Exit 13A; stay in the left lane where Hwy. 78 becomes Hwy. 99 (Kamehameha Hwy.); turn right on Kaonohi St., entry on the right. Bus: 32 (stops at Pearlridge Shopping Center at Kaonohi and Moanalua sts.; you'll have to walk about ½ mile uphill from here).

BICYCLING

Bicycling is a great way to see Oahu. Most streets here have bike lanes. For information on bikeways and maps, contact the **Honolulu City and County Bicycle Coordinator** (© 808/527-5044) or go to www.state.hi.us/dot/highways/bike/oahu.

If you're in Waikiki, you can rent a bike for as little as $10 for a half-day and $20 for 24 hours at **Big Kuhuna Rentals,** 407 Seaside Ave. (© **808/924-2736;** www.bigkahunarentals.com/sntmainbikes.htm). On the North Shore, for a full-suspension mountain bike, try **Raging Isle,** 66–250 Kamehameha Hwy., Haleiwa (© **808/637-7707;** www.ragingisle.com), which rents bikes for $40 for 24 hours.

For a bike-and-hike adventure, call **Bike Hawaii** (© **877/MTV-RIDE** or 808/734-4214; www.bikehawaii.com). It has a variety of group tours, like its Mountain Biking Ka'a'awa Valley at Kualoa. This guided mountain bike tour consists of dirt roads and single track meandering through the 1,000-acre Kaaawa Valley on Oahu's northeast shore, with stops at a reconstructed Hawaiian hale (house) and kalo lo'i (taro terrace) for some cultural narrative and an old military bunker that has been converted into a movie museum for films shot within here (*Jurassic Park, Godzilla, Mighty Joe Young, Windtalkers,* and more). The 6-mile trip, which takes 2 to 3 hours of riding, includes van transportation from your hotel, continental-style breakfast, bike, helmet, snacks, water bottle, and guide—it's $96 for adults and $72 for children 13 and under.

If you'd like to join in on some club rides, contact the **Hawaii Bicycle League** (© **808/735-5756;** www.hbl.org), which offers rides every weekend, as well as several annual events, plus great maps for bike outings. The league can also provide a schedule of upcoming rides, races, and outings.

HORSEBACK RIDING

You can gallop on the beach at the **Turtle Bay Resort,** 57–091 Kamehameha Hwy., Kahuku (© **808/293-8811;** www.turtlebayresort.com; bus no. 52 or 55), where 45-minute rides along sandy beaches with spectacular ocean views and through a forest of ironwood trees cost $50 for adults and $30 for children 7 to 12 (they must be at least 4 ft., 4 in. tall). Romantic evening rides are $80 per person. Advanced riders can sign up for a 60-minute trot-and-canter ride along Kawela Bay ($100).

TENNIS

Oahu has 181 free public tennis courts. To get a complete list of all facilities or information on upcoming tournaments, send a self-addressed, stamped envelope to the **Department of Parks and Recreation,** Tennis Unit, 650 S. King St., Honolulu, HI 96813. In Waikiki, if you want to check on the Diamond Head courts, 3908 Paki Ave., across from the Kapiolani Park, call © **808/971-7150.** The courts are available on a first-come, first-served basis; playing time is limited to 45 minutes if others are waiting.

If you're staying in Waikiki, try the **Wikiki Tennis Court and Lessons,** at the Aqua Marina Hotel, 1700 Ala Moana Blvd. (© **808/551-9438;** bus no. 19 or 20), which has one lighted court (open 9am–9pm daily), with court rental for $10 per person per hour, racket rental for $5 person per day, private lessons for $60 per hour and semi-private lessons for $75 per hour for two or more.

If you're on the North Shore, head to the **Turtle Bay Resort,** 57–091 Kamehameha Hwy., Kahuku (© **808/293-8811;** www.turtlebayresort.com; bus no. 52 or 55), which has 10 courts, four of which are lit for night play. You must reserve the night courts in advance; they're very popular. Court time is $10 per person (complimentary for guests); equipment rental and lessons are also available.

10 Orientation Tours

GUIDED SIGHTSEEING TOURS

If your time is limited, you might want to consider a guided tour. These tours are informative, can give you a good overview of Honolulu or Oahu in a limited amount of time, and are surprisingly entertaining.

E Noa Tours, 1141 Waimanu St., Suite 105, Honolulu (© **800/824-8804** or 808/ 591-2561; www.enoa.com), offers a range of tours, from island loops to explorations of historic Honolulu. These narrated tours are on air-conditioned, 27-passenger minibuses. The Royal Circle Island tour ($61 for adults, $50 for children 6–11, $44 for children under 6) stops at Diamond Head Crater, Hanauma Bay, Byodo-In Temple, Sunset Beach, Waimea Valley (admission included), and various beach sites along the way. Other tours go to Pearl Harbor/USS *Arizona* Memorial and the Polynesian Cultural Center.

Waikiki Trolley Tours ⊛, 1141 Waimanu St., Suite 105, Honolulu (© **800/824-8804** or 808/596-2199; www.waikikitrolley.com), offers three fun tours of sightseeing, entertainment, dining, and shopping. These tours are a great way to get the lay of the land. You can get on and off the trolley as needed (trolleys come along every 2–20 min.). An all-day pass (8:30am–11:35pm) is $25 for adults, $18 for seniors, and $12 for children (4–11); a 4-day pass is $45 for adults, $27 for seniors, and $18 for children. For the same price, you can experience the 2-hour narrated Ocean Coastline tour of the southeast side of Oahu, an easy way to see the stunning views.

Polynesian Adventure Tours, 1049 Kikowaena Place, Honolulu (© **808/833-3000;** www.polyad.com), offers several excursions. The all-day island tour starts at $58 for adults, $33 for children under 12; the half-day scenic shore and rainforest tour

---

Moments **A Bird's-Eye View**

To understand why Oahu was the island of kings, you need to see it from the air. **Island Seaplane Service** ⊛⊛ (© **808/836-6273;** www.islandseaplane. com) operates flights departing from a floating dock in the protected waters of Keehi Lagoon in either a six-passenger DeHavilland Beaver or a four-passenger Cessna 206. There's nothing quite like feeling the slap of the waves as the plane skims across the water and then effortlessly lifts into the air.

The half-hour tour ($119) gives you aerial views of Waikiki Beach, Diamond Head Crater, Kahala's luxury estates, and the sparkling waters of Hanauma and Kaneohe bays; the 1-hour tour ($220) continues on to Chinaman's Hat, the Polynesian Cultural Center, and the rolling surf of the North Shore. The flight returns across the island, over Hawaii's historic wartime sites: Schofield Barracks and the Pearl Harbor memorials.

Capt. Pat Magie, company president and chief pilot, has logged more than 32,000 hours of flight time without an accident (26,000 hr. in seaplanes in Alaska, Canada, the Arctic, and the Caribbean). Any day now, he'll break the world record for seaplane hours.

Moments **Rolling through Waikiki on a Segway**

One of my favorite ways to tour Waikiki is on a Segway Personal Transporter, the silly-looking two-wheeled machine that looks like an old push lawn mower (big wheels and a long handle). But amazingly enough, within just a few minutes, you get the hang of this contraption, which works through a series of high-tech stabilization mechanisms that read the motion of your body to turn or go forward or backward, and is propelled forward through twisting the hand throttle. It's lots of fun—think back to the first time you rode your bicycle, and the incredible freedom of zipping through space without walking. **Glide Ride Tours and Rentals,** located in the Hawaii Tapa Tower of the Hilton Hawaiian Village Beach Resort & Spa, 2005 Kalia Rd. (*©* **808/941-3151;** www.segwayofhawaii.com), will instruct you on the Segway (they make sure that you are fully competent before you leave their training area) and then take you on a series of tours ranging from a 40-min. introduction tour for $49 per person to a 2½-hour tour of Waikiki, Kapiolani Park, and Diamond Head for $125 per person.

is $25 for adults, $18 for children 3 to 11; the half-day USS *Arizona* Memorial Excursion is $26 for adults and $20 for children 3 to 11.

For those who'd prefer a self-guided driving tour, **TourTalk-Oahu** (*©* **877/585-7499;** www.tourtalkhawaii.com) offers a complete package of 2½-hour narrated compact discs (or cassettes), driving instructions, and a 72-page booklet containing color maps, photos, cultural and historical information, and Hawaii facts for $25.

WAIKIKI & HONOLULU WALKING TOURS

The **Hawaii Geographic Society** (*©* **808/538-3952**) presents numerous interesting and unusual tours, such as "A Temple Tour," which includes Chinese, Japanese, Christian, and Jewish houses of worship; an archaeology tour in and around downtown Honolulu; and others. Each is guided by an expert from the Hawaii Geographic Society and must have a minimum of three people; the cost is $10 per person. The society's brochure, *Historic Downtown Honolulu Walking Tour,* is a fascinating self-guided tour of the 200-year-old city center. If you'd like a copy, send $3 to **Hawaii Geographic Maps and Books,** 49 S. Hotel St. (P.O. Box 1698), Honolulu, HI 96808 (*©* **808/538-3952**).

CHINATOWN HISTORIC DISTRICT   Three-hour guided tours of Chinatown are offered Monday at 9:30am by the **Chinese Chamber of Commerce** *⋆*, 42 N. King St., at Smith Street (*©* **808/533-3181;** www.ccchi.org; bus no. 2). The cost is $10 per person; call to reserve.

For a self-guided walking tour of the neighborhood, see p. 210.

GUIDED ECO-TOURS

Oahu isn't just high-rises in Waikiki or urban sprawl in Honolulu, but extinct craters, hidden waterfalls, lush rainforests, forgotten coastlines, and rainbow-filled valleys. To experience the other side of Oahu, contact **Oahu Nature Tours** (*©* **808/924-2473;** www.oahunaturetours.com). It offers seven different eco-tours, starting at $24 per person, and provides everything: expert guides (geologists, historians, archaeologists), round-trip transportation, entrance fees, bottled water, snacks, and use of day packs, binoculars, flashlights, and rain gear.

If you want to explore a hidden, ancient Hawaii that even most lifelong residents have never seen, book a tour with **Mauka Makai Excursions** ⟨★, 350 Ward Ave., Honolulu (© **808/255-2206;** www.hawaiianecotours.net), a Hawaiian-owned and -operated eco-tour company specializing in field trips to off-the-beaten-path (and sometimes hidden-in-the-jungle) ancient temples, sea caves, sacred stones, petroglyphs, and other cultural treasures. Tours range from a half-day ($50 adults, $40 children 6–17) to a full day ($80 adults, $60 children). They provide bottled water, insect repellent, rain gear, beach gear, fishing tackle, and hotel pickup; you bring your imagination.

11 Attractions in & Around Honolulu & Waikiki

HISTORIC HONOLULU

The Waikiki you see today bears no resemblance to the Waikiki of yesteryear, a place of vast taro fields extending from the ocean to deep into Manoa Valley, dotted with numerous fish ponds and gardens tended by thousands of people. This picture of old Waikiki can be recaptured by following the emerging **Waikiki Historic Trail** ⟨★ (www.waikikihistorictrail.com), a meandering 2-mile walk with 20 bronze surfboard markers (standing 6 ft., 5 in. tall—you can't miss 'em), complete with descriptions and archival photos of the historic sites. The markers note everything from Waikiki's ancient fish ponds to the history of the Ala Wai Canal. The trail begins at Kuhio Beach and ends at the King Kalakaua statue, at the intersection of Kuhio and Kalakaua avenues.

Bishop Museum ⟨★★★ ⟨Kids⟩   Even if you do not have kids, this is a must-see on your vacation. Not only does this multibuilding museum have the world's greatest collection of natural and cultural artifacts from Hawaii and the Pacific, but recently it added a terrific new 16,500-square-foot Richard T. Mamiya Science Adventure Center, specializing in volcanology, oceanography, and biodiversity. You'll become a kid again in this interactive, fun environment where you walk down a "Hawaiian origins" tunnel into the deep ocean zone, stopping along the way to play with all the cool, high-tech toys, and then explore the interior of a volcano and climb to the top to get a bird's-eye view of an erupting caldera (it looks like the real thing!).

As we went to press, the Hawaiian Hall, the original cut-stone building (built in 1889) was undergoing a $20-millon massive renovation on the world's only museum dedicated to telling Hawaii's history. The plan called for updating the 19th-century-type displays to 21st-century technology with computers, new lighting, surround sounds, and prerecored Hawaiian voices and chants to give the museumgoer the experience of being back in old Hawaii. The renovations are expected to be complete at the end of 2008. It's a great rainy-day diversion; plan to spend at least half a day here. The museum was founded by a Hawaiian princess, Bernice Pauahi, who collected priceless artifacts and, in her will, instructed her husband, Charles Reed Bishop, to establish a Hawaiian museum "to enrich and delight" the people of Hawaii.

Hawaii's story will be told from the ground up, so to speak. The first floor will feature what Hawaii was like before Westerners arrived. The next floor will explain the importance to Hawaiians of land and nature, and the top floor will have changing exhibits that center around issues relating to Hawaii.

Kids Especially for Kids

Seeing an Erupting Volcano (p. 198)   It looks like the real thing (only you are standing just a few feet away)—a real molten-spewing, roaring, rock-launching volcano—and it's in the Bishop Museum. It's the new 16,500-square-foot Science Adventure Center, specializing in volcanology, oceanography, and biodiversity. The kids will be spellbound wandering through the "Hawaiian origins" tunnel into the deep ocean, stopping along the way to play with all the cool, high-tech toys, then exploring the interior of a volcano and climbing to the top to get a bird's-eye view of an erupting caldera.

Visiting the Honolulu Zoo (p. 206)   Visit Africa in Hawaii at Waikiki's Kapiolani Park. The lions, giraffes, zebras, and elephants delight youngsters and parents alike. But the great new thrill is the "Zoo by Moonlight" tour—so kids can see what really goes bump in the night.

Shopping the Aloha Flea Market   Most kids hate to shop. But the Aloha Flea Market, a giant outdoor bazaar at Aloha Stadium every Wednesday, Saturday, and Sunday, is more than shopping. It's an experience akin to a carnival, full of strange food, odd goods, and bold barkers. Nobody ever leaves this place empty-handed—or without having had lots of fun.

Flying a Kite at Kapiolani Park   Great open expanses of green and constant trade winds make this urban park one of Hawaii's prime locations for kite flying. You can watch the pros fly dragon kites and stage kite-fighting contests, or join in the fun after checking out the convenient kite shop across the street in New Otani's arcade.

Spending a Day at Waimea Beach Park (p. 180)   What many think is only a botanical garden tucked away on the North Shore is really a child's garden of delight. There are waterfalls and pools for swimming, and much more. Try kayaking the Waimea River or hiking through a junglelike forest.

Eating Shave Ice at Haleiwa (p. 236)   No visit to Hawaii is complete without an authentic shave ice. You can find shave ice in all kinds of tropical flavors throughout the islands, but for some reason, it tastes better in this funky North Shore surf town.

Beating Bamboo Drums in a Fijian Village (p. 219)   The Polynesian Cultural Center introduces kids to the games played by Polynesian and Melanesian children. The activities, which range from face painting to Hawaiian bowling, go on every day from 12:30 to 5:30pm.

Pounding a Shark-Skin Drum (p. 198)   The Bishop Museum at Kalia (in the heart of Waikiki) is made for kids. The interactive minimuseum features a host of activities, from lei making to thumping an ancient Hawaii drum made from shark skin. Cool surfing movies, too.

Other buildings on the grounds are jam-packed with acquisitions—from insect specimens and ceremonial spears to calabashes and old photos of topless hula dancers. A visit here will give you a good basis for understanding Hawaiian life and culture.

Honolulu Attractions

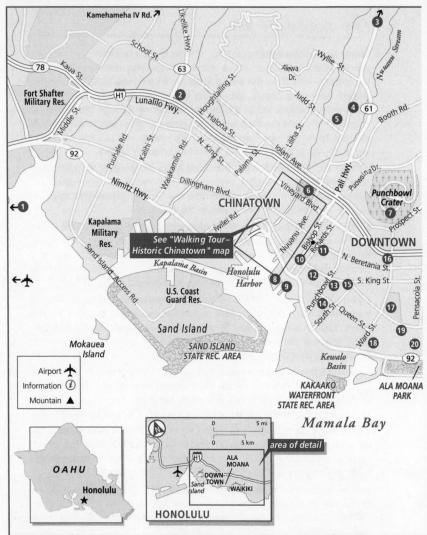

Kamehameha IV Rd.

School St.

Likelike Hwy.

78

Kaua St.

Fort Shafter
Military Res.

H1

Lunalilo Fwy.

63

Houghtailing St.

Halona St.

Wyllie St.

Alewa Dr.

Judd St.

Nuuanu Stream

3

4

61

Booth Rd.

5

92

Middle St.

Puuhale Rd.

Kalihi St.

Waiakamilo Rd.

N. King St.

Palama St.

Liliha St.

Iolani Ave.

Dillingham Blvd.

Nimitz Hwy.

Vineyard Blvd.

Pali Hwy.

Puowaina Dr.

Punchbowl Crater

7

Prospect St.

Kapalama Military Res.

Sand Island Access Rd.

Iwilei Rd.

CHINATOWN

See "Walking Tour–Historic Chinatown" map

Nuuanu Ave.

Bishop St.

Richards St.

DOWNTOWN

N. Beretania St.

16

Kapalama Basin

Honolulu Harbor

10

8

9

11

12

Punchbowl St.

13

15

S. King St.

Pensacola St.

U.S. Coast Guard Res.

14

South St.

Queen St.

17

Ward St.

19

Sand Island

18

20

92

Mokauea Island

SAND ISLAND STATE REC. AREA

Kewalo Basin

ALA MOANA PARK

Airport ✈
Information ⓘ
Mountain ▲

KAKAAKO WATERFRONT STATE REC. AREA

Mamala Bay

0   5 mi
0   5 km

area of detail

OAHU

Honolulu ★

H1

ALA MOANA

DOWN-TOWN

Sand Island

WAIKIKI

HONOLULU

Restaurant Row **14**
Royal Hawaiian Shopping Center **26**
Royal Mausoleum **4**
U.S. Army Museum **25**
USS *Arizona* Memorial at Pearl Harbor **1**
USS *Bowfin* Submarine Museum & Park **1**

USS *Missouri* Memorial **1**
Waikiki Aquarium **30**
Ward Centre **20**
Ward Entertainment Center **19**
Ward Warehouse **18**

You'll see the great feathered capes of kings, the last grass shack in Hawaii, preindustrial Polynesian art, even the skeleton of a 50-foot sperm whale.

Hula performances 🔆 take place weekdays at 11am and 2pm. This daily cultural event is worth making time for. Other tours include the **Na Mea Makamae Tour** (the story of the creation of the museum and the treasures of the Hawaiian culture) at 10am and 12:30pm, the **Na Hulu Ali'i** tour (tour of the elaborate feather art work of ancient Hawaiians) at 10:30am and 1:30pm, the **Plants of Paradise Garden Tour** at 11:30am, and **Meet Me at the Hot Spot—Lava Melting Demo** at noon and 2:30pm.

Personally, I would plan my trip around the shows in the planetarium: **The Sky Tonight** at 11:30am, **Explorers of Mauna Kea** at 1:30pm, and (my favorite) **Explorers of Polynesia** at 3:30pm daily.

1525 Bernice St., just off Kalihi St. (aka Likelike Hwy.). © **808/847-3511.** www.bishopmuseum.org. Admission $16 adults, $13 children 4–12 and seniors. Daily 9am–5pm. Bus: 2.

Hawaii Maritime Center 🔆 *Finds* You can easily spend a couple of hours here, wandering around and learning the story of Hawaii's rich maritime past, from the ancient journey of Polynesian voyagers to the nostalgic days of the *Lurline,* which once brought tourists from San Francisco on 4-day cruises. Inside the Hawaii Maritime Center's Kalakaua Boat House, patterned after His Majesty King David Kalakaua's own canoe house, are more than 30 exhibits, including Matson cruise ships (which brought the first tourists to Waikiki), flying boats that delivered the mail, and the skeleton of a Pacific humpback whale that beached on Kahoolawe. Outside, the *Hokulea,* a double-hulled sailing canoe that in 1976 reenacted the Polynesian voyage of discovery, is moored next to the *Falls of Clyde,* a four-masted schooner that once ran tea from China to the West Coast of the U.S. mainland.

Pier 7 (next to Aloha Tower), Honolulu Harbor. © **808/536-6373.** www.bishopmuseum.org. Admission $7.50 adults, $4.50 children 6–17. Daily 8:30am–5pm. Bus: 19 or 20.

Iolani Palace 🔆 If you want to really "understand" Hawaii, this 45-minute tour is well worth the time. The Iolani Palace was built by King David Kalakaua, who spared no expense. The 4-year project, completed in 1882, cost $360,000—and nearly bankrupted the Hawaiian kingdom. This four-story Italian Renaissance palace was the first electrified building in Honolulu (it had electricity before the White House and Buckingham Palace). Royals lived here for 11 years, until Queen Liliuokalani was deposed and the Hawaiian monarchy fell forever, in a palace coup led by U.S. Marines on January 17, 1893, at the demand of sugar planters and missionary descendants.

Cherished by latter-day royalists, the 10-room palace stands as an architectural statement of the monarchy period. Iolani attracts 60,000 visitors a year in groups of 15; everyone must don denim booties to scoot across the royal floors. Tours are either a comprehensive **Guided Tour** 🔆, which offers visitors a brief video about the history of the palace, adocent-guided tour of the inside of the Palace and a self-guided tour of thebasement;; an **Audio Tour,** which provides guests with an audio wand for a tour through the first floor and second floors and concludes with a self-guided tour of the Gallery; or the **Galleries Tour,** a self-guided tour of the Palace Galleries, complete with crown jewels, the ancient feathered cloaks, the royal china, and more.

At S. King and Richards sts. © **800/532-1051** or 808/522-0832. www.iolanipalace.org. Grand Tour $20 adults, $5 children 5–17; Audio Tour $12 adults, $5 children ages 5–17; Galleries Tour $6 adults, $3 children 5–17. Tues–Sat 8:30am–2pm; call ahead to reserve the Guided Tour. Children under 5 not permitted. Extremely limited parking on palace grounds; try metered parking on the street. Bus: 2.

Kawaiahao Church ⚜ In 1842 Kawaiahao Church stood complete at last, the crowning achievement of missionaries and Hawaiians working together for the first time on a common project. Designed by Rev. Hiram Bingham and supervised by Kamehameha III, who ordered his people to help build it, the project took 5 years. Workers quarried 14,000 coral blocks weighing 1,000 pounds each from the offshore reefs and cut timber in the forests for the beams.

This proud stone church, complete with bell tower and colonial colonnade, was the first permanent Western house of worship in the islands. It became the church of the Hawaiian royalty and remains in use today. Some fine portraits of Hawaiian royalty hang inside. I recommend seeing this edifice at the **Hawaiian-language services** ⚜⚜ (which probably set old Rev. Bingham spinning in his grave), conducted on Sundays at 9am.

957 Punchbowl St. (at King St.). ⓒ **808/522-1333.** Free admission (donations appreciated). Mon–Fri 8am–4pm; Sun services 9am. Bus: 2.

Mission Houses Museum This museum tells the dramatic story of cultural change in 19th-century Hawaii. American Protestant missionaries established their headquarters here in 1820. Included in the complex are a visitor center and three historic mission buildings, which have been restored and refurnished to reflect the daily life and work of the missionaries.

553 S. King St. (at Kawaiahao St.). ⓒ **808/531-0481.** www.missionhouses.org. Admission $10 adults, $8 military personnel and seniors, $6 students (age 6 to college age), free for children 5 and under. Tues–Sat 9am–4pm. Bus: 2.

Queen Emma Summer Palace Hanaiakamalama, the name of the country estate of Kamehameha IV and Queen Emma, was once in the secluded uplands of Nuuanu Valley. These days it's adjacent to a six-lane highway full of speeding cars. This simple seven-room New England–style house, built in 1848 and restored by the Daughters of Hawaii, is worth about an hour of your time to see the interesting blend of Victorian furniture and hallmarks of Hawaiian royalty, including feather cloaks and *kahili,* the feathered standards that mark the presence of *alii* (royalty). Other royal treasures include a canoe-shaped cradle for Queen Emma's baby, Prince Albert, who died at the age of 4. (Kauai's ultraritzy Princeville Resort is named for the little prince.)

2913 Pali Hwy. (at Old Pali Rd.). ⓒ **808/595-3167.** www.daughtersofhawaii.org. Admission $6 adults, $4 seniors, $1 children 11 and under. Daily 9am–4pm. Bus: 4, 55, 56, 57, or 65.

WARTIME HONOLULU

USS *Arizona* Memorial at Pearl Harbor ⚜⚜⚜ On December 7, 1941, the USS *Arizona,* while moored here in Pearl Harbor, was bombed in a Japanese air raid. The 608-foot battleship sank in 9 minutes without firing a shot, taking 1,177 sailors and Marines to their deaths—and catapulting the United States into World War II.

Nobody who visits the memorial will ever forget it. The deck of the ship lies 6 feet below the surface of the sea. Oil still oozes slowly up from the Arizona's engine room to stain the harbor's calm, blue water; some say the ship still weeps for its lost crew. The memorial is a stark, white, 184-foot rectangle that spans the sunken hull of the ship; it was designed by Alfred Pries, a German architect interned on Sand Island during the war. It contains the ship's bell, recovered from the wreckage, and a shrine room with the names of the dead carved in stone.

Today free U.S. Navy launches take visitors to the *Arizona.* Try to arrive at the visitor center, operated by the National Park Service, no later than 1:30pm to avoid the huge crowds; waits of 1 to 3 hours are common, and they don't take reservations at this time. While you're waiting for the free shuttle (operated by the U.S. Navy) to take you out to the ship, get the **Audio Tour** ✶✶✶. This is will make the trip even more meaningful. The tour (on an MP3 player) is about 2½ hours long and is like having your own personal park ranger as your guide. It costs $5 and is worth every nickel. The tape is narrated by Ernest Borgnine and features stories told by actual Pearl Harbor survivors—both American and Japanese. Plus, while you are waiting for the launch, the tour will take you step by step through the museum's personal mementos, photographs, and historic documents. You can pause the tour for the moving 20-minute film that precedes your trip to the ship. The tour continues on the launch, describing the shore line and letting you know what's in store at the Memorial itself. At the Memorial, the tour gives you a mental picture of that fateful day, and the narration continues on your boat ride back. Allow a total of at least 4 hours for your visit.

Due to increased security measures, visitors cannot carry purses, handbags, fanny packs, backpacks, camera bags (but you can carry your camera or video camera with you), diaper bags, or other items that offer concealment on the boat. However, there is a storage facility to store carry-on-size items (no bigger than 30×30×18 in.), for a fee. Also, you must wear **closed-toed shoes;** no sandals allowed.

Parents: Note that baby strollers, baby carriages, and baby backpacks are not allowed in the theater, on the boat, or on the USS *Arizona* Memorial. All babies must be carried. *One last note:* Most unfortunately, the USS *Arizona* Memorial is a high-theft area—leave your valuables at the hotel.

Pearl Harbor. ☎ **808/422-0561** (recorded info) or 808/422-2771. www.nps.gov/usar. Free admission. Daily 7:30am–5pm (programs run 7:45am–3pm). Children under 12 should be accompanied by an adult. Shirts and closed-toed shoes required; no swimsuits or flip-flops allowed (shorts are okay). Wheelchairs gladly accommodated. Drive west on H-1 past the airport; take the USS *Arizona* Memorial exit and follow the green-and-white signs; there's ample free parking. Bus: 20; or *Arizona* Memorial Shuttle Bus VIP (☎ **808/839-0911**), which picks up at Waikiki hotels 6:50am–1pm ($9/person round-trip).

USS *Bowfin* Submarine Museum & Park ✶

The USS *Bowfin* is one of only 15 World War II submarines still in existence today. You can go below deck of this famous submarine—nicknamed the "Pearl Harbor Avenger" for its successful attacks on the Japanese—and see how the 80-man crew lived during wartime. The *Bowfin* Museum has an impressive collection of submarine-related artifacts. The Waterfront Memorial honors submariners lost during World War II.

11 Arizona Memorial Dr. (next to the USS *Arizona* Memorial Visitor Center). ☎ **808/423-1341.** www.bowfin.org. Admission $10 adults, $6 active-duty military personnel and seniors, $3 children 4–12 (children under 4 are not permitted for safety reasons). Daily 8am–5pm. See USS *Arizona* Memorial, above, for driving, bus, and shuttle directions.

USS *Missouri* Memorial ✶

On the deck of this 58,000-ton battleship (the last one the Navy built), World War II came to an end with the signing of the Japanese surrender on September 2, 1945. The *Missouri* was part of the force that carried out bombing raids over Tokyo and provided firepower in the battles of Iwo Jima and Okinawa. In 1955 the Navy decommissioned the ship and placed it in mothballs at the Puget Sound Naval Shipyard, in Washington State. But the *Missouri* was modernized and called back into action in 1986, eventually being deployed in the Persian Gulf War, before retiring once again in 1992. Here it sat until another battle ensued, this time over who would get the right to keep this living legend. Hawaii won that battle and brought the ship to Pearl Harbor in 1998. The 887-foot ship is now open to visitors as a museum memorial.

If you have the time, take the tour, which begins at the visitor center. Guests are shuttled to Ford Island on military-style buses while listening to a 1940s-style radio program (complete with news clips, wartime commercials, and music). Once on the ship, guests watch an informational film and are then free to explore on their own or take a guided tour. Highlights of this massive (more than 200-ft. tall) battleship include the forecastle (or *fo'c's'le*, in Navy talk), where the 30,000-pound anchors are "dropped" on 1,080 feet of anchor chain; the 16-inch guns (each 65 ft. long and weighing 116 tons), which can accurately fire a 2,700-pound shell some 23 miles in 50 seconds; and the spot where the Instrument of Surrender was signed as Douglas MacArthur, Chester Nimitz, and "Bull" Halsey looked on.

Battleship Row, Pearl Harbor. ✆ 808/423-2263. www.ussmissouri.com. Admission $16 adults, $8 children 4–12. Guided tours (60 min.) $22 adults, $14 children (admission included). Daily 9am–5pm; guided tours 9:30am–4:30pm. Check in at the visitor center of the USS *Bowfin* Memorial, next to the USS *Arizona* Memorial. Drive west on H-1 past the airport, take the USS *Arizona* Memorial exit, and follow the green-and-white signs; there's ample free parking. Bus: 20 or 47.

National Cemetery of the Pacific   The National Cemetery of the Pacific (also known as "the Punchbowl") is an ash-and-lava tuff cone that exploded about 150,000 years ago—like Diamond Head, only smaller. Early Hawaiians called it Puowaina, or "hill of sacrifice." The old crater is a burial ground for 35,000 victims of three American wars in Asia and the Pacific: World War II, Korea, and Vietnam. Among the graves, you'll find many unmarked ones with the date December 7, 1941, carved in stone. Some will be unknown forever; others are famous, like that of war correspondent Ernie Pyle, killed by a Japanese sniper in April 1945 on Okinawa; still others buried here are remembered only by family and surviving buddies. The white stone tablets known as the Courts of the Missing bear the names of 28,788 Americans missing in action in World War II.

Survivors come here often to reflect on the meaning of war and to remember those, like themselves, who stood in harm's way to win peace a half-century ago. Some fight back tears, remembering lost buddies, lost missions, and the sacrifices of those who died.

Punchbowl Crater, 2177 Puowaina Dr. (at the end of the road). ✆ 808/541-1434. Free admission. Daily 8am–5:30pm (Mar–Sept to 6:30pm). Bus: 15.

JUST BEYOND PEARL HARBOR

Hawaiian Railway *(Kids)*   All aboard! This is a train ride back into history. Between 1890 and 1947, the chief mode of transportation for Oahu's sugar mills was the Oahu Railway and Land Co.'s narrow-gauge trains. The line carried not only equipment, raw sugar, and supplies, but also passengers from one side of the island to the other. You can relive those days every Sunday with a 1½-hour narrated ride through Ko Olina Resort and out to Makaha. As an added attraction, on the second Sunday of the month, you can ride on the nearly 100-year-old custom-built parlor-observation car belonging to Benjamin F. Dillingham, founder of the Oahu Railway and Land Co.; the fare is $20 (no kids under 13), and you must reserve in advance.

Ewa Station, Ewa Beach. ✆ 808/681-5461. www.hawaiianrailway.com. Admission $10 adults, $7 seniors and children 2–12. Departures Sun 1 and 3pm and weekdays by appointment. Take H-1 west to exit 5A; take Hwy. 76 south for 2½ miles to Tesoro Gas; turn right on Renton Rd. and drive 1½ miles to end of paved section. The station is on the left. Bus: C-Express to Kapalei, then transfer to no. 41, which goes through Ewa and drops you off outside the gate.

Hawaiian Waters Adventure Park *(Kids)*   Kids love this 29-acre water-theme amusement park, which opened in spring 1999 with some $14 million in attractions. Plan to spend the day. Highlights are a football field–size wave pool for bodysurfing, two 65-foot-high free-fall slides, two water-toboggan bullet slides, inner-tube slides, body flume slides, a continuous river for floating inner tubes, and separate pools for adults, teens, and children. In addition, there are restaurants, Hawaiian performances, and shops.

400 Farrington Hwy., Kapolei. ⓒ 808/674-9283. www.hawaiianwaters.com. Admission $35 adults, $15 seniors, $25 children 3–11, free for children under 3. Hours vary, but generally the park is open daily 10:30am–4 or 5pm in peak season (summer); during off-peak season 10:30am–3:30 or 4pm; closed some weekdays. Take H-1 west to exit 1 (Campbell Industrial Park). Make an immediate left turn to Farrington Hwy., and you will see the park on your left.

Hawaii's Plantation Village   The hour-long tour of this restored 50-acre village offers a glimpse back in time to when sugar planters shaped the land, economy, and culture of Hawaii. From 1852, when the first contract laborers arrived here from China, to 1947, when the plantation era ended, more than 400,000 men, women, and children from China, Japan, Portugal, Puerto Rico, Korea, and the Philippines came to work the sugar-cane fields. The "talk story" tour brings the old village alive with 30 faithfully restored camp houses, Chinese and Japanese temples, the Plantation Store, and even a sumo-wrestling ring.

Waipahu Cultural Garden Park, 94–695 Waipahu St. (at Waipahu Depot Rd.), Waipahu. ⓒ 808/677-0110. www. hawaiiplantationvillage.org. Admission (including escorted tour) $13 adults; $10 seniors; $7 military personnel; $5 children 4–11; children 3 and under free. Mon–Sat 10am–2pm. Take H-1 west to Waikele-Waipahu exit (Exit 7); get in the left lane on exit and turn left on Paiwa St.; at the 5th light, turn right onto Waipahu St.; after the 2nd light, turn left. Bus: 47.

FISH, FLORA & FAUNA

Foster Botanical Garden 𝄢𝄢 *(Finds*   You could spend days in this unique historic garden, a leafy oasis amid the high-rises of downtown Honolulu. Combine a tour of the garden with a trip to Chinatown (just across the street) to maximize your time. The giant trees that tower over the main terrace were planted in the 1850s by William Hillebrand, a German physician and botanist, on royal land leased from Queen Emma. Today this 14-acre public garden, on the north side of Chinatown, is a living museum of plants, some rare and endangered, collected from the tropical regions of the world. Of special interest are 26 "Exceptional Trees" protected by state law, a large palm collection, a primitive cycad garden, and a hybrid orchid collection.

50 N. Vineyard Blvd. (at Nuuanu Ave.). ⓒ 808/522-7066. www.co.honolulu.hi.us/parks/hbg/fbg.htm. Admission $5 adults, $1 children 6–12. Daily 9am–4pm; guided tours Mon–Sat at 1pm (reservations recommended). Bus: 2, 4, or 13.

Honolulu Zoo 𝄢 *(Kids*   Nobody comes to Hawaii to see an Indian elephant or African lions and zebras. Right? Wrong. This 43-acre municipal zoo in Waikiki attracts visitors in droves. If you've got kids, allot at least half a day. The highlight is the new African Savannah, a 10-acre exhibit with more than 40 African critters roaming around in the open. The zoo also has a rare Hawaiian nene goose, a Hawaiian pig, and mouflon sheep. (Only the goose, an evolved version of the Canadian honker, is considered to be truly Hawaiian; the others are imported from Polynesia, India, and elsewhere.)

For a real treat, take the **Zoo by Twilight Tour** 𝄢, which offers a rare behind-the-scenes look into the lives of the zoo's nocturnal residents. Tours are Saturday from 5:30 to 7:30pm; the cost is $12 for adults and $8 for children ages 4 to 12 years. Other great family programs include **Snooze in the Zoo,** in which you discover "who is roaring and who is snoring" during the night with pizza, tours, and campfire time with s'mores, plus breakfast and a morning stroll (check website for dates); and **Star Gazing at the Zoo,** an evening tour of the zoo that also explores the night sky above Hawaii with astronomer Dr. Michael Chauvin ($12 adults, $8 children 4–12).

151 Kapahulu Ave. (between Paki and Kalakaua aves.), at entrance to Kapiolani Park. ℂ 808/971-7171. www. honoluluzoo.org. Admission $8 adults, $1 children 6–12. Family Pass $25. Daily 9am–4:30pm. The Zoo parking lot entrance is on Kapahulu Ave and charges 25¢ per hour. The Shell parking lot across the street on Monsarrat Ave has free parking. Bus: 2, 8, 19, 20, or 47.

Lyon Arboretum ✿   The Lyon Arboretum dates back to 1918, when the Hawaiian Sugar Planters Association wanted to demonstrate the value of watershed for reforestation. In 1953 it became part of the University of Hawaii, where they continued to expand the extensive collection of tropical plants. Six-story-tall breadfruit trees, yellow orchids no bigger than a bus token, ferns with fuzzy buds as big as a human head . . . . These are just a few of the botanical wonders you'll find at the 194-acre Lyon Arboretum. A whole different world opens up to you along the self-guided 20-minute hike through the arboretum to Inspiration Point. You'll pass more than 5,000 exotic tropical plants full of singing birds in this cultivated rainforest (a University of Hawaii research facility) at the head of Manoa Valley.

3860 Manoa Rd. (near the top of the road). ℂ 808/988-0456. www.hawaii.edu/lyonarboretum. No admission fee, but donations accepted. Mon–Fri 9am–4pm. Bus: 5.

Sea Life Park (Kids)   This 62-acre ocean theme park, located in East Oahu, is one of the island's top attractions. The price, however, has been creeping up the past few years, and now I feel it is way overpriced (two adults and two children will cost nearly $100, which is just not worth it). Yes, it does feature whales from Puget Sound, Atlantic bottle-nosed dolphins, California sea lions, and penguins going through their hoops to the delight of kids of all ages. If you do go, allow all day to take in the sights, see the shows (hey, at these prices, get your money's worth). There's also a Hawaiian reef tank full of tropical fish; a "touch" pool, where you can touch a real sea cucumber (commonly found in tide pools); and a bird sanctuary, where you can see birds like the red-footed booby and the frigate bird. The chief curiosity, though, is the world's only "wholphin"—a cross between a false killer whale and an Atlantic bottle-nosed dolphin. On-site, marine biologists operate a recovery center for endangered marine life; during your visit, you may be able to see rehabilitated Hawaiian monk seals and seabirds.

41–202 Kalanianaole Hwy. (at Makapuu Point), Honolulu. ℂ 808/259-7933. www.sealifeparkhawaii.com. Admission $29 adults, $19 children 4–12. Daily 9:30am–5pm. Parking $3. Shuttle buses from Waikiki $5. Bus: 22 or 58.

Waikiki Aquarium ✿✿✿ (Kids)   Do not miss this! Half of Hawaii is its underwater world; plan to spend at least 2 hours discovering it. Behold the chambered nautilus, nature's submarine and inspiration for Jules Verne's *20,000 Leagues Under the Sea*. You may see this tropical spiral-shelled cephalopod mollusk—the only living one born in captivity—any day of the week here. Its natural habitat is the deep waters of Micronesia, but aquarium director Bruce Carlson not only succeeded in trapping the pearly shelled creature in 1,500 feet of water (by dangling chunks of raw tuna), he also managed to breed this ancient relative of the octopus. There are also plenty of other fish in this small but first-class aquarium, located on a live coral reef. The Hawaiian reef habitat features sharks, eels, a touch tank, and habitats for the endangered Hawaiian monk seal and green sea turtle. Recently added: a rotating biodiversity exhibit and interactive displays focusing on corals and coral reefs.

2777 Kalakaua Ave. (across from Kapiolani Park). ℂ 808/923-9741. www.waquarium.org. Admission $9 adults; $6 active military, seniors, and college students; $4 children 13–17; $2 children 5–12; free for children under 5. Daily 9am–5pm. Bus: 2.

Oahu's Vibrant Art Scene

Passionate art lovers should head straight to Hawaii's three top cultural resources: The Contemporary Museum, the Honolulu Academy of Arts, and the State Art Museum.

The acclaimed **Honolulu Academy of Arts** ✵✵, 900 S. Beretania St. (② **808/ 532-8700,** or 808/532-8701 for recording; www.honoluluacademy.org), is the state's only general fine-arts museum. It boasts one of the top Asian art collections in the country. Also on exhibit are American and European masters and prehistoric works of Mayan, Greek, and Hawaiian art. The museum's award-winning architecture is a paragon of graciousness, featuring magnificent courtyards, lily ponds, and sensitively designed galleries. Open Tuesday through Saturday from 10am to 4:30pm, Sunday from 1 to 5pm; tours 11am Tuesday through Saturday and 1:15pm on Sunday. Admission is $7 for adults and $4 for students, seniors, and military personnel; children under 12 enter free.

Set up on the slopes of Tantalus, one of Honolulu's upscale residential communities, **The Contemporary Museum,** 2411 Makiki Heights Dr. (② **808/ 526-0232;** www.tcmhi.org), is renowned for its 3 acres of Asian gardens (with reflecting pools, sun-drenched terraces, views of Diamond Head, and stone benches for quiet contemplation). Equally prominent is the presence of contemporary Hawaii artists in the museum's programs and exhibitions. Open Tuesday through Saturday from 10am to 4pm, Sunday from noon to 4pm. A 1-day membership is $5 for adults, $3 for seniors and students, and free for children 12 and under. The third Thursday of each month is free. Ask about the daily docent-led tours, and check out the excellent cafe and shop.

The **Hawaii State Art Museum** is housed in the original Royal Hawaiian Hotel, at 250 S. Hotel St. (at Richards St.; ② **808/586-0900;** www.state.hi. us/sfca), which was built in 1872 during the reign of King Kamehameha V. All of the 360 works currently displayed were created by artists who live in Hawaii. The pieces were all purchased by the state, thanks to a 1967 law that says that 1% of the cost of state buildings must be used to acquire works of art. Nearly 4 decades later, the state has amassed some 5,000 pieces. Open Tuesday to Saturday from 10am to 4pm; admission is free. Take the no. 2 bus from Waikiki. If you are driving, look for street (metered) parking.

OTHER NATURAL WONDERS & SPECTACULAR VIEWS

In addition to the attractions listed below, check out "Diamond Head Crater" under "Nature Hikes," earlier in this chapter; almost everybody can handle this hike, and the 360-degree views from the top are fabulous.

Nuuanu Pali Lookout ✵ *Moments*   Gale-force winds sometimes howl through the mountain pass at this 1,186-foot-high perch guarded by 3,000-foot peaks, so hold on to your hat—and small children. But if you walk up from the parking lot to the precipice, you'll be rewarded with a view that'll blow you away. At the edge, the dizzying panorama of Oahu's windward side is breathtaking: Clouds low enough to pinch scoot by on trade winds; pinnacles of the pali (cliffs), green with ferns, often disappear in the mist. From on high, the tropical palette of green and blue runs down to the sea. Combine this 10-minute stop with a trip over the pali to the windward side.

Near the summit of Pali Hwy. (Hwy. 61); take the Nuuanu Pali Lookout turnoff.

Nuuanu Valley Rain Forest *(Finds)* It's not the same as a peaceful nature walk, but if time is short and hiking isn't your thing, Honolulu has a rainforest you can drive through. It's only a few minutes from downtown Honolulu in verdant Nuuanu Valley, where it rains nearly 300 inches a year. And it's easy to reach: As the Pali Highway leaves residential Nuuanu and begins its climb though the forest, the last stoplight is the Nuuanu Pali Road turnoff; turn right for a jungley detour of about 2 miles under a thick canopy strung with liana vines, past giant bamboo that creaks in the wind, Norfolk pines, and wild shell ginger. The road rises and the vegetation clears as you drive, blinking in the bright light of day, past a small mountain reservoir.

Soon the road rejoins the Pali Highway. Kailua is to the right and Honolulu to the left—but it can be a hair-raising turn. Instead, turn right, go ½ mile to the Nuuanu Pali Lookout (see above), stop for a panoramic view of Oahu's windward side, and return to the town-bound highway on the other side.

Take the Old Nuuanu Pali Rd. exit off Pali Hwy. (Hwy. 61).

Puu Ualakaa State Park *(Moments)* The best **sunset view** of Honolulu is from a 1,048-foot-high hill named for sweet potatoes. Actually, the poetic Hawaiian name means "rolling sweet potato hill" and was named such because of how early planters used gravity to harvest their crop. The panorama is sweeping and majestic. On a clear day—which is almost always—you can see from Diamond Head to the Waianae Range, almost the length of Oahu. At night, several scenic overlooks provide romantic spots for young lovers who like to smooch under the stars with the city lights at their feet. It's a top-of-the-world experience—the view, that is.

At the end of Round Hill Dr. Daily 7am–6:45pm (to 7:45pm in summer). From Waikiki, take Ala Wai Blvd. to McCully St., turn right, and drive mauka (inland) beyond the H-1 on-ramps to Wilder St.; turn left and go to Makiki St.; turn right, and continue onward and upward about 3 miles.

MORE MUSEUMS

For details on Honolulu's three wonderful art museums, **The Contemporary Museum,** the **Honolulu Academy of Arts,** and the **Hawaii State Art Museum,** see the box "Oahu's Vibrant Art Scene," above.

Aliiolani Hale Don't be surprised if this place looks familiar: You probably saw it on *Magnum, P.I.* This gingerbread Italianate building, designed by Australian Thomas Rowe in Renaissance revival style, was built in 1874 and was originally intended to be a palace. Instead, Aliiolani Hale ("chief unto heavens") became the Supreme Court and Parliament government office building. Inside, there's a **Judiciary History Center** *(꿏)*, which features a multimedia presentation, a restored historic courtroom, and exhibits tracing Hawaii's transition from precontact Hawaiian law to Western law.

417 S. King St. (between Mililani and Punchbowl sts.). © **808/539-4999.** Fax 808/539-4996. www.jhchawaii.org. Free admission. Mon–Fri 9am–4pm; reservations for group tours only. Limited parking; metered parking on street. Bus: 1, 2, 3, 4, 8, 11, or 12.

U.S. Army Museum This museum, a former military fort built in 1909 and used in defense of Honolulu and Pearl Harbor, houses military memorabilia ranging from ancient Hawaiian warfare items to modern-day, high-tech munitions. On the upper deck, the Corps of Engineers Pacific Regional Visitors Center shows how the corps works with the civilian community to manage water resources in an island environment.

Fort DeRussy Park, Waikiki. © **808/438-2822**. Free admission. Tues–Sun 10am–4:30pm. Bus: 8.

WALKING TOUR	A STROLL THROUGH HISTORIC CHINATOWN

Getting There:	From Waikiki, take bus no. 2 or 20 toward downtown; get off on North Hotel Street (after Maunakea St.). If you're driving, take Ala Moana Boulevard and turn right on Smith Street; make a left on Beretania Street and a left again at Maunakea. The city parking garage (50¢ per half-hour) is on the Ewa (west) side of Maunakea Street, between North Hotel and North King streets.
Start and Finish:	North Hotel and Maunakea streets.
Time:	1 to 2 hours, depending on how much time you spend browsing.
Best Times:	Daylight hours.

Chinese laborers from the Guangdong Province first came to work on Hawaii's sugar and pineapple plantations in the 1850s. They quickly figured out that they would never get rich working in the fields; once their contracts were up, some started up small shops and restaurants in the area around River Street.

Chinatown was twice devastated by fire, once in 1886 and again in 1900. The second fire still intrigues historians. In December 1899 bubonic plague broke out in the area, and the Board of Health immediately quarantined its 7,000 Chinese and Japanese residents. But the plague continued to spread. On January 20, 1900, the board decided to burn down plague-infected homes, starting at the corner of Beretania Street and Nuuanu Avenue. But the fire department wasn't quite ready; a sudden wind quickly spread the flames from one wooden building to another in the densely built area, and soon Chinatown's entire 40 acres were leveled. Many historians believe that the "out-of-control" fire may have been purposely set to drive Chinese merchants—who were becoming economically powerful and controlled prime real estate—out of Honolulu. If this was indeed the case, it didn't work: The determined merchants built a new Chinatown in the same spot.

Chinatown reached its peak in the 1930s. In the days before air travel, visitors arrived here by cruise ship. Just a block up the street was the pier where they disembarked—and they often headed straight for the shops and restaurants of Chinatown, which mainlanders considered an exotic treat. In the 1940s, military personnel on leave flocked here looking for different kinds of exotic treats—in the form of pool halls, tattoo joints, and brothels.

Today Chinatown is again rising from the ashes. After deteriorating over the years into a tawdry district of seedy bars, drug dealing, and homeless squatters, the neighborhood recently underwent extensive urban renewal. There's still just enough sleaze on the fringes (a few peep shows and a couple of topless bars) to keep it from being some theme-park-style tourist attraction, but Chinatown is poised to relive its glory days.

It's not exactly a microcosm of China, however. What you'll find is a mix of Asian cultures, all packed into a small area where tangy spices rule the cuisine, open-air markets have kept out the mini-malls, and the way to good health is through acupuncture and herbalists. The jumble of streets comes alive every day with bustling residents and

Walking Tour: Historic Chinatown

area of detail

FOSTER BOTANICAL GARDEN 9

Vineyard Blvd.

1 Hotel Street
2 Bank of Hawaii
3 Yat Tung Chow
   Noodle Factory
4 Viet Hoa Chinese
   Herb Shop
5 Oahu Market Place
6 River Street
   Pedestrian Mall
7 Chinatown Cultural
   Plaza
8 Izumo Taisha
   Mission
   Cultural Hall
9 Kuan Yin Temple
10 Maunakea Street
11 Nuuanu Avenue
12 Hawaii Theatre

"Take a Break"

N. Kukhui S. Kukhui
N. Beretania St.
Pauahi St.
N. Hotel St. **start here** S. Hotel St. **finish here**
N. King St.
S. King St.
Merchant St.
Queen St.
PIER 14
Nimitz Hwy.
Honolulu Harbor PIER 13

visitors from all over the world; a cacophony of sounds, from the high-pitched bleating of vendors in the market to the lyrical dialects of the retired men "talking story" over a game of mah-jongg; and brilliant reds, blues, and greens trimming buildings and goods everywhere you look. No trip to Honolulu is complete without a visit to this exotic historic district.

Start your walk on the Ewa (west) side of Maunakea Street at:

❶ Hotel Street

During World War II, Hotel Street was synonymous with good times. Pool halls and beer parlors lined the blocks, and prostitutes were plentiful. Nowadays, the more nefarious establishments have been replaced with small shops, from art galleries to specialty boutiques, and urban professionals and recent immigrants look for bargains where the sailors once roamed.

Once you're done wandering through the shops, head to the intersection with Smith Street. On the Diamond Head (east) side of Smith, you'll notice stones in the sidewalk; they were taken from the sandalwood ships, which came to Hawaii empty of cargo except for these stones, which were used as ballast on the trip over. The stones were removed and the ships' hulls were filled with sandalwood for the return to the mainland.

From Hotel Street, turn toward the ocean on Maunakea and proceed to the corner of King Street to the:

② Bank of Hawaii

This unusual-looking bank is not the conservative edifice you'd expect—it's guarded by two fire-breathing-dragon statues.

Turn right onto King Street, where you'll pass the shops of various Chinese herbalists. Stop at 150 N. King St., where you'll find the:

③ Yat Tung Chow Noodle Factory

The delicious, delicate noodles that star in numerous Asian dishes are made here, ranging from threadlike noodles (literally no thicker than embroidery thread) to fat udon. There aren't any tours of the factory, but you can look through the window, past the white cloud of flour that hangs in the air, and watch as dough is fed into rollers at one end of the noodle machines; perfectly cut noodles emerge at the other end.

Proceed to 162 N. King St., to the:

④ Viet Hoa Chinese Herb Shop

Here Chinese herbalists act as both doctors and dispensers of herbs. Patients come in and tell the herbalist what ails them; the herbalist then decides which of the myriad herbs to mix together. Usually, there's a wall of tiny drawers all labeled in Chinese characters; the herbalist quickly pulls from the drawers various objects that range from dried flowers and ground-up roots to such exotics as mashed antelope antler. The patient then takes the concoction home to brew into a strong tea.

Cross to the south side of King Street, where, just west of Kekaulike Street, you'll come to the most-visited part of Chinatown, the open-air market known as:

⑤ Oahu Market Place

Those interested in Asian cooking will find all the necessary ingredients here, including pigs' heads, poultry (some still squawking), fresh octopi, salted jellyfish, pungent fish sauce, fresh herbs, and thousand-year-old eggs. The friendly vendors are happy to explain their wares and give instructions on how to prepare these exotic treats. The market, which has been at this spot since 1904, is divided into meats, poultry, fish, vegetables, and fruits. Past the open market are several grocery stores with fresh produce on display on the sidewalk. You're bound to spot some goodies here that you're not used to seeing at your local supermarket.

Follow King down to River Street and turn right toward the mountains. A range of inexpensive restaurants lines River Street from King to Beretania. You can get the best Vietnamese and Filipino food in town in these blocks, but go early—lines for lunch start at 11:15am.

Beyond Beretania Street is the:

⑥ River Street Pedestrian Mall

Here River Street ends and the pedestrian mall begins with the **statue of Chinese revolutionary leader Sun Yat-sen.** The wide mall, which borders the Nuuanu Stream, is lined with shade trees, park benches, and tables where seniors gather to play mah-jongg and checkers. There are plenty of takeout restaurants nearby if you'd like to eat lunch outdoors. If you're up early (5:30am in summer and 6am in winter), you'll see seniors practicing tai chi.

Along the River Street Mall, extending nearly a block over to Maunakea Street, is the:

⑦ Chinatown Cultural Plaza

This modern complex is filled with shops featuring everything from tailors to calligraphers (most somewhat more expensive than their street-side counterparts), as well as numerous restaurants—a great idea, but in reality, people seem to prefer wandering Chinatown's crowded streets to venturing into a modern mall. A couple of interesting shops here specialize in Asian magazines; there's also a small post office tucked away in a corner of the plaza, for those who want to mail cards home with the "Chinatown" postmark.

Bargaining: A Way of Life in Chinatown

In Chinatown, nearly every purchase—from chicken's feet to an 18-karat gold necklace—is made by bargaining. It's the way of life for most Asian countries—and part of the fun and charm of shopping in Chinatown.

The main rule of thumb when negotiating a price is **respect**. The customer must have respect for the merchant and understand that he's in business to make money. This respect is coupled with the understanding that the customer does not want to be taken advantage of and would like the best deal possible.

Keep in mind two rules when bargaining: **cash** and **volume**. Don't even begin haggling if you're not planning to pay cash. The second you pull out a credit card (if the merchant or vendor will even accept it), all deals are off. And remember, the more you buy, the better the deal the merchant will extend to you.

Significant savings can be realized for high-ticket items like jewelry. The price of gold in Chinatown is based on the posted price of the tael (a unit of weight slightly more than an ounce), which is listed for 14-, 18-, and 24-karat gold, plus the value of the labor. There's no negotiating on the tael price, but the cost of the labor is where the bargaining begins.

The best feature of the plaza is the **Moongate Stage** in the center, the site of many cultural presentations, especially around the Chinese New Year.

Continue up the River Street Mall and cross the Nuuanu Stream via the bridge at Kukui Street, which will bring you to the:

8 Izumo Taisha Mission Cultural Hall

This small, wooden Shinto shrine, built in 1923, houses a male deity (look for the X-shaped crosses on the top). Members of the faith ring the bell out front as an act of purification when they come to pray. Inside the temple is a 100-pound sack of rice, symbolizing good health. During World War II, the shrine was confiscated by the city of Honolulu and wasn't returned to the congregation until 1962.

If temples interest you, walk a block toward the mountains to Vineyard Boulevard; cross back over Nuuanu Stream, past the entrance of Foster Botanical Gardens, to:

9 Kuan Yin Temple

This Buddhist temple, painted in a brilliant red with a green ceramic-tiled roof, is dedicated to Kuan Yin Bodhisattva, the goddess of mercy, whose statue towers in the prayer hall. The aroma of burning incense is your clue that the temple is still a house of worship, not an exhibit, so enter with respect and leave your shoes outside. You may see people burning paper "money" for prosperity and good luck, or leaving flowers and fruits at the altar (gifts to the goddess). A common offering is the pomelo, a grapefruitlike fruit that's a fertility symbol as well as a gift, indicating a request for the blessing of children.

Continue down Vineyard and then turn right (toward the ocean) on:

10 Maunakea Street

Between Beretania and King streets are numerous **lei shops** (with lei makers working away right on the premises). The air is heavy with the aroma of flowers being woven into beautiful treasures. Not only is this the best place in all of Hawaii to get a deal on leis, but the size, color, and design of the leis made here are exceptional. Wander through the shops before you decide which lei you want.

TAKE A BREAK
If you have a sweet tooth, stop in at **Shung Chong Yuein** (食), 1027 Maunakea St. (near Hotel St.), for delicious Asian pastries like moon cakes and almond cookies, all at very reasonable prices. The shop also has a wide selection of dried and sugared candies (like ginger, pineapple, and lotus root) that you can eat as you stroll or give as an exotic gift to friends back home.

everything from precious antiques to god-awful knickknacks, to rare Hawaiian postcards from the early 1900s—but it has built its reputation on its fabulous selection of Chinese silks, brocades, and custom dresses.

Between Hotel and Pauahi streets is the **Pegge Hopper Gallery,** 1164 Nuuanu Ave., where you can admire Pegge's well-known paintings of beautiful Hawaiian women.

Turn left on Hotel Street and walk in the Diamond Head (east) direction to:

⑪ Nuuanu Avenue

You may notice that the sidewalks on Nuuanu are made of granite blocks; they came from the ballasts of ships that brought tea from China to Hawaii in the 1800s. On the corner of Nuuanu Avenue and Hotel Street is **Lai Fong Department Store,** a classic Chinatown store owned by the same family for more than 75 years. Walking into Lai Fong is like stepping back in time. The old store sells

At Pauahi Street, turn toward Diamond Head and walk up to Bethel Street and the:

⑫ Hawaii Theatre

This restored 1920 Art Deco theater is a work of art in itself. It hosts a variety of programs, from the Hawaii International Film Festival to beauty pageants (see "Oahu After Dark," later in this chapter, for more information).

Turn right onto Bethel and walk toward the ocean. Turn right again onto Hotel Street, which will lead you back to where you started.

12 Beyond Honolulu: Exploring the Island by Car

The moment always arrives—usually after a couple of days at the beach, snorkeling in the warm blue-green waters of Hanauma Bay, enjoying sundown mai tais—when a certain curiosity kicks in about the rest of Oahu, largely unknown to most visitors. It's time to find the rental car in the hotel garage and set out around the island. You can also explore Oahu using **TheBus** (see "Getting Around," earlier in this chapter).

OAHU'S SOUTHEAST COAST

From the high-rises of Waikiki, venture down Kalakaua Avenue through tree-lined Kapiolani Park to take a look at a different side of Oahu, the arid south shore. The landscape here is more moonscape, with prickly cacti onshore and, in winter, spouting whales cavorting in the water. Some call it the South Shore, others Sandy's (after the mile-long beach here), but Hawaiians call it **Ka Iwi,** which means "the bone"— no doubt because of all the bone-cracking shore breaks along this popular bodyboarding coastline. The beaches here are long, wide, and popular with local daredevils.

To get to this coast, follow Kalakaua Avenue past the multitiered Dillingham Fountain and around the bend in the road, which now becomes Poni Moi Road. Make a right on Diamond Head Road and begin the climb up the side of the old crater. At the top are several lookout points, so if the official Diamond Head Lookout is jammed with cars, try one of the other lookouts just down the road. The view of the rolling waves is spectacular; take the time to pull over.

Diamond Head Road rolls downhill into the ritzy community of **Kahala.** At the V in the road at the triangular Fort Ruger Park, veer to your right and continue on the

ATTRACTIONS ●

Halona Blowhole **1**
Heeia Pier **20**
Heeia State Park / Heeia Fish Pond **21**
Hoomaluhia Botanical Gardens **13**
Kailua Beach **11**
Kualoa Regional Park **23**
Kualoa Ranch and Activity Club **24**
Lanikai Beach **8**
Makapuu Beach Park **5**
Makapuu Point **4**
Nuuanu Pali Lookout **12**
Pele's Chair **3**
Polynesian Cultural Center **25**
Sandy Beach **2**
Sea Life Park **6**
Senator Fong's Plantation & Gardens **22**
Valley of the Temples **19**
Waimanalo Beach **7**

ACCOMMODATIONS ■

Alii Bluffs Winward Bed & Breakfast **17**
Indrid's **10**
Lanikai Bed & Breakfast **9**
Schrader's Windward Marine Resort **18**
Sheffield House **14**

DINING ◆

Assaggio **16**
Lucy's Grill 'n Bar **15**

palm tree–lined Kahala Avenue. Make a left on Hunakai Street, then a right on Kilauea Avenue, and look for the sign H-1 WEST—WAIMANALO. Turn right at the sign, although you won't get on the H-1 freeway; instead, get on the Kalanianaole Highway, a four-lane highway interrupted every few blocks by a stoplight. This is the suburban bedroom community to Honolulu, marked by malls on the left and beach parks on the right.

One of these parks is **Hanauma Bay** ✸✸ (p. 173); you'll see the turnoff on the right when you're about half an hour from Waikiki. This marine preserve is a great place to stop for a swim; you'll find the friendliest fish on the island here. *A reminder:* The beach park is closed on Tuesday.

Around mile marker 11, the jagged lava coast itself spouts sea foam at the **Halona Blowhole.** Look out to sea from Halona over Sandy Beach and across the 26-mile gulf to neighboring Molokai and the faint triangular shadow of Lanai on the far horizon. **Sandy Beach** (p. 178) is Oahu's most dangerous beach; it's the only one with an ambulance always standing by to whisk injured wave catchers to the hospital. Body boarders just love it.

The coast looks raw and empty along this stretch, but the road weaves past old Hawaiian fish ponds and the famous formation known as **Pele's Chair,** just off Kalanianaole Highway (Hwy. 72) above Queen's Beach. From a distance, the lava-rock outcropping looks like a mighty throne; it's believed to be the fire goddess's last resting place on Oahu before she flew off to continue her work on other islands.

Ahead lies 647-foot-high **Makapuu Point,** with a lighthouse that once signaled safe passage for steamship passengers arriving from San Francisco. The automated light now brightens Oahu's south coast for passing tankers, fishing boats, and sailors. You can take a short hike up here for a spectacular vista (p. 187).

Turn the corner at Makapuu and you're on Oahu's windward side, where cooling trade winds propel windsurfers across turquoise bays; the waves at **Makapuu Beach Park** (p. 178) are perfect for bodysurfing.

Ahead, the coastal vista is a profusion of fluted green mountains and strange peaks, edged by golden beaches and the blue, blue Pacific. The 3,000-foot-high sheer green Koolau Mountains plunge almost straight down, presenting an irresistible jumping-off spot for hang-glider pilots, who catch the thermals on hours-long rides.

Winding up the coast, Kalanianaole Highway (Hwy. 72) leads through rural **Waimanalo,** a country beach town of nurseries and stables, fresh-fruit stands, and some of the island's best conch- and triton-shell specimens at roadside stands. Nearly 4 miles long, **Waimanalo Beach** is Oahu's longest beach and the most popular for body-surfing. Take a swim here or head on to **Kailua Beach** ✸✸, one of Hawaii's best (p. 179).

If it's still early in the day, you can head up the lush, green Windward Coast by turning right at the Castle Junction, where Highway 72 meets Highway 61 (which is called Kailua Rd. on the makai [seaward] side of the junction, and Kalanianaole Hwy. on the mauka [inland] side of the junction), and continuing down Kailua Road (Hwy. 61). After Kailua Road crosses the Kaelepulu Stream, the name of the road changes to Kuulei Road. When Kuulei Road ends, turn left onto Kalaheo Avenue, which becomes Kaneohe Bay Drive after it crosses the Kawainui Channel. Follow this scenic drive around the peninsula until you get to Kamehameha Highway (Hwy. 83); turn right and continue on Kamehameha Highway for a scenic drive along the ocean.

If you're in a hurry to get back to Waikiki, turn left at Castle Junction and head over the Pali Highway (Hwy. 61), which becomes Bishop Street in Honolulu and ends at Ala Moana. Turn left for Waikiki; it's the second beach on the right.

THE WINDWARD COAST

From the **Nuuanu Pali Lookout** ⭐, near the summit of the Pali Highway (Hwy. 61), you get the first hint of the other side of Oahu, a region so green and lovely that it could be an island sibling of Tahiti. With its many beaches and bays, the scenic 30-mile Windward Coast parallels the corduroy-ridged, nearly perpendicular cliffs of the Koolau Range, which separates the windward side of the island from Honolulu and the rest of Oahu. As you descend on the serpentine Pali Highway beneath often gushing waterfalls, you'll see the nearly 1,000-foot spike of **Olomana,** the bold pinnacle that always reminds me of Devils Tower National Monument in Wyoming, and, beyond, the Hawaiian village of **Waimanalo.**

From the Pali Highway, to the right is Kailua, Hawaii's biggest beach town, with more than 50,000 residents and two special beaches, **Kailua** (p. 179) and **Lanikai** (p. 178). Funky little Kailua is lined with million-dollar houses next to tarpaper shacks, antiques shops, and bed-and-breakfasts. Although the Pali Highway (Hwy. 61) proceeds directly to the coast, it undergoes two name changes, becoming first Kalanianaole Highway—from the intersection of Kamehameha Highway (Hwy. 83)—and then Kailua Road as it heads into Kailua town; but the road remains Highway 61 the whole way. Kailua Road ends at the T intersection at Kalaheo Drive, which follows the coast in a northerly and southerly direction. Turn right on South Kalaheo Drive to get to Kailua Beach Park and Lanikai Beach. No signs point the way, but you can't miss them.

If you spend a day at the beach here, stick around for sunset, when the sun sinks behind the Koolau Range and tints the clouds pink and orange. After a hard day at the beach, you'll work up an appetite, and Kailua has several great inexpensive restaurants (see "Where to Dine," earlier in this chapter).

If you want to skip the beaches this time, turn left on North Kalaheo Drive, which becomes Kaneohe Bay Drive as it skirts Kaneohe Bay and leads back to Kamehameha Highway (Hwy. 83), which then passes through Kaneohe. The suburban maze of Kaneohe is one giant strip mall of retail excess that mars one of the Pacific's most picturesque bays. After clearing this obstacle, the place begins to look like Hawaii again.

Incredibly scenic Kaneohe Bay is spiked with islets and lined with gold-sand beach parks like **Kualoa** (p. 179), a favorite picnic spot. The bay has a barrier reef and four tiny islets, one of which is known as Moku o loe, or Coconut Island. Don't be surprised if it looks familiar—it appeared in *Gilligan's Island.*

At Heeia State Park is **Heeia Fish Pond,** which ancient Hawaiians built by enclosing natural bays with rocks to trap fish on the incoming tide. The 88-acre fish pond, which is made of lava rock and had four watchtowers to observe fish movement and several sluice gates along the 5,000-foot-long wall, is now in the process of being restored.

Stop by the **Heeia Pier,** which juts onto Kaneohe Bay. You can take a snorkel cruise here, or sail out to a sandbar in the middle of the bay for an incredible view of Oahu that most people, even those who live here, never see. If it's Tuesday through Sunday between 7am and 5pm, stop in at the **Deli on Heeia Kea Pier** (© **808/235-2192**), serving fishermen, sailors, and kayakers the town's best omelets and plate lunches at reasonable prices since 1979.

Everyone calls it **Chinaman's Hat,** but the tiny island off the eastern shore of Kualoa Regional Park is really named **Mokolii.** It's a sacred *puu honua,* or place of refuge, like the restored Puu Honua Honaunau on the Big Island of Hawaii. Excavations have unearthed evidence that this area was the home of ancient *alii* (royalty). Early Hawaiians believed that Mokolii ("fin of the lizard") is all that remains of a *mo'o,* or lizard, slain by Pele's sister, Hiiaka, and hurled into the sea. At low tide you can swim out to the island, but keep watch on the changing tide, which can sweep you out to sea. The islet has a small, sandy beach and is a bird preserve, so don't spook the red-footed boobies.

Little poly-voweled beach towns like **Kahaluu, Kaaawa, Punaluu,** and **Hauula** pop up along the coast, offering passersby shell shops and art galleries to explore. Famed hula photographer **Kim Taylor Reece** lives on this coast; his gallery at 53–866 Kamehameha Hwy., near Sacred Falls (© **808/293-2000;** www.kimtaylorreece.com), is open Thursday to Saturday from noon to 5pm. You'll also see working cattle ranches, fishermen's wharves, and roadside fruit and flower stands vending ice-cold coconuts (to drink) and tree-ripened mangoes, papayas, and apple bananas (short bananas with an apple aftertaste).

Sugar, once the sole industry of this region, is gone. But **Kahuku,** the former sugar-plantation town, has found new life as a small aquaculture community with prawn farms that supply island restaurants.

From here, continue along Kamehameha Highway (Hwy. 83) to the North Shore.

ATTRACTIONS ALONG THE WINDWARD COAST

The attractions below are arranged geographically as you drive up the coast from south to north.

Hoomaluhia Botanical Gardens ★
This 400-acre botanical garden at the foot of the steepled Koolau Mountains is the perfect place for a picnic. Its name means "a peaceful refuge," and that's exactly what the Army Corps of Engineers created when they installed a flood-control project here, which resulted in a 32-acre freshwater lake and garden. Just unfold a beach mat, lie back, and watch the clouds race across the rippled cliffs of the majestic Koolau Range. This is one of the few public places on Oahu that provides a close-up view of the steepled cliffs. The park has hiking trails and—best of all—the island's only free inland campground (p. 189). If you like hiking and nature, plan to spend at least a half-day here.

45–680 Luluku Rd., Kaneohe. © 808/233-7323. www.co.honolulu.hi.us/parks/hbg/hmbg.htm. Free admission. Daily 9am–4pm. Guided nature hikes Sat 10am and Sun 1pm. Take H-1 to the Pali Hwy. (Hwy. 61); turn left on Kamehameha Hwy. (Hwy. 83); at the 4th light, turn left onto Luluku Rd. Bus: 55 or 56 will stop on Kamehameha Hwy.; it's a 2-mile walk to the visitor center.

Valley of the Temples
This famous cemetery in a cleft of the pali is stalked by wild peacocks and about 700 curious people a day, who pay to see the 9-foot meditation Buddha, acres of ponds full of more than 10,000 Japanese koi carp, and a replica of Japan's 900-year-old Byodo-in Temple of Equality. The original, made of wood, stands in Uji, on the outskirts of Kyoto; the Hawaiian version, made of concrete, was erected in 1968 to commemorate the 100th anniversary of the arrival of the first Japanese immigrants to Hawaii. It's not the same as seeing the original, but it's worth a detour. A 3-ton brass temple bell brings good luck to those who can ring it—although the gongs do jar the Zen-like serenity of this little bit of Japan. If you are in a rush, you can sail through here in an hour, but you'll probably want to stay longer.

47–200 Kahekili Hwy. (across the street from Temple Valley Shopping Center), Kaneohe. © 808/239-8811. Admission $2 adults, $1 children under 12 and seniors 65 and over. Daily 8:30am–4:30pm. Take the H-1 to the Likelike Hwy. (Hwy. 63); after the Wilson Tunnel, get in the right lane and take the Kahekili Hwy. (Hwy. 63); at the 6th traffic light is the entrance to the cemetery (on the left). Bus: 65.

Senator Fong's Plantation & Gardens   Sen. Hiram Fong, the first Chinese American elected to the U.S. Senate, served 17 years before retiring to this 725-acre tropical garden years ago. This land originally belonged to King Lunalilo. In 1950 Senator Fong purchased it. The landscape you see today is relatively the same as what early Polynesians saw hundreds of years ago, with forests of kukui, hala, koa, and ohia-'ai (mountain apple). Ti and pili grass still cover the slopes. It's definitely worth an hour—if you haven't already seen enough flora to last a lifetime.

47–285 Pulama Rd., Kaneohe. ✆ **808/239-6775**. www.fonggarden.net. Admission $15 adults, $13 seniors, $9 children 5–12, with 1-hr. guided nature walk. Daily 10am–2pm. Take the H-1 to the Likelike Hwy. (Hwy. 63); turn left at Kahekili Hwy. (Hwy. 83); continue to Kaneohe and turn left on Pulama Rd. Bus: 55; it's a mile walk uphill from the stop.

Kualoa Ranch and Activity Club   This once-working ranch now has various different adventure packages covering numerous activities on its 4,000 acres. Activities include horseback riding, ATV rides, ranch tours, and more.

49–560 Kamehameha Hwy., Kaaawa. ✆ **800/231-7321** or 808/237-7321. www.kualoa.com. Reservations required. Various activity packages: single activities $19–$87; ½ day of various activities $65 adults, $39 children 3–11; full-day $95 adults, $59 children ages 3–11 years. Daily 9:30am–3pm. Take H-1 to the Likelike Hwy. (Hwy. 63), turn left at Kahekili Hwy. (Hwy. 83), and continue to Kaaawa. Bus: 52.

Polynesian Cultural Center ✿ *Kids*   Even if you never leave Hawaii, you can still experience the natural beauty and culture of the vast Pacific in a single day at the Polynesian Cultural Center, a kind of living museum of Polynesia. Here you can see firsthand the lifestyles, songs, dance, costumes, and architecture of seven Pacific islands or archipelagos—Fiji, New Zealand, Marquesas, Samoa, Tahiti, Tonga, and Hawaii—in the re-created villages scattered throughout the 42-acre lagoon park. A recent $1.1-million renovation project remodeled the front entrance and added an exhibit on the story of the Polynesian immigration.

You "travel" through this museum by foot or in a canoe on a man-made freshwater lagoon. Each village is "inhabited" by native students from Polynesia who attend Hawaii's Brigham Young University. The park, which is operated by the Mormon Church, also features a variety of stage shows celebrating the music, dance, history, and culture of Polynesia. There's a luau every evening. Because a visit can take up to 8 hours, it's a good idea to arrive before 2pm. Just beyond the center is the **Hawaii Temple** of the Church of Jesus Christ of Latter-Day Saints, which is built of volcanic rock and concrete in the form of a Greek cross and includes reflecting pools, formal gardens, and royal palms. Completed in 1919, it was the first Mormon temple built outside the continental United States. An optional tour of the Temple Visitors Center, as well as neighboring Brigham Young University, Hawaii, is included in the package admission prices.

55–370 Kamehameha Hwy., Laie. ✆ **800/367-7060**, 808/293-3333, or 808/923-2911. www.polynesia.com. Admission $50 adults, $35 children 3–11. Admission, IMAX, luau, and nightly show $80 adults, $56 children. Ambassador VIP (deluxe) tour $110–$200 adults, $76–$150 children. Mon–Sat 12:30–9:30pm. Take H-1 to Pali Hwy. (Hwy. 61) and turn left on Kamehameha Hwy. (Hwy. 83). Bus: 55. Polynesian Cultural Center coaches $19 round-trip; call numbers above to book.

CENTRAL OAHU & THE NORTH SHORE

If you can afford the splurge, rent a bright, shiny convertible—the perfect car for Oahu because you can tan as you go—and head for the North Shore and Hawaii's surf city: **Haleiwa** ✿, a quaint sugar-plantation town designated a historic site. A collection of faded clapboard stores with a picturesque harbor, Haleiwa has evolved into a surfer outpost and major roadside attraction with art galleries, restaurants, and shops that sell hand-decorated clothing, jewelry, and sports gear (see "Shopping A to Z," below).

Getting here is half the fun. You have two choices: The first is to meander north along the lush Windward Coast, through country hamlets with roadside stands selling mangoes, bright tropical pareu, fresh corn, and pond-raised prawns. Attractions along that route are discussed in the previous section.

The second choice is to cruise up the H-2 through Oahu's broad and fertile central valley, past Pearl Harbor and the Schofield Barracks of *From Here to Eternity* fame, and on through the red-earthed heart of the island, where pineapple and sugar-cane fields stretch from the Koolau to the Waianae mountains, until the sea reappears on the horizon. If you take this route, the tough part is getting on and off the H-1 freeway from Waikiki, which is done by way of convoluted routing on neighborhood streets. Try McCully Street off Ala Wai Boulevard, which is always crowded but usually the most direct route.

Once you're on H-1, stay to the right side; the freeway tends to divide abruptly. Keep following the signs for the H-1 (it separates off to Hwy. 78 at the airport and reunites later on; either way will get you there), and then the H-1/H-2. Leave the H-1 where the two highways divide; take the H-2 up the middle of the island, heading north toward the town of Wahiawa. That's what the sign will say not North Shore or Haleiwa, but Wahiawa.

The H-2 runs out and becomes a two-lane country road about 18 miles outside downtown Honolulu, near Schofield Barracks (see below). The highway becomes Kamehameha Highway (Hwy. 99 and later Hwy. 83) at Wahiawa. Just past Wahiawa, about a half-hour out of Honolulu, the **Dole Pineapple Plantation,** 64–1550 Kamehameha Hwy. (© **808/621-8408;** fax 808/621-1926; www.dole-plantation.com; bus no. 52), offers a rest stop with pineapples, pineapple history, pineapple trinkets, and pineapple juice, open daily from 9am to 6pm. This agricultural exhibit/retail area also features a maze kids will love to wander through, open daily from 9am to 5pm; admission is $5 for adults and $3 for children 4 to 12 (free for ages 3 and under). The latest attraction is the Pineapple Express, a single-engine diesel locomotive with four cars that takes a 22-minute tour around 2¼ miles of the plantation's grounds, with an educational spiel on the legacy of the pineapple and agriculture in Hawaii. The first tour departs at 9:30am, and the last tour gets back to the station at 5:20pm. Cost is $7.50 for adults, $5.50 for children 4 to 12 (free for ages 3 and under). The latest attraction is the Plantation Garden tour, a self-guided tour through the various crops that have been grown on Oahu's North Shore. The tour costs $3.75 for adults and $3 for children. "Kam" Highway, as everyone calls it, will be your road for most of the rest of the trip to Haleiwa.

CENTRAL OAHU ATTRACTIONS

On the central plains of Oahu, tract homes and malls with factory-outlet stores are now spreading across abandoned sugar-cane fields, where sandalwood forests used to stand at the foot of Mount Kaala, the mighty summit of Oahu. Hawaiian chiefs once sent commoners into thick sandalwood forests to cut down trees, which were then sold to China traders for small fortunes. The scantily clad natives caught cold in the cool uplands, and many died.

On these plains in 1908, the U.S. Army pitched a tent that later became a fort. And on December 7, 1941, Japanese pilots came screaming through Kolekole Pass to shoot

0 5 mi
0 5 km

Kaena
Point
1
930
Farrington Hwy.
Yokohama
Bay
930
Makua
Beach
Mokuleia
Haleiwa
Waialua
83
MAKAHA
BEACH
PARK
803
Kamehameha Hwy.
Makaha
Mt. Kaala
(4,020 feet)
Kaukonahua Rd.
99
93
Pokai
Bay
Wilikina Dr.
2
Waianae
Waianae Valley Rd.
99 80
3
Whitmore
Village
Maili
Kolekole Rd.
4
Wahiawa
Lualualei Naval Rd.
780
Kunia Rd.
Wheeler Air
Force Base
Nanakuli
750
Mililani
Kamehameha Hwy.
H2
99
9
93
Makakilo
Waipahu
H1
6
5
Waipio
Malakole Rd.
Ko Olina
10
8
Farrington Hwy.
Kalaeloa Blvd.
Kapolei
90
Pearl City
95
Ewa
Fort Weaver Rd.
Pearl Harbor
H1
Aiea
Barbers Point
Lighthouse
Barbers Point
Naval Air Station
76
Pearl Harbor
Naval Station
Pearl Harbor
Moanalua Fwy.
7
Ewa Beach
USS Arizona
Memorial
Salt Lake Blvd.
78
Hickam
Air Force
Base

Dole Pineapple Plantation **2**
Hawaii's Plantation Village **6**
Hawaiian Railway **7**
Hawaiian Waters Adventure Park **8**
J.W. Marriott Ihilani Resort & Spa **9**
Kaena Point State Park **1**
Kukaniloko Birthing Stones **3**
Roy's Ko Olina **10**
Tropic Lighting Museum **4**
U.S. Army Schofield Barracks **4**
Waikele Premium Outlets **5**

OAHU

Honolulu

Beach
Lighthouse
Mountain ▲

up the Art Deco barracks at Schofield, sending soldiers running for cover, and then flew on to sink ships at Pearl Harbor.

U.S. Army Schofield Barracks & Tropic Lightning Museum James Jones, author of *From Here to Eternity,* called Schofield Barracks "the most beautiful army post the U.S. has or ever had." The *Honolulu Star Bulletin* called it a country club. More than a million soldiers have called Schofield Barracks home. With its broad, palm-lined boulevards and Art Deco buildings, this old army cavalry post is still the largest operated by the U.S. Army outside the continental United States. And it's still one of the best places to be a soldier.

You can no longer visit the barracks themselves, but the history of Schofield Barracks and the 25th Infantry Division is told in the small **Tropic Lightning Museum.** Displays range from a 1917 bunker exhibit to a replica of Vietnam's infamous Cu Chi tunnels.

Schofield Barracks, Building 361, Waianae Ave. ℂ 808/655-0497. www.25idl.army.mil/Tropic%20Lightning%20 Museum/history.htm. Free admission. Tues–Sun 1–4pm. Bus: 52 to Wahiawa; transfer at California Ave. to no. 72, Schofield Barracks Shuttle.

Kukaniloko Birthing Stones This is the most sacred site in central Oahu. Two rows of 18 lava rocks once flanked a central birthing stone, where women of ancient Hawaii gave birth to potential *alii* (royalty). The rocks, according to Hawaiian belief, held the power to ease the labor pains of childbirth. Birth rituals involved 48 chiefs who pounded drums to announce the arrival of newborns likely to become chiefs. Children born here were taken to the now-destroyed Holonopahu Heiau in the pineapple field, where chiefs ceremoniously cut the umbilical cord.

Used by Oahu's *alii* for generations of births, the *pohaku* (rocks), many in bowl-like shapes, now lie strewn in a grove of trees that stands in a pineapple field here. Some think the site also may have served ancient astronomers—like a Hawaiian Stonehenge. Petroglyphs of human forms and circles appear on some of the stones. The Wahiawa Hawaiian Civic Club recently erected two interpretive signs, one explaining why this was chosen as a birth site and the other telling how the stones were used to aid in the birth process.

Off Kamehameha Hwy. between Wahiawa and Haleiwa, on Plantation Rd. opposite the road to Whitmore Village.

SURF CITY: HALEIWA

Only 28 miles from Waikiki is Haleiwa, the funky ex–sugar plantation town that's the world capital of big-wave surfing. This beach town really comes alive in winter, when waves rise up, light rain falls, and temperatures dip into the 70s (low to mid-20s Celsius); then, it seems, every surfer in the world is here to see and be seen.

Officially designated a historic cultural and scenic district, Haleiwa thrives in a time warp recalling the early 20th century, when it was founded by sugar baron Benjamin Dillingham, who built a 30-mile railroad to link his Honolulu and North Shore plantations in 1899. He opened a Victorian hotel overlooking Kaiaka Bay and named it Haleiwa, or "house of the Iwa," the tropical seabird often seen here. The hotel and railroad are gone, but Haleiwa, which was rediscovered in the late 1960s by hippies, resonates with rare rustic charm. Tofu, not taro, is a staple in the local diet. Arts and crafts, boutiques, and burger stands line both sides of the town. There's also a busy fishing harbor full of charter boats and captains who hunt the Kauai Channel daily for tuna, mahimahi, and marlin. The bartenders at **Jameson's by the Sea** ℛ, 62–540

Kamehameha Hwy. (© **808/637-6272**), make the best mai tais on the North Shore; they use the original recipe by Trader Vic Bergeron.

Once in Haleiwa, the hot and thirsty traveler should report directly to the nearest shave-ice stand, like **Matsumoto Shave Ice** 😿😿, 66–087 Kamehameha Hwy. (© **808/ 637-4827**). For 40 years, this small, humble shop operated by the Matsumoto family has served a popular rendition of the Hawaii-style snow cone flavored with tropical tastes. The cooling treat is also available at neighboring stores, some of which still shave the ice with a hand-crank device.

Just down the road are some of the fabled shrines of surfing—**Waimea Beach, Banzai Pipeline, Sunset Beach**—where some of the world's largest waves, reaching 20 feet and more, rise up between November and January. They draw professional surfers as well as reckless daredevils and hordes of onlookers, who jump in their cars and head north when word goes out that "surf's up." Don't forget your binoculars. For more details on North Shore beaches, see the "Beaches" section, earlier in this chapter.

North Shore Surf and Cultural Museum   Even if you've never set foot on a surfboard, you'll want to visit Oahu's only surf museum to learn the history of this Hawaiian sport of kings. This collection of memorabilia traces the evolution of surfboards from an enormous, weathered redwood board made in the 1930s for Turkey Love, one of Waikiki's legendary beach boys, to the modern-day equivalent—a light, sleek, racy foam-and-fiberglass board made for big-wave surfer Mark Foo, who drowned while surfing in California in 1994. Other items include classic 1950s surf-meet posters, 1960s surf-music album covers, old beach-movie posters with Frankie Avalon and Sandra Dee, the early black-and-white photos by legendary surf photographer LeRoy Grannis, and trophies won by surfing's greatest. Curator Steve Gould is working on a new exhibit of surfing in the ancient Hawaiian culture, complete with Hawaiian artifacts.

North Shore Marketplace, 66–250 Kamehameha Hwy. (behind Kentucky Fried Chicken), Haleiwa. © 808/637-8888. www.captainrick.com/surf_museum.htm. Free admission. Tues–Sun noon–5pm (unless the surf is up).

MORE NORTH SHORE ATTRACTIONS

Puu o Mahuka Heiau 😿 *(Moments)*   Go around sundown to feel the *mana* (sacred spirit) of this Hawaiian place. The largest sacrificial temple on Oahu, it's associated with the great Kaopulupulu, who sought peace between Oahu and Kauai. This prescient kahuna predicted that the island would be overrun by strangers from a distant land. In 1794 three of Capt. George Vancouver's men of the *Daedalus* were sacrificed here. In 1819, the year before New England missionaries landed in Hawaii, King Kamehameha II ordered all idols here to be destroyed.

A national historic landmark, this 18th-century *heiau,* known as the "hill of escape," sits on a 300-foot bluff overlooking Waimea Bay and 25 miles of Oahu's wave-lashed north coast—all the way to Kaena Point, where the Waianae Range ends in a spirit leap to the other world. The heiau appears as a huge rectangle of rocks twice as big as a football field, with an altar often covered by the flower and fruit offerings left by native Hawaiians.

1 mile past Waimea Bay. Take Pupukea Rd. mauka (inland) off Kamehameha Hwy. at Foodland, and drive 1 mile up a switchback road. Bus: 52, then walk up Pupukea Rd.

Waimea Valley Audubon Center 😿 *(Kids)*   For nearly 3 decades, Waimea Falls Park has hosted visitors to the 1,875-acre park (home to some 6,000 species of plants and trees) and activity center (from cliff diving and hula performances to kayaking and ATV tours). In 2003 the City and County of Honolulu awarded the lease to the valley

Oahu's North Shore

ACCOMMODATIONS ■
Ke Iki Beach Bungalows **14**
Laie Inn **20**
Santa's by the Sea **15**
Turtle Bay Resort **18**

ATTRACTIONS ●
Banzai Pipeline (Ehukai Beach Park) **16**
Haleiwa Beach Park **8**
Malaekahana Bay State Recreation Area **19**
North Shore Surf and Cultural Museum **4**
Polynesian Cultural Center **21**
Puu o Mahuka Heiau **12**
Shark's Cove, Pupukea Beach Park **13**
Sunset Beach **17**
Waimea Beach **10**
Waimea Valley Audubon Center **11**

DINING ◆
Cafe Haleiwa **2**
Cholos Homestyle Mexican **4**
Haleiwa Joe's **7**
Jameson's by the Sea **9**
Kua Aina **5**
Matsumoto Shave Ice **6**
Ola at Turtle Bay Resort **18**
Paradise Found Cafe **3**
Shrimp trucks **1**
21 Degrees North **18**

to the National Audubon Society. The Audubon Society has renamed the park Waimea Valley Audubon Center and is focusing on protecting and interpreting the valley's cultural, botanical, and ecological resources. Activities (kayaking, ATV tours, and others) have been eliminated, along with the cliff diving and hula; instead, the emphasis is on education and preservation. The public is invited to hike the trails, wander through, and spend a day in this quiet oasis. Admission prices have been lowered and parking now is free.

59–864 Kamehameha Hwy. ℂ **808/638-9199**. www.audubon.org. Admission $8 adults, $5 children 4–12 and seniors. Daily 10am–5:30pm. Bus: 52.

13 Shopping A to Z

Shopping competes with golf, surfing, and sightseeing as a bona fide Honolulu activity. And why not? The proliferation of top-notch made-in-Hawaii products, the vitality of the local crafts scene, and the unquenchable thirst for mementos of the islands lend respectability to shopping here.

Oahu is also a haven for mall mavens. More than 1,000 stores occupy the 11 major shopping centers on this island. From souvenir T-shirts to high fashion, posh European to down-home local, avant-garde to unspeakably tacky, Oahu's offerings are wide-ranging indeed. But you must sometimes wade through oceans of schlock to arrive at the mother lode. Nestled amid the Louis Vuitton, Chanel, and Tiffany boutiques on Waikiki's Kalakaua Avenue are plenty of tacky booths hawking air-brushed T-shirts, gold by the inch, and tasteless aloha shirts.

The section that follows is not about finding cheap souvenirs or tony items from designer fashion chains; you can find these on your own. Rather, I offer a guide to finding those special treasures that lie somewhere in between.

SHOPPING IN & AROUND HONOLULU & WAIKIKI
ALOHA WEAR

One of Hawaii's lasting afflictions is the penchant tourists have for wearing loud, matching aloha shirts and muumuu. I applaud such visitors' good intentions (to act local), but no local resident would be caught dead in such a get-up. Muumuu and aloha shirts are wonderful, but the real thing is what island folks wear on Aloha Friday (every Fri), to the Brothers Cazimero Lei Day Concert (every May 1), or to work (where allowed). It's what they wear at home and to special parties where the invitation reads "Aloha Attire."

Aside from the vintage Hawaiian wear (1930s–1950s) found in collectibles shops and at swap meets, my favorite contemporary aloha-wear designer is Hawaii's **Tori Richards. Tommy Bahama,** which never calls its shirts "aloha shirts" but claims, instead, a Caribbean influence, is another Hawaii shirt icon, and so is the up-and-coming **Tiki** brand, quirky and distinctive, with elements that hearken back to 1950s bowling shirts and Jimmy Dean charisma.

The best aloha shirts are pricey these days, going for $80 to $125. For the vintage look, **Avanti** has a corner on the market with its stunning line of silk shirts and dresses in authentic 1930s-to-1950s patterns. These shirts ($60–$105) boast all the qualities of a vintage silky, but without the high price or the web-thin fragility of an authentic antique. The dresses and other styles are the epitome of comfort and nostalgic good looks. The line is distributed in better boutiques and department stores throughout Hawaii or www.avantishirts.com.

Also popular is **Kahala Sportswear,** a well-known local company established in 1936. Kahala has faithfully reproduced, with astounding success, the linoleum-block prints of noted Maui artist Avi Kiriaty and the designs of other contemporary artists. Kahala is sold in department stores, surf shops, and stylish boutiques throughout Hawaii and the mainland.

Reyn Spooner is another source of attractive aloha shirts and muumuu in traditional and contemporary styles, with stores in Ala Moana Center, Kahala Mall, and the Sheraton Waikiki.

Well-known muumuu labels in Hawaii include **Mamo Howell,** with a boutique in Ward Warehouse, and **Princess Kaiulani** and **Bete** for the dressier muus, sold along with many other lines at Macy's and other department stores. **Hilo Hattie's** Ala Moana store (© **808/973-3266;** www.hilohattie.com) is a gold mine of affordable aloha wear. Hilo Hattie's also offers free daily shuttle service from Waikiki to its retail outlet on Nimitz Highway (© **808/537-2926**), and to Aloha Tower Marketplace, Ala Moana Center, and Waikiki. You'll also find macadamia nuts, Hawaii coffees, and other souvenirs at these Hilo Hattie's stores, as well as live Hawaiian entertainment.

ANTIQUES & COLLECTIBLES

Antique Alley   This narrow shop is chockablock with the passionate collections of several vendors. With its expanded collection of old Hawaiian artifacts and surfing and hula nostalgia, it's a sure winner for eclectic tastes. The showcases include estate jewelry, antique silver, Hawaiian bottles, collectible toys, pottery, cameras, Depression glass, linens, plantation photos and ephemera, and a wide selection of nostalgic items from Hawaii and across America. At the rear is a small, attractive selection of Soiree clothing, made by Julie Lauster, including antique kimonos and obis. Located behind Mattress Outlet. 1347 Kapiolani Blvd. © 808/941-8551.

Bailey's Antiques & Aloha Shirts   A large selection (thousands) of vintage, secondhand, and nearly new aloha shirts and other collectibles fills this eclectic emporium. It looks as though the owners regularly scour Hollywood movie costume departments for oddball gowns, feather boas, fur stoles, leather jackets, 1930s dresses, and scads of other garments from periods past. Bailey's has one of the largest vintage aloha-shirt collections in Honolulu, with prices ranging from inexpensive to sky-high. Old Levi's jeans, mandarin jackets, vintage vases, household items, shawls, purses, and an eye-popping assortment of bark-cloth fabrics (the real thing, not repros) are among the mementos in this monumental collection. 517 Kapahulu Ave. © 808/734-7628.

T. Fujii Japanese Antiques   This is a long-standing icon in Hawaii's antiques world and an impeccable source for ukiyo-e prints, scrolls, obis, Imari porcelain, tansus, tea-ceremony bowls, and screens, as well as contemporary ceramics from Mashiko and Kasama, with prices from $25 to $18,000. 1016 Kapahulu Ave. © 808/732-7860.

BOOKSTORES

Barnes & Noble   With more than 150,000 titles, a respectable music department, and strong Hawaiiana, fiction, and new-release departments, as well as a popular coffee bar, Barnes & Noble has become the second home of Honolulu's casual readers and bibliophiles. Kahala Mall, 4211 Waialae Ave. © 808/737-3323.

Bestsellers Books & Music   Hawaii's largest independent bookstore, located in downtown Honolulu, has a complete selection of nonfiction and fiction titles with an emphasis on Hawaiian books and music. There's another Bestsellers in the Hilton Hawaiian Village (2005 Kalia Rd.; © **808/953-2378**). 1001 Bishop St. © **808/528-2378.**

Borders   Borders is a beehive of literary activity, with weekly signings, prominent local and mainland musicians at least monthly, and special events almost daily that make this store a major Honolulu attraction. There are six Borders on Oahu: Waikiki, 2250 Kalakaua Ave. (© **808/922-4154**); Ward Centre, 1200 Ala Moana Blvd. (© **808/ 591-8995**); Waikele Center, 94–821 Lumiaina St. (© **808/676-6699**); 98-1005 Moanalua Rd., Aiea (© **808/487-1818**); Windward Mall, 46-056 Kamehameha Hwy., Kaneohe, (© **808/235-8044**); and Miilani Town Center, 95-1249 Meheula Pkway., Mililani (© **808/623-2138**).

Rainbow Books and Records   A little weird but totally lovable, especially among students and eccentrics (and insatiable readers), Rainbow Books is notable for its selection of popular fiction, records, and Hawaii-themed books, secondhand and reduced. It's about the size of a large closet, but you'll be surprised by what you'll find. Located next to Bank of Hawaii at the corner of King and University. 1010 University Ave. © 808/955-7994.

EDIBLES

In addition to the stores listed below, I recommend **Executive Chef** (© **808/596-2433**), in the Ward Warehouse, and **Islands' Best** (© **808/949-5345**), in the Ala Moana Center. Both shops contain wide-ranging selections that include Hawaii's specialty food items.

If you're looking for a bakery, **Saint-Germain,** in Shirokiya at Ala Moana Shopping Center (© **808/955-1711**), and near Times Supermarket, 1296 S. Beretania St. (© **808/593-8711**), sells baguettes, country loaves, and oddball delicacies such as mini mushroom-and-spinach pizzas. The reigning queen of bakers, though, is **Cafe Laufer,** 3565 Waialae Ave. (© **808/735-7717;** p. 167). Nearby, old-timers still line up at **Sconees,** 1117 12th Ave. (© **808/734-4024**), formerly Bea's Pies. Sconees has fantastic scones, pumpkin-custard pies, and Danishes. And don't forget **Mary Catherine's,** 2820 S. King St. (© **808/946-4333**), a great place for quality cakes and European pastries.

Asian Grocery   Asian Grocery supplies many of Honolulu's Thai, Vietnamese, Chinese, Indonesian, and Filipino restaurants with authentic spices, rice, noodles, produce, sauces, herbs, and adventurous ingredients. Browse among the kafir lime leaves, tamarind and fish pastes, red and green chiles, curries, chutneys, lotus leaves, gingko nuts, jasmine and basmati rice, and shelf upon shelf of medium to hot chile sauces. 1319 S. Beretania St. © 808/593-8440. www.asianfoodtrading.com.

Don Quijote   Stands offering takeout sushi, Korean *kal bi,* pizza, Chinese food, flowers, Mrs. Fields cookies, and other items for self and home surround this huge emporium. Inside you'll find household products, a pharmacy, and inexpensive clothing, but it's the prepared foods and produce that excel. The fresh-seafood section is

---

Fish Markets

Tamashiro Market, 802 N. King St., Kalihi (© 808/841-8047), is the grandfather of fish markets and the ace in the hole for home chefs with bouillabaisse or paella in mind. A separate counter sells seaweed salad, prepared poke, Filipino and Puerto Rican ti-wrapped steamed rice, and dozens of other ethnic foods.

For more mainstream shoppers, **Safeway** on Beretania Street (© 808/591-8315) has a seafood counter with fresh choices and a staff that takes pride in its deftness with prepared foods (like fresh ahi poke, seaweed salad, shrimp cocktail, and marinated crab—don't be shy about asking for a taste).

Neighbor islanders have been known to drive directly from the airport to **Yama's Fish Market**, 2203 Young St., Moiliili (© 808/941-9994), for one of the best plate lunches in town. But Yama's is also known for its inexpensive fresh fish, tasty poke, and lomi salmon. Chilled beer, boiled peanuts, and fresh ahi sliced into sashimi are popular for local-style gatherings, sunset beach parties, and festive *pau hana* (end-of-work) celebrations. New standouts include a fabulous assortment of chocolate biscotti and chocolate chip cookies, sweet-potato and custard mochi, and a haupia (coconut pudding) pie layered with bright-purple Okinawa sweet potato.

one of Honolulu's best, not far from where regulars line up for the bento lunches and individually wrapped sushi. When Kau navel oranges, macadamia nuts, Kona coffee, Chinese taro, and other Hawaii products are on sale, savvy locals arrive in droves to take advantage of the high quality and good value. Additional branches are at 345 Hahani St., Kailua (© **808/266-4400**); 850 Kam Hwy., Pearl City (© **808/453-5509**); and 94-144 Farrington Hwy., Waipahu (© **808/678-6800**). 801 Kaheka St. © 808/973-4800.

Fujioka's Wine Merchants   Oenophiles flock here for a mouthwatering selection of wines, single-malt Scotches, excellent Italian wines, and affordable, farm-raised caviar—food and libations for all occasions. Everyday wines, special-occasion wines, and esoteric wines are priced lower here than at most places. The wine-tasting bar at the rear of the store is a new attraction. Market City Shopping Center, 2919 Kapiolani Blvd., lower level. © 808/739-9463.

Honolulu Chocolate Co.   Life's greatest pleasures are dispensed here with abandon: expensive gourmet chocolates made in Honolulu, Italian and Hawaiian biscotti, boulder-size turtles, truffles, chocolate-covered coffee beans, and jumbo apricots in white and dark chocolate, to name a few. You pay dearly for them, but the dark-chocolate-dipped macadamia-nut clusters are beyond compare. Ward Centre, 1200 Ala Moana Blvd. © 808/591-2997.

It's Chili in Hawaii   This is *the* oasis for chile-heads, a house of heat with endorphins aplenty and good food to accompany the hot sauces from around the world, including a fabulous selection of made-in-Hawaii products. Scoville units (measurements of heat in food) are the topic of the day in this shop, lined with thousands of bottles of hot sauces, salsas, and other chile-based food products. Not everything is scorching, however; some products, like Dave's Soyabi and the limu-habañero sauce called Makai, are everyday flavor enhancers that can be used on rice, salads, meats, and pasta. If you're eating in, the fresh-frozen tamales, in several varieties (including meatless), are now in regular supply. Every Saturday free samples of green-chile stew are dished up to go with the generous hot-sauce tastings. Located by McCully Street, across the street from McDonald's. 2080 S. King St., Suite 105. © 808/945-7070.

Mauna Kea Marketplace Food Court   Hungry patrons line up for everything from pizza and plate lunches to quick, authentic, and inexpensive Vietnamese, Thai, Italian, Chinese, Japanese, and Filipino dishes. The best seafood fried rice comes from the woks of **Malee Thai/Vietnamese Cuisine**—it's perfectly flavored, with morsels of fish, squid, and shrimp. Tandoori Chicken Cafe serves a fount of Indian culinary pleasures, from curries and jasmine-chicken rice balls to spiced rounds of curried potatoes and a wonderful lentil dal. **Masa's** serves bento and Japanese dishes, such as miso eggplant, that are famous. You'll find the best dessert around at **Pho Lau,** which serves haupia (coconut pudding), tapioca, and taro in individual baskets made of pandanus. Join in the spirit of discovery at the produce stalls (pungent odors, fish heads, and chicken feet on counters—not for the squeamish). Vendors sell everything from fresh ahi and whole snapper to yams and taro, seaweed, and fresh fruits and vegetables. 1120 Maunakea St., Chinatown. © 808/524-3409.

Mazal's Kosherland Israeli Grocery Store   Now it is possible to keep kosher while in Hawaii with this tiny two-aisle (950-sq. ft.) shop, run by Ifat Sharabi, who grew up in Israel. She stocks the familiar, like Angel Bakery products, Ossem Passover foods, Pereq spices, tzfatit (a soft Israeli cheese), stuffed bureka pastries, canned goods

Health-Food Stores

In the university district, **Down to Earth,** 2525 S. King St., Moiliili (© 808/
947-7678), sells organic vegetables and vegetarian bulk foods, with good
prices, a strong selection of supplements and herbs, and a vegetarian juice-
and-sandwich bar. But my favorite is nearby **Kokua Market,** 2643 S. King St.
(© 808/941-1922), a health-food cooperative and Honolulu's best source for
organic vegetables. It also has an excellent variety of cheeses; pastas and
bulk grains; sandwiches, salads, and prepared foods; organic wines; and an
expanded vitamin section.

Tiny but powerful, with a loyal clientele, **House of Health,** 1541 S. Beretania St. (© 808/955-6168), has competitive prices and a wide selection of
health-food supplements. There's no produce, but there are frozen vegetarian foods, bulk grains, and healthful snacks. In Nuuanu Valley, mauka
(inland) of downtown Honolulu, **Huckleberry Farms,** 1613 Nuuanu Ave.
(© 808/524-7960), has a wide range of produce, vitamins, cosmetics, books,
and prepared vegetarian foods. A few doors down, the beauty and vitamin
retail outlet is stocked with cosmetics, nutritional supplements, and nonper-
ishable, nongrocery health products.

from Israel, frozen kosher meats and chilled dairy products from the Mainland. 555 N.
King, Kingsgate Plaza (at Dillingham Blvd.). © 808/848-1700.

People's Open Markets   Truck farmers from all over the island bring their produce to Oahu's neighborhoods in regularly scheduled, city-sponsored open markets,
held Monday through Saturday at various locations. Among the tables of ong choy,
choi sum, Okinawan spinach, opal basil, papayas, mangoes, seaweed, and fresh fish,
you'll find homemade banana bread, Chinese pomelo (like large grapefruit), fresh fid-
dleheads (fern shoots) when available, and colorful, bountiful harvests from land and
sea. Various sites around town. © 808/527-5167. www.honolulu.gov/parks/programs/pom/sked.htm.
Call to find the open market nearest you.

R. Field Wine Co.   Foodland has won countless new converts since Richard Field—
oenophile, gourmet, and cigar aficionado—moved his wine shop here. The thriving
gourmet store offers gemlike vine-ripened tomatoes and juicy clementines, sparkling
bags of Nalo gourmet greens, designer cheeses, caviar, Langenstein Farms macadamia
nuts, vegetarian and salmon mousses, vinegars, and all manner of epicurean delights,
including wines and single-malt Scotches. The warm, just-baked breads (rosemary–
olive oil, whole-wheat, organic wheat, and others) baked on the premises with dough
flown in from Los Angeles's famous La Brea Bakery are a huge hit. Foodland Super Market, 1460 S. Beretania St. © 808/596-9463.

Sushi Company   It's not easy to find premium-grade *hamachi* (yellowtail), ahi,
ikura (salmon roe), *ika* (cuttlefish), and other top-grade fresh ingredients in anything
but a bona fide sit-down sushi bar. But here it is, a small sparkling gem of a sushi
maker that sells fast-food sushi of non-fast-food quality, at great prices. Order ahead
or wait while they make it. The combinations range from minisets (27 pieces) to large-
variety sets (43–51 pieces), ideal for picnics and potlucks. Sushi Company has one

small two-person table; most of the business is takeout. 1111 McCully St. (at Young St.).
© 808/947-5411.

FLOWERS & LEIS

At most lei shops, simple leis sell for $10 and up, deluxe leis for $25 and up. For a
special-occasion designer bouquet or lei, you can't do better than Michael Miyashiro
of **Rainforest Plantes et Fleurs** (© 808/591-9999). He's an ecologically aware,
highly gifted lei maker—his leis are pricey but worth it. He custom-designs the lei for
the person and occasion. Order by phone or stop by the Ward Warehouse, where his
tiny shop is an oasis of green and beauty. Upon request, Miyashiro's leis will come in
ti-leaf bundles called *pu'olo,* custom gift baskets (in woven green coconut baskets), and
special arrangements. You can even request the card sentiments in Hawaiian, with
English translations.

The other primary sources for flowers and leis are the shops lining the streets of
Moiliili and Chinatown. Moiliili favorites include **Rudy's Flowers,** Isenburg at Beretania (© 808/944-8844), a local institution with the best prices on roses, Microne-
sian ginger lei, and a variety of cut blooms. Across the street, **Flowers for a Friend,**
2739 S. King St. (© 808/955-4227), has good prices on leis, floral arrangements, and
cut flowers. Nearby, **Flowers by Jr. and Lou,** 2652 S. King St. (© 808/941-2022),
offers calla lilies, Gerber daisies, a riot of potted orchids, and the full range of cut flowers along with its lei selection.

In Chinatown, lei vendors line Beretania and Maunakea streets, and the fragrances
of their wares mix with the earthy scents of incense and ethnic foods. My top picks
are **Lita's Leis,** 59 N. Beretania St. (© 808/521-9065), which has fresh puakenikeni,
gardenias that last, and a supply of fresh and reasonable leis; **Poohala Lei and Flowers,** 69 N. Beretania St. (© 808/537-3011), with a worthy selection of the classics at
fair prices; **Lin's Lei Shop,** 1017-A Maunakea St. (© 808/537-4112), with creatively
fashioned, unusual leis; and **Cindy's Lei Shoppe,** 1034 Maunakea St. (© 808/536-
6538), with terrific sources for unusual leis such as feather dendrobiums, firecracker
combinations, and everyday favorites like ginger, tuberose, orchid, and pikake. "Curb
service" is available with phone orders. Just give them your car's color and model, and
you can pick up your lei curbside—a great convenience on this busy street.

HAWAIIANA & GIFT ITEMS

My top recommendations are the **Academy Shop,** at the Honolulu Academy of Arts,
900 S. Beretania St. (© 808/523-8703), and the **Contemporary Museum Gift
Shop,** 2411 Makiki Heights Rd. (© 808/523-3447), two of the finest shopping stops
on Oahu and worth a special trip whether or not you want to see the museums themselves. (And you will want to see the museums, especially the recently expanded
Honolulu Academy of Arts.) The Academy Shop offers art books, jewelry, basketry,
ethnic fabrics, native crafts from all over the world, posters and books, and fiber vessels and accessories. The Contemporary Museum shop focuses on arts and crafts such
as avant-garde jewelry, cards and stationery, books, home accessories, and gift items
made by artists from Hawaii and across the country. I love the glammy selection of
jewelry and novelties, such as the twisted-wire wall hangings.

Hula Supply Center   Hawaiiana meets kitsch in this shop's marvelous selection of
Day-Glo cellophane skirts, bamboo nose flutes, T-shirts, hula drums, shell leis, feathered rattle gourds, lauhala accessories, fiber mats, and a wide assortment of pareu fabrics. Although hula dancers shop here for their dance accouterments, it's not all serious

shopping. This is fertile ground for souvenirs and memorabilia of Hawaii, rooted somewhere between irreverent humor and cultural integrity. 2346 S. King St. (at Isenbery), Moiliili. ⓒ 808/941-5379.

Native Books & Beautiful Things *(Finds* This *hui* (association) of artists and craftspeople is a browser's paradise featuring a variety Hawaiian items from musical instruments to calabashes, jewelry, leis, and books. You'll find contemporary Hawaiian clothing; handmade koa journals; Hawaii-themed home accessories; lauhala handbags and accessories; jams, jellies, and food products; etched glass; hand-painted fabrics and clothing; stone poi pounders; and other high-quality gift items. Some of Hawaii's finest artists in all craft media have their works available here on a regular basis, and the Hawaiian-book selection is tops. Ward Warehouse, 1050 Ala Moana Blvd. ⓒ 808/596-8885. Another location opening soon at the Waikiki Beach Walk.

Nohea Gallery A fine showcase for contemporary Hawaii art, Nohea celebrates the islands with thoughtful, attractive selections like pit-fired raku, finely turned wood vessels, jewelry, hand-blown glass, paintings, prints, fabrics (including Hawaiian-quilt cushions), and furniture. Nohea's selection is always evolving and growing, with 90% of the works by Hawaii artists. Ward Warehouse, 1050 Ala Moana Blvd. ⓒ 808/596-0074; Ward Center, 1200 Ala Moan Blvd. (ⓒ 808/591-9001) and Moana Surfrider Hotel, 2365 Kalakaua Ave. (ⓒ 808/923-6644). www.noheagallery.com.

Shop Pacifica Local crafts, lauhala and Cook Island woven coconut, Hawaiian music tapes and CDs, pareu, and a vast selection of Hawaii-themed books anchor this gift shop. Hawaiian quilt cushion kits, jewelry, glassware, seed and Niihau shell leis, cookbooks, and many other gift possibilities will keep you occupied between stargazing in the planetarium and pondering the shells and antiquities of the esteemed historical museum. In the Bishop Museum, 1525 Bernice St. ⓒ 808/848-4158.

SHOPPING CENTERS

Ala Moana Center Many of the shops here are the familiar names of mainland chains, such as **DKNY, Old Navy,** and **Eddie Bauer.** The three-story, superluxe **Neiman Marcus,** which opened in September 1998, was a bold move in Hawaii's troubled economy and has retained its position as the shrine of the fashionistas. But there are practical touches in the center, too, such as banks, a foreign-exchange service **(Thomas Cook),** a U.S. Post Office, several optical companies (including 1-hr. service by **LensCrafters**), **Foodland Supermarket, Longs Drugs,** and a handful of photo-processing services. The smaller locally owned stores are scattered among the behemoths, mostly on the ground floor. Nearly 400 shops and restaurants sprawl over several blocks (and 1.8 million sq. ft. of store space), catering to every imaginable need, from over-the-top upscale **(Tiffany, Chanel, Versace)** to mainland chains such as **Gap** and **Banana Republic.** Department stores such as **Macy's** sell fashion, food, cosmetics, shoes, and household needs. Need shoes? They're a kick at **Nordstrom,** and **Walking Co.** has first-rate comfort styles by Mephisto, Ecco, and Naot.

A good stop for gifts is **Islands' Best,** which spills over with Hawaiian-made foodstuffs, ceramics, fragrances, and more. **Splash! Hawaii** is a good source for women's swimwear. For aloha shirts and men's swimwear, try **Macy's, Town & Country Surf, Reyn's,** or the terminally hip **Hawaiian Island Creations.** Lovers of Polynesian wear and pareu shouldn't miss **Tahiti Imports.** The **food court** is abuzz with dozens of stalls purveying Cajun food, ramen, pizza, plate lunches, vegetarian fare, green tea and fruit freezes (like frozen yogurt), panini, and countless other treats. Open Monday

through Saturday 9:30am to 9pm, Sunday 10am to 7pm. 1450 Ala Moana Blvd. © 808/
955-9517. www.alamoanacenter.com. Bus: 8, 19, or 20. For Ala Moana Shuttle Bus runs and Waikiki Trolley information, see "Getting Around," earlier in this chapter.

Aloha Tower Marketplace   There is a perpetual parking shortage here, and if you
do manage to find a parking spot, the rates are sky high. Take the trolley if you can.
The refurbished Aloha Tower, once the tallest structure in Honolulu, still stands high
over the complex.

   Hawaiian House is a hit with its Island-style interiors and home accents. Dining
and shopping prospects abound: **Martin & MacArthur** gift shop, **Hawaiian Ukulele
Company, Sunglass Hut, Don Ho's Island Grill, Chai's Island Bistro,** and **Gordon
Biersch Brewery Restaurant** (see "Where to Dine," earlier in this chapter). Retail
shops are open Monday through Saturday 9am to 9pm, Sunday 9am to 6pm; dining
and entertainment daily 8am to midnight. 1 Aloha Tower Dr., on the waterfront between piers
8 and 11, Honolulu Harbor. © 808/528-5700. www.alohatower.com. Aloha Tower Entertainment Hotline © 808/566-2333. Various Honolulu trolleys stop here; if you want a direct ride from Waikiki, take
the free Hilo Hattie's trolley or the Waikiki Red Line trolley, which continues on to Hilo Hattie's in Iwilei.

DFS Galleria   "Boat days" is the theme at this newly renovated (to the tune of $65
million) Waikiki emporium, a three-floor extravaganza of shops ranging from the
superluxe (like **Givenchy** and **Coach**) to the very touristy. There are some great
Hawaii food products, though, ranging from the incomparable **Big Island Candies'**
shortbread cookies to a spate of coffees and preserves. **The Tube,** a walk-through
aquarium, is a big attraction. There are multitudes of aloha shirts and T-shirts, a virtual golf course, surf and skate equipment, a terrific Hawaiian music department, and
a labyrinth of fashionable stores once you get past the Waikiki Walk. Fragrances and
cosmetics make a big splash at **DFS. Starbucks** and **Jamba Juice** serve up coffee and
smoothies, and **Kalia Grill** features rotisserie and deli items for casual dining. *Caveat:*
Some sections are duty-free and, therefore, restricted to international travelers only.
Free live Hawaiian entertainment, featuring hula styles from the 1920s through the
1940s, takes place nightly at 7pm. Open daily 9am to 11pm. 330 Royal Hawaiian Ave. (corner of Kalakaua and Royal Hawaiian aves.). © 808/931-2655. www.dfsgalleria.com.

Kahala Mall   Chic, manageable, and unfrenzied, Kahala Mall is home to some of
Honolulu's best shops. Located east of Waikiki in the posh neighborhood of Kahala,
the mall has everything from a small **Macy's** to chain stores such as **Banana Republic** and **Gap**—nearly 100 specialty shops (including dozens of eateries and eight movie
theaters) in an enclosed, air-conditioned area. Java-magnet **Starbucks** sits a stone's
throw from the **Gourmet Express** with its fast, healthy salads; tortilla wraps; and fresh
juices. Smoothie lovers form long lines at **Jamba Juice.** For gift, fashion, and specialty
stores, my picks of the mall's best and brightest are **Riches,** a tiny kiosk with a big,
bold selection of jewelry; the **Compleat Kitchen;** the **Paperie,** with an impressive
selection of stationery, cards, napkins, and paper goods; and the sprawling **Hawaiian
House.** Open Monday through Saturday 10am to 9pm, Sunday 10am to 5pm. 4211
Waialae Ave., Kahala. © 808/732-7736. www.kahalamallcenter.com.

Royal Hawaiian Shopping Center   After 2 years and $84 million in remodeling
and renovations a new, larger, upscale shopping center opened in 2007 with new
shops, restaurants, a nightclub and theater, entry porte-cochere, and even a garden
grove of 70 coconut trees with entertainment area. The result is a 293,000-square foot
open-air mall (17,000 sq. ft. larger than before) with 110 stores, restaurants, and

entertainment on four levels. One of the flagship stores is **Hilo Hattie,** with some 30,000 square feet. The center also has a garden grove in the center of the mall with a pond, artesian fountain, stream running through, and performance area. The most exciting addition is the $15-million, 760-seat theater, with moving stages and acrobatic rigging. Then after the show, half of the theater's seating will retract to create a nightclub that can hold up to 1,000 people. *Upscale* is the operative word here. Although there are drugstores, lei stands, restaurants, and food kiosks, the most conspicuous stores are the European designer boutiques (**Chanel, Cartier, Hermès, L'Occitane, Fendi, Kate Spade, Bvlgari, Salvatore Ferragamo,** and more) that cater largely to visitors from Japan. Open daily 10am to 10pm. 2201 Kalakaua Ave., Honolulu. ✆ 808/922-0588. www.shopwaikiki.com.

Waikele Premium Outlets   Just say the word *Waikele* and my eyes glaze over. So many shops, so little time! There are two sections to this sprawling discount shopping mecca: the **Waikele Premium Outlets,** some 51 retailers offering designer and namebrand merchandise, and the **Waikele Value Center** across the street, with another 25 stores more practical than fashion oriented (**Eagle Hardware, Sports Authority**). The 64-acre complex has made discount shopping a travel pursuit in itself, with tours for visitor groups and carloads of neighbor islanders and Oahu residents making pilgrimages from all corners of the state. They come to hunt down bargains on everything from perfumes, luggage, and hardware to sporting goods, fashions, vitamins, and china. Examples: **Geoffrey Beene, Donna Karan, Saks Fifth Avenue, Anne Klein, Mikasa, Kenneth Cole, Banana Republic,** and the ultrachic **Barneys.** Open Monday through Friday 9am to 9pm, Sunday 10am to 6pm. 94–790 Lumiaina St., Waikele (about 20 miles from Waikiki). ✆ 808/676-5656. www.premiumoutlets.com. Take H-1 west toward Waianae and turn off at Exit 7. Bus: 42 from Waikiki to Waipahu Transit Center, then 433 from Transit Center to Waikele. To find out which companies offer shopping tours with Waikiki pickups, call the **Information Center** at ✆ 808/678-0786; www.premiumoutlets.com/waikele.

Ward Centre   Although it has a high turnover and a changeable profile, Ward Centre is a standout for its concentration of restaurants and shops. **Ryan's** and **Kakaako Kitchen** are as popular as ever, the former looking out over Ala Moana Park and the latter with lanai views of the sprawling **Pier 1 Imports** across the street. **Nordstrom Rack** and **Office Depot** have sprouted in a new development area that also includes a 16-theater movie megaplex now being built. All these establishments are part of developer Victoria Ward's Kakaako projects, which take up several blocks in this area: Ward Centre, Ward Farmers Market, Ward Village Shops, Ward Gateway Center, and Ward Warehouse.

Ward Centre's gift shops and galleries include **Crazy Shirts Factory Outlet** for Tshirts, **Paper Roses** for wonderful paper products, **Honolulu Chocolate Co.** (see "Edibles," earlier in this chapter), and the very attractive **The Gallery. Borders** is action central, bustling with browsers. Open Monday through Saturday 10am to 9pm, Sunday 10am to 5pm. 1200 Ala Moana Blvd. ✆ 808/591-8411. www.victoriaward.com.

Ward Entertainment Center   This large, multiblock complex includes Ward Centre, mentioned above, and Ward Warehouse, mentioned below, at the corner of Auahi and Kamakee streets. The complex has undergone enormous expansion, beginning with a new 16-movie megaplex and a new retail-and-restaurant complex, with eateries like **Dave & Buster's** (with virtual golf, games, interactive entertainment, bars, and a restaurant), **Buca di Beppo, Wolfgang Puck Express,** and **Cold Stone**

Creamery. Open Monday through Saturday 10am to 10pm, Sunday 10am to 9pm. Auahi and Kamakee sts. ℂ **808/591-8411.** www.victoriaward.com.

Ward Warehouse   Older than its sister property, Ward Centre, and endowed with an endearing patina, Ward Warehouse remains a popular stop for dining and shopping. **Native Books & Beautiful Things** and the **Nohea Gallery** (see "Hawaiiana & Gift Items," above, for both) are excellent sources for quality Hawaii-made arts and crafts.

Other recommended stops include **C. June Shoes** for designer footwear; **Mamo Howell** for distinctive aloha wear; **Private World** for sachets, linens, and fragrances; and **Little People Hawaii,** brimming with tasteful gifts for kids and babies. For T-shirts and swimwear, check out the **Town & Country Surf Shop,** and for an excellent selection of sunglasses, knapsacks, and footwear, don't miss **Thongs 'N Things.** Open Monday through Saturday 10am to 9pm, Sunday 10am to 5pm. 1050 Ala Moana Blvd. ℂ **808/591-8411.** www.victoriaward.com.

SURF & SPORTS

The surf-and-sports shops scattered throughout Honolulu are a highly competitive lot, with each trying to capture your interest (and dollars). The top sources for sports gear and accessories in town are **McCully Bicycle & Sporting Goods,** 2124 S. King St. (ℂ **808/955-6329**), with everything from bicycles and fishing gear to athletic shoes and accessories, along with a stunning selection of sunglasses; and **The Bike Shop,** 1149 S. King St., near Piikoi Street (ℂ **808/596-0588**), excellent for cycling and backpacking equipment for all levels, with major camping lines such as North Face, MSR, and Kelty. Avid cyclists coming to Oahu should make this a definite stop; it's the hub of cycling news on the island, offering night tours of downtown Honolulu by bicycle and other cycling activities islandwide. The **Sports Authority,** at 333 Ward Ave. (ℂ **808/596-0166**) and at Waikele Center (ℂ **808/677-9933**), is a discount megaoutlet offering clothing, cycles, and equipment.

Surf shops, centers of fashion as well as definers of daring, include **Local Motion** in Waikiki and Windward Mall (ℂ **808/979-7873**), **Town and Country** in Ala Moana Center and Ward Warehouse, and **Hawaiian Island Creations** at Ala Moana Center (ℂ **808/941-4491**). Local Motion is the icon of surfers and skateboarders, both professionals and wannabes; the shop offers surfboards, T-shirts, aloha and casual wear, boogie boards, and countless accessories for life in the sun. Hawaiian Island Creations is another supercool surf shop offering sunglasses, sun lotions, surf wear, and accessories galore.

SHOPPING IN WINDWARD OAHU

Windward Oahu's largest shopping complex is **Windward Mall,** 46–056 Kamehameha Hwy., in Kaneohe (ℂ **808/235-1143;** www.windwardmall.com), open Monday through Saturday from 10am to 9pm and Sunday from 10am to 5pm. The 100 stores and services at this standard suburban mall include **Macy's** and **Sears,** health stores, airline counters, surf shops, **LensCrafters,** and a 10-screen theater complex. A small food court serves pizza, Chinese fare, tacos, and other morsels.

All of the listings below can be found in the town of **Kailua,** whose shopping nexus is formed by **Long's Drugs** and **Macy's** department store, located side by side on Kailua Road.

The *malassada* mecca of Oahu is **Agnes Portuguese Bake Shop,** 46 Hoolai St. (ℂ **808/262-5367**). (*Malassadas* are sugary Portuguese dumplings, like doughnuts without holes.) With its abundance of free parking and a menu of homemade soups, artisan breads, and unique pastries, Agnes is a Kailua treasure.

Alii Antiques of Kailua II   Abandon all restraint, particularly if you have a weakness for vintage Hawaiiana. Koa lamps and rattan furniture from the 1930s and 1940s, hula nodders, rare 1940s koa tables, Roseville vases, Don Blanding dinnerware, and a breathtaking array of vintage etched-glass vases and trays are some of the items in this unforgettable shop. Across the street, the owner's wife runs **Alii Antiques of Kailua,** which is chockablock with jewelry, clothing, Bauer and Fiesta Ware, linens, Bakelite bracelets, and floor-to-ceiling collectibles. 9-A Maluniu Ave., Kailua. ℂ 808/261-1705.

BookEnds   BookEnds is the quintessential neighborhood bookstore, run by a pro who buys good books and knows how to find the ones she doesn't have. There are more than 60,000 titles here, new and used, from *Celtic Mandalas* to C. S. Lewis's *Chronicles of Narnia* and the full roster of current bestsellers. Volumes on child care, cooking, and self-improvement; a hefty periodicals section; and mainstream and off-beat titles are among the treasures to be found. 600 Kailua Rd., Kailua. ℂ 808/261-1996.

Heritage Antiques & Gifts   This Kailua landmark is known for its selection of Tiffany-style lamps ($200–$2,000). The mind-boggling inventory also includes European, Asian, American, local, and Pacific Island collectibles. The shop is fun, the people friendly, and the selection diverse enough to appeal to the casual as well as serious collector. Glassware, china, and estate, costume, and fine jewelry are among the items of note. Heritage has its own jeweler who does custom designs and repairs, plus a stable of woodworkers who turn out custom-made koa rockers and hutches to complement the antique furniture selection. 767 Kailua Rd. ℂ 808/261-8700.

SHOPPING ON THE NORTH SHORE: HALEIWA

Like Hilo on the Big Island and Maui's upcountry Makawao, Haleiwa means serious shopping for those who know that the unhurried pace of rural life can conceal vast material treasures. Ask the legions of townies who drive an hour each way just to stock up on wine and clothes at Haleiwa stores. (Of course, a cooler is de rigueur for perishables.) Below are some Haleiwa highlights.

ARTS, CRAFTS & GIFT ITEMS

Haleiwa's shops and galleries display a combination of marine art, watercolors, sculptures, and a plethora of crafts trying to masquerade (quite transparently) as fine art. This is the town for gifts, fashions, and surf stuff—mostly casual, despite some very high price tags. **Haleiwa Gallery,** next door to the North Shore Marketplace, displays a lot of local art of the nonmarine variety, and some of it is very appealing.

Global Creations Interiors, 66–079 Kamehameha Hwy. (ℂ 808/637-1505), offers casual clothes as well as international imports for the home, including Balinese bamboo furniture and colorful Yucatan hammocks. There are gifts and crafts by 115 local potters, painters, and artists of other media.

North Shore Glass Blowers, in the North Shore Marketplace (ℂ 808/637-4853), is an art glass studio featuring the work of Tracy and Denise Jacob. Additional glass art can be found in the same shopping center at **Oceans in Glass** (ℂ 808/637-3366), which has sculptures of dolphins, sea turtles, humpback whales, sharks, and colorful reef fish. You can watch as local artists create these beautiful sea life sculptures in their studios within the gallery.

EDIBLES

Haleiwa is best known for its roadside shave-ice stands: the famous **Matsumoto Shave Ice** ⚝⚝, 66–087 Kamehameha Hwy. (© **808/637-4827**), with the perennial queue snaking along Kamehameha Highway, and nearby **Aoki's.** Shave ice is the popular island version of a snow cone, topped with your choice of syrups, such as strawberry, rainbow, root beer, vanilla, or passion fruit. For a real exotic treat, order the *li hing mui* flavor. Aficionados order it with a scoop of ice cream and sweetened black adzuki beans nestled in the middle.

Tiny, funky **Celestial Natural Foods,** 66–443 Kamehameha Hwy. (© **808/637-6729**), is the health foodies' Grand Central for everything from wooden spine-massagers to health supplements, produce, cosmetics, and bulk foods.

FASHION

Although Haleiwa used to be an incense-infused surfer outpost where zoris and tank tops were the regional uniform and the Beach Boys and Ravi Shankar the music of the day, today it's one of the top shopping destinations for those with unconventional tastes. Specialty shops abound.

Top-drawer **Silver Moon Emporium,** North Shore Marketplace, 66–250 Kamehameha Hwy. (© **808/637-7710**), features the terrific finds of owner Lucie Talbot-Holu. Exquisite clothing and handbags, reasonably priced footwear, hats straight out of *Vogue,* jewelry, scarves, and a full gamut of other treasures pepper the attractive boutique. The entire line of chic Brighton accessories—shoes, handbags, fragrance, belts, and jewelry—are a prized addition.

In addition to Silver Moon, highlights of the prominent North Shore Marketplace include **Patagonia** (© **808/637-1245**), for high-quality surf, swim, hiking, kayaking, and all-around adventure wear; **North Shore Swimwear** (© **808/637-6859**), for excellent mix-and-match bikinis and one-piece suits, custom-ordered or off the rack; **Hawaiian Surf** (© **808/637-8316**), which specializes in custom-designed surf boards but also has hand-made clothing for men and women and "island-style" jewelry; and **Jungle Gems** (© **808/637-6609**), the mother lode of gemstones, crystals, silver, and beadwork.

Nearby **Oogenesis Boutique,** 66–249 Kamehameha Hwy. (© **808/637-4580**), in the southern part of Haleiwa, features a storefront lined with vintage-looking dresses that flutter prettily in the North Shore breeze.

SURF SHOPS

Haleiwa's ubiquitous surf shops are the best on earth, surfers say. At the top of the heap is **Northshore Boardriders Club,** North Shore Marketplace, 66–250 Kamehameha Hwy. (© **808/637-5026**), the mecca of the board-riding elite, with sleek, fast, elegant, and top-of-the-line boards designed by North Shore legends such as long-board shapers Barry Kanaiaupuni, John Carper, Jeff Bushman, and Pat Rawson. The store is also a testing ground for the newest and hottest trends in surf wear put out by retail giant Quicksilver.

In the North Shore Marketplace, **Raging Isle Sports** (© **808/637-7707**) is the surf-and-cycle center of the area, with everything from wet suits and surfboards to surf gear and clothing for men, women, and children. The adjoining surfboard factory puts out custom-built boards of high renown. There's also a large inventory of mountain bikes for rent.

A longtime favorite among old-timers is the newly expanded **Surf & Sea Surf Sail & Dive Shop,** 62–595 Kamehameha Hwy. (© **808/637-9887**), a flamboyant road-side structure just over the bridge, with old wood floors and a tangle of surf- and swimwear, T-shirts, surfboards, boogie boards, fins, watches, sunglasses, and more; you can also rent surf and snorkel equipment here.

Tropical Rush, 62–620-A Kamehameha Hwy. (© **808/637-8886**), has a huge inventory of surf and swim gear: surfboards, long boards, body boards, Sector 9 skate-boards, and slippers and swimwear for men and women. T-shirts, hats, sunglasses, and visors are among the scads of cool gear, and you can rent equipment and arrange surf lessons, too. An added feature is the shop's surf report line for the up-to-the-minute lowdown on wave action (© **808/638-7874**); it covers the day's surf and weather details for all of Oahu.

14 Oahu After Dark

Nightlife in Hawaii begins at sunset, when all eyes turn westward to see how the day will end. Sunset viewers always seem to bond in the mutual enjoyment of a natural spectacle. People in Hawaii are fortunate to have an environment that encourages this cultural ritual.

On Friday and Saturday at 6:30pm in the winter and at 7pm in the summer, as the sun casts its golden glow on the beach, **Kuhio Beach,** where Kalakaua Avenue inter-sects with Kaiulani, eases into evening with hula dancing and a torch-lighting cere-mony. This is a thoroughly delightful, free weekend offering. Start off earlier with a picnic basket and walk along the ocean-side path fronting Queen's Surf, near the Waikiki Aquarium. (You can park along Kapiolani Park or near the zoo.) There are few more pleasing spots in Waikiki than the benches at water's edge at this Diamond Head end of Kalakaua Avenue. A short walk across the intersection of Kalakaua and Kapahulu avenues, where the seawall and daring boogie boarders attract hordes of spectators, takes you to the Duke Kahanamoku statue on Kuhio Beach and the nearby Wizard Stones. Here you can view the torch-lighting and hula, and gear up for the strolling musicians who amble down Kalakaua Avenue every Friday from 8 to 10pm. The musicians begin at Beachwalk Avenue at the Ewa (western) end of Waikiki and end up at the statue.

BARS

ON THE BEACH   Waikiki's beachfront bars also offer many possibilities, from the **Mai Tai Bar** (© **808/923-7311**) at the Royal Hawaiian hotel (p. 121), a few feet from the sand, to the unfailingly enchanting **House Without a Key** (© **808/923-2311**), at the Halekulani (p. 119), where the breathtaking **Kanoelehua Miller** dances hula to the riffs of Hawaiian steel-pedal guitar under a century-old kiawe tree with the sunset and ocean glowing behind her—a romantic, evocative, nostalgic scene. It doesn't hurt, either, that the Halekulani happens to make the best mai tais in the world. This place has the after-dinner hours covered, too, with light jazz by local artists from 10:15pm to midnight nightly (see "Jazz" below).

Another great bar for watching the sun sink into the Pacific and enjoying a liquid libation is **Duke's Canoe Club** (© **808/922-2268;** www.dukeswaikiki.com), in the Outrigger Waikiki on the Beach hotel (p. 120). The outside Barefoot Bar is perfect for sipping a tropical drink, watching the waves and sunset, and listening to music. It can get crowded, so get there early. Hawaii sunset music is usually from 4 to 6pm on weekends, and there's live entertainment nightly from 10pm to midnight.

ALOHA TOWER MARKETPLACE   The landmark Aloha Tower at Honolulu Harbor, once Oahu's tallest building, has always occupied Honolulu's prime downtown location—on the water, at a naturally sheltered bay, near the business and civic center of Honolulu. Since its construction, the Aloha Tower Marketplace, 1 Aloha Tower Dr. (on the waterfront between Piers 8 and 11, Honolulu Harbor; © 808/528-5700), has gained popularity as an entertainment and nightlife spot, with more than 100 shops and restaurants, including several venues for Honolulu's leading musical groups.

Various venues in the marketplace offer live music. There's live music nightly at the popular open-air **Pier Bar** (© 808/536-2166): contemporary Hawaiian, swing, alternative rock, and jazz. At the recently expanded **Gordon Biersch Brewery Restaurant** (p. 157), where a new stage area was added, diners swing to jazz, blues, and island riffs. Most notable, however, are **Don Ho's Island Grill** (p. 157) and **Chai's Island Bistro,** Honolulu's hottest nightspots (see "Hawaiian Music," below, for more on Chai's).

Across the street from Aloha Tower Marketplace, the bar and lounge of **Palomino** (© 808/528-2400) is a magnet for revelers, often two deep at the bar. You'll find great appetizers, pizzas, service, and drinks, and you can order from the full dinner menu as well.

DOWNTOWN   The downtown scene is awakening from a long slumber, thanks to the performances at the Hawaii Theatre and the popular Nuuanu Avenue block parties, courtesy of some tenacious entrepreneurs who want everyone to love Nuuanu as much as they do. **Hanks Café,** on Nuuanu between Hotel and King streets (© 808/526-1410), is a tiny, kitschy, friendly pub with live music nightly, open-mic nights, and special events that attract great talent and a supportive crowd. On some nights, the music spills out into the streets and it's so packed you have to press your nose against the window to see what you're missing. At the makai end of Nuuanu, toward the pier, **Murphy's Bar & Grill** (© 808/531-0422) is a popular downtown ale house and media haunt that have kept Irish eyes smiling for years.

CLUB SCENE

The nightclub scene in Waikiki and Honolulu is just as hot as the sun-kissed beaches during the day. It's more laid-back than in big cities like New York; dress is casual (no slippers, tank tops, or athletic wear), and there's no point to even showing up until midnight. The **Wave Waikiki,** 1877 Kalakaua Ave. (between Ala Wai Blvd. and Ena Rd.; © 808/941-0424; www.wavewaikiki.com), is one of Hawaii's top dance clubs, with two levels (and two bars), featuring a huge variety of live music and every type of DJ you can think of. Open nightly from 9pm to 4am; the weekday cover is $5 and weekends $7 (except for special events, then expect to pay more). Dress code is so laid-back, all they care about is you have something on your back and on your feet.

Twice the size of the Wave and filled with dancing, darts, pool, and a sports bar with huge TV screens is the **Pipeline,** 805 Pohukaina St., in Kakaako (© 808/589-1999; www.pipelinecafe.net). Patrons here tend to be younger than at the Wave (you can get in at 18 years old) and they are dressed to go clubbing. Cover charge generally is $1 to $3; concerts are around $15.

The 20-something crowd, visitors, and military tend to head to **Moose McGilly-cuddy's,** 310 Lewers in Waikiki (© **808/923-0751;** www.maui.net/~mooses/mooses_waikiki). Downstairs is a cafe serving breakfast, lunch, and dinner; upstairs is a happening live entertainment and dance club. Open nightly with bikini contests on Sunday, Ladies' Night on Wednesday, and $1 drink night on Tuesday.

At the edge of Chinatown is something from a 1940s film noir: **Indigo's,** 1121 Nuuanu Ave. (© **808/521-2900;** www.indigo-hawaii.com), serves sizzling food during the day, turns to cool jazz in the early evening, and progresses to late-night DJs spinning Top 40, disco, rock, funk, and more.

The college-age crowd flocks to **Blue Tropix,** 1700 Kapiolani Blvd. (© **808/944-0001**), which features a small, 100-square-foot dance floor and lively DJ jams of Top 40, hip-hop, and R&B dance music. There's a $5 cover charge. Open daily from 10pm to 2am.

Downstairs in the lobby of the Ala Moana Hotel, **Rumours Nightclub** (© **808/955-4811**) is the disco of choice for those who remember Paul McCartney as something other than Stella's father. The theme changes by the month, but generally, it's the "Big Chill" '60s, '70s, and '80s music on Friday; the "Little Chill" on Saturday; ballroom dancing from 5 to 9pm on Sunday; Top 40 on Tuesday; karaoke on Wednesday; and an "after-work office party" to midnight on Thursday. A spacious dance floor, a good sound system, and Top 40 music draw a mix of generations.

At Restaurant Row, **Ocean Club,** 500 Ala Moana Blvd. (© **808/526-9888;** www.oceanclubonline.com), is the Row's hottest and hippest spot. Good seafood appetizers, attractive happy-hour prices, a fabulous quirky interior, and passionate DJs in alternative garb make up a dizzyingly successful formula. The minimum age is 23 (except on Thurs), and the dress code calls for "smart-casual"—no T-shirts, slippers, hats, athletic wear, ripped jeans, or beachwear (see also the dining review on p. 159).

For the more mature set, **Aaron's Atop the Ala Moana,** in the Ala Moana Hotel, 410 Atkinson Dr. (© **808/955-4466**), has the best view in town. From the 36th floor of the hotel (take the express elevator), watch the Honolulu city lights wrap around the room and cha-cha-cha to the vertigo! There's live music and dancing nightly, a great dinner menu, and an appetizer menu nightly from 5pm.

Get Down with ARTafterDark

The last Friday of every month (except Nov and Dec), the place to be after the sun goes down is the **Honolulu Academy of Arts' ARTafterDark,** a *pau-hana* (after-work) mixer in the art museum, at 900 S. Beretania St., that brings residents and visitors together around a theme combining art with food, music, and dancing. In addition to the exhibits in the gallery, ARTafterDark features visual and live performances. Last year the themes ranged from "Plant Rice" with rice and sake-tastings, rice dishes, and Asian beers with live Asian fusion music and a tour of the *Art of Rice* exhibit to "'80s Night," "Turkish Delights," "Cool Nights, Hot Jazz and Blues," and "Havana Heat."

Entry fee is $7, the party gets going about 6pm and lasts to 9pm; the crowd ranges from 20s to 50s, and the dress is everything from jeans and T-shirts to designer cocktail party attire. For more information, © **808/532-6091.**

HAWAIIAN MUSIC

Oahu has several key spots for Hawaiian music. A delightful addition to the Waikiki music scene is Hawaii's queen of falsetto, **Genoa Keawe,** who fills the Lobby Bar of the Waikiki Beach (© **808/922-6611**) with her larger-than-life voice. You'll find her here from 5:30 to 8:30pm every Thursday; the rest of the week, except Monday, other contemporary Hawaiian musicians fill in.

Brothers Cazimero remain one of Hawaii's most gifted duos (Robert on bass, Roland on 12-string guitar), appearing every Wednesday at 7pm at a leading venue for Hawaiian entertainment, **Chai's Island Bistro** (© **808/585-0011;** www.chais islandbistro.com), in the Aloha Tower Marketplace. Also at Chai's: Robert Cazimero plays by himself on the piano on Tuesday at 7pm, and **Jerry Santos** and **Olomana** perform on Monday at 7pm. If you're here on May 1, Lei Day, try to make it to the special concert the Brothers Caz give every year at the Waikiki Shell. Locals dress up in their leis and best aloha shirts, the air smells like pikake and pakalana, and you might even see the moon rise over Diamond Head.

Impromptu hula and spirited music from the family and friends of the performers are an island tradition at places such as the Hilton Hawaiian Village's **Paradise Lounge** (© **808/949-4321**), which serves as a large living room for the full-bodied music of **Olomana.** The group plays Friday and Saturday from 8pm to midnight (no cover, one-drink minimum).

Nearby, the Moana Surfrider offers a regular nightly program of live Hawaiian music and piano in its **Banyan Veranda** (© **808/922-3111**), which surrounds an islet-size canopy of banyan tree and roots where Robert Louis Stevenson loved to linger. The Veranda serves afternoon tea, a sunset buffet, and cocktails.

My best advice for lovers of Hawaiian music is to scan the local dailies or the *Honolulu Weekly* (www.honoluluweekly.com) to see if and where the following Hawaiian entertainers are appearing: **Kekuhi Kanahele,** an accomplished, award-winning chanter and *kahiko* (ancient hula) dancer; **Ho'okena,** a symphonically rich quintet featuring **Manu Boyd,** one of the most prolific songwriters and chanters in Hawaii; **Keali'i Reichel,** premier chanter, dancer, and award-winning recording artist; **Robbie Kahakalau,** another award-winning musician; **Kapena,** for contemporary Hawaiian music; **Na Leo Pilimehana,** a trio of angelic Hawaiian singers; the **Makaha Sons of Niihau,** pioneers in the Hawaiian cultural renaissance; **Fiji,** the stage name of artist George Veikoso, one of the most popular entertainers in Hawaii, with a unique blend of Hawaiian, Fijian, and other Polynesian music; and slack-key guitar master **Raymond Kane.**

Consider the gods beneficent if you happen to be here when the hula halau of **Frank Kawaikapuokalani Hewett** is holding its annual fundraiser. It's a rousing, inspired, family effort that always features the best in ancient and contemporary Hawaiian music. For the best in hula, check the dailies for halau fundraisers, which are always authentic, enriching, and local to the core.

SHOWROOM ACTS & REVUES

Showroom acts that have maintained a following include *The Magic of Polynesia* (© **808/971-4321;** www.magicofpolynesia.com), a show with illusionist **John Hirokana** at 8pm: dinner $77 adults, $54 children ages 4 to 11; show only $50 adults, $33 children ages 4 to 11. This was also the home of Hawaiian entertainer Don Ho, until, sadly, he passed away in 2007.

Across Kalakaua Avenue in the **Outrigger Waikiki on the Beach,** the **Society of Seven**'s nightclub act (a blend of skits, Broadway hits, popular music, and costumed musical acts) is into its third decade, no small feat for performers. Shows are Tuesday through Sunday at 8pm. Dinner costs $75 to $89 adults, $66 ages 2 to 20; show only is $49 adults and $38 children 2 to 20 (© **888/349-7888;** www.societyofseven.com).

Still sizzling in the Polynesian revue world is the Sheraton Princess Kaiulani's **"Creation—A Polynesian Odyssey"** (© **808/922-5811**), in the hotel's second-floor Ainahau Showroom. Produced by **Tihati,** the state's largest entertainment company, the show is a theatrical journey of fire dancing, special effects, illusions, hula, and Polynesian dances from Hawaii and the South Pacific. Shows are Tuesday, Thursday, Friday, Saturday, and Sunday, and cost $68 to $105 adults and $51 to $79 for kids 5 to 12 years for dinner; $38 for just the show.

The best in comedy is **Andy Bumatai,** who performs local stand-up sketches that will have you not only understanding local residents, but also screaming with laughter. Another excellent comic is **Frank Delima.** If he's playing anywhere on Oahu, it's worth the drive to see this comic genus, who sings, dances, and performs comic routines that will have you laughing until your sides hurt.

THE BLUES

The blues are alive and well in Hawaii, with quality acts (both local and from the mainland) drawing enthusiastic crowds. Past performers include **Junior Wells, Willie & Lobo, War,** with surprise appearances by the likes of **Bonnie Raitt.** The best-loved Oahu venue is **Anna Bannana's,** 2440 S. Beretania St., between University Avenue/Isenberg Street(© **808/946-5190**), still rocking after 30 years in the business, with reggae, blues, and rock—plus video games and darts.

JAZZ

Jazz lovers should watch for the Great Hawaiian Jazz Blow-Out every March at Mid-Pacific Institute's Bakken Hall, at the south end of Honolulu, near Diamond Head. To find out what's happening in the jazz scene while you're in town, check out www.honolulujazzscene.net. **Diamond Head Grill** (© **808/922-3734;** p. 142) features live music nightly, and **Duc's Bistro** (© **808/531-6325;** p. 158), downtown, presents live jazz nightly except Thursday, when vocalist Mihana Souza performs Hawaiian music. **Nick's Fishmarket,** Waikiki Gateway Hotel, 2070 Kalakaua Ave. (© **808/955-6333**), still offers live entertainment nightly in its lounge—mild jazz or Top 40 contemporary hits.

Tops in taste and ambience is the perennially alluring **Lewers Lounge,** in the Halekulani, 2199 Kalia Rd. (© **808/923-2311;** www.halekulani.com). Recent renovations (including comfy intimate seating around the pillars) make this a great spot for contemporary jazz nightly from 8:30pm to midnight, and with expert mixologist Dale DeGroff (the "king of cocktails") now the hotel's director of beverages, the drinks are better than ever. Be sure to try the Hpnotiq Liqueur, a blend of premium vodka, cognac, and fruit juices from France.

Outside of Waikiki, the **Veranda,** at the Kahala Hotel & Resort, 5000 Kahala Ave. (© **808/739-8888;** www.kahalaresort.com), is a popular spot for the over-40 crowd, with nightly jazz music and a dance floor.

Around town, watch for **Sandy Tsukiyama,** a gifted singer (Brazilian, Latin, jazz) and one of Honolulu's great assets, and jazz singers **Rachel Gonzales** and **Loretta**

Ables. Other groups in jazz, blues, and R&B include **Blue Budda, Bongo Tribe, Secondhand Smoke, Bluzilla, Piranha Brothers,** and the **Greg Pai Trio.**

THE PERFORMING ARTS

"Aloha shirt to Armani" is how I describe the night scene in Honolulu—mostly casual but with ample opportunity to part with your flip-flops and dress up.

Audiences have grooved to the beat of off-Broadway percussion hit *Stomp* and have enjoyed the talent of *Tap Dogs,* Momix, the Jim Nabors Christmas show, the Hawaii International Jazz Festival, the American Repertory Dance Company, barbershop quartets, and John Ka'imikaua's halau—all at the **Hawaii Theatre,** 1130 Bethel St., downtown (© **808/528-0506**). The theater is still basking in its renaissance following a 4-year, $22-million renovation. The neoclassical Beaux Arts landmark features a 1922 dome, 1,400 plush seats, a hydraulically elevated organ, breathtaking murals, and gilt galore, all working to create an atmosphere that's making the theater a leading multipurpose center for the performing arts.

The **Honolulu Symphony Orchestra** has booked some of its performances at the new theater, but it still performs at the Waikiki Shell and the **Neal Blaisdell Concert Hall** (© **808/591-2211**). Meanwhile, the highly successful **Hawaii Opera Theatre,** in its 41st season (past hits have included *La Bohème, Carmen,* and *Aïda*), still draws fans to the Neal Blaisdell Concert Hall, as do Hawaii's four ballet companies: **Hawaii Ballet Theatre, Ballet Hawaii, Hawaii State Ballet,** and **Honolulu Dance Theatre.** Contemporary performances by **Dances We Dance** and the **Iona Pear Dance Company,** a strikingly creative group performing Butoh (a contemporary dance form that originated in Japan), are worth tracking down if you love the avant-garde.

Hawaii, the Big Island

The Big Island of Hawaii—the island that lends its name to the entire 1,500-mile-long Hawaiian archipelago—is where Mother Nature pulled out all the stops. Simply put, it's spectacular.

The Big Island has it all: fiery volcanoes and sparkling waterfalls, black-lava deserts and snowcapped mountain peaks, tropical rainforests and alpine meadows, a glacial lake and miles of golden, black, and even green-sand beaches. The Big Island has an unmatched diversity of terrain and climate. A 50-mile drive will take you from snowy winter to sultry summer, passing through spring or fall along the way. The island looks like the inside of a barbecue pit on one side and a lush jungle on the other.

The Big Island is the largest island in the Hawaiian chain (4,038 sq. miles—about the size of Connecticut), the youngest (800,000 years), and the least populated (with 30 people per sq. mile). It has the highest peaks in the Pacific, the most volcanoes of any Hawaiian island, and the newest land on earth.

Five volcanoes—one still erupting—have created this continental island, which is growing bigger daily. At its heart is snowcapped Mauna Kea, the world's tallest sea mountain (measured from the ocean floor), complete with its own glacial lake. Mauna Kea's nearest neighbor is Mauna Loa (or "Long Mountain"), creator of one-sixth of the island; it's the largest volcano on earth, rising 30,000 feet out of the ocean floor (of course, you can see only the 13,796 ft. that are above

sea level). Kilauea's eruptions make the Big Island bigger every day—and, if you're lucky, you can stand just a few feet away and watch it do its work.

Steeped in tradition and shrouded in the primal mist of creation, the Big Island radiates what the Hawaiians call *mana,* a sense of spirituality that's still apparent in the acres of petroglyphs etched in the black lava, the numerous *heiau* (temples), burial caves scattered in the cliffs, sacred shrines both on land and in the sea, and even the sound the wind makes as it blows across the desolate lava fields.

The Big Island is not for everyone, however. It refuses to fit the stereotype of a tropical island. Some tourists are taken aback at the sight of stark fields of lava or black-sand beaches. You must remember that it's *big* (expect to do lots of driving). And you may have to go out of your way if you're looking for traditional tropical beauty, such as a quintessential white-sand beach.

On the other hand, if you're into watersports, this is paradise. The two tall volcanoes mean the water on the leeward side is calm 350 days a year. The underwater landscape of caves, cliffs, and tunnels attracts a stunning array of colorful marine life. The island's west coast is one of the best destinations in the world for big-game fishing. And its miles of remote coastline are a kayaker's dream of caves, secluded coves, and crescent-shaped beaches reachable only by sea.

On land, hikers, bikers, and horseback riders can head up and down a volcano,

The Big Island

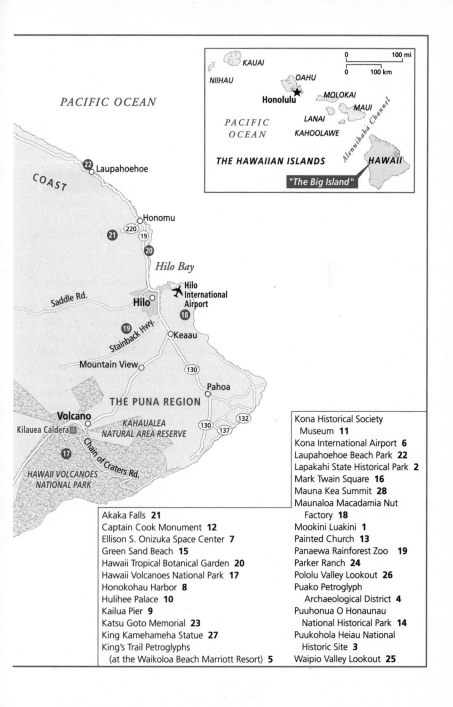

PACIFIC OCEAN

THE HAWAIIAN ISLANDS

KAUAI

NIIHAU

OAHU

Honolulu

MOLOKAI

MAUI

PACIFIC OCEAN

LANAI

KAHOOLAWE

Alenuihaha Channel

HAWAII

"The Big Island"

0   100 mi
0   100 km

COAST

Laupahoehoe **22**

Honomu

220 **19**

21

20

Hilo Bay

Hilo International Airport

Saddle Rd.

Hilo

Stainback Hwy.

19

18

Keaau

Mountain View

130

Pahoa

THE PUNA REGION

Volcano

Kilauea Caldera

KAHAUALEA NATURAL AREA RESERVE

130 **137** **132**

Chain of Craters Rd.

17

HAWAII VOLCANOES NATIONAL PARK

Akaka Falls **21**
Captain Cook Monument **12**
Ellison S. Onizuka Space Center **7**
Green Sand Beach **15**
Hawaii Tropical Botanical Garden **20**
Hawaii Volcanoes National Park **17**
Honokohau Harbor **8**
Hulihee Palace **10**
Kailua Pier **9**
Katsu Goto Memorial **23**
King Kamehameha Statue **27**
King's Trail Petroglyphs
   (at the Waikoloa Beach Marriott Resort) **5**

Kona Historical Society
   Museum **11**
Kona International Airport **6**
Laupahoehoe Beach Park **22**
Lapakahi State Historical Park **2**
Mark Twain Square **16**
Mauna Kea Summit **28**
Maunaloa Macadamia Nut
   Factory **18**
Mookini Luakini **1**
Painted Church **13**
Panaewa Rainforest Zoo **19**
Parker Ranch **24**
Pololu Valley Lookout **26**
Puako Petroglyph
   Archaeological District **4**
Puuhonua O Honaunau
   National Historical Park **14**
Puukohola Heiau National
   Historic Site **3**
Waipio Valley Lookout **25**

across beaches, into remote valleys, and through rainforests without seeing another soul. Bird-watchers are rewarded with sightings of the rare, rapidly dwindling native birds of Hawaii. Golfers can find nirvana on a wide variety of courses.

This is the least-explored island in the Hawaiian chain, but if you're looking to get away from it all and back to nature in its most primal state, that might be the best thing about it. Where else can you witness fiery creation and swim with dolphins, ponder the stars from the world's tallest mountain and catch a blue marlin, downhill-ski and surf the waves in a single day? You can do all this and more on only one island in the world: the Big Island of Hawaii.

1 Orientation

Most people arrive on the Big Island at Kona International Airport, on the island's west coast. From the airport, Kilauea volcano is to the right (counterclockwise), and the ritzy Kohala Coast is to the left (clockwise). (If you land in Hilo, of course, the volcano is clockwise and Kohala is counterclockwise.)

ARRIVING

The Big Island has two major airports for jet traffic between the islands: **Kona International Airport** and **Hilo International Airport.**

The **Kona Airport** receives direct overseas flights from Japan on **Japan Airlines** (© **800/525-3663;** www.jal.co.jp/en) and Vancouver on **Air Canada** (© **888/ 247-2262;** www.aircanada.com). Carriers from the mainland include **Aloha Airlines** (© **800/367-5250;** www.alohaairlines.com), with nonstop flights to Oakland and Orange County, both in California; **American Airlines** (© **800/433-7300;** www. aa.com), with flights to Los Angeles; **Delta Airlines** (© **800/221-1212;** www.delta. com), with nonstop flights from Salt Lake City (originating in Atlanta); **Northwest Airlines** (© **800/225-2525;** www.nwa.com), with flights from Seattle; **U.S. Airways/ American West** (© **800/428-4322;** www.usairways.com), with flights from Phoenix; and **United Airlines** (© **800/241-6522;** www.united.com), with nonstop flights from Denver, Los Angeles and San Francisco, and a direct flight to Chicago.

Hilo Airport has a direct flight from Oakland via **ATA** (© **800/435-9282;** www. ata.com), which code-shares with **Southwest Airlines.**

If you cannot get a direct flight to the Big Island, you'll have to pick up an interisland flight in Honolulu: **Aloha Airlines** (see above), **Hawaiian Airlines** (© **800/ 367-5320;** www.hawaiianair.com), and **go!** (© **888/IFLYGO2;** www.iflygo.com) offer jet service to both Big Island airports. All major rental companies have cars available at both airports. See "Getting Around Hawaii" in chapter 2 for more details on interisland travel and car rentals.

VISITOR INFORMATION

The **Big Island Visitors Bureau** has two offices on the Big Island: one at 250 Keawe St., Hilo, HI 96720 (© **808/961-5797;** fax 808/961-2126), and on the other side of the island at 250 Waikoloa Beach Dr., Waikoloa, HI 96738 (© **808/886-1652**). Its website is www.bigisland.org.

On the west side of the island, there are two additional sources to contact for information: the **Kona-Kohala Resort Association,** 68–1310 Mauna Lani Dr., suite 101, Kahala Coast, HI 96743 (© **800/318-3637** or 808/885-6414; fax 808/885-6145; www.kohalacoastresorts.com); and **Destination Kona,** P.O. Box 2850, Kailua-Kona,

---

Quake Update

Since the Oct 15, 2006 earthquake, most of the Big Island, and especially the Kona-Kohala coast (where the quake was centered), has been repaired and is back to normal. The main exception is the Mauna Kea Beach Hotel, which had extensive damage and as we went to press was still renovating. The hotel and all its restaurants are closed, but the golf course is still open.

HI 96745 (© **808/322-6809;** fax 808/322-8899). On the east side, you can contact **Destination Hilo,** P.O. Box 1391, Hilo, HI 96721 (© **808/935-5294;** fax 808/969-1984). And in the middle, contact the **Waimea Visitor Center,** P.O. Box 6570, Kamuela, HI 96743 (© **808/885-6707;** fax 808/885-0885).

The Big Island's best free tourist publications are *This Week,* the *Beach and Activity Guide,* and *101 Things to Do on Hawaii the Big Island.* All three offer lots of useful information, as well as discount coupons on a variety of island adventures. Copies are easy to find all around the island.

The *Beach and Activity Guide* is affiliated with the **Activity Connection,** Bougainvillea Plaza, Suite 102, 75–5656 Kuakini Hwy., Kailua-Kona (© **800/459-7156** or 808/329-1038; fax 808/327-9411; www.beachactivityguide.com), a discount activities desk offering real savings (no fees, no timeshares) of up to 15% on activities including island tours, snorkel and dive trips, submarine and horseback rides, luau, and more. The office is open daily from 7:30am to 5:30pm.

THE ISLAND IN BRIEF

The Kona Coast ★★

Kona is synonymous with great coffee and big fish—both of which are found in abundance along this 70-mile-long stretch of black-lava-covered coast.

A collection of tiny communities devoted to farming and fishing along the sun-baked leeward side of the island, the Kona Coast has an amazingly diverse geography and climate for such a compact area. The oceanfront town of **Kailua-Kona,** a quaint fishing village that now caters more to tourists than boat captains, is its commercial center. The lands of Kona range from stark, black, dry coastal desert to cool, cloudy upcountry where glossy green coffee, macadamia nuts, tropical fruit, and a riotous profusion of flowers cover the steep, jagged slopes. Among the coffee fields, you'll find the funky, artsy village of **Holualoa.** Higher yet in elevation are native forests of giant trees filled with tiny, colorful birds, some perilously close to extinction. About 7 miles south of Kailua-Kona, bordering the ocean, is the resort area of **Keauhou,** a suburban-like series of upscale condominiums, a shopping center, and million-dollar homes.

Kona means "leeward side" in Hawaiian—and that means full-on sun every day of the year. This is an affordable vacation spot; an ample selection of midpriced condo units, peppered with a few older hotels and B&Bs, lines the shore, which is mostly rocky lava reef, interrupted by an occasional pocket beach. Here, too, stand two world-class resorts: Kona Village, the site of one of the best luau in the islands, and one of Hawaii's luxury retreats, the Four Seasons at Hualalai.

Away from the bright lights of the town of Kailua lies the rural **South Kona Coast,** home to coffee farmers, macadamia-nut growers, and people escaping to the country. The serrated South Kona Coast is indented with numerous bays, from **Kealakekua,** a marine-life preserve that's the island's best diving spot, down to **Honaunau,** where a national historic park recalls the days of old Hawaii. Accommodations in this area are mainly B&Bs. This coast is a great place to stay if you want to get away from crowds and experience peaceful country living. You'll be within driving distance of beaches and the sites of Kailua.

The Kohala Coast 🌀🌀

Fringes of palms and flowers, brilliant blankets of emerald green, and an occasional flash of white buildings are your only clues from the road that this black-lava coast north of Kona is more than bleak and barren. But, oh, is it! Down by the sea, pleasure domes rise like palaces no Hawaiian king ever imagined. This is where the Lear jet–set escapes to play in world-class beachfront hotels set like jewels in the golden sand. But you don't have to be a billionaire to visit the Waikoloa, Mauna Lani, and Mauna Kea resorts: The fabulous beaches and abundant historic sites are open to the public, with parking and other facilities, including restaurants, golf courses, and shopping, provided by the resorts.

North Kohala 🌀🌀

Seven sugar mills once shipped enough sugar from three harbors on this knob of land to sweeten all the coffee in San Francisco. **Hawi,** the region's hub and home to the Kohala Sugar Co., was a flourishing town. Today Hawi's quaint, 3-block-long strip of sun-faded, false-fronted buildings and 1920s vintage shops lives on as a minor tourist stop in one of Hawaii's most scenic rural

regions, located at the northernmost reaches of the island. North Kohala is most famous as the birthplace of King Kamehameha the Great; a statue commemorates the royal site. It's also home to the islands' most sacred site, the 1,500-year-old **Mo'okini Heiau.**

Waimea (Kamuela) 🌀🌀

This old upcountry cow town on the northern road between the coasts is set in lovely country: rolling green pastures, wide-open spaces dotted by *puu* (hills), and real cowpokes who ride mammoth **Parker Ranch,** Hawaii's largest working ranch. The town is also headquarters for the **Keck Telescope,** the largest and most powerful in the world. Waimea is home to several affordable B&Bs, and Merriman's restaurant is a popular foodie outpost at Opelo Plaza.

The Hamakua Coast 🌀🌀

This emerald coast, a 52-mile stretch from Honokaa to Hilo on the island's windward northeast side, was once planted with sugar cane; it now blooms with flowers, macadamia nuts, papayas, and marijuana, also known as *pakalolo* (still Hawaii's number-one cash crop). Resort-free and virtually without beaches, the Hamakua Coast still has a few major destinations. Picture-perfect **Waipio Valley** has impossibly steep sides, taro patches, a green riot of wild plants, and a winding stream leading to a broad, black-sand beach; and the historic plantation town of **Honokaa** is making a comeback as the B&B capital on the coastal trail. **Akaka Falls** and **Laupahoehoe Beach Park** are also worth seeking out.

Hilo 🌀🌀

When the sun shines in Hilo, it's one of the most beautiful tropical cities in the Pacific. Being here is an entirely different kind of island experience: Hawaii's largest metropolis after Honolulu is a quaint, misty, flower-filled city of

Victorian houses overlooking a half-moon bay, with a restored historic downtown and a clear view of Mauna Loa's often snowcapped peak. Hilo catches everyone's eye until it rains—it rains a lot in Hilo, and when it rains, it pours.

Hilo is one of America's wettest towns, with 128 inches of rain annually. It's ideal for growing ferns, orchids, and anthuriums, but not for catching a few rays. But there's lots to see and do in Hilo, so grab your umbrella. The rain is warm (the temperature seldom dips below 70°F/21°C), and there's usually a rainbow afterward.

Hilo's oversize airport and hotels are remnants of a dream: The city wanted to be Hawaii's major port of entry. That didn't happen, but the facilities here are excellent. Hilo is also Hawaii's best bargain for budget travelers. It has plenty of hotel rooms—most of the year, that is. Hilo's magic moment comes in spring, the week after Easter, when hula *halau* (schools) arrive for the annual Merrie Monarch Hula Festival hula competition (see "Hawaii Calendar of Events," in chapter 2). This is a full-on Hawaiian spectacle and a wonderful cultural event. Plan ahead if you want to go: Tickets are sold out by the first week in January, and the hotels within 30 miles are usually booked solid.

Hilo is also the gateway to Hawaii Volcanoes National Park; it's just an hour's drive up-slope.

Hawaii Volcanoes National Park ★★★

This is America's most exciting national park, where a live volcano called Kilauea erupts daily. If you're lucky, it will be a spectacular sight. At other times, you may not be able to see the molten lava at all, but there's always a lot to see and learn. Ideally, you should plan to spend 3 days at the park

exploring the trails, watching the volcano, visiting the rainforest, and just enjoying this spectacular place. But even if you have only a day, get here—it's worth the trip. Bring your sweats or jacket (honest!); it's cool up here, especially at night.

If you plan to dally in the park, plan to stay in the sleepy hamlet of Volcano Village, just outside the National Park entrance. Several terrifically cozy B&Bs, some with fireplaces, hide under tree ferns in this cool mountain hideaway. The tiny highland community (elev. 4,000 ft.), first settled by Japanese immigrants, is now inhabited by artists, soul-searchers, and others who like the crisp air of Hawaii's high country. It has just enough civilization to sustain a good life: a few stores, a handful of eateries, a gas station, and a golf course.

Ka Lae: South Point ★★

This is the Plymouth Rock of Hawaii, where the first Polynesians arrived in seagoing canoes, probably from the Marquesas Islands or Tahiti, around A.D. 500. You'll feel like you're at the end of the world on this lonely, windswept place, the southernmost point of the United States (a geographic claim that belonged to Key West, Florida, before Hawaii became a state). Hawaii ends in a sharp, black-lava point. Bold 500-foot cliffs stand against the blue sea to the west and shelter the old fishing village of Waiahukini, which was populated from A.D. 750 until the 1860s. Ancient canoe moorings, shelter caves, and *heiau* (temples) poke through wind-blown pili grass. The east coast curves inland to reveal a green-sand beach, a world-famous anomaly that's accessible only by foot or four-wheel-drive. For most, the only reason to venture down to the southern tip is to experience the empty vista of land's end.

Everything in **Naalehu** and **Waio-hinu,** the two wide spots in the road that pass for towns at South Point, claims to be the southernmost this or that. Except for a monkeypod tree planted by Mark Twain in 1866, there's not much else to crow about. There is, thankfully, a gas station, along with a couple of places to eat, a fruit stand, and a few B&Bs. These end-of-the-world towns are just about as far removed from the real world as you can get.

2 Getting Around

BY CAR   You'll need a rental car on the Big Island; not having one will really limit you. All the major car-rental firms have agencies at the airports and at the Kohala Coast resorts; for a complete list, as well as tips on insurance and driving rules, see "By Car," under "Getting Around Hawaii," in chapter 2.

There are more than 480 miles of paved road on the Big Island. The highway that circles the island is called the **Hawaii Belt Road.** On the Kona side of the island, you have two choices: the scenic "upper" road, **Mamalahoa Highway** (Hwy. 190), or the speedier "lower" road, **Queen Kaahumanu Highway** (Hwy. 19). The road that links east to west is called the **Saddle Road** (Hwy. 200). Saddle Road looks like a shortcut from Kona to Hilo, but it usually doesn't make for a shorter trip. It's rough, narrow, and plagued by bad weather; as a result, most rental-car agencies forbid you from taking their cars on it.

BY TAXI   Taxis are readily available at both Kona and Hilo airports. In Hilo call **Ace-1** (© **808/935-8303**). In Kailua-Kona call **Kona Airport Taxi** (© **808/329-7779**). Taxis will take you wherever you want to go on the Big Island, but it's prohibitively expensive to use them for long distances.

BY BUS & SHUTTLE   For transportation from the Kona Airport, there are three options: two shuttle services that will come when you call them, and a discount shuttle that leaves the airport every hour on the hour and drops you at your hotel. Door-to-door service is provided by **SpeediShuttle** (© **808/329-5433;** www.speedishuttle. com). Some sample rates: From the airport to Kailua-Kona, the fare is $21 per person; to the Four Seasons, it's $21; and to Mauna Lani Resort, it's $46.

The islandwide bus system is the **Hele-On Bus** (© **808/961-8744;** www.co. hawaii.hi.us/mass_transit/heleonbus.html); as we went to press, the Hele-On Bus had the best deal on the island: ride free. The recently created Kokua Zone allows riders in West Hawaii to travel from as far south as Ocean View to as far north as Kawaihae for free; in East Hawaii, riders can ride free from Pahoa to Hilo. Visitors to Hawaii can pick up the free, air-conditioned bus from the Kohala hotels or from the Kona International Airport and ride the bus south to shopping centers like Costco, Lanihau Center, Kmart, Wal-Mart, and Keauhou Shopping Center. The Hele-On Bus also stops at the Kona Community Hospital and provides wheelchair access.

In the Keauhou Resort area, there's a free, open-air, 44-seat **Keauhou Resort Trolley,** with stops at the Keauhou Bay, Sheraton Keauhou Bay Resort & Spa, Kona Country Club, Keauhou Shopping Center, Outrigger Keauhou Beach Resort, and Kahaluu Beach Park. In addition, three times a day the Trolley travels round-trip, via Alii Drive to Kailua Village, stopping at White Sands Beach on the way. For information, contact concierges at either the Sheraton Keauhou Bay Resort & Spa (© **808/930-4900**) or the Outrigger Keauhou Beach Hotel (© **808/322-3411**).

FAST FACTS: The Big Island

American Express There's an office on the Kohala Coast at the **Hilton Waikoloa Village** (© 808/886-7958) and **The Fairmont Orchid** in Mauna Lani Resort (© 808/885-2000). To report lost or stolen traveler's checks, call © 800/221-7282.

Dentists In an emergency, contact **Dr. Craig C. Kimura** at Kamuela Office Center (© 808/885-5947); in Kona, call **Dr. Frank Sayre,** Frame 10 Center, behind Lanihau Shopping Center on Palani Road (© 808/329-8067); in Hilo, call **Hawaii Smile Center,** Hilo Lagoon Center, 101 Aupuni St. (© 808/961-9181).

Doctors In Hilo, the **Hilo Medical Center** is at 1190 Waianuenue Ave. (© 808/974-4700); on the Kona side, call **Hualalai Urgent Care,** 75–1028 Henry St., across the street from Safeway (© 808/327-HELP).

Emergencies For ambulance, fire, and rescue services, dial © 911 or call © 808/961-6022. The **Poison Control Center** hot line is © 800/362-3585.

Hospitals Hospitals offering 24-hour urgent-care facilities include the **Hilo Medical Center,** 1190 Waianuenue Ave., Hilo (© 808/974-4700); **North Hawaii Community Hospital,** Waimea (© 808/885-4444); and **Kona Community Hospital,** on the Kona Coast in Kealakekua (© 808/322-9311).

Police Dial © 911 in case of emergency; otherwise, call the **Hawaii Police Department** at © 808/326-4646 in Kona, © 808/961-2213 in Hilo.

Post Office All calls to the U.S. Post Office can be directed to © 800/275-8777. There are local branches in Hilo at 1299 Kekuanaoa Ave., in Kailua-Kona at 74–5577 Palani Rd., and in Waimea on Lindsey Road.

Weather For conditions in and around Hilo, call © 808/935-8555; for the rest of the Big Island, call © 808/961-5582. For marine forecasts, call © 808/935-9883.

3 Where to Stay

Before you reach for the phone to book your accommodations, refer back to "Tips on Accommodations," in chapter 2, to make sure you book the kind of place you want. Also remember that the Big Island is really big; see "The Island in Brief," above, to decide where to base yourself.

If you're interested in additional information on bed-and-breakfasts, contact the **Hawaii Island B&B Association,** P.O. Box 1890, Honokaa, HI 96727 (no phone; **www.stayhawaii.com**).

In the listings below, all rooms come with a full private bathroom (with tub or shower) and free parking unless otherwise noted. Remember to add Hawaii's 11.42% in taxes to your final bill.

If you would like to go "on the road," contact **Island RV and Safari Activities** (© 800/406-4555 or 808/334-0464; www.islandrv.com). They offer weekly rentals of a 22-foot class-C motor home, which sleeps up to four, for $2,100. Included in the package are airport pickup, all linens, barbecue grill, all park registration fee permits, your last night in a hotel (Royal Kona Resort), and help with planning your itinerary and booking activities.

THE KONA COAST
IN & AROUND KAILUA-KONA

For a detailed map of central Kailua-Kona, see p. 317.

Very Expensive

Four Seasons Resort Hualalai at Historic Kaupulehu ★★★ *Kids*   This is a great place to relax in the lap of luxury. Low-rise clusters of oceanview villas nestle between the sea and the greens of a new golf course. The Four Seasons has no concrete corridors and no massive central building—it looks like a two-story town-house project, clustered around three seaside swimming pools and a snorkeling pond. The rooms are furnished in Pacific tropical style: light gold walls, hand-knotted rugs over clay-colored slate, and rattan-and-bamboo settees. The ground-level rooms have bathrooms with private outdoor gardens (surrounded by black-lava rock and a bamboo roof), so you can shower under the tropical sun or nighttime stars. All rooms have new flatscreen plasma TVs.

If you can afford it, this is the place to go to be pampered—sit back and relax as the pool attendants bring you ice-cold water, chilled towels, and fresh fruit kabobs. Other pluses include a Hawaiian history and cultural interpretive center, complimentary scuba lessons, a complimentary valet, twice-daily maid service, and a multilingual concierge. The spa has been selected by *Condé Nast Traveller* magazine as the world's best resort spa. One of the five pools is a saltwater pond carved out of black-lava rock with reef fish swimming about. The new Lava Lounge offers exotic martinis, entertainment, and the best view for watching the sun sink into the Pacific.

Your kids will be pampered, too—the complimentary Kids for All Seasons program features plenty of activities to keep the little ones busy. The resort also offers children's menus in all restaurants, a game room, videos, complimentary infant gear (cribs, highchairs, and so on), and more.

72-100 Ka'upulehu Dr., Kailua-Kona, HI 96745. (*C*) **888/340-5662** or 808/325-8000. Fax 808/325-8053. www.four seasons.com/hualalai. 243 units. $695–$995 double; from $1,300 suite. Extra person $170. Children under 18 stay free in parent's room (maximum occupancy is 3 people; couples with more than one child must get 2 rooms). AE, DC, DISC, MC, V. **Amenities:** 3 restaurants (including Pahu i'a, p. 274, and Beach Tree Bar & Grill, p. 276); 3 bars (nightly entertainment ranging from contemporary Hawaiian to pianist); 5 exquisite outdoor pools (including a giant infinity pool and a lap pool); 18-hole Jack Nicklaus signature golf course exclusively for guests and residents; 8 tennis courts (4 lit for night play); complete fitness center; award-winning spa; 6 whirlpools; watersports equipment rentals; complimentary year-round children's program; game room; concierge; activities and car rental through the concierge; business center; salon; room service; both in-room and spa massage; babysitting; complimentary washer/dryers; same-day laundry service and dry cleaning; Wi-Fi Internet access in lobby, guest rooms, pools, and other places on property. *In room:* A/C, plasma TV, dataport, fridge, coffeemaker, hair dryer, iron, safe.

Kona Village Resort ★ *Kids*   This fabulous resort, which had begun to fall into disrepair in the past few years, was recently sold (to computer magnate Michael Dell) and it appears that the new owners are pouring some much-needed funds into maintenance of this oceanside Polynesian village. Since 1965, those seeking a great escape have crossed the black-lava fields to find refuge at this exclusive, one-of-a-kind haven by the sea with its wonderful dark-sand beach. Yes, the blissful languor still settles in as you surrender to the peaceful, low-key atmosphere, but make sure that you request one of the "renovated" thatched-roof, island-style bungalows, and, if money is no object, ask for my favorite bungalows, Lava Tahitian, which have a hot tub on the deck overlooking the ocean. Long time guests of the Village have noted a remarkable decline in the once sterling aloha service. Veteran employees still have that gracious

Where to Stay on the Kona Coast

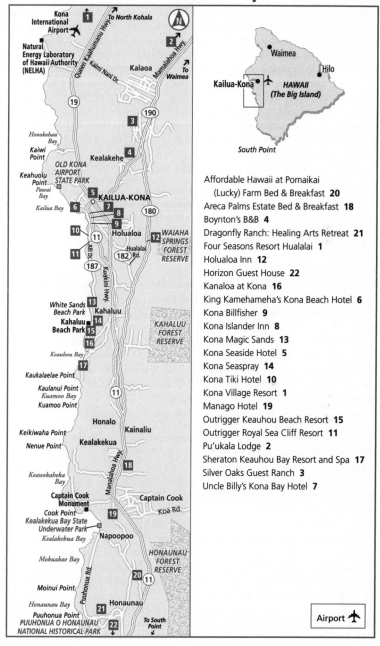

Affordable Hawaii at Pomaikai
  (Lucky) Farm Bed & Breakfast **20**
Areca Palms Estate Bed & Breakfast **18**
Boynton's B&B **4**
Dragonfly Ranch: Healing Arts Retreat **21**
Four Seasons Resort Hualalai **1**
Holualoa Inn **12**
Horizon Guest House **22**
Kanaloa at Kona **16**
King Kamehameha's Kona Beach Hotel **6**
Kona Billfisher **9**
Kona Islander Inn **8**
Kona Magic Sands **13**
Kona Seaside Hotel **5**
Kona Seaspray **14**
Kona Tiki Hotel **10**
Kona Village Resort **1**
Manago Hotel **19**
Outrigger Keauhou Beach Resort **15**
Outrigger Royal Sea Cliff Resort **11**
Pu'ukala Lodge **2**
Sheraton Keauhou Bay Resort and Spa **17**
Silver Oaks Guest Ranch **3**
Uncle Billy's Kona Bay Hotel **7**

Airport ✈

welcoming attitude, but the newer employees (which are quickly becoming a majority) don't seem to match the high standards of service which made the Village famous. Dining service is rushed and in some cases, practically non-existent for a luxury resort.

The resort resembles an eclectic Polynesian village, with historic sites and beaches. It's no longer located on a secluded cove (the guests at nearby Four Seasons can now walk the beach) and will likely get even more crowded—houses and condominiums are scheduled to be built around the "village." On the plus side: The room rate includes breakfast, lunch, and dinner—the Friday-night luau here is fabulous—plus all snorkeling equipment and other beach toys. It also includes scheduled activities throughout the day for kids and teens (there's even a special dinner seating for kids so parents can have a quiet dinner alone).

P.O. Box 1299, Kailua-Kona, HI 96745. ℂ 800/367-5290 or 808/325-5555. Fax 808/325-5124. www.konavillage. com. 125 units. $625–$1,130 double. Extra person $240 adults (13 and older), $50 children 3–5, $175 children 6–12 (no extra charge for children 2 and under). Rates include all meals for 2 adults, tennis, watersports, walking tours, and a Fri-night luau. Packages available. AE, DC, MC, V. **Amenities:** 2 restaurants; 2 bars (w/live entertainment most nights); 2 outdoor pools; tennis courts; fitness room; 2 Jacuzzis; complimentary watersports; extensive children's program (especially during the summer, when it extends past dinner); concierge; activities desk; Polynesian general store; babysitting; complimentary washer/dryers; laundry service; dry cleaning. *In room:* Fridge, coffeemaker, hair dryer, iron, safe, no phone.

Expensive

Outrigger Royal Sea Cliff Resort (Kids) Families will love these luxuriously appointed apartments and their affordable rates. The architecturally striking, five-story white buildings that make up this resort/condo complex, 2 miles from Kailua-Kona, are stepped back from the ocean for maximum views and privacy. (The downside is that there's no ocean swimming here, but the waves are near enough to lull you to sleep, and there's a decent swimming beach about a mile away.) Atrium gardens and hanging bougainvillea soften the look. Spacious units are furnished in tropical rattan with a large, sunny lanai, a full kitchen, and a washer/dryer, and there are barbecue and picnic facilities for oceanfront dining.

75–6040 Alii Dr., Kailua-Kona, HI 96740. ℂ 800/688-7444 or 808/329-8021. Fax 808/326-1887. www.outrigger. com. 148 units. $215–$255 studio double; $249–$415 1-bedroom apt for 4; $289–$459 2-bedroom apt for 6. AE, DC, DISC, MC, V. **Amenities:** 2 outdoor pools; complimentary tennis courts; Jacuzzi; activities desk. *In room:* A/C, TV, wireless Internet access, kitchen, fridge, coffeemaker, hair dryer, iron, safe, washer/dryer.

Moderate

King Kamehameha's Kona Beach Hotel The location is terrific, downtown Kailua Kona, right on the ocean. The problem here is this is a 30-plus-years-old hotel that looks tired. Rooms are showing their age, but they are clean and can have views of an ancient banyan tree, the Kailua Pier, or sparkling Kailua Bay. The hotel's own small, gold-sand beach is right out the front door. The hotel's restaurant is forgettable, but you're within walking distance of dozens of other options. The best deal here is the Paradise on Wheels, which comes with a double room, a compact car, and breakfast for two starting at just $170—a price that makes the "King Kam" (as locals call it) attractive to travelers on a budget.

75–5660 Palani Rd., Kailua-Kona, HI 96740. ℂ 800/367-6060 or 808/329-2911. Fax 808/922-8061. www.konabeach hotel.com. 460 units. $170–$250 double. Room, car, and breakfast packages from $170 (subject to availability). Extra person $30. AE, DC, DISC, MC, V. Parking $7. **Amenities:** Restaurant; outdoor bar w/Hawaiian entertainment; outdoor pool; 4 tennis courts; Jacuzzi; watersports equipment rentals; activities desk; shopping arcade; salon; room service; coin-op washer/dryers; laundry service; dry cleaning. *In room:* A/C, TV, dataport, fridge, coffeemaker, hair dryer, iron, safe.

Silver Oaks Guest Ranch ★★ *Finds*   Book this place! This is a true "guest ranch," consisting of two cottages spread over a 10-acre working ranch complete with friendly horses (no riding, just petting), the cutest Nigerian dwarf goats, chickens, and wild turkeys. The ranch sits at 1,300 feet, where the temperatures are in the 70s (low to middle 20s Celsius) year-round. The views are spectacular, some 40 miles of coastline from the ocean to Mauna Loa, yet it's just 5 miles from the airport and 5 miles from downtown Kailua-Kona. Hosts Amy and Rick Decker have impeccable taste, and each unit is uniquely decorated. You'll get breakfast items (cereals, milk, yogurt, coffee, fruit, and bread) for your first day. They have a closet full of beach gear for guests, not to mention books, videos, binoculars, even a couple of backpacks.

Reservations: 75–1027 Henry St., Suite 310, Kailua-Kona, HI 96740. © 877/325-2300 or 808/325-2000. Fax 808/325-2200. www.silveroaksranch.com. 2 units, plus additional space available for large groups. $175 double. Extra person $15. 5-night minimum. MC, V. **Amenities:** Outdoor pool; Jacuzzi; washer/dryers. *In room:* TV/VCR, high-speed Internet access, kitchen, fridge, coffeemaker.

Inexpensive

Interested in a B&B? Call **Pu'ukala Lodge** ★ (© **808/325-1729;** www.puukala-lodge. com), a five-room lodge (but only three rooms are rented at one time) on the slopes of Hualalai with sweeping views; rates start at $95, which includes full gourmet breakfast.

Boynton's B&B ★ *Kids*   Just 3 miles from Kailua-Kona, but up in the cooler, rolling hills, is this quaint two-bedroom B&B, perfect for a family vacation. The house perches at 1,000 feet in a quiet country neighborhood; guests can enjoy views of the coastline from the lanai. A private entrance leads you into the complete kitchen, which is stocked with breakfast fixings (including eggs, cereals, muffins, and juice). One bedroom looks out on tropical greenery, the other has an ocean view. Hosts Peter and Tracy Boyton have lovingly created a little bit of heaven here, complete with a hot tub on the deck outside. The beach is just a 5-minute drive away.

74–4920-A Palani Rd., Kailua-Kona, HI 96740. © **808/329-4178.** Fax 808/326-1510. www.konabandb.com. 1 unit. $120 double. Extra person $15. 3-night minimum. No credit cards. **Amenities:** Hot tub. *In room:* TV, kitchen, fridge, coffeemaker, hair dryer, iron.

Kona Billfisher *Kids*   The pluses here are: It's within walking distance of downtown Kailua-Kona, and the big, blue Pacific is just across the street. (The ocean here is not good for swimming or snorkeling, but there's a pool on-site, and you can swim at the Kailua Pier, just a mile away.) The property is very well maintained. Each unit comes with a full kitchen and a balcony, and features new furnishings and king-size beds. The one-bedroom units have sliding-glass doors that allow you to close off the living room and make it into another private bedroom, so for the price of a one-bedroom unit, you can have a two-bedroom—a real deal and a great setup for families. Other on-site facilities include a barbecue area. However, I am sad to report that the management of this condo has insisted that its booking agency add quite a few charges for these units: a $35 booking fee, a $35 to $45 cleaning fee, and a ridiculous fee for using the air-conditioning. Do the math—these additional charges add up.

Alii Dr. (across from the Royal Kona Resort), c/o Hawaii Resort Management, P.O. Box 39, Kailua-Kona, HI 96745. © **800/622-5348** or 808/329-3333. Fax 808/326-4137. www.konahawaii.com. 60 units. High season $105 1-bedroom, $135 2-bedroom; low season $90 1-bedroom, $115 2-bedroom; plus $35 booking fee, $35–$45 cleaning fee and $5–$6 a day for using the A/C. 3-night minimum. DC, DISC, MC, V. **Amenities:** Outdoor pool; nearby coin-op washer/dryer. *In room:* A/C, TV, kitchen, fridge, coffeemaker, iron.

Kona Islander Inn *Value*   This is the most affordable place to stay in Kailua-Kona. These plantation-style, three-story buildings are surrounded by lush, palm-tree-lined gardens with torch-lit pathways that make it hard to believe you're smack-dab in the middle of downtown. The central location—across the street from the historic Kona Inn Shops—is convenient but can be noisy. Built in 1962, the complex is showing some signs of age, but the units were recently outfitted with new appliances, new bedspreads and curtains, and a fresh coat of paint. The studios are small, but extras like lanais and kitchenettes outfitted with microwaves, minifridges, and coffeemakers make up for the lack of space.

75–5776 Kuakini Hwy. (south of Hualalai Rd.), Kailua-Kona. c/o Hawaii Resort Management, P.O. Box 39, Kailua-Kona, HI 96745. ☎ **800/622-5348** or 808/329-3333. Fax 808/326-4137. www.konahawaii.com. 80 units. $70–$100 double. DC, DISC, MC, V. **Amenities:** Outdoor pool; hot tub; activities desk; coin-op washer/dryers. *In room:* A/C, TV, kitchenette, fridge, coffeemaker.

Kona Magic Sands *Value*   If you want to stay right on the ocean without spending a fortune, this is the place to do it—it's one of the best oceanfront deals you'll find on a Kona condo, and the only one with a beach for swimming and snorkeling right next door. Every unit in this older complex has a lanai that steps out over the ocean and sunset views that you'll dream about long after you return home. These studio units aren't luxurious; they're small (two people max) and cozy, great for people who want to be lulled to sleep by the sound of the waves crashing on the shore. Each consists of one long, narrow room with a small kitchen at one end and the lanai at the other, with a living room/dining room/bedroom combo in between.

77–6452 Alii Dr. (next to Magic Sands Beach Park). c/o Hawaii Resort Management, P.O. Box 39, Kailua-Kona, HI 96745. ☎ **800/622-5348** or 808/329-3333. Fax 808/326-4137. www.konahawaii.com. 37 units, shower only. High season $135 double; low season $105 double; plus $60 cleaning fee. 3-night minimum. DC, DISC, MC, V. **Amenities:** Excellent restaurant; bar; oceanfront outdoor pool. *In room:* TV, kitchen, fridge, coffeemaker.

Kona Seaside Hotel   The best deal at this budget hotel is to get the room-and-car package; it's cheaper than the rack rates. Located in the heart of Kailua-Kona, the Kona Seaside is just steps away from Kailua Bay and Kailua-Kona's shopping, restaurants, and historic sites. The rooms are large and comfy (even if they don't have fancy soaps and extra amenities), but they can be noisy (ask for one away from the road). You may want to splurge on one of the 14 rooms with kitchenettes.

75–5646 Palani Rd. (at Kuakini Hwy.), Kailua-Kona, HI 96740. ☎ **800/560-5558** or 808/329-2455. Fax 808/329-6157. www.sand-seaside.com. 225 units. $125–$165 double. Extra person $20. Children under 12 stay free in parent's room. Internet specials at press time available from $88. AE, DC, MC, V. Parking $5. **Amenities:** Restaurant; bar; 2 small outdoor pools; coin-op washer/dryers; laundry service; dry cleaning. *In room:* A/C, TV, dataport (some units), kitchenette (some units), fridge.

Kona Tiki Hotel *Finds*   It's hard to believe that places like this still exist. The Kona Tiki, located right on the ocean, away from the hustle and bustle of downtown Kailua-Kona, is one of the best budget deals in Hawaii. All of the rooms are tastefully decorated and feature queen-size beds, ceiling fans, minifridges, and private lanais overlooking the ocean. Although it's called a hotel, this small, family-run operation is more like a large B&B, with lots of aloha and plenty of friendly conversation at the morning breakfast buffet around the pool. The staff is helpful in planning activities. There are no TVs or phones in the rooms, but there's a pay phone in the lobby. If a double with a kitchenette is available, grab it—the extra few bucks will save you a bundle in food costs. Book way in advance.

75–5968 Alii Dr. (about a mile from downtown Kailua-Kona), Kailua-Kona, HI 96740. © **808/329-1425**. Fax 808/327-9402. www.konatiki.com. 15 units. $66–$79 double; $88 double with kitchenette. Rates include continental breakfast. Extra person $8; children 2–12 $6. 3-night minimum. No credit cards. **Amenities:** Outdoor pool. *In room:* Kitchenette (in some rooms), fridge, no phone.

Uncle Billy's Kona Bay Hotel   An institution in Kona, Uncle Billy's is where visitors from the other islands stay. A thatched roof hangs over the lobby area, and a Polynesian longhouse restaurant is next door. The rooms are old but comfortable and come with large lanais; most also have minifridges (request one at booking), and 16 are condo-style units with kitchenettes. This budget hotel is a good place to sleep, but don't expect new furniture or carpets, or fancy soap in the bathroom. It can be noisy at night when big groups book in; avoid Labor Day weekend, when all the canoe paddlers in the state want to stay here and rehash the race into the wee morning hours.

75–5739 Alii Dr., Kailua-Kona, HI 96740. © **800/367-5102** or 808/961-5818. Fax 808/935-7903. www.unclebilly. com. 139 units. $119–$129 double; Check the website for specials starting at $99 and car/room deals for just $30 more a night. Extra person $14. Children 18 and under stay free in parent's room. AE, DC, DISC, MC, V. **Amenities:** Restaurant; bar (w/Hawaiian entertainment); 2 outdoor pools (1 just for children); watersports equipment rentals; activities desk; coin-op washer/dryers. *In room:* A/C, TV, dataport, kitchenette (in some rooms), fridge, hair dryers (in some rooms).

UPCOUNTRY KONA: HOLUALOA
Expensive

Holualoa Inn ★★ *(Finds)*   The quiet, secluded setting of this B&B—40 pastoral acres just off the main drag of the artsy village of Holualoa, 1,350 feet above Kailua-Kona—provides stunning panoramic views of the entire coast. Recently sold to Sandy Hazen, a local Kona coffee farmer, this contemporary 7,000-square-foot Hawaiian home has six private suites and window-walls that roll back to embrace the gardens and views. Sandy resorted the guest rooms with new furnishings and upgraded bathrooms, and put lahala matting on the ceilings. Plus, the Inn now has a renowned chef cooking your gourmet breakfast. Cows graze on the bucolic pastures below the garden Jacuzzi and pool, and the 30-acre estate includes 3,000 coffee trees, which are the source of the morning brew. The inn offers a gas grill for a romantic dinner beside the pool, a telescope for stargazing, and a billiard table. It's a 15-minute drive down the hill to busy Kailua-Kona and about 20 minutes to the beach, but the pool has a stunning view of Kailua-Kona and the sparkling Pacific below.

P.O. Box 222 (76–5932 Mamalahoa Hwy.), Holualoa, HI 96725. © **800/392-1812** or 808/324-1121. Fax 808/322-2472. www.holualoainn.com. 6 units, 1 with shower only. $225–$475 double. Rates include full breakfast. 2-night minimum. If you mention Frommer's when you book, they promise a discount. 15% discount for 7 nights or more. AE, DC, DISC, MC, V. On Mamalahoa Hwy., just after the Holualoa Post Office, look for Paul's Place General Store; the next driveway is the inn. Children must be 13 or older. **Amenities:** Huge outdoor pool; Jacuzzi. *In room:* Hair dryer, no phone.

KEAUHOU
Very Expensive

Sheraton Keauhou Bay Resort and Spa ★ *(Kids)*   In 2005, nearly 6 years after the old Kona Surf Resort closed, and after $70 million in renovations, the Sheraton Keauhou Bay Resort had a formal opening. The complete overhaul of this 1970s resort is remarkable: Walls were torn out in the lobby and the main dining room to allow access to the incredible view of Keauhou Bay, and the 420-square-foot rooms were completely redone to bring them into the 21st century. The best addition to the rooms is Sheraton's "Sweet Sleeper" bed, with a cushy mattress top, a feather-weight duvet, and five pillows to choose from. The next biggest change to the resort is the mammoth pool: Tucked in around the tropical gardens and splashing waterfalls, this enormous freshwater pool includes its own small man-made beach, the island's largest water slide, bubbling whirlpool spas, and a children's play area. Speaking of kids, there's a children's center and program on property and plenty of activities to keep the little ones occupied (water activities, cultural games and arts and crafts, video games, and so on). Plus, the Sheraton has a golf course next door, tennis courts on-property, and a shopping center (with restaurants) close by.

78–128 Ehukai St., Kailua-Kona, HI 96740. ⓒ **888/488-3535** or 808/930-4900. Fax 808/930-4800. www.sheraton keauhou.com. 522 units. $350–$460 double. Children 18 and younger stay free in parent's room with existing bedding. $60 extra person. AE, DC, DISC, MC, V. Self-parking $5, valet parking $10. **Amenities:** 2 restaurants (luau twice a week); bar; multilevel pool w/200-ft. water slide; 36-hole golf course nearby w/preferred guest rate; 2 tennis courts; fitness center; spa; whirlpool; year-round children's program; concierge; activities desk; business center; room service; babysitting; coin-op washer/dryers; laundry service; dry cleaning; sand volleyball court; basketball court. *In room:* A/C, TV, dataport, high-speed Internet (additional fee), fridge, coffeemaker, hair dryer, iron, safe.

Expensive

Kanaloa at Kona ★★ *Kids*   These big, comfortable, well-managed, and spacious vacation condos, on 16 landscaped acres, border the rocky coast beside Keauhou Bay, 6 miles south of Kailua-Kona. They're exceptional units, ideal for families, with comforts such as huge bathrooms with whirlpool bathtubs, dressing rooms, and bidets. In addition, the spacious lanais, tropical decor, and many appliances make for free and easy living. It's easy to stock up on supplies at the supermarket at the new mall just up the hill, but the oceanfront restaurant offers an alternative to your own cooking. Guests receive discounted golf rates at a nearby country club.

78–261 Manukai St., Kailua-Kona, HI 96740. ⓒ **800/688-7444** or 808/322-9625. Fax 800/622-4852. www.outrigger. com. Managed by Outrigger Resorts. 76 units. $239–$349 1-bedroom apt (sleeps up to 4); $259–$429 2-bedroom apt (up to 6); $395–$479 2-bedroom apt with loft (up to 8). AE, DC, DISC, MC, V. **Amenities:** Restaurant; ocean-side bar; 3 outdoor pools (1 for adults only); 2 tennis courts (lit); 3 Jacuzzis; concierge; activities desk; babysitting; coin-op washer/dryers. *In room:* TV, kitchen, fridge, coffeemaker, hair dryer, iron, safe.

Outrigger Keauhou Beach Resort ★ *Value*   Located on 10 acres, this former Ohana Keauhou Beach Hotel, still owned by the same company, has been upgraded to the more upscale Outrigger brand. The setting is perfect, on a large reef system (where sea turtles come ashore for a brief nap), and next door to one of Kona's best white-sand beaches, Kahuluu. Lush tropical gardens of native plants and flowers surround the hotel, and it's just a mile from the Kona Country Club's 36 holes of golf. The rooms are small (you could fit a crib in there, but a family of four should get two rooms); the oceanview rooms are well worth the extra money. We have gotten some complaints about cleanliness of the rooms, bug problems, and air-conditioning malfunctions. Management said they are working on these issues. The main dining room is forgettable, but you're just minutes from other restaurants and shopping at the nearby Keauhou Shopping Center. Rates are much cheaper than the nearby Sheraton Keauhou (see above).

78–6740 Alii Dr., Kailua-Kona, HI 96740. ⓒ **800/OUTRIGGER** or 808/322-3441. Fax 808/322-3117. www.outrigger. com. 309 units. $239–$399 double; suites from $449. Additional person $50. AE, DC, DISC, MC, V. Parking $5 per day. **Amenities:** 2 restaurants; 4 bars; outdoor pool; 36-hole golf course nearby; 6 tennis courts, 2 lighted for night play; fitness center; spa; whirlpool; year-round children's program; concierge; activities desk; business center; room service; coin-op washer/dryers; laundry service; dry cleaning; shuttle to shopping center. *In room:* A/C, TV, fridge, coffeemaker, hair dryer, iron, safe.

Moderate

Kona Seaspray ★ *Value*   The Kona Seaspray has a couple of great things going for it: location and price. It's just across from the Kahaluu Beach Park, possibly the best snorkeling area in Kona. The rates are a great deal when you consider that the one-bedroom apartments easily sleep four and the two-bedroom unit can sleep six. It's under new ownership, and all the units are undergoing renovations that include upgraded furniture and new carpets. All apartments have a full kitchen, and there's also a barbecue area. Every unit has a lanai and fabulous ocean view. Golf and tennis are nearby. This is the place to book if you are going to spend a lot of time lounging around, or if you need the extra space.

78–6671 Alii Dr. (reservations c/o Johnson Resort Properties, 78–6665 Alii Dr.), Kailua-Kona, HI 96740. ℭ 808/322-2403. Fax 808/322-0105. www.konaseaspray.com. 12 units. $115–$140 1-bedroom double; $125–$155 1-bedroom/2-bathroom double; $140–$180 2-bedroom/2-bathroom; plus $55–$75 cleaning fee. 3-night minimum. Extra person $20. AE, DISC, MC, V. **Amenities:** Gorgeous outdoor pool w/waterfall; whirlpool hot tub; washer/dryers. *In room:* TV/VCR, kitchen, full-size fridge, coffeemaker, hair dryer, iron.

SOUTH KONA
Expensive

Horizon Guest House ★★ *Finds*   If you're planning to stay in South Kona, get on the phone right now and book this place—this is the Hawaiian hideaway of your dreams. Host Clem Classen spent 2 years researching the elements of a perfect B&B, and the Horizon Guest House is the result. Its 40 acres of pastureland are located at an altitude of 1,100 feet. You can see 25 miles of coastline, from Kealakekua to just about South Point, yet you cannot see another structure or hear any sounds of civilization. The carefully thought-out individual units (all under one roof but positioned at an angle to one another so you don't see any other units) are filled with incredible Hawaiian furnishings, including hand-quilted Hawaiian bedspreads. Units also include private lanais with coastline views. The property features barbecue facilities, gardens everywhere, an outdoor shower, and plenty of beach toys. Clem whips up a gourmet breakfast in the main house, which also features a media room with library, video collection, TV (which you can take to your room if you use headphones so you won't disturb other guests), DVD, VCR, and cordless phone. At first glance, the rate may seem high, but once you're ensconced on the unique property, I think you'll agree it's worth every penny.

P.O. Box 268, Honaunau, HI 96726. ℭ 888/328-8301 or 808/328-2540. Fax 808/328-8707. www.horizonguesthouse.com. 4 units. $250 double. Rates include full gourmet breakfast. 2-night minimum. MC, V. 21 miles south of Kailua-Kona on Hwy. 11, just before mile marker 100. Children must be 14 or older. **Amenities:** Large outdoor pool worthy of a big resort; Jacuzzi perfectly placed to watch the sunset behind Kealakekua Bay; complimentary washer/dryers; dataport; wireless Internet access. *In room:* Fridge, coffeemaker, hair dryer, no phone.

Inexpensive
Affordable Hawaii at Pomaikai (Lucky) Farm Bed & Breakfast *Value*   True to its name, Affordable Hawaii offers an inexpensive perch from which to explore the South Kona Coast. Come share ex-California resident Nita Isherwood's century-old 4-acre farm, which is overflowing with macadamia-nut trees, coffee, tropical fruits, avocados as big as footballs, and even *jaboticaba*, an exotic fruit that makes a zingy jam and local wine. The least expensive room is inside the old farmhouse (hey, at $70 a night, this is a deal!). The Greenhouse wing has two rooms with wooden floors, big windows, and private entrances. The most unusual accommodation is the old coffee barn, updated into a rustic room for two with a raised queen-size bed, a fabulous view

of the coastline, and an outdoor shower. Guests can use a common kitchen with a refrigerator, microwave, hot plate, and barbecue grill.

83–5465 Mamalahoa Hwy. (south of Kailua-Kona, after mile marker 107), Captain Cook, HI 96704. © **800/325-6427** or 808/328-2112. Fax 808/328-2112. www.luckyfarm.com. 4 units. $80–$95 double high season; $70–$85 double low season. Rates include full farm breakfast. Extra person $10, kids under 6 are $5. 2-night minimum. AE, DISC, MC, V. *In room:* No phone.

Areca Palms Estate Bed & Breakfast ⭐ (Finds)
Everything about this upcountry B&B is impeccable: the landscaping, the furnishings, the fresh flowers in every room—even breakfast is served with attention to every detail. This charming cedar home, surrounded by immaculate parklike landscaping, sits above the Captain Cook–Kealakekua area, close to beaches, shopping, and restaurants. Guests enjoy watching the sun sink into the ocean from the large lanai or gazing at the starry sky as they soak in the hot tub. Hosts Janice and Steve Glass serve memorable breakfasts (orange-oatmeal quiche, tropical stuffed French toast, tree-ripened banana cakes), offer daily maid service, provide guests with beach equipment, and gladly help with reservations for activities and dinner.

P.O. Box 489, Captain Cook, HI 96704. © **800/545-4390** or 808/323-2276. Fax 808/323-3749. www.konabedand breakfast.com. 4 units. $110–$145 double. Rates include full breakfast. Extra person $25. 2-night minimum. MC, V. From Hwy. 11, make a left at the Pacific Island Tire dealer (after mile marker 111) and follow the signs. **Amenities:** Outdoor Jacuzzi. *In room:* TV, hair dryer, no phone.

Dragonfly Ranch: Healing Arts Retreat
Some may find the Dragonfly Ranch too rustic. But if you want to enjoy Hawaii's tropical outdoors and you're thrilled by the island's most unique architecture—structures that bring the outdoors inside—this may be the place for you. Cabins range from one room (with screens only, no drapes) to suites; you might describe the style as "early hippie." Breakfast includes healthy hot cereal such as amaranth, quinoa, and oatmeal with assorted toppings such as toasted pecans, sunflower seeds, walnuts, raisins, and golden flax seed; fresh homegrown organic fruit (like apple bananas and strawberry papayas); wheat-free granola and waffles; and sprouted grain bread. The location is ideal, with Puuhonua O Honaunau National Historic Park just down the road and five bays offering great swimming and diving just minutes away. The place itself, with free-standing cabins tucked away on 2 acres of fruit trees and exotic flowers, truly is a tropical fantasy.

P.O. Box 675 (19 miles south of Kailua-Kona on Hwy. 160), Honaunau, HI 96726. © **800/487-2159** or 808/328-2159. Fax 808/328-9570. www.dragonflyranch.com. 5 units, 4 with private bathroom, 1 with shower only. $100–$250 double. Rates include continental breakfast. Extra person $20. 3-night minimum. MC, V. From Hwy. 11, turn onto Hwy. 160 (the road to Puuhonua O Honaunau National Historic Park), between mile markers 103 and 104; after 1½ miles, look for the Dragonfly Ranch mailbox. **Amenities:** Yoga studio and fitness room; watersports equipment rentals; activities desk; car-rental desk; massage; babysitting; laundry service. *In room:* TV, wireless high-speed Internet access, kitchenette (in some rooms), fridge, coffeemaker, hair dryer, iron.

Manago Hotel (Value)
If you want to experience the history and culture of the 50th state, the Manago Hotel may be the place for you. This living relic is still operated by the third generation of the same Japanese family that opened it in 1917. It offers clean accommodations, tasty home cooking, and generous helpings of aloha, all at budget prices. The older rooms (with community bathrooms) are ultraspartan—strictly for desperate budget travelers. The rooms with private bathrooms in the new wing are still pretty sparse (freshly painted walls with no decoration and no TV), but they're spotlessly clean and surrounded by Japanese gardens with a koi pond. The room prices increase as you go up; the third-floor units have the most spectacular views of the

Kona coastline. Adventuresome travelers might want to try the Japanese rooms with tatami mats to sleep on and *furo* (deep hot tubs) in each room to soak in. By the end of your stay, you may leave with new friends (the Manago family is very friendly).

P.O. Box 145, Captain Cook, HI 96704. © 808/323-2642. Fax 808/323-3451. www.managohotel.com. 63 units, some with shared bathroom. $33 double with shared bathroom; $54–$59 double with private bathroom; $73 double Japanese room with small *furo* tub and private bathroom. Extra person $3. DISC, MC, V. **Amenities:** Restaurant (Manago Hotel Restaurant, p. 282); bar. *In room:* No phone.

THE KOHALA COAST
Note: You'll find Kohala coast accommodations on the "Where to Stay & Dine in North Kohala & Waimea" map on p. 263.

VERY EXPENSIVE
Hapuna Beach Prince Hotel ✿✿ This hotel enjoys one of the best locations on the Kohala Coast, adjacent to the magnificent white sands of Hapuna Beach. The Hapuna Beach Prince is more formal than other hotels on the Kohala Coast; guests, many from Japan, dress up here, some in the latest Tokyo fashions. You won't feel comfortable parading around in your T-shirt and flip-flops.

The rooms are comfortable, all attuned to the fabulous ocean view and the sea breezes. Although the rooms are small for a luxury hotel, the sprawling grounds make up for it (some guests, however, complain about the long walk from the lobby to their rooms). Service is friendly and caring.

There is also a wealth of activities on the property, from the 18-hole championship golf course (designed by Arnold Palmer and Ed Seay, and reserved for guests and residents) to the state-of-the-art fitness center and world-class Paul Brown Salon and Spa, one of the state's top salons.

At Mauna Kea Resort, 62–100 Kaunaoa Dr., Kohala Coast, HI 96743. © 800/882-6060 or 808/880-1111. Fax 808/880-3112. www.princeresortshawaii.com. 350 units. $395–$690 double; from $1,300 suite. Extra person $60. Children 17 and under stay free in parent's room using existing bedding. AE, DC, MC, V. **Amenities:** 5 restaurants (including the Coast Grille, p. 283); 2 bars (1 is an open-air beachfront bar w/live evening entertainment); huge outdoor pool; golf course; 13 tennis courts; fitness center; salon and spa; Jacuzzi; watersports equipment rentals; year-round Keiki Kamp children's program; concierge; activities desk; car-rental desk; business center; shopping arcade; room service; massage; babysitting; same-day laundry service and dry cleaning. *In room:* A/C, TV, high-speed Internet access, fridge, coffeemaker, hair dryer, iron, safe.

Mauna Kea Beach Hotel ✿✿ Just as we were going to press, this grande dame of hotel resorts in Hawaii was closed for extensive renovations due to the 2006 earthquake. The construction was estimated to be complete by 2008, but rates were not available; call for an update on reopening. The weekly outdoor clambake will continue during renovations, and the golf course and tennis courts both are open.

This resort dates back to the early 1960s. Laurance S. Rockefeller was sailing around Hawaii when he spotted a perfect crescent of gold sand and dropped anchor. In 1965 he built the Mauna Kea on the spot. Over the years, new luxury hotels have eclipsed the Mauna Kea in architectural style and amenities, but the beach out front is divine, the landscaped grounds have a maturity seen nowhere else on this coast, and its loyal old-money guests keep returning to savor the relaxed clubby ambience, remote setting, world-class golf course, and old Hawaii ways.

The two championship golf courses—Robert Trent Jones, Sr.'s, famous Mauna Kea course and the Arnold Palmer–designed Hapuna course—are both award winners.

The rooms are huge by today's standards. The hotel is positioned to catch the cooling trade winds, and the views from the large lanais are breathtaking.

62–100 Mauna Kea Beach Dr., Kohala Coast, HI 96743. © 800/882-6060 or 808/882-7222. Fax 808/880-3112. www.princeresortshawaii.com. 310 units. Call for update on reopening and rates. AE, DC, MC, V. **Amenities:** 6 restaurants; 3 bars w/live music; large outdoor pool; 2 championship golf courses; 13-court ocean-side tennis complex; excellent fitness center; Jacuzzi; watersports equipment rentals; children's program; concierge; activities desk; car-rental desk; shopping arcade; salon; room service; massage; babysitting; coin-op washer/dryers; laundry service; dry cleaning. *In room:* A/C, TV, high-speed Internet access, minibar, hair dryer, iron, safe.

Mauna Lani Bay Hotel & Bungalows ⟨⟨ (Kids)   Burned out? In need of tranquillity and gorgeous surroundings? Look no further. Sandy beaches and lava tide pools are the focus of this serene seaside resort, where gracious hospitality is dispensed in a historic setting. From the lounge chairs on the pristine beach to the turndown service at night, everything here is done impeccably.

Louvered doors open onto the plush guest rooms, which are outfitted in natural tones with teak accents, each with a lanai. They're arranged to capture maximum ocean views, and they surround interior atrium gardens and pools in which endangered baby sea turtles are raised. A shoreline trail leads across the whole 3,200-acre resort, giving you an intimate glimpse into the ancient past, when people lived in lava caves and tended the large complex of fish ponds.

The hotel offers a very complete children's program, plus "kid-friendly" restaurants, but in addition to that, this is just a great place for kids to explore. The saltwater stream that meanders through the hotel and out onto the property outside is filled with reef fish and even a shark. The fish ponds on the property are a great educational experience for *keiki,* and the beach has plenty of room for the youngsters to run and play. Next door to the resort are ancient Hawaiian petroglyph fields, where older kids can learn about Hawaii's past.

The Sports and Fitness Club (one of the best on the island) was just renovated, and The Shops at Mauna Lani recently opened with great retail-therapy opportunities and several food options.

68–1400 Mauna Lani Dr., Kohala Coast, HI 96743. © 800/367-2323 or 808/885-6622. Fax 808/885-1484. www.maunalani.com. 342 units. $430–$920 double; from $980 suite; $620–$1,860 villa (3-day minimum); $5,500–$6,225 bungalow (sleeps up to 4). AE, DC, DISC, MC, V. **Amenities:** 5 excellent restaurants (including CanoeHouse, p. 283); bar (live music nightly); large outdoor pool; 2 celebrated 18-hole championship golf courses; 10 Plexipave tennis courts; full-service fitness facility; range of massage treatments at the spa; Jacuzzi; watersports equipment rentals; bike rentals; year-round children's program; concierge; activities desk; business center; shopping arcade; salon; room service; massage; babysitting; laundry service; dry cleaning. *In room:* A/C, TV, dataport, fridge, coffeemaker, hair dryer, iron, safe.

Waikoloa Beach Marriott Resort & Spa ⟨   There have been big, big changes here. First they gutted all the guest rooms (back down to the bare concrete) and redesigned them, added 27-inch flatscreen TVs, put in glass lanai railings (which actually glow at sunset), and topped everything off with a very comfy Marriott "Revive" bed. This resort has always had one outstanding attribute: an excellent location on Anaehoomalu Bay (or A-Bay, as the locals call it), one of the best ocean-sports bays on the Kohala Coast. The gentle sloping beach has everything: swimming, snorkeling, diving, kayaking, windsurfing, and even old royal fish ponds. The property still isn't as posh as other luxury hotels along the Kohala Coast, but it also isn't nearly as expensive. The size and layout of the guest rooms remain the same—perfectly nice, but not luxurious. Families might want to book the deluxe rooms, which are oversized. A new adults-only infinity swimming pool was added in 2006, and the Mandara Spa was expanded to 5,000 sq. ft on two levels. The main dining room, Hawaii Calls, also was expanded with a new patio area outside and has a new menu. Guests may use the two championship golf courses at the adjacent Hilton Waikoloa Village.

Where to Stay & Dine in North Kohala & Waimea

DINING ◆

Aioli's **13**

Bamboo Restaurant **11**

Brown's Beach House **7**

Cafe Pesto **10**

Canoe House **6**

Charlie's Thai Cuisine **1**

Coast Grille **8**

Daniel Thiebaut Restaurant **13**

Island's Fine Burgers & Drinks **1**

Kings' Kitchen **1**

Kohala Rainbow Café **12**

Merriman's **13**

Merriman's Market Cafe **3**

Noodle House **1**

Norio's Sushi Bar & Restaurant **7**

Roy's Waikoloa Bar & Grill **3**

Sansei Seafood Restaurant & Sushi Bar **1**

Tako Taco Taqueria **13**

Waikoloa Beach Grill **4**

ACCOMMODATIONS ■

Aaah, the Views B&B **14**

Aloha Vacation Cottages **14**

Belle Vue **14**

The Cliff House **15**

Fairmont Orchid Hawaii **7**

Hapuna Beach Prince Hotel **8**

Hilton Waikoloa Village **5**

Luana Ola B&B **15**

Mountain Meadow **15**

Mauna Kea Beach Hotel **9**

Mauna Lani Bay Hotel & Bungalows **6**

Waianuhea **14**

Waikoloa Beach Marriott **2**

Waimea Garden Cottages **14**

Waipio Wayside B&B Inn **16**

69–275 Waikoloa Beach Dr., Waikoloa, HI 96738. ⓒ 877/359-3696 or 808/886-6789. Fax 808/886-3601. www.marriotthawaii.com. 555 units. $425–$565 double; cabana from $600 suite. Extra person $40. Children 17 and under stay free in parent's room. Resort fee $16 for overnight self-parking, daily mai tais for 2, 1 child meal (11 years and under) with purchase of adult entree (dinner), half-day snorkel rental for 2, 1-hr. daily tennis court time, free local calls (Big Island), and high-speed wireless Internet access. AE, DC, DISC, MC, V. Valet parking $15. **Amenities:** 2 restaurants; 1 bar w/nightly live entertainment; outdoor swimming pools (a huge pool w/water slide and separate children's pool); 2 tennis courts; fitness center; full-service Mandara Spa; Jacuzzi; watersports equipment rentals; year-round children's program; concierge; activities desk; business center; salon; room service; babysitting; coin-op washer/dryers; laundry service; dry cleaning; Hawaiian cultural activities, including petroglyphs tour and evening luau. *In room:* A/C, flatscreen TV, dataport, fridge, coffeemaker, hair dryer, iron, safe.

Expensive

The Fairmont Orchid, Hawaii ★★★ (Kids) Located on 32 acres of oceanfront property, the Orchid is the place for watersports nuts, cultural explorers, families with children, or someone who just wants to lie back and soak up the sun. This elegant beach resort takes full advantage of the spectacular ocean views and historical sites on its grounds. The sports facilities here are extensive, and there's an excellent Hawaiiana program: The "beach boys" demonstrate how to do everything from creating drums from the trunks of coconut trees to paddling a Hawaiian canoe or strumming a ukulele.

I recommend spending a few dollars more to book a room on The Fairmont's Gold Floor, which offers personalized service, a lounge (serving complimentary continental breakfast, finger sandwiches in the afternoon, and appetizers in the evening), and exquisite ocean views. All 540 guest rooms in this luxury hotel underwent complete renovation in 2006 (to the tune of $9.3 million) and sport new carpets, paint, artwork, lani furniture, and amenities. All guest rooms feature big lanais, sitting areas, and marble bathrooms, each with a double vanity and separate shower. The Spa Without Walls allows you to book a massage just about anywhere on the property—overlooking the ocean, nestled deep in the lush vegetation, or in your room. The Orchid's four restaurants are all wonderful, with a casual, relaxed atmosphere.

The Keiki Aloha program, for kids 5 to 12, features supervised activities like watersports and Hawaiian cultural activities. Some special money-saving family packages are also available.

The award-winning Norio's Sushi Bar & Restaurant has expanded, with three sushi chefs chopping, rolling, and performing magic at the sushi bar. The recently opened Polynesian revue ("The Gathering of Kings") and luau is making a big splash with everything from fire-knife dancing performances to culinary creations from Samoa, Tahiti, and New Zealand.

I applaud The Fairmont Orchid for dropping the obnoxious "resort fee" and allowing guests to pay for the extra services they want.

1 N. Kaniku Dr., Kohala Coast, HI 96743. © 800/845-9905 or 808/885-2000. Fax 808/885-1064. www.fairmont. com/orchid. 540 units. $359–$799 double; $799–$1,499 double Gold Floor; from $999 suite. Extra person $75. Children 17 and under stay free in parent's room. AE, DC, DISC, MC, V. Valet parking $15; self-parking $8. **Amenities:** 4 restaurants (including Norio's Sushi Bar & Restaurant, p. 283, and Brown's Beach House, p. 283); 5 bars (w/evening entertainment in the Paniolo Lounge); large outdoor pool; 2 championship golf courses; 10 award-winning Plexipave tennis courts (7 lit for night play); well-equipped fitness center; outstanding spa; 2 lava rock whirlpools; watersports equipment rentals; bike rentals; year-round children's program; concierge; activities desk; car-rental desk; business center; shopping arcade; salon; room service; babysitting; same-day laundry service and dry cleaning. *In room:* A/C, TV, high-speed Internet access $15/day, minibar, hair dryer, iron, safe.

Hilton Waikoloa Village 🐦

This hotel is a fantasy world all its own, perfect for those who love Vegas and Disneyland. Its high-rise towers are connected by silver-bullet trams, boats, and museum-like walkways lined with $7 million in Asian/Pacific reproductions. The kids will love it, but Mom and Dad may get a little weary waiting for the tram or boat to take them to breakfast (sometimes a 20-min. ordeal or a mile-long walk). The 62 acres feature tropical gardens, cascading waterfalls, exotic wildlife, exaggerated architecture, a 175-foot water slide twisting into a 1-acre pool, hidden grottoes, and man-made lagoons, including a dolphin lagoon (you can swim with the dolphins for a fee).

The contemporary guest rooms are spacious and luxurious, with built-in platform beds, lanais, and loads of amenities, from spacious dressing areas to a second phone line in all units. All rooms and bathrooms have recently undergone renovations from top to bottom, including new drapes, new beds and bedding, bigger televisions, and new furniture, carpet, and tile. With nine restaurants to choose from, you'll never lack for culinary choices, and golfers can choose from one of the two championship golf courses, one designed by Robert Trent Jones, Jr., and the other by Tom Weiskopf.

Even if you aren't staying here, drop by for the Kohala Spa, one of the best spas on the Kohala Coast, with 25,000 square feet of treatment rooms, saunas, whirlpools, and a host of treatments, including acupuncture and Eastern medicine practices—there's even an astrologer on staff!

69-425 Waikoloa Beach Dr., Waikoloa, HI 96738. © **800/HILTONS** or 808/886-1234. Fax 808/886-2900. www.hilton waikoloavillage.com. 1,240 units, including 57 suites. $249–$599 double; from $1,095 suite. Daily resort fee $15 for seaside putting course, access to Kohala spa, 1 hr. of tennis court time, and $25 beach toy credit. Extra person $40. Children 18 and under stay free in parent's room. AE, DC, DISC, MC, V. Valet parking $15; self-parking $7. **Amenities:** 9 restaurants; 9 bars (many w/entertainment); 3 huge outdoor pools (w/waterfalls, slides, whirlpools, and an adults-only pool); 2 18-hole golf courses; 8 tennis courts; excellent spa w/cardio machines, weights, and a multitude of services; Jacuzzi; watersports equipment rentals; bike rentals; fabulous children's program; game room; concierge; activities desk; car-rental desk; business center; shopping arcade; salon; room service; in-room massage; babysitting; coin-op washer/dryers; same-day laundry service and dry cleaning; concierge-level rooms; art gallery. *In room:* A/C, TV, dataport, high-speed Internet ($14/day), minibar/fridge, coffeemaker, hair dryer, iron, safe.

WAIMEA
MODERATE
Waimea Garden Cottages ★★ *Finds*   Imagine rolling hills on pastoral ranch land. Then add a babbling stream and two cozy Hawaiian cottages. Complete the picture with mountain views, and you have Waimea Garden Cottages. One unit has the feel of an old English country cottage, with oak floors, a fireplace, and French doors opening onto a spacious brick patio. The other is a remodeled century-old Hawaiian wash house, filled with antiques, eucalyptus-wood floors, and a full kitchen. Extra touches keep guests returning again and again: plush English robes, sandalwood soaps in the bathroom, mints next to the bed, and fresh flower arrangements throughout. Hosts Barbara and Charlie Campbell live on the spacious property.

Off Mamalahoa Hwy., 2 miles west of Waimea town center. Reservations c/o Hawaii's Best Bed & Breakfasts, P.O. Box 758, Volcano, HI 96785. © **800/262-9912** or 808/263-3100. Fax 808/962-6360. www.bestbnb.com. 2 units. $150–$160 double. Rates include continental breakfast. Extra person $20. 3-night minimum. No credit cards. *In room:* TV/VCR, kitchen, fridge, coffeemaker, hair dryer, iron, whirlpool bathtub (in 1 unit), fireplace (in 1 unit).

INEXPENSIVE
Aaah, the Views Bed & Breakfast ★ *Value*   This quiet B&B, just 15 minutes from the fabulous beaches of the Kohala Coast and 5 minutes from the cowboy town of Waimea, lives up to its name—each of the four units has huge picture windows from which you can watch the sun rise or set, or gaze out over green pastureland to the slopes of Mauna Kea. New owners Erika and Derek Stuart recently took over this B&B and have added a new deck to the stream-side property. One unit is a studio apartment, complete with kitchen. Two rooms share one bathroom, and the fourth unit has its own private bathroom down the hall.

P.O. Box 6593, Kamuela, HI 96743. © **808/885-3455.** Fax 808/885-4031. www.aaahtheviews.com. 4 units. $85–$165 double. Rates include continental breakfast. Extra person $20. 2-night minimum. MC, V. *In room:* TV/VCR, high-speed Internet access, kitchenette, fridge, coffeemaker, hair dryer, iron.

Aloha Vacation Cottages ★ *Finds*   You'll find these two rental units in a residential area in the cool climate of Waimea. The small, intimate guesthouse has a full kitchen, a separate bedroom, a washer/dryer, and all the comforts of home, including a selection of pillows and a mattress with an adjustable "comfort level" on each side. The larger stand-alone cottage has all the same amenities, plus more space. Guests are

greeted with a fruit basket, and barbecue facilities are available. The cottages are on the "dry" side of Waimea, just about a 10- to 15-minute drive to the beach and just a few minutes to the restaurants of Waimea.

P.O. Box 1395, Kamuela, HI 96743. © **877/875-1722** or 808/885-6535. www.alohacottages.net. 2 units. $120–$145. Extra person $15. 5-night minimum. MC, V. *In room:* TV/VCR, free high-speed Internet, hair dryer, iron, washer/dryer, beach gear.

Belle Vue ⟨★⟩   This two-story vacation rental has a truly beautiful view. Sitting in the hills overlooking Waimea and surrounded by manicured gardens, the charming home is just 15 minutes from the Kohala Coast beaches. The penthouse unit is a large, cathedral-ceilinged studio apartment with a small kitchen, huge bedroom, luxurious bathroom, and view of Mauna Loa and Mauna Kea mountains down to the Pacific Ocean. The one-bedroom apartment has a full kitchen and sofa bed. Each unit has a separate entrance. The rates include breakfast fixings (toast, juice, fruit, cereal, coffee) inside the kitchenettes.

1351 Konokohau Rd., off Opelo Rd. (P.O. Box 1295), Kamuela, HI 96743. © **800/772-5044** or ©/fax 808/885-7732. www.hawaii-bellevue.com. 3 units. $95–$185 double. Extra person $25. 2-night minimum. AE, MC, V. *In room:* TV, dataport, kitchenette, fridge, coffeemaker, hair dryer, iron.

THE HAMAKUA COAST

In addition to those listed below, another B&B in this area, in Ahualoa, a mountain community a short drive from Waipio, is **Mountain Meadow Ranch Bed & Breakfast,** 46–3895 Kapuna Rd., Honokaa, HI 96727 (© **808/775-9376;** www.mountain meadowranch.com), offering both a private cottage ($135 for four) and rooms in a house for $95 double.

Note: You'll find the following hotels on the "Where to Stay & Dine in North Kohala & Waimea" map on p. 263.

EXPENSIVE

Waianuhea ⟨★★⟩ *Finds*   Located in the rural rolling hills above Honokaa, totally off the grid, and nestled in seven beautifully landscaped acres (with a lily pond, fruit trees, a vegetable garden, and a bucolic horse pasture) lies this oasis of luxury and relaxation. Just off a narrow country road, this two-story inn features five posh rooms with soaking tubs, gas or wood stoves, phones, and flatscreen LCD satellite TV, all on photovoltaic solar power. The sumptuous main room has highly polished wood floors, a rock fireplace, and custom Italian sofas. The "Great Room" has wrap-around glass windows with multicolored glass balloons hanging from the ceiling. There are five guest rooms, but splurge a little and ask for the Malamalama suite with a cherrywood sleigh bed, extra-large soaking tub, glass-enclosed shower, and separate living room. Other amenities are nightly wine tasting (featuring different wines every month) with gourmet hors d'oeuvres, an outdoor hot tub, a guest minikitchen stocked with a range of goodies (enough to make a meal), and beverages at surprisingly reasonable prices. Complete multicourse gourmet breakfasts are served every morning.

45-3503 Kahana Dr. (P. O. Box 185), Honokaa, Hi 96727. © **888/775-2577** or 808/77-1118, fax 888/296-6302. www.waianuhea.com. 5 units. $195–$400. Includes full breakfast. AE, MC, V. **Amenities:** Hot tub, minikitchen. *In room:* TV/DVD, hair dryer, iron.

MODERATE

The Cliff House ⟨★★⟩ *Finds*   Perched on the cliffs above the ocean is this romantic two-bedroom getaway, surrounded by horse pastures and million-dollar views. A large deck takes in the ocean vista, where whales frolic offshore in winter. Impeccably decorated (the owner also owns Waipio Valley Artworks), the unit features a very well-equipped kitchen, two large bedrooms, and a full bathroom. Lots of little touches make this property stand out from the others: an answering machine for the phone, a pair of binoculars, a chess set, and even an umbrella for the rain squalls. Four people could comfortably share this unit.

P.O. Box 5070, Kukuihaele, HI 96727. © 800/492-4746 or 808/775-0005. Fax 808/775-0058. www.cliffhouse hawaii.com. 1 unit. $195 double. Extra person $35. 2-night minimum. MC, V. *In room:* TV, dataport, kitchen, fridge, coffeemaker, hair dryer, iron.

INEXPENSIVE

Luana Ola B&B Cottages ★ *Finds* These off-the-beaten-path, plantation-style, open-room cottages hearken back to the romantic 1940s. Furnished in rattan and wicker, each features a kitchenette and sleeps up to four. One unit has a spectacular ocean view; the ocean view from the other unit isn't as panoramic, but a satellite TV helps make up for it. Hostess Marsha Tokareff leaves all the fixings for a continental breakfast (fruit, pastries, and coffee) in your kitchen so you can get up at your leisure. The cottages are within walking distance to Honokaa town, yet far enough away to feel the peace and quiet of this bucolic area. Use of laundry facilities is available.

P.O. Box 1967, Honokaa, HI 96727. © 800/357-7727 or 808/775-1150. www.stayhawaii.com. 2 units. $125 double. Extra person $15. 2-night minimum. Rates include continental breakfast. MC, V. **Amenities:** Laundry service. *In room:* TV in 1 unit and DVD in other unit, CD/DVD, kitchenette, fridge, coffeemaker, hair dryer, iron.

Waipio Wayside B&B Inn ★★ *Finds* Jackie Horne's restored Hamakua Sugar supervisor's home, built in 1938, sits nestled among fruit trees, surrounded by sweet-smelling ginger, fragile orchids, and blooming birds-of-paradise. The comfortable house, done in old Hawaii style, abounds with thoughtful touches, such as the help-yourself tea-and-cookies bar with 26 different kinds of tea. A sunny lanai with hammocks overlooks a yard lush with banana, lemon, lime, tangerine, and avocado trees; the cliff-side gazebo has views of the ocean 600 feet below. There are five vintage rooms to choose from: My favorite is the master bedroom suite (dubbed the "bird's-eye" room), with double doors that open onto the deck; I also love the Library Room, which has an ocean view, hundreds of books, and a skylight in the shower. There's a shared living room with a TV (including VCR and DVD). Jackie's friendly hospitality and excellent continental breakfasts round out the experience.

P.O. Box 840, Honokaa, HI 96727. © 800/833-8849 or 808/775-0275. www.waipiowayside.com. 5 units. $99–$190 double. Rates include full organic tropical continental breakfast with coffee, fruit (sunrise papayas, mangoes, fresh tangerines), granola, yogurts, and muffins. Extra person $25. MC, V. On Hwy. 240, 2 miles from the Honokaa Post Office; look on the right for a long white picket fence and sign on the ocean side of the road; the 2nd driveway is the parking lot. **Amenities:** Concierge. *In room:* TV/VCR/DVD in living room.

HILO

Just outside Hilo is a terrific B&B, **Lihi Kai,** 30 Kahoa St., Hilo, HI 96720 (© **808/ 935-7865**), a beautifully designed house with mahogany floors, perched on the edge of a cliff with a wide-angle view of Hilo Bay; rooms start at $65 double (with a 3-night minimum; otherwise, it is $70 a night).

Note: You'll find the following accommodations on the "Hilo" map on p. 331.

EXPENSIVE

The Palms Cliff House Inn ★★ *Finds* This inn is a 15-minute drive north of Hilo town, at Honomu (where Akaka Falls is located). Perched on the side of a cliff, this grand old Victorian-style inn is surrounded by manicured lawns and macadamia-nut, lemon, banana, lime, orange, avocado, papaya, star fruit, breadfruit, grapefruit, and mango trees. Eight oversize suites, filled with antiques and equipped with DVD players, fireplaces, and private lanais, all overlook the ocean. Four rooms have private Jacuzzis; other extras include custom-made Italian-lace sheets, cooking classes, yoga classes, and private massage and other spa treatments. A gourmet hot breakfast (entrees range from banana–mac nut pancakes to asparagus–sweet potato quiche) is served on the wraparound lanai overlooking the rolling surf. Lots of activities on-site, from gourmet cooking classes to hula lessons to high tea. A magnificent getaway.

P.O. Box 189, Honomu, 96728. (℃ **866/963-6076** or 808/963-6076. Fax 808/963-6316. www.palmscliffhouse.com. 8 units. $250–$395 double. Rates include full gourmet breakfast. AE, DC, DISC, MC, V. **Amenities:** Hot tub. *In room:* A/C (only upper units), TV/DVD, dataport, fridge, hair dryer, iron, Jacuzzi (some units).

MODERATE

Shipman House Bed & Breakfast 🖈🖈 *Finds*   Built in 1900, the Shipman House is on both the national and state registers of historic places. This Victorian mansion has been totally restored by Barbara Andersen, the great-granddaughter of the original owner, and her husband, Gary. Despite the home's historic appearance, Barbara has made sure that its conveniences are strictly 21st century, including full bathrooms with all the amenities. All five guest bedrooms are large, with 10- to 12-foot ceilings and touches like heirloom furnishings and hand-woven lauhala mats. Wake up to a large continental homemade (with fresh fruit from the garden) breakfast buffet. On Wednesdays, guests can join in with the hula class practicing on the lanai. Recently they've added lei making and other cultural activities.

131 Kaiulani St., Hilo, HI 96720. (℃ **800/627-8447** or 808/934-8002. Fax 808/934-8002. www.hilo-hawaii.com. 5 units. $205–$225 double. Rates include continental breakfast. Extra person $25. AE, MC, V. From Hwy. 19, take Waianuenue Ave.; turn right on Kaiulani St. and go 1 block over the wooden bridge; look for the large house on the left. *In room:* No phone.

INEXPENSIVE

The Bay House 🖈 *Finds*   Overlooking Hilo Bay, this B&B offers immaculate rooms (each with oak floors, king-size bed, sofa, private bathroom, and oceanview lanai) at reasonable prices. A continental breakfast (tropical fruit, pastries, Kona coffee) is set out in a common area every morning (which also has a refrigerator, coffeemaker, toaster, and microwave for common use); you can take all you want to eat back to your lanai and watch the sun rise over Hilo Bay. In the evening, relax in the cliff-side Jacuzzi as the stars come out.

42 Pukihae St., Hilo, HI 96720. (℃ **888/235-8195** or (℃/fax 808/961-6311. www.bayhousehawaii.com. 3 units. $125 double. Rates include continental breakfast. Extra person $15. AE, MC, V. **Amenities:** Hot tub. *In room:* TV, hair dryer.

Dolphin Bay Hotel 🖈 *Value*   This two-story, motel-like building, 4 blocks from downtown, is a clean, family-run property that offers good value in a quiet garden setting. Ripe star fruit hang from the trees, flowers abound, and there's a junglelike trail by a stream. The tidy concrete-block apartments are small and often breezeless, but they're equipped with ceiling fans and jalousie windows. Rooms are brightly painted and outfitted with rattan furniture and Hawaiian prints. There are no phones in the rooms, but there's one in the lobby. You're welcome to all the papayas and bananas you can eat.

333 Iliahi St., Hilo, HI 96720. (℃ **808/935-1466.** Fax 808/935-1523. www.dolphinbayhilo.com. 18 units. $99–$109 studio double; $129 1-bedroom apt double; $149 2-bedroom apt double. Extra person $10. From Hwy. 19, turn mauka (toward the mountains) on Hwy. 200 (Waianuenue St.), and then right on Puueo St.; go over the bridge and turn left

on Iliahi St. MC, V. **Amenities:** Concierge; car-rental desk; coin-op washer/dryer. *In room:* TV, high-speed Internet access, kitchenette, fridge, coffeemaker, hair dryer (on request), iron, no phone.

Hale Kai Hawaii ★ (Value)

An eye-popping view of the ocean runs the entire length of this house; you can sit on the wide deck and watch the surfers slide down the waves. All rooms have that fabulous ocean view through sliding-glass doors. There's one suite, with a living room, kitchenette, and separate bedroom. Guests have access to a pool, hot tub, and small guest area with fridge, telephone, and library. Breakfast is a treat, with entrees like homemade mac-nut waffles or double cheese soufflé. New owners Maria Macias and Ricardo Zepeda have breathed new life into this B&B: The rooms are now all painted in vibrant tropical colors, Maria has improved the landscaping, and they've installed privacy barriers between each room.

111 Honolii Pali, Hilo, HI 96720. © 808/935-6330. Fax 808/935-8439. www.halekaihawaii.com. 4 units. $125–$139 double; $155 suite. Rates include gourmet breakfast. Extra person $20. 2-night minimum. MC, V. **Amenities:** Oceanfront outdoor pool; Jacuzzi. *In room:* TV, no phone.

Hilo Seaside Hotel

This family-operated hotel is located across the Hilo Bay on historic Banyan Drive. Surrounded by lush tropical gardens and a spring pond filled with Japanese carp, this hotel isn't fancy, but it's great for those on a budget. The rooms were updated and repainted in 2006. The location is terrific for exploring East Hawaii: a 45-minute scenic drive to Hawaii's Volcano National Park, a few minutes by car to downtown, and close to a 9-hole golf course and tennis courts.

126 Banyan Dr. (off Hwy. 19), Hilo, HI 96720. © 800/560-5557 or 808/965-0821. Fax 808/969-9195. www.hilo seasidehotel.com. 135 units. $110–$160 double. Extra person $20. Internet rates from $78. AE, DC, MC, V. **Amenities:** Restaurant; bar; outdoor pool; 18-hole golf course nearby; coin-op washer/dryers. *In room:* A/C, TV, fridge, hair dryer (some rooms), iron (on request), safe.

The Inn at Kulaniapia ★ (Finds)

The view from this off-the-beaten-track inn is worth the price alone: the 120-foot Kulaniapia Waterfall in one direction and the entire town of Hilo sprawled out 850 feet below in another direction. This is *the* place for a romantic getaway. In addition to luxury accommodations, you get a royal breakfast with egg dishes, fresh fruit grown on the 22-acre property, and just-baked breads. Wander along the 2-mile pathways that follow the Waiau River (check out the exotic bamboo garden) or swim at the base of the waterfall in the 300-foot pond. The rooms are well appointed, with balconies. It's just 15 minutes from Hilo but feels a zillion miles away from everything in the peaceful surroundings of a 2,000-acre macadamia-nut grove.

P.O. Box 11338, Hilo, HI 96720. © 866/935-6789 or 808/935-6789. Fax 808/935-6789. www.waterfall.net. 4 units. $109 double. Rates include breakfast. Extra person $20. AE, MC, V. **Amenities:** Hot tub; high-speed Internet access. *In room:* TV.

The Old Hawaiian B&B (Value)

Bargain hunters, take note: This old plantation house from the 1930s has been renovated and offers great room rates that include breakfast. Located on the Wailuku River, the house features a large lanai, where guests have use of a phone, refrigerator, and microwave. The rooms range from tiny to a large unit with its own sitting area and sunken bathtub and separate shower. All have their own private entrances and private bathrooms. Hosts Stewart and Lory Hunter prepare a beautiful breakfast of fruit cup, fruit smoothie, juice, coffee/tea, and two types of homemade bread (you'll want seconds of Lory's mac-nut scones). The Hunters happily help guests with sightseeing plans.

1492 Wailuku Dr., Hilo, HI 96720. © 877/961-2816 or 808/961-2816. www.thebigislandvacation.com. 3 units. $110 double. Extra person $10. MC, V. *In room:* Wireless Internet access, hair dryer, iron (on request).

Uncle Billy's Hilo Bay Hotel   Uncle Billy's is one of the least expensive place to stay along Hilo's hotel row, Banyan Drive. This oceanfront budget hotel boasts a dynamite location, and the car/room package offers an extra incentive to stay here. You enter via a tiny lobby, gussied up Polynesian style; it's slightly overdone, with sagging fishnets and tapa (bark cloth) on the walls. The guest rooms are simple: bed, TV, phone, closet, and bathroom—that's about it. The walls seem paper thin, and it can get very noisy at night (you may want to bring ear plugs), but at these rates, you're still getting your money's worth.

87 Banyan Dr. (off Hwy. 19), Hilo, HI 96720. (℃) 800/367-5102 or 808/961-5818. Fax 808/935-7903. www.unclebilly. com. 144 units. $104–$114 double; $119 studio with kitchenette. Car/room packages and special senior rates available. Extra person $14. Internet specials from $89. Children 18 and under stay free in parent's room. AE, DC, DISC, MC, V. **Amenities:** Restaurant; bar w/hula show nightly; oceanfront outdoor pool; activities desk; coin-op washer/dryers. *In room:* A/C, TV, kitchenette (some rooms), fridge, coffeemaker (some rooms), hair dryer (some rooms), iron (some rooms).

HAWAII VOLCANOES NATIONAL PARK

As a result of Hawaii Volcanoes being officially designated a National Park in 1916, a village has popped up at its front door. Volcano Village isn't so much a town as a wide spot in Old Volcano Road, with two general stores, a handful of restaurants, a post office, a coffee shop, a new firehouse, and a winery.

Except for Volcano House (see below), which is within the national park, all of the accommodations in this section are in Volcano Village. It gets cool here at night—Volcano Village is located at 3,700 feet—so a fireplace might be an attractive amenity. It also rains a lot in Volcano—100 inches a year—which makes everything grow Jack-and-the-Beanstalk style.

I recommend spending at least 3 days to really see and enjoy the park. The best way to do this is to rent a cottage or house, and the best rental agency is **Hawaii Volcano Vacations** ๑๑ (P.O. Box 913, Volcano, HI 96785; ℃ 800/709-0907 or 808/967-7271; www.hawaiivolcanovacations.com). Manager Aurelia Gutierrez selects only the top cottages, cabins, and houses in Volcano and makes sure that they are perfect for you. Her reasonably priced units range from $99 to $200, and each one is outfitted with a full kitchen, plus an outdoor grill, cooler, flashlight, umbrella, and fresh flower arrangement for your arrival. Many of them are great options for families traveling with kids.

On the way to the park is **Bed & Breakfast Mountain View** (℃ 888/698-9896 or 808/968-6868; www.bbmtview.com), a 7,000-square-foot home overlooking a 10,000-square-foot fish pond with teahouse, spa, and patio; rooms start at $65. It's located on South Kulani Road, between mile markers 13 and 14 off Highway 11.

The **Volcano Guest House** ๑ (P.O. Box 6, Volcano HI 96785; ℃ 808/967-7775; fax 808/985-7056; www.volcanoguesthouse.com) has four terrific units from a one-bedroom apartment for $85 to a stand-alone cottage for $105. (I recommend the cottage as an ideal place to stay with the kids: it's completely childproofed and stocked with toys—even a basketball hoop.) The cottage has two twin beds and a queen in the upstairs bedroom, a sofa bed in the living room, a full kitchen, and a backyard forest trail that goes all the way through 2 miles of tropical rainforest to the Thurston Lava Tube in Hawaii Volcanoes National Park.

The **Log Cabin** (℃ 808/262-7249; www.crubinstein.com/cabin.html) is a century-old ohia log cabin for the young at heart, for just $125 double, $150 for four, and $175 for six. And the **Volcano Teapot Cottage** (P.O. Box 511, Volcano, HI

Where to Stay & Dine in the Volcano Area

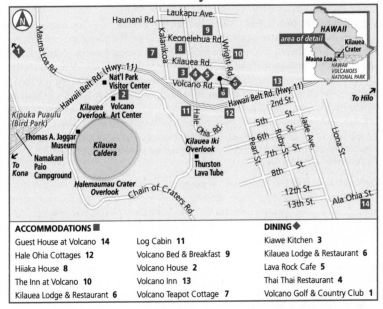

96785; © **808/967-7112;** www.volcanoteapot.com) is a quaint 1914 two-bedroom cottage, decorated with one-of-a-kind antiques, complete with hot tub spa in the forest out back, and renting for $195 double.

EXPENSIVE

The Inn at Volcano Formerly called Chalet Kilauea, this is the most expensive B&B in Volcano. It has a storybook, enchanting quality to it. I found some rooms, although exquisitely decorated, were not very practical for things like hanging clothes, storing toiletries, and so on. The least expensive room is decorated in memorabilia from the owners' extensive travels to eastern and southern Africa. Other rooms include an Oriental Jade room with collectibles from the Far East, a Continental Lace suite with Victorian decor, a treetop suite, and a separate cabin located next door to The Inn.

P.O. Box 998, Volcano, HI 96785. © **800/937-7786** or 808/967-7786. Fax 808/967-8660. www.volcano-hawaii.com. 5 units. $170–$400 double. Rates include full gourmet breakfast and afternoon tea. AE, DC, DISC, MC, V. **Amenities:** Hot tub; 3 of the rooms share a fridge, microwave, and coffeemaker on the porch. *In room:* TV/VCR, fridge (some rooms), coffeemaker (some rooms), microwave (some rooms).

MODERATE

Kilauea Lodge ☆ This popular roadside lodge, built in 1938 as a YMCA camp, sits on 10 wooded and landscaped acres. Its rooms offer heating systems and hot-towel warmers, beautiful art on the walls, fresh flowers, and, in some, fireplaces. There's also a 1929 two-bedroom cottage with a fireplace and a full kitchen, just a couple of blocks down the street. A full gourmet breakfast is served to guests at the restaurant.

P.O. Box 116 (1 block off Hwy. 11 on Old Volcano Rd.), Volcano, HI 96785. © **808/967-7366.** Fax 808/967-7367. www.kilauealodge.com. 17 units. $150–$165 double room; $180–$190 cottages. Rates include full breakfast. Extra person $20. AE, MC, V. **Amenities:** Restaurant (p. 294); hot tub. *In room:* Coffeemaker, no phone.

INEXPENSIVE

Hale Ohia Cottages ★ *Finds*   Take a step back in time to the 1930s. Here you'll have a choice of suites, each with private entrance. There are also four guest cottages, ranging from one bedroom to three. The surrounding botanical gardens contribute to the overall tranquil ambience of the estate. They were groomed in the 1930s by a resident Japanese gardener, who worked with the natural volcanic terrain but gently tamed the flora into soothing shapes and designs. The lush grounds are just a mile from Hawaii Volcanoes National Park. The latest addition is a romantic, cozy cottage with fireplace, hot tub, and unusual bedroom made from a 1930s redwood water tank.

P.O. Box 758 (Hale Ohia Rd., off Hwy. 11), Volcano, HI 96785. © 800/455-3803 or 808/967-7986. Fax 808/967-8610. www.haleohia.com. 8 units. $95–$179 double. Rates include continental breakfast. Extra person $20. MC, V. *In room:* Fridge, coffeemaker, hair dryer, no phone.

Volcano Bed & Breakfast *Value*   If you're on a tight budget, check into this charming restored 1912 historic home offering comfortable, clean, quiet rooms, all with shared bathrooms. The restored house sits on beautifully landscaped grounds and has new carpeting throughout and new furnishings in the common area. The rooms are tiny but clean and inviting. The common rooms include a living room with TV/VCR, a reading room, and a sunroom.

P.O. Box 998 (on Keonelehua St., off Hwy. 11 on Wright Rd.), Volcano, HI 96785. © 800/937-7786 or 808/967-7779. Fax 808/967-8660. www.volcano-hawaii.com. 6 units, none with private bathroom. $65–$85 double. Rates include continental breakfast. Extra person $15. AE, DC, DISC, MC, V. From Hwy. 11, turn north onto Wright Rd.; go 1 mile to Chalet Kilauea on the right, where you'll check in. *In room:* No phone.

Volcano House   Volcano House has a great location—inside the boundaries of the national park—and that's about all. This mountain lodge, which evolved out of a grass lean-to in 1865, is Hawaii's oldest visitor accommodations. It stands on the edge of Halemaumau's bubbling crater, and although the view of the crater is still an awesome sight, don't expect the Ritz here—rooms are very plain and heated with volcanic steam. *Tip:* Book only if you can get a room facing the volcano; if they are filled, don't bother—you can do better elsewhere.

P.O. Box 53, Hawaii Volcanoes National Park, HI 96718. © 808/967-7321. Fax 808/967-8429. www.volcanohouse hotel.com. 42 units. $130–$250 double. Extra person $20. AE, DC, DISC, MC, V. **Amenities:** Restaurant w/great view; bar.

Volcano Inn   Located in the rainforest, this property is a combination of two inns, one with four rooms and one with three, plus a separate cabin with kitchenette, all in the heart of Volcano Village. The rooms at the inn are quite luxurious for the price; each comes with a fireplace and daily maid service. The amenities here include complimentary use of the bicycles, a great video library at one inn and a regular book library at the other, and coffee service daily.

19–3820 Old Volcano Rd., Volcano, HI 96785. © 800/997-2292 or 808/967-7293. Fax 808/985-7349. www.volcano inn.com. 8 units. $105–$145 double. AE, DC, DISC, MC, V. *In room:* TV/VCR/DVD, fridge, hair dryer, iron, no phone.

SOUTH POINT

Bougainvillea Bed & Breakfast ★ *Finds*   Don and Martie Jean Nitsche bought this 3-acre property in the Hawaiian Rancho subdivision of Ocean View and had a *Field of Dreams* experience: They decided that if they built a bed-and-breakfast, people would come. Where some people just saw lava, the Nitsches saw the ancient Hawaiian path that went from the mountain to the sea. So they built. And out of the lava came gardens—colorful bougainvillea, a pineapple patch, and a fish pond to add to the pool and hot tub. Word got out. Martie's breakfast—her secret-recipe banana and mac-nut pancakes, sausage, fruit, and coffee—drew people from all over. Things got so good, they had to add more rooms (all with their own private entrances) and expand the living room (complete with TV, VCR, and video library) and dining room. Guests usually take their breakfast plates out to the lanai, which boasts ocean views. Or you can wander over to the pavilion, located next to the pool, which has a big barbecue area (with a minikitchen, including a microwave), a game area (darts, Ping-Pong table, and so on), a satellite TV, some exercise equipment, even a horseshoe pit. You can borrow snorkeling gear, beach mats, coolers, and other beach equipment.

P.O. Box 6045, Ocean View, HI 96737. © 800/688-1763 or 808/929-7089. Fax 808/929-7089. www.hawaii-inn.com. 4 units. $89 double. Rates include full breakfast. Extra person $15. AE, DC, DISC, MC, V. **Amenities:** Big outdoor pool; concierge; car-rental desk; massage in-room or outdoors; hot tub; satellite TV; minikitchen in pavilion; game area; microwave. *In room:* TV/VCR, hair dryer, no phone.

Macadamia Meadows Bed & Breakfast *Kids*   Near the southernmost point in the United States and just 45 minutes from Volcanoes National Park lies one of the Big Island's most welcoming B&Bs. It's located on an 8-acre working macadamia-nut farm, in a great place for stargazing, and the warmth and hospitality of host Charlene Cowan is unsurpassed. This is an excellent place for children; because the owner has children herself, the entire property is very kid-friendly. In addition to exploring the groves of mac-nut trees, kids can swim in the pool or play tennis. Charlene also has puzzles, games, and other "rainy day" items to entertain children. Two of the units can be reserved together as a two-bedroom suite. All rooms have private entrances and are immaculately clean. Ask Charlene about the free orchid tours.

94–6263 Kamaoa Rd., Waiohinu. Reservations: P.O. Box 756, Naalehu, HI 96772. © 888/929-8118 or 808/929-8097. Fax 808/929-8097. www.macadamiameadows.com. 5 units. $89–$139 double. Rates include continental breakfast. Extra person $10 children under 18, $15 adults; children under 5 stay free in parent's room. AE, DISC, MC, V. **Amenities:** Resort-size outdoor pool; tennis courts; activities desk. *In room:* TV, fridge, microwave, no phone.

South Point Banyan Tree House *Finds*   Couples looking for an exotic place to nest should try this tree house nestled inside a huge Chinese banyan tree. The cottage comes complete with see-through roof that lets the outside in, plus a comfy, just-for-two hot tub on the wraparound deck. Inside there's a queen-size bed and a kitchen with microwave and two-burner stove. The scent of ginger brings you sweet dreams at night, and the twitter of birds greets you in the morning.

At Hwy. 11 and Pinao St., Waiohinu. ©715/302-8180. www.southpointbth.com. 1 unit. $185 double. 2-night minimum. MC, V. **Amenities:** Hot tub; washer/dryer; outside grill. *In room:* TV/VCR, kitchen, fridge, coffeemaker.

4 Where to Dine

So many restaurants, so little time. What's a traveler to do? The Big Island's delicious dilemma is its daunting size and abundant offerings. Its gastronomic environment—the fruitful marriage of creative chefs, good soil, and rich cultural traditions—has made this island as much a culinary destination as a recreational one. And from the Kona Coffee Festival to the Aloha Festival's Poke Recipe Contest, the Big Island is host to extraordinary world-renowned culinary events.

The Big Island's volcanic soil produces fine tomatoes, lettuces, beets, beans, fruit, and basic herbs and vegetables that were once difficult to find locally. Southeast Asian fruit, such as mangosteen and rambutan, are beginning to appear in markets, along with the sweet white pineapple that is by now a well-established Big Island crop.

Along with the lamb and beef from Big Island ranches and seafood from local fishermen, this fresh produce forms the backbone of ethnic cookery and Hawaii Regional Cuisine.

Kailua-Kona is teeming with restaurants for all pocketbooks, while the haute cuisine of the island is concentrated in the Kohala Coast resorts. Waimea, also known as Kamuela, is a thriving upcountry community, a haven for yuppies, techies, and retirees who know a good place when they see one. In Hawi, North Kohala, expect bakeries, neighborhood diners, and one tropical-chic restaurant that's worth a special trip. In Hilo in eastern Hawaii, you'll find pockets of trendiness among the precious old Japanese and ethnic restaurants that provide honest, tasty, and affordable meals in unpretentious surroundings.

Warning: Big Island restaurants, especially along the Kona coast, seem to have a chronic shortage of waitstaff. Come prepared for a leisurely meal; sit and enjoy the warm moonlit night, sip a liquid libation, and realize time is relative here.

In the listings below, reservations are not necessary unless otherwise noted.

THE KONA COAST
IN & AROUND KAILUA-KONA

Note: Hualalai Club Grille, Pahu i'a, and Beach Tree Bar & Grill are located north of Kailua-Kona, 6 miles north of the airport and just south of the Kohala Coast.

Very Expensive

Hualalai Grille 𝒢𝒢 CONTEMPORARY PACIFIC   This open-air oasis of koa, marble, and island artwork just got better. Chef Alan Wong, who put the Canoe-House restaurant (p. 283) on the map and was one of the founders of Hawaii Regional Cuisine, has taken the helm at this popular golf club restaurant, which overlooks the course and has an ocean view. (Wong also has two restaurants on Oahu: Alan Wong's Restaurant, p. 163, and The Pineapple Room at Macy's, p. 151.) Lunch features soups (including Wong's famous chilled red-and-yellow-tomato soup poured in a yin-yang design), sandwiches (like grass-fed Kamuela beef burgers with bacon, cheese, avocado, and salsa), and daily specials (seared peppered ahi over crispy Asian slaw). Dinner entrees include ginger-crusted onaga, steamed moi (raised on property at Hualalai Resort), mac nut–crusted lamb chops, and a host of other mouthwatering offerings. Save room for dessert: chocolate crunch bars, caramel sea salt cheesecake, and other tempting delights. The only thing missing is good service. I have had two kinds of service here—service with an attitude and very bad service.

In the Hualalai Resort, Queen Kaahumanu Hwy., Kaupulehu-Kona. (C) 808/325-8525. www.hualalairesort.com. Reservations recommended. Main courses $12–$21 lunch, $36–$56 dinner. AE, DC, MC, V. Daily 11:30am–2:30pm and 5:30–9pm; bar menu served 11:30am–9:00pm.

Pahu i'a 𝒢 CONTEMPORARY PACIFIC CUISINE   You can't find a better oceanfront location on the Big Island (maybe in the entire state)—Pahu i'a sits just feet from the lapping waves. A small bridge of natural logs leads to this enchanting oceanfront dining room, where views on three sides expand on the aquatic theme (*pahu i'a* is Hawaiian for "aquarium," and there's a large one at the entrance). The food features fresh produce and seafood from the island—and even from the resort's own aquaculture ponds, which teem with shrimp and moi (threadfin), a rich Island fish. The day begins with the coast's most elegant breakfast buffet, featuring excellent omelets, meats, fresh fruit, and regional specialties. At dinner, part of the menu changes daily and always includes several fresh seafood preparations; the Pahu i'a

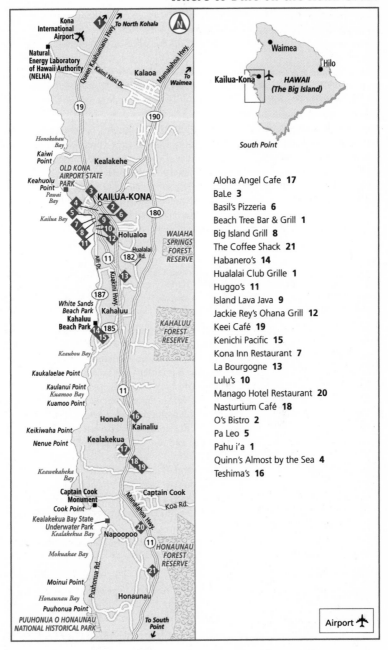

Aloha Angel Cafe **17**
BaLe **3**
Basil's Pizzeria **6**
Beach Tree Bar & Grill **1**
Big Island Grill **8**
The Coffee Shack **21**
Habanero's **14**
Hualalai Club Grille **1**
Huggo's **11**
Island Lava Java **9**
Jackie Rey's Ohana Grill **12**
Keei Café **19**
Kenichi Pacific **15**
Kona Inn Restaurant **7**
La Bourgogne **13**
Lulu's **10**
Manago Hotel Restaurant **20**
Nasturtium Café **18**
O's Bistro **2**
Pa Leo **5**
Pahu i'a **1**
Quinn's Almost by the Sea **4**
Teshima's **16**

bento box, a tasting of the specials of the day; crispy skin opakapaka meunière; mac nut–crusted lamb rack; veal Oscar; dry-aged prime New York steak; and Hawaiian whole lobster Thermidor. From ambience to execution to presentation, Pahu i'a is top-drawer.

In the Four Seasons Resort Hualalai, Queen Kaahumanu Hwy., Kaupulehu-Kona. ⓒ 808/325-8000. Reservations recommended. Breakfast buffet $28; dinner main courses $30–$60. AE, DC, DISC, MC, V. Daily 6:30–11:30am (buffet 7–11:30am); dinner 5:30–9:30pm.

Expensive
Beach Tree Bar & Grill ✿ CASUAL GOURMET   Here's an example of outstanding cuisine in a perfect setting, without being fancy, fussy, or prohibitively expensive. The bar on the sand is a sunset paradise, and the sandwiches, seafood, and grilled items at the casual outdoor restaurant (a few feet from the bar) are in a class of their own—simple, excellent, and imaginatively prepared. The menu, which varies, includes items like grilled fresh fish sandwiches, steaks, alternative healthy cuisine, and vegetarian specialties. On Saturday the "Surf, Sand and Stars" feast offers an array of buffet-style items from fresh fish to grilled New York sirloin, and on Wednesday there's a special "Viva Italia" menu. An added attraction is entertainment from 5 to 8pm nightly.

In the Four Seasons Resort Hualalai, Queen Kaahumanu Hwy., Kaupulehu-Kona. ⓒ 808/325-8000. Reservations recommended for Sat-night buffet. Lunch main courses $17–$22; dinner main courses $42–$47; Sat buffet: "Surf, Sand and Stars" $78 adults, $37 kids 5–12; Wed "Viva Italia" menu entrees $17–$35. AE, DC, DISC, MC, V. Daily 11:30am–8:30pm.

Huggo's ✿ PACIFIC RIM/SEAFOOD   The main Huggo's dining room still hums with diners murmuring dreamily about the view, but it's the thatched-bar fantasy that's *really* on the rocks. **Huggo's on the Rocks** ✿, a mound of thatch, rock, and grassy-sandy ground right next to Huggo's, is a sunset-lover's nirvana. At sundown it's packed with people sipping mai tais and noshing on salads, poke, sandwiches, plate lunches, sashimi, and fish and chips. For lunch the new menu ranges from a spicy grilled mahi taco plate to a huge burger with barbecue sauce. From 6:30 to 11am, this same location turns into the **Java on the Rocks** ✿✿ espresso bar, which is *not* to be missed—sip Kona coffee, enjoy your eggs, and watch the waves roll onto the shore.

At the senior Huggo's, fresh seafood remains the signature, as does the coral-strewn beach with tide pools just beyond the wooden deck. The tables are so close to the water you can see the entire curve of Kailua Bay. Feast on sautéed mahimahi, steamed clams, seared ahi, or imu-style chicken cooked in ti leaves. At lunch, specialties include *kalua* chicken quesadillas, brick-oven pizzas, and sandwiches ranging from hot turkey to prime rib and fresh fish.

75–5828 Kahakai Rd. ⓒ 808/329-1493. www.huggos.com. Reservations recommended. Main courses $9–$19 lunch, $21–$49 dinner. AE, DC, DISC, MC, V. Daily 6–11am; 11:30am–2:30pm and 5:30–10pm.

Kona Inn Restaurant ✿ AMERICAN/SEAFOOD   This is touristy, but it can be a very pleasant experience, especially if the sun is setting. The wide-ranging menu and fresh seafood in the open-air oceanfront setting remind you why you have come to Kailua-Kona. The large, open room and panoramic view of the Kailua shoreline are the most attractive features, especially for sunset cocktails and appetizers. It's a huge menu—everything from nachos and chicken Caesar salad to sandwiches, pasta, stir-fried dishes, and the highlight: the fresh fish served Cajun style or broiled and basted

Moments A Tasty Tour

Kona Joe Coffee Farm and Chocolate Company, 79–7346 Mamalahoa Hwy., between the 113 and 114 mile markers, in Kealakekua (© **808/322-2100;** www.konajoe.com), home of the world's first trellised coffee farm, offers free guided tours daily from 8:30am to 5pm, at the 20-acre estate in the "Gold Belt of Kona Coffee."

The tours begin with an excursion through the well-manicured fields of the unique coffee plants on a patented trellis technology developed by Joe Alban. When he began farming in 1997, Alban wanted a unique, top-of-the-line coffee, so he turned to his brother, John, who is a graduate of the viticulture and oenology program at University of California, Davis. Joe planted 5 acres of coffee in the traditional way and 5 acres of trellised coffee. The trellised coffee had a harvest of 35% more berries, which produced a sweeter, fuller-bodied coffee. With lots of pruning and uniform sun exposure, Kona Joe coffee took home the "Best New Roasted Coffee" blue ribbon by the Specialty Coffee Association in 2001, and in 2006, a local newspaper gave them the People's Choice Award for Best Coffee.

In the 10,000-square-foot visitor center on the plantation, the tour continues with live demonstrations on roasting, sorting, brewing, and panning. The tour ends with a sample of Kona Joe Coffee and the brownies, truffles, and chocolate-covered coffee beans (yum-yum!) also sold there.

in lemon butter. Watch for the daily specials on the less expensive Cafe Grill menu (coconut shrimp, stuffed mushrooms, fish and chips, and so on).

In Kona Inn Shopping Village, 75–5744 Alii Dr. © 808/329-4455. Reservations recommended at dinner. Main courses $16–$36; Cafe Grill $7–$13. AE, MC, V. Dinner menu daily 5:30–9pm; Cafe Grill daily 11:30am–9:30pm.

La Bourgogne 👧👧 *Finds* CLASSIC FRENCH   An intimate spot with 10 tables, La Bourgogne serves classic French fare with simple, skillful elegance. Baked brie in puff pastry is a taste treat, and the fresh Maine lobster salad, served on a bed of greens with mango slices and a passion-fruit vinaigrette, is a master stroke. Other offerings include classic onion soup, fresh catch of the day, *osso buco,* and New Zealand mussels steamed in apple cider, thyme, shallots, and cognac. The roast duck breast with raspberries and pine nuts is exactly the kind of dish that characterizes La Bourgogne—done to perfection, presented attractively, and with an unbeatable match of flavors and textures. Classically trained chef Ron Gallaher expresses his allegiance to *la cuisine Française* down to the last morsel of flourless chocolate cake and lemon tartlette.

Hwy. 11, 3 miles south of Kailua-Kona. © 808/329-6711. Reservations recommended. Main courses $28–$36. AE, DC, DISC, MC, V. Tues–Sat 6–10pm.

Moderate
Jackie Rey's Ohana Grill 👧👧 *Finds* ECLECTIC   This off-the-beaten-path eatery is hard to categorize: part sports bar, part family restaurant, part music/dancing (salsa, country western), part neighborhood cafe. No matter what you call it, you'll get great food at wallet-pleasing prices. Locals pile in at lunch for burgers, roasted turkey sandwiches, and

seared ahi poke. On weekdays, a happy-hour crowd downs a few brews and pupu (appetizers). Starting at 5pm, families with kids in tow show up for the delicious curry-crusted ahi (over organic greens), pork loin with coconut shrimp stuffing, seafood pasta, and beef short ribs (with a ko-chu-jang glaze). Weekends bring music and dancing starting at 8:30pm.

75–5995 Kuakini Hwy., Kailua-Koha. ℂ 808/327-0209. Reservations recommended for dinner. Lunch entrees $7–$12; dinner entrees $11–$24; pupu menu $5–$12. MC, V. Mon–Fri 11am–9pm; Sat 5–9pm.

Kenichi Pacific ★★★ *Finds* PACIFIC RIM FUSION/SUSHI BAR   Hidden in the Keauhou Shopping Center is this gem of a restaurant, decorated in muted tones and understated furnishings, featuring both Pacific Rim fusion cuisine and a sushi bar. The fantastic food and efficient service will leave you smiling. The appetizer menu is so tempting (ginger-marinated squid, blackened tuna, Dungeness crab cakes, fresh lobster summer rolls), you might just want to graze from one dish to the next. Entrees include pan-seared mahimahi with eggplant mousse, hearts of palm, and asparagus in a miso beurre blanc sauce; macadamia-crusted lamb accompanied by taro risotto; ono tataki; lemon grass ahi; and bamboo salmon. If you love duck, don't miss Kenichi's duck confit, which has Chinese five-spice cured duck leg with celeriac purée, ali'i mushrooms, pea tendrils, red-pepper coulis, and balsamic reduction. Leave room for the warm, flourless molten cake with Kona coffee-chip ice cream.

Keauhou Shopping Center, Keauhou. ℂ 808/322-6400. Reservations recommended for dinner. Entrees $19–$36. AE, DC, DISC, MC, V. Tues–Fri 11:30am–1:30pm; daily 5–9:30pm.

O's Bistro ★ NOODLES/PASTA   Chef Amy Ferguson-Ota's wildly popular gourmet noodle house Oodles of Noodles has been replaced by O's Bistro but offers nearly the same menu, with a staggering assortment of noodles from far-flung cultures and countries. Diners can tuck into udon, cake noodles, saimin, ramen, spaghetti, orzo, somen, and more. Plus there are entrees like fresh local-style steamed fish, Provençal-style fish, Peking duck in fresh plum sauce, and rib-eye steak with mashed potatoes. Breakfast (which starts at 10am) includes hearty egg and fish dishes, a healthful breakfast taco, and French toast with pecans.

In Crossroads Shopping Center, 75–1027 Henry St. ℂ 808/327-6565. Main courses $12–$16 lunch, $21–$34 dinner. DC, DISC, MC, V. Daily 10am–9pm.

Pa Leo PACIFIC RIM   Pa Leo dishes up very good fresh fish (crusted with taro and drizzled with lehua honey-lime tarter sauce), chicken (in a pineapple ginger-apple sauce), and meats (rack of lamb served with ginger cream). It overlooks the pier and Ahuena Heiau (King Kamehameha's temple). The new owners have painted the second-story restaurant with bold colors and filled it with orchids. The service is friendly, but when the place is busy, it can be slow, so have another liquid libation and enjoy the view. One very pressing problem is there is virtually no parking. Your options are to park in the pay lot at the King Kamehameha Hotel across the street or hope you luck into a spot on the street.

Alii Dr., Kailua-Kona. ℂ 808/329-5550. Reservations a must. Entrees $12–$32. AE, MC, V. Daily 11:00am–9pm.

Inexpensive

BaLe *Value* FRENCH-VIETNAMESE SANDWICHES & BAKERY   This statewide chain specializes in "fast" French-Vietnamese sandwiches, Vietnamese rice and noodle entrees, and bakery items. It's a nondescript place in a local shopping center, but with great deals like sandwiches on homemade French rolls from just $3.50, this family-run restaurant is the perfect place to stop before heading for the beach.

Kona Coast Shopping Center, 74–5588 Palani Rd. ℂ 808/327-1212. Entrees $7.50–$11; sandwiches $3.50–$6. MC, V. Mon–Sat 10am–9pm; Sun 11am–7pm.

Basil's Pizzeria PIZZA/ITALIAN Two dining rooms seat 100 in a garlic-infused atmosphere where pizza is king, sauces sizzle, and pasta is cheap. The oceanview restaurant, in a prime location in Kailua-Kona, is redolent with cheeses, garlic, and fresh organic herbs (a big plus). Shrimp pesto and the original barbecue-chicken pizzas are long-standing favorites, as is the artichoke-olive-caper version, a Greek-Italian hybrid. Recently they have expanded the menu to included sandwiches and burgers. Very popular with the 20-something crowd.

75–5707 Alii Dr. ℂ 808/326-7836. Individual pizzas $9.95–$12; main courses $9–$15. MC, V. Daily 11am–9:30pm.

Big Island Grill *(Finds* AMERICAN One of the best-kept secrets among local residents is the Big Island Grill, where you get huge servings of home cooking at 1970s prices. The place is always packed, from the first cup of coffee at breakfast to the last bite of dessert at night. Chef Bruce Gould has been cooking in Kona for decades and has a loyal following for his localized American cuisine. This is a place to take the family for dinner (excellent fresh salmon, generous salads, and the world's tastiest mashed potatoes) without having to go into debt. *Warning:* You'll likely have to wait (no reservations), and once you finally land a table, service can sometimes be slow. Relax, it's Hawaii and people are not in much of a hurry.

75–5702 Kuakini Hwy. ℂ 808/326-1153. Reservations not accepted. Main courses $6.25–$20. AE, MC, V. Mon–Sat 6–10am, 11am–9pm.

Habanero's *(Value* MEXICAN There's no leisurely dining at this small eatery, just great, fast Mexican food at budget prices. You order at one counter and pick up at another. Habanero's starts off with huevos rancheros and other egg dishes, such as a chorizo-egg burrito, for breakfast. Lunch and dinner items include burritos (the fish with black bean is my favorite), soft and hard tacos (the veggie is surprisingly tasty and filling), nachos, tostadas, quesadillas, enchiladas, and daily specials (Fri night is shrimp Vallarta). Bring cash.

Keauhou Shopping Center, Keauhou. ℂ 808/324-HOTT. All items under $7.75. No credit cards. Mon–Sat 9am–9pm.

Island Lava Java *(Value* ☆ AMERICAN Perched directly across the street from the ocean with an unimpaired view of the water activities in Kailua Bay, this inexpensive outdoor coffee shop started as a small espresso joint with a few pastries a few years ago. Eventually they added lunch and then dinner. Today Lava Java is the "in" place to sip espresso drinks, chow down on good food, and enjoy the ocean view. A handful of tables ring the small shop outside, and a few more tiny tables are located inside at this counter service-only restaurant. The breakfast menu features stacks of pancakes and eggs in various preparations, such as in a massive omelet, wrapped in a tortilla, or on an English muffin or bagel. The lunch menu is big on sandwiches, burgers, and salads. Dinners can be small (sandwiches or salads) or big (New York steak with all the trimmings, veggie lasagna, and fresh fish). Be sure to come with a laid-back attitude; service can be slow or forgetful (I once had to reorder a couple of times because the counter person kept getting my order wrong), but the price and the view more than make up for it.

75–5799 Alii Dr., Kailua-Kona. ℂ 808/327-2161. Breakfast $3.75–$13; lunch $6.25–$15; dinner $6.95–$17. AE, DISC, MC, V. Daily 6am–10pm.

Lulu's AMERICAN   As it often is with joints that are popular, Lulu's has fallen prey to the deadly sin of self-importance. Service is brisk and can be downright rude. It is casual, noisy, and corny (black velvet paintings at the entrance), but it's undeniably popular, with open-air dining, ocean views, and a sports-bar atmosphere. Other elements include Capiz-shell lamps, clamshell sconces, and hula girl replicas. The offerings include appetizers, sandwiches, salads, burgers, fresh fish tacos, and fresh fish and meats in the evening.

In the Coconut Grove Market Place, 75–5819 Alii Dr. ℂ **808/331-2633.** Reservations not accepted. Main courses $9–$15. AE, DC, DISC, MC, V. Daily 11am–10pm; bar until 2am Mon–Sun.

Quinn's Almost by the Sea ⭐ STEAK/SEAFOOD   Late-night noshers, take note: This is one of the few places you can grab a bite to eat in Kona after 9pm. Quinn's, located at the northern gateway to town, has a nautical/sports-bar atmosphere and offers casual alfresco dining on a garden lanai, with an air-conditioned, nonsmoking area also available. The menu is surf-and-turf basic: burgers, sandwiches, and a limited dinner menu of dependably good fresh fish, filet mignon, and a few shrimp dishes. There are eight burger selections and, when available, fresh ahi or ono sandwiches.

75–5655A Palani Rd. ℂ **808/329-3822.** Main courses $7.95–$24. MC, V. Daily 11am–11pm.

SOUTH KONA
Moderate
Aloha Angel Cafe ISLAND CUISINE   The former Aloha Cafe is under new management, but it kept the trademark large servings, heroic burgers and sandwiches, and a home-style menu for vegetarians and carnivores alike. Breakfast and lunch are served on the veranda that wraps around the old Aloha Theatre, with sweeping views down from the coffee fields to the shoreline. Dinner is in the tiny dining room (which, unfortunately, has no view); space is limited, so phone ahead to ensure that you get a table. The cheaper daytime staples include omelets, burritos, tostadas, quesadillas, and home-baked goods (breakfast is served all day). Most of the produce is organic, and fresh-squeezed orange juice and fresh-fruit smoothies are served daily. Sandwiches, from turkey to tofu-avocado and a wonderful fresh ahi, are heaped with vegetables on tasty whole-wheat buns. The dinner entrees cover the basics, from fresh catch to grilled New York steak and Cajun chicken with tropical salsa.

Hwy. 11, Kainaliu. ℂ **808/322-3383.** Reservations recommended for dinner. Breakfast $6.95–$9.95; dinner main courses $13–$22. AE, MC, V. Thurs–Mon 7:30am–8pm, Tues–Wed 7:30am–2:30pm.

Keei Cafe *Overrated* MEDITERRANEAN/LATINO/ISLAND   When this bistro cafe opened in a former fish market in Keei, it was fabulous in every respect—delicious food at frugal prices, friendly service, and quirky decor. The restaurant became so popular it moved a few years ago to a new location with hardwood floors, first-class artwork, and a view of the coast. It got really big really fast and didn't seem to keep up with the rapid growth. The first thing that went was seating people on time. On my last visit, I waited more than an hour for a 7:30pm reservation (the staff was unapologetic). Then the food, once the draw, was no longer dependably good. I'm including the restaurant in this guide because it's so popular, but I can no longer recommend it—not only because of the not-up-to-par food and the slow service, but more because of the cavalier attitude: The owners are making money (right now) and don't really care how they treat their clientele.

By the 113 mile marker on Hwy. 11, in Kalakekua. ℂ **808/322-9992.** Main courses $9–$12 lunch, $14–$23 dinner. No credit cards. Tues–Sat 10:30am–2:00pm and 5:15–9pm.

Kona Coffee Craze!

Coffeehouses are booming on the Big Island—this is, after all, the home of Kona coffee, with dozens of vendors who want to compete for your loyalty and dollars.

Most of the farms are concentrated in the North and South Kona districts, where coffee remains a viable industry. Notable among them is the **Kona Blue Sky Coffee Company,** in Holualoa (© 877/322-1700 or 808/322-1700; www.konablueskycoffee.com), which handles its own beans exclusively. The Christian Twigg-Smith family and staff grow, handpick, sun-dry, roast, grind, and sell their coffee on a 400-acre estate. You can buy coffee on the farm itself and see the operation from field to final product. You can also find Blue Sky at the Waikoloa Beach Marriott Resort and at KTA in Kailua-Kona and Keauhou, open Wednesday through Sunday.

Also in Holualoa, 10 minutes above Kailua-Kona, **Holualoa Kona Coffee Company** (© 800/334-0348 or 808/322-9937; www.konalea.com) purveys organic Kona from its own farm and other growers. Not only can you buy premium, unadulterated Kona coffee here, but you can also witness the hulling, sorting, roasting, and packaging of beans on a farm tour Monday through Friday from 8am to 3pm. Also in this upcountry village, the **Holuakoa Cafe,** Highway 180 (© 808/322-2233), is famous for high-octane espresso, ground from fresh-roasted Kona Blue Sky beans.

Some other coffees to watch for: **Bong Brothers** (© 808/328-9289; www.bongbrothers.com) thrives with its coffees, roadside fruit stand, and natural-foods deli that sells smoothies and healthful foods. Aficionados know that **Langenstein Farms** (© 808/328-8356; www.kona-coffee.com/konastore), a name associated with quality and integrity, distributes excellent Kona coffee and distinctively tasty macadamia nuts in the town of Honaunau. They also have great tours of the farm; just give them a call and they'll set something up. **Rooster Farms,** also in Honaunau (© 808/328-9173; www.roosterfarms.com), enjoys an excellent reputation for the quality of its organic coffee beans. The **Bad Ass Coffee Company** (www.badasscoffee.com) has franchises in Kainaliu, Kawaihae, Honokaa, Keauhou, and Kailua-Kona (and even a number of branches on the mainland), all selling its 100% Kona as well as coffees from Molokai, Kauai, and other tropical regions.

A good bet in Hilo is **Bears' Coffee,** 106 Keawe St. (© 808/935-0708), the quintessential sidewalk coffeehouse and a Hilo stalwart. Regulars love to start their day here, with coffee and specialties such as souffléed eggs, cooked light and fluffy in the espresso machine and served in a croissant. It's a great lunchtime spot as well, and recently they added a dinner menu.

Inexpensive

The Coffee Shack ★★ Kids COFFEEHOUSE/DELI   Great food, crisp air, and a sweeping ocean view make The Coffee Shack one of South Kona's great finds. It's an informal place with counter service, pool chairs, and white trellises on the deck, which is framed by ferns, palms, and banana and avocado trees. The fare is equally inviting: French toast made with homemade poi bread, lemon bars and carrot cake, and eggs Benedict with a delectable hollandaise. At lunch you'll find an assortment of imported beers, excellent sandwiches on home-baked breads, and fresh, hearty salads made with organic lettuces. Let the kids order peanut-butter-and-jelly or grilled-cheese sandwiches while you head for the smoked Alaskan salmon sandwich or the hot, authentic Reuben.

Hwy. 11, 1 mile south of Captain Cook. ⊘ 808/328-9555. Most items less than $8.95; pizzas $9–$13. DISC, MC, V. Daily 7:30am–3pm.

Manago Hotel Restaurant *(Value)* AMERICAN   The dining room of the decades-old Manago Hotel is a local legend, greatly loved for its unpretentious, tasty food at bargain prices. At breakfast, $5 buys you eggs, bacon, papaya, rice, and coffee. At lunch or dinner, you can dine on a 12-ounce T-bone, fried ahi, opelu, or the house specialty, pork chops—the restaurant serves nearly 1,500 pounds monthly. When the akule or opelu are running, count on a rush by the regular customers. This place is nothing fancy, and lots of things are fried, but the local folks would riot if anything were to change after so many years.

In the Manago Hotel, Hwy. 11, Captain Cook. ⊘ 808/323-2642. Reservations recommended for dinner. Main courses $8–$14. DISC, MC, V. Tues–Sun 7–9am, 11am–2pm, and 5–7:30pm.

Nasturtium Café *(Finds)* HEALTHY GOURMET   This once-tiny cafe recently expanded into the space next door and now has plenty of seating. It's a true find for those who love healthy gourmet food with an international flair—and, best of all, it comes at budget prices. Chef Diane Tomac-Campogan cooks up interesting dishes like Moroccan chicken wrap (with range-fed, hormone- and antibiotic-free chicken), a to-die-for fresh fish wrap, a very unusual ostrich burger, and a mean Mexican corn soup. Save room for dessert: ginger macadamia-nut tart (wheat- and dairy-free), fresh ginger spice cake, homemade fruit crisp a la mode, or the very yummy chocolate mousse (which chef Diane claims is cholesterol-free). Takeout is available, so you can take your mouthwatering treats and go to the beach for a picnic.

79–7491-B Mamalahoa Hwy. (Hwy. 11), Kainaliu. ⊘ 808/322-5083. Lunch under $15. MC, V. Tues–Fri 11am–4pm; Sat 11am–2:30pm. Live guitar music Wed–Sat.

Teshima's JAPANESE/AMERICAN   This is local style all the way. Shizuko Teshima has a strong following among those who have made her miso soup and sukiyaki an integral part of their lives. The early morning crowd starts gathering for omelets or Japanese breakfasts (soup, rice, and fish) while it's still dark outside. As the day progresses, the orders pour in for shrimp tempura and sukiyaki. By dinner, Number 3 teishoku trays—miso soup, sashimi, sukiyaki, shrimp, pickles, and other delights—are streaming out of the kitchen. Other combinations include steak and shrimp tempura, beef teriyaki and shrimp tempura, and the deep-sea trio of shrimp tempura, fried fish, and sashimi.

Hwy. 11, Honalo. ⊘ 808/322-9140. Reservations recommended. Complete dinners $19 and under. No credit cards. Daily 6:30am–1:45pm and 5–9pm.

THE KOHALA COAST

Note: You'll find the following restaurants on the "Where to Stay & Dine in North Kohala & Waimea" map on p. 263.

VERY EXPENSIVE

Brown's Beach House ✸✸ BIG ISLAND CUISINE   The nearby lagoon takes on the pink-orange glow of sunset, while torches flicker between the coconut trees. With white tablecloths, candles, and seating near the lagoon, this is a spectacular setting, complemented by a menu that keeps getting better by the year. The chef de cuisine, David Abrahams, serves up Big Island cuisine with a flare that includes unusual dishes like kiawe-grilled fresh island catch with tomato fondue, quinoa and almond–crusted free-range chicken paillarde, Big Island swordfish poached in seasoned olive oil, sizzling ahi tataki with local exotic mushrooms, and crab-crusted sautéed opakapaka. Next door is **Brown's Deli,** with freshly made breads, pastries, and espresso coffees for breakfast, and pizza, salads, and sandwiches for lunch and dinner.

At The Fairmont Orchid, Hawaii, 1 N. Kaniku Dr., Mauna Lani Resort. ✆ **808/885-2000.** www.fairmont.com/orchid. Reservations recommended for dinner. Lunch main courses $15–$22; dinner main courses $29–$59. AE, DC, DISC, MC, V. Daily 11:30am–2:30pm and 5:30–9:30pm.

CanoeHouse ✸✸ HAWAII REGIONAL   The setting is as gorgeous as ever, but it is not the same restaurant as it was when Alan Wong was the chef and the food coming out of the kitchen was nothing short of extraordinary. However, Wong didn't take the ambience with him, and the legendary sunset views remain, along with a koa canoe hanging from the ceiling in the open-air dining room. *Tip:* Ask for a table outside and go at sunset to get the real flavor of this incredible setting. The menu, which changes seasonally, includes great fish items (Shanghai lobster, sautéed moi, steamed opakapaka), meats (honey-roasted rack of lamb, grilled beef tenderloin, and braised short rib of beef), and even vegetarian items (spice-lacquered tofu). Save room for dessert!

At Mauna Lani Bay Hotel and Bungalows, 68–1400 Mauna Lani Dr. ✆ **808/881-7911.** Reservations recommended. Main courses $29–$45. AE, DC, DISC, MC, V. Summer daily 6–9pm; winter daily 5:30–9pm.

Coast Grille ✸✸ STEAK/SEAFOOD/HAWAII REGIONAL   It's a 3-minute walk from the main lobby to the open-air Grille, but the view along the way is nothing to complain about and will help you work up an appetite. The split-level dining room has banquettes and wicker furniture, open-air seating, and an oyster bar that is famous. The extensive seafood selection includes poke, clams, and fresh oysters from all over the world, as well as fresh seafood from island waters, served in multicultural preparations.

In the Hapuna Beach Prince Hotel, 62–100 Kaunaoa Dr. ✆ **808/880-1111.** www.hapunabeachprincehotel.com. Reservations recommended. Main courses $28–$55. AE, DISC, MC, V. Daily 6–9:30pm.

Expensive

Norio's Sushi Bar & Restaurant ✸ JAPANESE   This new upscale sushi bar and restaurant at The Fairmont Orchid features master sushi chef Norio Yamamoto, who trained in Tokyo and most recently worked at the sushi bar at the Ritz-Carlton Kapalua on Maui. His menu reflects a reverence for traditional Japanese delicacies like sushi and tempura dishes, plus a few signature items like *kushi katsu* (a panko-fried pork loin and onion skewer served with sesame katsu sauces), or *sukiyaki* (thinly sliced beef and vegetables). Also on the menu are a selection of sakes, Japanese beers, and green teas. Sushi lovers can sit at the newly expanded 15-seat sushi bar to watch the master and his team of three at work.

Fairmont Orchid, Mauna Lani Resort, Kohala Coast, Mauna Lani Resort. ✆ **808/885-2000.** www.fairmont.com/orchid. Reservations recommended. Entrees $32–$50. AE, DC, DISC, MC, V. Daily 6–9:30pm.

Coming Soon to a Restaurant Near You

As we went to press, the Queen's MarketPlace, located across the street from the Kings' Shops in the Waikioloa Beach Resort, was set to open with several wonderful eateries, including:

- **Sansei Seafood Restaurant & Sushi Bar** The award-winning restaurant by well-known chef D. K. Kodama (who has two other Sansei restaurants, one on Maui and one in Waikiki) features innovative Asian-influenced dishes such as spicy Japanese BLT Rolls and Asian rock shrimp cakes with ginger-lime-chile butter.
- **Island's Fine Burgers & Drinks** A great family restaurant featuring Hawaiian-style hamburgers, salads, and tacos in a very lush, tropical atmosphere.
- **Charlie's Thai Cuisine** Upscale Thai food with some unique dishes you don't usually see.
- **Kings' Kitchen** Chinese specialties (from roast duck to chow mein) prepared to go or to eat in the food pavilion.
- **The Noodle House** A range of Asia noodle dishes, from gau gee mein to Hawaiian Saimin.

Roy's Waikoloa Bar & Grill ★★★ PACIFIC RIM/EURO-ASIAN   Don't let the strip mall location fool you—Roy's Waikoloa has several distinctive and inviting features, such as a golf-course view, large windows overlooking a 10-acre lake, and the East-West cuisine and upbeat service that are Roy Yamaguchi signatures. This is a clone of his Oahu restaurant, offering favorites like Szechuan baby back ribs, blackened island ahi, hibachi-style salmon, and six other types of fresh fish prepared charred, steamed, or seared, and topped with exotic sauces such as shiitake miso and gingered lime-chile butter. Yamaguchi's tireless exploration of local ingredients and world traditions produces food that keeps him at Hawaii's culinary cutting edge. *Be warned:* Roy's is always packed (make reservations) and always noisy, but the food is always great and the service is excellent.

Kings' Shops, Waikoloa Beach Resort, 250 Waikoloa Beach Dr. ℂ 808/886-4321. www.roysrestaurant.com. Reservations recommended. Main courses $26–$33 dinner. AE, DC, DISC, MC, V. Daily 5–9:30pm.

Moderate

Cafe Pesto ★★ MEDITERRANEAN/ITALIAN   Fans drive miles for the gourmet pizzas, calzones, and fresh organic greens grown from Kealakekua to Kamuela. The herb-infused Italian pies are adorned with lobster from the aquaculture farms on Keahole Point, shiitake mushrooms from a few miles mauka (inland), and fresh fish, shrimp, and crab. Honey-miso crab cakes, Santa Fe chicken pasta, and sweet roasted peppers are other favorites.

In Kawaihae Shopping Center, at Kawaihae Harbor, Pule Hwy. and Kawaihae Rd. ℂ 808/882-1071. Main courses $8.95–$20 lunch, $15–$32 dinner. AE, DC, DISC, MC, V. Sun–Thurs 11am–9pm; Fri–Sat 11am–10pm.

Merriman's Market Cafe ★ MEDITERRANEAN/DELI   Peter Merriman, who has long reigned as king of Hawaii Regional Cuisine with Merriman's restaurant in Waimea (p. 286), has opened this tiny "market cafe" featuring cuisines of the Mediterranean made with fresh local produce, house-made sausages, artisan-style breads, and great cheese and wines. This is a fun place for lunch or a light dinner. The 3,000-square-foot restaurant and deli features full-service indoor and outdoor dining in a casual atmosphere and a gourmet deli with daily specials. Lunch ranges from salads to sandwiches. Dinner has small plate dishes, pizzas, and entrees from grilled fish to large salads.

Kings' Shops, Waikoloa Beach Resort, 250 Waikoloa Beach Dr., Waikoloa. © **808/886-1700.** Main courses $9.95–$16 lunch, $14–$29 dinner. AE, MC, V. Daily 11am–9:30pm.

Waikoloa Beach Grill ECLECTIC   Two well-known chefs have teamed up to take over the old golf course clubhouse restaurant. Their combined expertise translates to a range of eclectic dishes from local fish (done Asian style with a broth, Oriental veggies, and jasmine rice) to a traditional tomato curry with marinated chicken with nan bread. They also serve a lunch to hungry golfers. But the real reason to come here is chef David Brown's exquisite desserts. Brown, who served as the executive pastry chef at the Hilton Waikoloa, makes the most delectable pies, cobblers, and other incredible not-to-be-missed works of art. Other desserts include chocolate marquis, a Tahitian vanilla crème brûlée, a tiramisu, and a *lilikoi* cheesecake.

69–1022 Keana Pl., Waikoloa Beach Resort. © **808/886-6131.** Dinner reservations recommended. Lunch $8.95–$19; dinner entrees $23–$39; desserts under $10. AE, DC, DISC, MC, V. Daily 11am–4pm and 5–9pm.

NORTH KOHALA

Note: You'll find the following restaurants on the "Where to Stay & Dine in North Kohala & Waimea" map on p. 263.

Bamboo ★★ *Finds* PACIFIC RIM   Serving fresh fish and Asian specialties in a historic building, Hawaii's self-professed "tropical saloon" is a major attraction on the island's northern coastline. The exotic interior is a nod to nostalgia, with high wicker chairs from Waikiki's historic Moana Hotel, works by local artists, and old Matson liner menus accenting the bamboo-lined walls. The fare, island favorites in sophisticated presentations, is a match for all this style: imu-smoked pork quesadillas, fish prepared several ways, sesame nori-crusted or tequila-lime shrimp, and selections of pork, beef, and chicken. There are even some local faves, such as teriyaki chicken and fried noodles served vegetarian, with chicken, or with shrimp. Produce from nearby gardens and fish fresh off the chef's own hook are among the highlights. Hawaiian music wafts through Bamboo from 6:30pm to closing on weekends.

Hwy. 270, Hawi. © **808/889-5555.** Reservations recommended. Main courses $7.95–$18 lunch, $13–$38 dinner (full- and half-size portions available at dinner). MC, V. Tues–Sat 11:30am–2:30pm and 6–8:30pm; Sun 11:30am–2:30pm (brunch).

Tropical Dreams of Ice Cream

Tropical Dreams ice creams have spread out over the island but got their start in North Kohala. Across the street from Bamboo, **Kohala Coffee Mill and Tropical Dreams Ice Cream,** Highway 270, Hawi (© **808/889-5577**), serves upscale ice creams along with sandwiches, pastries, and a selection of Island coffees. The Tahitian vanilla and litchi ice creams are local legends, but I also love the macadamia-nut torte and *lilikoi* bars, made by a local pastry chef. Jams, jellies, herb vinegars, Hawaiian honey, herbal salts, and macadamia-nut oils are among the gift items for sale. It's open Monday to Friday from 6am to 6pm, and Saturday and Sunday from 7am to 5:30pm.

Kohala Rainbow Cafe *(Value)* GOURMET DELI   This place is known for its healthful fare and made-with-care wraps. It serves fresh soups, giant salads, and home-made sandwiches and burgers, but the wraps are most popular—herb-garlic flatbread filled with local organic baby greens and vine-ripened organic tomatoes, cheese, and various fillings. The Kamehameha Wrap features *kalua* pork, two different cheeses, and a Maui onion dressing. My favorite is the Mexican veggie wrap: greens, tomatoes, avocado, roasted peppers, cheese, and refried beans. There are a few seats outdoors next to a striking mural.

Hwy. 270, Kapaau, in front of the King Kamehameha Statue. © **808/889-0099.** Main courses under $10. MC, V. Mon–Fri 11am–5pm.

WAIMEA

Note: You'll find the following restaurants on the "Where to Stay & Dine in North Kohala & Waimea" map on p. 263.

EXPENSIVE

Daniel Thiebaut Restaurant *(★★)* FRENCH-ASIAN   This restaurant features Big Island products (Kamuela Pride beef, Kahua Ranch lettuces, Hirabara Farms field greens, herbs and greens from Adaptations in South Kona) as interpreted by the French-trained Thiebaut, formerly executive chef at Mauna Kea Beach Resort. High-lights include a Hunan-style rack of lamb, wok-fried scallops, vegetarian specials (such as crispy avocado spring rolls with a smoked tomato coulis), and fresh fish. The recently remodeled restaurant is full of intimate enclaves and has a gaily lit plantation-style veranda. In recent years, unfortunately, the quality of this once-sterling restau-rant has varied wildly. If Chef Daniel is in, you will most likely get an excellent meal, but if he is not cooking that night, service may suffer. My other complaint is the alarming rise in prices and simultaneous decrease in the amount of food on your plate.

65–1259 Kawaihae Rd. (the Historic Yellow Building). © **808/887-2200.** www.danielthiebaut.com. Reservations recommended. Entrees $25–$50. AE, DISC, MC, V. Daily 3:30–9pm; Sun brunch 10am–1:30pm.

Merriman's *(★★)* HAWAII REGIONAL   Merriman's is peerless. Although founder/owner/chef Peter Merriman now commutes between the Big Island and Maui, where he runs the Hula Grill, he manages to maintain the sizzle that has made Merriman's a premier Hawaii attraction. Order anything from Chinese short ribs to a goat-cheese-and-eggplant sandwich for lunch; at dinner, choose from the signature wok-charred ahi, kung pao shrimp, lamb from nearby Kahua Ranch, and a notewor-thy vegetarian selection. Among my many favorites are the Caesar salad with sashimi, Pahoa corn and shrimp fritters, and the sautéed, sesame-crusted fresh catch with spicy *lilikoi* sauce. *Kalua* pig quesadillas and the famous platters of seafood and meats are among the many reasons this is still the best, and busiest, dining spot in Waimea.

In Opelu Plaza, Hwy. 19. © **808/885-6822.** Reservations recommended. Main courses $12–$24 lunch, $23–$45 din-ner (market price for ranch lamb or ahi). AE, MC, V. Mon–Fri 11:30am–1:30pm; daily 5:30–9pm.

Inexpensive

Tako Taco Taqueria HEALTHY MEXICAN   Once a tiny "hole in the wall" with the most delicious (and healthy) Mexican food, Tako Taco recently moved to the other side of Waimea into bigger quarters and added margaritas, beer, and wine to the menu. Alas, the food is not what it once was. There's plenty of room to eat there, or you can take out. Most items fall between $6.50 and $12. The fresh fish burrito (with beans, rice, cheese, guacamole, sour cream, slaw, and salsa) is a hot deal at $8.50.

Epicurean Farm Tour & Dinner

Get a behind-the-scenes look at the making of a meal at Merriman's with **Merriman's Farm Visits & Dinner.** Monday through Thursday, a group of 10 leaves Waimea at noon for a 4-hour tour of two farms that sell produce, coffee, and meat to Merriman's, followed by a four-course dinner at the restaurant.

Tours include stops at such farms as the Hamakua Heritage Farm, which grows gourmet mushrooms; Long Ears Coffee Company, which has a 400-tree farm in Ahualoa; Kahua Ranch, an 8,500-acre ranch with cattle and sheep; and Honopua Farms, featuring organic vegetables, fresh cut flowers, and renowned master lei-maker Marie McDonald, a Smithsonian National Treasure.

At the conclusion of the farm tour, participants are bused back to Merriman's restaurant to enjoy the products that they have just seen in the form of a four-course meal, which includes a salad course (Honopua farm spinach salad with herb-roasted beets and Maui onions, topped by warm mac-nut, pear vinegar, and ginger dressing), a fish course (grilled fresh fish with lemon and arugula pesto), a meat course (braised Kahua Ranch lamb), and dessert (Long Ears coffee cheesecake).

The price for the tour and meal is $155; for reservations and information, contact Hawaii Forest & Trail, © **808/331-8505** or www.hawaii-forest.com.

There are plenty of vegetarian selections. If the Mexican wedding cookies or chocolate chip cookies are available, grab one (they're huge and only $1 each).

64–1066 Mamalahoa Hwy., Waimea. © **808/887-1717.** All items $14 and under. AE, MC, V. Mon–Sat 11am–9pm, Sun noon–9pm.

THE HAMAKUA COAST

Cafe Il Mondo ✿ PIZZA/ESPRESSO BAR   A tiny cafe with a big spirit has taken over the Andrade Building in the heart of Honokaa. Tropical watercolors and local art, the irresistible aromas of garlic sauces and pizzas, and a 1924 koa bar meld gracefully in Sergio and Dena Ramirez's tribute to the Old World. A classical and flamenco guitarist, Sergio occasionally plays solo guitar in his restaurant while contented diners tuck into the stone oven–baked pizzas. Try the Sergio pizza—pesto with marinated artichokes and mushrooms—or one of the calzones. Sandwiches come cradled in fresh French, onion, or rosemary buns. There's fresh soup daily, roasted chicken, and other specials; all greens are fresh, local, and organic.

Mamane St., Honokaa. © **808/775-7711.** Pizzas $10–$19; sandwiches $6.50; pasta $12. No credit cards. Tues–Sat 10am–8pm.

Jolene's Kau Kau Korner AMERICAN/LOCAL   This place is nothing fancy, but it's homey and friendly, with eight tables and windows overlooking a scene much like an Old Western town but for the cars. Choose from saimin, stir-fried tempeh with vegetables, sandwiches (including a good vegetarian tempeh burger), plate lunches (mahimahi, fried chicken, shrimp, beef stew), and familiar selections of local food.

At Mamane St. and Lehua, Honokaa. ☎ **808/775-9498.** Plate lunches $7–$9.50; dinner main courses $8.95–$19. No credit cards. Mon, Wed, and Fri 10am–8pm; Tues and Thurs 10am–3pm.

Simply Natural ✦ *Value* HEALTH FOOD/SANDWICH SHOP   Simply Natural is a superb find on Honokaa's main street. I love this charming deli with its friendly staff, wholesome food, and vintage interior. It offers a counter and a few small tables with bright tablecloths and fresh anthuriums. Don't be fooled by the unpretentiousness of the place; I had the best smoked-chicken sandwich I've ever tasted here. The owner's mother proudly displayed the gloriously plump whole chicken, smoked by her neighbor in Honokaa, before slicing and serving it on freshly baked onion bread from the Big Island Bakery. The wholesome menu features flavorful items such as sautéed mushroom-onion sandwich (on squaw, onion, or rosemary bread), tempeh burgers, and breakfast delights that include taro-banana pancakes. Top it off with premium ice cream by Hilo Homemade (another favorite) or a smoothie. The mango-pineapple-banana-strawberry version is sublime.

Mamane St., Honokaa. ☎ **808/775-0119.** Deli items $3.50–$7.95. No credit cards. Mon–Sat 8am–3:30pm.

Tex Drive In & Restaurant AMERICAN/LOCAL ETHNIC   When Ada Lamme bought the old Tex Drive In, she made significant changes, such as improving upon an ages-old recipe for Portuguese *malassadas,* a cakelike doughnut without a hole. Tex sells tens of thousands of these sugar-rolled morsels a month, including ones filled with pineapple/papaya preserves, pepper jelly, or Bavarian cream. The menu has a local flavor and features ethnic specialties: Korean chicken, teriyaki meat, *kalua* pork with cabbage, and Filipino specials. New on the menu are Tex wraps, served with homemade sweet-potato chips. With its gift shop and visitor center, Tex is a roadside attraction and a local hangout; residents have been gathering here for decades over early morning coffee and breakfast.

Hwy. 19, Honokaa. ☎ **808/775-0598.** Main courses $7.95–$12. DC, DISC, MC, V. Daily 6:30am–8:30pm.

What's Shakin' ✦ *Finds* HEALTH FOOD   Look for the cheerful, plantation-style, wooden house in yellow and white with a green roof, 2 miles north of the Hawaii Tropical Botanical Garden. Many of the bananas and papayas from Patsy and Tim Withers's 20-acre farm end up here, in fresh-fruit smoothies like the Papaya Paradise, an ambrosial blend of pineapples, coconuts, papayas, and bananas. If you're in the mood for something more substantial, try the blue-corn tamale with homemade salsa, the teriyaki-ginger tempeh burger, or one of the wraps. There are several lunch specials daily, and every plate arrives with fresh fruit and a green salad topped with Patsy's Oriental sesame dressing. You can sit outdoors in the garden and enjoy the staggering ocean view.

27–999 Old Mamalahoa Hwy. (on the 4-mile scenic drive), Pepeekeo. ☎ **808/964-3080.** Most items less than $8.50; smoothies all $5.75. MC, V. Daily 10am–5pm.

HILO

Note: You'll find the following restaurants on the "Hilo" map on p. 331.

EXPENSIVE

Harrington's ✦ SEAFOOD/STEAK   This is arguably the prettiest location in Hilo, on a clear rocky pool teeming with koi (carp) at Reeds Bay, close to the waterfront but not on it. The house specialty, thinly sliced Slavic steak swimming in butter and garlic, is part of the old-fashioned steak-and-seafood formula that makes the Harrington's experience a predictable one. But the Caesar salad is zesty and noteworthy,

Moments **A Lunch for All Five Senses**

Hidden in the tall eucalyptus trees outside of the old plantation community of Paauilo lies the **Hawaiian Vanilla Company,** on Paauilo Mauka Road, (© **808/776-1771;** www.hawaiivanilla.com). Located next to a gulch, surrounded by wild coffee, guava, loquats, and avocado trees, the company hosts one of the truly sensuous experiences on the Big Island—a multicourse Vanilla Luncheon. Before you even enter the huge Vanilla Gallery and Kitchen, you will be embraced by the heavenly sent of vanilla. You'll see vanilla orchid vines, and if you're truly lucky, you may see the elusive blossoms. One of the real treats is listening to owner Jim Reddekopp's presentation (and video) on how vanilla is grown, how it's used in the meal you will be eating, and just about everything else you ever wanted to know about this magical orchid and bean. The four-course, 2-hour lunch is $39 and worth every penny. The lunch is usually offered Wednesday and Thursday, and also sometimes on Tuesday and Friday; reservations are required. Other activities at the Hawaiian Vanilla Company are formal tea service, vanilla tastings, brunch, or just wandering through the mill. Myriad vanilla products, from beans to extracts, teas to lotions, are for sale.

and for those oblivious to calories, the escargots—baked en casserole on a bed of spinach and topped with lightly browned cheeses—are a rewarding choice. The meunière-style fresh catch, sautéed in white wine and topped with a lightly browned lemon-butter sauce, is also popular. The strongest feature of Harrington's is the tranquil beauty of Reeds Pond (also known as Ice Pond), one of Hilo's visual wonders. The open-air restaurant perches on the pond's shores, creating a sublime ambience.

135 Kalanianaole Ave. © **808/961-4966.** Reservations recommended. Lunch main courses $9.95–$16; dinner main courses $17 to market price. MC, V. Mon–Fri 11am–2pm; Mon–Sun 5:30–9pm.

Pescatore �285 SOUTHERN ITALIAN   In a town of ethnic eateries and casual mom-and-pop diners, this is a special-occasion restaurant, dressier and pricier than most Hilo choices. It's ornate, especially for Hilo, with gilded frames on antique paintings, chairs of vintage velvet, koa walls, and a tile floor. The fresh catch is offered in several preparations, including reduced-cream and Parmesan or capers and wine. The paper-thin ahi carpaccio is garnished with capers, red onion, garlic, lemon, olive oil, and shaved Parmesan—and it's superb. Chicken, veal, and fish Marsala; a rich and garlicky scampi Alfredo; and the *fra diavolo* (a spicy seafood marinara) are among the dinner offerings, which come with soup or salad. Lighter fare, such as simple pasta marinara and chicken Parmesan, prevails at lunch. Breakfast is terrific, too.

235 Keawe St. © **808/969-9090.** Reservations recommended for dinner. Breakfast $5–$8; lunch main courses $5–$12; dinner main courses $16–$29. AE, DC, DISC, MC, V. Mon–Fri 8:30am–2pm and 5–9pm; Sat–Sun 7:30am–2pm and 5–9pm.

Restaurant Kaikodo �285�285 ECLECTIC   Hilo's most elegant restaurant is housed in a 100-year-old Toyama Building (listed on the National Register of Historic Buildings) that was transformed by owners Howard and Mary Ann Rogers into a light-filled space with such historic details as a 19-foot mahogany bar from England and 100-year-old cut-glass doors from China. Chef Shae Catrett's menu ranges from meat (filet mignon, spice-crusted rack of lamb or grilled pork chop) to fish (blackened ahi), to vegetarian (eggplant stuffed with a medley of vegetables with chile rice cake).

60 Keawe St., Hilo. ⓒ 808/961-2558. www.restaurantkaikodo.com. Reservations recommended. Main courses lunch $9.50–$17, dinner $14–$34. AE, MC, V. Mon–Fri 11am–2pm; dinner Sun–Thurs 5:30–9pm, Fri–Sat 5:30–9:30pm.

MODERATE

Hilo Bay Café 🌺🌺 *Finds* PACIFIC RIM   *Foodie alert:* In the midst of a suburban shopping mall is this upscale, elegant eatery. It was created by the people from the Island Naturals Market and Deli, located on the other side of the shopping center. When you enter, the cascade of orchids sitting on the marble bar is the first thing you see. Mellow jazz wafts from speakers, and plush chairs at low tables fill out the room. The creative menu ranges from house-made ravioli (stuffed with artichoke hearts, roasted garlic, and cream cheese) to potato-crusted fresh catch, to grilled pork loin with bordelaise sauce. Lunch features salads (such as seared ahi Caesar), sandwiches (think grilled free-range chicken breast), and entrees (such as flaky-crust vegetarian potpie, slow-cooked pork barbecue ribs, and crispy spanakopita). There's also a terrific wine list and great martinis. Don't miss eating here.

Waiakea Center, 315 Makaala St. ⓒ 808/935-4939. Reservations recommended for dinner. Lunch $8–$15; dinner entrees $9–$26. AE, DISC, MC, V. Mon–Sat 11am–9pm; Sun 5–9pm.

Nihon Restaurant & Cultural Center 🌺 *Value* JAPANESE   This restaurant offers a beautiful view of Hilo Bay on one side and the soothing green sprawl of Liliuokalani Gardens on the other. This is a magnificent part of Hilo that's often overlooked because of its distance from the central business district. The menu features steak-and-seafood combination dinners and selections from the sushi bar, including the innovative poke and lomi salmon hand rolls. The "Businessman's Lunch," a terrific deal, comes with sushi, potato salad, soup, vegetables, and two choices from the following: butterfish, shrimp tempura, sashimi, chicken, and other morsels. This isn't inexpensive dining, but the value is sky-high, with a presentation that matches the serenity of the room and its stunning view of the bay.

Overlooking Liliuokalani Gardens and Hilo Bay, 123 Lihiwai St. ⓒ 808/969-1133. Reservations recommended. Main courses $9–$20; combination dinner $19. AE, DC, DISC, MC, V. Mon–Sat 11am–1:30pm and 5–8pm.

Ocean Sushi Deli 🌺 *Finds* SUSHI   Hilo's nexus of affordable sushi: Local-style specials stretch purist boundaries but are so much fun: lomi salmon, oyster nigiri, opihi nigiri, unagi avocado hand roll, ahi poke roll, and special new rolls that use thin sheets of tofu skins and cooked egg. For traditionalists, there are ample shrimp, salmon, *hamachi,* clam, and other sushi delights—a long menu of them, including handy ready-to-cook sukiyaki and *shabu-shabu* sets.

239 Keawe St. ⓒ 808/961-6625. Sushi boxes $4.75–$50; sushi family platters $20–$50. MC, V. Mon–Sat 10:30am–2pm and 5–9pm.

Queen's Court Restaurant AMERICAN/BUFFET   Many of those with a "not me!" attitude toward buffets have been disarmed by the Hilo Hawaiian's generous and well-rounded offerings at budget-friendly prices. A la carte menu items are offered Monday through Thursday, but it's the Hawaiian, seafood, and Dungeness crab/prime rib buffets throughout the week that draw throngs of local families. Lovers of Hawaiian food also come for the Friday Hawaiian lunch buffet.

> **Moments** **Bet You Can't Just Eat One**
>
> **Hawaii Island Gourmet Products,** which, under the brand Atebara Chips, has been making potato and taro- and shrimp-flavored chips in Hilo for 70 years, recently added a couple of new products that you just cannot miss: purple sweet potato chips and the delicious sweet potato, taro, and regular potato chips covered in chocolate (the first-place winner at the Taste of Hilo). You can find them at most stores on the Big Island (or at the major resorts on the Big Island) or contact them directly (© **808/969-9600;** www. hawaiichips.com). *Warning:* As we say in Hawaii, these chips are so *ono* (delicious) that you will be mail-ordering more when you get home.

In the Hilo Hawaiian Hotel, 71 Banyan Dr. © **808/935-9361.** Reservations recommended. Fri Hawaiian lunch buffet $16; Mon–Thurs prime rib/crab buffet $27; Fri–Sun seafood buffet $30. AE, DC, DISC, MC, V. Mon–Sat 6:30–9:15am and 11:15am–1:15pm; Sun 6:30–9:15am and 10:30am–1:30pm (brunch); daily 5:30–9pm.

Restaurant Miwa ☆ JAPANESE   Come to the Hilo Shopping Center to discover sensational seafood in a quintessential neighborhood sushi bar. This self-contained slice of Japan is a pleasant surprise in an otherwise unremarkable mall. *Shabu-shabu* (you cook your own ingredients in a heavy pot), tempura, fresh catch, and a full sushi selection are among the offerings. At dinner, you can splurge on the steak and lobster combination without dressing up. The haupia (coconut pudding) cream-cheese pie is a Miwa signature but is not offered daily; blueberry cream cheese is the alternative.

In the Hilo Shopping Center, 1261 Kilauea Ave. © **808/961-4454.** Reservations recommended. Main courses $9–$37 (most $10–$15). AE, DC, DISC, MC, V. Mon–Sat 11am–2pm and 5–10pm; Sun 5–9pm.

Seaside Restaurant ☆☆ STEAK/SEAFOOD   This is a casual local favorite—a Hilo signature with a character all its own. The mullet and *aholehole* (a silvery mountain bass) are fished out of the pond shortly before you arrive—you can't get much fresher than that. The restaurant has large windows overlooking the glassy ponds that spawned your dinner. Colin Nakagawa and his family cook the fish in two unadorned styles: fried or steamed in ti leaves with lemon juice and onions. Daily specials include steamed opakapaka, onaga (snapper), steak and lobster, *paniolo*-style prime rib, salmon encrusted with a nori-wasabi sprinkle, New York steak, and shrimp. If you are here on Wednesday through Sunday, they serve very fresh sushi. *Note:* If you want fish from the pond, *you must call ahead.* The outdoor tables are fabulous at dusk when the light reflects on the ponds with an otherworldly glow.

1790 Kalanianaole Ave. © **808/935-8825.** Reservations recommended. Main courses $15–$30. AE, DC, MC, V. Tues–Thurs and Sun 5–8:30pm; Fri–Sat 5–9pm.

INEXPENSIVE

Cafe Pesto Hilo Bay ☆☆ PIZZA/PACIFIC RIM   Cafe Pesto's Italian brick oven burns many bushels of ohia and kiawe wood to turn out its toothsome pizzas, topped with fresh organic herbs and island-grown produce. The high-ceilinged 1912 room looks out over Hilo's bay. It's difficult to resist the wild mushroom–artichoke pizza or the chipotle and tomato-drenched Southwestern. But go with the Four Seasons, dripping with prosciutto, bell peppers, and mushrooms—it won't disappoint. Some of my other favorites are the Milolii, a crab-shrimp-mushroom sandwich with basil pesto; the chile-grilled shrimp pizza; and the flash-seared poke and spinach salad.

In the S. Hata Building, 308 Kamehameha Ave. © 808/969-6640. Pizzas $8.95–$18. AE, DC, DISC, MC, V. Sun–Thurs 11am–9pm; Fri–Sat 11am–10pm.

Ken's House of Pancakes AMERICAN/LOCAL   The only 24-hour coffee shop on the Big Island, Ken's fulfills basic dining needs simply and efficiently, with a good dose of local color. Lighter servings and a concession toward health-conscious meals and salads have been added to the menu, a clever antidote to the numerous pies available. Omelets, pancakes, French toast made with Portuguese sweet bread, saimin, sandwiches, and soup stream out of the busy kitchen. Other affordable selections include fried chicken, steak, prime rib, and grilled fish. Tuesday is taco night, Wednesday is prime-rib night, Thursday is Hawaiian plate, and Sunday is all-you-can-eat-spaghetti night. Very local, very Hilo.

1730 Kamehameha Ave. © 808/935-8711. Most items less than $8. AE, DC, DISC, MC, V. Daily 24 hr.

Kuhio Grille AMERICAN/HAWAIIAN   The "home of the 1-pound *laulau*" is quite the local hangout, a coffee/saimin shop with a few tables outdoors and a bustling business indoors. Taro and taro leaves from Waipio Valley are featured in the popular Hawaiian plate, but there are other local specialties: saimin, miso-saimin, taro-corned-beef hash, chicken yakitori, burgers, and their famous fried rice. The "Kanak Atak" is a 1-pound lau and includes *kalua* pig, lomi salmon, pickled onions, haupia, rice, and poi, all for $17. Habitués make a beeline for the counter, where breakfast is served all day.

In Prince Kuhio Plaza. © 808/959-2336. Main courses $7–$20. AE, DISC, MC, V. Sun–Thurs 6am–10pm; Fri–Sat 6am–midnight.

Miyo's JAPANESE   Often cited by local publications as the island's "best Japanese restaurant," Miyo's offers home-cooked, healthy food (no MSG) served in an open-air room on Wailoa Pond, where curving footpaths and greenery fill the horizon. Sliding shoji doors bordering the dining area are left open so you can take in the view, which includes Mauna Kea on clear days. The sesame chicken (deep-fried and boneless with a spine-tingling sesame sauce) is a bestseller, but the entire menu is appealing. For vegetarians, there are specials such as vegetable tempura, vegetarian *shabu-shabu* (cooked in a chafing dish at your table, then dipped in a special sauce), and noodle and seaweed dishes. Other choices include mouthwatering sashimi, beef teriyaki, fried oysters, tempura, ahi *donburi* (seasoned and steamed in a bowl of rice), sukiyaki, and generous combination dinners. All orders are served with rice, soup, and pickled vegetables. The miso soup is a wonder, and the ahi tempura plate is one of Hilo's best buys. Special diets (low-sodium, sugarless) are cheerfully accommodated.

In Waiakea Villas, 400 Hualani St. © 808/935-2273. Lunch main courses $6–$13, combinations $9–$11; dinner main courses $6–$13, combinations $10–$15. MC, V. Mon–Sat 11am–2pm and 5:30–8:30pm.

Naung Mai *Value* THAI   This quintessential hole in the wall has gained an extra room, but even with 26 seats, it fills up quickly. In a short time, Naung Mai has gained the respect of Hilo residents for its curries and pad Thai noodles, and its use of fresh local ingredients. The flavors are assertive, the produce comes straight from the Hilo Farmers Market, and the prices are good. The four curries—green, red, yellow, and Mussaman (Thai Muslim)—go with the jasmine, brown, white, and sticky rice. The pad Thai rice noodles, served with tofu and fresh vegetables, come with a choice of chicken, pork, or shrimp, and are sprinkled with fresh peanuts. You can order your curry Thai-spicy (incendiary) or American-spicy (moderately hot), but even mild, the flavors are outstanding. Owner-chef Jirawan Onmai also makes wonderful spring rolls and a Tom Yum spicy soup that is legendary. Lunch specials are a steal. Naung Mai is obscured behind the Garden Exchange, so it may take some seeking out.

86 Kilauea Ave. ℂ **808/934-7540.** Reservations recommended. Main dishes $10–$14. MC, V. Mon–Fri 11am–2pm; Mon–Thurs 5–8:30pm; Fri–Sat 5–9pm.

Nori's Saimin & Snacks ⭐ *Finds* SAIMIN/NOODLE SHOP Like Naung Mai, Nori's requires some searching out, but it's worth it. Unmarked and not visible from the street, it's located across from the Hilo Lanes bowling alley, down a short driveway into an obscure parking lot. You'll wonder what you're doing here, but stroll into the tiny noodle house with the neon sign of chopsticks and a bowl, grab a plywood booth or Formica table, and prepare to enjoy the best saimin on the island. Saimin comes fried or in a savory homemade broth—the key to its success—with various embellishments, from seaweed to won-ton dumplings. Ramen, soba, udon, and *mundoo* (a Korean noodle soup) are among the 16 varieties of noodle soups. Barbecued chicken or beef sticks are smoky and marvelous. Plate lunches (teriyaki beef, ahi, Korean short ribs) and sandwiches give diners ample choices from morning to late night, but noodles are the star. The "big plate" dinners feature ahi, barbecued beef, fried noodles, kal bi ribs, and salad—not for junior appetites. The desserts at Nori's are also legendary, with its signature haupia and sweet-potato pies flying out the door almost as fast as the famous chocolate mochi cookies and cakes.

688 Kinoole St. ℂ **808/935-9133.** Most items less than $8.50; "big plate" dinner for 2 $19. AE, DC, MC, V. Mon 10:30am–3pm; Tues–Sat 10:30am–3pm and 4pm–midnight; Sun 10:30am–10pm.

Royal Siam Thai Restaurant ⭐ THAI A popular neighborhood restaurant, the Royal Siam serves consistently good Thai curries in a simple room just off the sidewalk. Fresh herbs and vegetables from the owner's gardens add an extra zip to the platters of noodles, soups, curries, and specialties, which pour out of the kitchen in clouds of spicy fragrance. The Buddha Rama, a wonderful concoction of spinach, chicken, and peanut sauce, is a scene-stealer and a personal favorite. The Thai garlic chicken, in sweet basil with garlic and coconut milk, is equally superb.

70 Mamo St. ℂ **808/961-6100.** Main courses $9–$13. AE, DC, DISC, MC, V. Mon–Sat 11am–2pm and 5–9pm; Sun 5–9pm.

HAWAII VOLCANOES NATIONAL PARK

Note: You'll find the following restaurants on the "Where to Stay & Dine in the Volcano Area" map on p. 271.

EXPENSIVE

Kiawe Kitchen PIZZA/MEDITERRANEAN Although it has a somewhat limited menu, this small eatery is a great place to stop for hot soup or fresh salad after viewing the volcano, and, recently, they added a full bar. The pizza is excellent (all fresh ingredients) but pricey; I'd recommend the insalada caprese and a bowl of soup for lunch. Dinners include lamb (both rack and shank), pasta dishes, a vegetarian item, and usually beef. The menu changes daily (whatever they can get fresh that day). There's an interesting beer list (all from Hawaii) and yummy espresso drinks (including Kona coffees). You can eat on the lanai or inside the restaurant.

19–4005 Haunani Rd., Volcano. ℂ **808/967-7711.** Main courses lunch $10–$13, dinner $16–$25. MC, V. Daily noon–2:30pm and 5:30–9:30pm.

Kilauea Lodge & Restaurant ⚐ CONTINENTAL   Diners travel long distances to escape from the crisp upland air into the warmth of this high-ceilinged lodge. The decor is a cross between chalet-cozy and volcano-rugged; the sofa in front of the 1938 fireplace is especially inviting when a fire is roaring. The European cooking is a fine culinary act. Favorites include the fresh catch, hasenpfeffer, potato-leek soup (all flavor and no cream), and Alsatian soup. All dinners come with soup, a loaf of freshly baked bread, and salad.

Hwy. 11 (Volcano Village exit). ✆ **808/967-7366.** Reservations recommended. Main courses $20–$40. AE, MC, V. Daily 5:30–9pm.

INEXPENSIVE

Lava Rock Cafe ⚐ ECLECTIC/LOCAL   Volcano Village's newest favorite spot is a cheerful, airy oasis with tables and booths indoors and semioutdoors, under a clear corrugated-plastic ceiling. The cross-cultural menu includes everything from chow fun to fajitas. The choices include three-egg omelets and pancakes with wonderful house-made *lilikoi* butter, teriyaki beef and chicken, serious desserts (like mango cheesecake), fresh catch, T-bone steak, and steak-and-shrimp combos. The lunchtime winners are the "seismic sandwiches" (which the cafe will pack for hikers), chili, quarter-pound burgers, salads, plate lunches, and "volcanic" heavies such as Southern-fried chicken and grilled meats.

Hwy. 11 (Volcano Village exit, next to Kilauea Kreations). ✆ **808/967-8526.** Main courses $4.50–$9 lunch, $7–$18 dinner. MC, V. Sun 7:30am–4pm; Mon 7:30am–5pm; Tues–Sat 7:30am–9pm.

Thai Thai Restaurant THAI   Volcano's first Thai restaurant adds warming curries to the chill of upcountry life. The menu features spicy curries (five types, rich with coconut milk and spices), satays, coconut-rich soups, noodles and rice, and sweet-and-sour stir-fries of fish, vegetables, beef, cashew chicken, and garlic shrimp. A big hit is the green papaya salad made with tomatoes, crunchy green beans, green onions, and a heap of raw and roasted peanuts—a full symphony of color, aroma, texture, and flavor.

19–4084 Old Volcano Rd. ✆ **808/967-7969.** Main courses $9–$15. AE, DISC, MC, V. Daily 5–9pm.

Volcano Golf & Country Club AMERICAN/LOCAL   One of the first two eateries in the area, this golf-course clubhouse has a reputation as a low-key purveyor of local favorites. The food ranges from okay to good, while the room—looking out over a fairway—is cordial. It's not as clichéd as it sounds, especially when the mists are rolling in and the greens and grays assume an eye-popping intensity; I've even seen nene geese from my table. In the typically cool Volcano air, local favorites such as chicken or fish sandwiches, hamburgers, pastas, saimin, and Hawaiian stew with rice become especially comforting. Also featured are teriyaki beef or chicken, and stir-fry.

Hwy. 11 (at mile marker 30). ✆ **808/967-8228.** Reservations recommended for large groups. Breakfast items under $9; lunch items under $9.75. AE, DC, DISC, MC, V. Mon–Fri 8am–3pm; Sat–Sun 7am–3pm.

NAALEHU/SOUTH POINT
MODERATE

Shaka Restaurant *(Kids)* AMERICAN/LOCAL   You can't miss the Shaka sign from the highway. This welcome addition to the Naalehu restaurant scene has white tile floors, long tables, an espresso machine, and a friendly, casual atmosphere. The serviceable menu of plate lunches and American fare will seem like gourmet cuisine after a long drive through the Ka'u desert. The servings are humongous, and the prices are kind to your wallet. Locals come here for the plate lunches, sandwiches (the Shaka burger is very popular), and honey-dipped fried chicken, and for the fresh catch at dinner—grilled, deep-fried, or prepared in a special panko crust with a ginger-mango sauce. Bring the kids; they'll love the pizza.

Hwy. 11. Naalehu. © 808/929-7404. Main courses $4.50–$8.95 lunch, $4.50–$22 dinner. MC, V. Daily 10am–9pm.

5 Beaches

Too young geologically to have many great beaches, the Big Island instead has a collection of unusual ones: brand-new black-sand beaches, green-sand beaches, salt-and-pepper beaches, and even a rare (for this island) white-sand beach.

THE KONA COAST
KAHALUU BEACH PARK ⭐⭐

This is the most popular beach on the Kona Coast; these reef-protected lagoons attract 1,000 people a day almost year-round. Kahaluu is the best all-around beach on Alii Drive, with coconut trees lining a narrow salt-and-pepper sand shore that gently slopes to turquoise pools. The schools of brilliantly colored tropical fish that weave in and out of the reef make this a great place to snorkel. In summer, it's also an ideal spot for children and beginning snorkelers; the water is so shallow that you can just stand up if you feel uncomfortable. But in winter, there's a rip current when high surf rolls in; look for the lifeguard warnings.

Kahaluu isn't the biggest beach on the island, but it's one of the best equipped, with off-road parking, beach-gear rentals, a covered pavilion, restrooms, barbecue pits, and a food concession. It gets crowded, so come early to stake out a spot.

KEKAHA KAI STATE PARK (KONA COAST STATE PARK) ⭐

This beach is about 2 miles north of the airport on Queen Kaahumanu Highway; turn left at a sign pointing improbably down a bumpy road. You won't need a four-wheel-drive vehicle to make it down here—just drive slowly and watch out for potholes. At the end you'll find 5 miles of shoreline with a half-dozen long, curving beaches and a big cove on Mahaiula Bay, as well as archaeological and historical sites. The series of well-protected coves is excellent for swimming, and there's great snorkeling and diving offshore; the big winter waves attract surfers.

Facilities include restrooms, picnic tables, and barbecue pits; you'll have to bring your own drinking water. The beach is open daily from 8am to 8pm (the closing is strictly enforced, and there's no overnight camping).

WHITE SANDS BEACH ⭐

Don't blink as you cruise Alii Drive, or you'll miss White Sands Beach. This small, white-sand pocket beach about 4½ miles south of Kailua-Kona is sometimes called Disappearing Beach because it does just that, especially at high tide or during storms. It vanished completely when Hurricane Iniki hit in 1991, but it's now back in place (at least, it was the last time I looked). On calm days, the water is perfect for swimming and snorkeling. Locals use the elementary waves to teach their children how to surf and boogie-board. In winter the waves swell to expert levels, attracting surfers and spectators. Facilities include restrooms, showers, lifeguards, and a small parking lot.

THE KOHALA COAST
ANAEHOOMALU BAY (A-BAY) ⭐⭐

The Big Island makes up for its dearth of beaches with a few spectacular ones, like Anaehoomalu, or A-Bay, as the locals call it. This popular gold-sand beach, fringed by

Beaches & Outdoor Activities on the Big Island

PACIFIC OCEAN

COAST

Laupahoehoe

Honomu

220
19

Hilo Bay

Saddle Rd.

Hilo

24 23

Hilo
International
Airport

22

Stainback Hwy.

Keaau

Mountain View

130

Pahoa

THE PUNA REGION

130   137   132

16   21   20   19   KAHAUALEA
NATURAL AREA RESERVE

Volcano

Kilauea Caldera   18

17

Chain of Craters Rd.

HAWAII VOLCANOES
NATIONAL PARK

14

BEACHES

Anaehoomalu Bay (A-Bay) **8**
Green Sand (Papakolea) Beach **13**
Hapuna Beach **4**
Kahuluu Beach Park **12**
Kaunaoa (Mauna Kea) Beach **1**
Kekaha Kai State Park **9**
Leleiwi Beach Park **23**
White Sands Beach **11**

CABINS & CAMPGROUNDS

Halape Shelter **14**
Kilauea Military Camp **21**
Namakani Paio Campground **16**
Waimanu Valley Campground **27**

HIKES

Devastation Trail **18**
Halemaumau Trail **17**
Kilauea Iki Trail **19**
Kipuka Puaulu (Bird Park) Trail **16**
Mauna Loa Trail **15**
Waimanu Valley's Muliwai Trail **26**

GOLF COURSES

Hamakua Country Club **25**
Hapuna Golf Course **3**
Hilo Municipal Golf Course **22**
Hualalai Golf Course **10**
Mauna Kea Beach Golf Course **2**
Mauna Lani Frances I'i Brown
    Championship Courses **5**
Naniloa Country Club **24**
Volcano Golf and
    Country Club **20**
Waikoloa Beach Course **7**
Waikoloa Kings' Course **7**
Waikoloa Village Golf Club **6**

a grove of palms and backed by royal fish ponds still full of mullet, is one of Hawaii's most beautiful. It fronts the Waikoloa Beach Marriott Resort and is enjoyed by guests and locals alike (it's busier in summer but doesn't ever get truly crowded). The beach slopes gently from shallow to deep water; swimming, snorkeling, diving, kayaking, and windsurfing are all excellent here. Equipment rental and snorkeling, scuba, and windsurfing instruction are available at the north end of the beach. At the far edge of the bay, snorkelers and divers can watch endangered green sea turtles line up and wait their turn to have small fish clean them. Facilities include restrooms, showers, picnic tables, and plenty of parking.

HAPUNA BEACH ☆☆☆

Just off Queen Kaahumanu Highway, south of the Hapuna Beach Prince Hotel, lies this crescent of gold sand—big, wide, and ½ mile long. In summer, when the beach is widest, the ocean calmest, and the crowds biggest, this is the island's best beach for swimming, snorkeling, and bodysurfing. But beware of Hapuna in winter, when its thundering waves, strong rip currents, and lack of lifeguards can be dangerous. Facilities include A-frame cabins for camping, pavilions, restrooms, showers, and plenty of parking.

KAUNAOA BEACH (MAUNA KEA BEACH) ☆☆☆

Everyone calls this gold-sand beach Mauna Kea Beach (it's at the foot of Mauna Kea Beach Hotel), but its real name is Hawaiian for "native dodder," a lacy, yellow-orange vine that once thrived on the shore. A coconut grove sweeps around this golden crescent, where the water is calm and protected by two black-lava points. The sandy bottom slopes gently into the bay, which often fills with tropical fish, sea turtles, and manta rays, especially at night, when the hotel lights flood the shore. Swimming is excellent year-round, except in rare winter storms. Snorkelers prefer the rocky points, where fish thrive in the surge. Facilities include restrooms, showers, and ample parking, but there are no lifeguards.

HILO
LELEIWI BEACH PARK ☆

Hilo's beaches may be few, but Leleiwi is one of Hawaii's most beautiful. This unusual cove of palm-fringed black-lava tide pools fed by freshwater springs and rippled by gentle waves is a photographer's delight—and the perfect place to take a plunge. In winter, big waves can splash these ponds, but the shallow pools are generally free of currents and ideal for families with children, especially in the protected inlets at the center of the park. Leleiwi often attracts endangered sea turtles, making this one of Hawaii's most popular snorkeling spots. The beach is 4 miles out of town on Kalanianaole Avenue. Facilities include restrooms, showers, lifeguards, picnic pavilions, and paved walkways. There's also a marine-life exhibit here.

SOUTH POINT
GREEN SAND BEACH (PAPAKOLEA BEACH) ☆

Hawaii's famous green-sand beach is located at the base of Puu o Mahana, an old cinder cone spilling into the sea. The place has its problems: It's difficult to reach; the open bay is often rough; there are no facilities, fresh water, or shade from the relentless sun; and howling winds scour the point. Nevertheless, each year the unusual green sands attract thousands of oglers, who follow a well-worn four-wheel-drive-only road for 2½ miles to the top of a cliff, which you have to climb down to reach the beach.

The sand is crushed olivine, a green semiprecious mineral found in eruptive rocks and meteorites. If the surf's up, check out the beach from the cliff's edge; if the water's calm, it's generally safe to swim.

To get to Green Sand Beach from the boat ramp at South Point, follow the four-wheel-drive trail; even if you have a four-wheel-drive vehicle, you may want to walk because the trail is very, very bad in parts. Make sure you have appropriate closed-toed footwear: tennis shoes or hiking boots. The trail is relatively flat, but you're usually walking into the wind as you head toward the beach. The beginning of the trail is lava. After the first 10 to 15 minutes of walking, the lava disappears and the trail begins to cross pastureland. After about 30 to 40 minutes more, you'll see an eroded cinder cone by the water; continue to the edge, and there lie the green sands below.

The best way to reach the beach is to go over the edge from the cinder cone. (It looks like walking around the south side of the cone would be easier, but it's not.) From the cinder cone, go over the overhang of the rock, and you'll see a trail.

Going down to the beach is very difficult and treacherous, as you'll be able to see from the top. You'll have to make it over and around big lava boulders, dropping down 4 to 5 feet from boulder to boulder in certain spots. And don't forget that you'll have to climb back up. Look before you start; if you have any hesitation, don't go down (you get a pretty good view from the top anyway).

Warning: When you get to the beach, watch the waves for about 15 minutes and make sure they don't break over the entire beach. If you walk on the beach, always keep one eye on the ocean and stick close to the rock wall. There can be strong rip currents here, and it's imperative to avoid them. Allow a minimum of 2 to 3 hours for this entire excursion.

6 Watersports

For general advice on the activities listed below, see "Special-Interest Trips," in chapter 2.

If you want to rent beach toys, like snorkel gear or boogie boards, the beach concessions at all the big resorts, as well as tour desks and dive shops, offer equipment rentals and sometimes lessons for beginners. The cheapest place to get great rental equipment is **Snorkel Bob's,** in the parking lot of Huggo's Restaurant at 75–5831 Kahakai Rd., at Alii Drive, Kailua-Kona (© **808/329-0770;** www.snorkelbob.com).

BOATING

For fishing charters, see "Sportfishing: The Hunt for Granders," later in this chapter.

Body Glove **Cruises** 🐾🐾   The *Body Glove,* a 55-foot trimaran that carries up to 100 passengers, runs an adventurous sail-snorkel-dive cruise at a reasonable price. You'll be greeted with fresh Kona coffee, fruit, and breakfast pastries; you'll then sail north of Kailua to Pawai Bay, a marine preserve where you can snorkel, scuba-dive, swim, or just hang out on the deck for a couple of hours. After a buffet deli lunch spread, you might want to take the plunge off the boat's waterslide or diving board before heading back to Kailua Pier. The boat departs daily from the pier at 9am and returns at 1:30pm. The only thing you need to bring is a towel; snorkeling equipment (and scuba equipment, if you choose to dive) is provided. *Money-saving tip:* The afternoon trip is cheaper.

Kailua Pier. © 800/551-8911 or 808/326-7122. Morning cruise $112 adults, $72 children 6–12, free for children 5 or under; afternoon cruise $73 adults, $53 children 6–12, free for children 5 or under; additional $59 for certified scuba divers with own equipment ($69 without own equipment) and $79 additional for introductory scuba; whale-watching (Dec–Apr) $73 adults, $53 children 6–12, free for children 5 or under.

Frommer's Favorite Big Island Experiences

Creeping Up to the Ooze (p. 307)   Since Kilauea's ongoing eruption began in 1983, lava has been bubbling and oozing in a mild-mannered way that lets you walk right up to the creeping flow for an up-close encounter.

Going Underwater at Kealakekua Bay (p. 320)   The islands have lots of extraordinary snorkel and dive sites, but none is so easily accessible as mile-wide Kealakekua Bay, an uncrowded marine preserve on the South Kona Coast. Here you can swim with dolphins, sea turtles, octopuses, and every species of tropical fish that calls Hawaii's waters home.

Discovering Old Hawaii at Puuhonua O Honaunau National Historical Park (p. 320)   Protected by a huge rock wall, this sacred Honaunau site was once a refuge for ancient Hawaiian warriors. Today you can walk the consecrated grounds and glimpse a former way of life in a partially restored 16th-century village, complete with thatched huts, canoes, forbidding idols, and a temple that holds the bones of 23 Hawaiian chiefs.

Stargazing from Mauna Kea (p. 324)   A jacket, beach mat, and binoculars are all you need to see every star and planet in this ultraclean atmosphere, where the visibility is so keen that 11 nations have set up telescopes (two of them the biggest in the world) to probe deep space.

Watching for Whales   Humpback whales pass through waters off the Kona Coast every December through April. To spot them from shore, head down to the Natural Energy Laboratory of Hawaii Authority (p. 317), just south of Kona Airport, and keep your eyes peeled as you walk the shoreline. To get here, follow Queen Kaahumanu Highway (Hwy. 19) toward the Keahole airport; 6 miles outside of town, look for the sign NATURAL ENERGY LAB and turn left. Just after the road takes a sharp turn to the right, there's a small paved parking area with restrooms; a beach trail is on the ocean side of the lot.

Savoring a Cup of Kona Coffee   It's just one of those things you have to do while you're on the Big Island. For a truly authentic cup of java, head

Captain Beans' Cruises   Captain Beans' runs Kona's most popular dinner cruise on a 150-foot catamaran, which can accommodate about 290 passengers. The 2-hour cruise includes dinner, cocktails, dancing, and Hawaiian entertainment.

Kailua Pier. © 800/831-5541 or 808/329-2955. www.robertshawaii.com. $61 adults, $34 children ages 4–11.

Captain Dan McSweeney's Year-Round Whale-Watching Adventures ★★★
Hawaii's most impressive visitors—45-foot humpback whales—return to the waters off Kona every winter. Capt. Dan McSweeney, a whale researcher for more than 25 years, works daily with the whales, so he has no problem finding them. Frequently, he drops an underwater microphone into the water so you can listen to their songs, or uses an underwater video camera to show you what's going on. In humpback season—roughly December to April—Dan makes two 3-hour trips daily. From July 1 to December 20, he schedules one morning trip on Tuesday, Thursday, and Saturday to

upcountry to **Holuakoa Cafe,** on Mamalahoa Highway (Hwy. 180) in Holualoa (© **808/322-2233**), where owner Meggi Worbach buys green coffee beans from local farmers, roasts and grinds them, and pours you the freshest cup of coffee you've ever had.

Hanging Out in Waipio Valley (p. 329)   Pack a picnic and head for this gorgeously lush valley that time forgot. Delve deep into the jungle on foot, comb the black-sand beach, or just laze the day away by a babbling stream, the tail end of a 1,000-foot waterfall.

Chasing Rainbows at Akaka Falls (p. 327)   When the light is right, a perfect prism is formed and a rainbow leaps out of this spectacular 442-foot waterfall, about 11 miles north of Hilo. Take time to roam through the surrounding rainforest, where you're sure to have close encounters with exotic birds, aromatic plumeria trees, and shocking red-torch ginger.

Gawking at the Day's Catch in Honokohau Harbor   Every afternoon between 4 and 5pm, local fishermen pull into the fuel dock to weigh in their big-game fish: 1,000-pound blue marlins, 150-pound yellowfin tunas, and plenty of scale-tipping mahimahi, ono (also known as wahoo), and others. Sit in the bleachers and check out these magnificent creatures.

Hunting for Petroglyphs   The majority of Hawaii's ancient rock carvings are found in the 233-acre Puako Petroglyph Archaeological District (p. 321), near Mauna Lani Resort. The best time to go looking is in the cool early morning or late afternoon. There are more than 3,000 petroglyphs in this area alone—see how many you can spot.

Shopping at the Hilo Farmers Market (p. 349)   For a handful of dollars, you can buy a pound of rambutan (a sweet Indonesian fruit), a bouquet of tropical orchids, and a couple of tasty foot-long Hawaiian *laulau* (pork, chicken, or fish steamed in ti leaves). But be sure to arrive early—the market opens at sunrise—because many of the 60 or so vendors quickly sell out.

look for pilot, sperm, false killer, melon-headed, pygmy killer, and beaked whales. Captain Dan guarantees a sighting, or he'll take you out again for free. No cruises in May and June.

Honokohau Harbor. © **888/WHALE6** or 808/322-0028. www.ilovewhales.com. $70 adults, $60 children under 11.

Captain Zodiac   If you'd prefer to take a **snorkel cruise to Kealakekua Bay** in a small boat, go in Captain Zodiac's 16-passenger, 24-foot inflatable rubber life raft. The boat takes you on a wild ride 14 miles down the Kona Coast to Kealakekua, where you'll spend about an hour snorkeling in the bay and then enjoy snacks and beverages at the picnic snorkel site. Trips are twice daily, from 8am to 12:15pm and from 12:45 to 5pm. *Warning:* Pregnant women and those with bad backs should avoid this often-bumpy ride.

Gentry's Marina, Honokohau Harbor. © **808/329-3199.** www.captainzodiac.com. $87 adults, $72 children 3–12 (book on the Internet for better rates).

Fair Wind Snorkeling and Diving Adventures ★★★ *(Kids)* One of the best ways to snorkel Kealakekua Bay, the marine-life preserve that's one of the best snorkel spots in Hawaii, is on Fair Wind's half-day **sail-and-snorkel cruise to Kealakekua.** Recently the company has added the latest (state-of-the-art) luxury 55-foot foil-assist catamaran (the first on the Big Island) for an upscale experience that promises a faster and smoother ride on a boat full of luxury. We recommend the *Hula Kai* cruise, a 5-hour morning snorkel and dive cruise that includes a light breakfast, a gourmet barbecue lunch, two snorkeling sites, a guided tour, and optional scuba diving for $149 adults (minimum age 8). Hula Kai also has an afternoon snorkeling and sunset barbecue for $125 (minimum age 8). Fair Wind also has a 60-foot catamaran that holds up to 100 passengers. The morning cruise leaves from Keauhou Bay at 9am and returns at 1:30pm, and includes a light breakfast, lunch, snorkel gear, and lessons; it goes for $115 for adults, $69 for kids 4 to 12 years, and $29 for toddlers. The afternoon snack cruise is a little shorter and a little cheaper: It runs from 2 to 5:30pm and includes snacks, sailing, and snorkeling, at a cost of $75 for adults, $45 for 4-12 year olds, and free for kids 3 and under. During whale season, the *Hula Kai* has a 3-hour whale-watching trip for $69.

78-7130 Kaleiopapa St., Kailua-Kona. ℂ **800/677-9461** or 808/322-2788. www.fair-wind.com. Snorkel cruises $65–$139 adults, $39–$59 children 4–12 (prices vary depending on cruise).

Kamanu Charters ★★ This sleek catamaran, 36 feet long and 22 feet wide, provides a laid-back sail-snorkel cruise from Honokohau Harbor to Pawai Bay. The 3½-hour trip includes a tropical lunch (deli sandwiches, chips, fresh island fruit, and beverages), snorkeling gear, and personalized instruction for first-time snorkelers. The *Kamanu* sails Monday through Saturday (weather permitting) at 9am and 1:30pm; it can hold up to 24 people.

Honokohau Harbor. ℂ **800/348-3091** or 808/329-2021. www.kamanu.com. $75 adults, $45 children under 12.

BODY BOARDING (BOOGIE BOARDING) & BODYSURFING

On the Kona side of the island, the best beaches for body boarding and bodysurfing are **Hapuna Beach, White Sands Beach,** and **Kekaha Kai State Park.** On the east side, try **Leleiwi Beach.**

KAYAKING

OCEAN KAYAKING Imagine sitting at sea level, eye to eye with a turtle, a dolphin, even a whale—it's possible in an oceangoing kayak. Anyone can kayak in calm waters: Just get in, find your balance, and paddle. After a few minutes of instruction and a little practice in a calm area (like the lagoon in front of the **King Kamehameha's Kona Beach Hotel**), you'll be ready to explore. Beginners can practice their skills in **Kailua** and **Kealakekua bays;** intermediates might try paddling from **Honokohau Harbor** to **Kekaha Kai Beach Park;** the **Hamakua Coast** is a challenge for experienced kayakers.

You can rent one- and two-person kayaks (and other ocean toys) from **Aloha Kayak** ★★★ (ℂ **877/322-1441** or 808/322-2868; www.alohakayak.com) for $20 for a half-day single and $30 double ($25 for a full-day single and $40 for a full-day double). They also have a unique tour from Keauhou Bay and the Captain Cook Monument, with Hawaiian guides showing you sea caves and snorkeling areas full of fish and turtles. The tours are either 4 hours ($65 adults, $33 for children ages 12 and under) or 2½ hours ($50 adults, $25 children 12 and under) and include all equipment, beverages, snorkeling gear, and snacks.

PARASAILING

Get a bird's-eye view of Hawaii's pristine waters with **UFO Parasail** (© **800/FLY-4UFO** or 808/325-5836; www.ufoparasail.net). UFO offers parasail rides daily from 8am to 2pm from Kailua Pier. The cost is $56 for the standard flight of 7 minutes of air time at 400 feet, and $65 for a deluxe 10-minute ride at 800 feet. You can go up alone or with a friend; no experience is necessary. *Tip:* Take the early-bird special (when the light is fantastic and the price is right) at 8am for just $51 (for 400 ft.) and $61 (for 800 ft.).

SCUBA DIVING

The Big Island's leeward coast offers some of the best diving in the world; the water is calm, warm, and clear. Want to swim with fast-moving game fish? Try **Ulua Cave** at the north end of the Kohala Coast. There are nearly two dozen dive operators on the west side of the Big Island, plus a couple in Hilo. They offer everything from scuba-certification courses to guided boat dives.

"This is not your mother or father's dive shop," says Jeff Kirschner, of the newly opened **BottomTime,** 74–5590 Luhia St. (© **866/GO-DIVEN** or 808/331-1858; www.bottomtimehawaii.com). "This is a dive shop for today's diver." Kirschner claims what sets BottomTime apart is their willingness to take their 34-foot catamaran (complete with showers, TV, and restrooms) to unusual dive sites, and "not those sites just 2 minutes from the mouth of the harbor." BottomTime also offers introductory dives in enriched air (Nitrox) for $170 and two-tank dives for $130.

One of Kona's oldest dive shops, **Jack's Diving Locker,** 75–5819 Alii Dr. (© **800/345-4807** or 808/329-7585; www.jacksdivinglocker.com), has recently purchased another longtime dive shop, Kona Coast Divers, and has combined the two businesses into one. Plus, it has expanded its former 600-square-foot retail store into an 8,000-square-foot dive center with swimming pool (with underwater viewing windows), retail store, classrooms, full-service rentals, and a full-service sports diving and technical diving facility. They offer the classic two-tank dive for $125 and a two-tank manta ray night dive for $145.

HOT-LAVA DIVES Hilo's **Nautilus Dive Center,** 382 Kamehameha Ave., between Open Market and the Shell Gas Station (© **808/935-6939;** www.nautilusdivehilo. com), offers a very unusual opportunity for advanced divers: diving where the lava flows into the ocean. "Sometimes you can feel the pressure from the sound waves as the lava explodes," owner Bill De Rooy says. "Sometimes you have perfect visibility to the color show of your life." As we went to press, these hot lava dives were on hold (an unstable collapse of a recent lava field sent 20 acres of lava into the ocean; fortunately, no one was injured). Call to see if the dives have resumed ($150–$200 for a two-tank dive).

NIGHT DIVING WITH MANTA RAYS 😊😊 A little less risky—but still something you'll never forget—is swimming with manta rays on a night dive. These giant, harmless creatures, with wingspans that reach up to 14 feet, glide gracefully through the water to feed on plankton. **Jack's Diving Locker,** 75–5819 Alii Dr. (© **800/345-4807** or 808/329-7585; www.jacksdivinglocker.com) offers a "Manta Ray Madness" dive for $145 for a two-tank dive and $95 for snorkelers. Everyone from beginners through experts will love this dive. They do not guarantee that these wild creatures will show up every night, but they do boast a more than 90% sightings record. If they are booked, try **Sandwich Isle Divers,** 75–5729 Alii Dr., in the back of the Kona Market Place (© **888/743-3483** or 808/329-9188; www.sandwichisledivers.com). It offers one-tank nighttime manta dives for $85, including equipment ($75 if you have your own gear), and two tanks for $100 if you have all your gear or $115 if you need to rent gear.

WEEKLONG DIVES   If you're looking for an all-diving vacation, you might think about spending a week on the 80-foot *Kona Aggressor II* ✹ (✆ **800/344-5662** or 808/329-8182; www.aggressor.com), a live-aboard dive boat that promises to provide you with unlimited underwater exploration, including day and night dives, along 85 miles of the Big Island's coastline. You might spot harmless 70-foot whale sharks, plus not-so-harmless tiger and hammerhead sharks, as well as dolphins, whales, monk seals, and sea turtles. Ten divers are accommodated in five staterooms. Guided dives are available, but as long as you're certified, just log in with the dive master and you're free to follow the limits of your dive computer. It's $2,295 for 7 days (without gear), double occupancy, which includes excellent accommodations and all meals. Rental gear, from cameras (starting at $100 a week) to dive gear ($120) to computers ($125), is available.

SNORKELING

If you come to Hawaii and don't snorkel, you'll miss half the fun. The year-round calm waters along the Kona and Kohala coasts are home to spectacular marine life. Some of the best snorkeling areas on the Kona-Kohala coasts include **Hapuna Beach Cove,** at the foot of the Hapuna Beach Prince Hotel, a secluded little cove where you can snorkel with schools of yellow tangs, needlefish, and green sea turtles. But if you've never snorkeled in your life, **Kahaluu Beach Park** is the best place to start. Just wade in and look down at the schools of fish in the bay's black-lava tide pools. Another "hidden" snorkeling spot is off the rocks north of the boat launch ramp at **Honaunau Bay.** Other great snorkel sites include **White Sands Beach, Kekaha Kai State Park,** and **Ho'okena, Honaunau, Puako,** and **Spencer** beach parks.

In addition to **Snorkel Bob's,** mentioned in the intro to this section, you can rent gear from **Kona Coast Divers** ✹, Honokohau Marina, Kailua-Kona (✆ **808/329-8802;** www.konacoastdivers.com).

SNORKELING CRUISES TO KEALAKEKUA BAY ✹✹✹   Probably the best snorkeling for all levels can be found in **Kealakekua Bay.** The calm waters of this underwater preserve teem with a wealth of marine life. Coral heads, lava tubes, and underwater caves all provide an excellent habitat for Hawaii's vast array of tropical fish, making mile-wide Kealakekua the Big Island's best accessible spot for snorkeling and diving. Without looking very hard, you can see octopuses, free-swimming moray eels, parrotfish, and goat fish; once in a while, a pod of spinner dolphins streaks across the bay. Kealakekua is reachable only by boat; in addition to **Fair Wind** (p. 302) and **Captain Zodiac** (p. 301), check out **Sea Quest Snorkeling and Rafting Adventures** (✆ **808/329-RAFT;** www.seaquesthawaii.com), which offers unique coastal adventures through sea caves and lava tubes on the Kona Coast, as well as snorkeling plunges into the ocean at the Historic Place of Refuge in Honaunau and at the Captain Cook Monument at Kealakekua. The six-passenger, rigid-hull, inflatable rafts can go where larger boats can't. The 4-hour morning tour is $85 adults and $72 children, while the 3-hour afternoon tour goes for $64 adults and $54 children. During whale season, they have a 3-hour whale-watching cruise for $53 adults and children. They do not allow children under 6 years old, pregnant women, or people with bad backs.

SNUBA

If you're not quite ready to make the commitment to scuba but you want more time underwater than snorkeling allows, **Big Island Snuba Tours** (© 808/326-7446; www.snubabigisland.com) may be the answer. Just like in scuba, the diver wears a regulator and mask; however, the tank floats on the surface on a raft and is connected to the diver's regulator by a hose that allows the diver to go 20 to 25 feet down. You need only 15 minutes of instruction before you're ready to go. Snuba can actually be easier than snorkeling, as the water is calmer beneath the surface. It costs $79 for a 1½-hour dive from the beach, $125 for one dive from a boat, and $150 for two dives from a boat; children must be at least 8 years old.

SPORTFISHING: THE HUNT FOR GRANDERS ★★

If you want to catch fish, it doesn't get any better than the Kona Coast, known internationally as the marlin capital of the world. Big-game fish, including gigantic blue marlin and other Pacific billfish, tuna, mahimahi, sailfish, swordfish, ono (also known as wahoo), and giant trevallies (ulua), roam the waters here. When anglers here catch marlin that weigh 1,000 pounds or more, they call them *granders;* there's even a "wall of fame" on Kailua-Kona's Waterfront Row, honoring 40 anglers who've nailed more than 20 tons of fighting fish.

Nearly 100 charter boats with professional captains and crew offer fishing charters out of **Keauhou, Kawaihae, Honokohau,** and **Kailua Bay harbors.** If you're not an expert angler, the best way to arrange a charter is through a booking agency like the **Charter Desk at Honokohau Marina** (© 888/KONA-4-US or 808/329-5735; www.charterdesk.com) or **Charter Services Hawaii** (© 800/567-2650 or 808/334-1881; www.konazone.com). Either one will sort through the more than 40 different types of vessels, fishing specialties, and personalities to match you with the right boat. Prices range from $590 to $1,200 or so for a full-day exclusive charter (you and up to five of your friends have the entire boat to yourselves), or for $80 you can share a boat with others and rotate your turn at pulling in the big one.

Serious sportfishers should call the boats directly. They include *Anxious* (© 808/326-1229; www.alohazone.com), *Marlin Magic* (© 808/325-7138; www.marlinmagic.com), and *Ihu Nui* (© 808/325-1513; www.charterdesk.com/ihunui.html). If you aren't into hooking a 1,000-pound marlin or 200-pound tuna and just want to go out to catch some smaller fish and have fun, I recommend **Reel Action Light Tackle Sportfishing** ★★ (© 808/325-6811; www.charternet.com/flyfish/hawaii.html). Light-tackle anglers and saltwater fly-fishermen should contact *Sea Genie II* ★★ (© 808/325-5355; www.seageniesportfishing.com), which has helped several anglers set world records. All of the above outfitters operate out of Honokohau Harbor.

Most big-game charter boats carry six passengers max, and the boats supply all equipment, bait, tackle, and lures. No license is required. Many captains now tag and release marlins; other fish caught belong to the boat (not to you, the charter)—that's Island style. If you want to eat your catch or have your trophy marlin mounted, arrange it with the captain before you go.

SUBMARINE DIVES

This is the stuff movies are made of: venturing 100 feet below the sea in a high-tech, 65-foot submarine. On a 1-hour trip, you'll be able to explore a 25-acre coral reef that's teeming with schools of colorful tropical fish. Look closely and you might catch glimpses of moray eels—or even a shark—in and around the reef. On selected trips, you'll watch as divers swim among these aquatic creatures, luring them to the view ports for face-to-face observation. Call **Atlantis Submarines** ✶, 75–5669 Alii Dr. (across the street from Kailua Pier), Kailua-Kona (© **800/548-6262;** www.atlantis adventures.com). Trips leave daily between 10am and 3pm. The cost is $84 for adults and $42 for children under 12, or book on the website for $76 adults and $38 kids. *Note:* The ride is safe for everyone, but skip it if you suffer from claustrophobia.

SURFING

Most surfing off the Big Island is for the experienced only. As a general rule, the beaches on the north and west shores of the island get northern swells in winter, while those on the south and east shores get southern swells in summer. Experienced surfers should check out the waves at **Pine Trees** (north of Kailua-Kona), **Lyman's** (off Alii Dr. in Kailua-Kona), and **Banyan's** (also off Alii Dr.); reliable spots on the east side of the island include **Honolii Point** (outside Hilo), **Hilo Bay Front Park,** and **Keaukaha Beach Park.** But there are a few sites where beginners can catch a wave, too: You might want to try **Kahuluu Beach,** where the waves are manageable most of the year, other surfers are around to give you pointers, and there's a lifeguard on shore.

Ocean Eco Tours (© **808/324-SURF;** www.oceanecotours.com), owned and operated by veteran surfers, is one of the few companies on the Big Island that teaches surfing. Private lessons cost $150 per person (including all equipment) and usually last a minimum of 2 hours; 2- to 3-hour group lessons go for $95 (also including all equipment), with a maximum of four students. Both teachers love this ancient Hawaiian sport, and their enthusiasm is contagious. The minimum age is 8, and you must be a fairly good swimmer.

Your only Big Island choice for surfboard rentals is **Pacific Vibrations,** 75–5702 Likana Lane (just off Alii Dr., across from the pier), Kailua-Kona (© **808/329-4140;** www.laguerdobros.com/pacvib/pacificv.html), where they rent short boards for $10 for 24 hours and long boards for $10 to $20.

WINDSURFING

The constant 5- to 25-knot winds blowing toward the beach make **Anaehoomalu Bay (A-Bay),** on the Kohala Coast, one of the best beaches for windsurfing. If you get into trouble, the wind brings you back to shore instead of taking you out to sea. **Ocean Sports,** at the Waikoloa Beach Marriott Resort (© **808/885-5555;** www. hawaiioceansports.com), starts beginners on a land simulator to teach them how to handle the sail and "come about" (turn around and come back). Instruction is $60 an hour; after a half-hour or so of instruction on land, you're ready to hit the water. If you already know how to windsurf, equipment rental is $30 an hour. Advanced windsurfers should head to **Puako** and **Hilo Bay.**

7 Hiking & Camping

For information on camping and hiking, contact **Hawaii Volcanoes National Park,** P.O. Box 52, Hawaii National Park, HI 96718 (© **808/985-6000;** www.nps.gov/ havo); **Puuhonua O Honaunau National Historic Park,** Honaunau, HI 96726 (© **808/328-2288;** www.nps.gov/puho); the **State Division of Forestry and Wildlife,** P.O. Box 4849, Hilo, HI 96720 (© **808/947-4221;** www.hawaii.gov); the **State Division of Parks,** P.O. Box 936, Hilo, HI 96721 (© **808/974-6200;** www.hawaii.gov); the **County Department of Parks and Recreation,** 25 Aupuni St., Hilo, HI 96720

(© 808/961-8311; www.hawaii-county.com); or the **Hawaii Sierra Club** (© 808/ 959-0452; www.hi.sierraclub.org). For other sources and general tips on hiking and camping in Hawaii, see "Special-Interest Trips," in chapter 2.

Camping equipment is *not* available for rent on the Big Island. Plan to bring your own or buy it at **Hilo Surplus Store** (© 808/935-6398).

GUIDED DAY HIKES   A guided day hike is a great way to discover natural Hawaii without having to sleep under a tree to do it. Call the following outfitters ahead of time (before you arrive) for a schedule of trips; they fill up quickly.

A longtime resident of Hawaii, Dr. Hugh Montgomery of **Hawaiian Walkways** ✪, Honokaa (© 800/457-7759 or 808/775-0372; www.hawaiianwalkways.com), former "Tour Operator of the Year" by the Hawaii Ecotourism Association of Hawaii, offers a variety of options, ranging from excursions that skirt the rim of immense valleys to hikes through the clouds on the volcano. Hikes are $95 for adults, $75 for kids, to $135 for adults and $95 for kids. Custom hikes are available for $95 each for six hikers. Prices include food, beverages, and equipment.

Naturalist and educator Rob Pacheco of **Hawaii Forest & Trail** ✪✪, 74–5035-B Queen Kaahumanu Hwy. (behind the Chevron Station), Kailua-Kona (© 800/464-1993 or 808/331-8505; www.hawaii-forest.com), offers day trips to some of the island's most remote, pristine, natural areas, some of which he has exclusive access to. Rob's fully trained staff narrates the entire trip, offering extensive natural, geological, and cultural commentary (and more than a little humor). Tours are limited to 10 people and are highly personalized to meet the group's interests and abilities. Options include waterfall adventures, rainforest discovery hikes, birding tours, volcanoes, and even an off-road adventure in a 6×6 Pinzgauer Scrambler that allows you to explore hard-to-reach places. Each tour involves 2 to 4 hours of easy-to-moderate walking, over terrain manageable by anyone in average physical condition. Half-day trips, including snacks, beverages, water, and gear, range from $109 to $165 for adults, $89 to $115 for children ages 8 to 12.

GUIDED NIGHT HIKES   For an off-the-beaten-track experience, **Arnott's Lodge,** 98 Apapane Rd., Hilo (© 808/969-7097; www.arnottslodge.com), offers a daylong tour of Hawaii Volcanoes National Park, followed by a night lava hike right up to the fiery flow. The 9½-hour tour leaves the lodge at noon and spends most of the afternoon in the park. The lava hike (a 4-hr., somewhat strenuous round-trip hike) takes place as the sun is setting, so you can see the glow of the flow both during and after sunset. The cost is $80.

HAWAII VOLCANOES NATIONAL PARK ✪✪✪

This national park is a wilderness wonderland. Miles of trails not only lace the lava, but also cross deserts, rainforests, beaches, and, in winter, snow at 13,650 feet. Trail maps (highly recommended) are sold at park headquarters. Check conditions before you head out. Come prepared for sun, rain, and hard wind any time of year. Always wear sunscreen and bring plenty of drinking water.

Warning: If you have heart or respiratory problems or if you're pregnant, don't attempt any hike in the park; the fumes will bother you.

TRAILS IN THE PARK

KILAUEA IKI TRAIL   You'll experience the work of the volcano goddess, Pele, firsthand on this hike. The 4-mile trail begins at the visitor center, descends through a forest of ferns into still-fuming Kilauea Iki Crater, and then crosses the crater floor past the vent where a 1959 lava blast shot a fountain of fire 1,900 feet into the air for 36 days. Allow 2 hours for this fair-to-moderate hike.

HALEMAUMAU TRAIL   This moderate 3.5-mile hike starts at the visitor center, goes down 500 feet to the floor of Kilauea Crater, crosses the crater, and ends at Halemaumau Overlook.

DEVASTATION TRAIL   Up on the rim of Kilauea Iki Crater, you can see what an erupting volcano did to a once-flourishing ohia forest. The scorched earth with its ghostly tree skeletons stands in sharp contrast to the rest of the lush forest. Everyone can take this .5-mile hike on a paved path across the eerie bed of black cinders. The trail head is on Crater Rim Road at Puu Puai Overlook.

KIPUKA PUAULU (BIRD PARK) TRAIL   This easy, 1.5-mile, hour-long hike lets you see native Hawaiian flora and fauna in a little oasis of living nature in a field of lava. For some reason, the once red-hot lava skirted this miniforest and let it survive. At the trail head on Mauna Loa Road is a display of plants and birds you'll see on the walk. Go early in the morning or in the evening (or, even better, just after a rain) to see native birds like the *apapane* (a small, bright-red bird with black wings and tail) and the iiwi (larger and orange-vermilion colored, with a curved orange bill). Native trees along the trail include giant ohia, koa, soapberry, kolea, and mamani.

MAUNA LOA TRAIL   Probably the most challenging hike in Hawaii, this trail goes 7.5 miles from the lookout to a cabin at 10,035 feet and then 12 more miles up to the primitive Mauna Loa summit cabin at 13,250 feet, where the climate is subarctic and overnight temperatures are below freezing year-round. This 4-day round-trip requires advance planning, great physical condition, and registration at the visitor center. Call ⓒ 808/985-6000 for maps and details. The trail head begins where Mauna Loa Road ends, 14 miles north of Highway 11.

CAMPGROUNDS & WILDERNESS CABINS IN THE PARK

The only park campground accessible by car is **Namakani Paio,** which has a pavilion with picnic tables and a fireplace (no wood is provided). Tent camping is free; no reservations are required. Stays are limited to 7 days per year. Backpack camping at hiker shelters and cabins is available on a first-come, shared basis, but you must register at the visitor center.

Kilauea Military Camp, a mile from the visitor center, is a rest-and-recreation camp for active and retired military personnel. Facilities include 75 one- to three-bedroom cabins with fireplaces (some with a Jacuzzi), cafeteria, bowling alley, bar, general store, weight room, and tennis and basketball courts. Rates are based on rank, ranging from $73 to $159 a night. Call ⓒ 808/967-8333 on the Big Island, or 808/438-6707 on Oahu (www.kmc-volcano.com).

The following cabins and campgrounds are the best of what the park and surrounding area have to offer:

HALAPE SHELTER   This backcountry site, about 7 miles from the nearest road, is the place for those who want to get away from it all and enjoy their own private white-sand beach. The small, three-sided stone shelter, with a roof but no floor, can accommodate two people comfortably, but four's a crowd. You could pitch a tent inside, but if the weather is nice, you're better off setting up outside. There's a catchment water tank, but check with rangers on the water situation before hiking in (sometimes they don't have accurate information on the water level; bring extra water just in case). The only other facility is a pit toilet. Go on weekdays if you're really looking for an escape. It's free to stay here, but you're limited to 3 nights. Permits are available at the visitor center on a first-come, first-served basis, no earlier than noon on the day before your trip. For more information, call © **808/985-6000.**

NAMAKANI PAIO CAMPGROUNDS & CABINS   Just 5 miles west of the park entrance is a tall eucalyptus forest where you can pitch a tent in an open grassy field. The trail to Kilauea Crater is just a ½ mile away. No permit is needed, but stays are limited to 7 days. Facilities include pavilions with barbecues and a fireplace, picnic tables, outdoor dish-washing areas, restrooms, and drinking water. There are also 10 cabins that accommodate up to four people each. Each cabin has a covered picnic table at the entrance and a fireplace with a grill. Toilets, sinks, and hot showers are available in a separate building. You can get groceries and gas in the town of Volcano, 4 miles away. Make cabin reservations through **Volcano House,** P.O. Box 53, Hawaii National Park, HI 96718 (© **808/967-7321**); the cost is $40 per night for two adults (and two children), $48 for three adults, and $56 for four adults.

WAIMANU VALLEY'S MULIWAI TRAIL

This difficult 2- to 3-day backpacking adventure—only for the hardy—takes you to a hidden valley some call Eden, with virgin waterfalls and pools and spectacular views. The trail, which goes from sea level to 1,350 feet and down to the sea again, takes more than 9 hours to hike in and more than 10 hours to hike out. Be prepared for clouds of bloodthirsty mosquitoes, and look out for wild pigs. If it's raining, forget it: You'll have 13 streams to cross before you reach the rim of Waimanu Valley, and rain means flash floods.

You must get permission to camp in Waimanu Valley from the **Division of Forestry and Wildlife,** P.O. Box 4849, Hilo, HI 96720-0849 (© **808/974-4221**). Permits to the nine designated campsites are assigned by number. They're free, but you're limited to a 7-day stay. Facilities are limited to two composting pit toilets. The best water in the valley is from the stream on the western wall, a 15-minute walk up a trail from the beach. All water must be treated before drinking. The water from the Waimanu Stream drains from a swamp, so skip it. Be sure to pack out what you take in.

To get to the trail head, take Highway 19 to the turnoff for Honokaa; drive 9½ miles to the Waipio Valley Lookout. Unless you have four-wheel-drive, this is where your hike begins. Walk down the road and wade the Wailoa Stream; then cross the beach and go to the northwest wall. The trail starts here and goes up the valley floor, past a swamp, and into a forest before beginning a series of switchbacks that parallel the coastline. These switchbacks go up and down about 14 gulches. At the ninth gulch, about two-thirds of the way along the trail, is a shelter. After the shelter, the trail descends into Waimanu Valley, which looks like a smaller version of Waipio Valley but without a sign of human intrusion.

8 Golf & Other Outdoor Activities

The not-for-profit group **Friends for Fitness,** P.O. Box 1671, Kailua-Kona, HI 96745 (© **808/322-0033**), offers a free brochure on physical activities (from aerobics to yoga) in West Hawaii; they will gladly mail it to you upon request.

GOLF

For last-minute and discount tee times, call **Stand-by Golf** (© **888/645-BOOK** or 808/322-BOOK) between 7am and 11pm. Stand-by Golf offers discounted (10%–40%), guaranteed tee times for same-day or next-day golfing.

If your game's a little rusty, head for the **Swing Zone,** 74–5562 Makala Blvd. (corner of Kuikuni Hwy., by the Old Airport Park), Kailua-Kona (© **808/329-6909**). The driving range has 27 mats and 10 grass tee spaces, the practice putting green and chipping area is free with a bucket of balls (60 balls for $6), and the pro shop sells limited supplies (rental clubs are available, too, for just $2). For $6, including a putter and a ball, you can play a round on the 18-hole, all-grass putting course built in the shape of the Big Island.

In addition to the courses below, I love the fabulous **Hualalai Golf Course** ★★★ at Four Seasons Resort Hualalai (p. 252). Unfortunately, it's open only to resort guests—but for committed golfers, this Jack Nicklaus–designed championship course is reason enough to pay the sky-high rates.

THE KOHALA COAST

Hapuna Golf Course ★★★ Since its opening in 1992, this 18-hole championship course has been named the most environmentally sensitive course by *Golf* magazine, as well as "Course of the Future" by the U.S. Golf Association. Designed by Arnold Palmer and Ed Seay, this 6,027-yard, links-style course extends from the shoreline to 700 feet above sea level, with views of the pastoral Kohala Mountains and the Kohala coastline. The elevation changes on the course keep it challenging (and windy at the higher elevations). There are a few elevated tee boxes and only 40 bunkers. Facilities include putting greens, driving ranges, lockers, showers, a pro shop, and restaurants.

Hapuna Beach Prince Hotel, off Hwy. 19 (near mile marker 69). © **808/880-3000.** www.hapunabeachprincehotel. com. Greens fees $145 ($120 for resort guests).

Mauna Kea Golf Course ★★★ This breathtakingly beautiful par-72, 7,114-yard championship course, designed by Robert Trent Jones, Jr., is consistently rated one of the top golf courses in the United States. The signature 3rd hole is 175 yards long; the Pacific Ocean and shoreline cliffs stand between the tee and the green, giving every golfer, from beginner to pro, a real challenge. Another par-3 that confounds duffers is the 11th hole, which drops 100 feet from tee to green and plays down to the ocean, into the steady trade winds. When the trades are blowing, 181 yards might as well be 1,000 yards. The Mauna Kea Beach Hotel, which fronts the golf course, is temporarily closed for repairs due to the 2006 earthquake, but facilities currently open include putting greens, a driving range, lockers and showers, a pro shop, and a restaurant. Book ahead; the course is very popular, especially for early weekend tee times.

Mauna Kea Beach Resort, Hwy. 19 (near mile marker 68). © **808/882-5400.** www.maunakeabeachhotel.com. Greens fees $210 ($150 for resort guests).

Mauna Lani Frances I'i Brown Championship Courses ★★★ The **Mauna Lani South Course,** a 7,029-yard par-72, has an unforgettable ocean hole: the downhill, 221-yard, par-3 7th, which is bordered by the sea, a salt-and-pepper sand dune, and lush kiawe trees. The **North Course** may not have the drama of the oceanfront holes, but because it was built on older lava flows, the more extensive indigenous vegetation gives the course a Scottish feel. The hole that's cursed the most is the 140-yard, par-3 17th: It's absolutely beautiful but plays right into the surrounding lava field.

Improve Your Golf Game in 2½ Hours

Darrin Gee's Spirit of Golf Academy ⚑⚑⚑, P.O. Box 2308, Kohala (© **866-GOLF-433** or 808/887-6800; www.spiritofgolfhawaii.com), has developed a program for the inner, mental game of golf that will improve your score in just 2½ hours, whether you're a beginner or you've been swinging clubs for years. Unlike the majority of golf schools, which focus on the mechanics of the golf swing, for just $250 you will learn how to improve your mental game, using his Seven Principals of golf, which means learning how to increase your focus and concentration, how to relax under pressure, and how to play to your potential. The small clinics (four players to one instructor) are available at championship golf courses on the Big Island.

Facilities include two driving ranges, a golf shop (with teaching pros), a restaurant, and putting greens.

Mauna Lani Dr., off Hwy. 19 (20 miles north of Kona Airport). © **808/885-6655.** www.maunalani.com. Greens fees $205 ($140 for resort guests); twilight rates $90.

Waikoloa Beach Course ⚑   This pristine 18-hole, par-70 course certainly reflects the motto of designer Robert Trent Jones, Jr.: "Hard par, easy bogey." Most golfers remember the par-5, 505-yard 12th hole, a sharp dogleg left with bunkers in the corner and an elevated tee surrounded by lava. Facilities include a golf shop, restaurant, and driving range.

1020 Keana Place (adjacent to the Waikoloa Beach Marriott Resort and Hilton Waikoloa Village), Waikoloa. © **877/WAIKOLOA** or 808/886-6060. www.waikoloagolf.com. Greens fees: $195 ($130 for resort guests); twilight rates $75.

Waikoloa Kings' Course ⚑   This sister course to the Waikoloa Beach Course is about 500 yards longer. Designed by Tom Weiskopf and Jay Morrish, the 18-hole links-style tract features a double green at the 3rd and 6th holes, and several carefully placed bunkers that often come into play due to the ever-present trade winds. Facilities include a pro shop and showers.

600 Waikoloa Beach Dr. (adjacent to the Waikoloa Beach Marriott Resort and Hilton Waikoloa Village), Waikoloa. © **877/WAIKOLOA** or 808/886-7888. www.waikoloabeachresort.com. Greens fees: $175 ($125 for resort guests); twilight rates $75.

Waikoloa Village Golf Club   This semiprivate 18-hole course, with a par-72 for each of the three sets of tees, is hidden in the town of Waikoloa and usually overshadowed by the glamour resort courses along the Kohala Coast. Not only is it a beautiful course with great views, but it also offers some great golfing. The wind can play havoc with your game here (like most Hawaii golf courses). Robert Trent Jones, Jr., designed this challenging course, inserting his trademark sand traps, slick greens, and great fairways. I'm particularly fond of the 18th hole: This par-5, 490-yard thriller doglegs to the left, and the last 75 yards up to the green are water, water, water. Enjoy the fabulous views of Mauna Kea and Mauna Loa, and—on a very clear day—Maui's Haleakala in the distance.

Waikoloa Rd., Waikoloa Village, off Hwy. 19 (18 miles north of Kona Airport). © **808/883-9621.** www.waikoloa.org. Greens fees: $75. Turn left at the Waikoloa sign; it's about 6 miles up, on your left.

THE HAMAKUA COAST

Hamakua Country Club *Value*   As you approach the sugar town of Honokaa, you can't miss this funky 9-hole course, built in the 1920s on a very steep hill overlooking the ocean. It's a par-33, 2,520-yard course. Architect Frank Anderson managed to squeeze in 9 holes by crisscrossing holes across fairways—you may never see a layout like this again. But the best part about Hamakua is the price—just $20 for 18 holes (you play the course twice). The course is open to nonmembers on weekdays only; you don't need a tee time. Just show up, and if no one's around, drop your $20 in the box and head out. Carts aren't allowed because of the steep hills.

On the ocean side of Hwy. 19 (41 miles from Hilo), Honokaa. (**808/775-7244**. Greens fees: $20 for 18 holes (you play the 9-hole course twice).

HILO

Hilo Municipal Golf Course   This is a great course for the casual golfer: It's flat, scenic, and often fun. *Warning:* Don't go after a heavy rain (especially in winter), when the fairways can get really soggy and play can slow way down. The rain does keep the course green and beautiful, though. Wonderful trees (monkeypods, coconuts, eucalyptus, banyans) dot the grounds, and the views—of Mauna Kea on one side and Hilo Bay on the other—are breathtaking. There are four sets of tees, with a par-71 from all; the back tees give you 6,325 yards of play. Getting a tee time can be a challenge; weekdays are your best bet.

340 Haihai St. (between Kinoole and Iwalani sts.), Hilo. (**808/959-7711**. Greens fees: $29 weekdays; $34 Sat–Sun and holidays. From Hilo, take Hwy. 11 toward Volcano; turn right at Puainako St. (at Prince Kuhio Shopping Center), left on Kinoole, and then right on Haihai St.

Naniloa Country Club   At first glance, this semiprivate, 9-hole course looks pretty flat and short, but once you get beyond the 1st hole—a wide, straightforward 330-yard par-4—things get challenging. The tree-lined fairways require straight drives, and the huge lake on the 2nd and 5th holes is sure to haunt you. This course is very popular with locals and visitors alike. Rental clubs are available.

120 Banyan Dr. (at the intersection of Hwy. 11 and Hwy. 19). (**808/935-3000**. Greens fees: $25 ($15 Naniloa Hotel guests) Mon–Fri; $35 ($25 Naniloa Hotel guests) Sat–Sun (if you can get a tee time); twilight rates are $10 less.

VOLCANO VILLAGE

Volcano Golf and Country Club   Located at an altitude of 4,200 feet, this public course got its start in 1922, when the Blackshear family put in a green using old tomato cans for the holes. It now has three sets of tees to choose from, all with a par of 72. The course is unusually landscaped, making use of the pine and ohia trees scattered throughout. It's considered challenging by locals. *Some tips from the regulars:* Because the course is at such a high altitude, the ball travels farther than you're probably used to, so club down. If you hit the ball off the fairway, take the stroke—you don't want to look for your ball in the forest and undergrowth. Also, play a pitch-and-run game—the greens are slick.

Hwy. 11, on the right side, just after the entrance to Hawaii Volcanoes National Park. (**808/967-7331**. www. volcanogolfshop.com. Greens fees: $64.

BICYCLING & MOUNTAIN BIKING

For mountain-bike and cross-training bike rentals in Kona, go to **Dave's Bike and Triathlon Shop,** 75–5669 Alii Dr., across from the Kailua Pier, behind Atlantis Submarine ((**808/329-4522**). Dave rents brand-name mountain bikes (with full suspension) for $15 a day or $60 a week (including helmet and water bottle). Feel free to ask Dave for route advice and local weather reports. You can also rent a bike rack for your car ($10 a week).

Hawaiian Pedals *(*, Kona Inn Shopping Village, Alii Drive, Kailua-Kona (© **808/ 329-2294**), and **Hawaiian Pedals Bike Works,** Hale Hana Centre, 74–5583 Luhia St., Kailua-Kona (© **808/326-2453;** www.hawaiianpedals.com), have a huge selection of bikes: cruisers ($20 a day), mountain bikes and hybrids ($35 a day), and racing bikes and front-suspension mountain bikes ($45 a day). Bike racks go for $5 a day, and you pay only for the days you actually use it (the honor system): If you have the rack for a week but use it for only 2 days, you'll be charged just $10. The folks at the shops are friendly and knowledgeable about cycling routes all over the Big Island.

GUIDED TOURS   Kona Coast Cycling (© **877/592-BIKE** or 808/327-1133; www.cyclekona.com) offers half-day (3–4 hr.) and full-day (4–6 hr.) bicycling tours, ranging from a casual ride to intense mountain biking at its best. The locations are diverse, from the rolling hills of a Kona coffee farm to awesome views of the Waipio Valley Lookout. Most tours include round-trip transportation from hotels, van support, tour guide, helmets, gloves, water, snacks, and lunch on the full-day trips. Prices range from $70 to $230 for adults and $60 to $100 for children (ages 6–15).

Contact the **Big Island Mountain Bike Association,** P.O. Box 6819, Hilo, HI 96720 (© **808/961-4452;** www.interpac.net/~mtbike), for its free brochure, *Big Island Mountain Biking,* which has useful safety tips on biking as well as great off-road trails for both beginner and advanced riders.

BIRDING

Native Hawaiian birds are few—and dwindling. But Hawaii still offers extraordinary birding for anyone nimble enough to traverse tough, mucky landscape. And the best birding is on the Big Island; birders the world over come here hoping to see three Hawaiian birds, in particular: akiapolaau, a woodpecker wannabe with a war club–like head; nukupuu, an elusive little yellow bird with a curved beak, one of the crown jewels of Hawaiian birding; and alala, the critically endangered Hawaiian crow that's now almost impossible to see in the wild.

Good spots to see native Hawaiian and other birds include the following:

HAWAII VOLCANOES NATIONAL PARK   The best places for accomplished birders to go on their own are the ohia forests of this national park, usually at sunrise or sunset, when the little forest birds seem to be most active. The Hawaiian nene goose can be spotted at the park's Kipuka Nene Campground, a favorite nesting habitat. Geese and pheasants sometimes appear on the Volcano Golf Course in the afternoon.

HAKALAU FOREST NATIONAL WILDLIFE REFUGE   The first national wildlife refuge established solely for forest bird management is on the eastern slope of Mauna Kea above the Hamakua Coast. It's open for birding on Saturday, Sunday, and state holidays, using the public access road only. You must call ahead of time to get the gate combinations of the locked gates and to register. Contact Refuge Manager Richard Wass, Hakalau Forest, 154 Waianuenue Ave., Room 219, Hilo, HI 96720 (© **808/933-6915;** Richard_Wass@mail.fws.gov).

HILO PONDS   Ducks, coots, herons (night and great blue), cattle egrets, and even Canada and snow geese fly into these popular coastal wetlands in Hilo, near the airport. Take Kalanianaole Highway about 3 miles east, past the industrial port facilities to Loko Waka Pond and Waiakea Pond.

BIRDING TOURS

If you don't know an apapane from a nukupuu, go with someone who does. Contact **Hawaii Forest & Trail,** 74–5035-B Queen Kaahumanu Hwy. (behind the Chevron Station), Kailua-Kona (© **800/464-1993** or 808/331-8505; www.hawaii-forest.com), to sign up for the **Rainforest and Dry Forest Adventure tour** ☆☆, led by naturalist Rob Pacheco. On this tour you'll venture into pristine rainforest to see rare and endangered Hawaiian birds. Immersed in this world of giant ferns and crisp mountain air, the guide will also point out Hawaii's unique botany and evolution. This full-day tour costs $155 and includes pickup, midmorning snack with coffee, lunch, beverages, daypacks, binoculars, walking sticks, and rain gear.

HORSEBACK RIDING

Kohala Na'alapa ☆, on Kohala Mountain Road (Hwy. 250) at mile marker 11 (ask for directions to the stables at the security-guard station; © **808/889-0022;** www.naalapastables.com), offers unforgettable journeys into the rolling hills of Kahua and Kohala ranches, past ancient Hawaiian ruins, through lush pastures with grazing sheep and cows, and along mountaintops with panoramic coastal views. The horses and various riding areas are suited to everyone from first-timers to experienced equestrians. There are two trips a day: a 2½-hour tour at 9am for $89 and a 1½-hour tour at 1:30pm for $68. No riders over 230 pounds, no pregnant riders, and no children under 8 permitted.

Experienced riders should sign up for a trip with **King's Trail Rides, Tack, and Gift Shop** ☆☆, Highway 11 at mile marker 111, Kealakekua (© **808/323-2388;** www.konacowboy.com). These 4-hour trips, with 2 hours of riding, are limited to four people. The trip heads down the mountain along Monument Trail to the Captain Cook Monument in Kealakekua Bay, where you'll stop for lunch and an hour of snorkeling. The $135 weekday ($150 weekends) price tag includes lunch and gear.

To see Waipio Valley on horseback, call **Waipio Na'alapa Trail Rides** ☆ (© **808/ 775-0419;** www.naalapastables.com). The 2½-hour tours of this gorgeous tropical valley depart Monday through Saturday at 9:30am and 1pm (don't forget your camera). The guides are well versed in Hawaiian history and provide running commentary as you move through this historic place. The cost is $89 for adults. No kids under 8, pregnant riders, or riders over 230 pounds.

RIDING PARKER RANCH Visitors can explore **Parker Ranch** (© **808/885-7655;** www.parkerranch.com/horseback.html) and its vast 175,000-acre working cattle ranch. You'll learn firsthand about Parker Ranch, its history, and its variety of plant life, and you may even catch glimpses of pheasant, francolins, or wild pigs. Rides (suitable for beginners) are available three times daily at 8:15am, 12:15pm, and a sunset ride at 4pm for $79 per person. Morning and noon rides are 2 hours, and the sunset ride is 1½ hours. Kids must be at least 7 years old. Riders will feel like Hawaiian *paniolo* (cowboys) as they ride through stone corrals where up to 5,000 Hereford cattle were rounded up after being brought down from the slopes of Mauna Kea. A visit to the racetrack where Parker Ranch thoroughbreds were trained and still hold the record for speed is included in the excursion. The rides all begin at the Blacksmith Shop on Pukalani Road.

TENNIS

You can play for free at any Hawaii County tennis court; for a detailed list of all courts on the island, contact **Hawaii County Department of Parks and Recreation,** 25

Aupuni St., Hilo, HI 96720 (© **808/961-8720;** www.hawaii-county.com/parks/ parks.htm). The best courts in Hilo are at the Hoolulu Tennis Stadium, located next to the Civic Auditorium on Manono Street. Most resorts in the Kona-Kohala area do not allow nonguests to use their tennis facilities.

9 Seeing the Sights

THE KONA COAST

GUIDED WALKING TOURS   The **Kona Historical Society** (© **808/323-2005;** www.konahistorical.org) hosts two historical walking tours in the Kona region. All walks must be booked in advance; call for reservations and departure locations. The 75-minute **Historic Kailua Village Walking Tour** ⚔ (© **808/323-3222;** www.kona historical.org/tours/walking.shtml) is the most comprehensive tour of the Kona Coast. It takes you all around Kailua-Kona, from King Kamehameha's last seat of government to the summer palace of the Hawaiian royal family and beyond, with lots of Hawaiian history along the way. Tickets are $20 for adults, $10 for children ages 5 to 12.

The 1-hour **Living History Tour** takes you through the everyday life of a Japanese family on the Uchida Coffee Farm during the 1920s to 1940s. Interact with costumed interpreters as they go about life on a coffee farm. The tour is offered Monday through Friday on the hour from 9am to 3pm, for $15 adults and $7.50 kids ages 5 to 12. Meet at the Kona Historical Society office, 81–6551 Mamalahoa Hwy. (next to Kona Specialty Meats), across from mile marker 110, Kealakekua. Call ahead for reservations (© **808/323-2006**).

SELF-GUIDED DRIVING TOURS   **Big Island Audio Tour** (© **808/896-4275;** www.bigislandaudiotour.com), a self-guided audio tour on CD, features 36 tracks of information, including directions to the well-known sites plus tracks on beaches, short hikes, side trips, and information on Hawaiian language, history, and culture. The cost is $20 plus $2 for shipping.

If you're interested in seeing how your morning cup of joe goes from beans to brew, get a copy of the **Coffee Country Driving Tour.** This self-guided drive will take you farm by farm through Kona's famous coffee country; it also features a fascinating history of the area, the lowdown on coffee-making lingo, some insider tips on how to make a great cup, and even a recipe for Kona coffee macadamia-nut chocolate-chunk pie (goes great with a cup of java). The free brochure is available at the **Big Island Visitors Bureau,** 250 Waikoloa Beach Dr., Waikoloa, HI 96738 (© **808/886-1652;** www.gohawaii.com/bigisland).

IN & AROUND KAILUA-KONA ⚔⚔⚔

Ellison S. Onizuka Space Center *Kids*   This small museum has a real moon rock and memorabilia in honor of Big Island–born astronaut Ellison Onizuka, who died in the 1986 *Challenger* space shuttle disaster. Displays include a gravity well, which illustrates orbital motion, and an interactive rocket-propulsion exhibit, where you can launch your own miniature space shuttle.

At Kona International Airport, Kailua-Kona. © 808/329-3441. www.hawaiimuseums.org/mc/ishawaii_astronaut.htm. Admission $3 adults, $1 children 18 and under. Daily 8:30am–4:30pm. Parking in airport lot, $2 per hour.

Hulihee Palace ⚔⚔   This two-story New England–style mansion of lava rock and coral mortar, built in 1838 by the Big Island's governor, John Adams Kuakini, overlooks the harbor at Kailua-Kona. The largest, most elegant residence on the island when it was erected, Hulihee became a home to Hawaii's royalty, making it the other royal palace in the United States (the most famous being Oahu's Iolani Palace). Now run by Daughters of Hawaii, it features many 19th-century mementos and gorgeous koa furniture. You'll get lots of background and royal lore on the guided tour. No photography is allowed. There was some damage to this historic structure in the 2006 earthquake, but by the time you read this, all is scheduled to be repaired.

The palace hosts 12 **Hawaiian music and hula concerts** a year, each dedicated to a Hawaiian monarch, at 4pm on the last Sunday of the month (except June and Dec, when the performances are held in conjunction with King Kamehameha Day and Christmas).

Across the street is **Mokuaikaua Church** (© **808/329-1589**), the oldest Christian church in Hawaii. It's constructed of lava stones, but its architecture is New England style all the way. The 112-foot steeple is still the tallest man-made structure in Kailua-Kona.

75–5718 Alii Dr., Kailua-Kona. © **808/329-1877**. www.huliheepalace.org. Admission $6 adults, $4 seniors, $1 children. Daily 9am–4pm. Daily tours held throughout the day (arrive at least an hour before closing).

Kailua Pier This is action central for water adventures. Fishing charters, snorkel cruises, and party boats all come and go here. Stop by around 4pm, when the captains weigh in with the catch of the day, usually huge marlin—the record-setters often come in here. It's also a great place to watch the sunset.

On the waterfront outside Honokohau Harbor, Kailua-Kona. © **808/329-7494**.

Kamehameha's Compound at Kamakahonu Bay 🌺🌺 On the ocean side of the Kona Beach Hotel is a restored area of deep spiritual meaning to Hawaiians. This was the spot that King Kamehameha the Great chose to retreat to in 1812 after conquering the Hawaiian Islands. He stayed until his death in 1819. The king built a temple, **Ahuena Heiau,** and used it as a gathering place for his kahuna (priests) to counsel him on governing his people in times of peace. In 1820 it was on this sacred ground that Kamehameha's son Liholiho, as king, sat down to eat with his mother, Keopuolani, and Kamehameha's principal queen, Kaahumanu, thus breaking the ancient *kapu* (taboo) against eating with women; this act established a new order in the Hawaiian kingdom. The temple grounds are now just a third of their original size, but still impressive. You're free to come and wander the grounds, envisioning the days when King Kamehameha appealed to the gods to help him rule with the spirit of humanity's highest nature.

On the grounds of King Kamehameha's Kona Beach Hotel, 75–5660 Palani Rd., Kailua-Kona. © **808/329-2911**. www.konabeachhotel.com/history.cfm. Free admission. Daily 9am–4pm; guided tours Mon–Fri at 1:30pm.

Kona Brewing Co. and Brewpub This microbrewery is the first of its kind on the Big Island. Spoon and Pops, a father-and-son duo from Oregon, brought their brewing talents here and now produce about 25 barrels (about 124,000 gal.) per year. Drop by any time during their business hours and take a quick, informal tour of the brewery, after which you get to taste the product. A brewpub on the property serves gourmet pizza, salads, and fresh-brewed Hawaiian ales.

75–5629 Kuakini Hwy., Kailua-Kona. (Entry on Pawai Place: Turn north on Kuakini Hwy [from Palani Rd.] and drive approximately ½ mile to the first stop sign, Kaiwi Street, and turn right. Take your first right on Pawai Place and follow it until it ends at the brewery parking lot. Watch for directional signs along the way.) © **808/334-BREW**. www.konabrewingco.com. Free tours and tastings. Tours Mon–Fri 10:30am and 3pm.

Kailua-Kona Town

ATTRACTIONS ●
Ahuena Heiau **9**
Coconut Grove Market Place **25**
Huihee Palace **14**
Kailua Pier **10**
Kamehameha's Compound at Kamakahonou Bay **9**
Kona Brewing Co. **5**
Kona Coast Shopping Center **2**
Kona Inn Shopping Village **16**
Lanihau Shopping Center **4**
Mokuaikaua Church **13**
Old Industrial Area **1**
Snorkel Bob's **23**
Waterfront Row **18**

ACCOMMODATIONS ■
King Kamehameha's Kona Beach Hotel **8**
Kona Billfisher **24**
Kona Islander Inn **19**
Kona Seaside Hotel **6**
Uncle Billy's Kona Bay Hotel **17**

DINING ◆
BaLe **2**
Basil's Pizzeria **12**
Big Island Grill **15**
Huggo's **22**
Island Lava Java **20**
Jackie Rey's Ohana Grill **26**
Kona Inn Restaurant **16**
La Bourgogne **26**
Lulu's **21**
O's Bistro **3**
Pa Leo **11**
Quinn's Almost by the Sea **7**

Natural Energy Laboratory of Hawaii Authority (NELHA) Technology buffs should consider a visit to NELHA, where the hot tropical sun, in combination with a complex pumping system that brings 42°F (6°C) ocean water from 2,000 feet deep up to land, is used to develop innovations in agriculture, aquaculture, and ocean conservation. The interesting 1½-hour tour takes in all areas of the high-tech ocean science and technology park, including the seawater delivery system, the energy-conversion process, and some of the park's more interesting tenants, from Maine lobsters to giant clams.

73–4460 Queen Kaahumanu Hwy. (at mile marker 94), Kailua-Kona. ✆ **808/329-8073.** www.nelha.org. Public presentation tours $8 adults, free for children 8 and under. Tues–Thurs 10am; reservations required.

UPCOUNTRY KONA: HOLUALOA 🎭🎭

On the slope of Hualalai volcano above Kailua-Kona sits the small village of Holualoa, which attracts travelers weary of super-resorts. Here you'll find a little art and culture—and shade.

This funky upcountry town, centered on two-lane Mamalahoa Highway, is nestled amid a lush, tropical landscape where avocados grow as big as footballs. Little more than a wide spot in the road, Holualoa is a cluster of brightly painted, tin-roofed plantation shacks enjoying a revival as B&Bs, art galleries, and quaint shops (see "Shops & Galleries," later in this chapter, for details). In 2 blocks, it manages to pack in two first-rate galleries, a frame shop, a potter, a glassworks, a goldsmith, an old-fashioned general store, a vintage 1930s gas station, a tiny post office, a Catholic church, and the **Kona Hotel,** a hot-pink clapboard structure that looks like a Western movie set—you're welcome to peek in, and you should.

The cool up-slope village is the best place in Hawaii for a coffee break. That's because Holualoa is in the heart of the coffee belt, a 20-mile-long strip at an elevation of between 1,000 and 1,400 feet, where all the Kona coffee in the world is grown in the rich volcanic soil of the cool uplands (see the box "Kona Coffee Craze!" on p. 281). Everyone's backyard seems to teem with glossy green leaves and ruby-red cherries (which contain the seeds, or beans, used to make coffee), and the air smells like an espresso bar. The **Holuakoa Cafe,** on Mamalahoa Highway (Hwy. 180) in Holualoa (© **808/322-2233**), is a great place to get a freshly brewed cup.

To reach Holualoa, follow narrow, winding Hualalai Road up the hill from Highway 19; it's about a 15-minute drive.

SOUTH KONA 🎭🎭🎭

Kona Historical Society Museum 🎭🎭   This well-organized museum is housed in the historic Greenwell Store, built in 1875 by Henry Nicholas Greenwell out of native stone. Antiques, artifacts, and photos tell the story of this fabled coast. The museum is filled with items that were common to everyday life here when coffee growing and cattle raising were the main industries. Stocked with accurate reproductions of goods that filled the shelves and hung from the ceiling joists, the store will offer a glimpse of the past, complete with storekeepers, dressed in period costumes, offering visitors St. Jacobs Oil to cure your arthritis or rheumatism. Before you leave, the shopkeeper may share some gossip about local people and events. The Historical Society has another project in the works: the Kona Heritage Ranch, an outdoor museum on the daily life of a rancher in 1890, which will be located next door to the Greenwell Store. As part of the project, the Kona Historical Society has created a replica of an 1890 Portuguese Stone Oven, the first of several structures and programs planned for the Kona Heritage Ranch. Portuguese from the Azores or Madeira started coming to Kona in the 1870s to help develop and manage dairies, a key phase of the ranching industry in Hawaii. The outdoor hive-type oven, made with cemented stone, was a constant presence wherever the Portuguese dairymen (and sugar industry workers) settled. They brought with them both their knowledge of dairying on tropical islands and their love of freshly baked stone-oven bread. An informal group gathers every Thursday to learn about wood-fired baking techniques. Coming is a $1-million visitor center to be completed by the end of 2008. Serious history buffs should sign up for one of the museum's walking tours; see "Guided Walking Tours," above.

Hwy. 11, between mile markers 111 and 112, Kealakekua. © **808/323-3222** or 808/323-2006. www.konahistorical. org. Free admission (donations accepted). Mon–Fri 9am–3pm. Parking on grassy area next to Kona Specialty Meats parking lot.

Kids Especially for Kids

Walking through Thurston Lava Tube at Hawaii Volcanoes National Park (p. 337) It's scary, it's spooky, and most kids love it. You hike downhill through a rainforest full of little chittering native birds to enter this huge, silent black hole full of drips, cobwebs, and tree roots that stretch underground for almost ½ mile.

Snorkeling Kahaluu Beach Park (p. 295) The shallow, calm waters off Kahaluu Beach are the perfect place to take kids snorkeling. The waters are protected by a barrier reef, and the abundance of fish will keep the kids' attention. You can pick up a fish identification card at any dive shop and make a game out of seeing how many fish the kids can find.

Riding a Submarine into the Underwater World (p. 306) The huge viewing windows on Atlantis' 48-passenger sub will have the kids enthralled as the high-tech craft leaves the surface and plunges 120 feet down through the mysterious Neptunian waters. The trip isn't too long—just an hour—and there are plenty of reef fish and prehistoric-looking corals to hold the young ones' attention.

Launching Your Own Space Shuttle (p. 315) Okay, it's a model of a space shuttle, but it's still a real blast. The Ellison S. Onizuka Space Center has dozens of interactive displays to thrill budding young astronauts, such as a hands-on experience with gyroscopic stabilization. Great video clips of astronauts working and living in space may inspire your kids as well.

Hunting for Petroglyphs (p. 321) There's plenty of space to run around and discover ancient stone carvings at either the Puako Petroglyph Archaeological District at Mauna Lani Resort, or the King's Trail, by the Waikoloa Beach Marriott Resort. And finding the petroglyphs is only part of the game—once you find them, you have to guess what the designs mean.

Watching the Volcano (p. 333) Any kid who doesn't get a kick out of watching a live volcano set the night on fire has been watching too much television. Take snacks, bottled water, flashlights, and sturdy shoes and follow the ranger's instructions on where to view the lava safely.

Kula Kai Caverns and Lava Tubes ★★ *Finds* Before you trudge up to Pele's volcanic eruption, take a look at her underground handiwork. Ric Elhard and Rose Herrera have explored and mapped out the labyrinth of lava tubes and caves, carved out over the past 1,000 years or so, that crisscross their property on the southwest rift zone on the slopes of Mauna Loa near South Point. Tour choices range from an easy half-hour tour on a well-lit underground route ($15 for adults, $8 for children ages 5–12) to a more adventuresome 2-hour caving trip ($65 per person; recommended minimum age is 8). Helmets, lights, gloves, and knee pads are all included. Sturdy shoes are recommended for caving.

Off Hwy. 11, Ocean View. ☎ 808/929-7539. www.kulakaicaverns.com. Half-hour tour $15 adults, $8 children 5–12; 2-hr. tour $65 adults and children; 3-hr. tour $95. Tours by appointment. Between mile markers 79 and 78 off Hwy. 11.

The Painted Church ★ *Finds*   Oh, those Belgian priests—what a talented lot. In the late 1800s, Father John Berchman Velghe borrowed a page from Michelangelo and painted biblical scenes inside St. Benedict's Catholic Church so the illiterate Hawaiians could visualize the white man's version of creation.

Hwy. 19, Honaunau. ② 808/328-2227.

Puuhonua O Honaunau National Historical Park ★★★   With its fierce, haunting idols, this sacred site on the black-lava Kona Coast certainly looks forbidding. To ancient Hawaiians, however, Puuhonua O Honaunau served as a 16th-century place of refuge, providing sanctuary for defeated warriors and *kapu* (taboo) violators. A great rock wall—1,000 feet long, 10 feet high, and 17 feet thick—defines the refuge where Hawaiians found safety. On the wall's north end is Hale O Keawe Heiau, which holds the bones of 23 Hawaiian chiefs. Other archaeological finds include burial sites, old trails, and a portion of an ancient village. On a self-guided tour of the 180-acre site—which has been restored to its precontact state—you can see and learn about reconstructed thatched huts, canoes, and idols, and feel the *mana* (power) of old Hawaii.

A cultural festival, usually held in June, allows you to join in games, learn crafts, sample Hawaiian food, see traditional hula, and experience life in precontact Hawaii. Every Labor Day weekend, one of Hawaii's major outrigger canoe races starts here and ends in Kailua-Kona. Call for details on both events.

Hwy. 160 (off Hwy. 11 at mile marker 104), Honaunau. ② 808/328-2288. www.nps.gov/puho. Admission $5 per vehicle, good for 7 days. Visitor center daily 8am–4:30pm; park Mon–Thurs 6am–8pm, Fri–Sun 6am–11pm. From Hwy. 11, it's 3½ miles to the park entrance.

SOUTH POINT: LAND'S END ★★★

At the end of 11 miles of bad road that peters out at Kaulana Bay, in the lee of a jagged, black-lava point, you'll find Land's End—the tail end of the United States. From the tip (beware of the big waves that lash the shore if you walk out there), the nearest continental landfall is Antarctica, 7,500 miles away.

It's a 2½-mile four-wheel-drive trip and a hike down a cliff from South Point to the anomaly known as **Green Sand Beach** ★ (see "Beaches," earlier in this chapter).

Back on the Mamalahoa Highway (Hwy. 11), about 20 miles east, is the small town of Pahoa; turn off the highway and travel about 5 miles through this once-thriving sugar plantation and beyond to the **Wood Valley Temple and Retreat Center** ★ (② 808/928-8539; www.nechung.org), also known as *Nechung Drayang Ling* ("Island of Melodious Sound"). It's an oasis of tranquillity tucked into the rainforest. Built by Japanese sugar-cane workers, the temple, retreat center, and surrounding gardens were rededicated by the Dalai Lama in 1980 to serve as a spiritual center for Tibetan Buddhism. You can walk the beautiful grounds, attend services, and breathe in the quiet mindfulness of this serene area.

THE KOHALA COAST ★★★

Puukohola Heiau National Historic Site ★★★   This seacoast temple, called "the hill of the whale," is the single most imposing and dramatic structure of the ancient Hawaiians. It was built by Kamehameha I from 1790 to 1791. The temple stands 224 feet long by 100 feet wide, with three narrow terraces on the seaside and an amphitheater to view canoes. Kamehameha built this temple after a prophet told him he would conquer and unite the islands if he did so; 4 years later, he fulfilled his kingly goal. The site also includes an interactive visitor center, the house of John Young, a trusted advisor of Kamehameha, and, offshore, the submerged ruins of Hale O Ka Puni, a shrine dedicated to the shark gods.

Hwy. 270, near Kawaihae Harbor. © 808/882-7218. www.nps.gov/puhe. Free admission. Tours $2. Daily 7:30am–4pm. The visitor center is on Hwy. 270; the *heiau* is a short walk away. The trail is closed when it's too windy, so call ahead if you're in doubt.

ANCIENT HAWAIIAN FISH PONDS

Like their Polynesian forebears, Hawaiians were among the first aquaculturists on the planet. Scientists still marvel at the ways they used the brackish ponds along the shoreline to stock and harvest fish. There are actually two different types of ancient fish ponds (or *loko i'a*). Closed ponds, located inshore, were closed off from the ocean. Open ponds used rock walls as a barrier to the ocean and sluice gates that connected the ponds to the ocean. The gates were woven vines, with just enough room for juvenile fish to swim in at high tide while keeping the bigger, fatter fish from swimming out. Generally, the Hawaiians kept and raised mullet, milkfish, and shrimp in these open ponds; juvenile manini, papio, eels, and barracuda occasionally found their way in, too.

The **Kalahuipuaa Fish Ponds,** at Mauna Lani Resort (© **808/885-6622**), are great examples of both types of ponds in a lush tropical setting. South of the Mauna Lani Resort are **Kuualii** and **Kahapapa Fish Ponds,** at the Waikoloa Beach Marriott Resort (© **808/885-6789**). Both resorts have taken great pains to restore the ponds to their original states and to preserve them for future generations; call ahead to arrange a free guided tour.

KOHALA COAST PETROGLYPHS

The Hawaiian petroglyphs are a great enigma of the Pacific—no one knows who made them or why. They appear at 135 different sites on six inhabited islands, but most of them are found on the Big Island.

At first glance, the huge slate of pahoehoe looks like any other smooth black slate of lava on the seacoast of the Big Island—until gradually, in slanting rays of the sun, a wonderful cast of characters leaps to life before your eyes. You might see dancers and paddlers, fishermen and chiefs, hundreds of marchers all in a row. Pictures of the tools of daily life are everywhere: fish hooks, spears, poi pounders, canoes. The most common representations are family groups. There are also post–European contact petroglyphs of ships, anchors, horses, and guns.

The largest concentration of these stone symbols in the Pacific lies within the 233-acre **Puako Petroglyph Archaeological District** ⊕, near Mauna Lani Resort. The 1.5-mile **Malama Trail** starts north of Mauna Lani Resort; take Highway 19 to the resort turnoff and drive toward the coast on North Kaniku Drive, which ends at a parking lot; the trail head is marked by a sign and interpretive kiosk. Go in the early morning or late afternoon, when it's cool. A total of 3,000 designs have been identified.

The **Kings' Shops** (© **808/886-8811**), at the Waikoloa Beach Resort, offers a free tour of the surrounding petroglyphs Tuesday through Friday at 10:30am and Saturday at 8:30am; it meets in front of the Food Pavilion. For the best viewing, go Saturday morning.

Visitors with disabilities, as well as others, can explore petroglyphs at **Kaupulehu Petroglyphs** ⊕ in the **Kona Village Resort,** Queen Kaahumanu Highway (© **808/ 325-5555**). Free guided tours are offered three times a week, but reservations are required (or you won't get past the gatehouse). Here you can see some of the finest images in the Hawaiian Islands. There are many petroglyphs of sails, canoes, fish, and chiefs in headdresses, plus a burial scene. Kite motifs—rare in rock art—similar to those found in New Zealand are also here. This is Hawaii's only ADA-accessible petroglyph trial.

Warning: The petroglyphs are thousands of years old and easily destroyed. Do not walk on them or attempt to take a "rubbing" (there's a special area in the Puako Preserve for doing so). The best way to capture a petroglyph is with a photo in the late afternoon, when the shadows are long.

NORTH KOHALA 𝒦𝒦𝒦

Lapakahi State Historical Park 𝒦 (Kids) This 14th-century fishing village, on a hot, dry, dusty stretch of coast, offers a glimpse into the lifestyle of the ancients. Lapakahi is the best-preserved fishing village in Hawaii. Take the self-guided 1-mile loop trail past stone platforms, fish shrines, rock shelters, salt pans, and restored *hale* (houses) to a coral-sand beach and the deep blue sea (good snorkeling). Wear good hiking shoes or tennies; it's a hearty 45-minute walk. Go early in the morning or late in the afternoon to beat the heat.

Hwy. 270, Mahukona. ℂ **808/889-5566**. www.hawaii.gov/dlnr/dsp/hawaii.html. Free admission. Daily 8am–4pm. Guided tours by appointment.

Mo'okini Luakini Heiau 𝒦𝒦 (Moments) The 1,500-year-old Mo'okini Heiau, once used by kings to pray and offer human sacrifices, is Hawaii's oldest, largest, and most sacred religious site (and now a national historic landmark). The massive three-story stone temple, dedicated to Ku, the Hawaiian god of war, was erected in A.D. 480; each stone is said to have been passed hand to hand from Pololu Valley, 14 miles away, by 18,000 men who worked from sunset to sunrise. Kamehameha, born nearby under Halley's Comet, sought spiritual guidance here before embarking on his campaign to unite Hawaii. You can see the temple only on the third Saturday of every month, when volunteers pull weeds and clean up property surrounding the temple. If you'd like to help out, call the Mo'okini Preservation Foundation, on Oahu (ℂ **808/373-8000**).

On the north shore, near Upolu Point Airport.

The Original King Kamehameha Statue 𝒦𝒦 Here stands King Kamehameha the Great, right arm outstretched, left arm holding a spear, as if guarding the seniors who have turned a century-old New England–style courthouse into an airy center for their golden years. The center is worth a stop just to meet the town elders, who are quick to point out the local sights, hand you a free *Guide to Historic North Kohala*, and give you a brief tour of the courthouse, whose walls are covered with the faces of innocent-looking local boys killed in World War II, Korea, and Vietnam.

But the statue's the main attraction here. There's one just like it in Honolulu, across the street from Iolani Palace, but this is the original: an 8-foot, 6-inch bronze by Thomas R. Gould, a Boston sculptor. It was cast in Europe in 1880 but was lost at sea on its way to Hawaii. A sea captain eventually recovered the statue, which was placed here, near Kamehameha's Kohala birthplace, in 1912.

Kamehameha was born in 1750, became ruler of Hawaii in 1810, and died in Kailua-Kona in 1819. His burial site remains a mystery.

Hwy. 270, Kapaau.

Pololu Valley Lookout 𝒦𝒦𝒦 At this end-of-the-road scenic lookout, you can gaze at the vertical jade-green cliffs of the Hamakua Coast and two islets offshore. The view may look familiar once you get here—it often appears on travel posters. Linger if you can; adventurous travelers can take a switchback trail (a good 45-min. hike) to a secluded black-sand beach at the mouth of a wild valley once planted in taro; bring water and bug spray.

At the end of Hwy. 270, Makapala.

Pua Mau Place *(Kids)*   Perched on the sun-kissed western slopes of the Kohala Mountains and dotted with deep, craggy ravines, lies one of Hawaii's most unusual botanical gardens, Pua Mau Place, a 45-acre oasis with breathtaking views of both the ocean and the majestic mountains. It's dedicated to plants that are "ever blooming," an expansive collection of continuously flowering tropical flowers, trees, and shrubs. The gardens also have an aviary of exotic birds and a unique hibiscus maze planted with some 200 varieties of hibiscus. This is a great place for families (children are invited to feed the birds in the aviary). Visitors can take the self-guided tour (along with a booklet filled with the names and descriptions of all the plants) along mulched pathways meandering through the gardens, where every plant is clearly marked.

10 Ala Kahua, Kawaihae. © 808/882-0888. www.puamau.com. Admission $10 adults, $8 seniors and students, free for children 12 and under. Daily 9am–4pm. Located off Hwy. 270 on Ala Kahua Dr. (in Kohala Estates) just north of Kawaihae. Turn at the 6-mile marker, ½ mile up the hill to the gate at a lava rock wall.

WAIMEA (KAMUELA) ☆☆☆

Kamuela Museum   It takes only about an hour to explore tiny Kamuela Museum. Its eclectic collection includes an early Hawaiian dogtooth death cup, a piece of rope used on the *Apollo* mission, and ancient artifacts from the royal family.

At the junction of Hwy. 19 and Hwy. 250, Waimea. © 808/885-4724. www.hawaiimuseums.org/mc/ishawaii_kamuela.htm. Admission $5 adults, $2 children under 12. Daily 8am–5pm.

Parker Ranch ☆   The *paniolo* (cowboy) tradition began here in 1809, when John Parker, a 19-year-old New England sailor, jumped ship and rounded up wild cows for King Kamehameha. There's some evidence that Hawaiian cowboys were the first to be taught by the great Spanish horsemen, the *vaqueros;* they were cowboying 40 years before their counterparts in California, Texas, and the Pacific Northwest. The Parker Ranch, after six generations of cowboys, is smaller today than in its glory, but it still is a working ranch; some 12 cowboys work 250 horses and over 30,000 head of cattle on 175,000 acres.

The **Visitor Center,** located at the Parker Ranch Shopping Center on Highway 190 (© 808/885-7655), is open daily from 9am to 5pm and houses the **Parker Ranch Museum,** which displays items that have been used throughout the ranch's history and illustrates six generations of Parker family history. An interesting video captures the essence of day-to-day life on a working ranch.

You can also tour two historic homes on the ranch. In 1989 the late Richard Smart—a sixth-generation heir—opened his 8,000-square-foot yellow Victorian home, **Puuopelu,** to art lovers. The French Regency gallery here includes original works by Renoir, Degas, Dufy, Corot, Utrillo, and Pissarro. Next door is **Mana Hale,** a little New England saltbox built from koa wood 140 years ago.

If you want to get out and see the ranch itself, take the 45-minute narrated **Kohala Carriage Tour** (Tues–Sat), which takes place in an old-fashioned wagon pulled by two large Belgian draft horses, with seating for 20, roll-down protection from the elements, and warm blankets for the upcountry temperatures. The tour rolls past ancient Hawaiian artifacts, 19th-century stone corrals (still in use), and miles of vast rolling hills; it stops at a working cowboy station, where visitors can get out, take photos, and stretch their legs.

See "Horseback Riding," under "Golf & Other Outdoor Activities," earlier in this chapter, for details on riding tours of Parker Ranch. Allow about 1½ hours to see the ranch.

Parker Ranch Center, Waimea. © 808/885-7655 for visitor center. www.parkerranch.com. Admission to museum $7 adults, $4.50 children younger than 12; tour of ranch homes $8.50 adults, $6 children; Kohala Carriage Tour $15 adults, $12 children. Visitor center and museum Mon–Sat 9am–5pm. If you're seeing the museum only, you can arrive as late as 4pm; the last museum/ranch homes tickets are sold at 4pm; the final museum/carriage tour tickets are sold at 2pm.

MAUNA KEA ✸✸✸

The summit of Mauna Kea, the world's tallest mountain if measured from its base on the ocean floor, is the best place on earth for astronomical observations because its mid-Pacific site is near the Equator and because it enjoys clear, pollution-free skies and pitch-black nights with no urban light to interfere. That's why Mauna Kea is home to the world's largest telescope, but the stargazing from here is fantastic even with the naked eye.

SETTING OUT   You'll need a four-wheel-drive vehicle to climb to the peak, **Observatory Hill.** A standard car will get you as far as the visitor center, but check your rental agreement before you go; some agencies prohibit you from taking your car on the Saddle Road, which is narrow and rutted, and has a soft shoulder.

SAFETY TIPS   Always check the weather and Mauna Kea road conditions before you head out (© 808/969-3218). Dress warmly; the temperatures drop into the 30s (around 0°C) after dark. Drink as much liquid as possible, avoiding alcohol and coffee, in the 36 hours surrounding your trip to avoid dehydration. Don't go within 24 hours of scuba diving—you could get the bends. The day before you go, avoid gas-producing foods, such as beans, cabbage, onions, soft drinks, or starches. If you smoke, take a break for 48 hours before to allow the carbon monoxide in your bloodstream to dissipate—you need all the oxygen you can get. Wear dark sunglasses to avoid snow blindness, and use lots of sunscreen and lip balm. Pregnant women and anyone under 13 or with a heart condition or lung ailment are advised to stay below. Once you're at the top, don't overexert yourself; it's bad for your heart. Take it easy up here.

ACCESS POINTS & VISITOR CENTERS   It's about an hour from Hilo or Waimea to the visitor center and another 30 to 45 minutes from here to the summit. Take the Saddle Road (Hwy. 200) from Highway 190; it's about 19 miles to Mauna Kea State Recreation Area, a good place to stop and stretch your legs. Go another 9 miles to the unmarked Summit Road turnoff, at mile marker 28 (about 9,300 ft.), across from the Hunter's Check-in Station. People usually start getting lightheaded after the 9,600-foot marker (about 6¼ miles up the Summit Rd.), the site of the last comfort zone and the **Onizuka Visitor Information Station** (© 808/961-2180; www.ifa.hawaii.edu/info/vis). Named in memory of Hawaii's fallen astronaut, a native of the Big Island and a victim of the *Challenger* explosion, the center is open daily from 9am to 10pm.

TOURS & PROGRAMS   If you'd rather not go it alone to the top, you can caravan up as part of a **free summit tour,** offered Saturday and Sunday at 1pm from the visitor center (returns at 5pm). You must be 16 or older and in good health (no cardiopulmonary problems), not be pregnant, and have a four-wheel-drive vehicle. The tours

---

Everything You've Always Wanted to Know about Mauna Kea

One of the best books on Mauna Kea, written by Onizuka Visitor Information Station manager David Byrne and Big Island writer Leslie Lang, is *Mauna Kea: A Guide to Hawaii's Sacred Mountain,* published by Watermark Publishing (✆ 866/900-BOOK; www.bookshawaii.net). The book has everything from the cultural history of the sacred mountain to her natural history, even great insights on the scientific value of the dormant volcano. Plus, the authors give you valuable tips on how to make the most of your visit to truly one of the wonders of the world.

---

explain the development of the facilities on Mauna Kea and include a walking tour of an observatory at 13,796 feet. Call ✆ **808/961-2180** if you'd like to participate.

Every night from 6 to 10pm, you can do some serious **stargazing** from the **Onizuka Visitor Information Station.** There's a free lecture at 6pm, followed by a video, a question-and-answer session, and your chance to peer through 11-inch, 14-inch, and 16-inch telescopes. Bring a snack and, if you've got them, your own telescope or binoculars, along with a flashlight (with a red filter). Dress for 30° to 40°F (–1° to 4°C) temperatures, but call for the weather report first (✆ **808/961-5582**). Families are welcome.

Another telescope tour is offered, free, during the day, by the **Subaru Telescope** (✆ **808/934-5056;** www.subarutelescope.org). You must book the 30-minute tour a week in advance, as they offer only 15 tours a month: Monday through Friday, at 10:30am, 11:30am, and 1:30pm on a first-to-sign-up basis. The Subaru Telescope is one of 13 world-class telescopes on the summit of Mauna Kea. You will need a four-wheel-drive car to make the trip up. They recommend that you stop for at least 30 minutes at the Onizuka Visitor Center at 9,000 feet to acclimate. Because of the risk of altitude sickness, the 30-minute tour is closed to pregnant women, children under 16, and anyone with health concerns that could be aggravated by the high altitude. Scuba divers are advised to schedule dives on a day separate from the tour.

At the **Keck Telescope Control Center,** 65–1120 Mamalahoa Hwy. (Hwy. 19), across from the North Hawaii Community Hospital, Waimea (✆ **808/885-7887;** www.keckobservatory.org), you can see a model of the world's largest telescope, which sits atop Mauna Kea. The center is open Monday through Friday from 8am to 4:30pm. A 12-minute video explains the Keck's search for objects in deep space.

The W.M. Keck Observatory does not offer tours at the summit, but it does provides a visitor's gallery with a 12-minute video, informational panels on the observatory layout and science results, two public restrooms, and a viewing area with partial views of the Keck telescope and dome. Gallery hours are 10am to 4pm Monday to Friday.

MAKING THE CLIMB If you're heading up on your own, stop at the visitor center for about a half-hour to get acquainted with the altitude. Walk around, eat a banana, and drink some water before you press onward and upward in low gear, engine whining. It takes about 30 to 45 minutes to get to the top from here. The trip is a mere 6 miles, but you climb from 9,000 to nearly 14,000 feet.

AT THE SUMMIT Up here, 11 nations, including Japan, France, and Canada, have set up peerless infrared telescopes to look into deep space. Among them sits the

---

Moments **Experiencing Where the Gods Live**

"The ancient Hawaiians thought of the top of Mauna Kea as heaven, or at least where the gods and goddess lived," according to Monte "Pat" Wright, owner and chief guide of **Mauna Kea Summit Adventures.**

Wright, the first guide to take people up to the top of the Mauna Kea, world's tallest mountain when measured from the base and an astonishing 13,796 feet when measured from sea level, says he fell in love with this often-snowcapped peak the first time he saw it.

Mauna Kea Summit Adventures offers a luxurious trip to the top of the world. The 7- to 8-hour adventure begins midafternoon, when guests are picked up along the Kona-Kohala coast in a brand-new $65,000 custom four-wheel-drive turbo-diesel van.

As the passengers make the drive up the mountain, the extensively trained guide discusses the geography, geology, natural history, and Hawaiian culture along the way.

The first stop is at the Onizuka Visitor Information Station, at 9,000 feet.

"We let people out to stretch, get acclimatized to the altitude, and eat dinner," Wright says.

As guests gear up with Mauna Kea Summit's heavy, arctic-style hooded parkas and gloves (30°F/–1°C is the average temperature on the mountain), the guide describes why the world's largest telescopes are located on Mauna Kea and also tells stories about the lifestyle of astronomers who live for a clear night sky.

After a dinner of gourmet sandwiches, vegetarian onion soup, and hot chocolate, coffee, or tea, everyone climbs back into the van for the half-hour ride to the summit.

Keck Telescope, the world's largest. Developed by the University of California and the California Institute of Technology, it's eight stories high, weighs 150 tons, and has a 33-foot-diameter mirror made of 36 perfectly attuned hexagon mirrors, like a fly's eye, rather than one conventional lens.

Also at the summit, up a narrow footpath, is a cairn of rocks; from it, you can see across the Pacific Ocean in a 360-degree view that's beyond words and pictures. When it's socked in, you get a surreal look at the summits of Mauna Loa and Maui's Haleakala poking through the puffy white cumulus clouds beneath your feet.

Inside a cinder cone just below the summit is **Lake Waiau,** the only glacial lake in the mid-Pacific, and at 13,020 feet above sea level, one of the highest lakes in the world. The lake never dries up, even though it gets only 15 inches of rain a year and sits in porous lava where there are no springs. Nobody quite knows what to make of this, but scientists suspect the lake is replenished by snowmelt and permafrost from submerged lava tubes. You can't see the lake from Summit Road; you must take a brief high-altitude hike. But it's easy: On the final approach to the summit area, upon regaining the blacktop road, go about 200 yards to the major switchback and make a hard right turn. Park on the shoulder of the road (which is at 13,200 ft.). No sign

As the sun sinks into the Pacific nearly 14,000 feet below, the guide points out the various world-renowned telescopes as they rotate into position for the night viewing.

After the last trace of sunset colors has disappeared from the sky, the tour again descends down to midmountain, where the climate is more agreeable, for stargazing. Each tour has Celestron Celestar 8 deluxe telescopes, which are capable of 30-175× magnification and gather up to 500 times more light than the unaided eye.

Wright does caution people to book the adventure early in their vacation.

"Although we do cancel about 25 trips a year due to weather, we want to be able to accommodate everyone," he says. If guests book at the beginning of their holiday and the trip is canceled due to weather, then Mauna Kea Summit will attempt to reschedule another day.

Wright also points out that due to the summit's low oxygen level (40% less oxygen than sea level) and the diminished air pressure (also 40% less air pressure than sea level), the lack of oxygen can be a serious problem for people with heart or lung problems or for scuba divers who have been diving in the previous 24 hours.

Pregnant woman, children under 13, and obese people should not travel to the summit due to the decreased oxygen. Because the roads to the summit are bumpy, anyone with a bad back might want to opt out.

The cost for this celestial adventure is $185 including tax (15% discounted if you book online at www.maunakea.com, 2 weeks in advance). For more information, call © 888/322-2366 or 808/322-2366, or go to www.maunakea.com.

points the way, but there's an obvious .5-mile trail that goes down to the lake about 200 feet across the lava. Follow the base of the big cinder cone on your left; you should have the summit of Mauna Loa in view directly ahead as you walk.

THE HAMAKUA COAST ✦✦✦

The sugar industry's rich 117-year history, along the scenic 45-mile coastline from Hilo to Hamakua, comes alive in the interpretive *Hilo-Hamakua Heritage Coast* drive guide, produced by the **Hawaii Island Economic Development Board,** 117 Kiawe St., Hilo, HI 96720 (© **808/935-2180;** www.hiedb.org).

The free guide not only points out the historic sites and museums, scenic photo opportunities, restaurants and stores, and even restrooms along the Hawaii Belt Road (Hwy. 19), but also has corresponding brown-and-white points-of-interest signs on the highway. Visitor information centers anchored at either end in Hilo and in Hamakua offer additional information on the area.

NATURAL WONDERS ALONG THE COAST

Akaka Falls ✦✦✦   See one of Hawaii's most scenic waterfalls via an easy 1-mile paved loop through a rainforest, past bamboo and ginger, and down to an observation

Co-KEY, Co-KEY: What Is That Noise?

That loud noise you hear after dark especially on the eastern side of the Big Island, is the cry of the male coqui frog looking for a mate. A native of Puerto Rico, where the frogs are kept in check by snakes, the coqui frog came to Hawaii in some plant material, found no natural enemies, and spread across the Big Island (and Maui). A chorus of several hundred coqui frogs is deafening (up to 163 decibels, or the noise level of a jet engine from 100 feet). In some places, like Akaka Falls, there are so many frogs that they now are chirping during daylight hours.

point. You'll have a perfect view of 442-foot Akaka and nearby Kahuna Falls, which is a mere 100-footer. Keep your eyes peeled for rainbows. The noise you hear is the sound of coqui frogs, an alien frog from Puerto Rico that has become a pest on the Big Island.

On Hwy. 19, Honomu (8 miles north of Hilo). Turn left at Honomu and head 3½ miles inland on Akaka Falls Rd. (Hwy. 220).

Hawaii Tropical Botanical Garden ✯✯   More than 1,800 species of tropical plants thrive in this little-known Eden by the sea. The 40-acre garden, nestled between the crashing surf and a thundering waterfall, has the world's largest selection of tropical plants growing in a natural environment, including torch gingers (which tower on 12-ft. stalks), a banyan canyon, an orchid garden, a banana grove, a bromeliad hill, and a golden bamboo grove, which rattles like a jungle drum in the trade winds. Some endangered Hawaiian specimens, such as the rare *Gardenia remyi,* are flourishing in this habitat. The gardens are seldom crowded; you can wander around by yourself all day.

Off Hwy. 19 on the 4-mile Scenic Rte., Onomea Bay (8 miles north of Hilo). ✆ **808/964-5233.** www.htbg.com. Admission $15 adults, $5 children 6–16, free for children 5 and younger. Daily 9am–4pm.

Laupahoehoe Beach Park ✯   This idyllic place holds a grim reminder of nature's fury. In 1946 a tidal wave swept across the village that once stood on this lava-leaf (that's what *laupahoehoe* means) peninsula and claimed the lives of 20 students and four teachers. A memorial in this pretty little park recalls the tragedy. The land here ends in black sea stacks that resemble tombstones. It's not a place for swimming, but the views are spectacular.

Laupahoehoe Point exit off Hwy. 19.

World Botanical Garden ✯✯   Just north of Hilo is Hawaii's largest botanical garden, with some 5,000 species. When the fruits are in season, the staff hands out free chilled juices. One of the most spectacular sites is the .25-mile rainforest walk (wheelchair accessible), along a stream on a flower-lined path to the viewing area of the three-tiered, 300-foot Umauma Falls. Parents will appreciate the large children's maze, where the "prize" is a playing field near the exit. The mock-orange hedge, which defines the various paths in the maze, is only 5 feet tall, so most parents can peer over the edge to keep an eye on their *keiki.* Other terrific walks include one through a wellness garden with medicinal Hawaiian plants and the "rainbow walk" (an ethno-botanical garden rainbow walk). There's also an arboretum. Still under construction as we went to press is a phylogenetic garden with plants and trees arranged in roughly the same sequence they first appeared on earth.

Off Hwy. 19 near the 16-mile marker in Umauma. P.O. Box 411, Honomu, HI 96728. ℂ 808/963-5427. www.world botanicalgardens.com. Admission $13 adults, $6 teens 13–19 years, $3 children 5–12 years, free for children under 5. Guided tours $40 adults, $30 teens, $20 children. Daily 9am–5:30pm.

HONOKAA ✫✫✫

Honokaa is worth a visit to see the remnants of plantation life, when sugar was king. This is a real place that hasn't yet been boutiqued into a shopping mall; it looks as if someone has kept it in a bell jar since 1920. There's a real barbershop, a real Filipino store, some good shopping (see "Shops & Galleries," later in this chapter), and a hotel with creaky floorboards that dishes up hearty food. The town also serves as the gateway to spectacular Waipio Valley (see below).

Honokaa has no attractions, per se, but you might want to check out the **Katsu Goto Memorial,** next to the library at the Hilo end of town. Katsu Goto, one of the first indentured Japanese immigrants, arrived in Honokaa in the late 1800s to work on the sugar plantations. He learned English, quit the plantation, and aided his fellow immigrants in labor disputes with American planters. On October 23, 1889, he was hanged from a lamppost in Honokaa, a victim of local-style justice.

THE END OF THE ROAD: WAIPIO VALLEY ✫✫✫

Long ago, this lush, tropical place was the valley of kings, who called it the valley of "curving water" (which is what *Waipio* means). From the black-sand bay at its mouth, Waipio sweeps 6 miles between sheer, cathedral-like walls that reach almost a mile high. Once 40,000 Hawaiians lived here, amid taro, red bananas, and wild guavas in an area etched by streams and waterfalls. Only about 50 Hawaiians live in the valley today, tending taro, fishing, and soaking up the ambience of this old Hawaiian place.

The sacred valley is steeped in myth and legend. Many of the ancient royals are buried here; some believe they rise up to become Marchers of the Night, whose chants reverberate through the valley. The caskets of Hawaiian chiefs Liloa and Lono Ika Makahiki, stolen from the Bishop Museum, are believed to have been brought here by Hawaiians.

To get to Waipio Valley, take Highway 19 from Hilo to Honokaa, and then Highway 240 to **Waipio Valley Lookout** ✫✫✫, a grassy park on the edge of Waipio Valley's sheer cliffs with splendid views of the wild oasis below. This is a great place for a picnic; you can sit at old redwood picnic tables and watch the white combers race along the black-sand beach at the mouth of the valley.

From the lookout, you can hike down into the valley. *Warning:* Do not attempt to drive your rental car down into the valley (even if you see someone else doing it). The problem is not so much going down as coming back up. Every day, rental cars have to be "rescued" and towed back up to the top, at great expense to the driver. Instead, take the **Waipio Valley Shuttle** (ℂ 808/775-7121) on a 90- to 120-minute guided tour (Mon–Sat 9am–4pm). Get your tickets at **Waipio Valley Art Works,** on Highway 240, 2 miles from the lookout (ℂ 808/775-0958). Tickets are $45 for adults, $20 for kids 11 and under.

You can also explore the valley on a narrated 90-minute **Waipio Valley Wagon Tour** (ℂ 808/775-9518; www.waipiovalleywagontours.com), a historical ride by mule-drawn surrey. Tours are offered Monday through Saturday at 9:30am, 11:30am, 1:30pm, and 3:30pm. It costs $55 for adults, $50 for seniors, $25 for children ages 4 to 12; call for reservations.

If you want to spend more than a day in the valley, plan ahead. A few simple B&Bs are situated on the ridge overlooking the valley and require advance reservations (see "Where to Stay," earlier in this chapter).

HILO 𝕬𝕬𝕬

Contact or stop by the **Downtown Hilo Improvement Association,** 252 Kamehameha Ave., Hilo, HI 96720 (© **808/935-8850;** www.downtownhilo.com), for a copy of its very informative self-guided walking tour of Hilo, which focuses on 18 historical sites dating from the 1870s to the present.

ON THE WATERFRONT

Old banyan trees shade **Banyan Drive** 𝕬𝕬, the lane that curves along the waterfront to the Hilo Bay hotels. Most of the trees were planted in the mid-1930s by memorable visitors like Cecil B. DeMille (who was here in 1933 filming *Four Frightened People*), Babe Ruth (his tree is in front of Hilo Hawaiian Hotel), King George V, Amelia Earhart, and other celebrities whose fleeting fame didn't last as long as the trees themselves.

It's worth a stop along Banyan Drive—especially if the coast is clear and the summit of Mauna Kea is free of clouds—to make the short walk across the concrete-arch bridge in front of the Naniloa Hotel to **Coconut Island** 𝕬, if only to gain a panoramic sense of the place.

Also along Banyan Drive is **Liliuokalani Gardens** 𝕬𝕬, the largest formal Japanese garden this side of Tokyo. This 30-acre park, named for Hawaii's last monarch, Queen Liliuokalani, is as pretty as a postcard, with bonsai, carp ponds, pagodas, and a moongate bridge. Admission is free; open 24 hours.

OTHER HILO SIGHTS

Lyman Museum & Mission House 𝕬 *Kids*   The oldest wood-frame house on the island was built in 1839 by David and Sarah Lyman, a missionary couple who arrived from New England in 1832. This hybrid combined New England– and Hawaiian-style architecture and is built of hand-hewn koa planks and native timbers. Here the Lymans received such guests as Mark Twain and Hawaii's monarchs. The well-preserved house is the best example of missionary life and times in Hawaii. You'll find lots of artifacts from the 19th century, including furniture and clothing from the Lymans and one of the first mirrors in Hilo.

The **Earth Heritage Gallery** in the complex next door continues the story of the islands with geology and volcanology exhibits, a mineral rock collection that's rated one of the best in the country, and a section on local flora and fauna. The **Island Heritage Gallery** features displays on Hawaiian culture, including a replica of a grass *hale* (house), as well as on other cultures transplanted to Hawaii's shores. A special exhibit gallery features changing exhibits on the history, art, and culture of Hawaii.

276 Haili St. (at Kapiolani St.), Hilo. © **808/935-5021.** www.lymanmuseum.org. Admission $10 adults, $8 seniors over 60, $3 children 6–17, $21 per family. Mon–Sat 9:30am–4:30pm. Tours 10am, 11am, 1pm, 2pm, and 3pm.

Maunaloa Macadamia Nut Factory   Explore this unique factory to learn how Hawaii's favorite nut is grown and processed. And, of course, you'll want to try a few samples.

Macadamia Nut Rd. (8 miles from Hilo, off Hwy. 11), Hilo. © **888/MAUNA LOA** or 808/966-8618. www.maunaloa. com. Free admission; self-guided factory tours. Daily 8:30am–5pm. From Hwy. 11, turn on Macadamia Nut Rd.; go 3 miles down the road to the factory.

Hilo

ATTRACTIONS ●

Banyan Drive **28**
Coconut Island **34**
Hilo Farmers Market **15**
Imiloa: Astronomy Center **19**
Leleiwi Beach Park **26**
Liliuokalani Gardens **32**
Lyman Museum
& Mission House **8**
Makupapapoi
Discovery Center **12**
Naha Stone **9**
Nani Mau Gardens **22**
Pacific Tsunami Museum **16**
Rainbow Falls **1**

ACCOMMODATIONS ■

The Bay House **6**
Dolphin Bay Hotel **5**
Hale Kai Hawaii **6**
Hilo Seaside **30**
The Inn at Kulaniapia **4**
Lihi Kai **6**
The Old Hawaiian B&B **3**
The Palms Cliff House **6**
Shipman House Bed & Breakfast **2**
Uncle Billy's Hilo Bay Hotel **29**

DINING ◆

Cafe Pesto Hilo Bay **14**
Harrington's **27**
Hilo Bay Café **23**
Ken's House of Pancakes **24**
Kuhio Grille **23**
Miyo's **21**
Naung Mai **17**
Nihon Restaurant & Cultural Center **33**
Nori's Saimin & Snacks **18**
Ocean Sushi Deli **11**
Pescatore **10**
Queen's Court Restaurant **31**
Restaurant Kaikodo **7**
Restaurant Miwa **20**
Royal Siam Thai Restaurant **13**
Seaside Restaurant **25**

Moments **Imiloa: Exploring the Unknown**

Absolutely do *not* miss the recently opened **Imiloa: Astronomy Center of Hawaii.** The 300 exhibits in the 12,000-square-foot gallery make the connection between the Hawaiian culture and its explorers, who discovered the Hawaiian Islands, and the astronomers who explore the heavens from the observatories atop Mauna Kea. *Imiloa,* which means "explorer" or "seeker of profound truth," is the perfect name for this architecturally stunning center, located on 9.1 landscaped acres overlooking Hilo Bay in the University of Hawaii at Hilo Science and Technology Park campus, 600 Imiloa Pl. (© 808/969-9700; www.imiloahawaii.org). Plan to spend at least a couple of hours here; a half a day would be better, to allow time to browse the excellent interactive exhibits as well as take in one of the planetarium shows, which boast a state-of-the-art digital projection system. Open Tuesday to Sunday from 9am to 4pm; admission is $15 for adults and $7.50 for children ages 4 to 12.

Mokupapa: Discovery Center for Hawaii's Remote Coral Reef *Kids Value*
This 4,000-square-foot center is perfect for kids, who can explore the Northwest Hawaiian Islands coral reef ecosystem. Through interactive displays, engaging three-dimensional models, and an immersion theater, the kids can learn natural science, culture, and history while having a great time. A 2,500-gallon saltwater aquarium provides a habitat for a collection of fish from the Northwest Hawaiian Islands reefs. Lots of fun at a terrific price: free!

308 Kamehameha Ave., Suite 109, Hilo. © 808/933-8198. www.hawaiireef.noaa.gov. Free admission. Tues–Sat 9am–4pm.

Naha Stone This 2½-ton stone was used as a test of royal strength: Ancient legend said that whoever could move the stone would conquer and unite the islands. As a 14-year-old boy, King Kamehameha the Great moved the stone—and later fulfilled his destiny. The Pinao stone, next to it, once guarded an ancient temple.

In front of Hilo Public Library, 300 Waianuenue Ave.

Nani Mau Gardens *Just outside Hilo is Nani Mau ("forever beautiful"), where Makato Nitahara, who turned a 20-acre papaya patch into a tropical garden, claims to have every flowering plant in Hawaii. His collection includes more than 2,000 varieties, from fragile hibiscus, whose blooms last only a day, to durable red anthuriums imported from South America. There are also Japanese gardens, an orchid walkway, a botanical museum, a house full of butterflies, and a restaurant that's open for lunch and dinner.

421 Makalika St., Hilo. © 808/959-3500. www.nanimau.com. Admission $10 adults, $5 children 4–10. Tram tours $5 extra for adults, $3 extra for children. Daily 9am–4:30pm. Go 3 miles south of Hilo Airport on Hwy. 11, turn on Makalika St., and continue ¾ mile.

Pacific Tsunami Museum * The most interesting artifacts here are not the exhibits, but the volunteers who survived Hawaii's most deadly "walls of water" in 1946 and 1960, both of which reshaped the town of Hilo. Visitors can listen to their stories of terror and view a range of exhibits, from interactive computers to a children's section, to a display on what happens when a local earthquake triggers a seismic wave, as it did in 1975 during the Big Island's last tsunami.

130 Kamehameha Ave., Hilo. © **808/935-0926**. www.tsunami.org. Admission $7 adults, $6 seniors, $5 ages 6–17 years, 5 and under free. Mon–Sat 9am–4pm.

Panaewa Rainforest Zoo 🌟 *Kids*   This 12-acre zoo, nestled in the heart of the Panaewa Forest Reserve south of Hilo, is the only outdoor rainforest zoo in the United States. Some 50 species of animals from rainforests around the globe call Panaewa home—including several endangered Hawaiian birds. All of them are exhibited in a natural setting. This is one of the few zoos where you can observe Sumatran tigers, Brazilian tapirs, and the rare pygmy hippopotamus, an endangered "minihippo" found in Western Africa.

Stainback Hwy. (off Hwy. 11), Hilo. © **808/959-7224**. www.hilozoo.com. Free admission. Daily 9am–4pm. Petting zoo Sat 1:30–2:30pm; tiger feeding 3:30pm daily.

Rainbow Falls 🌟 *Moments*   Go in the morning, around 9 or 10am, just as the sun comes over the mango trees, to see Rainbow Falls at its best. The 80-foot falls spill into a big round natural pool surrounded by wild ginger. According to legend, Hina, the mother of Maui, lives in the cave behind the falls. Unfortunately, swimming in the pool is no longer allowed.

West on Waianuenue Ave., past Kaumana Dr.

HAWAII VOLCANOES NATIONAL PARK 🌟🌟🌟

Yellowstone, Yosemite, and other national parks are spectacular, no doubt about it. But in my opinion, they're all ho-hum compared to this one: Here nothing less than the miracle of creation is the daily attraction.

In the 19th century, before tourism became Hawaii's middle name, the islands' singular attraction for world travelers wasn't the beach, but the volcano. From the world over, curious spectators gathered on the rim of Kilauea's Halemaumau crater to see one of the greatest wonders of the globe. Nearly a century after it was named a national park (in 1916), Hawaii Volcanoes remains the state's premier natural attraction.

Hawaii Volcanoes has the only rainforest in the U.S. National Park system—and it's the only park that's home to an active volcano. Most people drive through the park (it has 50 miles of good roads, some of them often covered by lava flows) and call it a day. But it takes at least 3 days to explore the whole park, including such oddities as **Halemaumau Crater** 🌟🌟🌟, a still-fuming pit of steam and sulfur; the intestinal-looking **Thurston Lava Tube** 🌟🌟🌟; **Devastation Trail** 🌟🌟🌟, a short hike through a desolated area destroyed by lava; and, finally, the end of **Chain of Craters Road** 🌟🌟🌟,

---

A Desert Crossing

If you follow Highway 11 counterclockwise from Kona to the Volcano, you'll get a preview of what lies ahead in the national park: hot, scorched, quake-shaken, bubbling-up new/dead land. This is the great Kau Desert, layer upon layer of lava flows, fine ash, and fallout. As you traverse the desert, you cross the Great Crack and the Southwest Rift Zone, a major fault zone that looks like a giant groove in the earth, before you reach Kilauea Volcano.

where lava regularly spills across the man-made two-lane blacktop to create its own red-hot freeway to the sea. In addition to some of the world's weirdest landscapes, the park has hiking trails, rainforests, campgrounds, a historic old hotel on the crater's rim, and that spectacular, still-erupting volcano.

NOTES ON THE ERUPTING VOLCANO   Volcanologists refer to Hawaii's volcanic eruptions as "quiet" eruptions because gases escape slowly instead of building up and exploding violently all at once. Hawaii's eruptions produce slow-moving, oozing lava that provides excellent, safe viewing most of the time.

Even so, the volcano has still caused its share of destruction. Since the current eruption of Kilauea began on January 3, 1983, lava has covered some 16,000 acres of lowland and rainforest, threatening rare hawks, honeycreeper birds, spiders, and bats, while destroying power and telephone lines and eliminating water service possibly forever. Some areas have been mantled repeatedly and are now buried underneath 80 feet of lava. At last count, the lava flow had destroyed nearly 200 homes and businesses, wiped out Kaimu Black Sand Beach (once Hawaii's most photographed beach) and Queen's Bath, obliterated entire towns and subdivisions (Kalapana, Royal Gardens, Kalapana Gardens, and Kapaahu Homesteads), and buried natural and historic landmarks (a 12th-c. *heiau*, the century-old Kalapana Mauna Kea Church, Wahaulu Visitor Center, and thousands of archaeological artifacts and sites). The cost of the destruction—so far—is estimated at $100 million. But how do you price the destruction of a 700-year-old temple or a 100-year-old church?

However, Kilauea hasn't just destroyed parts of the island; it has also added to it—more than 560 acres of new land. The volume of erupted lava over the last 2 decades measures nearly 2 billion cubic yards—enough new rock to pave a two-lane highway 1¼ million miles long, circling the earth some 50 times. Or, as a spokesperson for the park puts it: "Every 5 days, there is enough lava coming out of Kilauea volcano's eruption to place a thin veneer over Washington, D.C.—all 63 square miles."

The most prominent vent of the eruption has been Puu Oo, a 760-foot-high cinder-and-spatter cone. The most recent flow—the one you'll be able to see, if you're lucky—follows a 7-mile-long tube from the Puu Oo vent area to the sea. This lava flow has extended the Big Island's shoreline seaward and added hundreds of acres of new land along the steep southern slopes. Periodically, the new land proves unstable, falls under its own weight, and slides into the ocean. (These areas of ground gained and lost are not included in the tally of new acreage—only the land that sticks counts.)

Scientists are also keeping an eye on Mauna Loa, which has been swelling since its last eruption in 1983. If there's a new eruption, there could be a fast-moving flow down the southwest side of the island, possibly into South Kona or Kau.

WHAT YOU'RE LIKELY TO SEE   With luck, the volcano will still be streaming rivers of red lava when you visit the park, but a continuous eruption of this length (more than 2 decades) is setting new ground, so to speak. Kilauea continues to perplex volcanologists because most major eruptions in the past have ended abruptly after only several months.

But neither Mother Nature nor Madame Pele (the volcano goddess) runs on a schedule. The volcano could be shooting fountains of lava hundreds of feet into the air on the day you arrive, or it could be completely quiet—there are no guarantees. On many days, the lava flows right by accessible roads, and you can get as close as the heat will allow; sometimes, however, the flow is in underground tubes where you can't

Hawaii Volcanoes National Park

Legend

🏠 Cabin   🎋 Picnic Area

△ Campground   📷 Scenic Overlook

P Parking   🏠 Shelter

Tips A Volcano-Visiting Tip

Thanks to its higher elevation and windward (rainier) location, this neck of the woods is always colder than it is at the beach. If you're coming from the Kona side of the island in summer, expect it to be at least 10° to 20° cooler at the volcano; bring a sweater or light jacket. In the winter months, expect temperatures to be in the 40s or 50s (single digits to midteens Celsius), and dress accordingly. Always have rain gear on hand, especially in winter.

---

see it, or miles away from the nearest access point, visible only in the distance. Always ask the park rangers for advice before you set out on any lava-viewing expeditions.

VOLCANO VOCABULARY   The volcano has its own unique, poetic vocabulary that describes in Hawaiian what cannot be said so well in English. The lava that looks like swirls of chocolate cake frosting is called **pahoehoe** (pa-*hoy*-hoy); it results from a fast-moving flow that curls artistically as it moves. The big, blocky, jumbled lava that looks like a chopped-up parking lot is called **aa** (ah-ah); it's caused by lava that moves slowly, pulling apart as it overruns itself.

Newer words include **vog,** which is volcanic smog made of volcanic gases and smoke from forests set on fire by aa and pahoehoe. **Laze** results when sulfuric acid hits the water and vaporizes and mixes with chlorine to become, as any chemistry student knows, hydrochloric acid. Both vog and laze sting your eyes and can cause respiratory illness; don't expose yourself to either for too long. Anyone with heart or breathing trouble, or women who are pregnant, should avoid both vog and laze.

JUST THE FACTS

WHEN TO GO   The best time to go is when Kilauea is really pumping. If you're lucky, you'll be in the park when the volcano is active and there's a fountain of lava; mostly, the lava runs like a red river downslope into the sea. If you're on another part of the island and hear a TV news bulletin that the volcano is acting up, head to Hilo to see the spectacle. You won't be sorry—and your favorite beach will still be there when you get back.

ACCESS POINTS   Hawaii Volcanoes National Park is 29 miles from Hilo, on Hawaii Belt Road (Hwy. 11). If you're staying in Kailua-Kona, it's 100 miles, or about a 2½-hour drive, to the park. At press time, admission was still $10 per vehicle, but the park was proposing to double that to $20 per car in 2008; once you pay the fee, you can come and go as often as you want for 7 days. Hikers and bicyclists pay $5; bikes are allowed only on roads and paved trails.

VISITOR CENTERS & INFORMATION   Contact **Hawaii Volcanoes National Park,** P.O. Box 52, Hawaii Volcanoes National Park, HI 96718 (© **808/985-6000;** www.nps.gov/havo). **Kilauea Visitor Center** is at the entrance to the park, just off Highway 11; it's open daily from 7:45am to 5pm.

ERUPTION UPDATES   Everything you wanted to know about Hawaii's volcanoes, from what's going on with the current eruptions to where the next eruption is likely to be, is now available on the Hawaiian Volcano Observatory's new website, **http://hvo.wr.usgs.gov/kilauea/update/main.html**. The site is divided into areas on Kilauea (the currently erupting volcano), Mauna Loa (which last erupted in 1984), and Hawaii's other volcanoes. Each section provides photos, maps, eruption summaries, and historical information.

You can also get the latest on volcanic activity in the park by calling the park's **24-hour hot line** (© **808/985-6000**). Updates on volcanic activity are also posted daily on the bulletin board at the visitor center.

HIKING & CAMPING IN THE PARK   Hawaii Volcanoes National Park offers a wealth of hiking and camping possibilities. See "Hiking & Camping," earlier in this chapter, for details.

ACCOMMODATIONS IN & AROUND THE PARK   If camping isn't your thing, don't worry. There's a hotel, **Volcano House,** within the park boundary, on the rim of Halemaumau Crater. Volcano Village, just outside the park, has plenty of comfortable and convenient hotels and restaurants (see "Where to Stay" and "Where to Dine," earlier in this chapter).

SEEING THE HIGHLIGHTS

Your first stop should be **Kilauea Visitor Center** ⊛⊛, a rustic structure in a shady grove of trees just inside the entrance to the park. Here you can get up-to-the-minute reports on the volcano's activity, learn how volcanoes work, see a film showing blasts from the past, get information on hiking and camping, and pick up the obligatory postcards.

Filled with a new understanding of volcanology and the volcano goddess, Pele, you should then walk across the street to **Volcano House;** go through the lobby and out the other side, where you can get a look at **Kilauea Caldera** ⊛⊛⊛, a 2½-mile wide, 500-foot-deep pit. The caldera used to be a bubbling pit of fountaining lava; today you can still see wisps of steam that might, while you're standing there, turn into something more.

Now get out on the road and drive by the **Sulphur Banks** ⊛, which smell like rotten eggs, and the **Steam Vents** ⊛⊛⊛, where trails of smoke, once molten lava, rise from within the inner reaches of the earth. This is one of the places where you feel that the volcano is really alive. Stop at the **Thomas A. Jaggar Museum** ⊛⊛⊛ (open daily 8:30am–5pm; free admission) for a good look at Halemaumau Crater, which is½ mile across and 1,000 feet deep. On a clear day, you might also see Mauna Loa, 20 miles to the west. The museum shows video from days when the volcano was really spewing, explains the Pele legend in murals, and monitors earthquakes (a precursor of eruptions) on a seismograph.

Once you've seen the museum, drive around the caldera to the south side, park, and take the short walk to Halemaumau Crater's edge, past stinky sulfur banks and steam vents, to stand at the overlook and stare in awe at this once-fuming old fire pit, which still generates ferocious heat out of vestigial vents.

If you feel the need to cool off now, go to the **Thurston Lava Tube** ⊛⊛⊛, the coolest place in the park. You'll hike down into a natural bowl in the earth, a forest preserve the lava didn't touch—full of native birds and giant tree ferns. Then you'll see a black hole in the earth; step in. It's all drippy and cool here, with bare roots hanging down. You can either resurface into the bright daylight or, if you have a flashlight, poke on deeper into the tube, which goes for another ½ mile or so.

If you're still game for a good hike, try **Kilauea Iki Crater** ⊛, a 4-mile, 2-hour hike across the floor of the crater, which became a bubbling pool of lava in 1959 and sent fountains of lava 1,900 feet in the air, completely devastating a nearby ohia forest and leaving another popular hike ominously known as **Devastation Trail** ⟨⟨⟨. This .5-mile walk is a startling look at the powers of a volcanic eruption on the environment. (See "Hiking & Camping," earlier in this chapter, for details on these and other park hikes.)

Check out ancient Hawaiian art at the **Puu Loa Petroglyphs** ⟨, around mile marker 15 down Chain of Craters Road. Look for the stack of rocks on the road. A brief .5-mile walk will bring you to a circular boardwalk where you can see thousands of mysterious Hawaiian petroglyphs carved in stone. *Warning:* It's very easy to destroy these ancient works of art. Do not leave the boardwalk, and do not walk on or around the petroglyphs. Rubbings of petroglyphs will destroy them; the best way to capture them is by taking a photo.

This area, Puu Loa, was a sacred place for generations. Fathers came here to bury their newborns' umbilical cords in the numerous small holes in the lava, thus ensuring a long life for the child.

THE VOLCANO AFTER DARK   If the volcano is erupting, be sure to see it after dark. Brilliant red lava snakes down the side of the mountain and pours into the sea, creating a vivid display you'll never forget. About 1½ hours before sunset, head out of the park and back down Volcano Highway (Hwy. 11). Turn onto Highway 130 at Keaau; go past Pahoa to the end of the road. (The drive takes the better part of an hour.) From here (depending on the flow), it's about a mile walk over sharp crusted lava; park rangers will tell you how to get to the best viewing locations, or you can call ahead (© **808/985-6000**) to check where the current eruption is and how to get there. Be forewarned that the flow changes constantly and, on some days, may be too far from the road to hike, in which case you'll have to be content with seeing it from a distance. Be sure to heed the rangers: In the past, a handful of hikers who ignored these directions died en route; new lava can be unstable and break off without warning. Take water, a flashlight, and your camera, and wear sturdy shoes.

A BIRD'S-EYE VIEW   The best way to see Kilauea's bubbling caldera is from on high, in a helicopter. This bird's-eye view puts the enormity of it all into perspective. I recommend **Blue Hawaiian Helicopter** ⟨⟨⟨ (© **800/745-BLUE** or 808/886-1768; www.bluehawaiian.com), a professionally run, locally based company with an excellent safety record; comfortable, top-of-the-line copters; and pilots who are extremely knowledgeable about everything from volcanology to Hawaii lore. The company flies out of both Hilo and Waikoloa (Hilo is cheaper because it's closer). From Hilo, the 45-minute **Circle of Fire tour** ⟨⟨ takes you over the boiling volcano and then on to a bird's-eye view of the destruction the lava has caused and remote beaches ($210 per person, or $169 online). From Waikoloa, the 2-hour **Big Island Spectacular** ⟨⟨⟨ stars the volcano, tropical valleys, Hamakua Coast waterfalls, and the Kohala Mountains (from $424, or $364 online), but worth every penny).

10 Shops & Galleries

While chefs and farmers tout this island as fertile ground for crops and food, artists point to its primal, volcanic energy as a boost to their creative endeavors. Art communities and galleries are sprinkled across the Big Island, in villages like Holualoa and Volcano, where fine works in pottery, wood-turning, handmade glass, and other two- and three-dimensional media are sold in serene settings.

Although the visual arts are flourishing on this island, the line between shop and gallery can often be too fine to determine. Too many self-proclaimed "galleries" sell schlock or a mixture of arts, crafts, and tacky souvenirs. T-shirts and Kona coffee mugs are a souvenir staple in many so-called galleries.

The galleries and shops below offer a broad mix in many media. Items for the home, jewelry and accessories, vintage Hawaiiana, and accouterments at various prices and for various tastes can make great gifts to go, as can locally made food products such as preserves, cookies, flowers, Kona coffee, and macadamia nuts. You'll find that bowls made of rare native woods such as koa are especially abundant on the Big Island. This is an area in which politics and art intersect: Although reforestation efforts are underway to plant new koa trees, the decline of old-growth forests is causing many artists to turn to equally beautiful, and more environmentally sensitive, alternative woods.

THE KONA COAST
IN & AROUND KAILUA-KONA

Kailua-Kona's shopping prospects pour out into the streets in a festival atmosphere of T-shirts, trinkets, and dime-a-dozen souvenirs, with Alii Drive at the center of this activity. But the **Coconut Grove Market Place,** on Alii Drive, across the street from the seawall, has changed that image and added some great new shops around a sand volleyball court. Next door in the **Alii Sunset Plaza,** next to the Hard Rock Cafe, beaders can make a beeline for **Kona Beads** (© **808/331-2161**) to peruse a dizzying collection of beads from all over the world.

Shopping stalwarts in Kona are the **Kona Square,** across from **King Kamehameha's Kona Beach Hotel;** the hotel's shopping mall, with close to two dozen shops; and the **Kona Inn Shopping Village,** on Alii Drive. All include the usual assortment of T-shirt shops. One highlight is **Alii Gardens Marketplace** at the southern end of Kailua-Kona, a pleasant, tented outdoor marketplace with fresh fruit, flowers, imports, local crafts, and a wonderful selection of orchid plants. There's cheesy stuff there, too, but somehow it's less noticeable outdoors.

The newly opened **Kona International Market,** 74-5533 Luhia St (near Kaiwi St.), in the Old Industrial Area, is a great idea, a series of small open-air shops in a large pavilion with food vendors, similar to Waikiki's International Market. Unfortunately, with just a few exceptions, I am very disappointed in this "market." I searched all the vendors looking for something made in Hawaii, and with very few exceptions (some jewelry), most of the trinkets sold here were not from the Big Island, and not even from Hawaii, and prices were not that attractive. However, a major exception is **Emma's Flowers** (© 808/329-7746), a great place for leis and just-cut tropical flowers, at reasonable prices.

Honolua Surf Company   This shop targets the surf-and-sun enthusiast with good things for good times: towels, flip-flops, body boards, sunglasses, swimsuits, and everything else you need for ocean and shore action. Quiksilver, Tommy Bahama, Roxy, Billabong, and Kahala are among the top menswear labels here, but I also like the quirky, colorful Toes on the Nose. Also popular is the full line of products with the Honolua Surf Co. label, including T-shirts, hats, bags, dresses, sweatshirts, aloha shirts, and swimwear. At Kona Inn Shopping Village, Alii Dr. © **808/329-1001.**

Kailua Village Artists Gallery   A co-op of four dozen Hawaii island artists, plus a few guest artists, display their works in various media: watercolors, paintings, prints, hand-blown and blasted glass, and photography. Books, pottery, and an attractive

Art Appreciation

The finest art on the Kona Coast hangs in, of all places, a bank. Award-winning **First Hawaiian Bank,** 74–5593 Palani Rd. (© **808/329-2461**), has art lovers making special trips to view Hiroki Morinoue's mural, John Buck's prints, Chiu Leong's ceramic sculpture, Franco Salmoiraghi's photographs, Setsuko Morinoue's abstract fiber wall piece, and other works that were incorporated as part of the bank's design. Artists Yvonne Cheng and Sharon Carter Smith, whose works are included, assembled this exhibition, a sterling example of corporate sponsorship of the arts.

assortment of greeting cards are among the lower-priced items. In King Kamehameha's Kona Beach Hotel, 75–5660 Palani Rd. (© **808/329-6653**) and 78–6740 Alii Dr. (© **808/324-7060**).

Edibles & Everyday Things

The Big Island's **green markets** are notable for the quality of produce and the abundance of island specialties at better-than-usual prices. Look for the cheerful green kiosks of the **Alii Gardens Marketplace,** 75–6129 Alii Dr. (at the south end), where local farmers and artists set up their wares daily from 8am to 5pm. This is not your garden-variety marketplace; some vendors are permanent, some drive over from Hilo, and the owners have planted shade trees and foliage to make the 5-acre plot a Kona landmark. There are 40 to 50 vendors on any given day, selling jewelry, woodcrafts, produce, macadamia nuts, orchids, and—my favorite—the fresh juices of Kay Reeves, owner of Wau, who gets up before dawn to make her sensational fresh *lilikoi* and lime juices. Kona Blue Sky Coffee is also here, as is Lynn Cappell, a fine painter of island landscapes, and Laura de Rosa's sensational A'ala Dreams lotions and oils.

Java junkies jump-start their day at **Island Lava Java** (© **808/327-2161**), the hot new magnet for coffee lovers at the Coconut Grove Market Place, on Alii Drive. At the other end of Kailua-Kona, in the new New Industrial Area, between Costco and Home Depot, the handmade candies of the **Kailua Candy Company,** 73-5612 Kauhola St. (© **808/329-2522,** or 800/622-2462 for orders), also beckon, especially the macadamia-nut clusters with ground ginger or the legendary macadamia-nut *honu* (turtle). Other products include truffles, pure Kona coffee, shortbread cookies, toffee, T-shirts, mugs, mustards, and other gift items.

Kona Wine Market, in the King Kamehameha Mall (© **808/329-9400**), has a noteworthy selection, including some esoteric vintages, at prices you'll love. This is a wine lover's store, with selections from California, Europe, and points beyond, as well as gift baskets, cheeses, cigars, oils and vinegars, specialty pastas and condiments, Riedel glassware, and friendly, knowledgeable service.

For everyday grocery needs, **KTA Stores** (in the Kona Coast Shopping Center, at Palani Rd. and the Queen Kaahumanu Hwy., and in the Keauhou Shopping Village, on Alii Dr.) are always my first choice. Through its Mountain Apple brand, KTA sells hundreds of top-notch local products—from Kona smoked marlin and Hilo-grown rainbow trout to cookies, breads, jams and jellies, taro chips, and *kulolo*, the decadently dense taro-coconut steamed pudding—by dozens of local vendors. The fresh fish department is always an adventure; if anything esoteric is running, such as the flashy red aweoweo, it's sure to be on KTA's counters, along with a large spread of prepared foods for sunset picnics and barbecues.

My other favorite is **Kona Natural Foods,** in the Crossroads Center (② **808/329-2296**). It's been upgraded from a health-food store to a full-on healthful supermarket. And it's the only full-service health-food store for miles, selling bulk grains and cereals, vitamins, snacks, fresh-fruit smoothies, and sandwiches and salads from its takeout deli. Organic greens, grown in the South Kona area, are a small but strong feature of the produce section.

UPCOUNTRY KONA: HOLUALOA

Charming Holualoa, 1,400 feet and 10 minutes above Kailua-Kona at the top of Hualalai Road, is a place for strong espresso, leisurely gallery hopping, and nostalgic explorations across several cultural and time zones. One narrow road takes you across generations and cultures.

Paul's Place is Holualoa's only all-purpose general store, a time warp tucked between frame shops, galleries, and studios.

Prominent Holualoa artists include the jewelry maker/sculptor Sam Rosen, who years ago set the pace for found-object art and today makes beautiful pieces at the rear of Chestnut Gallery; the furniture maker and wood sculptor Gerald Ben; the printmaker Nora Yamanoha; the glass artist Wilfred Yamazawa; the sculptor Cal Hashimoto; and Hiroki and Setsuko Morinoue of Studio 7 gallery. All galleries listed are on the main street, Mamalahoa Highway, and all are within walking distance of each other.

Antiques by Cinderella's *(Finds* Most of the treasures here are tucked away, so don't be shy about asking the owner, Cindi Nespor, where she keeps her prized antique engravings or her out-of-print naturalists' books of hand-painted engravings. There are also rare prints and vases, kimonos, lamps, and home accessories. The rare books will quicken a book lover's heart, while the estate jewelry, vintage linens, rattan furniture, and hats make this a brilliant browse. Gorgeous antique shawls, long-extinct Chanel perfumes, and 1940s Garbo-style hats are among the treasures found here. Call ahead, though; the owner keeps flexible, Island-style hours. Mamalahoa Hwy. ② **808/322-2474.**

Dovetail Gallery and Design Located behind the old historic post office, Dovetail features contemporary and abstract art, and the works of high-end, fine craftsmen and furniture makers. But the gallery's custom woodworking shop separates it from all the other galleries lining the Mamalahoa Highway. It features top craftsmen and the design work of Gerald Ben, who not only is a skilled ceramicist, but also has been a custom woodworker for 22 years. His expertise is designing furniture and wood accessories for his clients, which include collectors, home owners, interior designers, and architects. 76–5942 Mamalahoa Hwy. ② **808/322-4046.**

Holualoa Gallery Owners Matthew and Mary Lovein show their own work as well as the work of selected Hawaii artists in this roadside gallery in Holualoa. Sculptures, paintings, koa furniture, fused-glass bowls, raku ceramics, and creations in paper, bronze, metal, and glass are among the gallery's offerings. 76–5921 Mamalahoa Hwy. ② **808/322-8484.**

Kimura Lauhala Shop Everyone loves Kimura's and the masterpieces of weaving that spill out of the tiny shop. It's lined with lauhala, from rolled-up mats and wide-brimmed hats to tote bags, coasters, and coin purses. The fragrant, resilient fiber, woven from the spiny leaves of the *hala* (pandanus) tree, is smooth to the touch and becomes softer with use. Lauhala also varies in color, according to region and growing conditions. Although Kimura employs a covey of local weavers who use the renowned

Farmers Market, Fruit Stands & Espresso Bar

South Kona, one of the best growing regions on the Big Island, has a weekly **Farmers Market** every Saturday from 8am to noon at the **Keauhou Shopping Village** parking lot, near Ace Hardware. It's a true farmers market, selling only produce grown on the Big Island. Another great vegetable and fruit stand down south is the **South Kona Fruit Stand,** 84–4770 Mamalahoa Hwy., Captain Cook (*C* **808/328-8547),** which sells some of the most unusual tropical produce from the Big Island. Way down south, the **Kau Tropical Espresso Bar and Organic Fruitstand** (*C* **808/929-8785)** has not only organic fruit, but also locally grown, organic coffee to go, or take a moment and "talk story" with Elizabeth or Barney, who can tell you about the fruits, vegetables, and coffee of the Big Island.

---

hala leaves of Kona, some South Pacific imports bolster the supply. At Mamalahoa Hwy. and Hualalai Rd. *C* 808/324-0053.

Studio 7 *(Finds* Some of Hawaii's most respected artists, among them gallery owners Setsuko and Hiroki Morinoue, exhibit their works in this serenely beautiful studio. Smooth pebbles, stark woods, and a garden setting provide the backdrop for Hiroki's paintings and prints, and Setsuko's pottery, paper collages, and wall pieces. The Main Gallery houses multimedia art, the Print Gallery sculptural pieces and two-dimensional works, and the Ceramic Gallery features the works of Clayton Amemiya, Chiu Leong, and Gerald Ben. This is the hub of the Holualoa art community; activities include workshops, classes, and special events by visiting artists. Mamalahoa Hwy. *C* 808/324-1335.

SOUTH KONA

In Kealakekua, the **Kamigaki Market,** on Highway 11, also called Mamalahoa Highway, is a reliable source of food items, especially for regional specialties such as macadamia nuts and Kona coffee.

In Honaunau, farther south, keep an eye out for the **Bong Brothers Store,** on Highway 11, and its eye-catching selections of fresh local fruit—from cherimoya (in season) to star fruit and white Sugarloaf pineapples. The Bongs are known for their deli items, produce, and Kona coffee fresh from their own roasting room, but I think their black, very hip Bong Brothers and Bong Sistah T-shirts are the find of the region. The juice bar offers homemade soups and smoothies made with fresh local fruit.

In the town of Captain Cook, look for the big BANANA BREAD sign (you can't miss it) across the street from the fire station on Highway 11, and you'll come across the **Captain Cook Baking Company,** which bakes excellent banana bread with macadamia nuts, under the "Auntie Helen's" label. The bread is made with Big Island bananas and macadamia-nut honey, and baked right there in the kitchen. This bakery-sandwich shop also sells Lilikoi Gold passion butter, cheesecake brownies, and submarine sandwiches on its own house-made breads.

Antiques and Orchids Beverly Napolitan and her husband took over Captain Cook's oldest building (built in 1906) and filled it with an eclectic array of antiques, collectibles, and fresh orchids. There are a few vintage Hawaiian items, lots of teacups, raspberry-colored walls, linens, old kimonos, celadon, etched glass and crystal lamps, a Queen Liliuokalani lanai sofa from the 1800s, and a red wooden veranda where high tea is served on Saturday (11am–4pm), complete with homemade scones, Devonshire cream, and English teacups. You can't miss this green building with white trim, on the mauka side of the highway in Captain Cook. Hwy. 11, Captain Cook. © 808/323-9851.

The Grass Shack   The Grass Shack has been here for more than 3 decades, with its large selection of local woodcrafts, Niihau shell and wiliwili-seed leis, packaged coffee, pahu drums, nose flutes, and lauhala (woven pandanus leaves) in every form. Bowls, boxes, and accessories of Norfolk pine, the rare kou, and other local woods also take up a sizable portion of the shop. Lauhala baskets, made of fiber from the region and the Hamakua Coast, are among the Shack's finest offerings, as are the custom ukuleles and feather gourds for hula dancing. Hwy. 11, Kealakekua. © 808/323-2877.

Island Framing Company and Gifts   The owners of this tiny frame shop have great taste, and they've filled their shop with their favorite things: excellent soaps and candles (including Votivo, very chichi), Japanese lanterns, framed prints, koa frames, Indonesian imports, umbrellas, and household accessories and accents that would liven up any home. The shop is in a charming green plantation house with a small veranda, on the ocean side of the street at the border of Kainaliu and Kealakekua. 79–7506 Hwy. 11, Kealakekua. © 808/322-4397.

Kimura Store *Finds*   This old-fashioned general store is one of those places you'll be glad you found—a store with spirit and character, plus everything you need and don't need. You'll see Hawaii's finest selection of yardage, enough cookware for a multicourse dinner, aspirin, Shiseido cosmetics, and an eye-popping assortment of buttons, zippers, and quilting materials. Irene Kimura, the family matriarch, who presided over the store for more than 60 years until she passed away recently, said she quit counting the fabric bolts at 8,000 but estimated there were more than 10,000. Kimura's is the spot for pareu and Hawaiian fabrics, brocades, silks, and offbeat gift items, such as Japanese china and *tabi,* the comfortable cloth footwear. Hwy. 11, Kainaliu. © 808/322-3771.

THE KOHALA COAST

Shops on the Kohala Coast are concentrated in and around the resorts, listed below.

HILTON WAIKOLOA VILLAGE   Among the hotel's shops, **Sandal Tree** carries footwear with style and kick: Italian sandals at non-Italian prices, designer pumps, and other footwear to carry you from dockside to dance floor.

KINGS' SHOPS   These stores are located at the entrance to Waikoloa Resort. A recent find here is **Walking in Paradise** (© 808/886-2600). The footwear—much of it made in France (Mephisto, Arche)—can be expensive, but it's worthwhile for anyone seeking comfort while exploring the harsh lava terrain of this island or the pedestrian culture of Kailua's Alii Drive. Toward the mauka (mountainside) end is **Noa Noa,** filled with exotic artifacts from Java and Borneo, and tropical clothing for easygoing life on the Pacific Rim. At **Under the Koa Tree,** some of the island's finest artists display their prints, woodcrafts, and paintings. For snacks, ice, sunscreen, wine, postcards, newspapers, and everyday essentials, there's the **Whalers General Store,** and for dining on the run, a small Food Court with pizza, plate lunches, and the **Wild Boar Juice & Java** bar for fresh-pressed carrot/ginger juice or a steaming cup of brew.

As we went to press, under construction was the $95-million **Queens' MarketPlace** (© 808/886-8811; www.waikoloabeachresort.com), located across the street from the Kings' Shops, with a range of shops from Giggles, Island Pearls, Local Motion to Sansei Seafood Restaurant & Sushi Bar, Island Gourmet Markets, and Starbucks.

HUALALAI RESORT **Ka'upulehu Store,** in the Four Seasons Resort Hualalai, is a perfect blend of high quality and cultural integrity. Located within the award-winning Ka'upulehu Cultural Center, the store carries items made in Hawaii: handmade paper, hand-painted silks, seed leis, greeting cards, koa bowls, wreaths, John Kelly prints, and a selection of Hawaii-themed books. **Hualalai Sports Club and Spa,** in the same resort, has a winning retail section of beauty, aromatherapy, and treatment products, including Hana Nai'a Aromatherapy Products. The products include mango and jasmine perfumes, Bulgarian rose water, and herbal lotions and potions.

MAUNA LANI RESORT The recently opened **The Shops at Mauna Lani** is a high-end cluster of well-known name stores and a sprinkle of local, homegrown places such as terrific eateries Kenichi and Dara's Authentic Thai Cuisine. Shops include Lahaina Galleries, Caché, Kohala Goldsmith, Black Perl Gallery, Tori Richards, A'ama Surf and Sport, and The Market at Mauna Lani. Chain restaurants include Ruth's Chris Steak House, Tommy Bahama, and Starbucks.

NORTH KOHALA

Ackerman Gallery Crafts and fine arts are housed in two separate galleries a few blocks apart. Artist Gary Ackerman and his wife, Yesan, display gifts, crafts, and the works of award-winning Big Island artists, including Ackerman's own Impressionistic paintings. There are Kelly Dunn's hand-turned Norfolk pine bowls, Jer Houston's heirloom-quality koa-and-ebony desks, and Wilfred Yamazawa's hand-blown-glass perfume bottles and sculptures. Primitive artifacts, Asian antiques, jewelry, and Cal Hashimoto's bamboo sculptures are also among the discoveries here. The crafts-and-gifts gallery, across from the King Kamehameha statue, has recently doubled in size; it features gift ideas in all media and price ranges. Hwy. 270 (across from the Kamehameha statue; also 3 blocks away, on the opposite side of the street), Kapaau. ℂ 808/889-5971.

As Hawi Turns You never know what you'll find in this whimsical, delightful shop of women's clothing and accessories. The windows might be filled with painted paper lanterns in the shapes of stars, or retro-painted switch plates, or kicky straw hats paired with bias-cut silk dresses and quirky jewelry. This is the perfect place to pamper yourself with such fripperies as tatami zoris and flamboyant accessories for a colorful, tropical life. Hwy. 270 (Akoni Pule Hwy.), Hawi. ℂ 808/889-5023.

Elements John Flynn designs jewelry, and his wife, Prakash, assembles fountains and other treasures, and together they've filled their quiet gallery with an assortment of arts and crafts from the Big Island, including local artist Margaret Ann Hoy's wonderful watercolors of island scenes. The lauhala accessories, jewelry, and fountains—simple bowls filled with smooth gemstones such as amethyst and rose quartz—make great gifts and accessories. Hwy. 270 (Akoni Pule Hwy.), Kapaau. ℂ 808/889-0760.

Harbor Gallery 👁️👁️ Formerly Kohala Kollection, this two-story gallery seems to have made a seamless transition, remaining a big draw next to the Cafe Pesto in this industrial harbor area of Kawaihae. Harry Wishard paintings, Miles Fry's museum-quality model canoes and ships, Kathy Long's pencil drawings, and Frances Dennis' painted island scenes on canvas are among the works by more than 150 artists, primarily from the Big Island. The range is vast—from jewelry to basketry, to ceramics, to heirloom-quality koa furniture. In Kawaihae Shopping Center, Hwy. 270, just north of Hwy. 19. ℂ 808/882-1510.

Kohala Book Shop 👁️👁️ Jan and Frank Morgan's new and used bookstore—the largest such store in Hawaii—is a huge success and a major attraction in the town's historic Hotel Nanbu building. The yellow building with red-and-green trim is beautifully and faithfully restored, all the better to house a priceless collection that includes out-of-print first editions, the $22,500 set of *Captain Cook's Journals*, *The Morals of Confucius* (dated 1691 and priced at $350), and thousands of other treasures. You'll see popular fiction and everyday books, too, along with titles on Hawaii and Oceania; at last count, the inventory was 20,000 and climbing. Thoughtful signs, good prices, and an attractive and welcoming environment are only some of the winning features. Hwy. 270 (Akoni Pule Hwy.), a block from the Kamehameha statue, Kapaau. ℂ 808/889-6732.

WAIMEA

Waimea is lei country as well as the island's breadbasket, so look for protea, vegetables, vine-ripened tomatoes, and tuberose stalks here at reasonable prices. Mainstays include **Honopua Farm** and **Hufford's Farm,** side by side, selling freshly cut flowers and organic vegetables.

Small and sublime, the **Waimea Farmers Market,** Highway 19, at mile marker 55 on the Hamakua side of Waimea town (on the lawn in front of the Department of Hawaiian Home Lands, West Hawaii office), draws a loyal crowd from 7am to noon on Saturday.

At the other end of Waimea, the **Parker School Farmers Market,** held Saturday from 7:30am to noon, is smaller and more subdued, but with choice items as well. The Kalopa macadamia nuts are the sweetest and tastiest I've ever had. Hilo's wonderful **Dan De Luz Woods** (p. 348) has a branch at 64–1013 Mamalahoa Hwy., in front of the True Value hardware store.

Other shops in Waimea range from the small roadside storefronts lining Highway 19 and Highway 190, which intersect in the middle of town, to complexes such as **Waimea Center,** where you'll find the trusty old **KTA Super Store,** the one-stop shop for all your basic necessities, plus a glorious profusion of interesting local foods. Across the street, with its upscale galleries and shops, **Parker Square** will likely be your most rewarding stop.

Bentley's Home & Garden Collection   To its lavish list of glassware, linens, chenille throws, home fragrances, stuffed animals, and Wild West gift-wraps, Bentley's has added casual country clothing in linens and cottons. Dresses, sweaters, raffia hats, top-drawer Western shirts, handbags, and woven shoes adorn this fragrant, gardenlike shop. In Parker Sq., Hwy. 19. ℂ 808/885-5565.

Gallery of Great Things   Here's an eye-popping assemblage of local art and Pacific Rim artifacts. Browse under the watchful gaze of an antique Tongan war club (not for sale) and authentic rhinoceros- and deer-horn blowguns from Borneo, among the plethora of treasures from Polynesia, Micronesia, and Indonesia. You'll find jewelry, glassware, photographs, greeting cards, fiber baskets, and hand-turned bowls of beautifully grained woods. Photos by Victoria McCormick, the sketches of Kathy Long, feather masks by Bety McCormick, and the paintings of Yvonne Cheng are among the treasures by local artists. There are a few pieces of etched glass and vintage clothing, too, along with a small, gorgeous collection of antique kimonos. In Parker Sq., Hwy. 19. ℂ 808/885-7706.

Mauna Kea Galleries *Finds*   This is the new and expanded version of the gallery I've come to know and love in Hilo, which is now open by appointment only. Mark Blackburn, who wrote *Hawaiiana: The Best of Hawaiian Design,* has made this his showcase for the treasures he loves to collect. He and his wife, Carolyn, amass vintage

Hawaiiana in mint condition and then respectfully display it. Their collection includes monarchy and Ming jewelry; mint-condition Santa Anita and Don Blanding dinnerware, including very rare pieces; adz-hewn koa and kou bowls; and vintage photography and menus, all individually stored in plastic sleeves ($10–$300). Rare books and prints, including hand-colored 1870s lithographs; old koa furniture; original Hawaiian fish prints from the early 1900s; and limited-edition, museum-quality reproductions of hula-girl photos from the 1890s are also among the finds. 65–1298 Kawaihae Rd. (across the street from Edelweiss Restaurant), Waimea. © 808/969-1184.

Silk Road Gallery   Silk Road offers a rare experience of beauty in a large corner of Parker Square. It's worth a special stop if you love Asian antiques: porcelain teacups, jade cups, kimonos, lacquerware, Buddhas, tansus, bronze bells and chimes, Indonesian woven baskets, Japanese screens, and all manner of delights for elevated living. Fine textiles and baskets, antique dolls, rare woodblock prints, and books, cards, and prints are some of its offerings. You can part with $15 for a bronze bell, thousands for an antique tansu, or something in between. In Parker Sq., Hwy. 19. © 808/885-7474.

Sweet Wind   Because the owner loves beauty and harmonious things, you'll find chimes, carved dolphins, crystals, geodes, incense (an excellent selection), beads, jewelry, gems, essential oils, and thoughtfully selected books worth more than a casual glance. The books cover self-help, health, metaphysics, Hawaiian spirituality, yoga, meditation, and other topics for wholesome living. In Parker Sq., Hwy. 19. © 808/885-0562.

Waimea General Store   This charming, unpretentious country store offers a superb assortment of Hawaii-themed books, soaps and toiletries, cookbooks and kitchen accessories, candles, linens, greeting cards, dolls, Japanese hapi coats, island teas, rare kiawe honey, preserves, cookies, and countless gift items from the practical to the whimsical. In Parker Sq., Hwy. 19. © 808/885-4479.

THE HAMAKUA COAST

Waipio Valley Artworks *Finds*   Housed in an old wooden building at the end of the road before the Waipio Valley, this gallery/boutique offers treasures for the home. The focus here is strictly local, with a strong emphasis on woodwork—one of the largest selections, if not the largest, in the state. A recent expansion has brought more chests and tables and gift items by Big Island artists. All the luminaries of wood-turning have works here: Jack Straka, Robert Butts, Scott Hare, Kevin Parks. Their bowls, rocking chairs, and jewelry boxes exhibit flawless craftsmanship and richly burnished grains. More affordable are the pens and hair accessories. Deli sandwiches and Tropical Dreams ice cream are served in the expanded cafe. In Kukuihaele. © 808/775-0958.

HONOKAA

Mamane Street Bakery, on the main drag (45–3625 Mamane St.; © 808/775-9478), will fill all your coffee-shop needs. Fresh-baked breads, pies, and pastries (including melt-in-your-mouth Danishes) are served with good coffee in a tiny cafe lined with old photographs.

Honokaa Market Place   I've noticed a proliferation of Balinese imports (not a good sign) mingling with the old and new Hawaiiana. The eclectic selection of Hawaiian, Asian, and Indonesian handicrafts includes wood crafts, Hawaiian prints, and Hawaiian quilts, from wall hangings and pillows to the full-size quilts, plus a few pieces of jewelry. 45–3321 Mamane St. © 808/775-8255.

Honokaa Trading Company "Rustic, tacky, rare—there's something for everyone," says owner Grace Walker. Every inch of this labyrinthine 2,200-square-foot bazaar is occupied by antiques and collectibles, new and used goods, and countless treasures. You'll find plantation memorabilia, Hawaiiana, bark-cloth fabrics from the 1940s, rhinestone jewelry and rattan furniture from the 1930s, vintage ukuleles, Depression glass, dinnerware from Honolulu's landmark Willows restaurant, koa lamps, Francis Oda airbrush paintings, vintage kimonos, and linens. It's an unbelievable conglomeration, with surprises in every corner. Vigilant collectors make regular forays here to scoop up the 1950s ivory jewelry and John Kelly prints. Mamane St. (✆ 808/775-0808.

Kamaaina Woods The showroom is adjacent to the workshop, so visitors can watch the craftspeople at work on the other side of the glass panel. Local woods are the specialty here, with a strong emphasis on koa and milo bowls. Boxes, carvings, albums, and smaller accessories are also included in the mix, but bowl-turning is clearly the focus. Prices begin at about $10. Lehua St. (down the hill from the post office). (✆ 808/775-7722.

Maya's Clothing and Gifts The Hawaiian-print table runners and locally made soaps and ceramics are only part of the growing selection at this Honokaa newcomer. Napkins, place mats, hula girl lamps, koa accessories, quilted Hawaiian pot holders, aloha shirts, jams and jellies, T-shirts, sportswear, jewelry boxes—it's an eclectic selection for all tastes. Mamane St. (✆ 808/775-1016.

Seconds to Go Elaine Carlsmith spends a lot of time collecting vintage pottery, glassware, kimonos, fabrics, and other treasures to sell to eager seekers of nostalgia. Many beautiful things have passed through her doors, including antique koa furniture, old maps, music sheets, and rare and out-of-print books. The vintage ivory jewelry and Don Blanding dinnerware are grabbed up quickly. The main store is a few doors away from the warehouse, where furniture and larger pieces are displayed. Mamane St. (✆ 808/775-9212.

Starseed Shop here for offbeat holographic bumper stickers, jewelry, beads, incense, and New Age amulets. The selection of crystals is impressive, and there are hundreds of boxes of beads, some of them rare European and Asian imports. The owner also has a special camera that purportedly photographs people's auras, or electromagnetic fields, so you can find out what your colors are. 45–3551 A-2 Mamane St. (✆ 808/775-9344.

Taro Patch Gifts Taro Patch carries an eclectic assortment of Hawaiian music tapes and CDs, switch plates printed with Hawaiian labels, Ka'u coffee, local jams and jellies, soaps, pareu, books, ceramics, sushi candles, essential oils, and sportswear, such as Hawaiian-print cowboy shirts. The Hawaiian seed lei selection is the best in town: kamani, blue marble, wiliwili, double sheep eye, betel nut, and several other attractive native species. 45–3599 Mamane St. (✆ 808/775-7228.

HILO

Shopping in Hilo is centered on the **Kaiko'o Hilo Mall,** 777 Kilauea Ave., near the state and county buildings; the **Prince Kuhio Shopping Plaza,** 111 E. Puainako, just off Highway 11 on the road north to Volcano, where you'll find a supermarket, drugstore, Macy's, and other standards; the **Bayfront area** downtown, where the hippest new businesses have taken up residence in the historic buildings lining Kamehameha

A Special Arts Center & Gallery

Part gallery, part retail store, and part consortium of the arts, the **East Hawaii Cultural Center,** 141 Kalakaua St., across from Kalakaua Park ((C) **808/961-5711**), is run by volunteers in the visual and performing arts. Keep it in mind for gifts of Hawaii, or if you have any questions regarding the **Hawaii Concert Society, Hilo Community Players, Big Island Dance Council,** or **Big Island Art Guild.** The art gallery and gift shop exhibit locally made cards, jewelry, books, sculptures, and wood objects, including museum-quality works.

Avenue; and the new **Waiakea Plaza,** where the big-box retailers (Ross, Office Max, Borders, Wal-Mart) have moved in. For practical needs, there's a **KTA Super Store** at 323 Keawe St. and another at 50 E. Puainako St.

Basically Books   This bookstore, affectionately called "the map shop," is a sanctuary for lovers of books, maps, and the environment. They have expanded their selection of Hawaii-themed gift items while they maintain the engaging selection of printed materials covering geology, history, topography, botany, mythology, and more. Get your bearings by browsing among the nautical charts, U.S. Geological Survey maps, street maps, raised relief maps, atlases, and compasses, and books on travel, natural history, music, spirituality, and much more. This bountiful source of information, specializing in Hawaii and the Pacific, will enhance any visit. 160 Kamehameha Ave. (C) **808/961-0144.**

Dan De Luz Woods   The unstoppable Dan De Luz has been turning bowls for more than 30 years. His studio, on the highway on the way to Volcano, is a larger, more stunning showcase than his previous location in Hilo. He turns koa, milo, mango, kamani, kou, sandalwood, hau, and other island woods, some very rare, into bowls, trays, and accessories of all shapes and sizes. You can find bookmarks, rice and stir-fry paddles, letter openers, and calabashes, priced from $3 to $1,000. Hwy. 11, Kurtistown. (C) **808/935-5587.**

Dragon Mama *(Finds)*   For a dreamy stop in Hilo, head for this haven of all-natural comforters, cushions, futons, meditation pillows, hemp yarns and shirts, antique kimonos and obi, tatami mats sold by the panel, and all manner of comforts in the elegantly spare Japanese esthetic. The bolts of lavish silks and pure, crisp cottons, sold by the yard, can be used for clothing or interior decorating. Dragon Mama also offers custom sewing, and you know she's good: She sewed the futon and bedding for the Dalai Lama when he visited the island a few years ago. 266 Kamehameha Ave. (C) **808/934-9081.**

Hana Hou *(Finds)*   Michele Zane-Faridi has done a superlative job of assembling, designing, and collecting objects of beauty that evoke old and new Hawaii. If you are looking for Hawaiian lauhala weaving, this is the place for mats, hats, purses, place mats, slippers, and even tissue box covers. But that's not all: Vintage shirts, china, books, women's dresses, jewelry, handbags, accessories, Mundorff prints, 1940s sheet music, and fabrics are displayed in surprising corners. The feathered leis and collectibles— such as vintage silver-and-ivory jewelry by Ming—disappear quickly. 164 Kamehameha Ave. (C) **808/935-4555.**

Hawaiian Force   Artist Craig Neff and his wife, Luana, hang their shingle at the original location of Sig Zane Designs (good karma), where they sell bold, wonderful

T-shirt dresses, mamaki tea they gather themselves, lauhala fans and trivets, surf wear, aloha shirts, and jewelry made of opihi and Niihau shells. Everything here is Hawaiian, most of it made or designed by the Neffs. Their handsome two-toned T-shirt dresses are a Hawaiian Force signature, ideal for island living, and very popular. 140 Kilauea Ave. ℂ **808/934-7171.**

Sig Zane Designs *Finds* My favorite stop in Hilo, Sig Zane Designs evokes such loyalty that people make special trips from the outer islands for this inspired line of authentic Hawaiian wear. The spirit of this place complements the high esthetic standards; everyone involved is completely immersed in Hawaiian culture and dance. The partnership of Zane and his wife, the revered hula master Nalani Kanaka'ole, is stunningly creative. The shop is awash in gleaming woods, lauhala mats, and clothing and accessories—handmade house slippers, aloha shirts, pareu, muumuu, T-shirts, and high-quality crafts. They all center on the Sig Zane fabric designs. The Sig Zane bedcovers, cushions, fabrics, clothing, and custom-ordered upholstery bring the rainforest into your room. To add to the delight, Sig and his staff take time to talk story and explain the significance of the images, or simply chat about Hilo, hula, and Hawaiian culture. 122 Kamehameha Ave. ℂ **808/935-7077.**

EDIBLES

Abundant Life Natural Foods Stock up here on healthful snacks, fresh organic produce, vitamins and supplements, bulk grains, baked goods, and the latest in health foods. There's a sound selection of natural remedies and herbal body, face, and hair products. The takeout deli makes fresh-fruit smoothies and sprout- and nutrient-rich sandwiches and salads. Seniors get a 10% discount. 292 Kamehameha Ave. ℂ **808/935-7411.**

Big Island Candies Abandon all restraint. The chocolate-dipped shortbread and macadamia nuts, not to mention the free samples, will make it very hard to be sensible. Owner Alan Ikawa has turned cookie making into a spectator sport. Large viewing windows allow you to watch the hand-dipping from huge vats of chocolate while the aroma of butter fills the room. Ikawa uses eggs straight from a nearby farm, pure butter, Hawaiian cane sugar, no preservatives, and premium chocolate. Gift boxes are carted interisland—or shipped all over the country—in staggering volumes. The Hawaiian Da Kine line is irrepressibly local: mochi crunch, fortune cookies, animal crackers, and other morsels—all dipped in chocolate. By far the best are the shortbread cookies, dipped in chocolate, peanut butter, and white chocolate. If you get thirsty, there's a juice-and-smoothie bar. Outside are picnic tables on the manicured grounds. 585 Hinano St. ℂ **800/935-5510** or **808/935-8890. www.bigislandcandies.com** for mail orders.

Hilo Farmers Market *Finds* This has grown into the state's best farmers market, embodying what I love most in Hawaii: local color, good soil and weather, the mixing of cultures, and new adventures in taste. More than 120 vendors from around the island bring their flowers, produce, and baked goods to this teeming corner of Hilo every Wednesday and Saturday from sunrise to 4pm. Because many of the vendors sell out early, go as early as you can. Expect to find a stunning assortment: fresh, homegrown oyster mushrooms from Kona; the creamy, sweet, queenly Indonesian fruit called mangosteen; warm breads, from focaccia to walnut; an array of flowers; fresh aquacultured seaweed; corn from Pahoa; Waimea strawberries; taro and taro products; foot-long, miso-flavored, and traditional Hawaiian laulau; made-from-scratch tamales; and fabulous ethnic vegetables. The selection changes by the week, but it's always reasonable, fresh, and appealing, with a good cross-section of the island's specialties. Although it's open daily, Wednesday and Saturday are the days when all the vendors are there. Kamehameha Ave. at Mamo St. ✆ 808/933-1000.

O'Keefe & Sons   You can enjoy O'Keefe's breads throughout the island, served in the best delis, coffee shops, and restaurants. But come to the source, this friendly Hilo bakery, for the full selection of artisan breads and pastries hot from the oven: Hilo nori bread, black-pepper/cilantro bread, focaccia in many flavors, cracked rye, challah, three types of sourdough, carrot-herb bread, and the classic French country loaf. Located opposite the *Hawaii Tribune Herald* building, O'Keefe's serves sandwiches, soups, and quiche for lunch. 374 Kinoole St. ✆ 808/934-9334.

HAWAII VOLCANOES NATIONAL PARK

Kilauea Kreations   This is the quilting center of Volcano, a co-op made up of local Volcano artists and crafters who make quilts, jewelry, feather leis, ceramics, baskets, and fiber arts. Gift items made by Volcano artists are also sold here, but it's the quilts and quilting materials that distinguish the shop. Starter kits are available for beginners. I also like the Hawaiian seed leis and items made of lauhala, as well as the locally made soaps and bath products and the greeting cards, picture frames, and candles. Old Volcano Rd. ✆ 808/967-8090.

Volcano Art Center   The Volcano Island's frontier spirit and raw, primal energy have spawned a close-knit community of artists, and the Volcano Art Center (VAC) is the hub of the island's arts activity. Housed in the original 1877 Volcano House, VAC is a not-for-profit art-education center that offers exhibits and shows that change monthly, as well as workshops and retail space. Marian Berger's watercolors of endangered birds, Dietrich Varez oils and block prints, Avi Kiriaty oils, Kelly Dunn and Jack Straka woods, Brad Lewis photography, Harry Wishard paintings, Ira Ono goddess masks, and Mike Riley furnishings are among the works you'll see. Of the 300 artists represented, 90% come from the Big Island. The fine crafts include baskets, jewelry, mixed-media pieces, stone and woodcarvings, and the wood diaries of Jesus Sanchez, a third-generation Vatican bookbinder who has turned his skills to the island woods. In Hawaii Volcanoes National Park. ✆ 808/967-8222.

Volcano Store   Walk up the wooden steps into a wonderland of flowers and local specialties. Tangy *lilikoi* butter (transportable, and worth a special trip) and flamboyant sprays of cymbidiums, tuberoses, dendrobiums, anthuriums, hanging plants, mixed bouquets, and calla lilies make a breathtaking assemblage in the enclosed front porch. Volcano residents are lucky to have these blooms at such prices. The flowers can also be shipped (orders are taken by phone); Marie and Ronald Onouye and their staff pack them meticulously. If mainland weather is too humid or frosty for reliable shipping, they'll let you know. Produce, stone cookies (as in hard-as-stone) from Mountain View, Hilo taro chips, bottled water (a necessity in Volcano), local *poha* (gooseberry) jam, and bowls of chile rice (a local favorite) round out the selection. Even if you're just visiting the park for the day, it's worth turning off to stop for gas here; kindly clerks give directions. At Huanani and Old Volcano Hwy. ✆ 808/967-7210.

Volcano Winery   Lift a glass of Volcano Blush or Macadamia Nut Honey and toast Pele at this boutique winery, where the local wines are made from tropical honey (no grapes) and tropical fruit blends (half-grape and half-fruit). It's open daily from 10am to 5:30pm; tastings are free. No tours yet, but plans are in the works to expand the winery to accommodate tours. You can order wines online at www.volcanowinery. com. Pii Mauna Dr., off Hwy. 11 at mile marker 30, all the way to the end. © 808/967-7479.

STUDIO VISITS

The airy Volcano studio/showroom of **Phan Barker** (© 808/985-8636), an international artist, is a mountain idyll and splendid backdrop for her art, which includes batik paintings on silk, acrylic painting on wood, oil on paper, dye on paper, and mixed-media sculptures. Her work has been exhibited in galleries and museums ranging from the Smithsonian to Saigon. In addition to studio visits (by appointment only), she also offers beginner classes in silk painting and drawing.

Adding to the vitality of the Volcano arts environment are the studio visits offered by the **Volcano Village Art Studios.** Several respected artists in various media open their studios to the public by appointment. Artists in the hui include **Ira Ono** (© 808/967-7261), who makes masks, water containers, fountains, paste-paper journals, garden vessels, and goddesses out of clay and found objects; **Pam Barton** (© 808/967-7247), who transforms vines, leaves, roots, bark, and tree sheddings into stunning fiber sculptures and vessels, from baskets to handmade paper and books; raku and jewelry artist **Zeke Israel** (© 808/965-8820); and sculptor **Randy Takaki** (© 808/985-8756), who works in wood, metal, and ceramics.

11 The Big Island After Dark

Jokes abound about neighbor-island nightlife being an oxymoron, but there are a few pockets of entertainment here, largely in the Kailua-Kona and Kohala Coast resorts. Your best bet is to check the local newspapers—*Honolulu Advertiser* and *West Hawaii Today*—for special shows, such as fundraisers, that are held at local venues. Other than that, regular entertainment in the local clubs usually consists of mellow Hawaiian music at sunset, small hula groups, or jazz trios.

Some of the island's best events are held at **Kahilu Theatre,** in Waimea (© 808/885-6017; www.kahilutheatre.org), so be on the lookout for any mention of it during your stay. Hula, the top Hawaiian music groups from all over Hawaii, drama, and all aspects of the performing arts use Kahilu as a venue.

BIG ISLAND LUAU

Kona Village Luau ✸✸✸ *(Moments)*   The longest continuously running luau on the island is still the best—a combination of an authentic Polynesian venue with a menu that works, impressive entertainment, and the spirit of old Hawaii. The feast begins with a ceremony in a sandy kiawe grove, where the pig is unearthed after a full day of cooking in a rock-heated underground oven. In the open-air dining room, next to prehistoric lagoons and tropical gardens, you'll sample a Polynesian buffet: *poisson cru,* poi, laulau (butterfish, seasoned pork, and taro leaves cooked in ti leaves), lomi salmon, squid luau (cooked taro leaves with steamed octopus and coconut milk), ahi poke, opihi (fresh limpets), coconut pudding, taro chips, sweet potatoes, chicken long rice, steamed breadfruit, and the shredded *kalua* pig. The Polynesian revue, a fast-moving, mesmerizing tour of South Pacific cultures, manages—miraculously—to avoid being clichéd or corny. The luau takes place Wednesday and Friday at 5pm. In Kona Village Resort. © 808/325-5555. www.konavillage.com. Reservations required. Part of the Full American Plan for Kona Village guests; for nonguests, $95 adults, $56 children 6–12, $30 children 2–5. AE, DC, MC, V.

Moments   An Evening under the Stars

This is one of those "unique Hawaii experiences" that you will remember long after your tan has faded. Perched from the vantage point of 3,200 feet on the slopes of the Kohala Mountains, **"An Evening at Kahua Ranch"** is a night under the stars with wonderful food, great entertainment, fun activities, and storytelling around a traditional campfire.

The evening begins when you are picked up at your hotel. As you relax in the air-conditioned van, enjoying the scenic coastline, your guide spins stories about this historic area. Arriving at the 8,500-acre working cattle ranch, you are personally greeted by the ranch owner, John Richards. When the sun starts to sink into the Pacific, beer, wine, and soft drinks are served as John talks about how cattle ranching came to Hawaii and how they manage the ranch in the 21st century.

A traditional ranch-style barbecue of sirloin steak, chicken, locally grown potatoes, Waimea corn-on-the-cob, baked beans, Big Island green salad, Kona coffee, and dessert is served shortly after sunset.

After dinner the fun and games begin: Local entertainers pull out guitars, line dancing gets going on the dance floor, and several *paniolo* (cowboy) activities take place. You can choose from learning how to rope, playing a game of horse shoes, or trying your hand at branding (a cedar shingle, yours to take home as a souvenir).

When the stars come out, there's an 8-inch telescope to gaze into the moon or search for distant planets. A campfire gets started, and the ranch's cowboys come over and start telling stories as you toast marshmallows for old-fashioned s'mores over a crackling campfire.

The entire experience from transportation to dinner and entertainment is only $89 per person (20% less if you book online). For more information call ℭ **808/987-2108** (www.EveningAtKahua.com).

You may have so much fun that you'll want to come back to see the working cattle ranch during the day. The best way to experience ranching in Hawaii is to see the ranch like the cowboys do: on an ATV. Each guest on the **ATV Adventure at Kahua Ranch** (www.kahuaranch.com/profile.html) is given a top-of-the-line 15–350 Polaris ATV; helmet, gloves, and goggles; and a safety-oriented training session. Although it is a guided tour, with a guide for every six guests, it is not a single-file/stay-on-the-road type of ATV experience. You travel across range lands and cattle pastures of the 8,500-acre ranch, from the Kehena rainforest to the Pohakuloa desert and from 2,500 to 4,500 feet. Novices have the assurance of a guide to watch over their safety, while experienced riders have the freedom to ride the rolling hills. Cost is $85 adults and $60 for children under 16.

Fairmont Orchid   "A Gathering of Kings" is the luau/Polynesian show at the Fairmont. The show, a series of traditional Polynesian dance and music, blended with modern choreography, island rhythms, and high-tech lighting and set design, tells the story of the Polynesians' journey across the Pacific to Hawaii, featuring the culture and arts of the islands of Samoa, Tahiti, New Zealand, and Hawaii. Complimenting the show, the luau also highlights the cuisine of these Pacific islands. Fairmont Orchid, One North Kohala Dr., Kohala Coast. (C) 808/329-8111. www.islandbreezeluau.com/gotk. $65 adults, $29 children 4–12, 3 and under free. AE, MC, V. Tues and Sat 5pm.

Sheraton Keauhou Bay Resort & Spa   If you are unable to get into the Kona Village Resort luau, this is my second pick. The food is fine, but you really come here for the show: Kamaha'o, The Wondrous Myths of Hawaii. Filled with lavish theatrics woven into Hawaiian chants, legends, hula, with acrobatic performing arts. This is definitely not your tired Polynesian revue. Sheraton Keauhou Bay Resort, 78-128 Ehukai St. (C) 808/930-4828. www.kaikehawaii.com. $80 adults, $40 children 5–12. AE, MC, V. Mon, Wed, and Fri 6pm. Reservations required.

MUSIC, DANCING & COMEDY IN KAILUA-KONA

A host of bars and restaurants feature dancing and live music when the sun goes down, all of them on Alii Drive in Kailua-Kona. Starting from the south end of Alii Drive, **Huggo's on the Rocks** ((C) 808/329-1493) has dancing and live music on weekends, and next door at **Huggo's Restaurant** there's jazz and blues and a piano bar. Across the street from Huggo's, **Durty Jake's Café & Bar** ((C) 808/329-7366), in the Coconut Marketplace, has live rock 'n' roll on Saturday and karaoke on weeknights. Upstairs, **Lulu's** ((C) 808/321-2633) draws a 20-something crowd with music and dancing Friday and Saturday until 1am.

Just down the street, the **Hard Rock Cafe** ((C) 808329-8866), in the **Alii Sunset Plaza,** has music most nights. Sometimes it's live, sometimes it's DJ, but it's always a happening kind of place.

If you are in the mood for a few laughs, the **Big Island Comedy Club** usually has a live performance once a week of stand-up comedians on tour. Performances are at the Royal Kona Resort; for information, call (C) **808/329-4368.**

THE KOHALA COAST RESORTS

Evening entertainment here usually takes the form of a luau or indistinctive lounge music at scenic terrace bars with scintillating sunset views. But newcomer Waikoloa Beach Marriott's **Clipper Lounge** is a bright new venue for local musicians, with live music nightly from 8:30 to 11:30pm.

The Wednesday and Friday luau at the **Kona Village Resort** (see above) is the best choice on the island. Otherwise, the resort roundup includes the **Hilton Waikoloa Village's Legends of the Pacific** ((C) 808/885-1234) Tuesday and Friday dinner show ($78 adults, $39 children 5–12, 4 and under free), and the Tuesday luau at the **Mauna Kea Beach Hotel** ((C) 808/882-7222; $86 adults, $43 children 5–12, 4 and under free).

A popular nightspot on the Kohala Coast is the **Honu Bar** ((C) 808/885-6622) at the Mauna Lani Bay Hotel, a sleek, chic place for light supper, live light jazz with dancing, gourmet desserts, fine wines, and after-dinner drinks. You can also order toothsome pastas and light suppers when most other restaurants are closing.

If you get a chance to see the **Lim Family,** don't miss them. Immensely talented in hula and song, members of the family perform in the intimate setting of the Mauna Lani Bay Hotel's **Atrium Bar** ((C) 808/885-6622) and at the Hapuna Beach Prince Hotel's open-air **Reef Lounge** ((C) 808/880-1111).

Moments   Old-Style Hawaiian Entertainment

The plaintive drone of the conch shell pierces the air, calling all to assemble. A sizzling orange sun sinks slowly toward the cobalt waters of the Pacific. In the distance, the majestic mountain, Mauna Kea, reflects the waning sun's light with a fiery red that fades to a hazy-purple and finally to an inky black as a voluptuous full moon dramatically rises over her shoulder.

It's **Twilight at Kalahuipua'a,** a monthly Hawaiian cultural celebration that includes storytelling, singing, and dancing on the oceanside, grassy lawn at Mauna Lani Bay Resort (© 808/885-6622). These full-moon events, created by Daniel Akaka, Jr., who is Mauna Lani Resort's director of cultural affairs, hark back to another time in Hawaii, when family and neighbors would gather to sing, dance, and "talk story."

Each month guests, ranging from the ultra-well-known in the world of Hawaiian entertainment to the virtually unknown local *kupuna* (elder), gather to perpetuate the traditional folk art of storytelling, with plenty of music and dance thrown in.

Twilight at Kalahuipua'a, always set on a Saturday closest to the full moon, really gets underway at least an hour before the 5:30pm start, when people from across the island and guests staying at the hotel begin arriving. They carry picnic baskets, mats, coolers, babies, and cameras. A sort of ocean-side, premusic tailgate party takes place with kamaaina (local resident) families sharing their plate lunches, sushi, and beverages with visitors, who have catered lunches, packaged sandwiches, and taro chips, in a truly old-fashioned demonstration of aloha.

The Hilton Waikoloa Beach's newly opened **Malolo Lounge** (© 808/886-1234; www.hiltonwaikoloavillage.com) has nightly live entertainment of Hawaiian music (5–8pm) and jazz (9pm–midnight).

Just beyond the resorts lies a great music spot—the **Blue Dolphin Restaurant,** 61–3616 Kawaihae Rd., Kawaihae (© 808/882-7771), where you can enjoy an eclectic mix of music (jazz, rock, swing, Hawaiian, even big-band music) Wednesday through Saturday.

HILO

Hilo's most notable events are special or annual occasions such as the **Merrie Monarch Hula Festival,** the state's largest, which continues for a week after Easter Sunday. The festivities include hula competitions from all over the world, demonstrations, and crafts fairs. A staggering spirit of pageantry takes over the entire town. Tickets are always hard to come by; call © 808/935-9168 well ahead of time, and see the "Hawaii Calendar of Events," in chapter 2, for further information.

A special new venue is the old **Palace Theater,** 38 Haili St. (© 808/934-7010; www.hilopalace.com), restored and back in action thanks to the diligent Friends of the Palace Theater. The neoclassical wonder first opened in 1925, was last restored in

1940, and has reopened for first-run movies while restoration continues. Film festivals, art movies, hula, community events, concerts (including the Slack Key Guitar Festival), and all manner of special entertainment take place here.

Special concerts are also held at the **Hawaii Naniloa Hotel's Crown Room** (© **808/ 969-3333**), the Hilo venue for performers from Oahu and the outer islands. You can always count on a great act here, whether it's the Brothers Cazimero or Willie K.

VOLCANO

Tucked into the rainforest of Volcano Village, on a 25-acre parcel of land, close to the Hawaii Volcanoes National Park, lies Jason Scott Lee's latest work of art, the **Ulua Theatre** (© **808/936-1193;** www.ulua.org). Lee is a Hawaii resident who has starred in films (*Map of the Human Heart, Dragon, Jungle Book, Rapa Nui,* and *Lilo & Stitch*) and performed on stage (the lead in *The King and I* in London). He built his dream theater on his land in Volcano.

"While I was traveling in England and Czechoslovakia, I saw small villages, hamlets really, with theaters, just lodges with candlelight and kerosene light," he said. "I wanted to bring back that sort of storytelling."

His list of upcoming productions ranges from music concerts to poetry slams, to plays. He just finished the one-man show from Los Angeles *Shadow Boxing,* with Grant Sullivan, who was nominated for an Ovation Award for Best One-Man Show.

Also new in Volcano is the **Hawaii at the Volcano Art Center's Niaulani Campus** in Volcano Village (© **808/967-8222;** www.volcanoartcenter.org). The name Niaulani, which means "brushed by the heavens" or "billowing heavens," actually describes the way the clouds and fog move through the rainforest. The new 4,400-square-foot administration building houses an intimate Great Room with a fireplace, sofas, and large windows looking out to the fern forest outside. Check local listings for the free events ranging from cultural talks to music and dance performances.

6

Maui, the Valley Isle

Maui meets all the criteria for a tropical paradise: swaying palm trees bordering perfect white-sand coves, free-falling waterfalls etching the faces of mountains, voluptuous jungles bursting with bright color and birdsong, and moonlight sparkling on calm, turquoise seas.

And everybody, it seems, knows it. Next to Waikiki, Maui is Hawaii's most popular destination, welcoming 2.5 million people each year to its sunny shores. As soon as you arrive at Kahului Airport, a huge banner will tell you that readers of *Condé Nast Traveller* voted Maui the best island *in the world*—and they've done so more than a dozen years running. *Travel + Leisure*'s readers also ranked Maui as their favorite island and top travel destination.

Maui has become *the* hip travel destination. Indeed, sometimes it feels a little too well-known—especially when you're stuck in bumper-to-bumper traffic or the wall-to-wall boat jam at Maui's popular snorkeling-diving atoll, Molokini Crater. However, the congestion here pales in comparison to big-city Honolulu; Maui is really just a casual collection of small towns. Once you move beyond the resort areas, you'll find a slower, more peaceful way of life, where car horns are used only to greet friends, posted store hours mean nothing if the surf's up, and taking time to watch the sunset is part of the daily routine.

Warm and friendly Maui has an easygoing lifestyle that's perfect for relaxing. But Maui also has an underlying energy that can nudge devout sunbathers right off the beach. People get inspired to do things they might not do otherwise, like rise before dawn to catch the sunrise over Haleakala Crater and then mount a bicycle to coast 37 miles down to sea level; head out to sea on a kayak to look for wintering humpback whales; or swim in the clear pool of a waterfall.

The island of Maui is the result of a marriage of two shield volcanoes, 10,023-foot-high Haleakala and 5,788-foot-high Puu Kukui, that spilled enough lava between them to create a valley—and inspire the island's nickname, the Valley Isle. Thanks to this unusual makeup, Maui packs a lot of nature in and around its landscape. The 727-square-mile island has two peaks more than a mile high, thousands of waterfalls, 120 miles of shoreline, and more than 80 golden-sand beaches. Its microclimates offer distinct variations on the tropical-island theme: The island's as lush as an equatorial rainforest in Hana, as dry as the Arizona desert in Makena, as hot as Mexico in Lahaina, and as cool and misty as Oregon up in Kula.

1 Orientation

ARRIVING

If you think of the island of Maui as the shape of a person's head and shoulders, you'll probably arrive near its neck, at **Kahului Airport.**

Try to fly directly to Maui—otherwise, you will be stuck with flying into Honolulu, with the likelihood of a 2-hour layover between flights. As of press time, these airlines fly directly from the mainland to Maui: **United Airlines** (© 800/241-6522; www.united.com) has nonstop service from Chicago, Los Angeles and San Francisco; **Hawaiian Airlines** (© 800/367-5320; www.hawaiianair.com) offers direct flights from Portland and Seattle; **American Airlines** (© 800/433-7300; www.aa.com) has direct service from Los Angeles, Oakland, and Phoenix; **Delta Airlines** (© 800/221-1212; www.delta.com) flies direct from Los Angeles/Atlanta and Salt Lake City; **Aloha Airlines** (© 800/367-5250 or 808/484-1111; www.alohaair.com) has direct flights from Oakland, San Diego, and Orange County, California; **Continental Airlines** (© 800/231-0856; www.continental.com) has flights from Los Angeles; **Northwest Airlines** (© 800/221-1212; www.nwa.com) travels from Seattle; **U.S. Airways/American West** (© 800/428-4322; www.usairways.com) flies from Phoenix and Las Vegas; and **American Trans Air** (© 808/435-9282; www.ata.com), which code-shares with **Southwest Airlines,** offers direct flights from Los Angeles, Oakland, and Phoenix several times a week.

Direct flights from Canada include **Air Canada** (© 888/247-2262; www.aircanada.com), with flights from Vancouver; **Harmony Airways** (© 866/868-6789; www.harmonyairways.com), with service from Calgary and Vancouver; and **West Jet** (© 888-937-8538; www.westjet.com), with flights from Vancouver.

The other major carriers fly to Honolulu, where you'll have to pick up an interisland flight to Maui. **Aloha Airlines** (© 800/367-5250 or 808/484-1111; www.alohaair.com), **Hawaiian Airlines** (© 800/367-5320 or 808/838-1555; www.hawaiianair.com), and **go!** (© 888/IFLYGO2; www.iflygo.com) offer jet service from Honolulu and the other neighbor islands.

LANDING AT KAHULUI   If there's a long wait at baggage claim, step over to the state-operated **Visitor Information Center** and pick up brochures and the latest issue of *This Week Maui,* which features great regional maps of the islands. After collecting your bags, proceed to the rental-car pickup area (at the ocean end, to your right as you stand with your back to the terminal, behind the rental-car desks) and wait for the appropriate rental-agency shuttle van to take you a half-mile away to the rental-car checkout desk. (All the major rental companies have branches at Kahului; see "Getting Around Hawaii," in chapter 2, for details on renting in Hawaii.)

If you're not renting a car, the cheapest way to get to your hotel is via **SpeediShuttle** (© 800/977/2605 or 808/661-6667; www.speedishuttle.com), which can take you between Kahului Airport and all the major resorts between 6am and 11pm daily. Rates vary, but figure on $30 for one to Wailea (one-way), $41 one-way to Kaanapali, and $56 one-way to Kapalua. Be sure to call ahead of time to arrange pickup.

If possible, avoid landing between 3 and 6pm, when Maui's working stiffs are "pau work" (finished with work) and a major traffic jam occurs.

AVOIDING KAHULUI   If you're planning to stay at any of the hotels in Kapalua or at the Kaanapali resorts, you might consider flying **Island Air** (© 800/323-3345; www.islandair.com) from Honolulu to **Kapalua–West Maui Airport.** From this airport, it's only a 10- to 15-minute drive to most hotels in West Maui, as opposed to an hour from Kahului. However, my experience with Island Air has not been stellar; they've left me stranded midroute not once, but twice.

As we went to press, go! airline (© 888/IFLYGO2; www.iflygo.com) announced the signing of a memorandum of understanding with Mokulele Airlines (a small charter

Maui

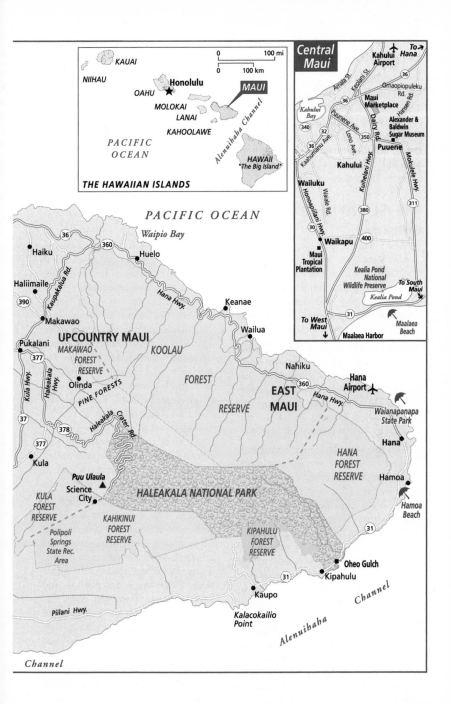

THE HAWAIIAN ISLANDS

KAUAI

NIIHAU

OAHU

Honolulu

MOLOKAI

LANAI

KAHOOLAWE

MAUI

PACIFIC OCEAN

Alenuihaha Channel

HAWAII "The Big Island"

Central Maui

To Hana

Kahului Airport

36

Amala St

Keolani St

Omaopiopuleku Rd.

Maui Marketplace

Hansen Rd.

36

Puunene Ave

Dairy Rd.

Alexander & Baldwin Sugar Museum

Kahului Bay

340

32

Lono Ave

350

Puunene

36

Kaahumanu Ave

Kahului

Mokulele Hwy.

Wailuku

Waiale Rd.

Honoapiilani Hwy.

311

30

380

Waikapu

400

Maui Tropical Plantation

Kealia Pond National Wildlife Preserve

To South Maui

To West Maui

31

Kealia Pond

Maalaea Beach

Maalaea Harbor

PACIFIC OCEAN

Waipio Bay

36

Haiku

360

Huelo

Haliimaile

Hana Hwy.

Keanae

390

Kaupakalua Rd.

Makawao

UPCOUNTRY MAUI

Wailua

Pukalani

MAKAWAO FOREST RESERVE

KOOLAU

Nahiku

Hana Airport

377

Haleakala Hwy.

Olinda

PINE FORESTS

FOREST

EAST MAUI

360

Hana Hwy.

Waianapanapa State Park

37

Haleakala

Crater Rd.

RESERVE

Hana

378

Hamoa

377

Kula

Puu Ulaula

Science City

HALEAKALA NATIONAL PARK

HANA FOREST RESERVE

Hamoa Beach

KULA FOREST RESERVE

KAHIKINU FOREST RESERVE

Polipoli Springs State Rec. Area

KIPAHULU FOREST RESERVE

31

Oheo Gulch

Kipahulu

Kaupo

Piilani Hwy.

Channel

Kalacokailio Point

Alenuihaha

Channel

service airline on the Big Island) to provide service from Honolulu to Kapalua under the name go!Express, on their new fleet of Cessna Grand Caravan 208B planes. Currently, go!Express offers the best rates and deals among Hawaii's airline carriers.

VISITOR INFORMATION

The **Maui Visitors Bureau** is at 1727 Wili Pa Loop, Wailuku, Maui, HI 96793 (© **800/525-MAUI** or 808/244-3530; fax 808/244-1337; www.visitmaui.com). To get here from the airport, go right on Highway 36 (Hana Hwy.) to Kaahumanu Avenue (Hwy. 32); follow it past Maui Community College and Wailuku War Memorial Park onto East Main Street in Wailuku. At North Market Street, turn right and then right again on Mill Street; go left on Imi Kala Street and left again onto Wili Pa Loop.

THE ISLAND IN BRIEF

Central Maui

Maui's main airport lies in this flat, windy corridor between Maui's two volcanoes, and this is where most of the island's population lives. You'll find good shopping and dining bargains here, as well as the heart of the business community and the local government.

Kahului This is "Dream City," home to thousands of former sugar-cane workers whose dream in life was to own their own home away from the sugar plantation. There's wonderful shopping here (especially at discount stores), but this is not a place to spend your vacation.

Wailuku Wailuku is like a time capsule, with its faded wooden storefronts, old plantation homes, shops straight out of the 1950s, and relaxed way of life. While most people race through on their way to see the natural beauty of **Iao Valley,** this quaint little town is worth a brief visit, if only to see a real place where real people actually appear to be working at something other than a suntan. This is the county seat, so you'll see people in suits on important missions in the tropical heat. The town has a spectacular view of Haleakala Crater, great budget restaurants, some interesting bungalow architecture, a Frank Lloyd Wright building, a wonderful historic B&B, and the always-endearing Bailey House Museum.

West Maui

This is the fabled Maui you see on postcards. Jagged peaks, green velvet valleys, a wilderness full of native species—the majestic West Maui Mountains are the epitome of earthly paradise. The beaches here are some of the islands' best. And it's no secret: This stretch of coastline along Maui's "forehead," from Kapalua to the historic port of Lahaina, is the island's most bustling resort area (with South Maui close behind). Expect a few mainland-style traffic jams.

If you want to book into a resort or condo on this coast, first consider what community you'd like to base yourself in. Starting at the southern end of West Maui and moving northward, the coastal communities look like this:

Lahaina This old seaport is a tame version of its former self, a raucous whaling town where sailors swaggered ashore in search of women and grog. Today the village teems with restaurants, T-shirt shops, and galleries, and parts of it are downright tacky, but there's still lots of real history to be found. Lahaina is a great place to stay; accommodations include a few old hotels (such as the newly restored 1901 Pioneer Inn on the harbor), quaint bed-and-breakfasts, and a handful of oceanfront condos.

Kaanapali ⟨⟩ Farther north along the West Maui coast is Hawaii's first master-planned family resort. Pricey midrise hotels line nearly 3 miles of gold-sand beach; they're linked by a landscaped parkway and a walking path along the sand. Golf greens wrap around the slope between beachfront and hillside properties. **Whalers Village**—a seaside mall with 48 shops and restaurants, plus the best little whale museum in Hawaii—and other restaurants are easy to reach on foot along the oceanfront walkway or by resort shuttle, which also serves the small West Maui airport just to the north. Shuttles also go to Lahaina (see above), 3 miles to the south, for shopping, dining, entertainment, and boat tours. Kaanapali is popular with meeting groups and families—especially those with teenagers, who like all the action.

Honokowai, Kahana & Napili In the building binge of the 1970s, condominiums sprouted along this gorgeous coastline like mushrooms after a rain. Today these older ocean-side units offer excellent bargains for astute travelers. The great location—along sandy beaches, within minutes of both the Kapalua and Kaanapali resort areas, and close enough to the goings-on in Lahaina town—makes this area an accommodations heaven for the budget-minded.

In **Honokowai** and **Mahinahina,** you'll find mostly older units that tend to be cheaper. There's not much shopping here (mostly convenience stores), but you'll have easy access to the shops and restaurants of Kaanapali.

Kahana is a little more upscale than Honokowai and Mahinahina. Most of its condos are big high-rise types, newer than those immediately to the south. You'll find a nice selection of shops and restaurants (including the

Maui branch of Roy's) in the area, and Kapalua–West Maui Airport is nearby.

Napili is a much-sought-after area for condo seekers: It's quiet; has great beaches, restaurants, and shops; and is close to Kapalua. Units are generally more expensive here (although I've found a few hidden gems at affordable prices).

Kapalua ⟨⟩⟨⟩ North beyond Kaanapali and the shopping centers of Napili and Kahana, the road starts to climb and the vista opens up to fields of golden-green pineapple and manicured golf fairways. A country lane lined with Pacific pines that leads toward the sea brings you to Kapalua. It's the very exclusive domain of two gracious—and expensive—hotels set on one of Hawaii's best white-sand beaches, next to two bays that are marine-life preserves (with fabulous surfing in winter).

Even if you don't stay here, you're welcome to come and enjoy Kapalua. Both of the fancy hotels here provide public parking and beach access. The resort also has an art school where you can learn local crafts, as well as three golf courses, historic features, swanky condos and homes (many available for vacation rental at astronomical prices), and wide-open spaces that include a rainforest preserve—all open to the general public.

South Maui

This is the hottest, sunniest, driest, most popular coastline on Maui for sun lovers—Arizona by the sea. Rain rarely falls here, and temperatures stick around 85°F (29°C) year-round. On this former scrubland from Maalaea to Makena, where cacti once grew wild and cows grazed, there are now four distinctive areas—Maalaea, Kihei, Wailea, and Makena—and a surprising amount of traffic.

Maalaea If West Maui is the island's head, Maalaea is just under the chin. This windy, oceanfront village centers on the small boat harbor (with a general store and a couple of restaurants) and the **Maui Ocean Center** 𝕲𝕲, an aquarium/ocean complex. Visitors staying here should be aware that it's almost always very windy. All the wind from the Pacific is funneled between the West Maui Mountains and Haleakala, and comes out in Maalaea.

Kihei Kihei is less a proper town than a nearly continuous series of condos and mini-malls lining South Kihei Road. This is Maui's best vacation bargain. Budget travelers swarm like sun-seeking geckos over the eight sandy beaches along this scalloped, condo-packed, 7-mile stretch of coast. Kihei is neither charming nor quaint; what it lacks in aesthetics, though, it more than makes up for in sunshine, affordability, and convenience. If you want a latte in the morning, the beach in the afternoon, and Hawaii Regional Cuisine in the evening—all at budget prices—head to Kihei.

Wailea 𝕲𝕲 Just 3 decades ago, this was wall-to-wall scrub kiawe trees, but now Wailea is a manicured oasis of multimillion-dollar resort hotels along 2 miles of palm-fringed gold coast. Wailea has warm, clear water full of tropical fish; year-round golden sunshine and clear blue skies; and hedonistic pleasure palaces on 1,500 acres of black-lava shore indented by five beautiful beaches. Amazing what a billion dollars can do.

This is the playground of the stretch-limo set. The planned resort development—practically a well-heeled town—has a shopping village, three prized golf courses of its own and three more in close range, and a tennis complex. A growing number of large homes sprawl over the upper hillside, some offering excellent bed-and-breakfast units at reasonable prices. The resorts along this fantasy coast are spectacular, to say the least. Next door to the Four Seasons, the most elegant, is the Grand Wailea Resort Hotel & Spa, a public display of ego by Tokyo mogul Takeshi Sekiguchi, who dropped $600 million in 1991 to create his own minicity. Stop in and take a look—it's so gauche you've gotta see it.

Appealing natural features include the coastal trail, a 3-mile round-trip path along the oceanfront with pleasing views everywhere you look. The trail's south end borders an extensive garden of native coastal plants, as well as the ruins of ancient lava-rock houses juxtaposed with elegant oceanfront condos. But the chief attractions, of course, are those five outstanding beaches (the best is Wailea).

Makena 𝕲𝕲 Suddenly, the road enters raw wilderness. After Wailea's overdone density, the thorny landscape is a welcome relief. Although beautiful, this is an end-of-the-road kind of place: It's a long drive from Makena to anywhere on Maui. If you're looking for an activity-filled vacation, you might want to try somewhere else, or you'll spend most of your vacation in the car. But if you want a quiet, relaxing respite, where the biggest trip of the day is from your bed to the beach, Makena is the place.

Beyond Makena, you'll discover Haleakala's last lava flow, which ran to the sea in 1790; the bay named for French explorer La Pérouse; and a chunky lava trail known as the King's Highway, which leads around Maui's empty south shore past ruins and fish camps. Puu Olai stands like Maui's Diamond Head on the shore, where a sunken crater shelters tropical fish, and empty golden-sand beaches stand at the end of dirt roads.

Upcountry Maui

After a few days at the beach, you'll probably take notice of the 10,000-foot mountain in the middle of Maui. The slopes of Haleakala ("House of the Sun") are home to cowboys, growers, and other country people who wave at you as you drive by. They're all up here enjoying the crisp air, emerald pastures, eucalyptus, and flower farms of this tropical Olympus—there's even a misty California redwood grove. You can see a thousand tropical sunsets reflected in the windows of houses old and new, strung along a road that runs like a loose hound from Makawao to Kula, where the road leads up to the crater and **Haleakala National Park** 𝆺𝅥𝆺𝅥𝆺𝅥. The rumpled, two-lane blacktop of Highway 37 narrows on the other side of Tedeschi Winery, where wine grapes and wild elk flourish on the Ulupalakua Ranch, the biggest on Maui. A stay upcountry is usually affordable and a nice contrast to the sizzling beaches and busy resorts below.

Makawao 𝆺𝅥𝆺𝅥 Until recently, this small, two-street upcountry town was little more than a post office, a gas station, a feed store, a bakery, and a restaurant/bar serving the cowboys and farmers living in the surrounding community; the hitching posts outside storefronts were really used to tie up horses. As the population of Maui started expanding in the 1970s, a health-food store sprang up, followed by boutiques, a chiropractic clinic, and a host of health-conscious restaurants. The result is an eclectic amalgam of old *paniolo* (cowboy) Hawaii and the baby-boomer trends of transplanted mainlanders. **Hui No'Eau Visual Arts Center** 𝆺𝅥, Hawaii's premier arts collective, is definitely worth a peek. The only accommodations here are reasonably priced bed-and-breakfasts, perfect for those who enjoy great views and don't mind slightly chilly nights.

Kula A feeling of pastoral remoteness prevails in this upcountry community of old flower farms, humble cottages, and new suburban ranch houses with million-dollar views that take in the ocean, the isthmus, the West Maui Mountains, and, at night, the lights that run along the gold coast like a string of pearls from Maalaea to Puu Olai. Everything flourishes at a cool 3,000 feet (bring a jacket), just below the cloud line, along a winding road on the way up to Haleakala National Park. Everyone here grows something—Maui onions, carnations, orchids, and proteas—and B&Bs cater to guests seeking cool tropic nights, panoramic views, and a rural upland escape. Here you'll find the true peace and quiet that only rural farming country can offer—yet you're still just 30 to 40 minutes away from the beach and an hour's drive from Lahaina.

East Maui

On the Road to Hana 𝆺𝅥𝆺𝅥𝆺𝅥 When old sugar towns die, they usually fade away in rust and red dirt. Not **Paia** 𝆺𝅥𝆺𝅥. The tangled spaghetti of electrical, phone, and cable wires hanging overhead symbolizes the town's ability to adapt to the times—it may look messy, but it works. Here, trendy restaurants, eclectic boutiques, and high-tech windsurf shops stand next door to a ma-and-pa grocery, a fish market, and stores that have been serving customers since plantation days. Hippies took over in the 1970s; although their macrobiotic restaurants and old-style artists' co-ops have made way for Hawaii Regional Cuisine and galleries featuring the works of renowned international artists, Paia still manages to maintain a pleasant granola vibe. The town's main attraction, though, is **Hookipa Beach Park** 𝆺𝅥𝆺𝅥, where the wind that roars through the isthmus of Maui brings windsurfers from around the world. A few B&Bs are located just outside Paia in the tiny community of **Kuau.**

Ten minutes down the road from Paia and up the hill from the Hana Highway—the connector road to the entire east side of Maui—is **Haiku.** Once a pineapple-plantation village, complete with a cannery (now a shopping complex), Haiku offers vacation rentals and B&Bs in a quiet, pastoral setting: the perfect base for those who want to get off the beaten path and experience the quieter side of Maui, but don't want to feel too removed (the beach is only 10 min. away).

About 15 to 20 minutes past Haiku is the largely unknown community of **Huelo** ⓐ. Every day, thousands of cars whiz by on the road to Hana; most barely glance at the double row of mailboxes overseen by a fading Hawaii Visitors Bureau sign. But down the gun-metal road lies a hidden Hawaii— a Hawaii of an earlier time, where Mother Nature is still sensual and wild,

where ocean waves pummel soaring lava cliffs, and where an indescribable sense of serenity prevails. Huelo isn't for everyone, but those who hunger for a place still largely untouched by "progress" should check into a B&B or vacation rental here.

Hana ⓐⓐ Set between an emerald rainforest and the blue Pacific is a village probably best defined by what it lacks: golf courses, shopping malls, and McDonald's. Except for a gas station and a bank with an ATM, you'll find little of what passes for progress here. Instead, you'll discover the simple joys of fragrant tropical flowers, the sweet taste of backyard bananas and papayas, and the easy calm and unabashed small-town aloha spirit of old Hawaii. What saved "Heavenly" Hana from the inevitable march of progress? The 52-mile **Hana Highway,** which winds around 600 curves and crosses more than 50 one-lane bridges on its way from Kahului. You can go to Hana for the day—it's 3 hours (and a half-century) from Kihei and Lahaina—but 3 days are better.

2 Getting Around

BY CAR The only way to really see Maui is by rental car; there's no island-wide public transit. All of the major car-rental firms have agencies on Maui (for a complete list as well as tips on insurance and driving rules, see "Getting Around Hawaii," in chapter 2).

Maui has only a handful of major roads, and you can expect to encounter a traffic jam or two in the major resort areas. Two of them follow the coastline around the two volcanoes that form the island, Haleakala and Puu Kukui (the West Maui Mountain); one road goes up to Haleakala's summit; one road goes to Hana; one goes to Wailea; and one goes to Lahaina. It sounds simple, right? Well, it isn't because the names of the few roads change en route. Study a map before you set out.

A traffic advisory: Be alert on the Honoapiilani Highway (Hwy. 30) en route to Lahaina because drivers who spot whales in the channel between Maui and Lanai often slam on the brakes and cause major tie-ups and accidents. Since this is the only main road connecting the west side to the rest of the island, if there is an accident, flooding, a rock slide, or any other road hazard, traffic can back up for 1 to 8 hours (no joking)—plan accordingly.

If you get into trouble on Maui's highways, look for the flashing blue strobe lights on 12-foot poles; at the base are emergency solar-powered call boxes (programmed to dial $\textcircled{C}$ 911 as soon as you pick up the handset). There are 29 emergency call boxes on the island's busiest highways and remote areas, including along the Hana and Haleakala highways and on the north end of the island in the remote community of Kahakuloa.

BY MOTORCYCLE   Feel the wind on your face and smell the salt air as you tour the island on a Harley, available for rent from **Maui Harley-Davidson,** 150 Dairy Rd., Kahului ($\textcircled{C}$ **808/877-1850;** www.mauicarsandbikes.com). Rentals start at $79 for 3 hours or $129 a day.

BY TAXI & SHUTTLE   Alii Taxi ($\textcircled{C}$ 808/661-3688) offers 24-hour service island-wide. You can also call **Kihei Taxi** ($\textcircled{C}$ **808/879-3000), Islandwide Taxi & Tours** ($\textcircled{C}$ **808/874-TAXI),** or **Sunshine Cabs of Maui** ($\textcircled{C}$ 808/879-2220) if you need a ride.

Holo Ka'a Public Transit is a public/private partnership that has convenient, economical, and air-conditioned shuttle buses. Maui Public Transit consists of seven public bus routes, all operated by Roberts Hawaii ($\textcircled{C}$ **808/871-4838;** www.mauicounty. gov/bus). These routes are funded by the County of Maui and provide service in and between various Central, South, and West Maui communities. All of the routes operate Monday through Saturday only. There is no service on Sundays. The routes go from as far south as Wailea up to as far north as Kapalua. Fares are $1 to $2.

FAST FACTS: Maui

American Express Offices are located in South Maui at the **Grand Wailea Resort** ($\textcircled{C}$ 808/875-4526), and in West Maui at the **Westin Maui** at Kaanapali Beach ($\textcircled{C}$ 808/661-7155).

Dentists Emergency dental care is available at **Kihei Dental Center,** 1847 S. Kihei Rd., Kihei ($\textcircled{C}$ 808/874-8401), or in Lahaina at **Aloha Lahaina Dentists,** 134 Luakini St. (in the Maui Medical Group Building), Lahaina ($\textcircled{C}$ 808/661-4005).

Doctors **West Maui Healthcare Center,** Whalers Village, 2435 Kaanapali Pkwy., Suite H-7 (near Leilani's on the Beach), Kaanapali ($\textcircled{C}$ 808/667-9721; fax 808/ 661-1584), is open 365 days a year until 10pm nightly; no appointment is necessary. In Kihei call **Urgent Care Maui,** 1325 S. Kihei Rd., Suite 103 (at Lipoa St., across from Star Market), Kihei ($\textcircled{C}$ 808/879-7781), which is open daily from 6am to midnight.

Emergencies Call $\textcircled{C}$ 911 for police, fire, and ambulance service. District stations are located in Lahaina ($\textcircled{C}$ 808/661-4441) and in Hana ($\textcircled{C}$ 808/248-8311).

Hospitals In Central Maui, **Maui Memorial Hospital** is at 221 Mahalani, Wailuku ($\textcircled{C}$ 808/244-9056). East Maui's **Hana Medical Center** is on Hana Highway ($\textcircled{C}$ 808/248-8924). In upcountry Maui, **Kula Hospital** is at 204 Kula Hwy., Kula ($\textcircled{C}$ 808/878-1221).

Post Office To find the nearest post office, call $\textcircled{C}$ 800/ASK-USPS. In Lahaina there are branches at the Lahaina Civic Center, 1760 Honoapiilani Hwy., and at the Lahaina Shopping Center, 132 Papalaua St. In Kahului there's a branch at 138 S. Puunene Ave.; and in Kihei there's one at 1254 S. Kihei Rd.

Weather For the current weather, call $\textcircled{C}$ 808/871-5054; for Haleakala National Park weather, call $\textcircled{C}$ 808/572-9306; for marine weather and surf and wave conditions, call $\textcircled{C}$ 808/877-3477.

3 Where to Stay

Maui has accommodations to fit every kind of vacation, from deluxe oceanfront resorts to reasonably priced condos, to historic bed-and-breakfasts. Before you book, be sure to read "The Island in Brief," earlier in this chapter, which will help you settle on a location. Also check out "Tips on Accommodations" in chapter 2.

Remember that Hawaii's 11.42% accommodations tax will be added to your final bill. Parking is free unless otherwise noted. Also, if you're booking a stay at an upscale hotel, be sure to ask if there is a "resort fee" ($12–$17 a day) tacked onto your bill.

For an even wider selection of places to stay, check out *Frommer's Maui.*

CENTRAL MAUI

If you're arriving late at night or you have an early morning flight out, the best choice near Kahului Airport is the **Maui Seaside Hotel,** 100 Kaahumanu Ave. (© **800/560-5552;** www.mauiseaside.com). The nondescript, motel-like rooms range from $140 to $180 (rates include continental breakfast). It's okay for a night, but not a place to spend your vacation.

WAILUKU
Moderate
Old Wailuku Inn at Ulupono ★★ *Finds*   This 1924 former plantation manager's home, lovingly restored by innkeepers Janice and Thomas Fairbanks, offers a genuine old Hawaii experience. The theme is Hawaii of the 1920s and 1930s, with decor, design, and landscaping to match. The spacious rooms are gorgeously outfitted with exotic ohia-wood floors, high ceilings, and traditional Hawaiian quilts. The mammoth bathrooms (some with claw-foot tubs, others with Jacuzzis) have plush towels and earth-friendly toiletries on hand. Recently, the Fairbanks added an additional building, the "Vagabond House," a modern three-room complex in the inn's lavishly landscaped backyard. The rooms are decorated in island-designer Sig Zane's floral prints with rare framed prints of indigenous Hawaiian flowers, plus plenty of modern amenities (including an ultraluxurious multihead shower). A full gourmet breakfast is served on the enclosed back lanai. You'll feel right at home lounging on the generously sized living-room sofa or watching the world go by from an old wicker chair on the lanai. The inn is located in the old historic area of Wailuku, just a few minutes' walk from the Maui County Seat Government Building, the courthouse, and a wonderful stretch of antiques shops.

2199 Kahookele St. (at High St., across from the Wailuku School), Wailuku, HI 96732. © **800/305-4899** or 808/244-5897. Fax 808/242-9600. www.mauiinn.com. 10 units. $140–$180 double. Rates include full breakfast. Extra person $20. 2-night minimum. MC, V. **Amenities:** Jacuzzi; laundry service; dry cleaning. *In room:* A/C, TV/VCR, dataport, high-speed Internet, coffeemaker.

Inexpensive
Happy Valley Hale Maui *Value*   The Kong family, owners of Nona Lani Cottages in Kihei (p. 385), have with loving care turned this old plantation home into a tiny oasis in the midst of this economically challenged area. Keep in mind these are frugal, budget accommodations—really an alternative to a youth hostel. However, it's immaculately clean, and the Kongs have made extensive renovations. The four bedrooms—each with twin beds, a small refrigerator, a dresser, and a closet—share two bathrooms. It's like staying in a family home, with a shared kitchen (no stove, but microwave, griddle, coffeemaker, and so on) and shared common room with television and comfy sofas. The front yard sports a barbecue and picnic area. The only drawback is that

Happy Valley is not exactly a resort area—public housing is just across the street. But for those on extremely tight budgets, it's a good option.

332 Alahe'e Dr., Wailuku, HI 96793. © **800/733-2688** or 808/357-3737. www.nonalanicottages.com. 4 units. $29 per bed shared room; $60 double private room. Extra person $15; $110 2-bedroom cottage for 4. 3-night minimum. MC, V. **Amenities:** Shared kitchen; coin-op washer/dryers. *In room:* Small fridge, no phone; kitchen in cottages.

WEST MAUI

In addition to the following choices, you may want to consider the oceanfront condos at **Lahaina Shores Beach Resort,** 475 Front St. (© **800/642-6284;** www.lahaina shores.com). Rates are $200 to $260 studio double, $275 to $325 one-bedroom double, and $325 to $360 one-bedroom penthouse double. Value-priced **Old Lahaina House,** P.O. Box 10355 (© **800/847-0761** or 808/667-4663; fax 808/667-5615; www.oldlahaina.com), features comfy twin- and king-bedded doubles for just $69 to $139; it's about a 2-minute walk to the water just across Front Street.

Expensive

Outrigger Aina Nalu Resort ✿   Set on 9 acres in the middle of Lahaina, this property was totally rebuilt, renovated, and remodeled in 2005. Then the units were sold off to private owners and put into a rental pool. The result is a brand-new first-class property, with all the latest appliances, new furniture, and 21st-century conveniences. The property is on a quiet side street (a rarity in Lahaina) and within walking distance of restaurants, shops, attractions, and the beach (just 3 blocks away). All of the good-size rooms, decorated in tropical-island style, are comfortable and quiet. The complex includes a sun deck and swimming pool, a barbecue, and a picnic area. The aloha-friendly staff will take the time to answer all of your questions.

660 Wainee St. (between Dickenson and Prison sts.), Lahaina, HI 96761. © **800/OUTRIGGER** or 808/667-9766. Fax 808/661-3733. www.outrigger.com. 197 units. $209–$229 studio with kitchenette; $269–$299 1-bedroom with kitchen (sleeps up to 4); $339–$359 2-bedroom with 1 bathroom and kitchen (sleeps 6); $349–$369 2-bedroom with 2 bathrooms and kitchen (sleeps 6). Extra rollaway bed $18. AE, DC, DISC, MC, V. Parking $5. **Amenities:** Outdoor pool; whirlpool; activity desk; laundry service; dry cleaning. *In room:* A/C, TV, kitchenettes (in studio), full kitchen in 1- and 2-bedroom units, fridge, coffeemaker, hair dryer, iron, safe, washer and dryer in 1- and 2-bedroom units.

The Plantation Inn ✿✿ *Finds*   Attention, romance-seeking couples: Look no further. This charming Victorian-style inn, located a couple of blocks from the water, looks like it's been here 100 years or more, but it's actually of 1990s vintage—an artful deception. The rooms are romantic to the max, tastefully done with period furniture, hardwood floors, stained glass, and ceiling fans. There are four-poster canopy beds in some rooms, brass beds and wicker in others. All units are soundproof (a plus in Lahaina) and come with a private lanai; the suites have kitchenettes. The rooms wrap around the large pool and deck. Also on the property are a pavilion lounge and an outstanding French restaurant (guests get a discount). Breakfast is served around the pool and in the elegant pavilion lounge.

174 Lahainaluna Rd. (between Wainee and Luakini sts., 1 block from Hwy. 30), Lahaina, HI 96761. © **800/433-6815** or 808/667-9225. Fax 808/667-9293. www.theplantationinn.com. 19 units, some bathrooms with shower only. $160–$225 double; suites from $245. Check the website for great package deals. Rates include full breakfast. Extra person $25. AE, DC, DISC, MC, V. **Amenities:** Acclaimed restaurant and bar (Gerard's, p. 401); large outdoor pool; Jacuzzi; concierge; activity desk; coin-op washer/dryers. *In room:* A/C, TV/VCR, kitchenettes (in suites), fridge, hair dryer, iron, safe.

Puamana   These 28 acres of town houses set right on the water are ideal for those who want to be able to retreat from the crowds and cacophony of downtown Lahaina into the serene quiet of an elegant neighborhood. Private and peaceful are apt descriptions for this complex: Each unit is a privately owned individual home, with no neighbors above or below. Most are exquisitely decorated, and all come with full kitchen, lanai, barbecue, and at least two bathrooms. Puamana was once a private estate in the 1920s, part of the sugar plantations that dominated Lahaina; the plantation manager's house has been converted into a clubhouse with an oceanfront lanai, library, card room, sauna, table-tennis tables, and office. I've found the best rates by booking through Klahani Travel (contact information below), but their office is not on-site, which has caused some problems with guests getting assistance. If you'd rather book directly with the Puamana association office, contact Puamana Community Association, 34 Puailima Place, Lahaina, HI 96761 (© **808/661-3423;** fax 808/667-0398; info@Puamana.info).

Front St. (at the extreme southern end of Lahaina, ½ mile from downtown). Reservations: c/o Klahani Travel, Lahaina Cannery Mall, 1221 Honoapiilani Hwy., Lahaina, HI 96761. © **800/669-6284** or 808/667-2712. Fax 808/661-5875. www.klahani.com. 40 units. $125–$200 1-bedroom; $150–$350 2-bedroom; $350–$500 3-bedroom. 3-night minimum. AE, DC, DISC, MC, V. **Amenities:** 3 pools (1 for adults only); tennis court; Jacuzzi; game room; activities desk; on-site laundry service. *In room:* TV, kitchen, fridge, coffeemaker, hair dryer, iron, washer/dryer (in some units).

Moderate

Best Western Pioneer Inn   This hotel is a two-story plantation-style structure with big verandas that overlook the streets of Lahaina and the harbor, which is just 50 feet away. All rooms have been totally remodeled, with vintage bathrooms and new curtains and carpets. The quietest rooms face either the garden courtyard—devoted to refined outdoor dining accompanied by live (but quiet) music—or the square-block-size banyan tree next door. I recommend room no. 31, over the banyan court, with a view of the ocean and the harbor. If you want a front-row seat for all the Front Street action, book no. 36 or 49.

658 Wharf St. (in front of Lahaina Pier), Lahaina, HI 96761. © **800/457-5457** or 808/661-3636. Fax 808/667-5708. www.pioneerinnmaui.com. 34 units. $165–$185 double; suites from $205. Extra person $15 (12 or older). AE, DC, DISC, MC, V. Parking included in room rate. **Amenities:** Restaurant (good for breakfast); bar w/live music; outdoor pool; big shopping arcade; laundry service. *In room:* A/C, TV, fridge, coffeemaker, hair dryer, iron.

Guest House 🌟🌟 *(Finds)*   This is one of Lahaina's great bed-and-breakfast deals: a charming house with more amenities than the expensive Kaanapali hotels just down the road. The roomy home features parquet floors and floor-to-ceiling windows; its swimming pool—surrounded by a deck and comfortable lounge chairs—is larger than some at high-priced condos. Every guest room has a quiet lanai and a romantic Jacuzzi. The large, fully equipped kitchen is available for guests' use. Scuba divers are welcome here (and well taken care of, with places to wash and store their gear). The Guest House also operates Trinity Tours and offers discounts on car rentals and other island activities. Tennis courts are nearby, and the nearest beach is about a block away.

1620 Ainakea Rd. (off Fleming Rd., north of Lahaina town), Lahaina, HI 96761. © **800/621-8942** or 808/661-8085. Fax 808/661-1896. www.mauiguesthouse.com. 4 units. $149 double; $129 single. Rates include full breakfast. MC, V. Take Fleming Rd. off Hwy. 30; turn left on Ainakea; it's 2 blocks down. **Amenities:** Huge outdoor pool; free watersports equipment usage; concierge; activity desk; car-rental desk; self-service washer/dryers. *In room:* A/C, TV/VCR/DVD, high-speed wireless Internet, fridge, Jacuzzi.

House of Fountains Bed & Breakfast *(Finds)*   This 7,000-square-foot contemporary home, in a quiet residential subdivision at the north end of town, is popular with visitors from around the world. This place is immaculate (hostess Daniela Atay provides daily maid service). The oversize rooms are fresh and quiet, with white ceramic-tile floors, handmade koa furniture, Hawaiian quilt bedspreads, and a Hawaiiana theme; the four downstairs rooms all open onto flower-filled private patios. In 2002, Daniela won the prestigious "Most Hawaiian Accommodation" award from the Hawaii

Lahaina & Kaanapali Accommodations & Attractions

Lahaina
Kaanapali
MAUI

ACCOMMODATIONS ■
Best Western Pioneer Inn **20**
Guest House **10**
House of Fountains
  Bed & Breakfast **11**
Hyatt Regency Maui **8**
Kaanapali Alii **7**
Kaanapali Beach Hotel **3**
Lahaina Inn **17**
Lahaina Roads **15**
Lahaina Shores Beach Resort **25**
Makai Inn **14**
Maui Eldorado Resort **2**
Old Lahaina House **23**
Outrigger Aina Nalu Resort **22**
Penny's Place **13**
The Plantation Inn **18**
Puamana **26**
Sheraton Maui **1**
The Spinnaker **16**
Wai Ola Vacation Paradise **12**
Westin Maui **6**
The Whaler **4**

ATTRACTIONS ●
Baldwin Home Museum **19**
Banyan Tree **21**
Lahaina Restoration Foundation **19**
Maluuluolele Park **24**
Master's Reading Room **19**
The Sugarcane Train **9**
Whale Center of the Pacific **5**

Golf
Parking **P**
Post Office ✉

Ahokoli Rd.

LK & P Sugar Cane Train

Kekaa Dr.

(30)

Kaanapali North
Golf Course

Whalers Village

Honoapiilani Hwy.

KAANAPALI

Kaanapali Parkway

Kaanapaii
Golf Courses
Club House

Nohea Ka Dr.

Kaanapali South
Golf Course

Hanakaoo
Beach Park

Wahikuli
Beach Park

Police

Lahania
Civic Center

Lahaina
Cannery Mall

Honoapiilani Hwy.

Kapunakea St.

Mala Wharf

Kahoma Stream

Lahainaluna
School
(1837) ■

Hilo Hattie
Lahaina Center

Train Depot
Pioneer
Sugar Mill

Lahainaluna Rd.

Papalaua St.

Lahaina
Shopping Center

LAHAINA

Front St.

Dickenson St.

Wainee St.

(30)

Luakini St.

Prison St.

Lahaina
Small Boat Harbor

505 Front St.
(Shops & Restaurants)

Shaw St.

Visitors and Convention Bureau. Guests share the fully equipped guest kitchen and barbecue area, and are welcome to curl up on the living-room sofa with a book from the library. The nearest beach is about a 5-minute drive away, and tennis courts are nearby. Around the pool is a thatch hut for weekly hula performances, an imu pit for luau, and an area that's perfect for Hawaiian weddings.

1579 Lokia St. (off Fleming Rd., north of Lahaina town), Lahaina, HI 96761. ℂ **800/789-6865** or 808/667-2121. Fax 808/667-2120. www.alohahouse.com. 6 units, shower only. $115–$160 double (2 people per room). Rates include full breakfast. AE, MC, V (additional 5% charge if using credit card). From Hwy. 30, take the Fleming Rd. exit; turn left on Ainakea; after 2 blocks, turn right on Malanai St.; go 3 blocks, and turn left onto Lokia St. **Amenities:** Outdoor pool; Jacuzzi; washer/dryers. *In room:* A/C, TV/VCR, fridge, hair dryer.

Lahaina Inn 𝕣   If you like old hotels that have genuine historic touches, you'll love this place. As in many old hotels, some of these Victorian antiques–stuffed rooms are small; if that's a problem for you, ask for a larger unit. All come with private bathrooms and lanais. The best room in the house is no. 7, which overlooks the beach, the town, and the island of Lanai. There's an excellent, though unaffiliated, restaurant in the same building (David Paul's Lahaina Grill, p. 401), and a bar downstairs.

127 Lahainaluna Rd. (near Front St.), Lahaina, HI 96761. ℂ **800/669-3444** or 808/661-0577. Fax 808/667-9480. www.lahainainn.com. 12 units, most bathrooms have shower only. $130–$170 double. AE, MC, V. Next-door parking $7 per day. **Amenities:** Bar; concierge; activity desk. *In room:* A/C, hair dryer, iron.

Lahaina Roads 𝑉𝑎𝑙𝑢𝑒   If you dream of an oceanfront condo but your budget is on the slim side, here's your place. This condominium complex offers small, reasonably priced units in an older building located in the quiet part of Lahaina, away from the noisy, crowded downtown area, overlooking the boats in the Mala Wharf roadstead (a protected place to anchor near the shore). The compact units come with full kitchens. The bedrooms face the road, while the living rooms and lanais overlook the ocean and the island of Lanai. The soundproof walls are a real plus. The building is about 35 years old but well maintained. The only drawbacks are no air-conditioning (it can be boiling hot in Lahaina) and no laundry facilities.

1403 Front St. (1 block north of Lahaina Cannery Shopping Center). Reservations: c/o Klahani Travel, Lahaina Cannery Mall, 1221 Honoapiilani Hwy., Lahaina, HI 96761. ℂ **800/669-MAUI** or 808/667-2712. Fax 808/661-5875. www.klahani.com. 17 units. $150 1-bedroom (sleeps up to 4); $225 2-bedroom (sleeps up to 6). 3-night minimum. AE, DC, DISC, MC, V. **Amenities:** Ocean-side outdoor pool. *In room:* TV, kitchen, fridge, coffeemaker, hair dryer, iron.

Wai Ola Vacation Paradise on Maui 𝕣 𝐹𝑖𝑛𝑑𝑠   Just 2 blocks from the beach, in a quiet residential development behind a tall concrete wall, lies this lovely retreat, with shade trees, sitting areas, gardens, a pool, an ocean mural, and a range of accommodations. You can book a small studio, a couple of suites inside the home, a separate honeymoon cottage, a 1-bedroom apartment, or the entire 5,000-square-foot house. Your hosts, Kim and Jim Wicker, gladly provide any information you need to make your vacation fabulous. Every unit has a welcome fruit basket when you arrive, plus coffee beans for the coffeemaker. Kim often surprises her guests with "a little something" from her kitchen, like cheesecake or heavenly brownies. You'll also find a deck, barbecue facilities, free wireless Internet, and an outdoor wet bar on the property; a great beach and tennis courts are nearby.

1565 Kuuipo St. (P.O. Box 12580), Lahaina, HI 96761. ℂ **800/492-4652** or 808/661-7901. Fax 808/661-1119. www.waiola.com. 5 units. Studio $129–$149; suite $139; 1-bedroom apt $139; honeymoon cottage $179; entire house $725–$900. Extra person $15. AE, DISC, MC, V. **Amenities:** Outdoor pool; Jacuzzi; complimentary use of watersports equipment; free self-service washer/dryers. *In room:* A/C, TV/DVD/VCR, dataport, kitchenette, fridge, coffeemaker, hair dryer, iron.

Inexpensive

Makai Inn *Value* ***Budget travelers, take note:*** Here's a small apartment complex located right on the water (okay, no white-sand beach out front, but what do you want at these eye-popping prices?). You can take a 10-minute stroll from this quiet neighborhood to the closest white-sand beach, or walk 20 minutes to the center of Lahaina town. The units are small (400 sq. ft.) but clean and have full kitchens, views of the ocean (in most units), and separate bedrooms. There are no phones or TVs, but there's a public phone by the office. In the middle of the complex is a tropical garden. I recommend the Ginger Hideaway unit with windows on two sides overlooking the ocean for just $156. Families will like the Pineapple Suite, the only two-bedroom unit (800 sq. ft.), for just $156.

1415 Front St., Lahaina, HI 96761. (℗ **808/662-3200.** Fax 808/661-9027. www.makaiinn.net. 18 units. $99–$156 double. Extra person $17. MC, V. **Amenities:** Coin-op washer/dryers. *In room:* Kitchen, no phone.

Penny's Place in Paradise *Finds* No attention to detail has been spared in this Victorian-style bed-and-breakfast, just 50 feet from the water with a fabulous view from the front porch of Molokai and Lanai. Each of the four rooms is uniquely decorated, with themes ranging from contemporary Hawaii to formal Victorian. Guests are welcome to use the balcony kitchenette (fridge, microwave, toaster, coffeemaker, and ice machine). Only the location is a problem—Penny's is located in a small island bounded by Honoapiilani Highway on one side and busy Front Street on the other. The house is soundproof, and air-conditioning in each room drowns out the noise inside. Recently Penny enclosed the outside lanai area so you can enjoy your breakfast without the highway noise.

1440 Front St., Lahaina, HI 96761. (℗ **877/431-1235** or 808/661-1068. Fax 808/667-7102. www.pennysplace.net. 4 units. $98–$147 double. Rates include continental breakfast Mon–Sat. 3-night minimum. AE, DISC, MC, V. *In room:* A/C, TV, wireless Internet, iron.

The Spinnaker *Value* Under the same management as the Makai Inn (see above), The Spinnaker is a residential complex on a side street in Lahaina town. One- and two-bedroom apartments are offered only by the week, but at extremely affordable prices. All units have full kitchens and all the comforts of home. There is a pool in the complex and a whirlpool and barbecue area. There's no maid service, but at these prices, you might not mind cleaning up on your own.

760 Wainae St., Lahaina, HI 96761. (℗ **808/870-9004.** Fax 808/661-9027. www.makaiinn.net/spinnaker. 7 units. $550 per week 1-bedroom; $650 per week 2-bedroom. 7-night minimum. MC, V. **Amenities:** Outdoor pool; whirlpool; coin-op washer/dryers. *In room:* A/C, TV, kitchen, iron.

KAANAPALI

If you stay at one of Starwood's Maui properties (Sheraton Maui Resort, Westin Maui Resort & Spa, or the Westin Kaanapali Ocean Resort Villas), there is a complimentary guest shuttle to Lahaina and back. ***Note:*** You'll find Kaanapali hotels on the "Lahaina & Kaanapali Accommodations & Attractions" map on p. 369.

Very Expensive

Hyatt Regency Maui *Kids* Spa-goers will love this resort. Hawaii's first oceanfront spa, the Spa Moana, opened here in 2000 with some 9,000 square feet of facilities, including an exercise floor with an ocean view, 11 treatment rooms, sauna and steam rooms, and a huge menu of massages, body treatments, and therapies. Book your treatment before you leave home—this place is popular.

The management has poured some $19 million in renovations into this fantasy resort, the southernmost of the Kaanapali beachfront properties. It certainly has lots of imaginative touches: a collection of exotic species (flaming pink flamingos, unhappy-looking penguins, and an assortment of loud parrots and macaws in the lobby), nine waterfalls, and an eclectic Asian and Pacific art collection. This huge place covers some 40 acres; even if you don't stay here, you might want to walk through the expansive tree-filled atrium and the parklike grounds, which contain a ½-acre outdoor pool with a 150-foot lava tube slide, a cocktail bar under the falls, a "honeymooner's cave," and a swinging rope bridge. There's even a children-only pool with its own beach and fountains.

The rooms, spread out among three towers, are pleasantly outfitted with an array of amenities and have very comfortable separate sitting areas and private lanais with eye-popping views. The latest, most comfortable bedding is now standard in every room (you will sleep like a baby in these fluffy feather beds), and you can splurge on a romantic dinner at the excellent restaurant. Two Regency Club floors have a private concierge, complimentary breakfast, sunset cocktails, and snacks.

Families will appreciate Camp Hyatt, a year-round program offering young guests a range of activities, from "Olympic Games" to a scavenger hunt. There's also a game room for kids with video games, pool, Ping-Pong, and air hockey.

200 Nohea Kai Dr., Lahaina, HI 96761. © 800/233-1234 or 808/661-1234. Fax 808/667-4498. www.maui.hyatt.com. 806 units. $385–$700 double; $580–$785 Regency Club; from $850 suite. Mandatory $15 resort fee for access to new Moana Athletic Club, daily local newspaper, local and toll-free phone calls, in-room coffee and tea, in-room safe, and 1-hr. tennis court time per day. Extra person $50 ($75 in Regency Club rooms). Children 18 and under stay free in parent's room using existing bedding. Packages available. AE, DC, DISC, MC, V. Valet parking $10, free self-parking. **Amenities:** 5 restaurants; 2 bars; ½-acre outdoor pool; 36-hole golf course; 6 tennis courts; health club w/weight room; state-of-the-art spa; Jacuzzi; watersports equipment rentals; bike rentals; year-round children's program; game room; concierge; activity desk; car-rental desk; business center; shopping arcade; salon; room service; in-room or spa massage; babysitting; coin-op washer/dryers; laundry service; dry cleaning; concierge-level rooms. *In room:* A/C, TV, dataport, high-speed Internet ($10/day), minibar, fridge, coffeemaker, hair dryer, iron, safe, 2-line phone.

Kaanapali Alii ★★ *Kids*   These luxurious oceanfront condominiums sit on 8 land-scaped acres right on Kaanapali Beach. Kaanapali Alii combines all the amenities of a luxury hotel (including a 24-hr. front desk) with the convenience of a condominium. Each of the one-bedroom (1,500 sq. ft.) and two-bedroom (1,900 sq. ft.) units is impeccably decorated and comes with all the comforts of home (fully equipped kitchen, washer/dryer, lanai, two full bathrooms) and then some (room service, daily maid service, complimentary local newspaper). The views from each unit include not only the ocean, but the island of Lanai in the distance. The beachside recreation area includes a swimming pool, a separate children's pool, a whirlpool, gas barbecue grills and picnic areas, exercise rooms, saunas, and tennis courts. You can even take yoga classes on the lawn.

50 Nohea Kai Dr., Lahaina, HI 96761. © 800/642-6284 or 808/661-3330. Fax 808/667-1145. www.kaanapali-alii. com. 264 units. $405–$675 1-bedroom for 4; $575–$830 2-bedroom for 6. AE, DC, DISC, MC, V. Free parking. **Amenities:** Poolside cafe; 2 outdoor pools; 36-hole golf course; 3 lighted tennis courts; fitness center; Jacuzzi; watersports equipment rentals; children's program; game room; concierge; activity desk; room service; in-room massage; babysitting; same-day dry cleaning. *In room:* A/C, TV, dataport, kitchen, fridge, coffeemaker, hair dryer, iron, safe, washer/dryer.

Sheraton Maui Resort ★★ *Kids*   Terrific facilities for families and fitness buffs and a premier beach location make this beautiful resort an all-around great place to stay. The grande dame of Kaanapali Beach is built into the side of a cliff on the curving,

white-sand cove next to Black Rock (a lava formation that rises 80 ft. above the beach), where there's excellent snorkeling. The resort comprises six buildings of six stories or less set in well-established tropical gardens. The lobby has been elevated to take advantage of panoramic views, and a lagoonlike pool features lava-rock waterways, wooden bridges, and an open-air whirlpool. Cliff divers swan-dive off the torch-lit lava-rock headland in a traditional sunset ceremony—a sight to see. And the views of Kaanapali Beach, with Lanai and Molokai in the distance, are some of the best around.

The new emphasis is on family appeal, with a class of rooms dedicated to those traveling with kids. Every unit is outfitted with amenities galore, right down to toothbrushes and toothpaste. The kids will love the new 32-inch flatscreen TVs. Other pluses include the Sweet Sleeper Bed, a private balcony, and a "no-hassle" check-in policy: The valet takes you and your luggage straight to your room.

The Seaside Salon and Day Spa is a tiny boutique spa offering quite an array of services; I recommend the "Beauty in a Blanket" treatment, which gives you a combination of everything from massage to a facial, with a wrap and a scrub thrown in.

2605 Kaanapali Pkwy., Lahaina, HI 96761. *C* **888/488-3535** or 808/661-0031. Fax 808/661-0458. www.sheraton-maui.com. 510 units. $470–$735 double; from $860 suite. Extra person $70. Children 17 and under stay free in parent's room using existing bedding. Resort fee of $17 plus tax for high-speed Internet access in guest rooms, self-parking, free local calls and credit card calls up to 60 minutes, free valet parking on the day of arrival. AE, DC, DISC, MC, V. Valet parking $5. **Amenities:** 2 restaurants; 2 poolside bars; indoor lounge; lagoon-style pool; 36-hole golf course; 3 tennis courts; fitness center; day spa; Jacuzzi; watersports equipment rentals; children's program; lobby and poolside concierge; car-rental desk; business center; room service; babysitting; coin-op washer/dryers; same-day laundry service and dry cleaning; nightly sunset cliff dive ceremony; beachfront snorkeling at Black Rock; weekly luau show. *In room:* A/C, TV, PlayStation, dataport, high-speed Internet, fridge, coffeemaker, hair dryer, iron, safe.

Westin Maui 🌟 *Kids* This 758-room hotel recently refurbished its Ocean Tower with new carpeting, wallpaper, furniture, and flatscreen TVs. I love the fabulous Westin beds: custom-designed, pillow-top "heavenly beds," plus a choice of five different pillows. If that doesn't give you sweet dreams, nothing will. The "aquatic playground"—an 87,000-square-foot pool area with five free-form heated pools joined by swim-through grottoes, waterfalls, and a 128-foot-long water slide—sets this resort apart from its peers along lovely Kaanapali Beach. This is the Disney World of waterpark resorts, and your kids will be in water-hog heaven. The fantasy theme extends from the estatelike grounds into the interior's public spaces, which are filled with the shrieks of tropical birds and the splash of waterfalls. The oversize architecture, requisite colonnade, and $2-million art collection make a pleasing backdrop for all the action. Most of the rooms in the two 11-story towers overlook the aquatic playground, the ocean, and the island of Lanai in the distance. The Westin no longer allows smoking in its guest rooms and suites.

2365 Kaanapali Pkwy., Lahaina, HI 96761. *C* **888/625-4949** or 808/667-2525. Fax 808/661-5764. www.westinmaui.com. 758 units. $485–$710 double; from $1,100 suite. Extra person $70. Resort fee of $18 for free local calls, use of fitness center and spa, coffee and tea, a souvenir shopping bag, a 4×6-in. photo, shuttle services to golf and tennis facilities, in-room high-speed Internet access, self-parking, and local paper. AE, DC, DISC, MC, V. Valet parking $15. **Amenities:** 5 restaurants; 3 bars; 5 free-form outdoor pools; 36-hole golf course; tennis courts; health club and spa w/aerobics, steam baths, sauna, massages, and body treatments; Jacuzzi; watersports equipment rentals; bike rental; children's program; game room; concierge; activity desk; car-rental desk; business center; shopping arcade; salon; room service; in-room and spa massage; babysitting; same-day laundry service and dry cleaning. *In room:* A/C, TV, dataport, high-speed Internet access, minibar, fridge, coffeemaker, hair dryer, iron, safe.

Expensive

Outrigger Maui Eldoradot 🌟 *Kids* These spacious condominium units—each with full kitchen, washer/dryer, and daily maid service—were built at a time when land in Kaanapali was cheap, contractors took pride in their work, and visitors expected spacious units with views from every window. You'll find it hard to believe that this was one of Kaanapali's first properties in the late 1960s; this first-class choice still looks like new. The Outrigger chain has managed to keep prices reasonable, especially in spring or fall. This is a great choice for families, with its big units, grassy areas that are perfect for running off excess energy, and a beachfront (with beach cabanas and a barbecue area) that's usually safe for swimming. Tennis courts are nearby.

2661 Kekaa Dr., Lahaina, HI 96761. ℰ 800/688-7444 or 808/661-0021. Fax 808/667-7039. www.outrigger.com. 204 units. $249–$299 studio double; $299–$349 1-bedroom (up to 4); $425–$539 2-bedroom (up to 6). Numerous packages available, including 5th night free, rental-car packages, senior rates, and more. Parking $5. AE, DC, DISC, MC, V. **Amenities:** 3 outdoor pools; 36-hole golf course; concierge/activity desk; car-rental desk; some business services; washer/dryers. *In room:* A/C, TV, dataport, kitchen, fridge, coffeemaker, hair dryer, iron, safe, washer/dryer.

The Whaler on Kaanapali Beach ⍟

In the heart of Kaanapali, right on the world-famous beach, lies this oasis of elegance, privacy, and luxury. The relaxing atmosphere strikes you as soon as you enter the open-air lobby, where light reflects off the dazzling koi in the meditative lily pond. No expense has been spared on these gorgeous accommodations; each unit has a full kitchen, washer/dryer, marble bathroom, 10-foot beamed ceilings, and blue-tiled lanai. Every unit boasts spectacular views of Kaanapali's gentle waves or the humpback peaks of the West Maui Mountains. Next door is Whalers Village, with numerous restaurants, bars, and shops; there's a barbecue area available to guests; and Kaanapali Golf Club's 36 holes are across the street.

2481 Kaanapali Pkwy. (next to Whalers Village), Lahaina, HI 96761. ℰ 866/77-Hawaii or 808/661-4861. Fax 808/661-8315. www.resortquesthawaii.com. 360 units. $255–$330 studio double; $360–$415 1-bedroom (up to 4 people); $305–$760 2-bedroom (up to 6 people). Check website for specials. AE, DC, DISC, MC, V. Parking $10 per day. **Amenities:** Outdoor pool; tennis courts; refurbished fitness room; Hinamana Salon & Spa (which offers massages, pedicures, and manicures); Jacuzzi; concierge desk; activity desk; coin-op washer/dryers. *In room:* A/C, TV/VCR/DVD, free dial-up Internet access (fee charged for wireless access), kitchen, fridge, coffeemaker, hair dryer, iron, safe, washer/dryer.

Moderate

Kaanapali Beach Hotel ⍟ 𝘝𝘢𝘭𝘶𝘦

It's older and less high-tech than its upscale neighbors, but the Kaanapali has an irresistible local style and a real Hawaiian warmth that's missing from many other Maui hotels. Three low-rise wings, bordering a fabulous stretch of beach, are set around a wide, grassy lawn with coco palms and a whale-shaped pool. The spacious, spotless motel-like rooms are done in wicker and rattan, with Hawaiian-style bedspreads and a lanai facing the courtyard and the beach. The beachfront rooms are separated from the water only by Kaanapali's landscaped walking trail.

Old Hawaii values and customs are always close at hand, and the service is some of the friendliest around. Tiki torches, hula, and Hawaiian music create a festive atmosphere every night in the expansive open courtyard. As part of the hotel's extensive Hawaiiana program, you can learn to cut pineapple, weave lauhala, even dance the real hula. The children's program is complimentary. There's also an arts-and-crafts fair 4 days a week, a morning welcome reception Monday through Saturday, and a farewell lei ceremony when you depart.

2525 Kaanapali Pkwy., Lahaina, HI 96761. ℰ 800/262-8450 or 808/661-0011. Fax 808/667-5978. www.kbhmaui. com. 430 units. $195–$335 double; from $275 suite. Extra person $30. Car, golf, bed-and-breakfast, and romance packages available, as well as senior discounts. AE, DC, DISC, MC, V. Valet parking $11, self-parking $9. **Amenities:** 2 restaurants; 1 bar (poolside; it fixes a mean piña colada); outdoor pool; 36-hole golf course nearby; access to tennis courts; watersports equipment rentals; children's program; concierge/guest services; activity desk; convenience shops; salon; babysitting; coin-op washer/dryers. *In room:* A/C, TV, fridge, coffeemaker, iron, safe.

HONOKOWAI, KAHANA & NAPILI
Expensive

Also consider **Sands of Kahana** (© **800/326-9874** or 808/669-0423; www.sands-of-kahana.com), an eight-story condo/timeshare complex that's great for families. The one- to three-bedroom units have small kitchens and washer/dryers. The property is loaded with kid-friendly extras, including a large children's pool, a playground, and a stretch of beach that's safe for swimming. Rates range from $150 to $225 for one bedroom, $265 to $325 for two bedrooms, and $325 to $365 for three bedrooms (7-night minimum).

Napili Kai Beach Resort ⋆⋆ *Finds*   This comfortable oceanfront complex lies just south of the Bay Club restaurant in Kapalua, nestled in a small white-sand cove. The one- and two-story units, with double-hipped Hawaii-style roofs, face a gold-sand beach, which is safe for swimming. Many units have a view of the Pacific, with Molokai and Lanai in the distance. Those who prefer air-conditioning should book into the Honolua Building, where you'll get a room set back from the shore around a grassy, parklike lawn and pool. Every unit (except eight hotel rooms) has a fully stocked kitchenette with full-size fridge, cook top, microwave, toaster oven, washer/dryer, and coffeemaker; some have dishwashers. On-site pluses include daily maid service; two shuffleboard courts; barbecue areas; complimentary morning coffee at the beach pagoda; free afternoon tea; weekly lei making, hula lessons, and horticultural tours; and a free weekly mai tai party. There are three nearby championship golf courses and excellent tennis courts at next-door Kapalua Resort.

5900 Honoapiilani Rd. (at the extreme north end of Napili, next to Kapalua), Lahaina, HI 96761. © **800/367-5030** or 808/669-6271. Fax 808/669-0086. www.napilikai.com. 162 units. $220–$260 hotel room double; $275–$360 studio double (sleeps 3–4); $415–$500 1-bedroom suite (sleeps up to 5); $585–$755 2-bedroom (sleeps up to 7). Packages available. AE, DISC, MC, V. **Amenities:** Restaurant; bar; 4 outdoor pools; 2 18-hole putting greens (w/free golf putters for guest use); tennis courts nearby (and complimentary use of tennis rackets); good-size fitness room; Jacuzzi; complimentary watersports equipment; free children's activities at Easter, June 15–Aug 31, and at Christmas; concierge; activity desk; babysitting; coin-op washer/dryers; laundry service; dry cleaning. *In room:* A/C (most units), TV, kitchenette (most units), fridge, coffeemaker, hair dryer, iron, safe.

Moderate

Hale Kai ⋆ *Kids*   This small, two-story condo complex is ideally located, right on the beach and next door to a county park—a great location for those traveling with kids. Shops, restaurants, and ocean activities are all within a 6-mile radius. The units are older but in excellent shape and come with well-equipped kitchens (with dishwasher, disposal, microwave, and blender) and louvered windows that open to the trade winds. Lots of guests clamor for the oceanfront pool units, but I find the park-view units cooler, and they still have ocean views (upstairs units also have cathedral ceilings). This place fills up fast, so book early.

3691 Lower Honoapiilani Rd. (in Honokowai), Lahaina, HI 96761. © **800/446-7307** or 808/669-6333. Fax 808/669-7474. www.halekai.com. 25 units. $160 1-bedroom double; $210 2-bedroom (up to 4 people); $310 3-bedroom (up to 6 people). Extra person $20. 5-night minimum. MC, V. **Amenities:** Outdoor pool; concierge; car-rental desk; coin-op washer/dryers. *In room:* TV/VCR, kitchen, fridge, coffeemaker, hair dryer, iron.

Kahana Sunset ⋆⋆ *Kids*   Lying in the crook of a sharp horseshoe curve on Lower Honoapiilani Road is this series of wooden condo units, stair-stepping down the side of a hill to a postcard-perfect white-sand beach. The unique location, nestled between the coastline and the road above, makes this a very private place to stay. In the midst of the buildings sits a grassy lawn with a small pool and Jacuzzi; down by the sandy beach are gazebos and picnic areas. The units feature full kitchens (complete with dishwashers), washer/dryers, large lanais with terrific views, and sleeper sofas. This is a great complex for families: The beach is safe for swimming, the grassy area is away from traffic, there's a barbecue area, and the units are roomy. The two-bedroom units have parking just outside.

4909 Lower Honoapiilani Hwy. (at the northern end of Kahana, almost in Napili). Book with Premier Properties, c/o P.O. Box 10219, Lahaina, HI 96761. ℂ **800/669-1488** or 808/669-8011. Fax 808/669-9170. www.kahanasunset. com. 79 units. $155–$275 1-bedroom (sleeps up to 4); $210–$440 2-bedroom (sleeps up to 6). AE, MC, V. From Hwy. 30, turn makai (toward the ocean) at the Napili Plaza (Napilihau St.), and then left on Lower Honoapiilani Rd. **Amenities:** 2 outdoor pools (1 just for children); concierge. In room: TV/VCR/DVD, kitchen, coffeemaker, iron, safe (in some units), washer/dryer.

Mauian Hotel on Napili Beach ⭐

The Mauian is perched above a beautiful ½-mile-long white-sand beach with great swimming and snorkeling; there's a pool with lounges, umbrellas, and tables on the sun deck; and the verdant grounds burst with tropical color. The rooms feature hardwood floors, Indonesian-style furniture, and big lanais with great views. Thoughtful touches include fresh flowers, plus chilled champagne for guests celebrating a special occasion. There are no phones or TVs in the rooms (this place really is about getting away from it all), but the large ohana (family) room does have a TV with a VCR and an extensive library if you need entertainment. There's complimentary coffee; phones and fax service are available in the business center. There's a barbecue area, plus great restaurants are just a 5-minute walk away, and Kapalua Resort is up the street. The nightly sunsets off the beach are spectacular.

5441 Lower Honoapiilani Rd. (in Napili), Lahaina, HI 96761. ℂ **800/367-5034** or 808/669-6205. Fax 808/669-0129. www.mauian.com. 44 units. $155–$230 double (sleeps up to 4). Extra person $10. Children under 5 stay free in parent's room. AE, DISC, MC, V. **Amenities:** Outdoor pool; golf course nearby; tennis courts nearby; activity desk; coin-op washer/dryers; shuffleboard court. In room: Kitchen, fridge, coffeemaker, no phone.

Napili Sunset (Value)

Housed in three buildings (two on the ocean and one across the street) and located just down the street from Napili Bay (see below), these clean, older, well-maintained units offer good value. At first glance, the plain two-story structures don't look like much, but the location, the bargain prices, and the friendly staff are the real hidden treasures here. In addition to daily maid service, the units all have full kitchens (with dishwashers), ceiling fans (no air-conditioning), sofa beds, small dining rooms, and small bedrooms. The beach—one of Maui's best—can get a little crowded. The studio units are all located in the building off the beach and a few steps up a slight hill; they're a good size, with a full kitchen and either a sofa bed or a Murphy bed, and they overlook the small pool and garden. The one- and two-bedroom units are all on the beach (the downstairs units have lanais that lead right to the sand). The staff makes sure each unit has the basics—paper towels, dishwasher soap, coffee filters, condiments—to get your stay off to a good start. There are restaurants within walking distance.

46 Hui Rd. (in Napili), Lahaina, HI 96761. ℂ **800/447-9229** or 808/669-8083. Fax 808/669-2730. www.napilisunset. com. 42 units. $140 studio double; $285 1-bedroom double; $435 2-bedroom (sleeps up to 4). Extra person $15. Children under 3 stay free in parent's room. 3-night minimum. MC, V. **Amenities:** Small outdoor pool; coin-op washer/dryers (free detergent supplied). In room: TV, kitchen, fridge, coffeemaker.

Noelani Condominium Resort ⭐⭐ (Kids)

This oceanfront condo is a great value, whether you stay in a studio or a three-bedroom unit (ideal for large families). Everything is first class, from the furnishings to the oceanfront location. Though it's on the water, there's no sandy beach here (despite the photos posted on their website)—but

Where to Stay & Dine in West Maui

MAUI

Mokuleia Bay

Plantation House **1**

Plantation Course

Fleming Beach Park

2 2

KAPALUA

Office Rd.

3 **4**

5

Village Course

Bay Course

Kapalua Dr.

6

7 7

Kapalua Bay

NAPILI

8

9

10

11

Lower Honoapiilani Rd.

HONOAPIILANI HIGHWAY

12

13 14

KAHANA

Hoohui Rd.

15

16

Akahele St.

Kapalua West-Maui Airport

17

18

Lower Honoapiilani Rd.

19

HONOKOWAI

20

21

30

right next door there's a sandy cove at the county park. There's good snorkeling off the cove, which is frequented by spinner dolphins and turtles in summer and humpback whales in winter. All units feature complete kitchens, entertainment centers, and spectacular views (all except the studio units also have their own washer/dryers and dishwashers). My favorites are in the Anthurium Building, where the condos have oceanfront lanais just 20 feet from the water. Frugal travelers will love the deluxe studios in the Orchid Building, with great ocean views. Guests are invited to a continental breakfast orientation on their first day and mai tai parties at night; there are also oceanfront barbecue grills for guest use.

4095 Lower Honoapiilani Rd. (in Kahana), Lahaina, HI 96761. ℂ 800/367-6030 or 808/669-8374. Fax 808/669-7904. www.noelani-condo-resort.com. 50 units. $125–$175 studio double; $167–$197 1-bedroom (sleeps up to 4); $257–$290 2-bedroom (sleeps up to 6); $317–$357 3-bedroom (sleeps up to 8). Rates include continental breakfast on 1st morning. Extra person $20. Children under 18 stay free in parent's room. Packages for honeymooners, seniors, and AAA members available. 3-night minimum. AE, MC, V. **Amenities:** 2 freshwater swimming pools (1 heated for night swimming); access to nearby health club; oceanfront Jacuzzi; concierge; activity desk; car-rental desk; coin-op washer/dryers. *In room:* TV/VCR, kitchen, fridge, coffeemaker, hair dryer, iron, safe, washer/dryer (in larger units).

Inexpensive

In addition to the choices below, consider **Hale Maui Apartment Hotel** (ℂ **808/669-6312;** fax 808/669-1302; www.maui.net/~halemaui), a wonderful tiny place run by Hans and Eva Zimmerman, whose spirit is 100% aloha. The one-bedroom suites, which run from $95 to $125 for a double, come with ceiling fans, private lanais, and complete kitchens. There's no pool, but a private path leads to a great swimming beach.

Kaleialoha This condo complex for the budget-minded has recently been upgraded, with new paint, bedspreads, and drapes in each apartment. Each one-bedroom unit has a sofa bed in the living room, which allows you to comfortably sleep four. All of the Island-style units feature fully equipped kitchens, with everything from dishwashers to washer/dryers (the only thing not supplied is beach towels; bring your own). There's great ocean swimming just off the rock wall (no sandy beach); a protective reef mows waves down and allows even timid swimmers to relax.

3785 Lower Honoapiilani Rd. (in Honokowai), Lahaina, HI 96761. ℂ 800/222-8688 or 808/669-8197. Fax 808/669-2502. www.mauicondosoceanfront.com. 21 units. High season $165–$180 1-bedroom double; low season $155–$175; plus $70 cleaning fee for less than 7-night stay. Extra person $10. Children under 2 stay free in parent's room. 3-night minimum. MC, V. **Amenities:** Outdoor pool; concierge; activity desk; coin-op washer/dryers. *In room:* TV/DVD, kitchen, fridge, coffeemaker, washer/dryer.

Maui Sands The Maui Sands was built back when property wasn't as expensive and developers took the extra time and money to surround their condos with lush landscaping. It's hard to get a unit with a bad view: All face either the ocean (with views of Lanai and Molokai) or tropical gardens blooming with brilliant heliconia, flowering hibiscus, and sweet-smelling ginger. Each roomy unit has a big lanai and a full kitchen. With two big bedrooms, plus space in the living room for a fifth person (or even a sixth), the larger units are good deals for families. There's a narrow beach out front.

Maui Resort Management, 3600 Lower Honoapiilani Rd. (in Honokowai), Lahaina, HI 96761. ℂ 800/367-5037 or 808/669-1900. Fax 808/878-8790. www.mauiresortmanagement.com. 76 units. $100–$165 1-bedroom (sleeps up to 3); $190–$220 2-bedroom (sleeps 5). 7-night minimum. MC, V. **Amenities:** Outdoor pool; coin-op washer/dryers. *In room:* A/C, TV, kitchen, fridge, coffeemaker.

Napili Bay *(Finds* One of Maui's best secret bargains is this small, two-story complex right on Napili's beautiful ½-mile white-sand beach. It's perfect for a romantic getaway:

The atmosphere is comfortable and relaxing, the ocean lulls you to sleep at night, and birdsong wakes you in the morning. The beach here is one of the best on the coast, with great swimming and snorkeling—people staying at much more expensive resorts down the road frequently come here. The studio apartments are definitely small, but they pack in everything you need to feel at home, from a full kitchen to a comfortable queen-size bed, and a roomy lanai that's great for watching the sun set over the Pacific. There's no air-conditioning, but louvered windows and ceiling fans keep the units fairly cool during the day. There are lots of restaurants and a convenience store within walking distance, and you're about 10 to 15 minutes away from Lahaina and some great golf courses.

33 Hui Dr. (off Lower Honoapiilani Hwy., in Napili). c/o Aloha Condos Hawaii, P.O. Box 396681, Keauhou, HI 96740. © 877/782-5642. www.alohacondos.com. 33 units. $120–$235 double, plus $85 cleaning fee. 5-night minimum. MC, V. **Amenities:** Coin-op washer/dryers. *In room:* TV, kitchen, fridge, coffeemaker.

KAPALUA

If you're interested in a luxurious condo or town house, consider **Kapalua Villas** (© 800/545-0018 or 808/669-8088; www.kapaluavillas.com). The palatial units dotting the oceanfront cliffs and fairways of this idyllic coast are a (relative) bargain, especially if you're traveling with a group. The one-bedroom condos go for $269 to $289; two bedrooms for $379 to $399; three bedrooms for $549 to $569, plus an $18-a-day resort fee (which covers parking; unlimited local, national and international phone calls; and high-speed Internet access). Numerous package deals (which include golf, tennis, honeymoon amenities, and car) can save you even more money.

Note: You'll find the following hotels on the "Where to Stay & Dine in West Maui" map on p. 377.

Very Expensive

Ritz-Carlton Kapalua 🦀🦀🦀 *Kids*   This Ritz is a complete universe, one of those resorts where you can happily sit by the ocean with a book for 2 whole weeks and never leave the grounds. It rises proudly on a knoll, in a singularly spectacular setting between the rainforest and the sea. During construction, the burial sites of hundreds of ancient Hawaiians were discovered in the sand, so the hotel was moved inland to avoid disrupting the graves. The setback gave the hotel a commanding view of Molokai.

The style is fancy plantation, elegant but not imposing. The public spaces are open, airy, and graceful, with plenty of tropical foliage and landscapes by artist Sarah Supplee that recall the island's not-so-long-ago agrarian past. Rooms are up to the usual Ritz standard, outfitted with marble bathrooms, private lanais, and in-room fax capability. If you can afford it, stay on the **Club Floor** 🦀🦀🦀—it offers the best amenities in the state, from French-roast coffee in the morning to a buffet at lunch, to cookies in the afternoon, to pupu and drinks at sunset. The Ritz Kids program offers a wide variety of activities, plus a weekly "Ritz Kids Night Out" program that allows parents to spend a quiet evening alone.

The Ritz has one of Maui's top restaurants, and the relaxing spa has just undergone extensive renovation and has a new menu of Hawaiian-influenced treatments. The resort's Hawaiian cultural program is one of Maui's best, with Hawaiian slack-key guitar concerts that are not to be missed, even if you are not staying here.

As we went to press, the investment partnership which recently purchased this property plans to sell 107 suites in the hotel to individual buyers, some of which will be available to vacationers and some of which will remain privately owned and occupied. The hotel announced that it would close the hotel until the end of 2007 to make some $95 million in renovations and hoped to reopen just before Christmas 2007. Contact the hotel for more details.

1 Ritz-Carlton Dr., Kapalua, HI 96761. © **800/262-8440** or 808/669-6200. Fax 808/669-1566. www.ritzcarlton.com. 548 units. $505–$675 double; $700–$875 Club Floor double; from $675 suite; from $815 Club Floor suites. Extra person $50 ($100 in Club Floor rooms). Resort fee of $18 for use of fitness center, steam room and sauna, selected wellness classes, preferred tee times, Aloha Friday festivities, cultural history tours, self-parking, resort shuttle service, signing privileges at selected restaurants and shops in the resort, tennis, morning coffee at the Lobby Lounge, use of the 9-hole putting green, tennis and basketball courts, and games of bocce ball on the lawn. Wedding/honeymoon, golf, and other packages available. AE, DC, DISC, MC, V. Valet parking $15, free self-parking. **Amenities:** 4 restaurants (including The Banyan Tree Restaurant, p. 409); 4 bars (including 1 serving drinks and light fare next to the beach); outdoor pool; access to the Kapalua Resort's 3 championship golf courses (each w/its own pro shop), golf teaching academy, and deluxe tennis complex; fitness room; spa; 2 outdoor hot tubs; watersports equipment rentals; bike rentals; children's program; game room; concierge; activity desk; car-rental desk; business center; shopping arcade; salon; room service; in-room and spa massage; babysitting; same-day laundry service and dry cleaning; concierge-level rooms (some of Hawaii's best). *In room:* A/C, TV, dataport, high-speed Internet ($14/day), coffeemaker, hair dryer, iron.

SOUTH MAUI

I recommend two booking agencies that rent a host of condominiums and vacation homes in the Kihei/Wailea/Maalaea area: **Kihei Maui Vacation** (© **800/541-6284** or 808/879-7581; www.kmvmaui.com) and **Condominium Rentals Hawaii** (© **800/367-5242** or 808/879-2778; www.crhmaui.com).

KIHEI

In addition to the choices below, consider the **ResortQuest at the Maui Banyan** (© **866/77-HAWAII** or 808/875-0004; www.resortquesthawaii.com), a condo property across the street from Kamaole Beach Park II. The large one- to three-bedroom units are very nicely done and feature full kitchens, air-conditioning, and washer/dryers. Rates start at $175 for hotel rooms, $205 for one-bedroom units, $265 for two-bedroom units, and $400 for three-bedroom/three-bathroom units; be sure to ask about packages.

Expensive

Maalaea Surf Resort 🌴   Enjoy a quiet, relaxing vacation on this well-landscaped property, with a beautiful white-sand beach right outside. Located at the quiet end of Kihei Road, this two-story complex sprawls across 5 acres of lush tropical gardens. The luxury town houses all have ocean views, big kitchens (with dishwashers), cable TV, and VCRs. Amenities include maid service (Mon–Sat), shuffleboard, barbecue grills, and discounts on tee times at nearby golf courses; restaurants and shops are within a 5-minute drive.

12 S. Kihei Rd. (at S. Kihei Rd. and Hwy. 350), Kihei, HI 96753. © **800/423-7953** or 808/879-1267. Fax 808/874-2884. www.maalaeasurfresort.com. 34 units. $250–$285 1-bedroom (sleeps up to 4 people); $330–$350 2-bedroom (sleeps up to 6); $350–$390 3-bedroom (sleeps up to 8). MC, V. **Amenities:** 2 outdoor pools; 2 tennis courts; concierge; activity desk; car-rental desk; coin-op washer/dryers. *In room:* A/C, TV/VCR/DVD, kitchen, fridge, coffeemaker, hair dryer, iron, safe.

Maui Coast Hotel 🌴🌴   This place stands out as one of the only moderately priced hotels in Kihei (which is largely full of affordable condo complexes rather than traditional hotels or resorts). That's big news—especially on Maui, where luxury abounds. The Maui Coast's Extra Value package gives you a rental car for just a few dollars more than your room rate. The other chief advantage of this hotel is its location, about a block from Kamaole Beach Park I, with plenty of bars, restaurants, and shopping

Where to Stay & Dine in South Maui

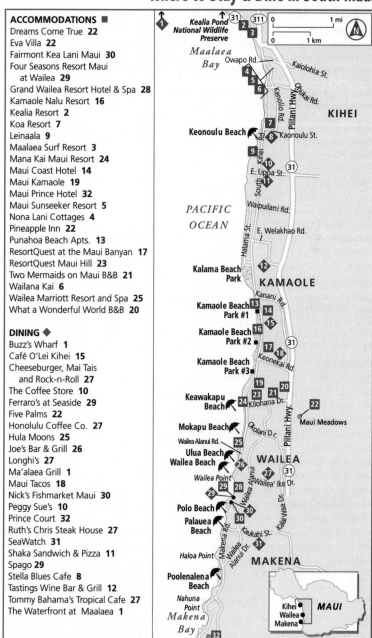

ACCOMMODATIONS ■
Dreams Come True **22**
Eva Villa **22**
Fairmont Kea Lani Maui **30**
Four Seasons Resort Maui
  at Wailea **29**
Grand Wailea Resort Hotel & Spa **28**
Kamaole Nalu Resort **16**
Kealia Resort **2**
Koa Resort **7**
Leinaala **9**
Maalaea Surf Resort **3**
Mana Kai Maui Resort **24**
Maui Coast Hotel **14**
Maui Kamaole **19**
Maui Prince Hotel **32**
Maui Sunseeker Resort **5**
Nona Lani Cottages **4**
Pineapple Inn **22**
Punahoa Beach Apts. **13**
ResortQuest at the Maui Banyan **17**
ResortQuest Maui Hill **23**
Two Mermaids on Maui B&B **21**
Wailana Kai **6**
Wailea Marriott Resort and Spa **25**
What a Wonderful World B&B **20**

DINING ◆
Buzz's Wharf **1**
Café O'Lei Kihei **15**
Cheeseburger, Mai Tais
  and Rock-n-Roll **27**
The Coffee Store **10**
Ferraro's at Seaside **29**
Five Palms **22**
Honolulu Coffee Co. **27**
Hula Moons **25**
Joe's Bar & Grill **26**
Longhi's **27**
Ma'alaea Grill **1**
Maui Tacos **18**
Nick's Fishmarket Maui **30**
Peggy Sue's **10**
Prince Court **32**
Ruth's Chris Steak House **27**
SeaWatch **31**
Shaka Sandwich & Pizza **11**
Spago **29**
Stella Blues Cafe **8**
Tastings Wine Bar & Grill **12**
Tommy Bahama's Tropical Cafe **27**
The Waterfront at Maalaea **1**

within walking distance and a golf course nearby. The rooms offer extras such as sitting areas, whirlpool tubs, ceiling fans, and private lanais.

2259 S. Kihei Rd. (1 block from Kamaole Beach Park I), Kihei, HI 96753. © **800/895-6284** or 808/874-6284. Fax 808/875-4731. www.mauicoasthotel.com. 265 units. $265 double; $295 suite; $325 1-bedroom (sleeps up to 4). Children 17 and under stay free in parent's room using existing bedding. Rollaway bed $20. Packages available. AE, DC, DISC, MC, V. **Amenities:** Restaurant; pool bar w/nightly entertainment; outdoor pool (plus children's wading pool); 2 night-lit tennis courts; fitness room; concierge; activity desk; room service; washer/dryers; laundry service; dry cleaning. *In room:* A/C, TV, fridge, coffeemaker, hair dryer, iron, safe.

ResortQuest Maui Hill ⭐ If you can't decide between the privacy of a condo and the conveniences of a hotel, try this place. Managed by the respected Aston chain, Maui Hill gives you the best of both worlds. Located on a hill above the heat of Kihei town, this large, Spanish-style resort (with stucco buildings, red-tile roofs, and arched entries) combines all the amenities and activities of a hotel—pool, hot tub, tennis courts, Hawaiiana classes, maid service, and more—with large luxury condos that have full kitchens and plenty of privacy. Nearly all units have ocean views, dishwashers, washer/dryers, queen-size sofa beds, and big lanais. Beaches, restaurants, and shops are within easy walking distance; a golf course is nearby; and barbecue grills are provided for guests' use. The management here goes out of its way to make sure your stay is perfect. *Note:* Some of the units have converted to timeshares, although no timeshare salesperson bothered me during my stay.

2881 S. Kihei Rd. (across from Kamaole Park III, between Keonekai St. and Kilohana Dr.), Kihei, HI 96753. © **866/77-HAWAII** or 808/879-6321. Fax 808/879-8945. www.resortquesthawaii.com. 140 units. $220–$325 1-bedroom apt; $275–$410 2-bedroom; $405–$525 3-bedroom. Extra person $30. AE, DC, DISC, MC, V. **Amenities:** Outdoor pool; putting green; tennis courts; Jacuzzi; concierge; activity desk; car-rental desk; coin-op washer/dryers; laundry service; dry cleaning. *In room:* A/C, TV/VCR, kitchen, fridge, coffeemaker, hair dryer, iron, safe, washer/dryer.

Moderate

Eva Villa on the Slopes of Haleakala ⭐⭐ *(Finds)* True to its name, this three-unit bed-and-breakfast is located on a ½ acre of lushly landscaped property at the top of the Maui Meadows subdivision. From the rooftop viewing lanai, guests have a spectacular view of the sunset behind Kahoolawe and Lanai, and in the distance the West Maui Mountains complete the 360-degree view. Hosts Rick and Dale Pounds have done everything to make this one of Maui's classiest vacation rentals. From the continental breakfast stocked in the unit's kitchen (fresh island fruit, juice, bread, muffins, jam, and coffee/tea) to the decor of the suites, to the heated pool, Jacuzzi, and individual barbecue facilities, this is a great place to stay. The location couldn't be better—just a few minutes' drive to Kihei's sunny beaches and Kihei and Wailea's restaurants, six golf courses, and plenty of tennis and shopping. All the units are a roomy 600 square feet. The separate cottage has a living room, full kitchen, and bedroom; the poolside studio is a one-room unit with a huge kitchen; and the poolside suite has two bedrooms and a kitchenette. You can't go wrong booking here.

815 Kumulani Dr., Kihei, HI 96753. © **800/824-6409** or 808/874-6407. Fax 808/874-6407. www.mauibnb.com. 3 units. $145–$175 double. Extra person $15. No credit cards. **Amenities:** Heated outdoor pool; Jacuzzi. *In room:* TV/DVD, CD, wireless Internet, kitchen or kitchenette, fridge, coffeemaker, washer/dryer in cottage.

Kamaole Nalu Resort This six-story condominium complex is located between two beach parks, Kamaole I and Kamaole II, and right across the street from a shopping complex. Units have fabulous ocean views, large living rooms, and private lanais; the kitchens are a bit small but come fully equipped. I recommend no. 306 for its wonderful bird's-eye view. The property also has an ocean-side pool and great barbecue facilities. Restaurants, bars, a golf course, and tennis courts are nearby; shopping is across the street. *Warning:* Because the building is right on Kihei Road, it can be noisy.

2450 S. Kihei Rd. (between Kanani and Keonekai rds., next to Kamaole Beach Park II), Kihei, HI 96753. ℂ 800/767-1497 or 808/879-1006. Fax 808/879-8693. www.kamaolenalu.com. 36 units. High season $215–$290 double; low season $150–$210 double. Extra child 5–18 years $15; adult 19 and over $25. 5-night minimum. MC, V. **Amenities:** Outdoor pool; activity desk; car-rental desk. *In room:* TV, kitchen, fridge, coffeemaker, hair dryer, iron, safe, washer/dryer.

Kealia Resort *Value*   This oceanfront property at the northern end of Kihei is well maintained and nicely furnished—and the price is excellent. As tempting as the lower-priced units may sound, don't give in: They face noisy Kihei Road and are near a major junction, so big trucks downshifting can be especially noisy at night. Instead, go for one of the oceanview units, which all have full kitchens and private lanais. The grounds face a 5-mile stretch of white-sand beach. The management goes out of its way to provide opportunities for guests to meet; social gatherings include free coffee-and-doughnut get-togethers every Friday morning and pupu parties on Wednesdays.

191 N. Kihei Rd. (north of Hwy. 31, at the Maalaea end of Kihei), Kihei, HI 96753. ℂ 800/265-0686 or 808/879-0952. Fax 808/875-1540. www.kealiaresort.com. 51 units. $100–$125 double studio; $150–$190 1-bedroom double; $215–$250 2-bedroom (sleeps up to 4). Extra person $10. Children 12 and under stay free in parent's room. 4-night minimum. MC, V. **Amenities:** Outdoor pool. *In room:* TV, kitchen, fridge, coffeemaker, hair dryer, iron, washer/dryer.

Leinaala *☆*   From Kihei Road, you can't see Leinaala amid the jumble of buildings, but this oceanfront boutique condo offers excellent accommodations at moderate prices. The building is set back from the water, with a county park—an oasis of green grass and tennis courts—in between. A golf course lies nearby. The units are compact but filled with everything you need: a full kitchen, sofa bed, and oceanview lanai. (Hideaway beds are available if you need one.)

998 S. Kihei Rd., Kihei, HI 96753. ℂ 800/822-4409 or 808/879-2235. Fax 808/874-6144. www.mauicondo.com. 24 units. $130–$160 1-bedroom double; $175–$205 2-bedroom (sleeps up to 4). 4-night minimum. No credit cards. **Amenities:** Outdoor pool; coin-op washer/dryers. *In room:* A/C, TV, kitchen, fridge, coffeemaker.

Mana Kai Maui Resort *☆ (Kids*   This eight-story complex, situated on a beautiful white-sand cove, is an unusual combination of hotel and condominium. The hotel rooms, which account for half of the total number of units, are small but nicely furnished. Families should consider the condo units, which feature full kitchens and open living rooms with sliding-glass doors that lead to small lanais overlooking the sandy beach and ocean. The building is more than 30 years old, and although some units are totally upgraded and look great, some still have that dreaded avocado green carpet, but they're all clean and comfortable. One of the best snorkeling beaches on the coast is just steps away; a golf course and tennis courts are nearby.

2960 S. Kihei Rd. (between Kilohana and Keonekai roads, at the Wailea end of Kihei), Kihei, HI 96753. ℂ 800/367-5242 or 808/879-2778. Fax 808/879-7825. www.crhmaui.com. 105 units. $132–$165 hotel room double; $212–$280 1-bedroom (sleeps up to 4); $267–$340 2-bedroom (up to 6). AE, MC, V. **Amenities:** Restaurant (Five Palms, p.441); bar; outdoor pool; concierge; coin-op washer/dryers. *In room:* A/C (hotel rooms only), TV, kitchen (condo units), fridge, coffeemaker, safe.

Maui Kamaole   You'll find this condo complex right across the street from the Kihei Public Boat Ramp and beautiful Kamaole Beach Park III, which is great for swimming, snorkeling, and beachcombing. Each roomy, fully furnished unit comes with a private lanai, two bathrooms (even in the one-bedroom units), and an all-electric kitchen. The one-bedroom units—which can comfortably accommodate four—are quite a deal, especially if you're traveling in the off season. The grounds are nicely landscaped and offer barbecues. Restaurants and bars are within walking distance; a golf course and tennis courts are also nearby.

2777 S. Kihei Rd. (between Keonekai and Kilohana rds., at the Wailea end of Kihei), Kihei, HI 96753. © **800/822-4409** or 808/874-8467. Fax 808/875-9117. www.mauikamaole.com. 62 out of the 210 units are in the rental pool. $160–$240 1-bedroom (sleeps up to 4); $210–$305 2-bedroom (sleeps up to 6). AE, MC, V. **Amenities:** 2 outdoor pools; tennis courts; Jacuzzi. *In room:* A/C, TV, kitchen, fridge, coffeemaker, iron, safe (in some units), washer/dryer.

Maui Sunseeker *Finds*

This former budget property, located just across the street from a terrific white-sand beach, has a new management team that "welcomes all but caters primarily to gay and lesbian travelers." The new owners have spiffed up the studio and one-bedroom units with custom furniture, and added air-conditioning and other amenities not usually seen at small properties (like high-speed Internet access and concierge services). The redone units have been tastefully decorated. The one-bedrooms, which have a pull-out sofa in the living room and new appliances in the kitchen, are a deal during low season. All units have private ocean-view lanais and the beach just a few steps away, and there's a gas barbecue for guests' use. The new owners of Maui Sunseeker also bought the apartment complex next door. They revamped everything and put slate in the bathrooms and new tile on the floor, bought new furniture, and repainted. The units are small, but the lanais are large and the price is right. There's also a gas barbecue available. Plus, there's a rooftop lanai where you can sit in the hot tub and enjoy great ocean views.

551 S. Kihei Rd., P.O. Box 276, Kihei, HI 96753. © **800/532-MAUI** or 808/879-1261. Fax 808/874-3877. www.maui sunseeker.com. 16 units. $120–$160 hotel room double; $120–$170 studio double; $150–$200 Jr. Suite double; $155–$205 Premium Jr. Suite double; $135–$225 1-bedroom double. Extra person $15. AE, DISC, MC, V. **Amenities:** Hot tub; concierge; coin-op washer/dryers; same-day laundry service. *In room:* A/C, TV/VCR, high-speed Internet, full kitchen (1 bedroom) or kitchenette (studio), coffeemaker, hair dryer, answering machine.

Inexpensive

Dreams Come True on Maui *Value*

This bed-and-breakfast (where "you are never just renting a room") was the dream come true for hosts Tom Croly and Denise McKinnon, who after several years of vacationing to Maui, opened this three-unit property in 2002. Centrally located in the Maui Meadows subdivision (just a few minutes' drive to golf courses, tennis courts, white-sand beaches, shopping, and restaurants in Kihei and Wailea), they offer a one-bedroom, oceanview cottage with its own (high-speed) Internet-connected computer, a gourmet kitchen, two TV sets, a washer/dryer, and wraparound decks. They also offer two rooms in the house (one with king-size bed, one with queen-size) with a TV, a private entrance, kitchenettes (plus outdoor cooking area with barbecue grill, sink, and microwave), use of washer/dryer, and lots of other amenities not usually found in B&Bs. Every guest is given personal concierge treatment, from the low-down on good snorkeling to a tour of the property. Guests are invited to use the centrally located oceanview deck and the living room in the house with its computer (with high-speed Internet connection). In the evenings, Tom shows movies on the 8-foot-wide movie screen and frequently helps guests transfer their digital images to a CD so they can go out and shoot more photos of Maui. They recently acquired a two-bedroom/two-bathroom condo, across the street from the beach, which they rent for $795 to $895 per week for one bedroom and $895 to $1,135 per week for two bedrooms.

3259 Akala Dr., Kihei, HI 96753. © **877/782-9628** or 808/879-7099. Fax 808/879-7099. www.dreamscometrueon maui.com. 3 units. $82–$109 rooms in house (3- to 4-night minimum); use of A/C additional $3/day; $125–$149 cottage (6-night minimum). MC, V. **Amenities:** Concierge service; washer/dryer. *In room:* A/C, TV/VCR, CD, kitchen or kitchenette, fridge, coffeemaker, hair dryer.

Koa Resort ☆ *(Kids)*   Located just across the street from the ocean, Koa Resort consists of five two-story wooden buildings on more than 5½ acres of landscaped grounds. The spacious, privately owned one-, two-, and three-bedroom units are decorated with care and come fully equipped, right down to the dishwasher and disposal in the kitchens. The larger condos have both showers and tubs; the smaller units have showers only. All feature large lanais, ceiling fans, and washer/dryers. For maximum peace and quiet, ask for a unit far from Kihei Road. Bars, restaurants, and a golf course are nearby.

811 S. Kihei Rd. (between Kulanihakoi St. and Namauu Place). c/o Bello Realty, P.O. Box 1776, Kihei, HI 96753. ℂ 800/541-3060 or 808/879-3328. Fax 808/875-1483. www.bellomaui.com. 54 units, some with shower only. High season $115 1-bedroom, $120–$130 2-bedroom, $180–$200 3-bedroom; low season $99 1-bedroom, $100–$110 2-bedroom, $160–$180 3-bedroom. MC, V. **Amenities:** Outdoor pool; 18-hole putting green; 2 tennis courts; Jacuzzi. *In room:* TV, kitchen, fridge, coffeemaker, iron, safe, washer/dryer.

Nona Lani Cottages ☆ *(Finds)*   Picture this: a grassy expanse dotted with eight cottages tucked among palm, fruit, and sweet-smelling flower trees, right across the street from a white-sand beach. This is one of the great hidden deals in Kihei. The cottages are tiny but probably contain everything you'll need: a small but complete kitchen, twin beds that double as couches in the living room, a separate bedroom with a queen-size bed, and a lanai with table and chairs. The cottages were renovated in 2002 with new ceramic flooring. The real attraction, however, is the garden setting next to the beach. There are no phones in the cabins, but there's a public one by the registration/check-in area. There's also a barbecue area.

If the cabins are booked, or if you want a bit more luxury, you might opt for one of the private guest rooms. These beautiful units feature plush carpet, koa bed frames, lanais, private entrances, and private bathrooms. The industrious Kong family, hosts here, also run Happy Valley Hale Maui, hostel accommodations on the other side of the island in Happy Valley, next to Wailuku.

455 S. Kihei Rd. (just south of Hwy. 31), P.O. Box 655, Kihei, HI 96753. ℂ 800/733-2688 or 808/879-2497. www.nonalanicottages.com. 11 units. $90–$100 double; $100–$120 cottage. Extra person $12–$15. 3-night minimum for rooms, 4-night minimum for cottages. No credit cards. **Amenities:** Coin-op washer/dryers. *In room:* A/C, TV, kitchen (in cottages), fridge, coffeemaker, no phone.

Pineapple Inn Maui ☆☆ *(Finds)*   Just opened at the end of 2004, this charming inn (four rooms, plus a two-bedroom cottage) is not only an exquisite find, but the prices are terrific. Located in the residential Maui Meadows area, with panoramic ocean views, this two-story inn is expertly landscaped in tropical flowers and plants, with a lily pond in the front and a giant saltwater pool and Jacuzzi overlooking the ocean. Each of the soundproof rooms (you won't hear the traffic by nearby Piilani Hwy.) is expertly decorated and contains a small kitchenette (fridge, coffeemaker, toaster, and microwave), which is stocked with juice, pastries, and drinks on your arrival. You'll also have an incredible view off your private lanai. There's also a darling two-bedroom, one-bathroom cottage (wood floors, beautiful artwork) that's landscaped for maximum privacy and has a full kitchen (even a dishwasher), separate bedrooms, phone and answering machine, and private lanai. There's a barbecue area for guests.

3170 Akala Dr., Kihei, HI 96753. ℂ 877/212-MAUI (6284) or 808/298-4403. www.pineappleinnmaui.com. 5 units. $109–$139 double; $185 cottage for 4. 3-night minimum for rooms, 6-night minimum for cottage. No credit cards. **Amenities:** Large saltwater pool; Jacuzzi; complimentary laundry facilities. *In room:* A/C, TV/VCR, wireless Internet access, kitchenette (in rooms), full kitchen (in cottage), fridge, coffeemaker, hair dryer, no phone (in rooms).

Punahoa Beach Apartments ⭐ *Value*   Book this place! I can't put it any more simply than that. The location—off noisy, traffic-ridden Kihei Road, on a quiet side street with ocean frontage—is fabulous. A grassy lawn rolls about 50 feet down to the beach, where there's great snorkeling just offshore and a popular surfing spot next door; shopping and restaurants are all within walking distance. All of the beautifully decorated units in this small, four-story building have fully equipped kitchens and lanais with great ocean views. Rooms go quickly in winter, so reserve early.

2142 Iliili Rd. (off S. Kihei Rd., 300 ft. from Kamaole Beach I), Kihei, HI 96753. (C) 800/564-4380 or 808/879-2720. Fax 808/875-9147. www.punahoabeach.com. 13 units. $116–$150 studio double; $160–$231 1-bedroom double; $198–$263 2-bedroom double; $188–$258 1-bedroom penthouse. Extra person $15. 5-night minimum. AE, MC, V. **Amenities:** Coin-op washer/dryer. *In room:* TV, kitchen, fridge, coffeemaker, iron.

Two Mermaids Maui B&B ⭐ *Finds*   The two mermaids, Juddee and Miranda, both avid scuba divers, have friendly accommodations, professionally decorated with brilliant, tropical colors and hand-painted art of the island. It sits in a quiet neighborhood just a 10-minute walk from the beach. My favorite unit is the Ocean Ohana, a large one-bedroom apartment (with option of a second connecting bedroom), complete with kitchenette, huge private deck, private entryway, and your own giant hot tub. Equally cute is the Poolside Suite, with private entry next to the outdoor pool. This studio (with the option of a separate connecting bedroom) is a living room during the day; at night it converts to a bedroom with a pull-down hide-a-bed. Continental breakfast, with some of the best homemade bread on the island, is placed on your doorstep every morning (so you can sleep in). Amenities include guitars in every unit, a range of complimentary beach equipment, microwave popcorn, and a barbecue area. Juddee is a licensed minister who can perform weddings.

2840 Umalu Place, Kihei, HI 96753. (C) 800/598-9550 or 808/874-8687. Fax 808/875-1833. www.twomermaids. com. 2 units. $95–$110 studio double ($135 with connecting bedroom); $125–$135 1-bedroom apt. ($175 with connecting 2nd bedroom). Rates include continental breakfast. 3-night minimum. No credit cards. **Amenities:** Outdoor pool; hot tub; golf nearby; tennis courts nearby; child care available; massage available. *In room:* TV, VCR/DVD (on request), kitchenette, fridge, coffeemaker, hair dryer, iron, free local phone calls.

Wailana Kai ⭐ *Value*   Bello Realty, which has searched out the best deals in Kihei, has added this renovated, two-story, 10-unit one- and two-bedroom apartment building to its collection. One-bedroom units currently start at $90—this is a deal that will not last long. Once they get a reputation, the prices most likely will go up. Located at the end of a cul-de-sac street, and just a 1-minute walk to the beach, the property was totally renovated in 2004 with two types of units: standard (perfectly acceptable and clean, with new paint, furniture, and so on) and deluxe (the ones I recommend, for only a few dollars more). All units have full kitchens and concrete soundproof walls, and the second floor has ocean views. There's also a barbecue area for guests.

34 Wailana Place. c/o Bello Realty, P.O. Box 1776, Kihei, HI 96753. (C) 800/541-3060 or 808/879-3328. Fax 808/ 875-1483. www.bellomaui.com. 10 units. $90–$110 1-bedroom; $110–$125 2-bedroom. MC, V. **Amenities:** Outdoor pool; coin-op washer/dryers. *In room:* TV/VCR, kitchen, fridge, coffeemaker, iron.

What a Wonderful World B&B ⭐ *Value*   I couldn't believe what I'd discovered here: an impeccably done B&B with a great location, excellent rates, and thought and care put into every room. Hostess Eva Tantillo not only has a full-service travel agency, but also a master's degree—along with several years of experience—in hotel management. The result? One of Maui's finest bed-and-breakfasts, centrally located in Kihei (½ mile to Kamaole II Beach Park, 5 min. from Wailea golf courses, and convenient to shopping and restaurants). Choose from one of four units: the master suite (with a barbecue grill on the lanai), a studio apartment, or two one-bedroom apartments. You're also welcome to use the communal barbecue. Eva serves a gourmet family-style breakfast (eggs Benedict, Alaskan waffles, skillet eggs with mushroom sauce, fruit blintzes, and more) on her lanai, which boasts views of white-sand beaches, the West Maui Mountains, and Haleakala.

2828 Umalu Place (off Keonakai St., near Hwy. 31), Kihei, HI 96753. *(C* 800/943-5804 or 808/879-9103. Fax 808/ 874-9352. www.amauibedandbreakfast.com. 4 units. $89–$135 suite double; $109–$135 studio double. 5% discount for cash. Rates include full breakfast. Children 11 and under stay free in parent's room. AE, MC, V. **Amenities:** Hot tub; laundry facilities. *In room:* TV, kitchen (in apartment units), fridge, coffeemaker, hair dryer, iron.

WAILEA

For a complete selection of condo units throughout Wailea and Makena, contact **Destination Resorts Hawaii** (*(C* **800/367-5246** or 808/879-1595; fax 808/874-3554; www.drhmaui.com). Its luxury units include studio doubles starting at $220, one-bedroom doubles from $235, two-bedrooms from $270, and three-bedrooms from $380. Those rates include free long-distance calls, high-speed Internet access, and parking; one property, the Polo Beach Club, is completely nonsmoking (indoors and out). Children under 12 stay free; minimum stays vary by property.

Note: You'll find the following hotels on the "Where to Stay & Dine in South Maui" map on p. 381.

Very Expensive

The Fairmont Kea Lani Maui 𝕂𝕂𝕂   At first glance, this blinding white complex of arches and turrets may look a bit out of place in tropical Hawaii (it's a close architectural cousin of Las Hadas, the Arabian Nights fantasy resort in Manzanillo, Mexico). But once you enter the flower-filled lobby and see the big blue Pacific outside, there's no doubt you're in Hawaii.

It's not cheap, but for the price of a hotel room in other luxury resorts, you get an entire suite—plus a few extras. Each unit in the all-suite hotel has a kitchenette (with microwave and coffeemaker), a living room with entertainment center and sofa bed (great if you have the kids in tow), a marble wet bar, an oversize marble bathroom with separate shower big enough for a party, a spacious bedroom, and a large lanai that overlooks the pools, lawns, and white-sand beach. Plus complimentary yoga classes, Hawaiian cultural canoe experience, and free transportation within the Wailea resort area.

The small boutique spa offers the latest in body work in intimate, relaxing surroundings—not to be missed, even if you're staying elsewhere.

The rich and famous stay in the villas—2,000-square-foot, two- and three-bedroom fantasy beach bungalows, each with its own plunge pool and gourmet kitchen.

4100 Wailea Alanui Dr., Wailea, HI 96753. *(C* 800/659-4100 or 808/875-4100. Fax 808/875-1200. www.fairmont. com/kealani. 450 units. $475–$1,000 suite (sleeps up to 4); from $1,900 villa. Valet parking $15, complimentary self-parking. AE, DC, DISC, MC, V. **Amenities:** 4 restaurants (including Nick's Fishmarket Maui, p.414), plus gourmet bakery and deli; 3 bars (w/sunset cocktails and entertainment at the Caffè Ciao Restaurant); 2 large swimming lagoons connected by a 140-ft. water slide and swim-up bar, plus an adult pool; closer by is Wailea Golf Club's 3 18-hole championship golf courses, as well as the nearby Makena and Elleair golf courses; use of Wailea Tennis Center's 11 courts (3 lit for night play and a pro shop); fine 24-hr. fitness center; excellent full-service spa; 2 whirlpools; water-sports equipment rentals; year-round children's program; seasonal (summer and holidays) game room; concierge; activity desk; business center; shopping arcade; full-service salon; 24-hr. room service; in-room and spa massage; babysitting; complimentary self-service laundry; same-day laundry service and dry cleaning. *In room:* A/C, TV/DVD/VHS, CD, dataport, high-speed Internet ($14/day), kitchenette, fridge, coffeemaker, hair dryer, iron, safe, microwave.

Four Seasons Resort Maui at Wailea ★★★ *Kids*   If money's no object, this is the place to spend it. It's hard to beat this modern version of a Hawaiian palace by the sea, with a relaxing, casual atmosphere. Although it sits on a glorious beach between two other hotels, you won't feel like you're on resort row: The Four Seasons inhabits its own world, thanks to an open courtyard of pools and gardens. Amenities are first-rate here, including outstanding restaurants and an excellent spa. This may be the most kid-friendly resort on the island. There's a complete activities program for kids (complimentary, of course); other perks for *keiki* include milk and cookies on arrival, kids' menus in all restaurants, free infant gear (cribs, strollers, and even toilet-seat locks), and a game room (video games, foosball, and more).

The spacious (about 600-sq.-ft.) rooms feature furnished lanais (nearly all with ocean views) that are great for watching whales in winter and sunsets year-round. The grand bathrooms contain deep marble tubs and showers for two.

Service is attentive but not cloying. At the pool, guests lounge in casbahlike tents, pampered with iced Evian and chilled towels. And you'll never see a housekeeping cart in the hall: The cleaning staff works in teams, so they're as unobtrusive as possible and in and out of your room in minutes.

The fabulous spa offers facial treatments and products by Kate Somerville Skin Health Experts, a pioneer in the fields of paramedical esthetics and medi-based skincare (with a list of prominent clients from Los Angeles including Felicity Huffman, Paris Hilton, Jessica Alba, Eva Mendes, and others). The spa also has an incredible menu of treatment ranging from traditional Hawaiian to craniosacral, to ayurvedic massage offered in 13 treatment rooms and three ocean-side *hales*.

The ritzy neighborhood surrounding the hotel is home to great restaurants and shopping, the Wailea Tennis Center (known as Wimbledon West), and six golf courses—not to mention that great beach, with gentle waves and islands framing the view on either side.

3900 Wailea Alanui Dr., Wailea, HI 96753. © **800/334-MAUI** or 808/874-8000. Fax 808/874-2222. www.four seasons.com/maui. 380 units. $425–$880 double; $960–$1,060 club floor; from $790 suite. Packages available. Extra person $100 ($250 in Club Floor rooms). Children under 18 stay free in parent's room. Valet parking $12. AE, DC, MC, V. **Amenities:** 3 restaurants (including Spago, p. 414); 3 bars (w/nightly entertainment); 3 fabulous outdoor pools; putting green; use of Wailea Golf Club's 3 18-hole championship golf courses, as well as the nearby Makena and Elleair golf courses; 2 on-site tennis courts (lit for night play); use of Wailea Tennis Center's 11 courts (3 lit for night play); health club featuring outdoor cardiovascular equipment (w/individual television/videoplayers); excellent spa; 2 whirlpools (1 for adults only); beach pavilion w/watersports gear rentals and 1-hr. free use of snorkel equipment; complimentary use of bicycles; fabulous year-round kids' program; one of Maui's best concierge desks; activity desk; car-rental desk; business center; shopping arcade; salon; room service; in-room spa, or ocean-side massage; babysitting; same-day laundry service and dry cleaning; concierge-level rooms. *In room:* A/C, TV, dataport, high-speed Internet ($10/day), minibar, fridge, coffeemaker, hair dryer, iron, safe.

Grand Wailea Resort Hotel & Spa ★★★   Spa aficionados, take note: Hawaii's largest (50,000 sq. ft.) and most elaborate spa is located here, with every kind of body treatment you can imagine. Treatments include use of the numerous baths, hot tubs, mineral pools, saunas, steam rooms, and other relaxation amenities in the his-and-her spa area.

Built at the pinnacle of Hawaii's brief fling with fantasy megaresorts, the Grand Wailea is extremely popular with families, incentive groups, and conventions; it's the grand prize in Hawaii vacation contests and the dream of many honeymooners. It has a Japanese restaurant decorated with real rocks hewn from the slopes of Mount Fuji;

10,000 tropical plants in the lobby; an intricate pool system with slides, waterfalls, rapids, and a water-powered elevator to take you up to the top; a restaurant in a man-made tide pool; a floating New England–style wedding chapel; and nothing but oceanview, amenity-filled rooms. It's all crowned with a $30-million collection of original art, much of it created expressly for the hotel by Hawaii artists and sculptors. Though minimalists may be put off, there's no denying that the Grand Wailea is plush, professional, and pampering, with all the diversions you could imagine. Oh, and did I mention the fantastic beach out front?

All the rooms and suites are now nonsmoking. All the former smoking rooms have undergone a thorough cleaning and have been deodorized. Smoking is limited to the private lanais outside the rooms.

3850 Wailea Alanui Dr., Wailea, HI 96753. (C) **800/888-6100** or 808/875-1234. Fax 808/874-2442. www.grand wailea.com. 780 units. $575–$950 double; from $1,800 suite; concierge (Na Pua) tower from $1,200. Resort fee $20 for lei greeting on arrival, welcome drink, local calls, coffee in room, use of spa, pools, admission to scuba-diving clinics and water aerobics, art and garden tours, nightly turndown service, high-speed Internet access, self-parking, and shuttle service to Wailea area. Extra person $50 ($100 in Na Pua Tower). AE, DC, DISC, MC, V. **Amenities:** 6 restaurants; 7 bars (including a nightclub w/laser-light shows); 2,000-ft.-long Activity Pool, featuring a swim/ride through mountains and grottoes; use of Wailea Golf Club's 3 18-hole championship golf courses, as well as the nearby Makena and Elleair golf courses; use of Wailea Tennis Center's 11 courts (3 lit for night play and a pro shop); complete fitness center; Hawaii's largest spa; Jacuzzi; watersports equipment rentals; children's program; game room; concierge; activity desk; car-rental desk; business center; shopping arcade; salon; room service; in-room and spa massage; babysitting; same-day laundry service and dry cleaning; concierge-level rooms; dive and windsurf lessons. *In room:* A/C, TV, dataport, high-speed Internet, kitchenette, minibar, fridge ($25 per stay fee), coffeemaker, hair dryer, iron, safe.

Wailea Beach Marriott Resort & Spa ⭐⭐ This classic, open-air, 1970s-style hotel in a tropical garden by the sea gives you a sense of what Maui was like before the big resort boom. It was the first resort built in Wailea (in 1976), and it remains the most Hawaiian of them all. Airy and comfortable, with touches of Hawaiian art throughout and a terrific aquarium that stretches forever behind the front desk, it just feels right.

What's truly special about this hotel is how it fits into its environment without overwhelming it. Eight buildings, all low-rise except for an eight-story tower, are spread along 22 gracious acres of lawns and gardens spiked by coco palms, with lots of open space and a half-mile of oceanfront property on a point between Wailea and Ulua beaches. The vast, parklike expanses are a luxury on this now-crowded coast.

The entire hotel (all rooms, the grounds, the restaurants, the spa, pools, and so on) has undergone a $60-million renovation, so it looks like it was just built. The small Mandara Spa offers a large list of treatments, from relaxing massages to aroma wraps to rejuvenating facials in a very Zen atmosphere. My only criticism is the lack (at this time) of a shower facility in the spa.

3700 Wailea Alanui Dr., Wailea, HI 96753. (C) **800/367-2960** or 808/879-1922. Fax 808/874-8331. www.wailea marriott.com. 545 units. $435–$800 single/double; from $850 suite. Extra person $40. Packages available. Resort fee $15 plus tax per night for self parking, high-speed Internet access, local phone calls, daily sunset appetizer, luau and snorkel gear rental discounts, and free kids' meals with purchase of adult entree. AE, DC, DISC, MC, V. **Amenities:** 2 restaurants; 2 bars; outdoor swimming pools; use of Wailea Golf Club's 3 18-hole championship golf courses; use of Wailea Tennis Center's 11 courts (3 lit for night play) and a pro shop; fitness center; full-service Mandara Spa & Salon w/steam rooms and whirlpools; watersports equipment rentals; children's program (plus kids-only pool and recreation center); concierge; activities desk; business center; shopping arcade; salon; room service; in-room or outdoor massages; babysitting; same-day laundry service and dry cleaning. *In room:* A/C, flatscreen TV, 4-outlet technology console, coffeemaker, hair dryer, iron, safe, ergonomic desk and chair, wet bar.

MAKENA

Maui Prince Hotel 🎄🎄 If you're looking for a vacation in a beautiful, tranquil spot with a golden-sand beach, here's your place. But if you plan to tour Maui, you might try another hotel. The Maui Prince is at the end of the road, far, far away from anything else on the island, so sightseeing in other areas would require a lot of driving.

When you first see the stark-white hotel, it looks like a high-rise motel stuck in the woods—but only from the outside. Inside you'll discover an atrium garden with a koi-filled waterfall stream, an ocean view from every room, and a simplicity to the furnishings that some find stark but others find blissfully clutter-free. Rooms are small but come with private lanais with great views.

5400 Makena Alanui, Makena, HI 96753. © **800/321-6284** or 808/874-1111. Fax 808/879-8763. www.mauiprince hotel.com. 310 units. $355–$525 double; from $700 suite. Extra person $60. Packages available. AE, DC, MC, V. **Amenities:** 4 restaurants (including Prince Court, p. 415); 2 bars w/local Hawaiian music nightly; 2 outdoor pools (adults' and children's); 36-hole golf course (designed by Robert Trent Jones, Jr.); 6 Plexipave tennis courts (2 lit for night play); fitness room; Jacuzzi; watersports equipment rentals; children's program; concierge; activity desk; shopping arcade; salon; room service; in-room massage; babysitting; same-day laundry service and dry cleaning. *In room:* A/C, TV, dataport, fridge, hair dryer, iron, safe.

UPCOUNTRY MAUI

You'll find it cool and peaceful up here; be sure to bring a sweater.

MAKAWAO & OLINDA

Here you'll be (relatively) close to Haleakala National Park; Makawao and Olinda are approximately 90 minutes from the entrance to the park at the 7,000-foot level (from there it's another 3,000 ft. and 30–45 min. to get to the top). Accommodations in Kula are the only ones closer to the park.

Banyan Tree House 🎄 *(Finds* Huge monkeypod trees (complete with swing and hammock) extend their branches over this 2½-acre property like a giant green canopy. The restored 1920s plantation manager's house is decorated with Hawaiian furniture from the 1930s. The house can accommodate a big family or a group of friends; it has three spacious bedrooms and three private, marble-tiled bathrooms. A fireplace stands at one end of the huge living room, a large lanai runs the entire length of the house, and the hardwood floors shine throughout. The four smaller guest cottages have been totally renovated and also feature hardwood floors and marble bathrooms. Floor plans vary; one has one queen-size bed, the others have two beds (a mix of queen-size, doubles, and twins).

The quiet neighborhood and old Hawaii ambience give this place a comfortable, easygoing atmosphere. Restaurants and shops are just minutes away in Makawao, and the beach is a 15-minute drive away—but this place is so relaxing that you may find yourself wanting to do nothing but lie in a hammock and watch the clouds float by.

3265 Baldwin Ave. (next to Veteran's Cemetery, less than a mile below Makawao), Makawao, HI 96768. © **808/572-9021.** Fax 808/573-5072. www.hawaii-mauirentals.com. 5 units. $155 rooms in house double; $150–$184 cottage for 2. Extra person $20. Children age 12 and under stay in parent's room for $10. 3-night minimum for house. No credit cards. **Amenities:** Outdoor pool; Jacuzzi; babysitting; small charge for washer/dryer. *In room:* TV (some cottages), kitchen or kitchenette, fridge, coffeemaker.

Olinda Country Cottages & Inn 🎄🎄 *(Finds* This charming property is set on the slopes of Haleakala in the crisp, clean air of Olinda, on an 8½-acre farm dotted with surreal protea plants and surrounded by 35,000 acres of ranchlands (with miles of great hiking trails). The 5,000-square-foot country home, outfitted with a professional

0 2 mi
0 2 km

N

County Park
Kuau **7**
36
7
Paia Bay
Pa'ia **4**
1 **3** **6**
5
364
Hamakua
Malik
Bay
Pa'uwela
Point
Opana
Point
Uaoa
Bay
8
Ha'iku
36
Ulumalu
9
365
360 **To Hana →**
Twin Falls **11**
12

2
Sugar Mill
← To Spreckelsville
Baldwin Ave.
398
10
Kaupakalua

37
Haleakala Highway
Hali'imaile **13**
371
14
15
16
Kokomo
Makawao **17**
365 394
Pukalani
390

18 377
37 **19**
372
370
21
Oma'opio
Kula Highway
Haleakala Highway
20
Olinda

Crater Road
22
23
Pulehu
Waiakoa
24
25
Kula
378 378
HALEAKALA
NATIONAL
PARK
378
MAUI
26 Waiohuli
27 Keokea
POLIPOLI
STATE
PARK

ATTRACTIONS ●
Alii Kula Lavender **19**
Kula Botanical Garden **18**
Tedeshi Vineyards & Winery **27**
Ulupalakua Ranch **27**

DINING ◆
Café 808 **25**
Café des Amis **2**
Casanova
  Italian Restaurant **17**
Charley's **6**
Colleen's at the Haiku
  Cannery **8**
Grandma's Coffee House **26**
Haliimaile General Store **13**
Jaques North Shore **5**
Kula Lodge **22**
Kula Sandlewoods **23**
Mama's Fish House **7**
Milagros Food Co. **4**
Moana Bakery & Café **3**
Paia Fish Market **1**
Pauwela Cafe **10**

ACCOMMODATIONS ■
Aloha Maui Cottages **11**
Banyan Tree House **16**
Huelo Point Flower Farm **12**
The Inn at Mama's Fish House **7**
Kili's Cottage **21**
Kula Cottage **24**
Maui Dream Cottages **9**
Olinda Country Cottages & Inn **20**
Pilialoha B&B Cottage **15**
Wild Ginger **14**

eye to detail, has large windows with incredible panoramic views of all of Maui. Upstairs are two guest rooms with country furnishings and separate entryways. Connected to the main house but with its own private entrance, the Pineapple Suite has a full kitchen, an antiques-filled living room, and a marble-tiled full bathroom. A separate 1,000-square-foot cottage is the epitome of cozy country luxury, with a fireplace, a queen-size bedroom, cushioned window seats (with great sunset views), and cathedral ceilings. My favorite, the 950-square-foot Hidden Cottage (located in a truly secluded spot surrounded by protea flowers), features three decks, 8-foot French glass doors, a full kitchen, a washer/dryer, and a private tub for two on the deck.

Restaurants are a 15-minute drive away in Makawao, and beaches are another 15 minutes beyond that. Once ensconced, however, you may never want to leave this enchanting inn.

2660 Olinda Rd. (near the top of Olinda Rd., a 15-min. drive from Makawao), Makawao, HI 96768. ℂ 800/932-3435 or 808/572-1453. Fax 808/573-5326. www.mauibnbcottages.com. 5 units. $140 double; $140 suite double; $195–$245 cottage for 2 (sleeps up to 5). Extra person $25. 2-night minimum for rooms and suite, 3-night minimum for cottages. No credit cards. *In room:* TV, kitchen (in cottages), fridge, coffeemaker, washer/dryer (in cottages).

KULA (AT THE BASE OF HALEAKALA NATIONAL PARK)

Lodgings in Kula are the closest options to the entrance of Haleakala National Park (about 60 min. away).

Kili's Cottage 🅚 *(Value* If you're looking for a quiet getaway in the cool elevation of Kula, this sweet cottage, situated on 2 acres, is the place. The amenities are numerous: large lanai, full kitchen, gas barbecue, washer/dryer, views, even toys for the kids. The hostess, Kili Namau'u, who is the director of a Hawaiian-language immersion school, greets each guest with royal aloha—from the flowers (picked from the garden) that fill the house to the welcome basket filled with tropical produce grown on the property.

Kula. Reservations c/o Hawaii's Best Bed & Breakfast, 571 Pauku St., Kailua, HI 96734. ℂ 800/262-9912 or 808/263-3100. Fax 808/967-8610. www.bestbnb.com. 1 unit. $115 double. Extra person $15. 2-night minimum. No credit cards. *In room:* TV, kitchen, fridge, coffeemaker, washer/dryer.

Kula Cottage 🅚 *(Finds* I can't imagine having a less-than-fantastic vacation here. Tucked away on a quiet street amid a large grove of blooming papaya and banana trees, Cecilia and Larry Gilbert's romantic honeymoon cottage is very private—it even has its own driveway and carport. The 700-square-foot cottage has a full kitchen (complete with dishwasher) and three huge closets that offer enough storage space for you to move in permanently. An outside lanai has a big gas barbecue and an umbrella table and chairs. Cecilia delivers a continental breakfast daily. Groceries and a small takeout lunch counter are within walking distance; it's a 30-minute drive to the beach.

40 Puakea Place (off Lower Kula Rd.), Kula, HI 96790. ℂ 808/878-2043 or 808/871-6230. Fax 808/871-9187. www.kulacottage.com. 1 unit. $95 double. Rate includes continental breakfast. 2-night minimum. No credit cards. *In room:* TV, kitchen, fridge, coffeemaker, washer/dryer.

EAST MAUI: ON THE ROAD TO HANA

Note: You'll find the accommodations in this section on the "Upcountry & East Maui" map on p. 391.

KUAU

The Inn at Mama's Fish House 🅚🅚 The fabulous location (nestled in a coconut grove on secluded Kuau Beach), beautifully decorated interior (with Island-style rattan furniture and works by Hawaiian artists), and extras (Weber gas barbecue, huge

27-in. TVs, and beach toys) make this place a gem for those seeking a centrally located vacation rental. All this, and the fabulous Mama's Fish House restaurant is just next door. The one-bedrooms are nestled in a tropical jungle (red ginger surrounds the garden patio), while the two-bedrooms face the beach. Both have terra-cotta floors, complete kitchens (even dishwashers), sofa beds, and laundry facilities.

799 Poho Place (off the Hana Hwy. in Kuau), Paia, HI 96779. (℃ 800/860-HULA or 808/579-9764. Fax 808/579-8594. www.mamasfishhouse.com. 6 units. $225 1-bedroom (sleeps up to 4); $475 2-bedroom (up to 6). 3-night minimum. AE, DISC, MC, V. **Amenities:** Restaurant. In room: A/C, TV/VCR, kitchen, fridge, coffeemaker, hair dryer, iron, washer/dryer.

HAIKU

Maui Dream Cottages (Value)   Essentially a vacation rental, this country estate is located atop a hill overlooking the ocean. The grounds are dotted with fruit trees (bananas, papayas, and avocados, all free for the picking), and the front lawn is comfortably equipped with a double hammock, chaise lounges, and table and chairs. One cottage has two bedrooms, the other just one (plus a sofa bed in the living room). They're both very well maintained and comfortably outfitted with furniture that's attractive but casual. The Haiku location is quiet and restful, and offers the opportunity to see how real islanders live. However, you'll have to drive a good 20 to 25 minutes to restaurants in Makawao or Paia. Hookipa Beach is about a 20-minute drive, and Baldwin Beach (good swimming) is 25 minutes away.

265 W. Kuiaha Rd. (1 block from Pauwela Cafe), Haiku, HI 96708. (℃ 808/575-9079. Fax 808/575-9477. www.maui dreamcottage.com. 2 units, shower only. $560 per week double. Extra person $10. 7-night minimum. MC, V. In room: TV, kitchen, fridge, coffeemaker, washer/dryer.

Pilialoha B&B Cottage 🌟   The minute you arrive at this split-level country cottage, located on a large lot with half-century-old eucalyptus trees, you'll see owner Machiko Heyde's artistry at work. Just in front of the quaint cottage (which is great for couples but can sleep up to five) is a garden blooming with some 200 varieties of roses. You'll find more of Machiko's handiwork inside. There's a queen-size bed in the master bedroom, a twin bed in a small adjoining room, and a queen-size sofa bed in the living room. A large lanai extends from the master bedroom. There's a great movie collection for rainy days or cool country nights, and a garage. Machiko delivers breakfast daily; if you plan on an early morning ride to the top of Haleakala, she'll make sure you go with a thermos of coffee and her homemade bread.

2512 Kaupakalua Rd. (½ mile from Kokomo intersection), Haiku, HI 96708. (℃ 808/572-1440. Fax 808/572-4612. www.pilialoha.com. 1 unit. $130 double. Rates include continental breakfast. Extra person $20. 3-night minimum. MC, V. **Amenities:** Complimentary use of beach toys (including snorkel equipment); washer/dryer. In room: TV, kitchenette, fridge, coffeemaker.

Wild Ginger Falls 🌟🌟 (Finds)   This cozy, romantic, intimate cottage, hidden in Miliko Gulch, overlooks a stream with a waterfall, bamboo, sweet-smelling ginger, and banana trees. It's perfect for honeymooners, lovers, and fans of Hawaiiana art. The moment you step into this 400-square-foot artistically decorated Hawaiian cottage, you will be delighted at the carefully placed memorabilia (ukulele tile, canoe paddle, and the like) found throughout. The cottage has a full kitchen with everything you should need for cooking. The Hawaiian theme carries into the living room, with a VCR behind a tropical painted cabinet and stereo. The comfy queen-size bed opens to the living area. The 156-square-foot screened porch has a table, chairs, and couch, perfect for curling up with a good book. Outside there's a barbecue, plus a large selection of beach toys. Your hosts are Bob, a ceramic artist (with his creations throughout the cottage), and his wife, Sunny, who manages Dolphin Galleries (where she has carefully selected artwork for the cottage).

355 Kaluanui Rd., Makawao, HI 96768. ©/fax **808/573-1173**. www.wildgingerfalls.com. 1 unit. $135–$145. double. 3-night minimum. No credit cards. *In room:* TV/VCR, kitchen, fridge, coffeemaker, hair dryer, iron, washer/dryer.

TWIN FALLS

Aloha Maui Cottages *(Finds* On 2 acres of jungle, tucked away in the Twin Falls area, sits this budget traveler accommodations. Three separate bungalows offer a back-to-nature experience. The rustic, clean, well-outfitted cabins are all landscaped to offer privacy and are a good value for the price. The cabins range from the Mango cottage, with hardwood floors, a full kitchen, and a big bedroom with an ocean view, to the Banana Room, a small room with a kitchenette. All rooms are stocked with coffee or tea and locally grown fruit (some comes from right outside your front door) in season, and have access to a gas barbecue. Host Ken knows all the hiking and biking trails (he will loan you his mountain bikes to go exploring) and secret waterfalls.

P.O. Box 790210, Paia, HI 96779. © **808/572-0298**. www.alohamauicottages.com. 3 units, 2 with shared bathroom. $70–$135 double. Extra person $5–$7. 3-night minimum. DISC, MC, V. *In room:* Kitchen or kitchenette.

HUELO

Huelo Point Flower Farm *(Finds* Here's a little Eden by the sea on a spectacular, remote, 300-foot sea cliff near a waterfall stream. This estate overlooking Waipio Bay has two guest cottages, a guesthouse, and a main house available for rent. The studio-size Gazebo Cottage has three glass walls that make the most of the cottage's oceanfront location, a koa-wood captain's bed, a private ocean-side patio, a private hot tub, and a half-bathroom with outdoor shower. The new 900-square-foot Carriage House apartment sleeps four and has glass walls facing the mountain and sea, plus a den, decks, and a loft bedroom. The two-bedroom main house contains an exercise room, a fireplace, a sunken Roman bath, cathedral ceilings, and other extras. On-site is a natural pool with a waterfall and an oceanfront hot tub. You're welcome to pick fruit, vegetables, and flowers from the extensive garden. Homemade scones, tree-ripened papayas, and fresh-roasted coffee start your day. The secluded location, off the crooked road to Hana, is just a half-hour from Kahului, or about 20 minutes from Paia's shops and restaurants.

Off Hana Hwy., between mile markers 3 and 4. P.O. Box 791808, Paia, HI 96779. © **808/572-1850**. www.maui flowerfarm.com. 4 units. $225 cottage double; $240 carriage house double; $395 guesthouse double; $495 main house for 4. Extra person $20–$35. 2-night minimum for smaller houses, 5-night minimum for main house. No credit cards. **Amenities:** Outdoor pool; 3 Jacuzzis; washer/dryer. *In room:* TV, kitchenette (in cottage), kitchen (in houses), fridge, coffeemaker, hair dryer.

AT THE END OF THE ROAD IN EAST MAUI: HANA

Note: You'll find Hana accommodations on the map on p. 463.

EXPENSIVE

Hotel Hana-Maui ★★★ *(Kids* This hotel sits on 66 rolling seaside acres and offers a wellness center, two pools, and access to one of the best beaches in Hana. This is the atmosphere, the landscape, and the culture of old Hawaii set in 21st-century accommodations. Every unit is excellent, but my favorites are the Sea Ranch Cottages (especially units 215–218 for the best views), where individual duplex bungalows look out over the craggy shoreline to the rolling surf. You step out of the oversize, airy units (with floor-to-ceiling sliding doors) onto a huge lanai with views that will stay with you long after your tan has faded. These comfy units have been totally redecorated with every amenity you can think of, and you won't be nickel-and-dimed for things like coffee and water—everything they give you, from the homemade banana bread to the bottled water, is complimentary. Cathedral ceilings, a plush feather bed, a giant-size soaking tub, Hawaiian artwork, bamboo hardwood floors—this is luxury. The white-sand beach (just a 5-min. shuttle away), top-notch wellness center with some of the best massage therapists in Hawaii, and numerous activities (horseback riding, mountain biking, tennis, pitch-and-putt golf) all add up to make this one of the top resorts in the state. There's no TV in the rooms, but the Club Room has a giant-screen TV, plus VCR and Internet access. I highly recommend this little slice of paradise.

Hana, Maui, HI 96713. (② **800/321-HANA** or 808/248-8211. Fax 808/248-7202. www.hotelhanamaui.com. 66 units. $475–$525 Bay Cottages double; $625–$1,075 Sea Ranch Cottages double; $1,575 2-bedroom suite for 4; 2-bedroom Plantation Guest House from $4,000. Extra person $140. AE, DC, DISC, MC, V. **Amenities:** Restaurant (w/Hawaiian entertainment twice a week); bar (entertainment 4 times a week); 2 outdoor pools; complimentary use of the 3-hole practice golf courses (clubs are complimentary); complimentary tennis courts; fitness center; full-service spa; game room; concierge; activity desk; car-rental desk; business center; small shopping arcade; salon; room service; babysitting; laundry service. *In room:* Dataport, kitchenette, fridge, coffeemaker, hair dryer, iron, safe.

MODERATE

Ekena 🏨 Just one glance at the 360-degree view, and you can see why hosts Robin and Gaylord gave up their careers on the mainland and moved here. This 8½-acre piece of paradise in rural Hana boasts ocean and rainforest views; the floor-to-ceiling glass doors in the spacious Hawaiian-style pole house bring the outside in. The elegant two-story home is exquisitely furnished, from the comfortable U-shaped couch that invites you to relax and take in the view to the top-of-the-line mattress on the king-size bed. The kitchen is fully equipped with high-tech conveniences (guests have made complete holiday meals here). Only one floor (and one two-bedroom unit) is rented at any one time to ensure privacy. The grounds are impeccably groomed and dotted with tropical plants and fruit trees. Hiking trails into the rainforest start right on the property, and beaches and waterfalls are just minutes away. Robin places fresh flowers in every room and makes sure you're comfortable; after that, she's available to answer questions, but she also respects your privacy.

P.O. Box 728 (off Hana Hwy., above Hana Airport), Hana, HI 96713. (② **808/248-7047.** Fax 808/248-7853. www.ekenamaui.com. 2 units. $225 for 2; $295–$400 for 4. Extra person $35. 3-night minimum. MC, V. **Amenities:** Washer/dryers. *In room:* TV/DVD, CD, kitchen, fridge, coffeemaker, iron.

Hamoa Bay Bungalow 🏨 *Finds* Down a country lane guarded by two Balinese statues stands a little bit of Indonesia in Hawaii: a carefully crafted bungalow and an Asian-inspired two-bedroom house overlooking Hamoa Bay. This enchanting retreat is just 2 miles beyond Hasegawa's general store on the way to Kipahulu. It sits on 4 verdant acres within walking distance of Hamoa Beach (which James Michener considered one of the most beautiful in the Pacific). The 600-square-foot Balinese-style cottage is distinctly tropical, with giant elephant bamboo furniture from Indonesia, batik prints, a king-size bed, a full kitchen, and a screened porch with hot tub and shower. Hidden from the cottage is a 1,300-square-foot home with a soaking tub and private outdoor stone shower. It offers an elephant bamboo king-size bed in one room, a queen-size bed in another, a screened-in sleeping porch, a full kitchen, and wonderful ocean views.

P.O. Box 773, Hana, HI 96713. (② **808/248-7884.** Fax 808/248-7853. www.hamoabay.com. 2 units. $225 cottage (sleeps only 2); $285 house for 2; $395 house for 4. 3-night minimum. MC, V. **Amenities:** Hot tub; washer/dryers. *In room:* TV/DVD, CD, kitchen, fridge, coffeemaker, iron.

Hana Ocean Front ★★   Just across the street from Hamoa Bay, Hana's premier white-sand beach, lie these two plantation-style units, impeccably decorated in old Hawaii decor and outfitted with everything you should need during your vacation. My favorite unit is the romantic cottage, complete with old-fashioned front porch where you can sit and watch the ocean; a separate bedroom (with a bamboo sleigh bed), plus pull-out sofa for extra guests; top-notch kitchen appliances; and comfy living room. The 1,000-square-foot vacation suite, located downstairs from hosts Dan and Sandi's home (but totally soundproof), has an elegant master bedroom with polished bamboo flooring, a spacious bathroom with custom hand-painted tile, and a fully appointed gourmet kitchen. Outside are a 320-square-foot lanai and a barbecue area. The units sit on the road facing Hana's most popular beach, so there is traffic during the day. At night the traffic disappears, the stars come out, and the sound of the ocean lulls you to sleep.

Hana, HI 96713. © 808/248-7558. Fax 808/248-8034. www.hanaoceanfrontcottages.com. 2 units. $250–$275 double. 3-night minimum. MC, V. *In room:* TV/VCR/DVD, stereo/CD, full gourmet kitchen, fridge, coffeemaker, hair dryer, iron.

Heavenly Hana Inn ★★ *(Finds*   Owners Robert Filippi and Sheryl Murray humbly describe their B&B as a "Japanese-style inn at secluded and beautiful Hana." That's like saying a Four Seasons Hotel is a big building with rooms. This place on the Hana Highway, just a stone's throw from the center of Hana town, is a little bit of heaven, where no attention to detail has been spared. Each suite has a sitting room with futon and couch, polished hardwood floors, and separate bedroom with a raised platform bed (with an excellent, firm mattress). The black-marble bathrooms have huge tubs. Flowers are everywhere, ceiling fans keep the rooms cool, and the delicious gourmet breakfast—worth the splurge—is served in a setting filled with art. The grounds are done in Japanese style with a bamboo fence, tiny bridges over a meandering stream, and Japanese gardens.

P.O. Box 790, Hana, HI 96713. ©/fax 808/248-8442. www.heavenlyhanainn.com. 3 units. $190–$260 suite. Full gourmet breakfast available for $17 per person. 2-night minimum. AE, DISC, MC, V. No children under age 15 accepted. *In room:* TV, no phone.

INEXPENSIVE

Mrs. Nakamura has been renting her **Aloha Cottages** (© **808/248-8420**) since the 1970s. Located in residential areas near Hana Bay, these five budget rentals are simply but adequately furnished, varying in size from a roomy studio with kitchenette to a three-bedroom, two-bathroom unit. They're all fully equipped, clean, and fairly well kept. Rates run from $65 to $100 double. Not all units have TVs, and none has a phone, but Mrs. N. is happy to take messages.

Baby Pigs Crossing Bed & Breakfast ★ *(Finds*   If you're looking for a quiet, romantic little cottage, nestled away from it all in old Hawaii but close enough to Hana to drive in for dinner, this is your place. International artist Arabella Gail Ark (formerly known as Gail Bakutis) has created a lovely retreat on her 1-acre parcel of land, which is landscaped in a "fragrance" garden with Hawaii's best sweet-smelling plants carefully planted throughout the property. The separate guesthouse, with an ocean view from the lanai, is professionally decorated with comfort in mind, from the very cozy rattan furniture to the king-size sofa bed. There's a separate bedroom with a queen-size bed and a small but utilitarian kitchenette. But the surprise is the unique bathroom with glass ceiling and walls (with privacy curtains), which opens out to a garden area.

P.O. Box 667, Hana, HI 96713. (C) **808/248-8890.** Fax 808/248-4865. www.mauibandb.com. 1 unit. $250 double for 1 night; $195 for two for 2 nights; $185 double for 3 nights. AE, MC, V. *In room:* TV/VCR, kitchenette, fridge, coffeemaker, cellphone.

Hana's Tradewinds Cottage ⭐ *Value* *Kids* Nestled among the ginger and heliconias on a 5-acre flower farm are two separate cottages, each with carport, barbecue, private hot tub, ceiling fans, and sofa bed. The studio cottage sleeps up to four; a bamboo shoji blind separates the sleeping area (with queen-size bed) from the sofa bed in the living room. The Tradewinds cottage has two bedrooms (with a queen-size bed in one room and two twins in the other), one bathroom (shower only), and a huge front porch. The atmosphere is quiet and relaxing, and hostess Rebecca Buckley, who has been in business for a decade, welcomes families (she has two children, a cat, and a very sweet golden retriever).

135 Alalele Place (the airport road), P.O. Box 385, Hana, HI 96713. (C) **800/327-8097** or 808/248-8980. Fax 808/248-7735. www.hanamaui.net. 2 units. $175 studio double; $175 2-bedroom double. Extra person $15. 2-night minimum. AE, DISC, MC, V. **Amenities:** Washer/dryer. *In room:* TV, kitchen, fridge, coffeemaker, no phone.

Waianapanapa State Park Cabins *Value* These 12 rustic cabins are the best lodging deal on Maui. Everyone knows it, too—so make your reservations early (up to 6 months in advance). The cabins are warm and dry, and come complete with kitchen, living room, bedroom, and bathroom with hot shower; furnishings include bedding, linens, towels, dishes, and very basic cooking and eating utensils. Don't expect luxury—this is a step above camping, albeit in a beautiful tropical jungle setting. The key attraction at this 120-acre state beach park is the unusual horseshoe-shaped black-sand beach on Pailoa Bay, popular for shore fishing, snorkeling, and swimming. There's a caretaker on-site, along with restrooms, showers, picnic tables, shoreline hiking trails, and historic sites. Bring mosquito protection—this is the jungle, after all.

Off Hana Hwy. c/o State Parks Division, 54 S. High St., Room 101, Wailuku, HI 96793. (C) **808/984-8109.** 12 units. $45 for 4 (sleeps up to 6). Extra person $5. 5-night maximum. No credit cards. *In room:* Kitchen, fridge, coffeemaker, no phone.

4 Where to Dine

With soaring visitor statistics and a glamorous image, the Valley Isle is fertile ground for Hawaii's famous enterprising chefs (like Roy Yamaguchi from Roy's, Gerard Reversade of Gerard's, James McDonald of I'O and Pacific'O, Peter Merriman of Hula Grill, Mark Ellman of Maui Taco and Mala Ocean Tavern, D. K. Kodama of Sansei Seafood Restaurant & Sushi Bar and Vino Italian Tapas & Wine Bar, and Beverly Gannon of Haliimaile General Store and Joe's Bar & Grill), as well as an international name or two (Wolfgang Puck of Spago). Plus a few newcomers who are cooking up a storm and getting a well-deserved following (Jennifer Nguyen of A Saigon Cafe, Dana Pastula of Café O'Lei and Ma'alaea Grill, and Don Ritchey of Moana Bakery & Cafe).

In this dizzying scenario, some things haven't changed: You can still dine well at Lahaina's open-air waterfront watering holes, where the view counts for 50% of the experience. There are still budget eateries, but not many; Maui's old-fashioned, multigenerational mom-and-pop diners are disappearing, eclipsed by the flashy newcomers, or clinging to the edge of existence in the older neighborhoods of central Maui, such as lovable Wailuku. Although you'll have to work harder to find them in the resort areas, you won't have to go far to find creative cuisine, pleasing style, and stellar dining experiences.

In the listings below, reservations are not necessary unless otherwise noted.

CENTRAL MAUI

The **Queen Kaahumanu Center,** the structure that looks like a white *Star Wars* umbrella in the center of Kahului, at 275 Kaahumanu Ave. (5 min. from Kahului Airport on Hwy. 32), has a very popular food court. **Edo Japan** teppanyaki is a real find, its flat Benihana-like grill dispensing marvelous, flavorful mounds of grilled fresh vegetables and chicken teriyaki for $5.70. **Maui Mixed Plate** dishes out "local style" cuisine of meat with rice and macaroni salad in the $4.45-to-$7 range. **Yummy Korean B-B-Q** offers the assertive flavors of Korea ranging from $4.75 to $7.50, **Panda Express** serves tasty Chinese food, and **Sushi Go** is a great place for fast sushi. Outside of the food court, but still in the shopping center, are **The Coffee Store** (p. 413); **Ruby's,** dishing out hamburgers, fries, and shakes; and **Starbucks.** There's also a branch of **Maui Tacos** (p. 408). When you leave Kaahumanu Center, take a moment to gaze at the West Maui Mountains to your left from the parking lot.

MODERATE

Class Act ⟨⟩ GLOBAL   Part of a program run by the distinguished Food Service Department of Maui Community College, now housed in a new state-of-the-art, $15-million culinary facility (with floor-to-ceiling windows at one end, exhibition kitchen at the other end) is this "classroom" restaurant with a huge following. Student chefs show their stuff with a flourish and pull out all the stops to give you a dining experience you will long remember. Linen, china, servers in ties and white shirts, and a four-course lunch make this a unique value. The appetizer, soup, salad, and dessert are set, but you can choose between the regular entrees and a heart-healthy main course prepared in the culinary tradition of the week. The menu roams the globe with highlights of Italy, Mexico, Maui, Napa Valley, France, New Orleans, and other locales. The filet mignon of French week is popular, as are the New Orleans gumbo and Cajun shrimp, the sesame-crusted mahimahi on taro leaf pasta, the polenta flan with eggplant, and the bean and green chile chilaquile.

Maui Community College, 310 Kaahumanu Ave., Wailuku. ⓒ **808/984-3280.** http://mauiculinary.com/academy/class_act.cfm. Reservations recommended. 4-course lunch $25. MC, V. Wed and Fri 11am–12:15pm (last seating). Closed June–Aug for summer vacation. Menu and cuisine type change weekly.

Ichiban *(Finds)* JAPANESE/SUSHI   What a find: An informal neighborhood restaurant that serves inexpensive, home-cooked Japanese food *and* good sushi at realistic prices. Local residents consider Ichiban a staple for breakfast, lunch, or dinner and a haven of comforts: egg-white omelets; great saimin; combination plates of teriyaki chicken, teriyaki meat, *tonkatsu* (pork cutlet), rice, and pickled cabbage; chicken yakitori; and sushi—everything from unagi and scallop to California roll. The sushi items may not be cheap, but like the specials, such as steamed opakapaka, they're a good value. I love the tempura, miso soup, and spicy ahi hand roll.

Kahului Shopping Center, 47 Kaahumanu Ave., Kahului. ⓒ **808/871-6977.** Main courses $5–$6 breakfast, $7.95–$12 lunch (combination plates $9.95), $6.95–$30 dinner (combination dinner $13, dinner specials from $8.95). AE, DC, MC, V. Mon–Fri 7am–2pm and 5–9pm; Sat 10:30am–2pm and 5–9pm. Closed 2 weeks around Christmas and New Year's.

Mañana Garage ⟨⟨ *(Finds)* LATIN AMERICAN   Chef Ed Santos is serving up some incomparable fare at this central Maui hot spot. The industrial motif features table bases like hubcaps, a vertical garage door as a divider for private parties, blown-glass chandeliers, and gleaming chrome and cobalt walls with orange accents. The menu is brilliantly conceived and executed. Fried green tomatoes are done just right and served with slivered red onions. Three different kinds of seviche perfectly balance flavors and textures: lime, cilantro, chile, coconut, and fresh fish. They even have barbecued ribs. Mañana Garage has introduced exciting new flavors to Maui's dining scene—if you are on this side of the island, don't miss this incredible experience.

33 Lono Ave., Kahului. ℂ 808/873-0220. Reservations recommended. Lunch main courses $7–$13; dinner main courses $16–$31. AE, DISC, MC, V. Mon, Wed, Sat 11am–1:30am; Tues and Thurs 11am–9pm; Fri 11am–10:30pm; Sun 5–9pm.

Marco's Grill & Deli ITALIAN   Located in the thick of central Maui, where the roads to upcountry, west, and South Maui converge, Marco's is popular among area residents for its homemade Italian fare and friendly informality. Everything—from the meatballs, sausages, and burgers to the sauces, salad dressings, and raviolis—is made in-house. The 35 different choices of hot and cold sandwiches and entrees are served all day; some favorites include vodka rigatoni with imported prosciutto and simple pasta with marinara sauce. This is one of those comfortable neighborhood fixtures favored by all generations. The antipasto salad and roasted peppers are taste treats, but the meatballs and Italian sausage are famous in central Maui. It also has a full bar.

Dairy Center, 395 Dairy Rd., Kahului. ℂ 808/877-4446. Main courses $11–$27. AE, DISC, MC, V. Daily 7:30am–10pm.

A Saigon Cafe 🎝🎝 *Finds* VIETNAMESE   Jennifer Nguyen has stuck to her guns and steadfastly refused to erect a sign, but diners find their way here anyway. That's how good the food is. Fans drive from all over the island for her crisped, spiced Dungeness crab, her steamed opakapaka with ginger and garlic, and her wok-cooked Vietnamese specials tangy with spices, herbs, and lemon grass. There are a dozen different soups, cold and hot noodles (including the popular beef noodle soup called *pho*), and chicken and shrimp cooked in a clay pot. You can create your own Vietnamese "burritos" from a platter of tofu, noodles, and vegetables that you wrap in rice paper and dip in garlic sauce. Among my favorites are the shrimp lemon grass, savory and refreshing, and the tofu curry, swimming in herbs and vegetables straight from the garden. The Nhung Dam—a hearty spread of basil, cucumbers, mint, romaine, bean sprouts, pickled carrots, turnips, and vermicelli, wrapped in rice paper and dipped in a legendary sauce—is cooked at your table.

1792 Main St., Wailuku. ℂ 808/243-9560. Main courses $6.50–$17. DC, MC, V. Mon–Sat 10am–9:30pm; Sun 10am–8:30pm. Heading into Wailuku from Kahului, go over the bridge and take the 1st right onto Central Ave.; then the 1st right on Nani St. At the next stop sign, look for the building with the neon sign that says OPEN.

INEXPENSIVE
AK's Café 🎝🎝 *Value* HEALTHY/PLATE LUNCHES   Chef Elaine Rothermel has a winner with this tiny cafe in the industrial district of Wailuku. It may be slightly off the tourist path, but it is well worth the effort to find this delicious eatery, with creative cuisine coming out of the kitchen—most dishes healthy, and a few dishes for those who just want to enjoy good food (forget about the calories). Prices are so eye-poppingly cheap, you might find yourself wandering back here during your vacation. Lunches feature everything from grilled chicken with Thai sauce to fish tacos, to hamburger steak, to seared ahi sandwich with tempura eggplant. Dinner specials include chicken marsala over noodles, crab cakes with papaya beurre blanc, tofu Napoleon with ginger basil sauce, and Hunan lamb chops. Plenty of heart-healthy options to choose from (low in sugar, salt and fat).

1237 Lower Main St., Wailuku. ℂ 808/244-8774. www.akscafe.com. Plate lunches $6.75–$9.50; dinners $11–$18. MC, V. Tues–Fri 10:30am–2pm; Tues–Sat 5–9pm. Live Hawaiian music Fri–Sat nights.

Down to Earth (*Value*) ORGANIC HEALTH FOOD   If you are looking for a healthy alternative to fast foods, here's your place. Healthful organic ingredients, 90% vegan, appear in scrumptious salads, lasagna, chili, curries, and dozens of tasty dishes, presented at hot and cold serve-yourself stations. Stools line the counters in the simple dining area, where a few tables are available for those who don't want takeout. The food is great: millet cakes, mock tofu chicken, curried tofu, and Greek salad, nearly everything organic and tasty, with herb-tamari marinades and pleasing condiments such as currants or raisins, apples, and cashews. (The fabulous tofu curry has apples, raw cashews, and raisins.) The food is sold by the pound, but you can buy a hearty, wholesome plate for $7. Vitamin supplements, health-food products, fresh produce, and cosmetics fill the rest of the store.

305 Dairy Rd., Kahului. (*C*) **808/877-2661.** Self-serve hot buffet and salad bar; food sold by the pound. Average $6–$8 for a plate. AE, MC, V. Mon–Sat 7am–9pm; Sun 8am–8pm.

Main Street Bistro (*Value*) AMERICAN   Formerly Who's the Boss restaurant, before that Iao Café, this popular eatery, located on the main street of Wailuku, is now owned by chef Tom Selman, well known in culinary circles on Maui. He was formerly the Chef du Cuisine at David Paul's Lahaina Grill and also was corporate chef for the Sansei/Vino restaurants. The restaurant is open only for lunch, but Selman also has added a pau hana tapa ("after-work small dishes") menu like crispy crab and shrimp gau gee, mini hamburgers, barbecue ribs, and an oli-braised salmon. Chef Selman calls his food "refined comfort food," with signature menu items that include onion rings with house-made smoky ketchup, roasted Chinese chicken salad, "mother's roast beef sandwich" (served open-faced on a French roll), Southern-fried chicken, Maryland-style crab cake, and a roasted veggie sandwich. The chef will happily customize any menu item for people who prefer low-calorie, low-fat, or low-carbohydrate options. Daily specials range from grilled steak to Asian risotto with shrimp, crab, and veggies.

2051 Main St., Wailuku. (*C*) **808/244-6816.** Entrees $8–$13; daily specials $6.95–$15. DC, MC, V. Mon–Fri 11am–3pm; tapas menu 3–7pm.

Maui Bake Shop BAKERY/DELI   Sleepy Vineyard Street has seen many a mom-and-pop business come and go, but Maui Bake Shop is here to stay. Maui native Claire Fujii-Krall and her husband, baker José Krall (who was trained in the south of France), are turning out buttery brioches, healthful nine-grain and two-tone rye breads, focaccia, strudels, sumptuous fresh-fruit gâteaux, puff pastries, and dozens of other baked goods and confections. The breads are baked in one of Maui's oldest brick ovens, installed in 1935; a high-tech European diesel oven handles the rest. The front window displays more than 100 bakery and deli items, among them salads, a popular eggplant marinara focaccia, homemade quiches, and an inexpensive calzone filled with chicken, pesto, mushroom, and cheese. Homemade soups (clam chowder, minestrone, cream of asparagus) team up nicely with sandwiches on freshly baked bread. Save room for the Ultimate Dessert: white-chocolate macadamia-nut cheesecake.

2092 Vineyard St. (at N. Church St.), Wailuku. (*C*) **808/242-0064.** Most items under $7. AE, DISC, MC, V. Tues–Fri 6:30am–2:30pm; Sat 7am–1pm.

Restaurant Matsu JAPANESE/LOCAL   Customers have come from Hana (more than 50 miles away) just for Matsu's California rolls, while regulars line up for the cold saimin (julienned cucumber, egg, Chinese-style sweet pork, and red ginger on noodles) and for the bento plates, various assemblages of chicken, teriyaki beef, fish, and rice. The nigiri sushi items are popular, especially among the don't-dally lunch crowd.

The katsu pork and chicken, breaded and deep-fried, are other specialties of this casual Formica-style diner. I love the tempura udon and the saimin, steaming mounds of wide and fine noodles swimming in homemade broths and topped with condiments. The daily specials are a changing lineup of home-cooked classics: oxtail soup, roast pork with gravy, teriyaki ahi, miso butterfish, and breaded mahimahi.

161 Alamaha St., Kahului. ⓒ 808/871-0822. Most items less than $7. No credit cards. Mon–Thurs 10am–3pm; Fri 10am–8pm; Sat 10am–2pm.

WEST MAUI
LAHAINA
There's a **Maui Tacos** (p. 408) in Lahaina Square (ⓒ **808/661-8883**). Maui's branch of the **Hard Rock Cafe** is in Lahaina at 900 Front St. (ⓒ **808/667-7400**).

Very Expensive
David Paul's Lahaina Grill ⟨⟨ NEW AMERICAN   Despite David Paul Johnson's departure, this Lahaina hot spot has maintained its popularity. It's still filled with chic, tanned diners in stylish aloha shirts, and there's still attitude aplenty at the entrance. The signature items remain: tequila shrimp and firecracker rice, Kona coffee–roasted rack of lamb, Maui onion–crusted seared ahi, and *kalua* duck quesadilla. As always, a special custom-designed chef's table can be arranged with 72-hour notice for larger parties. The ambience—black-and-white tile floors, pressed tin ceilings, eclectic 1890s decor—is striking, and the bar, despite not having an ocean view, is the busiest spot in Lahaina.

127 Lahainaluna Rd. ⓒ 808/667-5117. Reservations required. Main courses $29–$43; tasting menu $76. AE, DC, DISC, MC, V. Daily 6–10pm; Bar daily 5:30pm–midnight; earlier if it's slow.

The Feast at Lele ⟨⟨ POLYNESIAN   The owners of Old Lahaina Luau (see the box "A Night to Remember: Luau, Maui Style," later in this chapter), have teamed up with chef James McDonald's culinary prowess (I'O and Pacific'O), placed it in a perfect outdoor oceanfront setting, and added the exquisite dancers of the Old Lahaina Luau. The result: a culinary and cultural experience that sizzles. As if the sunset weren't heady enough, dances from Hawaii, New Zealand, Tahiti, and Samoa are presented, up close and personal, in full costumed splendor. Chanting, singing, drumming, dancing, the swish of ti-leaf skirts, the scent of plumeria—it's a full adventure, even for the most jaded luau aficionado. Guests sit at white-clothed, candlelit tables set on the sand (unlike the luau, where seating is en masse) and dine on entrees from each island: imu-roasted Kalua pig from Hawaii, Maori fishcake from New Zealand, poisson cru from Tahiti, and beef with breadfruit from Samoa. Particularly mesmerizing is the evening's opening: A softly lit canoe carries three people ashore to the sound of conch shells.

505 Front St. ⓒ 886/244-5353 or 808/667-5353. www.feastatlele.com. Reservations a must. Set 5-course menu $105 adults, $75 children 2–12. AE, DISC, MC, V. Apr 1–Sept 30 daily 6–9pm; Oct 1–Mar 31 daily 5:30–8:30pm.

Expensive
Gerard's ⟨⟨⟨ (Finds) FRENCH   The charm of Gerard's—soft lighting, Edith Piaf on the sound system, excellent service—is matched by a menu of uncompromising standards. After more than 2 decades in Lahaina, Gerard Reversade never runs out of creative offerings, yet stays true to his French roots. Roasted opakapaka with star anise, fennel fondue, and hints of orange and ginger is a stellar entree on a menu of winners. The Kona lobster and avocado salad promises ecstasy, and the spinach salad with scallops is among the finest I've tasted. Gerard's has an excellent appetizer menu, with

shiitake and oyster mushrooms in puff pastry, fresh ahi and smoked salmon carpaccio, and a very rich, highly touted escargot ragout with burgundy butter and garlic cream. The restaurant is a frequent winner of the *Wine Spectator* Award of Excellence and the *Wine Enthusiast* 2006 Award of Distinction.

In The Plantation Inn, 174 Lahainaluna Rd. © **808/661-8939**. www.gerardsmaui.com. Reservations recommended. Main courses $30–$50. AE, DC, DISC, MC, V. Daily 6–9pm.

I'O ⚔ PACIFIC RIM   I'O is a fantasy of sleek curves and etched glass, co-owned by chef James McDonald. He offers an impressive selection of appetizers (his strong suit) and some lavish Asian-Polynesian interpretations of seafood, such as his "rainbow catch"—fresh fish of the day topped with lemon grass pesto, tomatoes, truffle oil, and goat cheese fondue sauce—or his "scallops ala bondage"—scallops wrapped in sage and jalapeno bacon, served with roasted Japanese eggplant and a ponzu cream sauce. Unless you're sold on a particular entree, my advice is to go heavy on the superb appetizers, especially the blackened ahi tower (a tower of ahi, avocado, fruit, and tomatoes), shredded pork in a quesadilla with pepper-jack cheese, or the silken purse: wontons stuffed with roasted peppers, mushrooms, spinach, macadamia nuts, and tofu over a tomato coulis with creamy basil yogurt puree. Chef McDonald also owns Pacific'O Restaurant (see review below) and is the chef for The Feast at Lele (reviewed above).

505 Front St. © **808/661-8422**. www.iomaui.com. Reservations recommended. Main courses $28–$36. AE, DC, DISC, MC, V. Daily 5:30–10pm.

Pacific'O Restaurant ⚔ PACIFIC RIM/CONTEMPORARY PACIFIC   You can't get any closer to the ocean than the tables here, which are literally on the beach. With good food complementing this sensational setting, foodies and aesthetes have much to enjoy. The split-level dining starts near the entrance, with a long bar (where you can also order lunch or dinner) and a few tables along the railing. Steps lead down to the outdoor tables, where the award-winning seafood dishes come to you with the backdrop of Lanai across the channel. Favorites include the coconut and mac nut–crusted catch of the day or the pasta moana—fresh fish with bay scallops, rock shrimp, shiitake mushrooms, roasted peppers, and snap peas in a lobster Alfredo sauce poured over orecchiette pasta. If you like seafood, sunsets, and touches of India and Indonesia in your fresh-from-the-sea dining choices, you should be happy here.

505 Front St. © **808/667-4341**. www.pacificomaui.com. Reservations recommended. Main courses $9–$15 lunch, $26–$36 dinner. AE, DC, MC, V. Daily 11:30am–4pm and 5:30–10pm.

Moderate
Compadres Bar & Grill MEXICAN   Despite its concrete floor and high industrial ceilings, Compadres exudes good cheer. And that cheer has burgeoned lately with a new open-air seating area and a takeout taqueria window for diners on the run. The food is classic Tex-Mex, good any time of the day, beginning with huevos rancheros, egg burritos, hotcakes, and omelets (the Acapulco is heroic), and progressing to enchiladas and appetizers for the margarita-happy crowd. Stay spare (vegetable enchilada in fresh spinach tortilla) or get hefty (Texas T-bone and enchiladas). This is a carefree place with a large capacity for merrymaking. Don't miss Taco Tuesdays, from 4 to 8pm, when margaritas are just $3.

Lahaina Cannery Mall, 1221 Honoapiilani Hwy. © **808/661-7189**. Main courses $10–$23. AE, DC, DISC, MC, V. Daily 8am–10pm.

Where to Dine in Lahaina & Kaanapali

Aloha Mixed Plate **6**
Beachside Grill and
  Leilani's on the Beach **1**
Cheeseburger in Paradise **13**
Cilantro: Fresh Mexican Grill **8**
CJ's Deli & Diner **2**
Compadres Bar & Grill **5**
David Paul's Lahaina Grill **10**
E&O Trading Co **5**
The Feast at Lele **15**
Gerard's **11**
Hard Rock Café **7**
Hula Grill **1**
I'o **15**
Kimo's **9**
Lahaina Coolers **14**
Lahaina Fish Company **12**
Ma'alaea An Ocean Tavern **4**
Maui Taco **8**
Nikki's Pizza **1**
Pacific'o Restaurant **15**
Son'z Maui at Swan Court **3**

Golf
Parking
Post Office

E&O Trading Co. ★★ *Value* ECLECTIC SOUTHEAST ASIAN   From the wok fountain sculpture out front to the billowing tentlike fabrics lining the walls, you feel like you have entered another, more exotic world. Each branch of this tiny regional chain has its own unique signature and decor. The feel at the Lahaina Cannery location is straight out of the Arabian Nights. The menu, which has both small plates (so you can try a range of dishes) and larger portions, will have something for everyone, and the prices are easy on your wallet. My favorites are the sweet corn fritters with chili soy dipping sauce, any of the many assortments of satays, green papaya-ginger salad, mango-mustard glazed spare ribs, five-spice marinated duck breast (with sweet potato croquettes and plum wine sauce), and any of the five different kinds of naan (Indian flat bread). There's entertainment every evening from 4 to 6pm, and live music on Thursdays from 4:30 to 6:30pm. On Saturdays, the restaurant becomes the Feng Shui Lounge from 10pm to 2am with a DJ (and sometimes a cover—call to check).

Lahaina Cannery Mall, 1221 Honoapiilani Hwy. ℭ **808/667-1818.** www.eotrading.com. Reservations recommended. Small plates $4–$15; big plates $17–$30. MC, V. Daily 4–10pm.

Kimo's STEAK/SEAFOOD   Kimo's has a loyal following that keeps it from falling into the faceless morass of waterfront restaurants serving surf and turf with great sunset views. It's a formula restaurant (sibling to Leilani's on the Beach and Hula Grill) that works not only because of its oceanfront patio and upstairs dining room, but also because, for the price, there are some satisfying choices. It's always crowded, buzzing with people on a deck offering views of Molokai, Lanai, and Kahoolawe. Burgers and sandwiches are affordable and consistent, and the fresh catch in sweet-basil glaze is a top seller. The waistline-defying hula pie—macadamia-nut ice cream in a chocolate-wafer crust with fudge and whipped cream—originated here.

845 Front St. ℭ **808/661-4811.** www.kimosmaui.com. Reservations recommended for dinner. Main courses $9–$13 lunch, $20–$32 dinner. AE, DC, DISC, MC, V. Daily 11am–3:30pm and 5–10:30pm; bar 11am–1:30am; light menu from 3:30–5pm.

Lahaina Fish Company SEAFOOD   The open-air dining room is literally over the water, with flickering torches after sunset and an affordable menu that covers the seafood-pasta basics. Head to an oceanside table and order a cheeseburger, chicken burger, fish burger, generous basket of peel-and-eat shrimp, or sashimi—lingering is highly recommended. The light lunch/grill menu offers appetizers (sashimi, seared ahi, spring rolls, and pot stickers), salads, and soups. The restaurant has spiffed up its dinner selections to include hand-carved steaks, several pasta choices, and local fare such as stir-fry dishes, teriyaki chicken, and luau-style ribs. The specialty, though, remains the fresh seafood: Four types of fresh fish are offered nightly, in three preparations. Pacific Rim specials include fresh ahi, seared spicy or cooked in a sweet ginger-soy sauce.

831 Front St. ℭ **808/661-3472.** Main courses $8–$15 lunch, $10–$28 dinner. AE, MC, V. Daily 11am–midnight.

Mala Ocean Tavern ★★ *Value* LOCAL/SEAFOOD   Perched right on the ocean, this tiny "tavern" is the brain child of Mark and Judy Ellman, owners of Maui Tacos and Penne Pasta Café. Their philosophy is healthy, organically grown food and fresh fish used to make intriguing culinary dishes. The atmosphere could not be more enticing, with just a handful of tables out on the oceanfront lanai and several more tables in the warmly decorated interior. The staff is helpful and efficient, and the food is outstanding. If you are in the mood, ask for their exotic martini menu. You can pick from "tavern food" like an ahi burger or a cheeseburger, or one of the tempting salads (the beet and Kula goat cheese salad is divine), or something off the "big plate" menu (like wok-fried moi fish or hoisin-glazed baby back ribs). Don't miss the weekend brunches (I recommend the "killer" French toast). This is a popular place, so avoid prime lunch and dinner hours.

1307 Front St. (across from the Lahaina Cannery's Safeway Store). ℂ 808/667-9394. www.malaoceantavern.com. Small plates $5–$17; big plates $15–$26; brunch $6–12. MC, V. Mon–Fri 11am–10pm; Sat 9am–10pm; Sun 9am–9pm.

Inexpensive

Aloha Mixed Plate ⭐ *Value* PLATE LUNCHES/BEACHSIDE GRILL Look for the festive turquoise-and-yellow, plantation-style front with the red corrugated-iron roof and adorable bar, tiny and busy, directly across from the Lahaina Cannery Mall. Grab a picnic table at ocean's edge, in the shade of large kiawe and milo trees, where you can watch the bobbing sailboats and two islands on the near horizon. (On the upper level, there are umbrellas and plumeria trees—just as charming.) Then tuck into inexpensive mahimahi, *kalua* pig and cabbage, shoyu chicken, teriyaki beef, and other local plate-lunch specials, all at budget-friendly prices, served with macaroni salad and rice. The shoyu chicken is the best I've had, fork-tender and tasty, and the spicy chicken drumettes come from a fabled family recipe. (The best-sellers are the coconut prawns and Aloha Mixed Plate of shoyu chicken, teriyaki beef, and mahimahi.) I don't know of anywhere else where you can order a mai tai with a plate lunch and enjoy table service with an ocean view.

1285 Front St. ℂ 808/661-3322. www.alohamixedplate.com. Main courses $4.95–$14. MC, V. Daily 10:30am–10pm.

Cheeseburger in Paradise AMERICAN Wildly successful, always crowded, highly visible, and very noisy (especially when live music plays in the evenings), Cheeseburger is a shrine to the American classic. The home of three-napkin cheeseburgers with attitude, this is burger country, tropical style, with everything from tofu and garden burgers to the biggest, juiciest beef and chicken burgers, served on whole-wheat and sesame buns baked fresh daily. There are good reasons why the two-story green-and-white building next to the seawall is always packed: good value, good grinds, and a great ocean view. The Cheeseburger in Paradise—a hefty hunk with jack and cheddar cheeses, sautéed onions, lettuce, fresh tomatoes, and Thousand Island dressing—is a paean to the basics. You can build your own burger by adding sautéed mushrooms, bacon, grilled Ortega chiles, and other condiments for an extra charge. Onion rings, chile-cheese fries, and cold beer complete the carefree fantasy.

811 Front St. ℂ 808/661-4855. www.cheeseburgerland.com. Burgers $8.95–$13. AE, DISC, MC, V. Daily 8am–10pm.

Cilantro: Fresh Mexican Grill ⭐ *Finds* *Kids* MEXICAN This is Maui's best bet for fabulous Mexican food at frugal prices (and winner of the Taste of Lahaina Award each of the last 3 years). And, believe it or not, this fast-food restaurant serves fresh, healthy food. The chef and owner is Paris Nabavi, creator of Maui's Pizza Paradiso Italian Kitchen. He wanted the "challenge of something different," so he took off to Mexico to find out how the Mexicans used to cook in "the old days." He's back on Maui with this unbelievably delicious eatery where everything is made from scratch. Even the corn tortillas are handmade daily. Signature dishes include the citrus-and-herb-marinated chipotle rotisserie chicken, the veggie Mariposa salad, and the popular mother clucker flautas. Plus lip-smacking "al pastor" style adobo pork. All this at budget-pleasing prices. It's a great place to take the kids; Los Niños menu items are under $4.75.

170 Papalaua Ave. ℂ 808/667-5444. www.cilantrogrill.com. Entrees $3.95–$13. DISC, MC, V. Mon–Sat 11am–9pm; Sun 11am–8pm.

Lahaina Coolers (★ AMERICAN/INTERNATIONAL   A huge marlin hangs above the bar, epic wave shots and wall sconces made of surfboard fins fill the walls, and open windows line three sides of this ultracasual indoor/outdoor restaurant. This is a great breakfast joint, with feta-cheese Mediterranean omelets, huevos rancheros, and fried rice made with jasmine rice, Kula vegetables, and Portuguese sausage. There are three types of eggs Benedict: the classic, a vegetarian version (with Kula vegetables—excellent), and the Local, with Portuguese sausage and sweetbread. At lunch, burgers rule and the sandwiches, from grilled portobellos to the classic tuna melt, are ideal for casual Lahaina. Made fresh daily, the pasta is prepared Asian style (with chicken and spicy Thai peanut sauce), with pesto, or vegetarian (in a spicy Creole sauce). Pizzas, pastas, fresh catch, steak, and enchiladas round out the entrees. Everything can be prepared vegetarian upon request.

180 Dickensen St. ⓒ **808/661-7082.** www.lahainacoolers.com. Breakfast $8.25–$10; lunch main courses $7.50–$11; dinner main courses $10–$22. AE, DC, DISC, MC, V. Daily 8am–2am (full menu until midnight).

KAANAPALI

Whalers Village has a food court where you can buy pizza, very good Japanese food (including tempura soba and other noodle dishes), Korean plates, and fast-food burgers at serve-yourself counters and courtyard tables. It's an inexpensive alternative and a quick, handy stop for shoppers and Kaanapali beachgoers.

Expensive

Son'z Maui at Swan Court (★★★ CONTEMPORARY EUROPEAN/HAWAIIAN REGIONAL   For 30 years the Swan Court was *the* dining experience at the Hyatt Regency Maui. When Tri-Star Restaurant Group CEO Aaron Placourakis (who also owns Nick's Fishmarket, see p. 414) took over this restaurant, he and executive chef Geno Sarmiento knew they wanted to hit a home run every night with the cuisine. The restaurant already had perhaps the most romantic location in Maui, overlooking a man-made lagoon with white and black swans swimming by and the rolling surf of the Pacific in the distance. The culinary team's creative dishes, coupled with fresh local ingredients (Kula corn and strawberries, Ono Farms avocados, Hana hearts of palm, Maui Cattle Company beef, fresh Hawaiian fish, and sweet Maui onions), top-notch service, and the relaxing atmosphere makes this "gem" one of Maui's best restaurants. My personal picks from the very tempting menu are the Maui Surfing Goat Cheese ravioli appetizer with Kula corn, edamame, Hamakua mushrooms, prosciutto, and a sherry vinegar pan sauce and, for a main course, either the Hawaiian opakapaka picatta (with artichokes, caperberries, Lison lemon, sweet potato hash browns, and tomato purée) or the seared scallops BLT (with bacon and poached cherry tomatoes in a Caesar salad emulsion, served with truffled potato chips). They also serve a beautiful breakfast buffet.

Hyatt Regency Maui Resort & Spa, 200 Nohea Kai Dr. ⓒ **808/667-4506.** www.sonzmaui.com. Reservations necessary for dinner. Breakfast buffet $25, entrees $14–$22; Dinner entrees $30–$42. AE, DC, DISC, MC, V. Breakfast daily 6:30–11am; dinner daily 5:30–10pm.

Moderate

Beachside Grill and Leilani's on the Beach STEAK/SEAFOOD   The Beachside Grill is the informal, less-expensive room downstairs on the beach, where folks wander in off the sand for a frothy beer and a beachside burger. Leilani's is the dinner-only room, with more expensive but still not outrageously priced steak and seafood offerings. At Leilani's, you can order everything from fresh fish to filet mignon, to barbecued ribs, to fried coconut prawns. All of this, of course, comes with an ocean view. There's live Hawaiian music every afternoon except Friday, when the Rock 'n' Roll Aloha Friday set gets those decibels climbing. Free concerts are usually offered on a stage outside the restaurant on the last Sunday of the month.

In Whalers Village, 2435 Kaanapali Pkwy. ⓒ 808/661-4495. www.leilanis.com. Reservations suggested for dinner. Lunch and dinner (Beachside Grill) $8–$15; dinner (Leilani's) $18–$31. AE, DC, DISC, MC, V. Beachside Grill daily 11am–11pm (bar daily until 12:30am); Leilani's daily 5–10pm.

Hula Grill ⊛ HAWAII REGIONAL/SEAFOOD   Who wouldn't want to tuck into a wood-grilled ahi steak or a lemon-ginger roasted chicken at this bistro on the beach at Kaanapali. If you aren't that hungry, you have a choice of sandwiches, entrees, pizza, appetizers, and salads. There's happy-hour entertainment and Hawaiian music daily. For those wanting a more casual atmosphere, the Barefoot Bar, located on the beach, offers burgers, fish, pizza, and salads.

In Whalers Village, 2435 Kaanapali Pkwy. ⓒ 808/667-6636. www.hulagrill.com. Reservations recommended for dinner. Lunch and Barefoot Bar menus $8–$18; dinner main courses $18–$34. AE, DC, DISC, MC, V. Grill: Daily 11am–3pm and 5–9:30pm. Barefoot Bar: Daily 11am–10:30pm.

Inexpensive

CJ's Deli and Diner ⊛ (Value) AMERICAN/DELI   If you are staying in Kaanapali, this restaurant is walking distance from your resort; if you're not staying in Kaanapali, it's worth the drive to sample the "comfort food" (as they call it) at this hip, happening eatery with prices so low you won't believe you're still on Maui (most items under $12). A huge billboard menu hangs from the yellow-and-gold textured wall, and highly polished wooden floors give the roadside eatery a homey feeling. You can eat in or take out (you can even get a "chef-to-go" to come to your accommodations and cook for you), the atmosphere is friendly, and there's even a computer with high-speed Internet connection to keep the techies humming. Huge, delicious breakfasts start at 7am (check out the $4.95 early-bird special of two eggs, bacon or sausage, rice, and coffee) and is served until 11am. They have a wide selection of egg dishes, plus pancakes and waffles, and don't forget the tempting delights from the bakery. Lunch ranges from deli sandwiches, burgers, and hot sandwiches to pot roast, ribs, and fish dishes. If you are on your way to Hana or up to the top of Haleakala, stop by and get a box lunch. CJ's even has a menu for the kids.

Kaanapali Fairway Shops, 2580 Keka'a Dr. (just off the Honoapiilani Hwy.), Kaanapali Resort. ⓒ 808/667-0968. Breakfast items $3–$9.50; lunch $7–$12; Hana Lunch Box and Air Travel Lunch Box $12 each. AE, MC, V. Daily 7am–8pm.

Nikki's Pizza PIZZA   Formerly Pizza Paradiso, Nikki's has a full menu of pastas, pizzas, and desserts, including smoothies, coffee, and ice cream. This is a welcome addition to the Kaanapali scene, where casual is king and good food doesn't have to be fancy. The pizza reflects a simple and effective formula that has won acclaim through the years: good crust, true-blue sauces, and toppings loyal to tradition but with just enough edge for those who want it. Create your own pizza with roasted eggplant, mushrooms, anchovies, artichoke hearts, sausage, and a slew of other toppings. Nikki's offers some heroic choices, from the veggie to the Hawaiian (ham and Maui pineapple), to the Sopranos (roasted chicken, artichoke hearts, sun-dried tomatoes).

In Whalers Village, 2435 Kaanapali Pkwy. ⓒ 808/667-0333. Gourmet pizza $3.85–$4.65 by the slice; whole pizzas $12–$27. MC, V. Daily 11am–10pm.

HONOKOWAI, KAHANA & NAPILI

Note: You'll find the restaurants in this section on the "Where to Stay & Dine in West Maui" map on p. 377.

Moderate

Roy's Kahana Bar & Grill ★★ EURO-ASIAN   Despite the lack of dramatic view and an upstairs location in a shopping mall, Roy's remains crowded and extremely popular for one reason—fabulous food. It bustles with young, hip, impeccably trained servers delivering wasabi-pistachio crusted ahi steak, hibachi grilled salmon (with Japanese-style citrus ponzu), Asian jade pesto–steamed kampachi, and glazed honey-mustard short ribs. You could make a meal on the incredibly creative appetizers, such as Roy's original Hawaiian blackened ahi, crab cakes, seared shrimp sticks, crispy shrimp and pork lumpia, or Kula baby spinach salad. Large picture windows open up Roy's Kahana but don't quell the noise, another tireless trait long ago established by Roy's Restaurant in Honolulu, the flagship of Yamaguchi's burgeoning empire.

In the Kahana Gateway Shopping Center, 4405 Honoapiilani Hwy. ℂ **808/669-6999**. www.roysrestaurant.com. Reservations strongly recommended. Main courses $27–$37. AE, DC, DISC, MC, V. Daily 5:30–10pm.

Sea House Restaurant ASIAN/PACIFIC   The Sea House is not glamorous, famous, or hip, but it's worth mentioning for its spectacular view of Napili Bay. The Napili Kai Beach Club, where Sea House is located, is a charming throwback to the days when hotels blended in with their surroundings, had lush tropical foliage, and were sprawling rather than vertical. Dinner entrees range from "Uncle Frank's" banana Hawaiian snapper (with Hawaiian vanilla bean and coconut curry essence) to seafood chioppino, to veal piccata. There's even a menu for the keiki (kids), with items such as hamburgers and chicken nuggets.

In Napili Kai Beach Resort, 5900 Honoapiilani Hwy. ℂ **808/669-1500**. Reservations required for dinner. Main courses $25–$42; appetizer menu $5–$24. AE, DISC, MC, V. Daily 8am–9pm.

Inexpensive

Maui Brewing Company and Fish & Game Rotisserie SEAFOOD/STEAK This restaurant consists of a bar, a retail section, and tables. The small retail section sells fresh seafood, and the sit-down menu covers basic tastes: salads, fish and chips, fresh fish sandwiches, cheeseburgers, and beer—lots of it. At dinner, count on heavier meats and the fresh catch of the day (maybe ahi, mahimahi, or ono), with rotisserie items such as grilled chicken, steaks, and duck. The late-night menu offers shrimp, cheese fries, quesadillas, and lighter fare.

In the Kahana Gateway Shopping Center, 4405 Honoapiilani Hwy. ℂ **808/669-3474**. www.mauibrewingco.com. Reservations recommended for dinner. Main courses $8–$14 lunch, $12–$36 dinner. AE, DC, DISC, MC, V. Daily 11am–10pm; late-night menu 10:30pm–1am. During football season (Sept–Jan), brunch Sun 7:30am–3pm.

Maui Tacos MEXICAN   Mark Ellman's Maui Tacos chain has grown faster than you can say "Haleakala." Ellman put gourmet Mexican on paper plates and on the island's culinary map long before the island became known as Hawaii's center for salsa and chimichangas. Barely more than a takeout counter with a few tables, this and the six other Maui Tacos in Hawaii (five on Maui alone) are popular with hungry surfers, discerning diners, burrito buffs, and Hollywood glitterati, like Sharon Stone, whose picture adorns a wall or two. Choices include excellent fresh fish tacos (garlicky and flavorful), chimichangas, and mouth-breaking compositions such as the Hookipa (a personal favorite): a "surf burrito" of fresh fish, black beans, and salsa. The spinach burrito contains four kinds of beans, rice, and potatoes—it's a knockout, requiring a siesta afterward. Expect good food but not very fast service.

In Napili Plaza, 5095 Napili Hau St. © 808/665-0222. www.mauitacos.com. Items $1.75–$7.95. AE, DISC, MC, V Daily 9am–9pm. Also in Lahaina Sq., Lahaina. © 808/661-8883. Kamaole Beach Center, Kihei. © 808/879-5005. Kaahumanu Center, Kahului. © 808/871-7726. Piilani Village Shopping Center, Kihei, © 808/875-9340.

Pizza Paradiso Italian Caffe PIZZA/ITALIAN   Order at the counter (pastas, gourmet pizza whole or by the slice, paninis, salads, and desserts) and find a seat at one of the few tables. The pasta sauces—marinara, pescatore, Alfredo, Florentine, and pesto, with options and add-ons—are as popular as the pizzas (which took best pizza in the 2005 *Maui News*' Reader Poll). The Massimo, a pesto sauce with artichoke hearts, sun-dried tomatoes, and capers, comes with a choice of chicken, shrimp, or clams, and is so good it was a Taste of Lahaina winner in 1999. Recent new additions to the menu include gyros, souvlaki, hummus, and cheese steak sandwiches. Takeout, dine in, or delivery (free!), this is a hot spot in the neighborhood.

In the Honokowai Marketplace, 3350 Lower Honoapiilani Rd. © 808/667-2929. www.pizzaparadiso.com. Pastas $9.95–$11; pizzas $14–$28. DISC, MC, V. Daily 11am–10pm.

KAPALUA
Note: You'll find the restaurants in this section on the "Where to Stay & Dine in West Maui" map on p. 377.

Very Expensive
The Banyan Tree Restaurant ASIAN INFLUENCED   The most recent chef de cuisine, in a long line of outstanding chefs chosen from the stables of the Ritz-Carlton resorts around the globe, is Jojo Vasquez. His distinctive menu includes sautéed Kona kampachi with mustard greens, avocado, and poached shrimp salad; steamed onaga with Chinese black beans and pineapple emulsion; and roasted muscovy duck breast with sanke beans, enoki mushrooms, and pineapple gastrique. Plus a four- and five- course tasting menu incorporating Hawaiian gold Kapalua pineapple in every course (pineapple scallops, steamed onaga with spiced essence, crispy duck confit, and pineapple tiramisu). The atmosphere is extremely romantic, overlooking the ocean with the island of Molokai in the distance—get reservations for sunset.

Ritz-Carlton Kapalua Resort. © 808/669-6200. Reservations recommended for dinner. Dinner entrees $34–$55; 4-course meal $100; 5-course meal $125. AE, DC, DISC, MC, V. Tues–Sat 5:30–9:30pm.

Moderate
Pineapple Grill Kapalua ✦✦✦ PACIFIC ISLAND   If you had only 1 night to eat on the island of Maui, this would be the place to eat. Up-and-coming young chef Ryan Luckey (a local Lahaina boy) has taken the helm and is winning high praises from restaurant reviewers and the local residents who flock here nightly. My picks on this creative menu would be pistachio and wasabi pea–crusted ahi steak (with coconut-scented forbidden rice, Hamakua mushrooms, and wasabi ginger butter), sake-soy grilled mahimahi (in a ginger-carrot emulsion), or the wonderful Maui-style seafood paella (with a hint of Portuguese sausage and Kula herbs). An excellent list of wine pairings by the glass is available. Save room for dessert: the Maui gold-pineapple upside-down cake (with Whaler dark rum sauce and Maui-made Roselani gourmet mac-nut ice cream). There are also lots of tasty sandwiches and salads at lunch, and a continental-style breakfast in the morning. Plus, it's all served in a very Maui-like atmosphere, overlooking the rolling hills of the Kapalua Golf Course out to the Pacific Ocean.

200 Kapalua Dr. ⓒ **808/669-9600.** www.pineapplekapalua.com. Dinner reservations recommended. Lunch entrees $7–$17; dinner entrees $25–$35. AE, MC, V. Daily 8am–10pm.

Plantation House Restaurant 𝕲𝕲 SEAFOOD/HAWAIIAN-MEDITERRANEAN
With its teak tables, fireplace, and open sides, Plantation House gets stellar marks for atmosphere. The 360-degree view from high among the resort's pine-studded hills takes in Molokai and Lanai, the ocean, the rolling fairways and greens, the northwestern flanks of the West Maui Mountains, and the daily sunset spectacular. Readers of the *Maui News* have deemed this the island's Best Ambience—a big honor on an island of wonderful views. It's the best place for breakfast in West Maui, hands down, and one of my top choices for dinner. At breakfast, the eggs Mediterranean is superb, and at lunch, sandwiches (open-faced smoked turkey, roasted vegetable, and goat cheese wrap) and salads rule. When the sun sets, the menu expands to marvelous starters such as polenta and scampi-style shrimp, crab cakes, and Kula and Mediterranean salads. The menu changes constantly but may include fresh fish prepared several ways—among them, Mediterranean (on roasted Maui onions with couscous), Venice (pressed in panko, with a golden raisin–pine nut butter), Maui (pistachio-crusted), Plantation (with sautéed crab and lemon beurre blanc), and Italy (pepper-dusted with olives and caper-berry salsa). Plus numerous vegetarian entrees and wonderful Australian lamb, New Zealand lobster, and a Tuscan-style rib-eye steak you'll long remember.

2000 Plantation Club Dr. (at Kapalua Plantation Golf Course). ⓒ **808/669-6299.** www.theplantationhouse.com. Reservations recommended. Main courses $24–$32. AE, DC, MC, V. Daily 8am–3pm and 5:30–10pm.

Sansei Seafood Restaurant & Sushi Bar 𝕲𝕲 PACIFIC RIM   Perpetual award-winner Sansei offers an extensive menu of Japanese and East-West delicacies. Part fusion, part Hawaii Regional Cuisine, Sansei is tirelessly creative, with a menu that scores higher with adventurous palates than with purists (although there are endless traditional choices as well). If you don't like cilantro, watch out for those complex mango crab salad rolls. Other choices include panko-crusted ahi sashimi, sashimi trio, ahi carpaccio, noodle dishes, lobster, Asian shrimp cakes, traditional Japanese tempura, and sauces that surprise, in creative combinations such as ginger-lime chile butter and cilantro pesto. But there's simpler fare as well, such as shrimp tempura, noodles, and wok-tossed upcountry vegetables. Desserts are not to be missed. If it's autumn, don't pass up the Granny Smith apple tart with vanilla ice cream and home-made caramel sauce. In other seasons, opt for tempura-fried ice cream with chocolate sauce. There's karaoke Thursday and Friday nights from 10pm to 1am. *Money-saving tip:* Eat early; all food is 25% off between 5:30 and 6pm.

600 Office Rd. ⓒ **808/669-6286.** www.sanseihawaii.com. Reservations recommended. Main courses $16–$43. AE, DISC, MC, V. Daily 5:30–10pm. Also at Kihei Town Center, Kihei. ⓒ **808/879-0004.**

Vino Italian Tapas & Wine Bar 𝕲𝕲 *Finds* ITALIAN   Two Japanese guys, D. K. Kodama (chef and owner of Sansei Seafood Restaurant & Sushi Bar, reviewed above) and Chuck Furuya (Hawaii's only master sommelier), teamed up to create this culinary adventure for foodies. Vino opened in August 2003 to big, big accolades. Probably the best Italian food on Maui is served at this exquisite restaurant, overlooking the rolling hills of the Kapalua Golf Course. Always wanting to be on the cutting edge, the duo rebranded the restaurant in December 2004 to Vino Italian Tapas & Wine Bar. The new menu features more than two dozen tapas (small plates), ranging from the signature asparagus Milanese (just $7) to slow butter-poached Kona lobster

($20). Plus, they have retained the most popular large plate dishes, like fresh mahimahi with artichokes and grape tomatoes on capellini, crusted pan-fried veal stuffed with prosciutto, and *osso buco* with spinach risotto. Go to Vino's early during your stay on Maui; you most likely will want to return.

Kapalua Village Course Golf Club House, Kapalua Resort. (C) **808/661-VINO.** Reservations recommended. Tapas $6–$20; large plates $19–$38. AE, DISC, MC, V. Daily 11am–2pm and 5–9:30pm.

SOUTH MAUI
KIHEI/MAALAEA
There's a **Maui Tacos** at Kamaole Beach Center in Kihei ((C) **808/879-5005**). *Note:* You'll find the Kihei restaurants in this section on the "Where to Stay & Dine in South Maui" map on p. 381.

Expensive
Buzz's Wharf AMERICAN   Buzz's is another formula restaurant that offers a superb view, substantial sandwiches, meaty french fries, and surf-and-turf fare—in a word, satisfying but not sensational. Still, this bright, airy dining room is a fine way-station for whale-watching over a cold beer and a fresh mahimahi sandwich with fries. Some diners opt for several appetizers (stuffed mushrooms, steamer clams, clam chowder, onion soup) and a salad, and then splurge on dessert. Buzz's prize-winning Tahitian Baked Papaya is a warm, fragrant melding of fresh papaya with vanilla and coconut—the pride of the house.

50 Hauoli St., Maalaea Harbor. (C) 808/244-5426. www.buzzswharf.com. Reservations recommended. Main courses $20–$60. AE, DC, DISC, MC, V. Daily 11am–9pm.

Five Palms ✭ PACIFIC RIM   This is the best lunch spot in Kihei—open air, with tables a few feet from the beach and up-close-and-personal views of Kahoolawe and Molokini. You'll have to walk through a nondescript parking area and the modest entrance of the Mana Kai Resort to reach this unpretentious place. They feature a menu of breakfast and lunch items served from 8am to 2:30pm, so if you're jet-lagged and your stomach isn't on Hawaiian time, you can get a crab omelet at 2 in the afternoon or a juicy Kobe beef hamburger at 8 in the morning. At dinner, with the torches lit on the beach and the main dining room open, the ambience shifts to evening romantic but still casual. Just-caught fish is the star of the dinner menu.

In the Mana Kai Resort, 2960 S. Kihei Rd., Kihei. (C) 808/879-2607. www.fivepalmsrestaurant.com. Reservations recommended for dinner. Breakfast and lunch $7.95–$19; dinner $28–$45. AE, DC, MC, V. Daily 8am–2:30pm and 5–9:30pm, with pupu menu daily 2:45–6pm.

The Waterfront at Maalaea ✭✭ SEAFOOD   The family-owned Waterfront has won many prestigious awards for wine excellence, service, and seafood, but its biggest boost is word of mouth. Loyal diners rave about the friendly staff and seafood, fresh off the boat in nearby Maalaea Harbor and prepared with care. The bay and harbor view is one you'll never forget, especially at sunset. You have nine choices of preparations for the several varieties of fresh Hawaiian fish, ranging from *en papillote* (baked in buttered parchment) to Southwestern (smoked chile and cilantro butter), to Cajun spiced and Island style (sautéed, broiled, poached, or baked and paired with tiger prawns). Other choices: Kula onion soup, an excellent Caesar salad, the signature lobster chowder, and grilled eggplant layered with Maui onions, tomatoes, and spinach, served with red-pepper coulis and Feta Ravioli. Like the seafood, it's superb.

50 Hauoli St., Maalaea Harbor. (C) 808/244-9028. www.waterfrontrestaurant.net. Reservations recommended. Main courses $19–$41. AE, DC, DISC, MC, V. Daily 5pm–closing; last seating at 8:30pm.

Moderate

Café O'Lei Kihei ✦✦ STEAK/SEAFOOD   Chefs Michael and Dana Pastula have had a host of Café O'Lei restaurants on Maui (in Makawao, Lahaina, Maalaea, and Napili), and I've loved everyone of them. Their latest (in addition to the Ma'alaea Grill, reviewed below) is in an out-of-the-way location, the not-very-attractive Rainbow Mall. Never mind—you come here for the food, not the view (which is of congested Kihei Rd. and a small ocean view between the fence of high-rise condos across the street). Inside, the new location is an open and airy room, with floor-to-ceiling windows and hardwood floors; in the middle is a big circular bar and, on one side, an exhibition kitchen. The atmosphere is relaxing and inviting. The food is, as usual, not only outstanding, but a real bargain. You can't beat lunch with fresh fish, rice, and salad for under $12 (arrive early, as the locals are well aware of this wonderful gem and will book all the tables in advance). Dinners range from fresh fish to prime rib, mac nut–crusted chicken breast to roast duck, and even a mushroom-asparagus-pine-nut linguine for the vegetarians. Save room for dessert, such as pineapple upside-down cake or a fudge brownie sundae (yum, yum).

2439 South Kihei Rd., Kihei. ⓒ **808/891-1368.** Reservations recommended. Lunch entrees $7–$13; dinner entrees $15–$35. AE, DC, DISC, MC, V. Tues–Sun 10:30am–10pm.

Ma'alaea Grill ✦ ECLECTIC   This relaxing restaurant, with hardwood floors, bamboo dividers, and high ceilings, has one of the best views of the Pacific Ocean in Maalaea. There's a great lanai for sitting outside, but it's rarely used because the near-constant winds in Maalaea are wickedly strong. The lunch menu includes a yummy Asian Salad (oriental veggies and Chinese noodles over organic baby greens with a sesame vinaigrette) for $9, a mac nut–crusted ono with a ginger butter sauce for $12, and a range of burgers. At dinner, enjoy a terrific selection of fresh fish (prepared numerous ways), chicken, beef, and pasta—come before sunset. The restaurant is under the helm of Michael and Dana Pastula (who also own Café O'Lei, reviewed above). Their philosophy is "good food without hurting your pocketbook."

300 Maalaea Rd., Maalaea Harbor Village. ⓒ **808/243-2206.** Lunch entrees $7–$13; dinner entrees $15–$35. AE, DC, DISC, MC. V. Tues–Sun 10:30am–9pm; Mon 10:30am–3pm.

Stella Blues Cafe ✦ AMERICAN   Stella Blues gets going at breakfast and continues through to dinner with something for everyone—vegetarians, kids, pasta and sandwich lovers, hefty steak eaters, and sensible diners who go for the inexpensive fresh Maui greens salad. Grateful Dead posters line the walls, and a covey of gleaming motorcycles is invariably parked outside. It's loud and lively, irreverent and unpretentious. Sandwiches are the highlight, ranging from Tofu Extraordinaire to Mom's egg salad on a croissant, to garden burgers and grilled chicken. Tofu wraps and mountain-size Cobb salads are popular, as are large coffee shakes with mounds of whipped cream. Daily specials include fresh seafood and other surprises—all home-style cooking, made from scratch, down to the pesto mayonnaise and herb bread. At dinner, selections are geared toward good-value family dining, from affordable full dinners to pastas and burgers.

Azeka II Shopping Center, 1279 S. Kihei Rd., Kihei. ⓒ **808/874-3779.** Main courses $8–$26. AE, DC, DISC, MC, V. Daily 7:30am–10pm.

Tastings Wine Bar & Grill ✦✦ *Finds* AMERICAN   Hidden in a nondescript mini-mall (across the street from the Foodland in Kihei) lies a jewel of culinary creativity. Run by dynamic duo chef Derek McCarthy and his wife, Sandy Kim, this tiny bistro offers interesting, delicious "Island-inspired American cuisine," at excellent prices. I highly recommend the five-course menu with terrific wine pairings for $49. The regular menu includes such items as lettuce-wrapped prawn bundles with shaved carrots, cashews, cilantro, and mint for just $12; or spiced ahi seared rare ($14); or boat scallops on truffled cauliflower purée with a watercress salad ($15). The most expensive item on the menu is torchon of foie gras with grilled pineapple and lilikoi honey for $19. Don't leave without dessert: warm banana–mac nut bread with bananas Foster ice cream or bittersweet chocolate torte with hazelnut butter and caramelized bananas. Make reservations; this place is tiny and it's becoming popular.

Kihei Kalama Village, 1912 S. Kihei Rd. ℂ **808/879-8711.** Reservations highly recommended. Main courses $12–$19. 5-course meal with wine pairings $49. MC, V. Tues–Sun 5–10pm.

Inexpensive
The Coffee Store COFFEEHOUSE   This simple, classic coffeehouse for caffeine connoisseurs serves two dozen different types of coffee and coffee drinks, from mochas and lattes to cappuccinos, espressos, and toddies. Breakfast items include smoothies, lox and bagels, quiches, granola, and assorted pastries. Salads and sandwiches (tuna, turkey, ham, grilled veggie panini) also move briskly from the takeout counter. The turkey-and-veggie wraps are a local legend. There are only a few small tables, and they fill up fast, often with musicians and artists who've spent the previous evening entertaining at the Wailea and Kihei resorts.

In Azeka Place II, 1279 Kihei Rd., Kihei. ℂ **808/875-4244.** www.mauicoffee.com. All items less than $8.50. AE, MC, V. Mon–Sat 6am–7pm; Sun 6am–5pm.

Peggy Sue's AMERICAN   Just for a moment, forget that diet and take a leap. This 1950s-style diner has oodles of charm and is a swell place to spring for the best chocolate malt on the island. You'll also find sodas, shakes, floats, egg creams, milkshakes, and scoops of made-on-Maui Roselani brand gourmet ice cream. Old-fashioned soda-shop stools, an Elvis Presley Boulevard sign, and jukeboxes on every Formica table serve as a backdrop for the famous burgers (and garden burgers), brushed with teriyaki sauce and served with all the goodies. The fries are great, too.

In Azeka Place II, 1279 S. Kihei Rd., Kihei. ℂ **808/875-8944.** Burgers $8.45–$11; plate lunches $6.95–$16. AE, DISC, MC, V. Sun–Thurs 11am–9pm; Fri–Sat 11am–10pm.

Shaka Sandwich & Pizza PIZZA   How many "best pizzas" are there on Maui? It depends on which shore you're on, the west or the south. At this south-shore old-timer, which recently moved to a new (and much larger) location, they still are serving those award-winning pizzas, New York–style heroes, Philly cheese steaks, calzones, salads, and homemade garlic bread. Shaka uses fresh Maui produce, long-simmered sauces, and homemade Italian bread. Choose thin or Sicilian thick crust with gourmet toppings: Maui onions, spinach, anchovies, jalapeños, and a spate of other vegetables. Try the white pizza; with the perfectly balanced flavors of olive oil, garlic, and cheese, you won't even miss the tomato sauce. My favorite, the spinach pizza (with olive oil, spinach, garlic, and mozzarella), is a real treat.

1770 S. Kihei Rd., Kihei. ℂ **808/874-0331.** Sandwiches $6.35–$15; pizzas $17–$26. MC, V. Sun–Thurs 10:30am–9pm; Fri–Sat 10:30am–10pm.

WAILEA
The Shops at Wailea, a sprawling location between the Grand Wailea Hotel and Outrigger Wailea Resort, has added a spate of new shops and restaurants to this stretch of

South Maui. Five restaurants and dozens of shops, most of them upscale, are among the new tenants of this complex. **Ruth's Chris Steak House** is here, as well as **Tommy Bahama's Tropical Cafe & Emporium, Honolulu Coffee Company Café Wailea, Longhi's, Cheeseburger, Mai Tai's,** and **Rock-n-Roll.** Next door at the Wailea Beach Marriott Resort and Spa, **Hula Moons,** the retro-Hawaiian-themed restaurant, has reopened after a $3-million renovation and moved to the upper level of the lobby building, where it serves midpriced steak and seafood with an ocean view.

Note: You'll find the restaurants in this section on the "Where to Stay & Dine in South Maui" map on p. 381.

Very Expensive

Nick's Fishmarket Maui *ƙƙ* SEAFOOD Here's the place to bring your sweetie to enjoy the moon rise and the sweet smell of the stephanotis growing in on the terrace. Fans love this classic seafood restaurant that sticks to the tried and true. The few detractors complain that the food is too old style (ca. 1970s). Most agree that there is a high degree of professionalism in service and preparation. The Greek Maui Wowie salad gets my vote as one of the top salads in Hawaii. The menu features great fresh fish like opakapaka (one of their signature dishes), seared opah, and Hawaiian spiney lobster. For the non–fish eaters, rack of lamb, roasted chicken, and dry-aged New York steak offer ample choices for diners enjoying the fantasy setting on the South Maui shoreline.

In the Fairmont Kea Lani Hotel, 4100 Wailea Alanui. © **808/879-7224.** www.tri-star-restaurants.com. Reservations recommended. Main courses $30–$60; prix-fixe dinners $55–$85. AE, DC, DISC, MC, V. Daily 5:30–10pm; bar until 11pm.

Spago *ƙƙ* HAWAIIAN/CALIFORNIA/PACIFIC REGIONAL California meets Hawaii in this contemporary-designed eatery featuring fresh, local Hawaii ingredients prepared under the culinary watch of master chef Wolfgang Puck. The room, formerly Seasons Dining Room, has been stunningly transformed into a sleek modern layout using stone and wood in the open-air setting overlooking the Pacific Ocean. The cuisine lives up to Puck's reputation of using traditional Hawaiian dishes with his own brand of cutting-edge innovations. The menu features Hawaiian hapu'upu'u steamed in ti leaves; pineapple Thai red curry with onaga, mahi, and shrimp; grilled Chinois-style lamb chops; and caramelized pork chops with pineapple and papaya. The wine and beverage list is well thought out and extensive. Make reservations as soon as you land on the island (if not before); this place is popular. And bring plenty of cash or your platinum card.

Four Seasons Resort Maui, 3900 Wailea Alanui Dr., Wailea. © **808/879-2999.** www.fourseasons.com/maui. Reservations required. Main courses $37–$59. AE, DC, DISC, MC, V. Daily 5:30–9:30pm; bar with pupu daily 5–11pm.

Expensive

Ferraro's at Seaside *ƙ* ITALIAN This was a master stroke for Four Seasons: authentic Italian fare in a casual outdoor tropical setting, with a drop-dead gorgeous view of the ocean and the West Maui Mountains. Ferraro's is not inexpensive, but the food is first-rate. Lunch in the open-air restaurant features fabulous salads (my pick is the seared Hawaiian tuna and Nicoise salad), sandwiches (from a chicken pita to a grilled sirloin burger), and some Hawaiian classics (try the sesame-crusted salmon). At dinner, the romantic setting, with the sound of the ocean waves, makes for a memorable evening. The fish selection is noteworthy: grilled ahi with a crispy basil risotto roll, candied bell peppers, goat cheese, and a pine nut dressing, or pan-fried mahi with basil gnocchi. Make room for dessert; my favorite is the roasted Maui pineapple cobbler with buttermilk rum ice cream.

In the Four Seasons Resort Maui at Wailea, 3900 Wailea Alanui Dr. ✆ 808/874-8000. Reservations recommended. Lunch $15–$22; dinner courses $25–$46. AE, DC, DISC, MC, V. Daily 11:30am–4pm, 4–6pm (pupu menu), and 6–9pm.

Moderate
Joe's Bar & Grill ★★ AMERICAN GRILL   The 270-degree view spans the golf course, tennis courts, ocean, and Haleakala—a worthy setting for Beverly Gannon's style of American home cooking with a regional twist. The hearty staples include excellent mashed potatoes, lobster, fresh fish, and filet mignon, but the meatloaf (a whole loaf, like Mom used to make) seems to upstage them all. The Tuscan white bean soup is superb, and the tenderloin, with roasted portobellos, mashed potatoes with whole garlic, and a pinot noir demi-glace, is American home cooking at its best. Daily specials could be grilled ahi with white truffle–Yukon gold mashed potatoes or sautéed mahimahi with shrimp bisque and sautéed spinach. If chocolate cake is on the menu, you should definitely spring for it.

In the Wailea Tennis Club, 131 Wailea Ike Place. ✆ 808/875-7767. Reservations recommended. Main courses $26–$34. AE, DC, DISC, MC, V. Daily 5:30–9pm.

SeaWatch ★ ISLAND CUISINE   Under the same ownership as Kapalua's Plantation House Restaurant (p. 410), SeaWatch is a good choice from morning to evening, and it's one of the more affordable stops in tony Wailea. You'll dine on the terrace or in a high-ceilinged room, on a menu that carries the tee-off-to-19th-hole crowd with ease. From breakfast on, it's a celebration of island bounty: crab-cake eggs Benedict or smoked salmon Benedict is a great way to start your day. Lunch has a range of sandwiches (from a mango barbecue kalua pork sandwich to the traditional burgers, to fresh fish sandwiches), salads, and entrees (work stir-fried vegetables with grilled basil chicken to blackened fresh catch). Dinner, with that fabulous ocean view, has five different ways to prepare the fish of the day, roasted New Zealand lamb, muscovy duck, and free-range chicken breast.

100 Wailea Golf Club Dr. ✆ 808/875-8080. www.seawatchrestaurant.com. Reservations recommended for dinner. Breakfast $7–$12; lunch $8.50–$15; dinner main courses $28–$34. AE, DC, MC, V. Daily 8am–10pm.

MAKENA
Prince Court ★★ CONTEMPORARY ISLAND   Half of the Sunday brunch experience here is the head-turning view of Makena Beach, Molokini islet, and Kahoolawe island. The other half is the fabled Sunday buffet, bountiful and sumptuous, spread over several tables: pasta, omelets, cheeses, pastries, sashimi, crab legs, smoked salmon, fresh Maui produce, and a smashing array of ethnic and Continental foods, plus a few surprises: assorted dim sum, Thai-style beef curry, specialty pastas, and not-to-be-missed desserts. The dinner menu changes regularly but might include a rack of lamb, vegetable risotto, coquilles St. Jacques, or veal scaloppini ala marsala. On a recent visit, we dined on blackened ahi, pulehu teriyaki short ribs, and Asian seafood noodles. Don't miss the Friday night seafood and prime rib buffet, with one of the largest selections of seafood on ice (fresh sashimi, shrimp, Hawaiian poke, and oysters), a roast beef carving station, tons of salads (with a Caesar salad bar), and a range of other entrees (fresh fish, grilled chicken, etc.).

In the Maui Prince Hotel, 5400 Makena Alanui. ✆ 808/874-1111. Reservations recommended. Main courses $27–$45; Fri prime rib and seafood buffet $45 ($25 child, ages 5 and under eat free); Sun brunch $42. AE, MC, V. Sun 9am–1pm (with last seating at noon); Fri–Wed 6–9pm (Fri buffet 5 seatings, call for times).

UPCOUNTRY MAUI

Note: You'll find the restaurants in this section on the "Upcountry & East Maui" map on p. 391.

HALIIMAILE (ON THE WAY TO UPCOUNTRY MAUI)
Moderate

Haliimaile General Store ⭑⭑⭑ HAWAII REGIONAL/AMERICAN For More than a decade, Bev Gannon, one of the original Hawaii Regional Cuisine chefs, has been going strong at her foodie haven in the pineapple fields. You'll dine at tables set on old wood floors under high ceilings (sound ricochets fiercely here), in a peach-colored room emblazoned with works by local artists. The food, a blend of eclectic American with ethnic touches, puts an innovative spin on Hawaii Regional Cuisine. Even the fresh-catch sandwich on the lunch menu is anything but prosaic. Sip the *lilikoi* lemonade and nibble the sashimi napoleon or the house salad—island greens with mandarin oranges, onions, toasted walnuts, and blue-cheese crumble—all are notable items on a menu that bridges Hawaii with Gannon's Texas roots.

Haliimaile Rd. © **808/572-2666.** www.haliimailegeneralstore.com. Reservations recommended. Lunch $8–$22; dinner $22–$39. AE, DC, MC, V. Mon–Fri 11am–2:30pm; daily 5:30–9:30pm.

MAKAWAO & PUKALANI
Inexpensive

Casanova Italian Restaurant ⭑ ITALIAN Look for the tiny veranda with a few stools, always full, in front of a deli at Makawao's busiest intersection—that's the most visible part of the Casanova restaurant and lounge. Makawao's nightlife center contains a stage, dance floor, restaurant, and bar—and food to love and remember. This is pasta heaven; try the spaghetti *fra diavolo* or the spinach gnocchi in a fresh tomato-Gorgonzola sauce. Other choices include a huge pizza selection, grilled lamb chops in an Italian mushroom marinade, lots more pasta dishes, and luscious desserts. My personal picks on a stellar menu: garlic spinach topped with Parmesan and pine nuts, and tiramisu, the best on the island.

1188 Makawao Ave. © **808/572-0220.** www.casanovamaui.com. Reservations recommended for dinner. Main courses $22–$28; 12-in. pizzas $12–$20; pasta $12–$18. AE, DC, DISC, MC, V. Mon–Sat 11:30am–2pm and 5:30–9:30pm; Sun 5:30–9pm. Dancing Wed–Sat 9:45pm–1am. Lounge daily 5:30pm–12:30am or 1am. Deli Mon–Sat 7:30am–6pm; Sun 8:30am–6pm.

KULA (AT THE BASE OF HALEAKALA NATIONAL PARK)
Inexpensive

Cafe 808 AMERICAN/LOCAL Despite its out-of-the-way location (or perhaps because of it), Cafe 808 has become the universal favorite among upcountry residents of all ages. The breakfast coffee group, the lunchtime crowd, and dinner regulars all know it's the place for tasty home-style cooking with no pretensions: famous burgers (teriyaki, hamburger, cheeseburger, garden burger, mahimahi, taro), roast pork, smoked turkey, and a huge selection of local-style specials. Regulars rave about the chicken katsu, saimin, and beef stew. The few tables are sprinkled around a room with linoleum-tile floors, hardwood benches, plastic patio chairs, and old-fashioned booths—rough around the edges in a pleasing way, and very camp.

Lower Kula Rd., past Holy Ghost Church, across from Morihara Store. © **808/878-6874.** Burgers from $4; main courses $5.50–$9.95. No credit cards. Daily 6am–8pm.

Grandma's Coffee House COFFEEHOUSE/AMERICAN   Alfred Franco's grandmother started what is now a five-generation coffee business back in 1918, when she was 16 years old. Today this tiny wooden coffeehouse, still fueled by homegrown Haleakala coffee beans, is the quintessential roadside oasis. Grandma's offers espresso, hot and cold coffees, home-baked pastries, inexpensive pasta, sandwiches (including sensational avocado and garden burgers), homemade soups, fresh juices, and local plate-lunch specials that change daily. Rotating specials include Hawaiian beef stew, ginger chicken, chicken curry, lentil soup, and sandwiches piled high with Kula vegetables. The coffee is legendary, but I think the real standouts are the lemon squares and the pumpkin bread.

At the end of Hwy. 37, Keokea (about 6 miles before the Tedeschi Vineyards in Ulupalakua). ℂ 808/878-2140. Most items less than $8.95. AE, DC, MC, V. Daily 7am–5pm.

Kula Sandalwoods Restaurant ⭐ AMERICAN   Chef Eleanor Loui, a graduate of the Culinary Institute of America, makes hollandaise sauce every morning from fresh upcountry egg yolks, sweet butter, and Meyer lemons, which her family grows in the yard above the restaurant. This is Kula cuisine, with produce from the backyard and everything made from scratch, including French toast with home-baked Portuguese sweet bread; hotcakes or Belgian waffles with fresh fruit; open-faced country omelets; hamburgers drenched in a special cheese sauce made with grated sharp cheddar; a killer kalua pork sandwich; and an outstanding veggie burger. The grilled chicken breast sandwich is marvelous, served with soup of the day and Kula mixed greens. Dine in the gazebo or on the terrace, with dazzling views in all directions, including, in the spring, a yard dusted with lavender jacaranda flowers and a hillside ablaze with fields of orange akulikuli blossoms.

15427 Haleakala Hwy. (Hwy. 377). ℂ 808/878-3523. Breakfast $6.95–$12; lunch $7.25–$12; Sun brunch $6.95–$12. MC, V. Mon–Sat 6:30am–3pm; Sun brunch 6:30am–noon.

Moderate
Kula Lodge ⭐ HAWAII REGIONAL/AMERICAN   Don't let the dinner prices scare you; the Kula Lodge is equally enjoyable, if not more so, at breakfast and lunch, when the prices are lower and the views through the picture windows have an eye-popping intensity. The million-dollar vista spans the flanks of Haleakala, rolling 3,200 feet down to central Maui, the ocean, and the West Maui Mountains. The Kula Lodge has always been known for its breakfasts: fabulous eggs Benedict, including a vegetarian version with Kula onions, shiitake mushrooms, and scallions; legendary banana–mac nut pancakes; and a highly recommended tofu scramble with green onions, Kula vegetables, and garlic chives. If possible, go for sunset cocktails and watch the colors change into deep end-of-day hues. When darkness descends, a roaring fire and lodge atmosphere add to the coziness of the room. The dinner menu features "small plates" of Thai summer rolls, seared ahi, and other starters. Sesame-seared ono, leads the seafood attractions, but there's also pasta, rack of lamb, filet mignon, and free-range chicken breast.

Haleakala Hwy. (Hwy. 377). ℂ 808/878-2517. Reservations recommended for dinner. Breakfast $7.50–$16; lunch $11–$18; dinner $14–$29. AE, DC, DISC, MC, V. Daily 6:30am–9pm.

EAST MAUI
Note: You'll find the restaurants in this section on the "Upcountry & East Maui" map on p. 391.

PAIA
Inexpensive

Cafe des Amis 𝖋𝖋 *Finds* CREPES/MEDITERRANEAN/INDIAN This tiny eatery is a hidden delight: healthy and tasty breakfasts, lunches, and dinners that are easy on the wallet. Crepes are the star here, and they are popular: spinach with feta cheese, shrimp curry with coconut milk, and dozens more choices, including breakfast crepes and dessert crepes (like banana and chocolate or strawberries and cream). Equally popular are the Greek salads and smoothies. Dinners feature authentic Indian curries (service with rice, mango chutney, and tomato chutney), such as a vegetable curry with spinach, carrots, cauliflower, and potato with Tamil spices and tomato. It also serves the best coffee in Paia.

42 Baldwin Ave. © 808/579-6323. Breakfast crepes $8–$9; lunch crepes $7.25–$9; dinner entrees $11–$15. MC, V. Daily 8:30am–8:30pm.

Jacques North Shore 𝖋𝖋 *Value* SEAFOOD/SUSHI Of the numerous restaurants that have come and gone over the years at this location (right next to Charley's), this eclectic outdoor eatery is my favorite. Jacques is difficult to pin down; some have called it a hipper, cheaper version of the upscale Mama's Fish House (see review below) just down the road; others depict it as an atypical Maui dining experience with excellent food and great prices. The clientele tend to be trendy, hard-body windsurfers; blonde, tan surfers; and chic north-shore residents. Visitors who wander in generally leave with a smile. The decor is patio dining under a big circus tent. Some might be distracted by the hostess and servers (20-something beauty queens dressed in "barely there" clothes), but the main attraction is the food. Do not miss the North Shore pumpkin fish (fish, bananas, and oranges served with a ginger pumpkin sauce and miso butter), Greek pasta (roasted bell peppers, roasted garlic, and feta cheese over orecchiette pasta), or one of the fabulous vegetarian entrees like the vegetable curry (with tofu, bananas, and oranges). The sushi bar (closed Sun–Mon) whips out a mean spicy ahi roll and a died-and-gone-to-heaven California roll.

120 Hana Hwy. © 808/579-8844. Reservations not accepted. Main courses $11–$27. AE, DC, DISC, MC, V. Daily 5–10pm; sushi bar Tues–Sat 5–10pm.

Milagros Food Company 𝖋 SOUTHWESTERN/SEAFOOD Milagros has gained a following with its great home-style cooking, upbeat atmosphere, and highly touted margaritas. Sit outdoors and watch the parade of Willie Nelson look-alikes ambling by as you tuck into the ahi creation of the evening, a combination of Southwestern and Pacific Rim styles and flavors accompanied by fresh veggies and Kula greens. For breakfast, I recommend the Popeye spinach omelet or the huevos rancheros. Lunch ranges from ahi burgers to honey and mac-nut grilled salmon salad, to Clayton's One-Pound Burger. For dinner, options include a grilled ahi burrito, Mexican red enchiladas, seafood enchiladas, New York strip steak, shrimp pasta, and even Chesapeake Bay crab cakes. I love Paia's tie-dyes, beads, and hippie flavor, and this is the front-row seat for it all. Watch for happy hour, with cheap and fabulous margaritas.

Hana Hwy. and Baldwin Ave. © 808/579-8755. Breakfast $6–$9; lunch $7–$12; dinner $14–$25. AE, MC, V. Daily 8am–11pm.

Moana Bakery & Cafe 𝖋𝖋 LOCAL/EUROPEAN Moana gets high marks for its stylish concrete floors, high ceilings, booths and cafe tables, and fabulous food. Don Ritchey, formerly a chef at Haliimaile General Store, has created the perfect Paia eatery, a casual bakery-cafe that highlights his stellar skills. All the bases are covered: saimin, omelets, wraps, pancakes, and fresh-baked goods in the morning; soups, sandwiches, pasta, and satisfying salads for lunch; and, for dinner, varied selections with Asian and European influences and fresh island ingredients. The lemon grass–grilled prawns with green papaya salad is an explosion of flavors and textures; the roasted vegetable napoleon is gourmet fare; and the Thai red curry with coconut milk, served over vegetables, seafood, or tofu, comes atop jasmine rice with crisp rice noodles and fresh sprouts to cool the fire. Ritchey's Thai-style curries are richly spiced and intense. I also vouch for his special gift with fish: The nori sesame–crusted mahimahi with miso garlic tapioca pearls is cooked, like the curry, to perfection. There's live jazz most Friday nights.

71 Baldwin Ave. © **808/579-9999.** Reservations recommended for dinner. Breakfast $7–$14; lunch $6–$13; dinner main courses $7–$32. MC, V. Tues–Sun 8am–9pm; Mon 8am–2:30pm.

Paia Fish Market SEAFOOD   This is a true fish market, with fresh fish to take home and cooked seafood, salads, pastas, fajitas, and quesadillas to take out or enjoy at the few picnic tables inside the restaurant. It's an appealing selection: Cajun-style fresh catch, fresh fish specials (usually ahi or salmon), fresh fish tacos and quesadillas, and seafood and chicken pastas. You can also order hamburgers, cheeseburgers, fish and chips (or shrimp and chips), and wonderful lunch and dinner plates, cheap and tasty. Photos of the number-one sport here, windsurfing, adorn the walls.

110 Hana Hwy. © **808/579-8030.** Lunch and dinner plates $8–$22. DISC, MC, V. Daily 11am–9:30pm.

HAIKU
Colleen's at the Cannery ★★★ *Finds* ECLECTIC   Way, way, way off the beaten path lies this fabulous find in the rural Haiku Cannery Marketplace. Once through the doors, you'll swear you've dropped down in the middle of a hot, chic boutique restaurant in Soho in Manhattan (only, when you look around at the patrons, they are pure Haiku upcountry residents). It's worth the drive to enjoy Colleen's fabulous culinary creations, like a wild mushroom ravioli with sautéed portobello mushrooms, tomatoes, herbs, and a roasted pepper coulis for $14 (not New York City prices); pan-seared ahi for $15; or filet mignon with a side salad for $16. Colleen also serves up smaller meals, such as burgers and fish and chips. Breakfast includes mouth-watering bakery products such as French toast ($7.75) with Colleen's own homemade bread or the wonderful omelets ($9). Lunch stars baguette sandwiches, wraps, salads, and burgers and fries. I only wish they would take reservations.

Haiku Cannery Marketplace, 810 Haiku Rd. © **808/575-9211.** www.colleensinhaiku.com. Reservations not accepted. Breakfast $5.75–$9; lunch $7–15; dinner entrees $14–$24. MC, V. Daily 6am–10pm.

ON THE ROAD TO HANA
Very Expensive
Mama's Fish House ★★★ SEAFOOD   Okay, it's expensive (maybe the most expensive seafood house on Maui), but if you love fish, this is the place for you. The restaurant's entrance, a cove with windsurfers, tide pools, white sand, and a canoe resting under palm trees, is a South Seas fantasy worthy of Gauguin. The interior features curved lauhala-lined ceilings, walls of split bamboo, lavish arrangements of tropical blooms, and picture windows to let in the view. With servers wearing Polynesian prints and flowers behind their ears, and the sun setting in Kuau Cove, Mama's mood is hard to beat. The fish is fresh (the fishermen are even credited by name on the

menu) and prepared either Hawaiian style, with tropical fruit or baked in a crust of macadamia nuts and vanilla beans, or in a number of dishes involving ferns, seaweed, Maui onions, and roasted kukui nut. My favorite menu item is mahimahi laulau with luau leaves (taro greens) and Maui onions, baked in ti leaves and served with *kalua* pig and Hanalei poi. You can get deepwater ahi seared with coconut and lime, or ono "caught by Keith Nakamura along the 40-fathom ledge near Hana" in Hana ginger teriyaki with mac nuts and crisp Maui onion. Other special touches include the use of Molokai sweet potato, organic lettuces, Haiku bananas, and fresh coconut, which evoke the mood and tastes of old Hawaii.

799 Poho Place, just off the Hana Hwy., Kuau. ⓒ **808/579-8488**. Reservations recommended for lunch, required for dinner. Main courses $32–$48 lunch, $35–$55 dinner. AE, DC, DISC, MC, V. Daily 11am to last seating at 9pm (light menu 2:30–4:30pm).

Inexpensive
Nahiku Coffee Shop, Smoked Fish Stand, and Ti Gallery ⓡ *Finds* SMOKED KABOBS
What a delight to stumble across this trio of comforts on the long drive to Hana! The small coffee shop purveys locally made baked goods, several flavors of Maui-grown coffee, organic tropical fruit smoothies, and the Original and Best Coconut Candy made by Hana character Jungle Johnny. Next door, the Ti Gallery sells locally made Hawaiian arts and crafts, such as pottery and koa wood vessels.

The barbecue smoker, though, is my favorite part of the operation. It puts out superb smoked and grilled fish, fresh and locally caught, sending seductive aromas out into the moist Nahiku air. These are not jerkylike smoked meats; the process keeps the kabobs moist while retaining the smoke flavor. The breadfruit—sliced, wrapped in banana leaf, and baked—can be bland and starchy (like a baked potato), but it's a stroke of genius to give visitors a taste of this important Polynesian staple. The teriyaki-based marinade, made by the owner, adds a special touch to the fish (such as ono, ahi, and marlin). One of the biggest sellers is the *kalua* pig sandwich. Also a hit are the Island-style, two-hand tacos of fish, beef, and chicken, served with about six condiments, including cheese, jalapeños, and salsa. When available, fresh corn on the cob from Kipahulu is served and grabbed up apace. There are a few roadside picnic tables, or you can take your lunch to go for a beachside picnic in Hana.

Hana Hwy., ½ mile past mile marker 28. No phone. Kabobs $3 each. No credit cards. Fish stand Fri–Wed 10am–5pm; coffee shop daily 9am–5:30pm; gallery daily 10am–5pm.

Pauwela Cafe ⓡ *Finds* INTERNATIONAL
It's easy to get lost while searching out this wonderful cafe, but it's such a find. I never dreamed you could dine so well with such pleasing informality. The tiny cafe with a few tables indoors and out has a strong local following for many reasons. Three local boys purchased this well-loved cafe from the original owners in 2004. Brandon Shim is the chef (formerly with Tommy Bahamas in Wailea) and trained under previous owner Chris Speere at the Maui Community College Culinary Arts School. Chef Brandon certainly has learned well. Nearly everything in this tiny cafe is made from scratch. Breakfasts feature such scrumptious items as *pain perdu* (French bread in orange vanilla custard) and Belgian waffles. On Sunday, for brunch, Chef Brandon is whipping up eggs Benedict on cornbread with lemon hollandaise. Lunch is a great collection of salads and sandwiches, where the scene-stealing *kalua* turkey sandwich consists of moist, smoky shredded turkey with cheese on home-baked French bread and covered with a green-chile and cilantro sauce. For the vegetarians, there's a vegetarian taro burger and veggie burritos.

Because this cafe is located in an industrial center of sailboard and surfboard manufacturers, you may find a surf legend dining at the next table. The cafe is a little less than 1½ miles past the Haiku turnoff and a half-mile up on the left.

375 W. Kuiaha Rd., off Hana Hwy., past Haiku Rd., Haiku. ℭ 808/575-9242. Breakfast $4.25–$8.50; lunch $5.25–$9.50. AE, DISC, MC, V. Mon–Sat 7am–2:30pm; Sun 7am–1pm.

HANA

Hotel Hana-Maui ★★★ LOCAL/ECLECTIC   Not even Passport Resorts' executive chef, John Cox, who is in charge of developing the daily menu changes, can put his finger on the delicious type of cuisine served in the open, airy dining room. "I call it cuisine inspired by eastern Maui," he says, pointing to the ingredients-driven menu: the fresh fish caught by local fishermen, the produce brought in by nearby farmers, the fruits that are in season. The result is true Hawaiian food, grown right on the island. Breakfast features an omelet with local Maui onions and a Hana fern salad, almond-crusted French toast, or local papaya with yogurt and homemade granola. Lunch ranges from Maui Cattle Company burgers to just-caught fish sandwiches. Dinner, which changes daily, can include just-picked lettuce for salads (Kula-grown baby romaine with Gruyère crostini and sherry-thyme vinaigrette, or baby salad greens with Kula citrus, local radishes, and Kalamata olives); a range of soups (such as a chilled Kula cucumber soup); and entrees such as seared rare Hana-caught ahi with smoked bacon, forest mushrooms, and wilted greens, or oven-roasted chicken breast with crispy polenta, Nihiku bush beans, and mole sauce. Try the three- or four-course tasting menu or, even better, the Chef's Choice.

Hana Hwy. ℭ 808/248-8211. Reservations recommended for Fri–Sat dinner. Entrees $13–$18 breakfast, $10–$21 lunch, $31–$36 dinner; tasting menu $55 for 3 courses; $67 for 4 courses; $75 for Chef's Choice. AE, DISC, MC, V. Daily 7:30–10:30am, 11:30am–2:30pm, and 6–9pm. Friday buffet $50 and Hawaiian show 6–8:30pm.

5 Beaches

For beach toys and equipment, head to **Snorkel Bob's** (www.snorkelbob.com), which rents snorkel gear, boogie boards, and other ocean toys at four locations: 1217 Front St., Lahaina (ℭ 808/661-4421); Napili Village, 5425-C Lower Honoapiilani Hwy., Napili (ℭ 808/669-9603); in North Kihei at Azeka Place II, 1279 S. Kihei Rd. #310 (ℭ 808/875-6188); and in South Kihei/Wailea at Kamaole Beach Center, 2411 S. Kihei Rd. (ℭ 808/879-7449). All locations are open daily 8am to 5pm. If you're island hopping, you can rent from a Snorkel Bob's location on one island and return to a branch on another.

WEST MAUI

KAANAPALI BEACH ⌖

Four-mile-long Kaanapali is one of Maui's best beaches, with grainy gold sand as far as the eye can see. The beach parallels the sea channel through most of its length, and a paved walk links hotels and condos, open-air restaurants, and the Whalers Village shopping center. Because Kaanapali is so long and broad, and because most hotels have adjacent swimming pools, the beach is crowded only in pockets—there's plenty of room to find seclusion. Summertime swimming is excellent. The best snorkeling is around Black Rock, in front of the Sheraton, where the water's clear, calm, and populated with clouds of tropical fish.

Beaches & Outdoor Activities on Maui

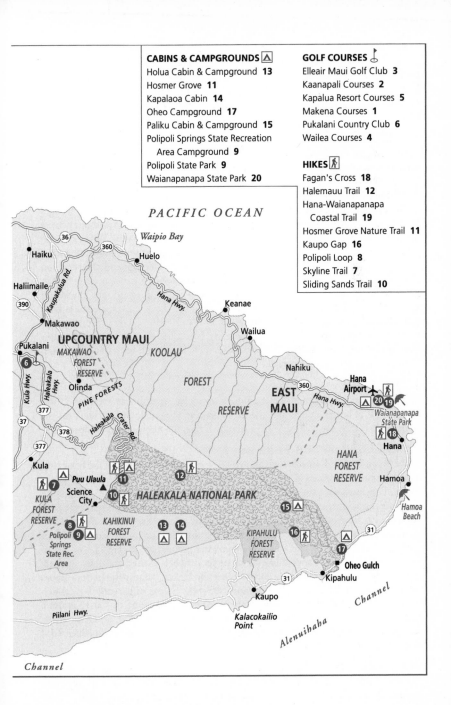

CABINS & CAMPGROUNDS △
Holua Cabin & Campground **13**
Hosmer Grove **11**
Kapalaoa Cabin **14**
Oheo Campground **17**
Paliku Cabin & Campground **15**
Polipoli Springs State Recreation
  Area Campground **9**
Polipoli State Park **9**
Waianapanapa State Park **20**

GOLF COURSES 🏌
Elleair Maui Golf Club **3**
Kaanapali Courses **2**
Kapalua Resort Courses **5**
Makena Courses **1**
Pukalani Country Club **6**
Wailea Courses **4**

HIKES 🚶
Fagan's Cross **18**
Halemauu Trail **12**
Hana-Waianapanapa
  Coastal Trail **19**
Hosmer Grove Nature Trail **11**
Kaupo Gap **16**
Polipoli Loop **8**
Skyline Trail **7**
Sliding Sands Trail **10**

PACIFIC OCEAN

Waipio Bay

Haiku

Huelo

Haliimaile

Makawao

UPCOUNTRY MAUI

Pukalani

MAKAWAO FOREST RESERVE

Olinda

PINE FORESTS

KOOLAU

FOREST

Keanae

Wailua

Nahiku

EAST MAUI

Hana Airport

Waianapanapa State Park

Hana

Kula

RESERVE

KULA FOREST RESERVE

Science City

Puu Ulaula

HALEAKALA NATIONAL PARK

KAHIKINUI FOREST RESERVE

Polipoli
Springs
State Rec.
Area

HANA FOREST RESERVE

Hamoa

Hamoa Beach

KIPAHULU FOREST RESERVE

Oheo Gulch

Kipahulu

Kaupo

Piilani Hwy.

Kalacokailio Point

Alenuihaha

Channel

Channel

Facilities include outdoor showers; you can also use the restrooms at the hotel pools. Various beach-activities vendors line up in front of the hotels. Parking is a problem, though. There are two public entrances: At the south end, turn off Honoapiilani Highway into the Kaanapali Resort and pay for parking here; or continue on Honoapiilani Highway, turn off at the last Kaanapali exit at the stoplight near the Maui Kaanapali Villas, and park next to the beach signs indicating public access.

KAPALUA BEACH 𝔊𝔊𝔊

The beach cove that fronts the Kapalua Bay Hotel and the Coconut Grove Villas is the stuff of dreams: a golden crescent bordered by two palm-studded points. The sandy bottom slopes gently to deep water at the bay mouth; the water's so clear that you can see it turn to green and then deep blue. Protected from strong winds and currents by the lava-rock promontories, Kapalua's calm waters are ideal for swimmers of all ages and abilities, and the bay is big enough to paddle a kayak around in without getting into the more challenging channel that separates Maui from Molokai. Waves come in just right for riding, and fish hang out by the rocks, making it great for snorkeling.

The beach is accessible from the hotel on one end, which provides shaded sun chairs and a beach-activities center for its guests, and a public access way on the other. It isn't so wide that you burn your feet getting in or out of the water, and the inland side is edged by a shady path and cool lawns. Outdoor showers are stationed at both ends. Parking is limited to about 30 spaces in a small lot off Lower Honoapiilani Road, by Napili Kai Beach Club, so arrive early. Next door is a nice but pricey oceanfront restaurant, Kapalua's Bay Club. Facilities include showers, restrooms, lifeguards, a rental shack, and plenty of shade.

SOUTH MAUI

Wailea's beaches may seem off-limits, hidden from plain view as they are by an intimidating wall of luxury resorts, but they're all open to the public by law. Look for the SHORELINE ACCESS signs along **Wailea Alanui Drive,** the resort's main boulevard.

KAMAOLE III BEACH PARK 𝔊

Three beach parks—Kamaole I, II, and III—stand like golden jewels in the front yard of the funky seaside town of Kihei, which, all of a sudden, is sprawling like suburban blight. The beaches are the best thing about Kihei. These three are popular with local residents and visitors alike because they're easily accessible. On weekends, they're jam-packed with fishermen, picnickers, swimmers, and snorkelers. The most popular is Kamaole III, or "Kam-3." It's the biggest of the three beaches, with wide pockets of gold sand, and the only one with a children's playground and a grassy lawn. Swimming is safe here, but scattered lava rocks are toe-stubbers at the water line, and parents should make sure their kids don't venture too far out because the bottom slopes off quickly. Both the north and south shores are rocky fingers with a surge big enough to attract fish and snorkelers; the winter waves appeal to bodysurfers. Kam-3 is also a wonderful place to watch the sunset. Facilities include restrooms, showers, picnic tables, barbecue grills, and lifeguards. There's plenty of parking on South Kihei Road across from the Maui Parkshore condos.

MALUAKA BEACH (MAKENA BEACH) 𝔊

On the southern end of Maui's resort coast, development falls off dramatically, leaving a wild, dry countryside of green kiawe trees. The Maui Prince sits in isolated splendor, sharing Makena Resort's 1,800 acres with only a couple of first-rate golf courses and a necklace of perfect beaches. The strand nearest the hotel is Maluaka Beach, often called Makena, notable for its beauty and its views of Molokini Crater, the offshore islet, and Kahoolawe, the so-called "target" island (it was used as a bombing target from 1945 until the early 1990s). This is a short, wide, palm-fringed crescent of golden, grainy sand set between two black-lava points and bounded by big sand dunes topped by a grassy knoll. The swimming in this mostly calm bay is considered the best on Makena Bay, which is bordered on the south by Puu Olai Cinder Cone and historic Keawalai Congregational Church. The waters around Makena Landing, at the north end of the bay, are particularly good for snorkeling. Facilities include restrooms, showers, a landscaped park, lifeguards, and roadside parking. Along Makena Alanui, look for the SHORELINE ACCESS sign near the hotel, turn right, and head down to the shore.

ONELOA BEACH (BIG BEACH) 🤿🤿

Oneloa, meaning "long sand" in Hawaiian, is one of the most popular beaches on Maui. Locals call it "Big Beach"—it's 3,300 feet long and more than 100 feet wide. Mauians come here to swim, fish, sunbathe, surf, and enjoy the view of Kahoolawe and Lanai. Snorkeling is good around the north end, at the foot of Puu Olai, a 360-foot cinder cone. During storms, however, big waves lash the shore, and a strong rip current sweeps the sharp drop-off, posing a danger for inexperienced open-ocean swimmers. There are no facilities except for portable toilets, but there's plenty of parking. To get here, drive past the Maui Prince Hotel to the second dirt road, which leads through a kiawe thicket to the beach.

On the other side of Puu Olai is **Little Beach,** a small pocket beach where assorted nudists work on their all-over tans, to the chagrin of uptight authorities. You can get a nasty sunburn and a lewd-conduct ticket, too.

ULUA BEACH 🤿

One of the most popular beaches in Wailea, Ulua is a long, wide, crescent-shaped gold-sand beach between two rocky points. When the ocean's calm, Ulua offers Wailea's best snorkeling; when it's rough, the waves are excellent for bodysurfers. The ocean bottom is shallow and gently slopes down to deeper waters, making swimming generally safe. The beach is usually occupied by guests of nearby resorts. In high season (Christmas–Mar and June–Aug), it's carpeted with beach towels and packed with sunbathers like sardines in cocoa butter. Facilities include showers and restrooms. Beach equipment is available for rent at the nearby Wailea Ocean Activity Center. Look for the blue SHORELINE ACCESS sign on South Kihei Road, near Renaissance Wailea Beach Resort; a tiny parking lot is nearby.

WAILEA BEACH 🤿

Wailea is the best golden-sand crescent on Maui's sun-baked southwestern coast. One of five beaches within Wailea Resort, Wailea is big, wide, and protected on both sides by black-lava points. It's the front yard of the Four Seasons Wailea and the Grand Wailea Resort Hotel & Spa, Maui's most elegant and outrageous beach hotels, respectively. From the beach, the view out to sea is magnificent, framed by neighboring Kahoolawe and Lanai and the tiny crescent of Molokini, probably the most popular snorkel spot in these parts. The clear waters tumble to shore in waves just the right size for gentle riding, with or without a board. From shore, you can see Pacific humpback whales in season (Dec–Apr) and unreal sunsets nightly. Facilities include restrooms, outdoor showers, and limited free parking at the blue SHORELINE ACCESS sign, which points toward Wailea Alanui Drive.

Frommer's Favorite Maui Experiences

Greeting the Rising Sun from atop Haleakala (p. 453). Bundle up, fill a thermos with hot java, and drive up the 37 miles from sea level to 10,000 feet to witness the birth of yet another day. Breathing in the rarefied air and watching the first rays of light streak across the sky makes the Haleakala sunrise a mystical experience.

Watching for Whales (p. 434). No need to head out in a boat—in winter you can see these majestic mammals breach and spy-hop from shore. One of the best places is scenic McGregor Point, at mile marker 9 along Honoapiilani Highway, just outside Maalaea in South Maui. The humpbacks arrive as early as November, but the majority travel through Maui's waters from mid-December to mid-April.

Snorkeling off Makena Landing. Calm waters and an abundance of marine life make Makena Bay one of Hawaii's best places to swim with the fishes. Don a mask and snorkel and paddle with turtles, watch clouds of butterfly fish flitter past, and search for tiny damselfish in the coral.

Taking a Dip in the Seven Sacred Pools (p. 462). There are actually more than seven of these fern-shrouded waterfall pools, and they're all beautiful. They spill seaward at Oheo Gulch, on the rainy eastern flanks of Haleakala. Some people try to swim in the pools nearest the ocean; if you do, keep an eye on the sky overhead so that a sudden cloudburst doesn't send you cascading out to sea.

Venturing Back in Time in a Historical Port Town (p. 449). In the 1800s, when whaling was at its height, seafarers swarmed into Lahaina and missionaries fought to stem the spread of their sinful influence. It was a wild time, and this tiny town was an exciting place. The Lahaina Restoration Foundation, in the Master's Reading Room on Front and Dickenson streets, will give you a free map that will let you discover those wild whaling days for yourself.

UPCOUNTRY & EAST MAUI
HAMOA BEACH ⚔

This half-moon-shaped, gray-sand beach (a mix of coral and lava) in a truly tropical setting is a favorite of sunbathers seeking rest and refuge. The Hotel Hana-Maui maintains the beach and acts as though it's private, which it isn't—so just march down the lava-rock steps and grab a spot on the sand. James Michener called it "a beach so perfectly formed that I wonder at its comparative obscurity." The 100-foot-wide beach is three football fields long and sits below 30-foot black-lava sea cliffs. Surf on this unprotected beach breaks offshore and rolls in, making it a popular surfing and body-surfing area. Hamoa is often swept by powerful rip currents, so be careful. The calm left side is best for snorkeling in summer. The hotel has numerous facilities for guests; there are outdoor showers and restrooms for nonguests. Parking is limited. Look for the Hamoa Beach turnoff from Hana Highway.

Watching Windsurfers Ride the Waves at Hookipa (below). Just off the Hana Highway past Paia is Hookipa Beach, known the world over as a windsurfing mecca. The great waves and consistent wind draw top windsurfers from around the globe. Watch spellbound as these colorful sailboarders ride, sail, and pirouette over the waves, turning into the wind and flipping into the air while rotating 360 degrees. It's the best free show in town.

Exploring Iao Valley (p. 448). When the sun strikes Iao Valley in the West Maui Mountains, an almost-ethereal light sends rays out in all directions. This really may be Eden.

Walking the Shoreline Trail at Waianapanapa (p. 441). A 6-mile trail follows the shoreline, bordered on one side by lava cliffs and a forest of lauhala trees, on the other by the open ocean. As you go, you'll pass an ancient *heiau* (temple), some fascinating caves, a pretty cool blowhole, jungley native Hawaiian plants, and the ever-changing sea.

Heading to Kula to Bid the Sun Aloha. Harold Rice Park, just off Kula Highway, is the perfect vantage point for watching the sun set over the entire island: down the side of Haleakala, out across the isthmus, and over to the West Maui Mountains, with Molokai and Lanai in the distance. As the sun sinks in the sky, the light shifts from bright yellow to mellow red. Once the sun drops below the horizon, the sky puts on its own Technicolor show in a dazzling array of colors.

Experiencing Art Night in Lahaina. Every Friday after the sun goes down, most of the town's galleries open their doors, serve pupu and refreshments, and hope you'll wander in. This is a fun, festive way to see what's going on in Maui's creative community. You may even be able to meet the artists; many are on hand to talk about their works.

HOOKIPA BEACH PARK &

Two miles past Paia, on the Hana Highway, is one of the most famous windsurfing sites in the world. Because of its hard, constant wind and endless waves, Hookipa attracts top windsurfers and wave jumpers from around the globe. Surfers and fishermen also enjoy this small, gold-sand beach at the foot of a grassy cliff, which provides a natural amphitheater for spectators. Except when competitions are being held, weekdays are the best times to watch the daredevils fly over the waves. When waves are flat, snorkelers and divers explore the reef. Facilities include restrooms, showers, pavilions, picnic tables, barbecues, and parking.

WAIANAPANAPA STATE PARK &

Four miles before Hana, off the Hana Highway, is this beach park, which takes its name from the legend of the Waianapanapa Cave, where Chief Kaakea, a jealous and cruel man, suspected his wife, Popoalaea, of having an affair. Popoalaea left her husband and hid herself in a chamber of the Waianapanapa Cave. She and her attendant ventured out only at night for food. Nevertheless, a few days later, Kaakea was passing by the area and saw the shadow of the servant. Knowing he had found his wife's hiding place, Kaakea entered the cave and killed her. During certain times of the year, the water in the tide pool turns red, commemorating Popoalaea's death. (Scientists claim, less imaginatively, that the water turns red due to the presence of small red shrimp.)

Waianapanapa State Park's 120 acres contain 12 cabins (p. 397), a caretaker's residence, a beach park, picnic tables, barbecue grills, restrooms, showers, a parking lot, a shoreline hiking trail, and a black-sand beach (actually, small black pebbles). This is a wonderful area for shoreline hikes (bring insect repellent—the mosquitoes are plentiful) and picnicking. Swimming is generally unsafe, though, due to strong waves and rip currents. Because Waianapanapa is crowded on weekends with local residents and their families, as well as tourists, weekdays are generally a better bet.

6 Watersports

For general advice on the activities listed below, see "Special-Interest Trips," in chapter 2.

Snorkel Bob's (www.snorkelbob.com) rents snorkel gear, boogie boards, and other ocean toys at four locations: 1217 Front St., Lahaina (© **808/661-4421**); Napili Village, 5425-C Lower Honoapiilani Hwy., Napili (© **808/669-9603**); in North Kihei at Azeka Place II, 1279 S. Kihei Rd. #310 (© **808/875-6188**); and in South Kihei/Wailea at Kamaole Beach Center, 2411 S. Kihei Rd. (© **808/879-7449**). All locations are open daily from 8am to 5pm. If you're island-hopping, you can rent from a Snorkel Bob's location on one island and return to a branch on another.

Boss Frog's Dive and Surf Shops (www.maui-vacation.net) has six stores for rental and other gear: Napili Plaza, next to Subway (© **808/669-4949**); Kahana Manor Shops, next to Dollies Pizza (© **808/669-6700**); Kaanapali, 3636 L. Honoapiilani Rd. (© **808/665-1200**); Lahaina, 150 Lahainaluna Rd. (© **808/661-3333**); North Kihei, 1215 Kihei Rd., Long's Drugs Shopping Center (© **808/891-0077**); and South Kihei, 2395 S. Kihei Rd., behind Pizza Hut at the Dolphin Plaza (© **808/875-4477**).

BOATING

Maui is big on snorkel cruises. The crescent-shaped islet called **Molokini** is one of the best snorkel and scuba spots in Hawaii. Trips to the island of **Lanai** (see chapter 8) are also popular for a day of snorkeling. Always remember to bring a towel, a swimsuit, sunscreen, and a hat on a snorkel cruise; everything else is usually included. If you'd like to go a little deeper than snorkeling allows, consider trying **Snuba,** a shallow-water diving system in which you are connected by a 20-foot air hose to an air tank that floats on a raft at the water's surface. Most of these snorkel boats offer it for an additional cost; it's usually around $50 for a half-hour or so. No certification is required for Snuba.

For fishing charters, see "Sportfishing," later in this chapter.

Maui Classic Charters 🐸🐸 Maui Classic Charters offers morning and afternoon **snorkel-sail cruises to Molokini** on *Four Winds II,* a 55-foot, glass-bottom catamaran, for $84 adults ($49 children 3–12 years) for the morning sail and $42 adults ($30 children) in the afternoon. *Four Winds* trips include a continental breakfast; a barbecue lunch; complimentary beer, wine, and soda; complimentary snorkeling gear and instruction; and sportfishing along the way.

Those looking for speed should book a trip on the fast, state-of-the-art catamaran *Maui Magic*. The company offers a 5-hour snorkel journey to both Molokini and La Pérouse for $99 for adults and $79 for children ages 5 to 12, including a continental breakfast; barbecue lunch; beer, wine, and soda; snorkel gear; and instruction. During **whale season** (Dec 22–Apr 22), the *Four Winds* has a whale-watch trip; a 3½-hour trip with beverages is $42 for adults and $30 for children ages 3 to 12.

Maalaea Harbor, slip 55 and slip 80. ℂ 800/736-5740 or 808/879-8188. www.mauicharters.com. Prices vary depending on cruise.

Pacific Whale Foundation   This not-for-profit foundation supports its whale research by offering **whale-watch cruises** and **snorkel tours,** some to Molokini and Lanai. It operates a 65-foot power catamaran called *Ocean Spirit,* a 50-foot sailing catamaran called *Manute'a,* and a fleet of other boats. There are 15 daily trips to choose from, offered from December through May, out of both Lahaina and Maalaea harbors.

101 N. Kihei Rd., Kihei. ℂ 800/942-5311 or 808/879-8811. www.pacificwhale.org. Trips from $20 adults, $17 children ages 7–12, free for ages 6 and under; snorkeling cruises from $80 adults, $30 children.

Pride of Maui   For a high-speed, action-packed snorkel-sail experience, consider the *Pride of Maui*. These 5½-hour **snorkel cruises** take in not only **Molokini,** but also Turtle Bay and Makena for more snorkeling; the cost is $90 for ages 13 and up and $56 for children ages 3 to 12. Continental breakfast, barbecue lunch, gear, and instruction are included. They also have an afternoon Molokini cruise ($42 for ages 13 and up and $27 for children ages 3 to 12, plus an optional lunch for an additional $7), an evening sunset cruise ($50 for ages 13 and up and $26 for children ages 3 to 12) and, during whale season, a whale-watching cruise ($26 for ages 13 and up and $17 for children ages 3 to 12).

Maalaea Harbor. ℂ 877/TO-PRIDE or 808/875-0955. www.prideofmaui.com. Prices vary; see above.

Scotch Mist Sailing Charters   This 50-foot Santa Cruz sailboat offers 2-hour sailing adventures. Prices include snorkel gear, juice, fresh pineapple spears, Maui chips, beer, wine, and soda.

Lahaina Harbor, slip 2. ℂ 808/661-0386. www.scotchmistsailingcharters.com. Sail trips $45 adults, $25 children ages 5–12; sunset sail $45.

Trilogy *Kids*   Trilogy offers my favorite **snorkel-sail trips.** Hop aboard one of the fleet of custom-built catamarans, from 54 to 64 feet long, for a 9-mile sail from Lahaina Harbor to **Lanai's Hulopoe Beach,** a terrific marine preserve, for a fun-filled day of sailing, snorkeling, swimming, and **whale-watching** (in season, of course). This is the only cruise that offers a personalized ground tour of the island and the only one with rights to take you to Hulopoe Beach. The full-day trip costs $179 for adults, half-price for children ages 3 to 12. Ask about overnighters to Lanai.

Trilogy also offers snorkel-sail trips to **Molokini,** one of Hawaii's best snorkel spots. This half-day trip leaves from Maalaea Harbor and costs $110 for adults, half-price for kids ages 3 to 12, including breakfast and a barbecue lunch. There's also a late-morning half-day snorkel-sail off Kaanapali Beach for the same price.

These are the most expensive sail-snorkel cruises on Maui, but they're worth every penny. The crews are fun and knowledgeable, and the boats comfortable and well equipped. All trips include breakfast (Mom's homemade cinnamon buns) and a very good barbecue lunch (shipboard on the half-day trip, on land on the Lanai trip). Note, however, that you will be required to wear a flotation device no matter how good your swimming skills are; if this bothers you, go with another outfitter.

Trilogy also offers sailing/snorkeling trips from Kaanapali to Honolua Bay, with lunch, for $110; a 1½-hour dolphin-watching excursion on a Zodiac for $60; a 2-hour whale-watching trip for $39; and a host of others.

© 888/MAUI-800 or 808/TRILOGY. www.sailtrilogy.com. Prices and departure points vary with cruise.

DAY CRUISES TO MOLOKAI

You can travel across the seas by ferry from Maui's Lahaina Harbor to Molokai's Kaunakakai Wharf on the *Molokai Princess* (© 800/275-6969 or 808/667-6165; www.mauiprincess.com). The 100-foot yacht, certified for 149 passengers, is fitted with the latest generation of gyroscopic stabilizers, making the ride smoother. The ferry makes the 90-minute journey from Lahaina to Kaunakakai daily; the round-trip cost is $85 adult and $43 children ages 3 to 12. Or you can choose to tour the island from two different package options: Cruise-Drive, which includes round-trip passage and a rental car for $191 for the driver, $76 per additional adult passenger, and $38 for children; or the Alii Tour, which is a guided tour in an air-conditioned van plus lunch for $191 for adults and $134 for children.

DAY CRUISES TO LANAI

You can also get to the island of Lanai by booking a trip with **Trilogy** (see above).

Expeditions Lahaina/Lanai Passenger Ferry ✿ *(Value)*   The cheapest way to Lanai is the ferry, which runs five times a day, 365 days a year. It leaves Lahaina at 6:45am, 9:15am, 12:45pm, 3:15pm, and 5:45pm; the return ferry from Lanai's Manele Bay Harbor leaves at 8am, 10:30am, 2pm, 4:30pm, and 6:45pm. The 9-mile channel crossing takes between 45 minutes and an hour, depending on sea conditions. Reservations are strongly recommended. Baggage is limited to two checked bags and one carry-on. Call **Lanai City Service** (© 800/800-4000 or 808/565-7227) to arrange a car rental or bus ride when you arrive.

Boat: Lahaina Harbor; office: 658 Front St., Suite 127, Lahaina. © 800/695-2624 or 808/661-3756. www.go-lanai.com. Round-trip from Maui to Lanai $50 adults, $40 children 2–11; children under 2 ride free.

BODY BOARDING (BOOGIE BOARDING) & BODYSURFING

In winter, Maui's best bodysurfing spot is **Mokuleia Beach,** known locally as Slaughterhouse because of the cattle slaughterhouse that once stood here, not because of the waves—although these waves are for expert bodysurfers only. Take Honoapiilani Highway just past Kapalua Bay Resort; various trails will take you down to the pocket beach.

Good body boarding can be found at **Baldwin Beach Park,** just outside Paia. Storms from the south bring fair bodysurfing conditions and great body boarding to the lee side of Maui: **Oneloa Beach** (or Big Beach) in Makena, **Ulua** and **Kamaole III** in Kihei, and **Kapalua** beaches are all good choices.

OCEAN KAYAKING

Gliding silently over the water, propelled by a paddle, seeing Maui from the sea the way the early Hawaiians did—that's what ocean kayaking is all about. One of Maui's best kayak routes is along the **Kihei Coast,** where there's easy access to calm water. Mornings are always best; the wind comes up around 11am, making seas choppy and paddling difficult.

For beginners, my favorite kayak-tour operator is **Makena Kayak Tours** ☆ (© 877/ **879-8426** or 808/879-8426; www.makenakayaks.com). Professional guide Dino Ventura leads a 2½-hour trip from Makena Landing and loves taking first-timers over the secluded coral reefs and into remote coves. His wonderful tour will be a highlight of your vacation. They've kept their low price of $55, which includes refreshments and snorkel and kayak equipment; the 4-hour tour (with lunch) costs $85.

South Pacific Kayaks, 2439 S. Kihei Rd., Kihei (© **800/776-2326** or 808/875-4848; www.mauikayak.com), is Maui's oldest kayak-tour company. Its expert guides lead ocean-kayak trips that include lessons, a guided tour, and snorkeling. Tours run from 2½ to 5 hours and range in price from $65 to $139.

In Hana, **Hana-Maui Sea Sports** (© 808/248-7711; www.hana-mauiseasports.com) runs 2-hour tours of Hana's coastline on wide, stable "no roll" kayaks, with snorkeling, for $89 per person. They also feature kayak surfing lessons for $89.

OCEAN RAFTING

If you're semiadventurous and looking for a more intimate experience with the sea, try ocean rafting. The inflatable rafts hold 6 to 24 passengers. Tours usually include snorkeling and coastal cruising. One of the best (and most reasonable) outfitters is **Hawaiian Ocean Raft** (© 888/677-RAFT or 808/667-2191; www.hawaiioceanrafting.com), which operates out of Lahaina Harbor. The best deal is the 5-hour morning tour, which is $74 for adults and $53 for children ages 5 to 12 (book online and save $11); it includes three snorkeling stops and time spent searching for dolphins, plus continental breakfast and midmorning snacks.

SCUBA DIVING

Everyone dives **Molokini,** a marine-life park and one of Hawaii's top dive spots. This crescent-shaped crater has three tiers of diving: a 35-foot plateau inside the crater basin (used by beginning divers and snorkelers), a wall sloping to 70 feet just beyond the inside plateau, and a sheer wall on the outside and backside of the crater that plunges 350 feet. This underwater park is very popular, thanks to calm, clear, protected waters and an abundance of marine life, from manta rays to clouds of yellow butterfly fish.

Stop by any location of **Maui Dive Shop** ☆ (www.mauidiveshop.com), Maui's largest diving retailer, with everything from rentals to scuba-diving instruction to diveboat charters, for a free copy of the 24-page *Maui Dive Guide.* Inside are maps of and details on the 20 best shoreline and offshore dives and snorkel sites, each ranked for beginner, intermediate, or advanced snorkelers/divers. Maui Dive Shop has branches in Kihei at Azeka Place II Shopping Center, 1455 S. Kihei Rd. (© **808/879-3388**), Kamaole Shopping Center (© **808/879-1533**), and Shops at Wailea (© **808/875-9904**); in Lahaina at Lahaina Cannery Mall (© **808/661-5388**); and in the Honokowai Market Place (© **808/661-6166**). Other locations include Whalers Village, Kaanapali (© **808/661-5117**); Kaanapali Fairway Shops (© **808/551-9663**); Maalaea Village (© **808/244-5514**); and Kahana Gateway, Kahana (© **808/669-3800**).

For personalized diving, **Ed Robinson's Diving Adventures** ☆ (© **800/635-1273** or 808/879-3584; www.mauiscuba.com) is the only Maui company rated one of *Scuba Diver* magazine's top five best dive operators for 7 years straight. Ed, a widely published underwater photographer, offers specialized charters for small groups. Two-tank dives are $126 ($137 with equipment); his dive boats depart from Kihei Boat Ramp.

If Ed is booked, call **Mike Severns Diving** (© **808/879-6596;** www.mikeseverns diving.com) for small (maximum 12 people, divided into two groups of 6), personal diving tours on a 38-foot Munson/Hammerhead boat with freshwater shower. Mike and his wife, Pauline Fiene-Severns, are both biologists who make diving in Hawaii educational as well as fun (they have a spectacular underwater photography book, *Molokini Island*). In their 25 years of operation, they have been accident-free. Two-tank dives are $140, including equipment rental, or $125 if you have your own equipment.

SNORKELING

Snorkeling on Maui is easy—there are so many great spots where you can just wade in the water with a face mask and look down to see the tropical fish. Mornings are best; local winds kick in around noon. Maui's best snorkeling beaches include **Kapalua Beach;** along the Kihei coastline, especially at **Kamaole Beach Park III;** and along the Wailea coastline, particularly at **Ulua Beach.** For an off-the-beaten-track experience, head south to **Makena Beach;** the bay is filled with clouds of tropical fish, and on weekdays, the waters are virtually empty.

The snorkeling at **Black Rock at Kaanapali** 𝓕 is worth the inflated rates at the parking lots that buffer this beach. The prominent craggy cliff at the Sheraton Maui Resort doesn't just end when it plunges into the ocean. Underwater, the sheer wall continues, creating one of the west side's best snorkeling areas: Turtles, rays, and a variety of snappers and goat fish cruise along the sandy bottom. In the crevices, ledges, and holes of the rock wall, you can find eels, shrimp, lobster, and a range of rainbowed tropical fish.

Two truly terrific snorkel spots are difficult to get to but worth the effort, as they're home to Hawaii's tropical marine life at its best:

MOLOKINI 𝓕𝓕   This sunken crater sits like a crescent moon fallen from the sky, almost midway between Maui and the uninhabited island of Kahoolawe. Molokini stands like a scoop against the tide and serves, on its concave side, as a natural sanctuary and marine-life preserve for tropical fish. Snorkelers commute daily in a fleet of dive boats. Molokini is accessible only by boat; see "Boating," above, for outfitters that can take you here. Expect crowds in the high season.

AHIHI-KINAU NATURAL PRESERVE 𝓕𝓕   In Ahihi Bay, you can't miss this 2,000-acre state natural area reserve in the lee of Cape Kinau, on Maui's rugged south coast, where, in 1790, Haleakala spilled red-hot lava that ran to the sea. Fishing is strictly forbidden here, and the fish know it; they're everywhere in this series of rocky coves and black-lava tide pools. To get here, drive south of Makena past Puu Olai to Ahihi Bay, where the road turns to gravel (and sometimes seems like it'll disappear under the waves). At Cape Kinau, three four-wheel-drive trails lead across the lava flow; take the shortest one, nearest La Pérouse Bay. If you have a standard car, drive as far as you can, park, and walk the remainder of the way. Après-snorkel, check out La Pérouse Bay on the south side of Cape Kinau, where the French admiral La Pérouse became the first European to set foot on Maui. A lava-rock pyramid known as Pérouse Monument marks the spot.

When the whales aren't around, **Capt. Steve's Rafting Excursions** (© **808/667-5565;** www.captainsteves.com) offers 7-hour snorkel trips from Mala Wharf in Lahaina to the waters around **Lanai** (you don't actually land on the island). Rates of $150 for adults and $115 for children 12 and under include breakfast, lunch, snorkel gear, and wet suits.

Snorkel Bob's (www.snorkelbob.com) will rent you everything you need; see the introduction to this section for locations. Also see "Scuba Diving," above, for information on Maui Dive Shop's free booklet on great snorkeling sites.

SPORTFISHING

Marlin, tuna, ono, and mahimahi await the baited hook in Maui's coastal and channel waters. No license is required; just book a sportfishing vessel out of Lahaina or Maalaea harbors. Most charter boats that troll for big-game fish carry six passengers max.

The best way to book a sportfishing charter is through the experts; the best booking desk in the state is **Sportfish Hawaii** (© **877/388-1376** or 808/396-2607; www.sportfishhawaii.com), which books boats not only on Maui, but on all islands. These fishing vessels have been inspected and must meet rigorous criteria to guarantee that you will have a great time. Prices range from $895 to $1,000 for a full-day exclusive charter (you, plus five friends, get the entire boat to yourself); it's $599 to $750 for a half-day exclusive.

SUBMARINE DIVES

Plunging 100 feet below the surface of the sea in a state-of-the-art, high-tech submarine is a great way to experience Maui's magnificent underwater world, especially if you're not a swimmer. **Atlantis Submarines** , 658 Front St., Lahaina (© **800/548-6262** or 808/667-2224; www.goatlantis.com), offers trips out of Lahaina Harbor every hour on the hour from 9am to 2pm; $84 for adults and $42 for children under 12 (children must be at least 3 ft. tall). Book online and save 10%. Allow 2 hours for this underwater adventure. This is not a good choice if you're claustrophobic.

SURFING

Expert surfers visit Maui in winter, when the surf's really up. The best surfing beaches include **Honolua Bay,** north of the Kapalua Resort (the third bay past the Ritz-Carlton Kapalua, off the Honoapiilani Hwy., or Hwy. 30); **Lahaina Harbor** (in summer, there'll be waves just off the channel entrance with a south swell); **Maalaea,** just outside the break wall of the Maalaea Harbor (a clean, world-class left); and **Hookipa Beach,** where surfers get the waves until noon (after that—in a carefully worked-out compromise to share this prized surf spot—the windsurfers take over).

Always wanted to learn to surf but didn't know whom to ask? Call the **Nancy Emerson School of Surfing,** 358 Papa Place, Suite F, Kahului (© **808/244-SURF** or 808/662-4445; fax 808/662-4443; www.surfclinics.com). Nancy has been surfing since 1961 and has even been a stunt performer for various movies, including *Waterworld.* She's pioneered a new instructional technique called "Learn to Surf in One Lesson"—you can, really. It's $75 per person for a 2-hour group lesson; private 2-hour classes are $175.

In Hana, **Hana-Maui Sea Sports** (© **808/248-7711;** www.hana-maui-seasports. com) has 2-hour long-board lessons taught by a certified ocean lifeguard for $89.

WHALE-WATCHING

The humpback is the star of the annual whale-watching season, which usually runs from about January to April (though it can begin as early as Dec and last until May).

WHALE-WATCHING FROM SHORE The best time to whale-watch is between mid-December and April: Just look out to sea. There's no best time of day, but it seems

An Expert Shares His Secrets: Maui's Best Dives

Ed Robinson, of Ed Robinson's Diving Adventures (see above), knows what makes a great dive. Here are some of his favorites on Maui:

Hawaiian Reef   This area off the Kihei-Wailea Coast is so named because it hosts a good cross-section of Hawaiian topography and marine life. Diving to depths of 85 feet, you'll see everything from lava formations and coral reef to sand and rubble, plus a diverse range of both shallow and deepwater creatures. It's clear why this area was so popular with ancient Hawaiian fishermen: Large helmet shells, a healthy garden of antler coral heads, and big schools of snapper are common.

Third Tank   Located off Makena Beach at 80 feet, this World War II tank is one of the most picturesque artificial reefs you're likely to see around Maui. It acts like a fish magnet: Because it's the only large solid object in the area, any fish or invertebrate looking for a safe home comes here. Surrounding the tank is a cloak of schooling snapper and goat fish just waiting for a photographer with a wide-angle lens. Despite its small size, the Third Tank is loaded with more marine life per square inch than any site off Maui.

Molokini Crater   The backside is always done as a live boat-drift dive. The vertical wall plummets from more than 150 feet above sea level to around 250 feet below. Looking down to unseen depths gives you a feeling for the vastness of the open ocean. Pelagic fish and sharks are often sighted, and living coral perches on the wall, which is home to lobsters, crabs, and a number of photogenic black-coral trees at 50 feet.

There are actually two great dive sites around Molokini Crater. Named after common chub or rudderfish, **Enenue Side** gently slopes from the surface to about 60 feet, and then drops rapidly to deeper waters. The shallower

that when the sea is glassy and there's no wind, the whales appear. Once you see one, keep watching in the same vicinity; they may stay down for 20 minutes. Bring a book. And binoculars, if you can.

Some good whale-watching spots on Maui are:

McGregor Point   On the way to Lahaina, there's a scenic lookout at mile marker 9 (just before you get to the Lahaina Tunnel); it's a good viewpoint to scan for whales.

Wailea Beach Marriott Resort & Spa   On the Wailea coastal walk, stop at this resort to look for whales through the telescope installed as a public service by the Hawaii Island Humpback Whale National Marine Sanctuary.

Olowalu Reef   Along the straight part of Honoapiilani Highway, between McGregor Point and Olowalu, you'll sometimes see whales leap out of the water. Their appearance can bring traffic to a screeching halt: People abandon their cars and run down to the sea to watch, causing a major traffic jam. If you stop, pull off the road so others may pass.

Puu Olai   It's a tough climb up this coastal landmark near the Maui Prince Hotel, but you're likely to be well rewarded: This is the island's best spot for offshore area is an easy dive, with lots of tame butterfly fish. It's also the home of Morgan Bentjaw, one of our friendliest moray eels. Enenue Side is often done as a live boat-drift dive to extend the range of the tour. Diving depths vary. Divers usually do a 50-foot dive, but on occasion, advanced divers drop to the 130-foot level to visit the rare boarfish and the shark condos.

Almost every kind of fish found in Hawaii can be seen in the crystalline waters of **Reef's End.** It's an extension of the rim of the crater, which runs for about 600 feet underwater, barely breaking the surface. Reef's End is shallow enough for novice snorkelers and exciting enough for experienced divers. The end and outside of this shoal drop off in dramatic terraces to beyond diving range. In deeper waters, there are shark ledges at varying depths and dozens of eels, some of which are tame, including moray, dragon, snowflake, and garden eels. The shallower inner side is home to Garbanzo, one of the largest and first eels to be tamed. The reef is covered with cauliflower coral; in bright sunlight, it's one of the most dramatic underwater scenes in Hawaii.

La Pérouse Pinnacle In the middle of scenic La Pérouse Bay, site of Haleakala's most recent lava flow, is a pinnacle rising from the 60-foot bottom to about 10 feet below the surface. Getting to the dive site is half the fun: The scenery above water is as exciting as that below the surface. Underwater, you'll enjoy a very diversified dive. Clouds of damselfish and triggerfish will greet you on the surface. Divers can approach even the timid bird wrasse. There are more porcupine puffers here than anywhere else, as well as schools of goat fish and fields of healthy finger coral. La Pérouse is good for snorkeling and long, shallow second dives.

whale-watching. On the 360-foot cinder cone overlooking Makena Beach, you'll be at the right elevation to see Pacific humpbacks as they dodge Molokini and cruise up Alalakeiki Channel between Maui and Kahoolawe. If you don't see one, you'll at least have a whale of a view.

WHALE-WATCHING CRUISES For a closer look, take a whale-watching cruise. Just about all of Hawaii's snorkel and dive boats become whale-watching boats in season; some of them even carry professional naturalists onboard so you'll know what you're seeing. For the best options, see "Boating," earlier in this chapter.

WHALE-WATCHING BY KAYAK & RAFT Seeing a humpback whale from an ocean kayak or raft is awesome. **Capt. Steve's Rafting Excursions** (© **808/667-5565;** www.captainsteves.com) offers 2-hour whale-watching excursions out of Lahaina Harbor for $49 adults, $35 for children ages 5 to 12. *Tip:* Save $10 by booking the "Early Bird" adventure, which leaves at 7:30am.

WINDSURFING

Maui has Hawaii's best windsurfing beaches. In winter, windsurfers from around the world flock to the town of **Paia** to ride the waves; **Hookipa Beach,** known all over the globe for its brisk winds and excellent waves, is the site of several world-championship contests. **Kanaha,** west of Kahului Airport, also has dependable winds. When the winds turn northerly, **Kihei** is the spot to be; some days, you can spot whales in the distance behind the windsurfers. The northern end of Kihei is best: **Ohukai Park,** the first beach as you enter South Kihei Road from the northern end, has not only good winds, but also parking, a long strip of grass to assemble your gear, and good access to the water. Experienced windsurfers here are found in front of the **Maui Sunset** condo, 1032 S. Kihei Rd., near Waipuilani Street (a block north of McDonald's), which has great windsurfing conditions but a very shallow reef (not good for beginners).

Hawaiian Island Surf and Sport, 415 Dairy Rd., Kahului (© **800/231-6958** or 808/871-4981; www.hawaiianisland.com), offers lessons (from $79), rentals, and repairs. Other shops that offer rentals and lessons are **Hawaiian Sailboarding Techniques,** 425 Koloa St., Kahului (© **800/968-5423** or 808/871-5423; www.hstwindsurfing.com), with 2½-hour lessons from $79; and **Maui Windsurf Co.,** 22 Hana Hwy., Kahului (© **800/872-0999** or 808/877-4816; www.maui-windsurf.com), which has complete equipment rental (board, sail, rig harness, and roof rack) from $45, and 1- or 2-hour lessons ranging from $75.

For daily reports on wind and surf conditions, call the **Wind and Surf Report** at © **808/877-3611.**

7 Hiking & Camping

In the past 3 decades, Maui has grown from a rural island to a fast-paced resort destination, but its natural beauty remains largely inviolate; there are still many places that can be explored only on foot. Those interested in seeing the backcountry—complete with virgin waterfalls, remote wilderness trails, and quiet, meditative settings—should head for Haleakala's upcountry or the tropical Hana Coast.

Camping on Maui can be extreme (inside a volcano) or benign (by the sea in Hana). It can be wet, cold, and rainy; or hot, dry, and windy—often all on the same day. If you're heading for Haleakala, remember that U.S. astronauts trained for the moon inside the volcano; bring survival gear. You'll need your swimsuit and rain gear if you're bound for Waianapanapa. Bring your own gear, as there are no places to rent camping equipment on Maui.

For more information on Maui camping and hiking trails, and to obtain free maps, contact **Haleakala National Park,** P.O. Box 369, Makawao, HI 96768 (© **808/572-4400;** www.nps.gov/hale); and the **State Division of Forestry and Wildlife,** 54 S. High St., Wailuku, HI 96793 (© **808/984-8100;** www.hawaii.gov). For information on trails, hikes, camping, and permits for state parks, contact the **Hawaii State Department of Land and Natural Resources,** State Parks Division, P.O. Box 621, Honolulu, HI 96809 (© **808/587-0300;** www.state.hi.us/dlnr); note that you can get information from the website but cannot obtain permits there. For Maui County Parks, contact the **Department of Parks and Recreation,** 1580-C Kaahumanu Ave., Wailuku, HI 96793 (© **808/243-7132;** www.mauimapp.com).

GUIDED HIKES   If you'd like a knowledgeable guide to accompany you on a hike, call **Maui Hiking Safaris** ✦ (© **888/445-3963** or 808/573-0168; fax 808/572-3037; www.mauihikingsafaris.com). Owner Randy Warner takes visitors on half- and full-day hikes into valleys, rainforests, and coastal areas. Randy's been hiking around Maui for more than 25 years and is wise in the ways of Hawaiian history, native flora and fauna, and volcanology. His rates are $59 to $79 for a half-day and $105 to $139 for a full day, and include day packs, rain parkas, snacks, water, and, on full-day hikes, sandwiches.

Maui's oldest hiking guide company is **Hike Maui** ✦ (ⓒ **808/879-5270;** fax 808/893-2515; www.hikemaui.com), headed by Ken Schmitt, who pioneered guided hikes on the Valley Isle. Hike Maui offers five different hikes a day, ranging from an easy 1-mile, 3-hour hike to a waterfall ($70), to a strenuous full-day hike in Haleakala Crater ($150). All prices include equipment and transportation.

Venture into the lush West Maui Mountains with an experienced guide on one of the numerous hikes offered by **Maui Eco-Adventures** (ⓒ **877/661-7720** or 808/661-7720; www.ecomaui.com). We love the Rainforest/Waterfall hike. After a continental breakfast, you'll hike by streams and waterfalls, through native trees and plants, and on to breathtaking vistas. The tour includes a picnic lunch, swims in secluded pools, and memorable photo ops. The 6-hour excursion costs $145 per person, including meals, a fanny pack with bottled water, and rain gear, if necessary. No children under 13 are allowed. For those more "on vacation," an easier jaunt costs just $80.

About 1,500 years ago, the verdant Kahakuloa Valley was a thriving Hawaiian village. Today only a few hundred people live in this secluded hamlet, but old Hawaii still lives on here. Explore the valley with **Ekahi Tours** (ⓒ **888/292-2422** or 808/877-9775; www.ekahi.com). Your guide, a Kahakuloa resident and a Hawaiiana expert, walks you through a taro farm, explains the mystical legends of the valley, and provides you with a peek into ancient Hawaii. The 7½-hour Kahakuloa Valley Tour is $80 for adults, $60 for children 11 and younger; snacks, beverages, and hotel pickup are included.

For information on hikes given by the **Hawaii Sierra Club** on Maui, call ⓒ **808/573-4147** (www.hi.sierraclub.org).

HALEAKALA NATIONAL PARK ✦✦✦
For complete coverage of the national park, see p. 453.

INTO THE WILDERNESS: SLIDING SANDS & HALEMAUU TRAILS
Hiking into Maui's dormant volcano is the best way to see it. The terrain inside the wilderness area of the volcano, which ranges from burnt-red cinder cones to ebony-black lava flows, is simply spectacular. There are some 27 miles of hiking trails, two camping sites, and three cabins.

Entrance to Haleakala National Park is $10 per car. The rangers offer free guided hikes, which are a great way to learn about the unusual flora and geological formations here. Briefing sessions on culture, history, and flora are given daily at 9:30, 10:30, and 11:30am at the Summit Visitors Building, 11 miles up from the Visitor's Information Center. Every Tuesday and Friday at 9am, there's a 2-hour, 2-mile guided cinder desert hike (meet at Sliding Sands Trailhead, next to the summit parking lot). Every Monday and Thursday at 9am, there's a 3-hour, 3-mile guided Waikamoi Cloud Forest hike (meet at Hosmer Grove) to view rare native birds and plants. Wear sturdy shoes and be prepared for wind, rain, and intense sun. Bring water and a hat. Additional options include full-moon hikes and star program hikes. *Always call in advance:* The hikes and briefing sessions may be canceled, so check first. For details, call the park at ⓒ **808/572-4400** or visit www.nps.gov/hale.

Try to arrange to stay at least 1 night in the park; 2 or 3 nights will allow you more time to explore the fascinating interior of the volcano (see below for details on the cabins and campgrounds in the wilderness area of the valley). If you want to venture out on your own, the best route takes in two trails: into the crater along **Sliding Sands Trail,** which begins on the rim at 9,800 feet and descends into the belly of the beast, to the valley floor at 6,600 feet; and back out along **Halemauu Trail.** Hardy hikers can consider making the 11-mile, one-way descent, which takes 9 hours, and the equally long returning ascent in a day. The rest of us can extend this steep hike to 2 days. The descending and ascending trails aren't loops; the trail heads are miles (and several thousand feet in elevation) apart, so you'll need to make transportation arrangements in advance. Before you set out, stop at park headquarters to get camping and hiking updates.

The trail head for Sliding Sands is well marked and the trail is easy to follow over lava flows and cinders. As you descend, look around: The view is breathtaking. In the afternoon, waves of clouds flow into the Kaupo and Koolau gaps. Vegetation is spare to nonexistent at the top, but the closer you get to the valley floor, the more vegetation you'll see: bracken ferns, pili grass, shrubs, even flowers. On the floor, the trail travels across rough lava flows, passing by rare silversword plants, volcanic vents, and multicolored cinder cones.

The Halemauu Trail goes over red and black lava and past vegetation, like evening primrose, as it begins its ascent up the valley wall. Occasionally, riders on horseback use this trail. The proper etiquette is to step aside and stand quietly next to the trail as the horses pass.

Some shorter and easier hiking options include the .5-mile walk down the **Hosmer Grove Nature Trail,** and the first mile or two down **Sliding Sands Trail,** which gives you a hint of what lies ahead. (Even this short hike is exhausting at the high altitude.) A good day hike is **Halemauu Trail** to Holua Cabin and back, an 8-mile, half-day trip.

STAYING IN THE WILDERNESS AREA   Most people stay at one of two tent campgrounds, unless they get lucky and win the lottery—the lottery, that is, for one of the three wilderness cabins. For more information, contact **Haleakala National Park,** P.O. Box 369, Makawao, HI 96768 (© **808/572-4400;** www.nps.gov/hale).

Cabins   It can get really cold and windy down in the valley (see "A Word of Warning about the Weather," above), so try for a cabin. They're warm, protected from the elements, and reasonably priced. Each has 12 padded bunks (but no bedding; bring

---

Tips A Word of Warning about the Weather

The weather at nearly 10,000 feet can change suddenly and without warning. Come prepared for cold, high winds, rain, and even snow in winter. Temperatures can range from 77°F (25°C) down to 26°F (–3°C), and high winds are frequent. Daytime temperatures can be 30° colder than at sea level. Sunrise and sunset temperatures average 30° to 40°F in winter (–1° to 4°C) and 40° to 50°F (4°–10°C) in summer. Rainfall varies from 40 inches a year on the western end of the crater to more than 200 inches on the eastern side. Bring boots, waterproof gear, warm clothes, extra layers, and lots of sunscreen—the sun shines very brightly up here. For the latest weather information, call © **808/871-5054.**

your own), a table, chairs, cooking utensils, a two-burner propane stove, and a wood-burning stove with firewood (you may also have a few cockroaches). The cabins are spaced so that each one is an easy walk from the other: Holua cabin is on the Hale-mauu Trail, Kapalaoa cabin on Sliding Sands Trail, and Paliku cabin on the eastern end by the Kaupo Gap. The rates are $55 a night for groups of one to six, $110 a night for groups of 7 to 12.

The cabins are so popular that the National Park Service has a lottery system for reservations. Requests for cabins must be made 3 months in advance (be sure to request alternate dates). You can request all three cabins at once; you're limited to 2 nights in one cabin and 3 nights total in the wilderness each month.

Campgrounds   If you don't win the cabin lottery, all is not lost—there are three tent-camping sites that can accommodate you: two in the wilderness and one just outside at Hosmer Grove. There is no charge for tent camping.

Hosmer Grove, located at 6,800 feet, is a small, open, grassy area surrounded by a forest. Trees protect campers from the winds, but nights still get very cold; sometimes there's ice on the ground up here. This is the best place to spend the night in a tent if you want to see the Haleakala sunrise. Come up the day before, enjoy the park, take a day hike, and then turn in early. The enclosed-glass summit building opens at sunrise for those who come to greet the dawn—a welcome windbreak. Facilities at Hosmer Grove include a covered pavilion with picnic tables and grills, chemical toilets, and drinking water. No permits are needed, and there's no charge—but you can stay for only 3 nights in a 30-day period.

The two tent-camping areas inside the volcano are **Holua,** just off Halemauu at 6,920 feet; and **Paliku,** just before the Kaupo Gap at the eastern end of the valley, at 6,380 feet. Facilities at both campgrounds are limited to pit toilets and nonpotable catchment water. Water at Holua is limited, especially in summer. No open fires are allowed inside the volcano, so bring a stove if you plan to cook. Tent camping is restricted to the signed area. No camping is allowed in the horse pasture. The inviting grassy lawn in front of the cabin is off-limits. Camping is free but limited to 2 consecutive nights, and no more than 3 nights a month inside the volcano. Permits are issued at Park Headquarters daily from 8am to 3pm, on a first-come, first-served basis on the day you plan to camp. Occupancy is limited to 25 people in each campground.

HIKING & CAMPING AT KIPAHULU (NEAR HANA)

In the East Maui section of Haleakala National Park, you can set up at **Oheo Campground,** a first-come, first-served, drive-in campground with tent sites for 100 near the ocean. It has a few tables, barbecue grills, and chemical toilets. No permit is required, but there's a 3-night limit. No food or drinking water is available, so bring your own. Bring a tent as well—it rains 75 inches a year here. Contact **Kipahulu Ranger Station,** Haleakala National Park, HI 96713 (© **808/248-7375;** www.nps.gov/hale), for information.

HIKING FROM THE SUMMIT   If you hike from the crater rim down **Kaupo Gap** to the ocean, more than 20 miles away, you'll pass through several climate zones. On a clear day, you can see every island except Kauai on the trip down.

APPROACHING KIPAHULU FROM HANA   If you drive to Kipahulu, you'll have to approach it from the Hana Highway because it's not accessible from the summit. From the ranger station, it's a short hike above the famous **Oheo Gulch** (which was misnamed the Seven Sacred Pools in the 1940s) to two spectacular waterfalls. The first, **Makahiku Falls,** is easily reached from the central parking area; the trail head begins near the ranger station. Pipiwai Trail leads you up to the road and beyond for .5 miles to the overlook. If you hike another 1.5 miles up the trail across two bridges and through a bamboo forest, you reach **Waimoku Falls.** It's a good uphill hike, but press on to avoid the pool's crowd. In hard rain, streams swell quickly. Always be aware of your surroundings.

SKYLINE TRAIL, POLIPOLI SPRINGS STATE RECREATION AREA

This is some hike—strenuous but worth every step if you like seeing the big picture. It's 8 miles, all downhill, with a dazzling 100-mile view of the islands dotting the blue Pacific, plus the West Maui Mountains, which seem like a separate island.

The trail is just outside Haleakala National Park at Polipoli Springs State Recreation Area; however, you access it by going through the national park to the summit. It starts just beyond the Puu Ulaula summit building on the south side of Science City and follows the southwest rift zone of Haleakala from its lunarlike cinder cones to a cool redwood grove. The trail drops 3,800 feet on a 4-hour hike to the recreation area in the 12,000-acre Kahikinui Forest Reserve. If you'd rather drive, you'll need a four-wheel-drive vehicle.

There's a campground at the recreation area at 6,300 feet. No fee or reservations are required, but your stay must be limited to 5 nights. Tent camping is free, but you'll need a permit. One 10-bunk cabin is available for $45 a night for one to four guests ($5 for each additional guest); it has a cold shower and a gas stove, but no electricity or drinking water (bring your own). To reserve, write the **State Parks Division,** 54 High St., Room 101, Wailuku, HI 96793, or call ⓒ **808/984-8109** Monday through Friday between 8am and 4pm.

POLIPOLI STATE PARK ⭐

One of the most unusual hiking experiences in the state can be found at Polipoli State Park, part of the 21,000-acre Kula and Kahikinui Forest Reserve on the slope of Haleakala. At Polipoli, it's hard to believe that you're in Hawaii: First of all, it's cold, even in summer, because the elevation is 5,300 to 6,200 feet; second, this former forest of native koa, ohia, and mamane trees, which was overlogged in the 1800s, was reforested in the 1930s with introduced species: pine, Monterey cypress, ash, sugi, red alder, redwood, and several varieties of eucalyptus. The result is a cool area, with muted sunlight filtered by towering trees.

The **Polipoli Loop** is an easy 5-mile hike that takes about 3 hours; dress warmly for it. Take the Haleakala Highway (Hwy. 37) to Keokea and turn right onto Highway 337; after less than a half-mile, turn on Waipoli Road, which climbs swiftly. After 10 miles, Waipoli Road ends at the Polipoli State Park campgrounds. The well-marked trail head is next to the parking lot, near a stand of Monterey cypresses; the tree-lined trail offers the best view of the island.

Polipoli Loop is really a network of three trails: Haleakala Ridge, Plum Trail, and Redwood Trail. After .5 mile of meandering through groves of eucalyptus, blackwood, swamp mahogany, and hybrid cypress, you'll join the Haleakala Ridge Trail, which, about a mile into the trail, joins with the Plum Trail (named for the plums that ripen in June–July). This trail passes through massive redwoods and by an old Conservation Corps bunkhouse and a run-down cabin before joining up with the Redwood Trail, which climbs through Mexican pine, tropical ash, Port Orford cedar, and—of course— redwood.

Camping is allowed with a $5-per-night permit from the **State Parks Division,** 54 S. High St., Room 101, Wailuku, HI 96793 (© **808/984-8109**).

KANAHA BEACH PARK CAMPING

One of the few Maui County camping facilities on the island is Kanaha Beach Park, located next to the Kahului Airport. The county has two separate areas for camping: 7 tent sites on the beach and an additional 10 tent sites inland. This well-used park is a favorite of windsurfers, who take advantage of the strong winds that roar across this end of the island. Facilities include a paved parking lot, portable toilets, outdoor showers, barbecue grills, and picnic tables. Camping is limited to no more than 3 consecutive days; the permit fee is $3 per adult and 50¢ for children per night, and can be obtained from the **Maui County Parks and Recreation Department,** 1580-C Kaahumanu Ave., Wailuku, HI 96793 (© **808/243-7389;** www.mauimapp.com/information/campingcounty.htm). The 17 sites book up quickly; reserve your dates far in advance (the county will accept reservations a year in advance).

WAIANAPANAPA STATE PARK 🐦🐦

Tucked in a tropical jungle, on the outskirts of the little coastal town of Hana, is Waianapanapa State Park, a black-sand beach set in an emerald forest.

The **Hana-Waianapanapa Coast Trail** is an easy 6-mile hike that takes you back in time. Allow 4 hours to walk along this relatively flat trail, which parallels the sea, along lava cliffs and a forest of lauhala trees. The best time to take the hike is either early morning or late afternoon, when the light on the lava and surf makes for great photos. Midday is the worst time; not only is it hot (lava intensifies the heat), but there's also no shade or potable water available.

There's no formal trail head; join the route at any point along the Waianapanapa Campground and go in either direction. Along the trail, you'll see remains of an ancient *heiau* (temple), stands of lauhala trees, caves, a blowhole, and a remarkable plant, naupaka, which flourishes along the beach. Upon close inspection, you'll see that the naupaka have only half-blossoms; according to Hawaiian legend, a similar plant living in the mountains has the other half of the blossoms. One ancient explanation is that the two plants represent never-to-be-reunited lovers: As the story goes, the couple bickered so much that the gods, fed up with their incessant quarreling, banished one lover to the mountain and the other to the sea.

Waianapanapa has 12 cabins and a tent campground. Go for the cabins (see "Where to Stay," earlier in this chapter), as it rains torrentially here, sometimes turning the campground into a mud-wrestling arena. Tent camping is $5 per night but limited to 5 nights in a 30-day period. Permits are available from the **State Parks Division,** 54 S. High St., Room 101, Wailuku, HI 96793 (© **808/984-8109**). Facilities include restrooms, outdoor showers, drinking water, and picnic tables.

HANA: THE HIKE TO FAGAN'S CROSS

This 3-mile hike to the cross erected in memory of Paul Fagan, the founder of Hana Ranch and Hotel Hana-Maui, offers spectacular views of the Hana Coast, particularly at sunset. The uphill trail starts across Hana Highway from the Hotel Hana-Maui. Enter the pastures at your own risk; they're often occupied by glaring bulls with sharp horns and cows with new calves. Watch your step as you ascend this steep hill on a jeep trail across open pastures to the cross and the breathtaking view.

8 Golf & Other Outdoor Activities

GOLF

For last-minute and discount tee times, call **Stand-by Golf** (© **888/645-BOOK** or 808/874-0600; www.stand-bygolf.com) between 7am and 9pm. Stand-by offers discounted (up to 50% off greens fees), guaranteed tee times for same-day or next-day golfing.

Golf Club Rentals (© **808/665-0800;** www.mauiclubrentals.com) has custombuilt clubs for men, women, and juniors (both right- and left-handed), which can be delivered island-wide; the rates are $20 to $25 a day.

WEST MAUI

Kaanapali Courses ✿   Both courses at Kaanapali offer a challenge to all golfers, from high handicappers to near-pros. The par-72, 6,305-yard **North Course** is a true Robert Trent Jones, Sr., design: an abundance of wide bunkers; several long, stretched-out tees; and the largest, most contoured greens on Maui. The tricky 18th hole (par 4, 435 yd.) has a water hazard on the approach to the green. The par-72, 6,250-yard **South Course** is an Arthur Jack Snyder design; although shorter than the North Course, it requires more accuracy on the narrow, hilly fairways. It also has a water hazard on its final hole, so don't tally up your scorecard until you sink the final putt.

Facilities include a driving range, putting course, and clubhouse with dining. You'll have a better chance of getting a tee time on weekdays.

Off Hwy. 30, Kaanapali. © **808/661-3691.** www.kaanapali-golf.com. Greens fees: $205 North Course, $175 South Course; Kaanapali guests pay $170 North, $130 South; twilight rates $110 North, $85 South for everyone. At the 1st stoplight in Kaanapali, turn onto Kaanapali Pkwy.; the 1st building on your right is the clubhouse.

Kapalua Resort Courses ✿✿✿   The views from these three championship courses are worth the greens fees alone. The par-72, 6,761-yard **Bay Course** (© **808/669-8820**) was designed by Arnold Palmer and Ed Seay. This course is a bit forgiving, with its wide fairways; the greens, however, are difficult to read. The often-photographed 5th overlooks a small ocean cove; even the pros have trouble with this rocky par-3, 205-yard hole. The par-71, 6,632-yard **Village Course** (© **808/669-8830**), another Palmer/Seay design, is the most scenic of the three courses. The hole with the best vista is the 6th, which overlooks a lake with the ocean in the distance. But don't get distracted by the view—the tee is between two rows of Cook pines. The **Plantation Course** (© **808/669-8877**), site of the Mercedes Championships, is a Ben Crenshaw/Bill Coore design. This 6,547-yard, par-73 course, set on a rolling hillside, is excellent for developing your low shots and precise chipping.

Facilities for all three courses include locker rooms, a driving range, and an excellent restaurant. Weekdays are your best bet for tee times.

Off Hwy. 30, Kapalua. © **877/KAPALUA.** www.kapaluamaui.com. Greens fees: Village Course $185 ($130 for hotel guests), twilight rate $85; Bay Course $200 ($140 for guests), twilight rate $90; Plantation Course $250 ($160 for guests), twilight rate $100.

SOUTH MAUI

Elleair Maui Golf Club (formerly Silversword Golf Club)   Sitting in the foothills of Haleakala, just high enough to afford spectacular ocean vistas from every hole, this is a course for golfers who love the views as much as the fairways and greens. It's very forgiving. *Just one caveat:* Go in the morning. Not only is it cooler, but, more important, it's also less windy. In the afternoon, the winds bluster down Haleakala with great gusto. This is a fun course to play, with some challenging holes; the par-5 2nd hole is a virtual minefield of bunkers, and the par-5 8th hole shoots over a swale and then uphill.

1345 Piilani Hwy. (near Lipoa St. turnoff), Kihei. (C) **808/874-0777.** www.elleairmauigolfclub.com. Greens fees: $120; twilight rate $90.

Makena Courses *(★★)*   Here you'll find 36 holes of "Mr. Hawaii Golf"—Robert Trent Jones, Jr.—at its best. Add to that spectacular views: Molokini islet looms in the background, humpback whales gambol offshore in winter, and the tropical sunsets are spectacular. The par-72, 6,876-yard **South Course** has a couple of holes you'll never forget. The view from the par-4 15th hole, which shoots from an elevated tee 183 yards downhill to the Pacific, is magnificent. The 16th hole has a two-tiered green that's blind from the tee 383 yards away (that is, if you make it past the gully off the fairway). The par-72, 6,823-yard **North Course** is more difficult and more spectacular. The 13th hole, located partway up the mountain, has a view that makes most golfers stop and stare. The next hole is even more memorable: a 200-foot drop between tee and green.

Facilities include a clubhouse, a driving range, two putting greens, a pro shop, lockers, and lessons. Beware of weekend crowds.

On Makena Alanui Dr., just past the Maui Prince Hotel. (C) **808/879-3344.** www.maui.net/~makena. Greens fees: $185 ($110–$115 for Makena Resort guests), twilight rate $115–$125 ($95–$100 for guests); guest rates vary seasonally, with higher rates in the winter.

Wailea Courses *(★★)*   There are three courses to choose from at Wailea. The **Blue Course,** a par-72, 6,758-yard course designed by Arthur Jack Snyder and dotted with bunkers and water hazards, is for duffers and pros alike. The wide fairways appeal to beginners, while the undulating terrain makes it a course everyone can enjoy. A little more difficult is the par-72, 7,078-yard championship **Gold Course,** with narrow fairways, several tricky dogleg holes, and the classic Robert Trent Jones, Jr., challenges: natural hazards, like lava-rock walls, and native Hawaiian grasses. The **Emerald Course,** also designed by Robert Trent Jones, Jr., is Wailea's newest, with tropical landscaping and a player-friendly design.

With 54 holes to play, getting a tee time is slightly easier on weekends than at other resorts, but weekdays are best (the Emerald Course is usually the toughest to book). Facilities include two pro shops, restaurants, locker rooms, and a complete golf training facility.

Wailea Alanui Dr. (off Wailea Iki Dr.), Wailea. (C) **888/328-MAUI** or 808/875-7450. www.waileagolf.com. Greens fees: Blue Course $135–$185 ($135–$155 resort guests), twilight rate $115–$125 everyone; Gold Course and Emerald Course $200 ($175 resort guests), no twilight rates.

UPCOUNTRY MAUI

Pukalani Country Club   This cool, par-72, 6,962-yard course at 1,100 feet offers a break from the resorts' high greens fees, and it's really fun to play. The 3rd hole offers golfers two different options: a tough (especially into the wind) iron shot from the tee, across a gully (yuck!) to the green; or a shot down the side of the gully across a second green into sand traps below. (Most people choose to shoot down the side of the gully; it's actually easier than shooting across a ravine.) High handicappers will love this course, and more experienced players can make it more challenging by playing from the back tees. Facilities include club and shoe rentals, practice areas, lockers, a pro shop, and a restaurant.

360 Pukalani St., Pukalani. (© 808/572-1314. www.pukalanigolf.com. Greens fees, including cart: $68 for 18 holes before 11am; $63 11am–2pm; $53 after 2pm; 9 holes $35. Take the Hana Hwy. (Hwy. 36) to Haleakala Hwy. (Hwy. 37) to the Pukalani exit; turn right onto Pukalani St. and go 2 blocks.

BICYCLING

If you want to venture out on your own, **Maui Sunriders Bike Company,** 71 Baldwin Ave., Paia (© **866/500-BIKE;** www.mauibikeride.com), rents bikes from $26.

For information on bikeways and maps, get a copy of the *Maui County Bicycle Map,* which has information on road suitability, climate, mileage, elevation changes, bike shops, safety tips, and various bicycling routes. The map is available for $7.50 ($6.25 for the map and $1.25 for postage), bank checks or money orders only, from **Tri Isle R, C, and D Council,** Attn: Bike Map Project, 200 Imi Kala St., Suite 208, Wailuku, HI 96793.

CRUISING HALEAKALA ☀ It's not even close to dawn, but here you are, rubbing your eyes awake, riding in a van up the long, dark road to the top of Maui's dormant volcano. It's colder than you ever thought possible for a tropical island. The air is thin. The place is crowded, packed with people. You stomp your chilly feet while you wait, sipping hot coffee. Then comes the sun, exploding over the yawning Haleakala Crater, big enough to swallow Manhattan—a moment you won't soon forget. Now you know why Hawaiians named the crater the House of the Sun. But there's no time to linger: Decked out in your screaming-yellow parka, you mount your mechanical steed and test its most important feature, the brakes—because you're about to coast 37 miles down a 10,000-foot volcano.

Cruising down Haleakala, from the lunarlike landscape at the top past flower farms, pineapple fields, and eucalyptus groves, is quite an experience—and just about anybody can do it. This is a safe trip that requires some stamina in the colder, wetter winter months but is fun for everyone in the warmer months—the key word being *warmer.* In winter and the rainy season, conditions can be harsh, especially on the top, with below-freezing temperatures and 40-mph winds.

Maui's oldest downhill company is **Maui Downhill** ☀ (© **800/535-BIKE** or 808/ 871-2155; www.mauidownhill.com), which offers a sunrise safari bike tour, including continental breakfast and brunch, starting at $125 (book online and save $21). If it's all booked up, try **Maui Mountain Cruisers** (© **800/232-6284** or 808/871-6014; www.mauimountaincruisers.com), which has sunrise trips for $144 and midday trips for $110. **Mountain Riders Bike Tours** (© **800/706-7700** or 808/242-9739; www.mountainriders.com) offers sunrise rides for $155 (book online for $125) and midday trips for $120. All rates include hotel pickup, transport to the top, bicycle, safety equipment, and meals. Wear layers of warm clothing—there may be a 30°F (17°C) change in temperature from the top of the mountain to the ocean. Generally, the tour groups will not take riders under 12, but younger children can ride along in the van that accompanies the groups. Pregnant women should also ride in the van.

If you want to avoid the crowd and go down the mountain at your own pace, call **Haleakala Bike Company** (© **888/922-2453;** www.bikemaui.com). They will outfit you with the latest gear and take you up Haleakala. *Note:* Not all tours go to the summit. If you want to start your bike ride at the summit, be sure to confirm. The cheapest trip starts at around the 6,500-foot level (about two-thirds up the mountain). After making sure you are secure on the bike, they will let you ride down by yourself at your own pace. Trips range from $60 to $105; they also have bicycle rentals to tour other parts of Maui on your own (from $30 a day).

HORSEBACK RIDING

Maui offers spectacular adventure rides through rugged ranchlands, into tropical forests, and to remote swimming holes. One of our favorites is **Piiholo Ranch,** in Makawao (© **866/572-5544** or 808/357-5544; www.piiholo.com). A working cattle ranch, owned by the kamaaina (long-time resident) Baldwin family, this is a horseback riding adventure with a variety of different rides to suit your ability, from the morning picnic ride, a 3½-hour ride on the ranch and a picnic lunch for $160 per person, to a 2-hour country ride through a working cattle ranch for $120.

If you're out in Hana, don't pass up the **Maui Stables** ★★, in Kipahulu (a mile past Oheo Gulch; © **808/248-7799;** www.mauistables.com). Not only do they offer two rides daily (9:30am and 1pm) through the mountains above Kipahulu Valley, but you also get a fantastic historical and cultural tour through the unspoiled landscape. It is an experience you will not forget. Both rides are $150. If you enjoy your ride, remember to kiss your horse and tip your guide.

For those horse lovers who are looking for the ultimate, check out Frank Levinson's **"Maui Horse Whisperer Experience"** (© **808/572-6211;** www.mauihorses.com), which includes a seminar on the language of the horse, $200 for half-day and $300 for full-day workshops. No horse aficionado should pass it up.

HALEAKALA ON HORSEBACK   If you'd like to ride down into Haleakala's crater, contact **Pony Express Tours** ★ (© **808/667-2200** or 808/878-6698; www. ponyexpresstours.com), which offers a variety of rides down to the crater floor and back up, from $169 to $195 per person. Shorter 1- and 2-hour rides are also offered at Haleakala Ranch, located on the beautiful lower slopes of the volcano, for $95 and $115. A 1-hour introductory ride is just $65. If you book via the Internet, you get 10% off. Pony Express provides well-trained horses and experienced guides, and accommodates all riding levels. You must be at least 10 years old, weigh no more than 230 pounds, and wear long pants and closed-toe shoes.

WAY OUT WEST ON MAUI: RANCH RIDES   I recommend riding with **Mendes Ranch & Trail Rides** ★, 3530 Kahekili Hwy., 4 miles past Wailuku (© **808/244-7320;** www.mendesranch.com). The 300-acre Mendes Ranch is a real-life working cowboy ranch that has the essential elements of an earthly paradise—rainbows, waterfalls, palm trees, coral-sand beaches, lagoons, tide pools, a rainforest, and its own volcanic peak (more than a mile high). Allan Mendes, a third-generation wrangler, will take you from the edge of the rainforest out to the sea. On the way, you'll cross tree-studded meadows where Texas longhorns sit in the shade and pass a dusty corral where Allan's father, Ernest, a champion roper, may be breaking in a wild horse. Allan keeps close watch, turning often in his saddle to make sure everyone is happy. He points out flora and fauna and fields questions, but generally just lets you soak up Maui's natural splendor in golden silence. A 2-hour morning or afternoon ride costs $110; add on a barbecue lunch at the corral for an additional $20.

TENNIS

Maui has excellent public tennis courts; all are free and available from daylight to sunset (a few are even lit for night play until 10pm). The courts are available on a first-come, first-served basis; when someone's waiting, limit your play to 45 minutes. For a complete list of public courts, call **Maui County Parks and Recreation** (© **808/243-7230**). Most public courts require a wait and are not conveniently located near the major resort areas, so most visitors are likely to play at their own hotels for a fee.

Kids Especially for Kids

Taking a Submarine Ride   Atlantis Submarines takes you and the kids down into the shallow coastal waters off Lahaina in a real sub, where you'll see plenty of fish (and maybe even a shark!). They'll love it, and you'll stay dry the entire time. Allow about 2 hours for the trip; see "Submarine Dives," under the "Watersports" section, earlier in this chapter for more information.

Riding the Sugar-Cane Train   Small kids love this ride, as do train buffs of all ages. A steam engine pulls open-passenger cars of the Lahaina/Kaanapali and Pacific Railroad on a 30-minute, 12-mile round-trip through sugar-cane fields between Lahaina and Kaanapali while the conductor sings and calls out the landmarks. Along the way, you can see the hidden parts of Kaanapali and the islands of Molokai and Lanai beyond. Tickets are $20 for adults, $14 for kids ages 3 to 12; call © 808/661-0080 or visit www.sugarcanetrain.com for details.

Searching for Stars   After sunset, the stars over Kaanapali shine big and bright because the tropical sky is almost pollutant-free and no big-city lights interfere with the cosmic view. Amateur astronomers can probe the Milky Way, see the rings of Saturn and Jupiter's moons, and scan the Sea of Tranquillity in a 60-minute star search on the world's first recreational computer-driven telescope. This cosmic adventure takes place nightly at the **Hyatt Regency Maui,** 200 Nohea Kai Dr. (© 808/661-1234), at 8, 9, and 10pm. The cost for hotel guests is $20 for adults and $10 for children 12 and under; nonguests pay $25 for adults and $15 for children.

The exceptions to this are in Kihei (which has courts in Kalama Park on South Kihei Rd., and in Waipualani Park on West Waipualani Rd., behind the Maui Sunset Condo), in Lahaina (courts are in Malu'uou o lele Park, at Front and Shaw sts.), and Hana (courts are in Hana Park, on the Hana Hwy.).

Private tennis courts are available at most resorts and hotels on the island. The **Kapalua Tennis Garden and Village Tennis Center,** Kapalua Resort (© 808/669-5677; www.kapaluamaui.com), is home to the Kapalua Open, which features the largest purse in the state, on Labor Day weekend. Court rentals are $14 per person for resort guests and $18 per person for nonguests. The staff will match you up with a partner if you need one. In Wailea, try the **Wailea Tennis Club,** 131 Wailea Iki Place (© 808/879-1958; www.waileatennis.com), with 11 Plexipave courts. Court fees are $15 per player.

9 Seeing the Sights

CENTRAL MAUI

Central Maui isn't exactly tourist central; this is where real people live. Most likely, you'll land here and head directly to the beach. However, there are a few sights worth checking out if you feel like a respite from the sun and surf.

KAHULUI

Under the airport flight path, next to Maui's busiest intersection and across from Costco and Kmart in Kahului's new business park, is a most unlikely place: the **Kanaha Wildlife Sanctuary,** Haleakala Highway Extension and Hana Highway (© 808/984-8100). Look for the parking area off Haleakala Highway Extension (behind the mall, across the Hana Hwy. from Cutter Automotive), and you'll find a 50-foot trail that meanders along the shore to a shade shelter and lookout. Look for the sign proclaiming this the permanent home of the endangered black-neck Hawaiian stilt, whose population is now down to about 1,000. Naturalists say this is a good place to see endangered Hawaiian Koloa ducks, stilts, coots, and other migrating shorebirds. For a quieter, more natural-looking wildlife preserve, see the **Kealia Pond National Wildlife Preserve** in Kihei (covered later).

WAILUKU & WAIKAPU

Wailuku, the historic gateway to Iao Valley, is worth a visit for a little antiquing and a visit to the **Bailey House Museum** *⟨⟩*, 2375-A Main St. (© **808/244-3326;** www.mauimuseum.org). Missionary and sugar planter Edward Bailey's 1833 home—an architectural hybrid of stones laid by Hawaiian craftsmen and timbers joined in a display of Yankee ingenuity—is a treasure trove of Hawaiiana. Inside you'll find an eclectic collection, from precontact artifacts like scary temple images, dogtooth necklaces, and a rare lei made of tree snail shells to latter-day relics like Duke Kahanamoku's 1919 redwood surfboard and a koa-wood table given to President Ulysses S. Grant, who had to refuse it because he couldn't accept gifts from foreign countries. There's also a gallery devoted to a few of Bailey's landscapes, painted from 1866 to 1896, which capture on canvas a Maui I can only imagine today. It's open Monday through Saturday from 10am to 4pm; admission is $5 for adults, $4 for seniors, and $1 for children ages 7 to 12.

About 3 miles south of Wailuku lies the tiny, one-street village of Waikapu, which has two attractions that are worth a peek. Relive Maui's past by taking a 40-minute narrated tram ride around fields of pineapple, sugar cane, and papaya trees at **Maui Tropical Plantation,** 1670 Honoapiilani Hwy. (© **800/451-6805** or 808/244-7643; www.mauitropicalplantation.com), a real working plantation open daily from 9am to 5pm. A shop sells fresh and dried fruit, and a restaurant serves lunch. Admission is

---

Moments Flying High: Helicopter Rides

Only a helicopter can bring you face to face with volcanoes, waterfalls, and remote places like Maui's little-known Wall of Tears, up near the summit of Puu Kukui in the West Maui Mountains. Today's pilots are part Hawaiian historian, part DJ, part amusement-ride operator, and part tour guide, telling you about Hawaii's flora, fauna, history, and culture. **Blue Hawaiian Helicopters** *⟨⟩⟨⟩⟨⟩* (© 800/745-BLUE or 808/871-8844; www.bluehawaiian.com) is the Cadillac of helicopter-tour companies. They have the latest high-tech, environmentally friendly (and quiet) Eco-Star helicopters, specially designed for air-tour operators. Flight times range from 30 to 100 minutes and cost $159 to $323. *Budget tip:* Book on the Internet for substantial savings!

free; the tram tours, which start at 10am and leave about every 45 minutes, are $9.50 for adults, $3.50 for kids ages 3 to 12.

IAO VALLEY 😊

A couple of miles north of Wailuku, where the little plantation houses stop and the road climbs ever higher, Maui's true nature begins to reveal itself. The transition from suburban sprawl to raw nature is so abrupt that most people who drive up into the valley don't realize they're suddenly in a rainforest. The moist, cool air and the shade are a welcome comfort after the hot tropic sun. This is Iao Valley, a 6¼-acre state park whose great nature, history, and beauty have been enjoyed by millions of people from around the world for more than a century. Iao ("Supreme Light") Valley, 10 miles long and encompassing 4,000 acres, is the eroded volcanic caldera of the West Maui Mountains. The head of the valley is a broad circular amphitheater where four major streams converge into Iao Stream. At the back of the amphitheater is rain-drenched Puu Kukui, the West Maui Mountains' highest point. No other Hawaiian valley lets you go from seacoast to rainforest so easily. This peaceful valley, full of tropical plants, rainbows, waterfalls, swimming holes, and hiking trails, is a place of solitude, reflection, and escape for residents and visitors alike.

To get here from Wailuku, take Main Street to Iao Valley Road to the entrance to the state park.

Two paved walkways loop into the massive green amphitheater, across the bridge of Iao Valley Stream, and along the stream itself. This paved .35-mile loop is Maui's easiest hike—you can take your grandmother on this one. The leisurely walk will allow you to enjoy lovely views of the Iao Needle and the lush vegetation. Others often proceed beyond the state park border and take two trails deeper into the valley, but the trails enter private land, and NO TRESPASSING signs are posted.

The feature known as **Iao Needle** is an erosional remnant consisting of basalt dikes. This phallic rock juts an impressive 2,250 feet above sea level. Youngsters play in **Iao Stream,** a peaceful brook that belies its bloody history. In 1790, King Kamehameha the Great and his men engaged in the battle of Iao Valley to gain control of Maui. When the battle ended, so many bodies blocked Iao Stream that the battle site was named Kepaniwai, or "damming of the waters." An architectural heritage park of Hawaiian, Japanese, Chinese, Filipino, and New England–style houses stands in harmony by Iao Stream at **Kepaniwai Heritage Garden.** This is a good picnic spot, with plenty of tables and benches. You can see ferns, banana trees, and other native and exotic plants in the **Iao Valley Botanic Garden** along the stream.

WHEN TO GO   The park is open daily from 7am to 7pm. Go early in the morning or late in the afternoon, when the sun's rays slant into the valley and create a mystical mood. You can bring a picnic and spend the day, but be prepared at any time for one of the frequent tropical cloudbursts that soak the valley and swell both waterfalls and streams.

INFORMATION & VISITOR CENTERS   For information, contact **Iao Valley State Park,** State Parks and Recreation, 54 High St., Room 101, Wailuku, HI 96793 (© **808/984-8100**). The **Hawaii Nature Center,** 875 Iao Valley Rd. (© **808/244-6500;** www.hawaiinaturecenter.org), home to the Iao Valley Nature Center, features hands-on, interactive exhibits and displays relating the story of Hawaiian natural history; it's an important stop for all who want to explore Iao Valley. Hours are daily from 10am to 4pm; admission is $6 for adults and $4 for children ages 4 to 12.

THE SCENIC ROUTE TO WEST MAUI: THE KAHEKILI HIGHWAY

The usual road to West Maui from Wailuku is the Honoapiilani Highway, which takes you across the isthmus to Maalaea and around to Lahaina, Kaanapali, and Kapalua. But those wanting a back-to-nature driving experience should go the other way, along the **Kahekili Highway** (Hwy. 340; *highway* is a bit of a euphemism for this paved but somewhat precarious road.)

Drive north from Wailuku to Waiehu and onto this road named for King Kahekili, who built houses out of the skulls of his enemies. The true wild nature of Maui is on full display here. The narrow and winding road weaves for 20 miles along an ancient Hawaiian coastal footpath to Honokohau Bay, at the island's northernmost tip, past blowholes, sea stacks, seabird rookeries, and the imposing 636-foot Kahakaloa headland. On the land side, you'll pass high cliffs, deep valleys dotted with plantation houses, cattle grazing on green plateaus, old wooden churches, taro fields, and houses hung with fishing nets. It's slow going (you can drive only about 10 mph along the road), but it's probably the most beautiful drive in Maui. Your rental-car company might try to deter you, and you shouldn't go if it's been raining, but otherwise it's not really a hard drive and the views are spectacular.

At Honokohau, pick up Highway 30 and continue on to the West Maui resorts; the first one you'll reach is Kapalua (see below).

WEST MAUI

For a map of attractions in Lahaina and Kaanapali, see p. 369.

KAPALUA

For generations, West Maui meant one thing: pineapple. Hawaii's only pineapple cannery today, **Maui Pineapple Co.** offers tours of its plantation through the Kapalua Resort Activity Center (© **808/669-8088;** www.kapaluamaui.com). Real plantation workers lead the 2½-hour tours. You'll learn about the history of West Maui, facts about growing and harvesting pineapple, and lots of trivia about plantation life; you can even pick your own pineapple. The tours, which depart from the Kapalua Villas Reception Center, 500 Office Rd., are offered twice a day Monday through Friday, at 9:30am and 12:30pm. It costs $29; children must be at least 10.

A WHALE OF A PLACE IN KAANAPALI

If you haven't seen a real whale yet, go to **Whalers Village,** 2435 Kaanapali Pkwy., an oceanfront shopping center that has adopted the whale as its mascot. You can't miss it: A huge, almost life-size metal sculpture of a mother whale and two nursing calves greets you. A few more steps, and you're met by the looming, bleached-white skeleton of a 40-foot sperm whale; it's pretty impressive.

On the second floor of the mall is the **Whale Center of the Pacific** (© **808/661-5992**), a museum celebrating the "Golden Era of Whaling" (1825–60). Harpoons and scrimshaw are on display; the museum has even re-created the cramped quarters of a whaler's seagoing vessel. It's open daily from 9:30am to 10pm; admission is free.

HISTORIC LAHAINA

Back when "there was no God west of the Horn," Lahaina was the capital of Hawaii and the Pacific's wildest port. Today it's a milder version of its old self—mostly a hustle-bustle of whale , ꞓ, timeshares, and "Just Got Lei'd" T-shirts. I'm not sure the rowdy whalers would be pleased. But if you look hard, you'll still find the historic port town they loved, filled with the kind of history that inspired James Michener to write his best-selling epic novel *Hawaii.*

Baldwin Home Museum ⟨ฅ⟩   The oldest house in Lahaina, this coral-and-rock structure was built in 1834 by Rev. Dwight Baldwin, a doctor with the fourth company of American missionaries to sail 'round the Horn to Hawaii. Like many missionaries, he came to Hawaii to do good—and did very well for himself. After 17 years of service, Baldwin was granted 2,600 acres in Kapalua for farming and grazing. His ranch manager experimented with what Hawaiians called *hala-kahiki,* or pineapple, on a 4-acre plot; the rest is history. The house looks as if Baldwin has just stepped out for a minute to tend a sick neighbor down the street.

Next door is the **Master's Reading Room,** Maui's oldest building (included with museum admission). This became visiting sea captains' favorite hangout once the missionaries closed down all of Lahaina's grog shops and banned prostitution. By 1844, once hotels and bars started reopening, it lost its appeal. It's now the headquarters of the **Lahaina Restoration Foundation** (⟨ℭ⟩ **808/661-3262;** www.lahainarestoration. org), a plucky band of historians who try to keep this town alive and antique at the same time. Stop in and pick up a self-guided walking-tour map, which will take you to Lahaina's most historic sites.

120 Dickenson St. (at Front St.). ⟨ℭ⟩ **808/661-3262.** Admission $3 adults, $2 seniors, $5 family. Daily 10am–4pm.

⟨*Moments*⟩   **Ho'omana'o: Step Back in Time to Old Hawaii**

As soon as the low wail from the Hawaiian conch shell fills the air, you know that you have entered another time. *Ho'omana'o* means "to remember," and this 3-hour feast and immersion into ancient Hawaii is something you will remember long after your tan has faded.

Brought to you by the same innovated team that stages the Old Lahaina Luau, the Ho'omana'o is located in the same oceanfront setting, surrounded by tropical native plants. The feast begins with a breakfast buffet ranging from island stuffed French toast to *kalua* pork with lomi salmon, to haupia (coconut) oatmeal. Hula dancers and chanters entertain, the sun sparkles off the calm ocean water, and a salty breeze is in the air. This is Hawaii at its finest.

Then the fun begins. You get to experience (not just look and listen, but experience hands-on) three aspects of Hawaii: hula, warfare, and ancient life.

At the *hula kulana* (ancient dances), you will actually be learning a few hula steps and how to play the traditional implements; at the warfare kulana, you will try your hand at tossing a spear, or, perhaps, put on a temporary, removable tattoo of a Hawaiian warrior; and at the ancient Hawaiian life station, you will sample freshly made poi and poke (small pieces of raw fish, salt, seaweed, and kukui nut), or practice throwing a fish net.

Ho'omana'o, in the Old Lahaina Luau grounds, 1251 Front St., Lahaina (⟨ℭ⟩ **800/248-5828;** www.oldlahainaluau.com), takes place 8:30 to 11:30am. Tickets are $69 adults and $49 children 12 and under. Don't miss it.

Day Trips to Molokai

It's possible to visit Molokai's famous leper colony (officially known as Kalau-papa National Historic Park) as a day trip from Maui. You won't be able to squeeze in the exhilarating mule ride down the 1,600-foot cliffs (they start at 8am), but you didn't want to sit on your ass all day long anyway, now did you? (Sorry, bad pun.) **Paragon Air** (© **808/244-3356**; www.paragon-air.com) offers a $240 package deal that includes round-trip airfare from Kahului Airport to Molokai's Kalaupapa airport, a 4-hour tour, lunch, and drinks. All visitors must be at least 16 years old.

Banyan Tree   Of all the banyan trees in Hawaii, this is the greatest of all—so big that you can't get it all in your camera's viewfinder. It was only 8 feet tall when it was planted in 1873 by Maui Sheriff William O. Smith to mark the 50th anniversary of Lahaina's first Christian mission. Today the big old banyan from India is more than 50 feet tall, has 12 major trunks, and shades two-thirds of an acre in Courthouse Square.

At the Courthouse Building, 649 Wharf St.

Maluuluolele Park   At first glance, this Front Street park appears to be only a hot, dry, dusty softball field. But under home plate is an edge of Mokuula, where a royal compound once stood more than 100 years ago, now buried under tons of red dirt and sand. Here, Prince Kauikeaolui, who ascended the throne as King Kamehameha III when he was only 10, lived with the love of his life, his sister, Princess Nahienaena. Missionaries took a dim view of incest, which was acceptable to Hawaiian nobles in order to preserve the royal bloodline. Torn between love for her brother and the new Christian morality, Nahienaena grew despondent and died at the age of 21. King Kamehameha III, who reigned for 29 years—longer than any other Hawaiian monarch—presided over Hawaii as it went from kingdom to constitutional monarchy, and as power over the islands began to shift from island nobles to missionaries, merchants, and sugar planters. Kamehameha died in 1854; he was 39. In 1918, his royal compound, containing a mausoleum and artifacts of the kingdom, was demolished and covered with dirt to create a public park. The baseball team from Lahainaluna School, the first American school founded by missionaries west of the Rockies, now plays games on the site of this royal place, still considered sacred to many Hawaiians.

Front and Shaw sts.

SOUTH MAUI

MAALAEA

Maui Ocean Center ★★★ *(Kids*   This 5-acre facility houses the largest aquarium in Hawaii and features one of Hawaii's largest predators: the tiger shark. As you walk past the three dozen or so tanks and countless exhibits, you'll slowly descend from the "beach" to the deepest part of the ocean without ever getting wet. Start at the surge pool, where you'll see shallow-water marine life like spiny urchins and cauliflower coral; then move on to the reef tanks, turtle pool, "touch" pool (with starfish and urchins), and eagle-ray pool before reaching the star of the show: the 100-foot-long, 600,000-gallon main tank featuring tiger, gray, and white-tip sharks, as well as tuna, surgeonfish, triggerfish, and numerous others. The most phenomenal thing about this tank is that the walkway goes right through it, so you're surrounded on three sides by marine creatures. A very cool place, and well worth the time. Some new additions are a hammerhead exhibit where juvenile scalloped hammerhead sharks are on display, and the Shark Dive Maui Program, where certified scuba divers plunge into the aquarium with sharks, stingrays, and tropical fish (yes, you, too, can dive with sharks), while friends and family watch safely from the other side of the glass.

Maalaea Harbor Village, 192 Maalaea Rd. (the triangle between Honoapiilani Hwy. and Maalaea Rd.) ✆ 808/270-7000. www.mauioceancenter.com. Admission $23 adults, $19 seniors, $16 children 3–12. Daily 9am–5pm (until 6pm July–Aug).

KIHEI

Capt. George Vancouver "discovered" Kihei in 1778, when it was only a collection of fishermen's grass shacks on the hot, dry, dusty coast (hard to believe, eh?). A **totem pole** stands today where he's believed to have landed, across from Aston Maui Lu Resort, 575 S. Kihei Rd. Vancouver sailed on to "discover" British Columbia, where a great international city and harbor now bear his name.

West of the junction of Piilani Highway (Hwy. 31) and Mokulele Highway (Hwy. 350) is **Kealia Pond National Wildlife Preserve** (✆ **808/875-1582**), a 700-acre U.S. Fish and Wildlife wetland preserve where endangered Hawaiian stilts, coots, and ducks hang out and splash. These ponds work two ways: as bird preserves and as sedimentation basins that keep the coral reefs from silting from runoff. You can take a self-guided tour along a boardwalk dotted with interpretive signs and shade shelters, through sand dunes, and around ponds to Maalaea Harbor. The boardwalk starts at the outlet of Kealia Pond on the ocean side of North Kihei Road (near mile marker 2 on Piilani Hwy.). Among the Hawaiian water birds seen here are the black-crowned high heron, Hawaiian coot, Hawaiian duck, and Hawaiian stilt. There also are shorebirds like sanderlings, Pacific golden plovers, ruddy turnstones, and wandering tattlers. From July to December, the hawksbill turtle comes ashore here to lay her eggs.

WAILEA

The best way to explore this golden resort coast is to rise with the sun and head for Wailea's 1.5-mile **coastal nature trail** ✦, stretching between the Kea Lani Hotel and the kiawe thicket just beyond the Renaissance Wailea. It's a great morning walk, a serpentine path that meanders uphill and down past native plants, old Hawaiian habitats, and a billion dollars' worth of luxury hotels. You can pick up the trail at any of the resorts or from clearly marked SHORELINE ACCESS points along the coast. The best time to go is when you first wake up; by midmorning, the coastal trail is too often clogged with pushy joggers, and it grows crowded with beachgoers as the day wears on. As the path crosses several bold black-lava points, it affords new vistas of islands and ocean; benches allow you to pause and contemplate the view across Alalakeiki Channel, where you may see jumping whales in season. Sunset is another good time to hit the trail.

MAKENA

A few miles south of Wailea, the manicured coast turns to wilderness; now you're in Makena. Once cattle were driven down the slope from upland ranches, lashed to rafts, and sent into the water to swim to boats that waited to take them to market. Now **Makena Landing** ✦ is the best place to launch kayaks bound for La Pérouse Bay and Ahihi-Kinau preserve.

From the landing, go south on Makena Road; on the right is **Keawalai Congregational Church** (© 808/879-5557), built in 1855, with walls 3 feet thick. Surrounded by ti leaves, which by Hawaiian custom provide protection, and built of lava rock with coral used as mortar, this church sits on its own cove with a gold-sand beach. It always attracts a Sunday crowd for its 9:30am Hawaiian-language service.

A little farther south on the coast is **La Pérouse Monument,** a pyramid of lava rocks that marks the spot where French explorer Adm. Comte de la Pérouse set foot on Maui in 1786. The first Westerner to "discover" the island, he described the "burning climate" of the leeward coast, observed several fishing villages near Kihei, and sailed on into oblivion, never to be seen again; some believe he may have been eaten by cannibals in what now is Vanuatu. To get here, drive south past Puu Olai to Ahihi Bay, where the road turns to gravel. Go another 2 miles along the coast to La Pérouse Bay; the monument sits amid a clearing in black lava at the end of the dirt road.

HOUSE OF THE SUN: HALEAKALA NATIONAL PARK ☆☆☆

At once forbidding and compelling, Haleakala ("House of the Sun") National Park is Maui's main natural attraction. More than 1.3 million people a year go up the 10,023-foot-high mountain to peer down into the crater of the world's largest dormant volcano. (Haleakala is officially considered active, even though it has not rumbled since 1790.) That hole would hold Manhattan.

But there's more to do here than stare into a big black hole: Just going up the mountain is an experience. Where else on the planet can you climb from sea level to 10,000 feet in just 37 miles, or a 2-hour drive? The snaky road passes through big, puffy cumulus clouds to offer magnificent views of the isthmus of Maui, the West Maui Mountains, and the Pacific Ocean.

Many drive up to the summit in predawn darkness to watch the **sunrise over Haleakala** ☆☆; others coast down the 37-mile road from the summit on a bicycle with special brakes (see "Bicycling," earlier in this chapter). Hardy adventurers hike and camp inside the crater's wilderness (see "Hiking & Camping," earlier in this chapter). Those bound for the interior should bring their survival gear, for the terrain is raw, rugged, and punishing—not unlike the moon.

JUST THE FACTS

Haleakala National Park extends from the summit of Mount Haleakala down the volcano's southeast flank to Maui's eastern coast, beyond Hana. There are actually two separate and distinct destinations within the park: **Haleakala Summit** and the **Kipahulu** coast (see "Tropical Haleakala: Oheo Gulch at Kipahulu," later in this chapter). The summit gets all the publicity, but Kipahulu draws crowds, too—it's lush, green, and tropical, and home to Oheo Gulch (also known as Seven Sacred Pools). No road links the summit and the coast; you have to approach them separately, and you need at least a day to see each place.

WHEN TO GO At the 10,023-foot summit, weather changes fast. With wind chill, temperatures can be freezing any time of year. Summer can be dry and warm; winter can be wet, windy, and cold. Before you go, get current weather conditions from the park (© 808/572-4400) or the **National Weather Service** (© 808/871-5054).

From sunrise to noon, the light is weak, but the view is usually free of clouds. The best time for photos is in the afternoon, when the sun lights the crater and clouds are few. Go on full-moon nights for spectacular viewing.

Impressions

There are few enough places in the world that belong entirely to themselves.
The human passion to carry all things everywhere, so that every place is
home, seems well on its way to homogenizing our planet, save for the odd
unreachable corner. Haleakala Crater is one of those corners.
                                        —Barbara Kingsolver, the *New York Times*

A note of caution: This is Mother Nature, not Disneyland, so there are no guarantees or schedules. Especially in winter, some mornings may be misty or rainy, and sunrise viewing may be obscured. It's the luck of the draw.

ACCESS POINTS   Haleakala Summit is 37 miles, or a 1½- to 2-hour drive, from Kahului. To get here, take Highway 37 to Highway 377 to Highway 378. For details on the drive, see "The Drive to the Summit," below. Pukalani is the last town for water, food, and gas.

The **Kipahulu** section of Haleakala National Park is on Maui's east end near Hana, 60 miles from Kahului on Highway 36 (Hana Hwy.). Due to traffic and rough road conditions, plan on 4 hours for the drive, one-way. For complete information, see "The Road to Hana," below, and "Tropical Haleakala: Oheo Gulch at Kipahulu," later in this chapter.

At both entrances to the park, the admission fee is $5 per person or $10 per car, good for a week of unlimited entry.

INFORMATION, VISITOR CENTERS & RANGER PROGRAMS   For information before you go, contact **Haleakala National Park,** Box 369, Makawao, HI 96768 (© **808/572-4400;** www.nps.gov/hale).

One mile from the park entrance, at 7,000 feet, is **Haleakala National Park Headquarters** (© **808/572-4400**), open daily from 7:30am to 4pm. Stop here to pick up information on park programs and activities, get camping permits, and, occasionally, see a Hawaiian nene bird. Restrooms, a pay phone, and drinking water are available.

The **Haleakala Visitor Center,** open daily from sunrise to 3pm, is near the summit, 11 miles past the park entrance. It offers a panoramic view of the volcanic landscape, with photos identifying the various features, and exhibits that explain the area's history, ecology, geology, and volcanology. Park staff members are often on hand to answer questions. Restrooms and water are available.

Rangers offer excellent, informative, and free **naturalist talks** at 9:30, 10:30, and 11:30am daily in the summit building. For information on **hiking** and **camping** possibilities, including wilderness cabins and campgrounds, see "Hiking & Camping" earlier in this chapter.

THE DRIVE TO THE SUMMIT

If you look on a Maui map, almost in the middle of the part that resembles a torso, there's a black wiggly line that looks like this: WWWWW. That's **Highway 378,** also known as **Haleakala Crater Road**—one of the fastest-ascending roads in the world. This grand corniche has at least 33 switchbacks; passes through numerous climate zones; goes under, in, and out of clouds; takes you past rare silversword plants and endangered Hawaiian geese sailing through the clear, thin air; and offers a view that extends for more than 100 miles.

Haleakala National Park

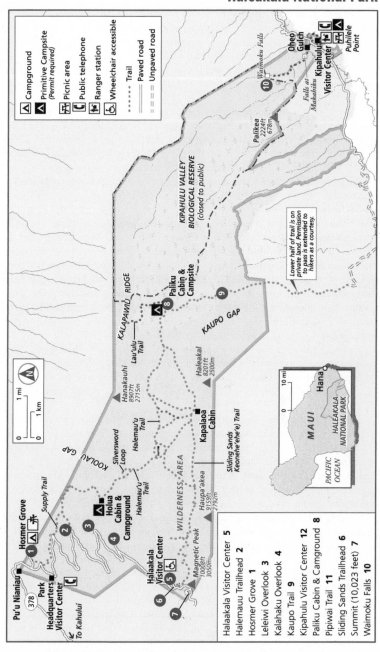

Legend:
- ▲ Campground
- ◣ Primitive Campsite *(Permit required)*
- 木 Picnic area
- ☎ Public telephone
- Ranger station
- ♿ Wheelchair accessible
- ⋯⋯ Trail
- ═══ Paved road
- ╪╪╪ Unpaved road

Waimoku Falls

Oheo Gulch

Kipahulu Visitor Center

Puhilele Point

Palikea 2224ft / 678m

KIPAHULU VALLEY BIOLOGICAL RESERVE (closed to public)

Lower half of trail is on private land. Permission to pass is extended to hikers as a courtesy.

Paliku Cabin & Campsite **8**

9

KAUPO GAP

KALAPAWILI RIDGE

Lau'ulu Trail

Hanakauhi 8907ft / 2715m

Haleakalā 8201ft / 2500m

Kapalaoa Cabin

Silversword Loop

Halemau'u Trail

Supply Trail

Hosmer Grove

1

2

3

4

Holua Cabin & Campground

Halemau'u Trail

KOOLAU GAP

WILDERNESS AREA

Haupa'akea 9159ft / 2792m

Magnetic Peak 10008ft / 3050m

Sliding Sands *Keonehe'ehe'e) Trail*

Haleakala Visitor Center

5

6

7

Pu'u Nianiau

Park Headquarters Visitor Center

378

To Kahului

N

0   1 mi
0   1 km

MAUI

Hana

HALEAKALA NATIONAL PARK

PACIFIC OCEAN

0   10 mi

Haleakala Visitor Center **5**
Halemauu Trailhead **2**
Hosmer Grove **1**
Leleiwi Overlook **3**
Kalahaku Overlook **4**
Kaupo Trail **9**
Kipahulu Visitor Center **12**
Paliku Cabin & Campground **8**
Pipiwai Trail **11**
Sliding Sands Trailhead **6**
Summit (10,023 feet) **7**
Waimoku Falls **10**

Going to the summit takes 1½ to 2 hours from Kahului. No matter where you start out, you'll follow Highway 37 (Haleakala Hwy.) to Pukalani, where you'll pick up Highway 377 (aka Haleakala Hwy.), which you'll take to Highway 378. Along the way, expect fog, rain, and wind. You may encounter stray cattle and downhill bicyclists. Fill up your gas tank before you go—the only gas available is 27 miles below the summit at Pukalani. There are no facilities beyond the ranger stations—not even a coffee urn in sight. Bring your own food and water.

Remember, you're entering a high-altitude wilderness area. Some people get dizzy due to the lack of oxygen; you might also suffer lightheadedness, shortness of breath, nausea, or worse: severe headaches, flatulence, and dehydration. People with asthma, pregnant women, heavy smokers, and those with heart conditions should be especially careful in the rarefied air. Bring water and a jacket or a blanket, especially if you go up for sunrise. Or you might want to go up to the summit for sunset, which is also spectacular.

At the **park entrance,** you'll pay an entrance fee of $10 per car (or $2 for a bicycle). About a mile from the entrance is **Park Headquarters,** where an endangered **nene,** or Hawaiian goose, may greet you with its unique call. With its black face, buff cheeks, and partially webbed feet, the gray-brown bird looks like a small Canada goose with zebra stripes; it brays out "nay-nay" (thus its name), doesn't migrate, and prefers lava beds to lakes. More than 25,000 nene once inhabited Hawaii, but habitat destruction and predators (hunters, pigs, feral cats and dogs, and mongooses) nearly caused their extinction. By 1951, there were only 30 left. Now protected as Hawaii's state bird, the wild nene on Haleakala number fewer than 250—the species remains endangered.

Beyond headquarters are **two scenic overlooks** on the way to the summit; stop at Leleiwi on the way up and Kalahaku on the way back down, if only to get out, stretch, and get accustomed to the heights. Take a deep breath, look around, and pop your ears. If you feel dizzy or drowsy, or get a sudden headache, consider turning around and going back down.

Leleiwi Overlook ⟨⟩ is just beyond mile marker 17. From the parking area, a short trail leads you to a panoramic view of the lunarlike crater. When the clouds are low and the sun is in the right place, usually around sunset, you may experience a phenomenon known as the "Specter of the Brocken"—you can see a reflection of your shadow, ringed by a rainbow, in the clouds below. It's an optical illusion caused by a rare combination of sun, shadow, and fog that occurs in only three places on the planet: Haleakala, Scotland, and Germany.

Two miles farther along is **Kalahaku Overlook** ⟨⟩, the best place to see a rare **silversword.** You can turn into this overlook only when you are descending from the top. The silversword is the punk of the plant world, its silvery bayonets displaying tiny purple bouquets—like a spacey artichoke with attitude. This botanical wonder proved irresistible to humans, who gathered them in gunnysacks for Chinese potions and British specimen collections, and just for the sheer thrill of having something so rare.

Tips **Descending from the Crater**

When driving down the Haleakala Crater Road, be sure to put your car in low gear so you don't destroy your brakes by riding them the whole way down.

Silverswords grow only in Hawaii, take from 4 to 50 years to bloom, and then, usually between May and October, send up a 1- to 6-foot stalk with a purple bouquet of sunflower-like blooms. They're very rare, so don't even think about taking one home.

Continue on, and you'll quickly reach **Haleakala Visitor Center,** which offers spectacular views. You'll feel as if you're at the edge of the earth, but the actual summit's a little farther on, at **Puu Ulaula Overlook** ✶✶✶ (also known as Red Hill), the volcano's highest point, where you'll find a cluster of buildings officially known as Haleakala Observatories, but unofficially called **Science City.** If you go up for sunrise, the building at Puu Ulaula Overlook, a triangle of glass that serves as a windbreak, is the best viewing spot. After the daily miracle of sunrise—the sun seems to rise out of the vast ocean—you can see all the way across Alenuihaha Channel to the often-snowcapped summit of Mauna Kea on the Big Island.

UPCOUNTRY MAUI

Come upcountry and discover a different side of Maui: On the slopes of Haleakala, cowboys, planters, and other country people make their homes in serene, neighborly communities like **Makawao** and **Kula,** a world away from the bustling beach resorts. Even if you can't spare a day or two in the cool, upcountry air, there are some sights that are worth a look on your way to or from the crater. Shoppers and gallery hoppers might want to spend more time here; see "Shops & Galleries," later in this chapter.

Kula Botanical Garden ✶ You can take a self-guided, informative, leisurely stroll through more than 700 native and exotic plants—including three unique collections of orchids, proteas, and bromeliads—at this 5-acre garden. It offers a good overview of Hawaii's exotic flora in one small, cool place.

Hwy. 377, south of Haleakala Crater Rd. (Hwy. 378), ½ mile from Hwy. 37. © **808/878-1715.** www.hawaiiweb.com/maui/html/sites/kula_botanical_gardens.html. Admission $5 adults, $1 children 6–12. Daily 9am–4pm.

Tedeschi Vineyards and Winery ✶ On the southern shoulder of Haleakala is **Ulupalakua Ranch,** a 20,000-acre spread once owned by legendary sea captain James Makee, celebrated in the Hawaiian song and dance *Hula O Makee.* Wounded in a

Honolulu waterfront brawl in 1843, Makee moved to Maui and bought Ulupalakua. He renamed it Rose Ranch, planted sugar as a cash crop, and grew rich. Still in operation, the ranch is now home to Maui's only winery, established in 1974 by Napa vintner Emil Tedeschi, who began growing California and European grapes here and producing serious still and sparkling wines, plus a silly wine made of pineapple juice. The rustic grounds are the perfect place for a picnic. Pack a basket before you go, but don't BYOB: There's plenty of great wine to enjoy at Tedeschi. Settle in under the sprawling camphor tree, pop the cork on a blanc de blanc, and toast your good fortune in being here.

Off Hwy. 37 (Kula Hwy.). ℂ **808/878-6058**. www.mauiwine.com. Free tastings. Daily 9am–5pm. Tours given 10:30am and 1:30pm.

EAST MAUI & HEAVENLY HANA

Hana is Paradise on Earth—or just about as close as you can get to it, anyway. In and around Hana, you'll find a lush tropical rainforest dotted with cascading waterfalls and sparkling blue pools, skirted by red- and black-sand beaches.

THE ROAD TO HANA ✿✿✿

Top down, sunscreen on, radio tuned to a little Hawaiian music on a Maui morning—it's time to head out to Hana along the Hana Highway (Hwy. 36), a wiggle of a road that runs along Maui's northeastern shore. The drive takes at least 3 hours from Lahaina or Kihei—but take all day. Going to Hana is about the journey, not the destination.

There are wilder roads, steeper roads, and more dangerous roads, but in all of Hawaii, no road is more celebrated than this one. It winds 50 miles past taro patches, magnificent seascapes, waterfall pools, botanical gardens, and verdant rainforests, and ends at one of Hawaii's most beautiful tropical places.

The outside world discovered the little village of Hana in 1926, when the narrow coastal road, carved by pickax-wielding convicts, opened. The mud-and-gravel road, often subject to landslides and washouts, was paved in 1962, when tourist traffic began to increase; it now sees 1,000 cars and dozens of vans a day, according to storekeeper Harry Hasegawa. That translates into half a million people a year, which is way too many. Go at the wrong time, and you'll be stuck in a bumper-to-bumper rental-car parade—peak traffic hours are midmorning and midafternoon year-round, especially on weekends.

In the rush to "do" Hana in a day, most visitors spin around town in 10 minutes and wonder what all the fuss is about. It takes time to take in Hana, play in the waterfalls, sniff the tropical flowers, hike to bamboo forests, and view the spectacular scenery. Stay overnight if you can, and meander back in a day or two. If you really must do the Hana Highway in a day, go just before sunrise and return after sunset.

Tips: Practice aloha. Give way at one-lane bridges, wave at oncoming motorists, let the big guys in 4×4s have the right of way—it's just common sense, brah. If the guy behind you blinks his lights, let him pass. And don't honk your horn—in Hawaii, it's considered rude.

THE JOURNEY BEGINS IN PAIA   Before you even start out, fill up your gas tank. Gas in Paia is expensive, and it's the last place for gas until you get to Hana, some 54 bridges and 600 hairpin turns down the road.

Paia was once a thriving sugar-mill town. The mill is still here, but the population shifted to Kahului in the 1950s when subdivisions opened there, leaving Paia to shrivel up and die. But the town refused to give up, and it has proven its ability to adapt to the times. Now chic eateries and trendy shops stand next door to the old ma-and-pa establishments. Plan to be here early, around 7am, when **Charley's** ✦, 142 Hana Hwy. (© **808/579-9453**), opens. Enjoy a big, hearty breakfast for a reasonable price.

WINDSURFING MECCA   Just before mile marker 9 is **Hookipa Beach Park** ✦, where top-ranked windsurfers come to test themselves against the forces of nature: thunderous surf and forceful wind. On nearly every windy day after noon (the board surfers have the waves in the morning), you can watch dozens of windsurfers twirling and dancing in the wind like colored butterflies. To watch them, do not stop on the highway, but go past the park and turn left at the entrance on the far side of the beach. You can either park on the high grassy bluff or drive down to the sandy beach and park alongside the pavilion. Facilities include restrooms, a shower, picnic tables, and a barbecue area.

INTO THE COUNTRY   Past Hookipa Beach, the road winds down into **Maliko Gulch** at mile marker 10. At the bottom of the gulch, look for the road on your right, which will take you out to **Maliko Bay.** Take the first right, which goes under the bridge and past a rodeo arena and on to the rocky beach. There are no facilities here except a boat-launch ramp. In the 1940s, Maliko had a thriving community at the mouth of the bay, but its residents rebuilt farther inland after a strong tidal wave wiped it out.

Back on the Hana Highway, for the next few miles, you'll pass through the rural area of **Haiku,** where you'll see banana patches, forests of guavas and palms, and avocados. Just before mile marker 15 is the **Maui Grown Market and Deli** (© **808/572-1693**), a good stop for drinks or snacks for the ride.

At mile marker 16, the curves begin, one right after another. Slow down and enjoy the view of bucolic rolling hills, mango trees, and vibrant ferns. After mile marker 16, the road is still called the Hana Highway, but the number changes from Highway 36 to Highway 360, and the mile markers go back to 0.

A GREAT PLUNGE ALONG THE WAY   A dip in a waterfall pool is everybody's tropical-island fantasy. A great place to stop is **Twin Falls** ✦, at mile marker 2. Just before the wide, concrete bridge, pull over on the mountain side and park. There is a NO TRESPASSING sign on the gate. Although you will see several cars parked in the area and a steady line of people going up to the falls, be aware that this is private property and trespassing is illegal in Hawaii. If you decide that you want to "risk it," you will walk about 3 to 5 minutes to the waterfall and pool, or continue on another 10 to 15 minutes to the second, larger waterfall and pool (don't go in if it has been raining).

HIDDEN HUELO   Just before mile marker 4 on a blind curve, look for a double row of mailboxes on the left side by the pay phone. Down the road lies a hidden Hawaii of an earlier time, where an indescribable sense of serenity prevails. Hemmed in by Waipo and Hoalua bays is the remote community of **Huelo** ✦. This fertile area once supported a population of 75,000; today only a few hundred live among the scattered homes here, where a handful of B&Bs and exquisite vacation rentals cater to a trickle of travelers (see "Where to Stay," earlier in this chapter).

The only reason Huelo is even marked is the historic 1853 **Kaulanapueo Church.** Reminiscent of New England architecture, this coral-and-cement church, topped with a plantation-green steeple and a gray tin roof, is still in use, although services are held just once or twice a month. It still has the same austere, stark interior of 1853: straight-backed benches, a no-nonsense platform for the minister, and no distractions on the walls to tempt you from paying attention to the sermon. Next to the church is a small graveyard, a personal history of this village in concrete and stone.

KOOLAU FOREST RESERVE   After Huelo, the vegetation seems more lush, as though Mother Nature had poured Miracle-Gro on everything. This is the edge of the **Koolau Forest Reserve.** *Koolau* means "windward," and this certainly is one of the greatest examples of a lush windward area: The coastline here gets about 60 to 80 inches of rain a year, as well as runoff from the 200 to 300 inches that falls farther up the mountain. Here you'll see trees laden with guavas, as well as mangoes, java plums, and avocados the size of softballs. The spiny, long-leafed plants are hala trees, which the Hawaiians used for weaving baskets, mats, and even canoe sails.

From here on out, there's a waterfall (and one-lane bridge) around nearly every turn in the road, so drive slowly and be prepared to stop and yield to oncoming cars.

DANGEROUS CURVES   About a half-mile after mile marker 6, there's a sharp U-curve in the road, going uphill. The road is practically one-lane here, with a brick wall on one side and virtually no maneuvering room. Sound your horn at the start of the U-curve to let approaching cars know you're coming. Take this curve, as well as the few more coming up in the next several miles, very slowly.

Just before mile marker 7 is a forest of waving **bamboo.** The sight is so spectacular that drivers are often tempted to take their eyes off the road. Be very cautious. Wait until just after mile marker 7, at the **Kaaiea Bridge** and stream below, to pull over and take a closer look at the hand-hewn stone walls. Then turn around to see the vista of bamboo.

A GREAT FAMILY HIKE   At mile marker 9, there's a small state wayside area with restrooms, picnic tables, and a barbecue area. The sign says KOOLAU FOREST RESERVE, but the real attraction here is the **Waikamoi Ridge Trail** ⋆, an easy .75-mile loop. The start of the trail is just behind the QUIET TREES AT WORK sign. The well-marked trail meanders through eucalyptus, ferns, and hala trees.

SAFETY WARNING   I used to recommend another waterfall, **Puohokamoa Falls,** at mile marker 11, but not anymore. Unfortunately, what once was a great thing has been overrun by hordes of not-so-polite tourists. You will see cars parking on the already dangerous, barely-two-lane Hana Highway half a mile before the waterfall. Slow down after the 10-mile marker. As you get close to the 11-mile marker, the road becomes a congested one-lane road due to visitors parking on this narrow highway. Don't add to the congestion by trying to park: There are plenty of other great waterfalls; just drive slowly and safely through this area.

CAN'T-MISS PHOTO OPS   Just past mile marker 12 is the **Kaumahina State Wayside Park** ⋆. This is not only a good pit stop (restrooms are available) and a wonderful place for a picnic (with tables and a barbecue area), but also a great vista point. The view of the rugged coastline makes an excellent shot—you can see all the way down to the jutting Keanae Peninsula.

Another mile and a couple of bends in the road, and you'll enter the Honomanu Valley, with its beautiful bay. To get to the **Honomanu Bay County Beach Park** ⋆, look for the turnoff on your left, just after mile marker 14, as you begin your ascent up the other side of the valley. The rutted dirt-and-cinder road takes you down to the rocky black-sand beach. There are no facilities here. Because of the strong rip currents offshore, swimming is best in the stream inland from the ocean. You'll consider the drive down worthwhile as you stand on the beach, well away from the ocean, and turn to look back on the steep cliffs covered with vegetation.

KEANAE PENINSULA & ARBORETUM At mile marker 17, the old Hawaiian village of **Keanae** ✿✿ stands out against the Pacific like a place time forgot. Here, on an old lava flow graced by an 1860 stone church and swaying palms, is one of the last coastal enclaves of native Hawaiians. They still grow taro in patches and pound it into poi, the staple of the old Hawaiian diet; and they still pluck opihi (limpet) from tide pools along the jagged coast and cast throw-nets at schools of fish.

At nearby **Keanae Arboretum,** Hawaii's botanical world is divided into three parts: native forest, introduced forest, and traditional Hawaiian plants, food, and medicine. You can swim in the pools of Piinaau Stream or press on along a mile-long trail into Keanae Valley, where a lovely tropical rainforest waits at the end.

WAIANAPANAPA STATE PARK ✿✿ On the outskirts of Hana, shiny black-sand Waianapanapa Beach appears like a vivid dream, with bright-green jungle foliage on three sides and cobalt blue water lapping at its feet. The 120-acre park on an ancient lava flow includes sea cliffs, lava tubes, arches, and that beach—plus a dozen rustic cabins. If you're interested in staying here, see "Where to Stay," earlier in this chapter. Also see "Beaches" and "Hiking & Camping," earlier in this chapter.

HANA ✿✿✿

Green, tropical Hana, which some call heavenly, is a destination all its own, a small coastal village in a rainforest inhabited by 2,500 people, many part-Hawaiian. Beautiful Hana enjoys more than 90 inches of rain a year—more than enough to keep the scenery lush. Banyans, bamboo, breadfruit trees—everything seems larger than life, especially the flowers, like wild ginger and plumeria. Several roadside stands offer exotic blooms for $1 a bunch. Just "put money in box." It's the Hana honor system.

The last unspoiled Hawaiian town on Maui is, oddly enough, the home of Maui's first resort, which opened in 1946. Paul Fagan, owner of the San Francisco Seals baseball team, bought an old inn and turned it into the **Hotel Hana-Maui,** which gave Hana its first and, as it turns out, last taste of tourism. Others have tried to open hotels and golf courses and resorts, but Hana, which is interested in remaining Hana, always politely refuses. There are a few B&Bs here, though; see "Where to Stay," earlier in this chapter.

A wood-frame 1871 building that served as the old Hana District Police Station now holds the **Hana Museum Cultural Center,** 4974 Uakea Rd. (© **808/248-8622**). The center tells the history of the area, with some excellent artifacts, memorabilia, and photographs. Also stop in at **Hasegawa General Store,** a Maui institution.

On the green hills above Hana stands a 30-foot-high white cross made of lava rock. The cross was erected by citizens in memory of Paul Fagan, who helped keep the town alive. The 3-mile hike up to **Fagan's Cross** provides a gorgeous view of the Hana coast, especially at sunset, when Fagan himself liked to climb this hill. See p. 441 for details.

Most day-trippers to Hana miss the most unusual natural attraction of all: **Red Sand Beach** ✿, officially named Kaihalulu Beach, which means "roaring sea." It's truly a sight to see. It's on the ocean side of Kauiki Hill, just south of Hana Bay, in a wild, natural setting in a pocket cove. Kauiki, a 390-foot-high volcanic cinder cone, lost its seaward wall to erosion and spilled red cinders everywhere, creating the red sands. To get here, walk south on Uakea Road, past the Hotel Hana-Maui to the end of the parking lot for Sea Ranch Cottages. Turn left, cross an open field past an old cemetery, and follow a well-worn path down a narrow cliff trail. In this private, romantic setting, some beachgoers shed their clothes, so try not to be offended.

TROPICAL HALEAKALA: OHEO GULCH AT KIPAHULU

If you're thinking about heading out to the so-called Seven Sacred Pools, out past Hana at the Kipahulu end of Haleakala National Park, let's clear this up right now: There are more than seven pools—about 24, actually—and *all* water in Hawaii is considered sacred. It's all a PR campaign that has spun out of control. Folks here call it by its rightful name, **Oheo Gulch** 🐸🐸🐸, and visitors sometimes refer to it as Kipahulu, which is actually the name of the area where Oheo Gulch is located. No matter what you call it, it's beautiful. This dazzling series of pools and cataracts is so popular that it has its own roadside parking lot.

From the ranger station, it's just a short hike above the famous Oheo Gulch to two spectacular **waterfalls.** Check with park rangers before hiking up to or swimming in the pools, and always keep an eye on the water in the streams. The sky can be sunny near the coast, but flood waters travel 6 miles down from the Kipahulu Valley, and the water level can rise 4 feet in less than 10 minutes. It's not a good idea to swim in the pools in winter.

Makahiku Falls is easily reached from the central parking area; the trail head begins near the ranger station. **Pipiwai Trail** leads up to the road and beyond for .5 mile to the overlook. If you hike another 1.5 miles up the trail across two bridges and through a bamboo forest, you reach **Waimoku Falls.** It's a hard uphill hike, but press on to avoid the pool's crowd.

ACCESS POINTS   Even though Oheo is part of Haleakala National Park, you cannot drive here from the summit. Oheo is about 30 to 50 minutes beyond Hana town, along Highway 31. The admission fee to enter is $5 per person or $10 per car. The Highway 31 bridge passes over some of the pools near the ocean; the others, plus magnificent 400-foot Waimoku Falls, are uphill, via an often-muddy but rewarding hour-long hike (see "Hiking & Camping," earlier in this chapter). Expect showers on the Kipahulu coast.

VISITOR CENTER   The **Kipahulu Ranger Station** (© **808/248-7375**) is staffed from 9am to 5pm daily. Restrooms are available, but there's no drinking water. Here you'll find park-safety information, exhibits, and books. Rangers offer a variety of walks and hikes year-round; check at the station for current activities. Tent camping is permitted in the park; see "Hiking & Camping," earlier in this chapter, for details.

BEYOND OHEO GULCH

A mile past Oheo Gulch on the ocean side of the road is **Lindbergh's Grave.** First to fly across the Atlantic Ocean, Charles A. Lindbergh (1902–74) found peace in the Pacific; he settled in Hana, where he died of cancer in 1974. The famous aviator is buried under river stones in a seaside graveyard behind the 1857 **Palapala Hoomau Congregational Church.**

Those of you who are continuing on around Maui to the fishing village of **Kaupo** and beyond should be warned that Kaupo Road, or Old Piilani Highway (Hwy. 31), is rough and unpaved, often full of potholes and ruts. There are no goods or services until you reach **Ulupalakua Ranch,** where there's a winery, a general store, and a gas

Fagan's Cross **6**
Hamoa Beach **10**
Hana Beach Park **3**
Hana Museum
 Cultural Center **2**
Hasegawa General
 Store **8**
Hotel Hana-Maui **5**
Hotel Hana-Maui
 Restaurant **7**
Oheo Gulch
 (Seven Sacred Pools) **9**
Red Sand Beach **4**
Waianapanapa State
 Park **1**

Beach
Church
Gas Station
Post Office

station, which is likely to be closed. Before you attempt this journey, ask around about road conditions, or call the **Maui Public Works Department** (© **808/248-8254**) or the **Police Department** (© **808/248-8311**). This road frequently washes out in the rain. Most rental-car companies forbid you from taking their cars on this road (they don't want to trek all the way out here to get you if your car breaks down), so you'd really be better off retracing your route back through Hana. But if conditions are good, it can be a pretty drive in the spring (it tends to be dry and boring in summer).

10 Shops & Galleries

The island of Maui is a shopaholic's dream as well as an arts center, with a large number of resident artists who show their works in dozens of galleries and countless gift shops. Maui is also the queen of specialty products, an agricultural cornucopia that includes Kula onions, upcountry proteas, Kaanapali coffee, world-renowned potato chips, and many other tasty treats that are shipped worldwide.

As with any popular visitor destination, you'll have to wade through bad art and mountains of trinkets, particularly in Lahaina and Kihei, where touristy boutiques line the streets between rare pockets of treasures. If you shop in South or West Maui, expect to pay resort prices, clear down to a bottle of Evian or sunscreen.

There are two upscale resort shopping malls: The Shops at Wailea in South Maui, and Whalers Village in Kaanapali. The 16-acre Shops at Wailea features more than 50 shops and numerous restaurants, everything from an ABC store to Louis Vuitton and Gap. Similarly, the Whalers Village in Kaanapali has shopping and restaurant activity concentrated in a single oceanfront complex.

Central Maui is home to some first-rate boutiques: Watch Wailuku, a quaint 1930-ish type of town, with its own antiques alleys, artsy Sig Zane Designs, a handful of cafes and ethnic restaurants, and a yummy bakery. The Kaahumanu Center, in neighboring Kahului, is *the* retail outlet for the island.

Upcountry, Makawao's boutiques are worth seeking out, despite some attitude and high prices. The charm of shopping on Maui has always rested in the small, independent shops and galleries that crop up in surprising places.

CENTRAL MAUI
KAHULUI

Kahului's best shopping is concentrated in two places. Almost all of the shops listed below are at one of the following centers:

The once-rough-around-the-edges **Maui Mall,** 70 E. Kaahumanu Ave. (© **808/ 877-7559**), is the place of everyday shopping, from **Long's Drugs** to **Star Market,** to **Tasaka Guri Guri** (the decades-old purveyor of inimitable icy treats that are neither ice cream nor shave ice, but something in between) and the location for Kahului's largest movie theater, a 12-screen megaplex that features current releases as well as art-house films.

Queen Kaahumanu Center, 275 Kaahumanu Ave. (© **808/877-3369**), a 10-minute drive from the Kahului Airport on Highway 32, offers more than 100 shops, restaurants, and theaters. Its second-floor Plantation District offers home furnishings and accessories, and gift and accessories shops. Kaahumanu covers all the bases, from the arts and crafts to a **Foodland Supermarket** and everything in between: a thriving food court; the island's best beauty supply, **Lisa's Beauty Supply & Salon** (© **808/ 877-6463**), and its sister store for cosmetics, **Madison Avenue Day Spa and Boutique** (© **808/873-0880**); mall standards like **Sunglass Hut, Radio Shack,** and **Local Motion** (surf- and beachwear); standard department stores like **Macy's** and **Sears;** and great specialty shops like **Sharper Image.**

Cost Less Imports Natural fibers are ubiquitous in this newly expanded corner of the Maui Mall, three times larger than before. Household accessories include lauhala, bamboo blinds, grassy floor and window coverings, shoji-style lamps, burlap yardage, baskets, Balinese cushions, Asian imports, and top-of-the-line, made-on-Maui soaps and handicrafts. Japanese folk curtains, called *noreng,* are among the diverse items you'll find here; it's a good source of tropical and Asian home decor. In the Maui Mall. © **808/877-0300.**

Maui Swap Meet The Maui Swap Meet is a large and popular event. After Thanksgiving and throughout December, the number of booths nearly explodes into the hundreds and the activity reaches fever pitch. The colorful Maui specialties include vegetables from Kula and Keanae, fresh taro, plants, proteas, crafts, household items, homemade ethnic foods, and baked goods, including some fabulous fruit breads. Every Saturday from 7am to noon, vendors spread out their wares in booths and under tarps, in a festival-like atmosphere that is pure Maui with a touch of kitsch. Between the cheap Balinese imports and New Age crystals and incense, you may find some vintage John Kelly prints and 1930s collectibles. Admission is 50¢, and if you go early while the vendors are setting up, no one will turn you away. The Swap Meet currently is located on S. Puunene Ave. (next to the Kahului Post Office), but in the spring of 2008, it will move to the back lot behind Maui Community College, Kahului Beach, and Weihnepo rds. Call for more info. © 808/877-3100.

Summerhouse Sleek and chic, tiny Summerhouse is big on style: casual and party dresses, separates by Russ Berens, FLAX, Kiko, and Tencel jeans by Signatur—the best. During the holiday season, the selection gets dressy and sassy, but it's a fun browse year-round. I adore the hats, accessories, easy-care clothing, and up-to-the-minute evening dresses that Summerhouse carries in abundance. The high-quality T-shirts are always a cut above. The casual selection is well suited to the Island lifestyle. In the Dairy Center, 395 Dairy Rd. © 808/871-1320.

WAILUKU

Wailuku's attractive vintage architecture, numerous antiques shops, and mom-and-pop eateries imbue the town with a charm noticeably absent in the resort areas of West, South, and upcountry Maui. There is no plastic aloha in Wailuku. Of course, there's junk, but a stroll along Main and Market streets usually turns up a treasure or two. It's a mixed bag, but a treasure hunt, too.

Bailey House Gift Shop For made-in-Hawaii items, Bailey House is a must-stop. It offers a thoroughly enjoyable browse through authoritative Hawaiiana, in a museum that's one of the finest examples of missionary architecture, dating from 1833. Gracious gardens, rare paintings of early Maui, wonderful programs in Hawaiian arts and culture, and a restored hand-hewn koa canoe await visitors. The shop, a small space of discriminating taste, packs a wallop with its selection of remarkable gift items, from Hawaiian music to exquisite woods, traditional Hawaiian games to pareu and books. Prints by the legendary Hawaii artist Madge Tennent, lauhala hats hanging in midair, hand-sewn pheasant hatbands, jams and jellies, Maui cookbooks, and an occasional Hawaiian quilt are some of the treasures to be found here. Bailey House Museum Shop, 2375-A Main St. © 808/244-3326.

Bird of Paradise Unique Antiques Owner Joe Myhand loves furniture, old Matson liner menus, blue willow china, kimonos for children, and anything nostalgic that happens to be Hawaiian. The furniture in the strongly Hawaiian collection ranges from 1940s rattan to wicker and old koa—those items tailor-made for informal island living and leisurely moments on the lanai. Myhand also collects bottles and mails his license plates all over the world. The collection ebbs and flows with his finds, keeping buyers waiting in the wings for his Depression glass, California pottery from the 1930s and 1940s, old dinnerware, perfume bottles, vintage aloha shirts, and vintage Hawaiian music on cassettes. 56 N. Market St. © 808/242-7699.

Brown-Kobayashi Graceful living is the theme here. Prices range from a few dollars to the thousands in this 750-square-foot treasure trove. The owners have added a fabulous selection of antique stone garden pieces that mingle quietly with Asian antiques and old and new French, European, and Hawaiian objects. Although the collection is eclectic, there is a strong cohesive aesthetic that sets Brown-Kobayashi apart from other Maui antiques stores. Japanese kimonos and obi, Bakelite and Peking glass beads, breathtaking Japanese lacquerware, cricket carriers, and cloisonné are among the delights here. Exotic and precious Chinese woods (purple sandalwood and huanghuali) glow discreetly from quiet corners, and an occasional monarchy-style lidded milo bowl comes in and flies out. 38 N. Market St. © 808/242-0804.

Maui's Own: OCEAN Vodka

If you are looking for a souvenir of your fabulous Maui trip to take home or a unique gift for friends, Maui has its own vodka, called OCEAN Vodka. Produced by Hawaii Sea Spirits, this ultrapremium brand is not only USDA certified to contain organic ingredients, but the water comes from 3,000 feet beneath the ocean off the Kona coast of the Big Island. The deep-sea water is harvested by KOYO USA, producers of MaHaLo Hawaii Deep Sea Water. The desalinated water has become widely popular in Japan, where people swear it has provided beneficial health effects (so far, no scientific studies have backed this claim up). The MaHaLo water is shipped to Maui, where it is blended with organic corn and rye to produce this one-of-a-kind vodka. Available at restaurants, bars, hotels, and retail shops (for a complete list, see www.oceanvodka.com).

Gottling Ltd.   Karl Gottling's shop specializes in Asian antique furniture, but you can also find smaller carvings, precious stones, jewelry, netsuke, opium weights, and finds in all sizes. I saw a cabinet with 350-year-old doors, and a 17th-century Buddha sitting serenely next to a 150-year-old Chinese cabinet. Ming dynasty ceramics, carved wooden apples ($15), and a Persian rug ($65,000) give you an idea of the range of possibilities here. 34 N. Market St. ℭ **808/244-7779.**

Sig Zane Designs Wailuku   Sig Zane is synonymous with the best in aloha wear. Whether it's a T-shirt, pareu, duffel bag, aloha shirt, or muumuu, a Sig Zane design has depth and sizzle. So when Hilo-based Sig Zane Designs opened in Wailuku, Maui retailers perked up. Zane and co-owner Punawai Rice have redefined Hawaiian wear by creating an inimitable style in clothing, textiles, furnishings, and bedding. The Maui store has already proven enormously successful. The staff is helpful and willing to share the background of each design so you will learn much about the culture, botany, mythology, and beauty of the Islands. 53 Market St. ℭ **808/249-8997.**

CENTRAL MAUI EDIBLES
Down to Earth Natural Foods, 305 Dairy Rd. (ℭ **808/877-2661**), has fresh organic produce, a bountiful salad bar, sandwiches and smoothies, vitamins and supplements, fresh baked goods, chips and snacks, whole grains, and more.

Maui's produce has long been a source of pride for islanders, and, on Tuesday, Wednesday, and Friday, **Ohana Farmers Market,** at Queen Kaahumanu Shopping Center (ℭ **808/878-3189**), is where you'll find a fresh, inexpensive selection of Maui-grown fruit, vegetables, flowers, and plants. Crafts and gourmet foods add to the event, and the large monkeypod trees provide welcome shade.

Located in the northern section of Wailuku, **Takamiya Market,** 359 N. Market St. (ℭ **808/244-3404**), is much loved by local folks and visitors with adventurous palates, who often drive all the way from Kihei to stock up on picnic fare and mouth-watering ethnic foods for sunset gatherings. Unpretentious home-cooked foods from East and West are prepared daily and served on plastic-foam plates. From the chilled-fish counter come fresh sashimi and poke, and in the renowned assortment of prepared foods are mounds of shoyu chicken, tender fried squid, roast pork, *kalua* pork, laulau, Chinese noodles, fiddlehead ferns, and Western comfort foods, such as corn bread and potato salad.

WEST MAUI
LAHAINA

Lahaina's merchants and art galleries go all out from 7 to 9pm on Friday, when **Art Night** ⚡ brings an extra measure of hospitality and community spirit. The Art Night openings are usually marked with live entertainment and refreshments, and a livelier-than-usual street scene.

If you're in Lahaina on the second or last Thursday of the month, stroll by the front lawn of the **Baldwin Home,** 120 Dickenson St. (at Front St.), for a splendid look at the craft of lei making (you can even buy the results).

What was formerly a big, belching pineapple cannery is now a maze of shops and restaurants at the northern end of Lahaina town, known as the **Lahaina Cannery Mall,** 1221 Honoapiilani Hwy. (② **808/661-5304**). Find your way through the T-shirt and sportswear shops to **Lahaina Printsellers,** home of antique originals, prints, paintings, and wonderful 18th- to 20th-century cartography, representing the largest collection of engravings and antique maps in Hawaii. Follow your nose to **Sir Wilfred's Coffee House,** where you can unwind with espresso and croissants, or head for **Compadres Bar & Grill,** where the margaritas flow freely and the Mexican food is tasty (p. 402). **Roland's** may surprise you with its selection of footwear, everything from Cole Haan sophisticates to inexpensive sandals. At the recently expanded food court, the new **Compadres Taqueria** sells Mexican food to go, while **L & L Drive-Inn** sells plate lunches near Greek, pizza, Vietnamese, and Japanese food booths. There's also a **Long's Drugs** and a **Safeway.**

The **Lahaina Center,** 900 Front St. (② **808/667-9216**), is fairly new and still a work in progress. It's located north of Lahaina's most congested strip, where Front Street begins. Across the street from the center, the seawall is a much-sought-after front-row seat to the sunset. There's plenty of free validated parking and easy access to more than 30 shops, a salon, restaurants, a nightclub, and a four-plex movie-theater complex. **Ruth's Chris Steak House** has opened its doors in Lahaina Center, and **Maui Brews** serves lunch and dinner and offers live music nightly except weekends. Among the shopping stops: **Banana Republic,** the **Hilo Hattie** (a dizzying emporium of aloha wear), **ABC Discount Store,** and a dozen other recreational, dining, and entertainment options.

The conversion of 10,000 square feet of parking space into the re-creation of a traditional Hawaiian village is a welcome touch of Hawaiiana at Lahaina Center. With the commercialization of modern Lahaina, it's easy to forget that it was once the capital of the Hawaiian kingdom and a significant historic site. The village, called **Hale Kahiko,** features three main *hale,* or houses: a sleeping house, the men's dining house, and the crafts house, where women pounded lauhala for mats and baskets. Construction of the houses consumed 10,000 feet of ohia wood from the island, 20 tons of pili grass, and more than 4 miles of hand-woven coconut sennit for the lashings. Artifacts, weapons, a canoe, and indigenous trees are among the authentic touches in this village; you can take a free guided tour daily between 9am and 6pm.

David Lee Galleries   This gallery is devoted to the works of David Lee, who uses natural powder colors to paint on silk. The pigments and technique create a luminous, ethereal quality. 712 Front St. ② **808/667-7740.**

Lahaina Arts Society Galleries　With its membership of more than 185 Maui artists, the nonprofit Lahaina Arts Society is an excellent community resource. Changing monthly exhibits in the Banyan Tree and Old Jail galleries offer a good look at the island's artistic well: two-dimensional art, fiber art, ceramics, sculpture, prints, jewelry, and more. In the shade of the humongous banyan tree in the square across from Pioneer Inn, "Art in the Park" fairs are offered every second and fourth weekend of the month. 648 Wharf St. (ⓒ 808/661-3228.

Lei Spa Maui　The Lei Spa Maui has expanded to include two massage rooms and shower facilities, making it a day spa offering facials and other therapies. It's a good sign that 95% of the beauty and bath products sold are made on Maui, and that includes Hawaiian Botanical Pikake shower gel, kukui and macadamia-nut oils, Hawaiian potpourris, mud masks with Hawaiian seaweed, and a spate of rejuvenating potions for hair and skin. Aromatherapy body oils and perfumes are popular, as are the handmade soaps and fragrances of torch ginger, plumeria, coconut, tuberose, and sandalwood. Scented candles in coconut shells, inexpensive and fragrant, make great gifts. 505 Front St. (ⓒ 808/661-1178.

Maggie Coulombe *Finds*　A haute couture store with the unique designs of Maggie Coulombe in the midst of Lahaina. You'll find Maggie's latest couture, jersey, linen, pareu, and shoes, plus accessories, jewelry, purses, and a few surprises. 505 Front St. (ⓒ 808/662-0696. www.maggiecoulombe.com.

The Old Lahaina Book Emporium　What a bookstore! Chockablock with used books in stacks, shelves, counters, and aisles, this bookstore is a browser's dream. More than 25,000 quality used books are lovingly housed in this shop, where owner JoAnn Carroll treats books and customers well. Prices are low, and the selection is diverse, everything from *Li'l Abner* to *Genius and Lust,* old *Mad* magazines, *Aphrodisiac Cookery, Bhagavad Gita, A History of Bicycles,* and *The Cockroach Combat Manual.* The store is 95% used books and 100% delight. Specialties include Hawaiiana, fiction, mystery, sci-fi, and military history, with substantial selections in cookbooks, children's books, and philosophy/religion. You could pay as little as $2 for a quality read, or a whole lot more for that rare first edition. Books on tape, videos, the classics, and old guitar magazines are among the treasures of this two-story emporium. 834 Front St. (ⓒ 808/661-1399.

Totally Hawaiian Gift Gallery　This gallery makes a good browse for its selection of Niihau shell jewelry, excellent Hawaiian CDs, Norfolk pine bowls, and Hawaiian quilt kits. Hawaiian quilt patterns sewn in Asia (at least they're honest about it) are labor-intensive, less expensive, and attractive, although not totally Hawaiian. Hawaiian-quilt-patterned gift wraps and tiles, perfumes and soaps, handcrafted dolls, and koa accessories are of good quality, and the artists, such as Kelly Dunn (Norfolk wood bowls), Jerry Kermode (wood), and Pat Coito (wood), are among the tops in their fields. Also in the Maui Marriott in Kaanapali (ⓒ **808/667-2171**). In the Lahaina Cannery Mall, 1221 Honoapiilani Hwy. (ⓒ 808/667-2558.

Village Galleries in Lahaina　The nearly 30-year-old Village Galleries is the oldest continuously running gallery on Maui, and it's esteemed as one of the few galleries with consistently high standards. Art collectors know this as a respectable showcase for regional artists; the selection of mostly original two- and three-dimensional art offers a good look at the quality of work originating on the island. The newer contemporary gallery offers colorful gift items and jewelry. An additional location is in the

Ritz-Carlton Kapalua, 1 Ritz-Carlton Dr. (© **808/669-1800**). 120 and 180 Dickenson St. © **808/661-4402** or 808/661-5559.

KAANAPALI

On a recent trip, I was somewhat disappointed with upscale **Whalers Village,** 2435 Kaanapali Pkwy. (© **808/661-4567**). Although it offers everything from whale blubber to Prada and Ferragamo, it is short on local shops, and parking at the nearby lot is expensive. The complex is home to the **Whalers Village Museum,** with its interactive exhibits, 40-foot sperm whale skeleton, and sand castles on perpetual display, but shoppers come for the designer thrills and beachfront dining.

My favorite shoe store, **Sandal Tree,** has its third store in Whalers Village. (The other two are at Hyatt Regency Maui and Grand Wailea Resort in Wailea.) **Martin & MacArthur,** a mainstay of the village, offers a dizzying array of Hawaii crafts: Hawaiian-quilt cushion covers, jewelry, soaps, books, and a stunning selection of woodworks. The always wonderful **Lahaina Printsellers** has a selection of antique prints, maps, paintings, and engravings, including 18th- to 20th-century cartography, all of which offer great browsing and gift potential. You can find award-winning **Kimo Bean** coffee at a kiosk, an expanded **Reyn's** for aloha wear, and **Cinnamon Girl,** a hit in Honolulu for its matching mother-daughter clothing. The return of **Waldenbooks** makes it that much easier to pick up the latest bestseller on the way to the beach. Once you've stood under the authentic whale skeleton at the Whalers Village Museum, you can blow a bundle at **Tiffany, Prada, Chanel, Coach, Dolphin Galleries,** or any of the more than 60 shops and restaurants that have sprouted in this open-air shopping center. The posh Euro trend continues; despite obvious efforts to offer more of a balance between Island-made and designer goods, it's still open season for the chain luxury stores.

Other mainstays: The **Eyecatcher** has an extensive selection of sunglasses; it's located just across from the busiest **ABC** store in the state. The former **Maui Yogurt Company** has been taken over by **Pizza Paradiso,** which sells ice cream and smoothies in a food court of other dine-and-dash goodies. Whalers Village is open daily from 9:30am to 10pm.

Ki'i Gallery   Some of the works are large and lavish, such as the Toland Sand prisms for just under $5,000 and the John Stokes hand-blown glass. Those who love glass in all forms, from hand-blown vessels to jewelry, will love a browse through Ki'i. I found Pat Kazi's work in porcelain and found objects, such as the mermaid in a teacup, inspired by fairy tales and mythology, both fantastic and compelling. The gallery is devoted to glass and original paintings and drawings; roughly half of the artists are from Hawaii. Also at the Grand Wailea Resort (© **808/874-3059**) and the Shops at Wailea (© **808/874-1181**). In the Hyatt Regency Maui, 200 Nohea Kai Dr. © **808/661-4456.**

Paul Ropp *Finds*   The Bali fashion designer's only store outside of Indonesia is found on the ground level at Whalers Village. Ropp sees fashion as a medium, and he calls his creations "sexual clothes." Stop by and check out his sense of fashion (lively and colorful) and eccentric style of dressing, which is perfect for Maui's tropical climate. Whalers Village. © **808/661-8000.**

Sandal Tree   It's unusual for a resort shop to draw local customers on a regular basis, but the Sandal Tree attracts a flock of footwear fanatics who come here from throughout the islands for rubber thongs and Top-Siders, sandals and dressy pumps, athletic shoes and hats, designer footwear, and much more. Sandal Tree also carries a generous selection of Mephisto and Arche comfort sandals, Donald Pliner, Anne Klein, Charles Jourdan, and beachwear and casual footwear for all tastes. Accessories range from fashionable knapsacks to avant-garde geometrical handbags—for town and country, day and evening, kids, women, and men. Prices are realistic, too. Also in Grand Wailea Resort, 3850 Wailea Alanui Dr., Wailea; and in the Hyatt Regency Maui, 200 Nohea Kai Dr. In Whalers Village, 2435 Kaanapali Pkwy. ✆ 808/667-5330.

HONOKOWAI, KAHANA & NAPILI

Those driving north of Kaanapali toward Kapalua will notice the **Honokowai Marketplace** on Lower Honoapiilani Road, only minutes before the Kapalua Airport. There are restaurants and coffee shops, a dry cleaner, the flagship **Star Market,** a few clothing stores, and the sprawling **Hawaiian Interiors.**

Nearby **Kahana Gateway** is an unimpressive mall built to serve the condominium community that has sprawled along the coastline between Honokowai and Kapalua. If you need women's swimsuits, however, **Rainbow Beach Swimwear** is a find. It carries a selection of suits for all shapes, at lower-than-resort prices, slashed even further during the frequent sales. **Hutton's Fine Jewelry** offers high-end jewelry from designers around the country (lots of platinum and diamonds), reflecting discerning taste for those who can afford it. Tahitian black pearls and jade (some hundreds of years old, all certified) are among Hutton's specialties.

KAPALUA

Honolua Store Walk on the old wood floors peppered with holes from golf shoes and find your everyday essentials: bottled water, stationery, mailing tape, jackets, chips, wine, soft drinks, paper products, fresh fruit and produce, and aisles of notions and necessities. With picnic tables on the veranda and a takeout counter offering deli items—more than a dozen types of sandwiches, salads, and budget-friendly breakfasts—there are always long lines of customers. Golfers and surfers love to come here for the morning paper and coffee. 502 Office Rd. (next to the Ritz-Carlton Kapalua). ✆ 808/669-6128.

Village Galleries Maui's finest exhibit their works here and in the other two Village Galleries in Lahaina. Take heart, art lovers: There's no clichéd marine art here. Translucent, delicately turned bowls of Norfolk pine gleam in the light, and George Allan, Betty Hay Freeland, Fred KenKnight, and Pamela Andelin are included in the pantheon of respected artists represented in the tiny gallery. Watercolors, oils, sculptures, hand-blown glass, Niihau shell leis, jewelry, and other media are represented.

A Creative Way to Spend the Day

Make a bowl from clay or paint a premade one, then fire it, and take it home. The **Art School at Kapalua** (✆ 808/665-0007; www.kapaluamaui.com), in a charming 1920s plantation building that was part of an old cannery operation, features local and visiting instructors and is open daily for people of all ages and skill levels. Projects, classes, and workshops at this not-for-profit organization highlight creativity in all forms, including photography, figure drawing, ceramics, landscape painting, painting on silk, and the performing arts (ballet, yoga, creative movement, Pilates). Classes are inexpensive. Call the school to see what's scheduled while you're on Maui.

The Ritz-Carlton's monthly Artist-in-Residence program features gallery artists in demonstrations and special hands-on workshops—free, including materials. In the Ritz-Carlton Kapalua, 1 Ritz-Carlton Dr. ℂ **808/669-1800.**

SOUTH MAUI
KIHEI
Kihei is one long strip of strip malls. Most of the shopping here is concentrated in the **Azeka Place Shopping Center** on South Kihei Road. Across the street, **Azeka Place II** houses several prominent attractions, including **The Coffee Store** and a cluster of specialty shops with everything from children's clothes to shoes, sunglasses, and swimwear.

Hawaiian Moons Natural Foods   Hawaiian Moons is an exceptional health-food store, as well as a mini-supermarket with one of the best selections of Maui products on the island. The tortillas are made on Maui (and good!), and much of the produce here, such as organic vine-ripened tomatoes and organic onions, is grown in the fertile upcountry soil of Kula. There's also locally grown organic coffee, gourmet salsas, Maui shiitake mushrooms, organic lemon grass and okra, Maui Crunch bread, free-range Big Island turkeys and chickens (no antibiotics or artificial nasties), and fresh Maui juices. Cosmetics are top-of-the-line: a staggering selection of sunblock, fragrant floral oils, kukui-nut oil from Waialua on Oahu, and Island Essence made-on-Maui mango-coconut and vanilla-papaya lotions, the ultimate in body pampering. The salad bar is one of the most popular food stops on the coast. 2411 S. Kihei Rd. ℂ **808/875-4356.**

WAILEA
Grand Wailea Shops   The sprawling Grand Wailea Resort is known for its long arcade of shops and galleries tailored to hefty pocketbooks. However, gift items in all price ranges can be found at Lahaina Printsellers (for old maps and prints), Dolphin Galleries, H. F. Wichman, Sandal Tree, and Napua Gallery, which houses the private collection of the resort owner. Ki'i Gallery is luminous with studio glass and exquisitely turned woods, and Sandal Tree (p. 469) raises the footwear bar. At Grand Wailea Resort, 3850 Wailea Alanui Dr. ℂ **808/875-1234.**

The Shops at Wailea   This is the big shopping boost that resort-goers have been awaiting for years. Chains still rule (Gap, Louis Vuitton, Banana Republic, Tiffany, Crazy Shirts, Honolua Surf Co.), but there is still fertile ground for the inveterate shopper in the nearly 60 shops in the complex. **Martin & MacArthur** (furniture and gift gallery; see "Kaanapali," above) has landed in Wailea as part of a retail mix that is similar to Whalers Village. The high-end resort shops sell expensive souvenirs, gifts, clothing, and accessories for a life of perpetual vacations.

One store of particular note in this complex is **CY Maui** (ℂ **808/891-0782**). Women who like washable, flowing clothing in silks, rayons, and natural fibers will love this shop, formerly the popular Manikin in Kahului. If you don't find what you want on the racks of simple bias-cut designs, you can have it made from the bolts of stupendous fabrics lining the shop. Except for a few hand-painted silks, everything in the shop is washable. 3750 Wailea Alanui. ℂ **808/891-6770.**

UPCOUNTRY MAUI
MAKAWAO
Besides being a shopper's paradise, Makawao is the home of the island's most prominent arts organization, the **Hui No'eau Visual Arts Center,** 2841 Baldwin Ave. (ℂ **808/ 572-6560**). Designed in 1917 by C. W. Dickey, one of Hawaii's most prominent

architects, the two-story, Mediterranean-style stucco home that houses the center is located on a sprawling 9-acre estate called Kaluanui. Its tree-lined driveway features two of Maui's largest hybrid Cook and Norfolk Island pines. A legacy of Maui's prominent kamaaina (old-timers), Harry and Ethel Baldwin, the estate became an art center in 1976. Visiting artists offer lectures, classes, and demonstrations, all at reasonable prices, in basketry, jewelry making, ceramics, painting, and other media. Classes on Hawaiian art, culture, and history are also available. Call ahead for schedules and details. The exhibits here are drawn from a wide range of disciplines and multicultural sources, and include both contemporary and traditional art from established and emerging artists. The gift shop, featuring many one-of-a-kind works by local artists and artisans, is worth a stop. Hours are Monday through Saturday from 10am to 4pm.

Collections   This longtime Makawao attraction is showing renewed vigor after more than 2 decades on Baldwin Avenue. It's one of my favorite Makawao stops, full of gift items and spirited clothing reflecting the ease and color of island living. Its selection of sportswear, soaps, jewelry, candles, and tasteful, marvelous miscellany reflects good sense and style. Dresses (including up-to-the-moment Citron in cross-cultural and vintage-looking prints), separates, home and bath accessories, sweaters, and a shop full of good things make this a Makawao must. 3677 Baldwin Ave. ℂ 808/572-0781.

Gallery Maui   Follow the sign down the charming shaded pathway to a cozy gallery of top-notch art and crafts. Most of the works here are by Maui artists, and the quality is outstanding. About 30 artists are represented: Wayne Omura and his Norfolk pine bowls, Pamela Hayes's watercolors, Martha Vockrodt and her wonderful paintings, a stunning Steve Hynson dresser of curly koa and ebony. The two- and three-dimensional original works reflect the high standards of gallery owners Deborah and Robert Zaleski (a painter), who have just added to their roster the talented ceramic artist David Stabley, a two-time American Craft Council juror. 3643-A Baldwin Ave. ℂ 808/572-8092.

Gecko Trading Co. Boutique   The selection here is eclectic and always changing: One day it's St. John's wort body lotion and mesh T-shirts in a dragon motif, the next it's Provence soaps and antique lapis jewelry. You never know what you'll find in this tiny boutique; I've seen everything from handmade crocheted bags from New York to Mexican hammered-tin candle holders. The prices are reasonable, the service is friendly, and it's more homey than glammy, and not as self-conscious as some of the other local boutiques. 3621 Baldwin Ave. ℂ 808/572-0249.

Holiday & Co.   Attractive women's clothing in natural fibers hangs from racks, while jewelry to go with it beckons from the counter. Recent finds include elegant fiber evening bags, luxurious bath gels, easygoing dresses and separates, Dansko clogs, shawls, shoes, soaps, aloha shirts, books, picture frames, and jewelry. 3681 Baldwin Ave. ℂ 808/572-1470.

Hot Island Glassblowing Studio & Gallery   You can watch the artist transform molten glass into works of art and utility in this studio in Makawao's Courtyard, where an award-winning family of glassblowers built its own furnaces. It's fascinating to watch the shapes emerge from glass melted at 2,300°F (1,260°C). The colorful works displayed range from small paperweights to large vessels. Four to five artists participate in the demonstrations, which begin when the furnace is heated, about a half-hour before the studio opens at 9am. 3620 Baldwin Ave. ℂ 808/572-4527.

Hurricane This boutique carries clothing, gifts, accessories, and books that are two steps ahead of the competition. Tommy Bahama aloha shirts and aloha print dresses; Sigrid Olsen's knitted shells, cardigans, and extraordinary silk tank dresses; hats; art by local artists; a notable selection of fragrances for men and women; and hard-to-find, eccentric books and home accessories are part of the Hurricane appeal. 3639 Baldwin Ave. © 808/572-5076.

Maui Hands Maui hands have made 90% of the items in this shop/gallery. Because it's a consignment shop, you'll find Hawaii-made handicrafts and prices that aren't inflated. The selection includes paintings, prints, jewelry, glass marbles, native-wood bowls, and tchotchkes for every budget. This is an ideal stop for made-on-Maui products and crafts of good quality. Makawao at the Courtyard, 3620 Baldwin Ave. © 808/572-5194. Another can be found in Paia, 84 Hana Hwy. © 808/579-9245.

The Mercantile The jewelry, home accessories (especially the Tiffany-style glass-and-shell lamps), dinnerware, Italian linens, plantation-style furniture, and clothing here are a salute to the good life. There's exquisite bedding, rugs, furniture including hand-carved armoires, down-filled furniture and slipcovers, and a large selection of Kiehl's products. The clothing—comfortable cottons and upscale European linens— is for men and women, as are the soaps, which include Maui Herbal Soap products and some unusual finds from France. Maui-made jams, honey, soaps, and ceramics, and Jurlique organic facial and body products are among the new winners. 3673 Baldwin Ave. © 808/572-1407.

Tropo Tropo is a magnet for stylish, sensitive, *and* rugged men searching for tasteful aloha wear and comfortable basics. Books, clothing, Tilley hats, and Crabtree & Evelyn products are among the finds here. Men can shop for Tommy Bahama trousers and shorts, tasteful T-shirts, stylish winter wovens by Toes on the Nose, and aloha shirts by Reyn Spooner, Tori Richards, Que, and Kahala. 3643 Baldwin Ave. © 808/573-0356.

Viewpoints Gallery Maui's only fine-arts cooperative showcases the work of 20 established artists in an airy, attractive gallery located in a restored theater with a courtyard, glassblowing studio, and restaurants. The gallery features two-dimensional art, jewelry, fiber art, stained glass, paper, sculpture, and other media. This is a fine example of what can happen in a collectively supportive artistic environment. 3620 Baldwin Ave. © 808/572-5979.

FRESH FLOWERS IN KULA

Like anthuriums on the Big Island, proteas are a Maui trademark and an abundant crop on Haleakala's rich volcanic slopes. They also travel well, dry beautifully, and can be shipped worldwide with ease. Among Maui's most prominent sources is **Sunrise Protea** (© 808/876-0200; www.sunriseprotea.com), in Kula. It offers a walk-through garden and gift shops, friendly service, and a larger-than-usual selection. Freshly cut flowers arrive from the fields on Tuesday and Friday afternoons. You can order individual blooms, baskets, arrangements, or wreaths for shipping all over the world. (Next door, the Sunrise Country Market offers fresh local fruits, snacks, and sandwiches, with picnic tables for lingering.)

Proteas of Hawaii (© 808/878-2533; www.proteasofhawaii.com), another reliable source, offers regular walking tours of the University of Hawaii Extension Service gardens across the street in Kula.

Outside of Kula, the Saturday-morning **Maui Swap Meet** (p. 464) is among the best and least expensive places for tropical flowers of every stripe.

UPCOUNTRY EDIBLES

Working folks in Makawao pick up spaghetti and lasagna, sandwiches, salads, and changing specials from the **Rodeo General Store,** 3661 Baldwin Ave. (© **808/572-7841**). At the far end of the store is the oenophile's bonanza, a superior wine selection housed in its own temperature-controlled cave.

Down to Earth Natural Foods, 1169 Makawao Ave. (© **808/572-1488**), always has fresh salads and sandwiches, a full section of organic produce (Kula onions, strawberry papayas, mangoes, and lychees in season), bulk grains, beauty aids, herbs, juices, snacks, tofu, seaweed, soy products, and aisles of vegetarian and health foods. Whether it's a smoothie or a salad, Down to Earth has fresh, healthful vegetarian offerings.

In the more than 6 decades that the **T. Komoda Store and Bakery,** 3674 Baldwin Ave. (© **808/572-7261**), has spent in this spot, untold numbers have creaked over the wooden floors to pick up Komoda's famous cream puffs. Old-timers know to come early or they'll be sold out. Then the cinnamon rolls, doughnuts, pies, and chocolate cake take over. Pastries are just the beginning; poi, macadamia-nut candies and cookies, and small bunches of local fruit keep the customers coming.

EAST MAUI

PAIA

Hemp House   Clothing and accessories made of hemp, a sturdy and sensible fiber, are finally making their way into the mainstream. The Hemp House has as complete a selection as you can expect to see in Hawaii, with "denim" hemp jeans, lightweight linenlike trousers, dresses, shirts, and a full range of sensible, easy-care wear. 16 Baldwin Ave. © 808/579-8880.

Maui Crafts Guild   The old wooden storefront at the gateway to Paia houses crafts of high quality and in all price ranges, from pit-fired raku to bowls of Norfolk pine and other Maui woods, fashioned by Maui hands. Artist-owned and -operated, the guild claims 25 members who live and work on Maui. Basketry, hand-painted fabrics, jewelry, beadwork, traditional Hawaiian stonework, pressed flowers, fused glass, stained glass, copper sculpture, banana bark paintings, pottery of all styles, and hundreds of items are displayed in the two-story gift gallery. Upstairs, sculptor Arthur Dennis Williams displays his breathtaking work in wood, bronze, and stone. Everything can be shipped. **Aloha Bead Co.** (© **808/579-9709**), in the back of the gallery, is a treasure trove for bead workers. 43 Hana Hwy. © 808/579-9697.

Moonbow Tropics   If you're looking for a tasteful aloha shirt, go to Moonbow. The selection consists of a few carefully culled racks of the top labels in aloha wear, in fabrics ranging from the finest silks and linens to Egyptian cotton and spun rayons. Silk pants, silk shorts, vintage-print neckwear, and an upgraded women's selection hang on colorful racks. The jewelry pieces, ranging from tanzanite to topaz, rubies to moonstones, are mounted in unique settings made on-site. 36 Baldwin Ave. © 808/579-8592.

HANA

Hana Coast Gallery *(Finds*   This gallery is a good reason to go to Hana: It's an aesthetic and cultural experience that informs as it enlightens. Tucked away in the posh hideaway hotel, the gallery is known for its high level of curatorship and commitment to the cultural art of Hawaii. There are no jumping whales or dolphins here—and except for a section of European and Asian masters (Renoir, Japanese woodblock prints), the 3,000-square-foot gallery is devoted entirely to Hawaii artists. Dozens of well-established local artists display their sculptures, paintings, prints, feather work, stone work, and carvings in displays that are so natural they could well exist in someone's home. Director-curator Patrick Robinson (of impeccable artistic integrity) has expanded the selection of koa-wood furniture in response to the ongoing revival of the American Crafts Movement with a Hawaiian/Japanese influence. Stellar artists Tai Lake from the Big Island and Randall Watkins from Maui are among those represented.

Connoisseurs of hand-turned bowls will find the crème de la crème of the genre here: J. Kelly Dunn, Ron Kent, Todd Campbell, Ed Perrira, and Gary Stevens. You won't find a better selection elsewhere under one roof. The award-winning gallery has won accolades from the top travel and arts magazines in the country (*Travel + Leisure, Arts & Antiques* magazine) and has steered clear of trendiness and unfortunate tastes. In the Hotel Hana-Maui. ℂ 808/248-8636.

Hasegawa General Store   Established in 1910, immortalized in song since 1961, burned to the ground in 1990, and back in business in 1991, this legendary store is indefatigable and more colorful than ever in its fourth generation in business. The aisles are choked with merchandise: coffee specially roasted and blended for the store, Ono Farms organic dried fruit, fishing equipment, every tape and CD that mentions Hana, the best books on Hana to be found, T-shirts, beach and garden essentials, baseball caps, film, baby food, napkins, and other necessities for the Hana life. Hana Hwy. ℂ 808/248-8231.

11 Maui After Dark

The island's most prestigious entertainment venue is the $28-million **Maui Arts and Cultural Center,** in Kahului (ℂ 808/242-7469; www.mauiarts.org). Bonnie Raitt has performed here, as have B. B. King, Hiroshima, Pearl Jam, Ziggy Marley, Lou Rawls, the American Indian Dance Theatre, Jonny Lang, and Tony Bennett, not to mention Keali'i Reichel and the finest in local and Hawaii talent. The center is as precious to Maui as the Met is to New York, with a visual-arts gallery, an outdoor amphitheater, offices, rehearsal space, a 300-seat theater for experimental performances, and a 1,200-seat main theater. Whether it's hula, the Iona Pear Dance Company, Willie Nelson, or the Maui Symphony Orchestra, only the best appear here. The center's activities are well publicized locally, so check the *Maui News* or ask your hotel concierge what's going on during your visit.

HAWAIIAN MUSIC   The best of Hawaiian music can be heard every Wednesday night at the indoor amphitheater at the Ritz-Carlton Kapalua with the **"Masters of Hawaiian Slack Key Guitar Series."** The weekly shows present a side of Hawaii that few visitors ever get to see. Host George Kahumoku, Jr., introduces a new slack key master every week. Not only is there incredible Hawaiian music and singing, but George and his guest "talk story" about old Hawaii, music, and Hawaiian culture. Not to be missed. Contact ℂ 888/669-3858 or www.slackkey.com. Tickets are $47. Beginning with the June 20, 2007 show, the Masters of Hawaiian Slack Key Guitar Concert Series will be performed at the Napili Kai Resort, while the Ritz Carlton is closed for renovations. They will be back at the Ritz in 2008, when the resort re-opens.

Moments **A Night to Remember: Luau, Maui Style**

Most of the larger hotels in Maui's major resorts offer luau on a regular basis. You'll pay about $65 to $70 to attend one. To protect yourself from disappointment, don't expect it to be a homegrown affair prepared in the traditional Hawaiian way. There are, however, commercial luau that capture the romance and spirit of the luau with quality food and entertainment in outdoor settings.

Maui's best luau is indisputably the nightly **Old Lahaina Luau** ★★ (© **800/248-5828** or 808/667-1998; www.oldlahainaluau.com). Located just ocean-side of the Lahaina Cannery, the Old Lahaina Luau maintains its high standards in food and entertainment, in an oceanfront setting that is peerless. Local craftspeople display their wares only a few feet from the ocean. Seating is provided on lauhala mats for those who wish to dine as the traditional Hawaiians did, but there are tables for everyone else. There's no fire dancing in the program, but you won't miss it (for that, go to The Feast at Lele, p. 401). This luau offers a healthy balance of entertainment, showmanship, authentic high-quality food, educational value, and sheer romantic beauty. (No watered-down mai tais, either; these are the real thing.)

The luau begins at sunset and features Tahitian and Hawaiian entertainment, including ancient hula, hula from the missionary era, modern hula, and an intelligent narrative on the dance's rocky course of survival into modern times. The entertainment is riveting, even for jaded locals. The food, which is served from an open-air thatched structure, is as much Pacific Rim as authentically Hawaiian: imu-roasted *kalua* pig, baked mahimahi in Maui onion cream sauce, guava chicken, teriyaki sirloin steak, lomi salmon, poi, dried fish, poke, Hawaiian sweet potato, sautéed vegetables, seafood salad, and the ultimate taste treat, taro leaves with coconut milk. The cost is $89 for adults, $59 for children 12 and under.

Except for **Casanova** in Makawao, **Maui Brews** in Lahaina, and **Hapa's** in Kihei, nightlife options on this island are limited. The major hotels generally have lobby lounges offering Hawaiian music, soft jazz, or hula shows beginning at sunset. If **Hapa, Willie K. and Amy Gilliom** or the soloist **Keali'i Reichel** are playing anywhere on their native island, don't miss them; they're among the finest Hawaiian musicians around today.

WEST MAUI: LAHAINA

The buzz in Lahaina is **Ulalena** ★, Maui Myth and Magic Theatre, 878 Front St. (© **877/688-4800** or 808/661-9913; www.ulalena.com), a riveting evening of entertainment that weaves Hawaiian mythology with drama, dance, and state-of-the-art multimedia capabilities in a brand-new multimillion-dollar theater. Polynesian dance, original music, acrobatics, and chant, performed by a local and international cast, combine to create an evocative experience that often leaves the audience speechless. It's interactive, with dancers coming down the aisles, drummers and musicians in surprising corners, and mind-boggling stage and lighting effects that draw the audience in. Some special moments: the goddesses dancing on the moon, the white sail of the first Europeans, the wrath of the volcano goddess Pele, the labors of the field-worker immigrants. The story unfolds seamlessly; at the end, you'll be shocked to realize that not a single word of dialogue was spoken. Performances are Tuesday through Saturday at 6:30pm. Tickets are $50 to $70 for adults and $30 to $50 for children 12 and under.

A very different type of live entertainment is **Warren & Annabelle's,** 900 Front St., Lahaina (© **808/667-6244;** www.warrenandannabelles.com), a magic/comedy cocktail show with illusionist Warren Gibson and "Annabelle," a ghost from the 1800s who plays the grand piano (even taking requests from the audience) as Warren dazzles you with his sleight-of-hand magic. Appetizers, desserts, and cocktails are available (either as a package or a la carte). Check-in is 5pm. Show-only price is $50. You must be 21 years old to attend, although they occasionally have a 4pm family show (minimum age is 6 years) without food or cocktails (generally during major school holidays); call for details.

The **Kaanapali Beach Hotel** has a wonderful show called *Kupanaha* that is perfect for the entire family. It features the renowned magicians Jody and Kathleen Baran and their entire family, including child prodigy magicians Katrina and Crystal. The dinner show features magic, illusions, and the story of the Hawaii fire goddess, Pele, presented through hula and chant performed by the children of the Kano'eau Dance Academy. The shows are Tuesday through Saturday; tickets are $75 to $85 for adults, $49 for teens (ages 13–20), and $35 for children ages 6 to 12 (free for children 5 and under). Included in the ticket price is dinner (entree choices include Island fish, roasted stuffed chicken, steak and shrimp, or a vegetarian dish, with a children's menu available). For reservations and tickets, call © **808/661-0011** or visit www.kbhmaui. com.

Maui Brews, 900 Front St. (© **808/667-7794**), draws the late-night crowd to its corner of the Lahaina Center with swing, salsa, reggae, and jams. There's live music Friday and Monday nights. Hours are daily from 11:30am, with happy hour from 3 to 6pm and nightclub hours from 9pm to 1:30am.

On Saturday nights, the hip, 20's and 30's crowd heads for **E&O Trading Co.,** in the Lahaina Cannery Mall, 1221 Honoapiilani Hwy., (© **808/667-1818;** www.eotrading.com), when the restaurant becomes the **Feng Shui Lounge** from 10pm to 2am with music by a DJ (and sometimes a cover—call to check).

You won't have to ask what's going on at **Cheeseburger in Paradise,** 811 Front St. (© **808/661-4855**), the two-story green-and-white building at the corner of Front and Lahainaluna streets. Just go outside and you'll hear it. Loud, live, and lively tropical rock blasts into the streets and out to sea nightly from 4:30 to 11pm.

Other venues for music in West Maui include the following:

- **B.J.'s Chicago Pizzeria,** 730 Front St. (© **808/661-0700**), offers live music from 7:30 to 10pm every night.
- **Cool Cat Café,** 658 Front St. (© **808/667-0909**), features live music Tuesday, Thursday, and Saturday from 2 to 4:30pm and 6:30 to 10pm.
- **Fish & Game Brewing Co.,** Kahana Gateway Center (© **808/669-3474**), has live music every night from 6:30 to 8:30pm (6–9pm in summer).
- **Hard Rock Cafe,** 900 Front St. (© **808/667-7400**), has live music at least twice a week from 10pm to 1am—reggae on Monday and various local bands on Saturday. On other nights, the entertainment varies (sometimes it's a DJ, sometimes

it's live). There's a cover charge of $5 Monday and Saturday (generally no cover the rest of the week).

- **Hula Grill,** Whalers Village (© **808/667-6636**), has live music (usually Hawaiian) from 3 to 5pm and again at 6:30 to 9pm nightly.
- **Kimo's,** 845 Front St. (© **808/661-4811**), has live musicians at various times; call for details.
- **Leilani's on the Beach,** Whalers Village (© **808/661-4495**), has live music from 4 to 6pm Wednesday through Sunday; the styles range from contemporary Hawaiian to rock.
- **Longhi's,** 888 Front St. (© **808/667-2288**), features a DJ on Friday nights from 9:45pm to 1:30am.
- **Moose McGillycuddy's,** 844 Front St. (© **808/667-7758**), offers a DJ some nights (the schedule varies; call for details) from 5:30 to 8:30pm.
- **Pacific'O,** 505 Front St. (© **808/667-4341**), offers live jazz Friday and Saturday from 9pm to midnight.
- **Paradise Bluz,** 744 Front St. (© **808/667-5299**), features live music or a DJ every night from 9pm to 2am. Look for special guests like Willie K.
- **Pineapple Grill,** 200 Kapalua Dr. (© **808/669-9600**), features Hawaiian music on Friday and jazz on Saturday from 7 to 10pm.
- **Pioneer Inn,** 658 Wharf St. (© **808/661-3636**), offers a variety of live music every night starting at 6pm.
- **Sansei,** Shops at Kapalua (© **808/669-6286**), has karaoke on Friday and Saturday from 10pm to 1am.
- **Sea Horse Restaurant,** Napili Kai Beach Resort (© **808/669-1500**), has live music from 7 to 9pm Wednesday through Monday and a Polynesian dinner show on Tuesday.
- **Spats,** Hyatt Regency, Kaanapali Resort (© **808/661-1234**), has dancing to a DJ on Saturday from 10pm to 3am.
- **Tropica,** Westin Maui (© **808/667-2525**), offers nightly music (call for times).

SOUTH MAUI—KIHEI

The Kihei area in South Maui also features music in a variety of locations:

- **Blue Marlin Harbor Front Bar & Grill,** Maalaea Harbor (© **808/244-8844**), has a variety of music Wednesday to Friday and Monday from 6:30 to 9pm.
- **Bocalino,** 1279 S. Kihei Rd. (© **808/874-9299**), has live music Monday through Saturday starting at 10pm.
- **Capischi,** Diamon Resort, 555 Kaukahi St., Wailea (© **808/879-2224**), has live music Friday and Saturday from 7 to 10pm.
- **Hapa's Night Club,** 41 E. Lipoa St. (© **808/879-9001**), has nightly music, generally Hawaiian; call for details.
- **Henry's Bar and Grill,** 41 E. Lipoa St. (© **808/87-2949**), offers live music Thursday through Saturday from 9pm to midnight.
- **Kahale's Beach Club,** 36 Keala Place (© **808/875-7711**), offers a potpourri of live music nightly; call for details.
- **Life's a Beach,** 1913 S. Kihei Rd. (© **808/891-8010**), has nightly live music; call for times.
- **Lobby Lounge,** Four Seasons Wailea (© **808/874-8000**), features nightly live music from 8:30 to 11:30pm.

Molokai

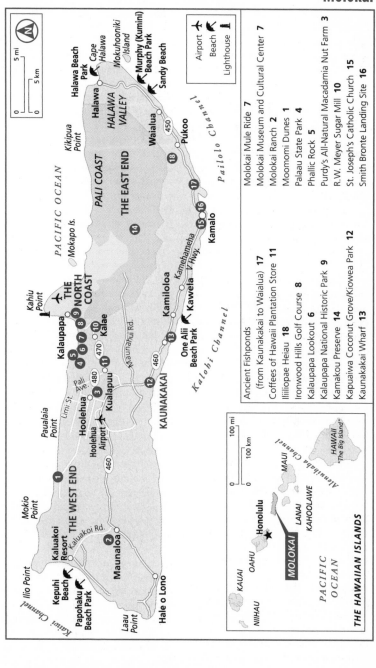

Airport ✈ Beach 🏖 Lighthouse 🗼

Molokai Mule Ride **7**
Molokai Museum and Cultural Center **7**
Molokai Ranch **2**
Moomomi Dunes **1**
Palaau State Park **4**
Phallic Rock **5**
Purdy's All-Natural Macadamia Nut Farm **3**
R.W. Meyer Sugar Mill **10**
St. Joseph's Catholic Church **15**
Smith Bronte Landing Site **16**

Ancient Fishponds
(from Kaunakakai to Waialua) **17**
Coffees of Hawaii Plantation Store **11**
Iliiliopae Heiau **18**
Ironwood Hills Golf Course **8**
Kalaupapa Lookout **6**
Kalaupapa National Historic Park **9**
Kamakou Preserve **14**
Kapuaiwa Coconut Grove/Kiowea Park **12**
Kaunakakai Wharf **13**

THE HAWAIIAN ISLANDS

KAUAI
NIIHAU
OAHU   Honolulu ★
         LANAI
         KAHOOLAWE
PACIFIC
OCEAN
MOLOKAI
MAUI
HAWAII
"The Big Island"

the rustic village of **Kaunakakai** ⚐ looks like the set of an old Hollywood Western, with sun-faded clapboard houses and horses tethered on the side of the road. Mile marker 0, in the center of town, divides the island into east and west.

Eastbound, along the **coastal highway** ⚐⚐⚐ named for King Kamehameha V, are Gauguin-like, palm-shaded cottages set on small coves or near fish ponds; spectacular vistas that take in Maui, Lanai, and Kahoolawe; and a fringing coral reef visible through the crystal-clear waves.

Out on the sun-scorched West End, overlooking a gold-sand beach with water usually too rough to swim in, is the island's lone destination resort, **Kaluakoi** (where the hotel is currently closed). The old hilltop plantation town of **Maunaloa** has been razed and rebuilt as a gentrified plantation community, complete with an expensive country lodge with a pricey dining room. Cowboys still ride the range on **Molokai Ranch,** a 65,000-acre spread, while adventure travelers and outdoor-recreation buffs stay at the tentalows on the ranch property and spend their days mountain biking, kayaking, horseback riding, sailing, hiking, snorkeling, and just vegetating on the endless white-sand beaches.

Elsewhere around the island, in hamlets like **Kualapuu,** old farmhouses with pickup trucks in the yards and sleepy dogs under the shade trees stand amid row crops of papaya, coffee, and corn—just like farm towns in Anywhere, USA.

But that's not all there is. The "backside" of Molokai is a rugged wilderness of spectacular beauty. On the outskirts of **Kaunakakai,** the land rises gradually from sea-level fish ponds to cool uplands and the Molokai Forest, long ago stripped of sandalwood for the China trade. All that remains is an indentation in the earth shaped like a ship's hull, a crude matrix that gave them a rough idea of

when they'd cut enough sandalwood to fill a ship (it's identified on good maps as *Luanamokuiliahi,* or Sandalwood Boat).

The land inclines sharply to the lofty mountains and the nearly mile-high summit of Mount Kamakou, and then ends abruptly with emerald-green cliffs, which plunge into a lurid aquamarine sea dotted with tiny deserted islets. These breathtaking 3,250-foot **sea cliffs** ⚐⚐, the highest in the world, stretch 14 majestic miles along Molokai's north shore, laced by waterfalls and creased by five valleys—Halawa, Papalaua, Wailau, Pelekunu, and Waikolu—once occupied by early Hawaiians who built stone terraces and used waterfalls to irrigate taro patches.

Long after the sea cliffs were formed, a tiny volcano erupted out of the sea at their feet and spread lava into a flat, leaflike peninsula called **Kalaupapa** ⚐⚐⚐—the 1860s leper exile where Father Damien de Veuster of Belgium devoted his life to care for the afflicted. A few people remain in the remote colony by choice, keeping it tidy for the visitors that arrive daily.

WHAT A VISIT TO MOLOKAI IS *REALLY* LIKE

There's plenty of aloha on Molokai, but the so-called "friendly island" remains ambivalent about vacationers. One of the least-visited Hawaiian islands, Molokai welcomes about 80,000 visitors annually on its own take-it-or-leave-it terms and makes few concessions beyond that of gracious host; it never wants to attract too big of a crowd, anyway. A sign at the airport offers the first clue: SLOW DOWN, YOU ON MOLOKAI NOW—wisdom to heed on this island, where life proceeds at its own pace.

Rugged, red-dirt Molokai isn't for everyone, but those who like to explore remote places and seek their own adventures should love it. The best of the island can be seen only on foot, bicycle, mule, horseback, kayak, or boat. The sea cliffs are accessible only by sea in summer,

Molokai, the Most Hawaiian Isle

Born of volcanic eruptions 1.5 million years ago, Molokai remains a time capsule on the dawn of the 21st century. It has no deluxe resorts, no stoplights, and no buildings taller than a coconut tree. Molokai is the least developed, most "Hawaiian" of all the islands, making it especially attractive to adventure travelers and peace seekers.

Molokai lives up to its reputation as the most Hawaiian place chiefly through its lineage; there are more people here of Hawaiian blood than anywhere else. This slipper-shaped island was the cradle of Hawaiian dance (the hula was born here) and the ancient science of aquaculture. An aura of ancient mysticism clings to the land here, and the old ways still govern life. The residents survive by taking fish from the sea and hunting wild pigs and axis deer on the range. Some folks still catch fish for dinner by throwing nets and trolling the reef.

Modern Hawaii's high-rise hotels, shopping centers, and other trappings of tourism haven't been able to gain a foothold here. The lone low-rise resort on the island, Kaluakoi—a now-closed, empty hotel built 30 years ago—was Molokai's token attempt at contemporary tourism. The only "new" developments since Kaluakoi are the Molokai Ranch's eco-tourism project of upscale "camping" in semipermanent "tentalows" (a combination of a bungalow and a tent) and a 22-room lodge on the 65,000-acre ranch. The focus of both is on outdoor recreation and adventure, with all the comforts of home.

Not everyone will love Molokai. The slow-paced, simple life of the people and the absence of contemporary landmarks attract those in search of the "real" Hawaii. I once received a letter from a New York City resident who claimed that any "big city resident" would "blanche" at the lack of "sophistication." But that is exactly the charm of Molokai. This is a place where Mother Nature is wild and uninhibited, with very little intrusion by man. Forget sophistication; this is one of the few spots on the planet where one can stand in awe of the island's diverse natural wonders: Hawaii's highest waterfall and greatest collection of fish ponds; the world's tallest sea cliffs; sand dunes, coral reefs, rainforests, and hidden coves; and gloriously empty beaches.

EXPLORING THE "MOST HAWAIIAN" ISLE Only 38 miles from end to end and just 10 miles wide, Molokai stands like a big green wedge in the blue Pacific. It has an east side, a west side, a backside, and a topside. This long, narrow island is like yin and yang: One side is a flat, austere, arid desert; the other is a lush, green, tropical Eden. Three volcanic eruptions formed Molokai; the last produced the island's "thumb"—a peninsula jutting out of the steep cliffs of the north shore, like a punctuation mark on the island's geological story.

On the red-dirt southern plain, where most of the island's 7,000 residents live,

- **Lulu's,** 1945 S. Kihei Rd. (© **808/879-9944**), offers entertainment starting at 8pm; karaoke on Wednesday, live music Thursday through Sunday.
- **Maalaea Grill,** Maalaea Village Shops (© **808/243-2206**), features live music Thursday to Saturday from 6:30 to 9pm.
- **Mulligan's on the Blue,** 100 Kaukahi St., Wailea (© **808/874-1131**), has live music starting at 9pm Friday and Saturday.
- **Sansei Seafood Restaurant & Sushi Bar,** Kihei Town Center (© **808/879-0004**), has karaoke Thursday to Sunday from 10pm to 1am.
- **South Shore Tiki Lounge,** 1913 S. Kihei Rd. (© **808/874-6444**), has live Hawaiian music daily from 4 to 6pm; dancing from 10pm to 2am.
- **Sports Page Bar,** 2411 S. Kihei Rd. (© **808/879-0602**), has live music Monday through Saturday starting at 9pm.
- **Yorman's By the Sea,** 760 Kihei Rd. (© **808/874-8385**), generally features jazz Wednesday to Sunday from 6:30pm onward.

UPCOUNTRY MAUI

Upcountry in Makawao, the party never ends at **Casanova,** 1188 Makawao Ave. (© **808/572-0220**), the popular Italian ristorante where the good times roll with the pasta. The newly renovated bar area has large booths, all the better for socializing around the stage and dance floor. If a big-name mainland band is resting up on Maui following a sold-out concert on Oahu, you may find its members setting up for an impromptu night here. DJs take over on Wednesday (ladies' night), and on Thursday, Friday, and Saturday, live entertainment draws fun-lovers from even the most remote reaches of the island. Entertainment starts at 9:45pm and continues to 1:30am. Expect good blues, rock 'n' roll, reggae, jazz, Hawaiian, and the top names in local and visiting entertainment. Elvin Bishop, the local duo Hapa, Los Lobos, and many others have filled Casanova's stage. The cover is usually $5. Go Sunday afternoons, from 3 to 6pm, for excellent live jazz.

PAIA & CENTRAL MAUI

In Central Maui, Café Marc Aurel, 28 N. Market St., Wailuku (© **808/244-0852**), is the place for a range of eclectic music from folk to Hawaiian, to ethnic, and even some open-mic nights. Call for information. The **Kahului Ale House,** 355 E. Kamehameha Ave. (© **808/877-9001**), features karaoke on Sunday, Monday, and Wednesday (10pm–2am); live music on Thursday and Friday (call for times); and a DJ on Saturday from 10pm. At Sushi Go!, in the Queen Kaahumanu Shopping Center, in Kahului (© **808/877-8744**), there is live music Wednesday, Friday, and Saturday. In Paia, **Charley's Restaurant,** 142 Hana Hwy. (© **808/579-9453**), features an eclectic selection of music from country and western (Willie Nelson has been seen sitting in) to fusion/reggae, to rock 'n' roll; call for details. Also in Paia, the **Moana Baker & Café,** 71 Baldwin Ave. (© **808/579-9999**), has everything from Hawaiian to cool jazz, to sizzling Latin; call for details.

Molokai

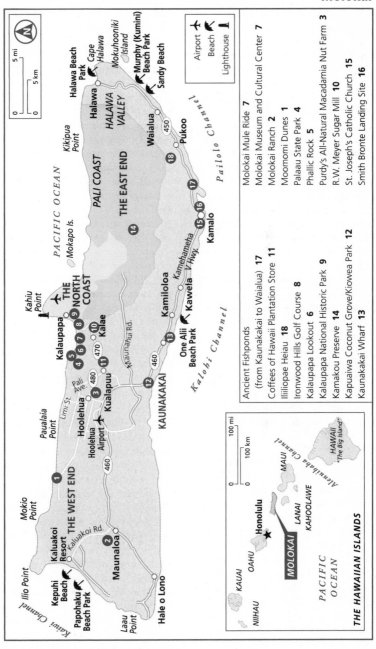

Airport ✈
Beach 🏖
Lighthouse 🗼

Molokai Mule Ride **7**
Molokai Museum and Cultural Center **7**
Molokai Ranch **2**
Moomomi Dunes **1**
Palaau State Park **4**
Phallic Rock **5**
Purdy's All-Natural Macadamia Nut Farm **3**
R.W. Meyer Sugar Mill **10**
St. Joseph's Catholic Church **15**
Smith Bronte Landing Site **16**

Ancient Fishponds
(from Kaunakakai to Waialua) **17**
Coffees of Hawaii Plantation Store **11**
Ililiopae Heiau **18**
Ironwood Hills Golf Course **8**
Kalaupapa Lookout **6**
Kalaupapa National Historic Park **9**
Kamakou Preserve **14**
Kapuaiwa Coconut Grove/Kiowea Park **12**
Kaunakakai Wharf **13**

THE HAWAIIAN ISLANDS

481

the rustic village of **Kaunakakai** ✸ looks like the set of an old Hollywood Western, with sun-faded clapboard houses and horses tethered on the side of the road. Mile marker 0, in the center of town, divides the island into east and west.

Eastbound, along the **coastal highway** ✸✸✸ named for King Kamehameha V, are Gauguin-like, palm-shaded cottages set on small coves or near fish ponds; spectacular vistas that take in Maui, Lanai, and Kahoolawe; and a fringing coral reef visible through the crystal-clear waves.

Out on the sun-scorched West End, overlooking a gold-sand beach with water usually too rough to swim in, is the island's lone destination resort, **Kaluakoi** (where the hotel is currently closed). The old hilltop plantation town of **Maunaloa** has been razed and rebuilt as a gentrified plantation community, complete with an expensive country lodge with a pricey dining room. Cowboys still ride the range on **Molokai Ranch,** a 65,000-acre spread, while adventure travelers and outdoor-recreation buffs stay at the tentalows on the ranch property and spend their days mountain biking, kayaking, horseback riding, sailing, hiking, snorkeling, and just vegetating on the endless white-sand beaches.

Elsewhere around the island, in hamlets like **Kualapuu,** old farmhouses with pickup trucks in the yards and sleepy dogs under the shade trees stand amid row crops of papaya, coffee, and corn—just like farm towns in Anywhere, USA.

But that's not all there is. The "backside" of Molokai is a rugged wilderness of spectacular beauty. On the outskirts of **Kaunakakai,** the land rises gradually from sea-level fish ponds to cool uplands and the Molokai Forest, long ago stripped of sandalwood for the China trade. All that remains is an indentation in the earth shaped like a ship's hull, a crude matrix that gave them a rough idea of

when they'd cut enough sandalwood to fill a ship (it's identified on good maps as *Luanamokuiliahi,* or Sandalwood Boat).

The land inclines sharply to the lofty mountains and the nearly mile-high summit of Mount Kamakou, and then ends abruptly with emerald-green cliffs, which plunge into a lurid aquamarine sea dotted with tiny deserted islets. These breathtaking 3,250-foot **sea cliffs** ✸✸, the highest in the world, stretch 14 majestic miles along Molokai's north shore, laced by waterfalls and creased by five valleys—Halawa, Papalaua, Wailau, Pelekunu, and Waikolu—once occupied by early Hawaiians who built stone terraces and used waterfalls to irrigate taro patches.

Long after the sea cliffs were formed, a tiny volcano erupted out of the sea at their feet and spread lava into a flat, leaflike peninsula called **Kalaupapa** ✸✸✸—the 1860s leper exile where Father Damien de Veuster of Belgium devoted his life to care for the afflicted. A few people remain in the remote colony by choice, keeping it tidy for the visitors that arrive daily.

WHAT A VISIT TO MOLOKAI IS *REALLY* **LIKE** There's plenty of aloha on Molokai, but the so-called "friendly island" remains ambivalent about vacationers. One of the least-visited Hawaiian islands, Molokai welcomes about 80,000 visitors annually on its own take-it-or-leave-it terms and makes few concessions beyond that of gracious host; it never wants to attract too big of a crowd, anyway. A sign at the airport offers the first clue: SLOW DOWN, YOU ON MOLOKAI NOW—wisdom to heed on this island, where life proceeds at its own pace.

Rugged, red-dirt Molokai isn't for everyone, but those who like to explore remote places and seek their own adventures should love it. The best of the island can be seen only on foot, bicycle, mule, horseback, kayak, or boat. The sea cliffs are accessible only by sea in summer, when the Pacific is calm, or via a 10-mile trek through the Wailau Valley—an adventure only a handful of hardy hikers attempt each year. The great **Kamakou Preserve** is open just once a month, by special arrangement with the Nature Conservancy. Even **Moomomi,** which holds bony relics of prehistoric flightless birds and other creatures, requires a guide to divulge the secrets of the dunes.

Those in search of nightlife have come to the wrong place; Molokai shuts down after sunset. The only public diversions are softball games under the lights of Mitchell Pauole Field, movies at Maunaloa, and the few restaurants that stay open after dark, often serving local brew and pizza.

The "friendly" island may enchant you as the "real" Hawaii of your dreams. On the other hand, you may leave shaking your head, never to return. Regardless of how you approach Molokai, remember our advice: Take it slow.

1 Orientation

ARRIVING

BY PLANE   Molokai has two airports, but you'll most likely fly into **Hoolehua Airport,** which everyone calls "the Molokai Airport." It's on a dusty plain about 6 miles from Kaunakakai town. Twin-engine planes offer daily service. Commuter airlines Pacific Wings started operating a discount airline, **PW Express** (© **888/866-5022** or 808/873-0877; www.flypwx.com) with 14 daily nonstop flights between Molokai and Honolulu, and four daily flights between Kahului, Maui, and Molokai. Their discount airfares are substantially cheaper than the twin-engine planes flown daily by **Island Air** (© **800/323-3345** from the mainland, or 800/652-6541 interisland; www.islandair.com), with eight direct flights a day from Honolulu. I must tell you that I have gotten less than sterling service from Island Air; their reservations system (or customer service, depending on who is blaming whom) has left me stranded in midroute, not once, but twice! **Molokai Air Shuttle** (© **808/545-4988**), which the local Molokai residents use, generally has six flights a day from Honolulu. However, they take reservations only 1 month in advance and do not have a website. **George's Aviation** (© **866/834-2120,** 808/834-2120 from Honolulu, or 808/893-2120 from Maui; www.georgesaviation.com) has "on-demand" charters every day from Honolulu and Maui to Molokai.

As we went to press, **go!** airline (© **888/IFLYGO2;** www.iflygo.com) announced the signing of a "memorandum of understanding" with Mokulele Airlines (a small charter service airline on the Big Island) to provide service from Honolulu to Molokai, under the name, **go!Express,** on their new fleet of Cessna Grand Caravan 208B planes. Currently, go!Express offers the best rates and deals among Hawaii's airline carriers.

BY BOAT   You can travel across the seas by ferry from Maui's Lahaina Harbor to Molokai's Kaunakakai Wharf on the *Molokai Princess* (© **800/275-6969** or 808/ 667-6165; www.mauiprincess.com). The 100-foot yacht, certified for 149 passengers, is fitted with the latest generation of gyroscopic stabilizers, making the ride smoother. The ferry makes the 90-minute journey from Lahaina to Kaunakakai daily; the round-trip cost is $85 adults and $43 children ages 3 to 12. Or you can choose to tour the island from two different package options: Cruise-Drive, which includes round-trip passage and a rental car for $191 for the driver, $76 per additional adult passenger, and $38 for children; or the Alii Tour, which is a guided tour in an air-conditioned van plus lunch for $191 for adults and $134 for children.

VISITOR INFORMATION

Contact the **Molokai Visitors Association,** P.O. Box 960, Kaunakakai, HI 96748 (© **800/800-6367** from the U.S. mainland and Canada, 800/553-0404 interisland, or 808/553-3876; www.molokai-hawaii.com), or stop by their office in The Moore Center, 2 Kamoi St., Suite 200, Kaunakakai. The staff can give you all the information you need on what to see and do while you're on Molokai.

THE ISLAND IN BRIEF

Kaunakakai ✦

Dusty vehicles—mostly pickup trucks—are parked diagonally along Ala Malama Street. You're in Kaunakakai, the closest thing Molokai has to a business district. Friendly Isle Realty and Friendly Isle Travel offer islanders dream homes and vacations; Rabang's Filipino Food posts bad checks in the window; antlered deer-head trophies guard the grocery aisles at Misaki's Market; and Kanemitsu's, the town's legendary bakery, churns out fresh loaves of onion-cheese bread daily.

Once an ancient canoe landing, Kaunakakai was the royal summer residence of King Kamehameha V. The port town bustled when pineapple and sugar were king, but those days, too, are gone. With its Old West–style storefronts laid out in a 3-block grid on a flat, dusty plain, Kaunakakai is a town from the past. At the end of Wharf Road is Molokai Wharf, a picturesque place to fish, photograph, and just hang out.

Kaunakakai is the dividing point between the lush, green East End and the dry, arid West End. On the west side of town stands a cactus and on the east side of town there's thick, green vegetation.

The North Coast ✦✦

Upland from Kaunakakai, the land tilts skyward and turns green, with scented plumeria in yards and glossy coffee trees all in a row, until it blooms into a true forest—and then abruptly ends at a great precipice, falling 3,250 feet to the sea. The green sea cliffs are creased with five V-shaped crevices so deep that light is seldom seen (to paraphrase a Hawaiian poet). The north coast is a remote, forbidding place, with a solitary peninsula—**Kalaupapa** ✦✦✦—that was once the home for exiled lepers (it's now a National Historic Park). This region is easy on the eyes but difficult to visit. It lies at a cool elevation, and frequent rain squalls blow in from the ocean. In summer the ocean is calm, providing great opportunities for kayaking, fishing, and swimming, but during the rest of the year, giant waves come rolling onto the shores.

The West End ✦

This end of the island, home to **Molokai Ranch,** is miles of stark desert terrain bordered by the most beautiful white-sand beaches in Hawaii. The rugged rolling land slopes down to Molokai's only destination resort, **Kaluakoi,** a cul-de-sac of condos clustered around a 3-decades-old seafront hotel (which closed in 2001 and was still closed when we went to press) near 3-mile-long Papohaku, the island's biggest beach. On the way to Kaluakoi, you'll find **Maunaloa,** a 1920s-era pineapple-plantation town that's in the midst of being transformed into a master-planned community, Maunaloa Village, with an upscale lodge, triplex theater, restaurants, and shops. The West End is dry, dry, dry. It hardly ever rains, but when it does (usually in the winter), expect a downpour and lots of red mud.

The East End 🎿🎿🎿

The area east of Kaunakakai becomes lush, green, and tropical, with golden pocket beaches and a handful of cottages and condos that are popular with thrifty travelers. With this voluptuous landscape comes rain. However, most storms are brief (15-min.) affairs. Winter is Hawaii's rainy season, so expect more rain during January to March, but even then, the storms usually are brief and the sun comes back out.

Beyond Kaunakakai, the two-lane road curves along the coast past piggeries, palm groves, and a 20-mile string of fish ponds as well as an ancient *heiau* (temple), Damien-built churches, and a few contemporary condos by the sea. The road ends in the glorious **Halawa Valley** 🎿, one of Hawaii's most beautiful valleys.

FAST FACTS

Molokai and Lanai are both part of Maui County. For **local emergencies,** call ℂ **911.** For nonemergencies, call the **police** at ℂ **808/553-5355,** the **fire department** at ℂ **808/553-5601,** or **Molokai General Hospital,** in Kaunakakai, at ℂ **808/553-5331.**

Downtown Kaunakakai has a **post office** (ℂ **808/553-5845**) and several banks, including the **Bank of Hawaii** (ℂ **808/553-3273**), which has a 24-hour ATM.

2 Getting Around

Getting around Molokai isn't easy if you don't have a rental car, and rental cars are often hard to find here. On holiday weekends (see "When to Go" in chapter 2), car-rental agencies simply run out of cars. Book before you go. There's no municipal transit or shuttle service, but a 24-hour taxi service is available (see below).

CAR-RENTAL AGENCIES Rental cars are available from **Budget** (ℂ **808/567-6877**) and **Dollar** (ℂ **808/567-6156**); both agencies are located at the Molokai Airport.

TAXI & TOUR SERVICES Molokai Off-Road Tours & Taxi (ℂ **808/553-3369;** www.molokai.com/offroad) offers regular taxi service, an airport shuttle ($34 for one to four people one-way to Molokai Ranch Lodge; $27 for one to three people one-way to Kaunakakai), and island tours (the half-day Molokai highlights tour is $95 per person).

3 Where to Stay

Molokai is Hawaii's most affordable island, especially for hotels. And because the island's restaurants are few, most hotel rooms and condo units come with kitchens, which can save you a bundle on dining costs.

The downside is that there aren't too many accommodations options on Molokai—mostly B&Bs, condos, a few quaint oceanfront vacation rentals, an aging resort, and a very expensive lodge. For camping on Molokai, you have two options: the upscale tentalows offered by The Beach Village at Molokai Ranch, or, for hardy souls, camping with your own tent at the beach or in the cool upland forest (see "Hiking & Camping," later in this chapter). We've listed our top picks below; for additional options, contact **Molokai Vacation Rentals,** P.O. Box 1979, Kaunakakai, HI 96748 (ℂ **800/367-2984** or 808/553-8334; fax 808/553-3783; www.molokai-vacation-rental.com). They have a range of vacation homes, from quaint oceanfront cottages for 2 from $105 a night to six-bedroom homes that sleep 12 for $750 a night. *Note:* Taxes of 11.42% will be added to your hotel bill. Parking is free.

KAUNAKAKAI

MODERATE

Hotel Molokai *(★) (Kids)*   This nostalgic Hawaiian motel complex is composed of a series of modified A-frame units, nestled under coco palms along a gray-sand beach that has a great view of Lanai but isn't good for swimming. In 2006 the entire hotel underwent a $1-million renovation, from repaving the parking lot to redoing the kitchen. The interiors of all the rooms have been upgraded and look clean and new. This is a modest budget hotel—the rooms have all the necessities but aren't fancy. Be sure to ask for a room with a ceiling fan; most rooms have a lanai. The mattresses are on the soft side, the sheets thin, and the bath towels rough, but you're on Molokai—and this is the only hotel in Kaunakakai. The kitchenettes have coffeemakers, toasters, pots, and a two-burner stove. The front desk is open only from 7am to 8pm; late check-ins or visitors with problems have to go to security.

Kamehameha V Hwy. (P.O. Box 1020), Kaunakakai, HI 96748. © **800/367-5004** on the mainland, 800/272-5275 in Hawaii, or 808/553-5347. Fax 800/477-2329. www.hotelmolokai.com. 54 units. $115–$155 double; $175 with kitchen; $195 suite. Extra bed/crib $20. AE, DC, DISC, MC, V. **Amenities:** Fairly good and reasonably priced restaurant w/bar; outdoor pool; watersports equipment rentals; bike rentals; activities desk; babysitting; coin-op washer/dryers. *In room:* A/C, TV, dataport, kitchenette (in some rooms), fridge, coffeemaker, hair dryer, iron, safe.

Molokai Shores Suites *(Kids)*   Basic units with kitchens and large lanais face a small gold-sand beach in this quiet complex of three-story Polynesian-style buildings, less than a mile from Kaunakakai. Alas, the beach is mostly for show (offshore, it's shallow mud flats underfoot), fishing, or launching kayaks, but the swimming pool and barbecue area come with an ocean view, and the spacious units make this a good choice for families. Well-tended gardens, spreading lawns, and palms frame a restful view of fish ponds, offshore reefs, and neighbor islands. The central location is a plus. There's no daily maid service. I have received some letters complaining about the lack of maintenance and cleanliness; the management swears that they are taking steps to correct these deficiencies. On my most recent visit to these individually owned condominiums, the grounds and units I saw were clean and well maintained. However, keep in mind that these units are individually owned (as well as managed by various management companies).

Kamehameha V Hwy. (P.O. Box 1037), Kaunakakai, HI 96748. © **800/535-0085** or 808/553-5954. Fax 808/553-5954. www.marcresorts.com. 102 units. $143 1-bedroom apt (sleeps up to 4); $188 2-bedroom apt (up to 6). Discounted rates for weekly and extended stays, plus corporate, military, and senior discounts and Internet-only specials. AE, DC, MC, V. **Amenities:** Putting green; salon; coin-op washer/dryers. *In room:* TV, kitchen, fridge, coffeemaker, iron.

INEXPENSIVE

A'ahi Place *(Value)*   Just outside of the main town of Kaunakakai and up a small hill lies this dream vacation cottage, complete with a wicker-filled sitting area, a kitchen, and two full-size beds in the bedroom. Two lanais make great places to just sit and enjoy the stars at night. The entire property is surrounded by tropical plants, flowers, and fruit trees. You can choose to forgo breakfast or, for $10 more per night (for two), get all the fixings for a continental breakfast (homegrown Molokai coffee, fresh-baked goods, and fruit from the property) placed in the kitchen. For those who seek a quiet vacation with no phone or TV to distract you, this is the place. And for those who wish to explore Molokai, the central location is perfect.

P.O. Box 2006, Kaunakakai, HI 96748. © **808/553-8033.** www.molokai.com/aahi. 1 unit. $75 double. Continental breakfast $10 extra. Extra person $20. 3-night minimum. No credit cards. *In room:* Kitchen, fridge, coffeemaker, no phone.

Where to Stay & Dine on Molokai

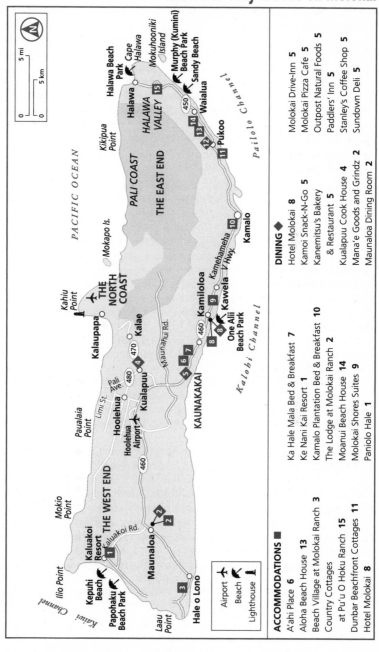

ACCOMMODATIONS ■

A'ahi Place **6**
Aloha Beach House **13**
Beach Village at Molokai Ranch **3**
Country Cottages
  at Pu'u O Hoku Ranch **15**
Dunbar Beachfront Cottages **11**
Hotel Molokai **8**

Ka Hale Mala Bed & Breakfast **7**
Ke Nani Kai Resort **1**
Kamalo Plantation Bed & Breakfast **10**
The Lodge at Molokai Ranch **2**
Moanui Beach House **14**
Molokai Shores Suites **9**
Paniolo Hale **1**

DINING ◆

Hotel Molokai **8**
Kamoi Snack-N-Go **5**
Kanemitsu's Bakery
  & Restaurant **5**
Kualapuu Cook House **4**
Mana'e Goods and Grindz **2**
Maunaloa Dining Room **2**

Molokai Drive-Inn **5**
Molokai Pizza Cafe **5**
Outpost Natural Foods **5**
Paddlers' Inn **5**
Stanley's Coffee Shop **5**
Sundown Deli **5**

Ka Hale Mala Bed & Breakfast *Value*   In a subdivision just outside town (off Kamehameha V Hwy., before mile marker 5) is this large four-room unit, with a private entrance through the garden and a Jacuzzi just outside. Inside you'll find white rattan furnishings, room enough to sleep four, and a full kitchen. The helpful owners, Jack and Cheryl, meet all guests at the airport like long-lost relatives. They'll happily share their homegrown organic produce; we recommend paying the extra $5 each for breakfast here. The owners can also supply a couple bikes and snorkel and picnic gear.

7 Kamakana Place (P.O. Box 1582), Kaunakakai, HI 96748. ©/fax **808/553-9009.** www.molokai-bnb.com. 1 unit. $80 double without breakfast, $90 double with breakfast. Extra person $15 without breakfast, $20 with breakfast. No credit cards. **Amenities:** Jacuzzi. *In room:* TV, kitchen, fridge, coffeemaker.

THE WEST END
VERY EXPENSIVE
The Lodge at Molokai Ranch ☞   This quaint 22-room inn is back in the hands of the Molokai Ranch and under new management (now it's a member of the Small Luxury Hotels of the World—Hotel Hana-Maui is the only other Hawaii hotel in this group). It's not cheap; not only is it the highest-priced hotel on Molokai, but it is the same price as luxury, oceanfront resorts on Maui. Only this property is *not* oceanfront. It's 6 miles and a 20- to 25-minute, bumpy drive down an unpaved gravel road to the closest beach. Nor is it in a resort, but in a sparsely populated community, with no other amenities (except the Big Kite Store) in the immediate area.

The attractive, two-story lodge sits on 8 nicely landscaped acres located in sometimes-windy and sometimes-cold Maunaloa Town. Designed to resemble a 1930s-style Hawaii ranch owner's private home, The Lodge features a giant fireplace, huge wooden beam construction, panoramic views, and details like cuffed cowboy boots beside the door that make it look and feel like a real ranch. Guests step back in time to a Hawaii of yesteryear.

The guest rooms, each with individual country decor, are of two types: deluxe and luxury. The luxury rooms are spacious corner units that feature either greenhouse-type skylights or a cozy king-size daybed nestled in a comfy alcove. My luxury room was wonderful, with a free-standing four-poster bed, a 270-degree view, and a TV that hydraulically lifted out of a credenza.

Other amenities include a dining room, the option of dining at buffets at the beach pavilion, and a small but practical spa (with massage treatments, men's and women's sauna, and locker facilities). The Lodge, along with the Beach Village at Molokai Ranch (p. 489), sits on the 65,000-acre Molokai Ranch and is geared toward outdoorsy types, with lots of activities available (horseback riding, mountain biking, hiking, kayaking, snorkeling, and more, ranging in price at $37–$275). There's also wonderful local entertainment in the Great Room in the evening; even if you don't stay here, come for the free entertainment.

P.O. Box 259, Maunaloa, HI 96770. © **888/627-8082** or 808/660-2824. Fax 808/552-2773. www.molokairanch.com. 22 units. $427–$518 double. $15 per day resort fee for transportation to beach, use of facilities at The Lodge, use of fitness center, safe, unlimited faxing and copying, and use of beach equipment at the beach camp. Extra person $50. Check online for money-saving packages. AE, DC, DISC, MC, V. **Amenities:** Restaurant (Maunaloa Dining Room, p. 495); bar w/entertainment Tues–Sat evenings; gorgeous heated outdoor infinity pool; workout room; small spa w/massage room; bike rentals; game room; concierge; activity desk; car-rental desk; shopping arcade; massage; laundry service. *In room:* A/C, TV, dataport, fridge, coffeemaker, hair dryer, iron, safe.

Believe It or Not: High-Priced Camping

This was a great idea: a unique eco-adventure that combines camping and outdoor activities with the amenities of a resort. The **Beach Village at Molokai Ranch** (ⓒ 888/627-8082 or 808/660-2824; fax 808/552-2773; www. molokairanch.com) features camping on an exclusive private beach, with very upscale "camping" accommodations. The Beach Village offers "tentalows"—safari-type tents mounted on wooden platforms. This is yuppie camping—with queen-size or twin beds, ceiling fans, solar-powered lights, private bathrooms with composting toilets, and solar hot-water showers, plus big decks with lounge chairs, hammocks, and picnic tables. There's even daily maid service! A big pavilion at the beach has all-you-can-eat buffet meals three times a day, plus nightly entertainment under the stars.

When the ranch first opened these camps in 1997, the price included airport pickup, meals, and a large menu of outdoor activities (horseback riding, mountain biking, hiking, sailing, snorkeling, kayaking, and other adventures). It was all-inclusive and quite a deal at $185 per person.

Today the prices have risen to an astounding $294 for garden tentalows, up to $386 for a tentalow directly on the beach (plus the ubiquitous resort fee of $15 a day for transportation to beach, use of facilities at The Lodge, use of fitness center, safe, unlimited faxing and copying, and use of beach equipment at the beach camp), and meals and activities are no longer included. Children 17 and under do stay free (with an adult), and children 12 and under also eat free, when accompanied by an adult. Meal prices are $15 for breakfast, $15 for lunch, and $31 for dinner. So the price for two adults staying in the least expensive room, including meals, tax, and the resort fee, comes to $471 a day—and that's not including any activities you may want to do. That's pretty expensive "camping."

MODERATE

Paniolo Hale 🏆 *Finds*   Tucked into a verdant garden on the dry West End, this condo complex has the advantage of being next door to a white-sand beach and a golf course. The two-story, old Hawaii ranch-house design is airy and homey, with oak floors and walls of folding-glass doors that open to huge screened verandas, doubling your living space. All are spacious and well equipped, with full kitchens and washer/dryers.

The whole place overlooks the Kaluakoi Golf Course, a green barrier that separates these condos from the rest of the rapidly fading Kaluakoi Resort. Out front, Kepuhi Beach is a scenic place for walkers and beachcombers, but the seas are too hazardous for most swimmers. A pool, paddle tennis, and barbecue facilities are on the property, which adjoins open grassland countryside.

As with most condominiums in a rental pool, the quality and upkeep of the individually owned units can vary widely. When booking, spend some time talking with the friendly people at Molokai Vacation Rentals so that you can get a top-quality condo that has been renovated recently.

Lio Place (next door to Kaluakoi Resort), Kaluakoi, HI 96770. Reservations c/o Molokai Vacation Rentals, P.O. Box 1979, Kaunakakai, HI 96748. ℂ 800/367-2984 or 808/553-8334. Fax 808/553-3783. www.molokai-vacation-rental.com. 77 units. $105–$145 double studio; $130–$195 1-bedroom apt (sleeps up to 4); $225–$300 2-bedroom apt (up to 6). 3-night minimum; 1-week minimum Dec 20–Jan 5. AE, MC, V. **Amenities:** Outdoor pool; nearby golf course. *In room:* TV, kitchen, fridge, coffeemaker, washer/dryer.

INEXPENSIVE

Ke Nani Kai Resort ⭐ (Kids)   This place is great for families, who will appreciate the space. The large apartments are set up for full-time living with real kitchens, washer/dryers, VCRs, attractive furnishings, and breezy lanais. There's a huge pool, a volleyball court, tennis courts, and golf on the neighboring Kaluakoi course. These condos are farther from the sea than other local accommodations but are still just a brief walk from the beach. The two-story buildings are surrounded by parking and garden areas. The only downside: Maid service is only every third day.

In the Kaluakoi Resort development, Kaluakoi Rd., off Hwy. 460 (P.O. Box 289), Maunaloa, HI 96770. Reservations c/o Molokai Vacation Rentals, P.O. Box 1979, Kaunakakai, HI 96748. ℂ 800/367-2984 or 808/553-8334. Fax 808/553-3783. www.molokai-vacation-rental.com. 100 units. $95–$125 1-bedroom apt (sleeps up to 4); $125–$175 2-bedroom apt (up to 6). 3-night minimum. AE, DC, DISC, MC, V. **Amenities:** Outdoor pool; golf course; 2 tennis courts; Jacuzzi. *In room:* TV, kitchen, fridge, coffeemaker, washer/dryer.

THE EAST END
MODERATE

Aloha Beach House ⭐⭐ (Finds) (Kids)   This is a great place to stay on Molokai. This Hawaiian-style beach house sits right on the white-sand beach of Waialua on the lush East End. In 2006 they put in new hardwood floors in the entire house. Perfect for families, this impeccably decorated, two-bedroom, 1,600-square-foot beach house has a huge open living/dining/kitchen area that opens out to an old-fashioned porch for meals or just sitting in the comfy chairs and watching the clouds roll by. It's fully equipped, from the complete kitchen (including a dishwasher) to a VCR (plus a library of videos), to all the beach toys you can think of. It's located close to Mana'e Goods and Grindz (p. 495).

Located just after mile marker 19. Reservations c/o The Rietows, P.O. Box 79, Kilauea, HI 96754. ℂ 888/828-1008 or 808/828-1100. Fax 808/828-2199. www.molokaivacation.com. 1 unit. $240–$280 double; $280 3–5 people; plus $150 cleaning fee. 3-night minimum. No credit cards. *In room:* TV, kitchen, fridge, coffeemaker, washer/dryer.

Country Cottage at Pu'u O Hoku Ranch ⭐ (Kids)   *Pu'u o Hoku* ("Star Hill") Ranch, which spreads across 14,000 acres of pasture and forests, is the last place to stay before Halawa Valley—it's at least an hour's drive from Kaunakakai along the shoreline. Two acres of tropically landscaped property circle the ranch's rustic cottage, which boasts breathtaking views of rolling hills and the Pacific Ocean. The wooden cottage features comfortable country furniture, a full kitchen, two bedrooms (one with a double bed, one with two twins), two bathrooms, and a separate dining room on the enclosed lanai. TVs and VCRs are available on request. Stargaze at night, watch the sunrise in the morning, and hike, swim, or play croquet in the afternoon. For larger parties, there's a four-bedroom, three-bathroom house (sleeps up to eight) on the property. Horseback riding is available at the ranch; see "Horseback Riding" under "Golf & Other Outdoor Activities," later in this chapter. Kids will have plenty of room to run around and explore.

Kamehameha V Hwy., at mile marker 25. Reservations: P.O. Box 1889, Kaunakakai, HI 96748. ℂ 808/558-8109. Fax 808/558-8100. www.puuohoku.com. 2 units. $140 double. Extra person $20. 2-night minimum. No credit cards. **Amenities:** Swimming pool. *In room:* TV/VCR (available on request), kitchen, fridge, coffeemaker.

Dunbar Beachfront Cottages *Kids*   This is one of the most peaceful, comfortable, and elegant properties on Molokai's East End, and the setting is simply stunning. Each of these two green-and-white plantation-style cottages sits on its own secluded beach (good for swimming)—you'll feel like you're on your own private island. Each cottage sleeps up to four (great for a family) and comes with a full kitchen, VCR, ceiling fans, comfortable tropical furniture, a large furnished deck (perfect for whale-watching in winter), and views of Maui, Lanai, and Kahoolawe across the channel.

Kamehameha V Hwy., past mile marker 18. Reservations c/o Kip and Leslie Dunbar, HC01 Box 738, Kaunakakai, HI 96748. ✆ 800/673-0520 or 808/558-8153. Fax 808/558-8153. www.molokai-beachfront-cottages.com. 2 units. $170 cottage (sleeps up to 4), plus 1-time $75 cleaning fee. 3-night minimum. No credit cards. *In room:* TV, kitchen, fridge, coffeemaker, washer/dryer.

Moanui Beach House *Kids*   If you're looking for a quiet, remote beach house, this is it. The genial Fosters, who have lived on the islands for many years, run the popular Kamalo Plantation Bed & Breakfast (see below). They recently renovated the kitchen in this two-bedroom beach house, right across the street from a secluded white-sand cove beach. The A-frame has a shaded lanai facing the ocean, a screened-in lanai on the side of the house, a full kitchen, and an ocean view that's worth the price alone—it's a great place for families to spread out and relax. The Fosters leave a "starter supply" of breakfast foods for guests (fruit basket, home-baked bread, tropical fruit juices, tea, and coffee).

Kamehameha V Hwy., at mile marker 20. Reservations c/o Glenn and Akiko Foster, HC01, Box 300, Kaunakakai, HI 96748. ✆/fax 808/558-8236. www.molokai.com/kamalo. 1 unit. $150 double. Extra person $50. 3-night minimum. No credit cards. *In room:* TV, kitchen, fridge, coffeemaker, hair dryer, iron, washer/dryer.

INEXPENSIVE

Kamalo Plantation Bed & Breakfast *Value*   Glenn and Akiko Foster's (no relation to the author) 5-acre spread includes an ancient *heiau* ruin in the front yard, plus leafy tropical gardens and a working fruit orchard. Their Eden-like property is easy to find: It's right across the East End road from Father Damien's historic St. Joseph church. The plantation-style cottage is tucked under flowering trees and surrounded by swaying palms and tropical foliage. It has its own lanai, a big living room with a queen-size sofa bed, and a separate bedroom with a king-size bed, so it can sleep four comfortably. The kitchen is fully equipped (it even has spices), and there's a barbecue outside. A breakfast of fruit and freshly baked bread is served every morning. There's no TV reception, but the cottage does have a VCR, a radio, and a CD and cassette player.

Kamehameha V Hwy., just past mile marker 10 (HC01, Box 300), Kaunakakai, HI 96748. ✆/fax 808/558-8236. www.molokai.com/kamalo. 1 unit. $100 cottage double. Rate includes continental breakfast. Extra person $10. 2-night minimum. No credit cards. *In room:* Kitchen, fridge, coffeemaker, hair dryer.

4 Where to Dine

The good news is that, on Molokai, you won't find long lines at overbooked, self-important restaurants. But when it comes to dining, Molokai is not nirvana. Even with the first upscale hotel and dining room open in Maunaloa, Molokai's culinary offerings are spare.

A lot of people like it that way and acknowledge that the island's character is unchangeably rugged and natural. But a few years ago, when the renovated Hotel Molokai unveiled a tropical fantasy of an oceanfront dining room, the islanders thought this was the height of culinary pleasure. And it quickly became the island's busiest restaurant.

In 1999, when the Molokai Ranch opened The Lodge, it introduced the concept of Molokai having its own gourmet culinary cuisine, using local ingredients in not only traditional Molokai preparations, but also other ethnic styles of cooking.

Even with these new developments, Molokai has retained its glacial pace of change. The culinary offerings of the island are dominated by mom-and-pop eateries, most of them fast-food or takeout places, and many of them with a home-cooked touch. Personally, I like the unpretentiousness of the island; it's an oasis in a state where plastic aloha abounds. But sybarites, foodies, and pampered oenophiles had best lower their expectations upon arrival, or turn around and leave the island's natural beauty to nature lovers.

You'll even find a certain defiant stance against the trappings of modernity. Although some of the best produce in Hawaii is grown on this island, you're not likely to find much of it served in its restaurants, other than in the takeout items at Outpost Natural Foods, or at the Molokai Pizza Cafe (one of the most pleasing eateries on the island), and the Hotel Molokai. The rest of the time, content yourself with ethnic or diner fare—or by cooking for yourself. The many visitors who stay in condos find that it doesn't take long to sniff out the best sources of produce, groceries, and fresh fish to fire up at home when the island's other dining options are exhausted. The "Edibles" sections in "Shopping" (later in this chapter) will point you to the places where you can pick up foodstuffs for your own Island-style feast.

Molokai's restaurants are inexpensive or moderately priced, and several of them do not accept credit cards. Regardless of where you eat, you certainly won't have to dress up. In most cases, we've listed just the town rather than the street address because, as you'll see, street addresses are as meaningless on this island as fancy cars and sequins. Reservations are not accepted unless otherwise noted.

Note: You'll find the restaurants reviewed in this chapter on the "Where to Stay & Dine on Molokai" map on p. 487.

KAUNAKAKAI
INEXPENSIVE

Hotel Molokai 🐾 AMERICAN/ISLAND On the ocean, with a view of Lanai, torches flickering under palm trees, and tiny fairy lights lining the room and the neighboring pool area, the Hotel Molokai's dining room evokes the romance of a South Seas fantasy. It's a casual room and, since its 1999 reopening, provides the only nightlife in Kaunakakai (see "Molokai After Dark," later in this chapter) and the most pleasing ambience on the island. Lunch choices consist of the basics; most promising are salads (Big Island organic greens) and sandwiches, from roast beef to grilled mahimahi. As the sun sets and the torches are lit for dinner, the menu turns to heavier meats, ribs, fish, and pasta. Try the fresh catch, kalbi ribs, barbecued pork ribs, New York steak, or lip-smacking coconut shrimp. Temper your expectations of culinary excellence, and you're sure to enjoy a pleasing dinner in an atmosphere that's unequaled on the island.

On Kamehameha V Hwy. ⓒ 808/553-5347. Reservations recommended for dinner. Main courses $7–$8 lunch, $12–$19 dinner. AE, DC, MC, V. Daily 7–10:30am, 11am–1:30pm, and 6–8:45pm (Fri 4–9pm); bar until 10:30pm.

Kamoi Snack-N-Go ICE CREAM/SNACKS The Kamoi specialty: sweets and icy treats. Ice cream made by Dave's on Oahu comes in flavors such as green tea, litchi sherbet, *ube* (made from Okinawan sweet potato), haupia, mango, and many others. Lines form for the cones, shakes, sundaes, and popular Icee floats served at this tiny snack shop. If the ice cream doesn't tempt you, maybe something in the aisles full of candies will. It's takeout only; no tables.

In Kamoi Professional Center. 🕐 **808/553-3742.** Ice cream $2.25–$4.15; sundaes $3.60–$6.40. MC, V. Mon–Fri 10am–9pm; Sat 9am–9pm; Sun noon–9pm.

Kanemitsu's Bakery & Restaurant 🕊 BAKERY/DELI   Morning, noon, and night, this local legend fills the Kaunakakai air with the sweet smells of baking. Taro lavosh is the hot seller, joining Molokai bread—developed in 1935 in a cast-iron, kiawe-fired oven—as a Kanemitsu signature. Flavors range from apricot-pineapple to coconut or strawberry, but the white, wheat, cheese, sweet, and onion-cheese breads are classics. The bread mixes offer a way to take Molokai home. In the adjoining coffee shop/deli, the hamburgers and egg-salad sandwiches are popular and cheap.

Kanemitsu's has a life after dark, too. Whenever anyone on Molokai mentions "hot bread," he's talking about the hot-bread run at Kanemitsu's, the surreal late-night ritual for die-hard bread lovers. Those in the know line up at the bakery's back door beginning at 10pm, when the bread is whisked hot out of the oven and into waiting hands. You can order your fresh bread with butter, jelly, cinnamon, or cream cheese, and the bakers will cut the hot loaves down the middle and slather on the works so it melts in the bread. The cream cheese and jelly bread makes a fine substitute for dessert.

79 Ala Malama St. 🕐 **808/553-5855.** Most items less than $5.50. AE, MC, V. Restaurant Wed–Mon 5:30am–noon; bakery Wed–Mon 5:30am–6:30pm.

Molokai Drive-Inn AMERICAN/TAKEOUT   It is a greasy spoon, but it's one of the rare drive-up places with fresh akule (mackerel) and ahi (when available), plus fried saimin at budget-friendly prices. The honey-dipped fried chicken is a favorite among residents, who also come here for the floats, shakes, and other artery-clogging choices. But don't expect much in terms of ambience: This is a fast-food takeout counter, and it doesn't pretend to be otherwise.

Kaunakakai. 🕐 **808/553-5655.** Most items less than $7.75. No credit cards. Mon–Fri 5:30am–10pm; Sat–Sun 6am–10:30pm.

Molokai Pizza Cafe 🕊 PIZZA   This gathering place serves excellent pizzas and sandwiches that have made it a Kaunakakai staple as well as one of my favorite eateries on the island. The best-selling pies are the Molokai (pepperoni and cheese), the Big Island (pepperoni, ham, mushroom, Italian sausage, bacon, and vegetables), and the Molokini (plain cheese slices). Pasta, sandwiches, and the new addition of "gourmet" hamburgers on homemade buns round out the menu. My personal fave is the vegetarian Maui pizza, but others tout the fresh-baked submarine and pocket sandwiches and the gyro pocket with spinach pie. Sunday is prime-rib day and Wednesday is Mexican. Coin-operated cars and a toy airplane follow the children's theme, but adults should feel equally at home with the very popular barbecued baby back rib plate and the fresh fish dinners.

In Kahua Center, on the old Wharf Rd. 🕐 **808/553-3288.** Large pizzas $14–$24. No credit cards. Sun 11am–10pm; Mon–Thurs 10am–10pm; Fri–Sat 10am–11pm.

Outpost Natural Foods 🕊 VEGETARIAN   The healthiest and freshest food on the island is served at the lunch counter of this health-food store, around the corner from the main drag on the ocean side of Kaunakakai town. The tiny store abounds in

Molokai papayas, bananas, herbs, potatoes, watermelon, and other local produce, complementing its selection of vitamins, cosmetics, and health aids, as well as bulk and shelf items. The salads, burritos, tempeh sandwiches, tofu-spinach lasagna, and mock chicken, turkey, and meatloaf served at the lunch counter are testament to the fact that vegetarian food need not be boring. A must for health-conscious diners and shoppers.

70 Makaena Place. ℂ **808/553-3377.** Most items less than $6. AE, DISC, MC, V. Sun–Fri 10am–3pm.

Paddlers' Inn AMERICAN/LOCAL   This local diner, with everything from burgers to steak, recently added breakfast (with specials like homemade sausage sauce and biscuits). If you want to meet local residents, come to this friendly place. Lunch is generally filled with hungry diners grinding on ⅓-pound all-beef burgers, big sandwiches, or plate lunches. Vegetarians will find a few items here, but not a lot. Call ahead for dinner specials; when we went to press, they were serving a New York steak and shrimp special on Wednesday for just $17 from 5 to 7pm. Later the small cafe becomes a hot spot for Molokai entertainment (p. 514).

10 Mohala St. ℂ **808/553-5256.** www.paddlersinnmolokai.com. Breakfast $5–$12; lunch $6–$20; dinner entrees $10–$25. AE, DC, DISC, MC, V. Mon–Fri 7am–8:30pm; Sat–Sun 8am–8:30pm.

Stanley's Coffee Shop and Gallery COFFEE SHOP   Breakfast, coffee, and sandwiches are on tap at this tiny cafe, located across the street from the Triangle Park and next door to St. Sophia Catholic Church. If you need an Internet connection or computer, it can supply that, too (at 10¢ per minute). Upstairs is the small gallery, which also does framing. Breakfast items range from Belgian waffles ($3.50) to eggs ($1.50 for two); lunch has a host of sandwiches (all under $5.95) and the strongest espresso coffees in Kaunakakai.

125 Puali St. ℂ **808/553-9966.** Breakfast under $6; lunch less than $9. MC, V on $20 or more. Mon–Fri 6:30am–4pm; Sat 6:30am–2pm.

Sundown Deli ✪ DELI   From "gourmet saimin" to spinach pie, Sundown's offerings are home-cooked and healthful, with daily specials that include vegetarian quiche, vegetarian lasagna, and club sandwiches. The sandwiches (like smoked turkey and chicken salad) and several salads (Caesar, Oriental, stuffed tomato) are served daily, with a soup that changes by the day (clam chowder, Portuguese bean, cream of broccoli). Vitamins, T-shirts, and snacks are sold in this tiny cafe, but most of the business is takeout.

145 Puali St. (across the street from Veteran's Memorial Park). ℂ **808/553-3713.** Sandwiches, soups, and salads $3.95–$7.50. No credit cards. Mon–Fri 7:30am–3:30pm.

EN ROUTE TO THE NORTH COAST
INEXPENSIVE

Kualapuu Cook House AMERICAN   Unfortunately this former plantation house, now under new ownership, is no longer the yummy diner it once was. Not only was I disappointed in the quality of our food, but the restaurant's poor sanitation (filled with flies) was a very unpleasant surprise. To top it all off, the once-friendly service has disappeared and a not-so-happy waitstaff grudgingly takes your order.

Farrington Hwy., 1 block west of Hwy. 470, Kualapuu. ℂ **808/567-9655.** Breakfast under $8.50; lunch under $10; dinner under $20. No credit cards. Tues–Sat 7am–8pm; Mon 7am–2pm.

THE WEST END
MODERATE

Maunaloa Dining Room ⚑ MOLOKAI REGIONAL   Molokai has never had anything resembling fine dining, but this restaurant changes the picture, with fresh Molokai ingredients in cross-cultural preparations. Breakfast features banana-stuffed French toast made from Molokai sweetbread or eggs with taro hash. Dinner entrees include fresh fish with saffron seafood risotto, mahimahi with spicy corn and black bean relish, country-smoked meatloaf, and fettuccine with Molokai Ranch sausage. The Sunday night all-you-can-eat buffet features a wok station with stir-fried vegetables and meats. Wednesday's buffet features salads and a pasta station (with a range of toppings). The room's ambience fits the *paniolo* surroundings.

The Lodge at Molokai Ranch, Maunaloa. ✆ **888/627-8082** or 808/660-2824. Reservations recommended for dinner. Breakfast entrees $7.50–$16; dinner main courses $19–$29; Sun buffet $22, kids under 12 $10; Wed pasta buffet $20. AE, DC, DISC, MC, V. Mon–Sat 7–10am and 6–9pm; Sun 7–10am and 5–9pm buffet. Lunch served 10am–4pm in the bar, most sandwiches under $12.

THE EAST END
INEXPENSIVE

Mana'e Goods and Grindz ⚑ AMERICAN   Formerly the Neighborhood Store, this place has a new name, but it's still the same quick stop market/lunch counter. It's nothing fancy, and that's what I love about it. Near mile marker 16 in the Pukoo area en route to the East End, this tiny store appears like a mirage, complete with a large parking area and picnic tables. The place serves omelets, Portuguese sausage, and other breakfast specials (brunch is very popular); it then segues into sandwiches, salads, mahimahi plates, and varied over-the-counter lunch offerings, served on paper plates with plastic utensils. Favorites include the mahimahi plate lunch, the chicken katsu, and the Mexican plate, each one with a tried-and-true home-cooked flavor. There are daily specials, ethnic dishes, and some vegetarian options, as well as burgers (including a killer veggie burger), saimin, and legendary desserts. Made-on-Maui Roselani ice cream is a featured attraction. A Molokai treasure, this is the only grocery store on the East End (see "Shopping," later in this chapter).

Pukoo. ✆ **808/558-8498.** Most items less than $10. MC, V. Daily store hours 8am–5pm; food service Mon–Fri 9am–5pm and Sat–Sun 8am–5pm.

5 Beaches

With imposing sea cliffs on one side and lazy fish ponds on the other, Molokai has little room for beaches along its 106-mile coast. Still, a big gold-sand beach flourishes on the West End, and you'll find tiny pocket beaches on the East End. The emptiness of Molokai's beaches is both a blessing and a curse: The seclusion means no lifeguards on any of the beaches. See the "Molokai" map on p. 481 for locations of these beaches.

KAUNAKAKAI
ONE ALII BEACH PARK

This thin strip of sand, once reserved for the *alii* (chiefs), is the oldest public beach park on Molokai. You'll find One Alii Beach Park (*One* is pronounced *o*-nay, not *won*) by a coconut grove on the outskirts of Kaunakakai. Safe for swimmers of all ages and abilities, it's often crowded with families on weekends, but it can be all yours on weekdays. Facilities include outdoor showers, restrooms, and free parking.

THE WEST END
KEPUHI BEACH

Golfers see this picturesque golden strand in front of the Kaluakoi Resort and Golf Course as just another sand trap, but sunbathers like the semiprivate grassy dunes; they're seldom, if ever, crowded. Beachcombers often find what they're looking for here, but swimmers have to dodge lava rocks and risk riptides. And look out for errant golf balls. There are no facilities or lifeguards, but cold drinks and restrooms are handy at the resort.

PAPOHAKU BEACH 𝕽𝕽

Nearly 3 miles long and 300 feet wide, gold-sand Papohaku Beach is one of the biggest in Hawaii (17-mile-long Polihale Beach on Kauai is the biggest). It's great for walking, beachcombing, picnics, and sunset watching year-round. The big surf and riptides make swimming risky except in summer, when the waters are calmer. Go early in the day, when the tropic sun is less fierce and the winds are calm. The beach is so big that you may never see another soul. Facilities include outdoor showers, restrooms, picnic grounds, and free parking.

THE EAST END
HALAWA BEACH PARK 𝕽

At the foot of scenic Halawa Valley is this beautiful black-sand beach with a palm-fringed lagoon, a wave-lashed island offshore, and a distant view of the West Maui Mountains across the Pailolo Channel. The swimming is safe in the shallows close to shore, but where the waterfall stream meets the sea, the ocean is often murky and unnerving. A winter swell creases the mouth of Halawa Valley on the north side of the bay and attracts a crowd of local surfers. Facilities are minimal; bring your own water. To get here, take King Kamehameha V Highway (Hwy. 450) east to the end.

MURPHY BEACH PARK (KUMIMI BEACH PARK)

In 1970 the Molokai Jaycees wanted to create a sandy beach park with a good swimming area for the children of the East End. They chose a section known as Kumimi Beach, which was owned by the Pu'u o Hoku Ranch. The beach was a dump—literally. The ranch owner, George Murphy, gave his permission to use the site as a park, and the Jaycees cleaned it up and built three small pavilions, plus picnic tables and barbecue grills. Officially, the park is called the George Murphy Beach Park (or just Murphy Beach Park), but some old-timers still call it Kumimi Beach, and, just to make things really confusing, some people call it Jaycees Park.

It's a small park shaded by ironwood trees that line a white-sand beach. It's generally a very safe swimming area, and on calm days snorkeling and diving are great outside the reef. Fishermen also frequently come here to look for papio and other Island fish.

SANDY BEACH 𝕽

Molokai's most popular swimming beach—ideal for families with small kids—is a roadside pocket of gold sand protected by a reef, with a great view of Maui and Lanai. You'll find it off the King Kamehameha V Highway (Hwy. 450) at mile marker 20. There are no facilities—just you, the sun, the sand, and the surf.

6 Watersports

The best place to rent beach toys (snorkels, boogie boards, beach chairs, fishing poles, and more) is **Molokai Outdoors Activities,** in the lobby of Hotel Molokai, just outside Kaunakakai (© **877/553-4477** or 808/553-4477; www.molokai-outdoors.com). They have everything you'll need for a day at the beach and can also give you advice on where to find a great swimming beach or where the waves are breaking. Another good place to check out is **Molokai Fish & Dive,** Kaunakakai (© **808/553-5926;** www.molokaifishanddive.com). You can rent snorkeling gear, fishing gear, even ice chests here. This is also a hot spot for fishing news and tips on what's running where.

For general advice on the activities listed below, see "Special-Interest Trips" in chapter 2.

BODY BOARDING (BOOGIE BOARDING) & BODYSURFING

Molokai has only three beaches that offer ridable waves for body boarding and bodysurfing: Papohaku, Kepuhi, and Halawa. Even these beaches are only for experienced bodysurfers, due to the strength of the rip currents and undertows. You can rent boogie boards with fins for just $5 a day or $20 a week at **Molokai Outdoors Activities** (© **877/553-4477** or 808/553-4477; www.molokai-outdoors.com).

OCEAN KAYAKING

During the summer months, when the waters on the north shore are calm, Molokai offers some of the most spectacular kayaking in Hawaii. However, most of Molokai is for the experienced kayaker only. You must be adept in paddling through open ocean swells and rough waves.

Molokai Outdoors Activities (© **877/553-4477** or 808/553-4477; www.molokai-outdoors.com) has sunset tours ($48 per person) of the ancient Hawaii fish ponds and a coastline tour ($63 per person). They also rent kayaks; rates start at $12 an hour and $26 a day.

SCUBA DIVING

Want to see turtles or manta rays up close? How about sharks? Molokai resident Bill Kapuni has been diving the waters around the island his entire life; he'll be happy to show you whatever you're brave enough to encounter. You can book him through **Molokai Fish & Dive** (© **808/553-5926;** www.molokaifishanddive.com), which offers scuba-diving trips from $135 to $275.

SNORKELING

When the waters are calm, Molokai offers excellent snorkeling; you'll see a wide range of butterfly fish, tangs, and angelfish. Good snorkeling can be found—when conditions are right—at many of Molokai's beaches (see the box titled "Molokai's Best Snorkel Spots," below). **Molokai Outdoors Activities** (© **877/553-4477** or 808/553-4477; www.molokai-outdoors.com) has the best prices on snorkeling rentals ($6 a day or $24 a week for fins, mask, and snorkel). Molokai Outdoors also offers snorkel/kayak tours for $63 per person.

For snorkeling tours on a boat, Walter Naki of **Molokai Action Adventures** (© **808/558-8184**) offers leisurely snorkeling, diving, and swimming trips in his 21-foot Boston whaler for $125 per person for a 4- to 6-hour custom tour.

SPORTFISHING

Molokai's waters can provide prime sporting opportunities, whether you're looking for big-game sportfishing or bottom fishing. The number-one person we recommend is

Molokai's Best Snorkel Spots

Most Molokai beaches are too dangerous for snorkeling in winter, when big waves and strong currents are generated by storms that sweep down from Alaska. From mid-September to April, stick to Murphy Beach Park (also known as Kumimi Beach Park) on the East End. In summer, roughly May to mid-September, the Pacific Ocean turns into a flat lake, and the whole west coast of Molokai opens up for snorkeling. Mike Holmes, of Molokai Ranch & Fun Hogs Hawaii, says the best spots are as follows:

Kawaikiunui, Ilio Point, and **Pohaku Moiliili** (West End) These are all special places seldom seen by even those who live on Molokai. You can reach Kawaikiunui and Pohaku Moiliili on foot after a long, hot, dusty ride in a four-wheel-drive vehicle, but it's much easier and quicker to go by sea. See above for places to rent a kayak and get advice. It's about 2 miles as the crow flies from Pohaku Moiliili to Ilio Point.

Kapukahehu (Dixie Maru) Beach (West End) This gold-sand family beach is well protected, and the reef is close and shallow. The name *Dixie Maru* comes from a 1920s Japanese fishing boat stranded off the rocky shore. One of the Molokai Ranch cowboys hung the wrecked boat's nameplate on a gate by Kapukahehu Beach, and the name stuck. To get here, take Kaluakoi Road to the end of the pavement, and then take the footpath 300 feet to the beach.

Murphy (Kumimi) Beach Park ⊛ (East End) This beach is located between mile markers 20 and 21, off Kamehameha V Highway. The reef here is easily reachable, and the waters are calm year-round.

Captain Clay, of **Hallelujah Hou Fishing** (② 808/336-1870; www.hallelujahhou fishing.com). Captain Clay, who also is a minister and the nicest guy you may ever meet, leads light tackle guided fishing trips on his 24-foot power catamaran. The price is $295 to $395 for up to four adults for a half-day. He provides all tackle and bottled water; you bring the sunscreen. If you catch something, he'll even filet it for dinner. A warning—there is no "head" (toilet) on the boat.

When customers are scarce, Capt. Joe Reich goes commercial fishing, so he always knows where the fish are biting. He runs **Alyce C Sportfishing** out of Kaunakakai Harbor (② 808/558-8377; ace@aloha.net). A full day of fishing for up to six people is $450, three-quarters of a day is $400, and half a day is $350. You can usually persuade him to do a whale-watching cruise during the winter months.

For fly-fishing or light-tackle reef-fish trolling, contact Walter Naki at **Molokai Action Adventures** (② 808/558-8184). A full-day trip in his 21-foot Boston whaler, for up to four people, is $125 per person.

For deep-sea fishing, contact **Fun Hogs Hawaii,** who books through Molokai Outdoors Activities (see below) for fishing excursions on a 27-foot, fully equipped sportfishing vessel. Prices are $365 for six passengers for 4 hours, $417 for 6 hours, and $521 for 8 hours.

If you just want to try your luck casting along the shoreline, **Molokai Outdoors Activities** (© 877/553-4477 or 808/553-4477; www.molokai-outdoors.com) offers the least expensive fishing poles for rent ($5 a day or $24 for the week) and can tell you where they're biting.

SURFING

Depending on the time of year and the wave conditions, Molokai can offer some great surfing for the beginner as well as the expert. **Molokai Outdoors Activities** (© 877/553-4477 or 808/553-4477; www.molokai-outdoors.com) not only will know where the waves are, but also rent soft surfboards for $13 a day. Good surfing spots include Kaunakakai Wharf in town, Hale O Lono Beach and Papohaku Beach on the West End, and Halawa Beach on the East End.

7 Hiking & Camping

HIKING MOLOKAI'S PEPEOPAE TRAIL

Molokai's most awesome hike is the **Pepeopae Trail** 🌺🌺, which takes you back a few million years. On the cloud-draped trail (actually a boardwalk across the bog), you'll see mosses, sedges, native violets, knee-high ancient ohia, and lichens that evolved in total isolation over eons. Eerie intermittent mists blowing in and out will give you an idea of this island at its creation.

The narrow boardwalk, built by volunteers, protects the bog and keeps you out of the primal ooze. Don't venture off it; you could damage this fragile environment or get lost. The 3-mile round-trip takes about 90 minutes to hike—but first you have to drive about 20 miles from Kaunakakai, deep into the Molokai Forest Preserve on a four-wheel-drive road. *Warning:* Don't try this with a regular rental car. Plan a full day for this outing. Better yet, go on a guided nature hike with the **Nature Conservancy of Hawaii,** which guards this unusual ecosystem. For information, write to the Nature Conservancy at 1116 Smith St., Suite 201, Honolulu, HI 96817. No permit is required for this easy hike. Call ahead (© **808/537-4508** or 808/553-5236; www.nature.org/wherewework/northamerica/states/hawaii/travel/art16727.html) to check on the condition of the ungraded, four-wheel-drive, red-dirt road that leads to the trail head and to let people know that you'll be up there.

To get here, take Highway 460 west from Kaunakakai for 3½ miles and turn right before the Maunawainui Bridge onto the unmarked Molokai Forest Reserve Road (sorry, there aren't any road signs). The pavement ends at the cemetery; continue on the dirt road. After about 2 to 2½ miles, you'll see a sign telling you that you are now in the Molokai Forest Reserve. At the Waikolu Lookout and picnic area, which is just over 9 miles on the Molokai Forest Reserve Road, sign in at the box near the entrance. Continue on the road for another 5 miles to a fork in the road with the sign PUU KOLEKOLE pointing to the right side of the fork. Do not turn right; instead, continue straight at the fork, which leads to the clearly marked trail head. The drive will take about 45 minutes.

HIKING TO KALAUPAPA 🌺🌺

This hike to the site of Molokai's famous leper colony is like going down a switchback staircase with what seems like a million steps. You don't always see the breathtaking view because you're too busy watching your step. It's easier going down (surprise!)—in about an hour, you'll go 2½ miles, from 2,000 feet to sea level. The trip up sometimes takes twice as long. The trail head starts on the mauka (inland) side of Highway

Frommer's Favorite Molokai Experiences

Riding a Mule into a Leper Colony. Don't pass up the opportunity to see this hauntingly beautiful peninsula. Buzzy Sproat's mules (p. 506) go up and down the 3-mile Kalaupapa Trail to Molokai's famous leper colony. The views are breathtaking: You'll see the world's highest sea cliffs (over 300 stories tall) and waterfalls plunging thousands of feet into the ocean. If you're afraid of heights, catch the views from the Kalaupapa Lookout.

Venturing into the Garden of Eden. Drive the 30 miles along Molokai's East End. Take your time. Stop to smell the flowers and pick guavas by the side of the road. Pull over for a swim. Wave at every car you pass and every person you see. At the end of the road, stand on the beach at Halawa Valley and see Hawaii as it must have looked in A.D. 650, when the first people arrived on the islands.

Celebrating the Ancient Hula. Hula is the heartbeat of Hawaiian culture, and Molokai is its birthplace. Although most visitors to Hawaii never get to see the real thing, it's possible to see it here—once a year, on the third Saturday in May, when Molokai celebrates the birth of the hula at its **Ka Hula Piko Festival.** The daylong affair includes dance, music, food, and crafts. For details, contact the Moloka`i Visitor Association (© **800/800-6367** or 808/553-3876; www.molokai-hawaii.com).

Strolling the Sands at Papohaku. Go early, when the tropical sun isn't so fierce, and stroll this 3-mile stretch of unspoiled golden sand on Molokai's West End. It's one of the longest beaches in Hawaii. The big surf and riptides make swimming somewhat risky, but Papohaku is perfect for walking, beachcombing, and, in the evening, sunset watching.

Traveling Back in Time on the Pepeopae Trail. This awesome hike takes you through the Molokai Forest Reserve (p. 499) and back a few million years in time. Along the misty trail (actually a boardwalk across the bog), expect close encounters of the botanical kind: mosses, sedges, violets, lichens, and knee-high ancient ohia.

Soaking in the Warm Waters off Sandy Beach. On the East End, about 20 miles outside Kaunakakai—just before the road starts to climb to Halawa Valley—lies a small pocket of white sand known as Sandy Beach. Submerging yourself here in the warm, calm waters (an outer reef protects the cove) is a sensuous experience par excellence.

470, just past the Mule Barn. Check in here at 7:30am, get a permit, and go before the mule train departs. You must be 16 or older (it's an old state law that kept kids out of the leper colony) and should be in good shape. Wear good hiking boots or sneakers.

HIKING THE WEST END

Molokai Outdoors Activities (© **877/553-4477** or 808/553-4477; www.molokai-outdoors.com) offers an all-day (6–8 hr.) Halawa Cultural hike full of historical information on East Molokai. The hike is rated intermediate to advanced, with a distance

Snorkeling among Clouds of Butterfly Fish. The calm waters off Murphy (Kumimi) Beach, on the East End, are perfect for snorkelers. Just don your gear and head to the reef, where you'll find lots of exotic tropical fish, including long-nosed butterfly fish, saddle wrasses, and convict tangs.

Kayaking along the North Shore. This is the Hawaii of your dreams: waterfalls thundering down sheer cliffs, remote sand beaches, miles of tropical vegetation, and the wind whispering in your ear. The best times to go are late March and early April, or in summer, especially August to September, when the normally galloping ocean lies down flat.

Watching the Sunset from a Coconut Grove. Kapuaiwa Coconut Grove/ Kiowea Park (p. 503), off Maunaloa Highway (Hwy. 460), is a perfect place to watch the sunset. The sky behind the coconut trees fills with a kaleidoscope of colors as the sun sinks into the Pacific. Be careful where you sit, though: Falling coconuts could have you seeing stars well before dusk.

Sampling the Local Brew. Saunter up to the Espresso Bar at the Coffees of Hawaii Plantation Store (p. 512) in Kualapuu for a fresh cup of java made from beans that were grown, processed, and packed on this 450-acre plantation. While you sip, survey the vast collection of native crafts.

Tasting Aloha at a Macadamia Nut Farm. It could be the owner, Tuddie Purdy, and his friendly disposition that make the macadamia nuts here taste so good. Or it could be his years of practice in growing, harvesting, and shelling them on his 1½-acre farm. Either way, Purdy produces a perfect crop. See how he does it on a short, free tour of Purdy's All-Natural Macadamia Nut Farm (p. 504) in Hoolehua, just a nut's throw from the airport.

Talking Story with the Locals. The number-one favorite pastime of most islanders is "talking story," or exchanging experiences and knowledge. You can probably find residents more than willing to share their wisdom with you while fishing from the wharf at Kaunakakai, hanging out at Molokai Fish & Dive (p. 511), or having coffee at any of the island's restaurants.

Posting a Nut. Why send a picturesque postcard to your friends and family back home when you can send a coconut? The Hoolehua Post Office (p. 503) will supply the coconuts if you'll supply the $4.05 postage fee.

of 2.2 miles. It has two river crossings, and some rocky areas along the trails, with possible fallen trees after a storm. The cost is $188 per person and includes a picnic lunch.

Molokai Fish & Dive (© **808/553-5926;** www.molokaifishanddive.com) offers a hike into Halawa Valley for $75 (see p. 510).

CAMPING
Bring your own camping equipment, as none is available for rent on the island.

AT THE BEACH

One of the best year-round places to camp on Molokai is **Papohaku Beach Park** 🏕, on the island's West End. This drive-up seaside site makes a great getaway. Facilities include restrooms, drinking water, outdoor showers, barbecue grills, and picnic tables. Groceries and gas are available in Maunaloa, 6 miles away. Kaluakoi Resort is a mile away. Get camping permits by contacting **Maui County Parks Department,** P.O. Box 526, Kaunakakai, HI 96748 (② **808/553-3204;** www.co.maui.hi.us/parks/permits/parkspermits.htm). Camping is limited to 3 days, but if nobody else has applied, the time limit is waived. The cost is $3 a person per night.

IN AN IRONWOOD FOREST

At the end of Highway 470 is the 234-acre piney woods known as **Palaau State Park** 🏕🏕, home to the Kalaupapa Lookout (the best vantage point for seeing the historic leper colony if you're not hiking or riding a mule in). It's airy and cool in the park's ironwood forest, where many love to camp at the designated state campground. Camping fees for Hawaii State Parks are $5 per campsite per night, and you'll need a permit from the **State Division of Parks** (② **808/567-6618;** www.hawaii.gov/dlnr/dsp/fees. html). For more on the park, see p. 504.

8 Golf & Other Outdoor Activities

GOLF

Golf is one of Molokai's best-kept secrets; it's challenging and fun, tee times are open, and the rates are lower than your score will be. After being closed for a number of years for extensive renovations (repairs to irrigation, new grass planted, redesigned bunkers, and narrower fairways), the **Kaluakoi Golf Course** (② **808/552-0255**) is open again. Most of the work was cosmetic, and the Ted Robinson–designed course is still as challenging as ever. Using the natural terrain and narrow fairways, there are some tough bunkers and water hazards to maneuver around, plus a stiff wind to contend with. The first 9 holes are at sea level, with panoramic views over isolated white-sand Papohaku Beach, with the island of Oahu in the distance. The back 9 holes play up along lush green hillsides, over a tropical gulch, and back down to the shore. Kaluakoi offers a golf range, a practice area, and three sets of tees to accommodate all levels of golfers. Greens fees are $75 with cart.

Ironwood Hills Golf Course, off Kalae Highway (② **808/567-6000**), is located just before the Molokai Mule Ride Mule Barn, on the road to the Lookout. Built in 1929 by Del Monte Plantation for its executives, it's one of the oldest courses in the state. This unusual course, which sits in the cool air at 1,200 feet, delights with its rich foliage, open fairways, and spectacular views of the rest of the island. *Tip:* After teeing off on the 6th hole, just take whatever clubs you need to finish playing the hole and a driver for the 7th hole, and park your bag under a tree. The climb to the 7th hole is steep—you'll be glad that you're carrying only a few clubs. Greens fees are $18 for 9 holes or $24 for 18 holes. Club rentals are $7 for 9 holes and $12 for 18.

BICYCLING

Molokai is a great place to see by bicycle. The roads are not very busy, and there are great places to pull off the road and take a quick dip.

Molokai Outdoors Activities, in the lobby of Hotel Molokai, just outside Kaunakakai (② **877/553-4477** or 808/553-4477; www.molokai-outdoors.com), offers bike rentals for $13 an hour, $26 a day, and $113 a week, including a complimentary bicycle rack for your car.

The best mountain biking in the state is on the trails of **The Lodge at Molokai Ranch** (booked through **Molokai Fish & Dive;** © 808/553-5926; www.molokaifish anddive.com). Imagine 65,000 acres with intercrossing trails that weave up and down the West End to the beach—simply spectacular. Guided tours for a downhill "gravity ride" start at $59, and bike rentals start at $39 a day.

HORSEBACK RIDING

One of the most scenic places to go riding on Molokai is **Pu'u O Hoku Ranch** (© 808/558-8109; www.puuohoku.com), about 25 miles outside Kaunakakai on the East End. Guided trail rides pass through green pasture on one of the largest working ranches on Molokai and then head up into the high mountain forest. Don't forget your camera: There are plenty of scenic views of waterfalls, the Pacific Ocean, and the islands of Maui and Lanai in the distance. Rates are $55 for an hour-long ride, $75 for a 2-hour ride, and $120 for a beach adventure.

For those looking for a little more than just a horseback ride, **The Lodge at Molokai Ranch** (booked through **Molokai Fish & Dive;** © 808/553-5926; www. molokaifishanddive.com) offers a "Paniolo Roundup," where you can learn horsemanship from the ranch's working cowboys and compete in traditional rodeo games; the half-day adventure is $85. Two-hour trail rides also are $85.

TENNIS

The only two tennis courts on Molokai are located at the **Mitchell Pauole Center,** in Kaunakakai (© 808/553-5141). Both are lit for night play and are available free on a first-come, first-served basis, with a 45-minute time limit if someone is waiting. You can also rent tennis rackets ($5 a day, $24 a week) and balls ($3 a day, $12 a week) from **Molokai Outdoors Activities** (© 877/553-4477 or 808/553-4477; www. molokai-outdoors.com).

9 Seeing the Sights

Note: You'll find the following attractions on the "Molokai" map on p. 481.

IN & AROUND KAUNAKAKAI

Kapuaiwa Coconut Grove/Kiowea Park 🔅 *Kids*   This royal grove—1,000 coconut trees on 10 acres planted in 1863 by the island's high chief Kapua'iwa (later, King Kamehameha V)—is a major roadside attraction. The shoreline park is a favorite subject of sunset photographers and visitors, who delight in a hand-lettered sign that warns: DANGER: FALLING COCONUTS. In its backyard, across the highway, stands Church Row: seven churches, each a different denomination—clear evidence of the missionary impact on Hawaii.

Along Maunaloa Hwy. (Hwy. 460), 2 miles west of Kaunakakai.

Post-A-Nut 🔅   Postmaster Margaret Keahi-Leary will help you say "Aloha" with a Molokai coconut. Just write a message on the coconut with a felt-tip pen, and she'll send it via U.S. mail. Coconuts are free, but postage starts at $4.05 for a mainland-bound coconut.

Hoolehua Post Office, Puu Peelua Ave. (Hwy. 480), near Maunaloa Hwy. (Hwy. 460). © 808/567-6144. Mon–Fri 7:30–11:30am and 12:30–4:30pm.

Purdy's All-Natural Macadamia Nut Farm (Na Hua O'Ka Aina) ⍟ *Finds*   The Purdys have made macadamia-nut buying an entertainment event, offering tours of the homestead and giving lively demonstrations of nutshell-cracking in the shade of their towering trees. The tour of the 70-year-old nut farm explains the growth, bearing, harvesting, and shelling processes.

Lihi Pali Ave. (behind Molokai High School), Hoolehua. ☎ 808/567-6601. www.molokai-aloha.com/macnuts. Free admission. Mon–Fri 9:30am–3:30pm; Sat 10am–2pm. Closed on holidays.

THE NORTH COAST

Even if you don't get a chance to see Hawaii's most dramatic coast in its entirety—not many people do—you shouldn't miss the opportunity to glimpse it from the **Kalaupapa Lookout** at Palaau State Park. On the way, there are a few diversions (arranged here in geographical order).

EN ROUTE TO THE NORTH COAST

Coffees of Hawaii   The defunct Del Monte pineapple town of Kualapuu is rising again—only this time, coffee is the catch, not pineapple. Located in the cool foothills, Coffees of Hawaii has planted coffee beans on 600 acres of former pineapple land. The plantation irrigates the plants with a high-tech, continuous water-and-fertilizer drip system. You can see it all on the self-guided walking tour or the Morning Espresso Tour, which is lead by a guide from the plantation and gives you a tour of the sorting facility and processing procedures. The less physically motivated should try the Mule Drawn Wagon tour, great for a family. The 2-hour tour is lead by a guide and two mules (Moana and Leila or Lilo and Loke) through the coffee fields and around the reservoir. Afternoon hiking adventures include a 2½-hour hike through the coffee fields to the top of Kualapuu Hill for a terrific view of Molokai. The Plantation Store sells arts and crafts from Molokai. Stop by the Espresso Bar for a Mocha Mama, an intoxicating blend of coffee, ice cream, and chocolate that will keep you going all day—maybe even all night.

1630 Farrington Ave., (near the junction of Hwy. 470), Kualapuu. ☎ 877/322-FARM or 808/567-9490. Ext 26. www.coffeesofhawaii.com. Mon–Fri 8am–5pm; Sat 8am–4pm; Sun 8am–2pm. Self-guided tour free. Morning Espresso Tour Mon–Fri 10am; $20 adults, $10 kids 5–10 years, under 5 free. Mule Drawn Wagon Tour Mon–Fri 8am and 1pm, Sat–Sun 8am; $35 adults, $10 kids 5–10, under 5 free. Afternoon Hiking Adventures daily 3–5:30pm; free.

Molokai Museum and Cultural Center   En route to the California Gold Rush in 1849, Rudolph W. Meyer (a German professor) came to Molokai, married the high chieftess Kalama, and began to operate a small sugar plantation near his home. Now on the National Register of Historic Places, this restored 1878 sugar mill, with its century-old steam engine, mule-driven cane crusher, copper clarifiers, and redwood evaporating pan (all in working order), is the last of its kind in Hawaii. The mill also houses a museum that traces the history of sugar growing on Molokai and has special events, such as wine tastings, taro festivals, an annual music festival, and occasional classes in ukulele making, loom weaving, and sewing. Call for a schedule.

Meyer Sugar Mill, Hwy. 470 (just after the turnoff for the Ironwood Hills Golf Course and 2 miles below Kalaupapa Overlook), Kalae. ☎ 808/567-6436. Admission $3.50 adults, $1 students. Mon–Sat 10am–2pm.

Palaau State Park ⍟   This 234-acre piney-woods park, 8 miles out of Kaunakakai, doesn't look like much until you get out of the car and take a hike, which literally puts you between a rock and a hard place. Go right, and you end up on the edge of

Kids Especially for Kids

Flying a Kite (p. 513)   Not only can you get a guaranteed-to-fly kite at the **Big Wind Kite Factory** (© 808/552-2634) in Maunaloa, but kite designer Jonathan Socher offers free kite-flying classes to kids, who'll learn how to make their kites soar, swoop, and, most important, stay in the air for more than 5 minutes.

Spending the Day at Murphy (Kumimi) Beach Park (p. 496)   Just beyond Waialua on the East End is this small wayside park that's perfect for kids. You'll find safe swimming conditions, plenty of shade from the ironwood trees, and small pavilions with picnic tables and barbecue grills.

Renting Gear   You don't have to schlep your car seat, jogging stroller, regular stroller, or portable crib to Molokai. **Molokai Outdoors Activities**, in the lobby of Hotel Molokai, just outside Kaunakakai (© 877/553-4477 or 808/553-4477; www.molokai-outdoors.com), has all that equipment for rent at very reasonable prices (daily and weekly rates).

Molokai's magnificent sea cliffs, with its panoramic view of the well-known Kalaupapa leper colony; go left, and you come face to face with a stone phallus.

If you have no plans to scale the cliffs by mule or on foot (see "Hiking & Camping," earlier in this chapter), the **Kalaupapa Lookout** 𝕬𝕬𝕬 is the only place from which to see the former place of exile. The trail is marked, and historic photos and interpretive signs will explain what you're seeing.

It's airy and cool in the ironwood forest, where camping is free at the designated state campground. You'll need a permit from the **State Division of Parks** (© 808/ 567-6618). Not many people seem to camp here, perhaps because of the legend associated with the **Phallic Rock** 𝕬. Six feet high and pointed at an angle that means business, Molokai's famous Phallic Rock is a legendary fertility tool—according to Hawaiian legend, a woman who wishes to become pregnant need only spend the night near the rock and, *voilà!*

Phallic Rock is at the end of a well-worn uphill path that passes an ironwood grove and several other rocks that vaguely resemble sexual body parts. No mistaking the big guy, though. Supposedly, it belonged to Nanahoa, a demigod who quarreled with his wife, Kawahuna, over a pretty girl. In the tussle, Kawahuna was thrown over the cliff, and both husband and wife were turned to stone. Of all the phallic rocks in Hawaii and the Pacific, this is the one to see. It's featured on a postcard with a tiny, awestruck Japanese woman standing next to it.

At the end of Hwy. 470.

THE LEGACY OF FATHER DAMIEN: KALAUPAPA NATIONAL HISTORIC PARK 𝕬𝕬𝕬

Kalaupapa, an old tongue of lava that sticks out to form a peninsula, became infamous because of man's inhumanity to victims of a formerly incurable contagious disease.

King Kamehameha V sent the first lepers—nine men and three women—into exile on January 6, 1866. By 1874, more than 11,000 lepers had been dispatched to die in one of the world's most beautiful—and lonely—places. They called it Kalaupapa, "The Place of the Living Dead."

Leprosy is actually one of the world's least contagious diseases, transmitted only by direct, repetitive contact over a long period of time. It's caused by a germ, *Mycobacterium leprae*, that attacks the nerves, skin, and eyes, and is found mainly, but not exclusively, in tropical regions. American scientists found a cure for the disease in the 1940s.

Before science intervened, there was Father Damien. Born to wealth in Belgium, Joseph de Veuster traded a life of excess for exile among lepers, devoting himself to caring for the afflicted at Kalaupapa. Horrified by the conditions in the leper colony, Father Damien worked at Kalaupapa for 11 years, building houses, schools, and churches, and giving hope to his patients. He died on April 15, 1889, in Kalaupapa, of leprosy. He was 49.

A hero nominated for Catholic sainthood, Father Damien is buried not in his tomb next to Molokai's St. Philomena Church, but in his native Belgium. Well, most of him anyway. His hand was recently returned to Molokai and was reinterred at Kalaupapa as a relic of his martyrdom.

This small peninsula, at the base of ramparts that rise like temples against the Pacific, is probably the final resting place of more than 11,000 souls. The sand dunes are littered with grave markers, sorted by the religious affiliation—Catholic, Protestant, Buddhist—of those who died here. But so many are buried in unmarked graves that no accurate census of the dead exists.

Kalaupapa is now a National Historic Park (© **808/567-6802;** www.nps.gov/kala) and one of Hawaii's richest archaeological preserves, with sites that date from A.D. 1000. About 60 former patients chose to remain in this tidy village, where statues of angels stand in the yards of the whitewashed houses. The original name for their former affliction, leprosy, was officially banned in Hawaii by the state legislature in 1981. The name used now is "Hansen's disease," for Dr. Gerhard Hansen of Norway, who discovered the germ in 1873.

Kalaupapa welcomes visitors who arrive on foot, by mule, or by small plane. Father Damien's St. Philomena church, built in 1872, is open to visitors, who can see it from a yellow school bus driven by resident tour guide Richard Marks, an ex-seaman and sheriff who survived the disease. You won't be able to roam freely, and you'll be allowed to enter only the museum, the crafts shop, and the church.

MULE RIDES TO KALAUPAPA 🐎🐎🐎 The first turn's a gasp, and it's all downhill from there. You can close your eyes and hold on for dear life, or slip the reins over the pommel and sit back, letting the mule do the walking down the precipitous path to Kalaupapa National Historic Park.

Even if you have only 1 day to spend on Molokai, spend it on a mule. This is a once-in-a-lifetime ride. The cliffs are taller than a 300-story skyscraper, but Buzzy Sproat's mules go safely up and down the narrow 3-mile trail daily, rain or shine. Starting at the top of the nearly perpendicular ridge (1,600 ft. high), the surefooted mules step down the muddy trail, pausing often on the 26 switchbacks to calculate their next move—and always, it seems to me, veering a little too close to the edge. Each switchback is numbered; by the time you get to number four, you'll catch your breath, put the mule on cruise control, and begin to enjoy Hawaii's most awesome trail ride.

The mule tours are offered once a day Monday through Saturday (the park is closed on Sun) starting at 8am, and they last until about 3:30pm. It costs $165 per person for the all-day adventure, which includes the round-trip mule ride, a guided tour of the settlement, a visit to Father Damien's church and tomb, lunch at Kalawao, and souvenirs. Book in advance, as these tours do often fill up. To go, you must be at least 16 years old and physically fit, and weigh less than 250 pounds. Contact **Molokai Mule Ride** ✦✦✦, 100 Kalae Hwy., Suite 104, on Highway 470, 5 miles north of Highway 460 (© **800/567-7550,** or 808/567-6088 between 8am and 10pm; www. muleride.com). Advance reservations (at least 2 weeks ahead) are required.

SEEING KALAUPAPA BY PLANE The fastest and easiest way to get to Kalaupapa is by hopping on a plane and zipping to Kalaupapa airport. From here, you can pick up the same Kalaupapa tour that the mule riders and hikers take. **Molokai Mule Ride** (see above) will pick you up at the Kalaupapa airport and take you to some of the area's most scenic spots, including Kalawao, where Father Damien's church still stands, and the town of Kalaupapa. Package includes round-trip airfare from Honolulu, hotel pickup, guided mule tour, entry permits, Historical Park tour, and a picnic lunch for $319 per person, two-person minimum.

If you are coming from Maui, your choices are either by ferry (where you will hike in and back out in 1 day or take the mule ride, and then stay overnight due to the ferry's schedule) or by plane (call them and they can help set up a charter plane).

If you are on Molokai and want to fly directly into Kalaupapa, Molokai Mule Ride will book you from the Molokai Airport to Kalaupapa and include entry permits, a Historical Park tour with Damien Tours, and a light picnic lunch for $130 per person, two-person minimum.

SEEING KALAUPAPA BY FERRY/HIKING From Maui, take the *Molokai Princess* ferry to Molokai (© **800/275-6969** or 808/667-6165; www.mauiprincess.com), where you are met and transported by van to the top of the 1,700-foot sea cliffs. Here you hike down the 3-mile trail to the Kalaupapa National Historic Park; at the park, you are met by Damien Tours and given a van tour of the peninsula, during which you'll visit Father Damien's St. Philomena Church, see his early gravesite and hear the stories of struggle and courage of the residents of Kalaupapa. The only catch is you have to hike back up the 1,700-foot cliffs, where you are picked up by the van and returned to the ferry dock for the trip back to Maui. This fabulous experience really should be undertaken only by the physically fit (it will take about an hour hiking down and another 90 min. to hike back up). Cost for ferry, transportation, tour, and lunch is $277 (participants must be 16 years and older).

THE WEST END
MAUNALOA

In the first and only urban renewal on Molokai, the 1920s-era pineapple-plantation town of Maunaloa is being reinvented. Streets are getting widened and paved, and curbs and sidewalks are being added to serve a new tract of houses. Historic Maunaloa is becoming Maunaloa Village—there's already a town center with a park, restaurant, movie theater, gas station, KFC, and upscale lodge.

This master-planned village will also have a museum and artisans' studios—uptown stuff for Molokai. The downside is the constant clouds of red dust raised by construction crews.

ON THE NORTHWEST SHORE: MOOMOMI DUNES

Undisturbed for centuries, the Moomomi Dunes, on Molokai's northwest shore, are a unique treasure chest of great scientific value. The area may look like just a pile of sand as you fly over on the final approach to Hoolehua Airport, but Moomomi Dunes is much more than that. Archaeologists have found adz quarries, ancient Hawaiian burial sites, and shelter caves; botanists have identified five endangered plant species; and marine biologists are finding evidence that endangered green sea turtles are coming out from the waters once again to lay eggs here. The greatest discovery, however, belongs to Smithsonian Institute ornithologists, who have found bones of prehistoric birds—some of them flightless—that existed nowhere else on earth.

Accessible by jeep trails that thread downhill to the shore, this wild coast is buffeted by strong afternoon breezes. It's hot, dry, and windy, so take water, sunscreen, and a windbreaker.

At Kawaaloa Bay, a 20-minute walk to the west, there's a broad golden beach that you can have all to yourself. *Warning:* Due to the rough seas, stay out of the water. Within the dunes, there's a 920-acre preserve accessible via monthly guided nature tours led by the **Nature Conservancy of Hawaii;** call © **808/553-5236** or 808/524-0779 for an exact schedule and details.

To get here, take Highway 460 (Maunaloa Hwy.) from Kaunakakai; turn right onto Highway 470, and follow it to Kualapuu. At Kualapuu, turn left on Highway 480 and go through Hoolehua Village; it's 3 miles to the bay.

THE EAST END

The East End is a cool and inviting green place that's worth a drive to the end of King Kamehameha V Highway (Hwy. 450). Unfortunately, the trail that leads into the area's greatest natural attraction, Halawa Valley, is now off-limits.

A HORSEBACK RIDE TO ILIILIOPAE HEIAU

On horseback (where the elevated view is magnificent), you bump along a dirt trail through an incredible mango grove, bound for an ancient temple of human sacrifice. This temple of doom—right out of *Indiana Jones*—is Iliiliopae, a huge rectangle of stone made of 90 million rocks, overlooking the once-important village of Mapulehu and four ancient fish ponds. The horses trek under the perfumed mangoes and then head uphill through a kiawe forest filled with Java plums to the *heiau* (temple), which stands across a dry stream bed under cloud-spiked Kaunolu, the 4,970-foot island summit.

Hawaii's most powerful *heiau* attracted Kahuna (priests) from all over the islands. They came to learn the rules of human sacrifice at this university of sacred rites. Contrary to Hollywood's version, historians say that the victims here were always men, not young virgins, and that they were strangled, not thrown into a volcano, while priests sat on lauhala mats watching silently. Spooky, eh?

This is the biggest, oldest, and most famous *heiau* on Molokai. The massive 22-foot-high stone altar is dedicated to Lono, the Hawaiian god of fertility. The *heiau* resonates with *mana* (power) strong enough to lean on. Legend says Iliiliopae was built in a single night by a thousand men who passed rocks hand over hand through the Wailau Valley from the other side of the island; in exchange for the *ili'ili* (rock), each received a *'opae* (shrimp). Others say it was built by *menehune*, mythic elves who accomplished Herculean feats.

After the visit to the temple, your horse takes you back to the mango grove. Contact **Molokai Wagon Rides,** King Kamehameha V Highway (Hwy. 450), at mile marker 15, Kaunakakai, HI 96748 (© **808/558-8380**). The tour and horseback ride is $50 per person. The hour-long ride goes up to the *heiau,* then beyond it to the top of the mountain for those breathtaking views, and finally back down to the beach.

KAMAKOU PRESERVE

It's hard to believe, but close to the nearly mile-high summit here, it rains more than 80 inches a year—enough to qualify as a rainforest. The Molokai Forest, as it was historically known, is the source of 60% of Molokai's water. Nearly 3,000 acres, from the summit to the lowland forests of eucalyptus and pine, are now held by the Nature Conservancy, which has identified 219 Hawaiian plants that grow here exclusively. The preserve is also the last stand of the endangered *olomao* (Molokai thrush) and *kawawahie* (Molokai creeper).

To get to the preserve, take the Forest Reserve road from Kaunakakai. It's a 45-minute, four-wheel-drive trip on a dirt trail to Waikolu Lookout Campground; from here, you can venture into the wilderness preserve on foot across a boardwalk on a 1½-hour hike (see "Hiking Molokai's Pepeopae Trail," earlier in this chapter). For more information, contact the **Nature Conservancy** (© **808/553-5236;** www.nature.org).

EN ROUTE TO HALAWA VALLEY

No visit to Molokai is complete without at least a passing glance at the island's **ancient fish ponds,** a singular achievement in Pacific aquaculture. With their hunger for fresh fish and lack of ice or refrigeration, Hawaiians perfected aquaculture in A.D. 1400, before Christopher Columbus "discovered" America. They built gated, U-shaped stone and coral walls on the shore to catch fish on the incoming tide and then would raise them in captivity. The result: a constant, ready supply of fresh fish.

The ponds, which stretch for 20 miles along Molokai's south shore and are visible from Kamehameha V Highway (Hwy. 450), offer insight into the island's ancient population. It took something like a thousand people to tend a single fish pond, and more than 60 ponds once existed on this coast. Some are silted in by red-dirt runoff from south coast gulches; others are in use by folks who raise fish and seaweed.

The largest, 54-acre **Keawa Nui Pond,** is surrounded by a 3-foot-high, 2,000-foot-long stone wall. **Alii Fish Pond,** reserved for kings, is visible through the coconut groves at One Alii Beach Park (p. 495). From the road, you can see **Kalokoeli Pond,** 6 miles east of Kaunakakai on the highway.

Our Lady of Sorrows Catholic Church, one of five built by Father Damien on Molokai and the first outside Kalaupapa, sits across the highway from a fish pond. Park in the church lot (except on Sun) for a closer look.

St. Joseph's Catholic Church   The afternoon sun strikes St. Joseph's Church with such a bold ray of light that it looks as if God is about to perform a miracle. This little 1876 wood-frame church is one of four Father Damien built "topside" on Molokai. Restored in 1971, the church stands beside a seaside cemetery, where feral cats play under the gaze of a Damien statue amid gravestones decorated with flower leis.

King Kamehameha V Hwy. (Hwy. 450), just after mile marker 10.

Smith Bronte Landing Site   In 1927 Charles Lindbergh soloed the Atlantic Ocean in a plane called *The Spirit of St. Louis* and became an American hero. That same year, Ernie Smith and Emory B. Bronte took off from Oakland, California, on July 14, in a single-engine Travelair aircraft named *The City of Oakland,* headed across the Pacific Ocean for Honolulu, 2,397 miles away. The next day, after running out of fuel, they crash-landed upside-down in a kiawe thicket on Molokai, but emerged unhurt to become the first civilians to fly to Hawaii from the U.S. mainland. The 25-hour, 2-minute flight

Moments   Halawa Valley: A Hike Back in History

"There are things on Molokai, sacred things, that you may not be able to see or may not hear, but they are there," says Pilipo Solotario, who was born and raised in Halawa Valley and survived the 1946 tsunami that barreled into the ancient valley. "As Hawaiians, we respect these things." Solotario feels it is important that visitors learn about the history and culture of Molokai; that is part of the secret of appreciating the island.

"I see my role, and I'm nearly 70 years old, as educating people, outsiders, on our culture, our history," he said at the beginning of his cultural hike into his family property in Halawa Valley. "To really appreciate Molokai, you need to understand and know things so that you are *pono,* you are right with the land and don't disrespect the culture. Then you see the real Molokai."

Solotario and his family, who own the land in the valley, are the only people allowed to hike into Halawa. They lead daily tours, which begin at the County Park pavilion, with a history of the valley, a discussion of the Hawaiian culture, and a display of the fruits, trees, and other flora you will be seeing in the valley. Along the hike, Solotario stops to point out historical and cultural aspects, including chanting in Hawaiian before entering a sacred *heiau.* At the waterfalls, visitors can swim in the brisk pool water. Cost for the 4-hour tour is $75. Contact **Molokai Fish & Dive** (© **808/553-5926;** www. molokaifishanddive.com). Bring insect repellent, water, a snack, and a swimsuit. Don't forget your camera.

Note that if you venture away from the county park into the valley on your own, you are trespassing and can be prosecuted.

landed Smith and Bronte a place in aviation history—and on a roadside marker on Molokai.

King Kamehameha V Hwy. (Hwy. 450), at mile marker 11, on the makai (ocean) side.

HALAWA VALLEY ☆

Of the five great valleys of Molokai, only Halawa, with its two waterfalls, golden beach, sleepy lagoon, great surf, and offshore island, is easily accessible. Unfortunately, the trail through fertile Halawa Valley, which was inhabited for centuries, and on to the 250-foot Moaula Falls has been closed for some time. There is one operator who conducts hikes to the falls (see box below).

You can spend a day at the county beach park (described under "Beaches" earlier in this chapter), but do not venture into the valley on your own. In a kind of 21st-century *kapu,* the private landowners in the valley, worried about slip-and-fall lawsuits, have posted NO TRESPASSING signs on their properties.

To get to Halawa Valley, drive north from Kaunakakai on Highway 450 for 30 miles along the coast to the end of the road, which descends into the valley past Jersalema Hou Church. If you'd just like a glimpse of the valley on your way to the beach, there's a scenic overlook along the road: After Pu'u o Hoku Ranch at mile marker 25, the narrow two-lane road widens at a hairpin curve, and you'll find the overlook on your right; it's 2 miles more to the valley floor.

10 Shopping

KAUNAKAKAI

Molokai Surf, Molokai Island Creations, and **Lourdes** are clothing and gift shops close to one another in downtown Kaunakakai, where most of the retail shops sell T-shirts, muumuu, surf wear, and informal apparel. For food shopping, there are several good options. Because many visitors stay in condos, knowing the grocery stores is especially important. Other than that, serious shoppers will be disappointed, unless they love kites or native wood vessels. The following are Kaunakakai's notable stores.

Bamboo Pantry   It's hard to believe this creative kitchenware, cutlery, and specialty foods store is located in the heart of Kaunakakai. Molokai is changing, and this store proves it with "gifts for the home," with everything from dishes, woven baskets, glassware, and high-end pots and pans to gourmet food. 107 Ala Malama St., Kaunakakai. © 808/553-3300.

Imamura Store   Wilfred Imamura, whose mother founded this store, recalls the old railroad track that stretched from the pier to a spot across the street. "We brought our household things from the pier on a hand-pumped vehicle," he recalls. His store, appropriately, is a leap into the past, a marvelous amalgam of precious old-fashioned things. Rubber boots, Hawaiian-print tablecloths, Japanese tea plates, ukulele cases, plastic slippers, and even coconut bikini tops line the shelves. But it's not all nostalgia: The Molokai T-shirts, jeans, and palaka shorts are of good quality and inexpensive, and the pareu fabrics are a find. In Kaunakakai. © 808/553-5615.

Molokai Drugs   David Mikami, whose father-in-law founded this pharmacy in 1935, has made this more than a drugstore. It's a gleaming, friendly stop full of life's basic necessities, with generous amenities such as a phone and a restroom for passersby. Here you'll find the best selection of guidebooks, books about Molokai, and maps, as well as greeting cards, paperbacks, cassette players, flip-flops, and every imaginable essential. The Mikamis are a household name on the island, not only because of their pharmacy, but also because the family has shown exceptional kindness to the often economically strapped Molokaians. In Kamoi Professional Center. © 808/553-5790.

Molokai Fine Arts Gallery ★★ (Finds)   If you shop in only one store in Kaunakakai, make it this one. Featuring the very best of Molokai artists and crafts persons, this has a visitor-friendly layout that allows you to spend as much time as you want perusing the myriad forms of art, such as exquisite handmade jewelry (from contemporary gold earrings, necklaces, and rings to Molokai shell leis), scenic paintings, batik on wood, photos, etched glass, carved bowls, and even feather leis. 2 Kamoi St., Suite 300, Kaunakakai. © 808/553-8520. www.molokaifinearts.com.

Molokai Fish & Dive   Here you'll find the island's largest selection of T-shirts and souvenirs, crammed in among fishing, snorkeling, and outdoor gear that you can rent or buy. Find your way among the fish nets, boogie boards, diving equipment, bamboo rakes, beach towels, postcards, juices and soft drinks, disposable cameras, and staggering miscellany of this store. One entire wall is lined with T-shirts, and the selection of Molokai books and souvenirs is extensive. The staff is happy to point out the best snorkeling spots of the day. In Kaunakakai. © 808/553-5926. www.molokaifishanddive.com.

Molokai Surf   This wooden building now houses Molokai Surf and its selection of skateboards, surf shorts, sweatshirts, sunglasses, T-shirts, footwear, boogie boards, backpacks, and a broad range of clothing and accessories for life in the surf and sun. 130 Kamehameha V Hwy., Kaunakakai. © 808/553-5093.

The Perfect Molokai Souvenir

It's small, it's easy to pack and take back home, and it's made only on Molokai. It's Molokai salt. The Hawaii Kai Corporation (www.soulofthe sea.net) has two product lines featuring Molokai salt: the gourmet **Soul of the Sea** ($30 for 12 oz.) and the **Palm Island Gourmet** ($8 for 8 oz.). Soul of the Sea salt is hand-harvested from some of the cleanest ocean water in the state, hand-processed and hand-packed on Molokai. It comes in three varietals: Papohaku White, Kilauea Black, and Haleakala Red. While making Soul of the Sea salt, Hawaii Kai Corporation got a byproduct they call Ocean Essence, which they blend with Molokai salt to restore trace minerals lost in the heating process. The result is Palm Island Gourmet, which comes in White Silver, Red Gold, or Black Lava.

Take's Variety Store   If you need luggage tags, buzz saws, toys, candy, cloth dolls, canned goods, canteens, camping equipment, hardware, batteries, candles, pipe fittings, fishing supplies—whew!—and other products for work and play, this 54-year-old variety store is the answer. You may suffer from claustrophobia in the crowded, dusty aisles, but Take's carries everything. In Kaunakakai. ✆ **808/553-5442.**

EDIBLES
For fresh-baked goods, see the review of Kanemitsu's Bakery & Restaurant on p. 493.

Friendly Market Center   You can't miss this salmon-colored wooden storefront on the main drag of "downtown" Kaunakakai, where people of all generations can be found just talking story in the Molokai way. Friendly's has an especially good selection of produce and healthy foods—from local poi to Glenlivet. Blue-corn tortilla chips, soy milk, organic brown rice, a good selection of pasta sauces, and Kumu Farms macadamia-nut pesto, the island's stellar gourmet food, are among the items that surpass standard grocery-store fare. In Kaunakakai. ✆ **808/553-5595.**

Misaki's Grocery and Dry Goods   Established in 1922, this third-generation local legend is one of Kaunakakai's two grocery stores. Some of its notable items: chopped garlic from Gilroy, California; fresh luau leaves (taro greens); fresh okra; Boca Burgers; large Korean chestnuts in season; gorgeous bananas; and an ATM. The fish section includes akule and ahi, fresh and dried, but the stock consists mostly of meats, produce, baking products, and a humongous array of soft drinks. Liquor, stationery, candies, and paper products round out the selection of this full-service grocery. In Kaunakakai. ✆ **808/553-5505.**

Molokai Wines & Spirits   This is your best bet on the island for a decent bottle of wine. The shop offers 200 labels, including Caymus, Silver Oak, Joseph Phelps, Heitz, Bonny Doon, and a carefully culled European selection. *Wine Spectator* reviews are tacked to some of the selections, and the snack options include imported gourmet cheeses, salami, and Carr's biscuits. In Kaunakakai. ✆ **808/553-5009.**

EN ROUTE TO THE NORTH COAST
Coffees of Hawaii Plantation Store and Espresso Bar   This is a fairly slick— for Molokai—combination coffee bar, store, and gallery for more than 30 artists and

craftspeople from Hawaii. Sold here are the Malulani Estate and Muleskinner coffees that are grown, processed, and packed on the 500-acre plantation surrounding the shop. (See p. 504 for details on plantation tours.) The gift items are worth a look: pikake and plumeria soaps from Kauai, perfumes and pure beeswax candles from Maui, koa bookmarks and hair sticks, pottery, woods, and baskets. Hwy. 480 (near the junction of Hwy. 470), Kualapuu. (C) 800/709-BEAN or 808/567-9023.

Molokai Museum Gift Shop   This restored 1878 sugar mill sits 1,500 feet above the town of Kualapuu. It's a considerable drive from town, but a good cause for those who'd like to support the museum and the handful of local artisans who sell their crafts, fabrics, cookbooks, quilt sets, and other gift items in the tiny shop. There's also a modest selection of cards, T-shirts, coloring books, and, at Christmas, handmade ornaments made of lauhala and koa. Meyer Sugar Mill, Hwy. 470 (just after the turnoff for the Ironwood Hills Golf Course and 2 miles below Kalaupapa Overlook), Kalae. (C) 808/567-6436.

EDIBLES

Kualapuu Market   This market, in its third generation, is a stone's throw from the Coffees of Hawaii store. It's a scaled-down, one-stop shop with wine, food, and necessities—and a surprisingly presentable, albeit small, assortment of produce, from Molokai sweet potatoes to Ka'u navel oranges in season. The shelves are filled with canned goods, propane, rope, hoses, paper products, and baking goods, reflecting the uncomplicated, rural lifestyle of the area. In Kualapuu. (C) 808/567-6243.

THE WEST END

Big Wind Kite Factory & the Plantation Gallery 👁👁   Jonathan and Daphne Socher, kite designers and inveterate Bali-philes, have combined their interests in a kite factory/import shop that dominates the commercial landscape of Maunaloa, the reconstituted plantation town. Maunaloa's naturally windy conditions make it ideal for kite-flying classes, which are offered free when conditions are right. The adjoining Plantation Gallery features local handicrafts such as milo-wood bowls, locally made T-shirts, Hawaii-themed sandblasted glassware, baskets of lauhala and other fibers, and Hawaiian-music CDs. There are also many Balinese handicrafts, from jewelry to clothing and fabrics. In Maunaloa. (C) 808/552-2364.

Maunaloa General Store   Maunaloa's only general store sells everything from paper products to batteries, dairy products, frozen and fresh meats, wine, canned goods, and a cross-section of necessities. In Maunaloa. (C) 808/552-2346.

Molokai Ranch Logo Shop   Located next to the bike rentals in a wooden building across from the lodge, this shop can outfit you for life's great adventures. Heavy-duty sweatshirts, Bullfrog sunscreens, sandals, swimwear, T-shirts, walking sticks, and fashionable dresses line the shelves. The food items and souvenirs are also diverse: mugs, magnets, CDs and cassettes, Molokai jams and jellies, fine wines, cold beer, Muleskinner coffees, coconut-shell soap dishes, picture frames, and other attractive gifts to go. In Maunaloa. (C) 808/552-2791.

A Touch of Molokai 👁   Even though the Kalaukoi Hotel is closed, this fabulous shop remains open. It is well worth the drive. The surf shorts and aloha shirts sold here are better than the norm, with attractive, up-to-date choices by Jams, Quiksilver, and other name brands. Tencel dresses, South Pacific shell necklaces (up to $400), and a magnificent, hand-turned milo bowl also caught our attention. Most impressive are the wiliwili, kamani, and soap-berry leis and a handsome array of lauhala bags, all made on Molokai. At Kaluakoi Hotel & Golf Club. © **808/552-0133.**

THE EAST END
EDIBLES
Mana'e Goods and Grindz   Formerly the Neighborhood Store 'N Counter, this is the only grocery on the East End. Come here for batteries, film, aspirin, cookies, beer, Molokai produce, candies, paper products, and other sundries. There's good food pouring out of the kitchen at the breakfast and lunch counter, too. See p. 495 for a restaurant review. In Pukoo. © **808/558-8498.**

11 Molokai After Dark

Hotel Molokai, in Kaunakakai (© **808/553-5347**), offers live entertainment by local musicians poolside and in the dining room every night. On Friday from 4 to 6pm is Kupuna (seniors) Night, when the seniors of Molokai who have been performing here for decades show you why people love their music and hula. With its South Seas ambience and poolside setting, it has become the island's premier venue for local and visiting entertainers. The **Paddlers' Inn** (© **808/553-5256**), also in Kaunakakai, recently has become a nightspot for live Hawaii music, comedy acts, and other entertainment, such as Monday night football and Karaoke on Tuesdays.

Movie buffs finally have a place to call their own on Molokai. **Maunaloa Cinemas** (© **808/552-2707**) is a triplex theater that shows almost-first-run movies in the middle of Maunaloa town—four screenings a day at each of the three theaters.

Also in Maunaloa, the lounge at **The Lodge at Molokai Ranch** (© **888/627-8082** or 808/660-2824) offers live traditional Hawaiian music at 5pm on Sunday, and on Friday and Saturday from 7 to 9pm, a jazz combo plays.

8

Lanai, a Different Kind of Paradise

Lanai is not an easy place to reach. There are no direct flights from the mainland. It's almost as if this quiet, gentle oasis—known, paradoxically, for both its small-town feel and its celebrity appeal—demands that its visitors go to great lengths to get here in order to ensure that they will appreciate it.

Lanai (pronounced lah-*nigh*-ee), the nation's biggest defunct pineapple patch, now claims to be one of the world's top tropical destinations. It's a bold claim because so little is here; Lanai has even fewer dining and accommodations choices than Molokai. There are no stoplights and barely 30 miles of paved road. This almost virgin island is unspoiled by what passes for progress, except for a tiny 1920s-era plantation village—and, of course, the village's fancy new arrivals: two first-class luxury hotels where room rates average $400-plus a night.

As soon as you arrive on Lanai, you'll feel the small-town coziness. People wave to every car, residents stop to "talk story" with their friends, fishing and working in the garden are considered priorities in life, and leaving the keys in your car's ignition is standard practice.

For generations, Lanai was little more than a small village, owned and operated by the pineapple company, surrounded by acres of pineapple fields. The few visitors to the island were either relatives of the residents or occasional weekend hunters. Life in the 1960s was pretty much the same as in the 1930s. But all that changed in 1990, when The Lodge at Koele, a 102-room hotel resembling an opulent English Tudor mansion, opened its doors, followed a year later by the 250-room Manele Bay, a Mediterranean-style luxury resort overlooking Hulopoe Bay. Overnight the isolated island was transformed: Corporate jets streamed into tiny Lanai Airport, former plantation workers were retrained in the art of serving gourmet meals, and the population of 2,500 swelled with transient visitors and outsiders coming to work in the island's new hospitality industry. Microsoft billionaire Bill Gates chose the island for his lavish wedding, booking all of its hotel rooms to fend off the press—and uncomplicated Lanai went on the map as a vacation spot for the rich and powerful.

But this island is also a place where people come looking for dramatic beauty, quiet, solitude, and an experience with nature. The sojourners who find their way to Lanai come seeking the dramatic views, the tropical fusion of stars at night, and the chance to be alone with the elements.

They also come for the wealth of activities: snorkeling and swimming in the marine preserve known as Hulopoe Bay, hiking on 100 miles of remote trails, talking story with the friendly locals, and beachcombing and whale-watching along stretches of otherwise deserted sand. For the adventurous, there's horseback riding in the forest, scuba diving in caves, playing golf on courses with stunning ocean views, or renting a four-wheel-drive vehicle for the day and discovering wild plains where spotted deer run free.

In a single decade, a plain red-dirt pineapple patch has become one of Hawaii's top fantasy destinations. But the real Lanai is a multifaceted place that's so much more than a luxury resort—and it's the traveler who comes to discover the island's natural wonders, local lifestyle, and other inherent joys who's bound to have the most genuine island experience.

THE PINEAPPLE ISLAND'S UNUSUAL PAST

This old shield volcano in the rain shadow of Maui has a history of resisting change in a big way. Early Polynesians, fierce Hawaiian kings, European explorers, 20th-century farmers—the island has seen them all and sent most of them packing, empty-handed and broken. The ancient Hawaiians believed that the island was haunted by spirits so wily and vicious that no human could survive here. People didn't settle here until around A.D. 1400.

But those spirits never really went away, it seems. In 1778, the king of the Big Island, Kalaniopuu, invaded Lanai in what was called "the war of loose bowels." His men slaughtered every warrior, cut down trees, and set fire to all that was left except a bitter fern whose roots gave them all dysentery.

In 1802, Wu Tsin made the first attempt to harvest a crop on the island, but he ultimately abandoned his cane fields and went away. Charles Gay acquired 600 acres at public auction to experiment with pineapple as a crop, but a 3-year drought left him bankrupt. Others tried in vain to grow cotton, sisal, and sugar beets; they started a dairy and a piggery and raised sheep for wool. But all enterprises failed, mostly for lack of water.

Harry Baldwin, a missionary's grandson, was the first to succeed on Lanai. He bought Lanai for $588,000 in 1917, developed a 20-mile water pipeline between Koele and Manele, and sold the island 5 years later to Jim Dole for $1.1 million.

Dole planted and irrigated 18,000 acres of pineapple, built Lanai City, blasted out a harbor, and turned the island into a fancy fruit plantation. For a half-century, he enjoyed great success. Even Dole was ultimately vanquished, however; cheaper pineapple production in Asia brought an end to Lanai's heyday.

The island still resembles old photographs taken in the glory days of Dole. Any minute now, you half expect to look up and see old Jim Dole himself rattling up the road in a Model-T truck with a load of fresh-picked pineapples. Only now, there's a new lord of the manor, and his name is David Murdock.

Of all who have looked at Lanai with a gleam in their eye, nobody has succeeded quite like Murdock, a self-made billionaire who acquired the island in a merger more than a decade ago. About 97% of it is now his private holding.

Murdock spent $400 million to build two grand hotels on the island: The Lodge at Koele, which resembles an English country retreat, and the Four Seasons Resort Lana'i at Manele Bay, a green tile-roofed Mediterranean palazzo by the sea. Murdock recycled the former field hands into waitstaff, even summoning a London butler to school the natives in the fine art of service, and carved a pair of daunting golf courses, one in the island's interior and the other along the wave-lashed coast. He then set out to attract tourists by touting Lanai as "the private island."

Murdock is now trying to make all this pay for itself by selling vacation homes and condos, all in the million-dollar range, next door to the two resorts.

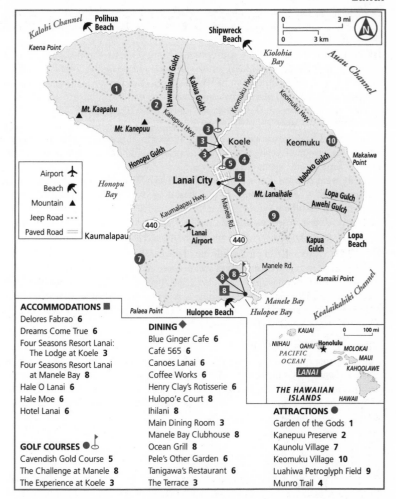

The redevelopment of this tiny rock should have been a pushover for the big-time tycoon, but island-style politics have continually thwarted his schemes. GO SLOW, a sun-faded sign at Dole's old maintenance shed once said. Murdock might have heeded the warning because his grandiose plans are taking twice as long to accomplish as he had expected. Lanai is under the political thumb of many who believe that the island's precious water supply shouldn't all be diverted to championship golf courses and Jacuzzis, and there remains opposition from Lanaians for Sensible Growth, who advocate affordable housing, alternative water systems, and civic improvements that benefit residents.

Lanai residents might have lived in a rural setting, but they certainly haven't been isolated. Having watched the other islands in Hawaii attempt the balancing act of economic growth and the maintenance of an island lifestyle, the residents of Lanai are cautiously welcoming visitors, but at a pace that is still easy for this former plantation community to digest.

1 Orientation

ARRIVING

BY PLANE   No matter where you're coming from, you'll have to make a connection in Honolulu or Kahului (on Maui), where you catch a plane for the 25-minute flight to Lanai's airport. You'll touch down in Puuwai Basin, once the world's largest pineapple plantation; it's about 10 minutes by car to Lanai City and 25 minutes to Manele Bay.

Twin-engine planes are the only air service to Lanai. **Island Air** (© **800/652-6541** or 808/565-6744; www.islandair.com) offers six flights a day from Honolulu. I must tell you that I have gotten less than sterling service from Island Air, their reservations system (or customer service, depending on who is blaming whom) has left me stranded in midroute—not once, but twice!

As we went to press, **go!** airline (© **888/IFLYGO2;** www.iflygo.com) announced the signing of a "memorandum of understanding" with Mokulele Airlines (a small charter service airline on the Big Island) to provide service from Honolulu to Lanai, under the name **go!Express,** on their new fleet of Cessna Grand Caravan 208B planes. Currently, go! offers the best rates and deals among Hawaii's airline carriers.

BY BOAT   A round-trip on **Expeditions Lahaina/Lanai Passenger Ferry** (© **808/ 661-3756;** www.go-lanai.com) takes you between Maui and Lanai for $26 each way. The ferry runs five times a day, 365 days a year, between Lahaina and Lanai's Manele Bay harbor. The 9-mile channel crossing takes 45 minutes to an hour, depending on sea conditions. Reservations are strongly recommended—call or book online. Baggage is limited to two checked bags and one carry-on.

VISITOR INFORMATION

Lanai Visitors Bureau, P.O. Box 631436, Lanai City, HI 96763; or 431 Seventh St., Suite A, Lanai City (© **800/947-4774** or 808/565-7600; fax 808/565-9316; www. visitlanai.net), and the **Hawaii Visitors and Convention Bureau** (© **800/GO-HAWAII** or 808/923-1811; www.gohawaii.com) provide brochures, maps, and island guides.

THE ISLAND IN BRIEF

Inhabited Lanai is divided into three parts—Lanai City, Koele, and Manele—and two distinct climate zones: hot and dry, and cool and misty.

Lanai City (pop. 3,200) sits at the heart of the island at 1,645 feet above sea level. It's the only place on the island where you'll find services. Built in 1924, this plantation village is a tidy grid of quaint tin-roofed cottages in bright pastels, with tropical gardens of banana, *lilikoi,* and papaya. Many of the residents are Filipino immigrants who worked the pineapple fields. Their clapboard homes, now worth $500,000 or more (for a 1,000-sq.-ft. home, built in 1935, on a tiny 5,000-sq.-ft. lot), are excellent examples of historic preservation; the whole town looks like it's been kept under a bell jar.

Around Dole Park Square, a charming village square lined with towering Norfolk and Cook Island pines, plantation buildings house general stores with basic necessities as well as a U.S. Post Office (where people stop to chat), two banks, three restaurants, an art gallery, an art center, a whimsical shop, and a coffee shop that outshines any Starbucks. A victim of "progress" was the local one-room police station with a jail that consisted of three blue-and-white wooden outhouse-size cells with padlocks. It's now a block from the square with "modern facilities," including regulation-size jail cells.

In the nearby cool upland district of **Koele** is The Lodge at Koele, standing alone on a knoll overlooking pastures and the sea at the edge of a pine forest, like a grand European manor. The other bastion of indulgence, the Four Seasons Resort Lana'i at Manele Bay, is on the sunny southwestern tip of the island at **Manele.** You'll get more of what you expect from Hawaii here—beaches, swaying palms, mai tais, and the like.

FAST FACTS

Lanai is part of Maui County. In case of **emergencies,** call the police, fire department, or ambulance services at (✆ 911, or the **Poison Control Center** at (✆ 800/362-3585. For nonemergencies, call the **police** ((✆ 808/565-6428).

For emergency dental care, call **Dr. James Sagawa** ((✆ 808/565-6418). If you need a doctor, contact the **Lanai Family Health Center** ((✆ 808/565-6423) or the **Lanai Community Hospital** ((✆ 808/565-6411).

For a weather report, call the **National Weather Service** at (✆ 808/565-6033.

2 Getting Around

With so few paved roads here, you'll need a four-wheel-drive vehicle if you plan to explore the island's remote shores, its interior, or the summit of Mount Lanaihale. Even if you have only a day on Lanai, rent one and see the island. Both standard cars and four-wheel-drive vehicles are available at the **Dollar Rent-A-Car** desk at **Lanai City Service/Lanai Plantation Store,** 1036 Lanai Ave. ((✆ 800/588-7808 for Dollar reservations, or 808/565-7227 for Lanai City Service). Expect to pay about $139 a day for a four-wheel-drive jeep.

Warning: Gas is expensive on Lanai, and those four-wheel-drive vehicles get terrible mileage. Because everything in Lanai City is within walking distance, it makes sense to rent a jeep only for the days you want to explore the island.

Though it's fun to rent a car and explore the island, it's possible to stay here and get to the beach without one. The two big resort hotels run shuttle vans to the Four Seasons Resort Lana'i at Manele Bay; from there, you walk to Hulopoe Beach. When you want to return, you just catch the hourly shuttle (it may run on the half-hour from Four Seasons Resort Lana'i at Manele Bay) back to Lanai City.

If you're staying elsewhere, you can walk to everything in Lanai City and take a taxi to the beach. **Lanai Plantation Store** ((✆ 808/565-7227) will provide transportation from Lanai City to Hulopoe Beach for $10 per person one-way (you can arrange in advance when you want to be picked up, or walk over to the Four Seasons Resort Lana'i at Manele Bay and phone them to come and get you—or you can most likely get a ride back up to Lanai City with a local). Whether or not you rent a car, sooner or later, you'll find yourself at Lanai City Service/Lanai Plantation Store. This all-in-one grocery store, gas station, rental-car agency, and souvenir shop serves as the island's Grand Central Station; here you can pick up information, directions, maps, and all the local gossip.

3 Where to Stay

The majority of the accommodations are located "in the village," as residents call Lanai City. Above the village is the luxurious Lodge at Koele, while down the hill at Hulopoe Bay are two options: the equally luxurious Four Seasons Resort Lana'i at Manele Bay or tent camping under the stars at the park.

In addition to the choices listed below, consider the B&B accommodations offered by **Delores Fabrao** (🕾 **808/565-6134;** dmfabrao@hotmail.com), who has two guest rooms in her home: a double with a shared bathroom and a family room that sleeps up to six with a private bathroom. This is the best deal on Lanai, with prices unchanged for the last 10 years ($55 double, $100 for four); she said she considers it a service to the community. She doesn't provide breakfast, but you'll have the run of the entire house, including the kitchen. If she has any of her homemade jams or jellies for sale, buy as many jars as you can! At **Hale Moe** (🕾 **808/565-9520** or 808/565-6656; www.staylanai.com), host and Lanai native Momi Suzuki makes three bedrooms in her Lanai City home available to guests; all have private bathrooms ($80–$90 double). Guests are welcome to use the entertainment center, the large deck, and her bicycle. She also has a vacation rental house for $300. **Hale O Lanai,** in Lanai City (🕾 **808/247-3637;** www.hibeach.com), has a fully equipped two-bedroom vacation rental that sleeps up to six; rates range from $115 to $135.

Don't forget to add 11.42% in taxes to all accommodations bills. Parking is free.

EXPENSIVE

Four Seasons Resort Lanai at Manele Bay ✿✿✿   The well-known luxury hotel chain Four Seasons took over management of this 236-unit resort after a $50-millon makeover at this oceanside resort. Every Four Season resort is spectacular, but this one really stands out. Located on a sun-washed southern bluff overlooking Hulopoe Beach, one of Hawaii's best stretches of golden sand, this U-shaped hotel steps down the hillside to the pool and the beach, and then fans out in oceanfront wings separated by gardens with lush flora, man-made waterfalls, lotus ponds, and streams. On the other side, it's bordered by golf greens. The place is a real oasis against the dry Arizona-like heat of Lanai's South Coast.

Designed as a traditional luxury beachfront hotel, it features open, airy rooms, each with a breathtaking view of the big blue Pacific. Murals depicting scenes from Hawaiian history, sea charts, potted palms, soft camel-hued club chairs, and hand-woven kilim rugs fill the lobby. Redone in a clean, crisp style of an elegant oceanside Hawaiian resort, the oversize guest rooms have 40-inch flatscreen LCD TVs, huge marble bathrooms, and semiprivate lanais. This resort is much less formal than The Lodge up the hill and attracts more families. Speaking of families, in addition to the "Kids for All Seasons" child-care programs, the hotel features a teen center with video games, computers, a small pool table, and a 54-inch LCD TV.

The new spa facility features a variety of massages, facials, wraps, and scrubs (don't miss the signature Ali'i banana coconut scrub). In addition, the Four Seasons has added a 1,500-square-foot fitness center (with one of the best ocean views in the resort) that features the latest cardiovascular and strength-training equipment, free weights, and a wood-floor studio for classes (spinning, yoga, Pilates, and meditation).

1 Manele Bay Rd., P.O. Box 631380, Lanai City, HI 96763. 🕾 **800/321-4666** or 808/565-2000. Fax 808/565-2483. www.fourseasons.com/manelebay. 236 units. $395–$1,040 double; $900 suite. Additional person $75. Children under 18 stay free in parent's room. Numerous packages available. AE, DC, MC, V. Airport shuttle $33 round-trip. **Amenities:** 4 restaurants (Ihilani, p. 522; Hulopo'e Court, p. 523; Ocean Grill, p. 523; and The Manele Bay Clubhouse, p. 524); bar w/breathtaking views; large outdoor pool; golf at the Jack Nicklaus–designed The Challenge at Manele; tennis courts; fitness center w/classes; full spa; Jacuzzi; complimentary snorkeling equipment; children's program; game room; concierge; activity desk; business center; retail store; salon; room service; massage; babysitting; laundry service; dry cleaning. *In room:* A/C, TV, DVD, dataport, wireless Internet ($10/day), coffeemaker, minibar, hair dryer, iron, safe.

Four Seasons Resort Lanai, The Lodge at Koele ★★★   The luxury resort chain Four Seasons has come to Lanai. After some $50 million in renovations, the Four Seasons took over the management of the former Lodge at Koele. All 102 guest rooms were totally renovated and now have new carpeting, glass bath partitions, signature Four Seasons beds, 42-inch LCD flatscreen televisions, new furniture, new fabrics, and high-speed Internet. This small inn, which resembles a grand English country estate, was built in 1991 and needed the renovation—the new look is spectacular. Also added were a game room and renovations to the Great Hall, including new furniture. The grounds have been spruced up, and a pagoda imported from China has been constructed on the sprawling English gardens grounds (not my taste, but I'm sure it will be the backdrop for hundreds of wedding photos).

The Four Seasons also retrained the staff to their level of excellent service. Don't expect the "sophisticated" service you find in most Four Seasons around the world—most of the staff have lived on Lanai for generations. Instead you'll find a wonderfully charming display of aloha spirit and a strong desire to make sure your vacation is perfect.

Before you reach for the phone, realize that this hotel is not at the beach (see the Manele Bay resort, above), but located in the cool mist of the mountains, on 21 acres at 1,700 feet above sea level, 8 miles inland from any beach. In the winter, temperatures can drop into the 50s (don't worry, the rooms have heat as well as air-conditioning). Most guests here are looking for relaxation: sitting on the rattan lawn chairs on the porch, reading, watching the turkeys mosey across the manicured lawns, strolling through the Japanese hillside garden, or watching the sun sink into the Pacific.

Inside, heavy timbers, beamed ceilings, and the two huge stone fireplaces of the Great Hall complete the look. Overstuffed furniture sits invitingly around the fireplaces, richly patterned rugs adorn the floor, and museum-quality art hangs on the walls. The guest rooms continue the English theme with four-poster beds, sitting areas (complete with window seats), formal writing desks, and single-sink bathrooms with oversize tubs. There are plenty of activities here and at the sister resort down the hill, Manele, so you'll get the best of both hotels. Other pluses include complimentary shuttle to the golf courses, beach, and Four Seasons Resort Lana'i at Manele Bay; complimentary coffee and tea in the lobby; formal afternoon tea; and twice-daily maid service. Additional activities include croquet lawns, horse riding, hiking trails, and garden walks.

Plans call for the addition of a free-standing Wellness Center and Spa, to open in 2008.

1 Keomoku Highway, P.O. Box 631380, Lanai City, HI 96763. ℂ **800/321-4666** or 808/565-4000. Fax 808/565-4561. www.fourseasons.com/koele. 102 units. $295–$595 double; from $695 suite. Extra person $75. Children under 18 stay free in parent's room. Numerous packages available. AE, DC, MC, V. Airport shuttle $33 round-trip. **Amenities:** 3 restaurants (including the Main Dining Room, p. 523, and The Terrace, p. 523); bar (w/live music); outdoor pool; golf at Greg Norman–designed Experience at Koele (p. 530); tennis courts; fitness room; Jacuzzi; complimentary snorkeling equipment rentals at Four Seasons Resort Lana'i at Manele Bay; bike rentals; children's program; game room; concierge; activity desk; retail store; room service; massage; babysitting; laundry service; dry cleaning. *In room:* A/C TV, DVD, dataport, wireless Internet ($10/day), minibar, fridge, coffeemaker, hair dryer, iron, safe.

MODERATE

Hotel Lanai ★ *(Kids)*   This hotel lacks the facilities of the two resorts described above, but it's perfect for families and other vacationers who can't afford to spend $400 (and up) a night. In fact, if you are looking for the old-fashioned aloha that Lanai City is famous for, this is the place to stay. Built in the 1920s for VIP plantation guests, this clapboard plantation-era relic has retained its quaint character and lives on as a country inn. A well-known chef from Maui, Henry Clay Richardson, is the inn's executive chef (see review of Henry Clay's Rotisserie on p. 524).

In 2005, the entire hotel underwent renovations—repainting, remodeling, and a general sprucing up. The guest rooms, although extremely small, are clean and newly decorated with Hawaiian quilts, wood furniture, and ceiling fans (but no air-conditioning or televisions). The most popular are the lanai units, which feature a shared lanai with the room next door. All rooms have ceiling fans and private, shower-only bathrooms. The small one-bedroom cottage, with a TV and bathtub, is perfect for a small family.

The hotel serves as a down-home crossroads where total strangers meet local folks on the lanai to drink beer and talk story or play the ukulele and sing into the dark, tropical night. Often a curious visitor in search of an authentic experience will join the party and discover Lanai's very Hawaiian heart. Guests have the use of the complimentary shuttle to The Lodge at Koele, the Four Seasons Resort Lana'i at Manele Bay, the golf courses (at which they get the same lower rates given to guests at the two resorts), and the beach.

828 Lanai Ave. (P.O. Box 630520), Lanai City, HI 96763. © **800/795-7211** or 808/565-7211. Fax 808/565-6450. www.hotellanai.com. 11 units. $125–$145 double; $175 cottage double. Rates include continental breakfast. Extra person $10. 2 nights minimum. AE, MC, V. Airport shuttle $33 round-trip. **Amenities:** Excellent restaurant (Henry Clay's Rotisserie, p. 524); intimate bar; access to 2 resort golf courses on the island; nearby tennis courts; complimentary snorkeling equipment.

INEXPENSIVE

Dreams Come True ✿ *Finds*   This quaint plantation house is tucked away among papaya, banana, lemon, and avocado trees in the heart of Lanai City, at 1,620 feet. Hosts Susan and Michael Hunter have filled their house with Southeast Asian antiques collected on their travels. Both are jewelers, and they operate a working studio on the premises. The four bedrooms offer everything from two single beds to queen-size beds. The common area looks out on the garden and is equipped with both TV and VCR. The use of the kitchen is available.

547 12th St. (P.O. Box 525), Lanai City, HI 96763. © **800/566-6961** or 808/565-6961. Fax 808/565-7056. www.dreams cometruelanai.com. 4 units. $112 double. Entire house $450 (sleeps 8–10). AE, DISC, MC, V. *In room:* No phone.

4 Where to Dine

Lanai is a curious mix of innocence and sophistication, with strong cross-cultural elements that liven up its culinary offerings. You can dine like a sultan on this island, but be prepared for high prices. The tony hotel restaurants require deep pockets, and there are only a handful of other options.

Note: You'll find the restaurants reviewed in this chapter on the map on p. 517.

VERY EXPENSIVE

Ihilani ✿✿✿ ITALIAN   A number of top Hawaii chefs (such as Phillippe Padovani and Edwin Goto) have each added bits of their own style to the inspiring menu, which melds Mediterranean with Island cuisine. The result is one of Lanai's top gourmet restaurants. The latest incarnation of this classy, formal restaurant, overlooking the resort and the ocean beyond, is traditional Italian cuisine. Try the perfect homemade spinach gnocchi or the lobster risotto. My other favorites include the osso buco, rare ahi alla caponata, and onaga alla puttanesca with artichoke purée and a spicy tomato and caper sauce. Be sure to leave room for the scrumptious desserts.

Four Seasons Resort Lana'i at Manele Bay. © **808/565-2296.** Reservations strongly recommended. Resort attire recommended. Main courses $25–$44. AE, MC, V. Tues–Sat 6–9:30pm.

Main Dining Room 𝖆𝖆𝖆 NEW AMERICAN   The former Formal Dining room has been revamped under the Four Seasons management and has a new menu. However, they did retain the relaxing setting, with a roaring fire, bountiful sprays of orchids, sienna-colored walls, and a team of waitstaff serving in hushed voices. The menu highlights American favorites. The appetizer menu is so tempting you could make a meal from the variety of choices: seared diver scallops with cauliflower purée, foie gras torchon with a toasted broche with roasted pineapple and vanilla compote, or the lava rock–seared Lanai venison. The entrees vary according to the season; when we dined there, the menu included Maui lavender honey–roasted duck breast, mustard and herb–roasted rack of lamb, and a buttered poached lobster from the Big Island. The service is impeccable, the atmosphere relaxing. But don't forget your platinum credit card—you'll need it.

The Lodge at Koele. © **808/565-4580.** Reservations required. Entrees $40–$51. AE, DC, MC, V. Daily 6–9:30pm.

EXPENSIVE

Hulopo'e Court 𝖆𝖆 HAWAII REGIONAL   This is the Manele Bay's informal dining room. It serves one of the best breakfast buffets I've seen in Hawaii, with everything from omelet station to breakfast meats, daily pancakes, potatoes, rice and local tropical fruit. The dinner menu showcases local ingredients—examples include the steamed Hawaiian seafood laulau (with mahimahi, sea bass, shrimp, Molokai sweet potatoes, and local vegetables), grilled opakapaka with Lanai greens and a mango sauce, and Hawaiian-style short ribs and pork chops.

Four Seasons Resort Lana'i at Manele Bay. © **808/565-2290.** Dinner reservations recommended. Resort attire recommended. Breakfast entrees $15–$18, buffet $28; dinner main courses $28–$42. AE, MC, V. Daily 7–11am and 6–9:30pm.

Ocean Grill 𝖆 SEAFOOD   The former Pool Grille has been remodeled and expanded, and is open for lunch and dinner. Located just off the pool, the casual, open-air, Hawaii-style bistro serves interesting lunches like wraps and sandwiches (such as a veggie wrap with portobello mushrooms, red bell peppers, provolone cheese, avocado, and roasted garlic hummus), a great selection of salads (including a yummy calamari salad), and a range of entrees such as *kalua* pork and cheese quesadilla, or mahimahi fish and chips. At dinner, watch the sun set and the stars come out as you dine on fresh local fish, steak, free-range chicken, or small plate entrees such as Hawaiian kampachi, crab cakes, lobster, and red curry chowder.

Four Seasons Resort Lana'i at Manele Bay. © **808/565-2092.** Lunch $13–$19; dinner $26–$46. AE, MC, V. Daily lunch 11am–5pm; Thurs–Mon dinner 5:30–9pm.

The Terrace 𝖆𝖆 AMERICAN   Located next to the Main Dining Room in The Lodge at Koele, between the 35-foot-high Great Hall and a wall of glass looking out over prim English gardens, this wonderful restaurant is the Lodge's "casual" dining room. The Terrace is far from your typical hotel dining room. The menu may be fancy for comfort food, but it does, indeed, comfort. Hearty breakfasts of waffles and cereals, fresh pineapple from the nearby Palawai Basin, frittata, and blue crab Benedict are a grand start to the day. Dinner choices include slow-roasted lamb shank, grilled beef fillet, roasted pork chops, fresh fish of the day, and a couple of vegetarian selections (garganelli pasta with sautéed mushrooms and white truffle butter, and a teriyaki-glazed vegetable and tofu brochette with zucchini couscous).

The Lodge at Koele. © **808/565-4580**. Reservations recommended. Breakfast $16–$27; dinner entrees $30–$44. AE, DC, MC, V. Daily 6am–2pm and 6–9pm.

MODERATE

The Experience at Koele Clubhouse AMERICAN   This tiny diner overlooks the verdant, rolling hills of the Experience at Kolele Golf Course. Soups, salads, and sandwiches rule here. You'll find most of your fellow diners have just finished a round of golf; you can join them at one of a handful of tables inside or on the lanai overlooking the pastoral view. Oversized sandwiches range from a delicious portabello mushroom on toasted focaccia bread to open-faced chicken salad (with a yummy mango-avocado salsa), smoked turkey club, or a charbroiled cheddar burger.

The Experience at Koele Golf Course. © **808/565-4580**. Lunch $10–$18. AE, DC, MC, V. Daily 10:30am–4:30pm.

Henry Clay's Rotisserie ⑥⑥ CAJUN/COUNTRY CUISINE   Henry Clay Richardson, a New Orleans native, has made some welcome changes to Lanai's dining landscape with his rustic inn in the middle of Lanai City. It's very popular and always full. Maybe that's because it's the only option on Lanai that occupies the vast gap between deli-diner and upscale-luxe.

The menu focuses on fresh meats, seafood, and local produce in assertive preparations. Appetizers and entrees reflect Cajun, regional, and international influences. Specialties include the Rajun Cajun Clay's shrimp, a fiery concoction of hefty shrimp in a spiced tomato broth, and the "Almost Grandma's Gumbo," straight from Clay's New Orleans roots. The meats, which could be duck, venison, lamb, beef, or chicken, are spit-roasted on the rotisserie. Diners rave about the fresh catch in lemon butter caper sauce; we loved the eggplant Creole. Don't leave without a piece of the New Orleans–style pecan pie. The decor consists of pine-paneled walls, chintz curtains, and fireplaces in both rooms.

In the Hotel Lanai. 828 Lanai Ave., Lanai City. © **808/565-7211**. www.hotellanai.com. Main courses $25–$36. AE, MC, V. Daily 5:30–9pm.

Manele Bay Clubhouse ⑥ PACIFIC RIM   The view from the alfresco tables here may be the best on the island, encompassing Kahoolawe, Haleakala (on Maui), and, on an especially clear day, the peaks of Mauna Kea and Mauna Loa on the Big Island. You can lunch on salads and sandwiches (Asian tuna salad with grilled ahi, turkey club sandwich, clubhouse burgers with caramelized onions and cheese) or on more substantial entrees, ranging from fish and chips to Kalbi barbeque beef. The clubhouse is casual, the view of the ocean is awe-inspiring, and it's a great gathering place.

In The Challenge at Manele Clubhouse. © **808/565-2232**. Reservations recommended. Lunch entrees $12–$20. AE, DC, MC, V. Daily 10:30am–4:30pm.

INEXPENSIVE

Blue Ginger Cafe COFFEE SHOP   Famous for its mahimahi sandwiches and inexpensive omelets, Blue Ginger is a very local, very casual, and very reasonably priced alternative to Lanai's fancy hotel restaurants. The four tables on the front porch face the cool Norfolk pines of Dole Park and are always filled with locals who talk story from morning to night. The offerings are solid, no-nonsense, everyday fare: fried saimin (no MSG), very popular hamburgers on homemade buns, and mahimahi with capers and mushrooms. Blue Ginger also serves a tasty French toast made with home-made bread and a surprisingly good stir-fried vegetable dish.

409 Seventh St. (at Ilima St.), Lanai City. ℂ 808/565-6363. Breakfast and lunch items under $13; dinner under $16. No credit cards. Daily 6am–8pm.

Café 565 PIZZA/SUBS   Diners at this colorful pizzeria (named after Lanai's phone prefix, 565) spill out of the old house and into the umbrella tables in the front yard. The pizzas here are the real thing, baked in pizza ovens. The sub sandwiches, in fresh-baked rolls, range from hot (like Philly cheese steak) to cold (Genoa salami, capicollo, mortadella, and provolone). Daily plate-lunch specials and great salads complete the menu.

408 Eighth St. (at Ilima St.), Lanai City. ℂ 808/565-6622. Sub sandwiches $5–$8.95; pizza $13–$20; most dinner entrees under $9. No credit cards. Mon–Fri 10am–3pm and 5–8pm; Sat 10am–3pm.

Canoes Lanai LOCAL   This ma-and-pa eatery may have changed its name (it used to be Tanigawa's), but it still remains the landmark that it's been since the 1920s. In those days, the tiny storefront sold canned goods and cigarettes; the 10 tables, ham-burgers, and Filipino food came later. This hole in the wall is a local institution, with a reputation for serving local-style breakfasts. The fare—fried rice, omelets, short stack, and simple ham and eggs—is more greasy spoon than gourmet, but it's budget-friendly.

419 Seventh St., Lanai City. ℂ 808/565-6537. Reservations not accepted. Breakfast less than $8.50; lunch sand-wiches $2.50–$8.50; burgers $2–$5. No credit cards. Thurs–Tues 6:30am–1pm.

Coffee Works ⍟ COFFEEHOUSE   Oahu's popular Ward Warehouse coffeehouse has opened a new branch in Lanai City with a menu of espresso coffees and drinks, ice cream (including local brands), and a small selection of pastries. It's Lanai City's new gathering place, a tiny cafe with tables and benches on a pleasing wooden deck just a stone's throw from Dole Park. Formerly a plantation house, the structure fits in with the surrounding plantation homes in the heart of Lanai City. There are some nice gift items available, including T-shirts, tea infusers, Chai, teapots, cookies, and gour-met coffees.

604 Ilima, Lanai City (across from Post Office). ℂ 808/565-6962. Most items under $5. AE, DC, DISC, MC, V. Mon–Sat 6am–4pm; Sun 6am–noon.

Pele's Other Garden ⍟⍟ DELI/BISTRO   This popular Lanai City eatery has added a patio with umbrella tables outside and expanded the kitchen in the back, so there's a lot more seating than there used to be—and a fuller menu to match. Own-ers Mark and Barbara have turned Pele's Other Garden from a small sandwich shop to a full-scale deli and bistro. Daily soup and menu specials, excellent pizza, fresh organic produce, and special items such as top-quality black-bean burritos, roasted red peppers, and stuffed grape leaves make Pele's Other Garden a Lanai City must. Sand-wiches are made with wraps or whole-wheat, rye, sourdough, or French bread, all baked on the island and delivered fresh daily. In the evening, you dine on china at cloth-covered tables, and the menu expands to include pastas (bow-tie pasta with but-terflied garlic shrimp, fettuccine with smoked salmon), pizza, and salads. Recently added are beer and wines by the glass (from $4.25).

Dole Park, 811 Houston St., Lanai City. ℂ 808/565-9628. Most lunch items less than $8; pizza from $7; dinner items $17–$20. AE, DISC, MC, V. Mon–Fri 10am–2:30pm and 5–8pm; Sat 5–8pm.

5 Beaches

If you like big, wide, empty, gold-sand beaches and crystal-clear, cobalt-blue water full of bright tropical fish—and who doesn't?—go to Lanai. With 18 miles of sandy shoreline, Lanai has some of Hawaii's least-crowded and most-interesting beaches.

HULOPOE BEACH ✿✿✿

In 1997, Dr. Stephen Leatherman of the University of Maryland (a professional beach surveyor who's also known as "Dr. Beach") ranked Hulopoe the best beach in the United States. It's easy to see why. This palm-fringed, gold-sand beach is bordered by black-lava fingers, protecting swimmers from ocean currents. In summer, Hulopoe is perfect for swimming, snorkeling, or just lolling about; the water temperature is usually in the mid-70s (mid-20s Celsius). Swimming is usually safe, except when swells kick up in winter. The bay at the foot of the Four Seasons Resort Lana'i at Manele Bay is a protected marine preserve, with schools of colorful fish and spinner dolphins. Humpback whales cruise by here in winter. Hulopoe is also Lanai's premier beach park, with a grassy lawn, picnic tables, barbecue grills, restrooms, showers, and ample parking. You can camp here, too.

HULOPOE'S TIDE POOLS Some of the best lava-rock tide pools in Hawaii are found along the south shore of Hulopoe Bay. These miniature Sea Worlds are full of

---

⌒Moments Frommer's Favorite Lanai Experiences

Snorkeling Hulopoe Beach. Crystal-clear waters teem with brilliant tropical fish off one of Hawaii's best beaches. There are tide pools to explore, waves to play in, and other surprises—like a pod of spinner dolphins that often makes a splashy entrance.

Exploring the Garden of the Gods. Eroded by wind, rain, and time, these geologic badlands (p. 531) are worth visiting at sunrise or sunset, when the low light plays tricks on the land—and your mind.

Hiking the Munro Trail. The 11-mile Munro Trail is a lofty, rigorous hike along the rim of an old volcano. You'll get great views of the nearby islands. Take a four-wheel-drive vehicle if you want to spend more time on top of the island.

Four-Wheeling It. Four-wheeling is a way of life on Lanai because there are only 30 miles of pavement on the whole island. Plenty of rugged trails lead to deserted beaches, abandoned villages, and valleys filled with wild game.

Camping under the Stars. The campsites (p. 529) at Hulopoe Beach Park are about as close to the heavens as you can get. The crashing surf will lull you to sleep at night, and chirping birds will wake you in the morning. If you're into roughing it, this is a great way to experience Lanai.

Watching the Whales at Polihua Beach. Located on the north shore, this beach—which gets its name from the turtles that nest here—is a great place to watch for whales during the winter months.

strange creatures such as asteroids (sea stars) and holothurians (sea cucumbers), not to mention spaghetti worms, Barber Pole shrimp, and Hawaii's favorite local delicacy, the opihi, a tasty morsel also known as the limpet. Youngsters enjoy swimming in the enlarged tide pool at the eastern edge of the bay. When you explore tide pools, do so at low tide. Never turn your back on the waves. Wear tennis shoes or reef walkers, as wet rocks are slippery. Collecting specimens in this marine preserve is forbidden, so don't take any souvenirs home.

POLIHUA BEACH 🐢

So many sea turtles once hauled themselves out of the water to lay their eggs in the sun-baked sand on Lanai's northwestern shore that Hawaiians named the beach here *Polihua*, or "egg nest." Although the endangered green sea turtles are making a comeback, they're seldom seen here now. You're more likely to spot an offshore whale (in season) or the perennial litter that washes up onto this deserted beach at the end of Polihua Road, a 4-mile jeep trail. There are no facilities except fishermen's huts and driftwood shelters. Bring water and sunscreen. Beware of the strong currents, which make the water unsafe for swimming. This strand is ideal for beachcombing (those little green-glass Japanese fishing-net floats often show up here), fishing, or just being alone.

SHIPWRECK BEACH 🐢

This 8-mile-long windswept strand on Lanai's northeastern shore—named for the rusty ship *Liberty* stuck on the coral reef—is a sailor's nightmare and a beachcomber's dream. The strong currents yield all sorts of flotsam, from Japanese handblown-glass fish floats and rare pelagic paper nautilus shells to lots of junk. This is also a great place to spot whales from December to April, when the Pacific humpbacks cruise in from Alaska. The road to the beach is paved most of the way, but you really need a four-wheel-drive to get down here.

6 Watersports

Lanai has Hawaii's best water clarity because it lacks major development, it has low rainfall and runoff, and its coast is washed clean daily by the sea current (known as "The Way to Tahiti"). But the strong sea currents pose a threat to swimmers, and there are few good surf breaks. Most of the aquatic adventures—swimming, snorkeling, scuba diving—are centered on the somewhat protected south shore, around Hulopoe Bay.

The only outfitter for watersports is **Trilogy Lanai Ocean Sports** 🐢🐢🐢 (© 888/MAUI-800; www.visitlanai.com).

SAILING/SNORKELING

Trilogy Lanai Ocean Sports (see contact information, above), which has built a well-deserved reputation as the leader in sailing/snorkeling cruises in Hawaii, has both a morning and an afternoon **snorkel sailing trip** on board its luxury custom sailing catamarans or its 32-foot jet-drive rigid aluminum-inflatable vessel. The trips along Lanai's protected coastline include sailing past hundreds of spinner dolphins and into some of the best snorkeling sites in the world. The prices range from $95 to $125 (half-price for children 3–15) and include lunch, sodas, snorkel gear, and instruction.

SCUBA DIVING

Two of Hawaii's best-known dive spots are found in Lanai's clear waters, just off the south shore: **Cathedrals I** and **II,** so named because the sun lights up an underwater grotto like a magnificent church. **Trilogy Lanai Ocean Sports** (see above for contact information) offers several different kinds of sailing, diving, and snorkeling trips on catamarans and from its new 32-foot high-tech jet-drive ocean raft. Trilogy has its own version of "sunrise services" at the Cathedrals. Not only is this the best time of day to dive this incredible area, but there are virtually no other dive boats in the water at this time. Cost is $169 to $199 for a two-tank dive and $79 for nondivers.

Beach dives are available for $95 (one-tank dive) for certified divers and $95 for an introductory dive for noncertified divers.

SNORKELING

Hulopoe is Lanai's best snorkeling spot. Fish are abundant in the marine-life conservation area. Try the lava-rock points at either end of the beach and around the lava pools.

SPORTFISHING

The **Four Seasons Resort Lana'i at Manele Bay** (© 808/565-2000; www.four seasons.com/lanai) charters a 53-foot Merritt sport fishing boat which will take up to six passengers for a full day of fishing ($1,200) or a half-day ($800).

SURFING

If you have ever wanted to learn how to surf, let instructor Nick Palumbo, a surfing champion, take you on a 4WD surfing safari to a secluded surf spot. He'll have you up and riding the waves in no time. His **Lanai Surf School & Surf Safari** (© 808/565-7258; www.lanaisurfsafari.com) features a package of a 2½-hour lesson with surfboard, 4WD transportation, refreshments, and "a really good time" for $185 per person.

WHALE-WATCHING

During whale season, from December to April, the **Trilogy** Crew takes passengers out on their 26-passenger, rigid-hulled inflatable boat, a 32-foot jet drive Zodiac named *Manele Kai,* for a 2-hour ocean adventure that explores some of the remote and unspoiled sites in Hawaii. Lanai is also home to one of Hawaii's largest schools of spinner dolphins and a haven to North Pacific humpback whales. The captains and crew are Certified Island Naturalists who make each trip educational as well as entertaining, and they can usually find these wonderful and playful mammals. The cost is $75 (half-price for children 3–15), and soft drinks are provided.

7 Hiking & Camping

HIKING

A LEISURELY MORNING HIKE

The 3-hour self-guided **Koele Nature Hike** starts by the reflecting pool in the backyard of The Lodge at Koele and takes you on a 5-mile loop through Norfolk Island pines, into Hulopoe Valley, past wild ginger, and up to Koloiki Ridge, with its panoramic view of Maunalei Valley and of Molokai and Maui in the distance. You're welcome to take the hike even if you're not a guest at The Lodge. The path isn't clearly marked—ask the concierge for a free map. We suggest doing this hike in the morning; by afternoon the clouds usually roll in, marring visibility at the top and increasing your chance of being caught in a downpour.

THE CHALLENGING MUNRO TRAIL

This tough 11-mile (round-trip) uphill climb through the groves of Norfolk pines is a lung-buster, but if you reach the top, you'll be rewarded with a breathtaking view of

Molokai, Maui, Kahoolawe, the peaks of the Big Island, and—on a really clear day—Oahu in the distance. Figure on 7 hours. The trail begins at Lanai Cemetery along Keomoku Road (Hwy. 44) and follows Lanai's ancient caldera rim, ending up at the island's highest point, Lanaihale. Go in the morning for the best visibility. After 4 miles, you'll get a view of Lanai City. The weary retrace their steps from here, while the more determined go the last 1.25 miles to the top. Die-hards head down Lanai's steep south-crater rim to join the highway to Manele Bay. For more details on the Munro Trail—including information on four-wheel-driving it to the top—see "Five Islands at a Single Glance: The Munro Trail" under "Seeing the Sights," below.

A SELF-GUIDED NATURE TRAIL
This self-guided nature trail in the Kanepuu Preserve (described below) is about a 10- to 15-minute walk through eight stations, with interpretive signs explaining the natural or cultural significance of what you're seeing. The trail head is clearly marked on the Polihua Road on the way to the Garden of the Gods. Kanepuu is one of the last remaining examples of the type of forest that once covered the dry lowlands throughout the state. There are some 49 plant species here that are found only in Hawaii. The **Nature Conservancy** (© **808/565-7430**) conducts guided hikes every month; call for details.

GUIDED HIKES
The Lodge at Koele (© **808/565-7300;** www.fourseasons.com/lanai) has a 2½-hour Koloiki Ridge Nature hike through 5 miles of the upland forests of Koele at 11am daily. Fee is $15.

The **Four Seasons Resort Lana'i at Manele Bay** (© **808/565-2000;** www.fourseasons.com/lanai) has a 1½-hour fitness hike along an old fisherman's trail at 9am Tuesday and Friday, led by Joe West, wildlife and outdoor photographer extraordinaire. Bring your camera and ask Joe for photographing tips. The fee is $15.

CAMPING AT HULOPOE BEACH PARK
There is only one legal place to camp on Lanai: Hulopoe Beach Park, which is owned by Castle and Cooke Resorts. To camp in this exquisite beach park, with its crescent-shaped white-sand beach bordered by kiawe trees, contact **Wendell Sarme–Park Manager,** Castle and Cooke Resorts, P.O. Box 630310, Lanai City, HI 96763 (© **808/565-2970**). There's a $5 registration fee, plus a charge of $5 per person, per night. Hulopoe has six campsites; each can accommodate up to six people. Facilities include restrooms, running water, showers, barbecue areas, and picnic tables.

8 Golf & Other Outdoor Activities
GOLF
Cavendish Golf Course *(finds)*   This quirky par-36, 9-hole public course not only has no clubhouse or club pros, but also no tee times, scorecards, or club rentals. To play, just show up, put a donation into the little wooden box next to the first tee, and hit away. The 3,071-yard, E. B. Cavendish–designed course was built by the Dole plantation in 1947 for its employees. The greens are a bit bumpy, but the views of Lanai are great and the temperatures usually quite mild.

Next to The Lodge at Koele in Lanai City. No phone. Greens fees $5–$10 donation suggested.

The Challenge at Manele ★★ This target-style, desert-links course, designed by Jack Nicklaus, is one of the most challenging courses in the state. Check out the local rules: "No retrieving golf balls from the 150-foot cliffs on the ocean holes 12, 13, or 17," and "All whales, axis deer, and other wild animals are considered immovable obstructions." That's just a hint of the unique experience you'll have on this course, which is routed among lava outcroppings, archaeological sites, kiawe groves, and ilima trees. The five sets of staggered tees pose a challenge to everyone from the casual golfer to the pro. Facilities include a clubhouse, a pro shop, rentals, a practice area, lockers, and showers.

Next to the Four Seasons Resort Lana'i at Manele Bay. ℂ **800/321-4666** or 808/565-2222. Greens fees $225 ($190 for guests).

The Experience at Koele ★★ This traditional par-72 course, designed by Greg Norman with fairway architecture by Ted Robinson, has very different front and back 9 holes. Mother Nature reigns throughout: You'll see Cook Island and Norfolk pines, indigenous plants, and lots of water—seven lakes, flowing streams, cascading waterfalls, and one green (the 17th) completely surrounded by a lake. All goes well until you hit the signature hole, number 8, where you tee off from a 250-foot elevated tee to a fairway bordered by a lake on the right and trees and dense shrubs on the left. After that, the back 9 holes drop dramatically through ravines filled with pine, koa, and eucalyptus trees. The grand finale, the par-5 18th, features a green rimmed by waterfalls that flow into a lake on the left side. To level the playing field, there are four different sets of tees. Facilities include a clubhouse, a pro shop, rentals, a practice area, lockers, and showers.

Next to The Lodge at Koele in Lanai City. ℂ **800/321-4666** or 808/565-4653. Greens fees $225 ($190 for guests).

BICYCLING
The Lodge at Koele (ℂ **808/565-7300**) rents mountain bikes for $8 an hour. You get a backpack and lunch with a 4-hour ($35) or 8-hour ($55) rental.

HORSEBACK RIDING
Horses can take you to many places in Lanai's unique landscape that are otherwise unreachable. The **Four Seasons Lanai Resort's Stables at Koele** (ℂ **808/565-4424**) offers various rides, including slow, gentle group rides starting at $85 for a 1½-hour **Paniolo Trail Ride,** which takes you into the hills surrounding Koele. You'll meander through guava groves and ironwood trees; catch glimpses of axis deer, quail, wild turkeys, and Santa Getrudis cattle; and end with panoramic views of Maui and Lanai. For $10 more, you can spend 2 hours in the saddle on the Mahana Ride. Private rides can be arranged for $95 per person for 1 hour and $150 per person for 2 hours. In the works is a 3-hour lunch ride; call for details. Long pants and shoes are required, and safety helmets are provided. Bring a jacket—the weather is chilly and rain is frequent. Children must be at least 9 years old and 4 feet tall, and riders cannot weigh more than 250 pounds.

TENNIS
Public courts, lit for night play, are available in Lanai City at no charge; call ℂ **808/565-6979** for reservations. Guests staying at The Lodge at Koele or the Four Seasons Resort Lana'i at Manele Bay have tennis privileges at either the Tennis Center at Manele, with its six Plexipave courts, a fully equipped pro shop, and tournament facilities; or the courts at Koele. Instruction is available for $25 for a clinic, $65 for a private 1-hour lesson. Courts are complimentary for hotel guests (not open to nonguests). For information, call ℂ **808/565-2072.**

9 Seeing the Sights

You'll need a four-wheel-drive vehicle to reach all the sights listed below. Renting a jeep is an expensive proposition on Lanai—from $139 to $179 a day—so we suggest that you rent one just for the day (or days) you plan on sightseeing; otherwise, it's easy enough to get to the beach and around Lanai City without your own wheels. For details on vehicle rentals, see "Getting Around," earlier in this chapter.

Note: You'll find the following attractions on the map on p. 517.

GARDEN OF THE GODS ⭐

A dirt four-wheel-drive road leads out of Lanai City, through the now uncultivated pineapple fields, past the Kanepuu Preserve (a dry-land forest preserve teeming with rare plant and animal life) to the so-called Garden of the Gods, out on Lanai's north shore. This rugged, barren, beautiful place is full of rocks strewn by volcanic forces and shaped by the elements into a variety of shapes and colors—brilliant reds, oranges, ochers, and yellows.

Ancient Hawaiians considered this desolate, windswept place an entirely supernatural phenomenon. Scientists, however, have other, less colorful explanations. Some call the area an "ongoing posterosional event"; others say it's just "plain and simple badlands." Take a four-wheel-drive ride out here and decide for yourself.

Go early in the morning or just before sunset, when the light casts eerie shadows on the mysterious lava formations. Drive west from The Lodge on Polihua Road; in about 2 miles, you'll see a hand-painted sign that'll point left down a one-lane, red-dirt road through a kiawe forest to the site.

FIVE ISLANDS AT A SINGLE GLANCE: THE MUNRO TRAIL ⭐

In the first golden rays of dawn, when lone owls swoop over abandoned pineapple fields, hop into a 4×4 and head out on the two-lane blacktop toward Mount Lanaihale, the 3,370-foot summit of Lanai. Your destination is the Munro Trail, the narrow, winding ridge trail that runs across Lanai's razorback spine to the summit. From

---

𝘒𝘪𝘥𝘴 Especially for Kids

Exploring Hulopoe Tide Pools (p. 526) An entire world of marine life lives in the tide pools on the eastern side of Hulopoe Bay. Everything in the water, including the tiny fish, is small—kid-size. After examining the wonders of the tide pool, check out the larger swimming holes in the lava rock, perfect for children.

Hunting for Petroglyphs (p. 532) The Luahiwa Petroglyph Field, located just outside Lanai City, is spread out over a 3-acre site. Make it a game: Whoever finds the most petroglyphs gets ice cream from the Pine Isle Market.

Listening to Storytellers Check with the Lanai Library, Fraser Avenue near Fifth Street, Lanai City (📞 **808/565-6996**), to see if any storytelling or other children's activities are scheduled. The events are usually free and open to everyone.

Perfect for a Rainy Day: Lanai Art Program

A perfect activity for a rainy day in Lanai City is the **Lanai Arts Program,** 333 Seventh St., located in the heart of the small town. Frequently, top artists from across Hawaii visit this homegrown art program and teach a variety of classes ranging from raku (Japanese pottery), silk printing, silk screening, pareu making (creating your own design on this islanders' wrap), gyotaku (printing a real fish on your own T-shirt), and watercolor drawing to a variety of other island crafts. The cost is usually in the $25 range for the 2- to 3-hour classes (materials cost extra). For more information, call © **808/565-7503** or visit www.lanaiart.org.

here, you may get a rare Hawaii treat: On a clear day, you can see all of the main islands in the Hawaiian chain except Kauai.

When it rains, the Munro Trail becomes slick and boggy with major washouts. Rainy-day excursions often end with a rental jeep on the hook of the island's lone tow truck—and a $250 tow charge. You could even slide off into a major gulch and never be found, so don't try it. But in late August and September, when trade winds stop and the air over the islands stalls in what's called a *kona* condition, Mount Lanaihale's suddenly visible peak becomes an irresistible attraction.

When you're on Lanai, look to the summit. If it's clear in the morning, rent a four-wheel-drive vehicle and take the Munro Trail to the top. Look for a red-dirt road off Manele Road (Hwy. 440), about 5 miles south of Lanai City; turn left and head up the ridge line. No sign marks the peak, so you'll have to keep an eye out. Look for a wide spot in the road and a clearing that falls sharply to the sea.

From here you can see Kahoolawe, Maui, the Big Island of Hawaii, and Molokini's tiny crescent. Even the summits show. You can also see the silver domes of Space City on Haleakala in Maui; Puu Moaulanui, the tongue-twisting summit of Kahoolawe; and, looming above the clouds, Mauna Kea on the Big Island. At another clearing farther along the thickly forested ridge, all of Molokai, including the 4,961-foot summit of Kamakou and the faint outline of Oahu (more than 30 miles across the sea), are visible. You actually can't see all five islands in a single glance anymore because a thriving pine forest blocks the view. For details on hiking the trail, see "Hiking & Camping," above.

LUAHIWA PETROGLYPH FIELD

Lanai is second only to the Big Island in its wealth of prehistoric rock art, but you'll have to search a little to find it. Some of the best examples are on the outskirts of Lanai City, on a hillside site known as Luahiwa Petroglyph Field. The characters you'll see incised on 13 boulders in this grassy 3-acre knoll include a running man, a deer, a turtle, a bird, a goat, and even a rare, curly-tailed Polynesian dog (a latter-day wag has put a leash on him—some joke).

To get here, take the road to Hulopoe Beach. About 2 miles out of Lanai City, look to the left, up on the slopes of the crater, for a cluster of reddish-tan boulders (believed to form a rain *heiau*, or shrine, where people called up the gods Ku and Hina to nourish their crops). A cluster of spiky century plants marks the spot. Look for the Norfolk pines on the left side of the highway, turn left on the dirt road that veers across the abandoned pineapple fields, and after about 1 mile, take a sharp left by the water tanks. Drive for another ½ mile and then veer to the right at the V in the road. Stay on this upper road for about ¼ mile; you'll come to a large cluster of boulders on the right side. It's just a short walk up the cliffs (wear walking or hiking shoes) to the petroglyphs. Exit the same way you came. Go between 3pm and sunset for ideal viewing and photo ops.

KAUNOLU VILLAGE

Out on Lanai's nearly vertical, Gibraltar-like sea cliffs is an old royal compound and fishing village. Now a national historic landmark and one of Hawaii's most treasured ruins, it's believed to have been inhabited by King Kamehameha the Great and hundreds of his closest followers about 200 years ago. It's a hot, dry, dusty, slow-going, 3-mile 4×4 drive from Lanai City to Kaunolu, but the mini-expedition is worth it. Take plenty of water, don a hat for protection against the sun, and wear sturdy shoes.

Ruins of 86 house platforms and 35 stone shelters have been identified on both sides of Kaunolu Gulch. The residential complex also includes the Halulu Heiau temple, named after a mythical man-eating bird. The king's royal retreat is thought to have stood on the eastern edge of Kaunolu Gulch, overlooking the rocky shore facing Kahekili's Leap, a 62-foot-high bluff named for the mighty Maui chief who leaped off cliffs as a show of bravado. Nearby are burial caves, a fishing shrine, a lookout tower, and many warrior-like stick figures carved on boulders. Just offshore stands the telltale fin of little Shark Island, a popular dive spot that teems with bright tropical fish and, frequently, sharks.

Excavations are underway to discover more about how ancient Hawaiians lived, worked, and worshipped on Lanai's leeward coast. Who knows? The royal fishing village may yet yield the bones of King Kamehameha. His burial site, according to legend, is known only to the moon and the stars.

KANEPUU PRESERVE

This ancient forest on the island's western plateau is so fragile you can visit only once a month, and even then only on a guided hike. Kanepuu, which has 48 species of plants unique to Hawaii, survives under the Nature Conservancy's protective wing. Botanists say the 590-acre forest is the last dry lowland forest in Hawaii; the others have all vanished, trashed by axis deer, agriculture, or "progress." Among the botanical marvels of this dry forest are the remains of *olopua* (native olive), *lama* (native ebony), *mau hau hele* (a native hibiscus), and the rare *'aiea* trees, which were used for canoe parts.

Due to the forest's fragile nature, guided hikes are led only 12 times a year, on a monthly, reservations-only basis. Contact the **Nature Conservancy Oahu Land Preserve** manager at 1116 Smith St., Suite 201, Honolulu, HI 96817 (© **808/537-4508**), to reserve.

OFF THE TOURIST TRAIL: KEOMOKU VILLAGE

If you're sunburned lobster red, have read all the books you packed, and are starting to get island fever, take a little drive to Keomoku Village, on Lanai's east coast. You'll really be off the tourist trail. All that's in Keomoku, a ghost town since the mid-1950s, is a 1903 clapboard church in disrepair, an overgrown graveyard, an excellent view across the 9-mile Auau Channel to Maui's crowded Kaanapali Beach, and some very empty beaches that are perfect for a picnic or a snorkel. This former ranching and fishing village of 2,000 was the first non-Hawaiian settlement on Lanai, but it dried up after droughts killed off the Maunalei Sugar Company. The village, such as it is, is a great little escape from Lanai City. Follow Keomoku Road for 8 miles to the coast, turn right on the sandy road, and keep going for 5¾ miles.

10 Shopping

Central Bakery ✪ *(Finds)* This is the mother lode of the island's baked delights, the bakery that is, well, central to Lanai's dining pleasure. If you've noshed on the fantastic sandwiches at The Lodge at Koele's The Terrace or any of the stellar desserts at its Formal Dining Room or at Four Seasons Resort Lana'i at Manele Bay, you've enjoyed goodies from Central Bakery. The bakery supplies all breads, all breakfast pastries, specialty ice creams and sorbets, all banquet desserts, and restaurant desserts on the island. Although it's not your standard retail outlet, you can call in advance, place your order, and pick it up. They prefer as much notice as possible (preferably 48 hours) but, in a pinch, will take a 24-hour order. Breads (most $4.50) range from walnut onion to roasted potato bacon to olive onion. They also have cookies (chocolate chip, oatmeal, coconut—all for 50¢), brownies, muffins, croissants (including chocolate croissants), Danish, and scones, plus an assortment of breakfast pastries (pineapple turnover, hazelnut roll, mascarpone apricot Danish, pistachio chocolate roll, and others). 1311 Fraser Ave., Lanai City. ⓒ 808/565-3920.

Dis 'N Dat ✪✪ *(Finds)* Dis (Barry) and Dat (Susie) visited Lanai from Florida to look at buying a retirement home. They found their home and moved to Lanai to retire. Retirement didn't last. A few years later, outgoing Barry and his wife started searching for unusual, finely crafted teak and exotic wood sculptures and carvings. Along the way, they took a shine to mobiles and wind chimes—the more outrageous, the better. Then they started collecting handmade jewelry, stained glass, and unique garden ornaments and home decor. All this led to this eclectic store, which you have to see to believe. Meeting Barry is worth the trip alone. This also is the biggest collection of Hawaii slipper necklaces, earrings, anklets, and bracelets. You'll also find T-shirts, pottery, ceramics, batik scarves, hula lamps and whimsical dragonfly lamps, woven baskets, and even waterfalls. You can't miss this vivid green shop with hanging chimes and mobiles leading the way to the front door. 418 Eighth Ave. (at Kilele St.), Lanai City. ⓒ 866/DISNDAT or 808/565-9170.

Gifts with Aloha ✪ Phoenix and Kimberly Dupree's store of treasures has blossomed since they moved to a larger location on the other side of Dole Park. They are now shipping minigardens and lamps to the mainland, and are selling fabulously stylish hats, locally made clothing, T-shirts, swimwear, quilts, Jams World dresses, children's clothes, toys, Hawaii-themed CDs, DVDs, music, books, pareu, candles, aloha shirts, picture frames, handbags, ceramics, and art by local artists (including some of the most beautiful jewelry in the islands). The sumptuous honey from the Big Island is available here, as are jams and jellies by Lanai's Fabrao House. The made-on-Maui soaps and bath products—in gardenia, pikake, and plumeria fragrances—make great gifts. Dole Park, 363 Seventh St. (at Ilima St.) ⓒ 808/565-6589.

Heart of Lanai Gallery Denise Hennig, the resident artist at Hotel Lanai, displays her own photographs and watercolors of landscapes, people, and the lifestyle of Lanai's plantation past, as well as the work of other local Lanai artists at her afternoon teas, Tuesday through Saturday from 2:30 to 4:30pm. You can drop by and enjoy a cup of tea with her as she shows you the art she is displaying that week. Her home/gallery is located behind the hospital in a bright yellow house. 758 Queens St., Lanai City. ⓒ 808/565-7815. www.lanaionline.com/Merchants/heart_of_lanai.htm.

High Lights   Located just a block off Seventh Street, across the street from Coffee Works, is this island-style beauty salon and supply store. Owner Katharina Oriol has been working in beauty salons since 1975 and offers a full-service salon with hair cuts, styling, highlighting, manicures, pedicures, waxing, and so on. She also carries a wide selection of beauty products for hair and skin, and cosmetics. She welcomes walk-ins. 617 Ilima Ave., Lanai City. *C* **808/565-7207.**

International Food & Clothing   This store sells the basics: groceries, housewares, T-shirts, hunting and fishing supplies, over-the-counter drugs, wine and liquor, paper goods, and hardware, and even offers a takeout lunch counter. I was pleasantly surprised by the extraordinary candy and bubble-gum section, the beautiful local bananas in the small produce section, the surprisingly extensive selection of yuppie soft drinks (Sobe, Snapple, and others), and the best knife-sharpener I've seen. 833 Ilima Ave. *C* **808/ 565-6433.**

Lanai Art Center *★* *(Finds*   This wonderful center was organized in 1989 to provide a place where both residents and visitors can come to create art. The center offers classes and studio time in ceramics, painting and drawing, calligraphy, woodworking, photography, silk and textile painting, watercolor, and glass. The center has an impressive schedule of visiting instructors from writers to folk artists (quilting, lei-making, and instrument-making) to oil painters. Check out their reasonably priced classes (generally in the $25 range) or browse in the gallery for excellent deals on works by Lanai residents. 333 Seventh St., Lanai City. *C* **808/565-7503.**

Lanai Marketplace   Everyone on Lanai, it seems, is a backyard farmer. From 7 to 11am or noon on Saturday, they all head to this shady square to sell their dewy-fresh produce, home-baked breads, plate lunches, and handicrafts. This is Lanai's version of the green market: petite in scale (like the island) but charming, and growing.

Dolores Fabrao's jams and jellies, under the **Fabrao House** label (*C* **808/565-6134** for special orders), are a big seller at the market and at resort gift shops. Flavors include pineapple-coconut, pineapple-mango, papaya, guaivi (strawberry guava), *poha* (gooseberry), passion fruit, Surinam cherry, and the very tart karamay jelly. All fruits are grown on the island. Dole Square.

The Local Gentry *★★* *(Finds*   Jenna (Gentry) Majkus's wonderful boutique, open since 1999, is the first of its kind on the island, featuring clothing and accessories that are not the standard resort-shop fare. (Visiting and local women alike make a beeline for this store.) You'll find fabulous silk aloha shirts by Tiki, mahogany wood lamps, mermaids and hula girls, inexpensive sarongs, and fabulous socks. There are also great T-shirts, jewelry, bath products, picture frames, jeans, and offbeat sandals. Its most recent additions are wonderful children's clothes. 363 Seventh St. (behind Gifs of Aloha, facing Ilima St.) *C* **808/565-9130.**

Mike Carroll Gallery   If he is on the island, you'll find Mike Carroll at work here on his original oil paintings. After a successful 22-year career as a professional artist in Chicago, Carroll moved to Lanai and has been painting the beauty and the lifestyle of the island ever since. You'll find an extensive selection of his original work, some limited editions, prints and note cards, plus a dozen or so of Maui and Lanai's top artists and even some locally made, one-of-a-kind jewelry. 443 Seventh St., Lanai City. *C* **808/565-7122.** www.mikecarrollgallery.com.

Pine Isle Market   A local landmark for two generations, Pine Isle specializes in locally caught fresh fish, but you can also find fresh herbs and spices, canned goods, electronic games, ice cream, toys, zoris, diapers, paint, cigars, and other basic essentials of work and play. The fishing section is outstanding, with every lure imaginable. 356 Eighth St. ⓒ **808/565-6488.**

Richard's Shopping Center The Tamashiros' family business has been on the square since 1946; not much has changed over the years. This "shopping center" is, in fact, a general store with a grocery section, paper products, ethnic foods, meats (mostly frozen), liquor, toys, film, cosmetics, fishing gear, sunscreens, clothing, kitchen utensils, T-shirts, and other miscellany. Half a wall is lined with an extraordinary selection of fish hooks and anglers' needs. Aloha shirts, aloha-print zoris, fold-up lauhala mats, and gourmet breads from the Central Bakery (see above) are among the countless good things at Richard's. 434 Eighth St. ⓒ **808/565-6047.**

11 Lanai After Dark

The only regular nightlife venues are the Lanai Playhouse, at the corner of Seventh and Lanai avenues in Lanai City, and the two resorts, The Lodge at Koele and Four Seasons Resort Lana'i at Manele Bay.

The **Lanai Playhouse** (ⓒ **808/565-7500**) is a historic 1920s building that has won awards for its renovations. When it opened in 1993, the 150-seat venue stunned residents by offering first-run movies with Dolby sound—quite contemporary for anachronistic Lanai. Lanai Playhouse usually, but not always, shows two movies each evening from Friday to Tuesday (to Wed in summer), at 6:30 and 8:30pm, with occasional Sunday and Monday matinees; if a 3-hour movie is on, it's shown at 7:30pm. Tickets are $8 for adults and $5 for kids and seniors, and $5 for matinees. The playhouse is also the venue for occasional special events.

The Lodge at Koele has stepped up its live entertainment. In the lodge's Great Hall, in front of its manorial fireplaces, local artists serenade listeners, who sip port and fine liqueurs while sinking into plush chairs, with contemporary Hawaiian, classical, and other genres of music. The special programs are on weekends, but throughout the week, some form of nightly entertainment takes place from 7 to 10pm.

Occasionally, special events will bring in a few more nightlife options. During the annual **Pineapple Festival,** generally the first weekend in July, some of Hawaii's best musicians arrive to show their support for Lanai (see "Hawaii Calendar of Events," in chapter 2). Other special events include the **Aloha Festival** (www.alohafestivals.com), which takes place either the end of September or the first week in October, and the **Christmas Festival,** the first Saturday in December (contact **Lanai Visitors Bureau,** P.O. Box 631436, Lanai City, HI 96763; or 431 Seventh St., Suite A, Lanai City; ⓒ **800/947-4774** or 808/565-7600; fax 808/565-9316; www.visitlanai.net).

9

Kauai, the Garden Isle

On any list of the world's most spectacular islands, Kauai ranks right up there with Bora Bora, Huahine, and Rarotonga. All the elements are here: moody rainforests, majestic cliffs, jagged peaks, emerald valleys, palm trees swaying in the breeze, daily rainbows, and some of the most spectacular golden beaches you'll find anywhere. Soft tropical air, birdsong, the smell of ginger and plumeria, golden sunsets, sparkling waterfalls—you don't just go to Kauai, you absorb it with every sense. It may get more than its fair share of tropical downpours, but that's what makes it so lush and green—and creates an abundance of rainbows. The readers of *Travel + Leisure Magazine* have voted Kauai as the best island in Hawaii several years in a row.

Kauai is essentially a single large shield volcano that rises 3 miles above the sea floor. The island lies 90 miles across the open ocean from Oahu but seems at least a half-century removed in time. It's often called "the separate kingdom" because it stood alone and resisted King Kamehameha's efforts to unite Hawaii. In the end, it required a royal kidnapping to take the garden isle. After King Kamehameha died, his son, Liholiho, ascended the throne. He gained control of Kauai by luring Kauai's king, Kaumualii, aboard the royal yacht and sailing to Oahu; once there, Kaumualii was forced to marry Kaahumanu, Kamehameha's widow, thereby uniting the islands.

Today the independent spirit lives on in Kauai, which refuses to surrender its island to wholesale tourism. A Kauai rule is that no building may exceed the height of a coconut tree—between three and four stories. As a result, the island itself, not its palatial beach hotels, is the attention-grabber. There's little nightlife here, no opulent shopping malls—just the beauty of the verdant jungle, the endless succession of spectacular beaches, the grandeur of Waimea Canyon, and the drama of the Na Pali Coast.

Kauai's beauty has played a supporting role in more than 50 Hollywood films, from *South Pacific* to *Jurassic Park*. But this island is not just another pretty face: Its raw wilderness is daunting, its seas challenging, its canyons forbidding—two-thirds of the island is impenetrable. This is the place for active visitors: There are watersports galore; miles of trails through rainforests and along ocean cliffs for hikers, bikers, and horseback riders; and golf options that range from championship links to local courses where chickens roam the greens and balls wind up in coconut trees.

But Kauai is also great for those who need to relax and heal jangled nerves. Here you'll find miles of sandy beaches and quiet spots in the forest, perfect for just sitting and meditating, and an endless supply of laid-back, lazy days that end with the sun sinking into the Pacific amid a blaze of glorious tropical color.

1 Orientation

ARRIVING

The final approach to Lihue Airport is dramatic; try to sit on the left side of the aircraft, where passengers are treated to an excellent view of the Haupu Ridge, Nawiliwili Bay, and Kilohana Crater. **United Airlines** (© 800/225-5825; www.ual.com) offers direct service to Kauai, with daily flights from Los Angeles and San Francisco. **American Airlines** (© 800/433-7300; www.aa.com) has direct flights from Los Angeles. **SunTrips** (© 800-SUN-TRIPS; www.suntrips.com) has a charter from San Francisco or Oakland once a week that is direct. **Pleasant Holidays** (© 800/742-9244; www.pleasantholidays.com), one of Hawaii's largest travel companies offering low-cost airfare and package deals, has two weekly nonstop flights from Los Angeles and San Francisco using American Trans Air. All other airlines land in Honolulu, where you'll have to connect to a 30-minute interisland flight to Kauai's Lihue Airport. Among the three interisland jet carriers, **Aloha Airlines** (© 800/367-5250, 808/245-3691, or 808/484-1111; www.alohaair.com), **go!** (© 888/IFLYGO2; www.iflygo.com), and **Hawaiian Airlines** (© 800/367-5320, 808/245-1813, or 808/838-1555; www.hawaiianair.com), there is a flight at least every hour to Lihue.

You'll land at the Lihue Airport, located 3 miles outside of the county seat of Lihue. There's a county visitor information kiosk located next to each baggage claim area. All of the major car-rental companies have branches at Lihue Airport; see "Getting Around," below, and "Getting Around Hawaii," in chapter 2, for details on renting in Hawaii. If you're not renting a car (although you should be), call **Kauai Taxi Company** (© 808/246-9554) for airport pickup.

VISITOR INFORMATION

The **Kauai Visitors Bureau** is located on the first floor of the Watumull Plaza, 4334 Rice St., Suite 101, Lihue, HI 96766 (© 808/245-3971; fax 808/246-9235; www.kauaivisitorsbureau.org). For a free official *Kauai Vacation Planner* or recorded information, call © 800/262-1400. The **Poipu Beach Resort Association,** P.O. Box 730, Koloa, HI 96756 (© 888/744-0888 or 808/742-7444; http://poipu-beach.org), will also send you a free guide to accommodations, activities, shopping, and dining in the Poipu Beach area.

If you'd like to learn more about Kauai before you go, contact the **Kauai Historical Society,** 4396 Rice St., Lihue, HI 96766 (© 808/245-3373; www.kauaihistoricalsociety.org). The group maintains a video-lending library that includes material on a range of topics, including Hawaiian legends, ghost stories, archaeology, and travelogues on individual areas around Kauai. Mainland residents can borrow tapes for up to 3 weeks. Rates are $1 for society members, $2.50 for nonmembers; shipping and handling costs $5.

You can now plan your vacation to Kauai around the island's festivals and local events by checking out the new website, www.kauaifestivals.com.

THE ISLAND IN BRIEF

Kauai's three main resort areas, where nearly all the island's accommodations are located, are all quite different in climate, price, and type of accommodations offered. On the south shore, dry and sunny **Poipu** is anchored by perfect beaches. This is the place to stay if you like the ocean, watersports, and plenty of sunshine. The **Coconut Coast,** on the east coast of Kauai, has the most condos, shops, and traffic—it's where all the action is. Hanalei, up on the **North Shore,** is rainy, lush, and quiet, with spectacular beaches and deep wilderness. Because of its remote location, the North Shore is a great place to get away from it all—but not a great place from which to explore the rest of the island.

Kauai

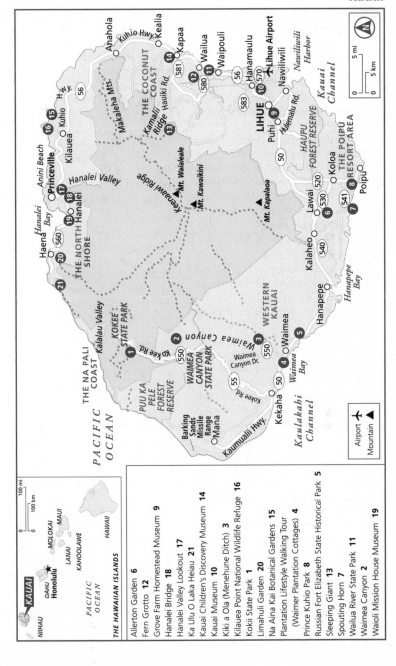

Anahola
Kuhio Hwy. Kealia
Kapaa
Wailua
Waipouli
Hanamaulu
Lihue Airport
Nawiliwili
Harbor
**Kauai
Channel**

THE COCONUT COAST
Makaleha Mts.
Kamalii Ridge Hauiki Rd.
581
580 56
583
570
LIHUE
Puhi 9
Hulemalu Rd.

56

Anini Beach
Princeville 17
Kilauea
Kuhio
16 15
Kuhio Hwy.
Hy.
56

Hanalei Valley

Hanalei Bay
18
Hanalei
19

Haena
560
20
21

THE NA PALI COAST

THE NORTH SHORE

Kalalau Valley

KOKEE STATE PARK

Koke Rd.
1
2
550

WAIMEA CANYON STATE PARK

PUU KA PELE FOREST RESERVE

Barking Sands Missile Range
Mana

Kaumualii Hwy.

Waimea Canyon

3
Waimea
550
4
Waimea Bay
Kekaha
50
Koke Rd.
55

WESTERN KAUAI

Mt. Waialeale
Mt. Kawaikini
Mt. Kapalaoa
Keaaawaii Ridge

5

HAUPU FOREST RESERVE

50
Lawai
530
520
6
540
541
7
8
Poipu
Koloa
THE POIPU RESORT AREA

Kalaheo

Hanapepe

Hanapepe Bay

Kaulakahi Channel

PACIFIC OCEAN

HAUPU FOREST RESERVE

Airport ✈
Mountain ▲

5 mi
5 km

13
12 11
14
580

THE HAUPU

Nawiliwili
10

Lihue & Environs

Lihue is where most visitors first set foot on the island. This red-dirt farm town, the county seat, was founded by sugar planters and populated by descendants of Filipino and Japanese cane cutters. It's a plain and simple place, with used-car lots and mom-and-pop shops. It's also the source of bargains: inexpensive lodging, great deals on dining, and some terrific shopping buys. One of the island's most beautiful beaches, **Kalapaki Beach** ✸✸, is just next door at **Nawiliwili,** by the island's main harbor.

The Poipu Resort Area

Poipu Beach ✸✸✸ On Kauai's sun-soaked south shore, this is a pleasant if sleepy resort destination of low-rise hotels set on gold-sand pocket beaches. Well-done, master-planned Poipu is Kauai's most popular resort, with the widest variety of accommodations, from luxury hotels to B&Bs and condos. It offers 36 holes of golf, 38 tennis courts, and outstanding restaurants. This is a great place for watersports and a good base from which to tour the rest of Kauai. The only drawback is that the North Shore is about 1 to 1½ hours away.

Koloa This tiny old town of gaily painted sugar shacks just inland from Poipu Beach is where the Hawaiian sugar industry was born more than a century and a half ago. The mill is closed, but this showcase plantation town lives on as a tourist attraction, with delightful shops, an old general store, and a vintage Texaco gas station with a 1930s Model A truck in place, just like in the good old days.

Kahaleo/Lawai Just a short 10- to 15-minute drive inland from the beach at Poipu lie the more residential communities of Lawai and Kalaheo. Quiet subdivisions line the streets, restaurants catering to locals dot the area, and life revolves around family and work. Good bargains on B&Bs and a handful of reasonably priced restaurants can be found here.

Western Kauai

This region, west of Poipu, is more remote than its eastern neighbor and lacks its terrific beaches. But it's home to one of Hawaii's most spectacular natural wonders, **Waimea Canyon** ✸✸✸ (the "Grand Canyon of the Pacific"), and, farther upland and inland, one of its best parks, **Kokee State Park** ✸✸.

Hanapepe For a quick trip back in time, turn off Highway 50 at Hanapepe, once one of Kauai's biggest towns. Founded by Chinese rice farmers, it's so picturesque that it was used as a backdrop for the miniseries *The Thornbirds.* Hanapepe makes a good rest stop on the way to or from Waimea Canyon. It has galleries selling antiques as well as local art and crafts, including Georgio's surfboard art and coconut-grams. It's also home to one of the best restaurants on Kauai, the Hanapepe Cafe & Espresso Bar (p. 573). Nearby, at **Salt Pond Beach Park** ✸ (p. 582), Hawaiians since the 17th century have dried a reddish sea salt in shallow, red-clay pans. This is a great place to swim, snorkel, and maybe even observe an ancient industry still in practice.

Waimea This little coastal town, the original capital of Kauai, seems to have quit the march of time. Dogs sleep in the street while old pickups rust in front yards. The ambience is definitely laid-back. A stay in Waimea is peaceful and quiet (especially at the Waimea Plantation Cottages on the beach; p. 553), but the remote location means this isn't the best base if you want to explore the other regions of Kauai, such as the North Shore, without a lot of driving.

Niihau: The Forbidden Island

Just 17 miles across the Kaulakahi Channel from Kauai lies the arid island of Niihau, "The Forbidden Island." Visitors are not allowed on this privately owned island, which is a working cattle-and-sheep ranch with about 200 residents living in the single town of Puuwai.

In 1864, after an unusually wet winter that turned the dry scrubland of the small island (18×6 miles) into green pasture, Eliza Sinclair, a Scottish widow, decided to buy Niihau and move her family here. King Kamehameha IV agreed to sell the island for $10,000. The next year, normal weather returned, and the green pastures withered into sparse semidesert vegetation.

Today Sinclair's great-great-grandson, Bruce Robinson, continues to run the ranching operation and fiercely protects the privacy of the island residents. Life on Niihau has not changed much in 140 years: There's no running water, indoor plumbing, or electric power. The Hawaiian language is still spoken. Most of the men work for the ranch when there is work, and fish and hunt when there is no work. The women specialize in gathering and stringing *pupu Niihau,* prized, tiny white seashells (found only on this island), into Niihau's famous leis, which fetch prices in the thousands of dollars.

On his search for the Northwest Passage in 1778, British explorer Capt. James Cook dropped anchor at Waimea and discovered a sleepy village of grass shacks. In 1815 the Russians arrived and built a fort here (now a national historic landmark), but they didn't last long: A scoundrel named George Anton Scheffer tried to claim Kauai for Russia, but he was exposed as an impostor and expelled by King Kamehameha I.

Today even Waimea's historic relics are spare and simple: a statue of Cook alongside a bas-relief of his ships, the rubble foundation of the Russian fort, and the remains of an ancient aqueduct unlike any other in the Pacific. Except for an overabundance of churches for a town this size, there's no sign that Waimea was selected as the first landing site of missionaries in 1820.

The Coconut Coast

The eastern shore of Kauai north of Lihue is a jumble of commerce and condos strung along the coast road named for Prince Kuhio, with several small beaches beyond. Almost anything you need, and a lot of stuff you can live without, can be found along this coast, which is known for its hundreds of coconut trees waving in the breeze. It's popular with budget travelers because of the myriad B&Bs and affordable hotels and condos to choose from, and it offers great restaurants and the island's major shopping areas.

Kapaa ✦ The center of commerce on the east coast and the capital of the Coconut Coast condo-and-hotel district, this restored plantation town looks just like an antique. False-front wooden stores line both sides of the highway; it looks as though they've been here forever—until you notice the fresh paint and new roofs and realize that everything has been rebuilt since Hurricane Iniki smacked the town flat in 1992. Kapaa has made an amazing comeback without losing its funky charm.

The North Shore

Kauai's North Shore may be the most beautiful place in Hawaii. Exotic seabirds, a half-moon bay, jagged peaks soaring into the clouds, and a mighty wilderness lie around the bend from the Coconut Coast, just beyond a series of one-lane bridges traversing the tail ends of waterfalls. There's only one road in and out, and only two towns, Hanalei and Kilauea—the former by the sea, the latter on a lighthouse cliff that's home to a bird preserve. Sun seekers may fret about all the rainy days, but Princeville Resort offers elegant shelter and two golf courses where you can play through rainbows.

Kilauea ✿ This village is home to an antique lighthouse, tropical-fruit stands, little stone houses, and Kilauea Point National Wildlife Refuge, a wonderful seabird preserve. The rolling hills and sea cliffs are hideaways for the rich and famous, including Bette Midler and Sylvester Stallone. The village itself has its charms: The 1892 Kong Lung Company, Kauai's oldest general store, sells antiques, art, and crafts; and you can order a jazzy Billie Holiday Pizza to go at Kilauea Bakery and Pau Hana Pizza.

Anini Beach ✿ This little-known residential district on a 2-mile reef (the biggest on Kauai) offers the safest swimming and snorkeling on the island. A great beach park is open to campers and day-trippers, and there's a boat ramp where locals launch sampans to fish for tuna. On Sunday there's polo in the park and the sizzle of barbecue on the green. Several residents host guests in nearby B&Bs.

Princeville ✿ A little overwhelming for Kauai's wild North Shore, Princeville Resort is Kauai's biggest project, an 11,000-acre development set on a high plain overlooking Hanalei Bay. This resort community includes a luxury Sheraton hotel, 10 condo complexes, new timeshare units around two championship golf courses, cliff-side access to pocket beaches, and one B&B right on the golf course.

Hanalei ✿✿✿ Picture-postcard Hanalei is the laid-back center of North Shore life and an escapist's dream; it's also a gateway to the wild Na Pali Coast. Hanalei is the last great place on Kauai yet to face the developer's blade of progress. At **Hanalei Bay,** sloops anchor and surfers play year-round. The 2-mile-long crescent beach, the biggest indentation on Kauai's coast, is ideal for kids in summer, when the wild surf turns placid. Hanalei still retains the essence of its original sleepy, end-of-the-road charm. On either side of two-lane Kuhio Highway, you'll find just enough shops and restaurants to sustain you for your visit—unless you're a hiker, surfer, or sailor, or have some other preoccupation that might keep you here the rest of your life.

Haena ✿✿ Emerald-green Haena isn't a town or a beach, but an ancient Hawaiian district, a place of exceptional natural beauty, and another gateway to the Na Pali Coast. It's the perfect tropical escape, and everybody knows it: Old house foundations and temples, now covered by jungle, lie in the shadow of new million-dollar homes of movie stars and musicians like Jeff Bridges and Graham Nash. This idyllic 4-mile coast has lagoons, bays, great beaches, spectacular snorkeling, a botanical garden, and the only North Shore resort that's right on the sand, the Hanalei Colony Resort (p. 562).

The Na Pali Coast ★★★

The road comes to an end, and now it begins: the Hawaii you've been dreaming about. Kauai's Na Pali Coast (*na pali* means "the cliffs") is a place of extreme beauty and Hawaii's last true wilderness. Its majestic splendor will forever remain unspoiled because no road will ever traverse it. You can enter this state park only on foot or by sea. Serious hikers—and we mean very serious—tackle the ancient 11-mile-long trail down the forbidding coast to Kalalau Valley (see "Hiking & Camping," later in this chapter). The lone, thin trail that creases these cliffs isn't for the faint of heart or anyone afraid of heights. Those who aren't up to it can explore the wild coast in an inflatable rubber Zodiac, a billowing sailboat, a high-powered catamaran, or a helicopter, which takes you for the ride of your life.

2 Getting Around

DRIVING AROUND KAUAI

You need a car to see and do everything on Kauai. Luckily, driving here is easy. However, there really is only one major road that circles the island, and during rush hour, from about 6 to 9am and 3 to 6pm, this road turns into a giant parking lot. A trip from the airport to Poipu could be as quick as 30 to 45 minutes during non-rush-hour times or as much as ½ hours during rush hour.

From Lihue Airport, turn right and you'll be on Kapule Highway (Hwy. 51), which eventually merges into Kuhio Highway (Hwy. 56) a mile down. This road will take you to the Coconut Coast and through the North Shore before reaching a dead end at Kee Beach, where the Na Pali Coast begins.

If you turn left from Lihue Airport and follow Kapule Highway (Hwy. 51), you'll pass through Lihue and Nawiliwili. Turning on Nawiliwili Road (Hwy. 58) will bring you to the intersection of Kaumualii Highway (Hwy. 50), which will take you to the south and southwest sections of the island. This road doesn't follow the coast, however, so if you're heading to Poipu (and most people are), take Maluhia Road (Hwy. 520) south.

Kaumualii Highway (Hwy. 50) continues to Waimea, where it then dwindles to a secondary road before reaching a dead end at the other end of the Na Pali Coast.

To get to Waimea Canyon, take either Waimea Canyon Road (Hwy. 550), which follows the western rim of the canyon and affords spectacular views, or Kokee Road (Hwy. 55), which goes up through Waimea Canyon to Kokee State Park (4,000 ft. above sea level); the roads join up about halfway.

CAR RENTALS   All of the major car-rental agencies are represented on Kauai; for a complete list, as well as tips on insurance and driving rules, see "Getting Around Hawaii," in chapter 2. The rental desks are just across the street from Lihue Airport, but you must go by van to collect your car. For deep discounts on weekly car-rental rates, call **Hookipa Haven Vacation Services** (✆ **800/398-6284;** www.hookipa.com). Rates in low season (Jan, Apr 16–June, and Aug 21–Dec 18) are $139 a week ($26 a day); they jump up to $200 a week ($34 a day) in high season.

MOTORCYCLE RENTALS   The best place to rent a motorcycle is from **Kauai Harley-Davidson,** 3-1866 Kaumualii Hwy., Lihue (✆ **808/241-7020;** www.kauai harley-davidson.com). Rates start at $179 for 24 hours.

OTHER TRANSPORTATION OPTIONS   Kauai Taxi Company (✆ **808/246-9554**) offers taxi, limousine, and airport shuttle service. **Kauai Bus** (✆ **808/241-6410;** www.kauai.gov) operates a fleet of 15 buses that serve the entire island. Taking the bus may be practical for day trips if you know your way around the island, but you can't take anything larger than a shopping bag aboard, and the buses don't stop at any of the resort areas—but they do serve more than a dozen coastal towns between Kekaha, on the southwest shore, all the way to Hanalei. Buses run more or less hourly from 5:30am to 6pm. The fare is $1.50, or 75¢ for seniors, students, and passengers with disabilities.

FAST FACTS: Kauai

Dentists Emergency dental care is available from **Dr. Mark A. Baird**, 4–9768 Kuhio Hwy., Kapaa (© 808/822-9393), and **Dr. Michael Furgeson**, 4347 Rice St., Lihue (© 808/246-6960).

Doctors Walk-ins are accepted at **Kauai Medical Clinic**, 3–3420 Kuhio Hwy., Suite B, Lihue (© 808/245-1500, or 808/245-1831 after-hours). You can also try the **North Shore Clinic**, Kilauea and Oka roads, Kilauea (© 808/828-1418); **Koloa Clinic**, 5371 Koloa Rd. (© 808/742-1621); **Eleele Clinic**, 3292 Waialo Rd. (© 808/335-0499); or **Kapaa Clinic**, 3–1105 Kuhio Hwy. (© 808/822-3431).

Emergencies Dial © 911 for police, fire, and ambulance service. The **Poison Control Center** can be reached at © 800/362-3585.

Hospitals **Wilcox Memorial Hospital**, 3420 Kuhio Hwy., Lihue (© 808/245-1100), has emergency services available 'round-the-clock.

Police For nonemergencies, call © 808/245-9711.

Post Office The main post office is at 4441 Rice St., Lihue. To find the branch office nearest you, call © 800/ASK-USPS.

Weather For current weather conditions, call © 808/245-6001. For marine conditions, call © 808/245-3564.

---

3 Where to Stay

You don't want to be stuck with long drives every day, so be sure to review "The Island in Brief," earlier, to choose the location that best fits your vacation needs.

Taxes of 11.42% are added to all hotel bills. Parking is free unless otherwise noted.

LIHUE & ENVIRONS
VERY EXPENSIVE
Kauai Marriott Resort & Beach Club 🌟🌟 *(Kids)* Once upon a time, this was a glitzy megaresort (the Westin Kauai) with ostentatious fantasy architecture, but then a hurricane (and new owners) toned it down. The result is grand enough to be memorable, but it's now grounded in reality—it looks like a Hawaiian hotel rather than a European palace. Water runs everywhere throughout the resort: lagoons, waterfalls, fountains, a 5-acre circular swimming pool (the largest on the island), and a terrific stretch of beach. The lagoons are home to six islands that serve as an exotic minizoo, which still lends an air of fantasy to the place and, along with the enormous pool and children's program (which includes such activities as exploring tropical gardens and learning about Hawaiian culture), makes the resort popular with families.

ACCOMMODATIONS ■
Garden Island Inn **11**
Kauai Beach Hotel & Resort **1**
Kauai Beach Villas **1**
Kauai Marriott Resort & Beach Club **13**

DINING ◆
Barbecue Inn **6**
Café Portofino **10**
Dani's Restaurant **8**
Duke's Canoe Club **13**
Gaylord's **9**
Hamura's Saimin Stand **7**
Hanamaulu Restaurant **2**
JJ's Broiler **12**
Kako's **5**
Kalapaki Beach Hut **14**
Restaurant Kiibo **4**
Tip Top Café/Bakery **3**

To Kapaa & the North Shore
Wilcox Memorial Hospital **56**
Kauai Museum
Police Station
LIHUE
Lihue Airport
Kilohana Plantation
Kukui Grove Center
Visitor Center
Vidinha Memorial Stadium
To Poipu & Waimea
Grove Farm Homestead
Nawiliwili
Menehune Gardens
KAUAI
Lihue
Lagoons Golf Course
Kalapaki Beach
Kiele Championship Golf Course
Nawiliwili Beach Park
Nawiliwili Bay
Niumalu Beach Park
Nawiliwili Harbor
HULEIA NATIONAL WILDLIFE REFUGE
Menehune Fishpond
Huleia Stream

Airport ✈
Information (i)
Post Office ✉

Guest rooms are comfortable, with fabulous views of gold-sand Kalapaki Beach, verdant gardens, and palm trees, and a recent refurbishment has them all looking brand new. The location allows for easy arrival and departure (Lihue Airport is only a mile away, and there's a free airport shuttle), but it also means you can hear the take-off and landing of every jet. Fortunately, air traffic stops by 9pm, but it begins bright and early in the morning.

Kalapaki Beach, Lihue, HI 96766. ⓒ **800/220-2925** or 808/245-5050. Fax 808/246-5148. www.marriott.com/lihhi. 356 units. $339–$454 double; from $664 suite. Paradise Plus Packages include deluxe accommodations and a choice of car or daily breakfast for 2 starting at $259. Extra person $40. AE, DC, DISC, MC, V. Valet parking $10, self-parking $7. **Amenities:** 4 restaurants (including Duke's Canoe Club, p. 565); 2 bars; the largest pool on the island; 36-hole Jack Nicklaus golf course; 8 tennis courts; state-of-the-art fitness center; 5 Jacuzzis; watersports equipment rentals; children's program; game room; concierge; activities desk; car-rental desk; business center; shopping arcade; salon; room service; massage; babysitting; coin-op washer/dryers; laundry service; dry cleaning. *In room:* A/C, TV/VCR, dataport, fridge, coffeemaker, hair dryer, iron, safe.

EXPENSIVE

Hilton Kauai Beach Hotel Resort   Formerly the Radisson Kauai, the hotel had a $7-million renovation in 2006 to convert it to a condo-hotel (which means that while the hotel will continue to operate as a full-service resort for visitors, a portion of the rooms in the hotel will be available for private ownership). Then the Hilton took over the management of the property and spent another $14 million to renovate and add such amenities as a 24-hour business center, an executive-club floor, Hilton's bedding and bath items, and an expanded fitness center. The 25-acre beachfront property, located 4 miles north of Lihue, commands a 3-mile stretch of the beach, but unfortunately, it's very windy and not safe for swimming. The resort is next door to a top-ranked municipal golf course, and there is a complimentary airport shuttle. The rooms have all been renovated and updated with plush new carpeting, a Balinese-style wood entry door, marble bath and floors, top-of-the-line bedding, and high-speed wireless Internet service. The Hilton also added a new quartzite stone decking at the resort's four-pool complex, a 12-foot waterfall cascading into the main pool, a flume and lava-tube waterslide at the sand-bottom pool, and a new whirlpool spa in a stone grotto surrounded by ferns and a waterfall. The location is good, about equidistant from both North Shore and south-shore activities, and also close to the Wailua River and its kayaking, water-skiing, river tours, historical sites, and waterfalls.

4331 Kauai Beach Dr., Lihue, HI 96766. © **800/HILTONS** or 808/245-1955. Fax 808/246-9085. www.hiltonkauai resort.com. 350 units. $179–$399 double; from $1,500 suite. Daily resort fee $11 for nightly sunset cocktail party and Polynesian dance show, coffee/tea service 6–7am, use of the Alolani Spa and Fitness Center, in-room coffee and tea service, in-room safe, local phone calls, in-room wireless access, shuttle service to airport, and parking. Numerous packages available, including car rentals, senior rates, and more. AE, DC, DISC, MC, V. Parking included in daily resort fee. **Amenities:** Restaurant; bar; 4 outdoor pools; tennis courts; fitness room; spa; Jacuzzi; watersports equipment rentals; concierge; activities desk; car-rental desk; business center; shopping arcade; salon; massage; babysitting; coin-op washer/dryers; laundry service; dry cleaning. *In room:* A/C, TV, dataport, Wi-Fi, fridge, coffeemaker, hair dryer, iron, safe.

MODERATE

Kauai Beach Villas   These beachfront condos are a good option for families and others seeking more space and privacy than they'd get elsewhere in Lihue. Located next door to the Hilton Kauai Beach Hotel Resort (see above), this property has the same drawback: unsafe swimming conditions on the beautiful but windy white-sand beach. All units are individually owned, although most are outfitted with tropical decor and bamboo-style furniture, a fully equipped kitchen, a washer/dryer, and a lanai big enough for two lounge chairs, a table, and four chairs. The two-bedroom units have lanais off each bedroom, too. Due to the individual ownership, the prices vary widely (you can get some deals here). The immaculately landscaped grounds contain pools, tennis courts, barbecue areas, and a volleyball court. The Wailua Municipal golf course is next door.

4330 Kauai Beach Dr., Lihue, HI 96766. Reservations c/o Kauai Vacation Rentals, 3–3311 Kuhio Hwy., Lihue. © **800/ 367-5025** or 808/245-8841. Fax 808/246-1161. www.kauaivacationrentals.com. 150 units. $162–$250 1-bedroom for 4; $119–$390 2-bedroom for 6. 3- to 7-night minimum. MC, V. **Amenities:** 1 outdoor pool; tennis courts; access to nearby health club; 1 hot tub; activities desk. *In room:* A/C (in bedrooms), TV/VCR, dataport, kitchen, fridge, coffeemaker, hair dryer, iron, safe, washer/dryer, answering machine.

INEXPENSIVE

Garden Island Inn ⭐ *(Finds)*   This bargain hunter's delight is located 2 miles from the airport, 1 mile from Lihue, and within walking distance of shops and restaurants. The spacious rooms are decorated with Island-style furniture, bright prints, and fresh tropical flowers (grown right on the grounds). Each unit contains a fridge, microwave, wet bar, TV, coffeemaker, and ocean view; some have private lanais, and the suites have sitting areas. The grounds are filled with flowers and banana and papaya trees (and you're welcome to help yourself to the fruit at the front desk). There's only one caveat:

The property does sit on a busy street, and some units can be noisy (bring ear plugs). Owner Steve Layne offers friendly service, lots of advice on activities (the entire staff happily uses their connections to get you discounts), and even complimentary use of beach gear, golf clubs (a course is nearby, as are tennis courts), and coolers. If they are booked, ask about their two-bedroom condo nearby ($150–$190 per night).

3445 Wilcox Rd. (across the street from Kalapaki Beach, near Nawiliwili Harbor), Lihue, HI 96766. (C) **800/648-0154** or 808/245-7227. Fax 808/245-7603. www.gardenislandinn.com. 21 units, private bathrooms have shower only. $95–$135 double. Extra person $5. AE, DISC, MC, V. **Amenities:** Complimentary watersports equipment; activities desk. *In room:* A/C, TV, fridge, coffeemaker, hair dryer, iron.

THE POIPU RESORT AREA

In addition to the accommodations listed below, you can try **Surf Song** ((C) **877/373-2331;** www.surfsong.com), with four units from $80 to $150 (3-night minimum), and, closer to the beach, **Pua Hale at Poipu** ((C) **800/745-7414** or 808/742-1700; www.kauai-puahale.com), with an intimate cottage within walking distance of the beach for $140 double (and a 4-night minimum). And at the **Garden Isle Cottages** ((C) **800/742-6711** or 808/742-6717; www.oceancottages.com), you'll overlook Koloa Landing and Waikomo Stream in an oceanfront, one-bedroom apartment for $198 to $220 double.

VERY EXPENSIVE

Grand Hyatt Kauai Resort & Spa ✦✦✦ *Kids*   It's hard to believe that this luxury hotel (one of Hawaii's best) could get any grander, but the recent multimillion-dollar renovations of this resort have done just that. This is one of Hawaii's best luxury hotels and one of the top-ranked tropical resorts in *Condé Nast Traveler*'s annual readers' poll. The four-story resort, built into the oceanside bluffs, spreads over 50 acres that overlook Shipwreck Beach (which is too rough for most swimmers) at the end of the road in Poipu. The $250-million Hyatt uses the Island architecture of the mid-1920s to recapture the old Hawaii of the Matson Line steamship era.

The airy atmosphere takes you back to the days of a grand plantation overlooking the sea. This is a comfortable, unostentatious place where you can bring the kids and Grandma. The rooms are large (nearly 600 sq. ft.) and elegantly outfitted. All have marble bathrooms and spacious private lanais; most have ocean views. Club floors have their own concierge and a lounge serving continental breakfast, drinks, and snacks. The hotel is next door to the Robert Trent Jones, Jr.–designed Poipu Golf Course. If you stay here, don't leave without a treatment from the **ANARA Spa,** the best spa on Kauai. (Also check out the large selection of classes—some of them free— at the fitness center.) There may be 23 Grand Hyatt hotels on the planet, but frankly, I can't image any of them could be better than this.

The collection of swimming pools here—freshwater and salt, with slides, waterfalls, and secret lagoons—makes this oceanfront Hyatt a real kids' paradise. The Camp Hyatt children's program offers arts and crafts, scavenger hunts, and other special activities. Plus, the Hyatt is one of the few hotels to offer "camp" in the evening, from 6 to 10pm.

1571 Poipu Rd., Koloa, HI 96756. (C) **800/55-HYATT** or 808/742-1234. Fax 808/240-6596. www.kauai-hyatt.com. 602 units. $430–$770 double; $810–$870 Regency Club; from $1,540 suite. Packages available. Extra person $50. Children 17 and under stay free in parent's room. Resort fee of $15 a day for local calls, self- and valet parking, 1 hr. at the tennis court free, fitness access to the ANARA Spa and to classes, and 10% off various shops on property. AE, DC, MC, V. **Amenities:** 6 restaurants (including Dondero's, p. 569); 6 bars (the partially open-air Stevenson's Library has mellow jazz Thurs–Sat nights); an elaborate freshwater fantasy pool complex, plus 2 more pools and 5 acres of saltwater swimming lagoons w/islands and a man-made beach; 4 tennis courts; one of the best fitness centers on the island; a 25,000-sq.-ft. ANARA Spa that is reason enough to stay here, w/lava-rock shower gardens, a 10-headed Swedish shower, and indoor-outdoor treatment rooms; 3 Jacuzzis; watersports equipment rentals; bike rental; extensive Camp Hyatt kids program; concierge; activities desk; car-rental desk; business center; shopping arcade; salon; room service; massage; babysitting; complimentary washer/dryers; same-day laundry and dry cleaning; concierge-level rooms. *In room:* A/C, TV/VCR (DVD players available for rent), high-speed Internet access ($15/day), minibar, fridge, coffeemaker, hair dryer, iron, safe.

Sheraton Kauai Resort 🌺🌺 (Kids)

This modern Sheraton has the feeling of old Hawaii and a dynamite location on one of Kauai's best beaches. It features buildings on both the ocean side and the mountain side of the road. The horseshoe-shaped, Polynesian-style lobby has shell chandeliers dangling from the ceiling. You have a choice of three buildings: one nestled in tropical gardens with koi-filled ponds; one facing the palm-fringed, white-sand beach (my favorite); or one looking across green grass to the ocean, with great sunset views. The rooms overlook either the tropical gardens or the rolling surf.

The bar here is fabulous. Even if you don't stay here, come by to order a cocktail and an appetizer, and take in the view and the Hawaiian music. A golf course is nearby. *Families, take note:* Kids eat free with a paying adult at the Shell Restaurant, at both breakfast and dinner.

2440 Hoonani Rd., Koloa, HI 96756. ℂ 800/782-9488 or 808/742-1661. Fax 808/742-9777. www.starwoodhotels. com/hawaii. 413 units. $370–$635 double (maximum 4 in room); from $700 suite for 4. Extra person $50. Resort fee of $15 for sunset mai tai punch hour (Sun, Mon, Wed, Fri) with a torch-lighting ceremony, guest library with daily newspapers and 4 computers with Internet access, and use of the fitness center and tennis courts. AE, DC, DISC, MC, V. **Amenities:** 3 restaurants; extraordinary bar; 2 outdoor pools (1 w/water playground, 1 for children); 3 tennis courts (2 night-lit); fitness room facing the ocean (one of the most scenic places to work out on Kauai); small massage-and-skin-care center; Jacuzzi; watersports equipment rentals; children's program; concierge; activities desk; shopping arcade; salon; room service; babysitting; coin-op washer/dryers; same-day laundry and dry cleaning. *In room:* A/C, TV, dataport, high-speed wireless Internet access ($15/day), fridge, coffeemaker, hair dryer, iron, safe.

EXPENSIVE

Kiahuna Plantation Resort 🌺🌺

This complex consists of several plantation-style buildings, loaded with Hawaiian style and sprinkled about a 35-acre garden setting with lagoons, lawns, and a gold-sand beach. Golf, shopping, and restaurants are within easy walking distance. All condo units are spacious, with full kitchens, daily maid service, and lanais. The Kiahuna Swim and Tennis Club (with the Casa Blanca at Kiahuna restaurant) is just across the street, and a championship golf course is nearby.

2253 Poipu Rd., Koloa, HI 96756. 333 units. ℂ 800/OUTRIGGER or 808/742-6411. Fax 808/742-1698. www.outrigger. com. $265–$499 1-bedroom apt (sleeps up to 4); $405–$545 2-bedroom apt (sleeps up to 6). Packages available, including 5th night free, car packages, senior rates, and more. AE, DC, DISC, MC, V. **Amenities:** Restaurant (Plantation Gardens, p. 570); bar; outdoor pool; tennis courts; watersports equipment rentals; children's program; activities desk; shopping arcade nearby; coin-op washer/dryers; barbecue areas. *In room:* TV/VCR, kitchen, fridge, coffeemaker, hair dryer, iron, safe.

MODERATE

Hideaway Cove Villas 🌺🌺 (Value)

Just a block from the beach, and next door to an excellent restaurant, are these gorgeous condominium units in a plantation setting. Amenities are top-drawer, and no expense was spared in the interior decorations. Units have hardwood floors, TV/VCR/DVD, comfy furniture, roomy beds (either four-poster beds or wood sleigh designs), spacious living areas, kitchenettes with the best appliances and granite countertops, and big outdoor lanais. You get all of this in a lush, landscaped tropical jungle at affordable prices. Owner Herb Lee is always on

Where to Stay & Dine in the Poipu Resort Area

ACCOMMODATIONS ■

Bamboo Jungle **2**
Garden Isle Cottages **11**
Grand Hyatt Kauai
   Resort & Spa **28**
Hideaway Cove Villas **26**
Kalaheo Inn **1**
Kauai Banyan Inn **8**
Kauai Cove **13**
Kiahuna Plantation Resort **17**
Marjorie's Kauai Inn **7**
Nini Kai Villas **24**
Poipu Crater Resort **27**
Poipu Kapili Resort **15**
Pua Hale at Poipu **21**
Sheraton Kauai Resort **16**
Surf Song **12**
Waikomo Stream Villas **14**

DINING ◆

The Beach House **10**
Brennecke's Beach Broiler **23**
Brick Oven Pizza **5**
Camp House Grill **6**
Casa Blanca at Kiahuna **20**
Casa di Amici **25**
Dondero's **28**
e.b.'s EATS **18**
Joe's on the Green **19**
Kalaheo Coffee Co. & Café **3**
Keoki's Paradise **18**
Plantation Gardens Restaurant **17**
Poipu Beach Broiler **22**
Pomodoro **4**
Roy's Poipu Bar & Grill **18**
Tidepool Restaurant **28**
Tomkats Grille **9**

Value The King of Condos

One of the easiest ways to find lodging in the Poipu Beach area is to contact **Grantham Resorts** (which recently sold to Jonathan Parrish), 3176 Poipu Rd., Koloa, HI 96756 (© **800/325-5701** or 808/742-2000; fax 808/742-9093; www.grantham-resorts.com). Grantham handles more than 100 "hand-picked" rental units for 12 different condo developments, plus dozens of vacation homes, ranging from quaint cottages to elite resort homes. Grantham Resorts has high standards for their rental units and offers extremely fair prices. If the properties are not maintained to their standards, they have no problem taking the units (and, in one case, an entire condominium project) out of their selected rentals. The condos start at $135 for a spacious two-bedroom, garden-view unit in low season, and vacation cottages start at $200 and go up to $1,400 for exquisite multimillion-dollar ocean estates. There's a 5-night minimum for condos and a 7-night minimum for homes.

If you're staying on Kauai for 5 days, ask Grantham Resorts about the **"Frommer's Value Rate."** You'll get a large one- or two-bedroom condo, well equipped (full kitchen, washer/dryer, wet bar, TV/DVD, and phone; most units have high-speed Internet), for as little as $105 a night for one-bedrooms and $135 for two-bedrooms with garden views, or $145 a night for oceanview condos (see the reviews for Nihi Kai Villas, Poipu Crater Resort, and Waikomo Stream Villas below). There's not a better deal on Kauai. Kudos to Grantham Resorts for these fabulous vacation bargains.

hand to guide you to Kauai's best spots and loan out his collection of beach toys and beach cruiser bicycles. A few of the units have Jacuzzis, so ask when you book.

2307 Nalo Rd. Reservations: P.O. Box 1113, Kaloa, HI 96756. © **866/849-2426** or 808/635-8785. www.hideaway cove.com. 7 units. $160–$185 studio double; $200 1-bedroom double; $265–$290 2-bedroom for 4; $395–$475 3-bedroom for 4; plus $90–$200 cleaning fee. Extra person $20. 2-night minimum. AE, DISC, MC, V. **Amenities:** Restaurant and bar next door; free beach toys and bicycles; washer/dryers. *In room:* TV/VCR/DVD, kitchen, fridge, coffeemaker, hair dryer, iron.

Poipu Kapili Resort 🏠🏠   This quiet, upscale oceanfront cluster of condos is outstanding in every area. I like the home-away-from-home comforts and special touches: a video and book library, a spacious pool, several barbecues, tennis courts lit for night play, and an herb garden (you're welcome to take samples if you're cooking). A golf course is also nearby. The apartments are large (one-bedroom/two-bathroom units are 1,150 sq. ft.; two-bedroom/three-bathroom units are 1,820 sq. ft.) and have fully equipped kitchens, tropical furnishings, ceiling fans, and private lanais. The ocean-front two-story town houses are my favorites because they catch the trade winds. The two-bedroom units also have washer/dryers (common laundry facilities are available on the property as well). Although the Pacific is right out your window, the nearest sandy beach is a block away (which can be a blessing because it means more privacy).

2221 Kapili Rd., Koloa, HI 96756. © **800/443-7714** or 808/742-6449. Fax 808/742-9162. www.poipukapili.com. 60 units. $230–$335 1-bedroom apt (sleeps up to 4); $320–$600 2-bedroom apt (up to 6). Discounts for longer stays;

package rates available; 7th night free May 1–Dec 20. Rates include Fri continental breakfast by the pool. MC, V. **Amenities:** Oceanside pool; championship tennis courts lighted for night use; activities desk; washer/dryers; barbecue area. *In room:* TV/VCR, high-speed Internet access, kitchen, fridge, coffeemaker, hair dryer (on request), iron.

INEXPENSIVE

Bamboo Jungle *(Finds)*   Lucy and Terry Ryan took over this property, a jungle of verdant plants, a quaint gazebo, an 82-foot lap pool, and an impeccably decorated old plantation-era house, and made the much-needed repairs and renovations to the rooms, each of which has a private entrance and French doors opening onto a private lanai with an ocean view. The netting over the beds creates a romantic mood and serves a functional purpose (it keeps Hawaii's insects on their side of the sleeping quarters). Accommodations range from a single room with deck to a studio with kitchenette. The house phone is available for guests' use. Breakfast is served in the "great room" inside the house. The next renovation will be to the gardens and yard. Golf and tennis courts are nearby. Note that there is no air-conditioning, which 350 days of the year is fine, but on the days the trade winds stop blowing, it's not so great.

3829 Waha Rd. Reservations: P.O. Box 737, Kalaheo, HI 96741. *©* **888/332-5115** or 808/332-5515. www.kauai-bed andbreakfast.com. 3 units. $130–$160 double. 3-night minimum (5-night minimum in Bamboo Garden Room). MC, V. From Hwy. 50, turn left at the traffic light onto Papalina Rd.; then right on Waha Rd. **Amenities:** Outdoor pool; Jacuzzi. *In room:* TV, kitchenette (in 1 room), coffeemaker, no phone.

Kalaheo Inn *(Value) (Kids)*   What a deal! Located in the town of Kalaheo, a 12-minute drive from world-famous Poipu Beach, a 5-minute drive from the Kukuiolono Golf Course, and within walking distance of shops and restaurants, the inn is a comfortable 1940s motel totally remodeled in 1999 and converted into apartment units with kitchenettes. In 2005, owners Chet and Tish Hunt replaced the beds with Simmons "Heavenly" mattresses, put hair dryers in the bathrooms and new refrigerators in all the rooms, and gave the place a polishing. The Hunts couldn't be friendlier, handing out complimentary beach towels, beach toys, and even golf clubs to guests (links are nearby). They love families and have a storeroom full of games to keep the kids entertained. This is a must-stay for vacationers on a budget.

4444 Papalina Rd. (just behind the Kalaheo Steakhouse), Koloa, HI 96756. *©* **888/332-6023** or 808/332-6023. Fax 808/332-5242. www.kalaheoinn.com. 15 units. $80 double studio; $90–$100 1-bedroom; $121 2-bedroom; $163 3-bedroom with full kitchen. AE, MC, V. **Amenities:** Watersports equipment; children's games; coin-op washer/dryers; complimentary Internet access. *In room:* TV, kitchen or kitchenette, fridge, coffeemaker, hair dryer, iron, no phone.

Kauai Banyan Inn *(Finds)*   On a hilltop overlooking an acre of landscaped property, a stream, and, of course, an old banyan tree is this five-room inn. Centered by a courtyard with a burbling fountain, this is a place of peace and quiet, great for relaxing and resting. The daughter of owner Lorna is a licensed massage therapist and can give you an in-room massage to relieve jet lag and built-up tension. Each room is good-size, with a kitchenette (a three-quarter-size refrigerator, microwave, two-burner stove, and coffeemaker). All the rooms have terrific pastoral views of the rolling countryside, lanais, private bathrooms, and private entrances. Breakfast is provided in your room and consists of homemade banana bread, fruit, coffee, and juice. Lorna welcomes kids and can dig up a portable crib and highchair for families. There's a barbecue area outside.

3528-B Mana Hema Pl., Lawai, HI 96765. *©* **888/786-3855**. www.kauaibanyan.com. 5 units. $90–$125, plus $30–$45 cleaning fee. MC, V. **Amenities:** Barbecue area; hot tub; beach equipment. *In room:* TV/DVD, free wireless Internet access, fridge, coffeemaker, hair dryer, iron/ironing board.

Moa Better: Chickens & Roosters

One of the first things that visitors notice about Kauai is there seems to be an unusually large number of *moa* (wild chickens). Kauai has always had a history of having more than its fair share of chickens and roosters running about, but after Hurricane Iniki picked up and scattered the fowl all over the island in 1992, they have been populating at a prodigious rate. Generally, having a few chickens scratching around in the dirt is quaint and downright picturesque. However, the "dark side" of the chicken population explosion is the increase in the number of roosters. In fact, a new industry has cropped up: rooster eradicators. Resorts hire these eradicators to remove the roosters from the well-manicured grounds because the large number of these male birds has led to, well, a sort of crowing contest. Generally roosters will crow as the sun comes up. But on Kauai, with the population increase, the roosters crow all day long and throughout the night in some places. Just be warned that part of the "charm" of Kauai is the rooster population, and you might want to consider bringing earplugs.

Kauai Cove ★ *Finds*   These immaculate cottages, located just 300 feet from the Koloa Landing, next to the Waikomo Stream, are the perfect private getaway. Each studio has a full kitchen, private lanai (with barbecue grill), and big bamboo four-poster bed. The cozy rooms feature beautiful hardwood floors, tropical decor, and cathedral ceilings. It's close enough that you can walk to sandy beaches, great restaurants, and shopping, yet far enough off the beaten path that privacy and quiet are assured. If the cottages are booked, ask about their two units in the Poipu Kai Resort.

2672 Puuholo Rd., Poipu, HI 96756. ©/fax **800/624-9945** or 808/742-2562. www.kauaicove.com. 3 units. $95–$165 double, plus $50–$65 cleaning fee. 3-night minimum. MC, V. **Amenities:** Use of pool, tennis courts, and hot tub nearby; wireless Internet access. *In room:* A/C, TV, dataport, kitchen, fridge, coffeemaker, CD.

Marjorie's Kauai Inn ★ *Finds*   This quiet property, perched on the side of a hill, is just 10 minutes from Poipu Beach and 5 minutes from Old Koloa Town. From its large lanai, it offers stunning views over the rolling pastures and the Lawai Valley. Every unit has a kitchenette, dining table, ceiling fan, and lanai. The new Sunset View unit has a separate sitting area and a futon sofa for extra guests. On the hillside is a huge 50-foot swimming pool, perfect for lap swimming. "Do more than one fun thing a day!" was the motto of the original owner, Marjorie Ketcher, who made sure that the guests were out diving, snorkeling, sightseeing, hiking, dining, dancing, or enjoying one of the hundreds of other things on Kauai. Marjorie has sold her B&B, and the new owners are continuing her philosophy of living each day in paradise to the fullest. As terrific as this property is, it is not recommended for families with children.

P.O. Box 866 (off Hailima Rd., adjacent to the National Tropical Botanical Garden), Lawai, HI 96765. © **800/717-8838** or 808/332-8838. www.marjorieskauaiinn.com. 3 units. $130–$160 double. Rates include continental breakfast. Extra person $20. 2-night minimum. No credit cards. **Amenities:** Pool; Jacuzzi; barbecue. *In room:* TV, kitchenette, fridge, coffeemaker, hair dryer.

Nihi Kai Villas ★ *Value*   Grantham Resorts (see the box "The King of Condos," above) is offering the deal of the decade on these large two-bedroom units about 600 feet from the beach. If you stay 7 nights, the rate for these well-equipped oceanview apartments starts at an unbelievable $145 a night (for four, which works out to just $73 a couple). You may not be getting new carpet, new furniture, new drapes, or a prime beachfront location, but you *are* getting a clean, well-cared-for unit with a full kitchen, washer/dryer, and TV/VCR; there's also a barbecue and picnic area on-site. The property is a 2-minute walk from world-famous Brennecke's Beach (great for bodysurfing) and a block from Poipu Beach Park. Within a 5-minute drive are two great golf courses, several restaurants, and loads of shopping.

1870 Hoone Rd. Reservations: c/o Grantham Resorts, 3176 Poipu Rd., Suite 1, Koloa, HI 96756. ⒸＰ 800/325-5701 or 808/742-2000. Fax 808/742-9093. www.grantham-resorts.com. 70 units. $145–$195 1-bedroom for up 6 guests; $145–$279 2-bedroom for up 6 guests. 5-night minimum. Ask about "Frommer's Value Rate" (5-night minimum). AE, DISC, MC, V. From Poipu Rd., turn toward the ocean on Hoowili Rd. and then left on Hoone Rd.; Nihi Kai Villas is just past Nalo Rd. on Hoone Rd. **Amenities:** Outdoor heated pool; nearby golf course; tennis courts; Jacuzzi; concierge; activities desk. *In room:* TV/DVD, free Internet access, kitchen, coffeemaker, iron, washer/dryer.

Poipu Crater Resort (Value   Here's a deal travelers on a budget can't beat: two-bedroom garden view units for just $119 a night in low season (and a still-unbelievable $139 in high season). This resort consists of 15 duplexes in a tropical garden setting. Each unit is about 1,500 square feet with living area, kitchen, large lanai, bathroom, and guest bedroom downstairs, and master bedroom and bathroom upstairs. Each has a full kitchen (with microwave), as well as a washer/dryer and VCR. The complex has a swimming pool, tennis and paddleball courts, sauna, Ping-Pong tables, and barbecues. Poipu Beach is about a 10-minute walk away, and the entire Poipu Beach resort area (offering everything from restaurants to golf courses) is within a 5-minute drive. The only caveats are no maid service and no air-conditioning.

2330 Hoohu Rd., Poipu. c/o Grantham Resorts, 3176 Poipu Rd., Suite 1, Koloa, HI 96756. ⒸＰ 800/325-5701 or 808/742-2000. Fax 808/742-9093. www.grantham-resorts.com. 30 units. $105–$139 2-bedroom garden view for up to 6 guests. 5-night minimum. Ask about "Frommer's Value Rate" (5-night minimum). AE, DISC, MC, V. From Poipu Rd., turn toward the ocean on Hoowili Rd., and then left on Hoone Rd.; continue on Hoone Rd., past the bends, where the road is now called Pee Rd.; turn left off Pee Rd. onto Hoohu Rd. **Amenities:** Outdoor pool; nearby golf course; tennis courts; sauna; barbecue area. *In room:* TV/DVD, kitchen, coffeemaker, iron, washer/dryer, CD.

Waikomo Stream Villas (Ｒ (Value   Grantham Resorts (see the box "The King of Condos," above) has one more fabulous trick up their sleeve: these 1,000-square-foot one-bedroom apartments, which comfortably sleep four, and larger two-bedroom units, which sleep six. Tucked into a lush tropical garden setting, these spacious, well-decorated units have everything you'll need on your vacation: full kitchen, VCR, washer/dryer, and private lanai. The complex—which has both adults' and children's pools, tennis courts, and a barbecue area—is adjacent to the Kiahuna Golf Club and just a 5-minute walk from restaurants, shopping, and Poipu's beaches and golf courses.

2721 Poipu Rd. (just after entry to Poipu, on ocean side of Poipu Rd.), Poipu. c/o Grantham Resorts, 3176 Poipu Rd., Suite 1, Koloa, HI 96756. ⒸＰ 800/325-5701 or 808/742-2000. Fax 808/742-9093. www.grantham-resorts.com. 60 units. $105–$159 1-bedroom for 4; $135–$189 2-bedroom for 6. 5-night minimum. Ask about "Frommer's Value Rates." AE, DISC, MC, V. **Amenities:** 2 outdoor pools (1 for children and 1 for adults); complimentary tennis courts; Jacuzzi; concierge; activities desk. *In room:* TV/DVD, free Internet access, kitchen, fridge, coffeemaker, washer/dryer.

WESTERN KAUAI
MODERATE
Waimea Plantation Cottages (Ｒ (Kids   This beachfront vacation retreat is like no other in the islands: Among groves of towering coco palms sit clusters of restored sugar-plantation cottages, dating from the 1880s to the 1930s and bearing the names

of their original plantation-worker dwellers. The lovely cottages have been transformed into cozy, comfortable guest units with period rattan and wicker furniture and fabrics from the 1930s, sugar's heyday on Kauai. Each has a furnished lanai and a fully equipped modern kitchen and bathroom; some units are oceanfront. Facilities include an oceanfront pool, tennis courts, and laundry. The seclusion of the village makes it a nice place for kids to wander and explore, away from traffic. The only downsides: the black-sand beach, which is lovely but not conducive to swimming (the water is often murky at the Waimea River mouth), and the location, at the foot of Waimea Canyon Drive—its remoteness can be very appealing, but the North Shore is 1½ hours away. Golf courses and tennis courts, however, are much closer.

9400 Kaumualii Hwy. (P.O. Box 367), Waimea, HI 96796. (℟ **800/9-WAIMEA** or 808/338-1625. Fax 808/338-2338. www.waimea-plantation.com. 48 units. $155–$175 studios with kitchenette double; $220–$360 1-bedroom double; $275–$425 2-bedroom (sleeps up to 4); $325–$475 3-bedroom (up to 5); $525 4-bedroom (up to 8); $800 5-bedroom (up to 9). Extra person $20. Children under 18 stay free in parent's room. AE, DC, DISC, MC, V. **Amenities:** Restaurant; bar; large outdoor pool; activities desk; coin-op washer/dryers; dry cleaning; wireless Internet access. *In room:* TV, dataport, kitchen, fridge, coffeemaker, iron, safe.

INEXPENSIVE

Kokee Lodge *(Value* This is an excellent choice, especially if you want to do some hiking in Waimea Canyon and Kokee State Park. There are two types of cabins here: The older ones have dormitory-style sleeping arrangements (and resemble a youth hostel), while the new ones have two separate bedrooms each. Both styles sleep six and come with cooking utensils, bedding, and linens. We recommend the newer units, which have wood floors, cedar walls, and more modern kitchen facilities (some are wheelchair-accessible as well). There are no phones or TVs in the units, but there is a pay phone at the general store. You can purchase firewood for the cabin stove at Kokee Lodge, where there's a restaurant that's open for continental breakfast and lunch every day. There's also a cocktail lounge, a general store, and a gift shop. *Warning for light sleepers:* This area is home to lots of roosters, which crow at dawn's first light.

P.O. Box 819, Waimea, HI 96796. (℟ 808/335-6061. 12 units. $90 double, plus $20 cleaning fee. Extra person $5. 5-night maximum. AE, DC, DISC, MC, V. *In room:* Kitchen, fridge, percolator, no phone.

THE COCONUT COAST

This is the land of B&Bs and inexpensive vacation rentals. In addition to those reviewed below, we recommend **Opaeka'a Falls Hale,** which has two exquisite units with pool and hot tub for $100; reservations are available through **Hawaii's Best Bed & Breakfasts** (℟ **800/262-9912;** www.bestbnb.com).

Another excellently priced choice is **Kakalina's B&B** (℟ **800/662-4330;** www. kakalina.com), on a 3-acre flower farm nestled in the foothills of Mount Waialeale, offering rates from $80. For a very reasonable $75 double, the intimate **Surf & Ski Cottage** (℟ **808/645-0592;** www.waterskisurfandkayak.com), right on the Wailua River, is the place for watersports nuts; it's owned by the people who run Kauai Water Ski & Surf Co., and guests get 20% off on rental of all water toys. And one of the very best deals on Kauai is **Hibiscus Hollow** (℟ **808/823-9004;** www.akauaivacation rental.com), a private studio for two for just $60 a night.

EXPENSIVE

Outrigger Waipouli Beach Resort & Spa 𝘬𝘬 *(Kids* This luxurious beach resort opened at the very end of December 2006 with a $200-million condominium project on 12.6 acres between the historic towns of Wailua and Kapaa. The resort features

Where to Stay & Dine on the Coconut Coast

KEALIA

To the North Shore

KAUAI
Princeville
Hanalei
Kapaa
Lihue

Kawaihau Rd.
Kapaa Stream
Hauaala Rd.
Kuhio Hwy.
Mailihuna Rd.
Kealia Beach
Scenic Lookout
Kaehulua Rd.
Laipo Rd.
Kanaela St.
Hauaala Rd.

Olehena Rd.
Olehana Rd.
581

KAPAA PARK
Lehua St.
Kapaa Beach Park
Waipouli Park

Kapaa Bypass Rd.
KAPAA

Sleeping Giant
Waikaea Canal

NONOU FOREST RESERVE
Kealia Stream

Kapaa Shopping Center
Waipouli Town Center

Kuhio Hwy.
56
Haleilio Rd.
Kinipopo Shopping Village
Nonou Rd.
Papaloa Rd.

Coconut Marketplace
Waipouli Beach

Opaekaa Falls
580
Kuamoo Rd.
Coco Palms Resort
WAILUA
Fern Grotto
Wailua River
Wailua River Marina
Wailua Beach Park
Wailua Bay
Lydgate State Beach Park
Kuhio Hwy.
Leho Dr.
Nukolii Beach Park
To Lihue

DINING ◆
Blossoming Lotus **10**
Bubba Burger **5**
The Bull Shed **16**
Café Coco **19**
Coconuts Island Style Grill **13**
The King & I **15**
Kountry Kitchen **6**
Mermaid **9**
Norberto's El Café **7**
Ono Family Restaurant **11**
Sukhothai Restaurant **8**
Wailua Family Restaurant **20**
Wailua Marina Restaurant **24**

ACCOMMODATIONS ■
Aloha Beach Resort **25**
Hibiscus Hollow **3**
Hotel Coral Reef **4**
Kakalina B&B **22**
Kapaa Shores **11**
Kauai Country Inn **1**
Lae Nani Outrigger
  Resort Condominium **18**
Lani-keha **22**
Mahina Kai **2**
Opaeka'a Falls Hale **22**
ResortQuest Kauai Beach
  at Makaiwa **17**
Rosewood B&B **22**
Surf & Ski Cottage **21**
Wailua Bay View **23**

six hotel rooms and 190 high-end condo units (153 two-bedroom/three-bath units and 37 one-bedroom/two-bath units), of which 130 units are in the rental pool (75% are the two-bedroom units). Each unit is furnished with the top-of-the-line materials like granite countertops; stainless steel appliances by Sub-Zero, Wolf, and Fisher/Paykel; a double dishwasher; a full-sized Whirlpool washer and dryer; whirlpool bath tubs in the master bathrooms; and 37-inch flatscreen TVs. The two-bedroom units are 1,300 square feet with floor-to-ceiling windows and two lanais.

The resort features a long list of amenities like complimentary high-speed Internet access, a 4,000-square-foot Aveda spa, a fitness center, and a 300,000-gallon heated saltwater fantasy pool, with flowing river, garden, dual serpentine waterslides, sand-bottom children's pool, and three sand-bottom whirlpool tubs. Plus, the entire property, all the guest rooms, and the common areas are nonsmoking.

The location, across the street from the Kauai Village Shopping Center and the Waipouli Town Center, means guests are within walking distance of restaurants and shops and, more importantly, just across the street from a Safeway grocery store and a Longs Drug Store and pharmacy.

4-820 Kuhio Hwy., Kapaa, HI 96746 ⓒ 800/OUTRIGGER or 808/823-8300. Fax 808/823-8301. www.outrigger.com. 196 units. $215–$245 hotel double; $265–$485 1-bed/2-bath for 4; $395–$755 2-bed/3-bath for 6. 2-night minimum. AE, DC, DISC, MC, V. **Amenities:** 2 restaurants; bar; huge oceanside outdoor pool; nearby golf course; nearby tennis courts; fitness center; spa; 3 outdoor whirlpools; activities desk; laundry service; dry cleaning. *In room:* A/C, TV/DVD, high-speed wireless Internet, full kitchen (condos only), fridge, coffeemaker, hair dryer, iron, safe, full-size washer and dryer (condos only).

MODERATE

Aloha Beach Resort ⓚ *Kids*
New ownership and management of this 10-acre property, located next door to a 57-acre beach park and playground on one side and a very sacred historic Hawaiian site on the other side, has brought back the feeling of old Hawaii at this moderately priced resort. After a $10-million renovation, the entire property is rich in Hawaiian culture from the historical presentation given by the general manager himself to the decor of the rooms, to the full-time *kupuna* (senior cultural expert) who gives classes to the guests in Hawaiian arts and crafts. Every room was renovated in 2006 with new carpet and furniture, oversized Balinese mahogany doors, upgraded bathrooms, and Hawaiian-style quilts on the beds. The result is a family-friendly choice located right next door to Lydgate Beach Park (with Kamalani Playground for the kids) and convenient to nearby golf. Restaurants and shopping are within minutes of the resort along the Coconut Coast.

3–5920 Kuhio Hwy., Kapaa, HI 96746 ⓒ 888/823-5111 or 808/823-6000. Fax 808/823-6666. www.abrkauai.com. 216 units. $149–$169 double; $240 1-bedroom cottages. Extra person $10. Rollaway beds/cribs $15. Children 18 and under stay free in parent's room. Check the Internet for specials. AE, DC, DISC, MC, V. **Amenities:** Restaurant; bar; 2 outdoor pools; complimentary tennis court; small fitness room; Jacuzzi; coin-op washer/dryers; laundry service. *In room:* A/C, TV, dataport, fridge, coffeemaker, hair dryer, iron, safe ($2/day).

Lae Nani Outrigger Resort Condominium ⓚ
The Lae Nani ("beautiful promontory point") offers a quiet, relaxing setting right on the beach, next door to restaurants and bars. On the point is the Kukui Heiau, where an ancient temple once stood. The one- and two-bedroom units are roomy, with large living rooms, separate dining rooms, complete kitchens, and generous lanais. The two-bedroom/two-bathroom units can easily fit a family of six. Maid service is provided daily. Extras include a lava-rock-protected swimming area and barbecue facilities. Next door is the Coconut Marketplace, with shops, restaurants, and nightlife; a golf course is nearby.

410 Papaloa Rd., Kapaa, HI 96746. ✆ 800/OUTRIGGER or 808/822-4938. Fax 808/822-1022. www.outrigger.com. 54 units. $175–$270 1-bedroom for 4; $219–$335 2-bedroom for 6. Rollaway bed/crib $20. 2-night minimum. AE, DC, DISC, MC, V. **Amenities:** Oceanfront outdoor pool; complimentary tennis courts; coin-op washer/dryers. *In room:* TV, dataport, kitchen, fridge, coffeemaker, iron.

Mahina Kai *Finds*   Mahina Kai ("moon over the water") is a traditional Japanese villa (complete with teahouse next door) on 2 landscaped acres just across the road from one of the most picturesque white-sand beaches on Kauai. There are three rooms in the main house with shoji-screen doors, private bathrooms and lanais, use of the gorgeous living room (with fish pond, vintage Hawaiian furniture, and views of Japanese gardens and Aliomanu Beach), and shared kitchenette. Although this place is undeniably unique, the rooms are tiny and sparsely furnished (no TVs or phones), and the walls paper thin. I'd suggest staying at the separate cottage (with kitchenette) next to the saltwater pool. Landscaped into the gardens are a lagoon-style pool and a hot tub. Guests are generally gay and lesbian couples, but anyone with a sense of humor and an open mind is welcome. Sitting in the hot tub, listening to the surf across the street, and gazing at the stars is pretty darn close to heaven on earth.

4933 Aliomanu Rd. (off Kuhio Hwy. at mile marker 14). P.O. Box 699, Anahola, HI 96703. ✆ 800/337-1134 or 808/822-9451. www.mahinakai.com. 5 units. $195–$345 double. Rates include continental breakfast. 3-night minimum. AE, MC, V. **Amenities:** Saltwater lagoonlike swimming pool; hot tub; massage available. *In room:* No phone.

ResortQuest Kauai Beach at Makaiwa 🏖   Just 10 minutes from Lihue Airport, in the town of Waipouli, this 311-room resort was totally refurbished in 2005 when Courtyard by Marriott rebranded the old Kauai Coconut Beach Resort. In 2006 ResortQuest took over the property, which sits on 10½ acres, nestled between a coconut grove and a white-sand beach, and made improvements to the landscaping, restaurants, and the open-air lobby, which now features a stained-glass depiction of a sailing canoe, a 2-story mural chronicling Kauai's sailing history, and a replica of a Hawaiian voyaging canoe. The convenient location is close to shopping and visitor attractions along the Coconut Coast, and also gives you easy access to the North Shore and the Poipu Beach area on the south shore.

The resort features a new swimming pool, hot tub, day spa, business center, fitness center, tennis courts, jogging paths, lounge (with nightly entertainment), and expanded restaurant. The resort has kept the award-winning Hawaiian luau by Tihati Productions, with dinner and show Tuesday through Sunday evenings. The large guest rooms have been gutted and redecorated with a Hawaiian theme, and include such amenities as hardwood furniture and a 27-inch television.

650 Aleka Loop, Kapaa, HI 96746. ✆ 866/77-HAWAII or 808/822-3455. Fax 808/822-0035. www.resortquest hawaii.com. 311 units. $285–$472 double; suites from $995. Extra person $30. Children 17 and under stay free in parent's room. Daily resort fee $12 for parking, high-speed Internet access, and local phone calls. AE, DC, DISC, MC, V. **Amenities:** Full-service restaurant; bar; outdoor pool; golf nearby; tennis nearby; Jacuzzi; activities desk; room service; coin-op washer/dryers; laundry service; dry cleaning; jogging path. *In room:* A/C, TV/VCR, dataport, wireless Internet access, fridge, coffeemaker, hair dryer, iron, safe.

INEXPENSIVE

Hotel Coral Reef *Value*   Here's a budget choice right on the beach. This small, unpretentious hotel faces a grassy lawn, coconut trees, and a white-sand beach. It offers economical rooms and friendly service in an ideal location, within walking distance of shops, restaurants, golf, and tennis. There's even an 8-mile bike path that starts right on the grounds. This is a budget hotel, not the Ritz, so expect clean, no-frills rooms. In 2005 and 2006, the rooms were renovated with new amenities and new beds, carpet, and drapes. The place is looking spiffier than ever. Of the two wings in the hotel, I prefer the oceanfront one, which has big rooms that overlook the beach through sliding-glass lanai doors. The two-room units have a separate bedroom and a living room with a sofa bed—perfect for families.

1516 Kuhio Hwy. (at the northern end of Kapaa, between mile markers 8 and 9), Kapaa, HI 96746. Ⓒ **800/843-4659** or 808/822-4481. Fax 808/822-7705. www.hotelcoralreef.com. 21 units. $125–$289 double; from $209 suite. Extra person $25. Children 12 and under stay free in parent's room. Room/car packages available. AE, MC, V. **Amenities:** Pool; activities desk; coin-op washer/dryers. *In room:* A/C, TV, fridge, coffeemaker, safe (in some oceanfront rooms).

Kapaa Shores ⒻⒶ These apartments are located right on the beach in the heart of Kapaa. Even the budget units have a partial view of the ocean, but oceanfront units are available for a bit more money. The one-bedrooms can comfortably sleep four, while the two-bedrooms can sleep as many as six (the sofa in each unit pulls out into a queen-size bed). All units are in excellent shape and come with fully equipped modern kitchens and large lanais, where you can enjoy a sunrise breakfast or sunset cocktails. On-site amenities include a large pool, a tennis court, a family-size hot tub, a shuffleboard court, laundry facilities, and barbecues. Golf courses, restaurants, and bars are nearby.

900 Kuhio Hwy. (between mile markers 7 and 8). Reservations c/o Garden Island Properties, 4–928 Kuhio Hwy., Kapaa, HI 96746. Ⓒ **800/801-0378** or 808/822-4871. Fax 808/822-7984. www.kauaiproperties.com. 84 units. $115–$160 1-bedroom; $122–$210 2-bedroom. 5- to 7-night minimum. AE, MC, V. **Amenities:** Outdoor pool; complimentary tennis courts; Jacuzzi; salon; coin-op washer/dryers. *In room:* TV/VCR or TV/DVD, dataport (Internet in some rooms), kitchen, fridge, coffeemaker, iron (washer/dryer in some rooms).

Kauai Country Inn ⒻⒶ *Finds* Book this place! It's hard to believe that nestled in the rolling hills behind Kapaa, this old-fashioned country inn exists. Hosts Mike and Martina Hough have taken their considerable creative talents and produced a slice of paradise on 2 acres. Each of the four suites is uniquely decorated in Hawaiian Art Deco with a touch of humor, complete with hardwood floors, a kitchen or kitchenette, your own computer with high-speed Internet connection, and lots of little amenities. Everything is top-drawer, from the furniture to the Sub-Zero refrigerator. They recently added a two-bedroom country cottage for families with young children. The grounds are immaculate, and you can pick as much organic fruit as you want from the abundance of mango, guava, *lilikoi*, star fruit, oranges, and lemons. Beatles fans, take note: Mike has been collecting memorabilia for decades and has the only private Beatles Museum in the state (including a Mini Cooper S car owned by Beatles manager Brian Epstein, original paintings by John Lennon, and a host of books, records, movies, tapes, T-shirts, and other interesting and unusual rare items). Annie, the house golden retriever, personally greets each guest.

6440 Olohena Rd., Kapaa, HI 96746. Ⓒ **808/821-0207.** www.kauaicountryinn.com. 5 units. $99–$159 1- and 2-bedroom suites double; $229–$250 2-bedroom cottage for 6. Extra person in suites $20. 4-night minimum suites; 4-night minimum cottage. Discount car rentals available. AE, MC, V. **Amenities:** Hot tub, laundry facilities. *In room:* TV/VCR/DVD, computer w/high-speed Internet, kitchen or kitchenette, fridge, coffeemaker, hair dryer, iron.

Lani-keha ⒻⒶ *Finds* Step back in time to the 1940s, when Hawaiian families lived in open, airy, rambling homes on large plots of land lush with fruit trees and sweet-smelling flowers. This gracious age is still alive and well in Lani-keha, a kamaaina (long-time resident) home with an open living/game/writing/dining room and over-size picture windows to take in the views. The house is elegant yet casual, with old-style rattan furniture—practicality and comfort outweigh design aesthetics. The large communal kitchen has everything a cook should need, even a dishwasher. All the guests share the TV/VCR and single phone in the living area.

848 Kamalu Rd. (Hwy. 581), Kapaa, HI 96746. © **800/821-4898** or 808/822-1605. Fax 808/822-2429. www.lani keha.com. 3 units. $65 double. Rates include continental breakfast. Extra person $15. 2-night minimum. No credit cards. From Kuhio Hwy. (Hwy. 56), turn left at the stoplight at Coco Palms onto Hwy. 580 (Kuamoo Rd.); go 3 miles; turn right at Hwy. 581 (Kamalu Rd.) and go 1 mile. **Amenities:** Washer/dryer. *In room:* No phone.

Rosewood Bed & Breakfast ✿ *Finds*   This lovingly restored century-old plantation home, set amid tropical flowers, lily ponds, and waterfalls, has accommodations to suit everyone. There's a Laura Ashley–style room in the main house along with two private cottages: one a miniature of the main house, with oak floors and the same Laura Ashley decor; the other a little grass shack set in a tropical garden, with an authentic thatched roof and an outside shower. There's also a bunkhouse with three separate small rooms with a shared shower and toilet. In 2006 all the beds were replaced with "Heavenly Beds," and computers with Internet access were installed in each room. Hostess Rosemary Smith also has a list of other properties she manages. *Note:* Smoking is not permitted on the property.

872 Kamalu Rd., Kapaa, HI. 96746. © **808/822-5216.** Fax 808/822-5478. www.rosewoodkauai.com. 7 units, 3 with shared bathroom. $85 double in main house (includes continental breakfast); $45–$55 double in bunkhouse; $125 1-bedroom cottage double (sleeps up to 4); $145 2-bedroom cottage (sleeps 4); $200 3-bedroom home (sleeps 6). Extra person $15. 3-night minimum. No credit cards. From Kuhio Hwy. (Hwy. 56), turn left at the stoplight at Coco Palms onto Hwy. 580 (Kuamoo Rd.); go 3 miles; at junction of Hwy. 581 (Kamalu Rd.), turn right; go 1 mile and look for the yellow house on the right with the long picket fence in front. *In room:* No phone. *In cottages:* TV, computer with Internet access, kitchen, fridge, coffeemaker, hair dryer, iron, no phone. *In bunkhouse:* Kitchenette, fridge, coffeemaker, no phone.

Wailua Bay View ✿ *Value*   Located right on the ocean, these spacious one-bedroom apartments offer excellent value. All units have ceiling fans, full kitchens (including microwave and dishwasher), washer/dryers, and large lanais. The bedrooms are roomy, and the sofa bed in the living room allows you to sleep up to four. Some of the $140 garden units are close to the road and can be noisy; ask for one with air-conditioning, which generally drowns out the street sounds. The oceanview units are more expensive but still a great deal. On-site facilities include a pool and barbecue area. Restaurants, bars, shopping, golf, and tennis are nearby.

320 Papaloa Rd., Kapaa, HI 96746. © **800/882-9007.** Fax 425/391-9121. www.wailuabay.com. 45 units. $140–$155 double, plus $95 cleaning fee $95. 7th night free Apr 15–June 14 and Sept 1–Dec 16. Discount car rentals available. AE, DISC, MC, V. **Amenities:** Small outdoor pool; washer/dryers; barbecue area. *In room:* A/C (most units), TV/VCR/DVD, dataport, wireless access (most rooms), kitchen, fridge, coffeemaker, iron.

THE NORTH SHORE

Want to rent a rock star's tree house? How about coochy-coochy entertainer Charo's beachfront estate? **Hanalei North Shore Properties** (© **800/488-3336** or 808/826-9622; fax 808/826-1188; www.hanaleinorthshoreproperties.com) handles all kinds of weekly rentals—from beachfront cottages and condos to romantic hideaways and ranch houses—along the North Shore. Renting a home is a great way to enjoy the area's awesome natural wonders, especially for those who like to avoid resorts and fend for themselves. Shopping, restaurants, and nightlife are abundant in nearby Hanalei. The company does not accept credit cards.

In addition to the B&Bs reviewed below, you might consider **North Country Farms** (© **808/828-1513;** www.northcountryfarms.com), which has two private,

Where to Stay & Dine on Kauai's North Shore

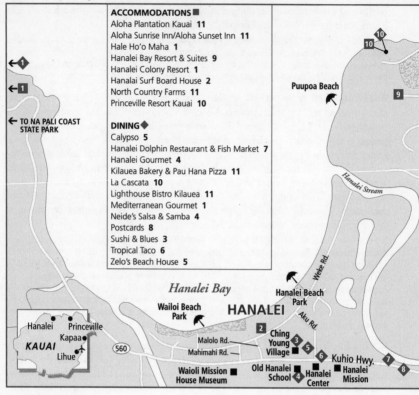

ACCOMMODATIONS ■
Aloha Plantation Kauai **11**
Aloha Sunrise Inn/Aloha Sunset Inn **11**
Hale Ho'o Maha **1**
Hanalei Bay Resort & Suites **9**
Hanalei Colony Resort **1**
Hanalai Surf Board House **2**
North Country Farms **11**
Princeville Resort Kauai **10**

DINING ◆
Calypso **5**
Hanalei Dolphin Restaurant & Fish Market **7**
Hanalei Gourmet **4**
Kilauea Bakery & Pau Hana Pizza **11**
La Cascata **10**
Lighthouse Bistro Kilauea **11**
Mediterranean Gourmet **1**
Neide's Salsa & Samba **4**
Postcards **8**
Sushi & Blues **3**
Tropical Taco **6**
Zelo's Beach House **5**

← TO NA PALI COAST
STATE PARK

Hanalei Bay

Puupoa Beach

Hanalei Stream

Wailoi Beach Park
HANALEI
Hanalei Beach Park
Wete Rd.
Aku Rd.

Hanalei
Princeville
Kapaa
KAUAI
Lihue
(560)

Malolo Rd.
Mahimahi Rd.
Ching Young Village
Kuhio Hwy.

Waioli Mission House Museum
Old Hanalei School
Hanalei Center
Hanalei Mission

handcrafted cottages on a 4-acre organic farm. It's a great place for families, and each cottage is $130 a night.

Note: You'll find the following accommodations on the "Where to Stay & Dine on Kauai's North Shore" map above.

VERY EXPENSIVE

Princeville Resort Kauai 🌟🌟🌟 *Kids*   This resort is the jewel in the Sheraton crown, a palace full of marble and chandeliers. It enjoys one of the world's finest settings, between Hanalei Bay and Kauai's steepled mountains. Nearby are outstanding surfing and windsurfing areas, as well as a wonderful reef for snorkeling. The panoramic view from the lobby has to be the most dramatic vista from any hotel in the state. The Princeville is Kauai's most popular setting for weddings; more than 300 a year are performed outdoors by the pool.

This grand hotel steps down a cliff; the entrance is actually on the ninth floor, and you take elevators down to your room and the beach. Each opulent room has such extras as a door chime, dimmer switches, bedside control panels, a safe, original oil paintings, an oversize bathtub, and a "magic" bathroom window: a liquid-crystal shower window that you can switch in an instant from clear to opaque. There are no lanais, but oversize windows allow you to admire the awesome view from your bed.

In addition to a great children's program, this property has oodles of activities for the entire family, from horseback riding to adventures exploring the island. The hotel grounds are a fantasyland for children (and some adults), with a huge swimming pool next to a sandy beach.

Other great amenities here: twice-daily fresh towels, daily newspaper, complimentary resort shuttle, comprehensive Hawaiiana program, riding stables, in-house cinema, arts program (from photography to painting), and a wealth of outdoor activities. Golfers may choose from two courses, both designed by Robert Trent Jones, Jr.; the whirlpools, steam baths, 115-foot lap pool, and multitude of treatments will delight spa-goers.

P.O. Box 3069 (5520 Kahaku Rd.), Princeville, HI 96722-3069. ☏ **800/826-4400** or 808/826-9644. Fax 808/826-1166. www.princevillehotelhawaii.com. 252 units. $565–$815 double; from $915 suite. Extra person $75. Children under 18 stay free in parent's room. AE, DC, DISC, MC, V. Parking $15. **Amenities:** 3 restaurants (1 w/excellent nightly entertainment; also see La Cascata, p. 578); 3 bars; huge oceanside outdoor pool; outstanding golf on 2 courses; 25 tennis courts; first-rate health club and spa; 3 outdoor Jacuzzis (including a really palatial one); watersports equipment rentals; bike rental; children's program; concierge; activities desk; car-rental desk; business center; shopping arcade; salon; 24-hr. room service; massage; babysitting; 24-hr. return laundry/dry cleaning. *In room:* A/C, TV, VCR available for rent, CD player, dataport, high-speed wireless Internet $13/day, minibar, fridge, coffeemaker, hair dryer, iron, safe.

EXPENSIVE

Hanalei Bay Resort & Suites ✸✸ This 22-acre resort is just up the street from ritzy Princeville Resort (see above), overlooking the fabled Bali Hai cliffs and Hanalei Bay. It has the same majestic view, but for as little as half the price. The place recaptures the spirit of old Hawaii, especially in the three-story stucco units that angle down the hill to the gold-sand, palm-fringed beach it shares with its neighbor. Rooms are decorated in Island style, with rattan furnishings and lanais overlooking the bay, the lush grounds, and the distant mountains. Shuttle service is available for those who may have problems walking on the steep hillside.

The Happy Talk Lounge is one of our favorite places on Kauai for sunset cocktails, while the open-air restaurant, Bali Hai, has a view that is so distractingly gorgeous that you can hardly concentrate on the food.

P.O. Box 220 (5380 Honoiki St.), Princeville, HI 96722. (☎) **800/827-4427** or 808/826-6522. Fax 808/826-6680. www. hanaleibayresort.com. 236 units. $205–$295 double; $250 studio with kitchenette (up to 4); $370–$410 1-bedroom apt (up to 4). Suites include full breakfast and afternoon cocktails. AE, DC, DISC, MC, V. **Amenities:** Restaurant; bar; 2 outdoor freshwater pools; complimentary shuttle to Princeville Resort's top-ranked golf courses; 8 tennis courts plus pro shop and tennis school; Jacuzzi; concierge; activities desk; massage; babysitting; coin-op washer/dryers; laundry service; dry cleaning. *In room:* A/C, TV, dataport (wireless access in some rooms), kitchenette, fridge, coffeemaker, hair dryer, iron, safe.

Hanalei Colony Resort ✸ *Kids* Picture this: a perfect white-sand beach just steps from your door, with lush tropical gardens, jagged mountain peaks, and fertile jungle serving as your backdrop. Welcome to Haena, Kauai's northernmost town and gateway to the famous Na Pali Coast, with miles of hiking trails, fabulous sunset views, and great beaches. This 5-acre resort is the place to stay if you're looking to experience the magic of the enchanting North Shore. The units are unbelievably spacious—six people could sleep here comfortably—making them great for families. Each has a private lanai (the less-expensive budget units face the garden), a full kitchen, a dining area, a living room, and ceiling fans (the area is blessed with cooling trade winds, so air-conditioning isn't necessary). The atmosphere is quiet and relaxing: no TVs, stereos, or phones. The property has a large pool, laundry facilities, and a barbecue and picnic area. Guests have access to complimentary beach mats and towels, a lending library, and children's toys, puzzles, and games (plus badminton and croquet for the entire family). A full spa and an award-winning restaurant are located next door.

P.O. Box 206 (5–7130 Kuhio Hwy.), Hanalei, HI 96714. (☎) **800/628-3004** or 808/826-6235. Fax 808/826-9893. www. hcr.com. 48 units. $230–$410 2-bedroom apt for 4. Rates include continental breakfast once a week. Minimum 5 nights June 1–Sept 8 and Dec 20–Jan 4. Extra person $15. AE, MC, V. **Amenities:** restaurant next door, Good-size outdoor pool; Jacuzzi; full-service spa next door; coin-op washer/dryers. *In room:* Kitchen, fridge, coffeemaker, no phone.

MODERATE

Aloha Sunrise Inn/Aloha Sunset Inn ✸✸ *Finds* Hidden on the North Shore are these two unique cottages nestled on a quiet 7-acre farm with horses, fruit trees, flowers, and organic vegetables. We highly recommend both of these darling bungalows. Each is fully furnished with hardwood floors, top-of-the-line bedding, tropical island–style decor, a complete kitchen, washer/dryer, and more (from all the great videos you have been meaning to watch to an excellent CD library). It's close to activities, restaurants, and shopping, yet far enough away to feel the peace and quiet of a Hawaii of yesteryear. Hosts Allan and Catherine Rietow, who have lived their entire lives on the islands, can help you plan your stay, give you money-saving tips, and even hand out complimentary masks, snorkels, and boogie boards and point you to their favorite beaches. *Note to parents:* These cottages are not appropriate for children.

P.O. Box 79, Kilauea, HI 96754. ℂ 888/828-1008 or 808/828-1100. Fax 808/828-2199. www.kauaisunrise.com. 2 units. $175–$185 double, plus a 1-time $95 cleaning fee. 3-night minimum. No credit cards. **Amenities:** Washer/dryer. *In room:* TV/VCR (in 1 cottage), cable TV (in other cottage), kitchen, fridge, coffeemaker, hair dryer, iron.

Hale Ho'o Maha *Finds*   For ever and ever, Kirby Guyer and her husband, Toby, ran a spacious four-bedroom, three-bathroom home on 5 acres. Then in 2006 they finished their own custom-designed B&B located on the North Shore in the Hanalei area known as Wainiha. Overlooking the mountains, waterfalls, and pristine Wainiha Bay, the Hawaiian antiques–filled home is just 110 steps to the beach (and a 10-min. drive to golf courses, shops, restaurants, and two riding stables). This spacious 5-bedroom/5½-bathroom home features an elevator (something you don't often see on Kauai). Guests are welcome to use the gourmet kitchen, gas barbecue, washer/dryer, refrigerator with ice maker/water, and TV/VCR/DVD in the "great room." Use of the boogie boards and snorkel equipment, beach chairs, towels, and coolers is complimentary. Each of the four-guest suites has hardwood floors, large closets, cable TV/DVD, ceiling fans, and high-speed Internet service. We recommend the Pineapple Room, with its 7-foot round bed (with custom quilted pineapple spread and matching handmade area rug). Breakfast might be macadamia-nut waffles with plenty of sausage or bacon, plus all the fresh island fruit and homemade granola you can eat. The best part is your hosts, Kirby and Toby, who know Kauai inside and out, and can give you great advice on what to do and how to save money.

7083 Alamihi Rd., Hanalei. Reservations: P.O. Box 82, Hanalei, HI 96714. ℂ 800/851-0291 or 808/826-7083. Fax 808/826-7084. www.aloha.net/~hoomaha. 4 units. $150–$175 double. Rates include full breakfast. DC, MC, V. **Amenities:** TV/VCR/DVD in great room; use of full kitchen; barbecue; complimentary use of laundry facilities and water toys. *In room:* TV/DVD, high-speed Internet, hair dryer.

Hanalei Surf Board House *✲✲ Finds*   Book well in advance: This place is so fabulous that it will go fast! Just a block from the beach, these two incredibly decorated studio units are a steal at $150. Host Simon Potts is a former record company executive from England who has "retired" to Hawaii (he's the hardest-working retired guy I've ever met). Potts has collected a bunch of surfboards from kids he coaches in soccer and lined them all standing up next to each other, creating the most unusual fenced-in yard in Hawaii. His imaginative decor choices extend to the studios, one of which sports a whimsical "cowgirl" theme and the other Elvis Presley memorabilia. Both units have kitchenettes, 300-channel televisions, DVD players, Bose Stereos, some 50 CDs (Simon still has connections in the music business), barbecues, and backyard lanais. But the best reason to stay here (besides a 2-min. walk to the beach or a 10-min. walk to downtown Hanalei) is Simon himself—his stories about the record industry will keep you howling with laughter for hours.

5459 Weke Rd., Hanalei, HI 96714. ℂ 808/826-9825. www.hanaleisurfboardhouse.com. 2 units. $150 double, plus $65 cleaning fee. 3-night minimum. No credit cards. *In room:* TV/DVD, high-speed Internet access, iPod dock, kitchenette, fridge, coffeemaker, hair dryer, iron, private barbecue.

INEXPENSIVE

Aloha Plantation Kauai *Finds*   Step back in history at this 1920s plantation home (the oldest in Kilauea Village), which hosts Paul and Laurie have decorated in impeccable old Hawaiian antiques. Located just off the highway (some highway noise, but not much), about 15 minutes from Princeville and 20 minutes from Hanalei, Aloha

Plantation Kauai offers three units. One of them is a 500-square-foot studio converted from an old garage; the other two are rooms in the main house. Both rooms have very comfortable wrought-iron beds and ceiling fans, and share a screen porch with coffeepot and an old 7-Up machine used as a refrigerator. One room has a half-bathroom and shares a shower with the owners; the other room has its own full bathroom. In the courtyard is a cooking area with a gas-burning stove, barbecue, microwave, rice cooker, and refrigerator. The studio has an air conditioner, TV, phone, and CD player, plus a private bathroom.

4481 Malulani St., Kilauea, HI 96754. ℂ 877-658-6977 or 808/828-6872. www.alohaplantation.com. 3 units. $69–$79 rooms double; $99 studio double. 2-night minimum. No credit cards. **Amenities:** Fridge; cooking area w/gas-burner stove, barbecue, microwave, and rice cooker; Jacuzzi; wireless Internet access. *In room:* No phone in rooms.

4 Where to Dine

Kauai's best dining spots ring the shores: Poipu on the south, Kapaa on the east, and Hanalei on the north. While Roy's in Poipu, Beach House in neighboring Lawai, and Gaylord's in Kilohana remain Kauai's foodie stalwarts, there are some excellent choices at all levels of the food chain. Most of the island's newcomers are moderately priced and have cropped up along the island's one main road.

On your jaunt across the island, you'll find affordable choices in every town, from hamburger joints to stands dishing up saimin (noodles in broth topped with scrambled eggs, onions, and sometimes pork), to busy neighborhood diners. As long as you don't expect filet mignon on a fish-and-chips budget, it shouldn't be difficult to please both your palate and your pocketbook. But if you're looking for lobster, rack of lamb, or risotto to write home about, you'll find those pleasures, too.

For condo dwellers who are preparing their own meals, we've featured a variety of markets and shops around Kauai—including some wonderful green markets and fruit stands—where you can pick up the island's best foodstuffs. These are listed in "Shops & Galleries," later in this chapter. If you're looking for fresh island fruit, also see the box "Fruity Smoothies & Other Exotic Treats," on p. 616.

In the listings below, reservations are not required unless otherwise noted.

LIHUE & ENVIRONS

You'll find the restaurants in this section on the "Where to Stay & Dine in Lihue" map on p. 545.

EXPENSIVE

Gaylord's 🐾🐾 CONTINENTAL/PACIFIC RIM One of Kauai's most splendid examples of kamaaina architecture, Gaylord's is the anchor of a 1930s plantation manager's estate on a 1,700-acre sugar plantation. You'll enter a complex of shops, galleries, and a living room of Hawaiian artifacts and period furniture. The main dining room, which winds around a flagstone courtyard overlooking rolling lawns and purple mountains, serves American classics (New York steak, rack of lamb, prime rib) along with pasta, fresh seafood, and lavish desserts. The ambience, historic surroundings, and soothing views from the terrace make Gaylord's a special spot for lunch—salads, soups, fresh fish, Oliver Shagnasty's signature baby back ribs, burgers, and sandwiches predominate. Daily specials include international dishes, such as *kalua* pork and Mexican fajitas, and fresh Island fish in various cross-cultural preparations.

At Kilohana, 3–2087 Kaumualii Hwy., Lihue. © **808/245-9593**. www.gaylordskauai.com. Reservations recommended. Main courses $9–$14 lunch, $19–$42 dinner. AE, DC, DISC, MC, V. Mon–Sat 7:45–9:45am (breakfast buffet) and 11am–3pm; daily 5:30–9pm; Sun 8am–2:30pm (brunch).

JJ's Broiler ✦ AMERICAN   Famous for its Slavonic steak (tenderloin in butter, wine, and garlic), herb-crusted ahi, and the lazy Susan of salad greens that's brought to your table, JJ's is a lively spot on Kalapaki Bay, with open-air dining and a menu that covers more than the usual surf and turf. I have found the service to range from laudable to lamentable, but the quality of the food is consistent. The coconut shrimp and Manila clams are big sellers, and the scallops Florentine are an imaginative twist on seafood. Lunchtime appetizers include potato skins, calamari rings, spring rolls, and won tons—the United Nations of pupu! The high ceilings, two-story dining, Kenwood Cup posters, and nautically designed rooms are enhanced by stellar views of the bay.

3416 Rice St., Nawiliwili. © **808/246-4422**. Reservations recommended for dinner. Lunch sandwiches $10–$15; dinner main courses $20–$30. DISC, MC, V. Daily 11am–10pm.

MODERATE

Café Portofino ✦✦ ITALIAN   This candlelit restaurant offers authentic Italian cuisine at reasonable prices in a relaxing atmosphere. It's a good pick for a romantic dinner, with a harpist or classical guitarist strumming softly in the background. Owner Giuseppe Avocadi personally greets every guest. The menu lists appetizers ranging from ahi (or beef) carpaccio to the house special antipasto (with five different daily choices). But it's the pasta that will bring you back here a second time: These homemade dishes are so light you'd swear you could keep on eating all night. There are a dozen different dishes to choose from, plus a few specials to make your decision all the harder. Also on the menu are fresh fish, a variety of chicken dishes, veal and beef dishes (from the traditional *osso buco* to scaloppini a la Marsala), and a few items for vegetarians. Live music is featured every night.

3481 Hoolaulea St., Nawiliwili. © **808/245-2121**. Reservations recommended. Main courses $14–$26. MC, V. Daily 5–9pm.

Duke's Canoe Club ✦ STEAK/SEAFOOD   It's hard to go wrong at Duke's. Part of a highly successful restaurant chain (including Duke's Canoe Club in Waikiki and three similar restaurants on Maui), this oceanfront oasis is the hippest spot in town, with a winning combination of a great view, an affordable menu, popular music, and a very happy happy hour. The noontime bestseller is stir-fried cashew chicken, but the fresh ahi burger and the grilled chicken quesadilla are front-runners, too. The inexpensive fish tacos are a major attraction, and the five or six varieties of fresh catch a night are a highlight, served in several different preparations—a great value. Hawaiian musicians serenade diners nightly, while downstairs in the Barefoot Bar, traditional and contemporary Hawaiian music adds to the cheerful atmosphere. On Tropical Fridays, tropical drinks go for $5.75 from 4 to 6pm, when live music stirs up the joint.

In the Kauai Marriott Resort & Beach Club, 3610 Rice St., Nawiliwili. © **808/246-9599**. Reservations recommended for dinner. Lunch $6–$13; dinner $15–$30. Taco Tuesdays 4–6pm, with $3 fish tacos and $3 draft beer. AE, DISC, MC, V. Barefoot Bar daily 11am–11pm; main dining room daily 5–10pm.

INEXPENSIVE

Dani's Restaurant AMERICAN/HAWAIIAN   Not a tourist spot, but a diner for local residents. Formica all the way and always packed for breakfast, Dani's is the pancake palace of Lihue: banana, pineapple, papaya, and buttermilk, plus sweet-bread

Plate-Lunch Pointers

If you haven't yet come face to face with the local phenomenon called the "plate lunch," Kauai is a good place to start. Like saimin, the plate lunch is more than a gastronomic experience—it's a part of the local culture. Lihue is peppered with affordable plate-lunch counters that serve this basic dish: two scoops of rice, potato or macaroni salad, and a beef, chicken, fish, or pork entree—all on a single plate. Although heavy gravies are usually de rigueur, some of the less traditional purveyors have streamlined their offerings to include healthier touches, such as lean grilled fresh fish. Pork cutlets and chicken or beef soaked in teriyaki sauce, however, remain staples, as does the breaded and crisply fried method called *katsu*, as in chicken katsu. Most of the time, *fried* is the operative word; that's why it's best to be ravenously hungry when you approach a plate lunch, or it can overpower you. At its best, a plate lunch can be a marvel of flavors; at its worst, it's a plate-size grease bomb. With the increasing popularity of such diets as Atkins and South Beach, many plate-lunch places are now happy to replace all those starches with a mixed green salad if you ask.

The following are the best plate-lunch counters on Kauai:

The **Koloa Fish Market** ⊛, 5482 Koloa Rd. (© **808/742-6199**), is in southern Kauai, on Koloa's main street. A tiny corner stand with plate lunches, prepared foods, and two stools on a closet-size veranda, it sells excellent fresh-fish poke, Hawaiian-food specials, and seared ahi to go. It's gourmet fare masquerading as takeout. Daily specials may include sautéed ahi or fresh opakapaka with capers. For a picnic or outing on the south shore, this is a good place to start.

On the Hanamaulu side of Lihue, across the street from Wal-Mart, look for the prim, gray building that reads **Fish Express** ⊛, 3343 Kuhio Hwy. (© **808/245-9918**). It's astonishing what you'll find here for under $12: Cajun-style grilled ahi with guava basil, fresh fish grilled in a passion-orange-tarragon sauce, fresh fish tacos in garlic and herbs, and many other delectables, all served with rice, salad, and vegetables. The Hawaiian plate lunch (laulau or *kalua* pork, lomi salmon, ahi poke, rice, or poi) is a top seller, as are the several varieties of smoked fish. The owners marinate the fish in soy sauce, sugar, ginger, and garlic (no preservatives), and smoke it with kiawe wood. The fresh fish specials, at $7.95, come in six preparations and are flavored to perfection. At the chilled counter you can choose freshly

French toast and *kalua*-pig omelets. Regulars know that fried rice is offered on Thursday only and that the papaya hotcakes are always a deal. At lunch, Hawaiian specials—laulau, *kalua* pig, lomi salmon, and beef stew in various combinations—dominate the otherwise standard American menu of fried foods and sandwiches.

4201 Rice St., Lihue. © 808/245-4991. Main courses $3.30–$8.50. MC, V. Mon–Fri 5am–1pm; Sat 5–11am.

Hamura's Saimin Stand ⊛ SAIMIN   If there were a saimin hall of fame, Hamura's would be it. It's a cultural experience, a renowned saimin stand where fans line up to sliced sashimi and many styles of poke, from scallop, ahi, and octopus to exotic marinated crab. This is a potluck bonanza that engages even new-comers, who point and order while regulars pick up sweeping assortments of seafood appetizers on large platters. They're all fresh and reasonably priced, great for Friday-afternoon *pau hana* (after-work) parties.

In east Kauai's Kapaa town, the indispensable **Pono Market,** 4–1300 Kuhio Hwy. (© **808/822-4581**), has similarly enticing counters of sashimi, poke, Hawaiian food, sushi, and a diverse assortment of takeout fare. It's known for its flaky *manju* (sweet potato and other fillings in baked crust), apple turnovers, sandwiches, excellent boiled peanuts, pork and chicken laulau, and plate lunches—shoyu chicken, sweet-and-sour spareribs, pineap-ple-glazed chicken, teriyaki fish, and so on. The potato-macaroni salad (reg-ulars buy it by the pound for barbecues and potlucks) and roast pork are top sellers. Pono Market is as good as they come. If they're available, pick up Taro Ko taro chips. They're made in Hanapepe, hard to find, and worth hand-carrying home.

At **Mark's Place,** 1610 Haleukana St. in Puhi Industrial Park (© **808/245-2722**), just southwest of Lihue, Island standards (Korean-style chicken, teriyaki beef, beef stew, chicken katsu) come with brown (or white) rice and salad for $6.25 to $7. The selection, which changes daily, always includes two salad and three entree choices, as well as hot sandwiches (chicken, beef, and hamburgers) and the ever-popular bento (rice with beef, chicken, or fish, arranged in a lidded box). Mark's is a takeout and catering operation, so don't expect table seating.

Lihue, the island's county and business seat, is full of ethnic eateries serv-ing inexpensive plate lunches. **Po's Kitchen,** 4100 Rice St. (© **808/246-8617**), offers Japanese specials: cone sushi, chicken katsu, teriyaki beef plates, and bentos. One block away, **Garden Island BBQ,** 4252-A Rice St. (© **808/245-8868**), is the place for Chinese plate lunches and local staples such as barbe-cued or lemon chicken and teriyaki steak, as well as soups and tofu dishes.

In the Kukui Grove Center, at Kaumualii Highway (Hwy. 50) and Old Naw-iliwili Road, **Joni-Hana** (© **808/245-5213**) is famous for its specials—nearly 20 a day! The tiny counter serves fried noodles, lemon-shoyu ono (wahoo), teriyaki everything, and many other local dishes.

take their place over steaming bowls of this Island specialty at a few U-shaped coun-ters that haven't changed in decades. The saimin and teriyaki barbecue sticks attract an all-day, late-night, pre- and post-movie crowd. The noodles come heaped with veg-etables, won tons, hard-boiled eggs, sweetened pork, vegetables, and several condi-ment combinations. I love the casualness of Hamura's and the simple pleasures it consistently delivers.

2956 Kress St., Lihue. © **808/245-3271**. Most items less than $7. No credit cards. Mon–Thurs 10am–10:30pm; Fri–Sat 10am–midnight; Sun 10am–9pm.

Hanamaulu Restaurant CHINESE/JAPANESE/SUSHI When passing this restaurant, you'd never know that serene Japanese gardens with stone pathways and tatami-floored teahouses are hidden within. You can dine at the sushi bar, American style, or in the teahouses for lunch or dinner, but you must call ahead for teahouse dining. At lunch, enter a world of chop suey, won tons, teriyaki chicken, and sukiyaki (less verve than value), with many other choices in budget-friendly Japanese and Chinese plate lunches. Special Japanese and Chinese menus can be planned ahead for groups of up to 60 people, who can dine at low tables on tatami floors in a Japanese-garden setting. Old-timers love this place, and those who came here when they were in diapers are now stopping in for after-golf pupu and beer.

3–4291 Kuhio Hwy., Hanamaulu. ⓒ 808/245-2511. Reservations recommended. Main courses $7–$18. MC, V. Tues–Fri 10am–1pm; Tues–Sun 5–8:30pm.

Kako's ⓡ SAIMIN Wonderful home-cooked broth and noodles are Kako's signature. Kako's saimin was a west-side phenomenon for years until Hurricane Iniki turned out the lights, so saimin aficionados are ecstatic that this former Hanapepe fixture has reopened, this time in Lihue. After a long absence, the new installation—just as tiny and just as good as the original—is cause for applause. Owner Dorothea Hayashi uses a secret recipe to make her broth from scratch, and the noodles, also house-made and fresh, are the perfect accompaniment. When teamed with her teriyaki chicken sticks, the saimin and won-ton min are pure heaven for noodle lovers. The saimin comes with a choice of toppings, such as barbecued chicken, cabbage, sliced eggs, and green onions. Old-fashioned, home-style hamburgers like Mom used to make, flavored with onions mixed into the patties, are flying out the door at a miraculous $1.75. Mrs. Hayashi told us that she has had so much business since she's been recommended in this guide that "maybe you should take us out of the book."

2980 Ewalu St. ⓒ 808/246-0404. Saimin $3–$5.50. No credit cards or checks. Mon–Sat 10:30am–2pm.

Kalapaki Beach Hut ⓚⓘⓓⓢ AMERICAN This place is tricky to find (look for the anchor chain out in front of the blue building), but the money you'll save makes it worth the hunt. Started in 1990 by Steve and Sharon Gerald as Kalapaki Beach Burgers, the tiny eatery started adding more items and then evolved into serving breakfast. This "hut" has window service and a few tables downstairs; sit upstairs for an ocean view. It's basic fare, served on paper plates with plastic cutlery at cheap, cheap prices. Breakfasts are hearty omelets, pancakes, and numerous egg dishes. Lunches are heavy on the hamburgers (prepared 10 different ways), lots of sandwiches, a few healthy salads, and fish and chips. The kids get their own menu. This casual restaurant welcomes people in their bathing suits and flip-flops.

3474 Rice St., Nawiliwili. ⓒ 808/246-6330. Breakfast $3.95–$6.95; lunch $3.50–$7.50. MC, V. Tues–Sun 7am–8pm; Mon 7am–9pm.

Restaurant Kiibo JAPANESE Neither a sleek sushi bar nor a plate-lunch canteen, Kiibo is a neighborhood staple with inexpensive, unpretentious, tasty, home-style Japanese food served in a pleasant room accented with Japanese folk art. You can dine on sushi, ramen, sukiyaki, tempura, teriyaki, or the steamed egg-rice-vegetable marvel called *oyako donburi*. There are satisfying, affordable lunch specials and teishoku specials of mackerel, salmon, soup, dessert, and other condiments.

299 Umi St., Lihue. ⓒ 808/245-2650. Main courses $6–$19. No credit cards. Mon–Fri 11am–1:30pm; Mon–Sat 5:30–9pm.

Tip Top Café/Bakery *(Kids* LOCAL   This small cafe/bakery (also the lobby for the Tip Top Motel) has been serving local customers since 1916. The best deal is their breakfasts: Most items are $5 or under, and their macadamia pancakes are known throughout Kauai. Lunch ranges from pork chops to teriyaki chicken, but their specialty is oxtail soup. For a real treat, stop by the bakery (where you pay your bill) and take something home. (We recommend the freshly baked *malasadas*.)

3173 Akahi St., Lihue. ℂ **808/245-2333.** Breakfast items under $5; lunch entrees under $6. MC, V. Tues–Sun 6:30am–2pm.

THE POIPU RESORT AREA

You'll find the restaurants in this section on the "Where to Stay & Dine in the Poipu Resort Area" map on p. 549.

EXPENSIVE

The Beach House *★★★* HAWAII REGIONAL   This is the place to go for a "splurge" meal: Celebrate a birthday, anniversary or any excuse for a romantic dinner on the beach with delicious food. The Beach House remains the south shore's premier spot for sunset drinks, appetizers, and dinner—a treat for all the senses. The oceanfront room is large, accented with oversize sliding-glass doors, with old Hawaii Regional favorites on the menu. Come for cocktails or early dinner, when you can still see the sunset and perhaps a turtle or two bobbing in the waves. Menus change daily and include Kauai asparagus salad, seared macadamia nut–crusted mahimahi with miso sauce, sea scallops with lemon grass and kafir lime, and the Beach House crab cake with mint sambal butter sauce and grilled tomato compote. Desserts shine, too, like the molten chocolate desire—a hot chocolate tart—and the mango crème brûlée.

5022 Lawai Rd., Poipu. ℂ **808/742-1424.** Reservations recommended. Main courses $20–$34. AE, DC, MC, V. Daily 5:30–9pm.

Casa di Amici *★* ITALIAN/INTERNATIONAL   Chef Randall Yates and his wife, Joanna, took over a free-standing wood-and-stone building in Poipu and turned it into a storybook restaurant with fairy lights, high ceilings, beveled glass, and a generous open deck where you can dine among palms and heliotropes. (There's live classical music Sat evenings 6:30–9:30pm on the baby grand piano.) It's worth seeking out: It's the third left turn past Brennecke's Beach, not more than 2 minutes from Poipu Beach Park, in an enclave of condos and vacation rentals.

The memorable Italian food has strong Mediterranean and cross-cultural influences. You'll find organic greens from Kilauea, several risotto choices (quattro formaggio and smoked salmon are outstanding), black tiger prawns in orange, saffron lobster sauce, and surprises such as Thai lobster bisque and duck in a sun-dried cherry Chambourd sauce. Among the nearly two dozen pasta selections is a classic fettuccine Alfredo for which Yates is deservedly famous. The set menu is Italian, but the specials showcase international influences, such as soy-sauce reductions, *furikake* (seaweed sprinkle), and assertive touches of jalapeño tequila aioli on salmon and grilled tiger prawns. This is flamboyant, joyful Italian fare. Plus, you can order either light- or regular-size entrees, a policy I love.

2301 Nalo Rd., Poipu. ℂ **808/742-1555.** Reservations recommended. Main courses $17–$20 light size, $22–$25 regular size. DC, MC, V. Daily 6pm–closing.

Dondero's *★★★* ITALIAN   If you are looking for a romantic dinner either under the stars overlooking the ocean or tucked away in an intimate table surrounded by inlaid marble floors, ornate imported floor tiles, and Franciscan murals, the Grand Hyatt's stellar Italian restaurant is the place for you. You get all this atmosphere at Dondero's, plus the best Italian cuisine on the island, served with efficiency. It's hard to have a bad experience here. My recommendations for a meal to remember: start with either the fresh mozzarella cheese with tomatoes and roasted peppers or the warm goat cheese tart. Then move on to the black-ink linguine with scallops, shrimp, mussels, salmon, clams, and lobster; the *osso buco* with risotto; or the sautéed Hawaiian onaga with a pineapple, ginger sauce. Save room for dessert, especially the crème brûlée with fresh berries. Dinners are pricey but worth every penny.

Grand Hyatt Kauai Resort & Spa, 1571 Poipu Rd., Poipu. ℂ 808/742-1234. Reservations a must. Main courses $22–$42. AE, DC, DISC, MC, V. Daily 6–10pm.

Plantation Gardens Restaurant HAWAII REGIONAL   I was very disappointed when I last ate here; it's still a mix of irresistible garden ambience and a well-executed menu fashioned around fresh local ingredients, but the portions are small, everything is a la carte, and the prices are outrageous ($104 for a dinner for two without drinks or dessert). The new menu comes from the culinary genius of chefs Tom Connolly and Teri McLeod. The seaweed, fish, and shellfish are from local waters, and many of the fruits, herbs, and vegetables are grown on the restaurant premises. The historic architecture includes a generous veranda, koa trim and Brazilian cherry floors, and gracious details of a 1930s estate that belonged to the manager of Hawaii's first sugar plantation. A sprawling horticultural marvel, the property includes koi ponds, coconut and kou trees, orchids, bromeliads, and a cactus and succulent garden.

In Kiahuna Plantation Resort, 2253 Poipu Rd. ℂ 808/742-2216. Reservations recommended. Main courses $18–$28. AE, DC, MC, V. Daily 5:30–9pm dinner (open at 5pm for pupu and cocktails).

Roy's Poipu Bar & Grill ★★ EURO-ASIAN   This is a loud, lively room with ceiling fans, marble tables, works by local artists, and a menu tailor-made for foodies. The signature touches of Roy Yamaguchi (of Roy's restaurants in Oahu, Big Island, Maui, Tokyo, New York, and Guam) are abundantly present: an excellent, progressive, and affordable wine selection; fresh local ingredients prepared with a nod to Europe, Asia, and the Pacific; and service so efficient it can be overbearing. Because appetizers (such as blackened ahi with mustard soy sauce, grilled Szechwan baby back ribs, and crispy crab cakes with butter sauce) are a major part of the menu, you can sample Roy's legendary fare without breaking the bank. The three dozen nightly specials invariably include eight fresh fish dishes, prepared at least five or six different ways.

In Poipu Shopping Village, 2360 Kiahuna Plantation Dr. ℂ 808/742-5000. www.roysrestaurant.com. Reservations highly recommended. Main courses $15–$45. AE, DC, DISC, MC, V. Daily 5:30–9:30pm.

Tidepool Restaurant ★★★ SEAFOOD   Here's another ultraromantic restaurant at the Grand Hyatt (see also Dondero's, above). A cluster of thatched bungalows overlook the lagoon in a dreamy open-aired restaurant with Tiki torches flickering in the moonlight. The atmosphere would be reason enough to book a table, but the cuisine is just as outstanding. Their specialty is fresh fish prepared a number of ways, but they also have juicy steaks and ribs, as well as entrees for vegetarians. My picks are the sautéed opakapaka with young spinach, roasted potato, and pumpkin; the wok-seared soy, sake, and ginger-marinated ahi; and the open-roasted black bean sea bass. Book early, and ask for a table overlooking the water.

Grand Hyatt Kauai Resort & Spa, 1571 Poipu Rd., Poipu. ℂ 808/742-1234. Reservations recommended. Main courses $23–$43. AE, DC, DISC, MC, V. Daily 5:30–10pm.

MODERATE

Brennecke's Beach Broiler ✪ AMERICAN/SEAFOOD   Cheerful petunias in window boxes and second-floor views of Poipu Beach are pleasing touches at this seafood/burger house, a favorite for more than 15 years. The view alone is worth the price of a drink and pupu, but it helps that the best hamburgers on the south shore are served here, as well as excellent vegetarian selections. It's casual, so drop in before or after the beach and dine on nachos and peppers, fresh fish sandwiches, kiawe-broiled fish and kabobs, prime rib, pasta, build-your-own gourmet burgers, and the salad bar. Look for happy-hour specials daily, and the Alaskan king crab and prime rib nights.

2100 Hoone Rd. (across from Poipu Beach Park). © 808/742-7588. www.brenneckes.com. Main courses $13–$40. AE, DC, DISC, MC, V. Daily 11am–10pm (street-side deli takeout daily 8am–8pm).

Casa Blanca at Kiahuna MEDITERRANEAN   This used to be one of my favorite dining places on Kauai; I planned my trips around eating here. But it has just gotten too unreliable in recent years—either you could have the meal of your life here with great service or it could be a total fiasco with bad service, to boot. Call in advance to see if owner Elizabeth "Liz" Foley, a culinary genius, will be on-site during your visit; of not, you might want to pass, as the quality of both service and food tends to suffer when she's not there. Lunch is a creative selection of sandwiches, salads, soups, and brochettes (Moroccan lamb, Algerian chicken skewers, and Moroccan vegetable with couscous), and even a kids' menu with such classics as PB&J and grilled cheese. They also have a delicious tapas menu of small items: Spanish shrimp, carpaccio, crostini with olive tapanade, spicy eggplant caponata, and more at Happy Hour. But it's at dinner that Liz's famous culinary talents really stand out, with zarzuela (Spanish stew with lobster, shrimp, mussels, tomato, and saffron), *Tangine al Dajaj* (traditional Moroccan street fare of stewed chicken with olives and spices served over couscous), *agnello* (New Zealand lamb with roasted red potatoes), and nightly specials. Whatever you order, do not miss the chocolate mousse with orange for dessert. After the sun has set, it is hard to find the unlit turnoff to the restaurant, but it's worth the search.

2290 Poipu Rd. (in the Kiahuna Swim and Tennis Club), Poipu. © 808/742-2929. Reservations recommended for dinner. Lunch $6–$12; tapas $5–$16; dinner entrees $14–$30. DISC, MC, V. Daily 11am–4pm and 5:30–9pm; happy hour 4–6:30pm.

Keoki's Paradise *(Kids)* STEAK/SEAFOOD   Great place to take the kids—they will love the tropical ambience here. Keoki's Paradise is sprawling and lively, and has improved with the years, with lunch favorites that include a fresh fish sandwich, fresh fish tacos, Thai shrimp sticks, and chicken Caesar salad—all good and affordable. In the evenings, regulars tout the fresh fish crusted in lemon grass, basil, and bread crumbs. When it's time for dessert, the original Hula pie from Kimo's in Lahaina is an ever-sinful winner. The cafe in the bar area serves lighter fare and features live Hawaiian music Sunday through Friday nights.

In Poipu Shopping Village, 2360 Kiahuna Plantation Dr. © 808/742-7534. Reservations recommended. Main courses $8–$12 lunch, $16–$27 dinner. AE, DC, DISC, MC, V. Daily 5–10pm in the main dining room; cafe menu daily 11am–11pm.

Poipu Beach Broiler *(Kids)* STEAK/SEAFOOD   Located in the former House of Seafood, this new casual eatery has a relaxing atmosphere, like an old beach house. We love their large appetizer menu. In fact, we recommend that you drop by at sunset, have a drink, and chow down on the great variety of pupu like vegetable summer rolls, sea scallops, seared ahi sashimi, or tender calamari. You can make a meal of the appe-tizers. Lunch is burgers, sandwiches, and salads; dinner entrees include fresh fish, prime rib, grilled sirloin, and baby back ribs. There's a menu for the kids.

1941 Poipu Rd., Poipu. © 808/742-6433. Lunch $8–$12; dinner $19–$35. AE, DC, DISC, MC. V. Daily 11:30am–10pm.

Pomodoro ★★ ITALIAN   Pomodoro is the Italian magnet of the west side, a small, casual, and intimate second-floor dining room with a bar, potted plants, soft lighting, and pleasing Italian music. It's a warm, welcoming place where Hawaiian hospitality meets European flavors: homemade garlic focaccia, homemade mozzarella, chicken saltimbocca, and homemade pastas (cannelloni, manicotti, and excellent lasagna, the house specialty). Whether you order the veal, chicken, scampi, calamari, or very fresh, organic green salads, you'll appreciate the wonderful home-style flavor and the polite, efficient servers.

In Rainbow Plaza, Kaumualii Hwy. (Hwy. 50), Kalaheo (inland from Poipu). © 808/332-5945. Reservations recom-mended. Main courses $14–$24. MC, V. Mon–Sat 5:30–9:30pm.

Tomkats Grille AMERICAN/GRILL   *Warning:* If you are on a low-fat or low-carb diet, this is not the place for you. Fried appetizers, inexpensive New York steak, rotis-serie chicken, seafood salad with fresh catch, and sandwiches and burgers are among the offerings at the Grille, in a serene garden setting in Old Koloa Town. Old-fashioned brews are big here—everything from local microbrews to Guinness Stout, plus two dozen others to help wash down the kalua pork quesadillas or the seared poke.

5404 Koloa Rd., Old Koloa Town. © 808/742-8887. Main courses $11–$37. MC, V. Daily 10:30am–11pm; happy hour daily 3–6pm; bar daily until 11:30pm.

INEXPENSIVE

Brick Oven Pizza PIZZA   A Kalaheo fixture for nearly 3 decades, Brick Oven is the quintessential mom-and-pop business, serving pizza cooked directly on the brick hearth, brushed with garlic butter, and topped with long-simmered sauces. You have a choice of whole-wheat or white crust, plus many toppings: house-made Italian sausage, Portuguese sausage, bay shrimp, anchovies, smoked ham, vegetarian options, and more. The result: very popular pizza, particularly when topped with fresh garlic and served with Gordon Biersch beer. The seafood-style pizza-bread sandwiches are big at lunch, and the "Super Pizza" with everything on it—that's *amore.*

2–2555 Kaumualii Hwy. (Hwy. 50), Kalaheo (inland from Poipu). © 808/332-8561. Sandwiches less than $8; pizzas $11–$32. MC, V. Tues–Sun 11am–10pm.

Camp House Grill (Kids) AMERICAN   Nick Morrison has been cooking up burgers, chicken, barbecue ribs, and spectacular breakfasts since he opened Camp House Grill in 1988. This down-home country place is *the* place for breakfast, with everything from pancakes to biscuits and gravy, to sweet-bread French toast, to dozens of differ-ent omelets. Low-priced specials offered before 8am include scrambled eggs, bacon, and toast for $4. Lunch and dinner range from burgers to deep-fried chicken, to fresh fish. (Prices are the same for lunch or dinner.) A kids' menu is available.

Kaumaualii Hwy. (across the street from the Menehune Foodmart), Kalaheo. © 808/332-9755. Breakfast $4–$9.95; lunch and dinner $4.95–$20. AE, DISC, MC, V. Daily 6:30am–9pm.

e.b.'s EATS AMERICAN/BAKERY   When this small bakery/cafe was in Lihue, it was a real find, but since their move to the not-so-great location in the Poipu Shop-ping Village, in a very dark corner, it's just not the cute little place it once was. This bakery/deli/cafe does serve up a healthy breakfast and lunch at low prices. The break-fast menu has an assortment of muffins, scones, and bagels. The offerings for lunch range from salads to sandwiches, with specials like pesto-crusted salmon, meatloaf, and rigatoni. Save room for dessert.

Poipu Shopping Village, 2360 Kiahuna Plantation Dr. Poipu. ℂ 808/742-1979. Lunch $6–$10; dinner $11–$26. AE, MC, V. Mon–Fri 9am–9pm; Sat–Sun 11am–5pm.

Joe's on the Green ⚘ (Finds AMERICAN   Psst! We'll let you in on a secret. This "hidden" eatery is mainly known to local residents, who flock here for breakfast or for lunch after a round of golf. They don't want the secret to get out because then their local hangout will be flooded with tourists. Breakfasts are a bargain, especially if you go before 8:30am and get the early-bird special for $6. This is the place to go for breakfast; not only do you have a great setting—outdoors overlooking the golf course—but the menu has everything from fluffy pancakes (banana–macadamia nut are the best) to biscuits 'n' gravy, to healthy tofu scramble. Lunch is popular because of a range of sandwiches (from fresh fish to Joe's Mama Burger, to a quarter-pound hot dog with sauerkraut and Cleveland stadium mustard), salads (build your own), and desserts (do not pass up the large, warm chocolate-chip cookie).

2545 Kiahuna Plantation Dr., at the Kiahuna Golf Club Clubhouse, Poipu. ℂ 808/742-9696. Breakfast $4.95–$9.50; lunch $5.50–$11. MC, V. Daily 7am–2:30pm; happy hour 3–5:30pm.

Kalaheo Coffee Co. & Cafe ⚘⚘ (Finds COFFEEHOUSE/CAFE   John Ferguson has long been one of our favorite Kauai chefs, and his cafe is a coffee lover's fantasy: Kauai Estate Peaberry, Kona dark roast, Guatemalan French roast, Colombian, Costa Rican, Sumatran, and African coffees—you can visit the world on a coffee bean! The coffeehouse also serves masterful breakfasts: Bonzo Breakfast Burritos (sautéed ham, peppers, mushrooms, onions, and olives scrambled with cheese and served with salsa and sour cream); veggie omelets with sun-dried tomatoes and mushrooms; and bagels. At lunch the fabulous grilled turkey burgers (heaped with grilled onions and mush-rooms on a sourdough bun) are the headliner on a list of winners that also includes fresh-from-the-garden salads and a tasty, inexpensive soup that changes daily. The cin-namon "knuckles" (baked fresh daily), fresh apple pie, and carrot cake are more rea-sons to stop by. And finally, by popular demand, they are serving dinner (Wed–Sat only): from pasta primavera (vegetarian $16, fresh fish $22, chicken $21) and home-made turkey meatloaf ($18) to a bourbon-orange glazed half-chicken ($16), a fresh fish seafood wrap ($23), and a grilled New York sirloin steak ($27).

2–2560 Kaumualii Hwy. (Hwy. 50), Kalaheo (across the street from Brick Oven Pizza). ℂ 808/332-5858. Most items less than $8; dinner entrees $16–$27. MC, V. Daily 6:30am–2pm; Wed–Sat 5:30–9pm.

WESTERN KAUAI

Hanapepe Cafe & Espresso Bar ⚘⚘ GOURMET VEGETARIAN/ITALIAN   The couple who used to own this delectable, wholesome vegetarian cafe with a casual, winning ambience sold it to Andrea Pisciotta, a former waitress in the restaurant who loved the place and wanted to continue the tradition. Pisciotta upgraded the facilities, painted the walls, put in new artwork, introduced fish to the menu, added dinners on Friday nights with live entertainment, and Monday through Friday added a bakery with wonderful baked goods and quiche. It's packed at lunchtime, when people come for the several varieties of garden burger. They have elevated this modest staple to gourmet status: You can top yours with sautéed mushrooms, grilled onions, pesto, fresh-grated Parmesan, and other choices. Other lunch notables: fresh red-skinned home fries, a heroic grilled vegetable sandwich, and whole roasted garlic heads. The Friday night dinner menu changes every week, but features Italian and fresh seafood specialties like lasagna quattro formaggio with spinach, mushrooms, and four cheeses; crepes; and the nightly special with the cafe's famous marinara sauce—terrific choices all. There's no liquor license, so if you want wine, bring your own.

3830 Hanapepe Rd., Hanapepe. **©** **808/335-5011.** Reservations recommended for dinner. Lunch main courses $6.50–$13; dinner main courses $16–$24. MC, V. Mon–Thurs 11am–3pm; Fri 11am–2pm and 6–9pm. Bakery Mon–Fri 7–11am.

Shrimp Station SHRIMP   Looking for a picnic lunch to take up to Waimea Canyon? Stop at this roadside eatery, which is nothing more than a kitchen with a few picnic tables outside. But the shrimp cooking up inside will make up for the lack of ambience. The shrimp is cooked a variety of ways, from shrimp taco to a shrimp burger, but the star attraction is the shrimp plates (choice of garlic shrimp, Cajun, Thai, or sweet chile garlic). If you get yours to go, make sure you grab plenty of napkins; you'll need them after munching these tasty but messy morsels.

9652 Kaumualii Hwy., Waimea. **©** **808/338-1242.** Shrimp platters $11–$12. AE, MC, V. Daily 11am–5pm.

Toi's Thai Kitchen THAI/AMERICAN   A west Kauai staple, Toi's has gained a following for its affordable, authentic Thai food and a casual atmosphere. Tucked into a corner of a small shopping complex (look for the McDonald's on the highway), Toi's serves savory dishes utilizing fresh herbs and local ingredients, many of them from the owner's garden. Popular items include the house specialty, Toi's Temptation (homegrown herbs, coconut milk, lemon grass, and your choice of seafood, meat, or tofu); the vegetable curries; shrimp satay; and ginger-sauce nua (your choice of seafood, meat, or tofu in a fresh ginger stir-fry). Most of the rice, noodle, soup, curry, and main-course selections allow you to choose from among pork, chicken, seafood, beef, and vegetarian options. Buttered garlic nua, peanut-rich satays, and stir-fried Basil Delight are among Toi's many tasty preparations. Lunch dishes come with green-papaya salad and a choice of jasmine, sticky, or brown rice; at dinner, they add dessert.

In the Eleele Shopping Center, Eleele. **©** **808/335-3111.** Main courses $10–$17. AE, MC, V. Tues–Sat 10:30am–2pm and 5:30–9pm.

Waimea Brewing Company ECLECTIC   This popular brewery in the Waimea Plantation Cottages is a welcome addition to the dry west side, serving pub fare with a multiethnic twist. "Small plates" for grazing are composed of ale-steamed shrimp, taro-leaf-and-goat-cheese dip with warm pita bread, or seafood chowder. "Big plates" come with steak with wasabi mashed potatoes, kalbi short ribs, or *kalua* pork. In between are soups, salads, and sandwiches, including fresh catch. The beer is brewed on the premises. It's a pleasant stop, one of the top two places in Waimea for dinner.

In Waimea Plantation Cottages, 9400 Kaumualii Hwy., Waimea. **©** **808/338-9733.** Main courses $10–$30. AE, DISC, MC, V. Daily 11am–9pm.

Wrangler's Steakhouse *Kids* STEAKHOUSE   Good service and pleasant veranda seating are among the pluses of this family-run operation. Western touches abound: a wagon in the loft, log-framed booths with gas lanterns, and lauhala *paniolo* (Hawaiian cowboy) hats in the made-in-Hawaii gift shop. Wrangler's serves steak, and lots of it—big, hand-selected cuts—and adds some Island touches, from vegetable tempura to grilled steak, to ahi with penne pasta. Families like Wrangler's because of its multi-course dinners that won't break the bank.

9852 Kaumualii Hwy., Waimea. (© **808/338-1218.** Lunch $8–$16; dinner main courses $18–$30. AE, DISC, MC, V. Mon–Thurs 11am–8:30pm; Fri 11am–9pm; Sat 5–9pm.

THE COCONUT COAST

You'll find the restaurants in this section on the "Where to Stay & Dine on the Coconut Coast" map on p. 555.

EXPENSIVE

The Bull Shed STEAK/SEAFOOD   The informality and oceanfront location are big pluses, but Kauai regulars also tout the steaks and chops—prime rib, Australian rack of lamb, garlic tenderloin—and the fresh catch. The seafood selection includes broiled shrimp, Alaskan king crab, and Parmesan-drenched scallops. Dinner orders include rice and the salad bar, and combination dinners target the ambivalent, with chicken, steak, seafood, and lobster pairings. The salad bar alone is a value, and the entrees are so big they're often shared.

796 Kuhio Hwy., Waipouli. (© **808/822-3791.** Reservations recommended for parties of 6 or more. Main courses $12–$38. AE, DC, DISC, MC, V. Daily 5:30–10pm.

MODERATE

Caffè Coco GOURMET BISTRO   This gets my vote for the most charming ambience on Kauai, with gourmet fare cooked to order, and at cafe prices. Food gets a lot of individual attention here. Caffè Coco appears just off the main road at the edge of a cane field in Wailua, its backyard shaded by pomelo, avocado, mango, tangerine, litchi, and banana trees, with a view of the Sleeping Giant Mountain. The trees provide many of the ingredients for the muffins, chutneys, and salsas that Ginger Carlson whips up in her kitchen. Seats are indoors (beyond the black-light art gallery) or on the gravel-floored back courtyard, where Tiki torches flicker at night. From interior design to cooking, this is clearly a showcase for Carlson's creativity. The food is excellent, with vegetarian and other healthful delights such as homemade chai, Greek salad, fish wraps, seared ahi with wasabi cream, and an excellent tofu-and-roast-veggie wrap. Although the regular menu is limited, there are many impressive specials. Service can be laid-back, to say the least.

4–369 Kuhio Hwy., Wailua. (© **808/822-7990.** Reservations recommended for 4 or more. Main courses $7–$21; specials usually less than $20. MC, V. Tues–Fri 11am–9pm; Sat–Sun 5–9pm.

Coconuts Island Style Grill AMERICAN/ECLECTIC   This is one of Kauai's newer sensations, located right on the highway (next to Taco Bell). Fans line up for the happy-hour pupu and affordable, tasty fare. Coconuts is upbeat and busy, with a cheerfully tropical dining room of bamboo ceilings and coconut everything: fixtures, furniture, and lights. There are lots of wines by the glass, good beers on tap, and a wide-ranging menu, including the popular teriyaki-dipped fresh salmon (oven-roasted, with kafir lime broth and mashed Okinawa sweet potatoes), and an excellent seafood chowder. The burgers and crab cakes are also popular. The appetizer menu (coconut-dusted shrimp, lobster ravioli) is a hit from the time the doors open at 4pm.

4–919 Kuhio Hwy. (© **808/823-8777.** Reservations accepted only for 5 or more. Main courses $12–$29. AE, DC, MC, V. Mon–Sat 4–10pm.

Wailua Family Restaurant *Kids* AMERICAN/LOCAL   The salad bars, efficient service, and family-friendly feeling here are legendary (seniors get discounts and there's a special menu for keiki). The cross-cultural salad bar includes a Mexican bar, pasta bar, sushi section, homemade soups, and ethnic samplings from Korean, Japanese, Filipino, and Hawaiian traditions. The papaya is always freshly sliced at breakfast (there's a breakfast buffet Sat–Sun), the cornbread is good, and the eggs Benedict comes with a choice of ham or turkey. You can also order mahimahi or ono with the eggs for a high-protein start. The all-you-can-eat buffet (soup, salad, pasta, taco, and desserts) is a steal for $12, and the American and ethnic classics on the menu include sandwiches, stir-fries, teriyaki steak, and seafood combos. There is outdoor seating now, too.

4361 Kuhio Hwy., across from Kinipopo Shopping Village. ✆ 808/822-3325. Reservations recommended for dinner. Breakfast $6–$8; lunch most items under $10; dinner main courses $11–$16. MC, V. Sun–Thurs 6:30am–9pm; Fri–Sat 6:30am–9:30pm.

Wailua Marina Restaurant AMERICAN   This is a strange but lovable place, anti-nouvelle to the end. I recommend the open-air seating along the Wailua River, where you can watch the riverboats heading for the Fern Grotto over sandwiches (mahimahi is a favorite) and salads. The interior is cavernous, with a high ceiling and stuffed fish adorning the upper walls—bordering on weird, but I love it anyway. The salad bar makes the place friendlier to dieters and vegetarians; otherwise, you'll find the Alaskan king crab legs with filet mignon (or filet paired with lobster tail), stuffed prawns, famous hot lobster salad, steamed mullet, teriyaki spareribs, baked stuffed Island chicken, and some 40 other down-home items heavy on the sauces and gravies. Although the open salad bar is a meal in itself, the more reckless can try the mayo-laden mini–lobster salad appetizer, or the crab-stuffed mushrooms. *Money-saving tip:* The early-bird specials (5–6pm) start at $11 for spaghetti dinner and go up to $13 for a mixed plate of shrimp tempura, chicken yakitori, and teriyaki top sirloin.

5971 Kuhio Hwy., Wailua. ✆ 808/822-4311. Reservations recommended. Lunch $8–$20; dinner main courses $12–$37. AE, MC, V. Tues–Sun 10:30am–2pm and 5–8:30pm.

INEXPENSIVE

Blossoming Lotus ★★ VEGETARIAN   This vegetarian restaurant has become so popular that it had to move into larger quarters just around the corner. In a tranquil atmosphere with plenty of light from the two-story dining room, stone floors, wooden tables, and muted music, this organic gourmet vegan restaurant even has carnivores raving about the incredible food here. You don't have to be a born-again vegetarian to find something on the creative menu to tempt you. Appetizers include spring rolls filled with fresh garden veggies and served with a Thai dipping sauce, and a cosmic corn bread packed with cilantro and chiles. Entrees range from a coconut curry to an enchilada casserole. Lots of salads and sinful-looking (but healthy) desserts round out the always-changing menu. A recent addition is an extensive organic beer and wine menu. There is live entertainment every night and a terrific vegan brunch on Sunday. If you want a quick drink or snack, the **Lotus Root**, 4-1384 Kuhio Hwy. (the previous location for this restaurant), offers just-baked goods, ice cream, juices, and smoothies.

Dragon Building, 4504 Kukui St., Kapaa. ✆ 808/822-7678. www.blossominglotus.com. Brunch $7–$15; dinner entrees $12–$19. AE, MC, V. Daily 5:30–9:30pm.

Bubba Burgers AMERICAN   Here at the house of Bubba, they dish out humor, great T-shirts, and burgers nonpareil, including tempeh burgers for vegetarians. Grilled, fresh fish sandwiches cater to the sensible, fish and chips to the carefree, and fish burgers to the undecided. But old-fashioned hamburgers are still the main attraction. You can order the Slopper (open-faced with chili), the half-pound Big Bubba (three patties), the Hubba Bubba (with rice, hot dog, and chili—a Bubba's plate lunch), and others. Chicken burgers, Bubba's famous Budweiser chili, and other American standards are also served up here, where the burger is king, attitude reigns, and lettuce and tomato cost extra. For a burger joint, it's big on fish, too, with a daily trio of fresh fish specials, fish burgers, and fish and chips.

4–1421 Kuhio Hwy., Kapaa. ℂ **808/823-0069.** All items less than $9. MC, V. Daily 10:30am–8pm.

The King and I THAI   This medium-size restaurant, in a small and nondescript roadside complex, serves reasonably priced specials and vegetarian selections, including spring rolls, salads, curries, and stir-fries. The owners grow their own herbs for the savory curries and seasonings on the menu. At dinner the pad Thai noodles with shrimp have a special touch and are a popular counterpoint to the red, green, and yellow curries. The vegetarian menu is generous—everything from noodles to spring rolls, to curries and eggplant/tofu—but most diners come back for the Evil Jungle Prince, your choice of veggies, chicken, or fish in a sauce of coconut milk, spices, and kafir-lime leaves.

In Waipouli Plaza, 4–901 Kuhio Hwy. ℂ **808/822-1642.** Reservations recommended. Main courses $7.50–$13. AE, DC, DISC, MC, V. Daily 4:30–9pm.

Kountry Kitchen AMERICAN   Forget counting calories when you sit down to the brawny omelets here. You can choose your own fillings from several possibilities, among them a kimchi omelet with cream cheese and several vegetable, meat, and cheese combinations. Sandwiches and American dinners (steak, fish, and chicken) are standard coffeehouse fare, but there are sometimes fresh fish specials that stand out. *Warning:* Sit as far away from the grill as possible; the smell of grease travels—and clings to your clothes.

1485 Kuhio Hwy., Kapaa. ℂ **808/822-3511.** Main courses $6–$9. MC, V. Daily 6am–1:30pm.

Mermaids Cafe ✦ HEALTHFUL/ISLAND STYLE   Don't you love these places that use fresh local ingredients, make everything to order, and barely charge anything for all that trouble? A tiny sidewalk cafe with brisk takeout and a handful of tables on Kapaa's main drag, Mermaids takes kafir lime, lemon grass, local lemons (Meyers when available), and organic herbs, when possible, to make the sauces and beverages to go with its toothsome dishes. Sauces are lively and healthful, such as the peanut satay made with lemon juice instead of fish sauce. It's served in the tofu or chicken satay, chicken coconut curry plate, and chicken satay wrap. The seared ahi wrap is made with the chef's special blend of garlic, jalapeño, lemon grass, kafir lime, basil, and cilantro, then wrapped in a spinach tortilla—fabulous. The fresh-squeezed lemonade is made daily, and you can choose white or organic brown rice. These special touches elevate the simple classics to dreamy taste sensations.

1384 Kuhio Hwy., Kapaa. ℂ **808/821-2026.** Main courses $8.95–$9.95. DC, MC, V. Daily 11am–9pm.

Norberto's El Cafe MEXICAN   The lard-free, home-style Mexican fare here includes top-notch chiles rellenos with homemade everything, vegetarian selections by request, and, if you're lucky, fresh fish enchiladas. All of the sauces are made from scratch, and the salsa comes red-hot with homegrown chile peppers fresh from the chef's garden. Norberto's signature is the spinachy Hawaiian taro-leaf enchiladas, a Mexican version of laulau, served with cheese and taro or with chicken.

4–1373 Kuhio Hwy., Kapaa. © **808/822-3362**. Reservations recommended for parties of 6 or more. Main courses $4.75–$9.45; complete dinners $14–$18. AE, DISC, MC, V. Mon–Sat 5–9pm.

Ono Family Restaurant AMERICAN   Breakfast is a big deal here, with eggs Florentine (two poached eggs, blanched spinach, and hollandaise sauce) leading the pack, and eggs Canterbury (similar to eggs Benedict) following close behind. The Garden Patch, fried rice topped with fresh steamed vegetables, scrambled eggs, and hollandaise sauce, is a real conscience-buster. Steak and eggs; banana, coconut, and macadamia-nut pancakes; and dozens of omelet choices also win fans.

Lunch is no slouch either, with scads of fish, veggie, steak, tuna, and turkey sandwiches to choose from, and beef burgers with various toppings highlighting the menu. The gourmet hamburger with fries and soup demands an after-lunch siesta.

4–1292 Kuhio Hwy., Kapaa. © **808/822-1710**. Most items less than $9. AE, DC, DISC, MC, V. Daily 7am–1:30pm.

Sukhothai Restaurant THAI/VIETNAMESE/CHINESE   Curries, saimin, Chinese soups, satays, Vietnamese pho, and a substantial vegetarian menu are a few of the features of this unobtrusive—but extremely popular—Thai restaurant. Menu items appeal to many tastes and include 85 Vietnamese, Chinese, and Thai choices, along with much-loved curries and the best-selling pad Thai noodles. The coconut/lemon grass/kafir lime soups (eight choices) are Sukhothai highlights, along with the red and green curries.

In the Kapaa Shopping Center (next to Kapaa's Big Save Market), 4–1105 Kuhio Hwy., Kapaa. © **808/821-1224**. Main courses $8–$17. AE, DC, DISC, MC, V. Daily 10am–9:30pm.

EN ROUTE TO THE NORTH SHORE

Duane's Ono-Char Burger HAMBURGER STAND   We can't imagine Anahola without this roadside burger stand; it's been serving up hefty all-beef burgers for generations. (And now there are Boca burgers, for vegetarians.) The teriyaki sauce and blue cheese are only part of the secret of Duane's beefy, smoky, and legendary ono-char burgers, which come in several styles: teriyaki, mushroom, cheddar, barbecue, and the Special, with grilled onions, sprouts, and two cheeses. The broiled fish sandwich (another marvel of the seasoned old grill) and the marionberry ice-cream shake, a three-berry combo, are popular as well.

On Kuhio Hwy., Anahola. © **808/822-9181**. Hamburgers $4.15–$6.45. MC, V. Mon–Sat 10am–6pm; Sun 11am–6pm.

THE NORTH SHORE

You'll find the restaurants in this section on the "Where to Stay & Dine on Kauai's North Shore" map on p. 560.

EXPENSIVE

La Cascata ★★★ MEDITERRANEAN/SOUTHERN ITALIAN   The North Shore's special-occasion restaurant is sumptuous—a Sicilian spree in Eden. Try to get here before dark so you can enjoy the views of Bali Hai, the persimmon-colored sunset, and the waterfalls of Waialeale, all an integral part of the feast. Click your heels on the terra-cotta floors, take in the *trompe l'oeil* vines, train your eyes through the concertina windows, and pretend you're being served on a terrazzo in Sicily. The menu dazzles quietly with its Mediterranean-inspired offerings and fresh local ingredients. Polenta, charred peppers, Kauai asparagus, organic Kauai vegetables, risottos, ragouts, grilled fresh fish, and vegetable napoleons are tasty and beautifully presented.

In the Princeville Resort, 5520 Ka Haku Rd. © **808/826-9644**. Reservations recommended for dinner. Main courses $28–$48; 3-course prix-fixe dinner $65. AE, DC, DISC, MC, V. Daily 6–10pm.

Lighthouse Bistro Kilauea ★ CONTINENTAL/PACIFIC RIM/ITALIAN

Even if you're not on your way to the legendary Kilauea Lighthouse, this bistro is so good it's worth a special trip. The charming green-and-white wooden building next to Kong Lung Store has open sides, old-fashioned plantation architecture, open-air seating, trellises, and high ceilings. The ambience is wonderful, with a retro feeling; it's not as polished as Poipu's Plantation Gardens but has its own casual appeal. (In fact, it's the North Shore version of Casa di Amici in Poipu, p. 569.) The food is excellent, an eclectic selection that highlights local ingredients in everything from fresh fish tacos and fresh fish burgers to mac nut–crusted chicken and four preparations of fresh catch. This is much more elegant than usual lunchtime fare.

In Kong Lung Center, Kilauea Rd. (off Hwy. 56 on the way to the Kilauea Lighthouse), Kilauea. © **808/828-0481**. Reservations recommended for 6 or more. Lunch $5–$11; dinner main courses $18–$39. MC, V. Mon–Sat 11am–2pm; daily 5:30–9pm.

MODERATE

Calypso ★ STEAK/SEAFOOD   Good food, concrete floors, window tables with flower boxes, seating on the deck with mountain views—what's not to like? Formerly Zelo's, this "beach house," spiced up with South Pacific kitsch, serves a wide variety of coffee drinks and excellent mai tais. The congenial bar area has a tin roof and ironwood poles, and a one-person canoe hangs overhead. Huge burgers, a variety of pastas, 50 different microbrews and 30 tropical drinks, a wonderful salad in a large clam-shaped bowl, warm bread, and a good seafood chowder are some of the attractions. The inexpensive tap beers and tacos ensure that visitors and locals alike pack the place during happy hour (3:30–5:30pm). If you can, snag a table on the deck.

Kuhio Hwy. and Aku Rd., Hanalei. © **808/826-9700**. Reservations recommended for parties of 6 or more. Main courses $8–$20 lunch, $9–$25 dinner. MC, V. Winter daily 11am–9:30pm; summer daily 11am–10pm.

Hanalei Dolphin Restaurant & Fish Market ★ SEAFOOD   Hidden behind a

gallery called Ola's are this fish market and adjoining steak-and-seafood restaurant, on the banks of the Hanalei River. Particularly inviting are the fresh fish sandwiches, served under umbrellas at river's edge. Most appealing (besides the river view) are the appetizers: artichokes steamed or stuffed with garlic, butter, and cheese; buttery stuffed mushrooms; and seviche fresh from the fish market, with a jaunty dash of green olives. From fresh catch to baked shrimp, to Alaskan king crab and chicken marinated in soy sauce, the Dolphin has stayed with the tried and true.

5-5016 Kuhio Hwy., Hanalei. © **808/826-6113**. Main courses $20–$36. MC, V. Daily 11am–10pm. (Fish market daily 10am–7pm in the winter and until 8pm in the summer.)

Hanalei Gourmet AMERICAN   The wood floors, wooden benches, and blackboards of the old Hanalei School, built in 1926, are a haven for today's Hanalei hipsters noshing on the Tu Tu Tuna (far-from-prosaic tuna salad with green beans, potatoes, niçoise olives, and hard-boiled eggs), fresh grilled ahi sandwiches, roasted eggplant sandwiches, chicken-salad boats (in papaya or avocado, with macadamia nuts and sans mayonnaise), and other selections. This is an informal cross-cultural tasting, from stir-fried veggies over udon to Oriental ahi-pasta salad, to artichoke hearts fried in beer batter. The sandwich selection, on fresh-baked bread, hits the timeless deli faves, from roast beef and pastrami to smoked turkey and chicken salad. The TV over the bar competes with the breathtaking view of the Hanalei mountains and waterfalls, and the wooden floors keep the noise level high (the music on the sound system can be almost deafening). Nightly live music adds to the fun.

In the Old Hanalei Schoolhouse, 5–5161 Kuhio Hwy., Hanalei. ☎ 808/826-2524. Main courses $7–$23. DC, DISC, MC, V. Daily 8am–9:30pm; bar open until 10:30pm.

Kilauea Bakery & Pau Hana Pizza ☆ PIZZA/BAKERY   When owner, baker, and avid diver Tom Pickett spears an ono and smokes it himself, his catch appears on the Billie Holiday pizza, guaranteed to obliterate the blues with its brilliant notes of Swiss chard, roasted onions, Gorgonzola-rosemary sauce, and mozzarella. And the much-loved bakery puts out guava sourdough; coconut cream–filled chocolate éclairs (yum!); blackberry–white chocolate scones; and other fine baked goods. The breads go well with the soups and hot lunch specials, and the pastries with the new full-service espresso bar, which serves not only the best of the bean, but also blended frozen drinks and such up-to-the-minute beverages as iced chai and Mexican chocolate smoothies (with cinnamon). We also love the fresh vegetables in olive oil and herbs, baked in a baguette; the olive tapenade; and the classic scampi pizza with tiger prawns, roasted garlic, capers, and cheeses. The Picketts have added a small dining room, and the few outdoor picnic tables under umbrellas are as inviting as ever. The macadamia-nut but-ter cookies and *lilikoi* fruit Danishes are sublime.

In Kong Lung Center, Kilauea Rd. (off Hwy. 56 on the way to the Kilauea Lighthouse), Kilauea. ☎ 808/828-2020. Pizzas $11–$30. MC, V. Daily 6:30am–9pm.

Mediterranean Gourmet ☆☆ *Finds* MIDDLE EASTERN   This "hidden" restau-rant, located next door to the Hanalei Colony Resort, nearly at the end of the road, was awarded Best New Restaurant on Kauai by a local magazine and is very deserving of the distinction. The oceanfront location is the perfect backdrop for chef/owner Imad Beydoun's Middle Eastern dishes, which he embellishes with an island twist. He and his wife, Yarrow, a local Hanalei girl (plus their kids), roll out the best Mediter-ranean food you will find in Hawaii. People on Kauai have long been buying Bey-doun's packaged products (hummus, babaganush, falafels, and tobouleh) at the local farmer's market, so when his family opened the restaurant, they already had a follow-ing. The menu has traditional Middle Eastern cuisine (stuffed grape leaves, hand-rolled fatayer, hummus, grilled kafta, Greek salads, and various kabobs), as well as more familiar dishes like chicken quesadilla, rack of lamb, New York strip steak, and fresh fish. Do not leave until you have had Chef Beydoun's homemade baklava and a cup of Turkish coffee. Go on Friday or Saturday to see belly-dancing performances.

Hanalei Bay Colony Resort, 5-7132 Kuhio Hwy., Hanalei. ☎ 808/826-9875. Lunch entrees $11–$17; dinner entrees $15–$35. MC, V. Mon-Sat 11am–9pm.

Neide's Salsa and Samba BRAZILIAN/MEXICAN   Tucked away in the very back of the Hanalei Center is a "hot" eatery dishing up Brazilian cuisine like *muqueca* (fresh fish with coconut sauce), *ensopado* (baked chicken and vegetables), and *bife ace-bolado* (beef steak with onions), plus the usual popular Mexican dishes like enchiladas and burritos. Big portions, friendly service, and reasonable prices make this a good bet.

Hanalei Center, Hanalei. ☎ 808/826-1851. Entrees $9–$15. MC, V. Daily 11:30am–2:30pm and 5–9pm.

Postcards Café ☆ GOURMET SEAFOOD/NATURAL FOODS   The charming plantation-style building that used to be the Hanalei Museum is now Hanalei's gour-met central. Postcards is known for its use of healthful ingredients, fresh from the island and creatively prepared and presented. My picks from the changing menu are the wasabi-crusted ahi, the sombrero (puff pastry filled with organic cheeses, green chilies, onions, mushrooms, and garlic), and the Shanghai (tofu with veggies and roasted cashews in a tamari ginger sauce). Save room for the yummy chocolate silk, a chocolate pie in a crust of graham crackers, dried cherries, and crusted cashews. In the front yard, an immense, mossy, hollowed-out stone serves as a free-standing lily pond and roadside landmark. Great menu, presentation, and ambience—a winner.

On Kuhio Hwy. (at the entrance to Hanalei town). © 808/826-1191. Reservations highly recommended for dinner. Main courses $15–$28. AE, DC, DISC, MC, V. Daily 6–9pm.

Sushi & Blues ✦ SUSHI/PACIFIC RIM This second-floor oasis has copper tables and a copper-topped bar, large picture windows for gazing at the Hanalei waterfalls, and, most important, chefs who know their sushi. Traditional sushi, fusion sushi, and hot Pacific Rim dishes for those who aren't sushi lovers please diners of every stripe. Big hits: the temaki hand rolls, the Las Vegas roll (a heroic composition of ahi, *hamachi,* and avocado dipped in tempura batter and quickly fried, hot on the outside and chilled on the inside), the Rainbow Roll (a super-duper California roll with eight different types of fish), and fresh fish prepared several ways, in fusion flavorings involving mango, garlic, sake, sesame, coconut, passion fruit, and other Pacific Rim preparations. The action fires up Wednesday, Thursday, Saturday, and Sunday from 8:30pm on with live music, from Hawaiian to blues, jazz to rock 'n' roll.

In Ching Young Village, Hanalei. © 808/826-9701. www.sushiandblues.com. Reservations recommended for parties of 6 or more. Main courses $18–$23; sushi rolls $4 and up. MC, V. Daily 6–10pm. Live music from 8:30pm on.

INEXPENSIVE
Tropical Taco ✦ MEXICAN For more than a quarter of a century Roger Kennedy has been making tacos and burritos in Hanalei. For years, you could find him working out of his green "taco wagon" parked along the road. He's still serving his tasty assortment of tacos and burritos, plus his signature "fat Jack" (a 10-inch deep-fried tortilla with cheese, beans, and beef or fish), but now from a permanent restaurant in the Hanalei building (with seating along the outside lanai). Roger does issue this warning about his tasty treats: "Not to be consumed 1 hour before surfing!" Just as he did with his taco wagon, Roger still offers "anything you want to drink, as long as it's lemonade."

Hale Lea Building, 5–5088 Kuhio Hwy., Hanalei. © 808/827-TACO. www.tropicaltaco.com. Most items under $8. No credit cards. Mon–Sat 11am–5pm.

5 Beaches

Eons of wind and rain have created this geological masterpiece of an island, with fabulous beaches like Hanalei, Kee, and Kalapaki. All are accessible to the public, as stipulated by Hawaii law, and many have facilities.

LIHUE'S BEST BEACH
KALAPAKI BEACH ✦
Any town would pay a fortune to have a beach like Kalapaki, one of Kauai's best, in its backyard. But little Lihue turns its back on Kalapaki; there's not even a sign pointing the way through the labyrinth of traffic to this graceful half-moon of golden sand at the foot of the Marriott Resort & Beach Club. One hundred and fifty feet wide and a quarter of a mile long, Kalapaki is protected by a jetty and patrolled by lifeguards,

making it very safe for swimmers. The waves are good for surfing when there's a winter swell, and the view from the sand of the steepled 2,200-foot peaks of the majestic Haupu Ridge that shield Nawiliwili Bay is awesome. Kalapaki is the best beach not only in Lihue, but also on the whole east coast. From Lihue Airport, turn left onto Kapule Highway (Hwy. 51) to Rice Street, turn left and go to the entrance of the Marriott, and pass the hotel's *porte-cochere* and turn right at the SHORELINE ACCESS sign. Facilities include lifeguards, free parking, restrooms, and showers; food and drink are available nearby at JJ's Broiler (p. 565).

THE POIPU RESORT AREA
MAHAULEPU BEACH 🎿🎿

Mahaulepu is the best-looking unspoiled beach in Kauai and possibly in the whole state. Its 2 miles of reddish-gold, grainy sand line the southeastern shore at the foot of 1,500-foot-high Haupu Ridge, just beyond the Grand Hyatt Kauai and McBryde sugar-cane fields, which end in sand dunes and a forest of casuarina trees. Almost untouched by modern life, Mahaulepu is a great escape from the real world. It's ideal for beachcombing and shell hunting, but swimming can be risky, except in the reef-sheltered shallows 600 feet west of the sandy parking lot. There's no lifeguard, no facilities—just great natural beauty everywhere you look. (This beach is where George C. Scott portrayed Ernest Hemingway in the movie *Islands in the Stream*.) While you're here, see if you can find the Hawaiian petroglyph of a voyaging canoe carved in the beach rock.

To get here, drive past the Grand Hyatt Kauai 3 miles east on a red-dirt road, past the golf course and stables. Turn right at the T intersection, go 1 mile to the big sand dune, turn left, and drive a half-mile to a small lot under the trees.

POIPU BEACH PARK 🎿

Big, wide Poipu is actually two beaches in one; it's divided by a sandbar, called a *tombolo*. On the left, a lava-rock jetty protects a sandy-bottom pool that's perfect for children; on the right, the open bay attracts swimmers, snorkelers, and surfers. And everyone likes to picnic on the grassy lawn graced by coconut trees. You'll find excellent swimming, small tide pools for exploring, great reefs for snorkeling and diving, good fishing, nice waves for surfers, and a steady wind for windsurfers. Poipu attracts a daily crowd, but the density seldom approaches Waikiki levels, except on holidays. Facilities include restrooms, showers, picnic areas, Brennecke's Beach Broiler nearby (p. 571), and free parking in the red-dirt lot. To get here, turn on Poipu Beach Road, and then turn right at Hoowili Road.

WESTERN KAUAI
SALT POND BEACH PARK

Hawaii's only salt ponds still in production are at Salt Pond Beach, just outside Hanapepe. Generations of locals have come here to swim, fish, and collect salt crystals to dry in sun beds. The tangy salt is used for health purposes and to cure fish and season food. The curved reddish-gold beach lies between two rocky points and features a protected reef, tide pools, and gentle waves. Swimming here is excellent, even for children; this beach is also good for diving, windsurfing, and fishing. Amenities include a lifeguard, showers, restrooms, a camping area, a picnic area, a pavilion, and a parking lot. To get here, take Highway 50 past Hanapepe and turn on Lokokai Road.

Beaches & Outdoor Activities on Kauai

Airport ✈
Mountain ▲

BEACHES 🏖
Anini Beach County Park **11**
Haena Beach Park **14**
Hanalei Beach **13**
Kalapaki Beach **8**
Kee Beach State Park **15**
Lydgate State Park **10**
Mahaulepu Beach **7**
Poipu Beach Park **3**
Polihale State Park **27**
Salt Pond Beach Park **1**
Tunnels Beach **14**

CABINS & CAMPGROUNDS △
Hanakapiai Beach Campground **16**
Hanakoa Valley Campground **17**
Kalalau Valley Campground **19**
Kawaikoi Campground **21**
Kokee Lodge & Campgrounds **24**
Kokee State Park Cabins **25**
Sugi Grove Campground **22**

GOLF COURSES ⛳
Kauai Lagoons Golf Courses **9**
Kiahuna Golf Club **6**
Kukuiolono Golf Course **2**
Poipu Bay Resort Golf Course **5**
Princeville Golf Club, Prince Course **12**

HIKES 🥾
Alakai Swamp Trail **20**
Kalalau Trail, Na Pali Coast
    State Park **18**
Kokee State Park Trails **26**
Makawehi Point **4**
Waimea Canyon Trail **23**

Frommer's Favorite Kauai Experiences

Snorkeling Kee Beach. Rent a mask, fins, and snorkel, and enter a magical underwater world. Face down, you'll float like a leaf on a pond, watching brilliant fish dart through water clear as day; a slow-moving turtle may even stop by to check you out. Face up, you'll contemplate green-velvet cathedral-like cliffs under a blue sky, with long-tailed tropical birds riding the trade winds. See p. 591.

Hiking Waimea Canyon, the Grand Canyon of the Pacific. Ansel Adams would have loved this ageless desert canyon, carved by an ancient river. Sunlight plays against its rustic red cliffs, burnt-orange pinnacles, and blue-green valleys. There's nothing else like it in the islands. See p. 595.

Wandering Around a High Mountain Forest. Kokee State Park, through Waimea Canyon at the end of Highway 550, is a combination rainforest and bog up around 4,000 feet. The park's 45 miles of trails offer everything from casual nature strolls to hardy camping and hiking adventures among the redwoods. See p. 596.

Strolling Through Hawaiian History. Old Waimea town looks so unassuming that you'd never guess it stood witness to a great many key events in Hawaii's history. This is the place where Capt. James Cook "discovered" the Hawaiian Islands, where Russians once built a fort, and where New England missionaries arrived in 1820 to save the heathens. A self-guided walking-tour guide is available at **Waimea Public Library,** Kaumualii Highway (© **808/ 338-6848**). See "Waimea Town" under "Seeing the Sights," later in this chapter.

Taking a Long Walk on a Short (but Historic) Pier. First built in 1910, Hanalei's Pier was once a major shipping port for local farmers. Today the rebuilt pier makes a great platform for swimming, fishing, and diving. It's at Black Pot Beach, where, in the olden days, local families would camp out all summer and always have something cooking in a "black pot" on the shore.

POLIHALE STATE PARK ♠

This mini-Sahara on the western end of the island is Kauai's biggest beach: 17 miles long and as wide as three football fields. This is a wonderful place to get away from it all, but don't forget your flip-flops—the midday sand is hotter than a lava flow. The golden sands wrap around Kauai's northwestern shore from Kekaha plantation town, just beyond Waimea, to where the ridgebacks of the Na Pali Coast begin. The state park includes ancient Hawaiian *heiau* (temple) and burial sites, a view of the "forbidden" island of Niihau, and the famed **Barking Sands Beach,** where footfalls sound like a barking dog. (Scientists say that the grains of sand are perforated with tiny echo chambers, which emit a "barking" sound when they rub together.) Polihale also takes in the Pacific Missile Range Facility, a U.S. surveillance center that snooped on Russian subs during the Cold War, and Nohili Dune, which is nearly 3 miles long and 100 feet high in some places.

Black Pot—and all of Hanalei Beach—is great for swimming, snorkeling, and surfing. See p. 586.

Watching for Whales. Mahaulepu Beach, in the Poipu area, offers excellent land-based viewing conditions to spot whales that cruise by from December through April. See p. 582.

Journeying into Eden. For a glimpse of the spectacularly remote Na Pali Coast, all you need to do is hike the first 2 miles along the well-maintained Kalalau Trail into the first tropical valley, Hanakapiai. Hardier hikers can venture another 2 miles to the Hanakapiai waterfalls and pools. *Warning:* Na Pali's natural beauty is so enticing that you may want to keep going—but the trail turns rugged and extremely challenging after the 2-mile mark. Contact the State Division of Parks for a permit if you want to camp along the trail. See "Hiking & Camping," later in this chapter.

Catching a Poipu Wave. Vividly turquoise, curling and totally tubular, big enough to hang ten yet small enough to bodysurf, the waves at Poipu are endless in their attraction. Grab a boogie board—you can rent one for just dollars a day—or simply jump in and go with the flow. See p. 589 and 592.

Watching the Hula. The Coconut Marketplace, on Kuhio Highway (Hwy. 56) between mile markers 6 and 7, hosts free shows every day at 5pm. Arrive early to get a good seat for the hour-long performances of both *kahiko* (ancient) and *auwana* (modern) hula. The real showstoppers are the *keiki* (children) who perform. Don't forget your camera!

Bidding the Sun Aloha. Polihale State Park hugs Kauai's western shore for some 17 miles. It's a great place to bring a picnic dinner, stretch out on the sand, and toast the sun as it sinks into the Pacific, illuminating the island of Niihau in the distance. Queen's Pond has facilities for camping, as well as restrooms, showers, picnic tables, and pavilions. See p. 584.

Be careful in winter, when high surf and rip currents make swimming dangerous. The safest place to swim is **Queen's Pond,** a small, shallow, sandy-bottom inlet protected from waves and shore currents. There are facilities for camping, as well as restrooms, showers, picnic tables, and pavilions. To get here, take Highway 50 past Barking Sands Missile Range and follow the signs through the sugar cane fields to Polihale. Local kids have been known to burgle rental cars out here, so don't leave tempting valuables in your car.

THE COCONUT COAST
LYDGATE STATE PARK

This seacoast park has a rock-wall fish pond that blunts the open ocean waves and provides the only safe swimming and the best snorkeling on the eastern shore. The 1-acre beach park, near the mouth of the Wailua River, is named for the Rev. J. M. Lydgate (1854–1922), founder and first pastor of Lihue English Union Church, who likely would be shocked at the public display of flesh here. This popular park is a great place

---

Moments   Stargazing

Any Kauai beach is great for stargazing, almost any night of the year. Once a month, on the Saturday nearest the new moon, when the skies are darkest, the **Kauai Educational Association for the Study of Astronomy** sponsors a star watch Kaumakani, at the softball field (follow Hwy. 50 west past Hanapepe, after mile marker 18, look for KEASA signs on the right for parking and the star watch location). For information on the next star watch, contact KEASA, P.O. Box 161, Waimea, HI 96796 (© **808/332-STAR [7827];** www.keasa.org). Video presentations start at 6pm, with star gazing on the ocean side of the resort to follow.

---

for a picnic or for kite flying on the green. It's 5 miles north of Lihue on Kuhio Highway (Hwy. 56); look for the turnoff just before the Kauai Resort Hotel. Facilities include a pavilion, restrooms, outdoor showers, picnic tables, barbecue grills, lifeguards, and parking.

THE NORTH SHORE

ANINI BEACH COUNTY PARK 🎦🎦

Anini is Kauai's safest beach for swimming and windsurfing. It's also one of the island's most beautiful: It sits on a blue lagoon at the foot of emerald cliffs, looking more like Tahiti than almost any other strand in the islands. This 3-mile-long gold-sand beach is shielded from the open ocean by the longest, widest fringing reef in Hawaii. With shallow water 4 to 5 feet deep, it's also the very best snorkel spot on Kauai, even for beginners; on the northwest side, a channel in the reef runs out to the deep blue water with a 60-foot drop that attracts divers. Beachcombers love it, too: Seashells, cowries, and sometimes even rare Niihau shells can be found here. Anini has a park, a campground, picnic and barbecue facilities, and a boat-launch ramp; several B&Bs and vacation rentals are nearby. Follow Kuhio Highway (Hwy. 56) to Kilauea; take the second exit, called Kalihiwai Road (the first dead-ends at Kalihiwai Beach), and drive a half-mile toward the sea; turn left on Anini Beach Road.

HANALEI BEACH 🎦

Gentle waves roll across the face of half-moon Hanalei Bay, running up to the wide, golden sand; sheer volcanic ridges laced by waterfalls rise to 4,000 feet on the other side, 3 miles inland. Is there any beach with a better location? Celebrated in song and hula, and featured on travel posters, this beach owes its natural beauty to its age—it's an ancient sunken valley with posterosional cliffs. Hanalei Bay indents the coast a full 1 mile inland and runs 2 miles point to point, with coral reefs on either side and a patch of coral in the middle—plus a sunken ship that belonged to a king, so divers love it. Swimming is excellent year-round, especially in summer, when Hanalei Bay becomes a big, placid lake. The aquamarine water is also great for body boarding, surfing, fishing, windsurfing, canoe paddling, kayaking, and boating (there's a boat ramp on the west bank of the Hanalei River). The area known as **Black Pot,** near the pier, is particularly good for swimming, snorkeling, and surfing. Facilities include a pavilion, restrooms, picnic tables, and parking. This beach is always packed with both locals and visitors, but you can usually find your own place in the sun by strolling down the shore; the bay is big enough for everyone.

To get here, take Kuhio Highway (Hwy. 56), which becomes Highway 560 after Princeville. In Hanalei town, make a right on Aku Road just after Tahiti Nui, and then turn right again on Weke Road, which dead-ends at the parking lot for the Black Pot section of the beach; the easiest beach access is on your left.

KEE BEACH STATE PARK 👙👙

Where the road ends on the North Shore, you'll find a dandy little reddish-gold beach almost too beautiful to be real. Don't be surprised if it looks familiar—it was featured in *The Thornbirds*. Kee (*kay*-ay) is on a reef-protected cove at the foot of fluted volcanic cliffs. Swimming and snorkeling are safe inside the reef but dangerous outside; those North Shore waves and currents can be killers. This park has restrooms, showers, and parking—but no lifeguard. To get here, take Kuhio Highway (Hwy. 56), which becomes Highway 560 after Princeville; Kee is about 7½ miles past Hanalei.

TUNNELS BEACH & HAENA BEACH PARK 👙👙

Postcard-perfect gold-sand Tunnels Beach is one of Hawaii's most beautiful. When the sun sinks into the Pacific along the fabled peaks of Bali Hai, there's no better-looking beach in the islands: You're bathed in golden rays that butter up the blue sky, bounce off the steeped ridges, and tint the pale clouds hot pink. Catch the sunset from the pebbly sand beach or while swimming in the emerald-green waters, but do catch it. Tunnels is excellent for swimming nearly year-round and is safe for snorkeling because it's protected by a fringing coral reef (the waters can get rough in winter, though). The long, curvy beach is sheltered by a forest of ironwoods that provides welcome shade from the tropic heat.

Around the corner is grainy-gold-sand Haena Beach Park, which offers excellent swimming in summer and great snorkeling amid clouds of tropical fish. But stay out of the water in winter, when the big waves are dangerous. Haena also has a popular grassy park for camping. Noise-phobes will prefer Tunnels.

Take Kuhio Highway (Hwy. 56), which becomes Highway 560 after Princeville. Tunnels is about 6 miles past Hanalei town, after mile marker 8 on the highway (look for the alley with the big wood gate at the end), and Haena is just down the road. Tunnels has no facilities, but Haena has restrooms, outdoor showers, barbecue grills, picnic tables, and free parking (no lifeguard, though).

6 Watersports

Several outfitters on Kauai not only offer equipment rentals and tours, but also give out expert information on weather forecasts, sea and trail conditions, and other important matters for hikers, kayakers, sailors, and other backcountry adventurers. For watersports questions and equipment rental, contact **Kayak Kauai,** 1 mile past Hanalei Bridge on Highway 560, in Hanalei, and now in Kapa'a (© **800/437-3507** or 808/826-9844; www.kayakkauai.com), the outfitters' center in Hanalei. They also have their own private dock (the only one on Kauai) for launching kayaks and canoes. In Kapaa contact **Kauai Water Ski & Surf Co.,** Kinipopo Shopping Village, 4–356 Kuhio Hwy. (on the ocean side of the highway), Kapaa (© **808/822-3574;** www. waterskisurfandkayak.com). In the Lihue and Poipu areas, go with **Snorkel Bob's** at 4–734 Kuhio Hwy. (just north of Coconut Plantation Marketplace), Kapaa (© **800/ 262-7725** or 808/823-9433; www.snorkelbob.com), and in Koloa at 3236 Poipu Rd. (just south of Poipu Shopping Village), near Poipu Beach (© **808/742-2206**).

For general advice on the activities listed below, see "Special-Interest Trips," in chapter 2.

BOATING

One of Hawaii's most spectacular natural attractions is Kauai's **Na Pali Coast.** Unless you're willing to make an arduous 22-mile hike (p. 599), there are only two ways to see it: by helicopter (see "Helicopter Rides over Waimea Canyon & the Na Pali Coast" under "Seeing the Sights," later in this chapter) or by boat. Picture yourself cruising the rugged Na Pali coastline in a 42-foot ketch-rigged yacht under full sail, watching the sun set as you enjoy a tropical cocktail, or speeding through the aquamarine water in a 40-foot trimaran as porpoises play off the bow.

When the Pacific humpback whales make their annual visit to Hawaii from December to March, they swim right by Kauai. In season, most boats on Kauai—including sail- and powerboats—combine **whale-watching** with their regular adventures.

Kauai has many freshwater areas that are accessible only by boat, including the Fern Grotto, Wailua State Park, Huleia and Hanalei national wildlife refuges, Menehune Fish Pond, and numerous waterfalls. If you want to strike out on your own, **Paradise Outdoor Adventures,** 4–1596 Kuhio Hwy., Kapaa (© **808/822-1112** or 415-420-6353), has a Boston whaler (six-person capacity) for $295 for a half-day and $590 for a full day (book on the website for only $248 for a half-day, $348 for a full day). Included are all the amenities, such as safety equipment, coolers, dry bags (for cameras, wallets, towels), and a comprehensive orientation on where to go. The staff will even deliver the boat to the Wailua River at no extra charge. They specialize in Wailua River tours, ranging in price from $68 to $88 per person.

For sportfishing charters, see "Fishing," below. For tours of the Fern Grotto, see p. 609.

Captain Andy's Sailing Adventures ⋆

Captain Andy operates a 55-foot, 49-passenger catamaran out of two locations on the south shore. The **snorkel/picnic cruise,** a 5½-hour cruise to the **Na Pali Coast**, costs $139 for adults and $99 for children 2 to 12, and includes a continental breakfast, deli-style lunch, snorkeling, and drinks. There's also a 4-hour Na Pali Coast **dinner sunset cruise** that sets sail for $105 for adults and $80 for children, and a 2-hour Poipu cocktail sunset sail with drinks and pupu for $69 adults and $50 children. A 6-hour Na Pali Zodiac cruise on inflatable boats costs $139 to $159 adults and $99 to $109 children 5 to 12 years old. *Tip:* Book on the website for $10 off.

Kukuiula Small Boat Harbor, Poipu; and Port Allen, Eleele. © 800/535-0830 or 808/335-6833. www.napali.com. Prices vary depending on trip.

Holoholo Charters

This outfitter has taken over several boats and features both swimming/snorkeling sailing charters as well as powerboat charters to the Na Pali Coast. The 5-hour sailing trips take place on a 48-foot catamaran called *Leila* and are offered in the morning (with a continental breakfast and lunch) year-round, with an additional afternoon trip (with munchies and a light evening meal) in the summer for $135 adults and $95 children (5–12 years). A 2-hour dinner sunset cruise costs $75 (passengers must be at least 18 years old). On a 7-hour trip on the 61-foot powerboat *Holoholo,* you cruise along the Na Pali Coast and then cross the channel to the forbidden island of Niihau, where you stop for snorkeling. A continental breakfast, buffet lunch, and snorkel equipment are included in the price: $175 adults, $125 children. Or choose a 3½-hour sunset cruise of the Na Pali Coast on a power catamaran for $95 adults, $75 kids ages 5 to 12. Complimentary shuttle service is provided to and from your hotel. *Tip:* Book online for $15 off.

Port Allen, Eleele. (© **800/848-6130** or 808/335-0815. www.holoholocharters.com. Prices and departure points vary depending on trip.

Liko Kauai Cruises 🏝 🄺ids   Liko offers more than just a typical whale-watching cruise; this is a 4-hour combination Na Pali Coast tour/deep-sea fishing/historical lecture/whale-watching extravaganza with lunch. It all happens on a 49-foot power catamaran (with only 24 passengers). In addition to viewing the whales, you'll glimpse sea caves, waterfalls, lush valleys, and miles of white-sand beaches; you'll also make stops along the way for snorkeling.

Kekaha Small Boat Harbor, Waimea. (© **888/SEA-LIKO** or 808/338-0333. Fax 808/356-0521. www.liko-kauai.com. Na Pali Trips $120 adults, $80 children 4–12 (lunch included).

BODY BOARDING (BOOGIE BOARDING) & BODYSURFING

The best places for bodysurfing and boogie boarding are **Kalapaki Beach** (near Lihue) and **Poipu Beach.** In addition to the rental shops listed above, one of the most inexpensive places to rent boogie boards is **Snorkel Bob's** (see above), where boards rent for just $15 a week.

FISHING

DEEP-SEA FISHING   Kauai's fishing fleet is smaller and less well recognized than others in the islands, but the fish are still out there. All you need to bring is your lunch and your luck. The best way to book a sportfishing charter is through the experts; the best booking desk in the state is **Sportfish Hawaii** 🏝 (© **877/388-1376** or 808/ 396-2607; www.sportfishhawaii.com), which books boats not only on Kauai, but on all the islands. These fishing vessels have been inspected and must meet rigorous criteria to guarantee that you will have a great time. Prices range from $1,500 for a full-day exclusive charter (you and five of your closest friends get the entire boat to yourself) to $925 for a three-quarter day, to $625 for a half-day exclusive. Frankly, the fishing is better off the Kona coast, and the prices are more reasonable, too.

FRESHWATER FISHING   Freshwater fishing is big on Kauai, thanks to its dozens of man-made reservoirs. They're full of largemouth, smallmouth, and peacock bass (also known as *tucunare*). The **Puu Lua Reservoir,** in Kokee State Park, also has rainbow trout and is stocked by the state every year. Fishing for rainbow trout in the reservoir has a limited season: It begins on the first Saturday in August and lasts for 16 days, after which you can fish only on weekends and holidays through the last Sunday in September.

Before you rush out and get a fishing pole, you have to have a **Hawaii Freshwater Fishing License,** available through the **State Department of Land and Natural Resources,** Division of Aquatic Resources, 3060 Eiwa St., Room 306, Lihue, HI 96766 (© **808/274-3344;** www.hawaii.gov/dlnr/dar/licenses.htm). You can also get a license through any fishing-supply store; try **Lihue Fishing Supply,** 2985 Kalena St., Lihue (© **808/245-4930**); **Waipouli Variety,** 4-901 1-A Kuhio Hwy., Kapaa (© **808/ 822-1014**); or **Westside Sporting Goods,** 9681 Kaumualii Hwy., Waimea (© **808/ 338-1411**). A 7-day tourist license costs $10. When you get your license, pick up a copy of the booklet *State of Hawaii Freshwater Fishing Regulations.* Another great little book to get is *The Kauai Guide to Freshwater Sport Fishing,* by Glenn Ikemoto, available for $2.50 plus postage from **Magic Fishes Press,** P.O. Box 3243, Lihue, HI

96766. If you would like a guide, **Sportfish Hawaii** (© **877/388-1376** or 808/396-2607; www.sportfishhawaii.com) offers guided bass-fishing trips starting at $265 for two for a half-day and $450 for two for a full day.

KAYAKING

Kauai is made for kayaking. You can take the Huleia River into **Huleia National Wildlife Refuge** (located along the eastern portion of the Huleia Stream where it flows into Nawiliwili Bay). It's the last stand for Kauai's endangered birds, and the only way to see it is by kayak. The adventurous can head to the Na Pali Coast, featuring majestic cliffs, empty beaches, open-ocean conditions, and monster waves. Or you can just go out and paddle around Hanalei Bay.

Kayak Kauai (★), a mile past Hanalei Bridge on Highway 560, in Hanalei (© **800/437-3507** or 808/826-9844; www.kayakkauai.com), has a range of tours for independent souls. The shop's experts will be happy to take you on a guided kayaking trip or to tell you where to go on your own. Equipment rental starts at $28 for a one-person kayak and $52 for a two-person ocean kayak per day. Kayak lessons are $50 per person per hour. Tours (some including snacks) start at $60 per person and include transportation up to the all-day excursion with lunch for $185 per person. Kayak Kauai also has its own private dock (the only one on Kauai) for launching kayaks and canoes.

Rick Haviland, who gained fame after he was mentioned in Paul Theroux's book *The Happy Isles of Oceania,* is the owner of **Outfitters Kauai** (★), 2827A Poipu Rd. (Poipu Plaza, a small five-shop mall before the road forks to Poipu/Spouting Horn), Poipu (© **888/742-9887** or 808/742-9667; www.outfitterskauai.com), which has a bunch of different kayaking tours. A full-day trip along the entire Na Pali Coast (summer only) costs $185 per person and includes a guide, lunch, drinks, and equipment. Another kayak tour takes you up a jungle stream and involves a short hike to waterfalls and a swimming hole; it's $94 for adults, $75 for children ages 5 to 14, including lunch, snacks, and drinks. Outfitters Kauai also rents river kayaks by the day ($40).

Other options to rent kayaks include **Kauai Water Ski & Surf Co.,** Kinipopo Shopping Village, 4–356 Kuhio Hwy. (on the ocean side), Kapaa (© **808/822-3574;** www.waterskisurfandkayak.com); and **Pedal 'n Paddle,** Ching Young Village Shopping Center, Hanalei (© **808/826-9069;** www.pedalnpaddle.com).

PADDLING INTO HULEIA NATIONAL WILDLIFE REFUGE   Ride the Huleia River through Kauai's 240-acre Huleia National Wildlife Refuge, the last stand of Kauai's endangered birds, with **True Blue,** Nawiliwili Harbor (© **888/245-1707** or 808/246-6333; www.kauaifun.com). You paddle up the picturesque Huleia (which appeared in *Raiders of the Lost Ark* and the remake of *King Kong*) under sheer pinnacles that open into valleys full of lush tropical plants, bright flowers, and hanging vines. Look for great blue herons and Hawaiian gallinules taking wing. The 4½-hour voyage, which starts at Nawiliwili Harbor, is a great trip for all—but especially for movie buffs, birders, and great adventurers under 12. It's even safe for nonswimmers. Wear a swimsuit, T-shirt, and boat shoes. The cost is $89 for adults, $69 for children 6 to 12. The prices include a picnic snack, juice, kayak, life vest, and guide services.

SCUBA DIVING

Diving on Kauai is dictated by the weather. In winter, when heavy swells and high winds hit the island, it's generally limited to the more protected south shore. Probably the best-known site along the south shore is **Caverns,** located off the Poipu Beach resort area. This site consists of a series of lava tubes interconnected by a chain of archways. A constant parade of fish streams by (even shy lionfish are spotted lurking in crevices), brightly hued Hawaiian lobsters hide in the lava's tiny holes, and turtles sometimes swim past.

In summer, when the north Pacific storms subside, the magnificent North Shore opens up, and you can take a boat dive locally known as the **Oceanarium,** northwest of Hanalei Bay, where you'll find a kaleidoscopic marine world in a horseshoe-shaped cove. From the rare (long-handed spiny lobsters) to the more common (taape, conger eels, and nudibranchs), the resident population is one of the more diverse on the island. The topography, which features pinnacles, ridges, and archways, is covered with cup corals, black-coral trees, and nooks and crannies enough for a dozen dives.

Because the best dives on Kauai are offshore, we recommend booking a two-tank dive off a dive boat. **Bubbles Below Scuba Charters,** 6251 Hauaala Rd., Kapaa (✆ **866-524-6268** or 808-332-7333; www.bubblesbelowkauai.com), specializes in highly personalized, small-group dives, with an emphasis on marine biology. The 35-foot boat *Kaimanu* is a custom-built Radon dive boat that comes complete with a hot shower. Two-tank boat dives cost $120 ($25 more if you need gear); nondivers can come along for the ride for $80. In summer (May–Sept) Bubbles Below offers a three-tank trip for experienced divers only to the "forbidden" island of Niihau, 90 minutes by boat from Kauai. You should be comfortable with vertical drop-offs, huge underwater caverns, possibly choppy surface conditions, and significant currents. You should also be willing to share water space with the resident sharks. The all-day, three-tank trip costs $275, including tanks, weights, dive computer, lunch, drinks, and marine guide (if you need gear, it's $25 more). On the south side, call **Fathom Five Adventures,** 3450 Poipu Rd. (next to the Chevron), Koloa (✆ **808/742-6991;** www. fathomfive.com).

GREAT SHORE DIVES FROM KAUAI   If you want a guided shore dive, **Fathom Five Adventures** (see above) will take you out for $70 for one tank and $85 for two tanks.

Spectacular shoreline dive sites on the North Shore include **Kee Beach/Haena Beach Park** (where the road ends), one of the most picturesque beaches on the island. On a calm summer day, the drop-off near the reef begs for underwater exploration. Another good bet is **Tunnels Beach,** also known as Makua Beach. It's off Highway 560, just past mile marker 8; look for the short dirt road (less than ½ mile) to the beach. The wide reef here makes for some fabulous snorkeling and diving, but again, only during the calm summer months. **Cannons Beach,** east of Haena Beach Park (use the parking for Haena, located across the street from the Dry Cave near mile marker 9 on Hwy. 560), has lots of vibrant marine life in its sloping offshore reef.

On the south shore, head to **Tortugas** (located directly in front of Poipu Beach Park) if you want to catch a glimpse of sea turtles. **Koloa Landing** has a horseshoe-shaped reef that's teeming with tropical fish. **Sheraton Caverns** (located off the Sheraton Kauai) is also popular, due to its three large underwater lava tubes, which are usually filled with marine life.

SNORKELING

See the introduction to this section for locations of **Snorkel Bob's.**

For great shoreline snorkeling, try the reef off **Kee Beach/Haena Beach Park,** located at the end of Highway 560. **Tunnels Beach,** about a mile before the end of

Highway 560 in Haena, has a wide reef that's great for poking around in search of tropical fish. Be sure to check ocean conditions—don't go if the surf is up or if there's a strong current. **Anini Beach,** located off the northern Kalihiwai Road (between mile markers 25 and 26 on Kuhio Hwy., or Hwy. 56), just before the Princeville Airport, has a safe, shallow area with excellent snorkeling. **Poipu Beach Park** has some good snorkeling to the right side of Nukumoi Point—the tombolo area, where the narrow strip of sand divides the ocean, is best. If this spot is too crowded, wander down the beach in front of the old Waiohai resort; if there are no waves, this place is also hopping with marine life. **Salt Pond Beach Park,** off Highway 50 near Hanapepe, has good snorkeling around the two rocky points, home to hundreds of tropical fish.

SURFING

Hanalei Bay's winter surf is the most popular on the island, but it's for experts only. **Poipu Beach** is an excellent spot to learn to surf; the waves are small and—best of all—nobody laughs when you wipe out. Check with the local surf shops or call the **Weather Service** (© 808/245-3564) to find out where surf's up.

Surf lessons are available for $60 for a 1½-hour session, including all-day use of equipment (board, wet-suit top, and carrying rack for your car), from **Windsurf Kauai,** in Hanalei (© 808/828-6838). Poipu is also the site of numerous surfing schools; the oldest and best is **Margo Oberg's School of Surfing,** at the Nukumoi Surf Shop, across from Brennecke's Beach (© 808/332-6100; www.surfonkauai.com). Margo charges $60 for 1½ hours of group instruction, including surfboard and leash; she guarantees that by the end of the lesson, you'll be standing and catching a wave.

Equipment is available for rent (ranging from $5 an hour or $20 a day for "soft" beginner boards to $7.50 an hour or $30 a day for hard boards for experienced surfers) from **Nukumoi Surf Shop,** across from Brennecke's Beach, Poipu Beach Park (© 888/384-8810 or 808/742-8019; www.brenneckes.com/nukumoi.html); **Hanalei Surf Co.,** 5–5161 Kuhio Hwy. (across from Zelo's Beach House Restaurant in Hanalei Center), Hanalei (© 808/826-9000); and **Pedal 'n Paddle,** Ching Young Village Shopping Center, Hanalei (© 808/826-9069).

TUBING

Back in the days of the sugar plantations, local kids would grab inner tubes and jump in the irrigation ditches crisscrossing the cane fields to get an exciting ride. Today you can enjoy this (formerly illegal) activity by "tubing" the flumes and ditches of the old Lihue Plantation through **Kauai Backcountry Adventures** (© 888/270-0555 or 808/245-2506; www.kauaibackcountry.com). Passengers are taken in four-wheel-drive vehicles high into the mountains above Lihue to look at vistas generally off-limits to the public. At the flumes, you will be outfitted with a giant tube, gloves, and headlamp (for the long passageways through the tunnels). All you do is jump in the water, and the gentle gravity-feed flow will carry you through forests, into tunnels, and finally to a mountain swimming hole, where a picnic lunch is served. The 3-hour tours are $92 and appropriate for anyone ages 5 to 95. Swimming is not necessary, as all you do is relax and drift downstream.

WATER-SKIING

Hawaii's only freshwater water-skiing is on the Wailua River. Ski boats launch from the boat ramp in Wailua River State Park, directly across from the marina. **Kauai Water Ski & Surf Co.,** Kinipopo Shopping Village, 4–356 Kuhio Hwy., Kapaa

Kids Especially for Kids

Surfing with an Expert (p. 592)   If seven-time world champ Margo Oberg, a member of the Surfing Hall of Fame, can't get your kid—or you—up on a board riding a wave, nobody can. She promises same-day results even for klutzes.

Paddling up the Huleia River (p. 590)   Indiana Jones ran for his life up this river to his seaplane in *Raiders of the Lost Ark.* You and the kids can venture down it yourself in a kayak. The picturesque Huleia winds through tropically lush Huleia National Wildlife Refuge, where endangered species like great blue herons and Hawaiian gallinules take wing. It's ideal for everyone.

Climbing the Wooden Jungle Gyms at Kamalani Playground (p. 585) Located in Lydgate State Park, Wailua, this unique playground has a maze of jungle gyms for children of all ages. You can whip down slides, explore caves, hang from bars, and climb all over. It's a great place to spend the afternoon.

Cooling Off with a Shave Ice (p. 571)   On a hot, hot day, stop by **Brennecke's Beach Broiler,** across from Poipu Beach Park (*(C)* **808/742-7588**), and order a traditional Hawaiian shave ice. This local treat consists of ice shavings stuffed into a paper cone and topped with a tropical-flavored syrup. If you can't decide on a flavor, go for the "rainbow"—three different flavors in one cone.

Exploring a Magical World (p. 614)   **Na Aina Kai Botanical Gardens** sits on some 240 acres, sprinkled with some 70 life-size (or larger-than-life-size) whimsical bronze statues, hidden off the beaten path of the North Shore. The tropical children's garden features a gecko hedge maze, a tropical jungle gym, a tree house in a rubber tree, and a 16-foot-tall Jack-in-the-Beanstalk giant with a 33-foot wading pool below. It's open only 3 days a week, so book before you leave for Hawaii, to avoid disappointment.

Experiencing a Hands-on Learning Adventure (p. 611)   The **Kauai Children's Discovery Museum,** located in Kapaa (*(C)* **808/823-8222;** www.kcdm. org), arose out of a grass-roots community effort. In addition to the exhibits, which range from playing with Hawaiian musical instruments to participating in virtual-reality television, to hiding out in a "magic treehouse" and reading a book (there's even a baby area for kids 4 and under), there are Keiki Camps (Children's Camps), where you can leave the kids all day; they'll participate in various outings to the beach and to points of interest.

(*(C)* **808/822-3574;** www.waterskisurfandkayak.com), rents equipment and offers lessons and guided tours; it's $70 for a half-hour trip and $140 for an hour.

WINDSURFING & KITESURFING

Anini Beach is one of the safest beaches for beginners to learn windsurfing. Lessons and equipment rental are available at **Anini Beach Windsurfing and Kitesurfing**

(© **808/826-WIND** or 808/826-9463). Owner Foster Ducker has been teaching windsurfing for nearly a decade; he has special equipment to help beginners learn the sport. A 2-hour lesson is $75 and includes equipment and instruction. If you fall in love with the sport and want to keep going, he'll rent the equipment for $25 an hour or $75 for the rest of the day. Serious windsurfers should head to **Hanalei Bay** or **Tunnels Beach** on the North Shore.

For the real adventurous, Ducker also is a certified instructor in kitesurfing; he claims he can get people up and on the water in just one lesson. His introduction to kitesurfing is 2 hours long and costs $200 for one person, and 3 hours at $400 for two.

7 Hiking & Camping

Kauai is an adventurer's delight. The island's greatest tropical beauty isn't easily reachable; you've got to head out on foot and find it. For more information on Kauai's hiking trails, contact the **State Division of Parks,** P.O. Box 1671, Lihue, HI 96766 (© **808/274-3446;** www.hawaii.gov/dlnr/dsp/kauai.html); the **State Division of Forestry and Wildlife,** 1151 Punchbowl St., Room 325, Honolulu, HI 96813 (© **808/587-0166;** www.dofaw.net); **Kauai County Parks and Recreation,** 4444 Rice St., Suite150, Lihui, HI 96766 (© **808/241-4463;** www.kauai.gov); or the **Kokee Lodge Manager,** P.O. Box 819, Waimea, HI 96796 (© **808/335-6061**).

Kayak Kauai ⟨⁂, a mile past Hanalei Bridge on Highway 560 in Hanalei (© **800/437-3507** or 808/826-9844; fax 808/822-0577; www.kayakkauai.com), is the premier all-around outfitter on the island. It's staffed by local experts who keep track of weather forecasts and sea and trail conditions; they have a lot more pertinent information that hikers, campers, and other backcountry adventurers need to know. Plus, they have guided hiking tours starting at $81 per person. If you don't plan to bring your own gear, you can rent it here or at **Pedal 'n Paddle,** in Hanalei (© **808/826-9069;** www.pedalnpaddle.com). If you want to buy camping equipment, head for **Ace Island Hardware,** at Princeville Shopping Center (© **808/826-6980**).

GUIDED HIKES You can join a guided hike with the Kauai chapter of the **Sierra Club,** P.O. Box 3412, Lihue, HI 96766 (© **808/246-9067;** www.hi.sierraclub.org), which offers four to seven different hikes every month, varying from an easy family moonlit beach hike to a moderate 4-mile trip up some 1,100 feet, to 8-mile-plus treks for serious hikers only. The club also does guided hikes of Kokee State Park (see below), usually on weekends. Because there's no staffed office, the best way to contact the chapter is to check the website; outings are usually listed 3 to 6 months in advance, with complete descriptions of the hike, the hike leader's phone number, and what to wear and bring. You can also check the daily newspaper, the *Garden Island,* for a list of hikes in the "Community Calendar" section. Generally, the club asks for a donation of $5 per person per hike for nonmembers, $1 for children under 18 and Sierra Club members. It also does service work (clearing trails, picking up trash) on the hikes, so you may spend an hour doing service work, and then 2 to 3 hours hiking. Last year, the club took three service-work trips along the Na Pali Coast trail to help maintain it.

Hawaiian Wildlife Tours ⟨⁂ (© **808/639-2968;** www.hawaiianwildlifetours.com) is environmental education in action. Biologist Dr. Carl Berg will take you out into the woods and down to the shoreline to see Kauai's native and vanishing species, from forest birds and flora to hoary bats, monk seals, and green sea turtles. His personalized tours last from 1 hour to a week and are tailored around the season and weather, your

> **Tips A Warning about Flash Floods**
>
> When it rains on Kauai, the waterfalls rage and rivers and streams overflow, causing flash floods on roads and trails. If you're hiking, avoid dry streambeds, which flood quickly and wash out to sea. Before going hiking, camping, or sailing, especially in the rainy season (Nov–Mar), check the weather forecast by calling © **808/245-6001.**

physical abilities, and what you want to see. He leads tours to Hanalei taro fields to see wetland birds, to Crater Hill to see nene geese, to Mahaulepu to see wildflowers in the sand dunes, to Kilauea Lighthouse to see oceanic birds, and much more. Rates are $45 per couple per hour.

Other options for guided hikes include **Princeville Ranch Hiking Adventures** (© **808/826-7669;** www.kauai-hiking.com), which offers various hikes on 2,000 acres of private property, such as a 4-hour hike to a waterfall (plus another hour swimming) for $129; and **Kauai Nature Adventures** (© **888/233-8365** or 808/742-8305; www.kauainaturetours.com), which leads a geological-history excursion, a tour of Kauai's environments from the mountain to the ocean, and a Mahaulepu coast hike, all led by scientists and costing $87 to $97 for adults and $54 to $64 for children ages 7 to 12, including lunch.

THE POIPU RESORT AREA
MAKAWEHI POINT ⚔

Like a ship's prow, Makawehi Point juts out to sea on the east side of Keoneloa Beach (known locally as Shipwreck Beach), which lies in front of the Grand Hyatt Kauai. This 50-foot-high sand-dune bluff attracts a variety of people: pole fishers, whale-watchers, those who just like the panoramic views of the Pacific, and daredevils who test their courage by leaping off the cliff into the waves (don't try it).

The trail head begins on the east end of Shipwreck Beach, past the Hyatt. It's an easy 10-minute walk up to Makawehi Point; after you take in the big picture, keep going uphill along the ridge of the sand dunes (said to contain ancient Hawaiian burial sites), past the coves frequented by green sea turtles and endangered Hawaiian monk seals, through the coastal pine forest, and past World War II bunkers to the very top. Now you can see Haupu Ridge and its 2,297-foot peak, the famously craggy ridgeline that eerily resembles Queen Victoria's profile, and, in the distance, Mahaulepu Beach, one of the best-looking in Hawaii. Inland, three red craters dimple the green fields; the one in the middle, the biggest, Pu'u Huni Huni, is said to have been the last volcano to erupt on Kauai—but it was so long ago that nobody here can remember when.

WESTERN KAUAI
WAIMEA CANYON TRAILS

On a wet island like Kauai, a dry hike is hard to find. But in the desert-dry gulch of Waimea Canyon, known as the Grand Canyon of the Pacific (once you get here, you'll see why—it's pretty spectacular), you're not likely to slip and slide in the muck as you go.

CANYON TRAIL   You want to hike Hawaii's Grand Canyon, but you don't think you have time? Take the Canyon Trail to the east rim for a breathtaking view into the

3,000-foot-deep canyon. Park your car at the top of Halemanu Valley Road (located between mile markers 14 and 15 on Waimea Canyon Rd., about a mile down from the museum). The 3.5-mile round-trip takes 2 to 3 hours and leads to Waipoo Falls (as does the hike described below) and back. I suggest going in the afternoon, when the light is best.

HIKE TO WAIPOO FALLS 𝒢   The 3-hour round-trip hike to Waipoo Falls is one of Kauai's best hikes. The two-tiered, 800-foot waterfall that splashes into a natural pool is worth every step it takes to get here. To find the trail, drive up Kokee Road (Hwy. 550) to the Puu Hina Hina Outlook; a quarter mile past the lookout, near a NASA satellite tracking station on the right, a two-lane dirt road leads to the Waipoo Falls trail head. From here, the trail winds through a jungle dotted with wild yellow orchids and flame-red torch ginger before it leads you out on a descending ridgeback that juts deep into the canyon. At the end of the promontory, take a left and push on through the jungle to the falls; at the end, reward yourself with a refreshing splash in the pool.

KOKEE STATE PARK 𝒢𝒢

At the end of Highway 550, which leads through Waimea Canyon to its summit, lies a 4,640-acre state park of high-mountain forest wilderness (3,600–4,000 ft. above sea level). The rainforest, bogs, and breathtaking views of the Na Pali coastline and Waimea Canyon are the draw at Kokee. This is the place for hiking—among the 45 miles of maintained trails are some of the best hikes in Hawaii. You can download a brochure of all the trails in Kokee from www.hawaii.gov/dlnr/dsp/brochures/Trails OfKokee.pdf. Official trail maps of all the park's trails are for sale for 50¢ at the **Kokee Natural History Museum** (© 808/335-9975).

A few words of advice: Always check current trail conditions; up-to-date trail information is available on a bulletin board at the Kokee Natural History Museum. Stay on established trails; it's easy to get lost here. Get off the trail well before dark. Carry water and rain gear—even if it's perfectly sunny when you set out—and wear sunscreen.

For complete coverage of the state park, see p. 607.

AWAAWAPUHI TRAIL   This 3.25-mile hike (6.5 miles round-trip) takes about 3 hours each way and is considered strenuous by most, but it offers a million-dollar view. Look for the trail head at the left of the parking lot, at mile marker 17 between the museum and Kalalau Lookout. The well-marked and well-maintained trail now sports .25-mile markers, and you can pick up a free plant guide for the trail at the museum. The trail drops about 1,600 feet through native forests to a thin precipice right at the very edge of the Na Pali cliffs for a dramatic and dizzying view of the tropical valleys and blue Pacific 2,500 feet below. It's not recommended for anyone with vertigo (although a railing will keep you from a major slip and fall). Go early, before clouds obscure the view, or late in the day—the sunsets are something to behold.

The Awaawapuhi can be a straight-out-and-back trail or a loop that connects with the **Nualolo Trail** (3.75 miles), which provides awesome views and leads back to the main road between the ranger's house and the Kokee cabins, which is about a mile and a half from where you started. So you can hike the remaining 1.5 miles along the road or hitch a ride if you decide to do the entire loop but can't make it all the way.

HALEMANU-KOKEE TRAIL   This trail takes you on a pleasant, easy-to-moderate 2.5-mile round-trip walk through a native koa-and-ohia forest inhabited by native

birds. The trail head is near mile marker 15; pick up the Faye Trail, which leads to this one. The Halemanu-Kokee links Kokee Valley to Halemanu Valley (hence the name); along the way, you'll see a plum orchard, valleys, and ridges.

PIHEA TRAIL   This is the park's flattest trail, but it's still a pretty strenuous 7.5-mile round-trip. A boardwalk that runs along about a third of the trail makes it easier, especially when it's wet. The trail begins at the end of Highway 550 at Puu o Kila Lookout, which overlooks Kalalau Valley; it goes down at first and then flattens out as it traces the back ridge of the valley. Once it enters the rainforest, you'll see native plants and trees. It intersects with the Alakai Swamp Trail (see below). If you combine both trails, figure on about 4 hours in and out.

ALAKAI SWAMP TRAIL ✦   If you want to see the "real" Hawaii, this is it—a big swamp that's home to rare birds and plants. The trail allows a rare glimpse into a wet, cloud-covered wilderness preserve where 460 inches of rainfall a year is common. This 7-mile hike used to take 5 hours of sloshing through the bog, with mud up to your knees. Now a boardwalk protects you from the shoe-grabbing mud. Come prepared for rain. (The only silver lining is that there are no mosquitoes above 3,000 ft.)

The trail head is off Mohihi (Camp 10) Road, just beyond the Forest Reserve entrance sign and the Alakai Shelter picnic area. From the parking lot, the trail follows an old World War II four-wheel-drive road. Stick to the boardwalk; this is a fragile eco-area. At the end of the 3.5-mile slog, if you're lucky and the clouds part, you'll have a lovely view of Wainiha Valley and Hanalei from Kilohana Lookout.

CAMPGROUNDS & WILDERNESS CABINS IN KOKEE

CABINS & TENT CAMPGROUNDS   Camping facilities include state campgrounds (one next to Kokee Lodge, and four more primitive backcountry sites), one private tent area, and the **Kokee Lodge,** which has 12 cabins for rent at very reasonable rates. At 4,000 feet, the nights are cold, particularly in winter, and no open fires are permitted at Kokee. The best deal is the cabins (see "Where to Stay," earlier in this chapter, for details). The **Kokee Lodge Restaurant** is open daily from 9am to 3:30pm for continental breakfast and lunch. Groceries and gas aren't available in Kokee, so stock up in advance; it's a long trip back down the mountain.

The **state campground** at Kokee allows tent camping only. Permits can be obtained from a state parks office on any island; on Kauai, it's at 3060 Eiwa St., Room 306, Lihue, HI 96766 (© **808/274-3444;** www.hawaii.gov/dlnr/dsp/fees.html). The permits are $5 per night; the time limit is 5 nights in a single 30-day period. Facilities include showers, drinking water, picnic tables, a pavilion with tables, restrooms, barbecues, sinks for dishwashing, and electric lights.

Tent camping at **Camp Sloggett,** owned by the Kauai YWCA, 3094 Elua St., Lihue, HI 96766 (© **808/245-5959;** fax 808/245-5961; http://campingkauai.com), is available for $10 per person per night (children under 5 stay free). The sites are on 1½ acres of open field, with a covered pit for fires and a barbecue area, plus volleyball and badminton nets. There's also hostel-style accommodations at the **Weinburg Bunkhouse,** with bunk beds, separate toilets, showers, and kitchenettes ($20 per person). To get here, continue on the highway past park headquarters and take the first right after the Kokee Lodge. Follow the dirt road and look for the wooden CAMP SLOGGETT sign; turn right and follow the bumpy road past the state cabins into a large clearing.

BACKCOUNTRY CAMPING   The more primitive backcountry campgrounds include **Sugi Grove** and **Kawaikoi,** located about 4 miles from park headquarters on the Camp 10 Road, an often-muddy and steep four-wheel-drive road. Sugi Grove is located across the Kawaikoi Stream from the Kawaikoi campsite. The area is named for the sugi pines, which were planted in 1937 by the Civilian Conservation Corps. This is a shady campsite with a single picnic shelter, a pit toilet, a stream, and space for several tents. The Kawaikoi site is a 3-acre open grass field, surrounded by Kokee plum trees and forests of koa and ohia. Facilities include two picnic shelters, a composting toilet, and a stream that flows next to the camping area. There is no potable water—bring in your own or treat the stream water.

Permits, which are $5 per night, are available through the **State Parks Office,** 3060 Eiwa St., Room 306 Lihue, HI 96766 (© **808/274-3444;** www.hawaii.gov/dlnr/dsp/ fees.html). You're limited to 5 nights in any 30-day period.

BEACH CAMPING AT POLIHALE STATE PARK

Polihale holds the distinction of being the westernmost beach in the United States. The beach is spectacular—some 300 feet wide in summer, with rolling sand dunes (some as high as 100 ft.) and the islands of Niihau and Lehua just offshore. Bordered by a curtain of Na Pali Coast cliffs on the north, razor-sharp ridges and steep valleys to the east, and the blue Pacific on the south and west, this is one of the most dramatic camping areas in the state.

The campgrounds for tent camping are located at the south end of the beach, affording privacy from the daytime beach activities. There's great swimming in summer (even then, be on the lookout for waves and rip currents—there are no lifeguards), some surfing (the rides are usually short), and fishing. The camping is on sand, although there are some kiawe trees for shade. (*Warning:* Kiawe trees drop long thorns, so make sure you have protective footwear.) Facilities include restrooms, showers, picnic tables, barbecues, and a spigot for drinking water. You can purchase supplies about 15 miles away in Waimea.

Permits, which are $5 per night, are available through the **State Parks Office,** 3060 Eiwa St., Lihue, HI 96766 (© **808/274-3444;** www.hawaii.gov/dlnr/dsp/fees.html). You're limited to 5 nights in any 30-day period. To reach the park from Lihue, take Highway 50 west to Barking Sands Pacific Missile Range. Bear right onto the paved road, which heads toward the mountains. There will be small signs directing you to Polihale; the second sign will point to a left turn onto a dirt road. Follow this for about 5 miles; at the fork in the road, the campgrounds are to the left and the beach park is to the right.

THE COCONUT COAST
THE SLEEPING GIANT TRAIL

This hardy hike takes you up the fabled mountain known as Sleeping Giant (which really does look like a giant resting on his back) to a fabulous view. The trail will gain 1,000 feet in altitude on a clearly marked trail (be sure to stay on the trail). The climb is steep and steadily uphill (remember, you are climbing up a mountain), but the view at the top is well worth the constant incline. To get to the trail head, turn mauka (toward the mountain) off Kuhio Highway (Hwy. 56) onto Haleilio Road (between Wailua and Kapaa, just past mile marker 6); follow Haleilio Road for 1.25 miles to the parking area, at telephone pole number 38. From here, signs posted by the State of Hawaii Division of Forestry and Wildlife lead you over the 1.75-mile trail, which ends at a picnic table and shelter. The panoramic view is breathtaking. Be sure to bring water—and a picnic, if you like.

THE NORTH SHORE
NA PALI COAST STATE PARK

Simply put, the Na Pali Coast is the most beautiful part of the Hawaiian Islands. Hanging valleys open like green-velvet accordions, and waterfalls tumble to the sea from the 4,120-foot-high cliffs; the experience is both exhilarating and humbling. Whether you hike in, fly over, or take a boat cruise past, be sure to see this park.

Established in 1984, Na Pali Coast State Park takes in a 22-mile stretch of fluted cliffs that wrap around the northwest shore of Kauai between Kee Beach and Polihale State Park. Volcanic in origin, carved by wind and sea, "the cliffs" (*na pali* in Hawaiian), which heaved out of the ocean floor 200 million years ago, stand as constant reminders of majesty and endurance. Four major valleys—Kalalau, Honopu, Awaawapuhi, and Nualolo—crease the cliffs.

Unless you boat or fly in (see "Boating" on p. 588 or "Helicopter Rides over Waimea Canyon & the Na Pali Coast" on p. 608), the park is accessible only on foot—and it's not easy. An ancient footpath, the **Kalalau Trail,** winds through this remote, spectacular 6,500-acre park, ultimately leading to Kalalau Valley. Of all the green valleys in Hawaii, and there are many, only Kalalau is a true wilderness—probably the last wild valley in the islands. No road goes here, and none ever will. The remote valley is home to long-plumed tropical birds, golden monarch butterflies, and many of Kauai's 120 rare and endangered species of plants. The hike into the Kalalau Valley is grueling and takes most people 6 to 8 hours one-way.

Despite its inaccessibility, this journey into Hawaii's wilderness has become increasingly popular since the 1970s. Overrun with hikers, helicopters, and boaters, the Kalalau Valley was in grave danger of being loved to death. Strict rules about access have been adopted. The park is open to hikers and campers on only a limited basis, and you must have a permit (though you can hike the first 2 miles, to Hanakapiai Beach, without a permit). Permits are $10 per night and are issued in person at the **Kauai State Parks Office,** 3060 Eiwa St., Room 306, Lihue, HI 96766 (© **808/274-3444;** www.hawaii.gov/dlnr/dsp/fees.html). You can also request one by writing **Kauai Division of State Parks** at the address listed above. For more information, contact **Hawaii State Department of Land and Natural Resources,** 1151 Punchbowl St., Room 130, Honolulu, HI 96813 (© **808/587-0320**).

HIKING THE KALALAU TRAIL 🛪🛪

The trail head is at Kee Beach, at the end of Highway 560. Even if you go only as far as Hanakapiai, bring water.

THE FIRST 2 MILES: TO HANAKAPIAI BEACH Do not attempt this hike unless you have adequate footwear (closed-toe shoes at least; hiking shoes are best), water, a sun visor, insect repellent, and adequate hiking clothes (shorts and a T-shirt are fine; your bikini is not). It's only 2 miles to Hanakapiai Beach, but the first mile is all uphill. This tough trail takes about 2 hours one-way and dissuades many, but everyone should attempt at least the first .5 mile, which gives a good hint of the startling beauty that lies ahead. Day hikers love this initial stretch, so it's usually crowded. The island of Niihau and Lehua Rock are often visible on the horizon. At mile marker 1, you'll have climbed from sea level to 400 feet; now it's all downhill to Hanakapiai Beach. Sandy in summer, the beach becomes rocky when winter waves scour the coast. There are strong currents and no lifeguards, so swim at your own risk. You can also hike another 2 miles inland from the beach to **Hanakapiai Falls,** a 120-foot cascade. Allow 3 hours for that stretch.

THE REST OF THE WAY Hiking the Kalalau is the most difficult and challenging hike in Hawaii, and one you'll never forget. Even the Sierra Club rates the 22-mile round-trip into Kalalau Valley and back as "strenuous"—this is serious backpacking. Follow the footsteps of ancient Hawaiians along a cliff-side path that's a mere 10 inches wide in some places, with sheer 1,000-foot drops to the sea. One misstep, and it's *limu* (seaweed) time. Even the hardy and fit should allow at least 2 days to hike in and out (see below for camping information). Although the trail is usually in good shape, go in summer when it's dry; parts of it vanish in winter. When it rains, the trail becomes very slippery, and flash floods can sweep you away.

A park ranger is now on-site full time at Kalalau Beach to greet visitors, provide information, and oversee campsites.

CAMPING IN KALALAU VALLEY & ALONG THE NA PALI COAST

You must obtain a camping permit; see above for details. The camping season runs roughly from May or June to September (depending on the site). All campsites are booked almost a year in advance, so call or write well ahead of time. Stays are limited to 5 nights. Camping areas along the Kalalau Trail include **Hanakapiai Beach** (facilities are pit toilets, and water is from the stream), **Hanakoa Valley** (no facilities, water from the stream), **Milolii** (no facilities, water from the stream), and **Kalalau Valley** (composting toilets, several pit toilets, and water is from the stream). Keep your camping permit with you at all times.

8 Golf & Other Outdoor Activities

GOLF

For last-minute and discount tee times, call **Stand-by Golf** (© **888/645-BOOK;** www.stand-bygolf.com) between 7am and 9pm. Stand-by offers discounted (up to 50% off greens fees), guaranteed tee times for same-day or next-day golfing.

In the listings below, the cart fee is included in the greens fee unless otherwise noted.

LIHUE & ENVIRONS

Kauai Lagoons Golf Courses Choose between two excellent Jack Nicklaus–designed courses: the **Mokihana Course** (formerly known as the Lagoons Course), for the recreational golfer, or the **Kauai Kiele Championship Course** ✮, for the low handicapper. The 6,942-yard, par-72 Mokihana is a links-style course with a bunker that's a little less severe than Kiele; emphasis is on the short game. The Kiele is a mixture of tournament-quality challenge and high-traffic playability; it winds up with one of Hawaii's most difficult holes, a 431-yard par-4 played straightaway to an island green.

Facilities include a driving range, lockers, showers, a restaurant, a snack bar, a pro shop, practice greens, a clubhouse, and club and shoe rental.

Kalapaki Beach, Lihue (less than a mile from Lihue Airport). © 800/634-6400 or 808/241-6000. www.kauailagoons golf.com. Greens fees at Mokihana Course: $120 ($80 for guests of the Kauai Marriott; $90 for guests of other hotels and condos on Kauai). For the Kiele Course: $195 ($140 for Marriott guests; $155 for guests of other hotels and condos on Kauai). From the airport, make a left on Kapule Hwy. (Hwy. 51) and look for the sign on your left.

THE POIPU RESORT AREA

Kiahuna Golf Club   In 2004 the front 9 holes of this par-70, 6,353-yard Robert Trent Jones, Jr.–designed course underwent complete renovation. The course plays around four large archaeological sites, ranging from an ancient Hawaiian temple to the remains of a Portuguese home and crypt built in the early 1800s. This Scottish-style course has rolling terrain, undulating greens, 70 sand bunkers, and near-constant winds. The 3rd hole, a par-3 185-yarder, goes over Waikomo Stream. At any given time, about half the players on the course are Kauai residents, the other half visitors. Facilities include a driving range, practice greens, and a snack bar.

2545 Kiahuna Plantation Dr. (adjacent to Poipu Resort area), Koloa. © 808/742-9595. www.kiahunagolf.com. Greens fees: $110; twilight rates $75. Take Hwy. 50 to Hwy. 520, bear left into Poipu at the fork in the road, and turn left onto Kiahuna Plantation Dr.

Kukuiolono Golf Course *Finds*   This is a fun 9-hole course in a spectacular location with scenic views of the entire south coast. You can't beat the price—$8 for the day, whether you play 9 holes or 90. The course is in Kukuiolono Park, a beautiful wooded area donated by the family of Walter McBryde. In fact, you'll see McBryde's grave on the course, along with some other oddities, like wild chickens, ancient Hawaiian rock structures, and Japanese gardens. Of course, there are plenty of trees to keep you on your game. When you get to the second tee box, check out the coconut tree dotted with yellow, pink, orange, and white golf balls that have been driven into the bark. Don't laugh—your next shot might add to the decor! This course shouldn't give you many problems—it's excellently maintained and relatively straightforward, with few fairway hazards. Facilities include a driving range, practice greens, club rental, a snack bar, and a clubhouse.

Kukuiolono Park, Kalaheo. © **808/332-9151.** Greens fees: $9 for the day; optional cart rental $8 for 9 holes. Take Hwy. 50 into the town of Kalaheo; turn left on Papaluna Rd., drive up the hill for nearly a mile, and watch for the sign on your right; the entrance has huge iron gates and stone pillars.

Poipu Bay Golf Course *★★*   This 6,959-yard, par-72 course with a links-style lay-out is the home of the PGA Grand Slam of Golf. Designed by Robert Trent Jones, Jr., this challenging course features undulating greens and water hazards on 8 of the holes. The par-4 16th hole has the coastline weaving along the entire left side. You can take the safe route to the right and maybe make par (but more likely bogey), or you can try to take it tight against the ocean and possibly make it in two. The most striking (and most disrespectful) hole is the 201-yard par-3 on the 17th, which has a tee built on an ancient Hawaiian stone formation. Facilities include a restaurant, a locker room, a pro shop, a driving range, and putting greens.

2250 Ainako St. (across from the Grand Hyatt Kauai), Koloa. © 808/742-8711. www.poipubaygolf.com. Greens fees: $200 ($135 Grand Hyatt guest) until noon; $125 noon–3pm ($110 Grand Hyatt guest); $75 after 3pm. Take Hwy. 50 to Hwy. 520; bear left into Poipu at the fork in the road; turn right on Ainako St.

THE NORTH SHORE

Princeville Golf Club, Prince Course *★★*   Here's your chance to play one of the best golf courses in Hawaii. This Robert Trent Jones, Jr.–designed devil of a course sits on 390 acres molded to create ocean views from every hole. Some holes have a water-fall backdrop to the greens, others shoot into the hillside, and the famous par-4 12th has a long tee shot off a cliff to a narrow, jungle-lined fairway 100 feet below. This is the most challenging course on Kauai; accuracy is key here. Most of the time, if you miss the fairway, your ball's in the drink. "The average vacation golfer may find the

Prince Course intimidating, but they don't mind because it's so beautiful," Jones says. Facilities include a restaurant, a health club and spa, lockers, a clubhouse, a golf shop, and a driving range.

Princeville. (℃ **800/826-1105** or 808/826-5070. www.princeville.com/play/prince_desc.html. Greens fees: $195 ($155 for Princeville resort guests and $135 for Princeville Hotel guests) for the Prince Course; $175 ($140 for Princeville resort guests and $125 for Princeville Hotel guests) for the Makai Course. Take Hwy. 56 to mile marker 27; the course is on your right.

BIKING

There are a couple of great places on Kauai for two-wheeling: the **Poipu area,** which has wide, flat roads and several dirt cane roads (especially around Mahaulepu); and the cane road (a dirt road used for hauling sugar cane) between **Kealia Beach** and **Anahola,** north of Kapaa.

The following places rent mountain bikes, from a low of $25 a day for cruisers to $45 a day for mountain bikes (with big discounts for multiple-day rentals): **Outfitters Kauai,** 2827A Poipu Rd. (look for the small five-shop mall before the road forks to Poipu/Spouting Horn), Poipu (℃ **808/742-9667;** www.outfitterskauai.com); and **Kauai Cycle and Tour,** 1379 Kuhio Hwy., Kapaa (℃ **808/821-2115;** www.bike hawaii.com/kauaicycle). For a great selection of high-quality mountain bikes at reasonable prices, it's worth the drive to **Pedal 'n Paddle,** in Hanalei (℃ **808/826-9069;** www.pedalnpaddle.com), which has not only high-grade Kona mountain bikes with Shimano components, but also bikes with front-end suspension systems. Rentals start at $10 a day or $30 a week and include helmet, bike lock, and car rack. The shop even has kids' 20-inch BMX bikes. The knowledgeable folks here are more than happy to provide you with free maps and tell you about the best biking spots on the island.

GUIDED BIKE TOURS   Outfitters Kauai ✦ (℃ **808/742-9667;** www.outfitters kauai.com) offers a fabulous downhill bike ride from Waimea Canyon to the ocean. The 12-mile trip (mostly coasting) begins at 6am, when the van leaves the shop in Poipu and heads up to the canyon. By the time you've scarfed down the fresh-baked muffins and coffee, you're at the top of the canyon, just as the sun is rising over the rim—it's a remarkable moment. The tour makes a couple of stops on the way down for short, scenic nature hikes. The tour lasts about 4 to 4½ hours. The sunset trip follows the same route. Both tours cost $98 per adult, $78 children 12 to 14.

BIRDING

Kauai provides some of Hawaii's last sanctuaries for endangered native birds and oceanic birds, such as the albatross. At **Kokee State Park,** a 4,345-acre wilderness forest at the end of Highway 550 in southwest Kauai, you have an excellent chance of seeing some of Hawaii's endangered native birds. You might spot the apapane, a red bird with black wings and a curved black bill; or the iwi, a red bird with black wings, orange legs, and a salmon-colored bill. Other frequently seen native birds are the honeycreeper, which sings like a canary; the amakihi, a plain olive-green bird with a long, straight bill; and the anianiau, a tiny yellow bird with a thin, slightly curved bill. The most common native bird at Kokee is the moa, or red jungle fowl, brought as domestic stock by ancient Polynesians. Ordinarily shy, they're quite tame in this environment. David Kuhn leads custom hikes, pointing out Hawaii's rarest birds on his **Terran Tours** (℃ **808/335-0398**), which range from a half-day to 3 days and feature endemic and endangered species.

Kilauea Point National Wildlife Refuge ★, a mile north of Kilauea on the North Shore (© **808/828-1413;** www.fws.gov/pacificislands/wnwr/kkilaueanwr.html), is a 200-acre headland habitat that juts above the surf and includes cliffs, two rocky wave-lashed bays, and a tiny islet that serves as a jumping-off spot for seabirds. You can easily spot red-footed boobies, which nest in trees, and wedge-tailed shearwaters, which burrow in nests along the cliffs. You may also see the great frigate bird, the Laysan albatross, the red-tailed tropic bird, and the endangered nene. Native plants and the Kilauea Point Lighthouse are highlights as well. The refuge is open from 10am to 4pm daily (closed on federal holidays); admission is $3. At press time, the refuge had suspended the popular 1-hour **guided hikes** up to the 568-foot summit of Crater Hill, which affords spectacular views. Call to see if they have resumed their hikes, which had taken place Monday through Thursday at 10am (the only fee is the $3 admission to the refuge), but you must make a reservation (© **808/828-0168**). To get here, turn right off Kuhio Highway (Hwy. 56) at Kilauea, just after mile marker 23; follow Kilauea Road to the refuge entrance.

Peaceful Hanalei Valley is home to Hawaii's endangered Koloa duck, gallinule, coot, and stilt. The **Hanalei National Wildlife Refuge** (© **808/828-1413;** www.fws. gov/pacificislands/wnwr/khanaleinwr.html) also provides a safe habitat for migratory shorebirds and waterfowl. It's not open to the public, but an interpretive overlook along the highway serves as an impressive vantage point. Along Ohiki Road, which begins at the west end of the Hanalei River Bridge, you'll often see white cattle egrets hunting crayfish in streams.

HORSEBACK RIDING

Only in Kauai can you ride a horse across the wide-open pastures of a working ranch under volcanic peaks and rein up near a waterfall pool. No wonder Kauai's *paniolo* smile and sing so much. Near the Poipu area, **CJM Country Stables,** 1731 Kelaukia St. (2 miles beyond the Grand Hyatt Kauai), Koloa (© **808/742-6096;** www.cjm stables.com), offers both 2- and 3-hour escorted Hidden Valley beach rides. You'll trot over Hidden Valley ranchland, past secluded beaches and bays, along the Haupu Ridge, across sugar-cane fields, and to Mahaulepu Beach; it's worth your time and money just to get out to this seldom-seen part of Kauai. The Secret Beach and Breakfast Ride costs $105 and includes breakfast. The 2-hour Hidden Beach Ride is $90. There's also a 3½-hour swim/beach/picnic ride for $115.

Princeville Ranch Stables, Highway 56 (just after the Princeville Airport), Hanalei (© **808/826-6777;** www.princevilleranch.com), has a variety of outings. The 1½-hour country ride takes in views of the Hanalei mountains and the vista of Anini Beach ($80), while the 3-hour ($125) or 4-hour ($135) Waterfall Picnic Ride crosses ranchland, takes you on a short (but steep) hike to swimming pools at the base of waterfalls, and then feeds you a picnic lunch. Riders must be in good physical shape, and don't forget to put your swimsuit on under your jeans. The Princeville Ranch Stables also offers other adventures, ranging from wagon rides to a cattle-drive ride.

TENNIS

The **Kauai County Parks and Recreation Department,** 4444 Rice St., Suite 150, Lihue (© **808/241-4463;** www.kauai.gov), has a list of the 12 county tennis courts around the island, all of which are free and open to the public. Private courts that are open to the public include the **Princeville Tennis Club,** Princeville (© **808/826-3620;** www.princeville.com), which has six courts available for $15 per person ($12 for guests) for 90 minutes. On the south side, try **Grand Hyatt Kauai Resort & Spa** (© 808/742-1234; www.kauai-hyatt.com), which has four courts, available for $30 an hour; and **Kiahuna Swim and Tennis Club,** Poipu Road (just past the Poipu Shopping Village on the left), Poipu Resort (© 808/742-9533), which has 10 courts renting for $10 per person for 90 minutes.

9 Seeing the Sights

No matter how much time you have on Kauai, make it a priority to see the North Shore. No doubt about it—this is Hawaii at its best.

A TOUR OF THE ISLAND

Four-Wheel-Drive Backroad Adventure ⭐ Great for getting off the beaten path and seeing the "hidden" Kauai, this 4-hour tour follows a figure-eight path around Kauai, from Kilohana Crater to the Mahaulepu coastline. The tour, done in a four-wheel-drive van, not only stops at Kauai's well-known scenic spots, but also travels on sugar-cane roads (on private property), taking you to places most people who live on Kauai have never seen. The guides are well versed in everything from native plants to Hawaiian history. Bring plenty of film for your camera.

Aloha Kauai Tours, 1702 Haleukana St., Lihue. © 800/452-1113 or 808/245-8809. www.alohakauaitours.com. Tours $70 adults, $50 children ages 12 and under. Tours offered daily 7:45am and 12:45pm; reservations required.

LIHUE & ENVIRONS

Grove Farm Homestead Museum You can experience a day in the life of an 1860s sugar planter on a visit to Grove Farm Homestead, which shows how good life was (for some, anyway) when sugar was king. This is Hawaii's best remaining example of a sugar-plantation homestead. Founded in 1864 by George N. Wilcox, a Hanalei missionary's son, Grove Farm was one of the earliest of Hawaii's 86 sugar plantations. A self-made millionaire, Wilcox died a bachelor in 1933, at age 94. His estate looks much like it did when he lived here, complete with period furniture, plantation artifacts, and Hawaiiana.

4050 Nawiliwili Rd. (Hwy. 58) at Pikaka St. (2 miles from Waapa Rd.), Lihue. © 808/245-3202. www.hawaiimuseums. org. Requested donation $5 adults, $2 children under 12. Tours offered Mon and Wed–Thurs at 10am and 1pm; reservations required.

Kauai Museum ⭐ (Kids) The history of Kauai is kept safe in an imposing Greco-Roman building that once served as the town library. This great little museum is worth a stop before you set out to explore the island. It contains a wealth of historical artifacts and information tracing the island's history from the beginning of time through contact (when Capt. James Cook "discovered" Kauai in 1778), the monarchy period, the plantation era, and the present. You'll hear tales of the *menehune* (the mythical elflike people who were said to build massive stoneworks in a single night) and see old poi pounders and idols, relics of sugar planters and *paniolo,* a nice seashell collection, old Hawaiian quilts, feather leis, a replica of a plantation worker's home, and much more—even a model of Cook's ship, the HMS *Resolution,* riding anchor in Waimea Bay. Vintage photographs by W. J. Senda, a Japanese immigrant, show old Kauai, while a contemporary video, shot from a helicopter, captures the island's natural beauty.

4428 Rice St., Lihue. © 808/245-6931. www.kauaimuseum.org. Admission $5 adults, $4 seniors, $3 students 13–17, $1 children 6–12. Mon–Fri 9am–4pm; Sat 10am–4pm. 1st Sat of every month is "Family Day," when admission is free.

(*Fun Fact* **Discover the Legendary Little People**

According to ancient Hawaiian legend, among Kauai's earliest settlers were the *menehune,* a race of small people who worked at night to accomplish magnificent feats. Above Nawiliwili Harbor, the **Menehune Fish Pond**—which at one time extended 25 miles—is said to have been built in just 1 night, with two rows of thousands of *menehune* passing stones hand to hand. The *menehune* were promised that no one would watch them work, but one person did; when they discovered the spy, they stopped working immediately, leaving two gaps in the wall. From Nawiliwili Harbor, take Hulemalu Road above Huleia Stream; look for the HAWAII CONVENTION AND VISITORS BUREAU marker at a turnoff in the road, which leads to the legendary fish pond. Kayakers can paddle up Huleia Stream to see it up close.

THE POIPU RESORT AREA

No Hawaii resort has a better entrance: On Maluhia Road, eucalyptus trees planted in 1911 as a windbreak for sugar cane fields now form a monumental **tree tunnel.** The leafy green, cool tunnel starts at Kaumualii Highway; you'll emerge at the golden-red beach.

Allerton Garden of the National Tropical Botanical Garden 🌺 Discover an extraordinary collection of tropical fruit and spice trees, rare Hawaiian plants, and hundreds of varieties of flowers at the 186-acre preserve known as **Lawai Gardens,** said to be the largest collection of rare and endangered plants in the world. Adjacent **McBryde Garden,** a royal home site of Queen Emma in the 1860s, is known for its formal gardens, a delicious kind of colonial decadence. It's set amid fountains, streams, waterfalls, and European statuary. Endangered green sea turtles can be seen here (their home in the sea was wiped out years ago by Hurricane Iniki). The tours are fascinating for green thumbs and novices alike.

Visitor Center, Lawai Rd. (across the street from Spouting Horn), Poipu. © 808/742-2623. www.ntbg.org. Admission $35 adults, $20 children 6–12 years. Guided 2½-hr. tours by reservation only Mon–Sat at 9am, 10am, 1pm, and 2pm; Sun 10am and 1pm. Self-guided tours of McBryde Garden Mon–Sat 9am–4pm, $20 adults and $10 children 6–12 years (trams into the valley leave once an hour on the half-hour, last tram 2:30pm); guided tour Sun 9:00am, $35 adults, $20 children 6–12 years. Reserve a week in advance in peak months of July–Sept.

Prince Kuhio Park This small roadside park is the birthplace of Prince Jonah Kuhio Kalanianaole, the "People's Prince," whose March 26 birthday is a holiday in Hawaii. He opened the beaches of Waikiki to the public in 1918 and served as Hawaii's second territorial delegate to the U.S. Congress. What remains here are the foundations of the family home, a royal fish pond, and a shrine where tributes are still paid in flowers.

Lawai Rd., Koloa. Just after mile marker 4 on Poipu Rd., veer to the right of the fork in the road; the park is on the right side.

Spouting Horn 🌺 *Kids* This natural phenomenon is second in regularity only to Yellowstone's Old Faithful. It's quite a sight—big waves hit Kauai's south shore with enough force to send a spout of funneled salt water 10 feet or more up in the air; in winter the water can get as high as six stories.

Spouting Horn is different from other blowholes in Hawaii, in that it has an additional hole that blows air that sounds like a loud moaning. According to Hawaiian legend, this coastline was once guarded by a giant female lizard (Mo'o); she would gobble up any intruders. One day, along came Liko, who wanted to fish in this area. Mo'o rushed out to eat Liko. Quickly, Liko threw a spear right into the giant lizard's mouth. Mo'o then chased Liko into a lava tube. Liko escaped, but legend says Mo'o is still in the tube, and the moaning sound at Spouting Horn is her cry for help.

At Kukuiula Bay, beyond Prince Kuhio Park (see above).

WESTERN KAUAI
WAIMEA TOWN
If you'd like to take a self-guided tour of this historic town, stop at the **Waimea Library,** at mile marker 23 on Highway 50, to pick up a map and guide to the sites.

Kiki a Ola (Menehune Ditch) Hawaiians were expert rock builders, able to construct elaborate edifices without using mortar. They formed long lines and passed stones hand over hand, and lifted rocks weighing tons with ropes made from native plants. Their feats gave rise to fantastic tales of *menehune,* elflike people hired by Hawaiian kings to create massive stoneworks in a single night—reputedly for the payment of a single shrimp (see the box "Discover the Legendary Little People," above). An excellent example of ancient Hawaiian construction is Kiki a Ola, the so-called Menehune Ditch, with cut and dressed stones that form an ancient aqueduct that still directs water to irrigate taro ponds. Historians credit the work to ancient Hawaiian engineers who applied their knowledge of hydraulics to accomplish flood control and irrigation. Only a 2-foot-high portion of the wall can be seen today; the rest of the marvelous stonework is buried under the roadbed.

From Hwy. 50, go inland on Menehune Rd.; a plaque marks the spot about 1½ miles up.

Russian Fort Elizabeth State Historical Park To the list of those who tried to conquer Hawaii, add the Russians. In 1815 a German doctor tried to claim Kauai for Russia. He even supervised the construction of a fort in Waimea, but he and his handful of Russian companions were expelled by Kamehameha I a couple of years later. Now a state historic landmark, the Russian Fort Elizabeth (named for the wife of Russia's Czar Alexander I) is on the eastern headlands overlooking the harbor, across from Lucy Kapahu Aukai Wright Beach Park. The fort, built Hawaiian-style with stacked lava rocks in the shape of a star, once bristled with cannons; it's now mostly in ruins. You can take a free, self-guided tour of the site, which affords a keen view of the west bank of the Waimea River, where Captain Cook landed, and of the island of Niihau across the channel.

Hwy. 50 (on the ocean side, just after mile marker 22), east of Waimea.

THE GRAND CANYON OF THE PACIFIC:
WAIMEA CANYON ✸✸✸
The great gaping gulch known as Waimea Canyon is quite a sight. This valley, known for its reddish lava beds, reminds everyone who sees it of the Grand Canyon. Kauai's version is bursting with ever-changing color, just like its namesake, but it's smaller—only a mile wide, 3,567 feet deep, and 12 miles long. A massive earthquake sent all the streams flowing into a single river that ultimately carved this picturesque canyon. Today the Waimea River—a silver thread of water in the gorge that's sometimes a

trickle, often a torrent, but always there—keeps cutting the canyon deeper, and nobody can say what the result will be 100 million years from now.

You can stop by the road and look at the canyon, hike down into it, or swoop through it in a helicopter. For more information, see "Hiking & Camping," earlier in this chapter, and "Helicopter Rides over Waimea Canyon & the Na Pali Coast," below.

THE DRIVE THROUGH WAIMEA CANYON & UP TO KOKEE

By car, there are two ways to visit Waimea Canyon and reach Kokee State Park, 20 miles up from Waimea. From the coastal road (Hwy. 50), you can turn up Waimea Canyon Drive (Hwy. 550) at Waimea town, or you can pass through Waimea and turn up Kokee Road (Hwy. 55) at Kekaha. The climb is very steep from Kekaha, but Waimea Canyon Drive, the rim road, is narrower and rougher. A few miles up, the two merge into Kokee Road.

The first good vantage point is **Waimea Canyon Lookout,** located between mile markers 10 and 11 on Waimea Canyon Road. From here, it's another 6 miles to Kokee. There are a few more lookout points along the way that also offer spectacular views, such as **Puu Hina Hina Lookout,** between mile markers 13 and 14, at 3,336 feet; be sure to pull over and spend a few minutes pondering this natural wonder. (The giant white object that looks like a golf ball and defaces the natural landscape is a radar station left over from the Cold War.)

KOKEE STATE PARK 🅰🅰

It's only 16 miles from Waimea to Kokee, but it's a whole different world because the park is 4,345 acres of rainforest. You'll enter a new climate zone, where the breeze has a bite and trees look quite continental. You're in a cloud forest on the edge of the Alakai Swamp, the largest swamp in Hawaii, on the summit plateau of Kauai. Days are cool and wet, with intermittent bright sunshine, not unlike Seattle on a good day. Bring your sweater, and, if you're staying over, be sure you know how to light a fire (overnight lows dip into the 40s/single digits Celsius).

The forest is full of native plants, such as mokihana berry, ohia lehua tree, iliau (similar to Maui's silversword), and imports like Australia's eucalyptus and California's redwood. Pigs, goats, and black-tailed deer thrive in the forest, but the moa, or Polynesian jungle fowl, is the cock of the walk.

Right next to Kokee Lodge (which lies on the only road through the park, about a mile before it ends) is the **Kokee Natural History Museum** 🅰 (© **808/335-9975;** www.kokee.org), open daily from 10am to 4pm (free admission). This is the best place to learn about the forest and Alakai Swamp before you set off hiking in the wild. The museum shop has great trail information and local books and maps, including the official park trail map. We recommend getting the *Pocket Guide on Native Plants on the Nature Trail for Kokee State Park* and the *Road Guide to Kokee and Waimea Canyon State Park.*

A **nature walk** is the best intro to this rainforest; it starts behind the museum at the rare Hawaiian koa tree. This easy self-guided walk of about .25 mile takes about 20 minutes if you stop and look at all the plants identified along the way.

Two miles above Kokee Lodge is **Kalalau Lookout** 🅰, the spectacular climax of your drive through Waimea Canyon and Kokee. When you stand at the lookout, below you is a work in progress that began at least 5 million years ago. It's hard to stop looking; the view is breathtaking, especially when light and cloud shadows play across the red-and-orange cliffs.

There's lots more to see and do up here: Anglers fly-fish for rainbow trout, and hikers tackle the 45 trails that lace the Alakai Swamp (see "Watersports" and "Hiking & Camping," earlier in this chapter). That's a lot of ground to cover, so you might want to plan on staying over. If pitching a tent is too rustic for you, the wonderful **cabins** set in a grove of redwoods are one of the best lodging bargains in the islands (see "Where to Stay," earlier in this chapter). The restaurant at **Kokee Lodge** is open for continental breakfast and lunch daily from 9am to 3:30pm.

For advance information, contact the **State Division of Parks,** 3060 Eiwa St., Room 306, Lihue, HI 96766 (© **808/274-3444**); and the **Kokee Lodge Manager,** P.O. Box 819, Waimea, HI 96796 (© **808/335-6061**). The park is open daily year-round. The best time to go is early in the morning, to see the panoramic view of Kalalau Valley from the lookout at 4,000 feet, before clouds obscure the valley and peaks.

HELICOPTER RIDES OVER WAIMEA CANYON & THE NA PALI COAST 🏵🏵🏵

Don't leave Kauai without seeing it from a helicopter. It's expensive but worth the splurge. You can take home memories of the thrilling ride up and over the Kalalau Valley on Kauai's wild North Shore and into the 5,200-foot vertical temple of Mount Waialeale, the most sacred place on the island and the wettest spot on earth (and, in some cases, you can even take home a video of your ride). All flights leave from Lihue Airport. *Money-saving tip:* You can save 15% to 37% by booking online.

Air Kauai Helicopters 🏵 Since 1988, Chuck DiPiazza has been flying visitors over Kauai without an incident. He flies custom-designed A-STAR helicopters with high-back leather seats and huge windows (37% larger than those on most other helicopters). The pilot sits on the left side of the helicopter (instead of the usual position on the right), which allows not only a better view, but also more legroom. Another plus: All his helicopters have BOSE Acoustic Noise Canceling Stereo Headsets. Ask for Captain Chuck; his commentaries are informative and down-to-earth, he welcomes questions, and he loves to show off his multi-CD disk player, which provides music for the tour.

3651 Ahukini Rd., Lihue. © **800/972-4666** or 808/246-4666. www.airkauai.com. The 60-min. tour is $219.

Blue Hawaiian 🏵🏵🏵 Blue Hawaiian has been the Cadillac of helicopter tour companies on Maui and the Big Island for more than a decade, and recently it has expanded its operations to Kauai. I strongly recommend that you try to book with Blue Hawaiian first. The operation is first class, and the equipment the state-of-the-art in Hawaii: American Eurocopter ECO-Star, which reduces noise in the helicopter by 50% and provides 23% more interior room. Plus, the craft has individual business class–style seats, two-way communication with the pilot, and expansive glass for incredible views. The 50-minute flight first journeys to Hanapepe Valley and then continues on to Mana Waiapuna, commonly referred to as "Jurassic Park Falls." Next it's up the Olokele Canyon, and then on to the Waimea Canyon, the famed "Grand Canyon of the Pacific." Most of the flight then will be along the Na Pali Coast, before heading out to the Bali Hai Cliffs and the pristine blue waters of Hanalei Bay and the Princeville Resort area. If the weather gods are on your side, you'll get to see the highest point on

Kauai: Mount Waialeale, the wettest spot on earth, with an average rainfall of 450 to 500 inches annually. Your flight will take you right into the center of the crater, with its 5,000-foot walls towering above and its 3,000-foot waterfalls surrounding you, something you will remember forever.

Harbor Mall staging area, 3501 Rice St., Lihue; take off from the Lihue Airport. ⓒ **800/745-2583** or 808/245-5800. www.bluehawaiian.com. 50-min. tour $219 ($199 if you book online).

Island Helicopters ⓚ Curt Lofstedt has been flying helicopter tours of Kauai for nearly 3 decades. He personally selects and trains professional pilots with an eye not only to their flying skills, but also to their ability to share the magic of Kauai. All flights are in the six-passenger Aerospatiale A-Star, with extra-large windows and stereo headsets to hear the pilot's personal narration.

Lihue Airport. ⓒ **800/829-5999** or 808/245-8588. www.islandhelicopters.com. 55-min. island tour $250. Mention Frommer's and receive 40% off ($150).

Jack Harter ⓚ The pioneer of helicopter flights on Kauai, Jack was the guy who started the sightseeing-via-helicopter trend. On the 60-minute tour, he flies a four-passenger Bell Jet Ranger Model 204 (with "scenic view" windows), a six-seater A-star, or a Eurocopter AS350BA A-star. The 90-minute tour (in the Bell Jet Ranger only) hovers over the sights a bit longer than the 60-minute flight so you can get a good look, but we found the shorter tour sufficient.

4231 Ahukini Rd., Lihue. ⓒ **888/245-2001** or 808/245-3774. www.helicopters-kauai.com. 60- to 65-min. tour $249; 90- to 95-min. tour $369 (book on the Internet and save $30–$40).

Will Squyres Helicopter Tours The 60-minute flight starts in Lihue and takes you through Waimea Canyon, along the Na Pali Coast, and over Waialeale Crater and the two sets of waterfalls that appeared in *Fantasy Island*. Will's A-star six-passenger copter has side-by-side seats (nobody sits backward, and everybody gets a window seat) and enlarged windows. A veteran pilot, Will has flown several thousand hours over Kauai since 1984 and knows the island, its ever-changing weather conditions, and his copters.

3222 Kuhio Hwy., Lihue. ⓒ **888/245-4354** or 808/245-8881. www.helicopters-hawaii.com. 60-min. Grand Tour of Kauai $219 (book online for $189).

THE COCONUT COAST

Fern Grotto This is one of Kauai's oldest (since 1946) and most popular tourist attractions. At press time, Fern Grotto is still closed due to flooding in early 2006. When it gets up and running again, Smith's operates a 157-passenger motorized barge which takes people up and down the river on a 45-minute cruise with a hula show on the return trip. The grotto is the source of many Hawaiian legends and a popular site for weddings.

Contact Smith's Motor Boats for tours. ⓒ 808/821-6892. www.smithskauai.com. Reservations recommended. Admission $15 adults, $7.50 children 2–12. Daily 9am–3:30pm. Wailua Marina, at the mouth of the Wailua River; turn off Kuhio Hwy. (Hwy. 56) into Wailua Marine State Park.

WAILUA RIVER STATE PARK

Ancients called the Wailua River "the river of the great sacred spirit." Seven temples once stood along this 20-mile river, which is fed by 5,148-foot Mount Waialeale, the wettest spot on earth. You can go up Hawaii's biggest navigable river by boat or kayak (see "Boating" and "Kayaking," earlier in this chapter), or drive Kuamoo Road (Hwy.

Hollywood Loves Kauai

More than 50 major Hollywood productions have been shot on Kauai since the studios discovered the island's spectacular natural beauty. Here are just a few:

- Manawaiopu Falls, Mount Waialeale, and other scenic areas around the island doubled for *Jurassic Park.*
- Kauai's lush rainforests formed a fantastic backdrop for Harrison Ford in both *Raiders of the Lost Ark* and *Indiana Jones and the Temple of Doom.*
- Mitzi Gaynor sang "I'm Gonna Wash That Man Right Outta My Hair" on Lumahai Beach in *South Pacific.*
- Elvis Presley married costar Joan Blackman near the Wailua River in *Blue Hawaii* (1961).
- Beautiful Kee Beach, on the North Shore, masqueraded as Australia in the miniseries *The Thornbirds,* starring Richard Chamberlain and Rachel Ward.
- Kauai appeared as the backdrop for *Outbreak,* the 1994 thriller about the spread of a deadly virus on a remote tropical island, starring Dustin Hoffman. Hoffman also appeared with Robin Williams and Julia Roberts in *Hook* (1991), in which Kauai appeared as Never-Never Land.
- James Caan, Nicolas Cage, Sarah Jessica Parker, and Pat Morita shared laughs on Kauai (which appeared as itself) in *Honeymoon in Vegas.*

Now you can visit these and other Kauai locations that made it to the silver screen, plus locations from such TV classics as *Fantasy Island* and *Gilligan's Island,* with **Hawaii Movie Tours** (© **800/628-8432** or 808/822-1192; www. hawaiimovietour.com). The commentary and sightseeing stops are supplemented by video clips of the location shots (complete with surround sound); in addition, a guide leads singalongs of movie and TV themes as you go from locale to locale in the new 14-passenger bus. All in all, there's a whole lot of fun to be had, especially for families. You'll see more of Kauai on this tour (including private estates not open to the public) than you would if you explored the island yourself. Tickets are $111 for adults and $92 for children 11 and under; lunch is included.

580, sometimes called the King's Highway), which goes inland along the north side of the river from Kuhio Highway (Hwy. 56)—from the northbound lane, turn left at the stoplight just before the ruins of Coco Palms Resort. Kuamoo Road goes past the *heiau* (temple) and historical sites to Opaekaa Falls and Keahua Arboretum, a State Division of Forestry attempt to reforest the watershed with native plants.

The entire district from the river mouth to the summit of Waialeale was once royal land. This sacred historical site was believed to be founded by Puna, a Tahitian priest who, according to legend, arrived in one of the first double-hulled voyaging canoes to come to Hawaii, established a beachhead, and declared Kauai his kingdom. All of Kauai's *alii* (royalty) are believed to be descended from Puna. Here, in this royal settlement, are remains of the seven temples, including a sacrificial *heiau,* a planetarium (a simple array of rocks in a celestial pattern), the royal birthing stones, and a stone bell to announce a royal birth. (You can still ring the bell—many people have—but make sure you have an announcement to make when it stops ringing.)

There's a nice overlook view of 40-foot **Opaekaa Falls** *ᴋᴋ* 1½ miles up Highway 580. This is probably the best-looking drive-up waterfall on Kauai. With the scenic peaks of the Makaleha Mountains in the background and a restored Hawaiian village on the riverbanks, these falls are what the tourist-bureau folks call an "eye-popping" photo op.

Near Opaekaa Falls overlook is **Poliahu Heiau,** the large lava-rock temple of Kauai's last king, Kaumualii, who died on Oahu in 1824 after being abducted by King Kamehameha II. If you stop here, you'll notice two signs. The first, an official 1928 bronze territorial plaque, says that the royal *heiau* was built by *menehune,* which it explains parenthetically as "Hawaiian dwarves or brownies." A more recent hand-painted sign warns visitors not to climb on the sacred rocks.

SLEEPING GIANT

If you squint your eyes just so as you pass the 1,241-foot-high Nounou Ridge, which forms a dramatic backdrop to the coastal villages of Wailua and Waipouli, you can see the fabled Sleeping Giant. On Kuhio Highway, just after mile marker 7, around the mini-mall complex Waipouli Town Center, look mauka (inland) and you may see what appears to be the legendary giant named Puni, who, as the story goes, fell asleep after a great feast. If you don't see it at first, visualize it this way: His head is Wailua and his feet are Kapaa. For details on an easy hike to the top of the Sleeping Giant, see "The Sleeping Giant Trail" on p. 598.

PARADISE FOUND: THE NORTH SHORE *ᴋᴋᴋ*
ON THE ROAD TO HANALEI

The first place everyone should go on Kauai is Hanalei. The drive along **Kuhio Highway** (Hwy. 56, which becomes Hwy. 560 after Princeville to the end of the road)

⸨Kids⸩ Kauai Children's Discovery Museum

This is every parent's dream: an enthralling, hands-on learning adventure to take kids to on rainy days (hey, it's so much fun, the kids will beg to come back even on sunny days). The **Kauai Children's Discovery Museum,** located under the Whale Tower in the Kauai Village Shopping Center, in Kapaa (© **808/823-8222;** www.kcdm.org), arose out of a grass-roots community effort to have a fun place where kids could learn about science, culture, arts, technology, and nature. Not only are the hands-on, interactive exhibits thrilling to kids, but it's a great place for your kids to meet and interact with children from Kauai. The 7,000-square-foot play center is open Tuesday to Saturday from 10am to 5pm. In addition to the exhibits, which range from playing with Hawaiian musical instruments to participating in virtual-reality television, to hiding out in a "magic treehouse" and reading a book (there's even a baby area for kids 4 and under), there are Keiki Camps (Children Camps) during school holidays, where you can leave the kids all day for various outings to the beach and to points of interest. Admission is $4 for kids (ages 1–17 years) and $5 for adults, with family memberships available.

Tips **Bridge Etiquette: Showing Aloha on Kauai's One-Lane Bridges**

Hawaii's drivers are much more laid-back and courteous than most mainland drivers. Hanalei has a series of one-lane bridges where it is not only proper etiquette to be courteous, but is also the law. When you approach a one-lane bridge, slow down and yield if a vehicle, approaching in the opposite direction, is either on the bridge or just about to enter the bridge. If you are in a long line of vehicles approaching the bridge, don't just join the train crossing the bridge. The local "rule of thumb" is about seven to eight cars over the bridge, then yield and give the cars waiting on the other side of the bridge a chance to come across. Of course, not everyone will adhere to these rules, but then, not everyone visiting Hawaii truly feels the spirit of aloha.

---

displays Kauai's grandeur at its absolute best. Just before Kilauea, the air and the sea change, the light falls in a different way, and the last signs of development are behind you. Now there are roadside fruit stands, a little stone church in Kilauea, two roadside waterfalls, and a long, stiltlike bridge over the Kalihiwai Stream and its green river valley.

If you don't know a guava from a mango, stop in Kilauea at the cool, shady **Guava Kai Plantation,** at the end of Kuawa Road (© **808/828-6121**), for a refreshing, free treat. After you take a walk through the orchards and see what a guava looks like on the tree, you can sample the juice of this exotic pink tropical fruit (which also makes a great jam or jelly—sold here, too). For other sweet treats along the way, check out the box "Fruity Smoothies & Other Exotic Treats" on p. 616. The plantation is open daily from 9am to 5pm.

Birders might want to stop off at **Kilauea Point National Wildlife Refuge,** a mile north of Kilauea, and the **Hanalei National Wildlife Refuge,** along Ohiki Road, at the west end of the Hanalei River Bridge. (For details, see "Birding," earlier in this chapter.) In the Hanalei Refuge, along a dirt road on a levee, you can see the **Hariguchi Rice Mill,** now a historic treasure.

Now the coastal highway heads due west and the showy ridgelines of Mount Namahana create a grand amphitheater. The two-lane coastal highway rolls through pastures of grazing cattle and past a tiny airport and the luxurious Princeville Hotel.

Five miles past Kilauea, just past the Princeville Shopping Center, is **Hanalei Valley Lookout.** Big enough for a dozen cars, this lookout attracts crowds of people who peer over the edge into the 917-acre Hanalei River Valley. Seldom will you see so many shades of green in one place: The green rice, taro, and streams lace a patchwork of green ponds that back up to green-velvet Bali Hai cliffs. Don't be put off by the crowds; this is definitely worth a look. You might even see an endangered Hawaiian black-necked stilt.

Farther along, a hairpin turn offers another scenic look at Hanalei town, and then you cross the **Hanalei Bridge.** The Pratt truss steel bridge, prefabbed in New York City, was erected in 1912; it's now on the National Registry of Historic Landmarks. If it ever goes out, the nature of Hanalei will change forever; currently, this rusty, one-lane bridge (which must violate all kinds of department of transportation safety regulations) isn't big enough for a tour bus to cross.

You'll drive slowly past the **Hanalei River banks** and Bill Mowry's **Hanalei Buffalo Ranch,** where 200 American bison roam in the tropical sun; you may even see buffalo grazing in the pastures on your right. The herd is often thinned to make buffalo patties. (You wondered why there was a buffalo burger on the Ono Family Restaurant menu, didn't you?)

Just past Tahiti Nui, turn right on Aku Road before Ching Young Village and then take a right on Weke Road; **Hanalei Beach Park,** one of Hawaii's most gorgeous, is a half-block ahead on your left. Swimming is excellent here year-round, especially in summer, when Hanalei Bay becomes a big, placid lake; for details, see "Beaches," earlier in this chapter.

If this exquisite 2-mile-long beach doesn't meet your expectations, head down the highway, where the next 7 miles of coast yield some of Kauai's other spectacular beaches, including **Lumahai Beach,** of *South Pacific* movie fame, as well as **Tunnels Beach** (p. 587), where the 1960s puka-shell necklace craze began, and **Haena Beach Park** (p. 587), a fabulous place to kick back and enjoy the waves, particularly in summer. Once you've found your beach, stick around until sundown and then head back to one of the North Shore's restaurants for a mai tai and a fresh seafood dinner (see "Where to Dine," earlier in this chapter). Another perfect day in paradise.

ATTRACTIONS ALONG THE WAY

Ka Ulu O Laka Heiau   On a knoll above the boulders of Kee Beach (p. 587) stands a sacred altar of rocks, often draped with flower leis and ti-leaf offerings, dedicated to Laka, the goddess of hula. It may seem like a primal relic from the days of idols, but it's very much in use today. Often dancers from Hawaii's hula *halau* (schools) climb the cliff, bearing small gifts of flowers. In Hawaiian myths, Lohiau, a handsome chief, danced here before the fire goddess Pele; their passion became *Haena,* which means "the heat." Sometimes, in a revival of the old Hawaiian ways, a mother of a newborn will deposit the umbilical cord of her infant at this sacred shrine. The site is filled with what Hawaiians call *mana,* or power.

From the west side of Kee Beach, take the footpath across the big rocks almost to the point; then climb the steep grassy hill.

Limahuli Garden of the National Tropical Botanical Garden 𝄐   Out on Kauai's far North Shore, beyond Hanalei and the last wooden bridge, there's a mighty cleft in the coastal range where ancestral Hawaiians lived in what can only be called paradise. Carved by a waterfall stream known as Limahuli, the lush valley sits at the foot of steepled cliffs that Hollywood portrayed as Bali Hai in the film classic *South Pacific.* This small, almost secret garden is eco-tourism at its best. It appeals not just to green thumbs, but to all who love Hawaii's great outdoors. Here botanists hope to save Kauai's endangered native plants. You can take the self-tour to view the plants, which are identified in Hawaiian and English. From taro to sugar cane, the mostly Polynesian imports tell the story of the people who cultivated the plants for food, medicine, clothing, shelter, and decoration. In addition, Limahuli's stream is sanctuary to the last five species of Hawaiian freshwater fish.

Visitor Center, ½ mile past mile marker 9 on Kuhio Hwy. (Hwy. 560), Haena. ✆ 808/826-1053. Fax 808/826-1394. www.ntbg.org. Admission $15 self-guided, $25 guided; free for children 12 and under. Tues–Fri and Sun 9:30am– 4pm. Advance reservations required for 2½-hr. guided tours. During peak season of July–Sept, book at least a week ahead.

Na Aina Kai Botanical Gardens *ᖶᖶᖶ (Finds* Do not miss this incredible, magical garden on some 240 acres, sprinkled with some 70 life-size (some larger than life-size) whimsical bronze statues, hidden off the beaten path of the North Shore. This is the place for both avid gardeners as well as people who think they don't like botanical gardens. They have everything: waterfalls, pools, arbors, topiaries, colonnades, gazebos, a maze you will never forget, a lagoon with spouting fountains, a Japanese teahouse, and an enchanting path along a bubbling stream to the ocean. The imaginary, fairy-tale creativity that has gone into these grounds will be one of your fondest memories of Kauai. A host of different tours is available, from 1½ hours ($25) to 5 hours ($70) long, ranging from casual, guided strolls to riding in the covered CarTram to treks from one end of the gardens to the ocean. Currently, the tours are open to adults and children 13 years and older. For younger kids, there is a magical tropical children's garden with a gecko hedge maze, a tropical jungle gym, a tree house in a rubber tree, and a 16-foot-tall Jack-in-the-Beanstalk giant with a 33-foot wading pool below. The 2-hour children's "Under the Rainbow" garden tour is $25 for adults and $15 for children ages 13 and under, and includes a tour of the formal gardens. Book a tour before you leave for Hawaii so you won't be disappointed.

4101 Wailapa Rd. (write: P.O. Box 1134), Kilauea. ℂ 808/828-0525. Fax 808/828-0815. www.naainakai.com. Tues–Thurs 8am–5pm and Fri 9am–noon. Tours vary. Advance reservations strongly recommended. To get there from Lihue, drive north past mile marker 21 and turn right on Wailapa Rd. At the road's end, drive through the iron gates. From Princeville, drive south 6½ miles and take the 2nd left past mile marker 22 on Wailapa Rd. At the road's end, drive through the iron gates.

Waioli Mission House Museum If you're lucky and time your visit just right, you can visit this 150-year-old mission house, which serves today as a living museum. It's a real treasure. Others in Honolulu are easier to see, but the Waioli Mission House retains its sense of place and most of its furnishings, so you can really get a clear picture of what life was like for the New England missionaries who came to Kauai to convert the heathens to Christianity.

Most mission houses are small, dark Boston cottages that violate the tropical sense of place. This two-story wood-frame house, built in 1836 by Abner and Lucy Wilcox of New Bedford, Massachusetts, is an excellent example of hybrid architecture. The house features a lanai on both stories, with a cookhouse in a separate building. It has a lava-rock chimney, ohia-wood floors, and Hawaiian koa furniture.

Kuhio Hwy. (Hwy. 560), just behind the green Waioli Huia Church, Hanalei. ℂ 808/245-3202. Free admission (donations gratefully accepted). Tours Tues, Thurs, and Sat 9am–3pm. Reservations required.

THE END OF THE ROAD
The real Hawaii begins where the road stops. This is especially true on Kauai—for at the end of Highway 56, the spectacular **Na Pali Coast** begins. To explore it, you have to set out on foot, by boat, or by helicopter. For details on experiencing this region, see "Hiking & Camping," "Boating," and "Helicopter Rides over Waimea Canyon & the Na Pali Coast," earlier in this chapter.

10 Shops & Galleries

Shopping is a pleasure on this island. Where else can you browse vintage Hawaiiana practically in a cane field, buy exquisite home accessories in an old stone building built in 1942, and get a virtual agricultural tour of the island through city-sponsored green markets that move from town to town throughout the week, like a movable feast? At

Kauai's small, tasteful boutiques, you can satisfy your shopping ya-yas in concentrated spurts around the island. This is a bonanza for the boutique shopper—particularly the one who appreciates the thrill of the hunt.

"Downtown" Kapaa continues to flourish, and Hanalei, touristy as it is, is still a shopping destination. (Ola's and Yellowfish make up for the hurricane of trinkets and trash in Hanalei.) Kilauea, with Kong Lung Store and the fabulous new Lotus Gallery, is the style center of the island. The Kauai Heritage Center of Hawaiian Culture & the Arts makes it possible for visitors to escape the usual imitations, tourist traps, and clichés in favor of authentic encounters with the real thing: Hawaiian arts, Hawaiian cultural practices, and Hawaiian elders and artists. What else can you expect on Kauai? Anticipate great shops in Hanalei, a few art galleries and boutiques, and a handful of shopping centers—not much to distract you from an afternoon of hiking or snorkeling. The gift items and treasures you'll find in east and north Kauai, however, may be among your best Hawaiian finds.

GREEN MARKETS & FRUIT STANDS   The county of Kauai sponsors regular weekly **Sunshine Markets** (© **808/241-6390;** www.kauai.gov) throughout the island, featuring fresh Kauai **Sunrise papayas** (sweeter, juicier, and redder than most), herbs and vegetables used in ethnic cuisines, exotic fruit such as rambutan and ate-moya, and the most exciting development in pineapple agriculture, the low-acid white pineapple called **Sugarloaf,** rarer these days but still spottily available. These markets, which sell the full range of fresh local produce and flowers at rock-bottom prices, present the perfect opportunity to see what's best and what's in season. Farmers sell their bounty from the backs of trucks or at tables set up under tarps.

The biggest market is at **Kapaa New Town Park,** in the middle of Kapaa town, on Wednesday at 3pm. The Sunshine Market in **Lihue,** held on Friday at 3pm at the Vidhina Stadium Parking Lot, is close in size and extremely popular. The schedule for the other markets: **Koloa Ball Park,** Monday at noon; **Kalaheo Neighborhood Center,** Papalina Road off Kaumualii, Tuesday at 3:30pm; **Hanapepe Park,** Thursday at 3pm; **Kilauea Neighborhood Center,** Keneke off Lighthouse Road, Thursday at 4:30pm; and **Kekaha Neighborhood Center,** Elepaio Road, Saturday at 9am. Especially at the Koloa Market, which draws hundreds of shoppers, go early and shop briskly.

On the North Shore, Kilauea is the agricultural heart of the island, with two weekly green markets: the county-sponsored **Sunshine Market,** Thursday at 4:30pm at the Kilauea Neighborhood Center; and the private Kilauea Quality Farmers Association (mostly organic growers) **Farmers Market,** Saturday from 11:30am to 1:00pm behind the Kilauea Post Office. Everything in the wide-ranging selection is grown or made on Kauai, from rambutan and long beans to sweet potatoes, corn, lettuce, and salsas and chutneys.

Also on the North Shore, about a quarter mile past Hanalei in an area called Waipa, the **Hawaiian Farmers of Hanalei**—anywhere from a dozen to 25 farmers—gather along the main road with their budget-friendly, just-picked produce. This market is held every Tuesday at 2pm. You'll find unbelievably priced papayas (in some seasons, several for a dollar, ready to eat), organic vegetables, inexpensive tropical flowers, avocados and mangoes in season, and, when possible, fresh seafood. The best of the best, in season, are rose apples, mountain apples, and the orange-colored papaya *lilikoi.*

On the south shore, we're hearing great things about the two adorable fruit stands in Lawai, where you can find inexpensive bananas (sometimes $1.25 a hand!), papayas, and avocados along an old country road. The fruit is cheerfully displayed,

Fruity Smoothies & Other Exotic Treats

Fruit stands have sprouted on this island, and smoothies are gaining ground as the milkshake of the new millennium. New crops of exotic trees imported from Southeast Asia are maturing on Kauai, creating anticipation among residents and fruitful ideas for the smoothie world. "Everyone's waiting for the mangosteens and durians," comments Joe Halasey, who, with his wife, Cynthia, runs **Banana Joe's** (© **808/828-1092**), the granddaddy of Kauai's roadside fruit-and-smoothie stands. "They take about 12 years to start bearing, so there are a lot of maturing trees. We're all waiting for the fruit. Rambutans [with a hairy, red exterior and a translucent, litchilike flesh] are good for the farmers here because they're available, and they're a winter fruit. In the summer, mangoes and litchis are always in high demand."

Banana Joe's has been a Kilauea landmark since it opened in 1986 at 52719 Kuhio Hwy., between mile markers 23 and 24 heading north, on the mauka (mountain) side of the street. Sapodilla, star apple (round, purple, and sweet, like a creamy Concord grape), macadamia nuts, Anahola Granola, and homemade breads—like banana and mango-coconut—are among Banana Joe's attractions. The Halaseys have expanded their selection of organic vegetables and exude a quiet aloha from their roadside oasis.

Mangosteens, reputedly the favorite fruit of Queen Victoria, have a creamy, custardy flesh of ambrosial sweetness. When mangosteens start appearing at Hawaii fruit stands, they will no doubt be in high demand, like

and sometimes it's sold on the honor system—leave the money if no one is there. This is country-style nonpareil. (From Kaumualii Hwy., turn at the corner where Mustard's Last Stand is—Lauoho Rd.—then take the first right.) In Kauai jargon, directions would be: "Go to that old road where the old post office was, near Matsuura Store, the old manju place . . . ."

Closer to the resorts, in Poipu, with a view across asparagus fields and the chiseled ridges of Haupu Mountain, the **Poipu Southshore Market** sells produce, some of it by Haupu Growers, daily from 10am to 6pm on Koloa Bypass Road. Haupu Growers is the major supplier of Kauai asparagus, and this is where you'll find it. Asparagus season begins in October.

LIHUE & ENVIRONS

DOWNTOWN LIHUE The gift shop of the **Kauai Museum,** 4428 Rice St. (© **808/245-6931**), is your best bet for made-on-Kauai arts and crafts, from Niihaushell leis to woodwork, lauhala and coconut products, and more. The master of lauhala weaving, Esther Makuaole, weaves regularly in the gallery on Monday and Wednesday from 9am to 1:30pm.

About a mile north of the Lihue Airport, on Highway 56 (Kuhio Hwy.), **Kauai Fruit & Flower** is a great stop for flowers, including the rare Kauai maile in season, coconut drums the owner makes himself, Hawaiian gourds *(ipu),* cut flowers for shipping, and Kauai fruit, such as papayas and pineapples. Other products include lauhala mangoes and litchis during their summer season. In the meantime, Banana Joe's has a hit on its hands with Sugarloaf, the white, nonacidic, ultrasweet, organically grown pineapple popularized on the Big Island. Whether made into smoothies or frostees (frozen fruit put through the Champion juicer), or just sold plain, fresh, and whole, the Sugarloaf is pineapple at its best. For litchi lovers, who must wait for their summer appearance, new varieties such as Kaimana and Brewster are adding to the pleasures of the season. In addition to fresh fruit, fruit smoothies, and frostees, Banana Joe's sells organic greens, tropical-fruit salsas, jams and jellies, drinking coconuts (young coconuts containing delicious drinking water), gift items, and baked goods such as papaya-banana bread. Its top-selling smoothies are papaya, banana, and pineapple.

Mango Mama's, 4660 Hookui St. (© 808/828-1020), is another favorite on the Kilauea roadside. Recently expanded, it's now a full-service cafe serving espresso, smoothies, fresh-squeezed juices, sandwiches, bagels, coffee, coffee smoothies, and fresh fruit. The Sweet Dreams (fresh mango, pineapple, passion fruit, and guava) is a big winner here.

Near the Lihue Airport, Pammie Chock at **Kauai Fruit & Flower** (© 808/ 245-1814; see below) makes a pineapple–passion fruit smoothie that gets my vote as the best on the island.

gift items, teas, Kauai honey, Kauai salad dressings, jams and jellies, and custom-made gift baskets.

In the **Kukui Grove Center,** at Kaumualii Highway (Hwy. 50) and Old Nawiliwili Road, is the **Kauai Products Store** (© 808/246-6753). It's a fount of local handicrafts (about 60% Kauai artists) and a respectable showcase for made-on-the-island products, such as soaps, paintings, clothing, coffee, Kukui guava jams, fabrics, and Niihau-shell leis. The Hawaiian quilts are made in the Philippines but designed by Kauai families. You'll find everything from a $10,750 bronze sculpture to bamboo chairs. Beware of the macadamia-nut fudge, found only at Kauai Products Store: It's rich, sweet, and irresistible. If you are a sandal aficionado, the place to shop is the **Island Sandal Company** in **The Anchor Cover Shopping Center,** Nawiliwili (© 808/246-4424). This is the place for every kind of sandal, from flip-flops to dress sandals, plus they have a huge selection of unusual handbags, sassy hats, and even toe rings.

KILOHANA PLANTATION Kilohana, the 35-acre Tudor-style estate that sprawls across the landscape in Puhi, on Highway 50 between Lihue and Poipu, is an architectural marvel that houses a sprinkling of galleries and shops. At the **Country Store,** on the ground level, you'll find Island and American crafts of decent quality, koa accessories, pottery, and Hawaii-themed gift items. On the other side of Gaylord's, the **Kilohana and Kahn galleries** offer a mix of crafts and two-dimensional art, from originals to affordable prints, at all levels of taste.

THE POIPU RESORT AREA

Expect mostly touristy shops in Poipu, the island's resort mecca; here you'll find T-shirts, souvenirs, black pearls, jewelry, and the usual quota of tired marine art and trite hand-painted silks.

Exceptions: The formerly characterless **Poipu Shopping Village,** at 2360 Kiahuna Plantation Dr., is shaping up to be a serious shopping stop. **Hale Mana** is a glorious collection of hard-to-find gift items of excellent taste: fabulous incense sticks from Provence (lavender, amber, vanilla), antique picture frames, lacquer boxes, beaded bags, unique candles, sterling-silver chopsticks, sake sets, pillows, masks, Hawaiian handmade paper, and jewelry by Kauai artist Adove. The staggering selection also includes dramatic acrylic jewelry that looks like elk horn, one-of-a-kind jewelry and purses by Maya, gemlike sake cups, cotton yukata, silk kimono, snuff bottles, and diaphanous silk dresses that you won't find elsewhere in Hawaii. Also in Poipu Shopping Village, the tiny **Bamboo Lace** boutique lures the fashionistas; its resort wear and accessories can segue from Hawaii to the south of France in one easy heartbeat. Across the courtyard, **Sand People** is great for understated resort wear (such as Tencel jeans) and Indonesian coconut picture frames, while the newly renovated **Overboard** rides the wave of popularity in aloha wear and surf stuff.

The shopping is surprisingly good at the **Grand Hyatt Kauai,** with the footwear mecca **Sandal Tree, Water Wear Hawaii** for swim stuff, **Reyn's** for top-drawer aloha shirts, **Kauai Kids** for the children, and **McInery,** an institution in Hawaii for aloha wear.

Across the street from Poipu Beach, on Hoone Road, **Nukumoi Surf Shop** is a pleasant surprise: an excellent selection of sunglasses, swimwear, surf equipment, and watersports regalia, and not just for the under-20 crowd.

In neighboring **Old Koloa Town,** you'll find everything from **Lappert's Ice Cream** and **Island Soap and Candle Works** (where you can watch them make soap and candles) to **Crazy Shirts** and **Sueoka Store** on Koloa's main drag, Koloa Road. Just walk the long block for gifts, souvenirs, sun wear, groceries, soaps and bath products, and everyday necessities, but don't expect dazzling temptations.

On Poipu Road between Koloa and Poipu, in the tiny Poipu Plaza mini-mall, nestled next to **Sea Sport Divers** and **Outfitters Kauai,** the **Kukuiula Store** is a stop for everything from produce and sushi to paper products, sunscreen, beverages, and groceries. Occasionally, when the fishermen drop by, the store offers fresh sliced sashimi and poke, quite delicious and popular for sunset picnickers and nearby condo residents. In Kalaheo, condo dwellers and locals are flocking to the nondescript, single-building

---

Send a Little Bit of Paradise Home

You can take paradise home with you—well, at least the outrageously beautiful flowers. The best place to order flowers to be sent home is **Tropical Flowers by Charles,** 3465 Lawailoa Lane, Koloa (© **800/699-7984** or 808/332-7984; www.a-tropical-flower.com). Not only is Charles a flower genius (he grows a range of tropical flowers, including some very rare and unusual varieties), but his hardy blooms and his skill at packing mean that your little bit of Kauai will live for a long, long time. All this, and extremely reasonable prices (bouquets start at just $15).

Medeiros Farms, 4365 Papalina Rd. (© **808/332-8211**), for everything they raise and make: chicken, range-fed beef, eggs, Italian pork, and Portuguese sausages. The meats are hailed across the island, and the prices are good. Medeiros Farms chicken is so good it's mentioned on some of the chichi menus on the island.

WESTERN KAUAI

HANAPEPE This West Kauai hamlet is becoming a haven for artists, but finding them requires some vigilance. The center of town is off Highway 50; turn right on Hanapepe Road just after Eleele if you're driving from Lihue. First, you'll smell the sumptuous lavender **Taro Ko Chips Factory** ✪, located in an old green plantation house at 3940 Hanapepe Rd. Cooking in a tiny, modest kitchen at the east end of town, these famous taro chips are handmade by the farmers who grow the taro in a nearby valley. Despite their breakable nature, these chips make great gifts to go. To really impress them back home, get the lihi mung–flavored chips.

Farther on, Hanapepe Road is lined with gift shops and galleries, including **Koa Wood Gallery** and its koa furniture, koa photo albums, and Norfolk pine bowls; and the corny but cherubic **Aloha Angels,** where everything is angel-themed or angel-related. The **Kauai Village Gallery** offers abstract and surreal paintings by Kauai artist Lew Shortridge, while nearby **Kauai Fine Arts** offers an odd mix that works: antique maps and prints of Hawaii, authentic Polynesian tapa, rare wiliwili-seed leis, old Matson liner menus, and a few pieces of contemporary Island art. Down the street, the **Kim Starr Gallery,** showing only Kim Starr's oil paintings, pastels, drawings, and limited-edition graphics, is a strong positive note in Hanapepe's art community. Taking a cue from Maui's Lahaina, where every Friday night is Art Night, Hanapepe's gallery owners and artists recently instituted the **Friday Night Art Walk** every Friday from 6 to 9pm. Gallery owners take turns hosting this informal event along Hanapepe Road.

A great treat to take home is **Kauai Kookies** (© 800/361-1126 or 808/335-5003; www.kauaikookie.com), with the factory outlet at 1–3959 Hwy. 50 in Hanapepe. Choose from eight delicious different kinds of cookies (Kona coffee mac-nut, chocolate chip mac-nut, peanut butter, guava mac-nut, and so on) to ship home, or carry a few around in your car.

WAIMEA Neighboring Waimea is filled more with edibles than art, with Kauai's favorite native supermarket, **Big Save,** serving as the one-stop shop for area residents and passersby heading for the uplands of Kokee State Park, some 4,000 feet above this sea-level village. A cheerful distraction for lovers of Hawaiian collectibles is **Collectibles and Fine Junque,** on Highway 50, next to the fire station on the way to Waimea Canyon. This is where you'll discover what it's like to be the proverbial bull in a china shop (even a knapsack makes it hard to get through the aisles). Heaps of vintage linens, choice aloha shirts and muumuu, rare glassware, books, ceramics, authentic 1950s cotton chenille bedspreads, and a back room full of bargain-priced secondhand goodies always capture my attention. You never know what you'll find in this tiny corner of Waimea.

Up in Kokee State Park, the gift shop of the **Kokee Natural History Museum** (© **808/335-9975**) is *the* stop for botanical, geographical, historical, and nature-related books and gifts, not only on Kauai, but on all the islands. Audubon bird books, hiking maps, and practically every book on Kauai ever written line the shelves.

THE COCONUT COAST

As you make your way from Lihue to the North Shore, you'll pass **Bambulei** (© 808/823-8641), bordering the cane field in Wailua next to Caffè Coco. Watch for the sign just past the Wailua intersection, across from Kintaro's Restaurant. Bambulei houses a charming collection of 1930s and 1940s treasures—everything from Peking lacquerware to exquisite vintage aloha shirts, to lamps, quilts, jewelry, parrot figurines, and zany salt and pepper shakers. If it's not vintage, it will look vintage, and it's bound to be fabulous. Vintage muumuu are often in perfect condition, and dresses go for $20 to $2,000.

Wood turner **Robert Hamada** (© 808/822-3229) works in his studio at the foot of the Sleeping Giant, quietly producing museum-quality works with unique textures and grains. His skill, his lathe, and more than 60 years of experience have brought luminous life to the kou, milo, kauila, camphor, mango, and native woods he logs himself. Hamada was honored by the Kauai Museum in May 2001 when his private collection of woods was displayed in the main lobby in honor of his 80th birthday.

KAPAA   Moving toward Kapaa on Highway 56 (Kuhio Hwy.), don't get your shopping hopes up; until you hit Kapaa town, quality goods are slim in this neck of the woods. The **Coconut Marketplace** features the ubiquitous Elephant Walk gift shop, Gifts of Kauai, and various other underwhelming souvenir and clothing shops sprinkled among the sunglass huts. Our favorite shop here is the unassuming **Overboard,** a small but tasteful boutique with great aloha shirts by Kahala, Tommy Bahama, Duke Kahanamoku, and other top labels for men and women.

Nearby, set back from the main road across from Foodland supermarket, **Marta's Boat** is one of the island's more appealing boutiques for children and women. The shop is a tangle of accessories, toys, chic clothing, and unusual gift items.

In the green-and-white wooden storefronts of nearby **Kauai Village,** you'll find everything from **Wyland Galleries'** trite marine art to *yin chiao* Chinese cold pills and organic produce at **Papayas Natural Foods.** Although its prepared foods are overpriced, Papayas carries the full range of health-food products and is your only choice in the area for vitamins, prepared health foods to go, health-conscious cosmetics, and bulk food items.

Less than a mile away on the main road, the **Waipouli Variety Store** is Kapaa's version of Maui's fabled Hasegawa General Store—a tangle of fishing supplies, T-shirts and thongs, beach towels, and souvenirs. Cookie lovers swear by nearby **Popo's Cookies,** the *ne plus ultra* of store-bought cookies on the island. Popo's chocolate-chip, macadamia-nut, chocolate–macadamia nut, chocolate-coconut, almond, peanut butter, and other varieties of butter-rich cookies are among the most sought-after food items to leave the island.

And Kapaa town is full of surprises. On the main strip, across from Sunnyside Market, you'll find the recently expanded **Kela's Glass Gallery** (© 808/822-4527), the island's showiest showplace for handmade glass in all sizes, shapes, and prices, with the most impressive selection in Hawaii. Go nuts over the vases and studio glass pieces, functional and nonfunctional, and then stroll along this strip of storefronts to **Hula Girl** (© 808/822-1950) and **South China Sea Trading Company** (© 808/823-8655), and see if you can resist their wares. South China's Asian accents make you want to move in for good. You'll find everything from inexpensive bead necklaces to coconut rice paddles and kitchen accessories, to the sumptuous Indonesian silk sarongs, all of high quality and reasonable prices; at their furniture store in the **Kauai**

Design Center (© 808/822-9444), it's mosquito netting to carved doors, to a coconut-inlaid armoire. I love the fragrance of rush and reed, the amber tones of Indonesian, Vietnamese, and Philippine crafts. Meanwhile, at **Hula Girl**, a wonderful whimsy prevails: aloha shirts (very pricey), vintage-looking luggage covered with decals of old Hawaii, Patrice Pendarvis prints, zoris, sunglasses, and shells.

Down the street, **Earth Beads**, on the main drag (Hwy. 56), sells beads, jewelry, gemstones, and craft materials, along with a small selection of gifts and accessories. Across the street is the town's favorite fashion stop, **Island Hemp & Cotton**, where Hawaii's most stylish selection of this miracle fabric is sold: gorgeous silk-hemp dresses, linen-hemp sportswear, hemp aloha shirts, Tencel clothing, T-shirts, and wide-ranging, attractive, and comfortable clothing and accessories that have shed the hippie image. It's also a great store for gift items, from Balinese leather goods to handmade paper, jewelry, luxury soaps, and natural-fiber clothing for men and women. A few doors to the north, **Orchid Alley** gets our vote for most adorable nursery on the island. A narrow alcove opens into a greenhouse of phalaenopsis, oncidiums, dendrobiums, and dozens of brilliant orchid varieties for shipping or hand-carrying.

THE NORTH SHORE

Kauai's North Shore is the premier shopping destination on the island. Stylish, sophisticated galleries and shops, such as **Kong Lung**, in a 1942 Kilauea stone building (the last to be built on the Kilauea Plantation) off Highway 56 on Kilauea Road (© **808/ 828-1822**), have launched these former hippie villages as top-drawer shopping spots. Save your time, energy, and, most of all, discretionary funds for this end of the island. Kong Lung, through all its changes, including pricier merchandise in every category, remains a showcase of design, style, and quality, from top-of-the-line dinnerware and bath products to aloha shirts, jewelry, ceramics, women's wear, stationery, and personal and home accessories. The book selection is fabulous, and the home accessories—sake sets, tea sets, lacquer bowls, hand-blown glass, pottery—are unequaled in Hawaii. It's expensive, but browsing here is a joy.

Directly behind Kong Lung is newcomer **Lotus Gallery** (© **808/828-9898**), a showstopper for lovers of antiques and designer jewelry. Good juju abounds here. The serenity and beauty will envelop you from the moment you remove your shoes to step in the door and onto the bamboo floor. There are gems, crystals, Tibetan art, antiques and sari clothing from India, 12th-century Indian bronzes, temple bells, Oriental rugs, pearl bracelets—items from $30 to $50,000. Owners Kamalia (jewelry designer) and Tsajon Von Lixfeld (gemologist) have a staggering sense of design and discovery that brings to the gallery such things as Brazilian amethyst crystal (immense and complex), emeralds, a fine 100-strand lapis necklace ($4,000), and Kamalia's 18-karat pieces, with clean, elegant lines and gemstones that soothe and elevate.

In Hanalei, at **Ola's**, by the Hanalei River on the Kuhio Highway (Hwy. 560) after the bridge and before the main part of Hanalei town (© **808/826-6937**), Sharon and Doug Britt, an award-winning artist, have amassed a head-turning assortment of American and Island crafts, including Doug's paintings and the one-of-a-kind furniture that he makes out of found objects, driftwood, and used materials. Britt's works—armoires, tables, lamps, bookshelves—often serve as the display surfaces for others' work, so look carefully. Lundberg Studio hand-blown glass, exquisite jewelry, intricately wrought pewter switch plates, sensational hand-blown goblets, and many other fine works fill this tasteful, seductive shop. Be on the lookout for the wonderful koa jewel boxes by local woodworker Tony Lydgate.

From health foods to groceries, to Bakelite jewelry, the **Ching Young Village Shopping Center,** in the heart of Hanalei, covers a lot of bases. It's more funky than fashionable, but Hanalei, until recently, has never been about fashion. People take their time here, and there are always clusters of folks lingering at the few tables outdoors, where tables of Kauai papayas beckon from the entrance of **Hanalei Health and Natural Foods.** Next door, **Hot Rocket** is ablaze with aloha shirts, T-shirts, Reyn Spooner and Jams sportswear, flamingo china, backpacks and pareu, swimwear, and, for collectors, one of the finest collections of Bakelite accessories you're likely to see in the islands.

Next door to Ching Young Village is **On the Road to Hanalei** (✆ **808/826-7360**), worth your time to wander around and check out the unusual T-shirts (great gifts to take home because they don't take up much suitcase space), scarves, pareu, jewelry, and other unique gifts.

Across the street in the **Hanalei Center,** the standout boutique is the **Yellowfish Trading Company** ✯ (✆ **808/826-1227**), where owner Gritt Benton's impeccable eye and zeal for collecting are reflected in the 1920s-to-1940s collectibles: menus, hula-girl nodders, hula lamps, rattan and koa furniture, vases, bark-cloth fabric, retro pottery and lamp bases, must-have vintage textiles, and wonderful finds in books and aloha shirts.

11 Kauai After Dark

Suffice it to say that you don't come to Kauai to trip the light fantastic—this is the island for winding down. But there are a few nightlife options.

As the former plantation community and now county seat, Lihue is a place where local residents live and work. For action after sunset, music, dancing, and bars, the hotels and resorts are the primary players. There are a few local places, but generally all is quiet in Lihue after dark.

The **Coconut MarketPlace,** 4–484 Kuhio Hwy., Kapaa (✆ **808/822-3641**), has a free hula show every Wednesday at 5pm.

The **Kauai Marriott Resort & Beach Club,** 3610 Rice St., Nawiliwili (✆ **808/245-5050**), has a host of nightlife activities, including a torch-lighting ceremony on the beach every Monday and Thursday. **Duke's Canoe Club's Barefoot Bar** (✆ **808/246-9599**) has traditional and contemporary Hawaiian music on Friday nights, when tropical drinks go for $5.50 from 4 to 6pm, when live music stirs up the joint.

In the town of Lihue, **Rob's Good Times Grill,** Rice Shopping Center, 4303 Rice St. (✆ **808/246-0315**), is great for dancing Thursday through Saturday nights, and Sunday to Tuesday they feature karaoke.

The south shore, with the sunset view and miles of white-sand beaches, is a great place for nightlife. At the far end of Poipu, the **Stevenson's Library** at the **Grand Hyatt Kauai Resort & Spa,** 1571 Poipu Rd., Koloa (✆ **808/742-1234;** www.kauai-hyatt.com), is the place for an elegant after-dinner drink with live jazz nightly from 8 to 11pm. Come dressed in resort casual wear (no tank tops or slippers) The koa-lined bar has comfy, overstuffed chairs, a big saltwater aquarium, and various activities like pool or chess. They've recently added Martini and Sushi nights every Friday, Saturday, and Sunday night, with fresh sushi made to order. For literary types, the Stevenson's

Library houses more than 1,000 books, most of which are available to borrow and take back to your room to read.

Also in Poipu, **Keoki's Paradise,** in the Poipu Shopping Village, 2360 Kiahuna Plantation Dr. (© **808/742-7534**), offers live music Monday through Friday evenings (call for times), with the cafe menu available from 11am to 11:30pm. Hawaiian, reggae, and contemporary music draws the 21-and-over dancing crowd.

The **Poipu Shopping Village** also offers free Tahitian dance performances every Tuesday and Thursday at 5pm in the outdoor courtyard.

Down the street at **Sheraton Kauai Resort,** 2440 Hoonani Rd. (© **808/742-1661**), **The Point,** on the water, is the Poipu hot spot. There's live music and dancing Thursday and Saturday, with a range of different artists from contemporary Hawaiian to good ol' rock 'n' roll.

Beyond Poipu, in the old plantation community of Hanapepe, every Friday is **Hanapepe Art Night** from 5 to 9pm. Each one is unique. Participating galleries take turns being the weekly "host gallery," offering original performances or demonstrations, which become the theme for that art night. All the galleries are lit up and decked out, giving the town a special atmosphere. Enjoy a stroll down the streets of quaint, historic Hanapepe Town and meet the local artists. Also in Hanapepe on Friday nights, the **Hanapepe Cafe & Espresso Bar,** 3830 Hanapepe Rd. (© **808/335-5011**), is open for dinner from 6 to 9pm and has live music.

Up on the North Shore, Hanalei has some action, primarily at **Sushi & Blues,** in Ching Young Village (© **808/826-4105**). Reggae, rhythm and blues, rock, and good music by local groups draw dancers and revelers Wednesday, Thursday, and Sunday from 8:30pm on. The format changes often here, so call ahead to see who's playing.

Across the street, the **Hanalei Gourmet,** in the Old Hanalei Schoolhouse, 5–5161 Kuhio Hwy. (© **808/826-2524**), has live music every night except Monday and Thursday. Down the road, **Tahiti Nui** (© **808/826-6277**) is a great place to "experience" old Hawaii. Stop by for an exotic drink and "talk story" with the owner, Louise Marston, who actually is from Tahiti. The restaurant/bar is family-friendly, and there always seems to be someone who drops in and starts singing and playing music, just like in the "old days."

Just down the road, Princeville has several nightlife spots. **Hanalei Bay Resort,** 5380 Honoiki St. (© **808/826-6522;** www.hanaleibayresort.com), is a music lover's gem, with a Sunday Jazz Jam in its **Happy Talk Lounge** from 4 to 7pm, and on Saturday from 7 to 9pm various artists playing light jazz. Al Jarreau and Quincy Jones are among those who have stopped by the Sunday Jazz Jam, and the evening crowd has had its share of well-known Hawaiian jammers.

Over at the **Princeville Resort Kauai,** 5520 Kahaku Rd. (© **808/826-9644;** www.princeville.com), in the main lobby, the **Living Room** (filled with comfy, overstuffed furniture) has a range of nightlife activities, like a Hawaiian ceremony of chanting, dancing, and an entertaining talk on Hawaiian culture, from 6:30 to 7pm on Sunday, and other Island-related entertainment from 7:30 to 10:30pm nightly.

Appendix:
Hawaii in Depth

As the sun rises on the 21st century, other tropical islands are closing in on the 50th state's position as the world's premier beach destination. But Hawaii isn't just another pretty place in the sun. There's an undeniable quality ingrained in the local culture and lifestyle—the quick smiles to strangers, the feeling of family, the automatic extension of courtesy and tolerance. It's the aloha spirit, and you won't find it anywhere else.

1 History 101

Paddling outrigger canoes, the first ancestors of today's Hawaiians followed the stars and birds across the sea to Hawaii, which they called "the land of raging fire." Those first settlers were part of the great Polynesian migration that settled the vast triangle of islands stretching between New Zealand, Easter Island, and Hawaii. No one is sure exactly when they came to Hawaii from Tahiti and the Marquesas Islands, some 2,500 miles to the south, but a bone fish hook found at the southernmost tip of the Big Island has been carbon-dated to A.D. 700. Chants claim that the Mo'okini Heiau, also on the Big Island, was built in A.D. 480.

An entire Hawaiian culture arose from these settlers. Each island became a separate kingdom. The inhabitants built temples, fish ponds, and aqueducts to irrigate taro plantations. Sailors became farmers and fishermen. The *alii* (high-ranking chiefs) created a caste system and established taboos. Ritual human sacrifices were common.

THE "FATAL CATASTROPHE" No ancient Hawaiian ever imagined a *haole* (a white person; literally, one with "no breath") would ever appear on one of these "floating islands." But then one day in 1778, just such a person sailed into Waimea Bay on Kauai, where he was welcomed as the god Lono.

The man was 50-year-old Capt. James Cook, already famous in Britain for "discovering" much of the South Pacific. Now on his third great voyage of exploration, Cook had set sail from Tahiti northward across uncharted waters to find the mythical Northwest Passage that was said to link the Pacific and Atlantic oceans. On his way, Cook stumbled upon the Hawaiian Islands quite by chance. He named them the Sandwich Islands, for the Earl of Sandwich, first lord of the admiralty, who had bankrolled the expedition.

Overnight, stone-age Hawaii entered the age of iron. Nails were traded for fresh water, pigs, and the affections of Hawaiian women. The sailors brought syphilis, measles, and other diseases to which the Hawaiians had no natural immunity, thereby unwittingly wreaking havoc on the native population.

After his unsuccessful attempt to find the Northwest Passage, Cook returned to Kealakekua Bay on the Big Island, where a fight broke out over an alleged theft, and the great navigator was killed by a blow to the head. After this "fatal catastrophe," the British survivors sailed home. But Hawaii was now on the sea charts, and traders on the fur route between Canada and China anchored in Hawaii to get fresh water. More trade—and more disastrous liaisons—ensued.

Two more sea captains left indelible marks on the islands. The first was American John Kendrick, who in 1791 filled his ship with sandalwood and sailed to China. By 1825, Hawaii's sandalwood forests were gone, enabling invasive plants to take charge. The second captain was Englishman George Vancouver, who in 1793 left cows and sheep, which spread out to the high-tide lines. King Kamehameha I sent for cowboys from Mexico and Spain to round up the wild livestock, thus beginning the islands' *paniolo* (cowboy) tradition.

The tightly woven Hawaiian society began to unravel after the death in 1819 of King Kamehameha I, who had used guns seized from a British ship to unite the islands under his rule. One of his successors, Queen Kaahumanu, abolished old taboos and opened the door for religion of another form.

STAYING TO DO WELL   In April 1820, missionaries bent on converting the pagans arrived from New England. The missionaries clothed the natives, banned them from dancing the hula, and nearly dismantled their ancient culture. They tried to keep the whalers and sailors out of the bawdy houses, where a flood of whiskey quenched fleet-size thirsts and the virtue of native women was never safe. They taught reading and writing, created the 12-letter Hawaiian alphabet, started a printing press, and began recording the islands' history, which until then was only an oral account in memorized chants.

Children of the missionaries became the islands' business leaders and politicians. They married Hawaiians and stayed on in the islands, causing one wag to remark that the missionaries "came to do good and stayed to do well." In 1848 King Kamehameha III proclaimed the Great Mahele (division), which enabled commoners and eventually foreigners to own crown land. In two generations,

more than 80% of all private land was in *haole* (foreign) hands. Sugar planters imported waves of immigrants (Chinese starting in 1852, Japanese in 1885, and Portuguese in 1878) to work the fields as contract laborers.

King David Kalakaua was elected to the throne in 1874. This popular "Merrie Monarch" built Iolani Palace in 1882, threw extravagant parties, and lifted the prohibitions on the hula and other native arts. For this, he was much loved. He also gave Pearl Harbor to the United States; it became the westernmost bastion of the U.S. Navy. In 1891 King Kalakaua visited chilly San Francisco, caught a cold, and died in the royal suite of the Sheraton Palace. His sister, Queen Liliuokalani, assumed the throne.

A SAD FAREWELL   On January 17, 1893, a group of American sugar planters and missionary descendants, with the support of U.S. Marines, imprisoned Queen Liliuokalani in her own palace, where she later penned the sorrowful lyric "Aloha Oe," Hawaii's song of farewell. The monarchy was dead.

A new republic was established, controlled by Sanford Dole, a powerful sugar-cane planter. In 1898, through annexation, Hawaii became an American territory ruled by Dole. His fellow sugar-cane planters, known as the Big Five, controlled banking, shipping, hardware, and every other facet of economic life on the islands.

Oahu's central Ewa Plain soon filled with row crops. The Dole family planted pineapple on its vast acreage. Planters imported more contract laborers from Puerto Rico (1900), Korea (1903), and the Philippines (1907–31). Most of the new immigrants stayed on to establish families and become a part of the islands. Meanwhile, the native Hawaiians became a landless minority.

For nearly a century on Hawaii, sugar was king, generously subsidized by the

U.S. government. The sugar planters dominated the territory's economy, shaped its social fabric, and kept the islands in a colonial plantation era with bosses and field hands. But the workers eventually went on strike for higher wages and improved working conditions, and the planters found themselves unable to compete with cheap third-world labor costs.

THE TOURISTS ARRIVE Tourism proper began in the 1860s. Kilauea volcano was one of the world's prime attractions for adventure travelers. In 1865 a grass Volcano House was built on the Halemaumau Crater rim to shelter visitors; it was Hawaii's first tourist hotel. But tourism really got off the ground with the demise of the plantation era.

In 1901 W. C. Peacock built the elegant Beaux Arts Moana Hotel on Waikiki Beach, and W. C. Weedon convinced Honolulu businessmen to bankroll his plan to advertise Hawaii in San Francisco. Armed with a stereopticon and tinted photos of Waikiki, Weedon sailed off in 1902 for 6 months of lecture tours to introduce "those remarkable people and the beautiful lands of Hawaii." He drew packed houses. A tourism promotion bureau was formed in 1903, and about 2,000 visitors came to Hawaii that year.

The steamship was Hawaii's tourism lifeline. It took 4½ days to sail from San Francisco to Honolulu. Streamers, leis, and pomp welcomed each Matson liner at downtown's Aloha Tower. Well-heeled visitors brought trunks, servants, and Rolls-Royces, and stayed for months. Hawaii amused visitors with personal tours, floral parades, and shows spotlighting that naughty dance, the hula.

Beginning in 1935 and running for the next 40 years, Webley Edwards's weekly live radio show, "Hawaii Calls," planted the sounds of Waikiki—surf, sliding steel guitar, sweet Hawaiian harmonies, drumbeats—in the hearts of millions of listeners in the United States, Australia, and Canada.

By 1936, visitors could fly to Honolulu from San Francisco on the *Hawaii Clipper,* a seven-passenger Pan American Martin M-130 flying boat, for $360 one-way. The flight took 21 hours, 33 minutes. Modern tourism was born, with five flying boats providing daily service. The 1941 visitor count was a brisk 31,846 through December 6.

WORLD WAR II & ITS AFTERMATH On December 7, 1941, Japanese Zeros came out of the rising sun to bomb American warships based at Pearl Harbor. This was the "day of infamy" that plunged the United States into World War II.

The attack brought immediate changes to the islands. Martial law was declared, stripping the Big Five cartel of its absolute power in a single day. Japanese Americans and German Americans were interned. Hawaii was "blacked out" at night, Waikiki Beach was strung with barbed wire, and Aloha Tower was painted in camouflage. Only young men bound for the Pacific came to Hawaii during the war years. Many came back to graves in a cemetery called Punchbowl.

The postwar years saw the beginnings of Hawaii's faux culture. Harry Yee invented the Blue Hawaii cocktail and dropped in a tiny Japanese parasol. Vic Bergeron created the mai tai, a drink made of rum and fresh lime juice, and opened Trader Vic's, America's first theme restaurant that featured the art, decor, and food of Polynesia. Arthur Godfrey picked up a ukulele and began singing *hapa-haole* tunes on early TV shows. In 1955 Henry J. Kaiser built the Hilton Hawaiian Village, and the 11-story high-rise Princess Kaiulani Hotel opened on a site where the real princess once played. Hawaii greeted 109,000 visitors that year.

STATEHOOD In 1959 Hawaii became the 50th of the United States. That year also saw the arrival of the first jet airliners, which brought 250,000 tourists to the state. The personal touch that had defined aloha gave way to the sheer force of numbers. Waikiki's room count nearly doubled in 2 years, from 16,000 units in 1969 to 31,000 in 1971, and kept increasing until city fathers finally clamped down on growth. By 1980, annual arrivals had reached four million.

In the early 1980s, the Japanese began traveling overseas in record numbers, and they brought lots of yen to spend. Their effect on sales in Hawaii was phenomenal: European boutiques opened branches in Honolulu, and duty-free shopping became the main supporter of Honolulu International Airport. Japanese investors competed for the chance to own or build part of Hawaii. Hotels sold so fast and at such unbelievable prices that heads began to spin with dollar signs.

In 1986 Hawaii's visitor count passed five million. Two years later, it went over six million. Expensive fantasy megaresorts bloomed on the neighbor islands like giant artificial flowers, swelling the luxury market with ever-swankier accommodations.

The visitor count was at a record 6.7 million in 1990 when the bubble burst in early 1991 with the Gulf War and worldwide recessions. In 1992 Hurricane Iniki devastated Kauai. Airfare wars sent Americans to Mexico and the Caribbean. Overbuilt with luxury hotels, Hawaii slashed its room rates, giving middle-class consumers access to high-end digs at affordable prices—a trend that continues as Hawaii struggles to stay atop the tourism heap.

Hawaii was finally back to record-breaking visitor counts (6.9 million) in 2000. Then September 11, 2001, sent a blow to Hawaii—tourism dropped abruptly, sending Hawaii's economy into a tailspin. But people eventually started traveling again, and in 2003, visitor arrivals were up to 6.3 million. By 2005, Hawaii's economy was recovering, the number of visitors to the state shot up to 6.75 million (continuing record-breaking number of tourists were expected in 2006), business was booming in construction, and real estate sales were higher than ever.

2 Hawaii Today

A CULTURAL RENAISSANCE A conch shell sounds, a young man in a bright feather cape chants, torchlight flickers at sunset on Waikiki Beach, and hula dancers begin telling their graceful centuries-old stories. It's a cultural scene out of the past come to life once again—for Hawaii is enjoying a renaissance of hula, chant, and other aspects of its ancient culture.

The biggest, longest, and most elaborate celebrations of Hawaiian culture are the Aloha Festivals, which encompass more than 500 cultural events from August to October. "Our goal is to teach and share our culture," says Gloriann Akau, who manages the Big Island's Aloha Festivals. "In 1946, after the war, Hawaiians needed an identity. We were lost and needed to regroup. When we started to celebrate our culture, we began to feel proud. We have a wonderful culture that had been buried for a number of years. This brought it out again. Self-esteem is more important than making a lot of money."

In 1985, native Hawaiian educator, author, and *kupuna* (respected elder) George Kanahele started integrating Hawaiian values into hotels like the Big Island's Mauna Lani and Maui's Kaanapali Beach Hotel. "You have the responsibility to preserve and enhance the Hawaiian culture, not because it's going to make money for you, but because it's the right thing to do," Kanahele told the Hawaii Hotel Association. "Ultimately, the only thing unique about Hawaii is its

Hawaiianess. Hawaiianess is our competitive edge."

From general managers to maids, resort employees went through hours of Hawaiian cultural training. They held focus groups to discuss the meaning of aloha—the Hawaiian concept of unconditional love—and applied it to their work and their lives. Now many hotels have joined the movement and instituted Hawaiian programs. No longer content with teaching hula as a joke, resorts now employ a real *kumu hula* (hula teacher) to instruct visitors and have a *kupuna* (elder) take guests on treks to visit *heiau* (temples) and ancient petroglyph sites.

THE QUESTION OF SOVEREIGNTY The Hawaiian cultural renaissance has also made its way into politics. Many *kanaka maoli* (native people) are demanding restoration of rights taken away more than a century ago when the U.S. overthrew the Hawaiian monarchy. Their demands were not lost on President Bill Clinton, who was picketed at a Democratic political fund-raiser at Waikiki Beach in July 1993. Four months later, Clinton signed a document stating that the U.S. Congress "apologizes to Native Hawaiians on behalf of the people of the United States for the overthrow of the Kingdom of Hawaii on January 17, 1893, with the participation of agents and citizens of the United States, and deprivation of the rights of Native Hawaiians to self-determination."

But even neo-nationalists aren't convinced that complete self-determination is possible. Each of the 30 identifiable sovereignty organizations (and more than 100 splinter groups) has a different stated goal, ranging from total independence to nation-within-a-nation status, similar to that of Native Indians. In 1993 the state legislature created a Hawaiian Sovereignty Advisory Commission to "determine the will of the native Hawaiian people." The commission plans to pose the sovereignty question in a referendum open to anyone over 18 with Hawaiian blood, no matter where they live. The question still remains unanswered.

3 Life & Language

Plantations brought so many different people to Hawaii that the state is now a rainbow of ethnic groups: Living here are Caucasians, African Americans, American Indians, Eskimos, Japanese, Chinese, Filipinos, Koreans, Tahitians, Vietnamese, Hawaiians, Samoans, Tongans, and other Asian and Pacific islanders. Add a few Canadians, Dutch, English, French, Germans, Irish, Italians, Portuguese, Scottish, Puerto Ricans, and Spaniards. Everyone's a minority here.

In combination, it's a remarkable potpourri. Many retain an element of the traditions of their homeland. Some Japanese Americans in Hawaii, generations removed from the homeland, are more traditional than the Japanese of Tokyo. And the same is true of many Chinese, Koreans, Filipinos, and others, making Hawaii a kind of living museum of various Asian and Pacific cultures.

THE HAWAIIAN LANGUAGE

Almost everyone here speaks English. But many folks in Hawaii now speak Hawaiian as well. All visitors will hear the words *aloha* and *mahalo* (thank you). If you've just arrived, you're a *malihini*. Someone who's been here a long time is a *kamaaina*. When you finish a job or your meal, you are *pau* (finished). On Friday it's *pau hana*, work finished. You eat *pupu* (Hawaii's version of hors d'oeuvres) when you go *pau hana*.

The Hawaiian alphabet, created by the New England missionaries, has only 12 letters: the five regular vowels (a, e, i, o, and u) and seven consonants (h, k, l, m, n, p, and w). The vowels are pronounced in the Roman fashion: that is, *ah, ay, ee, oh,* and *oo* (as in "too")—not *ay, ee, eye, oh,* and *you,* as in English. For example, *huhu* is pronounced *who-who*. Most vowels are sounded separately, though some are pronounced together, as in Kalakaua: Kah-lah-*cow*-ah.

WHAT *HAOLE* MEANS When Hawaiians first saw Western visitors, they called the pale-skinned, frail men *haole* because they looked so out of breath. In Hawaiian, *ha* means *breath,* and *ole* means an absence of what precedes it. Today the term *haole* is generally a synonym for a Caucasian or foreigner and is used without any intended disrespect. If uttered by an angry stranger who adds certain adjectives (like "stupid"), the term can be construed as a racial slur.

SOME HAWAIIAN WORDS Here are some basic Hawaiian words that you'll often hear in Hawaii and see throughout this book. For a more complete list of Hawaiian words, point your Web browser to www.geocities.com/~olelo/hltableofcontents.html or www.hisurf.com/hawaiian/dictionary.html.

alii Hawaiian royalty
aloha greeting or farewell
halau school
hale house or building
heiau Hawaiian temple or place of worship

kahuna priest or expert
kamaaina old-timer
kapa tapa, bark cloth
kapu taboo, forbidden
keiki child
lanai porch or veranda
lomilomi massage
mahalo thank you
makai a direction, toward the sea
mana spirit power
mauka a direction, toward the mountains
muumuu loose-fitting gown or dress
ono delicious
pali cliff
paniolo Hawaiian cowboy(s)
wiki quick

PIDGIN: 'EH FO'REAL, BRAH
If you venture beyond the tourist areas, you might hear another local tongue: pidgin English, a conglomeration of slang and words from the Hawaiian language. "Broke da mouth" (tastes really good) is the favorite pidgin phrase and one you might hear; "'Eh fo'real, brah" means "It's true, brother." You could be invited to hear an elder "talk story" (relating myths and memories). But because pidgin is really the province of the locals, your visit to Hawaii is likely to pass without your hearing much pidgin at all.

4 A Taste of Hawaii

TRIED & TRUE: HAWAII REGIONAL CUISINE
Peter Merriman, a founding member of Hawaii Regional Cuisine (HRC) and a recipient of the James Beard Award for Best Chef/Northwest/Hawaii (along with George Mavrothalassitis of Chef Mavro Restaurant), describes the current trend in Hawaii as a refinement, a tweaking upward, of everything from fine dining to down-home local cooking. This means sesame- or nori-crusted fresh catch on plate-lunch menus, and huli-huli chicken at five-diamond eateries, paired with Beaujolais and leeks and gourmet long rice.

At the same time, says Merriman, HRC, the style of cooking that put Hawaii on the international culinary map, has become watered down, a buzzword: "A lot of restaurants are paying lip service."

As it is with things au courant, it is easy to make a claim but another thing to live up to it. As Merriman points out, HRC was never solely about technique; it is equally about ingredients and the chef's creativity and integrity. "We continue to get local inspiration," says Merriman. "We've never restricted ourselves." If there is a fabulous French or Thai dish, chefs like Merriman will prepare it with local ingredients and add a creative edge that makes it distinctively Hawaii Regional.

HRC was established in the mid-1980s in a culinary revolution that catapulted Hawaii into the global epicurean arena. The international training, creative vigor, fresh ingredients, and cross-cultural menus of the 12 original HRC chefs have made the islands a dining destination applauded nationwide. (In a tip of the toque to island tradition, *ahi*—a word ubiquitous in Hawaii—has replaced *tuna* on many chic New York menus.)

While in Hawaii, you'll encounter many labels that embrace the fundamentals of HRC and the sophistication, informality, and nostalgia it encompasses. Euro-Asian, Pacific Rim, Indo-Pacific, Euro-Pacific, fusion cuisine—by whatever name, Hawaii Regional Cuisine has evolved as Hawaii's singular cooking style. It highlights the fresh seafood and produce of Hawaii's rich waters and volcanic soil, the cultural traditions of Hawaii's ethnic groups, and the skills of well-trained chefs, who broke ranks with their European predecessors to forge new ground in the 50th state.

Fresh ingredients are foremost here. Farmers and fishermen work together to provide steady supplies of just-harvested seafood, seaweed, fern shoots, vine-ripened tomatoes, goat cheese, lamb, herbs, taro, gourmet lettuces, and countless harvests from land and sea. These ingredients wind up in myriad forms on ever-changing menus, prepared in Asian and Western culinary styles. Exotic fruits introduced by recent Southeast Asian emigrants—such as sapodilla, soursop, and rambutan—are beginning to appear regularly in Chinatown markets. Aquacultured seafood, from seaweed to salmon to lobster, is a staple on many menus. Additionally, fresh-fruit sauces (mango, litchi, papaya, pineapple, guava), ginger-sesame-wasabi flavorings, sake sauces, tamarind and fish sauces, coconut-chile accents, tropical-fruit vinaigrettes, and other local and newly arrived seasonings from Southeast Asia and the Pacific impart unique qualities to the preparations.

Here's a sampling of what you can expect to find on a Hawaii Regional menu: seared Hawaiian fish with *lilikoi* shrimp butter; taro-crab cakes; Pahoa corn cakes; Molokai sweet-potato or breadfruit vichyssoise; Ka'u orange sauce and Kahua Ranch lamb; fern shoots from Waipio Valley; Maui onion soup and Hawaiian bouillabaisse, with fresh snapper, Kona crab, and fresh aquacultured shrimp; blackened ahi summer rolls; herb-crusted onaga; and gourmet Waimanalo greens, picked that day. You may also encounter locally made cheeses, squash and taro risottos, Polynesian imu-baked foods, and guava-smoked meats. If there's pasta or risotto or rack of lamb on the menu, it could be nori (red algae) linguine with opihi (limpet) sauce, or risotto with local seafood served in taro cups, or rack of lamb in cabernet and hoisin sauce (fermented soybean, garlic, and spices). Watch for ponzu sauce, too; it's lemony and zesty, much more flavorful than the soy sauce it resembles.

PLATE LUNCHES & MORE: LOCAL FOOD

At the other end of the spectrum is the vast and endearing world of "local food." By that I mean plate lunches and poke, shave ice and saimin, bento lunches and manapua—cultural hybrids all.

Reflecting a polyglot population of many styles and ethnicities, Hawaii's idiosyncratic dining scene is eminently inclusive. Consider Surfer Chic: Barefoot in the sand, in a swimsuit, you chow down on a **plate lunch** ordered from a lunch wagon, consisting of fried mahimahi, "two scoops rice," macaroni salad, and a few leaves of green, typically julienned cabbage. (Generally, teriyaki beef and shoyu chicken are options.) Heavy gravy is often the condiment of choice, accompanied by a soft drink in a paper cup or straight out of the can. Like **saimin**—the local version of noodles in broth topped with scrambled eggs, green onions, and sometimes pork—the plate lunch is Hawaii's version of high camp.

But it was only a matter of time before the humble plate lunch became a culinary icon in Hawaii. These days, even the most chichi restaurant has a version of this modest Island symbol (not at plate-lunch prices, of course), while vendors selling the real thing—carb-driven meals served from wagons—have queues that never end.

Because this is Hawaii, at least a few licks of poi—cooked, pounded taro (the traditional Hawaiian staple crop)—are a must. Other **native foods** include those from before and after Western contact, such as *laulau* (pork, chicken, or fish steamed in ti leaves), *kalua* pork (pork cooked in a Polynesian underground oven known here as an imu), lomi salmon (salted salmon with tomatoes and green onions), squid luau (cooked in coconut milk and taro tops), poke (cubed raw fish seasoned with onions and seaweed and the occasional sprinkling of roasted kukui nuts), haupia (creamy coconut pudding), and *kulolo* (steamed pudding of coconut, brown sugar, and taro).

Bento, another popular quick meal available throughout Hawaii, is a compact, boxed assortment of picnic fare usually consisting of neatly arranged sections of rice, pickled vegetables, and fried chicken, beef, or pork. Increasingly, however, the bento is becoming more health conscious, as in macrobiotic or vegetarian brown-rice bentos. A derivative of the modest lunch box for Japanese immigrants who once labored in the sugar and pineapple fields, bentos are dispensed everywhere, from department stores to corner delis and supermarkets.

Also from the plantations come **manapua,** a bready, doughy sphere filled with tasty fillings of sweetened pork or sweet beans. In the old days, the Chinese "manapua man" would make his rounds with bamboo containers balanced on a rod over his shoulders. Today you'll find white or whole-wheat manapua containing chicken, vegetables, curry, and other savory fillings.

The daintier Chinese delicacy **dim sum** is made of translucent wrappers filled with fresh seafood, pork hash, and vegetables, served for breakfast and lunch in Chinatown restaurants. The Hong Kong–style dumplings are ordered fresh and hot from bamboo steamers rolled on carts from table to table. Much like hailing a taxi in Manhattan, you have to be quick and loud for dim sum.

For dessert or a snack, particularly on Oahu's North Shore, the prevailing choice is **shave ice,** the island version of a snow cone. Particularly on hot, humid days, long lines of shave-ice lovers gather for heaps of finely shaved ice topped with sweet tropical syrups. (The sweet-sour *li hing mui* flavor is a current favorite.) The fast-melting mounds, which require prompt, efficient consumption, are quite the local summer ritual for sweet tooths. Aficionados order shave ice with ice cream and sweetened adzuki beans plopped in the middle.

AHI, ONO & OPAKAPAKA: A HAWAIIAN SEAFOOD PRIMER

The seafood in Hawaii has been described as the best in the world. And why not?

Without a doubt, the islands' surrounding waters, including the waters of the remote northwestern Hawaiian Islands, and a growing aquaculture industry contribute to the high quality of the seafood here.

The reputable restaurants in Hawaii buy fresh fish daily at predawn auctions or from local fishermen. Some chefs even catch their ingredients themselves. "Still wiggling" and "just off the hook" are the ultimate terms for freshness in Hawaii.

Although some menus include the Western description for the fresh fish used, most often the local nomenclature is listed, turning dinner for the uninitiated into a confusing, quasiforeign experience. To help familiarize you with the menu language of Hawaii, here's a basic glossary of island fish:

ahi   yellowfin or big-eye tuna, important for its use in sashimi and poke at sushi bars and in Hawaii Regional Cuisine

aku   skipjack tuna, heavily used by local families in home cooking and poke

ehu   red snapper, delicate and sumptuous, yet lesser known than opakapaka

hapuupuu   grouper, a sea bass whose use is expanding

hebi   spearfish, mildly flavored, and frequently featured as the "catch of the day" in upscale restaurants

kajiki   Pacific blue marlin, also called *au,* with a firm flesh and high fat content that make it a plausible substitute for tuna

kumu   goatfish, a luxury item on Chinese and upscale menus, served *en*

papillote or steamed whole, Oriental style, with scallions, ginger, and garlic

mahimahi   dolphin fish (the game fish, not the mammal) or dorado, a classic sweet, white-fleshed fish requiring vigilance among purists because it's often disguised as fresh when it's actually "fresh-frozen"—a big difference

monchong   bigscale or sickle pomfret, an exotic, tasty fish, scarce but gaining a higher profile on Hawaiian Island menus

nairagi   striped marlin, also called *au;* good as sashimi and in poke, and often substituted for ahi in raw-fish products

onaga   ruby snapper, a luxury fish, versatile, moist, and flaky

ono   wahoo, firmer and drier than the snappers, often served grilled and in sandwiches

opah   moonfish, rich and fatty, and versatile—cooked, raw, smoked, and broiled

opakapaka   pink snapper, light, flaky, and luxurious, suited for sashimi, poaching, sautéing, and baking; the best-known upscale fish

papio   jack trevally, light, firm, and flavorful and favored in island cookery

shutome   broadbill swordfish, of beeflike texture and rich flavor

tombo   albacore tuna, with a high fat content, suitable for grilling

uhu   parrotfish, most often encountered steamed, Chinese style

uku   gray snapper of clear, pale-pink flesh, delicately flavored and moist

ulua   large jack trevally, firm-fleshed and versatile

5 The Natural World: An Environmental Guide to the Islands

The first Hawaiian islands were born of violent volcanic eruptions that took place deep beneath the ocean's surface about 70 million years ago—more than 200 million years after the major continental land masses had been formed. As soon as the islands emerged, Mother Nature's fury began to carve beauty from barren rock.

Untiring volcanoes spewed forth rivers of fire that cooled into stone. Severe tropical storms, some with hurricane-force winds, battered and blasted the cooling lava rock into a series of shapes. Ferocious earthquakes flattened, shattered, and reshaped the islands into precipitous valleys, jagged cliffs, and recumbent flatlands. Monstrous surf and gigantic tidal waves rearranged and polished the lands above and below the reaches of the tide.

It took millions of years for nature to shape the familiar form of Diamond Head on Oahu, Maui's majestic peak of Haleakala, the waterfalls of Molokai's northern side, the reefs of Hulopoe Bay on Lanai, and the lush rainforests of the Big Island. The result is an island chain like no other—a tropical dreamscape of a landscape rich in flora and fauna, surrounded by a vibrant underwater world.

THE FLORA OF THE ISLANDS

Hawaii is filled with sweet-smelling flowers, lush vegetation, and exotic plant life.

AFRICAN TULIP TREES   Even from afar, you can see the flaming red flowers on these large trees, which can grow to be more than 50 feet tall. The buds hold water, and Hawaiian children use the flowers as water pistols.

ANGEL'S TRUMPETS   These small trees can grow up to 20 feet tall, with an abundance of large (up to 10 in. diameter) pendants—white or pink flowers that resemble, well, trumpets. The Hawaiians call them *nana-honua,* which means "earth gazing." The flowers, which bloom continually from early spring to late fall, have a musky scent. *Warning:* All parts of the plant are poisonous and contain a strong narcotic.

ANTHURIUMS   Anthuriums originally came from the tropical Americas and the Caribbean islands. There are more than 550 species, but the most popular are the heart-shaped red, orange, pink, white, and purple flowers with tail-like spathes.

Look for the heart-shaped green leaves in shaded areas. These exotic plants have no scent but will last several weeks as cut flowers. Anthuriums are particularly prevalent on the Big Island.

BANYAN TREES   Among the world's largest trees, banyans have branches that grow out and away from the trunk, forming descending roots that grow down to the ground to feed and form additional trunks, making the tree very stable during tropical storms. The banyan in the courtyard next to the old Court House in Lahaina, Maui, is an excellent example of a spreading banyan—it covers ⅔ acre.

BIRDS OF PARADISE   These natives of Africa have become something of a trademark of Hawaii. They're easily recognizable by the orange and blue flowers nestled in gray-green bracts, looking somewhat like birds in flight.

BOUGAINVILLEA   Originally from Brazil, these vines feature colorful, tissue-thin bracts, ranging in color from majestic purple to fiery orange, that hide tiny white flowers. A good place to spot them is on the Big Island, along the Queen Kaahumanu Highway stretching from Kona Airport to Kailua-Kona.

BREADFRUIT TREES   A large tree—more than 60 feet tall—with broad, sculpted, dark-green leaves, the famous breadfruit produces a round, head-size green fruit that's a staple in the diets of all Polynesians. When roasted or baked, the whitish-yellow meat tastes somewhat like a sweet potato.

BROMELIADS   There are more than 1,400 species of bromeliads, of which the pineapple plant is the best known. "Bromes," as they're affectionately called, are generally spiky plants ranging in size from a few inches to several feet in diameter. They're popular not only for their unusual foliage, but also for their strange and wonderful flowers. Used widely in landscaping and interior decoration, especially in resort areas, bromeliads are found on every island.

COFFEE   Hawaii is the only state that produces coffee commercially. Coffee is an evergreen shrub with shiny, waxy, dark-green, pointed leaves. The flower is a small, fragrant white blossom that develops into ½-inch berries that turn bright red when ripe. Look for coffee at elevations above 1,500 feet on the Kona side of the Big Island and on large coffee plantations on Kauai, Molokai, Oahu, and Maui.

GINGER   White and yellow ginger flowers are perhaps the most fragrant in Hawaii. Usually found in clumps growing 4 to 7 feet tall in areas blessed by rain, these sweet-smelling, 3-inch-wide flowers are composed of three dainty petal-like stamens and three long, thin petals. Ginger was introduced to Hawaii in the 19th century from the Indonesia-Malaysia area. Look for white and yellow ginger from late spring to fall. If you see ginger on the side of the road, stop and pick a few blossoms—your car will be filled with a divine fragrance the rest of the day.

Other members of the ginger family frequently seen in Hawaii include red, shell, and torch ginger. Red ginger consists of tall green stalks with foot-long red "flower heads." The red "petals" are actually bracts, which protect the 1-inch-long white flowers. Red ginger, which does not share the heavenly smell of white ginger, lasts a week or longer when cut. Look for red ginger from spring through late fall. Shell ginger, which originated in India and Burma, thrives in cool, wet mountain forests. These plants, with their pearly white, clamshell-like blossoms, bloom from spring to fall.

Perhaps the most exotic ginger is the red or pink torch ginger. Cultivated in Malaysia as seasoning, torch ginger rises directly out of the ground. The flower stalks, which are about 5 to 8 inches in length, resemble the fire of a lighted torch. This is one of the few types of ginger that can bloom year-round.

HELICONIA   Some 80 species of the colorful heliconia family came to Hawaii from the Caribbean and Central and South America. The bright yellow, red, green, and orange bracts overlap and appear to unfold like origami birds. The most obvious heliconia to spot is the lobster claw, which resembles a string of boiled crustacean pincers. Another prolific heliconia is the parrot's beak: Growing to about hip height, it's composed of bright-orange flower bracts with black tips. Look for parrot's beaks in spring and summer.

HIBISCUS   The 4- to 6-inch hibiscus flowers bloom year-round and come in a range of colors, from lily white to lipstick red. The flowers resemble crepe paper, with stamens and pistils protruding spire-like from the center. Hibiscus hedges can grow up to 15 feet tall. The yellow hibiscus is Hawaii's official state flower.

JACARANDA   Beginning around March and sometimes lasting until early May, these huge lacy-leaved trees metamorphose into large clusters of spectacular lavender-blue sprays. The bell-shaped flowers drop quickly, leaving a majestic purple carpet beneath the tree.

MACADAMIA   A transplant from Australia, macadamia nuts have become a commercial crop in recent decades in Hawaii, especially on the Big Island and Maui. The large trees—up to 60 feet tall—bear a hard-shelled nut encased in a leathery husk, which splits open and dries when the nut is ripe.

MONKEYPOD TREES   The monkeypod is one of Hawaii's most majestic trees; it grows more than 80 feet tall and 100 feet across. Seen near older homes and in parks, the leaves of the monkeypod drop in February and March. Its wood is a favorite of woodworking artisans.

NIGHT-BLOOMING CEREUS   Look along rock walls for this spectacular night-blooming flower. Originally from Central America, this vinelike member of the cactus family has green scalloped edges and produces foot-long white flowers that open as darkness falls and wither as the sun rises. The plant also bears an edible red fruit.

ORCHIDS   To many minds, nothing says Hawaii more than orchids. The most widely grown variety—and the major source of flowers for leis and garnish for tropical libations—is the vanda orchid. The vandas used in Hawaii's commercial flower industry are generally lavender or white, but they grow in a rainbow of colors, shapes, and sizes. The orchids used for corsages are the large, delicate cattleya; the ones used in floral arrangements—you'll probably see them in your hotel lobby—are usually dendrobiums. On the Big Island, don't pass up a chance to wander through the numerous orchid farms around Hilo.

PANDANUS (HALA)   Called *hala* by Hawaiians, pandanus is native to Polynesia. Thanks to its thick trunk, stiltlike supporting roots, and crown of long, swordlike leaves, the hala tree is easy to recognize. In what is quickly becoming a dying art, Hawaiians weave the *lau* (leaves) of the hala into hats, baskets, mats, bags, and the like.

PLUMERIA   Also known as frangipani, this sweet-smelling, five-petal flower, found in clusters on trees, is the most popular choice of lei makers. The Singapore plumeria has five creamy-white petals, with a touch of yellow in the center. Another popular variety, ruba—with flowers from soft pink to flaming red—is also used in leis. When picking plumeria, be careful of the sap from the flower—it's poisonous and can stain clothes.

PROTEA   Originally from South Africa, this unusual oversize shrub comes in more than 40 different varieties. The flowers of one species resemble pincushions; those of another look like a bouquet of feathers. Once dried, proteas will last for years.

SILVERSWORD   This very uncommon and unusual plant is seen only on the Big Island and in the Haleakala Crater on Maui. This rare relative of the sunflower family blooms between July and September. The silversword in bloom is a fountain of red-petaled, daisylike flowers that turn silver soon after blooming.

TARO   Around pools, near streams, and in neatly planted fields, you'll see these green heart-shaped leaves, whose dense roots are a Polynesian staple. The ancient Hawaiians pounded the roots into poi. Originally from Sri Lanka, taro is not only a food crop, but is also grown for ornamental reasons.

THE FAUNA OF THE ISLANDS

When the first Polynesians arrived in Hawaii between A.D. 500 and 800, scientists say they found some 67 varieties of endemic Hawaiian birds, a third of which are now believed to be extinct. They did not find any reptiles, amphibians, mosquitoes, lice, fleas, or even a cockroach.

There were only two endemic mammals: the hoary bat and the monk seal. The **hoary bat** must have accidentally blown to Hawaii at some point, from either North or South America. It can still be seen during its early evening forays, especially around the Kilauea Crater on the Big Island.

The **Hawaiian monk seal,** a relative of warm-water seals found in the Caribbean and the Mediterranean, was nearly slaughtered into extinction for its skin and oil during the 19th century. These seals have recently experienced a minor population explosion; sometimes they even turn up at various beaches throughout the state. They're protected under federal law by the Marine Mammals Protection Act. If you're fortunate enough to see a monk

636 APPENDIX · HAWAII IN DEPTH

Leapin' Lizards!

Geckos are harmless, soft-skinned, insect-eating lizards that come equipped with suction pads on their feet, enabling them to climb walls and windows to reach tasty insects such as mosquitoes and cockroaches. You'll see them on windows outside a lighted room at night or hear their cheerful chirp.

---

seal, just look; don't disturb one of Hawaii's living treasures.

The first Polynesians brought a few animals from home: dogs, pigs, and chickens (all were for eating), as well as rats (stowaways). All four species are still found in the Hawaiian wild today.

BIRDS

More species of native birds have become extinct in Hawaii in the last 200 years than anywhere else on the planet. Of 67 native species, 23 are extinct and 30 are endangered. Even the Hawaiian crow, the **alala,** is threatened.

The **aeo,** or Hawaiian stilt—a 16-inch-long bird with a black head, black coat, white underside, and long pink legs—can be found in protected wetlands like the Kanaha Wildlife Sanctuary on Maui (where it shares its natural habitat with the Hawaiian coot), the Kealia Pond on Maui, and the Hanalei National Wildlife Refuge on Kauai, which is also home to the Hawaiian duck. Other areas in which you can see protected birds are the Kipuku Puaulu (Bird Park) and the Olaa Rain Forest, both in Hawaii Volcanoes National Park on the Big Island, and at Goat Island bird refuge off Oahu, where you can see wedge-tailed shearwaters nesting.

Another great birding venue is Kokee State Park on Kauai. Various native birds that have been spotted include some of the 22 species of the native honey creepers. Frequently seen are the **apapane** (a red bird with black wings and a curved black bill), **iiwi** (also red with black wings but with orange legs and a salmon-colored bill), **amakihi** (a plain olive-green

bird with a long, straight bill), and **anianiau** (a tiny yellow bird with a thin, curved bill). Also in the forest is the **elepaio,** a small gray flycatcher with an orange breast and an erect tail. The most common native bird at Kokee—and the most easily seen—is the **moa,** or red jungle fowl, a chicken brought to Hawaii by the Polynesians.

To get a good glimpse of the seabirds that frequent Hawaii, drive to Kilauea Point on Kauai's north shore. Here you can easily spot **red-** and **white-footed boobies, wedge-tailed shearwaters, frigate birds, red-tailed tropic birds,** and the **Laysan albatross.**

The **nene** is Hawaii's state bird. It's being brought back from the brink of extinction through strenuous protection laws and captive breeding. A relative of the Canada goose, the nene stands about 2 feet high and has a black head and yellow cheeks. The approximately 500 nenes in existence can be seen in only three places: at Haleakala National Park on Maui, at Mauna Kea State Park bird sanctuary, and on the slopes of Mauna Kea on the Big Island.

The Hawaiian short-eared owl, the **pueo,** which grows to between 12 and 17 inches, can be seen at dawn and dusk on Kauai, Maui, and the Big Island. According to legend, spotting a pueo is a good omen.

SEA LIFE

Approximately 680 species of fish are known to inhabit the waters around the Hawaiian Islands. Of those, approximately 450 species stay close to the reef and inshore areas.

CORAL The reefs surrounding Hawaii are made up of various coral and algae. The living coral grows through sunlight that feeds a specialized algae, which, in turn, allows the development of the coral's calcareous skeleton. The reef, which takes thousands of years to develop, attracts and supports fish and crustaceans, which use it for food and habitat. Mother Nature can batter the reef with a strong storm, but humans have proven far more destructive.

The corals most frequently seen in Hawaii are hard, rocklike formations named for their familiar shapes: antler, cauliflower, finger, plate, and razor coral. Some coral appears soft, such as tube coral; it can be found in the ceilings of caves. Black coral, which resembles winter-bare trees or shrubs, is found at depths of more than 100 feet.

REEF FISH Of the approximately 450 types of reef fish here, about 27% are native to Hawaii and are found nowhere else in the world. During the millions of years it took for the islands to sprout up from the sea, ocean currents—mainly from Southeast Asia—carried thousands of marine animals and plants to Hawaii's reef; of those, approximately 100 species adapted and thrived. You're likely to spot one or more of the following fish while underwater:

Angelfish can be distinguished by the spine, located low on the gill plate. These fish are very shy; several species live in colonies close to coral.

Blennies are small, elongated fish, ranging from 2 to 10 inches long, with the majority in the 3- to 4-inch range. Blennies are so small that they can live in tide pools; you might have a hard time spotting one.

Butterfly fish, among the most colorful of the reef fish, are usually seen in pairs (scientists believe they mate for life) and appear to spend most of their day feeding. There are 22 species of butterfly fish, of which three (bluestripe, lemon or milletseed, and multiband or pebbled butterfly fish) are endemic. Most butterfly fish have a dark band through the eye and a spot near the tail resembling an eye, meant to confuse their predators (moray eels love to lunch on them).

Moray and **conger eels** are the most common eels seen in Hawaii. Morays are usually docile except when provoked or when there's food around. Unfortunately, some morays have been fed by divers and now associate divers with food; thus, they can become aggressive. But most morays like to keep to themselves. While morays may look menacing, conger eels look downright happy, with big lips and pectoral fins (situated so that they look like big ears) that give them the appearance of a perpetually smiling face. Conger eels have crushing teeth so they can feed on crustaceans; because they're sloppy eaters, they usually live with shrimp and crabs that feed off the crumbs they leave.

Parrotfish, one of the largest and most colorful of the reef fish, can grow up to 40 inches long. They're easy to spot—their front teeth are fused together, protruding like buck teeth that allow them to feed by scraping algae from rocks and coral. The rocks and coral pass through the parrotfish's system, resulting in fine sand. In fact, most of the white sand found in Hawaii is parrotfish waste; one large parrotfish can produce a ton of sand a year. Native parrotfish species include yellowbar, regal, and spectacled.

Scorpion fish are what scientists call "ambush predators": They hide under camouflaged exteriors and ambush their prey. Several kinds sport a venomous dorsal spine. These fish don't have a gas bladder, so when they stop swimming, they sink—that's why you usually find them "resting" on ledges and on the ocean bottom. They're not aggressive, but be very careful where you put your hands and feet in the water so as to avoid those venomous spines.

Surgeonfish, sometimes called *tang,* get their name from the scalpel-like spines located on each side of the body near the base of the tail. Several surgeonfish, such as the brightly colored yellow tang, are boldly colored; others are adorned in more conservative shades of gray, brown, or black. The only endemic surgeonfish—and the most abundant in Hawaiian waters—is the convict tang, a pale white fish with vertical black stripes (like a convict's uniform).

Wrasses are a very diverse family of fish, ranging in length from 2 to 15 inches. Wrasses can change gender from female to male. Some have brilliant coloration that changes as they age. Several types of wrasse are endemic to Hawaii: Hawaiian cleaner, shortnose, belted, and gray (or old woman).

GAME FISH Hawaii is known around the globe as *the* place for big-game fish—marlin, swordfish, and tuna. Six kinds of **billfish** are found in the offshore waters around the islands: Pacific blue marlin, black marlin, sailfish, broadbill swordfish, striped marlin, and shortbill spearfish. Hawaii billfish range in size from the 20-pound shortbill spearfish and striped marlin to the 1,805-pound Pacific blue marlin, the largest marlin ever caught with rod and reel in the world.

Tuna ranges in size from small (1 lb. or less) mackerel tuna used as bait (Hawaiians call them *oioi*) to 250-pound yellowfin ahi tuna. Other local species of tuna are big-eye, albacore, kawakawa, and skipjack.

Other types of fish, also excellent for eating, include **mahimahi** (also known as dolphin fish or dorado), in the 20- to 70-pound range; **rainbow runner,** from 15 to 30 pounds; and **wahoo** (ono), from 15 to 80 pounds. Shoreline fishermen are always on the lookout for **trevally** (the state record for a giant trevally is 191 lb.), **bonefish, ladyfish, threadfin, leatherfish,** and **goatfish.** Bottom fishermen pursue a range of **snapper**—red, pink, gray, and others—as well as **sea bass** (the state record is a whopping 563 lb.) and **amberjack** (which weigh up to 100 lb.).

WHALES Humpback whales are popular visitors who come to Hawaii to mate and calve every year, beginning in November and staying until spring (Apr or so), when they return to Alaska. On every island, you can take winter whale-watching cruises that will let you observe these magnificent leviathans up close. You can also spot them from shore—humpbacks grow to up to 45 feet long, so when one breaches (jumps out of the water), you can see it for miles.

Humpbacks are among the biggest whales found in Hawaiian waters, but other whales—such as pilot, sperm, false killer, melon-headed, pygmy killer, and beaked—can be seen year-round, especially in the calm waters off the Big Island's Kona Coast.

SHARKS Yes, there *are* sharks in Hawaii, but you more than likely won't see one unless you're specifically looking. About 40 different species of sharks inhabit the waters surrounding Hawaii, ranging from the totally harmless whale shark (at 60 ft., the world's largest fish), which has no teeth and is so docile that it frequently lets divers ride on its back, to the not-so-docile, extremely uncommon great white shark. The most common sharks seen in Hawaii are white-tip or gray reef sharks (about 5 ft. long) and black-tip reef sharks (about 6 ft. long).

HAWAII'S ECOSYSTEM PROBLEMS

Officials at Hawaii Volcanoes National Park on the Big Island saw a potential problem a few decades ago with people taking a few rocks home with them as "souvenirs." To prevent this problem from escalating, the park rangers created a legend that the fiery volcano goddess, Pele, would punish these souvenir-seekers with bad luck. There used to be a display case in the park's visitor center filled with letters from people who had taken rocks from the volcano, relating stories of all the bad luck that followed. Most begged Pele's forgiveness and instructed the rangers to please return the rock to the exact location that was its original home.

Unfortunately, Hawaii's other ecosystem problems can't be handled as easily.

MARINE LIFE   Hawaii's beautiful and abundant marine life has attracted so many visitors that they threaten to overwhelm it. A great example of this is Oahu's beautiful **Hanauma Bay.** Crowds flock to this marine preserve, which features calm, protected swimming and snorkeling areas loaded with tropical reef fish. Its popularity forced government officials to limit admissions and charge an entrance fee. Commercial tour operators have also been restricted.

Another marine-life conservation area that suffers from overuse is **Molokini,** a small crater off the coast of Maui. Twenty-five years ago, one or two small six-passenger boats made the trip once a day to Molokini; today it's not uncommon to sight 20 or more boats, each carrying 20 to 49 passengers, moored inside the tiny crater. One tour operator has claimed that, on some days, it's so crowded that you can actually see a slick of suntan oil floating on the surface of the water.

Hawaii's **reefs** have faced increasing impact over the years as well. Runoff of soil and chemicals from construction, agriculture, and erosion can blanket and choke a reef, which needs sunlight to survive. Human contact with the reef can also upset the ecosystem. Coral, the basis of the reef system, is very fragile; snorkelers and divers grabbing onto it can break off pieces that took decades to form. Feeding the fish can also upset the balance of the ecosystem (not to mention

upsetting the digestive systems of the fish). In areas where they're fed, the normally shy reef fish become more aggressive, surrounding divers and demanding food.

FLORA   The rainforests are among Hawaii's most fragile environments. Any intrusion—from hikers carrying seeds on their shoes to the rooting of wild boars— can upset the delicate balance of these complete ecosystems. In recent years, development has moved closer and closer to the rainforests. On the Big Island, people have protested the invasion of bulldozers and the drilling of geothermal wells in the Wao Kele O Puna rainforest for years.

FAUNA   The biggest impact on the fauna in Hawaii is the decimation of native birds by feral animals, which have destroyed the bird's habitats, and by mongooses that have eaten the birds' eggs and young. Government officials are vigilant about snakes because of the potential damage they can do to the remaining bird life.

A recent pest introduced to Hawaii is the coqui frog. That loud noise you hear after dark especially on the eastern side of the Big Island and various parts of Maui, including the Kapalua Resort area and on the windward side of the island, is the cry of the male coqui frog looking for a mate. A native of Puerto Rica, where the frogs are kept in check by snakes, the coqui frog came to Hawaii in some plant material, found no natural enemies, and has spread across the Big Island and Maui. A chorus of several hundred coqui frogs is deafening (it's been measured at 163 decibels, or the noise level of a jet engine from 100 feet). In some places, like Akaka Falls, on the Big Island, there are so many frogs that they now are chirping during daylight hours.

6 Recommended Reading

In addition to the books discussed below, those planning an extended trip to Hawaii should check out *Frommer's Maui 2008; Frommer's Honolulu, Waikiki & Oahu; Frommer's Kauai; Frommer's Maui Day by Day; Frommer's Honolulu & Oahu Day by Day;* and *Frommer's Hawaii with Kids* (all published by Wiley Publishing, Inc.).

FICTION

The first book people think about is James A. Michener's *Hawaii* (Fawcett Crest, 1974). This epic novel manages to put the island's history into chronological order, but remember, it is still fiction, and very sanitized fiction, too. For a more contemporary look at life in Hawaii today, one of the best novels is *Shark Dialogue,* by Kiana Davenport (Plume, 1995). The novel tells the story of Pono, the larger-than-life matriarch, and her four daughters of mixed races. Davenport skillfully weaves legends and myths of Hawaii into the "real life" reality that Pono and her family face in the complex Hawaii of today. Lois-Ann Yamanaka uses a very "local" voice and stark depictions of life in the islands in her fabulous novels *Wild Meat and the Bully Burgers* (Farrar, Straus, Giroux, 1996), *Blu's Hanging* (Avon, 1997), and *Heads by Harry* (Avon, 1999).

NONFICTION

Mark Twain's writing on Hawaii in the 1860s offers a wonderful introduction to Hawaii's history. One of his best books is *Mark Twain in Hawaii: Roughing It in the Sandwich Islands* (Mutual Publishing, 1990). Another great depiction of the Hawaii of 1889 is *Travels in Hawaii* (University of Hawaii Press, 1973), by Robert Louis Stevenson. For contemporary voices on Hawaii's unique culture, one of the best books to get is *Voices of Wisdom:*

Hawaiian Elders Speak, by M. J. Harden (Aka Press, 1999). Some 24 different Kahuna (experts) in their fields were interviewed about their talent, skill, or artistic practice. These living treasures talk about how Hawaiians of yesteryear viewed nature, spirituality and healing, preservation and history, dance and music, arts and crafts, canoes, and the next generation.

The recently rereleased *Native Planters in Old Hawaii: Their Life, Lore and Environment* (Bishop Museum Press, Honolulu, 2004) was originally published in 1972 but is still one of the most important ethnographic works on traditional Hawaiian culture, portraying the lives of the common folk and their relationship with the land before the arrival of Westerners. This revised edition, with a great index that allows you to find anything, is an excellent resource for anyone interested in Hawaii.

FLORA & FAUNA

Because Hawaii is so lush with nature and blessed with plants, animals, and reef fish seen nowhere else on the planet, a few reference books can help you identify what you're looking at and make your trip more interesting. In the botanical world, Angela Kay Kepler's *Hawaiian Heritage Plants* (A Latitude 20 Book, University of Hawaii Press, 1998) is the standard for plant reference. In a series of essays, Kepler weaves culture, history, geography, botany, and even spirituality into her vivid descriptions of plants. You'll never look at plants the same way. There are great color photos and drawings to help you sort through the myriad species. Another great plant book is *Tropicals* (Timber Press, 1988), by Gordon Courtright, which is filled with color photos identifying everything from hibiscus and heliconia to trees and palms.

The other necessary reference guide to have in Hawaii is a book identifying the colorful reef fish you will see snorkeling. The best reference book is John E. Randall's *Shore Fishes of Hawaii* (University of Hawaii Press, 1998). Two other books on reef fish identification, with easy-to-use spiral bindings, are *Hawaiian Reef Fish— The Identification Book* (Blue Kirio Publishing, 1993), by Casey Mahaney, and *Hawaiian Reef Fish* (Island Heritage, 1998), by Astrid Witte and Casey Mahaney.

To learn everything you need to identify Hawaii's unique birds, try H. Douglas Pratt's *A Pocket Guide to Hawaii's Birds* (Mutual Publishing, 1996).

For fans of the Hawaiian lei, *Na Lei Makamae: The Treasured Lei* (University of Hawaii Press, 2003), by Marie McDonald and Paul Weissich, is a comprehensive work on this incredible art form. McDonald is one of Hawaii's top lei makers, and Weissich is the director emeritus of Honolulu Botanical Gardens; together they cover some 88 flowers and plants used for leis.

HISTORY

There are many great books on Hawaii's history, but one of the best places to start is with the formation of the Hawaiian islands, vividly described in David E. Eyre's *By Wind, By Wave: An Introduction to Hawaii's Natural History* (Bess Press, 2000). In addition to chronicling the natural history of Hawaii, Eyre describes the complex interrelationships among the plants, animals, ocean, and people that are necessary. Eyre points out that Hawaii has become the "extinction capital of the world," but rather than dwelling on that fact, he urges readers to do something about it and carefully spells out how.

For an even more complete tome, get University of Hawaii Press's *Hawaiian Natural History, Ecology and Evolution,* by Alan C. Ziegler. Readers can trace the natural history of the Hawaiian archipelago through the book's 28 chapters or focus on specific topics such as island formation by plate tectonics, plant and animal evolution, flightless birds and their fossil sites, Polynesian migrational history and ecology, the effects of humans and exotic animals on the environment, current conservation efforts, and the contributions of the many naturalists who visited the islands over the centuries and the stories behind their discoveries.

For a history of "precontact" Hawaii (before Westerners arrived), David Malo's *Hawaiian Antiquities* (Bishop Museum Press, 1976) is the preeminent source. Malo was born around 1793 and wrote about the Hawaiian lifestyle at that time, as well as the beliefs and religion of his people. It's an excellent reference book, but not a fast read. For more readable books on old Hawaii, try *Stories of Old Hawaii* (Bess Press, 1997), by Roy Kakulu Alameide, on myths and legends; *Hawaiian Folk Tales* (Mutual Publishing, 1998), by Thomas G. Thrum; and *The Legends and Myths of Hawaii* (Charles E. Tuttle Company, 1992), by His Hawaiian Majesty King David Kalakaua.

The best story of the 1893 overthrow of the Hawaiian monarchy is told by Queen Liliuokalani, in her book *Hawaii's Story by Hawaii's Queen Liliuokalani* (Mutual Publishing, 1990). When it was written, it was an international plea for justice for her people, but it is a poignant read even today. It's also a "must-read" for people interested in current events and the recent rally in the 50th state for sovereignty. Two contemporary books on the question of Hawaii's sovereignty are Tom Coffman's *Nation Within—The Story of America's Annexation of the Nation of Hawaii* (Epicenter, 1998), and *Hawaiian Sovereignty: Do the Facts Matter?* (Goodale, 2000), by Thurston Twigg-Smith, which explores the opposite view. Twigg-Smith, former publisher of the statewide newspaper *The Honolulu Advertiser,* is the grandson of Lorrin A. Thurston, one of the architects of the 1893 overthrow of the monarchy. His so-called "politically incorrect" views present a different look on this hotly debated topic.

For more recent history, Lawrence H. Fuchs's *Hawaii Pono* (Bess Press, 1991) is a carefully researched tome on the contributions of each of Hawaii's main immigrant communities (Chinese, Japanese, and Filipino) between 1893 and 1959.

An insightful look at history and its effect on the Hawaiian culture is *Waikiki, A History of Forgetting and Remembering*, by Andrea Feeser (University of Hawaii Press, 2006). A beautiful art book (designed by Gaye Chan), this is not your normal coffee table book, but a different look at the cultural and environmental history of Waikiki. Using historical texts, photos, government documents, and interviews, this book lays out the story of how Waikiki went from a self-sufficient agricultural area to a tourism mecca, detailing the price that was paid along the way.

Another great cultural book just released is Davianna Pomaikai McGregor's *Na Kuaaina, Living Hawaiian Culture* (University of Hawaii Press, 2007). I love this book for so many reasons—first, it focuses not on the Hawaiian royalty, but on the common people of Hawaii and how they lived. McGregor, a professor of ethnic studies at UH, examines how people lived in rural lands and how they kept the Hawaiian traditions alive. She describes the cultural significance of each area (the island of Molokai; Hana, Maui; and Puna, Hawaii), the landscape, the Hawaiian gods who lived there, the chants and myths about the area, and how the westernization of the area has changed the land and the Hawaiian people.

Index

FROMMER'S® COMPLETE TRAVEL GUIDES

Alaska
Amalfi Coast
American Southwest
Amsterdam
Argentina & Chile
Arizona
Atlanta
Australia
Austria
Bahamas
Barcelona
Beijing
Belgium, Holland & Luxembourg
Belize
Bermuda
Boston
Brazil
British Columbia & the Canadian
 Rockies
Brussels & Bruges
Budapest & the Best of Hungary
Buenos Aires
Calgary
California
Canada
Cancún, Cozumel & the Yucatán
Cape Cod, Nantucket & Martha's
 Vineyard
Caribbean
Caribbean Ports of Call
Carolinas & Georgia
Chicago
China
Colorado
Costa Rica
Croatia
Cuba
Denmark
Denver, Boulder & Colorado Springs
Edinburgh & Glasgow
England
Europe
Europe by Rail
Florence, Tuscany & Umbria

Florida
France
Germany
Greece
Greek Islands
Hawaii
Hong Kong
Honolulu, Waikiki & Oahu
India
Ireland
Israel
Italy
Jamaica
Japan
Kauai
Las Vegas
London
Los Angeles
Los Cabos & Baja
Madrid
Maine Coast
Maryland & Delaware
Maui
Mexico
Montana & Wyoming
Montréal & Québec City
Moscow & St. Petersburg
Munich & the Bavarian Alps
Nashville & Memphis
New England
Newfoundland & Labrador
New Mexico
New Orleans
New York City
New York State
New Zealand
Northern Italy
Norway
Nova Scotia, New Brunswick &
 Prince Edward Island
Oregon
Paris
Peru
Philadelphia & the Amish Country

Portugal
Prague & the Best of the Czech
 Republic
Provence & the Riviera
Puerto Rico
Rome
San Antonio & Austin
San Diego
San Francisco
Santa Fe, Taos & Albuquerque
Scandinavia
Scotland
Seattle
Seville, Granada & the Best of
 Andalusia
Shanghai
Sicily
Singapore & Malaysia
South Africa
South America
South Florida
South Pacific
Southeast Asia
Spain
Sweden
Switzerland
Tahiti & French Polynesia
Texas
Thailand
Tokyo
Toronto
Turkey
USA
Utah
Vancouver & Victoria
Vermont, New Hampshire & Maine
Vienna & the Danube Valley
Vietnam
Virgin Islands
Virginia
Walt Disney World® & Orlando
Washington, D.C.
Washington State

FROMMER'S® DAY BY DAY GUIDES

Amsterdam
Chicago
Florence & Tuscany

London
New York City
Paris

Rome
San Francisco
Venice

PAULINE FROMMER'S GUIDES! SEE MORE. SPEND LESS.

Hawaii

Italy

New York City

FROMMER'S® PORTABLE GUIDES

Acapulco, Ixtapa & Zihuatanejo
Amsterdam
Aruba
Australia's Great Barrier Reef
Bahamas
Big Island of Hawaii
Boston
California Wine Country
Cancún
Cayman Islands
Charleston
Chicago
Dominican Republic

Dublin
Florence
Las Vegas
Las Vegas for Non-Gamblers
London
Maui
Nantucket & Martha's Vineyard
New Orleans
New York City
Paris
Portland
Puerto Rico
Puerto Vallarta, Manzanillo &
 Guadalajara

Rio de Janeiro
San Diego
San Francisco
Savannah
St. Martin, Sint Maarten, Anguila &
 St. Bart's
Turks & Caicos
Vancouver
Venice
Virgin Islands
Washington, D.C.
Whistler

FROMMER'S® CRUISE GUIDES

Alaska Cruises & Ports of Call | Cruises & Ports of Call | European Cruises & Ports of Call

FROMMER'S® NATIONAL PARK GUIDES

Algonquin Provincial Park
Banff & Jasper
Grand Canyon

National Parks of the American West
Rocky Mountain
Yellowstone & Grand Teton

Yosemite and Sequoia & Kings
   Canyon
Zion & Bryce Canyon

FROMMER'S® MEMORABLE WALKS

London
New York

Paris
Rome

San Francisco

FROMMER'S® WITH KIDS GUIDES

Chicago
Hawaii
Las Vegas
London

National Parks
New York City
San Francisco

Toronto
Walt Disney World® & Orlando
Washington, D.C.

SUZY GERSHMAN'S BORN TO SHOP GUIDES

France
Hong Kong, Shanghai & Beijing
Italy

London
New York

Paris
San Francisco

FROMMER'S® IRREVERENT GUIDES

Amsterdam
Boston
Chicago
Las Vegas

London
Los Angeles
Manhattan
Paris

Rome
San Francisco
Walt Disney World®
Washington, D.C.

FROMMER'S® BEST-LOVED DRIVING TOURS

Austria
Britain
California
France

Germany
Ireland
Italy
New England

Northern Italy
Scotland
Spain
Tuscany & Umbria

THE UNOFFICIAL GUIDES®

Adventure Travel in Alaska
Beyond Disney
California with Kids
Central Italy
Chicago
Cruises
Disneyland®
England
Florida
Florida with Kids

Hawaii
Ireland
Las Vegas
London
Maui
Mexico's Best Beach Resorts
Mini Mickey
New Orleans
New York City

Paris
San Francisco
South Florida including Miami &
   the Keys
Walt Disney World®
Walt Disney World® for
   Grown-ups
Walt Disney World® with Kids
Washington, D.C.

SPECIAL-INTEREST TITLES

Athens Past & Present
Best Places to Raise Your Family
Cities Ranked & Rated
500 Places to Take Your Kids Before They Grow Up
Frommer's Best Day Trips from London
Frommer's Best RV & Tent Campgrounds
   in the U.S.A.

Frommer's Exploring America by RV
Frommer's NYC Free & Dirt Cheap
Frommer's Road Atlas Europe
Frommer's Road Atlas Ireland
Great Escapes From NYC Without Wheels
Retirement Places Rated

FROMMER'S® PHRASEFINDER DICTIONARY GUIDES

French | Italian | Spanish

I don't speak sign language.

A hotel can close for all kinds of reasons.
Our Guarantee ensures that if your hotel's undergoing construction, we'll
let you know in advance. In fact, we cover your entire travel experience.
See www.travelocity.com/guarantee for details.

You'll never roam alone.

There's a parking lot where my ocean view should be.

 À la place de la vue sur l'océan, me voilà avec une vue sur un parking.

 Anstatt Meerblick habe ich Sicht auf einen Parkplatz.

 Al posto della vista sull'oceano c'è un parcheggio.

 No tengo vista al mar porque hay un parque de estacionamiento.

 Há um parque de estacionamento onde deveria estar a minha vista do oceano.

 Ett parkeringsområde har byggts på den plats där min utsikt över oceanen borde vara.

 Er ligt een parkeerterrein waar mijn zee-uitzicht zou moeten zijn.

 هنالك موقف للسيارات مكان ما وجب ان يكون المنظر الخلاب المطل على المحيط .

 眼前に広がる紺碧の海・・・じゃない。窓の外は駐車場！

 停车场的位置应该是我的海景所在。

— *I'm fluent in pig latin.*

Hotel mishaps aren't bound by geography.

Neither is our Guarantee. It covers your entire travel experience, including the price. So if you don't get the ocean view you booked, we'll work with our travel partners to make it right, right away. See www.travelocity.com/guarantee for details.

travelocity
You'll never roam alone.

©2007 Travelocity.com LP CST# 2056372-50